Methodological and Conceptual Issues in Applied Behavior Analysis

Second Edition
1968–1999

from the

Journal of Applied Behavior Analysis

Reprint Series, Volume 4

Editors

Brian A. Iwata, University of Florida
Nancy A. Neef, Ohio State University
David P. Wacker, University of Iowa
F. Charles Mace, University of Wales
Timothy R. Vollmer, University of Florida

Assistant Editor
Rachel H. Thompson, University of Florida

Published by the
Society for the Experimental Analysis of Behavior
Department of Human Development
University of Kansas
Lawrence, KS 66045
Telephone (785) 843-0008

Inquiries regarding subscriptions to the *Journal of Applied Behavior Analysis* and additional orders for this or other reprint volumes should be addressed to Mary Louise Wright, Business Manager, *JABA,* at the above address

ISBN 1-882018-01-X

Printed in the United States of America
by
Allen Press
1041 New Hampshire Street
Lawrence, KS 66044

Additional volumes in the *JABA* reprint series:

Behavior Analysis in Developmental Disabilities

Reprint Volume 1. The volume covers behavioral assessment and treatment in mental retardation and related disabilities, including reinforcer identification and effective usage, basic learning processes, self-care and daily living skills, language acquisition and communication, leisure and recreation, academic performance, vocational skills, community preparation, biobehavioral applications, severe behavior disorders, and parent and staff training. (ISBN 1-882018-03-6)
$35.00 (70 articles)

Behavior Analysis in the Community

Reprint Volume 2. The volume covers applications of behavior analysis in open-field settings, including crime prevention and intervention, health care, ecological/environmental preservation, community affairs, safety, and organizational/business practices.
$15.00 (54 articles)

Behavior Analysis in Education

Reprint Volume 3. The volume covers instructional processes and includes topics such as preschool applications, language and social behavior, academic performance, classroom management, peers as tutors, behaviorally disordered students, teacher and parent training, and health and safety. (ISBN 0-929018-00-1)
Forthcoming

PREFACE TO THE SECOND EDITION

Applied behavior analysis has often been described as both a methodological and conceptual enterprise. A common feature among its many applications is a unique approach to experimental research and program evaluation commonly referred to as "single-subject methodology." Used originally in operant conditioning laboratories, the single-subject approach represents a clear departure from traditional research methods typical of most areas of psychology and the social sciences. Greater emphasis is placed on the objective measurement of ongoing behavior, the collection of extended data samples for individual subjects, the use of a subject's behavioral "baseline" as a control condition for the purpose of conducting experimental comparisons, and the evaluation of experimental effects through direct visual examination of data. Through the application of this methodology, applied behavior analysis attempts to answer questions about environment–behavior relationships and to discover ways in which socially important behaviors (of children, students, clients, patients, etc.) may be improved. Thus, empirical relationships provide the basis for developing a behavior-change technology, both of which are derived from, and sometimes extend, principles of learning theory.

The present volume, *Methodological and Conceptual Issues in Applied Behavior Analysis,* focuses on a description of the single-subject research model as it is used in applied research, as well as on more general issues arising from such work. Three-hundred articles on these topics have been published in *JABA* from 1968 to 1999, and 67 of them are reprinted in this volume. This represents a significant increase from 49 articles in the first edition as well as a noticeable change in content. The first edition of this volume focused very heavily on methodology (38 of the articles). The present volume provides a somewhat even balance among methodological, conceptual, and professional aspects of our field.

The first section, *The Nature of Applied Behavior Analysis,* contains two seminal articles that define applied behavior analysis. The Baer, Wolf, and Risley (1968) article delineates seven methodological and conceptual characteristics (dimensions) of our field and provides an overview of issues examined in subsequent sections. Twenty years later, the same authors (1987) reanalyze these seven dimensions and suggest some interesting directions for future research.

The section on *Science, Theory, and Technology* addresses one of several criticisms that have been levied against applied research over the years, namely, that it places too much emphasis on the production of behavior change (or on the techniques used to effect change) and not enough emphasis on analytical investigation that integrates or extends theoretical concepts. Hayes, Rincover, and Solnick (1978) provide the most explicit statement of this concern, and the accompanying articles provide responses from several perspectives.

The *Measurement* section describes frequently used procedures for defining and quantifying behavioral data in applied research. In addition, several studies are presented that evaluate or compare observational procedures or identify variables that may affect the representativeness of data.

Because applied researchers so often rely on the use of human observers, numerous questions have arisen about the accuracy and reliability of measurement. Articles in the section on *Interobserver Agreement* present methods for calculating observer reliability and summarize some of their advantages and disadvantages.

Interobserver agreement traditionally has been associated with the measurement of dependent variables. The section on *Treatment Integrity* focuses on a related topic—consistent implementation of independent variables—and includes a general discussion of the issue and an illustrative empirical investigation.

The section on *Experimental Design* focuses on basic strategies for introducing, removing, and replicating the effects of experimental manipulations. Reversal, multiple baseline, changing criterion, and multielement (alternating treatments) designs are described, as are appropriate uses, contraindications, and interpretive problems.

Although visual analysis of behavioral data remains the most common method for evaluating experimental effects in applied behavior analysis research, a number of alternatives based on the use of inferential statistics have been proposed. Two frequently suggested models—analysis of variance and time-series analysis—are described in the section on *Data Analysis,* and critiques of both statistical and visual analysis approaches are presented.

Because our field is concerned not only with the objective outcome of an intervention program but also with its practical utility, consumer evaluations often play an important role in determining the relevance of intervention goals, the appropriateness of procedures, and the significance of the results. These processes necessarily introduce subjective elements into the research enterprise. Articles in the section on *Social Validity* present a convincing argument for the use of consumer evaluations, describe several methods for designing such evaluations, and summarize problems that arise from the interpretation of verbal reports.

Articles in the section on *Conceptual Issues* cover a variety of topics of general interest and were written from the perspectives of both basic and applied researchers. As a group, these articles represent good examples of attempts to integrate learning theory, basic principles, and applications with respect to a particular performance (e.g., choice behavior), procedure (e.g., shaping), or contingency (e.g., negative reinforcement).

The section on *Research, Training, and Professional Practice* contains a related series of articles on graduate training. Questions about the relative emphasis to be placed on research versus practice have been raised in clinical psychology training programs for years. These same questions are becoming increasingly important to applied behavior analysts as consumer demand for our technology increases and are considered by several leaders in our field.

The final section, *Trends in Applied Behavior Analysis,* contains articles that document and discuss characteristics of the field or changes in emphasis, as exemplified in research published across years in *JABA.*

Those who wish to examine any of the above areas in greater detail may consult the *Complete Bibliography* at the end of this volume, which lists all 300 articles published in *JABA* on methodological and conceptual issues since 1968. Space constraints prevented us from including many important articles, so we encourage instructors to examine the bibliography for supplementary readings.

Our initial plan in preparing this edition was to include study questions for each article. We succeeded in generating questions for most, but not all, of the articles. Rather than to delay publication further (and given the increased size of this edition), we decided to proceed without the questions. However, we remain committed to the completion of our task and plan to make the study questions available in the near future.

Brian A. Iwata
for the Editors

Table of Contents

Social Validity

Conceptual Issues

Research, Training, and Professional Practice

Trends in Applied Behavior Analysis

JOURNAL OF APPLIED BEHAVIOR ANALYSIS 1968, 1, 91-97 NUMBER 1 (SPRING, 1968)

SOME CURRENT DIMENSIONS OF APPLIED BEHAVIOR ANALYSIS[1]

DONALD M. BAER, MONTROSE M. WOLF, AND TODD R. RISLEY

THE UNIVERSITY OF KANSAS

The analysis of individual behavior is a problem in scientific demonstration, reasonably well understood (Skinner, 1953, Sec. 1), comprehensively described (Sidman, 1960), and quite thoroughly practised (*Journal of the Experimental Analysis of Behavior*, 1957 –). That analysis has been pursued in many settings over many years. Despite variable precision, elegance, and power, it has resulted in general descriptive statements of mechanisms that can produce many of the forms that individual behavior may take.

The statement of these mechanisms establishes the possibility of their application to problem behavior. A society willing to consider a technology of its own behavior apparently is likely to support that application when it deals with socially important behaviors, such as retardation, crime, mental illness, or education. Such applications have appeared in recent years. Their current number and the interest which they create apparently suffice to generate a journal for their display. That display may well lead to the widespread examination of these applications, their refinement, and eventually their replacement by better applications. Better applications, it is hoped, will lead to a better state of society, to whatever extent the behavior of its members can contribute to the goodness of a society. Since the evaluation of what is a "good" society is in itself a behavior of its members, this hope turns on itself in a philosophically interesting manner. However, it is at least a fair presumption that behavioral applications, when effective, can sometimes lead to social approval and adoption.

Behavioral applications are hardly a new phenomenon. Analytic behavioral applications, it seems, are. Analytic behavioral application is the process of applying sometimes tentative principles of behavior to the improvement[2] of specific behaviors, and simultaneously evaluating whether or not any changes noted are indeed attributable to the process of application—and if so, to what parts of that process. In short, analytic behavioral application is a self-examining, self-evaluating, discovery-oriented research procedure for studying behavior. So is all experimental behavioral research (at least, according to the usual strictures of modern graduate training). The differences are matters of emphasis and of selection.

The differences between applied and basic research are not differences between that which "discovers" and that which merely "applies" what is already known. Both endeavors ask what controls the behavior under study. Non-applied research is likely to look at any behavior, and at any variable which may conceivably relate to it. Applied research is constrained to look at variables which can be effective in improving the behavior under study. Thus it is equally a matter of research to discover that the behaviors typical of retardates can be related to oddities of their

[1]Reprints may be obtained from Donald M. Baer, Dept. of Human Development, University of Kansas, Lawrence, Kansas 66044.

[2]If a behavior is socially important, the usual behavior analysis will aim at its improvement. The social value dictating this choice is obvious. However, it can be just as illuminating to demonstrate how a behavior may be worsened, and there will arise occasions when it will be socially important to do so. Disruptive classroom behavior may serve as an example. Certainly it is a frequent plague of the educational system. A demonstration of what teacher procedures produce more of this behavior is not necessarily the reverse of a demonstration of how to promote positive study behaviors. There may be classroom situations in which the teacher cannot readily establish high rates of study, yet still could avoid high rates of disruption, if she knew what in her own procedures leads to this disruption. The demonstration which showed her that would thus have its value.

chromosome structure and to oddities of their reinforcement history. But (currently) the chromosome structure of the retardate does not lend itself to experimental manipulation in the interests of bettering that behavior, whereas his reinforcement input is always open to current re-design.

Similarly, applied research is constrained to examining behaviors which are socially important, rather than convenient for study. It also implies, very frequently, the study of those behaviors in their usual social settings, rather than in a "laboratory" setting. But a laboratory is simply a place so designed that experimental control of relevant variables is as easy as possible. Unfortunately, the usual social setting for important behaviors is rarely such a place. Consequently, the analysis of socially important behaviors becomes experimental only with difficulty. As the terms are used here, a non-experimental analysis is a contradiction in terms. Thus, analytic behavioral applications by definition achieve experimental control of the processes they contain, but since they strive for this control against formidable difficulties, they achieve it less often per study than would a laboratory-based attempt. Consequently, the rate of displaying experimental control required of behavioral applications has become correspondingly less than the standards typical of laboratory research. This is not because the applier is an easy-going, liberal, or generous fellow, but because society rarely will allow its important behaviors, in their correspondingly important settings, to be manipulated repeatedly for the merely logical comfort of a scientifically sceptical audience.

Thus, the evaluation of a study which purports to be an applied behavior analysis is somewhat different than the evaluation of a similar laboratory analysis. Obviously, the study must be *applied, behavioral,* and *analytic;* in addition, it should be *technological, conceptually systematic,* and *effective,* and it should display some generality. These terms are explored below and compared to the criteria often stated for the evaluation of behavioral research which, though analytic, is not applied.

Applied

The label applied is not determined by the research procedures used but by the interest which society shows in the problems being studied. In behavioral application, the behavior, stimuli, and/or organism under study are chosen because of their importance to man and society, rather than their importance to theory. The non-applied researcher may study eating behavior, for example, because it relates directly to metabolism, and there are hypotheses about the interaction between behavior and metabolism. The non-applied researcher also may study bar-pressing because it is a convenient response for study; easy for the subject, and simple to record and integrate with theoretically significant environmental events. By contrast, the applied researcher is likely to study eating because there are children who eat too little and adults who eat too much, and he will study eating in exactly those individuals rather than in more convenient ones. The applied researcher may also study bar-pressing if it is integrated with socially important stimuli. A program for a teaching machine may use bar-pressing behavior to indicate mastery of an arithmetic skill. It is the arithmetic stimuli which are important. (However, some future applied study could show that bar-pressing is more practical in the process of education than a pencil-writing response.[3])

In applied research, there is typically a close relationship between the behavior and stimuli under study and the subject in whom they are studied. Just as there seem to be few behaviors that are intrinsically the target of application, there are few subjects who automatically confer on their study the status of application. An investigation of visual signal detection in the retardate may have little immediate importance, but a similar study in radar-scope watchers has considerable. A study of language development in the retardate may be aimed directly at an immedi-

[3]Research may use the most convenient behaviors and stimuli available, and yet exemplify an ambition in the researcher eventually to achieve application to socially important settings. For example, a study may seek ways to give a light flash a durable conditioned reinforcing function, because the experimenter wishes to know how to enhance school children's responsiveness to approval. Nevertheless, durable bar-pressing for that light flash is no guarantee that the obvious classroom analogue will produce durable reading behavior for teacher statements of "Good!" Until the analogue has been proven sound, application has not been achieved.

ate social problem, while a similar study in the MIT sophomore may not. Enhancement of the reinforcing value of praise for the retardate alleviates an immediate deficit in his current environment, but enhancement of the reinforcing value of 400 Hz (cps) tone for the same subject probably does not. Thus, a primary question in the evaluation of applied research is: how immediately important is this behavior or these stimuli to this subject?

Behavioral

Behaviorism and pragmatism seem often to go hand in hand. Applied research is eminently pragmatic; it asks how it is possible to get an individual to do something effectively. Thus it usually studies what subjects can be brought to do rather than what they can be brought to say; unless, of course, a verbal response is the behavior of interest. Accordingly a subject's verbal description of his own non-verbal behavior usually would not be accepted as a measure of his actual behavior unless it were independently substantiated. Hence there is little applied value in the demonstration that an impotent man can be made to say that he no longer is impotent. The relevant question is not what he can say, but what he can do. Application has not been achieved until this question has been answered satisfactorily. (This assumes, of course, that the total goal of the applied researcher is not simply to get his patient-subjects to stop complaining to him. Unless society agrees that this researcher should not be bothered, it will be difficult to defend that goal as socially important.)

Since the behavior of an individual is composed of physical events, its scientific study requires their precise measurement. As a result, the problem of reliable quantification arises immediately. The problem is the same for applied research as it is for non-applied research. However, non-applied research typically will choose a response easily quantified in a reliable manner, whereas applied research rarely will have that option. As a result, the applied researcher must try harder, rather than ignore this criterion of all trustworthy research. Current applied research often shows that thoroughly reliable quantification of behavior can be achieved, even in thoroughly difficult settings. However, it also suggests that instrumented recording with its typical reliability will not always be possible. The reliable use of human beings to quantify the behavior of other human beings is an area of psychological technology long since well developed, thoroughly relevant, and very often necessary to applied behavior analysis.

A useful tactic in evaluating the behavioral attributes of a study is to ask not merely, was *behavior* changed? but also, *whose* behavior? Ordinarily it would be assumed that it was the subject's behavior which was altered; yet careful reflection may suggest that this was not necessarily the case. If humans are observing and recording the behavior under study, then any change may represent a change only in their observing and recording responses, rather than in the subject's behavior. Explicit measurement of the reliability of human observers thus becomes not merely good technique, but a prime criterion of whether the study was appropriately behavioral. (A study merely of the behavior of observers is behavioral, of course, but probably irrelevant to the researcher's goal.) Alternatively, it may be that only the experimenter's behavior has changed. It may be reported, for example, that a certain patient rarely dressed himself upon awakening, and consequently would be dressed by his attendant. The experimental technique to be applied might consist of some penalty imposed unless the patient were dressed within half an hour after awakening. Recording of an increased probability of self-dressing under these conditions might testify to the effectiveness of the penalty in changing the behavior; however, it might also testify to the fact that the patient would in fact probably dress himself within half an hour of arising, but previously was rarely left that long undressed before being clothed by his efficient attendant. (The attendant now is the penalty-imposing experimenter and therefore always gives the patient his full half-hour, in the interests of precise experimental technique, of course.) This error is an elementary one, perhaps. But it suggests that in general, when an experiment proceeds from its baseline to its first experimental phase, changes in what is measured need not always reflect the behavior of the subject.

Analytic

The analysis of a behavior, as the term is used here, requires a believable demonstration of the events that can be responsible for the occurrence or non-occurrence of that behavior. An experimenter has achieved an analysis of a behavior when he can exercise control over it. By common laboratory standards, that has meant an ability of the experimenter to turn the behavior on and off, or up and down, at will. Laboratory standards have usually made this control clear by demonstrating it repeatedly, even redundantly, over time. Applied research, as noted before, cannot often approach this arrogantly frequent clarity of being in control of important behaviors. Consequently, application, to be analytic, demonstrates control when it can, and thereby presents its audience with a problem of judgment. The problem, of course, is whether the experimenter has shown enough control, and often enough, for believability. Laboratory demonstrations, either by over-replication or an acceptable probability level derived from statistical tests of grouped data, make this judgment more implicit than explicit. As Sidman points out (1960), there is still a problem of judgment in any event, and it is probably better when explicit.

There are at least two designs commonly used to demonstrate reliable control of an important behavioral change. The first can be referred to as the "reversal" technique. Here a behavior is measured, and the measure is examined over time until its stability is clear. Then, the experimental variable is applied. The behavior continues to be measured, to see if the variable will produce a behavioral change. If it does, the experimental variable is discontinued or altered, to see if the behavioral change just brought about depends on it. If so, the behavioral change should be lost or diminished (thus the term "reversal"). The experimental variable then is applied again, to see if the behavioral change can be recovered. If it can, it is pursued further, since this is applied research and the behavioral change sought is an important one. It may be reversed briefly again, and yet again, if the setting in which the behavior takes place allows further reversals. But that setting may be a school system or a family, and continued reversals may not be allowed. They may appear in themselves to be detrimental to the subject if pursued too often. (Whether they are in fact detrimental is likely to remain an unexamined question so long as the social setting in which the behavior is studied dictates against using them repeatedly. Indeed, it may be that repeated reversals in some applications have a positive effect on the subject, possibly contributing to the discrimination of relevant stimuli involved in the problem.)

In using the reversal technique, the experimenter is attempting to show that an analysis of the behavior is at hand: that whenever he applies a certain variable, the behavior is produced, and whenever he removes this variable, the behavior is lost. Yet applied behavior analysis is exactly the kind of research which can make this technique self-defeating in time. Application typically means producing valuable behavior; valuable behavior usually meets extra-experimental reinforcement in a social setting; thus, valuable behavior, once set up, may no longer be dependent upon the experimental technique which created it. Consequently, the number of reversals possible in applied studies may be limited by the nature of the social setting in which the behavior takes place, in more ways than one.

An alternative to the reversal technique may be called the "multiple baseline" technique. This alternative may be of particular value when a behavior appears to be irreversible or when reversing the behavior is undesirable. In the multiple-baseline technique, a number of responses are identified and measured over time to provide baselines against which changes can be evaluated. With these baselines established, the experimenter then applies an experimental variable to one of the behaviors, produces a change in it, and perhaps notes little or no change in the other baselines. If so, rather than reversing the just-produced change, he instead applies the experimental variable to one of the other, as yet unchanged, responses. If it changes at that point, evidence is accruing that the experimental variable is indeed effective, and that the prior change was not simply a matter of coincidence. The variable then may be applied to still another response, and so on. The experimenter is attempting to show that he has a reliable experimental variable, in that each behavior changes maximally only when the experimental variable is applied to it.

How many reversals, or how many baselines, make for believability is a problem for the audience. If statistical analysis is applied, the audience must then judge the suitability of the inferential statistic chosen and the propriety of these data for that test. Alternatively, the audience may inspect the data directly and relate them to past experience with similar data and similar procedures. In either case, the judgments required are highly qualitative, and rules cannot always be stated profitably. However, either of the foregoing designs gathers data in ways that exemplify the concept of replication, and replication is the essence of believability. At the least, it would seem that an approach to replication is better than no approach at all. This should be especially true for so embryonic a field as behavioral application, the very possibility of which is still occasionally denied.

The preceding discussion has been aimed at the problem of *reliability:* whether or not a certain procedure was responsible for a corresponding behavioral change. The two general procedures described hardly exhaust the possibilities. Each of them has many variations now seen in practice; and current experience suggests that many more variations are badly needed, if the technology of important behavioral change is to be consistently believable. Given some approach to reliability, there are further analyses of obvious value which can be built upon that base. For example, there is analysis in the sense of simplification and separation of component processes. Often enough, current behavioral procedures are complex, even "shotgun" in their application. When they succeed, they clearly need to be analyzed into their effective components. Thus, a teacher giving M & M's to a child may succeed in changing his behavior as planned. However, she has almost certainly confounded her attention and/or approval with each M & M. Further analysis may be approached by her use of attention alone, the effects of which can be compared to the effects of attention coupled with candies. Whether she will discontinue the M & M's, as in the reversal technique, or apply attention with M & M's to certain behaviors and attention alone to certain others, as in the multiple baseline method, is again the problem in basic reliability discussed above. Another form of analysis is parametric: a demonstration of the effectiveness of different values of some variable in changing behavior. The problem again will be to make such an analysis reliable, and, as before, that might be approached by the repeated alternate use of different values on the same behavior (reversal), or by the application of different values to different groups of responses (multiple baseline). At this stage in the development of applied behavior analysis, primary concern is usually with reliability, rather than with parametric analysis or component analysis.

Technological

"Technological" here means simply that the techniques making up a particular behavioral application are completely identified and described. In this sense, "play therapy" is not a technological description, nor is "social reinforcement". For purposes of application, all the salient ingredients of play therapy must be described as a set of contingencies between child response, therapist response, and play materials, before a statement of technique has been approached. Similarly, all the ingredients of social reinforcement must be specified (stimuli, contingency, and schedule) to qualify as a technological procedure.

The best rule of thumb for evaluating a procedure description as technological is probably to ask whether a typically trained reader could replicate that procedure well enough to produce the same results, given only a reading of the description. This is very much the same criterion applied to procedure descriptions in non-applied research, of course. It needs emphasis, apparently, in that there occasionally exists a less-than-precise stereotype of applied research. Where application is novel, and derived from principles produced through non-applied research, as in current applied behavior analysis, the reverse holds with great urgency.

Especially where the problem is application, procedural descriptions require considerable detail about all possible contingencies of procedure. It is not enough to say what is to be done when the subject makes response R_1; it is essential also whenever possible to say what is to be done if the subject makes the alternative responses, R_2, R_3, *etc.* For example, one may read that temper tantrums in children are often extinguished by closing the child in his room for the duration of the tantrums plus ten minutes. Unless that procedure description also states what should be done if the child tries to leave the room early, or kicks out the window, or smears feces on the walls, or begins to make strangling sounds, *etc.*, it is not precise technological description.

Conceptual Systems

The field of applied behavior analysis will probably advance best if the published descriptions of its procedures are not only precisely technological, but also strive for relevance to principle. To describe exactly how a preschool teacher will attend to jungle-gym climbing in a child frightened of heights is good technological description; but further to call it a social reinforcement procedure relates it to basic concepts of behavioral development. Similarly, to describe the exact sequence of color changes whereby a child is moved from a color discrimination to a form discrimination is good; to refer also to "fading" and "errorless discrimination" is better. In both cases, the total description is adequate for successful replication by the reader; and it also shows the reader how similar procedures may be derived from basic principles. This can have the effect of making a body of technology into a discipline rather than a collection of tricks. Collections of tricks historically have been difficult to expand systematically, and when they were extensive, difficult to learn and teach.

Effective

If the application of behavioral techniques does not produce large enough effects for practical value, then application has failed. Non-applied research often may be extremely valuable when it produces small but reliable effects, in that these effects testify to the operation of some variable which in itself has great theoretical importance. In application, the theoretical importance of a variable is usually not at issue. Its practical importance, specifically its power in altering behavior enough to be socially important, is the essential criterion. Thus, a study which shows that a new classroom technique can raise the grade level achievements of culturally deprived children from D− to D is not an obvious example of applied behavior analysis. That same study might conceivably revolutionize educational theory, but it clearly has not yet revolutionized education. This is of course a matter of degree: an increase in those children from D− to C might well be judged an important success by an audience which thinks that C work is a great deal different than D work, especially if C students are much less likely to become drop-outs than D students.

In evaluating whether a given application has produced enough of a behavioral change to deserve the label, a pertinent question can be, how much did that behavior need to be changed? Obviously, that is not a scientific question, but a practical one. Its answer is likely to be supplied by people who must deal with the behavior. For example, ward personnel may be able to say that a hospitalized mute schizophrenic trained to use 10 verbal labels is not much better off in self-help skills than before, but that one with 50 such labels is a great deal more effective. In this case, the opinions of ward aides may be more relevant than the opinions of psycholinguists.

Generality

A behavioral change may be said to have generality if it proves durable over time, if it appears in a wide variety of possible environments, or if it spreads to a wide variety of related behaviors. Thus, the improvement of articulation in a clinic setting will prove to have generality if it endures into the future after the clinic visits stop; if the improved articulation is heard at home, at school, and on dates; or if the articulation of all words, not just the ones treated, improves. Application means practical improvement in important behaviors; thus, the more general that application, the better, in many cases. Therapists dealing with the development of heterosexual behavior may well point out there are socially appropriate limits to its generality, once developed; such limitations to generality are usually obvious. That generality is a valuable characteristic of applied behavior analysis which should be examined explicitly apparently is not quite that obvious, and is stated here for emphasis.

That generality is not automatically accomplished whenever behavior is changed also needs occasional emphasis, especially in the evaluation of applied behavior analysis. It is sometimes assumed that application has failed when generalization does not take place in any widespread form. Such a conclusion has no generality itself. A procedure which is effective in changing behavior in one setting may perhaps be easily repeated in other settings, and thus accomplish the generalization sought. Furthermore, it may well prove the case that a given behavior change need be programmed in only a certain number of settings, one after another, perhaps, to accomplish eventually widespread generalization. A child may have 15 techniques for disrupting his parents, for example. The elimination of the most prevalent of these may still leave the remaining 14 intact and in force. The technique may still prove both valuable and fundamental, if when applied to the next four successfully, it also results in the "generalized" loss of the remaining 10. In general, generalization should be programmed, rather than expected or lamented.

Thus, in summary, an *applied* behavior analysis will make obvious the importance of the behavior changed, its quantitative characteristics, the experimental manipulations which analyze with clarity what was responsible for the change, the technologically exact description of all procedures contributing to that change, the effectiveness of those procedures in making sufficient change for value, and the generality of that change.

REFERENCES

Journal of the Experimental Analysis of Behavior. Bloomington: Society for the Experimental Analysis of Behavior, 1957-.

Sidman, Murray. *Tactics of scientific research.* New York: Basic Books, 1960.

Skinner, B. F. *Science and human behavior.* New York: Macmillan, 1953.

Received 24 December 1967.

JOURNAL OF APPLIED BEHAVIOR ANALYSIS 1987, 20, 313–327 NUMBER 4 (WINTER 1987)

SOME STILL-CURRENT DIMENSIONS OF APPLIED BEHAVIOR ANALYSIS

DONALD M. BAER
MONTROSE M. WOLF
UNIVERSITY OF KANSAS

TODD R. RISLEY
UNIVERSITY OF ALASKA

Twenty years ago, an anthropological note described the current dimensions of applied behavior analysis as it was prescribed and practiced in 1968: It was, or ought to become, applied, behavioral, analytic, technological, conceptual, effective, and capable of appropriately generalized outcomes. A similar anthropological note today finds the same dimensions still prescriptive, and to an increasing extent, descriptive. Several new tactics have become evident, however, some in the realm of conceptual analysis, some in the sociological status of the discipline, and some in its understanding of the necessary systemic nature of any applied discipline that is to operate in the domain of important human behaviors.

DESCRIPTORS: application, dissemination, technology, terminology, history

---

Twenty years ago, an anthropologist's account of the group calling its culture Applied Behavior Analysis (ABA) had to begin by describing the relevant context (Baer, Wolf, & Risley, 1968): the existence and power of the disciplinary matrix (Kuhn, 1970, p. 175) within which the behavior of individuals was analyzed experimentally. That matrix was itself the characteristic behavior of a more inclusive, older group calling its culture The Experimental Analysis of Behavior (TEAB). The characteristic exemplary strategies (Kuhn, 1970, p. 189) of the TEAB group were their procedural emphases of reinforcement, punishment, and discriminative-stimulus contingencies as behavior-analytic environmental variables, their reliance on single-subject designs as the formats of analysis and proof, and their consistent use of the Skinner box as their arena. Within a decade, the ABA group outnumbered its originally overarching TEAB group, such that the inevitable debates about their actual and desirable conceptual cohesion and separateness took on some sociological urgency (but not very much urgency, especially from nonbehavior analytic points of view. At a conference on behavior analysis, steady-state argument led Nancy Datan to recount an Arab proverb about the nature of conflict: "I must defend my tribe against the world, my family against the tribe, my brothers against my family, and myself against my brothers.") (e.g., Baer, 1981; Deitz, 1978; Michael, 1980; Pierce & Epling, 1980). Even so, the ABA subgroup continued to show nearly the same strategies that characterized the TEAB group, but shifted their application exclusively to what the group called "socially important behaviors" in those behaviors' real-life Skinner boxes.

That shift in strategy required a considerable number of new tactics. At the most basic disciplinary-matrix level, measurement procedures were almost immediately opened to continuous interval-based response measures; the recording not of discrete-response occurrences but instead of intervals during which the response had occurred at least once or was ongoing solved the otherwise unmanageable problem of recording real-life behaviors with difficult-to-define onsets and offsets (Baer, 1986, but cf. Powell, 1984). These measures at first supplemented, and soon almost replaced, the rate-of-response measures characteristic of the parent TEAB group. In addition, seven classes of tactic labels were proposed as stimulus controls for appropriate behavior-analytic conduct in the new world of application (within which behavior-analytic logic is indeed difficult to defend—ironically, the part of the world that likes to call itself "real" usually prefers mentalistic explanations of its own behavior).

The stimulus controls proposed for behavior-analytic conduct in the world of application were the seven key words in a set of injunctions always to be: *applied, behavioral, analytic, technological, conceptual, effective,* and capable of appropriately *generalized* outcomes.

Today, those tactic labels remain functional; they still connote the current dimensions of the work usually called applied behavior analysis. The tactics for which they are stimulus controls have changed to some extent, however. (If they had not changed to some degree in two decades, we might well worry about the viability of their discipline; if they had changed too much, we might well wonder if there was any discipline in their viability. Thus, we would do well to estimate often how properly situated we are between those two extremes.)

Applied

Initially, the meaning of *applied* centered on vague concepts of social problems, social interest, and the immediate importance of the behavior or its functional stimuli to the behaver. Twenty years of experience, especially with what often is called social criticism, have begun to clarify what social problems, interest, and importance are. On the face of it, they are at least behaviors of a person called subject or client that trouble that person; but more often, they are also behaviors of people other than the one called subject or client. Social problems are those behaviors of the subject or client that result in counteraction, sometimes by the client, but more often by nonclients, sufficient to generate something called a solution, or at least a program. (In the world of application, attractive programs that do not solve the problem to which they are ostensibly applied sometimes are valuable even so. At least, they solve the sometimes more aversive problem of doing nothing about that problem. In addition, they very often solve some quite important related problem: They let the client or the counteracting nonclients discuss the problem with a sympathetic friend, they provide those people a platform, or both. Perhaps there is no such thing as a totally ineffective program. But when programs do not solve the target problem, it is typical—and functional—not to measure their ineffectiveness at that, yet it could be illuminating to measure their social validity.)

Thus, social problems are essentially the behaviors of displaying or explaining problems—one's own or someone else's. Problem displays are sometimes large-scale, sometimes small-scale. Perhaps the smallest scale display is seen when one client explains a personal problem to a therapist; the question is whether the client can explain well enough to secure the therapist's attempt at its solution. By contrast, sometimes an entire society can approach nuclear annihilation and technological illiteracy; the question then is whether its media can display and explain that problem effectively enough to secure the political behavior that will generate its government's attempt at solutions, or whether its government will try to solve other, smaller problems, exactly because the small-problem proponents are more effective at using the media, lobbying, and financial campaign support.

It is clear that the therapist's response is usually controlled not simply by the client's promise to pay a fee but also by the therapist's agreement that this problem deserves a solution—an agreement sometimes withheld. Thus, most therapists would consider teaching a self-instructional program aimed at improving a client's dart-throwing skill for social events at a favorite bar, but not at improving the client's rifle-shooting accuracy for a proposed murder. Similarly, the government's decision may (we hope) be controlled not simply by what will accomplish its reelection and the back-up reinforcers pursuant to that, but also by its analysis of its society's survival and prosperity.

The polarities of these two decisions seem to be, respectively, the client's problem display and willingness to pay versus the therapist's values (in other words, the historical and current contingencies controlling the therapist's agreement to program the necessary behavior changes), and the lobbyists' problem displays and willingness to support campaigns versus the government's analysis of societal survival and prosperity (in other words, the historical and current contingencies controlling the government's agreement to program the necessary behavior changes). Those polarities have not changed much in two decades (or in two millenia); what is grimly new in the discipline is the more widespread explicit recognition that all such polarities are themselves behaviors of displayers and displayees; that the behaviors of displaying and explaining problems always exist on continua of their effectiveness for a given displayee; and that whenever one agency displays and explains its problems effectively, its effectiveness can cause some other agency to display that very effectiveness as *its* problem, perhaps more effectively, and so on, *ad infinitum*.

The past two decades have not yielded a better public analysis of effective problem display and explanation (although its deliberate practice is surely one of the world's older professions). At best, they have shown us that we need analyses of (a) displaying and explaining problems so as to gain effective use of the media, (b) controlling the behavior of those other people who can function as decision-makers' constituencies (i.e., lobbying), (c) having or being able to recruit campaign support, and (d) recognizing events called *crises* as the setting events when those repertoires will be most effective. At least those analyses are necessary to understand fully what we most often mean by *applied*. We mean every form of countercontrol typically under the stimulus control of problem displays and explanations. That leaves us with a very large programmatic question: What do we know and what can we learn about effective stimulus control that can be applied in the domain of problem displays? It is clear that some people in our society know a great deal about that. If they know, then we can learn. The crucial behavior may be to establish the priority of that research area as essential to making us a truly applied discipline; clearly, the last two decades have prompted that priority with increasing urgency.

Behavioral

One mark of the success of applied behavior analysis in the last two decades is that its practitioners, researchers, and theorists have encountered so many invitations to become something other than behavioral, usually in the form of becoming something "more" than behavioral. In particular, their occasional mainstreaming with behavior therapy, education, developmental psychology, psycholinguistics, and sociobiology has given them the chance to entertain constructs of anxiety, attention, intelligence, disabilities, spontaneity, readiness, critical periods, innate releasers, storage and retrieval mechanisms, schemata, and the like. Some behavior analysts did entertain one or more of those constructs enough to be no longer behavioral; others were simply entertained by those constructs. The most fruitful task, however, is to recognize that each of those labels (and many others like them) often represents some behavioral reality not yet analyzed as such. The point is that these behavioral realities are not likely to be analyzed as such within their parent disciplines, and thus never will become truly applicable there, yet might well be analyzed behavior-analytically, perhaps with great profit to us and those disciplines, and thus to our roles within those disciplines.

Doing so will not jeopardize our ability to discriminate a behavioral discipline from a nonbehavioral discipline: The various professional behavior patterns that constitute a behavioral discipline, thoroughly described and analyzed by Zuriff (1985), can always be discriminated from the considerably more various patterns that constitute nonbehavioral disciplines, even if no one were any longer to display those behavior patterns. (In other words, Zuriff's analysis is essentially philosophical rather than anthropological.) However, it seems clear that behaviorism will be a small-minority approach, at least for the foreseeable future of this culture. Indeed, behavioral textbooks explaining the Premack principle might include in their lists of cultural reinforcers access to the use and consumption of inner, mentalistic explanations for behavior. Perhaps behavior-analytic language is the key to that. The past 20 years have shown us again and again that our audiences respond very negatively to our systematic explanations of our programs and their underlying assumptions, yet very positively to the total spectacle of our programs—their procedures and their results—as long as they are left "unexplained" by us.

Hineline (1980) has begun the analysis of how our systematic language affects our audiences, and how they use their own unsystematic language to explain behavior. Sometimes, for example, certain contexts actually do evoke attributions of behavior to environmental causes, yet even that kind of attribution and its contextual control can themselves be attributed to internal "personality" causes, and in a language culture like ours, they usually are (see Hineline, 1980, p. 84). Perhaps applied behavior analysis should consider much more carefully and much more explicitly the language options that might maximize its effectiveness in its culture: (a) find ways to teach its culture to talk behavior-analytically (or at least to value behavior-analytic talk); (b) develop nonbehavior-analytic talk for public display, and see if that talk will prove as useful for research and analysis as present behavior-analytic talk, or whether two languages must be maintained; or (c) let it be (we represent approximately 2% of American psychology, and we are currently stable at that level).

Some of the success of applied behavior analysis has led to its trial in office-practice contexts. In those contexts, the direct observation of behavior often seems impractical, and practitioners resort to more suspect forms of observation, for example, self-reports or ratings by participant-observers, both often in the form of answers to questionnaires, inventories, checklists, interviews, focused diaries, and the like. With such measures, it is considered safer to use many of them at the same time (see *Behavioral Assessment,* 1979–). The thesis that one behavior can be a measure of another behavior seems behavioral on its face; on analysis, it seems behavioral but extraordinarily risky, depending heavily on the choice of the "other" behavior.

Twenty years of practice have given applied behavior analysis a nearly standard measurement method: the direct observation and recording of a subject's target behaviors by an observer under the stimulus control of a written behavior code. Obviously, that is the measurement of some behavior of one person by some other behavior of another person. The strength of this particular method is the modifiability of the observer's behavior by careful, direct training, and the accessibility of the observer's behavior to direct and frequent reliability assessments. In particular, when those reliability assessments pair the observer with the code-writer, they accomplish the essential validity of any observation-based behavioral analysis: They allow the empirical revision of the code and thus of the stimulus control that it exerts over the observer's observing and recording behavior, until it satisfies the code-writer. That revision is accomplished by rewriting the code and retraining the observer's response to it until the observer's recordings of target behavior agree closely with those of the code-writer observing the same sample of the subject's behavior. Thus, the code-writer *controls* the observing and recording behavior of the observer, and in principle can assess and refine that control as often as the problem may require. In that the code-writer is (or ought to be) the person who finds the subject's behavior to be a problem (or is the surrogate of that person), then satisfying the code-writer that all and only the correct behaviors are being recorded is the *only* approach to valid measurement that makes complete systematic sense: Valid measurement is measurement of that behavior that has caused the problem-presenter to present it (cf. Baer, 1986). Clearly, this argument does not change if the observer is replaced by a recording instrument. This is a strong argument against the use of standardized codes: It is unlikely that a standardized code written in complaint of someone else's behavior can satisfy the present complainer as well as the code that this complainer would write about this specific complainee.

By contrast, it is risky to assume that the subject's self-report or a participant-observer's rating of the subject's target behavior would show a similar reliability with its direct observation by an observer under the code-writer's control. The observer's behavior can be controlled in a well-understood manner; the subject's self-reports and the participant-observer's ratings usually are uncontrolled by the practitioner-researcher. In principle, the subject's self-reports and the participant-observers' ratings might be controlled in the same way as are a standard observer's observation and recording behaviors, but we know relatively little about doing so, and although we often can maintain nearly exclusive control of the observer's relevant behavior, we rarely can even approach that exclusivity with the subject's or a participant-observer's behavior.

Of course, self-reports and participant-observers' ratings might be studied in their own right as behaviors for analysis, rather than as substitutes for the direct observation of the target behavior. Their analysis would almost certainly yield interesting knowledge of the large world of verbal behavior and the small world of professional ritual, but apart from that, it would not often seem to have applied significance, other than to document the already strongly suspected invalidity of such behaviors as substitutes for the target behavior. However, within that small world of professional ritual, it is worth noting that the use of such measures—often called psychometrics in the social sciences—has a certain social validity, especially for research-grant applications: Some role of conventional psychometrics in a research proposal increases the probability of that proposal being approved and funded when the proposal's reviewers are not behavior-analytic (which is almost always). It is true that any choice of Psychometric_1 versus Psychometric_2 will inevitably attract at least some reviewers' criticisms, but at least it will be criticism within the context of approval for playing the correct game. That might be considered applied significance.

Thus, applied behavior analysis most often still is, and most often always should be, the study of an observer's behavior that has been brought under the tight control of the subject's behavior. Sometimes, that is exactly what is meant by behavioral assessment. More often, it is either the study of how subjects talk about their own behavior or how other people talk about the subject's behavior, a kind of talk that usually is under complex, varied, and largely unknown control, only one component of which *may* be the subject's target behavior (what loosely is called the truth).

Sometimes, though (and increasingly in the past two decades), behavioral assessment has used those forms of psychometrics that are best described as *samples* of the target repertoire, notably IQ and achievement tests. The problems with such tests are much the same as with self-reports and participant-observers' ratings: We rarely know if the testing context controls those behaviors differently than they are controlled in everyday life, and we rarely know if those test samples are representative samples of the desired repertoire. The only way to know those facts with any certainty is again to resort to direct observation, but these tests represent (or fail to represent) repertoires that often are too large to allow practical direct observation. Thus they are often used as the only practicable alternative, despite their uncertainties (and sometimes they are used because they still command great social validity in this society).

That tactic is not a novel one in applied behavior analysis: In the analysis of accidents, for example, we can hardly deal with accident behaviors directly, because they are too infrequent, so we change the much more frequent behaviors that we suppose are precursors to accidents—we analyze not accidents, but risk-taking. Similarly, in the analysis of delinquency, we can hardly change delinquent acts directly, again because they are infrequent and also because they are systematically done in relative secrecy, so again we change not them but what we suppose their precursors are in various arenas of social control. If the guesses implicit in those areas of research do not disqualify them as examples of applied behavior analysis, then the analogous guesses implicit in the use of, say, achievement tests need not automatically disqualify them, either.

The applied question most often may be whether the uncertainties inherent in resorting to such measures are preferable to the status quo of knowledge in each problem area, and the answer, like most answers, will probably be under contextual control—sometimes uncertainty is preferable to status quo, sometimes it isn't.

Thus the term "behavioral assessment," a new category event of the past two decades, sometimes describes very pragmatic tactics and sometimes only the least valid measurement tactics of the very old pseudobehavioral disciplines against which behavior analysis rebelled. Clearly, its tactics can include exceptionally elegant and sophisticated concepts, techniques, and measures of reliability (see Cronbach, Glaser, Nanda, & Rajaratnam, 1972), which sometimes are applicable to direct observation (Hartmann, 1977); but when those tactics measure what we wish to analyze is problematic in both analytic and pragmatic ways. Ultimately, knowing when they do and when they do not will require very difficult studies based on direct observation.

Analytic and Conceptual

Twenty years ago, *analytic* meant a convincing experimental design, and *conceptual* meant relevance to a comprehensive theory about behavior. The two topics could be and often were discussed separately. Since then, it has become increasingly aversive to maintain that separation. Now, applied behavior analysis is more often considered an analytic discipline only when it demonstrates convincingly how to make specified behavior changes *and* when its behavior-change methods make systematic, conceptual sense. In the past 20 years, we have sometimes demonstrated convincingly that we had changed behavior as specified, but by methods that did not make systematic, conceptual sense—it was not clear *why* those methods had worked. Such cases let us see that we were sometimes convincingly applied and behavioral, yet even so, not sufficiently analytic. Similarly, we have sometimes changed behavior without even a convincing demonstration of how we did that, and so did not know if our methods made systematic, conceptual sense because we did not know clearly what the responsible methods were; those cases let us see how not to be a discipline, let alone an applied, behavioral, or analytic one.

Now, the theory that defines systematic, conceptual sense for us is pushed not only to be about behavior, but also about the behavior of changing behavior: More often now, we can see ourselves as the subjects of someone else, not just as Experimenter (recall the discussion of countercontrol under *Applied*). This fits well with the steadily emerging contextualism apparent in unapplied behavior analysis. A proper appreciation of context always implies that we are not merely studying or managing it, but also are part of it and therefore are being managed by it, even down to our studying and managing of it.

The emerging appreciation of context as the *setting events* that had better be understood and managed in truly effective application flows easily from Kantor's field approach to the study of behavior (Morris, 1982). But it also flows just as easily from our recently expanding knowledge and management of stimulus control and conditional stimulus control (see Sidman, 1986; and the special-issue Volume 6 of *Analysis and Intervention in Developmental Disabilities,* 1986). That development suggests strongly that we will rarely find an instance of stimulus control not modified drastically by some (and perhaps many) conditional stimulus controls. The relevance of that thesis to application is urgent: It begins the analysis of the generality of any intervention's effectiveness, in that it urges us to seek the contextual conditions under which the intervention has maximal and minimal effectiveness.

Thus, the first applied lesson of contextualism is that there will always be such conditions; the second is that many of them must be clarified as stimulus and response events, because that is rarely self-evident (cf. Wahler and Fox's [1982] discussion of "insularity" as a limiting condition in parent training); the third, most difficult yet most pragmatic, is that clarifying contextual controls is not enough: If we want widely effective interventions, we will have to manage these contextual controls; rather than stopping with the assessment of their roles as limiting factors, we will have to learn how to program around them or program them away.

Contextualism also implies a certain class of experimental designs. The simplest contextual statements are of the form, Behavior B is controlled differently by Variable V in Context 1 than in Context 2. To see that reliably, we need experimental control of at least two levels of Variable V, say V1 and V2; and we need experimental control of at least two contexts of interest, say Context X and Context Y. Given that, we need to see how

Behavior B relates to V1 and V2 in Context X, and we need to see if that control is reliable. Then we need to see how Behavior B relates to V1 and V2 in Context Y, and we need to see if that control is reliable. Finally, we need to see both of those relationships (how B relates to V1 and V2 in Context X, and how B relates to V1 and V2 in Context Y) again and again, so that we see whether the difference that Contexts X and Y make in how V1 and V2 control B is a reliable difference. The simplest reversal designs would look something like the following two, where CX and CY are Contexts X and Y (see diagram below). Both of these are minimal designs for the problem, yet each contains 16 conditions in which to examine the ongoing baseline of the behavior under study. The pace of the design had better be a rather fast one, suggesting that variant of the reversal design often called the multielement design (e.g., Ulman & Sulzer-Azaroff, 1975). Designs like these can be found in the literature of the field, but not often. To the extent that applied behavior analysis will analyze rather than assess the generality of its interventions, these designs and others capable of the same kind of demonstration will prove essential.

The last 20 years have seen considerable development of research designs. At the outset, it was sufficient to label only the reversal and multiple baseline designs: the examination of one behavior in repeated experimental conditions, and the examination of many behaviors, sometimes with some in one experimental condition while others are in a different experimental condition. These are the two fundamental analysis strategies, of course; their logic is seen in the multiple, mixed, and concurrent schedules that had so often served as experimental designs in TEAB. But in that world, schedules had names, yet designs did not: Researchers simply arranged those conditions (often, schedules) necessary to answer their experimental questions, refined the conditions as analytically as their knowledge of potential important confounding variables allowed, and did all that as often as conviction required. The value of their designs lay not in any category names that might be imposed on them but in the relation between the conditions that they had arranged and the question proposed.

Now, we have named so many designs that textbooks devoted to their taxonomy and their "rules" have emerged. The strategy underlying that development was probably like the one underlying the seven self-conscious guides to behavior analytic conduct posed in 1968 (applied, behavioral, analytic, etc.): In application, good design would often prove difficult to accomplish or maintain, and graduate training in application might not often plumb the depths of the topic; codification might help overcome those difficulties. The questions now are whether in fact the codification of research design into types and rules did help that purpose; if so, to what extent; and finally, whether that extent is worth the cost. The cost may be primarily that applied researchers increasingly transform questions to fit the known designs and their rules, rather than constructing a design that answers the original question. It might prove valuable to the field to recall its original designs and their logic—a good design is one that answers the question convincingly, and as such needs to be constructed in reaction to the question and then tested through argument in that context (sometimes called "thinking through"), rather than imitated from a textbook. For example, one convention paper evaluated a program training youths to fill out employment applications more effectively. The researchers asked several employers to read a sequence of applications, each written by

CX	CY	CX	CY
V1 V2 V1 V2	V1 V2 V1 V2	V1 V2 V1 V2	V1 V2 V1 V2

VI	V2	V1	V2
CX CY CX CY	CX CY CX CY	CX CY CX CY	CX CY CX CY

a different trainee, beginning with some written before training and ending with some written after training; the change from pre- to posttraining applications occurred at different points in each employer's sequence, in an apparent multiple baseline design across employers. The design was such that all applications, pre- and posttraining alike, were read. Almost without exception, the employers said "No" to trainee applications written before training and "Yes" to trainee applications written after training. This design is alluded to in an article by Mathews and Fawcett (1984), but is not described there in detail because of editorial insistence. Many in the convention audience, perhaps like the editor, ignored the fact that this design showed clearly that the training program was exceptionally effective, and argued instead that it was not a "proper" multiple baseline design. Perhaps the important point is that convincing designs should be more important than "proper" designs.

Technological

Twenty years ago, it was urgent to recommend that a new field aspiring to both effective application and stature as a science be both procedural and explicit about it. The point was to avoid the situation of so many clinical, management, and administrative disciplines in which, once discussions of theory and goals had ended, the procedures to be applied were specified no better than "work with." For the most part, that has happened; journal articles and textbooks do offer a complete list of their operative procedures, such that a reader has a fair chance of replicating the application with the same results. Indeed, collections of procedures have begun to emerge, such that readers now may choose among alternative procedures aimed at the same goal.

Still, three points deserve comment:

1. Some procedures, such as praise or incidental teaching, often are varied in what the researcher considers to be a desirably natural manner from occasion to occasion. Those topographies and their sequences rarely are specified; to do so in advance might often be considered unnatural, and to do so retrospectively (e.g., from a videotape) would be expensive for publishers and boring for readers. The underlying assumption is of course that those variations make no difference to the outcome. That assumption is rarely if ever tested empirically. It would be good for the discipline if a review 20 years from now could state that the assumption had proved correct, or that it had been found incorrect so often that current practice had remedied the problem, despite the expense. (Readers' boredom with such detail would have dissolved in the discovery that these variations could indeed make a difference in outcome.)

2. In application, those procedures carried out by people (which are most of the procedures of applied behavior analysis) usually are observed and recorded, just as are the subject's behaviors. This documents the extent to which the specified procedures are performed, and also describes any unspecified procedures that may occur. The process is probably reactive in many applications, creating greater adherence to specified procedures than might be secured otherwise. But these data are rarely presented outside of the group conducting the application, again probably because of publishers' expense and readers' presumed boredom: When such data show that the specified procedures are being carried out well enough, there is no problem; and when they show the opposite, the application usually stops until better adherence to procedure is obtained, whereupon there is again no problem. This argument is probably defensible on a cost-benefit basis, but it would be better for the discipline if its review 20 years from now could state that the relevant debate had occurred publicly. That debate is essentially a matter for journal and textbook editors and reviewers: They call for such data or fail to; they publish such data when supplied or recommend against doing so. Thus, they might well use one of their future journal symposia to consider this issue, which is mainly a matter of journal policy.

3. Dissemination is a practice much older than applied behavior analysis, but, in the realm of behavior, it is usually much less technological than applied behavior analysis. Even so, its literature and its practitioners debate (without resolution) an es-

sentially technological issue: When a program is disseminated, should its disseminators require that its procedures be followed faithfully, no matter where or when the program is used? Or should its users be allowed, and even encouraged, to modify those procedures to fit their local situations and contingencies? (We might first ask, functionally, when we have that choice. That is, when is the control requisite to maintain fidelity to original procedures available to us, and when not?) Fidelity to original procedures is recommended because those procedures have been studied and are known to be effective; their variations and alternatives usually have not been studied, so nothing can be said about their effectiveness. On the other hand, flexibility in application is recommended on the premise that the entire program will become aversive to people who cannot modify it to suit their situation and their contingencies, and if a program is not used, it cannot be effective.

These are both technological arguments; interestingly, contextualism, experience, and common sense seem to agree that each is likely to be correct in certain contexts but not in others. The empirical investigation of those controlling contexts obviously is crucial to future large-scale dissemination (which is certainly the essence of *applied*), as is the investigation of when we even have that choice. That research has largely not been done; presumably, now that a discipline as technological as applied behavior analysis has entered the domain of dissemination, it is more likely to be done, albeit expensively. The appropriate strategy was recommended by Sidman (1960) almost 30 years ago, in a different but relevant context: One criterion of important science is to explore the controlling conditions of any behavioral phenomenon. What is the range of variation of a program's procedures that still allows sufficient effectiveness? If it is large enough, flexible application can be encouraged, and the program's survival in diverse settings may well be enhanced. If it is narrow, fidelity will be required, or what survives will not be effective.

It will be interesting to see if a review of the discipline 20 years from now will be able to summarize some facts about those processes, or will instead have to report that applied behavior analysis is still entering its large-scale applications very much at risk for failure.

Capable of Appropriately Generalized Outcomes

Twenty years ago, the ability of the discipline to produce appropriately generalized outcomes was seen as crucial to its survival: An applied discipline that had to make every topographical variant of its desired behavior changes, and had to attach each of them to every appropriate stimulus control, across time, was intrinsically impractical. Today, the problem is still crucial, but now to the maximal effectiveness rather than the survival of the discipline. In the past 20 years, we have changed behavior as specified *and* shown experimental control of its appropriate generalization just often enough to make clear that the discipline is capable of such outcomes. What remains is the much more reassuring (and much larger) task of exploring the conditions that control appropriate generalization (i.e., appropriate stimulus control).

Fortunately, the problem is usually seen now as one that probably can be solved by suitable programming, rather than by good luck; thus, a good deal of research has systematically examined ways to teach from the outset so that appropriately generalized outcomes are established. (Yet a remarkable number of studies do not compare their generalization-facilitative teaching to any alternative teaching of the same target behavior that does not facilitate its generalization, and so we actually learn nothing about the problem from such studies.) The problem is far from solved; we still have no system for matching the most suitable generalization-promotion method to the behavior change at hand, and no certainty that there is such a system to be found. Our categorizations of generalization-promotion techniques are clearly nonanalytic; they have been proposed (see Stokes & Baer, 1977) in the same way that current dimensions (applied, behavioral, analytic, etc.) have been proposed—on the assumption that codification will evoke more of the necessary professional behavior, especially research (Baer, 1982). That assumption probably cannot be tested empirically: We can hardly conduct an experiment that compares our discipline's progress toward thorough control of generalization, with and without such codifications. Thus, there remains the obligation of continuing debate (see Johnston, 1979).

Effective

The hallmark of any applied discipline ought to be effectiveness; the case is no different for applied behavior analysis. However, in the realm of behavior change, the hallmark of effectiveness can be subtle: Sometimes, it seems to be simply the degree to which the target behavior has been changed; much more often, it is the degree to which something other than the target behavior has been changed, and that something other almost invariably is someone's countercontrol against the original behavior (see the earlier discussion of *Applied*). Thus, for example, if we look closely, we may find that in some cases, changing a student's grades from Fs to Cs satisfies the student, the student's family, and that segment of their society that will eventually read those grades and react to them—if the grades are Fs, these agents will see that as a problem; if the grades are Cs, they will not. But in some other cases, we may find that a student's grades must be changed from Bs to As before that student, that student's family, and that segment of their society that will eventually read those grades and react to them will stop reacting to them as a problem. The marker variable distinguishing these two cases may often seem to be social class, but that is neither analytic (see Baer, 1984, pp. 547–551) nor relevant to the point, which is that changing grades is not effective per se; stopping and avoiding the relevant references to these grades as a problem is the true criterion of our intervention's effectiveness.

Almost every successful study of behavior change ought to routinely present two outcomes—a measure of the changed target behaviors, of course, and a measure of the problem displays and explanations that have stopped or diminished in consequence. Yet very few studies do that. Perhaps their researchers assume that *they* are the only relevant problem-detectors or problem-detector surrogates. Indeed, that may sometimes be true, but it had better be both defensible and explicitly defended or it becomes arrogance (which may not further the social status of the discipline if it is widely noticed as such). On the other hand, the absence of that second measure may represent a crucial weakness in our current effectiveness. We may have taught many social skills without examining whether they actually furthered the subject's social life; many courtesy skills without examining whether anyone actually noticed or cared; many safety skills without examining whether the subject was actually safer thereafter; many language skills without measuring whether the subject actually used them to interact differently than before; many on-task skills without measuring the actual value of those tasks; and, in general, many survival skills without examining the subject's actual subsequent survival. Some of those measures will be controversial to define and expensive to collect, of course; but it may be true that the discipline has developed to the point at which they become crucial. (Children usually become more expensive as they grow.)

Perhaps this practice will become more widespread in the discipline as the calculation of cost–benefit ratios increases from its present near-zero rate—if we take the "benefit" side of the ratio seriously, rather than assume that the behavior change itself is the benefit. Cost–benefit ratios, on the face of it, are the essence of effectiveness, and ought to be routine in any applied discipline (e.g., Hill et al., 1987). They have proven problematic in this one, perhaps partly because the discipline is still so much in its research-trials phase, partly because behavioral benefits are not as clearly defined as most business benefits, and partly because the concepts and techniques of cost–benefit calculation are not yet clearly established themselves.

Fortunately, at least one second measure of effectiveness is beginning to become routine: social validity (Kazdin, 1977; Wolf, 1978), which is the extent to which all the consumers of an intervention like it (i.e., like its goals, targets, effects, procedures, and personnel). The point of social-validity measures is to predict (and thus avoid) rejection of an intervention, especially when it is disseminated (which, because of its large scale, may prove less tolerable to consumers than the initial small-scale research trials). If an intervention is socially invalid, it can hardly be effective, even if it changes its target behaviors thoroughly and with an otherwise excellent cost–benefit ratio; social validity is not sufficient for effectiveness but is necessary to effectiveness.

Unfortunately, social validity is sometimes assessed at present in very rudimentary ways that may too often find social validity where it does not actually operate. Perhaps the problem is that researchers are in the context of hoping for social validity, which is subtly different from and much more dangerous than the context of searching for any sources of social invalidity. In that the discipline is now moving into large-scale dissemination, valid social-validity assessments will soon become crucial to survival; yet this aspect of our measurement technique has seen very little inquiry and development.

Perhaps a review 20 years from now will report a great deal of progress in that dimension of effectiveness. If so, the problem will not have proved to be simple. For example, some measures of social validity are deliberately and pragmatically biased toward positive results, not to deceive their users but to prevent alarm in their consumers (e.g., governing boards) while at the same time alerting their users (the researcher-appliers) to detect and remedy the problems that must underlie scores that usually are 7 but now are 5 on a 7-point scale. Furthermore, it is entirely possible that even quite invalid queries into social validity are better than no queries at all: Giving consumers any opportunity to express complaints and discontents that otherwise would go unnoticed may save at least some programs from fatal backlashes, at least if the offended consumer is moved enough by simply the existence of the otherwise inadequate social-validity assessment form to write in its margins or talk to the appliers.

Perhaps equally significant is the recent development of assessment techniques that inquire about consumers' goals before the program is designed (Fawcett, Seekins, Whang, Muiu, & Suarez de Balcazar, 1982; Schriner & Fawcett, in press), so that the program has a chance to achieve all of those goals, thereby going far to guarantee validly high social validity when that dimension is eventually assessed. This technology, if pursued intensively enough, may become part of the pragmatic analysis of social validity, especially because it finds common themes emerging from its inquiries about the goals of different sets of consumers in what seem to be quite different problem situations (cf. Seekins, Mathews, Fawcett, & Jones, in press); thus the analysis of its validity may be one of the best priority targets for future research.

Perhaps the clearest measure of our discipline's effectiveness is the increasing number of ineffective applications that we have tried in recent years. By good judgment or good luck, we began with dramatic, troublesome, yet nevertheless crucially delimited cases, and our effectiveness with them strongly reinforced our disciplinary behaviors. Had it been otherwise, we might not be the recognized applied discipline that we are today. But having done that, we are of course moving on to a different class of problems, partly because those problems are there, partly because they are exceptionally important, and partly because we are still a research-based applied discipline, and because research ought not to be too repetitive, then, to the extent that we have done (or at least sampled) everything else, these problems are what is left to do.

But the problems of today are not as delimited as those of our beginnings. They are called lifestyles in recognition of their systemic nature. The behavior classes called delinquency, substance abuse, safety, exercise, and diet, for example, represent complex classes of topographies serving complex functions involving many agents of reinforcement/punishment and stimulus control, all of whom interact to constitute and maintain the system as such. Thus, entry at just one point of such systems is likely to yield only limited, short-term behavior changes before the inevitable countercontrol restores the prior status of the system, with us either frozen out or co-opted ineffectively within (see Wolf, Braukmann, & Ramp, 1987). The first remedy is recognition: The concept of systems analysis is now an important component of our effectiveness, and research that will show us how to do that better will prove exceptionally useful. The second remedy, following whatever analysis the first currently allows, is system-wide intervention: Thus, for example, obese children are dealt with not as simple therapist–client interactions, but within their life systems—at least within their families (Brownell, Kelman, & Stunkard, 1983) and better yet, within their families and their school systems (Brownell & Kaye, 1982). The third remedy may be the discrimination of those problems in which a single, short-duration intervention can be effective from those invariably systemic problems in which chronic presence will be required to maintain the effective intervention. Just as medicine recognizes that appendicitis needs only one intervention but that diabetes needs life-long treatment and educates its consumers to the inevitability of that and its costs, applied behavior analysis had better begin its validation and use of the same two categories.

Perhaps the most important remedy of all, however, will be to establish the proper context in which to respond to failures. The last 20 years have produced an increasing rate of them; the next 20 almost surely will see that rate continue and, very likely, increase even more. That fact and that probability have already been interpreted as an inadequacy of behavior-analytic principles. For example, Reppucci and Saunders (1974) responded to one of their failures in a delinquency institution with a broadly generalized principle:

> Finally, there is an issue the resolution of which will have enormous consequences for behavior modification as we know and apply it today. The issue inheres in the fact [sic] that the principles of behavior modification are insufficient and often inappropriate for understanding natural settings—their structure, goals, tradition, and intersetting linkages. (p. 569)

Its publication in the *American Psychologist* of course presented this new "fact" to potentially every APA member (most of whom would not know that it is the only kind of evaluation of behavior modification that their association's journal ever prints, and who might not ask how a "fact" like that can be established through one failure to install and maintain a program in a single institution).

It is worth asking first if technological failure is the same as theoretical failure. Quite likely, technological failure is an expected and indeed important event in the progress of *any* applied field, even those whose underlying theory is thoroughly valid. Thus, the step from the physics laboratory to engineering has been, and will continue to be, marked by occasional jammed elevators, fallen bridges, crashed airplanes, and exploded space shuttles. The engineers know that; they abandon only their designs, not their theories, with each such event. Petroski (1985), for example, sums up their history as follows:

> I believe that the concept of failure—mechanical and structural failure in the context of this discusson—is central to understanding engineering, for engineering design has as its first and foremost objective the obviation of failure. Thus the colossal disasters that do occur are ultimately failures of design, but the lessons learned from those disasters can do more to advance engineering knowledge than all the successful machines and structures in the world. Indeed, failures appear to be inevitable in the wake of prolonged success, which encourages lower margins of safety. Failures in turn lead to greater safety margins and, hence, new periods of success. To understand what engineering is and what engineers do is to understand how failures can happen and how they contribute more than successes to advance technology. (p. xii)

The same point is inherent in an understanding of medical progress—every death is, in a sense, a failure in our current designs for health maintenance, just as every fallen bridge is a failure in our current designs for balancing load against strength.

Applied behavior analysis must deal with phenomena at least as complex as loaded bridges and stressed physiologies, and perhaps, considering the domains of variables relevant to behavior, more complex. Then it will proceed at first with as many, or more, flawed designs as those fields have; but it will profit from those failures, as they have, and it will require time and repetition to do so, as they have.

How do we know that any given failure reflects bad design rather than inadequate principle? We never know that; but we can search for bad design immediately after every failure, and if we find it, that will give us something to try in the next application much more readily than will despair over our principles. For example, Reppucci and Saunders played the role only of outside consultants in their failure. Indeed, it is the *principles* of behavior analysis (as well as considerable experience) that suggest little potential for changing the behavior of overworked, underinterested staff and administrators with the few contingencies usually available to consultants (unless a severe crisis is ongoing). Liberman (1980), in response to a number of similar failures, has suggested not a new principle but merely a stronger design—that some of us combine research with administration:

> We cannot count on administrators' need for accountability and program evaluation to serve as "coattails" for our behavioral programs. . . . If we want our work to live beyond a library bookshelf, we will have to jump into the political mainstream and get our feet wet as administrator-researchers. (pp. 370–371)

If we survey those behavioral programs that have maintained themselves over impressive spans of time, we as often find the pattern Liberman recommends as we find impressive spans of time: Liberman himself at the Oxnard Mental Health Center, McClannahan and Krantz at the Princeton Child Development Institute, Cataldo at the Johns Hopkins' Kennedy Institute, and Christian at the May Institute, for examples. These cases are not proofs of anything, nor intended to be; they are simply worth considering as designs that might attract a proof and might yield a profit for our discipline if they did.

The Teaching-Family model is another example of a somewhat different and apparently durable design, one as old as this journal. It created 12 regional training centers to mediate 215 replications of the original Achievement Place delinquency program, and wrote not journal articles but plain-English training manuals for their use. The originators of that program also met Liberman's design prescription; they added to their research role those of administering the component programs and fighting their political battles, and of securing consistent enough grant support for the necessary 10 years of trial-and-failure-and-next-trial-and-success research necessary to understand and implement the essential quality control, staff training, and other support systems required for survival and dissemination. Indeed, even 20 years have not seen the completion of that research and development program, but its failures are now rare, despite greatly expanded opportunities (Wolf et al., 1987).

The point is that failures teach; the Teaching-Family model grew out of the Teaching-Failure model. Surely our journals should begin to publish not only our field's successes but also those of its failures done well enough to let us see the possibility of better designs than theirs.

In summary, effectiveness for the future will probably be built primarily on system-wide interventions and high-quality failures, as we continue to bring theory to the point of designs that solve problems. But it should be current theory that is built on, not some replacement of it—current theory has worked far too well to be abandoned in the face of what are more parsimoniously seen as technological rather than theoretical failures. Clearly, increasing our effectiveness will not be easy, and it will not happen quickly. We should expect a long period of difficult, expensive, repetitive, and sometimes ineffective research into these applications, and we should enter that research with our best social skills, because we shall require the cooperation of unusually many people, often in unusually exposed positions. However, even with relatively little reaction-to-failure work behind us, it seems clear that we can do it.

It seems clear that we can do what remains to be done. That we can is probably our most fundamental, most important, and most enduring dimension; that we will is simply logical.

REFERENCES

Analysis and Intervention in Developmental Disabilities. (1986). Special issue, **6.**

Baer, D. M. (1981). A flight of behavior analysis. *The Behavior Analyst,* **4,** 85–91.

Baer, D. M. (1982). The role of current pragmatics in the future analysis of generalization technology. In R. B. Stuart (Ed.), *Adherance, compliance, and generalization in behavioral medicine.* New York: Brunner/Mazel.

Baer, D. M. (1984). Future directions? Or, is it useful to ask, "Where did we go wrong?" before we go? In R. A. Polster & R. F. Dangel (Eds.), *Behavioral parent training: Where it came from and where it's at.* New York: Guilford Press.

Baer, D. M. (1986). In application, frequency is not the only estimate of the probability of behavior units. In M. D. Zeiler & T. Thompson (Eds.), *Analysis and integration of behavioral units* (pp. 117–136). Hillsdale, NJ: Lawrence Erlbaum Associates.

Baer, D. M., Wolf, M. M., & Risley, T. R. (1968). Some current dimensions of applied behavior analysis. *Journal of Applied Behavior Analysis,* 1968, **1,** 91–97.

Behavioral Assessment. (1979–). New York: Pergamon Press.

Brownell, K. D., & Kaye, F. S. (1982). A school-based behavior modification, nutrition education, and physical activity program for obese children. American Journal of Clinical Nutrition, **35,** 277–283.

Brownell, K. D., Kelman, J. H., & Stunkard, A. J. (1983). Treatment of obese children with and without their mothers. Changes in weight and blood pressure. *Pediatrics,* **71,** 515–523.

Cronbach, L. J., Glaser, G. C., Nanda, H., & Rajaratnam, N. (1972). *The dependability of behavioral measurements: Theory of generalizability for scores and profiles.* New York: Wiley.

Deitz, S. M. (1978). Current status of applied behavior analysis: Science vs. technology. *American Psychologist,* **33,** 805–814.

Fawcett, S. B., Seekins, T., Whang, P. L., Muiu, C., & Suarez de Balcazar, Y. (1982). Involving consumers in decision-making. *Social Policy,* **13,** 36–41.

Hartmann, D. P. (1977). Considerations in the choice of interobserver reliability estimates. *Journal of Applied Behavior Analysis,* **10,** 103–116.

Hill, M. L., Banks, P. D., Handrich, R. R., Wehman, P. H., Hill, J. W., & Shafer, M. S. (1987). Benefit-cost analysis of supported competitive employment for persons with mental retardation. *Research in Developmental Disabilities,* **8,** 71–89.

Hineline, P. N. (1980). The language of behavior analysis: Its community, its functions, and its limitations. *Behaviorism,* **8,** 67–86.

Johnston, J. M. (1979). On the relation between generalization and generality. *The Behavior Analyst,* **2,** 1–6.

Kazdin, A. E. (1977). Assessing the clinical or applied importance of behavior change through social validation. *Behavior Modification,* **1,** 427–452.

Kuhn, T. S. (1970). *The structure of scientific revolutions* (2nd Ed.). Chicago: University of Chicago Press.

Liberman, R. P. (1980). Review of: *Psychosocial treatment for chronic mental patients* by Gordon L. Paul and Robert J. Lentz. *Journal of Applied Behavior Analysis,* **13,** 367–371.

Mathews, R. M., & Fawcett, S. B. (1984). Building the capacities of job candidates through behavioral instruction. *Journal of Community Psychology,* **12,** 123–129.

Michael, J. (1980). Flight from behavior analysis. *The Behavior Analyst,* **3,** 1–22.

Morris, E. K. (1982). Some relationships between interbehavioral psychology and radical behaviorism. *Behaviorism,* **10,** 187–216.

Petroski, H. (1985). *To engineer is human: The role of failure in successful design.* New York: Saint Martin's Press.

Pierce, W. D., & Epling, W. F. (1980). What happened to analysis in applied behavior analysis? *The Behavior Analyst,* **3,** 1–9.

Powell, J. (1984). On the misrepresentation of behavioral realities by a widely practiced direct observation procedure: Partial interval (one-zero) sampling. *Behavioral Assessment,* **6,** 209–219.

Reppucci, N. D., & Saunders, J. T. (1974). Social psychology of behavior modification. *American Psychologist,* **29,** 649–660.

Schriner, K. F., & Fawcett, S. B. (in press). Development and validation of a community-concerns report method. *Journal of Community Psychology.*

Seekins, T., Mathews, R. M., Fawcett, S. B., & Jones, M. L. (in press). A market-oriented strategy for applied research in independent living. *Journal of Rehabilitation.*

Sidman, M. (1960). *Tactics of scientific research.* New York: Basic Books.

Sidman, M. (1986). Functional analysis of emergent verbal classes. In T. Thompson & M. D. Zeiler (Eds.), *Analysis and integration of behavioral units.* Hillsdale, NJ: Lawrence Erlbaum Associates.

Stokes, T. F., & Baer, D. M. (1977). An implicit technology of generalization. *Journal of Applied Behavior Analysis,* **10,** 349–367.

Ulman, J. D., & Sulzer-Azaroff, B. (1975). Multielement baseline design in educational research. In E. Ramp & G. Semb (Eds.), *Behavior analysis: Areas of research and application.* Englewood Clifs, NJ: Prentice-Hall.

Wahler, R. G., & Fox, J. J. (1982). Response structure in deviant parent-child relationships: Implications for family therapy. In D. J. Bernstein (Ed.), *Response struc-*

ture and organization: The 1981 Nebraska symposium on motivation. Lincoln, NE: University of Nebraska Press.

Wolf, M. M. (1978). Social validity: The case for subjective measurement, or how behavior analysis is finding its heart. *Journal of Applied Behavior Analysis,* **11,** 203–214.

Wolf, M. M., Braukmann, C. J., & Ramp, K. A. (1987). Serious delinquent behavior as part of a significantly handicapping condition: Cures and supportive environments. *Journal of Applied Behavior Analysis,* **20,** 347–359.

Zuriff, G. E. (1985). *Behaviorism: A conceptual reconstruction.* New York: Columbia University Press.

Received May 21, 1987
Revision received July 29, 1987
Final acceptance September 2, 1987
Action Editor, Jon S. Bailey

JOURNAL OF APPLIED BEHAVIOR ANALYSIS 1980, 13, 275-285 NUMBER 2 (SUMMER 1980)

THE TECHNICAL DRIFT OF APPLIED BEHAVIOR ANALYSIS

STEVEN C. HAYES, ARNOLD RINCOVER, AND JAY V. SOLNICK

UNIVERSITY OF NORTH CAROLINA AT GREENSBORO
AND UNIVERSITY OF KANSAS

Four dimensions (applied, analytic, general, conceptual) were selected from Baer, Wolf, and Risley's (1968) seminal article on the nature of applied behavior analysis and were monitored throughout the first 10 volumes of the *Journal of Applied Behavior Analysis*. Each of the experimental articles in Volumes 1 through 6 and the first half of Volumes 7 through 10 was rated on each of these dimensions. The trends showed that applied behavior analysis is becoming a more purely technical effort, with less interest in conceptual questions. We are using simpler experimental designs and are conducting fewer analogue studies. Although concern for maintenance is increasing, other forms of generality are being measured or analyzed less often. These trends are discussed in terms of a technical drift in applied behavior analysis.

DESCRIPTORS: characteristics and trends in applied behavior analysis, use of experimental designs, generalization, behavioral principles, analogue studies

A decade ago, the young discipline of applied behavior analysis emerged as a fully recognized subarea of behavioral science with the first publication of the *Journal of Applied Behavior Analysis*. In the inaugural issue, some of the distinctive features of the field were described by Baer, Wolf, and Risley (1968) in a seminal article entitled "Some Current Dimensions of Applied Behavior Analysis." This paper became perhaps the most highly referenced and reprinted article ever published in *JABA* and each of its three authors went on to become an editor of the journal, collectively guiding the first seven volumes. In that paper the methodology, strategy, language, settings, and problems of concern for applied behavior analysis were described. With the first 10 volumes of *JABA* now published it might be profitable to reexamine the dimensions of applied behavior analysis described by Baer et al. and to trace their development over the first decade. The purpose of such an enterprise is not just historical; delineating the trends of *JABA* over the last 10 years may help us to identify future directions of the field, and may serve as a cue for evaluating, promoting, or reshaping certain of these directions.

THE DIMENSIONS

Baer et al. pointed to seven main characteristics of applied behavior analysis research. They will be considered in turn with a description of each dimension and a rationale for its selection or exclusion from further study.

The first characteristic of applied behavior analysis research is that it should be *applied*. According to Baer et al. (1968, p. 92) applied behavior analysis should be concerned with socially significant behavior change, in problem settings, with the organisms displaying the problem behavior. Recently, however, this definition of applied, and the possible value of "applicable" and nonapplied research, have been the subject of some controversy in the field (e.g., Birnbrauer, 1979). Therefore, it seemed to us both interesting and important to document the trends in this area.

Applied behavior analysis research must also be *analytic:* There must be a demonstration of experimental control. Baer et al. (1968) de-

Reprint requests should be sent to Steven C. Hayes, Department of Psychology, University of North Carolina at Greensboro, Greensboro, North Carolina 27412. Preparation of this article was supported in part by Grant No. G007802084 from the U.S. Office of Education.

scribed several time series designs that might be used for such analysis. "Reliability analyses" are designs that ask whether or not a certain procedure is responsible for corresponding behavioral change. Component and parametric analyses respectively assess which elements of the procedure produce the change, and the relationship between the value of the independent variable and the resultant change. Interestingly, Baer et al. apparently expected a trend in *JABA* with regard to this dimension: "At this stage in the development of applied behavior analysis, primary concern is usually with reliability, rather than with parametric analysis or component analysis" (Baer et al., 1968, p. 95), perhaps implying that component and parametric analyses would increase as the field progressed. This dimension was included for further study in order that any such trends might be uncovered.

Baer et al. argued that applied behavior analysis should be *conceptual.* Authors should show how their procedures relate to basic principles of behavior: "The field of applied behavior analysis will probably advance best if the published descriptions of its procedures are not only precise technologically but also strive for relevance to principle. . . . This can have the effect of making a body of technology into a discipline rather than a collection of tricks. Collections of tricks historically have been difficult to expand systematically, and when they were extensive, difficult to learn and teach" (Baer et al., 1968, p. 96). Many authors, formally and in passing, have speculated about recent trends in *JABA* in regard to this dimension, and few issues have given rise to more spirited discussion (e.g., Azrin, 1977; Birnbrauer, 1979; Deitz, 1978; Hayes, 1978).

Finally, applied behavior analytic research must be concerned with the *generality* of behavioral change. Generality is assessed by examining the maintenance of behavior change over time, its generality across different settings or stimulus conditions, the degree to which it spreads to related behaviors, and the degree to which it occurs across individuals. This dimension has received considerable conceptual and experimental attention in recent years and is, in many quarters, viewed as the foremost problem of applied behavior analysis. It seems important to assess whether or not *JABA* has been responsive to this dimension.

The remaining three dimensions described by Baer et al. will not be assessed here either because their importance and use seem to be clear and apparent or because we could not reliably measure the dimension. There is relatively little disagreement about the *behavioral* dimension, that behaviors should be precisely and reliably measured. Kazdin (1975) reported that 79% of *JABA* articles published in Volumes 1-9 met appropriate standards of intrasubject replication and assessment of reliability. That applied behavior analysis must be *technological,* with procedures sufficiently detailed to allow replication, has also been one of the major strengths of *JABA* of has not been subject to much controversy.

Data for the final dimension, *effectiveness,* will not be presented because we were not able to measure reliably whether the behavior changes reported in *JABA* studies were large enough and/or of sufficient social significance to be of practical value. Wolf (1978) has recently anticipated our problem of measuring effectiveness with his call for social validation measures. The use of social validation measures in applied behavior analysis would seem to be an excellent aid in assessing effectiveness. Unfortunately, for purposes of this paper, we cannot evaluate post hoc the effectiveness of *JABA* studies.

METHOD

Every article in *JABA* published in Volumes 1-6 and in the first two issues of Volumes 7-10 was rated by the senior author. Only half of the latter volumes were read as they are nearly twice as long as the earlier volumes. Each article was scored on four dimensions—applied, analytic, conceptual, and generality. The scoring system used for each is described below. Only the results for experimental articles are reported here.

Applied

The applied dimension was scored in three parts. We first recorded whether the behavior studied was an *analogue behavior.* As a guideline, we asked whether the behavior was itself the problem behavior or had been selected on the basis of convenience. Second, we recorded whether the subjects used were *analogue subjects.* That is, were these subjects having difficulty with the problem behavior? Finally, we assessed whether the setting was an *analogue setting.* Was the study conducted in the problem setting or was it selected for convenience or for a controlled laboratory situation?

Analytic

This dimension was divided into four levels of analysis. In a *reliability analysis,* a relatively straightforward design, such as an A-B-A, simple group comparison, or multiple baseline design, is used simply to determine whether or not a particular intervention has reliably produced the behavior change. A second category is *comparative analysis* which aims to compare two distinct and relatively nonoverlapping treatment approaches. These include certain group comparison, alternating treatments, and B-C-B-C designs. Third, a *component analysis* compares elements of a particular treatment package, such as an A - B - B+C - B - A design. The final type is a *parametric analysis,* in which an independent variable is varied systematically along a dimension which is thought to relate to the behavior change. For example, the intensity or frequency of a particular independent variable might be systematically altered. For each study, every analysis reported was categorized in this manner. Thus, a single study could conceivably include several distinct types of analyses.[1]

Generality

Four types of generality were individually scored—generality across time (maintenance), settings, behaviors, and persons. For every study, we scored whether or not *each* type of generality was experimentally assessed, independent of whether it was achieved. A study was said to be concerned with a given kind of generality if there was a method of analysis specifically designed to assess it and if measures were taken, where no intervention was planned, in a second setting, on a second behavior, for a nontargeted person, or in a time period at least 1 month removed from the termination of treatment.

Conceptual

A four-part system was developed to describe the conceptual orientation of *JABA* research.[2] Some research is designed to develop scientific procedures, such as observation systems, and these were categorized as *methodology* studies. Research in the applied arena that concerns the development of helpful techniques was divided into three types. Some of this work is purely *technical.* It contains no reference to principles of behavior nor does it investigate new principles. Rather, the work is oriented exclusively toward "how to" questions of applied interest. For example, research that investigated the effects of police patrols on theft reduction and that contained no reference to behavioral principles (e.g., reinforcement or stimulus control) would be considered technical. Other research may refer to known principles of behavior and test the generality of known principles, such as

---

[1]Note that any type of experimental analysis must first be based upon a reliability analysis. One can hardly ask about the effects of components, for example, until the effect of the overall package is clear. For this reason reliability analyses were scored only if one part of the manuscript *explicitly* reported a purely reliability analysis. The reliability analyses which were *implicit* in other types of analyses were not scored.

[2]A fifth category was scored, but is not reported here due to its low frequency. Some research is oriented *solely* toward the development of scientific concepts (such as the type seen in *JEAB*). Only a few experimental studies of this sort were found in *JABA*. However, there has been a substantial increase in discussion (nonexperimental) articles of this sort.

studies that apply reinforcement principles to new behaviors, settings, or populations. These were labeled *direct applications.* Finally, some applied work shows an effort to advance our basic knowledge of some behavioral phenomena. In addition to "how to" questions, this type of research also asks "what is" questions, such as "what is the motivation for imitation in children?" or "what is a response class?" These types of studies were labeled *systematic applications.*[3]

Interobserver Agreement

Each article was read and scored by the senior author. Twenty randomly selected articles were also independently rated by one of the junior authors. There were three categories in the applied dimension and four in the generality dimension that were separately rated for each manuscript as well as the two single dimensions of analytic and conceptual. Thus, the reliability of nine separate categories was calculated. For each manuscript the correspondence between the ratings of the senior author and the junior authors was determined. Within each category the number of agreements and the number of disagreements were assessed. Agreements were defined as follows:

1. Applied. Agreement was scored if raters agreed that it was or was not an analogue. Agreement was calculated separately for each of the three types.

2. Analytic. An agreement was calculated if both raters indicated the presence of the particular analysis. If one rater indicated that an analysis was present while another did not, that was a disagreement.

3. Generality. Agreement was calculated separately for each of the four areas in a fashion identical to the "applied" categories above.

4. Conceptual. Each article received one of four summary labels. An agreement required that there be perfect correspondence between the raters as to the category. Reliability was calculated by dividing the number of agreements by the number of agreements and disagreements and multiplying that number by 100. Reliabilities ranged from 85% to 100% across the nine total categories.

RESULTS

Data Analysis

Each of the analyses below is expressed as the percentage of the experimentally based articles in the volumes of interest. If, for example, a given volume contained 50 experimental articles and 10 of these assessed setting generality, the resulting value would be 20%.

Applied

Subjects. Very little change has occurred over the years in the percentage of experimental manuscripts using analogue subjects. On the average, 22% of the first four volumes (range: 21% to 23%) and 24% of the last four volumes (range: 21% to 30%) used analogue subjects as is shown in Figure 1.

Settings. Figure 1 suggests a trend toward fewer analogue settings in *JABA.* Although the first four volumes averaged 21.3% (range: 11% to 27%), the latter four volumes averaged only 11.7% (range: 3% to 16%).

Behaviors. Figure 1 also shows a substantial decrease in analogue behaviors found in *JABA.* Only 4.2% (range: 0% to 10%) of the articles in the last four volumes of *JABA* have used analogue behaviors, compared to 14.3% (range: 6% to 21%) over the first four volumes.

Analytic

Reliability analyses. The form of the question in reliability analyses is simply: "Was there an effect of B?" These kinds of questions are as

[3]Sidman (1960) uses the terms *direct replication* and *systematic replication* to distinguish between simply repeating an experiment with new subjects and investigating the limiting conditions of an experimental manipulation. Systematic replication potentially provides more information about the generality of a behavioral phenomenon and may also uncover new phenomena. In this respect the distinction made here between *direct* and *systematic application* parallels that drawn by Sidman (1960). See also Deitz (1978).

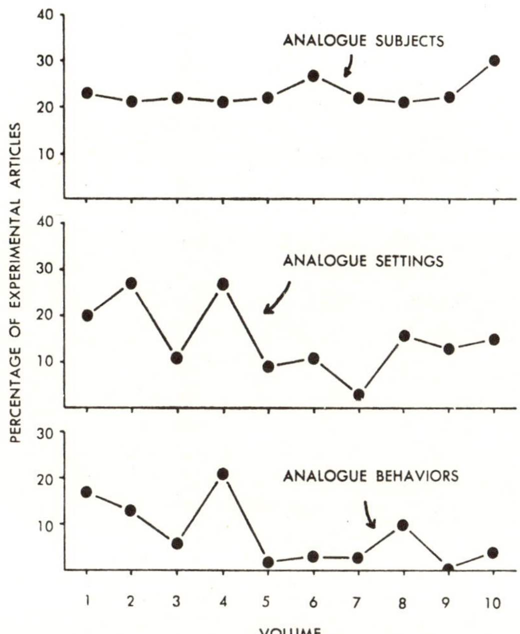

Fig. 1. The percentage of experimental articles using analogue subjects, settings, or behaviors.

popular today as they were in the earlier volumes and represent the major thrust of experimental work in *JABA*. The upper graph in Figure 2 reveals that, with the exception of the 29% found for Volume 5, 50% to 78% (mean: 65.7%) of the articles in *JABA* volumes have used reliability analyses.

Comparative analyses. The form of the experimental question in comparative analyses is: "Is B more (or less) effective than C?" There is clearly an increasing trend in the percentage of such questions in experimental articles in *JABA* over the years, as shown in Figure 2. Whereas the initial four volumes averaged 18.8% (range: 14% to 23%), the latest four volumes have averaged 32.7% (range: 26% to 41%).

Component analyses. The form of the experimental question in component analyses is: "What is it about B that makes it effective?" Surprisingly, these questions seem to be disappearing from *JABA* (Figure 2), gradually declining from an average of 22.3% in the first four volumes (range: 11% to 43%) to an average of 5.5% (range: 4% to 7%) in the last four volumes.

Parametric analyses. The questions posed in parametric analyses are of the form, "What are the effects of different levels (degrees) of B?" These questions have never been popular in *JABA* and they are declining further. Parametric analyses averaged 10.3% in the first four volumes (range: 6% to 13%), and 4% (range: 3% to 8%) for the most recent four volumes (Figure 2).

Generality

Maintenance. The first type of generality is that across time, or maintenance. For each study we ascertained whether at least a 1-month follow-up was conducted after treatment. Figure 3 shows a slight increase in *JABA*'s concern for maintenance from an average of 19.3% in the first four volumes (range: 9% to 24%), to an average of 24.8% in the last four volumes (range: 13% to 33%).[4]

Across settings/stimuli. In stimulus generalization a systematic assessment was made of the behavior gains in a nontraining setting or with untrained task stimuli. Figure 3 shows that assessments of this type have always been substantial in *JABA* (with the exception of Volume 5). However, it is surprising to note what appears to be a decreasing trend in these studies over the past decade. These articles averaged 36.8% (range: 27% to 44%) over the first four volumes, but only 26.8% (range: 19% to 37%) over the last four volumes.

Across responses. Response generalization

[4]The increasing trend toward measuring maintenance deserves some elaboration in view of seemingly contradictory findings by Kauffman, Nussen, and McGee (1977). They reported that reports of maintenance seem to be decreasing, at least in studies conducted in educational settings. They divided their literature review (which included several journals) into two time periods, 1968-1970 and 1971-1974, and found that information regarding maintenance (they used a less rigorous criterion than that used here) was present in 32% of the articles in the former period, and only 25% of the articles in the latter period. In using the same time intervals our data show a similar result—a decrease from the earlier period (18%) to the later period (16%). However, looking at all the data from 1968 to 1978, (Figure 3) suggests a slight increasing trend.

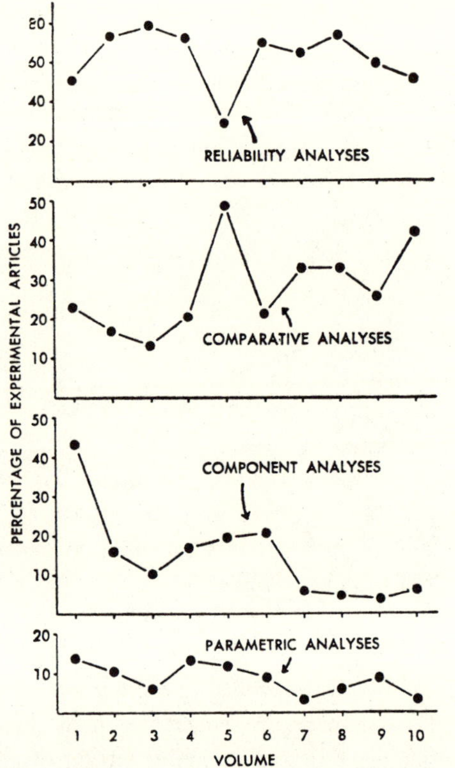

Fig. 2. The percentage of experimental articles conducting reliability, comparative, component, or parametric analyses. (Note that the ordinate differs in parts of the figure.)

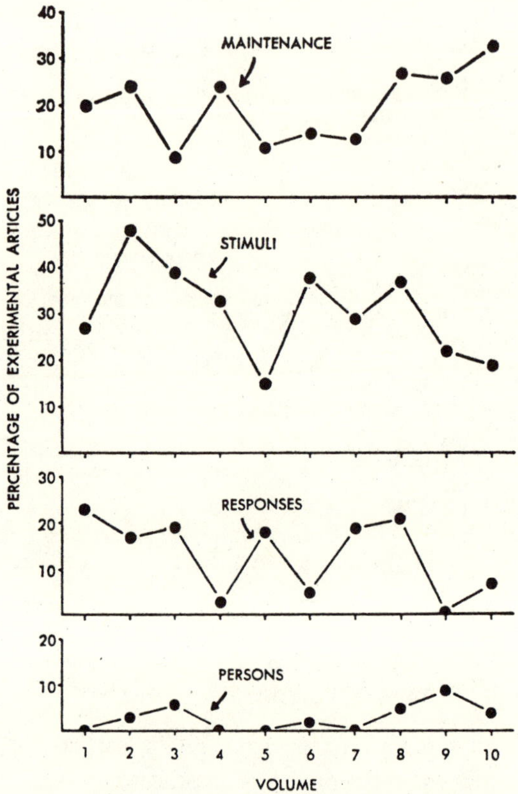

Fig. 3. The percentage of experimental articles assessing maintenance, generality across settings or stimuli, generality across responses, or generality across persons.

refers to the systematic assessment of the relationship between changes in the directly treated behaviors and changes in other, nontreated behaviors. Although the data (Figure 3) are quite variable there appears to be some decline, from 15.5% (range: 3% to 23%) in Volumes 1-4 to 11.8% (range: 0% to 21%) in the last four volumes.

Across persons. Person generalization is concerned with the relationship between behavior changes in the target individual and changes in nontargeted individuals. This type of assessment has been extremely rare in *JABA,* averaging only 2.3% for the first four volumes (range: 0% to 6%), and 4.5% for the last four volumes (range: 0% to 9%).

Conceptual

Methodological. Figure 4 reveals a clear rising trend in the proportion of *JABA* manuscripts concerned with methodological questions. There were few methodological articles in the first four years of *JABA* (mean: 1.5%; range: 0% to 3%), but they have gradually increased over the last four volumes (mean: 8%; range: 4% to 11%).

Purely technical articles. In early volumes of *JABA* it was virtually unknown for manuscripts to be published that contained no reference to behavioral principles, perhaps because of Baer et al.'s injunction against doing so (1968, p. 96). However, Figure 4 shows a dramatic rise in such articles over the last several volumes, from only .8% (range: 0% to 3%) in Volumes 1-4 to 18% (range: 10% to 22%) in Volumes 7-10.

Direct applications. The majority of *JABA* manuscripts have always been, and continue to be, simple applications, testing the applicability of known behavioral principles (Figure 4). Of

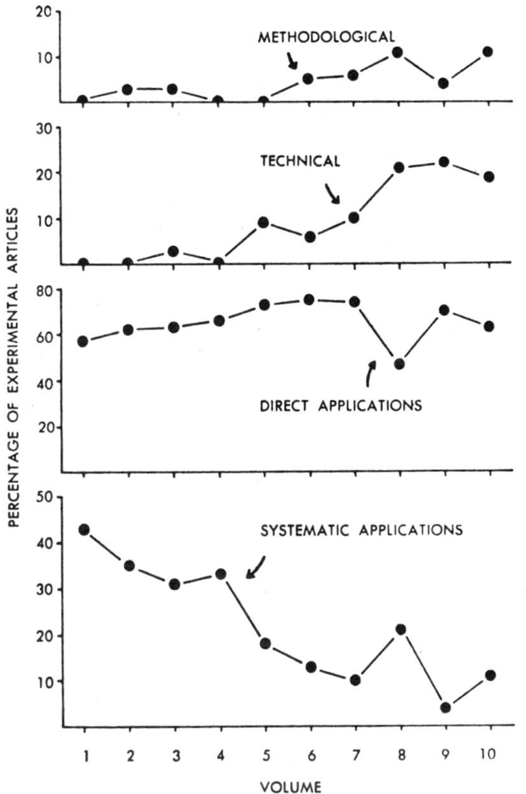

Fig. 4. The percentage of experimental articles which are methodological, purely technical, direct applications, or systematic applications. (Note that the ordinate differs in parts of the figure.)

the first four volumes, 62% (range: 57% to 66%) and of the last four volumes, 64% (range: 47% to 74%) were of this type.

Systematic applications. Conversely, whereas early issues of *JABA* were heavily devoted to the development and extension of behavioral principles in applied studies, this type of research is fast disappearing from *JABA* (Figure 4). In Volumes 1-4 these articles comprised 35.5% of the journal (range: 31% to 43%). They have gradually but systematically decreased and over the last four volumes represent 10.5% of the articles published in *JABA* (range: 4% to 21%).

DISCUSSION

Overall the data show that applied behavior analysis is becoming a more purely technical effort, with less and less interest in conceptual questions. To answer these technical questions we are using relatively simple experimental designs which determine if the technique had a reliable effect, or if it is better than another technique, with little interest in the components producing the effect or the parametric boundaries of the techniques. Our research is occurring less often in nonapplied situations and is using fewer analogue behaviors. Finally, we are a bit more careful to collect some maintenance data but our concern for the stimulus and response generality of behavior change seems to be lessening. Each of these trends deserves some elaboration.

The Applied Nature of Applied Behavior Analysis

The data show that applied behavior analysis is increasingly following Baer et al.'s recommendation that applied studies directly manipulate the problem behaviors, in natural settings, and with the troubled populations. However, this definition of applied has been labeled a "structural" one because it is based strictly upon the nature of the subjects, settings, and behavioral topography being studied. Alternatively, it is possible to define an applied study "functionally," as any study that increases the applied workers' ability to predict, understand, and control socially important behavior in the settings and with the clients they serve. Functionally speaking, then, basic or analogue studies may be very "applied" when they lead to widespread technological improvement.

The applied impact of a study cannot be known until we have tested the applicability of results in the social arena. It is by no means clear, however, that applied impact is necessarily or always enhanced by relying upon a structural definition of applied behavior analysis. Birnbrauer (1979) has argued that an insistence upon the structural trappings of applied work may at times be fundamentally at odds with the stated functionalism of applied behavior analysis and may be limiting the actual applied impact of our research. If, for example, one is interested in the control of academic behaviors in a classroom, it is often felt that applied impact is assured merely by doing the research in a classroom setting. Classrooms, however, are often relatively uncontrolled environments and may differ in important ways across schools, teachers, peer groups, and over time. What is important is not the *appearance* of similarity between the research setting and the setting in which the results are put to use but the *functional* similarity between the two.

To continue the example, if classrooms A and B differ in important ways, then research that is done in any environment that contains the set of functionally important variables characteristic of classroom A will be applicable to that classroom, regardless of the appearance of similarity. Conversely, research done in classroom B may not be applicable to classroom A despite the fact that they seem similar.

It seems to us that we do not yet know what type of research will yield the largest long-term benefit. While there seems to be obvious value in much work conducted in applied settings, there is also applied value in some analogue work. For example, discovering "stimulus overselectivity" in autistic children (Lovaas, Schreibman, Koegel, & Rehm, 1971) has led to the design of new, more effective teaching procedures (Rincover, 1978; Schreibman, 1975). It is too soon to know which approach will be more fruitful, and the decision is complicated by the fact that many of the people conducting structurally applied, outcome-oriented research, have had principles-oriented, conceptual training (e.g., Azrin, Risley, Wolf). We need to be aware of the drift toward cure-oriented research because it is too early, in our view, to drift too far. Whether a structural or analogue approach to applied behavior analysis is most functional remains to be seen. Probably, both approaches are useful, with their relative usefulness to a given case depending on factors such as the present state of knowledge of the determinants of the behavior under investigation, the current level of effectiveness, efficiency, and generality and public acceptance of existing treatments. If so, the present data may reveal a danger that the field is becoming too rigidly "applied," concentrating on what Birnbrauer (1979) called "cure-oriented demonstrations."

The Analytic Nature of Applied Behavior Analysis

Once one has adopted the view that the immediate and primary aim of applied behavior analysis is client cure, it follows that there is less need for component and parametric analyses. If one has an effective treatment program, the pressure to refine it may be quite low, and one need only compare it to others periodically (cf. Azrin, 1977). It is interesting to note that, although Baer et al. clearly expected more complicated analyses to be done as applied behavior analysis matured, the exact opposite has occurred.

As described by Baer et al. the term "analytic" means the clear demonstration of an effect: "An experimenter has achieved an analysis of a behavior when he can exercise control over it" (Baer et al., 1968, p. 94). The importance of component analyses, parametric analyses, and other more sophisticated analytic attempts are often to be found less in "control" (in an immediately applied sense) and more in "understanding" (in a scientific sense). One may easily control, say, aggressive behavior through the use of punishment without having contributed significantly to an understanding of aggression. Perhaps for this reason parametric and component analyses are seldom seen in the pages of *JABA.* Their immediate applied value is often not especially clear, although their ultimate applied and scientific value may be profound. For example, if one has a package program that is effective, there may be little obvious value in doing a component analysis. But these more complicated analyses may increase our knowledge of the actual functional variables and subsequently increase our ability to generate more efficient and general behavioral programs. Perhaps, we have gone too far in our attempt to be *immediately* applied at the expense of being *ultimately* more effective, in failing to encourage more analogue and analytical studies that have treatment implications.

Generalization and Maintenance

One might argue that generality is not so much an essential aspect of applied behavior analysis as it is one of the foremost challenges to it. Much of the early work in *JABA* was understandably devoted to demonstrating that operant methods could be effectively used with clinical problems, leaving the generality of those effects to future studies. Unfortunately, much of the current research continues to focus to an even greater degree on demonstrating effects without attending to their generality (Figure 3). Only in maintenance have we become somewhat more careful to assess it at least (this does not imply that we are better at producing it, however). There are hopeful signs, such as Stokes and Baer's (1977) review of the setting generality literature, yet setting generality remains a critical problem for the field.

It is also noteworthy that the large majority of generalization research has been concerned with generalization across settings and with maintenance, with relatively little attention given to response generalization or generalization across persons. Some clinical populations, such as autistic and retarded children, display behavioral deficits (and excesses) which are so extensive that one behavior at a time applications of behavior modification have not proven very fruitful (Lovaas, Koegel, Simmons, & Long, 1973). For such populations it would seem that we *must* investigate strategies that produce multiple or widespread behavior change—that is, a technology for promoting response generalization—if we are ever to socialize or normalize these clients (e.g., Rincover & Koegel, 1977). Similarly, if our parent or teacher training programs are ever to find homes and schools, it would seem that we must investigate dissemination procedures for promoting generalization across persons. In short, response and person generalization seem to be important, though as yet ignored, directions for applied behavior analysis.

Conceptual Systems

Baer et al. argue that the field will advance most rapidly if the description of procedures are not only precise and complete but demonstrate their relevance to principles of behavior. But there is another sense in which applied research may bear upon conceptual issues. It may frequently be the case that significant theoretical issues may be raised most clearly in the context of applied work. For example, the nature of response classes is an issue necessarily raised by a behavioral analysis of imitation, generative language, and other applied phenomena. The nature of response classes may be of less immediate concern in basic research, where less complex behaviors are selected on the basis of research convenience, and filling behavioral deficits is not the goal of the research. In the effort to distinguish between the experimental analysis of behavior and applied behavior analysis, Baer et al. may have overstated the case: "In application, the theoretical importance of a variable is usually not at issue" (Baer et al., 1968, p. 96).

The data reveal what might be termed a technical drift in *JABA.* We are becoming less concerned with basic principles of behavior, and more concerned with techniques per se. It may be, as some have stated, that additional principles are needed beyond those developed in basic operant psychology. The present data, however, not only show that the old concepts are being increasingly ignored but also that no new concepts are emerging. This decrease in conceptual analyses has been defended as indicating the proper use of inductive methodology in behavior analyses (e.g., Risley, Note 1). But it may have several undesirable effects. Technology can be, and often is, successfully developed without any particular conceptual interest. Applied behavior analysts often seem to generate their interventions by intuition, trial and error, informal observations, or common sense, rather than theoretical concepts and analysis. This approach *can* generate solutions or partial solutions relatively quickly. However, the speed of development in purely technical efforts may be illusory and may rely partly on the fact that many prominent behavior analysts doing technical research have had extensive theoretical training. Such an approach by persons not trained in behavior theory might actually slow progress of the field, since little attention might be paid to the functional variables which can be carried to different settings, subjects, and target behaviors. At this point, we do not know which approach will be more productive in the long run (Deitz, 1978).

Current Dimensions in Applied Behavior Analysis

The empirical data support the view that applied behavior analysis as reflected in *JABA* has shown a consistent relationship to the major criteria described by Baer et al. However, the trends are somewhat disturbing in several areas: the formalization of the meaning of the term "applied" to be limited to structural and topographical appearances and not necessarily to the functional realities; the lack of balance in the types of analyses we are conducting and a resultant loss of information; and the lack of concern for different types of generalization. Overall, we are seeing an increasing technical drift in applied behavior analysis.

It is not clear whether the trends documented here are due to changes in *JABA* editorial policies, promoted by the four editors represented here, to types of research conducted (and funded) in the field, or the types of manuscripts submitted to *JABA*. It may be that it is often easier simply to show that techniques work than to simultaneously make important conceptual contributions. Whatever their determinants, these trends may indicate a developing polarization in applied behavior analysis between its purely technical and more conceptual aspects. This would seem unfortunate because both types of endeavors seem clearly to have applied value. Perhaps what is needed are separate outlets for work of applied but not theoretical interest (such as a *Journal of Behavioral Technology*) and studies of applied plus theoretical interest. Alternately, perhaps recognition of this issue may contribute to a greater balance between the two approaches in *JABA*.

REFERENCE NOTE

1. Risley, T. R. In S. C. Hayes (Chair), *Some current dimensions of applied behavior analysis: Ten years later.* Symposium presented at the meeting of the Midwestern Association of Behavior Analysis, Chicago, May 1978.

REFERENCES

Azrin, N. H. A strategy for applied research: Learning based but outcome oriented. *American Psychologist,* 1977, **32,** 140-149.

Baer, D. M., Wolf, M., & Risley, T. R. Some current dimensions of applied behavior analysis. *Journal of Applied Behavior Analysis,* 1968, **1,** 91-97.

Birnbrauer, J. S. Applied behavior analysis, service, and the acquisition of knowledge. *The Behavior Analyst,* 1979, **2,** 15-21.

Deitz, S. M. Current status of applied behavior analysis: Science versus technology. *American Psychologist,* 1978, **33,** 805-814.

Hayes, S. C. Theory and technology in behavior analysis. *The Behavior Analyst,* 1978, **1,** 35-41.

Kauffman, J. M., Nussen, J. L., & McGee, C. S. Follow-up in classroom behavior modification: Survey and discussion. *Journal of School Psychology,* 1977, **15,** 343-348.

Kazdin, A. E. Characteristics and trends in applied behavior analysis. *Journal of Applied Behavior Analysis,* 1975, **8,** 332.

Lovaas, O. I., Koegel, R., Simmons, J. O., & Long, J. S. Some generalizations and follow-up measures on autistic children in behavior therapy. *Journal of Applied Behavior Analysis,* 1973, **6,** 131-164.

Lovaas, O. I., Schreibman, L. E., Koegel, R. L., & Rehm, R. Selective responding by autistic children to multiple sensory input. *Journal of Abnormal Psychology,* 1971, **77,** 211-222.

Rincover, A. Variables affecting stimulus fading and discriminative responding in psychotic children. *Journal of Abnormal Psychology,* 1978, **87,** 541-553.

Rincover, A., & Koegel, R. L. Research on the education of autistic children: Recent advances and future directions. In B. Lahey & A. Kazdin (Eds.), *Advances in clinical child psychology.* New York: Plenum Press, 1977.

Schreibman, L. E. Effects of within-stimulus and extra-stimulus prompting on discrimination learning in autistic children. *Journal of Applied Behavior Analysis,* 1975, **8,** 91-112.

Sidman, M. *Tactics of scientific research.* New York: Basic Books, 1960.

Stokes, T. F., & Baer, D. M. An implicit technology of generalization. *Journal of Applied Behavior Analysis,* 1977, **10,** 349-367.

Wolf, M. M. Social validity: The case for subjective measurement or how applied behavior analysis is finding its heart. *Journal of Applied Behavior Analysis,* 1978, **11,** 203-214.

Received December 5, 1978
Final acceptance September 21, 1979

JOURNAL OF APPLIED BEHAVIOR ANALYSIS 1991, 24, 411–416 NUMBER 3 (FALL 1991)

DECONSTRUCTING "TECHNOLOGICAL TO A FAULT"

EDWARD K. MORRIS
UNIVERSITY OF KANSAS

Is applied behavior analysis "technological to a fault"? This is not the first time the question has been posed, perhaps because we do not agree on (or understand) what it means. Perhaps the question means different things to different people or even to the same person at different times or in different settings. Sometimes the question is about the relationship between the experimental analysis of behavior and applied behavior analysis (e.g., Baer, 1978, 1987; Pierce & Epling, 1980; see also Deitz, 1987), sometimes between science and technology (e.g., Deitz, 1978), sometimes between theory and application (e.g., Azrin, 1977; Hayes, 1978, 1987; Hayes, Rincover, & Solnick, 1980), and sometimes about schisms in all of the above (e.g., Poling, Picker, Grossett, Hall-Johnson, & Holbrook, 1981; Ribes, 1977). Given this range of possibilities, perhaps we should approach the question in terms of what we understand "technological" and "to a fault" to mean—and thereby pursue a deconstruction of "technological to a fault."

Dictionaries

What of the meaning of "to a fault"? The first listing for "fault" in my *American Heritage Dictionary* (1985) is: "1. a. A weakness; defect. b. A mistake; error. c. A minor offense; misdeed" (p. 493). The final listing is idiomatic, where "to a fault" means "excessively." There seems not much to equivocate here about the meaning: some thing or some practice excessive to the point of weakness, defect, mistake, error, or misdeed.

What then of "technological"? Here, my dictionary defines "technological" as "pertaining to or involving technology, esp. scientific technology" (p. 1248), where "technology" means "1. a. The application of science, esp. to industrial or commercial objectives. b. The entire body of methods and materials used to achieve such objectives" (p. 1248). Given these dictionary definitions, what would "technological to a fault" mean? That the science, methods, and materials of behavior analysis are being applied excessively? I think not. By these definitions, technological seems not a fault, but a virtue.

The Dimensions of Applied Behavior Analysis

So much for dictionaries. Perhaps we should turn to Baer, Wolf, and Risley (1968), for it was they who offered "technological" as a defining dimension of applied behavior analysis:

> "Technological" here means simply that the techniques making up a particular behavioral application are completely identified and described. . . . The best rule of thumb for evaluating a procedure description as technological is probably to ask whether a typically trained reader could replicate that procedure well enough to produce the same results, given only a reading of the description. (p. 95)

Or, as stated in their conclusion: "an *applied* behavior analysis will make obvious the importance of the behavior changed . . . [and] the technologically exact description of all procedures contributing to the change . . ." (p. 97). I doubt that this meaning of "technological" is what is at fault, unless we make a sin of exactitude in procedural description. We might note in passing, though, that the typically trained reader of 1968 is different from today's. Today's readers may have to be more technically and sensitively trained, at least to be

I thank Scott Geller for inviting this commentary, and Steve Fawcett, Bryan Midgley, Ilene Schwartz, and Donna Wickham for commenting so wisely on its internal and external validity (or lack thereof). Correspondence should be addressed to the author at the Department of Human Development, Dole Human Development Center, University of Kansas, Lawrence, Kansas 66045-2133.

effective in some of the broader-scale interventions (e.g., Fawcett, Suarez de Balcazar, & Johnson, 1986; Greenwood, Delquadri, & Hall, 1989).

Some Stimulus Controls

This reductionistic line of etymological inquiry seems not very fruitful, so let me try something more behavior-analytic by asking: What are we *tacting* when speaking of "technological to a fault"? Or, to turn the question around: What are the stimulus controls over saying such a thing (see Day, 1969)? The answer is not to be found in dictionaries.

"Technological to a fault" would seem to have some "family of meanings" (Wittgenstein, 1953; see Deitz & Arrington, 1984) or common stimulus controls across the discipline. Without that, we would be unable to speak intelligibly with one another (or as intelligibly as we do). Still, those stimulus controls are multiple and variable—across and within individuals, as outlined at the start—to such an extent that a complete deconstruction of "technological to a fault" is a larger task than my comments can contend with. Thus, I address only what *one* of those stimulus controls might be. There are no doubt others.

Faults in context. To begin with, though, let me note that we should probably not judge applied behavior analysis as technological to a fault outside the context of the field as a whole. Given the definitions above, I think we can agree that being technological is not, in itself, inherently a fault (cf. Baer, 1981). Thus, applied behavior analysis may only be technological to a fault in the context of other applied behavior-analytic practices, or lack thereof. Indeed, we may even want more such technology, in the right context.

Looked at this way, the concern (or question or criticism) about technological to a fault turns into a broader concern about the conduct of applied behavior analysis as a whole. This is, if being technological at all (or at its current level) is not inherently a fault, then the fault (if any) lies in the relationship of the technology to the rest of applied behavior analysis. We must look not for the fault in the technology itself, but at the technology-in-context. Let me turn to what some of this context might be, and thus to one of the stimulus controls for tacting "technological to a fault."

Two Correct Meanings of "Analysis"

One answer to the question of "technological to a fault" depends, I think, on what we take the "analysis" in applied behavior analysis to mean (see Morris & Midgley, 1990; Pennypacker, 1981). Does analysis refer to the experimental *demonstration* of the effectiveness of a behavioral application, procedure, or technique for modifying socially important behavior (e.g., overcorrection, differential reinforcement of alternative behavior)? Or does analysis refer to the experimental *discovery* of the functions (or of some of the causes) of socially important behavior, followed by changing the variables of which it is a function so as to change the behavior?

Put another way: Are the independent variables in applied behavior analysis (a) our applied behavioral applications (i.e., techniques) or (b) the controlling variables over socially important behavior—or both, whenever they can be? The former yields an "analysis of behavioral applications." The latter yields an "analysis of behavior, applied." The former demonstrates the effects of behavioral applications (and nonbehaviorally based applications too, I am afraid). The latter discovers the functions (or some of the causes) of the behavior of concern.

Which of these two meanings is the correct one, if such a question can be asked? I once again invoke authority, and turn to Baer et al. (1968) because "analysis" is another of their defining dimensions. In some places, Baer et al. appear to embrace "analysis" in the sense of discovery:

> Both endeavors [applied and basic research] ask what controls the behavior under study. . . . Thus it is . . . a matter of research to discover that the behaviors typical of [people with developmental disabilities] can be related to oddities of their chromosomal structure and to oddities of their reinforcement history. (pp. 91–92)

In other places, they seem more equivocal, describing "analysis" in a manner that could fit either discovery or demonstration:

> The analysis of a behavior, as the term is used here, requires a believable demonstration of the events that can be responsible for the occurrence or non-occurrence of that behavior. An experimenter has achieved an analysis of a behavior when he can exercise control over it. (pp. 93–94)

Likewise, in summing up, they state:

> an *applied* behavior analysis will make obvious the importance of the behavior changed . . . [and] the experimental manipulations which analyze with clarity what was responsible for the change. (p. 97)

Two decades later, they offered that "*analytic* meant a convincing experimental design" (Baer, Wolf, & Risley, 1987, p. 318) but, I ask, in the service of what—discovery or demonstration? In sum, Baer et al. (1968, 1987) allow both meanings of (or stimulus controls over) "analysis"—demonstration and discovery. More than merely "allow" both meanings, though, we should probably embrace them both as equally correct (Baer, 1981; Deitz, 1983; Morris & Braukmann, 1987). In so doing, however, we should more clearly distinguish between them—applied research and technological application—so as to avoid confusion and clarify their interrelationship (see Birnbrauer, 1979; Deitz, 1982; Johnston, in press).

If both meanings are correct, then they should be equally accommodated and invited as applied behavior analyses, but they have not been, which is perhaps a stimulus control over "technological to a fault": The "analysis" in applied behavior analysis is much more a matter of demonstration than discovery. That is, the "demonstration" meaning is seemingly more equal than the "discovery" meaning. If this inequality is the stimulus control over "to a fault," then the problem is one of balance or, more behaviorally, a matter of consequences. It is this matter of consequences that must be addressed, for the consequences are the arbiter of the truth of "to a fault."

A Matter of Consequences

The matter of consequences may be parsed two ways: (a) the consequences in any individual instance and (b) the consequences for applied behavior analysis as a whole. In individual instances, applied behavior analysis may be technological to a fault when it is more concerned with demonstrating the effects of specific behavioral interventions than with discovering the functions of (i.e., performing a functional analysis of) the important social behaviors at hand (and then ameliorating them). By emphasizing demonstration only, few new or useful facts may be discovered about the behavior of the individual (e.g., Carr & Durand, 1985; Touchette, MacDonald, & Langers, 1985), about reasons for the behavior (e.g., Iwata, Dorsey, Slifer, Bauman, & Richman, 1982; Lovaas, Freitag, Gold, & Kassorla, 1965), or about how behavior change might best generalize and be maintained (e.g., Horner, Dunlap, & Koegel, 1988). Demonstrated solutions to individual problems may, of course, be necessary and desirable in many instances, especially in the short run when discovery wastes valuable time that harms our clients or when discovery seems impossible (see Baer, 1970; Horner et al., 1990).

As for applied behavior analysis as a whole, it may be technological to a fault when it demonstrates the effects of behavioral interventions at the expense of discovering (and then demonstrating) actual controlling relationships, as well as new facts about behavior and reasons for the social problems to begin with. Discovered (and then demonstrated) solutions seem necessary for the discipline as a whole—necessary for its continued development, as opposed to growth. But let me be clear again: My argument is not against the *growth* of effective technology through demonstration; rather, it is for the further *development* of applied behavior analysis through discovery. Growth and development are not the same thing.

This stimulus control over "technological to a fault" may seem overly abstract and relational, but abstract and relational may be exactly what it is, for no particular instance of applied behavior analysis identifies the stimulus control of the relationship between demonstration and discovery. An exemplar, though, might be useful—an exemplar of the stimulus control over tacting "to a fault." One of the best of these is probably the problem of generalization and maintenance (Marholin, Siegel, & Phillips, 1976; Stokes & Baer, 1977). "Technological to a fault" may be under the control of the imbalance between demonstration and discovery on (or across) those occasions when, lacking a functional analysis that discovers controlling variables, generalization and maintenance fail. To demonstrate change in problem behavior by applying a technology is not necessarily to discover the contingencies responsible for the problem in the first place, much less to discover the metacontingencies that control those contingencies—an even larger problem (see Glenn, 1988). With the contingencies left unchanged, they will likely reassert their influence when the demonstration is withdrawn. It is in this sense that we sometimes treat symptoms, not causes. (Freud was right for the wrong reasons.)

Rule-Governed and Contingency-Shaped Applied Behavior Analysis

Interestingly, the question of (and answer to) whether applied behavior analysis is technological to a fault has the same form and sense of: Is behavior rule governed to a fault? My answer is rhetorical: Is it inherently a fault that behavior be rule governed at all? No, the problem is again one of degree, balance, and context with respect to an individual's overall repertoire. More to the present point, however, perhaps we can analyze the emphasis on demonstration over discovery in applied behavior analysis in terms of the rule-governed and contingency-shaped behavior of applied behavior analysts. Here, I offer not a cause of tacting "technological to a fault," but a cause of those causes.

The contingencies that shape and maintain analysis-as-discovery are subtle, difficult to discern, and not well codified. Hence, analysis-as-discovery is difficult to teach and to learn (just as is shaping; Johnston & Pennypacker, 1980; Sidman, 1960). In contrast, the rules that govern analysis-as-demonstration are clearer, more obvious, and well codified. Hence, analysis-as-demonstration is easier to teach and learn, for instance, via established single-subject research designs (Michael, 1980, pp. 8–9; see, e.g., Barlow & Hersen, 1984). Even when both are well learned and practiced, the differential effort of demonstrating versus discovering may also produce "technological to a fault"—demonstrating is often easier than discovering (Hayes et al., 1980). (We should not overlook external control over the behavior of behavior analysts. Public and private funding sources and social agencies will often differentially prompt and reinforce demonstration over discovery.)

All of this relates to a larger issue in the philosophy of science: The distinction between the "context of discovery" and the "context of justification" (Reichenbach, 1938/1961; see Smith, 1986, pp. 44–46), the latter being "demonstration" in our present case. The context of discovery is the relationship between scientist and subject matter, and the contingencies that shape and maintain scientific discovery (e.g., effective action through prediction and control; see Skinner, 1956). The context of justification is the relationship between scientist and scientist, and the rules that govern justifications for their claims of discovery (e.g., truth-by-agreement). The former is poorly understood, and difficult to teach and learn; the latter is easy grist for instruction and application. It is no secret which of the two, discovery versus justification, most philosophers of science teach as *the* scientific method—justification.

In making justification the sine qua non of the scientific method, we are not made much more effective as scientists in coming to understand behavior via discovery; we become better at justifying what we have come to know. Moreover, predicting and controlling behavior on the basis of what we can demonstrate alone is weak ground for saying we "understand" behavior, especially when compared to predicting and controlling behavior on the basis of what we have discovered about it and then demonstrated. We should beware when applied behavior analysis is disproportionately concerned with demonstration as opposed to discovery.

Summing Up

I began with what was to be a definition of "technological to a fault," but had to turn to its stimulus controls, in particular, the imbalance between analysis as demonstration and analysis as discovery. For this, I offered a consequence (i.e., difficulties with generalization and maintenance) and a cause (i.e., the rule-governed nature of demonstration). I have now seemingly concluded with a brief discourse on the relationship of discovery and demonstration to behavior-analytic epistemology. Such are the consequences of deconstruction. There is not just one truth, but many. They are all variations on a theme—circumstances under which applied behavior analysis may be "technological to a fault."

REFERENCES

The American Heritage Dictionary (2nd col. ed.). (1985). Boston: Houghton-Mifflin.

Azrin, N. H. (1977). A strategy for applied research: Learning based but outcome oriented. *American Psychologist,* **32,** 140–149.

Baer, D. M. (1970). A case for the selective reinforcement of punishment. In C. Neuringer & J. Michael (Eds.), *Behavior modification in clinical psychology* (pp. 243–249). Englewood Cliffs, NJ: Prentice-Hall.

Baer, D. M. (1978). On the relation between basic and applied research. In T. A. Brigham & A. C. Catania (Eds.), *The handbook of applied behavior analysis* (pp. 11–16). New York: Irvington.

Baer, D. M. (1981). A flight of behavior analysis. *The Behavior Analyst,* **4,** 85–91.

Baer, D. M. (1987). The difference between basic and behavior analysis is one behavior. *Behavior Analysis,* **22,** 101–106.

Baer, D. M., Wolf, M. M., & Risley, T. R. (1968). Some current dimensions of applied behavior analysis. *Journal of Applied Behavior Analysis,* **1,** 91–97.

Baer, D. M., Wolf, M. M., & Risley, T. R. (1987). Some still-current dimensions of applied behavior analysis. *Journal of Applied Behavior Analysis,* **20,** 313–327.

Barlow, D. H., & Hersen, M. (1984). *Single case experimental designs: Strategies for studying behavior change* (2nd ed.). New York: Pergamon.

Birnbrauer, J. S. (1979). Applied behavior analysis, service, and the acquisition of knowledge. *The Behavior Analyst,* **2,** 15–21.

Carr, E. G., & Durand, V. M. (1985). Reducing behavior problems through functional communication training. *Journal of Applied Behavior Analysis,* **18,** 111–126.

Day, W. F. (1969). Radical behaviorism in reconciliation with phenomenology. *Journal of the Experimental Analysis of Behavior,* **12,** 315–328.

Deitz, S. M. (1978). Current status of applied behavior analysis: Science versus technology. *American Psychologist,* **33,** 805–814.

Deitz, S. M. (1982). Defining applied behavior analysis: An historical analogy. *The Behavior Analyst,* **5,** 53–64.

Deitz, S. M. (1983). Two correct definitions of "applied." *The Behavior Analyst,* **6,** 105–106.

Deitz, S. M. (1987). On the relation between the experimental analysis of human behavior and applied behavior analysis. *The Psychological Record,* **37,** 29–33.

Deitz, S. M., & Arrington, R. L. (1984). Wittgenstein's language games and the call to cognition. *Behaviorism,* **12,** 7–14.

Fawcett, S. B., Suarez de Balcazar, Y., & Johnson, M. (1986). Disabilities concerns emerge as a national pattern. *Independent Living Forum,* **4**(2), 11–13.

Glenn, S. S. (1988). Contingencies and metacontingencies: Toward a synthesis of behavior analysis and cultural materialism. *The Behavior Analyst,* **11,** 161–179.

Greenwood, C. R., Delquadri, J., & Hall, R. V. (1989). Longitudinal effects of classroom peer tutoring. *Journal of Educational Psychology,* **81,** 371–383.

Hayes, S. C. (1978). Theory and technology in behavior analysis. *The Behavior Analyst,* **1,** 25–33.

Hayes, S. C. (1987). The relation between "applied" and "basic" psychology. *Behavior Analysis,* **22,** 91–100.

Hayes, S. C., Rincover, A., & Solnick, J. V. (1980). The technical drift of applied behavior analysis. *Journal of Applied Behavior Analysis,* **13,** 275–285.

Horner, R. H., Dunlap, G., & Koegel, R. L. (Eds.). (1988). *Generalization and maintenance: Life-style changes in applied settings.* Baltimore: Brookes.

Horner, R. H., Dunlap, G., Koegel, R. L., Carr, E. G., Sailor, W., Anderson, J., Albin, R. W., & O'Neill, R. E. (1990). Toward a technology of "nonaversive" behavioral support. *Journal of the Association for Persons with Severe Handicaps,* **15,** 125–132.

Iwata, B. A., Dorsey, M. F., Slifer, K. J., Bauman, K. E., & Richman, G. S. (1982). Toward a functional analysis of self-injury. *Analysis and Intervention in Developmental Disabilities,* **2,** 3–20.

Johnston, J. M. (in press). A model for developing and evaluating behavioral technology. In S. Axelrod & R. Van Houten (Eds.), *Effective behavioral treatment: Issues and implications.* New York: Plenum.

Johnston, J. M., & Pennypacker, H. S. (1980). *Strategies and tactics of human behavioral research.* Hillsdale, NJ: Erlbaum.

Lovaas, O. I., Freitag, G., Gold, V. J., & Kassorla, I. C. (1965). Experimental studies in childhood schizophrenia: Analysis of self-destructive behavior. *Journal of Experimental Child Psychology,* **2,** 67–84.

Marholin, D., Siegel, L. J., & Phillips, D. (1976). Treatment and transfer: A search for empirical procedures. In M. Hersen, R. M. Eisler, & P. M. Miller (Eds.), *Progress in behavior modification* (Vol. 3, pp. 293–432). New York: Academic Press.

Michael, J. (1980). Flight from behavior analysis. *The Behavior Analyst,* **3,** 1–21.

Morris, E. K., & Braukmann, C. J. (1987). The dimensions of applied behavior analysis from crime and delinquency. In E. K. Morris & C. J. Braukmann (Eds.), *Behavioral approaches to crime and delinquency: A handbook of application, research, and concepts* (pp. 27–59). New York: Plenum.

Morris, E. K., & Midgley, B. D. (1990). Some historical and conceptual foundations of ecobehavioral analysis. In S. R. Schroeder (Ed.), *Ecobehavioral analysis and developmental disabilities: The twenty-first century* (pp. 1–32). New York: Springer-Verlag.

Pennypacker, H. S. (1981). On behavior analysis. *The Behavior Analyst,* **4,** 159–161.

Pierce, W. D., & Epling, W. F. (1980). What happened to analysis in applied behavior analysis? *The Behavior Analyst,* **3,** 1–9.

Poling, A., Picker, M., Grossett, D., Hall-Johnson, E., & Holbrook, M. (1981). The schism between experimental and applied behavior analysis: Is it real and who cares? *The Behavior Analyst,* **4,** 93–102.

Reichenbach, H. (1961). *Experience and prediction.* Chicago: University of Chicago Press. (Original work published 1938)

Ribes, E. (1977). Relationship among behavior theory, experimental research, and behavior modification techniques. *The Psychological Record,* **27,** 417–424.

Sidman, M. (1960). *Tactics of scientific research.* New York: Basic Books.

Skinner, B. F. (1956). A case history in scientific method. *American Psychologist,* **11,** 221–233.

Smith, L. D. (1986). *Behaviorism and logical positivism: A reassessment of the alliance.* Stanford, CA: Stanford University Press.

Stokes, T. F., & Baer, D. M. (1977). An implicit technology of generalization. *Journal of Applied Behavior Analysis,* **10,** 349–367.

Touchette, P. E., MacDonald, R. F., & Langers, S. N. (1985). A scatter plot for identifying stimulus control of problem behavior. *Journal of Applied Behavior Analysis,* **18,** 343–351.

Wittgenstein, L. (1953). *Philosophical investigations* [Trans. G. E. M. Anscombe]. Oxford: Blackwell.

Received March 12, 1991
Final acceptance May 29, 1991
Action Editor, E. Scott Geller

JOURNAL OF APPLIED BEHAVIOR ANALYSIS 1991, 24, 417–420 NUMBER 3 (FALL 1991)

THE LIMITS OF TECHNOLOGICAL TALK

STEVEN C. HAYES
UNIVERSITY OF NEVADA

Applied behavior analysts and behavior therapists have long prided themselves on their technological precision and methodological sophistication. Some even go so far as to *define* the field on the basis of its commitment to the "specification of treatment in operational . . . terms" (Kazdin & Hersen, 1980, p. 287). This emphasis is a proud component of the behavioral tradition, but along with it has come a deemphasis of theoretical and philosophical concerns.

Science can be divided into four levels of increasing scope (Hayes, 1978): technique (how to do it), method (how to know it has been done), theory (how to talk in a systematic fashion), and philosophy (assumptions about how to view the world). The first 10 years of *JABA* were characterized by an increasing loss of interest in theoretical development, even to the point of a failure to speak of interventions in terms of known principles (Hayes, Rincover, & Solnick, 1980). This trend, although it may have moderated somewhat, has seemingly not reversed in the last 10 years. Technological talk has occurred in a verbal vacuum, often without systematic efforts to connect a given finding with anything else.

In the current issue, the Editor of *JABA* has asked if we are technological to a fault. It is a good question. My answer is yes, in the sense that too many have felt that technology and method alone can serve as a basis for the development of the field.

WHAT ARE THE PRODUCTS OF RESEARCH?

The direct product of science—even at the level of technique—is words. The actual technique of, say, a token economy cannot be given away in a scientific sense. This is part of what distinguishes science and other areas such as craft or art. What is communicated in our research journals are words *about* this technique. Scientists, in that sense, are word makers. This observation, although obvious, has important implications.

The Meaning of Method

Viewing scientists as speakers casts a different light on their methods and analytic practices. These can be viewed simply as a means of refining and restricting sources of control over scientific talk. For example, behavior analysts commonly ask speakers to "show me your data." That is, there is an insistence that verbal formulations of relations among events be based on direct and verifiable contact with these phenomena. Similarly, editors and others may ask for the relevant reliability coefficients covering a given set of observations. That is, there is a concern that scientific talk not be based on contact with the world that is influenced too heavily by idiosyncratic features of a given individual's history.

These methods and practices help distinguish scientific talk from other forms of discourse. Many societal institutions produce verbal products: religion, law, literature, and so on. But in these institutions there are few attempts to limit the sources of control over verbalizations to direct, verifiable, and shared contact with the world, in contrast to audience factors, states of motivation, and so on. But science is more than a matter of method.

Why Speakers Speak

Behavior analysts have much to be proud of in their commitment to methodological rigor and technological clarity. Understanding that the product of scientific research is verbal, however, also leads to an interest in the behavior of the listener—the consumers of scientific products. It is here that the limits of technological talk become evident.

The properties of verbal constructions. Verbal

Reprints may be obtained from the author, Department of Psychology, University of Nevada, Reno, Nevada 89557-0062.

statements about relations among events can vary along four dimensions: precision, scope, organization, and depth. Precision has to do with the number of alternative verbal constructions that can be made about a given event. Scope has to do with the number of events that can be encompassed by a given verbal construction. Organization refers to the degree of systematization and coherence of given sets of verbal constructions. Depth refers to the degree to which constructions at one level of analysis (e.g., the psychological level) cohere with constructions at other levels (e.g., the anthropological or genetic level).

The nature of technological speech. The idea that what is important in applied science is the specification of empirically validated treatments in operational terms boils down to the idea that a scientific discipline can be based solely on statements high in precision but low in scope, depth, and organization. A technological statement is, if done properly, high in precision. If I say that I tested the effects of Technique X and if I have delineated the nature of Technique X carefully through the use of manuals, checks on the integrity of treatment, and so on, then there are very few alternative verbal constructions of this kind that could apply to the situation. It is unlikely, for example, that Technique X was really Technique Y. Such statements, however, are low in scope. Talk about Technique X will not necessarily apply directly to Techniques Y or Z.

Narrow constructions inherently lead to poor organization and little depth. Narrow constructions cannot become highly organized both because the number of verbal constructions proliferates and because there is little overlap between statements to guide their organization. The verbal products of other sciences will never cohere with such talk because irrelevant details are indistinguishable from fundamental processes.

An example may help. Suppose a cook experiments for several years and finally develops a new bread recipe. If this is done carefully we will have an instance of precise speech, based on verifiable experience. We could collect data on the outcome produced by the recipe, and even assess the reliability of the observations. Such a bread recipe exemplifies the characteristics of technological talk. It is highly precise, but it has little scope. It does not tell us how to bake pies or make beer. It may fail to mention or anticipate the effects of altitude, or different strains of wheat. Because recipes have little scope, cookbooks are merely collections. The total number of available recipes is always increasing. It is impossible to learn them all. There is no systematic and fundamental means to relate one recipe to another.

This same bread recipe could be described in terms of the way yeast breaks down certain compounds, the chemical properties of grain, the effect of carbon dioxide, and so on. Such constructions have much broader scope. They might indeed apply to baking pies or making beer, for example. They might suggest what the effects of altitude or grain variety might be. They could in turn be organized into systems of statements about the biological processes of organisms. Chemists or physicists would find links between their ways of speaking and that of biologists concerned with the transformation of energy.

The Limits of Technological Talk

Precision is always a plus in science. Talk that is broad in scope but very weak in precision is scientifically useless. For example, the statement "the world is the plaything of the Great Spirit" has enormous scope. Anything can be encompassed by it. But it has no precision and no scientific utility. Is it raining today because the Great Spirit is crying, or because the Great Spirit is washing? We have no way to tell, and thus an infinity of verbal constructions can apply to any given event.

Although precision is important, poor scope, depth, and organization also limit the usefulness of scientific talk for its consumers. There are several kinds of limitations such talk produces.

1. Without scientific statements with significant scope, we have no grounds to use our knowledge directly when confronted with a new problem or situation. The application of knowledge to new situations is an issue of scope, not precision. It is an issue of how many events (in this case, the new

problem itself) can be encompassed by a verbal construction. Without an adequate theory to guide us, techniques are simply thrown at new problems, without an appropriate scientifically validated rationale for their use in this new situation. An example is the rather pathetic way certain core techniques, such as relaxation training, are included in almost every package for almost every disorder.

Behavior analysts have paid an enormous amount of attention to internal validity—ways to ensure that scientific statements are based upon the data. But the consumption of scientific research is a matter of external validity. The external validity of research does not flow logically from internal validity (despite the arguments of textbooks to the contrary: see Hayes, 1988, for a discussion).

I often ask my students a key question the late Aaron Brownstein taught me to view in a different way: Why do we replicate research? Students almost invariably answer that the purpose is to see whether the same result will occur if we did the same thing. This is clearly false. We are not testing the consistency of the universe when we replicate research. If we did *exactly* the same thing in every detail, the same results would occur. Rather, our purpose is to see whether doing what the author said is doing the same thing. We are testing the functional adequacy of the researcher's verbalizations in guiding our behavior.

Unfortunately, in the applied arena even the most careful technological description cannot ensure this functional adequacy. No situation can be completely described—we have neither the language nor the time adequate to such a task. We would have to describe the dress of the experimenter, the temperature in the room, the intonations used when instructions were given, and so on, ad infinitum. Thus, any description of a study is a description only of a very small part of what was done.

The irony is that even if the technologist has no interest in the solution of *new* problems, we can never be certain that we are dealing with an *old* problem. All applications of research knowledge are applications to new problems to a degree. And there we are back to the problem of scope. The use of talk that is deliberately high in scope (e.g., talk in terms of principles of behavior) is an effort to ensure the functional adequacy or external validity of a researcher's verbalizations.

2. Without scientific statements that have significant scope, we have no systematic means to develop new techniques. Technological talk is a poor source of entirely new technology. Most of the well-known behavioral techniques were developed many years ago by persons well versed in behavioral principles. Three and four academic generations later, with more emphasis on technology and less on principles, we are seeing an almost self-stimulatory concern for technological refinements and little genuine technological innovation. Common sense is a poor source of true innovation, almost by definition: it is reasonable but expected. Whatever value common sense contains has probably already been extracted by persons with access to little else as a guide to reason. It is the uncommon sense provided by theory that is the major rational source of innovative technological development.

3. A science based purely on statements high in precision and low in scope becomes increasingly disorganized and incoherent. As we have already described, disorganization and shallowness are the natural concomitants of narrow constructions. We see the products all around us. Applied psychology is fracturing into subareas organized by commonsense categories such as patient population or clinical procedure, even though everything we know about behavior theory suggests that these divisions are scientifically trivial. Without theory, no other result is possible because no one can assimilate the mountain of seemingly disconnected bits of information that science-as-technology presents. The field becomes an incoherent mass, impossible to master and impossible to teach. In addition, the shallowness of the analysis means that other areas of science are impossible to relate to our techniques. A hole in the fabric of science opens that cannot be filled.

4. Without talk that is high in scope, the promise of behavior analysis cannot be kept. In my view, behavior analysis is that part of science studying whole organisms interacting in and with a context, and seeking the development of an increasingly organized set of empirically verified verbal rules

permitting the description, prediction, control, and interpretation of these interactions with precision, scope, and depth. From this point of view, behavior analysis is a field that spans basic and applied areas by its very nature. It is the only contemporary position in psychology that promises such an integration. Sadly, it is a promise that is being abandoned. Only a handful of people publish in both *JEAB* and *JABA*. Few even read both. In the last decade, *JEAB* has seen dozens of human studies on such extraordinary phenomena as stimulus equivalence, mutual exclusion, and rule governance, yet the *JABA* readership as a whole knows little about these developments. It is only talk that is broad in scope—theoretical talk—that permits the two areas to speak with and learn from each other.

5. Unless applied researchers show an interest in basic theoretical development, many key basic questions will never be asked. Even if applied behavior analysts carefully kept up with the basic research literature, it would not be enough. Even if *JABA* required some reasoned reference to relevant behavioral principles in every published article, it would not be enough. Applied behavior analysts cannot simply take the passive role.

Basic psychology produces a huge scientific output. As a result, there is a false sense that basic psychology is currently examining all major psychological issues of relevance to human functioning. It is not. Science is a social enterprise, subject to fads, fancies, and notable blind spots. Often, when research issues disappear, it is not because they have been solved. They simply were dropped. They went out of fashion. Other research issues are never raised, even if they might be important.

The conclusion this leads to is sobering. Even if basic behavior analysis proceeds rapidly and successfully on its agenda, there can be little reason to be confident that the issues dealt with there would be sufficient to support the full intellectual development of applied behavior analysis. If applied behavior analysis is to see the theoretical development it needs, it must not just *consume* theory but also *produce* it (see Hayes, 1987, for some reasons why). Applied behavior analysts themselves must take the responsibility to help develop the principles needed to describe ways of predicting and controlling the kinds of interactions they are studying.

There are, of course, trade-offs. Increases in scope almost always come at the cost of a loss in precision. That is best dealt with by developing both technological and theoretical constructions for given events. No loss in precision of the technological description is produced, and the considerable benefit of theory is gained: the promise of an integrated science that is systematically applicable to new situations. That's why theory is needed. *JABA* has advanced the first part of the equation. It should help advance the second.

REFERENCES

Hayes, S. C. (1978). Theory and technology in behavior analysis. *The Behavior Analyst,* **1**, 25–33.

Hayes, S. C. (1987). The relation between "applied" and "basic" psychology. *Behavior Analysis,* **22**, 91–100.

Hayes, S. C. (1988). The implications of external validity for strategies of treatment research. In E. R. Rahdert & J. Grabowski (Eds.), *Adolescent drug abuse: Analyses of treatment research,* Research Monograph 77 (pp. 113–127). Washington, DC: National Institute on Drug Abuse.

Hayes, S. C., Rincover, A., & Solnick, J. (1980). The technical drift of applied behavior analysis. *Journal of Applied Behavior Analysis,* **13**, 275–285.

Kazdin, A. E., & Hersen, M. (1980). The current status of behavior therapy. *Behavior Modification,* **4**, 283–302.

Received February 25, 1991
Final acceptance May 16, 1991
Action Editor, E. Scott Geller

JOURNAL OF APPLIED BEHAVIOR ANALYSIS 1991, 24, 421–424 NUMBER 3 (FALL 1991)

APPLIED BEHAVIOR ANALYSIS AS TECHNOLOGICAL SCIENCE

BRIAN A. IWATA

THE UNIVERSITY OF FLORIDA

Since its inception, the *Journal of Applied Behavior Analysis* (*JABA*) has emphasized the publication of research involving applications of the experimental analysis of behavior to problems of social importance. These features of *JABA* and the larger field that it represents were clearly described in the seminal article by Baer, Wolf, and Risley (1968) and have been reaffirmed numerous times subsequently (e.g., Azrin, 1977; Baer, 1978). Thus, there always has been a close link between basic and applied research in behavior analysis, even though that link may not be formally stated in every article published.

In examining the generality of behavioral principles with socially important responses, applied research has produced a methodology and technology of behavior change analogous to those found in other scientific endeavors having social impact. All fields of science that have produced methods for quantification of data and control over their subject matter also have shared a research orientation heavily emphasizing the development of technology and its translation into effective behavior (e.g., of the architectural, surgical, and airplane manufacturing sort). To the extent that applied behavior analysis represents a scientific *and* practical approach to the study of behavior, its technological character is essential.

But is our emphasis on technology excessive? Hayes, Rincover, and Solnick (1980) answered the question affirmatively. Independent of the data on which their conclusion was based (only one of 15 sets of data supported that conclusion[1]), it would be difficult to argue that technology in *any* field of science is excessive because the only direct consequence of improved technology is increased precision. Better precision leads to better experimental control that, in the case of applied behavior analysis, yields benefits in both application and extension of basic science. Our ability to both analyze behavior and develop consistently effective behavior-change procedures is entirely dependent upon further improvements in technology.

The critique of applied behavior analysis did not end with technology, however. Hayes et al. (1980) proposed that applied behavior analysis is not only "technological to a fault" but also "atheoretical to a fault." This criticism is more difficult to refute because it requires clarification of several issues: What is theoretically relevant research? Does applied behavior analysis research emphasize technology over theory? What is the role of theory in the further development of our field?

What Is Theoretically Relevant Research?

Hayes et al. (1980) defined theoretical research as that showing

> an effort to advance our basic knowledge of some behavioral phenomenon. In addition to "how to" questions, this type of research also asks "what is" questions, such as "what is the nature of imitation in children" or "what is a response class?" (p. 278)

Reprints may be obtained from the author, Psychology Department, the University of Florida, Gainesville, Florida 32611.

[1] The relevant data set was a small proportion of *JABA* studies in which procedural descriptions were not labeled with respect to their underlying basic principles. Hayes et al. defined these studies as "purely technical articles," in the sense that there was nothing theoretically relevant about the studies. Yet the definition has at least two limitations. First, "technical" was not described with respect to any inclusion criteria (i.e., what must a study contain in order to be considered technical?). Instead, the authors defined technical by exclusion; omitting reference to a basic principle is not the same as describing procedures in a clear and operational (technical) manner. Second, it seems that the authors used a structural or topographical definition for technical rather than a functional one; they later reprobated this very approach when discussing how analogue studies can be considered relevant to application if one uses a functional rather than procedural description for "applied."

Using this definition, it is difficult to determine "what is" or is not an instance of theoretical research. For example, consider the extent to which several types of research questions about imitation are "theoretical" in nature.

1. Is imitation an operant response? The answer is provided simply by arranging a contingency between imitation and a suitable consequence such as praise.

2. Is imitation sensitive to intermittent reinforcement? The answer is provided by arranging the contingency for a proportion of imitative responses.

3. Does reinforcement of imitative behavior produce generalization (e.g., to nonreinforced imitative responses)? The answer is provided by reinforcing some imitative topographies but not others, while taking data on both.

4. What techniques can be used to improve imitation in developmentally handicapped children? The answer is provided by performing any of the above operations with a particular individual serving as subject.

5. What can be done when procedures used to answer Question 4 sometimes are associated with behavior other than imitation (i.e., disruption)? The answer is provided by varying the consequences for imitation and/or disruption; alternatively, one can begin asking a series of questions about disruption per se (Is it an operant?, etc.).

Each of the five questions asks about the "nature" of imitation ("what is?") and related behaviors in a way that can only be answered through technological arrangement of the environment ("how to?"). Moreover, one could argue that none of the answers produces a new theoretical concept but that all extend operant theory. The first question is interesting and likely to be asked when little is known about imitation; the last is interesting when more is known about imitation. This seems like a reasonable developmental progression of research that can easily account for a predominance of the last question, and variations thereof, after the first question has been answered a few times. The only differences across questions are how the contingencies are arranged, how the data are collected, and how the subjects are selected. More effort, control, and technology are required as one moves from the first to the last question. Yet the first question might be regarded as theoretical but the last as purely technological, and the first question will remain theoretical even after it has been answered frequently enough to become uninteresting. It is not clear how asking less and doing less (technology) translate into more (theory).

If imitation as an example is too simple because it has been the subject of behavioral research for over 20 years, more recent topics can be substituted. In behavior analysis research with developmentally handicapped individuals, two areas of current interest are the establishment of conditional discriminations (i.e., stimulus equivalence classes) in response acquisition and functional analysis approaches to response reduction. Both are regarded as major theoretical as well as technological areas of research. Yet neither has produced new theory. Instead, previously identified functional relations—described as stimulus control and response maintenance—have been extended through technological refinement, and already we are seeing very rapid progression from "what is" to "how to" questions. Given the potential interchangeability between these types of questions, an alternative to the claim that "some research is less theoretical" can be proposed: "All behavioral research is theoretically relevant, but some research is more applied." Neither describes an ideal taxonomy, but the limited utility of the first statement may become apparent to some only when it is placed in contrast to the second.

Does Applied Behavior Analysis Research Emphasize Technology over Theory?

Another way to consider the issue of technological versus theoretical research is to ask whether there is too little theory. This question cannot be answered definitively because it assumes that the consequences of too much or too little are known. Nevertheless, when viewed in relationship to other fields of science, the ratio of technology to theory in behavior analysis is probably no larger than that seen in physics or biology, and perhaps considerably smaller. It is only when behavior analysis is viewed in relation to the rest of psychology that our emphasis on technology may seem excessive or our use of theory limited. The other major psychological systems—for example, psychoanalysis, which dominated the study of human behavior early in the century, and cognitivism, which has taken its place—have not produced a practical science of behavior precisely because their subject matter remains elusive. These fields are left with theory as an explanation of behavior in the absence of confirming data. By contrast, behavior analysts have shown repeatedly that it is possible to exert reliable control over behavior by systematically varying its consequences and events correlated with them. So, our "theories" (e.g., about reinforcement contingencies, schedules, stimulus control, etc.) are different from most psychological theories because they are not speculations about how uncontrolled phenomena *might be* controlled. Most of our theories exist as functional relations describing how phenomena *have been* controlled.

At the present time, there is still much about environment–behavior interactions that we do not know (i.e., that we have not been able to control), and all of what we do know has yet to be translated into effective application. Therefore, a small proportion of our field consists of "might be" theories, but these are often short-lived as vacant predictions about behavior because they are quickly replaced by technological data. Thus, our theories, like those in the physical sciences, are both derived from and extended by technological demonstrations of experimental control. In much of psychology, exciting theories—guesses about behavior—are offered instead of a technology of behavior based on experimental control. And psychoanalysis is dead not because of a lack of theory or theoretical research but because of a lack of useful technology.

What Is the Role of Theory in the Further Development of Our Field?

Hayes et al. (1980) suggested that "Applied behavior analysts often seem to generate their interventions by intuition, trial and error, informal observations, or common sense, rather than theoretical concepts and analysis. . . . Such an approach . . . might actually slow progress of the field" (p. 284). But has such research *really* slowed progress? Must applied research be theory driven in order to be useful? Moxley (1989) noted that scientific theory and technology are not necessarily related in a hierarchical manner (i.e., effective technology development need not follow from or rely on existing theory). Instead, there appears to be a symmetrical relationship: Technology can be derived from either theory or technology itself and vice versa. Skinner (1950) commented more specifically on the necessity of theory to research many years ago:

> It is argued that research would be aimless and disorganized without a theory to guide it. The view is supported by psychological texts which take their cue from the logicians rather than empirical science and describe thinking as necessarily involving stages of hypothesis, deduction, experimental test, and confirmation. But this is not the way most scientists actually work. It is possible to design significant experiments for other reasons, and the possibility to be examined is that such research will lead more directly to the kind of information which a science usually accumulates. (p. 194)

Skinner's view does not discount theory as a useful controlling variable for research behavior, but it suggests that theory is not the only legitimate controlling variable. Returning to the earlier example of imitation, it can be seen that different research questions suggest different controlling variables. The first question (reinforcement control) asks how imitation develops. The second and third questions (schedule control, generalization) ask what can be done with already developed imitation. Answers to all three questions are generally informative, but also are of limited immediate benefit to therapists working with nonimitative clients or to the clients themselves. The fourth and fifth questions (establishing imitation in handicapped individuals, and doing so while reducing competing behavior) ask about imitation in specific applied contexts; the answers are immediately beneficial to therapists and clients, but are such answers generally informative? I think so, because answers to the latter questions suggest how behaviors other than imitation might be examined in the same individuals, how imitation might be developed in other individuals, and how reinforcement procedures might be varied to examine other behaviors in other individuals.

There are, of course, additional controlling variables to consider, such as those promoting widespread adoption of technological innovation (Stolz, 1981). The point is that a multiplicity of controlling variables has advanced our field by promoting diversity. And the practical value of these diverse research efforts, not just for consumers but also for other researchers, has been a direct function of well-controlled experimentation (i.e., technology).

The Real Problem

The most serious problem evident in applied behavior analysis today is not the type of research being conducted; it is that not enough good research—of all types—is being conducted. We need studies that do nothing more than operationally define hypothetical constructs considered important in our society but not previously examined behaviorally. An example might be "healthy self-concept" in children. Once defined, we need studies that identify the environmental determinants of a healthy self-concept, the conditions under which self-concept fails to "emerge," and problems associated with "poor" self-concept. We need other studies developing methods for improving self-concept, increasing the effectiveness and efficiency of those methods, and examining the generality of those methods across subjects and settings. We need studies to identify the indirect or long-term benefits of intervention. Finally, we need to consider how our resulting technology for enhancing self-concept can be disseminated effectively.

Each of these types of research is theoretically relevant, heavily dependent on technology, and important to the further development of our field. There will always be questions about relative proportion: Some will call for more "real-world" application, whereas others call for more studies that "extend basic principles." These calls are relevant as attempts to increase the frequency of underrepresented types of research. In fact, most of us agree that more of both types of research is needed and feel that the goal can be achieved through careful prompting, modeling, and reinforcement. To reduce the frequency of one type of research in order to increase the other, however, seems imprudent. To reduce the frequency of one type of research by denigrating it or by punishing those who do it well seems foolish.

REFERENCES

Azrin, N. H. (1977). A strategy for applied research: Learning based but outcome oriented. *American Psychologist*, **32**, 140–149.

Baer, D. M. (1978). On the relation between basic and applied research. In T. A. Brigham & A. C. Catania (Eds.), *Handbook of applied behavior analysis* (pp. 11–16). New York: Irvington.

Baer, D. M., Wolf, M. M., & Risley, T. R. (1968). Some current dimensions of applied behavior analysis. *Journal of Applied Behavior Analysis*, **1**, 91–97.

Hayes, S. C., Rincover, A., & Solnick, J. V. (1980). The technical drift of applied behavior analysis. *Journal of Applied Behavior Analysis*, **13**, 275–285.

Moxley, R. A. (1989). Some historical relationships between science and technology with implications for behavior analysis. *The Behavior Analyst*, **12**, 45–57.

Skinner, B. F. (1950). Are theories of learning necessary? *Psychological Review*, **57**, 193–216.

Stolz, S. B. (1981). Adoption of innovations from applied research: "Does anybody care?" *Journal of Applied Behavior Analysis*, **14**, 491–505.

Received June 7, 1991
Final acceptance June 14, 1991
Action Editor, E. Scott Geller

JOURNAL OF APPLIED BEHAVIOR ANALYSIS 1991, 24, 425–427 NUMBER 3 (FALL 1991)

WE NEED A NEW MODEL OF TECHNOLOGY

J. M. JOHNSTON
AUBURN UNIVERSITY

I have long preferred the phrase *behavioral technology* to refer to the results of the science of experimental and applied behavior analysis. My reason for wanting to use the term *technology* is that this is how the natural sciences refer to their applied capabilities. Saying that our applied skills constitute a technology is a generous assessment, however, because references to technology in the natural sciences differ significantly from our use of the term. In the natural sciences, technology most often refers to consistently effective techniques whose mechanisms have been largely explained by the science.

These demanding criteria are infrequently met in the applied offerings of psychology or even behavior analysis. If we cannot explain our applied procedures with an experimental literature that fully details critical variables and how they work in terms of the basic laws of behavior, and if the effects have not been shown by experimental investigation to be consistently effective, then our procedures might be more appropriately called craft, skilled experience, professional lore, or common sense. It is not even enough that a behavior-change procedure may be effective for reasons unknown or merely suspected. In other words, this conception of technology says that the experimentally derived understanding of the way a procedure works is more important than its origins, the consistency of its effectiveness, or the effectiveness of competing approaches.

The experimental requirements of this approach to developing technology involve both learning about the origins and current sources of control over target behaviors as well as identifying and analyzing separately the elements of a procedure to determine the role of each in the overall effect. This information will clarify the environmental requirements and options contributed by the behaviors under study, as well as those elements critical to a procedure's effects that must not be tampered with and those that can be modified under certain conditions. The next step is to determine the mechanisms by which the elements contribute to the procedure's effects, both separately and collectively. These experimental requirements will generate a literature of thematic studies that explain fully the procedure's functions and mechanisms in terms of the basic laws of the science of behavior.

This conception of technology requires a second empirical process that candidates must survive. The procedure must be evaluated under realistic, applied conditions and shown to be consistently and practically effective. This may sometimes require only descriptive studies, but it usually calls for more than one or two demonstrations. It means that if the effects obtained under typical field conditions are in any way different than those already established in the analytical literature, they must be described and perhaps studied. It also means that the requirements and effects of population, setting, and administrative factors must be identified; this will often lead to more analytical research.

This approach to developing a technology is not a very accurate description of how applied behavior analysis has developed its procedures. Although we can boast a large applied literature, we have not focused on studying target behaviors, and our procedures have generally not received this kind of systematic experimental attention. Analytical efforts have tended to be fairly superficial, emphasizing procedures rather than behavior and falling well short of experimentally explicating procedural mechanisms at the level of basic principles of operant behavior.

We do a somewhat better job at evaluating procedures under field conditions. Successful demon-

Some of the points argued in this paper are presented more fully in Johnston (in press).

Reprints may be obtained from the author, Department of Psychology, Auburn University, Auburn, Alabama 36849.

strations are of limited usefulness, however, when our understanding of why they work is based primarily on superficial topographical similarities to basic operant principles. Without this understanding, we cannot be very confident about what it will take to produce effective results under other conditions. Although our description of procedures sometimes uses the terminology of basic conditioning processes, the exercise is more often nominal than experimentally functional (Johnston, 1988).

I believe we need to work toward a model for developing and evaluating behavioral technology consistent with the approach of the other natural sciences. I have proposed such a model (Johnston, in press), although it cannot be properly summarized here. Its focus is on developing an experimental literature that is comprehensive in both its attempt to understand target behaviors and its search for the how and why of applied procedures. With such an experimental data base, practitioners will be in a better position than at present to select procedures based on a set of clear behavioral and procedural requirements for effectiveness, with reasonable confidence that meeting those requirements will assure success.

Such a model has many important implications for our field; I would like to suggest a few that are especially relevant to the theme of this series of papers. First, it suggests that we should make a clear distinction between technological research and technological application. Instead of thinking of the field of behavior analysis in terms of a basic versus applied division of labor, we should further subdivide applied activities into research versus service. (Even better would be a major division of research versus service, with research subdivided into basic versus applied.)

Technological research focuses on developing ways of controlling behavior for practical purposes. Even so, its experimental methods should usually be indistinguishable from those of basic research. Most such studies should be thematic and analytical in style, answering questions about behavior, its controlling variables, procedural components, administrative influences, and so forth. Only a relatively small part of this literature should focus on evaluation per se.

Technological application should not have to focus on asking experimental questions at all, although these will sometimes arise when procedures fail to produce the desired effects. Efforts here should be on behalf of delivering a service and should primarily involve only assessment, selection and adjustment of procedures, and continuing field evaluation. The more successful a procedure's research history, the less likely it is that practitioners will have to turn a service intervention into an experiment in order to meet applied goals.

The importance of this distinction is in the requirements for conducting sound research versus offering effective service. The overriding goal of technological research is to discover the variables that influence certain forms of behavior, including those embedded in proposed intervention procedures; this challenge requires control. Control, however, often requires some degree of artificiality. On the other hand, technological application requires accommodating the circumstances of field settings, but this usually sacrifices control.

In other words, the goals and requisites of these activities often conflict, making one a poor opportunity for accomplishing the other. When we indiscriminately combine them, as in contemporary applied behavioral research, it may only constrain the effectiveness of both efforts. The methodological necessities for important and revealing technological research and the experimental questions they serve should not be routinely compromised by the practical needs of service delivery. Similarly, applications of established procedures do not necessarily need to be handicapped by all of the niceties of research method when no experiment is conducted.

This distinction suggests a second implication of this model. We should represent the different needs of applied research versus practice in how we accept students into graduate programs, how we train them, and how they are employed. Although the interests and skills needed for effectiveness in these two career directions have much in common, there are important differences. Technological researchers must be both inclined and trained to be good scientists above all else. They need to be expert in the applied and basic literatures, as well as being familiar with the populations and applied settings of interest. However, the applied components of their training must not compromise their training as researchers. On the other hand, practitioners-to-be must know not just the applied literature but must also acquire clinical expertise and other skills required for effectiveness in applied settings. It may be equally important that these students fully intend to be practitioners rather than researchers.

It might even be argued that practitioners should receive training that is more service oriented than research oriented. The scientist-practitioner philosophy we seem to have uncritically borrowed from clinical psychology (see Barlow, Hayes, & Nelson, 1984) may be counterproductive for this new model. There have been many debates about the scientist-practitioner approach to training practitioners, but it is easy to see that few careers fit its assumptions very well. Not only are most holders of the doctorate in psychology apparently uninterested in being both researchers and practitioners, it is difficult to do both well. The contingencies of service goals and employment often lead to compromises in the quality of both the conception and execution of applied research, which is reflected in a weak clinical literature. Although there will always be a few meritorious exceptions, as a general approach to training practitioners the scientist-practitioner model is easy to argue against. (We might remember that medicine and engineering give their practitioners narrowly professional training.)

The model I have suggested (Johnston, in press) should be seen as enhancing rather than diminishing the role of practitioners. Although practitioners would be selected and trained to be more narrowly service oriented than at present, we would no longer need to define their value by such academic credentials as research publications. In addition to their role in service delivery, they would communicate the demand for particular technologies, describe accidental discoveries from their field experience, and report shortcomings with new technologies. Of course, the state of our present skills falls short of this ideal, and practitioners will for years to come unavoidably find themselves conducting service in a research style in order to obtain desired results. This does not usually result in very rigorous research, however. Furthermore, it usually fails to answer the questions that must be addressed in order to understand the factors that influence target behaviors and how intervention procedures work, both of which are required to make procedures consistently effective.

These are provocative topics, and the brevity of my comments may make these points more vexing than intriguing. Many behavior analysts may even feel that we may never be able to create a technology in the style of the natural sciences because (a) behavior is different from other natural phenomena, (b) our ability to control important variables in applied environments will always be limited, or (c) we are doing pretty well already (i.e., better than anyone else). Such rebuttals seem highly debatable, but they do not seem like sound reasons for not trying. It is difficult to imagine convincing arguments for why we should not strive for technological capabilities as impressive as those offered by the physical and biological sciences.

I am worried that we do not seem to have a model or standard that presently guides our technological research questions. There is evidence for this concern throughout our literature. In the area of retardation, for example, we seem to have focused for years on changing behavior with powerful consequences until the recent "discovery" of functional analysis (i.e., what we used to call behavior analysis) suggested we ought to learn more about behavior and its causes. What worries me most, however, is that we may have lost our sense of what behavior analysis can accomplish, of what is possible, of where we are going. Maybe we have not yet decided.

REFERENCES

Barlow, D. H., Hayes, S. C., & Nelson, R. O. (1984). *The scientist practitioner: Research and accountability in clinical and educational settings.* New York: Pergamon.

Johnston, J. M. (1988). Strategic and tactical limits of comparison studies. *The Behavior Analyst,* **11,** 1–9.

Johnston, J. M. (in press). A model for developing and evaluating behavioral technology. In S. Axelrod & P. Van Houten (Eds.), *Effective behavioral treatment: Issues and implementation.* New York: Plenum.

Received February 26, 1991
Final acceptance March 27, 1991
Action Editor, E. Scott Geller

JOURNAL OF APPLIED BEHAVIOR ANALYSIS 1991, 24, 429–431 NUMBER 3 (FALL 1991)

TACTING "TO A FAULT"

DONALD M. BAER
UNIVERSITY OF KANSAS

The thesis is that behavior analysis is technological to a fault. Perhaps the simplest, most fundamental response is to note the proper meaning of the word *technology,* from which it follows that you cannot be technological to a fault. You *can* have a faulty technology. The way in which technology can be faulty is to be incomplete. An incorrect technology is an oxymoron. A technology that does things an audience dislikes is not a faulty technology; the point of a technology is to accomplish that at which it is aimed, and the point of an audience is to choose at what to aim.

I find two major functions of technology in the disciplines of empirical science. One is to make observation and measurement valid and reliable; the other is to make things work reliably. Some disciplines are not about making anything work, but instead are about noting regularity, order, and predictability. Astronomy and most of meteorology, sociology, and anthropology are examples; they need and develop mainly measurement technologies. Some disciplines are about making things work; they need and develop both technologies. Physics, chemistry, engineering, business administration, and medicine are notable examples. However, a few of the disciplines that must make things work cannot yet get all their things to work very reliably; perhaps the most notable examples for present purposes are the social, behavioral, and management sciences. The interesting question is what stimulus function that current partial failure of technology has in those sciences.

In the natural sciences, as best I know their histories, failures to control their subject matter have had two stimulus functions: One was to set the occasion for developing real-world procedures that would yield better control. When those procedures succeeded they were, of course, labeled technology. The second was to set the occasion for theorizing, mainly to explain why current technology was still as unreliable as it was. Of course, that was not the avowed function of theory, but I claim that it usually was the underlying function.

In my opinion, these two functions were most often inverses. The development of better control usually took time, effort, resources, and imagination; the development of a theoretical explanation of why current technology did not always succeed required less imagination, far less time, even less effort, and virtually no resources. Perhaps that was why theory development usually preceded technology development, and why theories that were developed in the absence of better experimental control so often faded away when that control was finally achieved. True, the stereotypic account of science says that good theory precedes and enables better experimental control. Clearly, that does happen sometimes. However, in my opinion, the reverse is much more common.

If the question is whether behavior analysis too often answers current failures of experimental control by striving for better experimental control, and too rarely answers current failures of experimental control by inventing theoretical explanations for that failure, then I must ask for a criterion of "too." I suspect the underlying question is about how variously we choose those criteria. I propose a behavior-analytic way of discussing them: Let us extrapolate how different proportions of those two endeavors (striving for better experimental control vs. inventing theories to explain why our current control is imperfect) will lead to different kinds of behavioral science; then we can ask ourselves and our audience if we recognize in those outcomes some reinforcers or some punishers. We can then recommend the proportions of theory and striving for

Reprints may be obtained from the author, Department of Human Development, 4001 Dole Human Development Center, University of Kansas, Lawrence, Kansas 66045-2133.

better control that maximize our reinforcers and minimize our punishers. And after that we can discover how little behavioral function recommendations have.

If that is my recommendation, then perhaps *I* should begin. I can report that my behavior is much better reinforced by achieving experimental control over what I study than by achieving a theoretical explanation of why I sometimes fail to achieve that experimental control. However, my behavior is also a little better reinforced by a theoretical explanation than by neither experimental control nor explanation. Thus, I have done a lot of the former and some of the latter (mainly when asked—e.g., the present case).

Should I invent reasons (theory?) as to why my reinforcers fall in that rank order? As if such reasons might better convince a reader than would the mere truth about my behavior? Try the following, but remember that they are only rationalizations.

History. I claim that natural science has advanced to the forms in which we now teach it, more through the achievement of better and better experimental control than through the development of theory.

Survival. I claim that our society is more likely to survive through the development of better behavioral technology than by the development of theory about why our current behavioral technology is still not saving us from self-destruction. In particular, I claim that when we strive for better experimental control over society's adoption of behavioral programs, the results will make it easier to choose among the many current theories about why society does not use knowledge to save itself.

Profession. I guess that the earth contains roughly 500,000 psychologists and 5,000 behavior analysts. I claim that the most distinctive feature of the behavior analysts is their devotion to achieving better and better experimental control of what they study, whereas the most distinctive feature of the psychologists is their devotion to achieving theoretical explanations for all current failure to do so (especially explanations that will bear their name) and that, among these, theories that blame the victim rather than the programmer are the more desired. In that case, why compete in a professional market already saturated with people better trained for that kind of production?

Victim blaming per se. Interestingly, theoretical reactions to incomplete technologies sometimes blame technology per se, as if to assert that the reason a technology is incomplete is that it is only a technology, and thus that we shall remain forever incomplete as long as we rely on technology. But for what do we rely on technology? Only to accomplish what we have decided to accomplish. If there is a flaw, it is either that the technology does not accomplish all of what we desire, or that we do not desire enough of the right things (the things desired by someone else), or that we desire the wrong things (the things disliked by someone else), or some of that, or all of that. That form of argument against technology is at least topographically similar to arguing that the powerless are powerless because they are not assertive, which we establish through questionnaires. Power can be asserted, and yet in their cases it is not. Thus, they are powerless because they are not assertive, which we know because they say so if asked, which we claim are valid measures because people who say that are typically powerless. Thus, some people are powerless because they are powerless. That is victim blaming (and also tautology).

Similarly, is the argument that we fail to accomplish all we wish because we are technological to a fault? And how do we know that we are technological to a fault? It had better not be simply that we say we are technological and also say we are not accomplishing all that we wish. But perhaps a certain amount of that kind of argument was the impetus for this particular journal symposium.

Logic. I claim that radical behaviorism is already an exceptionally thorough and comprehensive theoretical account of behavior, one that, more than any other, not only presses its students to value better and better experimental control over any behaviors amenable to it but also teaches them how to approach that goal—and then teaches them to analyze approach behavior, and then choice behavior, and then the verbal behavior we use when we tact goals. It seems to me that radical behaviorism recommends reserving merely conceptual control only for those behaviors not amenable to experimental control. I argue that radical behaviorism requires mainly internal elaboration of all that is logically implicit in its principles rather than addition and revision.

But I have no proof of any of that, as none of us has or will have, and so the readers of this symposium would do better not to be convinced by any of it. Which is to say, I would like it better if they did not tact conviction under these stimulus conditions. Which in turn is to say, I would respond to switch out of a chain in which the terminal link was that kind of tacting and into a concurrent chain in which the terminal link was tacting abstention from that kind of tacting. But for any audience not responsive to the tacts of concurrent chains, I return to "I would like it better if they did not tact conviction under those stimulus conditions."

If these critics were students in my research-methods class, I might arrange stimulus controls and contingencies to insure that they did not tact conviction under such stimulus conditions. If I knew how to do that effectively, I would be technological, wouldn't I? To a fault? Perhaps the critics who would say so mean only that they would teach research methods differently, or would teach different research methods, perhaps based on different standards of when to tact the word *proof*. But why blame teaching technology for that difference? A complete teaching technology would simply make the teaching of any such standards more effective. For those critics who decry effective teaching per se as either illiberal or poor preparation for life in the real world of having to teach yourself most things, a complete technology would also show them how to teach as ineffectively as controls their tacting of satisfaction.

Perhaps readers should simply see if any of this reminds them of how their reinforcers are rank-ordered. Then, if they are ever pressed for rationalizations of what they are going to do and not do anyway, rationalized or not, they can offer their individual choices from these and the many others this symposium offers.

Received March 10, 1991
Final acceptance May 7, 1991
Action Editor, E. Scott Geller

JOURNAL OF APPLIED BEHAVIOR ANALYSIS 1991, 24, 433–435 NUMBER 3 (FALL 1991)

TECHNOLOGICAL TO A FAULT OR FAULTY APPROACH TO TECHNOLOGY DEVELOPMENT?

F. CHARLES MACE

UNIVERSITY OF PENNSYLVANIA

Steve Hayes seems to hold the view that technology, in its proper place, is a vital organ in the body of behavioral science. It has an important role to play that is distinct from other body systems, namely theory development and basic research. However, in the context of this analogy, Hayes seems to contend that *JABA* became carcinogenic by overemphasizing technology, by becoming "technological to a fault." According to Hayes, the ensuing cancer infiltrated the organ and may metastasize to the entire body. This viewpoint seems to rest on the assumptions that (a) technology, theory, and basic science are purely separate endeavors and (b) emphasis on one area occurs at the expense of the others. In my opinion, the problem is not that we have become too technological. Indeed, it is hard to see how that is possible. If technology provides the tools for solving problems, how can we have too many tools? The absurdity of the adage, "too much knowledge is a dangerous thing," seems to hold true for technology as well. The problem as I see it is that we do not have a clear understanding of how technologies proficiently evolve. I suspect that Hayes would agree with this point. Where we differ, however, is in placing the blame on technology.

How is a technology developed? I think we can look to other fields for some excellent examples of the process of technology building. Technological advances in medicine, for example, are the result of continuous, and often purposeful, interaction among basic scientists, technology developers, clinical researchers, clinicians, and theory builders. There are well-trodden pathways connecting all of these areas that are essential to the ultimate goal of advancing medical technology. Some phases of the process are so well defined that they are regulated by the federal government. The process of developing AIDS drugs provides a good illustration. Until the advent of AIDS, the basic science of virology and, in particular, retrovirology had experienced modest growth. All of this changed, of course, with the discovery of HIV as the source of AIDS. The field of virology boomed in response to this acute human need as basic scientists worked feverishly to understand the life cycle of HIV at the genetic, cellular, and systemic levels. This surge of activity is providing the basic building blocks that will be essential to the development of effective pharmacological therapies. Moreover, advances in AIDS research have been greatly facilitated by ongoing technological developments in related subspecialties such as immunology and molecular genetics. Much of the work in these two areas has been directly applicable to basic AIDS research. Thus, the first stage of technology development is the accumulation of fundamental knowledge of the subject matter resulting from basic research in related disciplines. When this occurs in response to a specific human problem, as in the case of AIDS, basic research will have a focus that will more readily nurture technological developments in specific directions.

The second stage of the process entails experimental demonstrations of a drug's capacity to interrupt the life cycle of the virus. This is generally done with a small number of HIV specimens with replications across known viral strains. Drugs that show clear promise of inhibiting or preventing virus replication become candidates for further development and testing on animals and/or with hu-

---

I appreciate the insightful comments of Sandy Harris, Joyce Mauk, Nancy Neef, Mark Reber, and John Parrish on earlier versions of this manuscript.

Reprints may be obtained from the author, Children's Hospital of Philadelphia, University of Pennsylvania School of Medicine, 34th and Civic Center Blvd., Philadelphia, Pennsylvania 19104.

mans in clinical trials. Because there has been considerable difficulty in developing an HIV/AIDS animal model for testing drug efficacy, this stage of the process is often omitted for therapeutic drugs, although simian models have been useful for testing potential vaccines.

Phase I clinical trials consist of parametric investigations of drug dosages and regimen durations with human subjects. The primary goal of this phase is to determine whether the drug is safe for use with humans at different dosages. In general, this is accomplished with a relatively small number of subjects, with careful documentation of adverse side effects across time and dosages. Drugs that are tolerated at dosages that are anticipated to have therapeutic effects enter Phase II clinical trials. The principal goal of this second phase is to evaluate the clinical benefits of the drug under double-blind experimental conditions. Here again, a relatively small number of individuals receive the drug under a narrower range of dosages. Drugs that yield clinically significant improvement in the immune response or symptoms of opportunistic infection progress to the last phase of clinical trials. Phase III clinical trials are large-scale studies of drug effectiveness under less controlled conditions more typical of clinical medicine. The primary goals of this phase are to document (a) percentage effectiveness in the population; (b) the nature, range, and distribution of adverse side effects; and (c) possible differential effects among population subgroups. Drugs that pass successfully through all three phases of clinical trials are likely to win Federal Drug Administration (FDA) approval. However, the process of evaluation continues postapproval with additional parametric studies of effects with sub-groups and long-term clinical benefits, side effects, and mortality rates. Clinicians contribute in this final stage by reporting case studies and/or publishing clinical data as "Letters to the Editor."

What I hope this example illustrates is that the development of technologies in some fields is achieved through a deliberate progression of different types of research. These types of studies span a continuum from basic research to uncontrolled clinical reports, all of which are important for the development of technologies. I have believed for some time that behavior analysis would benefit greatly from the adoption of a deliberate strategy for technology building appropriate for our discipline. Looking at the discrepancy between our current practice and that of, say, medicine may help define the "problem" and suggest some solutions.

The first discrepancy concerns the relationship between basic and applied research in behavior analysis. After the initial infusion of fundamental knowledge of the principles of behavior (i.e., positive and negative reinforcement, schedules of reinforcement, stimulus control, punishment, and stimulus and response shaping), applied research has been essentially insulated from ongoing developments in basic behavioral science. This disconnection between basic and applied research has, in my view, slowed the pace of technological development and limited its complexity and specificity to the nature of human behavior problems. In addition, the responsiveness of basic researchers to specific human conditions that we see in other fields, such as medicine, is generally absent in behavior analysis. Were we able to foster this kind of relationship between experimental and applied research, I can envision its beneficial application to several research areas, including environmental protection. In the case of industrial pollution, we might begin by considering the possible contingencies operating to support acts of pollution. The choice to pollute or invest in ecologically sound disposal practices is probably influenced by factors such as (a) immediate versus delayed consequences, (b) the probability and severity of aversive contingencies, (c) the cost schedule associated with ecological alternatives, (d) the potency of reinforcement for responsible disposal, and (e) a company's short- and long-term profit margins (i.e., rates of reinforcement). There is much to be known about these factors in isolation and combination that could be addressed by experimental researchers.

A second major difference between our approach to technology building and that of medicine is the definition of the type and sequence of applied studies that need to be conducted to produce an effective and, hence, "adoptable" technology. In other words, what is our equivalent of phased clinical trials? An investigative sequence that seems generic to most applied areas is:

1. An initial experimental demonstration of the effects of a novel procedure or a method or process of investigation on a single subject.

2. Systematic replications that parametrically vary subject, setting, and response variables (four or five replications per experiment is probably sufficient).

3. Demonstration of the short- and long-term maintenance of the intervention effects with 4 or 5 subjects per experiment.

4. Detailed analysis of factors predicting favorable and unfavorable responses to the intervention with several subjects (i.e., specification of the conditions necessary and sufficient for the behavioral operation to invoke the behavioral process).

5. Large-scale studies documenting the percentage effectiveness in the population and consisting of single-case experiments in numbers sufficient for accurately estimating population success rates.

6. Large-scale studies comparing the effectiveness of alternative interventions, under optimal conditions and in numbers permitting comparative success rates in the population.

Many areas of applied research have completed this sequence (e.g., see Johnston and Pennypacker's, 1980, discussion of the replicative history of time-out research) and included many nuances that I have not mentioned. However, other promising areas are abandoned before a mature technology emerges. (E.g., the descriptive study on beer drinking among college students by Geller, Russ, and Altomari, 1986, may be a case in point. This study showed that alcohol consumption varied by gender, beverage vessel size, and the number of people in the patron's party, suggesting variables whose manipulation may reduce alcohol-related traffic crashes.) Medicine is assisted immeasurably in this process by regulation and the economic incentives for product development. Without this assistance, or until we acquire it, I believe we should begin thinking about ways to arrange the contingencies for programmatic research that will encourage completion of the process. One practical strategy may be for an editorial staff to require submitting authors to discuss where in the sequence their research falls, and what type of study needs to be conducted next in the progression toward a mature technology.

To return to the germinating point of this discussion, I believe the failure of some of our technologies to be adopted is not due to our being "technological to a fault." Instead, I believe the problem can be traced to our faulty approach to technology development. I believe the solution lies in the integration of our basic and applied sectors and the coordination of our efforts toward specific goals that are defined and valued by the culture. If such a strategy results in technologies that are more rapid in their development and more powerful in their effects, the problem of adoption will be diminished considerably.

REFERENCES

Geller, E. S., Russ, N. W., & Altomari, M. G. (1986). Naturalistic observations of beer drinking among college students. *Journal of Applied Behavior Analysis*, **19**, 391–396.

Johnston, J. M., & Pennypacker, H. S. (1980). *Strategies and tactics of human behavioral research*. Hillsdale, NJ: Erlbaum.

Received May 22, 1991
Final acceptance May 31, 1991
Action Editor, E. Scott Geller

JOURNAL OF APPLIED BEHAVIOR ANALYSIS 1968, 1, 175-191 NUMBER 2 (SUMMER 1968)

A METHOD TO INTEGRATE DESCRIPTIVE AND EXPERIMENTAL FIELD STUDIES AT THE LEVEL OF DATA AND EMPIRICAL CONCEPTS[1]

SIDNEY W. BIJOU, ROBERT F. PETERSON, AND MARION H. AULT

UNIVERSITY OF ILLINOIS

It is the thesis of this paper that data from descriptive and experimental field studies can be interrelated at the level of data and empirical concepts if both sets are derived from frequency-of-occurrence measures. The methodology proposed for a descriptive field study is predicated on three assumptions: (1) The primary data of psychology are the observable interactions of a biological organism and environmental events, past and present. (2) Theoretical concepts and laws are derived from empirical concepts and laws, which in turn are derived from the raw data. (3) Descriptive field studies describe interactions between behavioral and environmental events; experimental field studies provide information on their functional relationships. The ingredients of a descriptive field investigation using frequency measures consist of: (1) specifying in objective terms the situation in which the study is conducted, (2) defining and recording behavioral and environmental events in observable terms, and (3) measuring observer reliability. Field descriptive studies following the procedures suggested here would reveal interesting new relationships in the usual ecological settings and would also provide provocative cues for experimental studies. On the other hand, field-experimental studies using frequency measures would probably yield findings that would suggest the need for describing new interactions in specific natural situations.

Psychology, like the other natural sciences, depends for its advancement upon both descriptive accounts and functional analyses of its primary data. Descriptive studies answer the question "How?". They may, for example, report the manner in which a Bantu mother nurses her child, or the way in which the Yellow Shafted Flicker mates. Experimental studies, on the other hand, provide the "Why?". They might discuss the conditions which establish and maintain the relationships between the mother and infant, between the male and female birds.

It has been claimed that progress in the behavioral sciences would be enhanced by more emphasis on descriptive studies. This may be true, but one may wish to speculate on why descriptive accounts of behavior have been de-emphasized. One possibility is the difficulty of relating descriptive and experimental data. For example, a descriptive study of parent-child behavior in the home may have data in the form of ratings on a series of scales (Baldwin, Kalhorn, and Breese, 1949), while an experimental study on the same subject may have data in the form of frequencies of events (Hawkins, Peterson, Schweid, and Bijou, 1966). Findings from the first study cannot reasonably be integrated with the second at the level of data and empirical concepts. Anyone interested in relating the two must resort to imprecise theory or concepts like "permissive mother", "laissez-faire atmosphere", "controlling child", "negativism", *etc.* This practice is unacceptable to psychologists who believe that all concepts must be based on or linked to empirical events.

It is the thesis of this paper that descriptive field studies (which include cross-cultural, ecological, and normative investigations) and experimental field studies can be performed so that the data and empirical terms in each are continuous, interchangeable, and mutually interrelatable.

Barker and Wright (1955) state that one of the aims of their ecological investigations is to produce data that may be used by all investigators in child behavior and development.

---

[1]The formulation presented here was generated from the research conducted under grants from the U. S. Public Health Service, National Institute of Mental Health (M-2208, M-2232, and MH-12067), and from the U. S. Office of Education, Handicapped Children and Youth Branch (Grant No. 32-23-1020-6002, Proposal No. R-006). Reprints may be obtained from Sidney W. Bijou, Child Behavior Laboratory, University of Illinois, 403 East Healey, Champaign, Illinois 61820.

Their study of "Midwest" and its children (1955) is in part devoted to the development of a method which provides raw material (which they compared to objects stored in a museum) amenable to analyses from different theoretical points of view. There are two considerations which make this doubtful. First, their data consist of "running accounts of what a person is doing and his situation on the level of direct perception or immediate inference" with "minor interpretations in the form of statements *about* rather than descriptions *of* behavior or situations" (Wright, 1967). It would seem that the material they collect would be serviceable only to those who accept non-observables in the raw data defined according to their prescription. Investigators who prefer to define their hypothetical variables some other way or who wish to exclude non-observables will find it difficult to integrate their data with those in the Barker and Wright studies. Second, final data in the form of running narrations cannot readily be transformed into units describing interactions between behavioral and environmental events, such as duration, intensity, latency, or frequency. Any attempt to convert such verbal accounts into one or more of the interactional dimensions would require so many arbitrary decisions that it would be doubtful whether another investigator could even come close to producing the same operations and results.

If, however, frequency-of-occurrence measures of environmental and behavioral events were used in both descriptive and field experimental studies, data and empirical concepts could be made congruous. The measure of frequency is preferable to that of duration, intensity, and latency for several reasons (Skinner, 1953). First, this measure readily shows changes over short and long periods of observations. Second, it specifies the *amount* of behavior displayed (Honig, 1966). Finally, and perhaps most important, it is applicable to operant behaviors across species. Hence, a methodology based on frequency of events would be serviceable for both experimental and descriptive studies of both human and infra-human subjects. This versatility has been illustrated by Jensen and Bobbitt in a study on mother and infant relationships of the pig-tailed macaques (Jensen and Bobbitt, 1967).

With the use of frequency measures, the work of the ecological psychologist and the experimental psychologist would both complement and supplement each other. Descriptive studies would reveal interesting relationships among the raw data that could provide provocative cues for experimental investigations. On the other hand, field experimental studies would probably yield worthwhile leads for descriptive investigations by pointing to the need for observing new combinations of behavioral classes in specified situations. Ecological psychologists would show in terms of frequency of events, the practices of a culture, subculture, or an institutional activity of a subculture; experimental investigators working with the same set of data terms and empirical concepts would attempt to demonstrate the conditions and processes which establish and maintain the interrelationships observed.

Before considering the procedures for conducting a descriptive study using frequency measures, it might be well to make explicit three basic assumptions. The first: for psychology as a natural science, the primary data are the observable interactions between a biological organism and environmental events, past and present. These interrelationships constitute the material to be recorded. This means that the method does not include accounts of behavior isolated from related stimulus events ("Jimmy is a rejected child." "Johnny is a highly *autistic* child." "First Henry moved about by making swimming movements, later he crawled, now he can walk with support.") Furthermore, it means that it excludes statements of generalizations about behavior and environmental interactions. ("This is an extremely aggressive child who is always getting into trouble.") Finally, it means that it excludes accounts of interactions between behavioral and environmental events intertwined with hypothetical constructs. ("The preschool child makes errors in describing the water line in a jar because of his undeveloped cognitive structure.")

The second assumption: concepts and laws in psychology are derived from raw data. Theoretical concepts evolve from empirical concepts and empirical concepts from raw data; theoretical interactional laws are derived from empirical laws and empirical laws from relationships in the raw data.

The third assumption: descriptive studies provide information only on events and their occurrence. They do not provide information on the functional properties of the events or the functional relationships among the events. Experimental studies provide that kind of information.

We move on to consider the procedures involved in conducting a descriptive field investigation. They include: (1) specifications of the situation in which a study is conducted, (2) definitions of behavioral and environmental events in observable terms, (3) measurements of observer reliability, and (4) procedures for collecting, analyzing, and interpreting the data. We terminate the paper with a brief illustration of a study for the behavior of a 4-yr-old boy in a laboratory nursery school.

Specifying the Situation in which a Study is Conducted

We define the situation in which a study is conducted in terms of its physical and social setting and the *observable events* that occur within its bounds. The physical setting may be a part of the child's home, a hospital or residential institution, a store, or a playground in the city park. It may be a nursery school, a classroom in an elementary school, or a room in a child guidance clinic.

The specific part of the home selected as a setting may consist of the living room and kitchen if the design of the home precludes flexible observation (Hawkins, Peterson, Schweid, and Bijou, 1966). In a hospital it might be the child's bedroom, the dining room, or the day room (Wolf, Risley, and Mees, 1964). In a state school for the retarded, it may be a special academic classroom (Birnbrauer, Wolf, Kidder, and Tague, 1965); in a regular elementary school, a classroom (Becker, Madsen, Arnold, and Thomas, 1967); and in a nursery school, the schoolroom and the play yard (Harris, Wolf, and Baer, 1964).

During the course of a study, changes in the physical aspect of the situation may occur despite efforts to keep them constant. Some will be sufficiently drastic to prevent further study until restoration of the original conditions (*e.g.*, power failure for several days). Others will be within normal limits (*e.g.*, replacement of old chairs in the child's bedroom) and hence will not warrant disrupting the research.

The social aspect of the situation in a home might consist of the mother and the subject's younger sibling (Hawkins, *et al.*, 1966); in a child guidance clinic, the therapist and the other children in the therapy group. In a nursery school it might include the head teacher, the assistant teacher, and the children (Johnston, Kelley, Harris, and Wolf, 1966).

Sometimes the social situation changes according to routines and the investigator wishes to take records in the different situations created by the changes. For example, he may wish to describe the behavior of a preschool child as he engages in each of four activities in the morning hours of the nursery school: show and tell, music and games, snack, and pre-academic exercises. Each would be described as a field situation and data would be taken in each as if it were a separate situation. The events recorded could be the same for all the activities (*e.g.*, frequency of social contacts), or they could be specific to each depending upon the nature of the activity. They could also be a combination of both (*e.g.*, frequency of social contacts and sum total of prolonged productive activity in each pre-academic exercise).

Major variations in social composition in a home study that would be considered disruptive could include the presence of other members of the family, relatives, or friends. In a nursery school, it might be the absence of the head teacher, presence of the child's mother, or the absence of many of the children. These and other events like them would probably call a halt to data collection until the standard situation is returned.

Temporary social disruptions may take many forms. For example, in the home the phone may ring, a salesman may appear, a neighbor may visit; and in the nursery school it might be a holiday preparation, or a birthday party for a member of the group.

In summary, the physical and social conditions in which an ecological study is conducted is specified at the outset. Whether the variations occurring during the study are sufficient to disrupt data collection depends, in large measure on the interactions to be studied, practical considerations, and the investigator's experience in similar situations in the past. However, accounts of changes in physical and social conditions, whether major or minor, are described and noted on the data sheets.

Defining Behavioral and Stimulus Events in Observable Terms

In this method we derive definitions of behavioral and stimulus events from preliminary investigations in the actual setting. Such pilot investigations are also used to provide preliminary information on the frequencies of occurrences of the events of interest and the feasibility of the situation for study.

A miniature episode in the life of a preschool boy, Timmy, will serve as an example. We start with having the observer make a running description of Timmy's behavior in the play yard in the style she would use if she were a reporter for a magazine.

Timmy is playing by himself in a sandbox in a play yard in which other children are playing. A teacher stands nearby. Timmy tires of the sandbox and walks over to climb the monkeybars. Timmy shouts at the teacher, saying, "Mrs. Simpson, watch me." Timmy climbs to the top of the apparatus and shouts again to the teacher, "Look how high I am. I'm higher than anybody." The teacher comments on Timmy's climbing ability with approval. Timmy then climbs down and runs over to a tree, again demanding that the teacher watch him. The teacher, however, ignores Timmy and walks back into the classroom. Disappointed, Timmy walks toward the sandbox instead of climbing the tree. A little girl nearby cries out in pain as she stumbles and scrapes her knee. Timmy ignores her and continues to walk to the sandbox.

To obtain a clearer impression of the time relationships among antecedent stimulus events, responses, and consequent stimulus events, the objective aspects of the narrative account are transcribed into a three-column form and each behavioral and stimulus event is numbered in consecutive order.

Setting: Timmy (T.) is playing alone in a sandbox in a play yard in which there are other children playing. T. is scooping sand into a bucket with a shovel, then dumping the sand onto a pile. A teacher, Mrs. Simpson (S.), stands approximately six feet away but does not attend to T.

Time	*Antecedent Event*	*Response*	*Consequent Social Event*
9:14		1. T. throws bucket and shovel into corner of sandbox.	
		2. . . . stands up.	
		3. . . . walks over to monkeybars and stops.	
		4. . . . turns toward teacher.	
		5. . . . says, "Mrs. Simpson, watch me."	
			6. Mrs. S. turns toward Timmy.
	6. Mrs. S. turns toward Timmy	7. T. climbs to top of apparatus.	
		8. . . . looks toward teacher.	
		9. . . . says, "Look how high I am. I'm higher than anybody."	
9:16			10. Mrs. S. says, "That's good, Tim. You're getting quite good at that."

	10. Mrs. S. says, That's good, Tim. You're getting quite good at that."	11. T. climbs down	
		12. . . . runs over to tree.	
		13. . . . says, "Watch me climb the tree, Mrs. Simpson."	
			14. Mrs. S. turns and walks toward classroom.
	14. Mrs. S. turns and walks toward classroom.	15. T. stands, looking toward Mrs. S.	
9:18	16. Girl nearby trips and falls, bumping knee.		
	17. Girl cries.		
		18. T. proceeds to sandbox	
		19. . . . picks up bucket and shovel.	
		20. . . . resumes play with sand.	

Note that a response event (*e.g.*, 5. . . . says, "Mrs. Simpson, watch me.") may be followed by a consequent social event (*e.g.*, 6. Mrs. S. turns toward Timmy.) which may also be the antecedent event for the next response (*e.g.*, 7. T. climbs to top of apparatus.) Note, too, that the three-column form retains the temporal relationships in the narration. Note, finally, that only the child's responses are described. Inferences about feelings, motives, and other presumed internal states are omitted. Even words like "ignores" and "disappointed" do not appear in the table.

On the basis of several such running accounts and analyses a tentative set of stimulus and response definitives are derived and criteria for their occurrence are specified. This material serves as a basis for a provisional code consisting of symbols and definitions. Observers are trained to use the code and are tested in a series of trial runs in the actual situation.

Consider now the problems involved in defining behavioral and stimulus terms, devising codes, and recording events. But first let us comment briefly on the pros and cons of two recording methods.

When discussing the definitions of events and assessing reliability of observers, we refer to observers who record with paper and pencil. In each instance the same could be accomplished by electro-mechanical devices. The investigator must decide which procedure best suits his purpose. For example, Lovaas used instruments to record responses in studies on autistic behavior. He and his co-workers have developed apparatus and worked out procedures for recording as many as 12 responses in a setting. The following is a brief description of the apparatus and its operation (Lovaas, Freitag, Gold, and Kassorla, 1965*b*).

> The apparatus for quantifying behaviors involved two units: an Esterline-Angus 20-pen recorder and an operating panel with 12 buttons, each button mounted on a switch (Microswitch: "Typewriter pushbutton switch"). When depressed, these buttons activated a corresponding pen on the Esterline recorder. The buttons were arranged on a 7 by 14-in. panel in the configuration of the fingertips of an outstretched hand. Each button could be pressed independently of any of the others and with the amount of force similar to that required for an electric typewriter key (p. 109).

An electro-mechanical recording device has certain advantages over a paper-and-pencil system. It requires less attention, thus allowing the observer to devote more of his effort to watching for critical events. Furthermore, instruments of this sort make it possible to assess more carefully the temporal relationships between stimulus and response events, as well as to record a large number of responses within a given period. On the other hand, paper-and-pencil recording methods are more flexible. They can be used in any setting since they do not require special facilities, such as a power supply.

Defining and Recording Behavioral Events

The main problem in defining behavioral events is establishing a criterion or criteria in a way that two or more observers can agree on their occurrences. For example, if it is desired to record the number of times a child hits other children, the criteria of a hitting response must be clearly given so that the observer can discriminate hitting from patting or shoving responses. Or if it is desired to count the number of times a child says, "No", the criteria for the occurrence of "No" must be specified to discriminate it from other words the child utters, and from non-verbal forms of negative expressions. Sometimes definitions must include criteria of loudness and duration. For example in a study of crying behavior (Hart, *et al.*, 1964), crying was defined to discriminate it from whining and screaming and it had to be (a) "loud enough to be heard at least 50 feet away, and (b) of 5-sec or more duration".

The definitions of complex behavioral events are treated the same way. Studies concerned with such intricate categories of behavior as isolate behavior, fantasy-play, aggressive behavior, and temper-tantrums must establish objective criteria for each class of responses included in the category. We shall elaborate on defining multiple response classes in the following discussion on recording behavioral events.

There are two styles of recording behavioral events in field situations: one consists of logging the incidences of responses (and in many situations, their durations); the other of registering the frequencies of occurrences and non-occurrences within a time interval. Sometimes frequencies and their durations are recorded (Lovaas, Freitag, Gold, and Kassorla, 1965*b*).

Recording the frequencies of occurrences and non-occurrences in a time interval requires the observer to make a mark (and only one mark) in each time interval in which the response occurred. It is apparent that in this procedure the maximum frequency of a response is determined by the size of the time unit selected. If a 5-sec interval were used, the maximum frequency would be 12 per min; if a 10-sec interval were employed, the maximal rate would be six responses per minute, and so on. Thus, in studies with a high frequency of behavioral episodes, small time intervals are employed to obtain high correspondence between the actual and recorded frequencies of occurrences.

There are several approaches to defining and recording single and multiple class responses. One method consists of developing a *specific observational code* for each problem studied. For example, in studies conducted at the Child Behavior Laboratory at the University of Illinois, codes were prepared for attending-to-work behavior, spontaneous speech, and tantruming. The attending-to-work or time-on-task code was employed with a distractible 7-yr-old boy. It included: (1) counting words, (2) looking at the words, and (3) writing numbers or letters. When any of these behaviors occurred at any time during a 20-sec interval, it was scored as an interval of work. In a second study involving a 6-yr-old boy with a similar problem, this code was used with one additional feature: in order for the observer to mark occurrence in the 20-sec interval, the child had to engage in relevant behavior for a minimum of 10 sec. The reliability on both codes averaged 90% for two observers over 12 sessions. (See Section 3 for our method of determining reliability.)

A code for spontaneous speech was developed for a 4-yr-old girl who rarely spoke. Incidences of speech were recorded whenever she uttered a word or words which were not preceded by a question or a prompt by a peer or teacher. Although this class of behavior was somewhat difficult to discriminate, reliability averaged 80% for two observers over 15 sessions.

Tantrum behaviors exhibited by a 6-yr-old boy were defined as including crying, whining, sobbing, and whimpering. The average reliability for this class of behavior was 80% for two observers over 11 sessions.

In contrast to this more or less vocal form of tantrum behavior, a code developed in another study on temper-tantrums centered around gross motor responses of an autistic child (Brawley, Harris, Allen, Fleming, and Peterson, 1968, in press.) Here a tantrum was recorded whenever the child engaged in self-hitting in combination with any one of the following forms of behavior: (1) loud crying, (2) kicking, or (3) throwing himself or objects about.

Another method of defining and recording responses is to develop a *general observational code,* one that is inclusive enough to study many behaviors in a given field situation. An example of such a code is the one prepared by the nursery school staff at the University of Washington. In essence, verbal and motor responses are recorded in relation to physical and social events using a three or four track system. Tables 1 and 2 show sample lines from data sheets. Each box represents an interval of 15 sec.

In Table 1, which is a segment of a data sheet for a nursery school girl who changed activities with high frequency, entries were made in the boxes in the top row to indicate occurrences of vocalizations (V). Entries were made in the middle row to shop proximity (P) or physical contact (T) with another person, and in the bottom row to indicate contact with physical objects (E) or with children and whether the interaction was parallel play (A) or shared play (C). Other marks and symbols are added in accordance with the problem studied. For example, each single bracket in Table 1 indicates leaving of one activity and embarking on another. During the 6-min period in which records were taken (24 15-sec intervals), the child changed her activity 12 times. During that time the teacher gave approval five times contingent upon her verbal or proximity behavior as indicated by X's above the top line (10, 11, 16, 17, and 18). A tally of the data indicated that she spent most of the 6-min period alone or in close proximity to another child, sometimes on the same piece of play equipment. During three intervals (16, 17, and 18) she talked (V), touched (T), and engaged in physical interaction with another child (C). Even though rate of activity change, and not peer interaction, was the subject of the study, the other data on social behavior provided interesting information: decline in rate of activity change was related to an increase in rate of appropriate peer behavior.

This code can be readily modified to handle more complex interactions. For example, it was used to record the behavior of a nursery school boy who shouted epithets, kicked, and hit other children. Ordinarily these aggressive acts would appear in the record sheets undifferentiated from a non-aggressive interaction. To differentiate them from other behaviors the symbol letter was circled if the behavior met the criteria of an aggressive act. As shown in Table 2, intervals 13, 22, and 23 contain a "V" with a circle, Ⓥ, which indicates aggres-

Table 1

Sample line from a data sheet of nursery school girl who changed activities with high frequency.

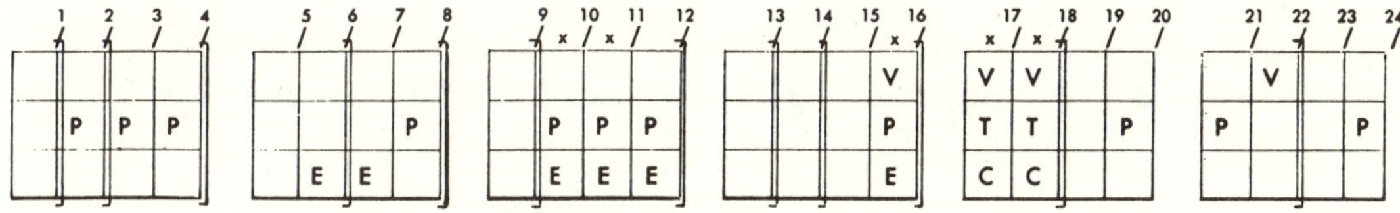

Table 2

Sample Line from a Data Sheet of Nursery School Boy Displaying Aggressive Behaviors

1	2	3	4	5	6	7	8	9	10	11	12	13	14	15	16	17	18	19	20	21	22	23	24	25	26	27	28	29	30
					x	x	x			x	x					x	x								x	x		x	
V					V							Ⓥ				V	V	V	V	V	Ⓥ	Ⓥ						V	
P	P				P	P	P	P								P	P	Ⓣ	Ⓣ	P		P	P	P	P	P	P	T	P
C	C		C	C	C	C	C	C	C	C	A	A	A	A	A	A	A	A	A	A	A	A			A	A	C	C	
					B	B	B	B	B	B	B					B	B	B	B	B	B	B	B	B	B	B	B	B	

sive verbalizations, while intervals 19 and 20 contain a "T" with a circle, Ⓣ, which indicates physical "attack" (actual hitting, kicking, or pinching). Another bit of information was incorporated in the recording system. The letter "B" was entered in the fourth row to indicate that the child was playing with or being aggressive to a specific nursery school boy named Bill. This additional notation was made midway in the study when teachers observed that the subject and Bill usually behaved aggressively toward each other. Data collected before this change served as a baseline against which to judge the effects of changing social contingencies. Subsequently, teachers gave approval contingent on nonaggressive interactions between these boys as shown by the X's above intervals 6, 7, 8, 11, 12, 17, 18, 26, 27, and 29.

Another general observational code, tailored for analysis of pupils' behavior in the elementary school classroom, has been devised by Thomas and Becker (1967). Like the nursery school code, it consists of symbols and definitions designed to cover the range of interactions that may take place in the field situation defined by the classroom.

Defining and Recording Stimulus Events

The ease or difficulty of defining a stimulus class is related to its source. It has been pointed out (*e.g.*, Bijou and Baer, 1961) that some stimuli originate in natural and man-made things, some in the biological make-up of the subject himself, and some in the behavior of people and other living organisms. Consider briefly each source in turn.

Defining stimuli from physical things does not pose a difficult problem since physical objects are usually available for all to see. All that is required is that these stimuli be described in the usual physical dimensions of space, time, size, velocity, color, texture, and the like.

Defining stimuli which originate in the biological make-up of the subject is beset with difficulty mostly because of their obscurity under any circumstance and particularly under field conditions. Consider what must be available to an observer if he is to record in objective terms the duration, intensity, or frequency of stimuli involved in a toothache, "butterflies" in the stomach, general bodily weakness, dizziness, and hunger-pangs. Instruments would be needed to make visible all sorts of internal biological events; and for the most part, these are not yet available in practical forms. It seems clear that at present, field methods of research, especially with human beings, are not appropriate for describing biologically anchored variables. Research on these variables must be postponed until it is practical to monitor physiological actions through cleverly designed telemetric devices. But it should be stressed that the exact role of specific biological variables *must* be studied at some time for a thorough functional analysis of psychological behavior (defined here as the interaction of a total functioning biological individual with environmental events).

Defining social stimuli, or stimuli which evolve from the action of people, ranges in difficulty between physical and biological events. This is so because social events, like physical and biological events, must in many instances be described in terms of their physical dimensions, and as is well known, the components of social stimuli can be terribly subtle and complex. For the reader interested in a further analysis of social events within the framework of a natural science, Skinner's discussion is recommended (1953, pp. 298-304).

In field studies, the procedure for defining and recording social stimuli is the same as that for defining and recording response events, since social events are treated as the responses of people in antecedent or consequent relationships to the behavior of the subject. Therefore, the entire previous section on defining and recording behavioral events pertains to defining and recording social events.

Some social stimuli, like response stimuli, may consist of a single class of behavior on the part of an adult or a child and may be recorded on the basis of frequency or its occurrence or nonoccurrence within a time interval. Examples of single-class antecedent stimuli are simple commands and requests, *e.g.*, "Start now," "Gather around in a circle," "Come, let's ride the trikes." Examples of single-class consequent stimuli are confirmations ("Right"), disconfirmations ("Wrong"), approval ("Good") and disapproval ("You play too rough.")

Other social stimuli may be composed of several classes of behavior stemming from one person or several in concert. As in the case of defining multiple response classes, criteria for each subclass in the group may constitute a code. A specific observational code may be developed to describe social events in a specific situation for a specific study. For example, in a study of autistic behavior, adult attention was defined as: "(1) Touching the child; (2) being within two feet of and facing the child; (3) talking to, touching, assisting or going to the child" (Brawley, *et al.* 1968). With such criteria the investigator catalogued the types of behaviors which constituted social interaction involving attention and excluded other stimuli originating in the behavior of an adult in contact with the subject.

General observational codes for social events, like those for response events, have also been devised to study many problems in a general type of field setting. For example, Becker and Thomas (1967) have developed a comprehensive code for recording the teacher's behavior in an elementary classroom situation.

Which classes of behavior-environmental interactions will be selected for study will depend on the purpose of the investigation; the maximum number, however, will be limited by the practical considerations. Studies requiring detailed analyses of many response classes may be planned as a series. The first dealing with grossly defined classes and the others with more and more progressively refined categories. For example, the first study may be concerned with the frequency of social contacts with adults and peers, and the second with specific verbal and motor responses directed to specific adults (teachers and parents) and peers (boys and girls).

Assessing Observer Reliability

Disagreements between observers may be related to inadequacies in (1) the observational code, (2) the training of the observers, or (3) the method of calculating reliability.

The observational code. Problems of defining and recording behavioral and stimulus events have been discussed in Section 2. Observer reliability is directly related to the comprehensiveness and specificity of the definitions in the observational code. Generally it is advisable to devise codes with mutually exclusive event categories, each definition having criteria that do not occur in any other definition.

Training of observers. Even when a code is completely serviceable, two observers may not necessarily record the occurrence of the same event at the same time unless each has been adequately trained in using the code and in controlling his behavior while observing and recording.

For example, training might begin by familiarizing the observer with the tools for recording, *e.g.*, the clipboard, stopwatch, and data sheets. This might be followed by an orientation to the code and exercises in recording behavioral events. A film or video tape of sequences similar to those in the actual situation might be used to provide supplementary experiences.

It is often helpful to have a second observer to record along with the first observer. During trial recordings the observers can indicate to each other the behaviors being scored and uncover misunderstandings regarding the nature of the code or ambiguities in the definition of particular responses. Such a procedure reduces interpretation on the part of the observer and can contribute to an improved code.

Since it is relatively easy for the observers to slip an interval in the course of a long recording session, they should be instructed to note the beginning of certain activities, *e.g.*, story time, snack, nap, *etc.* This allows them to determine easily when they are out of phase with one another. Slips may also result from inaccurate stopwatches. Watches should be periodically tested by starting them simultaneously and checking them a few hours later.

After training on the proficient use of the code the observer might then be given instruction on how to conduct himself while observing and recording. Thus, he might be told how to refrain from interacting with the subject, *e.g.*, ignore all questions, avoid eye-contact, and suppress reactions to the subject's activities as well as those associated with him. He might also be instructed in moving about to maintain a clear view of the subject yet not make it obvious that he is following him.

Method of calculating reliability. The reliability index is to some degree a function of how it is calculated. Suppose we have data from two observers showing the frequency of a class of events taken over 1 hr. Unless the sums obtained by each observer are equal, the smaller sum is divided by the larger to obtain a percentage of agreement. If the sums are identical the reliability index would be 100. This method is often used when the investigator is interested in frequencies *per se*, since the measure obtained gives only the amount of agreement over the total number of events observed. It does not indicate whether the two observers were recording the same event at exactly the same time. Thus, it might be possible that one observer was recording few behaviors during the first half hour and many during the second, while the second observer was doing just the opposite. To ascertain whether this is the case, one could divide the period of observation into small segments and calculate the reliability of each. Agreements over progressively smaller segments give confidence that the observers are scoring the same event at the same time. One may assess the agreement over brief intervals such as 5 or 10 sec. Reliability is calculated by scoring each interval as agree or disagree (match or mismatch) and dividing the total number of agreements by the number of agreements plus the number of disagreements. Note that one may score several agreements or disagreements in an interval if a number of events are being recorded simultaneously as shown in Tables 1 and 2. In this case the interval is broken down according to the number of different events recorded, with each event scored as a match or mismatch.

The reliability index may also be influenced by the frequency of response under study. When a behavior is displayed at a very low rate, the observer will record few instances of occurrence and many of nonoccurrence. In this situation the observers could disagree on the occurrence of the behavior yet still show high reliability due to their agreement on the large number of intervals where no behavior was recorded. A similar problem exists with regard to high-frequency behaviors. Here, however, the observers may disagree on the nonoccurrence of the behavior and agree on occurrence, because of the frequency of the latter. The problem may be resolved by computing not one but two reliability coefficients, one for occurrence and one for nonoccurrence.

In some cases the requirement of perfect matching of intervals may be relaxed slightly. Thus, behaviors recorded within one interval (especially if the interval is short) may also be considered as instances of agreement for reliability purposes. A technique of noncontinuous observing may also increase reliability (O'Leary, O'Leary, and Becker, 1967). In this procedure the observers record for shorter portions of time. For example, instead of taking continuous 10-sec observations, the observer might record for 10 out of every 15 sec, or for 20 out of every 30 sec. During the period in which the observer is not attending to the child, he should be recording the behaviors just observed.

The use of a second observer does not insure high reliability of recording; it is possible for both observers to agree on the scoring of certain events and at the same time be incorrect (Gewirtz and Gewirtz, 1964). Both observers might record some events which should not be noted and ignore others which should. Hence, a third observer might be used on occasion to determine if this possibility exists.

Collecting, Analyzing, and Interpreting Data

Data collection. Final data collection is begun as soon as it is evident that the observers are adequately trained, the field situation is feasible, and the subject has adapted to the presence of the observers.

Whether the investigator collects data during all of the time available for observation or takes time samples will depend upon many factors, including the purpose of the study, the nature of the data, and the practical considerations. Regardless of the frequency with which observations are made, it is recommended that the data be plotted at regular intervals to provide a kind of progress chart. A visual account of the fluctuations and trends can help the investigator make important decisions, *e.g.*, setting up the time for the next reliability evaluation or establishing the termination time for a phase of the study.

Data analysis. Up until now we discussed the investigators' activities in relation to the interactions between the observer and the field events. The investigator was viewed as a critic, watching the observer record the events in a natural ecology. Thus, in the data collection phase of a study the investigator's role is somewhat similar to that of a motion picture director evaluating what the camera is recording in relation to the scene as he sees it. In this section on data analysis and in the next on interpretation, we shall consider what the investigator does, not in relation to the recording equipment and field events, but in relation to the data collected.

Basically, in data analysis the investigator looks at the data collected to "see what is there". Usually he finds that making one or several transformations in the raw data helps him to see more clearly the relationships among the events observed. Transformational procedures might consist of converting the frequency counts into graphic, tabular, verbal, arithmetical, or statistical forms. Exactly which operations he performs on the data will depend on the purpose of the study, the nature of the data, and his theoretical assumptions about what can or cannot be demonstrated by a descriptive field study.

Usually, data analysis begins when data collection ends. However, as noted previously, an investigator might graph the data while the study is in progress. Under these circumstances data analysis might consist of revising and refining the graphs and making other transpositions to show the relationships among the subparts of the data.

Data collected in terms of rate are usually plotted in a graphic form with responses on the vertical axis and time of the horizontal axis. Points on the chart may represent either discrete or cumulative values. Discrete values are the sums or means for each successive session; cumulative values are the sums or means for all previous sessions. Therefore, curves with discrete values might go up, stay at the same level, or go down; cumulative curves might also go up or stay at the same level. Cumulative curves do not go down. A decrease in the frequency of a response is shown in the curve as a deceleration in rate (bends toward the horizontal axis); an increase in frequency as an acceleration (bends toward the vertical axis); a constant frequency as no change in rate; and a zero frequency as a horizontal line.

In most instances graphic presentations are made more meaningful when accompanied by percentage values. In addition, it is often advantageous to show percentages of occurrences in the different conditions and sub-conditions of the field situation.

Viewing the interactions in selected time periods (early morning, and late morning) or around certain events (before and after mealtime) as populations, statistical analyses may be made to assess the nature of and the reliability of differences observed.

Interpretation of findings. Essentially, interpretation of findings consists of the investigator's statements on what is "seen" in the data together with his conception of their generality. Such statements are the *raison-d'être* of an investigation.

Obviously, an investigator is free to interpret his findings in any way he chooses. The investigator who accepts the assumptions of a natural science approach to psychology seeks to limit his interpretations to empirical concepts and relationships consistent with his observations and the analytical operations made upon the products of his observations. Hence, in a descriptive field study his interpretations would usually consist of a discussion of what was found in the situation with comparisons to other findings obtained under functionally similar conditions. Conclusions on the similarities and differences between his findings and others would be incorporated in his argument for the generality of his findings. Interpretations in an experimental field study would depend on the number and type of manipulations employed and would usually be limited to describing the functional relationships obtained.

Illustrative Study

Using the procedures previously described, a study was undertaken to obtain a descriptive account of a boy in a laboratory nursery school at the University of Illinois. The nursery school curriculum and the practices of the teaching staff of this school were based on behavioral principles (Skinner, 1953, and Bijou and Baer, 1961).

Subject and field situation. The subject (Zachary) was typical of the children in the nursery school in the judgment of the teachers. He was 4.5 yr old, of high average intelligence (Peabody IQ 116) and from a middle socio-economic class family. On the Wide Range Achievement Test he scored kindergarten 3 in reading, pre-kindergarten 5 in spelling, and kindergarten 6 in arithmetic.

The nursery school consisted of a large room, approximately 21 by 40 ft. Evenly spaced along one wall were three doors which led to three adjacent smaller rooms. One of these rooms was a lavatory, the second contained paints, papers, and other equipment, and the third a variety of toys. Nearby was a large table and several chairs used for art activities and snack. Opposite these rooms along the other wall were several tables separated by brightly colored, movable partitions. In these booths, the children worked on academic subjects.

The school was attended by 12 children, six boys and six girls, between 4 and 5 yr of age. The teaching staff consisted of a full-time teacher and an assistant teacher, and depending on the time of day, one to three undergraduates who assisted in administering new programs in reading, writing, and arithmetic.

In general, the morning program was as follows:

9:00-10:00 Art, academic, and pre-academic work
10:00-10:30 Free play
10:30-11:00 Snack
11:00-12:00 Academic work, show-and-tell, and storytime.

A typical morning might begin with art. At this time, 8 to 10 children sat around a large table working with various materials. During this activity each child in turn left the group for 10 to 20 min to work on writing or arithmetic. While engaged in writing or arithmetic the child worked with a teacher in one of the booths. After completing his assigned units of work he returned to his art activity and another child left the group to work on his units of writing or arithmetic. After all the children had participated in these academic subjects, the art period was terminated and was followed by play. During play, the children were free to move about, often spending much of the time in either of the smaller nursery school rooms playing with blocks or other toys. After approximately 30 min of play, the youngsters returned to the large table for a snack of juice and cookies. While eating and drinking they talked spontaneously and informally with their teachers and peers. Following snack time some of the children participated in reading while the others gathered for show-and-tell or storytime. During storytime the children sat on the floor in a group while the teacher read and discussed the story. In show-and-tell, instead of the teacher leading the group, each child had a chance to stand by the teacher in front of the group, and show an object he had brought from home and tell about it. As they did during the art period the children left the group one at a time for a period of reading. Because of variations in the amount of time a child spent on academic subjects, a child did not engage in all of these activities every day.

Behavioral and stimulus events recorded. The behaviors recorded were of two general categories: social contacts and sustained activities. Social contacts included verbal interchanges and physical contacts with children and teachers. Sustained activities involved behaviors in relation to the school tasks. The specific observational code developed for the study is presented in Table 3.

Observation began 3.5 weeks after the start of the school year and covered a 3-hr period in the morning. The observations were taken on 28 school days. The observer sat a few feet from the subject and discretely followed him as he moved from one activity to another in the nursery school room. Every 10 sec the teacher recorded the occurrence or nonoccurrence of events defined in the code. The data sheet was similar to that shown in Table 1; however, only the first and second rows were used.

Observer reliability. The reliability of observation and the adequacy of the behavioral code was evaluated several times throughout the study by having a second observer record stimulus and response events. Reliability was calculated by scoring each interval as a match or mismatch and dividing the total number of agreements by the number of agreements plus disagreements. Four checks on social contacts showed agreements of 75, 82, 85, and 87%. Three checks on sustained activity yielded agreements of 94, 95, and 97%. Thus, average agreement on social contacts exceeded 82% while average agreement of sustained activity exceeded 95%.

Analysis of Data

Social contacts. Data were gathered on Zachary's social behaviors in informal activities of art, play, snack, storytime, and show-and-tell. They will be described and samples of the detailed accounts in art and snack will be presented in graphic form. The youngster's most dominant behavior during the art period, shown in Fig. 1, was talking to others (14% of the time).

Teachers and peers talked with him about equally, an average of 8 and 7% respectively. Physical contacts between Zachary, teachers, and peers were low, around 1 to 2%.

The child's verbal behavior to peers during the play period was higher than in the art

Table 3

Observational Code for Describing the Behavior of a Boy in a Laboratory Nursery School

Symbol	*Definition*
	First Row (Social Contacts)
	S verbalizes to himself. Any verbalization during which he does not look at an adult or child or does not use an adult's or child's name. Does not apply to a group situation.
	S verbalizes to adult. *S* must look at adult while verbalizing or use adult's name.
	S verbalizes to child. *S* must look at child while verbalizing or use child's name. If in a group situation, any verbalization is recorded as verbalization to a child.
S	Child verbalizes to *S*. Child must look at *S* while verbalizing or use *S*'s name.
△	Adult verbalizes to *S*. Adult must look at *S* while verbalizing or use *S*'s name.
S	Adult gives general instruction to class or asks question of class, or makes general statement. Includes storytelling.
	S touches adult. Physical contact with adult.
	S touches child with part of body or object. Physical contact with child.
V	Adult touches *S*. Physical contact with adult.
T	Child touches *S* with part of body or object. Physical contact with child.

Symbol	*Definition*
	Second Row (Sustained Activity)
•	*Sustained activity in art. S* must be sitting in the chair, facing the material and responding to the material or teacher within the 10-sec interval. Responding to the material includes using pencil, paint brush, chalk, crayons, string, scissors or paste or any implement on paper, or working with clay with hands on clay or hands on implement which is used with clay, or folding or tearing paper. Responding to the teacher includes following a command made by an adult to make a specific response. The behavior must be completed (child sitting in his chair again) within two minutes.
•	*Sustained activity in storytime. S* must be sitting, facing the material, or following a command given by the teacher or assistant. If the *S* initiates a verbalization to a peer, do not record sustained activity in the 10-sec interval.
•	*Sustained activity in show-and-tell. S* must be sitting, facing the material, or following a command given by the teacher. If the *S* initiates a verbalization to a peer, do not record sustained activity in that 10-sec interval.
•	*Sustained activity in reading. S* must be sitting in the chair, facing the material and responding to the material or the teacher within the 10-sec interval.
•	*Sustained activity in writing. S* must be sitting in the chair, facing the material and responding to the material or the teacher within the 10-sec interval. Responding to the material includes using the pencil (making a mark), or holding the paper or folder. Responding to the teacher includes responding verbally to a cue given by the teacher.
•	*Sustained activity in arithmetic. S* must be sitting in the chair, facing the material and responding to the material or the teacher within the 10-sec interval. Responding to the material or teacher includes using the pencil or eraser or holding the paper or folder or responding verbally to cue.
	Sustained activity did not occur in interval.

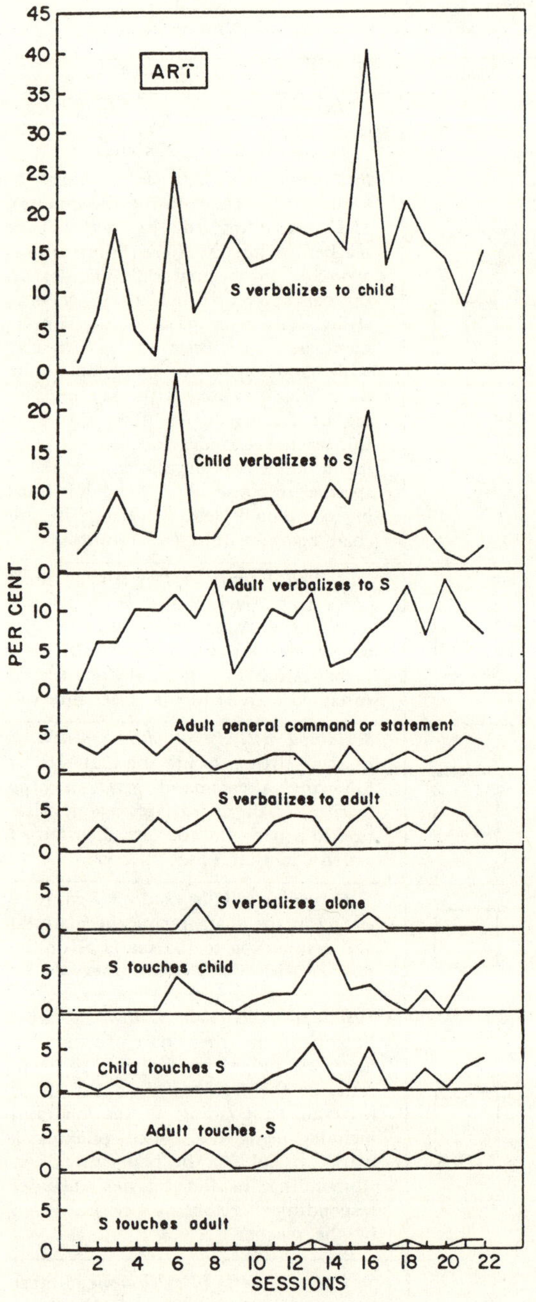

Fig. 1. Social contact during art.

period. He talked to his friends on an average of 38%; they talked to him on an average of only 10%. Verbal exchanges with teachers were low (an average of 2.5%). Zachary touched other children 7% of the time on the average and they reciprocated on an average of 3%. Physical contacts with teachers were relatively infrequent.

As in the art and play periods, Zachary's social interactions during snack time, shown in Fig. 2, consisted mostly of talking to his classmates, an average of 21%. They, in turn, talked to him only an average of 7%. During this period the teacher's general commands (instructions addressed to the group) were relatively high, averaging 7% in contrast to the 2% during art and play. Physical contacts with other children were low, as in art and play, about 3%.

Compared to the art, play, and snack peri-

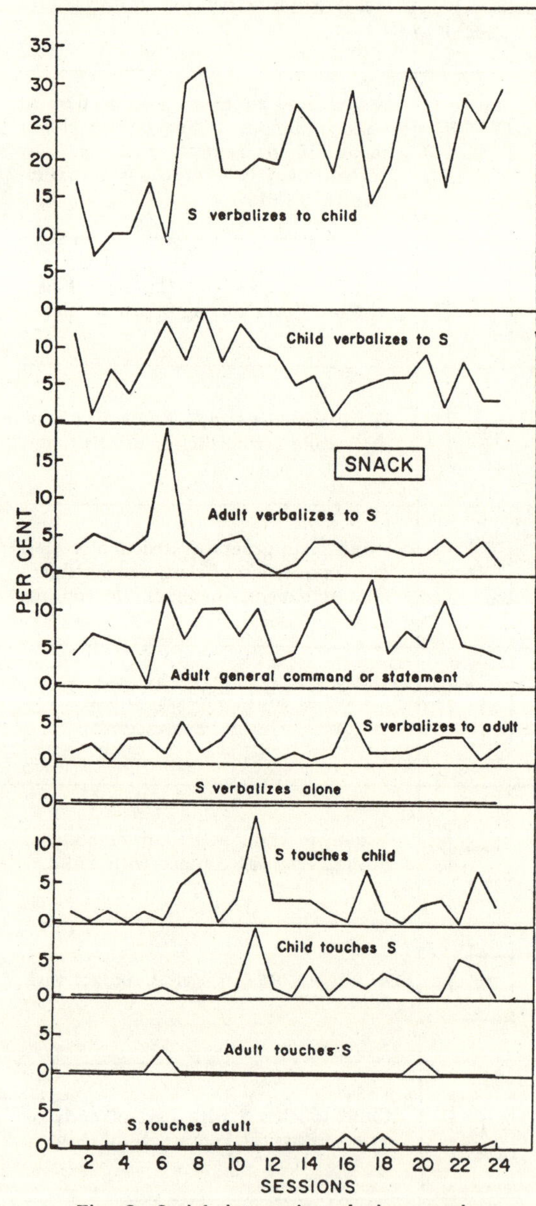

Fig. 2. Social interaction during snack.

ods, Zachary's verbalizations to peers and to teachers were low (8 and 4% respectively), and the number of times he touched children (10%), and children touched him were also relatively low (2%). Storytime had a high frequency of teacher's general commands and statements (average of 73%) since this category was scored when the teacher read and discussed the stories.

In show-and-tell, Zachary's social behavior was similar to that during storytime. He talked to other children 14% of the time and touched them 9% of the time. Zachary physically contacted teachers about 1% of the time and they reciprocated about 3% of the time.

In respect to Zachary's social behavior during the academic periods, these data clearly indicate that the teacher talked to Zachary a great deal during the reading (an average of 69%), writing (an average of 71%), and arithmetic periods (an average of 58%), and the child talked to the teacher with high frequency, particularly in reading (an average of 44%) and arithmetic (an average of 41%). In writing he talked to the teacher only 3% of the time. There were also a few instances in which the teacher touched Zachary and rare occasions in which Zachary interacted socially with other children. Figure 3 is a detailed graphic account of his social behavior during the writing period.

Sustained activity. For the observer to mark the occurrence of sustained activity, Zachary had to respond in a manner appropriate for a particular school activity. (See second part of Table 3). For example, during art, the child had to be sitting in his chair, facing the art materials and manipulating them during each 10-sec interval. Similar definitions were used for other situations and periods. Given these definitions, the results show a generally high level of sustained activity in all phases of the morning program. Daily rates of sustained activities in art, storytime, and show-and-tell range between 70 and 99% with an average of 89% for art, 95% for storytime, and 88% for show-and-tell. See Fig. 4 for variations from session to session in Zachary's sustained behavior during art. Sustained activity in reading, writing, and arithmetic, range from 90 to 100% over the days observed with an average of 97, 95, and 96% respectively. See Fig. 5 for variations in the child's sustained behavior in writing. Due to the limited availability of the observer, and the fact that not every activity occurred every day, the number of observations on each activity varied.

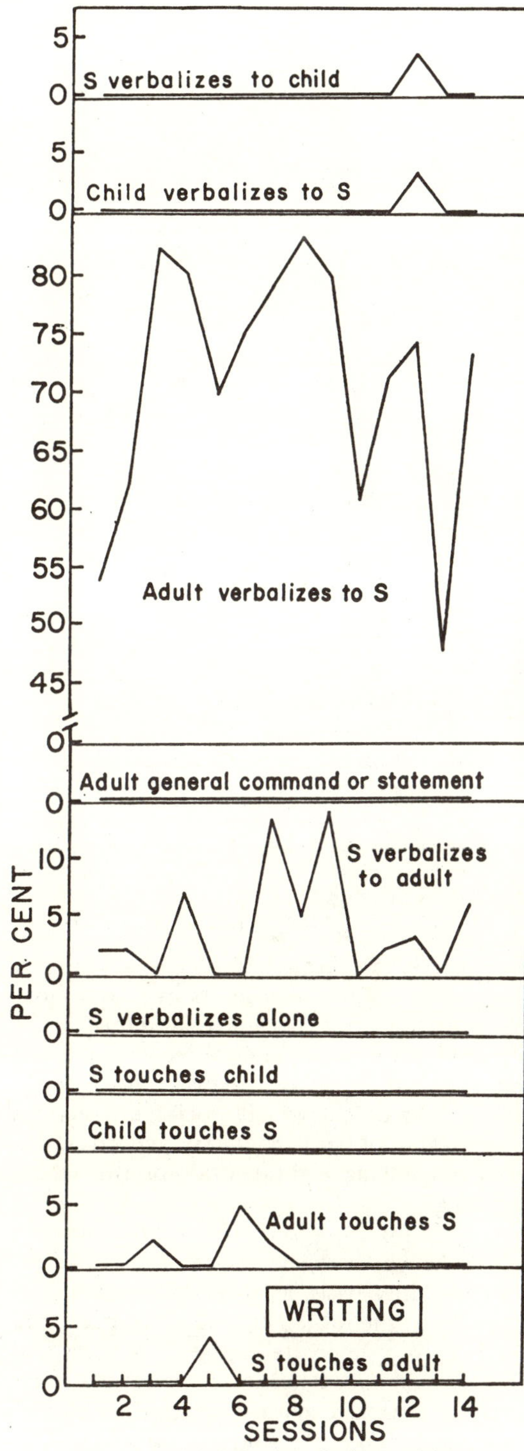

Fig. 3. Social behavior during writing.

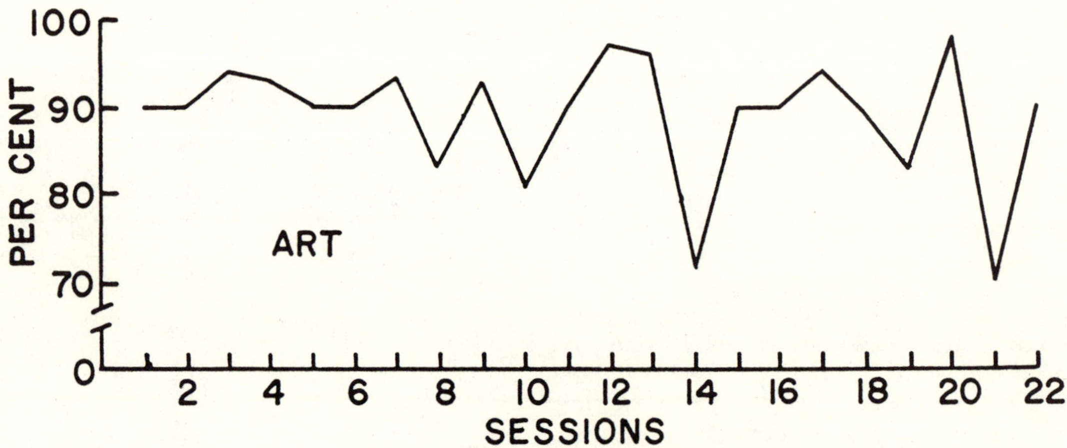

Fig. 4. Sustained activity during art.

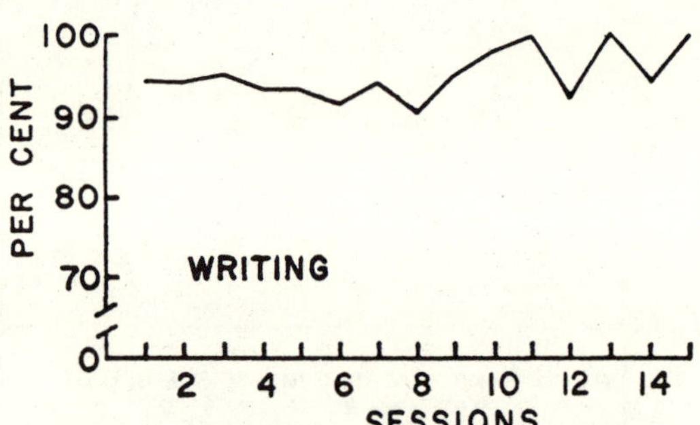

Fig. 5. Sustained activity during writing.

DISCUSSION

A descriptive account of the behaviors of a boy during the morning hours in a laboratory nursery school was obtained in terms of the frequency of occurrence of objectively defined stimulus and response events. The account shows rates of changes in social interactions (verbal and physical contacts) and sustained activities during eight periods of the school morning.

In the informal activities of the nursery school in which the youngster performed on an individual basis, as in art, free play, and snack time, the subject talked to his peers and teachers to a moderate degree. His peers and teachers responded to him verbally to a lesser extent. He talked more than he listened and over the period of the study, his verbal output increased. Physical interactions with peers and teachers in these situations were at a relatively low level. Finally, the youngster's sustained activity in the art period was high (between 70 and 98%) and became more variable, on a day-to-day basis, during the second half of the study. In the other two informal activities, storytime and show-and-tell, the child participated as a member of a group in which the teacher's verbal behavior was prominent, especially during storytime. In these two situations the child talked to others less, but as in art, free play, and snack time, he talked more than he listened. In storytime and show-and-tell he engaged in some body contacts with peers and teachers, yet his sustained activity on nursery school tasks was high, with a range of 90 to 99% for the former and 70 to 95% for the latter.

In the more structured activities of reading, writing, and arithmetic the teacher's verbal behavior to the child was high and his verbal behavior to her was correspondingly high, particularly in reading and arithmetic. During academic exercises all other social interactions were zero or near zero, and the child's sustained activities were consistently high over days, ranging from 90 to 100% of the time.

The data gathered in this study can serve two main purposes. First, they can provide normative information on behavior in a laboratory preschool. Thus, it might be interesting to compare this child's rates of response obtained in this study after 3.5 weeks of school with his rates during the last month of the school year. It might also be interesting to compare this child's behavior with another child's in the same nursery school. Such a comparison might be especially valuable if someone claimed that the second child's behavior was deviant. In addition, it might be informative to compare this child's behavior with a comparable child in a community-operated nursery school. Second, the data suggest certain relationships between the behavior of the subject, the teacher, and other children. Thus, the investigator might use the data as a baseline for an experimental study in which conditions are manipulated to test for possible functional relationships.

REFERENCES

Baldwin, A. L., Kalhorn, J., and Breese, F. H. The appraisal of parent behavior. *Psychological Monographs*, 1949, **63**, No. 299.

Barker, R. G. and Wright, H. F. *Midwest and its children: the psychological ecology of an American town*. New York: Harper & Row, 1955.

Becker, W. C., Madsen, C. H., Jr., Arnold, Carole R., and Thomas, D. R. The contingent use of teacher attention and praise in reducing classroom behavior problems. *Journal of Special Education*, 1967, **1**, 287-307.

Becker, W. C. and Thomas, D. R. A revision of the code for the analysis of a teacher's behavior in the classroom. Unpublished manuscript, 1967.

Bijou, S. W. and Baer, D. M. *Child development: a systematic and empirical theory*. Vol. 1, New York: Appleton-Century-Crofts, 1961.

Birnbrauer, J. S., Wolf, M. M., Kidder, J. D., and Tague, Cecilia. Classroom behavior of retarded pupils with token reinforcement. *Journal of Experimental Child Psychology*, 1965, **2**, 219-235.

Brawley, Eleanor R., Harris, Florence R., Allen, K. Eileen; Fleming, R. S., and Peterson, R. F. Behavior modification of an autistic child. *Behavioral Science*, 1968, in press.

Gewirtz, Hava and Gewirtz, J. L. A method for assessing stimulation behaviors and caretaker-child interaction. Unpublished manuscript, 1964.

Harris, Florence R., Wolf, M. M., and Baer, D. M. Effects of adult social reinforcement on child behavior. *Young Children*, 1964, **20**, 8-17.

Hawkins, R. P., Peterson, R. F., Schweid, Edda, and Bijou, S. W. Behavior therapy in the home: Amelioration of problem parent-child relations with the parent in a therapeutic role. *Journal of Experimental Child Psychology*, 1966, **4**, 99-107.

Honig, W. K. Introductory remarks. In W. K. Honig (Ed.) *Operant behavior: areas of research and application*. New York: Appleton-Century-Crofts, 1966.

Jensen, G. D. and Bobbitt, Ruth A. Implications of primate research for understanding infant development. *The exceptional child*, Vol. 1, J. Hellmouth (Ed.), Special Child Publications, Seattle, Washington, 1967.

Johnston, Margaret S., Kelley, C. Susan, Harris, Florence R., and Wolf, M. M. An application of reinforcement principles to development of motor skills of a young child. *Child Development*, 1966, **37**, 379-387.

Lovaas, O. I., Freitag, G., Gold, Vivian J., and Kassorla, Irene C. Recording apparatus and procedure for observation of behaviors of children in free play settings. *Journal of Experimental Child Psychology*, 1965, **2**, 108-120. (*b*)

Lovaas, O. I., Freitag, G., Gold, Vivian J., and Kassorla, Irene C. Experimental studies in childhood schizophrenia: analysis of self-destructive behavior. *Journal of Experimental Child Psychology*, 1965, **2**, 67-84. (*a*)

O'Leary, K. D., O'Leary, Susan G., and Becker, W. C. Modification of a deviant sibling interaction pattern in the home. *Behaviour Research and Therapy*, 1967, **5**, 113-120.

Skinner, B. F. *Science and human behavior*. New York: Macmillan, 1953.

Wolf, M. M., Risley, T. R., and Mees, H. L. Application of operant conditioning procedures to the behavior problems of an autistic child. *Behaviour Research and Therapy*, 1964, **1**, 305-312.

Wright, H. F. *Recording and analyzing child behavior*. New York: Harper & Row, 1967.

Received 22 April 1968.

JOURNAL OF APPLIED BEHAVIOR ANALYSIS 1978, **11**, 513-521 NUMBER 4 (WINTER 1978)

THE EFFECT OF WITNESSING CONSEQUENCES ON THE BEHAVIORAL RECORDINGS OF EXPERIMENTAL OBSERVERS

FRANCIS C. HARRIS AND ANTHONY R. CIMINERO[1]

UNIVERSITY OF GEORGIA

The cueing effects of interviewer praise contingent on a target behavior and expectation of behavior change were examined with six observers. Experiment I investigated the effect of cues in conjunction with expectation. Experiment II assessed the relative contributions of cues and expectation, and Experiment III examined the effect of cues in the absence of expectation. The frequencies of two behaviors, client eye contact and face touching, were held constant throughout a series of videotaped interviews between an "interviewer" and a "client". A within-subjects design was used in each experiment. During baseline conditions, praise did not follow eye contact by the client on the videotape. In all experimental conditions, praise statements from the interviewer followed each occurrence of eye contact with an equal number of praises delivered at random times when there was no eye contact. Three of the six observers dramatically increased their recordings of eye contact during the first experimental phase, but these increases were not replicated in a second praise condition. There were no systematic changes in recorded face touching. Witnessing the delivery of consequences, rather than expectation seemed to be responsible for the effect. This potential threat to the internal validity of studies using observational data may go undetected by interobserver agreement checks.

DESCRIPTORS: witnessing consequences, observer bias, reliability, interobserver agreement, human observers

---

Recent research has shown several ways that observational data may be inaccurate. Possible influencing factors include observer "drift" (Wildman, Erickson, and Kent, 1975), knowledge of experimental hypotheses in conjunction with contingent feedback on recordings congruent with the hypotheses (O'Leary, Kent, and Kanowitz, 1975), observer cheating (O'Leary and Kent, 1973), knowledge of agreement checking (Reid, 1970; Romanczyk, Kent, Diament, and O'Leary, 1973; Taplin and Reid, 1973), predictability of behavior (Mash and McElwee, 1974), complexity of behavior (Mash and Makohoniuk, 1975), and subject reactivity (Mash and Hedley, 1975; Roberts and Renzaglia, 1965; Surratt, Ulrich, and Hawkins, 1969; Zegiob and Forehand, 1978). Under some circumstances, however, subject reactivity has not been found (Dubey, Kent, O'Leary, and Broderick, 1977; Hagen, Craighead, and Paul, 1975; Johnson and Bolstad, 1973; Martin, Gelfand, and Hartmann, 1971; Mercatoris and Craighead, 1974). Such biased data may threaten internal validity and produce results that may be due to observational variables, rather than independent variables. Kazdin (1977) and Kent and Foster (1977) provided comprehensive reviews of the relevant literature on bias.

A potential type of bias that has not received attention concerns the influence of extraneous cues indicating the occurrence of target behaviors. The most obvious examples of these types of cues are the consequences often delivered immediately following target behaviors to the persons being observed. These cues could prompt an observer to score behaviors that would not otherwise have been scored, as in a previous baseline

[1]Reprints may be obtained from Anthony R. Ciminero, Department of Psychology, Universitiy of Georgia, Athens, GA 30602. Appreciation is expressed to Alice L. Harris and I. Daniel Turkat for their assistance in preparing the videotapes.

condition when no consequences were delivered, thus making data reported in experimental conditions artificially inflated or deflated.

The magnitude of this type of bias would, of course, differ from study to study, but if it were operating it could introduce one form of systematic bias. The danger of biased conclusions would be greatest in studies reporting small but systematic differences in behavior between experimental conditions.

The primary purpose of the present series of investigations was to determine the effects of witnessing the delivery of consequences on the recording behavior of observers. Since there is some evidence (O'Leary *et al.*, 1975) that knowledge of experimental hypotheses in conjunction with feedback to the observer can bias behavioral recordings, even though expectation alone does not seem to cause bias (Kent, O'Leary, Diament, and Dietz, 1974), expectancy effects were also investigated.

Experiment I investigated the effect of cues associated with the delivery of consequences in conjunction with expectation. Experiment II assessed the relative contributions of cues and expectation, and Experiment III examined the effect of cues in the absence of expectation.

GENERAL PROCEDURES

Videotape Preparation

A confederate "client" was provided with a written scenario describing several complaints typically associated with sleeping problems. She was instructed to use the scenario to guide her responses during the subsequent interviews.

Taping sessions were conducted in a 4-m by 3-m room furnished with two chairs. The interviewer and client sat facing each other, with the camera (Sony, AVC-3200) positioned behind the interviewer such that the back of his head and the face of the client were in the picture. The interviewer's face was not visible on the tapes to prevent cueing on his mouth movements. The experimenter sat out of camera range and operated the videotape recorder (Sony, AV-8600).

For each 10-min interview, eight 15-sec intervals were randomly designated for the occurrence of each of the following behaviors: (1) client touches her face; (2) client makes eye contact with the interviewer, followed by a praise statement from the interviewer; and (3) interviewer praises for eye contact in the absence of client eye contact. During the taping of each interview, the experimenter used an earphone to listen to an audiocassette on which the numbers 1 to 40 had been recorded at 15-sec intervals. Whenever the number for any of the designated intervals was heard, the experimenter immediately held up signs dictating the behavior of the participants. The client had been instructed previously to move her head about continuously and not touch her face except when instructed to do so. All the praise statements included a description of the behavior being praised (*e.g.*, "I'm glad you just looked at me."). The interviewer did not comment on the client's face-touching behavior.

After taping all 15 interviews, a copy of each tape was made using another videotape recorder (Sony, VO-1600) and a television set that monitored the original recording. None of the praise statements was transferred to the copy. This was accomplished by carefully viewing each original tape and recording the words spoken immediately before a praise statement. As the copy was being made, the recording volume on the machine being recorded onto was turned off just before each praise. It was turned back on immediately after each praise.

Recording System

Observations were conducted using a recording form divided into 40 numbered blocks, each representing a 15-sec interval. Symbols (EC and FT) were printed in each block. An all-or-none recording system was used such that if one or more occurrences of a target behavior was observed, the observer simply slashed through the appropriate symbol. Movement from block to blocked was cued by prerecorded numbers on the audiocassette previously used in the preparation of the videotapes. Before each observation session, the cassette was rewound as far as possible. The starting of the cassette player was synchronized with a spoken number at the beginning of each videotape to ensure uniform recording conditions across all sessions.

Eye contact was scored when the client positioned her face and head such that she appeared to make eye contact with the interviewer for approximately two or more consecutive seconds. The 2-sec period was approximated by instructing the observers to count, "One thousand one, one thousand two." The trainer modelled this at an approximately standard rate during initial training of each observer. Face touching was scored when any part of the client's hand touched any part of her head between her jaw and hairline.

Interobserver agreement between the criterion observers and between the experimental observers was calculated in two different ways for each session. Overall agreement was determined by taking total agreements (occurrence and nonoccurrences) and dividing by the number of observation intervals. Occurrence agreement was determined by taking occurrence agreements and dividing by occurrence agreements plus occurrence disagreements.

Check on Content of Videotapes

The tapes were made such that the number of eye contacts and face touches was constant across all sessions. To demonstrate this, a pair of experienced criterion observers, one male and one female, who were both experienced in making behavioral observations, observed a complete set of the tapes on which there were no praise statements. Thus, any systematic changes in the experimental observers' recorded levels of the target behaviors could be attributed to witnessing praises and/or expecting a change in behavior.

The criterion observers were given 15 min to study the instructions and definitions. All questions regarding recording procedures and definitions were answered by having the observer reread the appropriate section of the instructions. They were told that their recordings would be compared to each other's to check for agreement. They then observed the first 10-min interview. If 0.80 occurrence agreement was obtained on each behavior they observed the next tape. If not, the observer studied the instructions for 15 additional minutes and rescored the tape. This procedure was continued until all three training tapes had been scored with 0.80 or better occurrence agreement for each behavior. The criterion observers then scored the 12 experimental tapes from which the praise statements had been removed.

The criterion observers' recordings were used to prepare a criterion protocol for each tape. An interval was scored on the protocol for each of the two behaviors if the criterion observers agreed on the behavior's occurrence or nonoccurrence. Intervals in which there was disagreement were excluded from the protocol for the appropriate behavior.

Across sessions, overall agreement between the criterion observers for eye contact ranged from 0.98 to 1.00, with a mean of 0.99. Means for each condition were 1.00, 1.00, 1.00, and 0.98, respectively. Occurrence agreement for eye contact ranged from 0.88 to 1.00, with a mean of 0.98. Means for each condition were 1.00, 1.00, 1.00, and 0.92, respectively. Overall agreement for face touching ranged from 0.95 to 1.00, with a mean of 0.99. Means for each condition were 0.98, 0.99, 1.00, and 0.98, respectively. Occurrence agreement for face touching ranged from 0.75 to 1.00, with a mean of 0.97. Means for each condition were 0.86, 0.99, 1.00, and 0.98, respectively.

Figure 1 shows the mean percentage of intervals scored for each target behavior by the primary criterion observer during each condition. A coin toss determined the choice of the "primary" criterion observer. This distinction was made merely for convenience in plotting the data. Eye contact and face touching were scored at consistent levels, 17.5% to 22.5% for eye contact and 15% to 25% for face touching, across all sessions. Eye-contact means for each condition were 20%, 22%, 20%, and 20% respectively. Face-touching means were 17%, 23%, 19%, and 23%, respectively.

Experimental-Observer Training

The first three 10-min tapes, with the praises removed, were arbitrarily designated as observer training tapes. All the experimental observers were trained exactly as the criterion observers had been, except that their recordings were compared with the protocol instead of each other's recordings. The experimental observers were told once, at the start of training, that their recordings would be checked against the recordings of several other observers. During training, the experimental observers viewed the three training tapes, in turn, until 0.80 occurrence agreement with the protocol was achieved for each behavior on a tape seen for the first time. If criterion was not met on any tape, that tape was rescored until criterion was met before moving on. Observers 1 to 6 required, respectively, 3, 6, 4, 4, 3, and 4 observations of the first training tape before reaching 0.80 occurrence agreement on both behaviors. All six experimental observers met criterion on the first viewing of the second training tape.

Setting and Standard Procedures

Experimental observation sessions were conducted on 12 consecutive weekdays. A solid partition separated the adjacent observation stations. The experimental observers viewed the tapes in the same sequence in which they were presented to the criterion observers.

EXPERIMENT I

METHOD

Design

An A-B-A-B design was used to assess the effects of interviewer praise contingent on client eye contact in conjunction with the expectation of client improvement on observers' recording behavior. In each baseline (A) phase, experimental observers viewed three of the interviews from which the praises had been removed and recorded occurrences of client face-touches and eye contact with the interviewer. In each expectation plus praise (B) condition interview, the interviewer delivered praise following each occurrence of eye contact and at several other random times when there was no eye contact. During the B conditions, they were told that praise had been effective in increasing eye contact in previous research.

Subjects

Two female undergraduate psychology majors, 22 and 25 yr old, served as experimental observers. They were randomly chosen from a group of four students assigned to participate in the present project as part of their commitment to a summer institute in psychology at the University of Georgia. Students attending the institute received a stipend. None of the four students working on this project had previous experience as a behavioral observer.

Procedure

The experimenter announced each condition of which expectation was a component by stating that there was substantial experimental evidence that contingent praises had been successful in increasing a variety of behaviors, and that the interviewer would be using them to increase the client's eye contact. Subsequent sessions in the expectation plus praise condition were preceded by a shortened version of the original announcement.

RESULTS

Across sessions, overall agreement on eye contact between the experimental observers ranged from 0.80 to 1.00, with a mean of 0.90. Means for each condition were 0.93, 0.87, 0.90, and 0.90, respectively. Occurrence agreement for eye contact ranged from 0.41 to 1.00, with a mean of 0.64. Means for each condition were 0.72, 0.47, 0.64, and 0.72, respectively. Overall agreement on face touching ranged from 0.93 to

1.00, with a mean of 0.97. Means for each condition were 0.98, 0.97, 0.98, and 0.95, respectively. Occurrence agreement on face touching ranged from 0.70 to 1.00, with a mean of 0.87. Means for each condition were 0.89, 0.85, 0.92, and 0.80, respectively.

Figure 1 shows the percentage of intervals scored for each target behavior by each experimental observer. Observer 1 recorded eye contact at a mean frequency of 21% during the baseline condition. There was an immediate increase to a mean of 38.3% during the first expectation plus praise condition. This recovered to the previous level during the second baseline condition. Reinstitution of the expectation plus praise condition did not produce another increase in recorded eye contact. Observer 1 recorded face touching at a consistent level, 17.5% to 24%, across all sessions. Observer 2 recorded eye contact and face touching consistently, 15% to 23% and 15% to 25%, respectively, across all sessions.

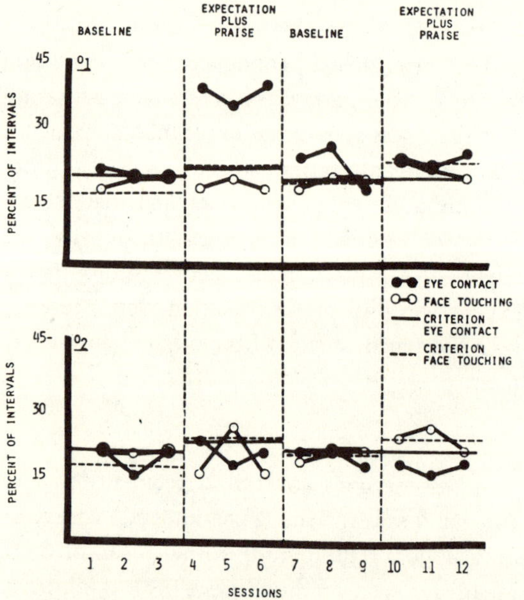

Fig. 1. Percentage of intervals in which Observers 1 and 2 scored eye contact (closed circles) and face touching (open circles). The horizontal (broken and solid) lines represent the mean percentages of intervals in each condition scored by the primary criterion observer.

EXPERIMENT II

Method

Design

Based on the results of Experiment I, Experiment II was designed to assess the relative contributions of expectation and witnessing praises to the increased recording of eye contact. An A-B-BC-B design was used to determine if expectation alone would be sufficient to increase recorded eye contact and if witnessing praises would increase recordings over the levels recorded during expectation alone. During the A condition, the observers viewed tapes from which all praises had been removed. During the B conditions, they also observed tapes with no praises, but were given the expectation that the client's eye contact would increase. During the BC condition, they were given the same expectation as in the previous B condition and they observed the tapes that contained correct and incorrect praises.

Subjects

The two undergraduate students participating in the summer institute who were not selected for the previous experiment served as experimental observers. One was a 23-yr-old male and the other a 24-yr-old female.

Procedure

The videotapes, recording system, observer training strategy, and general procedures were the same as those used in Experiment 1. When expectation was used alone, the observers were told that the client had experienced a praise session immediately before the observation session. Before each session in the expectation plus praise condition, the observers were told that the praises would be given during the session instead of before it.

Results

Across sessions, overall agreement on eye contact between the experimental observers ranged from 0.85 to 1.00, with a mean of 0.91. Means for each condition were 0.93, 0.89, 0.88, and 0.92, respectively. Occurrence agreement for eye contact ranged from 0.40 to 1.00, with a mean of 0.62. Means for each condition were 0.72, 0.50, 0.64, and 0.63, respectively. Overall agreement on face touching ranged from 0.93 to 1.00, with a mean of 0.97. Means for each condition were 0.99, 0.97, 0.99, and 0.94, respectively. Occurrence agreement on face touching ranged from 0.73 to 1.00, with a mean of 0.88. Means for each condition were 0.96, 0.85, 0.96, and 0.78, respectively.

Figure 2 shows the percentage of intervals scored by each experimental observer for each behavior. The data collected by the original criterion observers are shown again in this figure. Except for eye contact in the first session, Observer 3 recorded the target behaviors at consistent levels, 17.5% to 22.5% for eye contact and 17.5% to 25% for face touching, across all sessions. Observer 4 recorded face touching at a consistent level across all sessions. He recorded eye contact at a mean frequency of 17% during baseline.

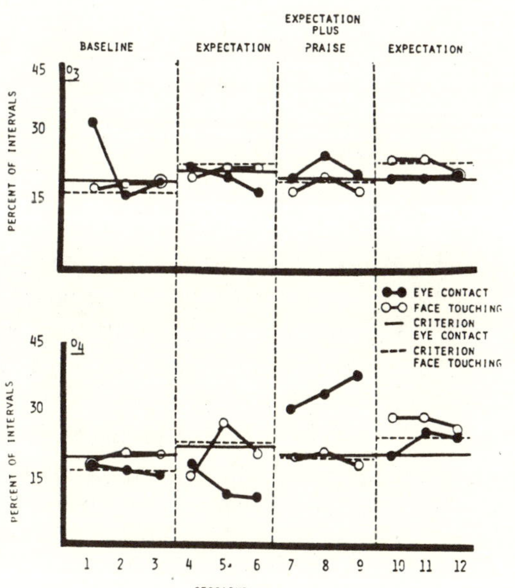

Fig. 2. Percentage of intervals in which Observers 3 and 4 scored eye contact (closed circles) and face touching (open circles). The horizontal (broken and solid) lines represent the mean percentage of intervals in each condition scored by the primary criterion observer.

Although there was a slight change in the direction opposite the expectation for Observer 4, there did not appear to be any systematic change as a result of the expectation procedures. However, there was an immediate increase to a mean of 29% during the subsequent expectation plus praise condition. This recovered to the previous expectation-only level in the final condition in which no praises were witnessed.

EXPERIMENT III

Method

Design

Based on the results of the previous experiments, Experiment III was designed to determine if witnessing praises in the absence of outcome expectations would be sufficient to increase the recording of eye contact. An A-B-A-B design was used. During the A conditions, the observers viewed the tapes from which all praises had been removed. During the B conditions, they viewed the tapes on which there were correct and incorrect praise statements.

Subjects

Two male undergraduate psychology majors enrolled in an introductory psychology course were the experimental observers. Each was 22 yr old. Neither had previous experience as an observer.

Procedure

The videotapes, recording system, and observer training strategy were the same as those used in Experiments I and II.

Results

Across sessions, overall agreement on eye contact between the experimental observers ranged from 0.68 to 1.00, with a mean of 0.89. Means for each condition were 0.96, 0.82, 0.88, and 0.90, respectively. Occurrence agreement on eye contact ranged from 0.40 to 1.00, with a mean of 0.61. Means for each condition were 0.78, 0.44, 0.46, and 0.53, respectively. Overall agreement on face touching ranged from 0.93 to 1.00. with a mean of 0.96. Means for each condition were 0.99, 0.97, 0.96, and 0.96, respectively. Occurrence agreement on face touching ranged from 0.70 to 1.00, with a mean of 0.87. Means for each condition were 0.96, 0.85, 0.87, and 0.83, respectively.

Figure 3 shows the percentage of intervals scored by each experimental observer and the criterion observers' data. Observer 5 recorded eye contact at a mean 16.5% level during baseline. This increased to 43.6% during the first praise condition and returned to the previous baseline level during the second baseline condition. Reinstitution of the praise procedures, however, did not produce another increase in recorded eye contact. Observer 5 recorded face touching at a consistent level across all conditions. Observer 6 recorded eye contact and face touching at consistent levels across all conditions.

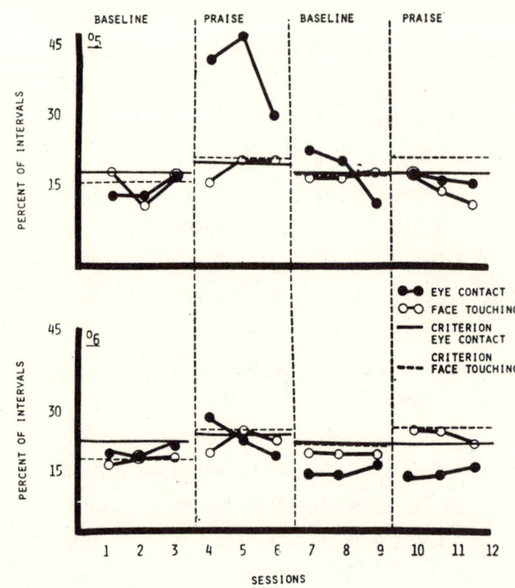

Fig. 3. Percentage of intervals in which Observers 5 and 6 scored eye contact (closed circles) and face touching (open circles). The horizontal (broken and solid) lines represent the mean percentage of intervals in each condition scored by the primary criterion observer.

GENERAL DISCUSSION

The present data suggest that witnessing consequences can influence the behavioral recordings of some observers. This was demonstrated by eye contact above the 20% level being recorded only during praise conditions. Behavior-specific effects of witnessing consequences are suggested by the absence of any systematic changes in recorded face touching. Expectation did not play any apparent role in the altered recordings. This is consistent with previous research (Kent *et al.,* 1974), suggesting that merely expecting a change in behavior does not lead to altered recordings of specific behaviors.

Even though the recordings of only three of the six experimental observers were influenced, it is important to note that the effect on those observers was quite obvious. Inflated eye-contact recordings occurred only during the initial praise condition for the affected observers. Although interval validity was not demonstrated with the affected observers by the variations of the A-B-A-B design, some internal validity was indicated by the fact that the control target behavior, face touching, was not influenced.

The failure to replicate the effect for either subject who showed an initial bias merits elaboration. Since half the consequences were delivered at random times during the interviews, they often occurred when the client was quite obviously looking away from the interviewer and not meeting the definition for eye contact. As time went by, the discrepancy between client behavior and interviewer comments was so great, it probably became obvious and rendered the praises ineffective in changing recording behavior. Informal discussions with the subjects after the study corroborated this speculation. Future research could investigate this phenomenon by having consequences delivered following close or distant approximations to the target behavior.

These results suggest that the interobserver agreement checks might not always detect the biasing effect of witnessing cues. For all three experimental observer pairs, all the condition means for overall eye contact agreement were above 0.80, even though one member of each pair recorded considerably more behavior than the other during each initial praise condition. This suggests the importance of plotting both observers' data before drawing conclusions and/or using conservative methods (occurrence or nonoccurrence agreement) to determine interobserver agreement (Hawkins and Dotson, 1975). In cases where only one observer was affected by extraneous cues, more conservative methods of calculating interobserver agreement probably would yield differentially low scores in certain conditions and cue the investigator and reader that a problem existed. For example, in the present series of investigations, occurrence agreement was systematically lower in conditions when one member of the pair was affected. In cases such as these when only one member of an observer pair is affected, occurrence agreement would be sensitive to the bias effect. The danger would arise when the primary observer and agreement checker were *both* affected. In that case, the data would be reliable (in terms of agreement scores) but inaccurate in reflecting the levels of the behavior under study.

The reduced interobserver agreement scores following the initial baseline condition for all three observer pairs appear to have been an indirect result of the experimental manipulation, rather than of a qualitative difference between the first three tapes and all the others. All observers were initially trained to 0.80 occurrence agreement with a criterion protocol. Occurrence agreement scores were above 0.70 for the initial baseline conditions but decreased substantially during each initial experimental condition. This did not occur with the criterion observers, thus making it unlikely that there was a difference in actual eye-contact behavior between the first three tapes and all the others. The decrease in occurrence agreement scores following the first baseline condition for all three pairs of experimental observers appears to be a result of only one member of each pair being affected by the experimental manipulation.

It also appears unlikely that inadequate training procedures could have accounted for the reduced interobserver agreement scores following the initial baseline condition. The observer training procedures in this series of experiments appear to be no less rigorous than are commonly reported in the literature. The observers viewed the initial training tape a mean of four times before achieving 0.80 occurrence agreement with the protocol on both behaviors. They all achieved 0.80 occurrence agreement with the protocol on the first viewing of the second training tape. This makes it likely that the present results are due to the independent variables, rather than to poorly trained observers.

The present results suggest that there might be important individual differences in observers with respect to their susceptibility to being influenced by extraneous cues regarding target behavior occurrence. This appears to contradict the widely held assumption (Baer, 1977) that the vast majority of observers, given the same behavioral definition, will be able to agree on the occurrence or nonoccurrence of the behavior regardless of any other factors. Future research could focus on identifying the relevant individual differences.

In many previous studies, no attention has been given to this particular form of bias caused by witnessing consequences. The present results might cast some doubt on conclusions of those studies demonstrating small but consistent differences in behavior between experimental conditions.

Until the parameters of observer reactivity are investigated using different consequences, target behaviors, observers, and experimental subjects, researchers might minimize it by: (1) cautioning observers to attend only to the behavior under study and disregard any extraneous cues; (2) incorporating training in correctly discriminating target behavior occurrence in the presence of consequences during initial observer training and subsequent recalibration sessions; or (3) if feasible, designing the experiment such that observers are never exposed to extraneous cues that a behavior has occurred. These suggestions are obviously tentative and await empirical validation to document their effectiveness in reducing this type of bias.

REFERENCES

Baer, D. M. Reviewer's comment: just because it's reliable doesn't mean that you can use it. *Journal of Applied Behavior Analysis,* 1977, **10**, 117-119.

Dubey, D. R., Kent, R. N., O'Leary, S. G., and Broderick, J. E. Reactions of children and teachers to classroom observers: A series of controlled investigations. *Behavior Therapy,* 1977, **8**, 887-897.

Hagen, R. L., Craighead, W. E., and Paul, G. L. Staff reactivity to evaluative behavioral observations. *Behavior Therapy,* 1975, **6**, 201-205.

Hawkins, R. P. and Dotson, V. A. Reliability scores that delude: An Alice in Wonderland trip through the misleading characteristics of interobserver agreement scores in interval recording. In E. Ramp and G. Semb (Eds), *Behavior analysis: areas of research and application.* Englewood Cliffs, New Jersey: Prentice-Hall, 1975. Pp. 359-376.

Johnson, S. M. and Bolstad, O. D. Methodological issues in naturalistic observation: Some problems and solutions for field research. In L. A. Hamerlynck, J. Handy, and D. A. Nash (Eds), *Behavior change: Methodology, concepts, and practice.* Champaign, Illinois: Research Press, 1973. Pp. 7-67.

Kazdin, A. E. Artifact, bias, and complexity of assessment: the ABCs of reliability. *Journal of Applied Behavior Analysis,* 1977, **10**, 141-150.

Kent, R. N. and Foster, S. L. Direct observational procedures: Methodological issues in naturalistic settings. In A. R. Ciminero, K. S. Calhoun, and H. E. Adams (Eds), *Handbook of behavioral assessment.* New York: John Wiley & Sons, 1977. Pp. 279-328.

Kent, R. N., O'Leary, K. D., Diament, C., and Dietz, A. Expectation biases in observational evaluation of therapeutic change. *Journal of Consulting and Clinical Psychology,* 1974, **42**, 774-780.

Martin, M. F., Gelfand, D. M., and Hartmann, D. P. Effects of adult and peer observers on boys' and girls' responses to an aggressive model. *Child Development,* 1971, **42**, 1271-1275.

Mash, E. J. and Hedley, J. Effect of observer as a function of prior history of social interaction. *Perceptual and Motor Skills,* 1975, **40**, 659-669.

Mash, E. J. and Makohoniuk, G. The effects of prior information and behavioral predictability on observer accuracy. *Child Development,* 1975, **46**, 513-519.

Mash, E. J. and McElwee, J. D. Situational effects on observer accuracy: Behavior predictability, prior experience, and complexity of coding categories. *Child Development,* 1974, **45**, 367-377.

Mercatoris, M. and Craighead, W. E. Effects of nonparticipant observation on teacher and pupil classroom behavior. *Journal of Educational Psychology,* 1974, **66**, 512-519.

O'Leary, K. D. and Kent, R. N. Behavior modification for social action: Research tactics and problems. In L. A. Hamerlynck, L. C. Handy, and E. J. Mash (Eds), *Behavior change: Methodology, concepts, and practice.* Champaign, Illinois: Research Press, 1973. Pp. 69-96.

O'Leary, K. D., Kent, R. N., and Kanowitz, J. Shaping data collection congruent with experimental hypotheses. *Journal of Applied Behavior Analysis,* 1975, **8**, 43-51.

Romanczyk, R. G., Kent, R. N., Diament, C., and O'Leary, K. D. Measuring the reliability of observational data: a reactive process. *Journal of Applied Behavior Analysis,* 1973, **6**, 175-184.

Reid, J. B. Reliability assessment of observation data: A possible methodological problem. *Child Development,* 1970, **41**, 1143-1150.

Roberts, R. R. and Renzaglia, G. A. The influence of tape recording on counseling. *Journal of Counseling Psychology,* 1965, **12**, 10-16.

Surratt, P. R., Ulrich, R. E., and Hawkins, R. P. An elementary student as a behavioral engineer. *Journal of Applied Behavior Analysis,* 1969, **2**, 85-92.

Taplin, P. S. and Reid, J. B. Effects of instructional set and experimenter influence on behavior reliability. *Child Development,* 1973, **44**, 547-554.

Wildman, B. G., Erickson, M. T., and Kent, R. N. The effect of two training procedures on observer agreement and variability of behavior ratings. *Child Development,* 1975, **46**, 520-524.

Zegiob, L. E., Arnold, S., and Forehand, R. An examination of observer effects in parent-child interactions. *Child Development,* 1975, **46**, 509-512.

Zegiob, L. and Forehand, R. Parent-child interactions: Observer effects and social class differences. *Behavior Therapy,* 1978, **9**, 118-123.

Received 20 December 1977.
(*Final Acceptance 13 July 1978.*)

JOURNAL OF APPLIED BEHAVIOR ANALYSIS 1979, 12, 501-516 NUMBER 4 (WINTER 1979)

THE FUNCTIONS OF ASSESSMENT: IMPLICATIONS FOR SELECTION AND DEVELOPMENT OF DEVICES FOR ASSESSING REPERTOIRES IN CLINICAL, EDUCATIONAL, AND OTHER SETTINGS

ROBERT P. HAWKINS

WEST VIRGINIA UNIVERSITY

An attempt is made to identify the many different functions that assessment of an individual's repertoire can serve. Implications of these functions for the character of and evidence about assessment devices are suggested. The functions fall into two general groups, those which influence decisions regarding an individual learner, and those which influence policy, program development, and scientific knowledge. The first group of functions is presented in a rough chronological sequence such that they form a "behavioral assessment funnel," beginning with functions involving broad-band assessment to identify likely persons and skill areas, and narrowing to the precise pinpointing, monitoring, and follow-up functions. The contribution of behavior analysis and behavior therapy to assessment methodology in this sequence is identified as well as the areas where more traditionally conceived methods are still useful. The second group of functions and behavioral contributions to it are then discussed.

DESCRIPTORS: behavioral assessment, functions of assessment, selection of assessment devices, traditional assessment, clinical assessment, educational assessment, phases of assessment, construction of assessment devices

---

Applied behavior analysis has made profound contributions to the technology for assessing repertoires. At the same time, behavior analysts have often rejected or ignored valuable existing ("traditional") knowledge and technology for clinical and educational assessment (Cone, 1977; Goldfried, 1977; Hawkins, 1975; Nelson and Bowles, 1975; Hartmann, Note 1). The purposes of the present paper are three. The first is to identify several different phases and functions in assessment. The second is to put the contributions of behavior analysis in context, showing where the contribution thus far has been greatest and where previously existing knowledge and technology can be of value to a behavior analyst. The third is to illustrate how the present analysis holds implications for selection and construction of assessment devices, including implications regarding generalizability (Cronbach, Gleser, Nanda, and Rajaratnam, 1972), type of output needed, and costs.

First, a discrimination that appears useful is between assessment designed to influence directly decisions regarding an individual and assessment designed for one or more of three other functions: classification for administrative records, research for evaluating interventions, and collection of normative data. Those functions serving the general purpose of influencing decisions regarding an individual will be presented first.

This paper is based partly on one presented at the meeting of the American Psychological Association, September 1976, Washington, D.C., under the title "Relevance for what? It depends on the assessment goal," in a symposium chaired by D. H. Barlow and entitled *Behavioral assessment: The relevance of traditional psychometric procedures.* Reprints may be obtained from the author at Psychology Department, West Virginia University, Morgantown, West Virginia 26506.

PHASES AND FUNCTIONS INVOLVED IN ASSESSMENT INFLUENCING DECISIONS REGARDING AN INDIVIDUAL

Texts on assessment generally are designed to help train professionals for work with individual students, clients, or other learners. The general goal of such work is usually improvement of the learner's adaptation to his or her environment in some way, such as through acquisition of academic skills, learning to interact more effectively with members of the opposite sex, or relearning functional speech or locomotion. Thus the general purpose of the individual assessment taught by such texts is, as Linehan (1977) has described, "to figure out what the client's problem is and how to change it for the better (p. 31)"; or, in terms more descriptive of educational assessment, "to figure out what the client's present skills are and what should be learned next."

But the process of figuring out "what the client's problem is" or "what should be learned next" is not a unitary process; it is one consisting of several sequential phases, each with a somewhat different function and each placing somewhat different requirements on the assessment methods employed. As Anastasi (1968) put it, speaking of validity, "No test can be said to have 'high' or 'low' validity in the abstract. Its validity must be determined with reference to the particular use for which the test is being considered" (p. 99). Yet assessment texts, including Anastasi's, generally do not distinguish between the different functions and their different implications, and most texts completely omit some of the functions.

THE "BEHAVIORAL ASSESSMENT FUNNEL" AND THE FUNCTIONS PREDOMINANT IN EACH PHASE

The phases of individual case assessment can be considered to form a funnel, with an initially broad scope and a subsequent narrow and constant focus (Cone and Hawkins, 1977). The five phases are as follows: (1) screening and general disposition, (2) definition and general quantifiication of problem or achievement, (3) pinpointing and design of intervention, (4) monitoring of progress, and (5) follow-up. Though these phases describe a typical chronological sequence, the functions attributed to them here are not so firmly limited in time. For example, the functions of the first phase are never totally eclipsed and an initial pinpointing of the problem in phase three might well be revised during a later phase.

Screening and General Disposition

Functions predominant in screening and disposition. When a potential learner (client or student) first appears at the door of a clinic or educational institution, the first assessment function to be performed is *determination of whether the case is appropriate* for the agency. The question is "Does this case belong here?" This assessment is often conducted partly or wholly by clerical staff and may take only a few minutes. In the schools the person's age and previous grade in school may suffice, though colleges often require a certain level of performance in previous schooling and/or on an entrance examination. In clinics the person answering the telephone will often obtain some gross description of the client's problem and will refer those clients who obviously need a different agency's service.

If the answer to the initial screening question is "No, the learner does not belong here," the assessor must make a *determination of where to refer the learner* for more appropriate services. But if the answer to the initial screening question is "Probably," the next assessment function is the *determination of what further assessment may be relevant.* In the clinic this second screening and disposition question might be phrased "What general kind(s) of problem(s) may this person be having (and thus what kinds of further assessment information will I need)?" In a school the question might be simply "Is it likely that this student's academic or social skills are unusual enough for his or her age that some program out of the ordinary might be called for?" The whole screening and disposition phase may take 5 minutes or several hours.

Characteristics desirable in methods used for screening and general disposition. The screening and disposition phase requires a broad-band assessment (Cronbach, 1970) capable of detecting any likely kind of problem, even if it does not satisfactorily specify the nature of the problem. Thus interviewing, a case study, a "mental status" examination, incomplete sentences, and the like might be appropriate for clinical cases, because each is very flexible and can readily survey a broad range of possible problems. For example, a clinician assessing a medically referred case involving complaint of chronic headache might initially attempt to determine what neurological assessment has been done, what dental assessment has been done, what consequences might normally ensue when the client complains of headache, and how demanding the client's job and home life have been. In educational environments, interviews, the Wide Range Achievement Test (Guidance Associates of Delaware, 1978), an AML (Cowen, Dorr, Clarfield, Kreling, McWilliams, Pokracki, Pratt, Terrell, and Wilson, 1973), the STS Youth Inventory (Scholastic Testing Service, 1971), or the Mooney Problem Check List (Psychological Corp., 1950) might be appropriate, depending on whether academic, personal, or social skills are of interest.

The functions of this phase of assessment are a crude sorting of people into "serve" or "send elsewhere," and "assess for X" or "do not assess for X." These are obviously predictions, and any assessment device that improves the accuracy of these predictions is worth considering. For example, if one had evidence that the MMPI improved detection of potential suicides in a particular population, it would seem foolish not to use the MMPI as part of the screening of a client representing that population. One need not subscribe to the theoretical assumptions regarding "personality" that typify users of a device like the MMPI in order to take advantage of any predictive value it may have.[1] On the other hand, neither must one accept the traditional correlation coefficient as the measure of predictive validity. A more satisfactory evaluation would be a series of contingency tables for each of several promising cutoff scores. Each table would show how many true positives, false positives, true negatives, and false negatives a particular cutoff score would produce with a given population.

The kind of output needed for screening and disposition functions is simple. The assessment must simply classify the learner as appropriate or inappropriate for the agency and identify further assessments that may be useful. Commensurate with the simplicity of output is the allowable cost. Usually screening and disposition devices must be inexpensive, particularly in terms of professional time.

Contributions of behavioral assessors to screening and disposition assessment. Of the five assessment phases, this one has probably received the least attention by both traditional and behavioral assessors. Certainly the SORC analysis of assessment by Kanfer and Saslow (1969) made a significant contribution to a behavioral conception of both this phase and the second phase of assessment. Interview guides (Holland, 1970) and descriptions (*e.g.,* Morganstern, 1976) similarly contribute to both phases. The computer-assisted clinical interview described by Angle, Hay, Hay, and Ellinwood (1977) is designed to determine in what areas of adjustment clients may be having sufficient difficulty to warrant further inquiry. This interview has the advantages of being inexpensive in terms of

[1]Suicide risk is intentionally used in the example to emphasize the fact that a cost, risk/benefit is implicit in deciding to conduct any assessment. In this case the risk is not detecting a high probability, negatively valued event. The magnitude of such risk and the magnitude of benefit from detecting a problem (*e.g.,* from ensuing treatment), would determine the cutoff scores used and the tolerable cost of the assessment.

professional time (though not the client's), very broad in scope, and completely standardized (and thus readily researchable).

Definition and General Quantification of the Problem or Achievement

Functions predominant in definition and quantification. This phase is the most familiar to clinical and educational assessors, and traditional texts on testing deal almost exclusively with it (*e.g.*, Anastasi, 1978). This phase is comparable to the aspects of assessment that Mash and Terdal (1976) label "diagnosis," in reference primarily to clinical problems. It takes up where screening and disposition left off, with rough hunches as to the nature of the problem. It proceeds with a careful evaluation of those hypotheses and ends with a commitment to certain hypotheses about the functional relations involved in the problem. Further assessment and treatment is then based on these hypotheses. In this process the problem will often have been quantified, if only in gross terms such as "mild" or "severe," or in terms of a prognosis.

Thus two major processes are required in this phase—hypothesis formation and measurement—and the clinician will often cycle repeatedly between hypothesizing and measuring (including probing for the simple presence or absence of hypothesized factors) until some tenable formulation of the problem is attained. In clinical settings a great deal of knowledge is often required about behavior pathologies if the assessor is to be effective in generating reasonable hypotheses.

The functions of this phase, then, are at least the following: (1) *identification of the skill or problem areas in which help is definitely to be offered,* (2) *quantification of the general level of skill in the relevant areas,* and finally (3) *determination of where and how, in general, the needed learning can best be accomplished.* Put more generally, the functions are to set the general goals of intervention and select the environment for their achievement.

The kinds of questions asked in this phase might include "How serious is this particular problem?" "What is this student's level of reading comprehension?" "Should intervention be attempted?" and "What program or person can be of greatest help?" Note that the outcome of this phase is *placement* in a general learning environment—such as a second-grade classroom or with an assertiveness training expert—and often, within that environment, at a particular level of skill, such as a third-grade reader or an advanced assertion group. Many clinicians and educators terminate serious assessment efforts here.

Characteristics desirable in methods used for definition and general quantification. The first outcome of this phase is definition of the general nature of the problem. This might be achieved through a series of assessment activities, each with its own validity requirements. For example, the problem of a client whose initial complaint was chronic headache might have been identified in this phase as one involving insufficiently assertive behavior on a job in which the new boss was unreasonably demanding. The devices used in arriving at this hypothesis might have included interviews that explored several questions, such as when the headaches began and how often they occur, whether there had been any trauma to the head, and what precedes and follows a headache. Ideally one would have evidence that these questions, individually or collectively, are good discriminators between persons known to have psychosomatic headaches and persons known to have headaches based on other factors. The assessment might also have included some form of neurological examination, and here again one would look for criterion-related validity showing that the type of examination given was a good discriminator between two groups, particularly between persons with neurologically based headaches and persons with headaches based on other factors. Finally, the assessor may have used a structured assertiveness test, in which case it would be desirable to have evidence that this test discriminates well between persons whose behavior is insufficiently assertive in the face of unreasonable demands in the natural environment and those whose behavior is effectively assertive (*e.g.*, McFall and Lillesand, 1971).

The final outcome of this phase is a recommended placement of the learner, which is essentially a prediction that that person (or perhaps others) will fare better with such a placement than with alternative placements, including no special treatment or education. Evidence for the validity of the placement could be program evaluation data showing that similar learners had performed better during placement in the similar programs than without those programs. The similarity of the present learner to those with whom such predictive validity was established might be on the basis of the type of problem to be remedied, demographic variables, or various traditional test scores. So long as there is good evidence that a particular variable predicts success in a program, the behavior analyst should feel free to use that variable as a predictor. The fact that it is a traditional assessment device with little value in *identifying the problem* should not dissuade the behavior analyst from using it in *determining placement.* Any assessment device may have high validity for one function and low validity for another.

The cost of conducting assessment in this second phase may be considerably higher than in the screening and disposition phase, particularly with complex clinical problems. The output from this phase may be as simple as the statement, "This student's academic skills are progressing at the expected rate, except in the area of written expression where they are beyond expectation; continuation of the present program is recommended." On the other hand, the output could be a complex formulation describing how the natural environment may have established a set of interrelated, maladaptive behavior patterns and may continue to maintain them. In addition, the output will include a general recommendation regarding the type of intervention suggested.

Contributions of behavioral assessors to definition and general quantification. Behavioral contributions to this phase of assessment have come primarily from behavior therapists whose interest is individual clinical problems. In contrast, contributions to the next three phases have come primarily from applied behavior analysts with a great diversity of interests.

Behavioral assessment for this phase may use a variety of methods, including indirect assessment of behavior, direct assessment in controlled environments, and direct methods in natural environments (Cone and Hawkins, 1977). The behavioral interview—both a direct and an indirect assessment method, depending on the behaviors of interest—has been developed by a number of behavior therapists. Morganstern (1976) provides analysis of the procedures used, while Goldfried and Pomeranz (1968), Kanfer and Saslow (1969) and others focus more on the content. The interview is used to assess a wide range of clinical problems, as are self-report questionnaires. Examples of self-report questionnaires used by behavior therapists are the Beck Depression Inventory (Beck, 1972), the Rathus Assertiveness Schedule (Rathus, 1973), and the Menstrual Symptom Questionnaire (Chesney and Tasto, 1975).

Direct assessment in controlled environments has been reviewed by McFall (1977) and by Nay (1977). It includes measurement of a client's avoidance of a feared object through the behavioral avoidance test, the assessment of a client's heterosocial skills through a contrived meeting with a confederate of the opposite sex, the assessment of how assertively a client behaves through a telephone call involving a series of demands, and measurement of sexual arousal to verbal descriptions of situations (Abel, Blanchard, Barlow, and Mavissakalian, 1975).

Direct assessment in the natural environment can be carried out by the behavior therapist or by his agent, as when Hawkins, Peterson, Schweid, and Bijou (1966) observed parent-child interaction in the home to determine what the problem was. But self-monitoring in the natural environment might also be considered direct assessment to the extent that one can have confidence in the reliability of the data. As Mahoney (1977) and Nelson (1977) have illustrated, self-monitoring can include immediate recording of a specified event, a structured diary in which antecedents and consequences are recorded along with a particular class of event, immediate ratings at preselected or random times, or tape recordings of verbal descriptions of behavior and associated events. Any of these could be very valuable in defining and quantifying a clinical problem to determine an appropriate type of intervention.

In educational settings the most familiar assessment device for these functions is the standardized, norm-referenced achievement test, such as the Iowa Test of Basic Skills (Houghton Mifflin, 1974). A norm-referenced test can assist in determining what group a student fits into best. Such a test describes the general level of a student's skills in each of several skill areas; however, it is of limited value in determining precisely what skills to teach the individual child next, a major function of the next phase of assessment. By contrast, a criterion-referenced test (Livingston, 1977) can perform both these functions.

It should be noted that one form of assessment in the definition and quantification phase can be to "short circuit" much of the process and to place the learner in a likely program for a trial period. If the costs and risks of such a placement are likely to be smaller than those of another form of assessment, the trial period approach seems advisable. It has the advantage of providing the best possible prediction as to how well the learner will perform in the program: his or her actual performance; but the assessor must actually monitor the learner's performance during the trial period and not prematurely rule out alternative placements. The trial period approach was employed by Hansen and Lovitt (1976) in deciding what reading text was the most appropriate for each child in a special classroom. They monitored both "words correct" and "words incorrect" per minute in oral reading from texts at each of several difficulty levels.

Pinpointing and Design of Intervention

This phase corresponds closely to the "design" aspect of assessment described by Mash and Terdal (1976). It involves functions that educational and psychological tradition have given relatively little attention. The functions are: (1) *selection of specific behavioral objectives,* (2) *analysis of specific existing contingencies that may be maintaining the subject's ineffective behavior or may otherwise impede achievement of the objectives,* (3) *identification of specific resources (social, physical, financial, behavioral) for achieving the objectives,* (4) *design or selection of a teaching sequence (curriculum, in education's terms) to achieve the objectives,* and (5) *determination of precise quantitative levels of key measurable events.*

The focus of this phase is very narrow and constitutes the apex of the behavioral assessment funnel. Baseline data on a learner would be a final outcome of this phase, as the phase ends the pre-intervention assessment.

Questions addressed in this phase include, "What would the stimulus control and topography of a more effective performance look like and how does this person's performance deviate from that?" "How regular and adequate are the current antecedent stimuli (opportunities and demands for performance) and consequences?" "What interfering behaviors are occurring and why?" "Under what antecedent and consequence contingencies is the desired performance to be maintained eventually?" and "What specific resources (*e.g.*, antecedents and consequences) promise to be useful in changing the repertoire?"

Characteristics desirable in methods used for pinpointing and design of intervention. The kind of generalizability that appears most important in this phase is content validity. If the definition of the problem in the previous phase has been correct, the assessor's job in pinpointing is to determine what specific behaviors truly make up that problem in this individual case (thus the relevance of task analysis; *cf.* Schwartz and Gottman, 1976). The assessor needs devices that sample the relevant behaviors, antecedents, and consequences in such a way that the typical quality of each is assessed.

The typical norm-referenced assessment device will be of little use. Instead the assessor needs devices that are criterion referenced in the sense that they assess how well relevant aspects of the repertoire approximate repertoires known to be *effective* at the tasks identified. Though the decision as to what levels of performance are effective may be based on data that are normative in the sense of describing a criterion group (*e.g.,* Walker and Hops, 1976), the ideal basis is experimental demonstration of the effectiveness of various levels of performance (Hawkins, 1975).

Because repertoires and environments are so individual in terms of what skills are critical and what levels of performance are effective, direct observation in the natural environment (Cone and Hawkins, 1977) or at least in controlled, naturalistic situations is very appealing.

The documentation of the content validity of such assessments would be difficult, at best. A very relevant body of information would be research validating task analyses like the one being used in pinpointing. For example, shy males were once taught to make greater eye contact while conversing with women, but it has been discovered in recent experiments that what is probably important is not the *amount* of eye contact but *when* it occurs (McFall, 1977). Through a number of such studies experimentally testing the effects of teaching certain skills to persons with a certain type of problem, we can discover an increasing number of the necessary and sufficient skills for effective performance.

Where contrived situations are used to pinpoint, evidence is also needed that the performance observed is related to the natural environment performance that the assessor assumes is being evaluated. This is particularly critical when neither the antecedent stimuli nor the form of response are identical to those in the natural environment. For example, Freedman (1974) (see also McFall, 1977) developed an Adolescent Problem Inventory in which a youth reports *verbally* what he or she would do in a series of problem situations that are *verbally* described. The specific situations described to the youth were selected by a series of judgments made by Freedman, by delinquent youth, and by experts. Freedman found the device to discriminate significantly between delinquents and nondelinquents, but that is weak evidence that the 44 items represent truly critical situations or that the verbal responses obtained represent the behavior that the subjects would actually emit in the natural environment. Thus the device seems of very limited promise for the pinpointing functions, though it may be useful for other functions.

A familiar form of validity evidence relevant in this phase is that involving the accuracy of the predictions involved. The intervention design generated in this phase is a prediction that if the design is implemented the behaviors and environmental factors will change. These predictions are at least partially verifiable. If the environment and behavior do not change, the decisions of this phase (and perhaps earlier ones) are invalid at least to the extent of being insufficient. If the desired changes do occur, the decisions receive at least partial support, though placebo and other effects may actually account for the changes.

Finally, interobserver agreement is relevant for this phase, though it will not be discussed further until the next phase. Here let me point out an interesting form of interobserver agreement that is particularly appropriate to the pinpointing and design phase. It is a form of social validation (*cf.* Wolf, 1978) and would consist of asking the learner to what extent the process and outcome objectives set during this phase seem appropriate to the problem or skill level with which he or she entered. This is common practice among some clinicians, but below the college level it appears to be rare among educators.

Contributions of behavioral assessors to pinpointing and design of intervention. Behaviorally oriented educators and clinicians have made innumerable and profound contributions to the functions of this phase. In education, learning hierarchies are being constructed (*e.g.,* Resnick, Wang, and Kaplan, 1973) that form the basis for assessment as well as curriculum development. Criterion-referenced tests for assessing such academic skills as reading are beginning to be commercially published (*e.g.,* Harcourt Brace Jovanovich, 1975). "Prescriptive" behavior checklists such as those of Popovich (1977) and Walls, Zane, and Werner (1978) are being developed that appear to perform all of the functions of this phase for certain types of learners.

Clinical assessment devices for this phase include a variety of direct observation procedures (Bijou, Peterson, and Ault, 1968; Hawkins, Axelrod, and Hall, 1976; Mahoney, 1977) applied to a wide range of problems. Barlow, Reynolds, and Agras (1973) directly observed the topography of sitting, standing, and walking behaviors in a young male transexual and, based on comparative observation of normals, targeted very specific aspects of these topographies. Schwarz and Hawkins (1970) videotaped a very shy adolescent in a classroom setting and selected three specific behaviors for modification: voice loudness, posture, and face-touching. Trap, Milner-Davis, Joseph, and Cooper (1978) used transparent overlays to assess seven different accuracy characteristics of cursive letter writing in first-grade students.

Oral and written verbal reports are also very useful in the pinpointing and design phase. LoPiccolo and Steger (1974) use a well-structured questionnaire to target specific sexual interactions of spouses having sexual adjustment problems. Stuart and Stuart (1976) designed a set of detailed questionnaires for families to assess positive and negative behavior change goals and the family resources for achieving them. Questionnaires have also been developed for assessing only potential reinforcers (*e.g.,* Daley, 1976).

Monitoring of Progress

Functions of monitoring. As the name implies, the primary function of assessment in this phase is *determination of the current level of performance* so that the intervention can be evaluated and changed as needed. Of all assessment functions this may be the one to which behavior analysts have made their greatest contribution. Being accustomed to precise, continuous measurement in the laboratory, pioneering behavior analysts addressing human problems developed methods for similarly measuring behavior in the field (*e.g.,* Ayllon and Michael, 1959; Ferster and DeMeyer, 1962; Hart, Allen, Buell, Harris, and Wolf, 1964; Lindsley, 1959). The precise, daily (or frequent) measurement procedures resulting from these pioneering efforts have many advantages over global, norm-referenced or infrequent measurement (Eaton and Lovitt, 1972; Hawkins, Axelrod, and Hall, 1976).

Another function that has recently emerged (Wolf, 1978) is *evaluating the palatability of the intervention to the learner and other consumers.* As Phillips, Phillips, Wolf, and Fixsen (1973) have indicated, the ideal program is one that is not only maximally effective but also *preferred* by the learners.

Because the measurement used to monitor progress is narrow band and constant over time (except when target behaviors change), this phase of assessment represents the long, narrow "neck" of the behavioral assessment funnel. The questions addressed in this phase include, "Are the desired changes in key events taking place?" "Are events whose change is undesirable staying stable?" and "Is this as humane a process as it can be?"

Characteristics desirable in assessment methods for monitoring progress. The devices useful in monitoring progress will be those that are criterion referenced or "edumetric" (Carver, 1974) in the sense that they assess only behaviors being taught (content validity) and are sensitive to change. If, in past research, a device has failed to show change when it is reasonable to expect change (*e.g.,* Lobitz and Johnson, 1975), it would not be a good candidate for monitoring progress. Further, the device should not be responsive to spurious influences such as retesting effects or instrument decay (*cf.* Baer, Wolf, and Risley, 1968; Kent and Foster, 1977; Wildman and Erickson, 1977).

As with almost any assessment device used in any phase, evidence of high interobserver (interexaminer, interscorer, interrater) agreement is desirable in the monitoring of progress. When progress is monitored through direct measurement of the target behaviors in the natural environment, this may seem to be the only relevant information, because there is no better criterion with which to compare the data. However, it is also desirable to know that the data represent the typical performance of the learner in situations and at times other than those in which the data are being obtained (Cone and Hawkins, 1977).

To the extent that a device differs from direct measurement in the natural environment, evidence of a high correlation between the device and such direct measurement becomes important. However, this should probably be qualified by pointing out that it is sometimes more efficient and more socially valid to measure the functional outcome or "impact" of the target behaviors, rather than the target behaviors themselves, such as measuring the frequency of dating in a client who has been taught several specific hetero-social skills to solve a problem he or she has identified as an inability to get dates. In fact, Gilbert (1978) would probably argue that measuring the behavior itself is trivial without assessment of what we might call the "impact" of the behavior change.

A further characteristic that is necessary if an assessment method is to be used routinely and repeatedly with all learners being served by a program (as opposed to use in time-limited research) is economy. Mahoney (1977) has described some economical methods for obtaining clinical data, and others (Hall, 1971; Hawkins, Axelrod, and Hall, 1976; Kubany and Sloggett, 1973) have described some for use by school personnel, but further development of economical, readily disseminated methods is needed.

In assessing the palatability of the intervention, perhaps the primary criterion a device should meet is that one index of palatability agree with another index from the same subjects. For example, if one is administering a questionnaire to assess a student's satisfaction with a learning program, it would be beneficial to know that the student gave a similar report when the same questions were posed by others not obviously connected with the program. Even more convincing would be evidence that when repeatedly given the choice to participate in that program as opposed to others, the learners would choose that program, as Phillips *et al.*'s (1973) youth did.

Contributions of behavioral assessors to monitoring. The technology of using repeated measurement, particularly daily (Eaton and Lovitt, 1972) or very frequent measurement (*e.g.,* Bushell, Jackson, and Weis, 1975), has been highly developed by applied behavior analysts. This technology is well illustrated throughout the *Journal of Applied Behavior Analysis.* Behavior analysts are working to make the technology practical for everyday use in clinical and educational settings, and the technology for maximizing causal interpretability of the results is well developed (*e.g.,* Hersen and Barlow, 1976).[2]

---

[2]The author would argue that the primary responsibility of the practitioner is to document the direction (favorable *vs.* unfavorable) and amount of change occurring in the repertoire *during* teaching or treatment, and, in many clinical cases, the durability of that change. The use of research designs implies a research and development function, to be discussed later, not service delivery. Documenting that the service being provided is causing the change, particularly through

Follow-up

Function predominant in follow-up. The primary function of a follow-up assessment is *evaluation of the durability and sufficiency of behavior changes.* Evaluation of durability is usually accomplished through continuing the measurement used during the previous phase, but making it less frequent so that follow-up can continue for an adequate period without excessive cost. Thus the end of the assessment funnel's "neck" would represent the durability evaluation.

The questions of interest include, "Is the effect lasting?" "Is it carrying over to the desired situations in which training did not occur?" "Is it satisfactory to the persons who requested the change?" and "Are there unexpected effects in the repertoire or the environment?"

The funnel simile may be violated somewhat when the sufficiency of the behavior change is evaluated. Because the monitoring might have sampled only parts of the problem for the sake of economy, the follow-up may be broader band in order to see whether the whole program has been solved. A more inclusive follow-up could also detect side effects of the intervention.

Characteristics desirable in devices used for follow-up. In general the same characteristics needed in the pinpointing and the monitoring phases are useful in follow-up, but at least two additional characteristics are often of value here. The first is breadth of coverage. To assess side effects, one must sample a wider range of behaviors and environmental factors than those assessed during the monitoring phase. Use of a broad-scan behavioral checklist before and after treatment might be useful, for example. A second useful characteristic is economy. Once a learner is no longer intensively engaged in a treatment or education program, he or she is unlikely to be willing to invest the needed time, labor, or inconvenience for frequent or difficult assessments.

One form of evaluation of the sufficiency of a behavior change is measurement of consumer satisfaction (Wolf, 1978). The learner and/or others who are in a position to be affected by the learner's behavior are asked such things as whether the behavior change was relevant and great enough. If their verbal reports on a consumer satisfaction questionnaire correlate with such measures as their verbal reports to others on the same topic, their referral of the learner for similar help again, their hiring the learner, or their admitting the learner to more advanced programs, the questionnaire is shown to be serving its purpose. Such validity evidence on consumer satisfaction measures does not seem to be available yet.

The Multiple-Phase Utility of Some Devices

It is interesting to note that many behavioral assessment devices appear to serve numerous functions that cross several phases. For example LoPiccolo and Steger's (1974) Sexual Interaction Inventory would probably be useful in every phase but screening and general disposition. Similarly, a comprehensive, criterion-referenced series of tests of mathematical skills organized according to a learning hierarchy (Resnick *et al.*, 1973) would be useful for all phases except screening and disposition. The characteristics that seem to make a device useful for so many functions appear to be these: (1) the device is designed to assess performance of a fairly well-defined task or task-sequence;[3] (2) the device samples most of the skills needed to perform that task; (3) it does not sample many other skills (or if it does they are clearly identified with a different task); (4) it includes quantification of each of the skills sampled; and (5) one can readily measure the targeted skills individually without constructing a new assessment device.

use of designs more complex than AB (Hersen and Barlow, 1976), goes beyond efficient service delivery and falls in the research and development function described later in this paper.

[3]The word "task" is used here to mean a combination of a stimulus array (situation) and a setting event (goal, motivational state; *cf.* Bijou and Baer, 1978).

FUNCTIONS THAT INFLUENCE POLICY, PROGRAM DEVELOPMENT, AND SCIENTIFIC KNOWLEDGE

Classification for Administrative Records

It is common practice in mental health institutions to classfy individuals for the sake of record keeping. Such information is not necessarily used to make decisions regarding the individual's treatment, and if it is used in this way, the earlier discussion regarding definition of an individual's problem is applicable. Though classification is often distasteful because of the oversimplification it entails, the shortcomings of most classification schemes, and the possible damage to the learner (Hobbs, 1975), some form of classification seems important because it is essential in epidemiological research, in prevention efforts, and in program description and evaluation. It is unfortunate that mental health has been burdened with a classification scheme—the American Psychiatric Association Diagnostic and Statistical Manual (1968)—in which it is difficult even to get agreement between experienced clinicians (Spitzer, Cohen, Fleiss, and Endicott, 1967); the ethics of using such a scheme is questionable.

Characteristics desirable in devices used for administrative classification. Perhaps the first requirement of devices for this purpose is interobserver agreement. Major policy decisions are often influenced by data from classifications. For example, if a federal agency is considering allocation of monies for education of "learning disabled" children, it is highly desirable that the agency have data first on the reliability with which children can be classified "learning disabled" and then on the incidence of learning disabilities among children. Similarly, it is desirable that a community mental health center have data on the incidence of developmental retardation or depression in its service area before launching programs to serve those problems.

It is also desirable that classification using different methods arrive at approximately the same result. Thus a device intended for identifying schizophrenics should be able to discriminate reliably between persons in a program for schizophrenics and persons in a general hospital, a program for alcoholics, or a program for sex offenders. It should be pointed out here that such concurrent validity is *not sufficient for clinical use in placing individuals,* even though it is often cited as evidence of "the validity" of a device, as though validity were unitary.

Contribution of behavioral assessors to classification. Three clearly behavioral efforts in this area are those of Adams, Doster, and Calhoun (1977), Cautela and Upper (1975), and Ross (1974). Perhaps one of these approaches will lead to a system sufficiently reliable to be worthy of widespread use.

Evaluating Interventions during Research and Development

During the development of new interventions it is important that they be evaluated extensively and intensively. The methods used for this can be ones that would be infeasible for use in routine delivery of the same intervention. For example, it is difficult to envision routine use of the facsimile cocktail lounge for assessment of alcoholic behaviors (Mills, Sobell, and Schaefer, 1971) in many clinics treating alcoholics or routine use of vaginal blood volume measurement of sexual arousal (Geer, Morokoff, and Greenwood, 1974; Geer, 1977) with women having sexual adjustment problems. Only if the benefits of such devices are repeatedly shown to far exceed those of other devices will their use become routine. Yet their use in research is quite appropriate.

Program evaluation—in which an ongoing program is evaluated in many of its dimensions, including learner variables, process variables, outcome variables, and cost variables—has its own set of questions and requirements. Typically measurement of many variables is desirable, thus making cost per individual assessment a critical factor. In addition, the risks from errors of individual measurement are greatly reduced, freeing the evaluator to use devices that would be unacceptable in individual evaluation for anything but screening.

The number of questions an evaluation researcher can address is infinite. Some examples are "What kinds of individual problems do the persons served by the program have?" "What kinds of environments do they come from?" "How much change in the target behaviors occurs while the learners are in the program?" "Is this due to the program or to other factors?" "What kinds of individuals are affected most readily by the program?" and "Under what circumstances do the effects endure?"

Characteristics desirable in assessment methods for research and development. In experimental research the most uniformly important characteristic of an assessment device is probably sensitivity to change. On the other hand, cost is usually of less concern than in the routine delivery of services. Other characteristics would be difficult to discuss because the research and development function is probably not one function. The value of including it here is to point out that many devices appropriate for research are not appropriate for individual case decisions.

In intensive study of a program it is appropriate to commit many more resources to assessment than in routine delivery of the same program, after it has been adequately developed and tested. In fact, it would probably be an unwise practice to revalidate continuously the program in any way that costs more than 5% of the program's resources, depending on such factors as how much the program is still developing and the number of factors militating against maintenance of quality programming (*i.e.*, social influences, response effort). Thus the investment that goes into assessment must depend upon the stage of the intervention's development, the sources of funding and their objectives, the size of the group being assessed, and similar factors.

In order to find learner or environmental variables that may *predict* success in a program, a researcher may be wise to use assessment devices that tap a rather broad range of variables or are norm-referenced. Personality test scores or IQ scores may be very good predictors of success during or after a program, for example, and if so, they should be considered for use in future admissions. Until more behaviorally conceived devices are developed that serve all such predictive functions well, traditionally conceived devices will be needed.

Contribution of behavioral assessors to research and development. In addition to the behavioral assessment devices already mentioned, behavioral assessors have devised a wide array that would be useful in research. They range from a checklist for assessing street-crossing skills taught at school (Yeaton and Bailey, 1978) to a simple textual change that assesses reading comprehension (Guthrie and Tyler, 1976), and from a nonverbal measure of activity as an index of depression (Williams, Barlow, and Agras, 1972) to a partially controlled social interaction as a measure of interpersonal skills (Goldsmith and McFall, 1975).

Obtaining Normative, Descriptive Data

Though this could probably be treated as part of the research and development function, it differs in that no evaluation of a program is implied. The researcher is simply attempting to describe, to answer the question "What normally happens?" Either learner behavior or environmental factors can be measured.

Characteristics desirable in devices for normative data. Any assessment device that is useful for other functions can be useful for describing repertoires or environments. There appear to be no characteristics that are unique to this function.

Contribution of behavioral assessors to normative, descriptive research. Behavior analysts have tended to devalue normative data while developing criterion-referenced approaches and functional analyses, but there is a legitimate place for norms in behavior analysis, as Nelson and Bowles (1975) and Kazdin (1977) have pointed out. For example, Jones and Eimers

(1975) obtained rather precise normative data on the behavior of some very successful teachers and used these norms to set criterion levels of performance for less successful teachers. Walker and Hops (1976) obtained precise data on the classmates of school children who were being phased out of a special treatment program to see how closely the treated children's behavior approximately these norms, and Busse (1974) did the same kind of thing for the same purpose, using a more general behavior checklist. Finally, White (1975) measured teachers' rates of approval and disapproval, finding, among other things, that approval rates decline rapidly after the primary grades.

In some cases normative information serves as a temporary substitute for a functional analysis. Knowing what effective persons do in a particular situation can suggest what responses are functional in making them effective (Goldfried and D'Zurilla, 1969; Hawkins, 1975), though the evidence is correlational and a functional analysis is preferable. Similarly, if educators and clinicians working with developmentally retarded individuals have data on the normal sequence in which specific skills were learned, they are in a better position to construct a tentative learning sequence.

In other cases normative data are important because social norms *define* effectiveness. "For example, a male's walking or sitting in a particular 'masculine' manner will receive social acceptance (reinforcement) because it is the *norm,* while walking or sitting in a feminine fashion will reduce the overall reinforcement available to the male" (Cone and Hawkins, 1977, p. 389).

CONCLUSIONS

The technical characteristics and evidence of generalizability required of an assessment device vary greatly according to the functions it is to serve. The same device may be appropriate for one function and inappropriate for another. If the functions of an assessment are carefully considered, behavior analysts will sometimes find legitimate use for traditionally conceived devices, though probably not traditional use. Previous presentations of assessment have provided little or no analysis of the functions and their implications, and the present one is only a crude beginning.

Behavioral assessors have not completely shaken their trait thinking, as Cone and Hawkins (1977, pp. 382-388) point out, but they have contributed a wealth of assessment devices and used them for a wide variety of functions. Some of these functions had been largely neglected by traditional assessors.

The number of different assessment devices that will be needed for the various functions in clinical and educational environments will be vastly greater as the behavioral approach to assessment grows. The traditional description of "personality," "intelligence," and general academic achievement required few devices in comparison to a functional skills approach. Computerized clearinghouses for behavioral assessment devices may become necessary (Cone and Hawkins, 1977). No doubt greater standardization in using some devices will be necessary (Goldfried, 1977), but it may be possible to put such standardization into the device by providing adequate procedural description. Certainly normative standardization seems unnecessary for most behavioral assessment, but descriptive data on a particular population may often be valuable.

REFERENCE NOTE

1. Hartmann, D. P. Must the baby follow the bathwater? Psychometric principles—behavioral data. In D. H. Barlow (Chair), *Behavioral assessment: The relevance of traditional psychometric procedures.* Symposium presented at the meeting of the American Psychological Association, Washington, D.C., September 1976.

REFERENCES

Abel, G. G., Blanchard, E. B., Barlow, D. H., and Mavissakalian, M. Identifying specific erotic cues in sexual deviations by audiotaped descriptions.

Journal of Applied Behavior Analysis, 1975, **8,** 247-260.

Adams, H. E., Doster, J. A., and Calhoun, K. S. A psychologically based system of response classification. In A. R. Ciminero, K. S. Calhoun, and H. E. Adams (Eds), *Handbook of behavioral assessment.* New York: Wiley, 1977.

American Psychiatric Association. *Diagnostic and statistical manual of mental disorders, II.* Washington, D.C.: American Psychiatric Association, 1968.

Anastasi, A. *Psychological testing* (3rd ed.), Toronto: Macmillan, 1968.

Anastasi, A. *Psychological testing* (4th ed.), Toronto: Macmillan, 1978.

Angle, H. V., Hay, L. R., Hay, W. M., and Ellinwood, E. H. Computer assisted behavioral assessment. In J. D. Cone and R. P. Hawkins (Eds), *Behavioral assessment: New directions in clinical psychology.* New York: Brunner/Mazel, 1977.

Ayllon, T. and Michael, J. The psychiatric nurse as a behavioral engineer. *Journal of the Experimental Analysis of Behavior,* 1959, **2,** 323-334.

Baer, D. M., Wolf, M. M., and Risley, T. R. Some current dimensions of applied behavioral analysis. *Journal of Applied Behavior Analysis,* 1968, **1,** 91-97.

Barlow, D. H., Reynolds, E. G., and Agras, W. S. Gender identity change in a transsexual. *Archives of General Psychiatry,* 1973, **28,** 569-579.

Beck, A. T. *Depression: Causes and treatment.* Philadelphia: University of Pennsylvania Press, 1972.

Bijou, S. W., Peterson, R. F., and Ault, M. A method to integrate descriptive and experimental field studies at the level of data and empirical concepts. *Journal of Applied Behavior Analysis.* 1968, **1,** 175-191.

Bijou, S. W. and Baer, D. M. *Behavior analysis of child development.* Englewood Cliffs, N.J.: Prentice-Hall, 1978.

Bushell, D., Jr., Jackson, D. A., and Weis, L. C. Quality control in the behavior analysis approach to Project Follow Through. In W. S. Wood (Ed), *Issues in evaluating behavior modification.* Champaign, Ill.: Research Press, 1975.

Busse, W. J. *A normative and validation study of the Behavior Problem Checklist.* Unpublished masters thesis, Western Michigan University, 1974.

Carver, R. P. Two dimensions of tests: Psychometric and edumetric. *American Psychologist,* 1974, **19,** 512-518.

Cautela, J. R. and Upper, D. The process of individual behavior therapy. In M. Hersen, R. M. Eisler, and P. M. Miller (Eds), *Progress in behavior modification,* Vol. 1. New York: Academic Press, 1975.

Chesney, M. A. and Tasto, D. L. The development of the menstrual symptom questionnaire. *Behaviour Research and Therapy,* 1975, **13,** 237-244.

Cone, J. D. The relevance of reliability and validity for behavioral assessment. *Behavior Therapy,* 1977, **8,** 411-426.

Cone, J. D. and Hawkins, R. P., (Eds), *Behavioral assessment: New directions in clinical psychology.* New York: Brunner/Mazel, 1977.

Cowen, E. L., Dorr, D., Clarfield, S., Kreling, B., McWilliams, S. A., Pokracki, F., Pratt, M., Terrell, D., and Wilson, A. The AML: A quick-screening device for early identification of school maladaptation. *American Journal of Community Psychology,* 1973, **1,** 12-35.

Cronbach, L. J. *Essentials of psychological testing* (3rd ed.). New York: Harper & Row, 1970.

Cronbach, L. J., Gleser, G. C., Nanda, H., and Rajaratnam, N. *The dependability of behavioral measures.* New York: Wiley, 1972.

Daley, M. F. The "Reinforcement Menu"—Finding effective reinforcers. In E. J. Mash & L. G. Terdal (Eds), *Behavior-therapy assessment: Diagnosis, design, and evaluation.* New York: Springer, 1976.

Eaton, M. D. and Lovitt, T. C. Achievement tests vs. direct and daily measurement. In G. Semb, D. R. Green, R. P. Hawkins, J. Michael, E. L. Phillips, J. A. Sherman, H. Sloane, and D. R. Thomas (Eds), *Behavior analysis and education—1972.* Lawrence: University of Kansas Center for Follow Through, 1972.

Ferster, C. B. and DeMeyer, M. K. A method of experimental analysis of the behavior of autistic children. *American Journal of Orthopsychiatry,* 1962, **32,** 89-98.

Freedman, B. J. An analysis of social-behavioral skill deficits in delinquent and non-delinquent adolescent boys. Unpublished doctoral dissertation, University of Wisconsin, 1974.

Geer, J. H. Sexual functioning: Some data and speculations on psychophysiological assessment. In J. D. Cone & R. P. Hawkins (Eds), *Behavioral assessment: New directions in clinical psychology.* New York: Brunner/Mazel, 1977.

Geer, J. H., Morokoff, D., and Greenwood, P. Sexual arousal in women. The development of a measurement device for vaginal blood volume. *Archives of Sexual Behavior,* 1974, **3,** 599-564.

Gilbert, T. F. *Human competence: Engineering worthy performance.* New York: McGraw-Hill, 1978.

Goldfried, M. R. Behavioral assessment in perspective. In J. D. Cone & R. P. Hawkins (Eds), *Behavioral assessment: New directions in clinical psychology.* New York: Brunner/Mazel, 1977.

Goldfried, M. R. and D'Zurilla, T. J. A behavioral-analytic model for assessing competence. In C. D. Spielberger (Ed), *Current topics in clinical and community psychology.* New York: Academic Press, 1969.

Goldfried, M. R. and Pomeranz, D. Role of assessment in behavior modification. *Psychological Reports,* 1968, **23,** 75-87.

Goldsmith, J. B. and McFall, R. M. Development and evaluation of interpersonal skill-training programs for psychiatric inpatients. *Journal of Abnormal Psychology,* 1975, **84,** 51-58.

Guidance Associates of Delaware, Inc. *Wide Range Achievement Test.* Wilmington: Guidance Assoc. of Delaware, 1978.

Guthrie, J. T. and Tyler, J. Operational definitions of reading. In T. A. Brigham, R. Hawkins, J. W. Scott, and T. F. McLaughlin (Eds), *Behavior analysis in education: Self-control and reading.* Dubuque, Iowa: Kendall/Hunt, 1976.

Hall, R. V. *Behavior modification, Vol. 1: The measurement of behavior.* Lawrence, Kans.: H & H Enterprises, 1971.

Hansen, C. L. and Lovitt, T. C. Reading: Round one—matching the child to the book. In T. A. Brigham, R. P. Hawkins, J. W. Scott, and T. F. McLaughlin (Eds), *Behavior analysis in education: Self-control and reading.* Dubuque, Iowa: Kendall/Hunt, 1976.

Harcourt Brace Jovanovich. *Skills Monitoring System.* New York: Harcourt Brace Jovanovich, 1975.

Hart, B. M., Allen, K. E., Buell, J. S., Harris, R. F., and Wolf, M. M. Effects of social reinforcement on operant crying. *Journal of Experimental Child Psychology,* 1964, **1,** 145-153.

Hawkins, R. P. Who decided *that* was the problem? Two stages of responsibility for applied behavior analysis. In W. S. Wood (Ed), *Issues in evaluating behavior modification.* Champaign, Ill.: Research Press, 1975.

Hawkins, R. P., Axelrod, S., and Hall, R. V. *Teachers as behavior analysts: Precisely monitoring student performance.* In T. A. Brigham, R. P. Hawkins, J. W. Scott, and T. F. McLaughlin (Eds), *Behavior analysis in education: Self control and reading.* Dubuque, Iowa: Kendall/Hunt, 1976.

Hawkins, R. P., Peterson, R. F., Schweid, E., and Bijou, S. W. Behavior therapy in the home: Amelioration of problem parent-child relations with the parent in a therapeutic role. *Journal of Experimental Child Psychology,* 1966, **4,** 99-107.

Hersen, M. and Barlow, D. H. *Single case experimental designs: Strategies for studying behavior change.* New York: Pergamon, 1976.

Hobbs, N. *The futures of children.* San Francisco: Jossey-Bass, 1975.

Holland, C. An interview guide for behavioral counseling with parents. *Behavior Therapy,* 1970, **1,** 70-79.

Houghton Mifflin. *Iowa Test of Basic Skills.* Boston: Houghton Mifflin, 1974.

Jones, F. H. and Eimers, R. C. Role playing to train elementary teachers to use a classroom management "skill package." *Journal of Applied Behavior Analysis,* 1975, **8,** 421-433.

Kanfer, F. H. and Saslow, G. Behavioral diagnosis. In C. M. Franks (Ed), *Behavior therapy: Appraisal and status.* New York: McGraw-Hill, 1969.

Kazdin, A. E. Assessing the clinical or applied importance of behavior change through social validation. *Behavior Modification,* 1977, **1,** 427-452.

Kent, R. N. and Foster, S. L. Direct observational procedures: Methodological issues in naturalistic settings. In A. R. Ciminero, K. S. Calhoun, and H. E. Adams (Eds), *Handbook of behavioral assessment.* New York: Wiley, 1977.

Kubany, E. S. and Sloggett, B. A. A coding procedure for teachers. *Journal of Applied Behavior Analysis,* 1973, **6,** 339-344.

Lindsley, O. R. Reduction in rate of vocal psychotic symptoms by differential positive reinforcement. *Journal of the Experimental Analysis of Behavior,* 1959, **2,** 269.

Linehan, M. Issues in behavioral interviewing. In J. D. Cone & R. P. Hawkins (Eds), *Behavioral assessment: New directions in clinical psychology.* New York: Brunner/Mazel, 1977.

Livingston, S. A. Psychometric techniques for criterion-referenced testing and behavioral assessment. In J. D. Cone & R. P. Hawkins (Eds), *Behavioral assessment: New directions in clinical psychology.* New York: Brunnel/Mazel, 1977.

Lobitz, G. K. and Johnson, S. M. Normal versus deviant children: A multimethod comparison. *Journal of Abnormal Child Psychology,* 1975, **3,** 353-374.

LoPiccolo, J. and Steger, J. C. The Sexual Interaction Inventory: A new instrument for assessment of sexual dysfunction. *Archives of Sexual Behavior,* 1974, **3,** 585-595.

Mahoney, M. J. Some applied issues in self-monitoring. In J. D. Cone & R. P. Hawkins (Eds), *Behavioral assessment: New directions in clinical psychology.* New York: Brunner/Mazel, 1977.

Mash, E. J. and Terdal, L. G. (Eds) *Behavior-therapy assessment.* New York: Springer, 1976.

McFall, R. M. Analogue methods of behavioral assessment: Issues and prospects. In J. D. Cone & R. P. Hawkins (Eds), *Behavioral assessment: New directions in clinical psychology.* New York: Brunner/Mazel, 1977.

McFall, R. M. and Lillesand, D. V. Behavior rehearsal with modeling and coaching in assertive training. *Journal of Abnormal Psychology,* 1971, **77,** 313-323.

Mills, K. C., Sobell, M. B., and Schaefer, H. H. Training social drinking as an alternative to abstinence for alcoholics. *Behavior Therapy,* 1971, **2,** 18-27.

Morganstern, K. P. Behavioral interviewing: The initial stage of assessment. In M. Hersen & A. S.

Bellack (Eds), *Behavioral assessment: A practical handbook.* New York: Pergamon, 1976.

Nay, W. R. Analogue measures. In A. R. Ciminero, K. S. Calhoun, & H. E. Adams (Eds), *Handbook of behavioral assessment.* New York: Wiley, 1977.

Nelson, R. O. Methodological issues in assessment via self-monitoring. In J. D. Cone & R. P. Hawkins (Eds), *Behavioral assessment: New directions in clinical psychology.* New York: Brunner/Mazel, 1977.

Nelson, R. O. and Bowles, P. E., Jr. The best of two worlds: Observations with norms. *Journal of School Psychology,* 1975, **13,** 3-9.

Phillips, E. L., Phillips, E. A., Wolf, M. M., and Fixsen, D. L. Achievement Place: Development of the elected manager system. *Journal of Applied Behavior Analysis,* 1973, **6,** 541-561.

Popovich, D. *A prescriptive behavioral checklist for the severely and profoundly retarded.* Baltimore: University Park Press, 1977.

Psychological Corporation. *Mooney Problem Checklist.* New York: Psychological Corporation, 1950.

Rathus, S. A. A 30-item schedule for assessing assertive behavior. *Behavior Therapy,* 1973, **4,** 398-406.

Resnick, L. B., Wang, M. C., and Kaplan, J. Task analysis in curriculum design: A hierarachically sequenced introductory mathematics curriculum. *Journal of Applied Behavior Analysis,* 1973, **6,** 679-709.

Ross, A. O. Psychological disorders of children: *A behavioral approach to theory, research, and therapy.* New York: McGraw-Hill, 1974.

Scholastic Testing Service. *STS youth inventory.* Bensenville, Ill.: Scholastic Testing Service, 1971.

Schwartz, R. M. and Gottman, J. M. Towards a task analysis of assertive behavior. *Journal of Consulting and Clinical Psychology,* 1976, **44,** 910-920.

Schwarz, M. L. and Hawkins, R. P. Application of delayed reinforcement procedures to the behavior problems of an elementary school child. *Journal of Applied Behavior Analysis,* 1970, **3,** 85-96.

Spitzer, R. L., Cohen, J., Fleiss, J. L., and Endicott, J. Quantification of agreement in psychiatric diagnosis. *Archives of General Psychiatry,* 1967, **17,** 83-87.

Stuart, R. B. and Stuart, F. M. Prestructuring behavior therapy through precounseling assessment. In E. J. Mash & L. G. Terdal (Eds), *Behavior-therapy assessment: Diagnosis, design, and evaluation.* New York: Springer, 1976.

Trap, J. J., Milner-Davis, P., Joseph, S., and Cooper, J. O. The effects of feedback and consequences on transitional cursive letter formation. *Journal of Applied Behavior Analysis,* 1978, **11,** 381-393.

Walls, R. T., Zane, T., and Werner, T. J. *The Vocational Behavior Checklist* (Experimental Edition). Morgantown, W. Va.: Rehabilitation Research and Training Center (509 Allen Hall, West Virginia University), 1978.

Walker, H. M. and Hops, H. Use of normative peer data as a standard for evaluating classroom treatment effects. *Journal of Applied Behavior Analysis,* 1976, **9,** 159-168.

White, M. A. Natural rates of teacher approval and disapproval in the classroom. *Journal of Applied Behavior Analysis,* 1975, **8,** 367-372.

Wildman, B. G. and Erickson, M. T. Methodological problems in behavioral observation. In J. D. Cone & R. P. Hawkins (Eds), *Behavioral assessment: New directions in clinical psychology.* New York: Brunner/Mazel, 1977.

Williams, J. G., Barlow, D. H., and Agras, W. S. Behavioral measurement of severe depression. *Archives of General Psychiatry,* 1972, **27,** 330-333.

Wolf, M. M. Social validity: The case for subjective measurement or how applied behavior analysis is finding its heart. *Journal of Applied Behavior Analysis,* 1978, **11,** 203-214.

Yeaton, W. H. and Bailey, J. S. Teaching pedestrian safety skills to young children: An analysis and one-year follow-up. *Journal of Applied Behavior Analysis,* 1978, 315-329.

Received 6 October 1978.
(Final Acceptance 20 July 1979.)

JOURNAL OF APPLIED BEHAVIOR ANALYSIS 1979, 12, 713-724 NUMBER 4 (WINTER 1979)

UNOBTRUSIVE MEASURES IN BEHAVIORAL ASSESSMENT

ALAN E. KAZDIN

THE PENNSYLVANIA STATE UNIVERSITY

A major distinguishing characteristic of behavioral assessment is the direct assessment of overt behavior. Direct assessment is assumed to provide a sample of behavior that reflects client performance in the situation in which behavior is assessed, even if the assessment procedures were not implemented. Yet, in the majority of investigations, behavioral assessment procedures are obtrusive, *i.e.*, subjects are aware that their behavior is being assessed. The potential problem with obtrusive assessment is that it may be reactive, *i.e.*, affect how subjects perform. Recent research has demonstrated that obtrusive observations often are reactive and that behaviors assessed under obtrusive and unobtrusive conditions bear little relation. From methodological and applied perspectives, additional attention needs to be given to unobtrusive measures of behavior change. The present paper illustrates unobtrusive measures in behavior modification including direct observations, archival records, and physical traces of performance. In addition, validation and assessment problems, questions about the obtrusiveness of the measures, and ethical issues are discussed.

DESCRIPTORS: assessment, methodology, observational technology, reactivity

---

Behavioral assessment has many distinguishing characteristics. A few of the significant features include direct assessment of overt behavior, interest in behavior as samples of performance rather than as signs of underlying personality, use of multiple modalities of assessment, and evaluation of such influences on performance as antecedents, consequences, and factors associated with the assessment procedures themselves (see Ciminero, Calhoun, and Adams, 1977; Cone and Hawkins, 1977; Hersen and Bellack, 1976).

Perhaps one of the most salient features of behavioral assessment is the direct observation of overt behavior. Direct observations may be one of the few central characteristics that unites many different areas within behavior therapy. Different methods are used to assess behavior directly depending upon the target problem, subjects, and setting. For example, assessment of such problems as anxiety or social skills often has relied upon contrived laboratory conditions to present actual or simulated cues to evoke the target behavior (*e.g.*, behavioral avoidance tests for fear of snakes or behavioral role-playing performance to measure dating skills). Investigations in applied settings, such as schools, the home, hospitals, and the community, have directly assessed overt behavior to measure the problems, skills, and deficits focused upon in training.

Notwithstanding many benefits, behavioral assessment has some limitations. In most research in behavior modification, assessment procedures are obtrusive. *Obtrusiveness of assessment refers to the fact that subjects may, in varying degrees, be aware that assessment is going on.* Different circumstances may contribute to the obtrusiveness of the measure. For example, with direct observation the subjects may be informed that specific behaviors are of interest, be placed in a simulated or contrived situation where their performance is directly ob-

Preparation of this paper was facilitated by a grant (MH31047) from the National Institute of Mental Health. Requests for reprints should be sent to the author, Department of Psychology, The Pennsylvania State University, University Park, Pennsylvania 16802.

served, see an observer who records their behavior, or indeed serve as an observer of their own behavior (self-monitoring).

Obtrusiveness of an assessment procedure is a matter of degree. Some measures (*e.g.*, questionnaires) may be more salient to the subject than others and may sustain continuous awareness that behavior is being evaluated. Other measures may be less salient (*e.g.*, observers at the back of a classroom), and subject awareness of assessment may decrease over time (as observers become part of the classroom environment and their activities are ignored).

The potential problem with obtrusive assessment is that it may be reactive. *Reactivity refers to the influence that the assessment procedure exerts on the subject's performance.* Obtrusive measures are not necessarily reactive. Just because subjects are aware that assessment is going on does not necessarily mean that their behavior will be affected. However, obtrusive assessment may influence subject behavior and lead to conclusions that would differ from those obtained if behavior were assessed without the subject's awareness.

As with obtrusiveness, reactivity of assessment is not an all or none matter. Subject behavior can be affected in varying degrees by the assessment procedures. For a given measurement strategy, reactivity may be a function of various conditions of assessment. For example, if subjects are informed that the results of assessment will be used to determine the reinforcers that they earn, assessment may be much more reactive than if subjects are told that the results have absolutely no bearing upon their performance.

REACTIVITY OF BEHAVIORAL ASSESSMENT

Reactivity of obtrusive assessment has been recognized as a problem both in traditional and behavioral assessment (Kent and Foster, 1977; Webb, Campbell, Schwartz, and Sechrest, 1966). Different lines of research have demonstrated the reactive effects of direct behavioral observations. For example, observations of client-therapist behavior in therapy sessions (Roberts and Renzaglia, 1965) and parent-child behavior in the home (Johnson, Christensen, and Bellamy, 1976) yield different results if gathered unobtrusively and obtrusively.

Research has demonstrated that the presence of observers in applied settings influences subject performance (Mercatoris and Craighead, 1974; Surratt, Ulrich, and Hawkins, 1969; White, 1977), although there are exceptions (Hagen, Craighead, and Paul, 1975). The reactivity of obtrusive assessment even has been evident in research on observer behavior (*e.g.*, Kent, O'Leary, Diament, and Dietz, 1974; Romanczyk, Kent, Diament, and O'Leary, 1973). When observers are monitored obtrusively by an experimenter, their interobserver agreement and use of particular behavioral categories differ from when they are monitored unobtrusively.

Other areas of behavioral research have suggested reactive influences of direct observations. Research on social skills training has recently examined interpersonal behaviors in obtrusive and unobtrusive assessment conditions where subjects provide role-play responses and are placed in a contrived situation while unaware that they are being observed (Bellack, Hersen, and Lamparski, 1979; Bellack, Hersen, and Turner, 1978). The results suggest very little relationship in social skill performance across different assessment conditions. Additional studies have shown that behaviors differ when assessed under obtrusive and unobtrusive conditions (*e.g.*, Carmody, 1978; Kazdin, 1974*a;* Hersen, Eisler, and Miller, 1974). The different results obtained in these latter studies cannot be attributed unambiguously to the obtrusiveness of the assessment conditions because other dimensions varied across conditions, such as when the measures were administered (posttest *vs.* follow-up) and the specific tasks presented (*e.g.*, self-report *vs. in vivo* test).

Perhaps the clearest demonstration that behavioral assessment can be reactive derives from research on self-monitoring (Kazdin, 1974*b;* Nelson, 1977). Observation of one's own behavior often influences the behavior that is recorded. The reactivity of self-assessment has been actively researched to identify variables that contribute to behavior change (see Ciminero, Nelson, and Lipinski, 1977). In general, research from several sources has suggested that obtrusive assessment conditions may influence overt performance.

For behavior modification, the reactivity of obtrusive assessment raises both methodological and clinical issues. From a methodological standpoint, obtrusive assessment conditions constitute a method factor associated with particular assessment procedures (Campbell and Fiske, 1959). Method factors may contribute in varying degrees to the results that are obtained. Ideally, behavior should be assessed with different methods so that the contribution of unique method factors of the particular assessment procedures can be separated from the behavior of interest. In fact, behavioral research has taken considerable pains to assess behavior with many different methods in various areas of treatment. Yet, even when different assessment procedures are used, the measures usually share one particular methodological characteristic, namely, obtrusiveness. In light of the reactivity often associated with obtrusive assessment, as noted above, it would seem important to evaluate behavior with both obtrusive and unobtrusive methods.

For a clinical perspective, there may be even greater reasons to be concerned with the reactive effects of assessment. Applied research is designed to produce behavior change in a person's everyday life, usually in situations when the person does not believe that his or her behavior is assessed. For example, one would like assurances that a parent is responding appropriately to a child when observers are not in the home or when tape recordings are not made. Showing appropriate behavior only when the observer is present runs the risk that changes in behavior are restricted to reactive assessment periods. Assessment would be desirable under conditions in which subjects were unaware that their behavior was being observed. Data obtained from unobtrusive measures provide important information about the generality of the results. In this context, *generality refers to the assessment of behavior under conditions which differ from obtrusive measures usually used for treatment evaluation.*

Unobtrusive methods of assessment need not replace any existing methods. Their major role is to supplement direct observations currently in use. Because of the specificity of behavior, the reactive effects of obtrusive observations, and the importance of assessing behavior free from observer influences, unobtrusive measures provide important information about behavior change and the assessment conditions of which behavior may be a function.

Unobtrusive measures have been used relatively infrequently in behavioral assessment. The purpose of the present paper is to illustrate various alternatives for unobtrusive measures in behavior modification research and to encourage the use of such measures in evaluating behavior-change programs. Unobtrusive assessment methods and considerations pertaining to their implementation and interpretation are discussed.

UNOBTRUSIVE ASSESSMENT TECHNIQUES

Different techniques have been used in behavior modification to assess behavior unobtrusively. Direct methods of observing behavior have been the most commonly used, but archival records and physical traces of behavior have been examined as well. The assessment methods themselves are likely to be quite familiar to most behavioral researchers because they are commonly used as obtrusive methods of assessment. Collecting data unobtrusively does not necessarily mean using entirely different assessment methods but rather ensuring that the subjects are unaware of assessment.

Direct Observation

With direct observation, behavior is observed by persons who categorize the subjects' performance according to various behavioral codes that reflect the target focus. Direct observations have been obtained unobtrusively in contrived as well as naturalistic situations.

Contrived situations. Many behaviors of interest in behavioral research might not be easily obtained in naturalistic situations because the responses are of low frequency, require special precipitating conditions, or would be prohibitive to observe in terms of available resources. Situations often are contrived to evoke responses so that the target behavior can be assessed without arousing the subject's awareness.

Contrived situations that assess behavior unobtrusively can be illustrated by programs evaluating social interaction. For example, Bellack *et al.* (1979) evaluated the social behaviors of college students by placing them in a situation with an opposite-sexed confederate. Subjects were told that a "slight scheduling mix-up" required them to wait. While waiting, the confederate precipitated social interaction which was videotaped unobtrusively and later evaluated for such measures as eye contact, duration of responding, smiles, and other measures. Similarly, social interaction among psychiatric patients has been evaluated by requiring patients to remain in a waiting room with another patient (actually an accomplice) who engaged in a prearranged sequence of behaviors to prompt social interaction (Gutride, Goldstein, and Hunter, 1973).

Hersen *et al.* (1974) developed assertive behavior among psychiatric patients and used a contrived task to evaluate treatment. Patients were short-changed, *i.e.,* presented with less money in canteen booklets after training than they were originally promised. Each patient's response to being short-changed was videotaped and later evaluated to assess overall assertiveness and latency to respond. Frederiksen, Jenkins, Foy, and Eisler (1976) evaluated the effects of treatment designed to train patients to avoid abusive verbal outbursts. Situations on the ward that previously had precipitated these outbursts were arranged to occur after treatment. When the contrived situations were implemented, the patient's responses (*e.g.,* hostile comments, inappropriate requests) were assessed unobtrusively by staff normally present on the ward.

Occasionally, contrived situations have included phone calls that are designed to appear completely unrelated to treatment. For example, McFall and Marston (1970) called subjects who completed an assertion training program. The caller posed as a magazine salesperson and completed a prearranged sequence of requests. The client's responses were evaluated unobtrusively to study refusal behavior. Phone call measures have been used frequently to evaluate how clients respond to seemingly unreasonable requests. The calls provide unobtrusive measures because the association between the treatment program and the phone call is concealed, at least until the client is debriefed after assessment.

Naturalistic observation. Direct observation of overt behavior in the setting in which clients normally function has been widely used in behavioral research, particularly applied behavior analysis. Assessment has been conducted in classrooms, day-care centers, homes, institutions, and many other settings in the natural environment. Although many studies have assessed behaviors directly, it is not always clear whether the observations were obtained unobtrusively.

In most programs, direct observations appear to have been obtrusive. For example, in many classroom programs, observers who are stationed at the back or side of the room may make the observations obtrusive. On the other hand, the observations may be unobtrusive if observers are not present, if the teacher observes behavior, if observers are placed in a booth behind a one-way mirror, or if videotaped records are obtained from a concealed camera. Even under these latter conditions, assessment may be reactive if it is part of an intervention program in which clients are informed that their behavior is being evaluated or that specific behaviors will be followed by various consequences.

Occasionally, the intervention program and observation procedures may facilitate unobtrusive assessment. A particularly interesting classroom example was provided by Hauserman, Walen, and Behling (1973) who increased interracial interaction among first graders in an integrated classroom. The teacher rewarded interaction with a "new friend' without specifying the need for interracial interaction during a lunch period and unobtrusively recorded whether interracial partners shared a lunch table. Observations during a free-play period were more obviously unobtrusive because of the absence of specific contingencies. Unobtrusive measures both in the lunchroom and during free-play periods afterwards tended to reflect the efficacy of the program.

Direct observations have been obtained unobtrusively in other settings. For example, Hollandsworth, Glazeski, and Dressel (1978) treated a male college graduate who was extremely anxious and deficient in verbal skills. Training improved speaking in an organized and fluent fashion, using self-corrective statements, and generating questions. An unobtrusive measure of verbal skills was obtained by having observers pose as shoppers in the store in which the client worked. Unobtrusive observations before and after treatment were made as the client interacted with customers. Observations of behaviors related to those altered in treatment corroborated the efficacy of training.

Products of Behavior

Occasionally, direct observations of overt behavior can be supplemented or even replaced by measuring various products of behavior such as administrative records or physical traces of performance. Products of behavior often are unobtrusive measures because subjects are not likely to be aware that these traces will be used for research purposes. Indeed, records and traces of behavior often are examined years after the behaviors leading to these products have been performed (Webb *et al*., 1966).

Archival records. Records of performance consist of information usually recorded by various administrative, governmental, and institutional agencies. Records of birth, crime, death, and marital status are examples of commonly used archival records in the social sciences. Archival records have been used in many applied behavioral programs because they can often be conveniently obtained. In addition, records of performance frequently serve as socially important criteria for evaluating intervention effects. For example, recidivism and records of arrest or contact with police have been used to evaluate behavioral interventions with prisoners (Jenkins, Witherspoon, DeVine, deValera, Muller, Barton, and McKee, Note 1), and days out of the hospital, discharge, and readmission rates have often been used to evaluate programs with psychiatric patients (*e.g.*, Paul and Lentz, 1977).

Achievement Place has used archival records as unobtrusive outcome measures, in addition to the extensive use of direct measures of overt behavior (*e.g.*, Phillips, Phillips, Fixsen, and Wolf, 1971) and self-report inventories (Eitzen, 1975). Fixsen, Phillips, Phillips, and Wolf (1976) compared the effectiveness of Achievement Place, institutional care, and probation in the rehabilitation of predelinquents. Several archival measures were used including recidivism, police and court contacts, grades and attendance at school, and records of school dropouts.

Social and community extensions of behavioral programs have frequently used archival records to evaluate performance. Programs designed to curb energy consumption in the home have obtained records from meters that register oil, gas, or electrical consumption (*e.g.*, Hayes and Cone, 1977; Seaver and Patterson, 1976). Conservation of automobile fuel has been evaluated unobtrusively by recording mileage from the odometers of cars (Foxx and Hake, 1977).

Applications in business and industry have evaluated punctuality by looking at daily time cards (Hermann, de Montes, Dominguez, Montes, and Hopkins, 1973). Cash shortages associated with particular employees who work at a cash register of a small business were evaluated by monitoring the internal record of the register that cumulates the sum of each transaction (Marholin and Gray, 1976). Research on the reduction of crime has used daily police records of burglaries as archival data (Schnelle, Kirchner, Macrae, McNees, Eck, Snodgrass, Casey, and Uselton, 1978; Schnelle, Kirchner, McNees, and Lawler, 1975). Each of these assessment methods provides the opportunity to obtain data unobtrusively.

Physical traces. Traces refer to material deposited in or removed from the environment, or to permanent physical products. Traces have been used relatively infrequently in behavioral research, presumably because many of the behaviors of interest in treatment (*e.g.*, anxiety, hyperactive behavior, depression, language, social skills) do not often leave physical traces in the environment. On the other hand, some behaviors are readily amenable to observation of trace measures, such as the number of job tasks that individuals complete or the number of items individuals may steal from each other (*e.g.*, Azrin and Wesolowski, 1974; Pierce and Risley, 1974). Yet, rarely are such measures obtained unobtrusively.

Physical traces have been used in a few areas of behavioral research. For example, research on littering has evaluated various interventions unobtrusively by assessing the number of pieces of litter or weight of accumulated litter across such settings as a zoo, athletic stadium, forest ground, movie theater, and urban community settings (*e.g.*, Burgess, Clark, and Hendee, 1971; Chapman and Risley, 1974). Hayes, Johnson, and Cone (1975) evaluated littering by marking and planting various pieces of litter among existing litter in a federal youth correctional facility. Pieces of litter were coded by making small tears, ink marks, folds and creases, and other procedures. Deposit of the marked items among other pieces of litter permitted evaluation of pickup of existing trash without the fear that individuals would generate new trash merely to receive reinforcers.

A procedure that also involved marking items was used to provide a trace measure of theft in a retail department store (McNees, Egli, Marshall, Schnelle, and Risley, 1976). Different types of merchandise were marked with coded tags that were removed and retained when the items were purchased. Accumulation of the number of tagged items remaining in the store plus those tags removed from purchased items provided a physical trace measure used to infer missing items, *i.e.*, shoplifting.

Physical trace measures of performance have been observed extensively in classroom research. Written products of behavior have been used to assess classroom interventions for reading, arithmetic, and creative writing, and constitute important traces of behavior.[1] In most programs, however, academic responses have not been observed unobtrusively.

CONSIDERATIONS IN USING UNOBTRUSIVE MEASURES

Unobtrusive measures represent an important addition to behavioral assessment. Behavioral assessment has extended traditional assessment in such ways as observing overt behavior and examining performance in the environment in which target behaviors normally occur. However, in both traditional and behavioral assessment, treatment effects have been evaluated primarily with obtrusive measures. Relatively little evidence is available attesting to the efficacy of treatment where subjects were not aware

[1]Insofar as physical traces are written records, they might be classified as an archival measure. However, archival records usually refer to governmental and institutional records. The distinction is not critical to the present discussion. For an elaboration of different categories of unobtrusive measures, the reader may wish to refer to other sources (Bouchard, 1976; Kazdin, 1980; Webb *et al.*, 1966).

of the assessment procedures. For programs that attempt to alter behaviors in the natural environment, direct unobtrusive assessment may provide important corroborative data assessing whether treatment effects generalize beyond possibly reactive assessment conditions.

The advantage of unobtrusive measures in behavioral research is not that they are free from potential problems of their own. Rather, the methodological problems of unobtrusive measures, where they exist, *differ* from those of other measures that are currently in wider use (Webb *et al.*, 1966). The strength of unobtrusive assessment methods is that they can corroborate other sources of data independently of reactivity. Yet, a number of issues need to be considered in evaluating the results of unobtrusive measures.

Validation of Unobtrusive Measures

In behavioral assessment in general, relatively little attention has been given to various types of validity discussed in traditional psychometric assessment (Goldfried and Linehan, 1977). As might be expected, the attention accorded validation of unobtrusive behavioral measures is even less. Part of the reason for the lack of validation research is that unobtrusive measures are usually improvised for a single study. Because the measures are not standardized or routinely included in an assessment battery, their assessment characteristics receive less attention than might otherwise be the case. The general lack of attention to various types of validity introduces problems in interpreting the results obtained from unobtrusive measures.

The interpretation of many measures may not seem to require comment because the measures have "face validity," *i.e.*, seem of obvious relevance. Yet, the validity of many unobtrusive measures can be questioned. For example, in one study, clients who completed assertion training were phoned and asked to volunteer to serve for a few hours at a new hospital (Kazdin, 1974*a*). The request was designed to elicit refusal behavior because of the unreasonable requests that were made (*e.g.*, volunteering at an inconvenient time). Although the measure was unobtrusive, one can seriously question whether the phone call request was an appropriate measure of assertive behavior. Requesting volunteers for hospital work may more readily assess altruism rather than assertion skills.

Investigations that employ unobtrusive measures, particularly in contrived situations, rarely provide supporting information to validate whether the construct of interest is assessed (construct validity). If the results on the unobtrusive measure reflect intervention effects and corroborate data from other measures, the interpretation of the measure is less ambiguous than if no effects are demonstrated. The latter results make it unclear whether treatment effects were weak or the assessment device was inappropriate or insensitive.

Archival records occasionally present problems in deciding what is measured. Measures of recidivism, discharge, and readmission, for example, may not reflect the behaviors of interest. For instance, contact with the police and courts after release may not necessarily reflect how well ex-prisoners are doing in terms of appropriate social behavior. Reduced contact with the law might reflect superior criminal skills or inferior police surveillance and detection. Similarly, discharge and readmission rates of psychiatric patients may reflect changes in hospital philosophy rather than treatment effects (Gripp and Magaro, 1974). Indeed, discharge and readmission may bear little relationship to the psychological status of the patient (Fairweather, Sanders, Crissler, and Maynard, 1969). Although archival data may be of interest in their own right, the information they convey may be determined by many factors other than the behavior of direct interest.

Another problem in interpreting unobtrusive measures results from the narrow range of stimulus conditions that are assessed. The difficulties in obtaining unobtrusive measures have caused investigators to sample few components of the responses of interest. For example, in contrived situations clients may be presented with a restricted sample of stimulus conditions, such as interacting in a room with a confederate or being short-changed. The measure presents a single task from which inferences are drawn about larger segments of behavior. Given the specificity of behavior (Mischel, 1968), it may be important to draw from a larger sample of stimulus conditions to make inferences about performance. Investigations using unobtrusive measures usually provide little information to suggest that the content of the measures represents the larger domain of interest (content validity).

Unobtrusive measures do not always present interpretive problems. For example, observations of family interaction or child play at school may directly assess the target focus. If assessment is unobtrusive, interpretive problems about the data would be reduced, if not eliminated completely. Additional issues may be relevant, such as whether behaviors extend to other than the assessed situations, but this is not a unique issue to the measurement device.

Assessment Problems

Many unobtrusive methods involve direct observations of overt behavior where observers classify behavior according to specific behavioral codes. Interobserver agreement is assessed to evaluate whether observations are obtained consistently over time and among different observers. Several factors may influence the data that observers collect including changes in how the codes are applied over time (observer drift), the number of behaviors or subjects that are observed simultaneously, feedback and expectancies conveyed by the investigator, and the kind of response sequence that observers received during training (Kazdin, 1977; Kent and Foster, 1977). These problems are not unique to unobtrusive measures of overt behavior and, hence, need not be elaborated here. However, it is important to mention the assessment problems of direct observation because they present special obstacles for the investigator using unobtrusive observations.

Direct and unobtrusive measures of client behavior may be difficult to obtain because the presence of an observer, as observer, should not be detected. Yet, it may be difficult to assess interobserver agreement and to keep the observations unobtrusive if two or more observers must simultaneously record behavior. Possibly, interobserver agreement might be assessed by comparing data from one observer with tape recordings or videotaped records that could be obtained unobtrusively. Indeed, if the primary data could be obtained through audio or videotaped records, observers would not be able to influence subject performance and agreement could be obtained when the records were played.

Aside from maintaining unobtrusive assessment conditions for the subjects, research has suggested the desirability of keeping reliability checks unobtrusive for observers as well. Reactive effects of checking reliability are difficult to control in ordinary circumstances, even when no attempt is made to observe subject behavior unobtrusively. Conducting unobtrusive reliability checks on unobtrusive measures of overt subject behavior presents a formidable task for the investigator.

Obtrusiveness of the Measures

Whether many measures that are designed to be unobtrusive are in fact is a question that warrants comment. Measures occasionally are referred to as "unobtrusive" to reflect the intent of the investigator. Whether the client was unaware of the assessment procedure is a matter of surmise. For example, a confederate and experimental ruse are often utilized in contrived situations. Yet, subjects might easily see through the ruse when they are "surprisingly" interrupted on a task (Friedman, 1971) or seated in a waiting room where an accomplice coincidentally prompts treatment-relevant behavior (Gutride *et al.*, 1973). In some cases, unobtrusive measurement takes place in the same room where the subjects have been assessed under obtrusive conditions which may further raise suspicions (Bellack *et al.*, 1979).

Investigators rarely assess whether subjects were aware of the "unobtrusive" measurement procedure. As an exception, Frederiksen *et al.* (1976) asked patients on the ward whether they had realized that situations to which they were previously exposed were contrived. The patients did not identify the situations as related to assessment. Part of the reason for this may have been that the situations were modeled after actual events that had previously precipitated abusive behavior prior to treatment. In general, if it is possible for subjects to see through the ruse, it might be useful to gather information to evaluate whether the measure was unobtrusive.

Ethical Issues

Although ethical issues arise in all human experimentation, special sensitivity to these issues may be required with the use of unobtrusive measures. Attempting to obtain measures that circumvent the subject's awareness might violate the requirements of informed consent. Obviously, from the standpoint of assessment, it would be of unclear value to request permission from the subject to obtain unobtrusive observations without sensitizing subjects to the assessment procedures that follow. Perhaps subjects could provide consent for several different types of assessment opportunities, only some of which would actually be utilized by the investigator. Occasionally, subjects have not been informed about the unobtrusive measure until after it has been administered. After assessment clients may be debriefed and provided with the option of having the information remain confidential and not be used.

Subjecting clients to assessment procedures prior to obtaining permission may not be adequately compensated by providing them with the option of not using the information. The mere act of assessment may be objectionable to many clients and would not be agreed to in advance. Also, once the information is obtained, it may provide a threat to privacy. The ethical issues of using unobtrusive measures may be attenuated or exacerbated by the specific conditions under which assessment is conducted, the extent to which the information normally would be available, the event to which the assessment procedures place the subject under stress or risk, and similar factors.

For many unobtrusive measures, ethical issues associated with deception may not arise. For example, many archival records and physical traces would not be deceptive or present special threats to individual privacy because the information is ordinarily available and the identity of individual persons may not be used (*e.g.*, crime records in a police precinct or theft of merchandise in a store). The purposes of research may not raise ethical issues with such measures over and above those issues raised in collecting the information in the first place. Of course, how the information is used may alter the ethical requirements from the subjects' perspective.

For present purposes, it is important merely to note that ethical issues raise considerations for using unobtrusive measures. Although the issues cannot be elaborated here, their importance should not be minimized. However, ethical issues and guidelines related to circumstances, such as those associated with unobtrusive measurement have been outlined elsewhere (Ad hoc Committee on Ethical Standards in Psychological Research, 1973).

CONCLUSIONS

Behavioral assessment has made remarkable gains. Assessment methods have been exemplary in looking at different channels or modalities of behavior. Many complex clinical responses (*e.g.*, anxiety) have been carefully elaborated in the course of treatment evaluation. In applied programs, intervention effects are routinely evaluated on those behaviors that served as the impetus for treatment.

Most assessment procedures in behavior modification research are obtrusive. Because subjects are aware that their behavior is assessed, they may perform differently than they would with unobtrusive assessment methods. The reactive effects of assessment in behavioral research need not be surmised. Several studies have shown that the "same" behavior may differ depending upon whether subjects are aware that their behavior is assessed. Interestingly, even behavior of observers has been shown to differ as a function of whether they believe they are being monitored.

The reactive effects of assessment are not necessarily artifacts or sources of bias. Indeed, many researchers have creatively researched reactivity of assessment to help produce changes in clinically relevant behavior (Ciminero, Nelson, and Lipinski, 1977; Nelson, 1977). Yet, from the standpoint of evaluating treatment gains, obtrusive assessment provides information that needs to be supplemented whenever possible with unobtrusive measures. Research suggesting little relationship across obtrusive and unobtrusive assessment conditions and the concerns over the specificity of behavior across situations argue for use of unobtrusive measures to supplement existing assessment strategies.

The use of unobtrusive measures is not the only solution that can resolve the problems created by reactive assessment. An alternative solution might be to elaborate the conditions of obtrusive assessment that contribute or lead to reactive effects. Research might elaborate the cues of the assessment situation, format of assessment, instructions to the client, and other factors that may make direct observation of behavior less reactive (see Kazdin, 1980). For example, influences of the testing situation have been researched for the behavioral assessment of fear. The level of fear that subjects evince on behavioral avoidance tests varies as a function of whether subjects are told their behavior is assessed in a clinic versus a research or laboratory setting (Bernstein, 1973), whether the measure is said to assess anxiety or physiological arousal (Bernstein and Nietzel, 1974), or whether subjects are encouraged to evince little fear (Kazdin, 1973).

Once the specific cues of the testing situation that influence subject performance are known, they can be minimized to generate performance that might closely approximate the information obtained with unobtrusive assessment. Obtrusive measures offer many advantages, such as convenience, relative standardization across experiments, and lack of the need for deception. Hence, research devoted to the conditions that may make obtrusive measures less reactive is quite worthwhile.

Whether improvements are made in understanding and minimizing the reactivity of obtrusive measures, the use of *un*obtrusive measures needs to increase as well. Unobtrusive measures provide a test of the generality of experimental results and answer an extremely important treatment outcome question, namely, how do clients perform when they do not know their performance is monitored? For many intervention techniques and client populations within behavior modification, the answer to the question remains to be provided.

REFERENCE NOTE

1. Jenkins, W. O., Witherspoon, A. D., DeVine, M. D., deValera, E. K., Muller, J. B., Barton, M. C., and McKee, J. M. *The post-prison analysis of criminal behavior and longitudinal follow-up evaluation of institutional treatment.* A report on the Experimental Manpower Laboratory for Corrections, February, 1974.

REFERENCES

Ad hoc Committee on Ethical Standards in Psychological Research, *Ethical principles in the conduct of research with human participants.* Washington, D.C.: American Psychological Association, 1973.

Azrin, N. H. and Wesolowski, M. D. Theft reversal: An overcorrection procedure for eliminating stealing by retarded persons. *Journal of Applied Behavior Analysis,* 1974, **7**, 577-581.

Bellack, A. S., Hersen, M., and Lamparski, D. Role-play tests for assessing social skills: Are they valid? Are they useful? *Journal of Consulting and Clinical Psychology,* 1919, **47**, 335-342.

Bellack, A. S., Hersen, M., and Turner, S. M. Role-play tests for assessing social skills: Are they valid? *Behavior Therapy,* 1978, **9**, 448-461.

Bernstein, D. A. Behavioral fear assessment: Anxiety or artifact? In H. Adams and I. P. Unikel

(Eds), *Issues and trends in behavior therapy.* Springfield, Illinois: Charles C Thomas, 1973.

Bernstein, D. A. and Nietzel, M. T. Behavioral avoidance tests: The effects of demand characteristics and repeated measures of two types of subjects. *Behavior Therapy,* 1974, **5**, 183-192.

Bouchard, T. J. Field research methods: Interviewing, questionnaires, participant observation, systematic observation, unobtrusive measures. In M. D. Dunnette (Ed), *Handbook of industrial and organizational psychology.* Chicago: Rand McNally, 1976.

Burgess, R. L., Clark, R. N., and Hendee, J. C. An experimental analysis of anti-litter procedures. *Journal of Applied Behavior Analysis,* 1971, **4**, 1-5.

Campbell, D. T. and Fiske, D. Convergent and discriminant validation by the multitrait-multimethod matrix. *Psychological Bulletin,* 1959, **56**, 81-105.

Carmody, T. P. Rational-emotive, self-instructional, and behavioral assertion training: Facilitating maintenance. *Cognitive Therapy and Research.* 1978, **2**, 241-253.

Chapman, C. and Risley, T. R. Anti-litter procedures in an urban high-density area. *Journal of Applied Behavior Analysis,* 1974, **7**, 377-383.

Ciminero, A. R., Calhoun, K. S., and Adams, H. E. (Eds) *Handbook of behavioral assessment.* New York: Wiley, 1977.

Ciminero, A. R., Nelson, R. O., and Lipinski, D. P. Self-monitoring procedures. In A. R. Ciminero, K. S. Calhoun, and H. E. Adams (Eds), *Handbook of behavioral assessment.* New York: Wiley, 1977.

Cone, J. D. and Hawkins, R. P. (Eds) *Behavioral assessment: New directions in clinical psychology.* New York: Brunner/Mazel, 1977.

Eitzen, D. S. The effects of behavior modification on the attitudes of delinquents. *Behaviour Research and Therapy,* 1975, **13**, 195-299.

Fairweather, G. W., Sanders, D. H., Crissler, D. L., and Maynard, A. *Community life for the mentally ill.* Chicago: Aldine, 1969.

Fixsen, D. L., Phillips, E. L., Phillips, E. A., and Wolf, M. M. The teaching-family model of group home treatment. In W. E. Craighead, A. E. Kazdin, and M. J. Mahoney (Eds), *Behavior modification: Principles, issues, and applications.* Boston: Houghton Mifflin, 1976.

Foxx, R. M. and Hake, D. F. Gasoline conservation: A procedure for measuring and reducing the driving of college students. *Journal of Applied Behavior Analysis,* 1977, **10**, 61-74.

Frederiksen, L. W., Jenkins, J. O., Foy, D. W., and Eisler, R. M. Social skills training to modify abusive verbal outbursts in adults. *Journal of Applied Behavior Analysis,* 1976, **9**, 117-125.

Friedman, P. H. The effects of modeling and role-playing on assertive behavior. In R. D. Rubin, H. Fensterheim, A. A. Lazarus, and C. M. Franks (Eds), *Advances in behavior therapy.* New York: Academic Press, 1971.

Goldfried, M. R. and Linehan, M. M. Basic issues in behavioral assessment. In A. R. Ciminero, K. S. Calhoun, and H. E. Adams (Eds), *Handbook of behavioral assessment.* New York: Wiley, 1977.

Gripp, R. F. and Magaro, P. A. Token economy program in the psychiatric hospital: Review and analysis. *Behaviour Research and Therapy,* 1974, **12**, 205-228.

Gutride, M. E., Goldstein, A. P., and Hunter, G. F. The use of modeling and role playing to increase social interaction among asocial psychiatric patients. *Journal of Consulting and Clinical Psychology,* 1973, **40**, 408-415.

Hagen, R. L., Craighead, W. E., and Paul, G. L. Staff reactivity to evaluative behavioral observations. *Behavior Therapy,* 1975, **6**, 201-205.

Hauserman, N., Walen, S. R., and Behling, M. Reinforced racial integration in the first grade: A study in generalization. *Journal of Applied Behavior Analysis,* 1973, **6**, 193-200.

Hayes, S. C. and Cone, J. D. Reducing residential electrical energy use: Payments, information, and feedback. *Journal of Applied Behavior Analysis,* 1977, **10**, 425-435.

Hayes, S. C., Johnson, V. S., and Cone, J. D. The marked item technique: A practical procedure for litter control. *Journal of Applied Behavior Analysis,* 1975, **8**, 381-386.

Hermann, J. A., de Montes, A. I., Dominguez, B., Montes, F., and Hopkins, B. L. Effects of bonuses for punctuality on the tardiness of industrial workers. *Journal of Applied Behavior Analysis,* 1973, **6**, 563-570.

Hersen, M. and Bellack, A. S. (Eds) *Behavioral assessment: A practical handbook.* New York: Pergamon, 1976.

Hersen, M., Eisler, R. M., and Miller, P. M. An experimental analysis of generalization in assertive training. *Behaviour Research and Therapy,* 1974, **12**, 295-310.

Hollandsworth, J. G., Glazeski, R. C., and Dressel, M. E. Use of social-skills training in the treatment of extreme anxiety and deficient verbal skills in the job-interview setting. *Journal of Applied Behavior Analysis,* 1978, **11**, 259-269.

Johnson, S. M., Christensen, A., and Bellamy, G. T. Evaluation of family intervention through unobtrusive audio recordings: Experiences in "bugging" children. *Journal of Applied Behavior Analysis,* 1976, **9**, 213-219.

Kazdin, A. E. The effect of suggestion and pretesting on avoidance reduction in fearful college students. *Journal of Behavior Therapy and Experimental Psychiatry,* 1973, **4**, 213-221.

Kazdin, A. E. Effects of covert modeling and model reinforcement on assertive behavior. *Journal of Abnormal Psychology,* 1974, **83**, 240-252. (*a*)

Kazdin, A. E. Self-monitoring and behavior change. In M. J. Mahoney and C. E. Thoresen (Eds), *Self-control: Power to the person.* Monterey, California: Brooks/Cole, 1974. (*b*)

Kazdin, A. E. Artifact, bias, and complexity of assessment: The ABC's of reliability. *Journal of Applied Behavior Analysis,* 1977, **10**, 141-150.

Kazdin, A. E. *Research design in clinical psychology.* New York: Harper & Row, 1980.

Kent, R. N. and Foster, S. L. Direct observational procedures: Methodological issues in naturalistic settings. In A. R. Ciminero, K. S. Calhoun, and H. E. Adams (Eds), *Handbook of behavioral assessment.* New York: Wiley, 1977.

Kent, R. N., O'Leary, K. D., Diament, C., and Dietz, A. Expectation biases in observational evaluation of therapeutic change. *Journal of Consulting and Clinical Psychology,* 1974, **42,** 774-780.

Marholin, D., II and Gray, D. Effects of group response cost procedures on cash shortages in a small business. *Journal of Applied Behavior Analysis,* 1976, **9,** 25-30.

McFall, R. M. and Marston, A. R. An experimental investigation of behavior rehearsal in assertive training. *Journal of Abnormal Psychology,* 1970, **76,** 295-303.

McNees, M. P., Egli, D. S., Marshall, R. S., Schnell, J. F., and Risley, T. R. Shoplifting prevention: Providing information through signs. *Journal of Applied Behavior Analysis,* 1976, **9,** 399-405.

Mercatoris, M. and Craighead, W. E. Effects of nonparticipant observation on teacher and pupil classroom behavior. *Journal of Educational Psychology,* 1974, **66,** 512-519.

Mischel, W. *Personality and assessment.* New York: Wiley, 1968.

Nelson, R. O. Assessment and therapeutic functions of self-monitoring. In M. Hersen, R. M. Eisler, and P. M. Miller (Eds), *Progress in behavior modification, Volume* 5. New York: Academic Press, 1977.

Paul, G. L. and Lentz, R. J. *Psychological treatment of chronic mental patients: Milieu versus social-learning programs.* Cambridge, Massachusetts: Harvard University Press, 1977.

Phillips, E. L., Phillips, E. A., Fixsen, D. L., and Wolf, M. M. Achievement Place: Modification of the behaviors of pre-delinquent boys within a token economy. *Journal of Applied Behavior Analysis,* 1971, **4,** 45-59.

Pierce, C. H. and Risley, T. R. Recreation as a reinforcer: Increasing membership and decreasing disruptions in an urban recreation center. *Journal of Applied Behavior Analysis,* 1974, **7,** 403-411.

Roberts, R. R. and Renzaglia, G. A. The influence of tape recording on counseling. *Journal of Counseling Psychology,* 1965, **12,** 10-16.

Romanczyk, R. G., Kent, R. N., Diament, C., and O'Leary, K. D. Measuring the reliability of observational data: A reactive process. *Journal of Applied Behavior Analysis,* 1973, **6,** 175-184.

Schnelle, J. F., Kirchner, R. E., Macrae, J. W., McNees, M. P., Eck, R. H., Snodgrass, S., Casey, J. D., and Uselton, P. H. Police evaluation research: An experimental and cost-benefit analysis of a helicopter patrol in a high crime area. *Journal of Applied Behavior Analysis,* 1978, **11,** 11-21.

Schnelle, J. F., Kirchner, R. E., McNees, P. M., and Lawler, J. M. Social evaluation research: The evaluation of two police patrolling strategies. *Journal of Applied Behavior Analysis,* 1975, **8,** 353-365.

Seaver, W. B. and Patterson, A. H. Decreasing fuel oil consumption through feedback and social commendation. *Journal of Applied Behavior Analysis,* 1976, **9,** 147-152.

Surratt, P. R., Ulrich, R. E., and Hawkins, R. P. An elementary student as a behavioral engineer. *Journal of Applied Behavior Analysis,* 1969, **2,** 85-92.

Webb, E. J., Campbell, D. T., Schwartz, R. C., and Sechrest, L. *Unobtrusive measures: Nonreactive research in the social sciences.* Chicago: Rand McNally, 1966.

White, G. D. The effects of observer presence on the activity level of families. *Journal of Applied Behavior Analysis,* 1977, **10,** 734.

Received 6 November 1978.
(Final Acceptance 6 April 1979.)

JOURNAL OF APPLIED BEHAVIOR ANALYSIS 1980, 13, 493-500 NUMBER 3 (FALL 1980)

AN EMPIRICAL METHOD FOR DETERMINING AN APPROPRIATE INTERVAL LENGTH FOR RECORDING BEHAVIOR

R. W. SANSON-FISHER, A. DESMOND POOLE, AND JOHN DUNN

THE UNIVERSITY OF WESTERN AUSTRALIA

The study sought to examine the effects of varying interval length on the representation of data obtained using modified frequency time sampling. A 7-category scale was used to observe reliably the behavior of eight psychiatric inpatients. Using electronic real time recording equipment, it was possible to computer analyze the obtained data at varying interval lengths, the shortest interval being 1.0 seconds. It was found that increasing the interval length had little effect on the percentage of total duration recorded within each behavioral category, suggesting that this is a relatively stable measure of behavior. Percentage total events for each category was less stable with increasing interval lengths. The number of recorded events within each category tended to decrease, while their average durations tended to increase, as a function of increasing the interval length. The data suggest that the current practice of determining interval length in an arbitrary fashion, or on the basis of convention, should be abandoned. Rather, such a decision should be empirically determined for each particular observation scale and subject group. One method by which this might be achieved is presented.

DESCRIPTORS: interval length, within-interval error, empirical method of determination

---

Johnson and Bolstad (1973) and Jones, Reid, and Patterson (1975) have suggested that the development of direct observational techniques may well be the single most important contribution of applied behavior analysis to the discipline of psychology. Certainly such techniques are widely used by behavioral scientists.

Reviewing studies published in the *Journal of Applied Behavior Analysis* between 1968 and 1975, Kelly (1977) found that 76% employed direct observation procedures. Of the recording techniques used in those studies, 29% involved event recording, 20% interval recording, and 21% time sampling. Each of these observation tactics seeks to record data that accurately represent the actual stream of behavior being observed. However, even when the problems of interobserver reliability (Kazdin, 1977) are satisfactorily overcome, the results obtained using the different recording procedures are not necessarily comparable and all introduce some degree of distortion (Powell, Martindale, & Kulp, 1975; Powell & Rockinson, 1978; Repp, Roberts, Slack, Repp, & Berkler, 1976). In particular, Powell and Rockinson (1978) have demonstrated that interval recording procedures do not permit the frequency of discrete behaviors to be recorded accurately.

Interval recording, however, is widely employed as a means of representing a subject's behavior, but as pointed out by Jones et al. (1975) and Sanson-Fisher, Poole, Small, and Fleming (1979), this procedure creates serious problems for the researcher attempting to interpret the obtained data. This is primarily a result of the fact that in interval recording each interval is treated as representing a discrete behavioral event. Therefore, if the same behavior is coded in a sequence of intervals, it is impossible to

The authors extend their thanks to all staff and patients who permitted this study to be undertaken. The research was partially supported by a grant from The Sir Charles Gairdner Hospital Clinical Services Research Fund. Requests for reprints should be sent to the Secretary, Department of Psychiatry and Behavioural Science, University of Western Australia, Nedlands, Western Australia 6009.

determine whether this represents one continuous behavior or a number of sequential occurrences of that event. As Jones et al. (1975) state: "This difficulty of interpretation affects the scoring of the behavioral record, as, for example, in computing rates-per-minute, simple frequencies of occurrence, and probabilities of sequential interactions" (p. 55). Repp et al. (1976) have also demonstrated that with such procedures the utilized interval length can give rise to differences in the rates at which behaviors are reported to occur and in estimates of the duration of those behaviors.

The foregoing problems may be considered "across interval" errors, but modified frequency recording may also miss events if their duration is less than the employed interval length (Sackett, 1978). For example, consider the situation where an interval has been set at 6 sec and coding priority is determined by time dominance. If behavior A occurs for 4 sec, changes to behavior B for 3 sec, and reverts to the original behavior for a further 5 sec, behavior A will be recorded in both intervals. This loss of the short duration behavior B can be referred to as a "within-interval" error, which is a consequence of the interval length. The duration of the recording interval can, therefore, be of critical importance in determining the accuracy, or representativeness, of the obtained data.

Currently, the determination of the length of an interval appears to be largely an arbitrary matter rather than an empirical one. Jones et al. (1975) stated: "There do not seem to be any set rules about appropriate time samples. . . . The particular goals of the observational system probably define time sampling periods more appropriately than any procedural rules of thumb" (p. 54). As described by Jones et al. their group used a 6-sec modified frequency interval length, but Kelly (1977) reported that the most frequently used interval length, in studies reported in the *Journal of Applied Behavior Analysis*, is of 10-sec duration.

A search of recent behavioral studies indicated that no study specified the manner of selection, or appropriateness, of the utilized interval length even though it has been demonstrated that this has an impact on the accuracy of data (Powell et al., 1975; Repp et al., 1976). It is likely that an appropriate interval size, one which does not distort data, will be a complex function of the observation scale and the behavioral repertoire of the subjects (Repp et al., 1976). If this is correct, it suggests that prior to every experiment, and/or change of observation scale, some method of determining an appropriate interval length needs to be established.

A major advantage of empirically determining an appropriate interval length is that it may allow the calculation of discrete behavioral events by eliminating the occurrence of within-interval errors. In traditional interval recording, each interval has to be treated as containing a discrete event because it cannot be assumed that other behaviors did not occur for brief periods within an interval. Consequently, because of the possibility of such within-interval error, it is not necessarily justified to treat sequential intervals containing the same behavioral codes as representing one continuous event, although this may be what was actually observed. However, if within-interval error is eliminated, it is possible to sum across intervals to obtain a more accurate representation of discrete behaviors and their durations.

Systems that permit the recording of behaviors in "real time" eliminate within-interval error (Sanson-Fisher et al., 1979). Such systems are now possible due to recent developments in electronic and computer technology (Celhoffer, Boukydis, Minde, & Muir, 1977; Fitzpatrick, 1977; Sackett, Stephenson, & Ruppenthal, 1973; Sanson-Fisher et al., 1979; Stephenson & Roberts, 1977; Stephenson, Smith, & Roberts, 1975; Torgerson, 1977; Hollenbeck, Smythe, & Sackett, Note 1). According to Sidowski (1977), the main advantages of these systems are that they "allow the researcher to record the occurrences of behaviors as well as their durations in real time (allowing for subsequent serial and time-series analyses) and to produce outputs that allow for easy transfer of data to storage devices (e.g., magnetic tape or disk) or for direct entry into a computer" (p. 403). Another pragmatic reason for their use is the ease with which they can be employed by observers, who do not have to learn a pacing technique, as is necessary in interval recording procedures. Instead, observers need only to press a button to record a behavior's onset and termination (Sanson-Fisher et al., 1979).

However, even when data have been collected using "real time" recording procedures, analysis of the data still requires that an interval length must be set. The lower limits of such an interval is usually not imposed by the hardware or computer facilities. For example, the Data Acquisition in Real Time (DART 1) recording system described by Sanson-Fisher et al. (1979) allows for an interval length of .1 sec. At this interval length, data representation would appear to be more than adequate, given that it is unlikely that many behaviors of interest would occur for less than .1 sec. However, the need for human observers introduces constraints on the interval length that may be reliably used. This occurs as a result of such factors as the observers' need to glance at the equipment, their reaction times, the complexity of the rating scale, and the behavior under observation. Thus, although the use of very brief intervals is possible with "real time" hardware, the need to obtain observer reliability places constraints on the shortest interval that may be used.

The objective of the present study is to demonstrate a method to determine objectively an interval length at which little information of interest is lost, given a prescribed observational system and subject group. The study also provides an opportunity to examine the effect of differing interval lengths on the interpretation of collected data.

METHOD

Procedure

Video observations were carried out in an acute short-stay psychiatric unit described in detail by Sanson-Fisher, Poole, and Thompson (1979). Three video recorders were installed in the main patient areas over 3 months prior to beginning the study. During that period all patients admitted to the unit were informed that evaluation studies were taking place and requested to consent to being observed. Staff had consented to the research over 1 year previously. To further minimize observer reactivity, neither staff nor patients were aware of the nature of the observations being undertaken.

Throughout the study the video recorders were automatically switched on three times per day between 9:00 a.m. and 5:00 p.m. The eight target subjects were selected, at random, from all inpatients in the unit and were observed on eight separate 5 min occasions over 4 consecutive week-days.

Behaviors were coded by research assistants who were extensively trained as observers. The coding of behavior was carried out while observing the video recordings and using the DART 1 equipment (Sanson-Fisher et al., 1979). The inpatients' behavior was coded using the following 7-category observation scale.

Observation Scale

Positive self-concept. Behavior coded in this category reflects patients' positive self evaluation, optimism about achieving a satisfactory posttreatment adjustment and/or motivation for change, e.g., "I think I can handle my problems"; "I feel good/happy/content/relaxed."

Independent altruism. Asking questions about others' illnesses, their past experiences and future expectations, and offering solutions to another's problems were coded as independent altruism. Also included were comments that indicated patients were asserting their independence and requesting information about their condition, treatment, or other aspects of their psychiatric care, i.e., "How is your family?"; "Why have my drugs been changed?"

On task. All occasions on which patients were observed to be engaged in appropriate activities, such as painting, pottery, woodwork, or reading were coded under this category.

Talk. General nonpsychiatric oriented conversation, not coded as positive or negative self-concept or independent altruism, was included in this category, e.g., talk about general issues, such as politics, movies, the weather, and other nonegocentric comments.

Negative self-concept. Comments reflecting a negative evaluation of self, life-style, coping skills, and derogatory conversations about close family members and friends were coded within this category, e.g., "I am worthless"; "I cannot cope."

Egocentricity. Behaviors included in this category were idle play and staring into space. Fixation on an object or person in a passive nonresponsive manner, self-stimulation, and sleeping were common examples of behavior coded as egocentric behavior.

Bizarre. Behavior coded bizarre was seen as inexplicable or irrational. It included such things as smiling, giggling, or weeping inappropriately; talking, muttering, or mumbling to oneself. Also included were bizarre movements, aggression in the absence of physical threat, claims of being controlled by other people or unusual forces, descriptions of phobic behavior and/or phobic avoidance behavior. The full definitions of this category were derived from traditional psychiatric scales.

In those situations in which the categories were not found to be mutually exclusive, previously determined priority rules were used. For example, if a patient was performing an on-task activity and also exhibiting bizarre behavior, the latter was coded.

The reliability of observations was assessed by having the same sequences of behavior independently coded by a second observer. Four 5-min sequences were randomly selected from observations made on days 1 to 3 and three from those obtained on day 4. The observers were not aware which sequences were selected for recording to assess reliability and, following the procedures recommended by Kazdin (1977), the sequences used for these checks were selected from the most complex available.

RESULTS

Reliability

Reliabilities were calculated separately for each observation category. Because of criticisms that percentage agreement, as a measure of reliability, fails to take account of chance agreements, the Kappa coefficient was used to estimate reliability (Hartmann, 1977). The levels of interobserver reliability, at the 1.0-sec interval length, are given in Table 1.

Data Analysis Procedure

The procedure for analyzing the data at the various interval lengths was identical throughout the study and will be described in relation to the 1.0-sec interval.

A specially developed software program scanned the data (stored on disk) on a second-by-second basis, and within each second determined which behavior dominated in terms of duration (i.e., time dominance). That is, if two behaviors occurred within a 1.0-sec period, behavior A for .4 sec and behavior B for .6 sec, behavior B was

Table 1

Level of interobserver agreement for each behavior category, at 1.0-sec interval length, using the Kappa coefficient.

Behavior category	*No. of reliability checks on which relevant category was coded*	*% occasions on which Kappa coefficient was significant at* $p < .05$
Positive self-concept	14	85.7
Independent altruism	8	87.5
On task	15	100.0
Talk	15	93.3
Negative self-concept	13	92.3
Egocentricity	12	83.3
Bizarre*	—	—

*Did not occur with sufficient frequency to calculate reliability.

coded as occurring within that interval. If behavior B again dominated within the next interval, it was treated as being the same event, and so on across all successive 1.0-sec intervals in which that behavior dominated. Once a different behavior dominated within a 1.0-sec interval, the occurrence of behavior B was considered to have terminated, and the duration of its occurrence was calculated, i.e., its duration equaled the sum of successive 1.0-sec intervals in which it dominated. Therefore, unless a behavior other than B occurred for less than .5 sec within an interval in this sequence, there was no within-interval error. Consequently, the representation of B as one event is an accurate representation of that behavior.

Using this procedure, the frequency with which each behavior category was recorded throughout the observation period was calculated, together with the average duration of those behaviors. The procedure was repeated using each of the longer interval lengths. However, as the interval increased so did the potential for within-interval error which is half the employed interval length, e.g., using the 5-sec interval behaviors occurring for less than 2.5 sec would be discounted in the determination of continuous behavioral events.

The Effects of Interval Length on the Representation of Behavior

Because 1.0 sec was the shortest interval at which satisfactory interobserver reliability could be achieved, these data were taken as criteria, i.e., the best estimate of the frequencies and durations of behaviors. The number of events and the average duration per event at 1.0 sec, together with those at interval lengths of 2.0, 3.0, 4.0, 5.0, 6.0, and 10.0 sec, are summarized in Table 2.

As can be seen, the effect of increasing the interval length is to decrease the number of occurrences of behavior recorded within each category. There is also a converse tendency for averaging duration per event to increase as a result of increasing the interval length. This effect is more clearly observed when the data obtained at each interval length are expressed as a percentage of those obtained at the criterion interval (i.e., 1.0 sec), as has been done in Table 3.

Table 2

Number of behavior events and their average duration for each behavior category as a function of interval length.

	Interval length						
Behavior category	*1 sec*	*2 sec*	*3 sec*	*4 sec*	*5 sec*	*6 sec*	*10 sec*
			NUMBER OF EVENTS				
Positive self-concept	55	49	39	34	31	27	18
Independent altruism	16	12	9	7	6	4	1
On task	219	193	171	155	143	134	108
Talk	80	66	59	54	44	38	28
Negative self-concept	53	50	49	43	42	40	35
Egocentricity	50	50	49	50	48	47	46
Bizarre	3	3	3	3	3	3	3
			AVERAGE DURATION PER EVENT (SEC)				
Positive self-concept	5.71	6.65	7.85	8.94	9.19	10.67	13.89
Independent altruism	2.94	3.17	4.00	5.14	6.67	6.00	10.00
On task	38.87	44.16	49.74	55.02	60.24	64.43	80.19
Talk	8.09	9.58	10.83	11.63	13.64	15.00	20.36
Negative self-concept	66.87	70.68	72.43	81.95	84.29	88.05	101.14
Egocentricity	108.02	108.20	110.39	108.48	112.50	115.28	119.78
Bizarre	144.00	143.33	145.00	142.67	143.33	144.00	146.67

Table 3

Number of behavior events recorded at each interval length as a percentage of those detected at 1.0 sec, and average durations as a percentage change from that obtained at 1.0 sec.

Behavior category	*Interval length* 2 sec	3 sec	4 sec	5 sec	6 sec	10 sec
	PERCENTAGE OF 1.0-SEC EVENTS					
Positive self-concept	89.1	70.9	61.8	56.4	49.1	32.7
Independent altruism	75.0	56.3	43.8	37.5	25.0	6.3
On task	88.1	78.1	70.8	65.3	61.2	49.3
Talk	82.5	73.8	67.5	55.0	47.5	35.0
Negative self-concept	94.3	92.5	81.1	79.2	75.5	66.0
Egocentricity	100.0	98.0	100.0	96.0	94.0	92.0
Bizarre	100.0	100.0	100.0	100.0	100.0	100.0
	PERCENTAGE CHANGE FROM 1.0-SEC DURATION DATA					
Positive self-concept	16.5	37.5	55.6	60.9	86.9	142.9
Independent altruism	7.8	36.1	74.8	126.8	104.1	240.1
On task	13.6	28.0	41.5	55.0	65.8	106.3
Talk	18.4	33.9	43.8	68.6	85.4	151.6
Negative self-concept	5.7	8.3	22.6	26.1	31.7	51.2
Egocentricity	.2	2.2	.4	4.1	6.7	10.9
Bizarre	−.5	.7	−.9	−.5	.0	1.9

This analysis indicates that the main effects of increasing the interval are to underestimate the number of events and to overestimate their average durations. It appears that, for the present data, the duration of an event has the greatest influence on the accuracy of its representation at the various interval lengths. Only in the case of the Bizarre category, which has an extremely long average duration per event, is there no loss of events and an extremely small percentage change in duration. Similar conclusions can be made about the Egocentricity category which is also characterized by a long average duration and again the effects of interval length appear to be small. On the other hand, Independent Altruism contains behaviors of short duration and, as a result, reflects the greatest variation with increasing interval lengths.

As interval recording techniques do not usually permit the reporting of a number of specific events, or their durations, because of the presence of within-interval errors, data are frequently reported in terms of either percentage total events or percentage total duration within each behavior category. The effects of varying the interval length on these measures are, therefore, summarized in Table 4.

As can be seen, the data obtained at the different interval lengths show little variation. However, Spearman rank order correlations were calculated between the ranks for percentage total events at the 1.0-sec interval and for those at the longer interval lengths, and a significant association ($p < .05$) between the 1.0-sec data and those at 2.0, 3.0, and 4.0 sec was found. This was not so for the other intervals. A similar analysis for percentage total duration revealed that the rank order correlations between the 1.0-sec data and those at the other interval length were throughout 1.0 ($p < .01$). It appears, therefore, that for the present data percentage total duration is the measure which is least susceptible to the effects of varying the interval length.

DISCUSSION

Consistent with previous research, the present study indicates that the choice of interval length may affect the accuracy with which observed behaviors are represented in the data. Although

Table 4

Percentage total events and percentage total duration, for each behavior category, as a function of interval length.

Behavior category	Interval length 1 sec	2 sec	3 sec	4 sec	5 sec	6 sec	10 sec
PERCENTAGE TOTAL EVENTS							
Positive self-concept	11.55	11.58	10.29	9.83	9.78	9.22	7.53
Independent altruism	3.36	2.84	2.37	2.02	1.89	1.37	.42
On task	46.01	45.63	45.12	44.08	45.11	45.73	45.19
Talk	16.81	15.68	15.57	15.61	13.88	12.97	11.72
Negative self-concept	11.13	11.82	12.93	12.43	13.25	13.65	14.64
Egocentricity	10.50	11.82	12.93	14.45	15.14	16.04	19.25
Bizarre	.63	.71	.79	.87	.93	1.02	1.26
r_s with 1.0 sec	—	.88*	.88*	.86*	.75	.68	.64
PERCENTAGE TOTAL DURATION							
Positive self-concept	1.66	1.73	1.62	1.61	1.51	1.52	1.32
Independent altruism	.25	.28	.19	.19	.21	.13	.05
On task	45.04	45.11	45.05	45.19	45.56	45.71	45.63
Talk	3.42	3.35	3.39	3.33	3.17	3.02	3.00
Negative self-concept	18.75	18.71	18.00	18.67	18.72	18.65	18.65
Egocentricity	28.58	28.64	28.65	28.74	28.56	28.68	29.03
Bizarre	2.29	2.28	2.30	2.27	2.27	2.29	2.32
r_s with 1.0 sec	—	1.00**	1.00**	1.00**	1.00**	1.00**	1.00**

*$p < .05$ (two-tailed).
**$p < .01$ (two-tailed).

the commonly used percentage events and percentage duration measures appear to be relatively unaffected by variations in interval length. this is not the case when information is required about discrete behaviors and their duration. This problem arises because of variability in the duration of discrete occurrences of the various categories of behavior. For example, in the present study, behaviors coded as Independent Altruism occurred for short durations (2.94 sec at the 1.0-sec interval length). Consequently, as the interval length was increased, an increasing number of such events were not recorded.

When the naturally occurring variability of different categories of behavior need to be accommodated within the constraints of an interval recording system, it appears necessary to determine the interval length so as not to lose short duration behaviors which may be of interest. By collecting data using a real time recording system, and then analyzing them at varying interval lengths, it is possible to examine the topography of the behavior so as to determine an optimum interval length, i.e., one at which within-interval error, caused by the missing of short duration behaviors, is minimized. This interval length may then be used to code behavior and still allow one to calculate discrete behaviors and their durations.

The results of the present study, for example, suggest that, given the same observation scale and subject group, the use of a 3.0-sec interval might be acceptable. Using this interval length, 79.6% of all events recorded at 1.0 sec are still represented in the data.

It is suggested that when data on frequency of events and/or their durations are required, the method described in this paper provides a possible technique for empirically determining an appropriate interval length.

REFERENCE NOTE

1. Hollenbeck, A. R., Smythe, L. E., & Sackett, G. P. BOSS: Behavioral Observation Scoring System—A

manual for computer-assisted observational research. Unpublished manuscript, University of Washington, 1975.

REFERENCES

Celhoffer, L., Boukydis, C., Minde, K., & Muir, E. The DCR-11 event recorder: a portable high-speed digital cassette system with direct computer access. *Behavior Research Methods and Instrumentation,* 1977, **9**, 442-446.

Fitzpatrick, L. J. Automated data collection for observed events. *Behavior Research Methods and Instrumentation,* 1977, **9**, 447-451.

Hartmann, D. P. Considerations in the choice of interobserver reliability estimates. *Journal of Applied Behavior Analysis,* 1977, **10**, 103-116.

Johnson, S. M., & Bolstad, O. D. Methodological issues in naturalistic observation: some problems and solutions for field research. In L. A. Hamerlynck, L. C. Handy, & E. J. Mash (Eds.), *Behavior change: Methodology, concepts and practice.* Champaign, Ill.: Research Press, 1973.

Jones, R. R., Reid, J. B., & Patterson, G. R. Naturalistic observation in clinical assessment. In P. McReynolds (Ed.), *Advances in psychological assessment* (Vol. 3). San Francisco: Jossey-Bass Inc., 1975.

Kazdin, A. Artifact, bias, and complexity of assessment: The ABC's of reliability. *Journal of Applied Behavior Analysis,* 1977, **10**, 141-150.

Kelly, M. B. A review of the observational data-collection and reliability procedures reported in the *Journal of Applied Behavior Analysis. Journal of Applied Behavior Analysis,* 1977, **10**, 99-101.

Powell, J., Martindale, A., & Kulp, S. An evaluation of time-sampling measures of behavior. *Journal of Applied Behavior Analysis,* 1975, **8**, 463-469.

Powell, J., & Rockinson, R. On the inability of interval time sampling to reflect frequency of occurrence data. *Journal of Applied Behavior Analysis,* 1978, **11**, 531-532.

Repp, A. C., Roberts, D. M., Slack, D. J., Repp, C. F., & Berkler, M. S. A comparison of frequency, interval and time-sampling methods of data collection. *Journal of Applied Behavior Analysis,* 1976, **9**, 501-508.

Sackett, G. P. Measurement in observational research. In G. P. Sackett (Ed.), *Observing behavior: Data collection and analysis methods* (Vol. 2). Baltimore: University Park Press, 1978.

Sackett, G. P., Stephenson, E., & Ruppenthal, G. G. Digital acquisition systems for observing behavior in laboratory and field settings. *Behavior Research Methods and Instrumentation,* 1973, **5**, 344-348.

Sanson-Fisher, R. W., Poole, A. D., Small, G. A., & Fleming, I. Data acquisition in real time—an improved system for naturalistic observation. *Behavior Therapy,* 1979, **10**, 543-554.

Sanson-Fisher, R. W., Poole, A. D., & Thompson, V. Behaviour patterns within a general hospital psychiatric unit: An observational study. *Behaviour Research and Therapy,* 1979, **17**, 317-332.

Sidowski, J. B. Observation research: Some instrumental systems for scoring and storing behavioral data. *Behavior Research Methods and Instrumentation,* 1977, **9**, 403-404.

Stephenson, G. R., & Roberts, T. W. The SSR system: A general encoding system with computerized transcription. *Behavior Research Methods and Instrumentation,* 1977, **9**, 434-441.

Stephenson, G. R., Smith, D. P. B., & Roberts, T. W. The SSR system: an open format event recording system with computerized transcription. *Behavior Research Methods and Instrumentation,* 1975, **7**, 497-515.

Torgerson, L. Datamyte 900. *Behavior Research Methods and Instrumentation,* 1977, **9**, 405-406.

Received March 16, 1979
Final acceptance February 22, 1980

JOURNAL OF APPLIED BEHAVIOR ANALYSIS 1986, 19, 73–77 NUMBER 1 (SPRING 1986)

METHODS OF TIME SAMPLING: A REAPPRAISAL OF MOMENTARY TIME SAMPLING AND PARTIAL INTERVAL RECORDING

ALEX HARROP AND MICHAEL DANIELS

LIVERPOOL POLYTECHNIC

We compared the accuracy of momentary time sampling (MTS) and partial interval recording (PIR) in estimating both absolute behavioral levels and relative change. A computer randomly generated runs of pseudobehavior varying in duration and rate and simulated MTS and PIR of each run. Results indicated that when estimating absolute behavioral levels, duration rather than rate should be used as the dependent measure, and MTS is more accurate than PIR. In contrast, PIR is the more sensitive method for detecting relative changes in behavioral levels, although, at high rates, PIR tends to underestimate the degree of change.

DESCRIPTORS: observation methods, momentary time sampling, partial interval recording, measurement error

---

Time sampling is a procedure that, although suffering from inherent limitations (Johnston & Pennypacker, 1980), is widely used in applied behavior analysis. The accuracy of time-sampling methods has been investigated by several researchers, in particular by Repp, Roberts, Slack, Repp, and Berkler (1976), and by Powell, Martindale, Kulp, Martindale, and Bauman (1977). The two methods that were compared in both investigations may be defined as (a) momentary time sampling (MTS), in which a response is scored if it occurs exactly at a predetermined moment, and (b) partial interval recording (PIR), in which an observation interval is scored if a response occurs during any part of the interval.

Repp et al. (1976) examined the accuracy of MTS and PIR in assessing rate of responding. They found MTS to be extremely inaccurate for all conditions investigated. PIR was found to be accurate for low and medium rates of responding, but to underestimate high-rate responding. Powell et al. (1977) examined the accuracy of MTS and PIR in assessing duration of responding. They found MTS to be superior to PIR, which overestimated duration. The work of Repp et al. therefore suggests that PIR is the better method for measuring rate of responding, whereas that of Powell et al. suggests that MTS is better for measuring duration.

An examination of these studies indicates, however, that neither adequately equated the conditions under which MTS and PIR were compared, and neither explored the possible independent influence of behavioral parameters (e.g., duration of behavioral episodes and rate of responding) on the accuracy of the techniques. Furthermore, the analyses applied to the data were, in both cases, limited to a comparison of accuracy in estimating absolute behavioral levels. Although such estimation is, in many situations, important (e.g., in determining whether an intervention is necessary), an equally important consideration, particularly in intervention research, is accuracy in the estimation of relative changes in behavioral level.

In view of the limitations in the studies by Repp et al. (1976) and Powell et al. (1977), we decided to examine further the accuracy of comparable MTS and PIR procedures in estimating both absolute behavioral levels and relative changes, for various durations and rates of behavior. We hope that our results may help to provide researchers and practitioners with clearer guidelines on the relative merits of the two techniques and on the conditions in which one method may be preferred.

Requests for reprints should be sent to Alex Harrop, Section of Psychology, Liverpool Polytechnic, C. F. Mott Campus, Liverpool Road, Prescot, Merseyside L34 1NP, United Kingdom. Michael Daniels is at the same address.

Table 1
Mean Percentage Error of Absolute Estimation for Momentary Time Sampling (MTS) and Partial Interval Recording (PIR)

Emitted duration (s)	Low to medium rates		Medium to high rates	
	MTS	PIR	MTS	PIR
	Estimated rate			
1	5.5	−8.5**	3.9	−36.5**
5	387.5**	32.0**	396.7**	2.7
10	900.5**	82.5**	891.9**	53.1**
20	1,871.6**	181.2**	1,883.4**	151.2**
	Estimated duration			
1	5.5	815.2**	3.9	535.0**
5	−2.5	164.0**	−0.7	105.4**
10	0.1	82.5**	−0.8	53.1**
20	−1.4	40.6**	−0.8*	25.6**

* $p < .01$.
** $p < .0001$.

METHOD

Design

To permit a fair comparison between MTS and PIR, we attempted to equate the costs, and the demands on the observer, of these techniques. A "time base" of 15 s defined the time between the start of successive observations. For MTS, this meant that behavior was observed for 1 s every 15 s. For PIR, the behavior was observed for a 10-s observation interval, with a nonobservation time (used in practice for recording) of 5 s. We chose a total sampling period of 1 hr for both methods, representing a period for which a human observer might realistically be expected to remain on task. For each method, therefore, 240 observations occurred in the session.

The emitted behavior was regulated into four constant durations (1, 5, 10, and 20 s), representing behaviors that were almost instantaneous, one-half, equal to, and twice the observation interval used for PIR. The use of a 20-s duration also permitted a behavior to span two observation instances or intervals. We chose constant duration behaviors because, although unlikely in practice, these permit a controlled parametric investigation.

The rates of emission were controlled by setting the probability of onset of a behavior (p) into two sequences: (a) "low to medium" rates, where p = 1:180, 1:90, 1:60, 1:45, 1:36, and 1:30, representing expected frequencies of 20, 40, 60, 80, 100, and 120 per hr for behaviors of 1-s duration, and (b) "medium to high" rates, where p = 1:30, 1:15, 1:10, 1:7.5, 1:6, and 1:5, representing expected frequencies of 120, 240, 360, 480, 600, and 720 per hr for behaviors of 1-s duration.

Computer Simulation

We chose computer simulation for our study because it offers the advantages of speed, accuracy, and precise parametric control. Simulation was based on the assumption that, when using human observers, 1 s represents the shortest time in which a behavior may occur and be observed. Accordingly, time was simulated in terms of successive discrete "moments" (considered, notionally, as seconds) in which a behavior may either occur or not occur.

For each combination of emitted duration and probability of onset, a BBC Model B microcomputer generated 20 runs of pseudobehavior, producing 880 separate behavioral records (20 runs × 4 durations × 11 probabilities). To produce these records, a Basic procedure randomly generated the pseudobehaviors into a single-dimension string array of 3,620 elements. This size covered the sampling period (3,600 s), preceded by a further 20 s that permitted behaviors to be initiated prior to the commencement of observation. The Basic random number function controlled the probability of onset of behavior. We appreciated inadequacies of the Basic function as a source of random numbers, but judged that this would not materially affect the validity of the simulation procedure. Once a behavior was initiated, another occurrence was not permitted until the first behavior was completed. This ensured that all behaviors were of constant duration, although successive occurrences could follow without pause.

Following the generation of each behavioral record, a further procedure sampled the array every 15 s, beginning with the 21st element, simulating

Table 2
Indices of Sensitivity and Linearity for Momentary Time Sampling (MTS) and Partial Interval Recording (PIR)

Emitted duration (s)	Low to medium rates				Medium to high rates			
	Sensitivity		Linearity[a]		Sensitivity		Linearity[a]	
	MTS	PIR	MTS	PIR	MTS	PIR	MTS	PIR
1	0.049	0.538	0.993	0.999	0.037	0.371	0.998	0.949**
5	0.397	0.863	0.995	0.999	0.340	0.729	0.997	0.969**
10	0.611	0.866	0.999	0.999*	0.390	0.688	0.999	0.977**
20	0.846	0.949	0.999	1.000	0.579	0.800	0.999	0.987**

[a] Significance levels are for curvilinearity.
* $p < .01$.
** $p < .0001$.

both MTS and PIR. For MTS, the procedure counted the number of observations that recorded behavior. For PIR, the procedure counted the number of intervals during which, at any time, behavior occurred.

RESULTS AND DISCUSSION

Estimating Absolute Levels

To examine the error that may be produced by MTS and PIR when estimating absolute behavioral levels, actual rate and total duration of behavior were compared with estimates derived from the recorded data. For rate, the actual frequency with which behavior occurred in the sampling period was compared with the frequency estimated per hour of observation time (recorded frequency × 3,600/seconds of observation). For duration, the actual proportion of the sampling period during which behavior occurred was compared with the proportion of observations that were scored.

Results indicate that error of estimation is a function of dependent measure, sampling method, emitted duration, and, for PIR (but not MTS), behavioral rate. Table 1 presents the mean percentage errors of estimation under the various conditions. To test for the presence of systematic overestimation or underestimation, the binomial test was applied to the estimates, following the procedure used by Brulle and Repp (1984).

When estimating absolute rate, considerable systematic error is, in general, produced by both sampling methods, with rates being progressively overestimated as emitted duration increases. For PIR, overestimation also increases with lower behavioral rates. With short duration behaviors, however, particularly if they are also of higher rates, PIR underestimates rate. It is pertinent to note here that Repp et al. (1976), who found that PIR was accurate in estimating rates or, with high rates, produced underestimation, used pseudobehaviors of very short duration (0.035 s). Our results demonstrate clearly the problems of using rate as the dependent measure with time-sampling procedures; problems due to the impossibility, given only information that, for example, 200 out of 240 observations are scored, of determining whether this represents behavior of high frequency and short duration or of low frequency and long duration.

When estimating absolute duration, MTS appears not to introduce systematic error, whereas PIR produces overestimation that increases with shorter emitted durations and lower rates. These results are consistent with those of Powell et al. (1977), who concluded that MTS offers clear advantages over PIR when duration is the measure of interest.

Estimating Relative Changes

To examine the accuracy of MTS and PIR in estimating relative changes in behavioral level, the criterion adopted was the regression of recorded on actual rates. Because emitted duration is constant

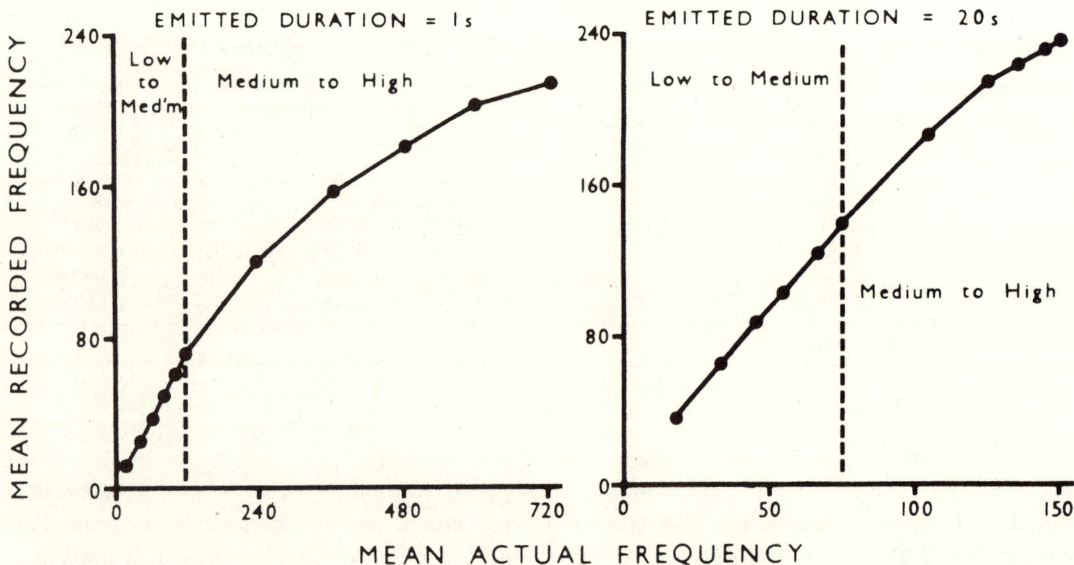

Figure 1. Mean recorded frequency obtained with partial interval recording as a function of mean actual frequency.

in each condition, regression analyses for rate are equivalent to those for total duration. Analysis of variance of regression was carried out on the data from each of the two probability sequences for each sampling method and emitted duration. An index of *sensitivity* is provided by the proportion of variance *within* probability levels accounted for by pooled regression. Sensitivity is a measure of the ability of a sampling method to reflect accurately small changes in the actual rate of behavior (randomly occurring within each probability level). An index of *linearity* is provided by the proportion of variance *between* probability levels accounted for by linear regression. Linearity is a measure of the degree to which a graph of the average recorded rates across probability levels would be similar in shape to a graph of the average actual rates. Table 2 presents the indices of sensitivity and linearity for both methods of recording in the various conditions.

With both sampling methods, sensitivity increases with lower rates and longer emitted durations. More importantly, in all conditions, sensitivity is significantly ($p < .005$) and substantially greater with PIR than with MTS. For low to medium rates, linearity with both sampling methods is high for all emitted durations. For medium to high rates, linearity with MTS is high for all emitted durations, whereas with PIR it is lower because of a significant curvilinear component. To examine curvilinearity, graphs were drawn to show the relationship between mean recorded frequency and mean actual frequency for each emitted duration (for examples, see Figure 1). Graphs indicate the presence of systematic error with PIR (attenuated at longer emitted durations) that is in the direction of underestimating change with high rates of behavior.

Conclusions

Although caution must be exercised in extrapolating our results beyond the range of values we selected for the sampling and behavioral parameters, several general conclusions are indicated. MTS (but not PIR) provides accurate average estimates of absolute duration. Estimates of absolute rate are inaccurate with both methods. PIR is more sensitive than MTS in detecting relative changes in behavioral level (rate or total duration), but PIR underestimates the magnitude of change with high-rate behaviors, particularly if they are also of short duration. Although MTS is the less sensitive method, it appears not to suffer from systematic error in estimating relative change. Because, however, the systematic error produced by PIR is always in the direction of providing a conservative estimate of change, researchers and practitioners may consider that this error is a price worth paying for the greater sensitivity of the method.

REFERENCES

Brulle, A. R., & Repp, A. C. (1984). An investigation of the accuracy of momentary time sampling procedures with time series data. *British Journal of Psychology,* **75,** 481–485.

Johnston, J. J., & Pennypacker, H. S. (1980). *Strategies and tactics of human behavioral research.* Hillsdale, NJ: Lawrence Erlbaum.

Powell, J., Martindale, B., Kulp, S., Martindale, A., & Bauman, R. (1977). Taking a closer look: Time sampling and measurement error. *Journal of Applied Behavior Analysis,* **10,** 325–332.

Repp, A. C., Roberts, D. M., Slack, D. J., Repp, C. F., & Berkler, M. S. (1976). A comparison of frequency, interval and time-sampling methods of data collection. *Journal of Applied Behavior Analysis,* **9,** 501–508.

Received April 8, 1985
Final acceptance October 29, 1985

JOURNAL OF APPLIED BEHAVIOR ANALYSIS 1990, 23, 323–331 NUMBER 3 (FALL 1990)

THE REPRESENTATIVENESS OF OBSERVATIONAL SAMPLES OF DIFFERENT DURATIONS

OLIVER C. MUDFORD AND IVAN L. BEALE
UNIVERSITY OF AUCKLAND, NEW ZEALAND

AND

NIRBHAY N. SINGH
VIRGINIA COMMONWEALTH UNIVERSITY

The representativeness of behavioral observation samples with durations of less than the whole time of interest was investigated. A real-time recording system was developed to quantify the behavior of 5 profoundly mentally retarded physically handicapped adult students in an institutional training setting. Behavior was observed using six mutually exclusive and exhaustive categories during 2.5-hr observation sessions. Sample observation sessions with durations ranging from 15 to 135 min were computer simulated from the whole-session (150-min) records. It was found that the representativeness of these samples, when compared to whole-session records, was a function of the relative duration of the behavioral categories and of sample duration. The occurrence of relatively high-duration behaviors (lasting for more than 50% of the session) was estimated to within 20% error by samples of less than 60 min, but low-duration behaviors (1 to 3% of the session) were inadequately quantified even from 135-min samples. Increasing irregularity of bouts of behavior in the low-duration behaviors is suggested as the cause of the functions obtained. Implications of the findings for applied behavior analysis are discussed, with the recommendation that the adequacy of observational session durations be empirically assessed routinely.

DESCRIPTORS: behavioral assessment, behavioral observation, measurement error, time sample, mentally retarded adults

---

Assessment of performance by direct observational methods is one of the distinguishing characteristics of applied behavior analysis. In contrast to psychometric measurement devices, there is generally no need to argue that what is being measured represents the behaviors of interest. However, it has long been recognized that the quality of observational measurement needs to be thoroughly investigated. At issue are the effects of superimposing sampling methods on ongoing streams of behavior when the components cannot, for practical reasons, be measured continuously, with known accuracy, in all settings, and through the whole time of interest.

The effects of noncontinuous measurement by interval and time sampling methods have received considerable attention (e.g., Harrop & Daniels, 1986; Repp, Roberts, Slack, Repp, & Berkler, 1976). The accuracy of measurement, whether estimated directly or through inference from interobserver agreement, has been extensively studied (e.g., Boykin & Nelson, 1981). The differential results of behavior assessment across settings have been noted and recognized by behavior analysts using multiple baseline across settings designs (e.g., Odom, Hoyson, Jamieson, & Strain, 1985). Scant attention, however, has been given to the effect of observation session duration within a setting, although the issue has often been raised (e.g., Altmann, 1974; Goldfried, 1983; Hartmann, 1984; Wildman & Erickson, 1977).

Some studies relevant to the question of duration of observation have been performed by educational

---

Some of the data were presented to the Applied Behavior Analysis symposium at the conference of the New Zealand Psychological Society at Dunedin, New Zealand in August 1986.

We thank Jane Penney (Templeton Hospital) for assistance in the conduct of the study and Mike Owen (Auckland University) for producing the figures.

Reprint requests should be sent to Ivan L. Beale, Department of Psychology, University of Auckland, Auckland, New Zealand.

researchers (e.g., Karweit & Slavin, 1982; Rowley, 1978). Their approach has been to use psychometric concepts of generalizability to assess the stability of classroom behavior across samples, rather than the degree to which the sample represents the whole. This approach may be invalidated by unwarranted assumptions about the distributions of the behaviors sampled and by the failure to test for trend (Rogosa, Floden, & Willett, 1984). The generality of their findings is further restricted by the measurement of only frequency data using momentary time sampling.

The validity of observational samples with respect to longer time periods has been investigated in assessing the behaviors of psychiatric patients (Alevizos, DeRisi, Liberman, Eckman, & Callahan, 1978). This study evaluated the representativeness of data obtained from two 15-s observations per day against a criterion measure obtained from 15 such observations over 12 hr. However, the representativeness of the criterion data was not assessed against the whole time of interest (i.e., the waking hours of the day). Further, the validity of the recording method was not assessed against a continuous record, so possible invalidity due to recording confounds interpretation of their results.

The problem of selecting a duration for observation sessions has yet to be solved, although some recommendations have been made. For instance, Bijou, Peterson, Harris, Allen, and Johnston (1969) and Kazdin (1984) have suggested 1-hr observation periods. Only Johnston and Pennypacker (1980) appear to have suggested that all responses may have to be observed, at least temporarily, to assess empirically the representativeness of samples smaller than the whole time of interest. This recommendation can be seen as analogous to that of Sanson-Fisher, Poole, and Dunn (1980) that appropriate interval lengths for interval recording ought to be empirically determined by simulated sampling of real-time records of behavior.

The present study used trained observers to take real-time continuous records of behavior for the whole time of interest. These records served as criteria for comparison with computer-simulated sample sessions of varying duration drawn from the whole-session records. Subsequently, sample sessions of adequate length were subjected to computer-simulated momentary time sampling to provide an example of the compounding of errors produced by sample length and interobservation interval length.

METHOD

Subjects and Setting

Five profoundly mentally retarded adults were selected from a class of 10 attending a training program in a residential facility. Selection was based only on regularity of attendance. Ages ranged between 26 and 35 years, and length of stay in the institution varied from 6 to 28 years. All subjects had impaired mobility and used wheelchairs or other assistance to move.

The 3 training staff were teachers of people with severe and profound handicaps. Observations were made in the training area (14 m by 7 m) throughout morning and afternoon training sessions (8:30 to 11:00 a.m. and 1:00 to 3:30 p.m.). Residents were generally provided with training materials more suited to an educational curriculum than a functional curriculum (Reid et al., 1985). Morning and afternoon sessions differed in that residents sat at individual tables in the morning and around a large table in the afternoon. Staff were not aware of the purpose of the study.

Apparatus

A portable IBM personal computer (PC) was programmed in BASIC to record real-time observational data.

Observation Categories

An exhaustive and mutually exclusive set of categories was developed to describe subjects' behaviors (Sackett, 1978). Six categories were selected that had face validity for assessing the subjects' activities: social interaction with peer (SP); social interaction with staff (SS); handling materials provided (HM); self-propelled movement (SM); inappropriate behaviors, including stereotyped and self-injurious behaviors (I); and passive (P). (Detailed definitions may be obtained from the authors.)

Mutual exclusivity was obtained through the use of a priority coding system. The categories have been listed in order of priority. In practice, the effect of this system was to make the categories SM, HM, and P independent of staff assistance or social interaction. It had been observed before formal observation that inappropriate behavior was never concurrent with behavior categories higher in priority. A single-digit code was assigned to each category for input to the PC.

Observers

Five pairs of undergraduate students (who were enrolled in a third-year course in applied behavior analysis) and the first author acted as observers. Each pair of observers was assigned to 1 subject. The observers were trained in the training room and from videotapes until interobserver agreement, assessed by kappa, exceeded 0.75 in two 10-min sessions in the training room (Cohen, 1960; Hollenbeck, 1978).[1] Student observers were not informed of the purpose of the study.

Observation Procedure

Each subject was observed for one entire training day (i.e., the 5 hr spent in the training area, divided into two 2.5-hr sessions). Thus, in total, there were 10 150-min sessions recorded. Neither staff nor subject reactivity to observation was apparent. The training staff had been informed that the behaviors of individual staff members were not being assessed.

At session onset, the primary observer began entering behavior codes on the numeric keypad to the right of the PC keyboard. A printed list of codes was available during observations. Whenever the subject's behavior changed to that defined by a different category the observer entered a new code. Because categories were mutually exclusive, only the time of the start of a bout of behavior was stored in the PC's solid-state memory along with the code entered. These raw data were filed on disk at the end of the observation session for later analysis. Alphanumeric codes, which had been entered, were displayed on the PC screen to provide a visual check. When possible, primary observers alternated each half hour as a safeguard against fatigue. If, during observations, the subject became obscured from the primary observer, another observer followed the subject and hand-signaled changes in code.

Interobserver Agreement

Reliability of observations was assessed by comparing the records of two observers recording simultaneously. The second observer sat to the left of the primary observer and used letter codes to represent behavioral categories. Neither observer was informed of the codes used by the other, although the senior author/observer sometimes acted in either capacity. Observers were asked not to discuss coding during observations and were not heard to do so. Agreement checks were immediately terminated if the observers' view of the subject was obscured.

Interobserver agreement assessments were spaced throughout sessions and occupied between 26% and 34% of the training day for each subject. As the measure for agreement between observers, kappa was computed using the second-by-second algorithm detailed by Hollenbeck (1978). In 29 of the 30 checks, kappa exceeded the criterion value of 0.75. The mean value of kappa across observations was 0.89: No feedback was provided to observers on their levels of agreement.

RESULTS

The Whole-Session Records

The primary observer's record of each code was taken as a whole-session record. There were 60

[1] Kappa was used to quantify interobserver agreement because it appeared to be an acceptable coefficient of agreement for continuous observational records at the time of data collection (1985) (e.g., Sanson-Fisher et al., 1980). In hindsight, modifications of the well-known percentage agreement formulae may be seen as more appropriate indices of agreement between observers (MacLean, Tapp, & Johnson, 1985; Repp, Harman, Felce, Van Acker, & Karsh, 1989). Kappa by Hollenbeck's method and percentage agreement cannot be formally (i.e., mathematically) related.

such records: six codes and two records per subject. The absolute duration of behavior in sessions was computed by cumulating the time differences between onsets and offsets of a code. Relative durations of the code in each record were computed by transforming the absolute duration into the percentage of the 2.5-hr session. Across subjects and sessions the average percentage of time taken up with social interactions with peers was 3.0% (range, <0.1% to 11.1%); for social interaction with staff, 15.9% (8.8% to 30.8%); for handling materials, 28.8% (1.7% to 56.6%); for self-propelled movement, 5.9% (0.1% to 13.8%); for inappropriate behavior, 0.4% (0.0% to 1.1%); and for passive behavior, 46.0% (11.1% to 85.5%). Thirteen records having a relative duration of <0.7% were not analyzed further because they were considered appropriate only for event recording. These included eight of the 10 records for inappropriate behavior.

To summarize the basic parameters of behavior other than relative duration, the records were grouped according to relative duration; however the 10 records for SS were excluded because it was suspected that these were qualitatively different from the residents' records. For behaviors occurring in more than 50% of a record, the mean absolute frequency was 62, the mean absolute duration of a bout was 109 s (maximum 1,825 s), and the average interbout time (IBT) was 49 s (maximum 895 s). For behaviors occurring for between 10% and 25% of sessions, the mean frequency was 36, the mean duration was 32 s (maximum 325 s), and the mean IBT was 203 s (maximum 4,355 s). For the lowest relative duration group warranting further consideration (relative duration of 0.7% to 2.9%), the mean frequency was 11, mean duration was 17 s (maximum 175 s), and mean IBT was 509 s (maximum 4,785 s). This summary has not included behaviors that occurred between 3% and 10%, nor those between 25% and 50%, nor SS behaviors, but the trends in data generally were consistent with those data reported, showing that relative duration, frequency, and mean duration increased together while IBT decreased.

Sample Sessions

The whole-session records were sampled by computer to permit inspection of the relation between sample sessions of various durations and the whole-session (150-min) records. The duration of the sample sessions ranged from 15 to 135 min, increasing from the lower figure by 15-min increments. At each of the nine sample session durations, three types of systematic samples were taken: centered on the midpoint of the whole session; beginning at the start of the whole session; and ending at the termination of the whole session. Subsequently, for five sample durations (15, 45, 75, 105, and 135 min) five random starting points were generated. The randomness was constrained by the sample duration.

Comparisons Between Sample Sessions and the Whole-Session Records

The relative duration of each code per sample was calculated as previously described for comparison with the whole-session relative duration. A percentage similarity statistic was computed by dividing the smaller of each pair by the larger and multiplying by 100. The resulting values were subtracted from 100 to yield a percentage difference score, in which zero indicates complete agreement and larger values indicate lesser agreement. When a relative duration value of zero was obtained for a sample, the resulting percentage difference score was 100.

For both systematic and random samples, percentage difference scores were grouped according to relative duration in the whole sessions (as above) and the mean percentage difference calculated. Again the records for SS were treated separately. Only data from samples centered on the midpoint of a session are included here (in Figure 1) because values obtained from all three systematic starting points were similar.

The functions plotted in Figure 1 show clear trends, with difference scores decreasing with increasing sample duration. There is also a clear effect of the relative duration parameter. The functions

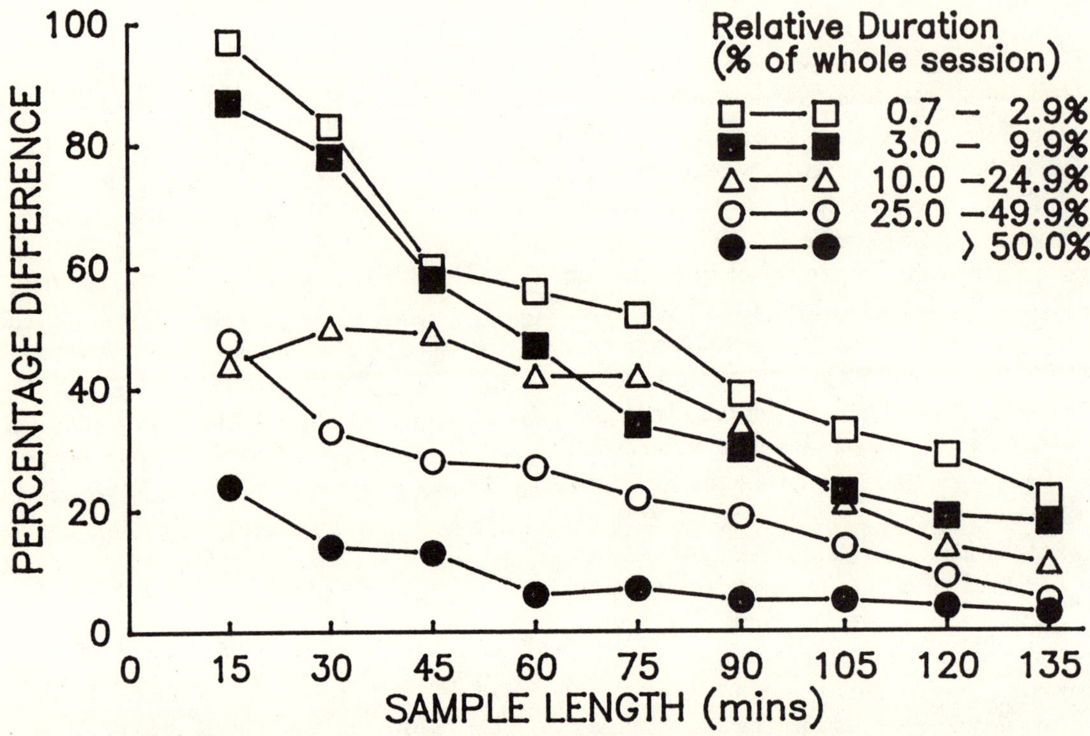

Figure 1. Percentage difference between relative duration from samples of increasing length and from the whole (150 min) sessions for subjects' codes grouped by whole-session relative duration. Samples were centered on the midpoint of the session.

tend to be vertically separated, percentage difference increasing with relative duration. There appears to be an interaction between relative duration and sample length, because values for the five relative duration groups differ more at short than at long sample durations.

Our next step was to explore the generality of the obtained effects of duration and session length across measures of difference. The random sample data were reanalyzed using a percentage error measure of correspondence between sample and whole-session records (Rojahn & Kanoy, 1985). This was computed by subtracting the sample value for relative duration from the whole-session value, dividing by the whole-session value, and multiplying by 100. Values of percentage error can range from +100% when the relative duration in the sample is zero to very large negative values when the sample provides a gross overestimate. The obtained values for percentage difference and percentage error are plotted in Figure 2. To facilitate comparison between the measures, the sign of the error score was made positive before averaging. Thus, only the magnitude, and not the direction, of the error is considered. Clearly, considering Figure 2, percentage error shows the same effects of relative duration and sample length revealed by the percentage dif-

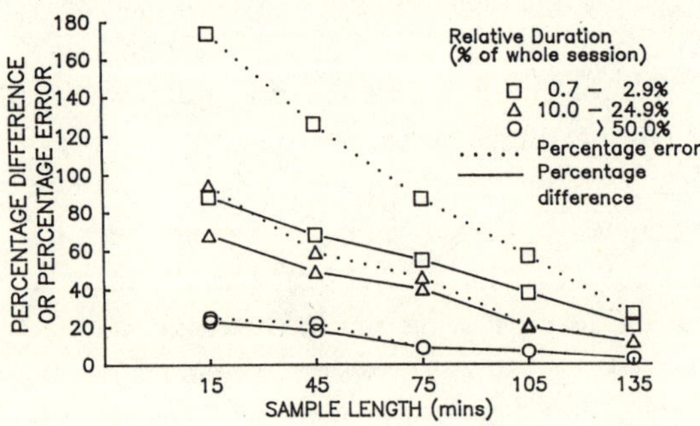

Figure 2. A comparison of the percentage difference and percentage error measures for groups of subjects' codes with low, moderate, and high relative durations.

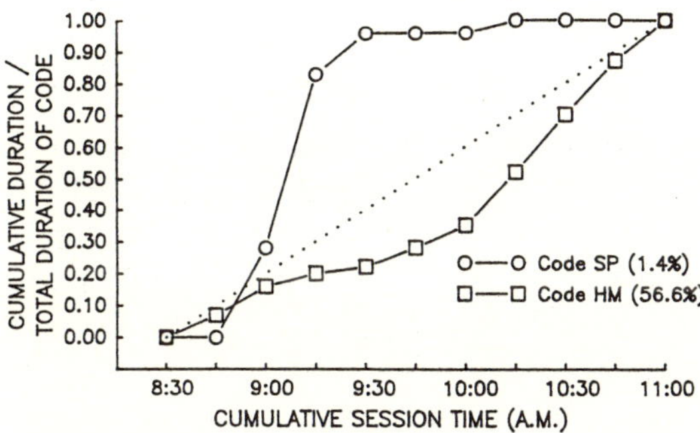

Figure 3. Cumulative duration/total duration for a high relative duration code (HM) and a low relative duration code (SP) from a morning session (8:30 to 11:00 a.m.). Proportion of code duration recorded is plotted against cumulative session time.

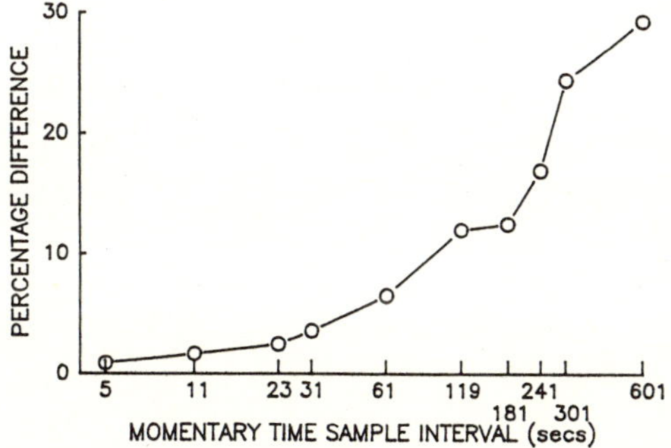

Figure 4. Percentage difference between real relative duration and relative duration derived from simulated momentary time samples of increasing interobservation intervals (seconds, logarithmic scale). Passive behavior was measured from three randomly selected hours in each session. Each data point represents the mean of 30 measures.

ference scores. However, both main effects and the interaction are magnified by the error measure.

In order that an explanation of the effects obtained may be offered, an analysis was made of the distributions of high and low relative duration behaviors in one observational session. The absolute duration of a high relative duration code (HM; relative duration = 56.6%) and of a low relative duration code (SP; 1.4%) was calculated in 15-min blocks throughout the session. Absolute durations were cumulated across successive blocks and divided by the total absolute duration of codes for that session. This produced a measure of cumulative duration as a proportion of total duration, which was plotted against cumulative session duration in Figure 3.

The dotted diagonal line in Figure 3 represents the theoretical cumulative function for a code, the occurrence of which is uniformly distributed across successive 15-min blocks of session time. Samples as small as a single block would accurately represent the relative duration of that code over the whole session. The low duration code occurs mainly between 8:45 and 9:30 a.m. Samples taken within that period would greatly overestimate the whole-session duration, and samples taken outside that period would grossly underestimate it. The high duration code is more uniformly distributed, however, and generally remains closer to the diagonal. Samples of the whole-session record of this code would generally be more representative than would samples of the low relative duration code.

A further analysis was conducted to explore the implications of these results for sampling methods not involving real-time recording. Momentary time sampling (MTS) was chosen because it is considered the least biased method for estimating duration (e.g., Harrop & Daniels, 1986) and is probably less demanding on the observer than most alternatives. Three randomly selected 60-min segments from some whole-session records were sampled by a computer program simulating MTS at intervals from 5 s to 601 s. Percentage difference between obtained MTS data and the real-time data for duration within the segment was computed for relative durations of the code for passive behavior, which had the highest average relative duration across sessions and subjects at 46%. The resulting function is plotted in Figure 4 and shows that difference scores increase with increasing intervals between observations. If up to 25% difference is taken as an acceptable level of representativeness, it can be seen that an observation every 301 s is sufficient for assessment of the duration of the behavior in that hour. If less than 20% difference is desired, this can be achieved by one observation every 241 s.

DISCUSSION

This study investigated the representativeness of data obtained from observational samples with durations shorter than the whole time of interest (2.5

hr). It was found that increasing sample duration produced reduced error or difference when relative durations obtained from the samples were compared with relative durations across the whole time of interest. Generally, at any given sample length, behaviors of greater relative duration were sampled in a more representative fashion than those of smaller relative duration. Data summarizing the basic parameters of the behaviors suggest that these results could be explained by examining the distribution of behaviors across the whole times of interest. Increased relative duration was accompanied by increased frequency of bouts of the behavior, increased average duration of bouts, and decreased average IBTs. Further, obtained maximum values of the parameters exceeded the means by a factor of 10 to 20.

Such results might be predicted by rational analysis of the effects of sampling when events are irregular in their distribution across time. Successful prediction could also have been achieved from study of the results of analogous studies investigating interval or time sampling within observation sessions. For example, Green and Alverson (1978) determined that bias in recording at a given interval length was related to mean duration of behavior and mean IBT. In other words, with the obtained uneven distributions (e.g., in Figure 3) the obtained effects on representativeness were to be expected. Without prior data, however, the actual distributions of behaviors through the whole time of interest cannot be predicted, nor can appropriate values for parameters be chosen for computer-generated pseudobehaviors (e.g., Green & Alverson, 1978; Rojahn & Kanoy, 1985).

Less predictable are the findings regarding the *absolute* degree of error in the sample sessions of shorter duration. If, for example, 20% error is taken as the maximum acceptable, samples of at least 105-min duration were required for behaviors occurring only for 10% to 25% of the whole session. On the other hand, samples of only 30 min were adequately representative for behaviors taking up over 50% of the session. Thus, there is no support for the recommendation of a standard 60-min observation session (Bijou et al., 1969; Kazdin, 1984), even when the total time of interest is as little as 2.5 hr. The alternative recommendation of Johnston and Pennypacker (1980), that adequate observation session length ought to be empirically determined through exhaustive observation, has been strengthened. This parallels the findings of Sanson-Fisher et al. (1980) concerning the selection of an appropriate interval size for partial interval recording.

There are some limited cases to which this general recommendation does not apply (e.g., when the regularity of behavior can be known a priori). For example, in observations of a teacher or other behavior change agent performing according to predetermined schedules of prompting and reinforcement with unvarying durations and IBTs, observation of as little as one cycle of events may be representative of the whole series.

When speculating on the generality of the levels of absolute error, the characteristics of the present subjects, settings, and measurement system need to be considered. These observations were of nonambulatory profoundly retarded adults in a training setting that could best be described as archaic (Reid et al., 1985). If the training staff had been teaching their clients chronological age-appropriate functional skills such as self-propelled movement and social interactions with peers, the parameters of behaviors may have been quite different. However, baseline settings and levels of behaviors such as those described may not be infrequent. The use of mutually exclusive categories of behaviors in the present study may suggest a source of lack of generality, in that behaviors lower in priority were recorded only if higher priority behaviors were not co-occurring. This could result in the underestimation of the relative durations of the lower priority behaviors, with the concurrent effects of increasing IBTs, reducing bout durations, and reducing representativeness of small samples. Although no data were collected to counteract this criticism, it was informally observed that the effects of priority coding were as anticipated and described in the method section. In other words, the face validity of the recording system was not reduced by the method of formal observations.

An aspect of the measurement method used that may have implications for both internal and external validity of the study is the interobserver agreement assessment procedure. The observers were seated side by side, which strongly suggests a lack of independence (Kazdin, 1977). Even though they used different codes for behaviors and the behaviors were explicitly defined, the high levels of agreement obtained (as estimated by kappa) could have been due to observers cuing one another by key pressing rather than to the relatively easy job they had distinguishing behavior changes. In retrospect, it would have been preferable to produce an accurate criterion record of behavior as the whole-session record to be sampled (Johnston & Pennypacker, 1980).

The problem of error produced by the method of sampling within sessions is illustrated in Figure 4. In that case a sample-length error of up to about 20% was present before MTS was imposed on the session. If an acceptable MTS error of 20% was also present, these two errors compound to produce a 44% error if the sign of the error was the same. That magnitude would probably not be acceptable. Further compounding of error may be produced by observer error although, unless an accurate criterion record was produced for comparison, the result could not be combined mathematically with the other sources of error.

In summary, this study shows that, except in some special cases, the representativeness of observation sessions with respect to the whole time of interest should be empirically assessed. The absolute levels of error in sample sessions will differ across subjects, settings, and behavioral recording systems. Consideration should be given to the compounding effects of error produced by observers, method, and session duration.

REFERENCES

Alevizos, P., DeRisi, W., Liberman, R., Eckman, T., & Callahan, E. (1978). The behavior observation instrument: A method for program evaluation. *Journal of Applied Behavior Analysis*, **11**, 243–257.

Altmann, J. (1974). Observational study of behaviour: Sampling methods. *Behaviour*, **49**, 227–267.

Bijou, S. W., Peterson, R. F., Harris, F. K., Allen, E., & Johnston, M. S. (1969). Methodology for experimental studies of young children in natural settings. *Psychological Record*, **19**, 143–150.

Boykin, R. A., & Nelson, R. O. (1981). The effects of instructions and calculation procedures on observers' accuracy, agreement, and calculation correctness. *Journal of Applied Behavior Analysis*, **14**, 479–489.

Cohen, J. (1960). A coefficient of agreement for nominal scales. *Educational and Psychological Measurement*, **20**, 37–46.

Goldfried, M. R. (1983). Behavioral assessment. In I. B. Weiner (Ed.), *Clinical methods in psychology* (2nd ed., pp. 233–281). New York: Wiley.

Green, S. B., & Alverson, L. G. (1978). A comparison of indirect measures for long duration behaviors. *Journal of Applied Behavior Analysis*, **11**, 530.

Harrop, A., & Daniels, M. (1986). Methods of time sampling: A reappraisal of momentary time sampling and partial interval recording. *Journal of Applied Behavior Analysis*, **19**, 73–77.

Hartmann, D. P. (1984). Assessment strategies. In D. H. Barlow & M. Hersen (Eds.), *Single case experimental design: Strategies for studying behavior change* (2nd ed., pp. 107–139). New York: Pergamon.

Hollenbeck, A. R. (1978). Problems of reliability in observational research. In G. P. Sackett (Ed.), *Observing behavior: Vol. 2. Data collection and analysis methods* (pp. 79–98). Baltimore, MD: University Park Press.

Johnston, J. M., & Pennypacker, H. S. (1980). *Strategies and tactics of human behavioral research.* Hillsdale, NJ: Erlbaum.

Karweit, N., & Slavin, R. E. (1982). Time-on-task: Issues of timing, sampling, and definition. *Journal of Educational Psychology*, **74**, 844–851.

Kazdin, A. E. (1977). Artifact, bias, and complexity: The ABCs of reliability. *Journal of Applied Behavior Analysis*, **10**, 141–150.

Kazdin, A. E. (1984). *Behavior modification in applied settings* (3rd ed.). Homewood, IL: Dorsey.

MacLean, W. E., Tapp, J. T., & Johnson, W. L. (1985). Alternate methods and software for calculating interobserver agreement for continuous observation data. *Journal of Psychopathology and Behavioral Assessment*, **7**, 65–73.

Odom, S. L., Hoyson, M., Jamieson, B., & Strain, P. S. (1985). Increasing handicapped preschoolers' peer social interactions: Cross-setting and component analysis. *Journal of Applied Behavior Analysis*, **18**, 3–16.

Reid, D. H., Parsons, M. B., McCarn, J. E., Green, C. W., Phillips, J. F., & Schepis, M. M. (1985). Providing a more appropriate education for severely handicapped persons: Increasing and validating functional classroom tasks. *Journal of Applied Behavior Analysis*, **18**, 289–301.

Repp, A. C., Harman, M. L., Felce, D., Van Acker, R., & Karsh, K. G. (1989). Conducting behavioral assessments on computer-collected data. *Behavioral Assessment*, **11**, 249–268.

Repp, A. C., Roberts, D. M., Slack, D. J., Repp, C. F., & Berkler, M. S. (1976). A comparison of frequency, interval, and time-sampling methods of data collection. *Journal of Applied Behavior Analysis*, **9**, 501–508.

Rogosa, D., Floden, R., & Willett, J. B. (1984). Assessing

the stability of teacher behavior. *Journal of Educational Psychology,* **76,** 1000–1027.

Rojahn, J., & Kanoy, R. C. (1985). Toward an empirically based parameter selection for time-sampling systems. *Journal of Psychopathology and Behavioral Assessment,* **7,** 99–120.

Rowley, G. L. (1978). The relationship of reliability in classroom research to the amount of observation: An extension of the Spearman-Brown formula. *Journal of Educational Measurement,* **15,** 165–180.

Sackett, G. P. (1978). Measurement in observational research. In G. P. Sackett (Ed.), *Observing behavior: Vol. 2. Data collection and analysis methods* (pp. 25–43). Baltimore, MD: University Park Press.

Sanson-Fisher, R. W., Poole, A. D., & Dunn, J. (1980). An empirical method for determining an appropriate interval length for recording behavior. *Journal of Applied Behavior Analysis,* **13,** 493–500.

Wildman, B. G., & Erickson, M. T. (1977). Methodological problems in behavioral observation. In J. D. Cone & R. P. Hawkins (Eds.), *Behavioral assessment* (pp. 255–273). New York: Brunner/Mazel.

Received October 19, 1988
Initial editorial decision February 23, 1989
Revisions received November 3, 1989; December 15, 1989
Final acceptance April 18, 1990
Action Editor, Terry J. Page

JOURNAL OF APPLIED BEHAVIOR ANALYSIS 1990, 23, 533–537 NUMBER 4 (WINTER 1990)

MOMENTARY TIME SAMPLING AS AN ESTIMATE OF PERCENTAGE TIME: A FIELD VALIDATION

RICHARD A. SAUDARGAS AND KATHLEEN ZANOLLI

UNIVERSITY OF TENNESSEE–KNOXVILLE

This study examined the percentage time estimates of momentary time sampling against the real time obtained with handheld computers in a natural setting. Twenty-two concurrent observations were conducted in elementary schools by one observer who used 15-s momentary time sampling and a second who used a handheld computer. Results for the six behaviors showed a close correspondence between the momentary time sampling percentage observation intervals and the real time percentage observation time, although 15-s momentary time sampling tended not to sample low-frequency short-duration behaviors. The results confirmed laboratory findings that short-interval momentary time sampling estimates percentage time accurately for a wide range of behavior frequencies and durations, and suggested that observers using momentary time sampling in a natural setting are able to obtain accurate data.

DESCRIPTORS: time sample, methodology, naturalistic observations

One of the most common measures of behavior is an estimate of the percentage of time a person engages in a behavior. The usual method of obtaining an estimate of this measure is to use some form of time sampling. Time sampling involves dividing time into discrete units and then coding the occurrence or nonoccurrence of behaviors within the defined time units. Two commonly used time sampling schemes are partial interval (PI) and momentary time sampling (MTS). Both PI and MTS involve dividing time into blocks of seconds and then coding the occurrence or nonoccurrence of behaviors based on a decision rule. The decision rule for PI is that a behavior will be coded if the behavior occurs at least once within the time block. The decision rule for MTS is that a behavior will be coded if it is occurring at the moment the time the block ends (or begins). In neither PI nor MTS is the frequency or duration of behavior within a time block considered. Conceptual and empirical articles examining PI and MTS have typically concluded that PI overestimates percentage time of behavior whereas MTS gives a reasonably accurate estimate of percentage time when brief intervals (30 s or less) are used (e.g., Powell, Martindale, Kulp, Martindale, & Bauman, 1977; Tyler, 1979). Two additional conclusions have been reached about MTS (Ary, 1984). First, the higher frequency of state changes, the greater the difference between the actual percentage of time and the MTS estimate. Second, MTS is equally likely to underestimate or overestimate the percentage of time a behavior occurs.

The conclusion that MTS is superior to PI in providing an accurate estimate of percentage time has been reached using computer simulation and laboratory videotapes of actual behaviors (e.g., Green & Alverson, 1978; McDowell, 1973; Powell, 1984; Powell et al., 1977; Tyler, 1979). In computer simulation research, behaviors of systematically varying rates and durations are programmed, whereas in videotape research, the behaviors are measured in real time. Both the computer simulation and the videotape studies then overlay PI and MTS of varying interval blocks onto the real time measures and make comparisons between the percentage of real time and the estimates obtained from PI and MTS.

Because MTS is accurate in laboratory settings, a next logical step is to make direct comparisons between a measure of real time and MTS with trained observers in a natural setting. Making such comparisons would answer two questions: (a) whether MTS accurately estimates percentage time

Correspondence and reprint requests should be sent to Richard Saudargas, Psychology Department, University of Tennessee, Knoxville, Tennessee 37996.

across a wide range of behavior frequencies and durations as they occur naturally in time and (b) whether trained observers can accurately record data using MTS in a single observation pass as is done in applied studies in the natural environment. Recent developments in computer technology have made such a comparison possible. This study examined the percentage time estimates of MTS obtained on a multibehavior observation code against the real percentage time obtained with handheld computers.

METHOD

Subjects and Setting

Sixteen elementary school children were observed (2 first graders, 1 second grader, 5 third graders, and 8 fourth graders). The students, from eight classrooms in six elementary schools, were observed while they engaged in independent activities that consisted of completing workbook pages, ditto sheets, and boardwork. The teachers conducted reading groups during this time. Observations occurred over 2 months.

State-Event Classroom Observation System

Observations were conducted using the State-Event Classroom Observation System (SECOS) (Saudargas & Fellers, 1986; Saudargas & Lentz, 1986). SECOS is a multibehavior observation system designed for use in classroom research and for assessments of handicapped children, and contains six state behaviors and 12 event behaviors. State behaviors are those of varying durations; the measure of interest is an estimate of the percentage of the observation time the state behavior occurred. Event behaviors have brief durations of approximately equal length; the measure of interest is frequency or rate of occurrence (Altman, 1974; Saudargas & Lentz, 1986). Research has shown that the behaviors observed with SECOS can differentiate among learning disabled children (Fellers & Saudargas, 1987; Slate & Saudargas, 1986a), seriously emotionally disturbed children (Slate & Saudargas, 1986b), gifted children (Fellers & Saudargas, 1988), and normal children at different grade levels (Saudargas & Zanolli, 1989).

The six state behaviors on SECOS for which percentage observation time is of interest were analyzed for this study: *schoolwork,* defined as the child attending to academic assignments; *looking,* defined as the child looking away from the academic assignment; *other activity,* defined as the child involved with objects or materials not part of the academic assignment such as sharpening pencils, getting out or putting away materials, and playing with toys; *child interaction,* defined as the child interacting with a peer; *teacher interaction,* defined as the child interacting with the classroom teacher; and *out of seat,* defined as the child's buttocks being off a chair. All the behaviors were mutually exclusive with the exception of out of seat (i.e., the child could engage in the other five behaviors while in seat or out of seat).

There are two versions of SECOS. The paper and pencil version (SECOS-MTS) uses 15-s MTS to estimate percentage observation time on the six state behaviors, and frequency counts are made on the 12 event behaviors. The coding procedure consists of combining MTS with frequency counting. At the beginning of each 15-s interval, the observer codes the occurrence or nonoccurrence of the six state behaviors. During the remaining time of the 15-s interval, the observer codes the frequency of the event behaviors as they occur. To obtain the percentage of intervals in which a state behavior occurred, the number of intervals a state behavior was coded is divided by the total number of intervals observed and multiplied by 100. The rate of each event behavior is obtained by dividing the frequency by the observation time.

On the handheld computer version (SECOS-C), the 18 SECOS behaviors are recorded on a Hewlett-Packard HP71-B handheld computer, which keeps track of real time and frequencies for all behaviors (Saudargas & Bunn, 1989). When a behavior occurs, the observer presses a computer key corresponding to the behavior. After an observation, the handheld computer data are transferred to a personal computer for data analyses. The percentage of observation time for each state behavior is obtained by dividing the total time the behavior occurred by the total observation time and multiplying by 100. Behavior rates are obtained by dividing the frequency of each behavior by the total observation time.

Observation Procedures

The observers were two graduate students trained in the use of SECOS. One conducted the observations using the SECOS-MTS, and the second used the SECOS-C. The observers entered each classroom during independent seatwork and conducted the observation. To facilitate communication about when to begin and end the observation, the observers stood next to each other while conducting the observation. The two observation methods are so different that the possibility of the observers cueing each other regarding occurrences and nonoccurrences of behavior was remote. To be certain that the observers began and ended each observation at exactly the same time, the SECOS-MTS observer signaled the beginning of the first observation interval and the end of the last observation interval. Each observation period lasted for 20 consecutive min. Two children were observed three times each, 2 children were observed twice each, and the remaining 12 children were observed once each.

Interobserver agreement had been obtained on the SECOS-MTS and SECOS-C for each observer on training videotapes and in ongoing field research at the time this study was conducted. Separate interobserver agreement was not obtained for this study because of the practical problems of having a third or fourth observer in the classroom. However, interobserver agreement data for each observer with observers in other studies were as follows: For the SECOS-MTS observer, interobserver agreement averaged for the six behaviors was 86% and ranged from 78% to 94% (agreements divided by agreements plus disagreements). For the SECOS-C observer, interobserver agreement averaged over the six behaviors was 83% and ranged from 72% to 91%.

RESULTS

The observation session comparison between percentage observation time for the computer data and the percentage observation intervals for each of the six behaviors is presented in Figure 1. Overall, the correspondence was very close between MTS percentage of intervals and the real time percentage obtained by the computers. In four of the 22 observations (Observations 4, 11, 14, 16), discrepancies of 9% or greater were obtained in the schoolwork category, and relatively large differences were also obtained for these same observations in the looking category.

One important outcome was the tendency for 15-s MTS not to detect behaviors that occurred for a very low percentage of time. During observations in which the computer observer coded a small amount of time for a behavior, the MTS observer often did not record the behavior at all. This pattern was especially noticeable for teacher interactions that tended to occur infrequently and for short durations. Teacher interactions were not scored by the MTS observer during 13 observations, but during 11 of these 13 observations, the computer observer coded some, albeit brief, teacher interactions.

DISCUSSION

The results of this field study confirmed the laboratory finding that 15-s MTS closely approximates actual percentage of time across a range of naturally occurring behaviors. The results suggest that trained observers using MTS in a multicategory observation system will obtain accurate data in the single observation pass available to them in field settings. Because we were interested in the accuracy of the SECOS (which uses 15-s MTS), no other time sampling intervals were selected for comparison. It is likely that longer MTS intervals would have replicated previous laboratory work showing that increasing MTS interval length increased error (Powell, 1984; Powell et al., 1977).

Although the data obtained from each method were very similar, measurement error occurred. During a few observations, relatively large differences between MTS and the computer were noted on the schoolwork category, with a corresponding opposite difference in the looking category. These discrepancies may have occurred because of observer disagreements about the category in which to code a behavior. Even though the observers were

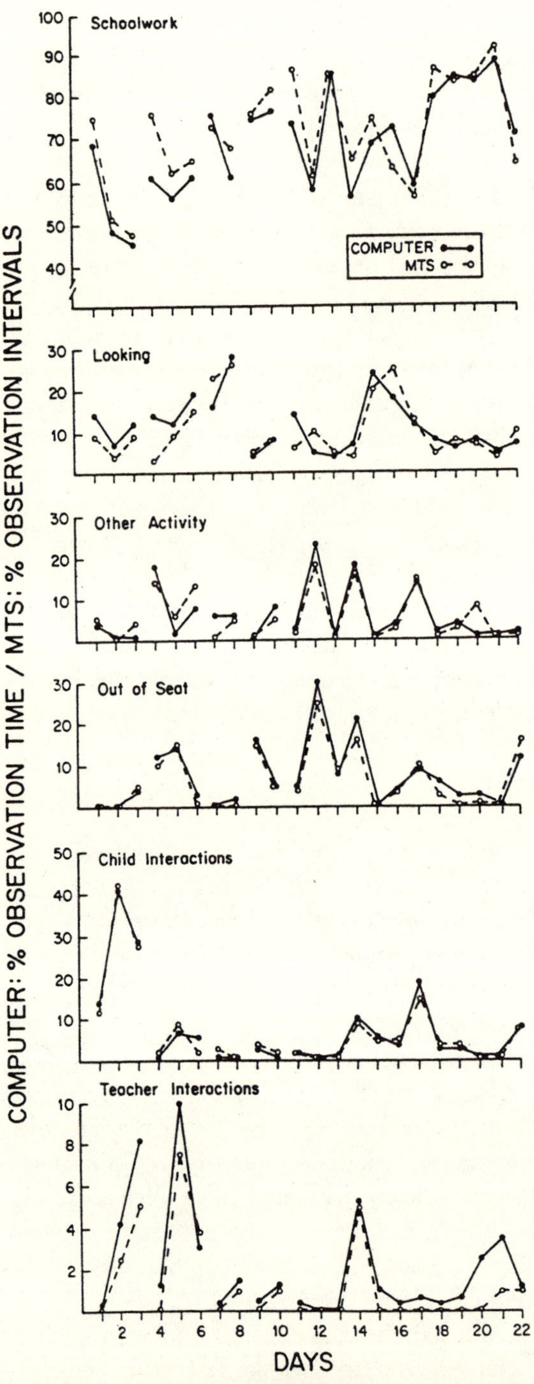

Figure 1. The 15-s MTS observation intervals and the computer percentage observation time for the six behaviors. Three observations were conducted on Student 1, three on Student 2, two each on Students 3 and 4, and one each on the remaining students. The data points are connected with lines to make the relationships easier to see. The data are plotted in the order in which they were obtained.

highly trained and had excellent reliability in other studies, obtaining interobserver agreement for this study might have helped to explain the differences. These differences also may have occurred because the frequency of state changes was higher during these observations (Ary, 1984). That is, the students alternated between attending to their schoolwork and looking at high rates. Although the computer would code these state changes and the resultant time accurately, MTS might not.

The finding that 15-s MTS tended not to detect short-duration behaviors is important if those behaviors are of interest and percentage observation time is the response dimension of interest. One way to increase the probability that important, yet infrequent, behaviors with very short durations are sampled would be to use a PI coding scheme in which the occurrence or nonoccurrence of the behavior at any time during the interval is coded. Such a strategy has been widely used in applied behavioral research. However, the use of PI time sampling systems is unacceptable, in our view, because they yield data that do not correspond with real behavior frequencies or durations (e.g., Powell, 1984). Although it may be possible to score the occurrences of low-frequency and short-duration behaviors with a PI time sampling system, the resultant data would be inaccurate and conclusions drawn from such data might be incorrect.

A more acceptable alternative for sampling short-duration behaviors would be to shorten the MTS interval. In the present study, a 5-s MTS interval might have detected the behaviors not sampled by the longer 15-s interval. Of course, a very brief interval might decrease the number of behaviors that could be coded reliably by a human observer using paper and pencil procedures. Nevertheless, it would be better to record fewer behaviors using MTS, because the percentage time data would be more accurate and the resulting conclusions would be more justifiable and replicable.

REFERENCES

Altman, J. (1974). Observational study of behavior sampling methods. *Behaviour*, **49**, 227–267.

Ary, D. (1984). Mathematical explanation of error in duration recording using partial interval, whole interval, and momentary time sampling. *Behavioral Assessment,* **6,** 221–228.

Fellers, G., & Saudargas, R. A. (1987). An analysis of the classroom behaviors of learning disabled and non-handicapped girls. *Learning Disability Quarterly,* **10,** 231–236.

Fellers, G., & Saudargas, R. A. (1988, April). *Classroom behavior of gifted elementary school children.* Paper presented at National Association of School Psychologists Convention, Chicago.

Green, S. B., & Alverson, L. G. (1978). A comparison of indirect measures for long-duration behaviors. *Journal of Applied Behavior Analysis,* **11,** 530.

McDowell, E. (1973). Comparison of time-sampling and continuous recording techniques for observing developmental changes in caretaker and infant behaviors. *The Journal of Genetic Psychology,* **123,** 99–105.

Powell, J. (1984). On the misrepresentation of behavioral realities by a widely practiced direct observation procedure: Partial interval (one-zero) sampling. *Behavioral Assessment,* **6,** 209–219.

Powell, J., Martindale, B., Kulp, S., Martindale, A., & Bauman, R. (1977). Taking a closer look: Time sampling and measurement error. *Journal of Applied Behavior Analysis,* **10,** 325–332.

Saudargas, R. A., & Bunn, R. D. (1989). A handheld computer system for classroom observation. *Journal of Special Education Technology,* **9,** 200–206.

Saudargas, R. A., & Fellers, G. (1986). *State-event classroom observation system (SECOS).* Unpublished manuscript, University of Tennessee, Knoxville.

Saudargas, R. A., & Lentz, F. E. (1986). Estimating percent of time and rate via direct observation: A suggested observational procedure and format. *School Psychology Review,* **15,** 36–48.

Saudargas, R. A., & Zanolli, K. (1989). *Classroom behavior during individual seatwork.* Manuscript submitted for publication.

Slate, J. R., & Saudargas, R. A. (1986a). Differences in classroom behaviors of learning disabled and average children. *Learning Disability Quarterly,* **9,** 61–68.

Slate, J. R., & Saudargas, R. A. (1986b, November). Differences in the classroom behaviors of behaviorally disordered and regular class children. *Behavior Disorders,* 45–53.

Tyler, S. (1979). Time sampling: A matter of convention. *Animal Behavior,* **27,** 801–810.

Received March 7, 1989
Initial editorial decision September 30, 1989
Revisions received December 20, 1989; June 29, 1990
Final acceptance August 28, 1990
Action Editor, Terry J. Page

JOURNAL OF APPLIED BEHAVIOR ANALYSIS 1998, **31,** 253–261 NUMBER 2 (SUMMER 1998)

COMPUTERIZED SYSTEMS FOR COLLECTING REAL-TIME OBSERVATIONAL DATA

SUNGWOO KAHNG AND BRIAN A. IWATA

THE UNIVERSITY OF FLORIDA

Advances in computer technology have led to the development of a number of semiautomated systems for collecting real-time observational data. We conducted a survey of 15 developers of computerized systems and summarized the features of each system. Many of these systems have incorporated laptop or handheld computers as well as bar-code scanners. Most systems used IBM-compatible (DOS or Windows) software, although a few were designed for either the MacOS or some other operating system. The range in prices started from free to more complete systems costing over $1,500. Data analysis programs were included with most programs; however, only about a third of the systems included a program to compute interobserver agreement.

DESCRIPTORS: computerized observation, data collection, data analysis, observation systems

---

Recent technological advances have led to a proliferation of computer applications in behavioral research (see Farrell, 1991, for a review). One area of particular interest to applied behavior analysts has been the development of semiautomated systems for collecting real-time observational data. These systems have the potential to facilitate the task of observation by improving the reliability and accuracy of recording relative to traditional but cumbersome methods based on paper and pencil, and to improve the efficiency of data calculation and graphing (Donát, 1991; Eiler, Nelson, Jensen, & Johnson, 1989). Thus, the use of computers for both recording and analyzing data has become increasingly important in clinical work as well as in research.

As the technology continues to improve, these systems have incorporated more advanced features while becoming increasingly user friendly. Unfortunately, information about available options is not widely accessible and is shared primarily through informal networks. Therefore, we conducted a survey of developers of computerized real-time observation systems. Fifteen developers responded to an initial request for information published in the *Journal of Applied Behavior Analysis* and subsequently completed more detailed surveys, the results of which are summarized in this report. A critical review of the systems, which would require comparisons under a number of different but standardized situations, was beyond the scope of this report. Therefore, our intent was merely to describe the key characteristics of each system, as reported by its developer. All summaries are presented in alphabetical order. A table listing the major features of each system, along with information for obtaining additional information, is presented in the Appendix. We recommend that potential users compare features and costs for systems having similar capabilities, contact several developers for more complete descriptions of their current systems, and query colleagues who use these specific systems or similar ones.

Behavioral Evaluation Strategy and Taxonomy (BEST)

BEST allows the user to record up to 36 different responses during a session. It has

Reprints may be obtained from Brian Iwata, Psychology Department, The University of Florida, Gainesville, Florida 32611.

the capability to record response frequency, duration, intervals (variable duration), time samples, latency, interresponse time (IRT), and discrete trials. A text feature allows the recording of notes for unique or atypical event occurrences. In addition, a pause feature permits the interruption of observation sessions if the need arises, and entry errors made while recording can be edited.

The data analysis program gives the user the option of calculating response frequency (total number and rate), duration, latency, IRT, percentage of intervals, percentage of trials, and conditional probabilities. The user can also define subgroups that contain various combinations of responses (A or B, A and B). BEST has the option to calculate central tendencies (mean and median), variability (range and frequency distribution), and statistical significance (*z* score transformations). A reliability program allows the comparison of interobserver agreement (overall agreement and kappa). BEST also has the option to create frequency, duration, rate, and percentage charts; percentage pie charts; and multiple behavior temporal graphs. In addition, the data and graphs can be exported to commercial graphics applications (e.g., Windows Paint, Delta Graph, etc.).

BEST requires an IBM-compatible personal computer (PC) with a minimum 386 processor running DOS or Windows. It has minimal RAM and hard disk requirements. Demonstration copies are available upon request for 90 to 120 days. Individual purchase of the software costs $750. Institutional purchases (i.e., site license), which include multiple copies of the software and a guarantee of free upgrades, are available for $1,250. Included with the package are instruction manuals and technical support.

Behavior Observer System (BOS)

BOS uses handheld computers (Apple Newton or US Robotic Pilot) to record behavioral data by touching "buttons" created on the screens. The user can access templates (i.e., code sets) already created for a number of observational contexts. Furthermore, the user can customize the templates or create new templates by choosing from a list of behaviors provided by the system or by writing directly on the buttons. These templates allow the recording of up to 24 different responses during a session. With BOS, the user can record response frequency, duration, intervals (minimum 3 s), time samples, latency, IRT, and discrete trials.

The data analysis option of BOS has the capability to calculate response frequency (total number and rate), duration, latency, IRT, percentage of intervals, and percentage of trials, using the handheld computer. The user can also define subgroups that contain various combinations of responses (A or B, A and B) for further analysis. Interobserver agreement (overall, occurrence, and nonoccurrence agreement) can be calculated when using Apple Newton handheld computers by linking them via their infrared data transfer systems. The raw data, as well as session and reliability statistics, can be downloaded to a MacOS or Windows-based PC for storage or further manipulation by spreadsheets, graphing programs, data bases, or statistical software.

BOS requires an Apple Newton or US Robotic Pilot handheld computer with at least 2 megabytes (MB) of RAM. The cost of the software alone is $199. However, Psychsoft offers grants of free software to students and faculty who wish to use the system at their academic institutions. Included with the purchase price are an instruction manual and technical support.

DATACAP, HARCLAG, HARCREL

DATACAP is software for real-time recording of observational data on Psion Series 3 or Workabout handheld computers. It allows recording of up to 40 different responses using frequency or duration measures. The data are saved as ASCII files for uploading to IBM-compatible PCs for storage or further analysis.

HARCLAG is a DOS-based program that can also run under Windows. It has the capability to calculate response frequency (total number and rate), duration, latency, IRT, and conditional probabilities. In addition, it has the capability to calculate cumulative frequency distributions as well as time-based lag sequential analyses. The user can also define subgroups that contain various combinations of responses (A or B, A and B) for further analysis. A Windows-based reliability program, HARCREL, permits the calculation of interobserver agreement (overall, occurrence, and nonoccurrence agreement as well as kappa).

Both HARCLAG and HARCREL have minimal memory requirements and require an IBM-compatible PC with a minimum 386 processor. All software is free and includes an instruction manual.

Data Collection Assistant (DCA)

DCA uses TimeWand I (TWI) or DuraTrax (DT) bar-code scanners to collect real-time data. Data can be recorded as frequency, duration, and discrete trials for an infinite number of different responses (over 2 million). In addition, the observer can use DCA to collect Likert scale data, prompt sequences, and yes-no entries. Customized templates can be created to facilitate data collection. Entry errors made while recording can be edited.

The data analysis option allows the user to calculate response frequency (total number and rate), duration, and percentage of trials. The user can also graph the data and identify central tendencies (mean and median) as well as determine the range and frequency distribution. The user can also annotate data collection and graphs with relevant comments.

DCA requires an IBM-compatible PC (Windows) with at least a 486/33 processor, 8 MB of RAM, and 8 to 10 MB of hard disk space. The costs of the TWI and DT scanners are $348 per unit and $625 per unit, respectively. An instruction manual and technical support are included with the package.

Direct Observation Data System (DODS)

Using separate programs, DODS has the capability of capturing frequency, duration, interval (variable duration), time sample, latency, and antecedent-behavior-consequences (ABC) data for three different responses. In addition, it can aid in the selection of data collection measures as well as interpreting student progress, refining an intervention, and confirming the mastery of an objective.

When the observation is complete, the program summarizes the data as response frequency (total number and rate), duration, latency, or percentage of intervals. The utilities program allows the user to retrieve files, graph data, and write and print reports or graphs. If the need arises to collect pencil-and-paper data, DODS has the option of constructing and printing data collection forms.

DODS requires a computer running MacOS (System 6.0.5 or later) and HyperCard. The user can also develop a remote recording device that consists of an adapted Macintosh mouse, radio transmitter, and radio receiver for use when a desktop computer is not available. The software is available free of charge.

Ecobehavioral Assessment System Software (EBASS)

EBASS is a series of three observational programs, each of which is designed specifically for a client's educational level. All allow the user to record interval data (10 to 20 s) for over 100 different responses.

The data analysis feature allows the user to calculate percentage of intervals, conditional probabilities, mean, range, and frequency distribution. In addition, responses can be combined (A and B) for further analysis. Interobserver agreement (overall and occurrence agreement) can also be calculated. The raw data, as well as session statistics, can be stored to disk or graphed.

EBASS requires an IBM-compatible PC (DOS or Windows) and has minimal memory requirements. The cost of the complete package is $750 and includes an instruction manual and instructional videotapes as well as technical support. Site licenses are also available.

EVENT-PC

EVENT-PC is designed for use with multiple platforms (DOS, MacOS, Windows, Commodore 64, and Tandy 100/102). The observer can record frequency, duration, latency, and IRT for 40 different responses.

The data analysis feature has the capability of calculating total number and duration of responding. EVENT-PC can also calculate means, ranges, and standard deviations. With a supplemental program, SEQ, the user can perform additional statistical tests (e.g., chi-square). All results can be printed, viewed on screen, or saved to disk. Disk outputs are compatible with most spreadsheets and statistical packages. EVENT-PC has the ability to graph interval relations for visual inspection.

All platform versions have minimal memory requirements. The DOS, MacOS, and Windows version of EVENT-PC are available for $50. The price includes an instruction manual and technical support.

Multi-Option Observation System for Experimental Studies (MOOSES)

MOOSES has the capability of capturing frequency, duration, interval (variable duration), and time-sampling data for 200 different responses. Code sets for individual projects are defined in a file by the user of the program. Entry errors can be edited at the end of the observation session.

The user can calculate response frequency (total number and rate), duration, percentage of intervals, percentage of trials, and conditional probabilities. The user can define subgroups that contain various combinations of responses (A and B, A or B). Furthermore, interobserver agreement (smaller-larger, overall, occurrence, and nonoccurrence agreement) can be calculated.

MOOSES requires an IBM-compatible PC (DOS) and has minimal memory requirements. The cost of the software system is $450. The package includes an instruction manual and technical support through E-mail. A program for recording data from video (PROCODER) is also available at an extra cost.

Observational Data Acquisition Program (ODAP)

ODAP allows simultaneous recording of up to 20 different responses in a given observation session. It permits the recording of response frequency, duration, intervals (variable duration), time samples, latency, and IRT. In addition, deletion of entry errors can be made while recording. Data output is provided in two formats: a raw data file and a summary file that is appended after each observation session with session identifiers as well as response frequency (total number and rate) and duration.

ODAP requires an IBM-compatible PC (DOS) and has minimal memory requirements. The software is free and includes an instruction manual.

Observational Data Collection & Analysis for Windows (ObsWin)

ObsWin is an integrated data collection and analysis software package. It has the capability to capture frequency and duration data for up to 86 different behaviors. The user can create up to seven mutually exclusive code sets to facilitate data collection. Errors in data collection can be marked for future editing, and notes may be written during an observation session and saved with data files.

The data analysis option allows the user to calculate response frequency (total number and rate), duration, latency, IRT, and conditional probabilities. The user can also define various combinations of responses (A or B, A and B) for further analysis. ObsWin has the capability to compute central tendencies (mean and median), variability (range and frequency distribution), lag sequential analyses, and interobserver agreement (smaller-larger, overall, occurrence, nonoccurrence, and exact agreement). It also has the option to read in data collected using other existing data collection programs.

All data (raw, session statistics, and reliability statistics) can be saved to disk or printed. The user can create occurrence graphs, cumulative onset graphs, frequency per interval graphs, and summary statistic bar charts. All graphs may be saved as Windows metafiles or bitmaps.

The basic data collection program requires an IBM-compatible computer (DOS) and has minimal memory requirements. The analysis program, which also includes a program for data collection from video, requires Windows 3.1, 4 MB RAM, and a 386 processor. The cost of the system is £500. The package includes an instruction manual and technical support. The purchaser is permitted to use one copy of the Windows-based program on a single computer, but the DOS-based program can be freely distributed on any number of computers.

The Observer

The Observer's program tasks are divided into several subprograms. Observers can collect frequency, duration, interval (variable duration), time sample, latency, and IRT data for a maximum of 999 different responses. Entry errors can be marked for later editing, and text notes for unique or atypical events can be written during an observation session. The user also has the option to pause the observation session if the need arises and to adjust the session timer during data collection. All observation sessions are stored to disk, and the user is notified when the threshold of disk space is about to be reached.

The data analysis feature has the capability to calculate the total number of responses, duration, latency, IRT, percentage of intervals, and conditional probabilities. The user can also define subgroups that contain various combinations of responses (A or B, A and B). The user also has the option of calculating other statistics such as interobserver agreement (overall and exact agreement, kappa), mean, range, standard deviation, and standard error as well as lag sequential analyses. In addition, the user can construct a graph of the observational data against elapsed time. All data can be saved to disk, printed, or exported to a number of spreadsheets, databases, or statistical packages.

The price of the base package, which includes the Observer software, is $1,740 and can be used on any PC running DOS (minimal memory requirements), Windows (minimum 4 MB RAM, 10 MB hard disk, 386DX processor), or MacOS (minimum 4 MB RAM, 10 MB hard disk, system 6.0.7). Supplemental software packages that allow the user to collect data on a variety of different handheld computers (Observational Research Kit), such as the Psion Organizer and Workabout, or from video (Video Tape Analysis System) are available for an additional cost. All packages include an instruction manual and technical support.

Portable Computer Systems (PCS)

PCS consists of separate data collection and analysis programs. The data collection program allows the observer to record response frequency, duration, latency, and IRT for up to 45 different events, and to capture discrete-trial data. Entry errors made while recording can be edited. The data collector has the option to temporarily disable the keys and timer if the need arises, as well as to enter text notes about the observation session.

The data analysis program can calculate response frequency (total number and rate), duration, latency, IRT, and conditional probabilities. In addition, PCS has the option to conduct lag sequential analyses. The user can define combinations of responses (A and B, A or B) for further analysis. A reliability program allows the comparison of data files using overall, occurrence, and nonoccurrence agreement.

PCS requires an IBM-compatible PC (DOS) and has minimal memory requirements. PCS is available for $400 and includes an instruction manual.

Professional Behavior Evaluation System (ProBES)

ProBES operates on a Psion Series 3a handheld computer. It enables the observer to collect frequency, duration, interval (1 s to 999 s), and time-sampling data for six different responses. The user can create templates for different types of observation sessions to facilitate data collection.

The data analysis option can calculate response frequency (total number and rate), duration, percentage of intervals, percentage of trials, conditional probabilities, and means. All of these can be viewed within ProBES immediately after completion of a session, downloaded to a desktop computer as a text file, or printed using any standard printer.

The cost of the system is $695. Included with the system are a Psion Series 3a handheld computer, all software, an instruction manual, and technical support.

Social Interaction Continuous Observation Program for Experimental Studies (SCOPE)

SCOPE permits the recording of up to 21 different responses during a given observation session and can capture response frequency and duration. In addition, entry errors made during collection can be edited.

The data analysis feature allows the user to calculate response frequency (total number and rate), duration, conditional probabilities, and lag sequential analyses. Interobserver agreement (overall, occurrence, nonoccurrence, and exact agreement) can also be calculated.

SCOPE requires an IBM-compatible PC (DOS or Windows) and has minimal memory requirements. The program is available free of charge.

Virtual Behavior Analyst (VBA)

VBA is a template used in Microsoft Word 6.0 that allows the collection of up to 16 different responses. VBA captures response frequency, duration, interval (1 s to 60 min), time-sample, latency, and IRT data. Entry errors can be edited while recording. A separate program (The Enabler Series) can be used to record discrete-trial data.

The data analysis option allows the user to calculate response frequency (total number and rate), duration, latency, IRT, percentage of intervals, and conditional probabilities. In addition, the raw data and session statistics can be stored to disk or imported into Microsoft Excel for further analysis or graphing.

VBA requires an IBM-compatible PC with at least 8 MB RAM, a 386 processor, and Microsoft Office. A stand-alone version is currently under production. VBA retails for $99 and includes an instruction manual and technical support. Interested users may download ScreenCam demos of the program from the Behavior Analysis Archive at the

University of Wisconsin–Madison (ftp:// alpha1.csd.uwm.edu/pub/Psychology/ BehaviorAnalysis/software/research).

REFERENCES

Donát, P. (1991). Measuring behaviour: The tools and the strategies. *Neuroscience & Biobehavioral Reviews, 15,* 447–454.

Eiler, J. M., Nelson, W. W., Jensen, C. C., & Johnson, S. P. (1989). Automated data collection using bar code. *Behavior Research Methods, Instruments, & Computers, 21,* 53–58.

Farrell, A. D. (1991). Computers and behavioral assessment: Current applications, future possibilities, and obstacles to routine use. *Behavioral Assessment, 13,* 159–179.

Received October 27, 1997
Initial editorial decision December 2, 1997
Final acceptance January 12, 1998
Action Editor, David P. Wacker

APPENDIX

Summary of Main Features of Computerized Observation Systems

Program	Behavioral Evaluation Strategy & Taxonomy	Behavior Observer System	DATACAP, HARCLAG, HARCREL
Address	Tom Sharpe Dept. of HKLS Lambert Fieldhouse Purdue University W. Lafayette, IN 47907	Sander Martin Psychsoft 1758 Timberidge Circle Corinth, TX 76205	Eric Emerson Hester Adrian Research Centre University of Manchester Manchester M13 9PL United Kingdom
Phone	(765)494-3178	(817)368-0345	0161 275 3335
FAX	(765)496-1239	(817)565-4682	0161 275 3333
Internet	tsharpe@sla.purdue.edu	smartin@terrill.unt.edu	eric.emerson@man.ac.uk
Data collection	user supplied (laptop computer)	user supplied (hand-held computer)	user supplied (hand-held computer)
Hardware operating system	DOS Windows	MacOS Windows	DOS Windows
Data collection[a]	F, D, I, S, L, IRT, T	F, D, I, S, L, IRT, T	F, D
Data analysis[a]	F, R, D, I, L, IRT, T, P	F, R, D, I, L, IRT, T	F, R, D, L, IRT, P
Reliability statistics[b]	OV, K	OV, OCC, NON	OV, OCC, NON, K
Price	$750	$199	free

[a] F = frequency, R = rate, D = duration, I = interval, S = time sample, L = latency, IRT = interresponse time, T = discrete trial, P = conditional probability.
[b] SL = smaller/larger, OV = overall, OCC = occurrence, NON = nonoccurrence, EX = exact, K = kappa.

APPENDIX
(Extended)

Program	Data Collection Assistant	Direct Observation Data System	Ecobehavioral Assessment System Software
Address	Jay Saunders Bluestem Technologies 1104 E. 25 Terrace Lawrence, KS 66046	Happy Johnson College of New Jersey Hillwood Lakes, CN 4700 Trenton, NJ 08650	Charles Greenwood Juniper Gardens Children's Project 650 Minnesota Ave., 2nd Floor Kansas City, KS 66101
Phone	(785)865-3804	(609)771-2998	(913)321-3143
FAX	(785)865-0158	(609)771-3434	(913)371-8522
Internet	bluestem@pchelponline.com	johnsha@tcnj.edu	greenwood@kuhub.cc. ukans.edu http://www.lsi.ukans. edu/jg/ebass.htm
Data collection	TimeWand I DuraTrax by Videx	user supplied (laptop computer or remote controlled device)	user supplied (laptop computer)
Hardware operating system	Windows	MacOS Windows	DOS Windows
Data collection[a]	F, D, T	F, D, I, S, L	I
Data analysis[a]	F, R, D, T	F, R, D, I, L, T	I, P
Reliability statistics[b]	none	none	OV, OCC
Price	\$348–\$625	free	\$750

APPENDIX
(Extended)

Program	EVENT-PC	Multi-Option Observation System for Experimental Studies	Observational Data Acquisition Program
Address	James Ha University of Washington RPRC Box 357330 Seattle, WA 98195	Jon Tapp Jon Tapp & Associates Box 43 Hampden-Sydney, VA 23943	William Hetrick Fairview Developmental Center 2501 Harbor Blvd., Box 5A Costa Mesa, CA 92626
Phone	(206)543-2420	(804)223-2928	
FAX			
Internet	jcha@u.washington.edu	jt@mail.hsc.edu http://panther.hsc.edu/ mooses.html	
Data collection	user supplied (laptop computer)	user supplied (laptop computer)	user supplied (laptop computer)
Hardware operating system	DOS MacOS Windows	DOS	DOS
Data collection[a]	F, D, L, IRT	F, D, I, S	F, D, I, S, L, IRT
Data analysis[a]	F, D	F, R, D, I, T, P	F, R, D
Reliability statistics[b]	none	SL, OV, OCC, NON	none
Price	\$50	\$450	free

APPENDIX
(Extended)

Program	Observational Data Collection & Analysis for Windows	The Observer 3.0	Portable Computer Systems
Address	Chris Oliver School of Psychology University of Birmingham, Edgbaston Birmingham, B15 2TT United Kingdom	Noldus Information Technology 6 Pidgeon Hill Dr., Suite 180 Sterling, VA 20165	Peggy Williams Communitech P.O. Box 425 Dekalb, IL 60115
Phone	0121 414 4909	(800)355-9541	(815) 753-8436
FAX	0121 414 4897	(703)404-5507	(815) 753-9250
Internet	c.oliver@bham.ac.uk	info@noldus.com http://www.noldus.com	arepp@niu.edu
Data collection	user supplied (laptop computer)	user supplied (hand-held or laptop computer)	user supplied (laptop computer)
Hardware operating system	DOS Windows	DOS MacOS Windows	DOS
Data collection[a]	F, D	F, D, I, S, L, IRT	F, D, L, IRT, T
Data analysis[a]	F, R, D, L, IRT, P	F, D, L, IRT, I, P	F, R, D, L, IRT, P
Reliability statistics[b]	SL, OV, OCC, NON, EX	OV, EX, K	OV, OCC, NON
Price	£500	$1,740	$400

APPENDIX
(Extended)

Program	Professional Behavior Evaluation System	Social Interaction Continuous Observation Program for Experimental Studies	Virtual Behavior Analyst
Address	Robert Ricketts 4150 Southwest Dr., Suite 250 Abilene, TX 79606	Richard Shores University of Kansas at Parsons 2601 Gabriel Parsons, KS 67357	Merrill Winston World Enabling Resources 5231 Pine Tree Rd. Coral Springs, FL 33067
Phone	(915) 692-3942	(316) 421-6550 x1859	(954) 341-2878
FAX	(915) 692-6433		(954) 977 0409
Internet	ricketts@abilene.com		drmrw@msn.com http://www.weru.com
Data collection	Psion Series 3a	user supplied (laptop computer)	user supplied (laptop computer)
Hardware operating system	OPL	DOS Windows	Windows (Microsoft Office)
Data collection[a]	F, D, I, S	F, D	F, D, I, S, L, IRT
Data analysis[a]	F, R, D, I, T, P	F, R, D, P	F, R, D, L, IRT, I, P
Reliability[b]	none	OV, OCC, NON, EX	none
Price	$695	free	$99

JOURNAL OF APPLIED BEHAVIOR ANALYSIS 1976, 9, 109-113 NUMBER 1 (SPRING) 1976

TECHNICAL ARTICLE

DIFFERENCES AMONG COMMON METHODS FOR CALCULATING INTEROBSERVER AGREEMENT

ALAN C. REPP,[1] DIANNE E. D. DEITZ, SHAWN M. BOLES, SAMUEL M. DEITZ,[2] AND CHRISTINA F. REPP

GEORGIA RETARDATION CENTER AND GEORGIA STATE UNIVERSITY

In most applied studies, experimenters attempt to increase the probability that data accurately reflect the subject's behavior by assessing the degree to which two observers agree that responding has occurred. While some authors report this comparison as an index of observer reliability, others report it as an index of observer or interobserver agreement.

Regardless of the term used, most authors who report agreement (instead of correlation) use variations of the same procedure. In general, each session is divided into a number of time blocks, the number of time blocks with interobserver agreement is divided by the sum of the agreements and disagreements, the quotient is multiplied by 100, and the result is reported as per cent agreement between observers. Although several variations exist within this general procedure, the most common are variations in the length of the time block and in the definition of an interval of agreement. The present experiment compared the results of computing interobserver agreement by these common methods and variations.

METHOD

General Procedure

Several methods for calculating interobserver agreement on the same data were compared. Two observers unaware of the purpose of the experiment recorded responding by five children in an early childhood program. Five response classes (each child emitted a different response) were recorded for varying numbers of sessions: R_1 (turning in seat, 13 sessions), R_2 (mouthing nonedibles, 12 sessions), R_3 (making eye contact, eight sessions), R_4 (screaming, nine sessions), and R_5 (touching objects, 21 sessions).

Although the responses, *per se,* were not of importance in this experiment, they were defined to make the data representative of field studies.[3] In the pre-experimental phase, both observers discussed and wrote definitions on each response class while observing the response and then independently recorded responding. After any session in which the per cent agreement calculated by the Whole-Session method (described below) was greater than 80%, the discussions stopped, and another recording session occurred. If a session resulted in an agreement score of less than 80%, another discussion and recording session occurred. After three consecutive sessions with agreement of at least 80%, the pre-experimental phase ended and the experimental phase began.

Three rooms were used. The children were in a classroom; the observers seated approximately 3 m apart were in a second room separated from the first by a one-way mirror; the equipment (an event recorder, timer, and power supply) was in a third room acoustically isolated from the other two rooms. Sessions varied from 5 to 12 minutes, and in each session two observers recorded the responding of one child by closing one of the two silent microswitches that controlled separate pens on an event recorder. These pens were deflected from the beginning to the end of a response. A third pen on the event recorder, momentarily deflected at 5-sec intervals by an electronic timer, provided a permanent record of time against which the data could be analyzed. As the observations were made during an ongoing educational program, sessions began and ended when the children's location in the room facilitated observations. At the end of the experiment, per cent agreement was calculated by the three methods described below.

1. *Whole-session method.* In this method, the time block was equivalent to the entire session. The number of responses recorded by each observer was summed, the smaller number divided by the larger, and the quotient multiplied by 100 to yield per cent agreement.

2. *Exact-agreement method.* In this method, the event recorder pen that deflected every 5 sec provided a means by which the number of responses recorded by each observer in each interval could be compared. Responses were defined as the deflection of an observer's pen or the continuance of a deflection that had begun in a preceding interval. An agreement was defined as an interval in which both observers recorded the same number of responses; disagreement as

---

[1]Georgia Retardation Center 4770 North Peachtree Road Atlanta, Georgia 30341.

[2]Georgia State University.

[3]More complete definitions are available on request.

an interval in which the observers did not record the same number of responses. Interobserver agreement was determined by dividing the number of intervals of agreement by the total number of intervals in the session.

There were two variations within this method. The first was the length of the interval—5, 10, 20, and 30 sec—with the three larger being made by combining consecutive 5-sec intervals. In the second variation, calculations were based either on all the intervals in a session (All-Intervals method) or only on those intervals in which at least one observer recorded responding (Response-Intervals-Only method).

3. *Category method.* Calculations were similar to the previous method, the difference being that an interval was defined as one of agreement either if both observers failed to record any responding or if both observers recorded at least one response. An interval of disagreement was defined as one in which one observer recorded responding and the other did not. The same two variations made within the Exact-Agreement method were made within the Category method.

Data analysis.[4] The per cent of interobserver agreement was used for each method. Analyses were conducted for the various calculation methods on each of the five response classes. The main comparisons were: (1) Whole Session *versus* Exact Agreement *versus* Category, (2) All Intervals *versus* Response Intervals Only, and (3) 5-sec *versus* 10-sec *versus* 20-sec *versus* 30-sec time intervals.

RESULTS

The rates of responding (1.4, 6.6, 3.7, 1.7, and 3.2 rpm for responses classes one through five, respectively) are representative of experiments dealing with moderate response rates.

Whole Session versus *Exact Agreement* versus *Category*

In the first analysis, data were combined in two ways: (1) across the All-Intervals and Response-Intervals-Only methods, and (2) across the four interval sizes so that the Exact-Agreement method and the Category method could be compared with the Whole-Session method for each of the five response classes. Means, which were calculated for each response class (Figure 1), indicated that: (1) the Category and Whole-Session methods produced similar results, with the former producing higher scores for three of the five response classes (mean difference = 2%), (2) the Category method produced higher percentages (mean difference = 14%) than the Exact-Agreement method for all five response classes, and (3) the Whole-Session method produced higher percentages than the Exact-Agreement method for four of the five response classes (mean difference = 12%).

All Intervals versus *Response Intervals Only*

In the second analysis, data were combined across the Exact Agreement, Category, and Interval Size factors so that the All-Intervals and Response-Intervals-Only methods could be compared. Means calculated for each method and for each response are plotted in Figure 1 (lower portion). For each response class, the Response-Interval-Only method consistently produced lower agreement percentages than the All-Intervals method. The mean difference across the five response classes was 7%.

Interval Size

Means for interobserver agreement calculated by the Exact-Agreement and Category methods were calculated for the four interval sizes (Figure 2) and indicate that: (1) as the interval size increased, the difference between the agreement percentages derived from the two methods increased; (2) as the interval size increased, the agreement percentages calculated by the Exact-Agreement method decreased; and (3) as the interval size increased, the agreement percentages calculated by the Category method increased.

Combined Methods

With the data from the five response classes at the smallest and at the largest intervals averaged, the results indicated that: (1) the Category—All-Intervals method produced the highest scores at both the 5-sec (mean = 94%) and the 30-sec intervals (mean = 94%), (2) the Exact-Agreement-Response-Intervals-Only method produced the lowest scores (means = 77% and 64%), (3) the Category-Response-Intervals Only method produced increasing scores with increasing interval size (means = 85% and 92%), and (4) the Exact-Agreement-All-Intervals method produced decreasing scores with increasing interval size (means = 91% and 71%).

DISCUSSION

Exact Agreement versus *Category*

For all five response classes, the data indicated considerable differences between these two methods of calculating interobserver agreement, with the Category method producing the highest scores. This difference occurred because the Category method is the limiting value of the Exact-Agreement method. That is, any interval that is scored as one of agreement in the Exact-Agreement method must be scored as one of agreement in the Category method, but not all intervals scored as agreement in the Category method are scored as agreement in the Exact-Agreement method (*e.g.*, if one observer recorded four responses and another observer recorded three).

---

[4]Appropriate statistical analyses were conducted on all comparisons and are available in an expanded version of this paper.

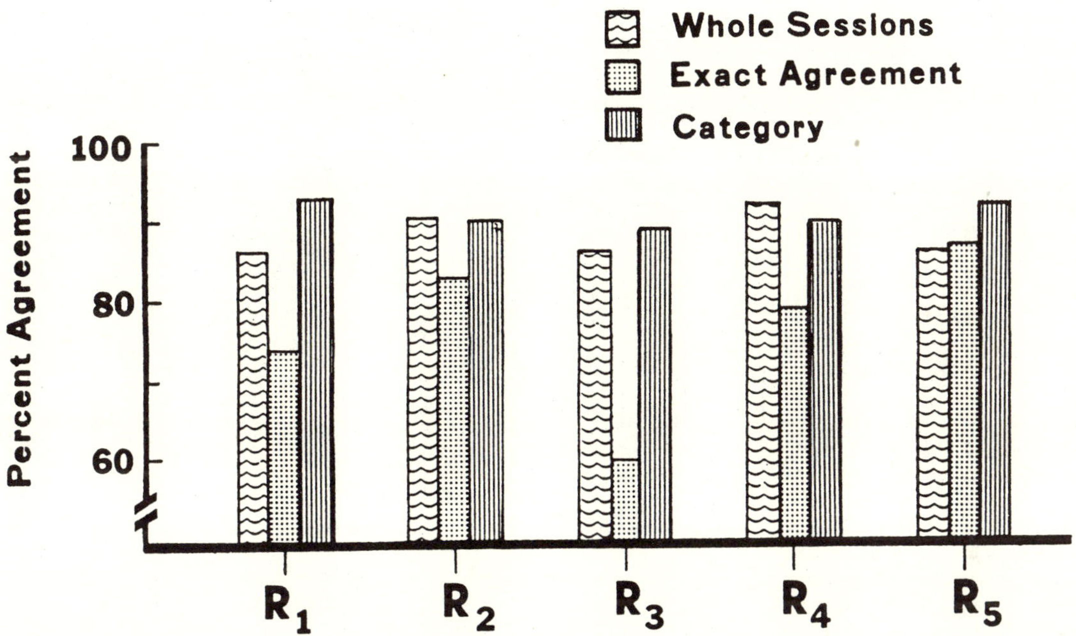

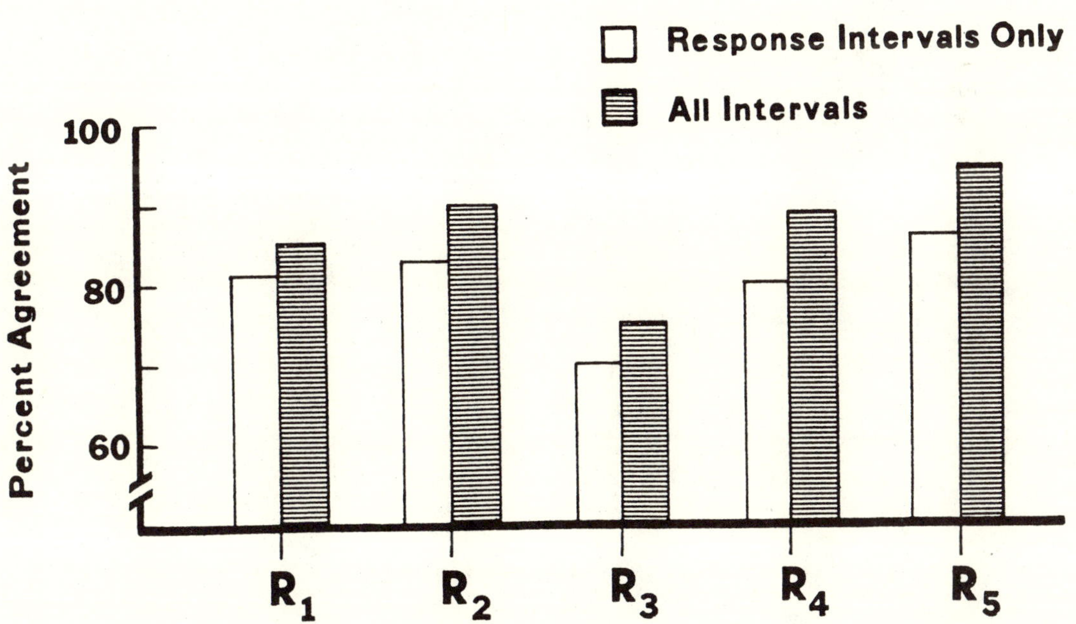

Fig. 1. The mean per cent of interobserver agreement for each method for each response class. All calculations were made on the same data.

All Intervals versus *Response Intervals Only*

For all response classes, the All-Intervals method produced higher agreement percentages than the Response-Intervals-Only method; and the formula for calculating per cent interobserver agreement is the reason for the difference. Any interval defined as one of agreement and any interval defined as one of disagreement within the Response-Intervals-Only method is defined in the same manner in the All-Intervals method. The difference between these two methods is the inclusion by the latter method of all intervals in which neither observer recorded any responding. These intervals, of course, are defined as intervals of agreement in the All-Intervals method but are excluded from calculations in the Response-Intervals-Only method.

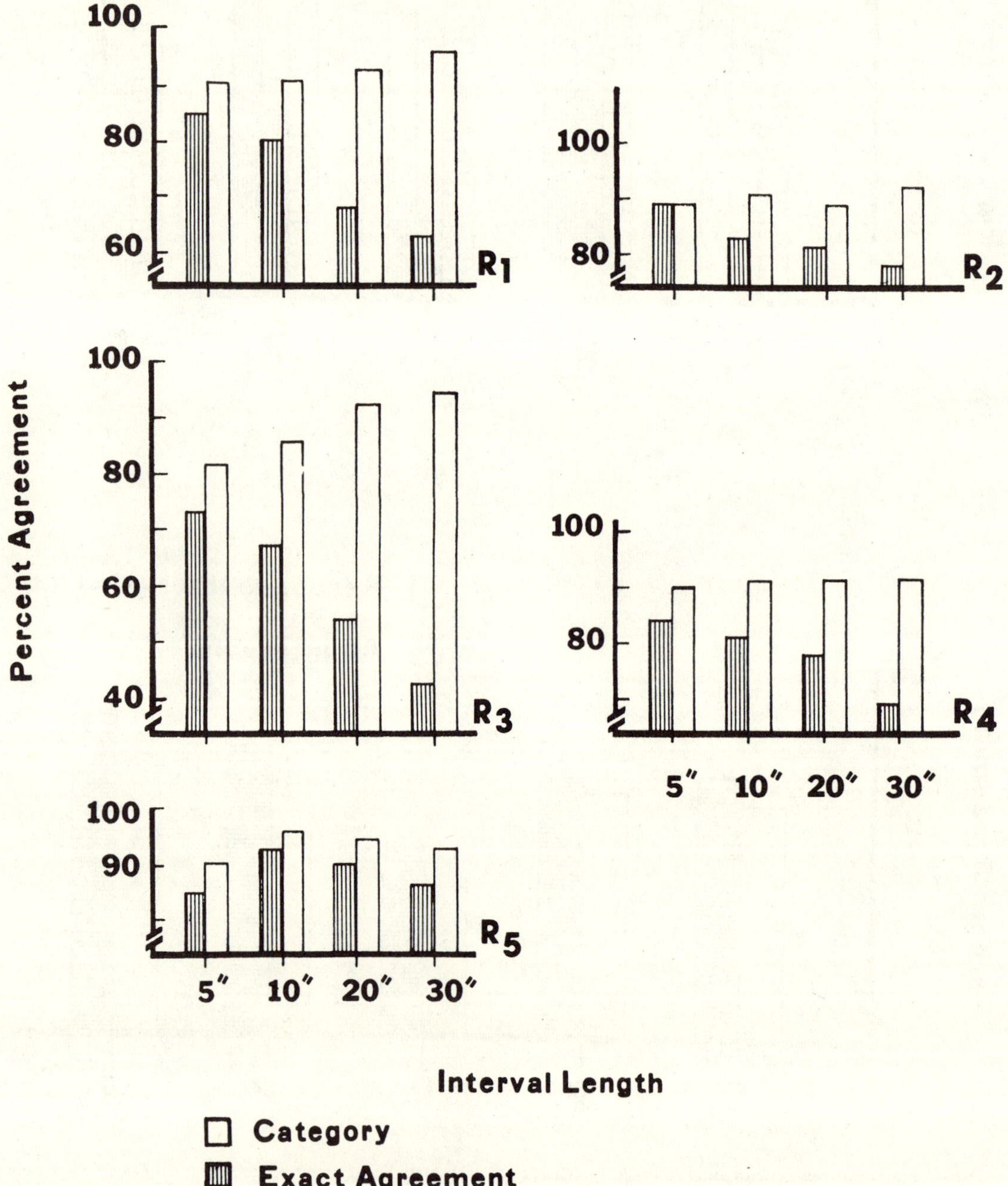

Fig. 2. The mean per cent of interobserver agreement calculated by the Category and Exact-Agreement methods for each response class. Data were collapsed across the time intervals and across the other methods.

Interval Size

Generally, as the interval size increased, the difference between the interobserver agreement percentages derived from the Exact-Agreement and Category methods increased. Figure 2 indicates that the increased differences resulted from two factors. The first was that as the interval size increased, the agreement percentages calculated by the Exact-Agreement method tended to decrease. As the interval size increased, the number of responses recorded by each observer in an interval increased, and the opportunity for and, hence, probability of disagreement between observers increased. The trend held in all but one case, 5-sec and 10-sec intervals for R_5. The reason for this exception was that errors could cancel each other. For example, Observer A might record two responses in the first 5 sec and no responses in the next 5 sec, while Observer B might do the obverse. With 5 sec as the interval size, both intervals would be scored as intervals of disagreement, and the agreement score would be 0%. However, with 10 sec as the interval size, the interval would be scored as one of agreement, and the agreement score would be 100%.

The second factor was that the agreement percentages calculated by the Category method generally increased as the interval size increased. The tapes indicated that as interval size increased, the probability of both observers recording at least one response increased. As this method defined agreement as an interval in which both observers recorded at least one response, the interobserver agreement percentage increased as interval size increased. This trend, however, did not occur in all cases (10, 20, and 30 sec for R_5, 30 sec for R_4). The reason for these exceptions appears to be the case in which neither observer recorded responding in a smaller interval while one observer recorded responding in the larger interval.

Whole Session

The Whole-Session method resulted in high, but not the highest, interobserver agreement percentages. Since the calculation of interobserver agreement by this method does not have the same basis as the other methods, there is no reason to expect similarity in the results of this and the other methods. Some investigators (*e.g.*, Johnson and Bolstad, 1973) have argued that this is the least justifiable of the common methods, since it does not indicate whether one observer recorded the same response (or at least responding during the same time period) as the other observer. Because of the argument that it is the least justifiable method, there is a common assumption that it would produce the most liberal interobserver agreement percentages. While the method may not be valid, the lack of an exaggerated agreement percentage is interesting and perhaps unexpected.

GENERAL DISCUSSION

Previous research has indicated several reasons for inaccuracy in recording data and in calculating interobserver agreement, and most of these reasons have been based on the observer's behavior. The present study has defined the behavior of another individual, the experimenter, as a cause of variation in reported interobserver agreement scores. The data indicated that the method chosen by the experimenter for calculating interobserver agreement has an effect on the percentages reported. In reporting agreement percentages, one can ensure higher scores by using the intervals in the recording period. Experimenters concerned with reporting more conservative scores can do so by calculating interobserver agreement based only upon those intervals in which responding occurred. In addition, more conservative agreement percentages also can be presented by using the Exact-Agreement method instead of the Category method (a common variation of which is usually labelled "time block"). However, this is not an argument for the exclusive use of the Exact-Agreement method, even though it is the most conservative, as the category method may occasionally be more appropriate (*e.g.*, when observers are recording multiple responses and using only pencil and paper).

The method of calculating interobserver agreement can have a considerable effect on the scores reported (overall means across responses on the same data varied from 64% to 94%). While 64% agreement may be insufficient for most experimenters and 94% agreement sufficient, the percentages themselves are misleading because they are a function of the method used to calculate interobserver agreement, rather than a function of data. Differences that one could reasonably expect would have arisen only from differences in the response data or from the comprehensiveness of the response definition may have arisen from differences in methods for calculating agreement, and one experimenter's report of 94% may reflect no more agreement between observers than another experimenter's report of 64%.

REFERENCES

Johnson, S. M. and Bolstad, O. D. Methodological issues in naturalistic observation: Some problems and solutions for field research. In L. A. Hamerlynck, L. C. Handy, and E. J. Mash (Eds.), *Behavior change: methodology, concepts, and practice.* Champaign, Illinoise: Research Press, 1973. Pp. 7-67.

JOURNAL OF APPLIED BEHAVIOR ANALYSIS 1977, **10**, 121-126 NUMBER 1 (SPRING) 1977

EVALUATING INTEROBSERVER RELIABILITY OF INTERVAL DATA[1]

B. L. HOPKINS AND JAIME A. HERMANN

UNIVERSITY OF KANSAS AND
UNIVERSIDAD NACIONAL AUTONOMA DE MEXICO

Previous recommendations to employ occurrence, nonoccurrence, and overall estimates of interobserver reliability for interval data are reviewed. A rationale for comparing obtained reliability to reliability that would result from a random-chance model is explained. Formulae and graphic functions are presented to allow for the determination of chance agreement for each of the three indices, given any obtained per cent of intervals in which a response is recorded to occur. All indices are interpretable throughout the range of possible obtained values for the per cent of intervals in which a response is recorded. The level of chance agreement simply changes with changing values. Statistical procedures that could be used to determine whether obtained reliability is significantly superior to chance reliability are reviewed. These procedures are rejected because they yield significance levels that are partly a function of sample sizes and because there are no general rules to govern acceptable significance levels depending on the sizes of samples employed.

DESCRIPTORS: interobserver reliability, interval data, statistical inference, chance agreement, reliability criteria

---

Much research involving applied behavior analyses employs data collected by observers who record the occurrence of responses during short time intervals (*e.g.,* Aylion and Roberts, 1974; Glynn and Thomas, 1974; Knapczyk and Livingston, 1974). Such research assesses the reliability of observations by having two observers simultaneously record the same responses. The two records are compared interval-by-interval to determine the percentage of intervals in which the two observers agree that the behavior did or did not occur.

This index might be called *overall reliability* and is defined by:

$$R_{overall} = \frac{O_{1\&2} + N_{1\&2}}{T} \times 100 \qquad (1)$$

where

$O_{1\&2}$ = the number of intervals in which *both* Observer 1 and Observer 2 record the response as occurring;

$N_{1\&2}$ = the number of intervals in which *both* Observer 1 and Observer 2 record the response as not occurring; and

T = the total number of intervals for which the two observers' records are compared.

For example, if two persons simultaneously observe for 100 intervals, and both record some response as occurring in the same 63 intervals and do not record the response as occurring in the same 17 intervals (during the remaining 20 intervals, one or the other, but not both, records the response as occurring), the overall index of reliability would be:

$$R_{overall} = \frac{63 + 17}{100} \times 100$$

$$R_{overall} = 80\%$$

The ratio of intervals of agreement to total intervals is commonly multiplied by 100 to yield a percentage.

[1]This manuscript is part of a paper, "Problems in Experimental Design and Data Analysis", presented at the American Psychological Association Meetings in Montreal, Canada, 1973. Preparation of this manuscript was supported in part by SRS grant 59-P-35116. Reprints may be obtained from B. L. Hopkins, Department of Human Development, University of Kansas, Lawrence, Kansas 66045.

Bijou, Peterson, and Ault (1968) mentioned that the above index of reliability may be difficult to interpret whenever responses are recorded as occurring in either a large percentage or a small percentage of intervals. Table 1 is a hypothetical example of the problem that can exist for responses recorded as occurring in only a few intervals. Each observer has recorded the response as occurring in one of the 10 intervals. The observers agreed by making similar observations in eight of the 10 intervals. However, they failed to agree on intervals in which the response is recorded as occurring. Such records would cause doubt that the observers are, in fact, agreeing on occurrences of the response.

Similar problems exist for responses recorded as occurring in most intervals. Table 2 is a hypothetical example of such a problem. The two observers recorded the response as occurring in 90% of the intervals. Moreover, the observers agreed that the behavior did or did not occur in 80% of the intervals. Nevertheless, the observers failed to agree on the intervals in which the response is not recorded as occurring. This discrepancy is crucial. The observers might be recording two entirely different but relatively high-rate behaviors, and interval-by-interval comparison of their records would yield many intervals of agreement simply because both are recording some response as occurring in most intervals.

Table 1

A hypothetical example of records obtained by two observers recording a behavior as occurring in a small percentage of intervals.

	Short Intervals									
Observer 1				B						
Observer 2								B		
Overall agreement	✓	✓	✓		✓	✓	✓		✓	✓
$O_{1\&2}$										
$O_{1 \text{ or } 2}$				✓				✓		

Table 2

A hypothetical example of records obtained by two observers recording a behavior as occurring in a large percentage of intervals.

	Short Intervals									
Observer 1	B	B		B	B	B	B	B	B	B
Observer 2	B	B	B	B	B	B	B	B		B
Overall Agreement	✓	✓		✓	✓	✓	✓	✓		✓
$N_{1\&2}$										
$N_{1 \text{ or } 2}$			✓						✓	

Because of these problems, Bijou *et al.* (1968) recommended that an index of *occurrence reliability* be computed for very low-rate behaviors and an index of *nonoccurrence reliability* for high-rate behaviors. However, as Hawkins and Dotson (1975) noted, their recommendations have not been widely adopted by researchers. The calculation definitions for these indices are:

$$R_{occurrence} = \frac{O_{1\&2}}{T} \times 100 \qquad (2)$$

and

$$R_{nonoccurrence} = \frac{N_{1\&2}}{T} \times 100 \qquad (3)$$

In the example of Table 1, there are no intervals in which both observers record the response as occurring and two intervals in which either observer records the behavior as occurring. Thus, there is 0% agreement on occurrences of the behavior. Similarly in Table 2, although there is 80% agreement on the overall reliability index, the two observers fail to agree on intervals in which the response does not occur and there is, therefore, 0% agreement on the nonoccurrence index.

Routine methods are available to compare obtained percentages of agreement to agreement that would be expected by a random-chance model. The chance model assumes that the two observers record the response as occurring in the same number of intervals as it is empirically determined to occur. However, the model further assumes that the recording of instances of the response are randomly distributed over intervals. It is then possible to determine whether the empirically determined reliability as obtained by two actual observers is superior to reliability that might be obtained by chance.

Computation formulae for these chance-reliability indices can be deduced from the basic theorems of probability theory for independent events (Feller, 1957). They are:

$$\text{Chance } R_{\text{overall}} = \frac{(O_1 \times O_2) + (N_1 \times N_2)}{(T)^2} \times 100 \quad (4)$$

$$\text{Chance } R_{\text{occurrence}} = \frac{O_1 \times O_2}{(T)^2} \times 100 \quad (5)$$

$$\text{Chance } R_{\text{nonoccurrence}} = \frac{N_1 \times N_2}{(T)^2} \times 100 \quad (6)$$

where

O_1 = the number of intervals in which Observer 1 records the response as occurring;

O_2 = the number of intervals in which Observer 2 records the response as occurring;

N_1 = the number of intervals in which Observer 1 records the response as not occuring;

N_2 = the number of intervals in which Observer 2 records the response as not occurring; and

T = the total number of intervals for which the two observers' records are compared.

Suppose that two observers are recording on-task behavior for a retarded child in a classroom and that they simultaneously observe for 100, 10-sec intervals. Further suppose that both record the response as occurring in 90 intervals and that the index of overall reliability, as calculated by formula (1) above, indicates that they agree on 80% of the intervals. We can employ formula (4) to determine if the obtained percentage of agreement is better than would be obtained by chance:

$$\text{Chance } R_{\text{overall}} = \frac{(90 \times 90) + (10 \times 10)}{(100)^2} \times 100 = 82\%$$

Indeed, the obtained percentage of agreement, 80, would be less than the 82% expected by chance.

Each of the three computational formulae, (4), (5), and (6), is constructed in such a way that chance agreement varies with the empirical per cent of intervals in which the response is recorded as occurring. By assuming various proportions of intervals in which a behavior is recorded as occurring, the entire chance functions can be developed. For example, if two observers are recording a behavior as occurring in 10% of the observation intervals,

$$\begin{aligned}\text{Chance } R_{\text{overall}} &= [(pO_1 \times pO_2) + (pN_1 \times pN_2)] \times 100 \\ &= [(0.10 \times 0.10) + (0.90 \times 0.90)] \times 100 \\ &= [0.01 + 0.81] \times 100 = 82\%. \end{aligned} \quad (7)$$

If the behavior is being recorded as occurring in 30% of the intervals,

$$\begin{aligned}\text{Chance } R_{\text{overall}} &= [(0.30 \times 0.30) + (0.70 \times 0.70)] \times 100 \\ &= [0.09 + 0.49] \times 100 = 58\%. \end{aligned}$$

Formula (7) is equivalent to formula (4) but has been transformed to deal with proportions of intervals, rather than actual numbers of intervals to allow for easy computations for the hypothetical cases. The terms pO_1, pO_2, *etc.*, are the proportion of intervals in which Observer 1 records the behavior as occurring, the proportion in which Observer 2 records the behavior as occurring, *etc.*

The entire function for chance overall reliability is plotted in Figure 1. The function is qualitatively similar to one published by Hawkins and Dotson (1975) but is more exact than theirs. To use this function, first determine the per cent of intervals in which the observers are recording the behavior as occurring. Find this per cent on the horizontal axis. Project a straight line vertically from that point. The point at which the projected line intercepts the function provides the per cent reliability that would be obtained by chance by projecting a horizontal line from that point on the function to the vertical axis. For example, as determined on Figure 1, chance agreement is about 73% for a response recorded

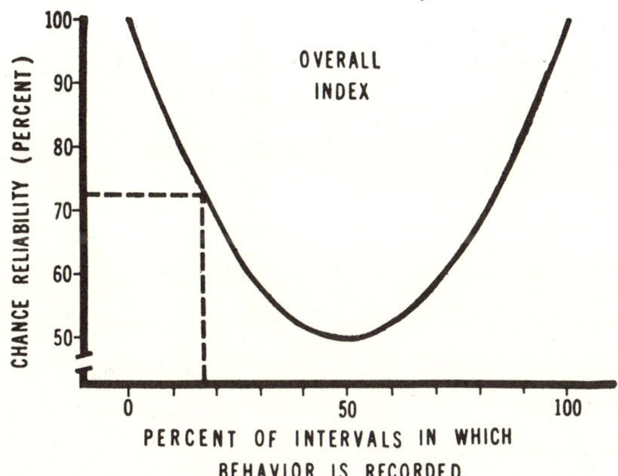

Fig. 1. Overall chance reliability as a function of the per cent of intervals in which a behavior is recorded as occurring.

as occurring in about 16% of the intervals of observation.

The function in Figure 1 assumes that the two observers are recording the response as occurring in about the same per cent of intervals. If there are discrepancies in the per cent of intervals in which the response is reported to occur by the two observers, then the calculation formula (4) should be employed, rather than Figure 1.

Figure 2 is the chance-reliability functions developed for the occurrence and nonoccurrence indices. The function for the overall index and the function for the occurrence index converge as the per cent of intervals in which the response is recorded approaches 100. Similarly, the overall and nonoccurrence functions converge as the per cent of intervals in which the response is recorded approaches zero.

The functions of Figure 2 are used in the same way as described above for the function for the overall index. Thus, chance occurrence reliability for observers recording a response as occurring in 10% of intervals is only 1%. Chance nonoccurrence reliability for observers recording a response as occurring in 70% of intervals is only 9%. Again, the calculation formulae (5) and (6) should be used instead of the figures unless both observers are recording the response as occurring in about the same percentage of intervals.

Inspection of Figures 1 and 2 indicates that all three functions are continuous for the entire range of the per cent of intervals in which a response is recorded as occurring. Therefore, contrary to the Bijou *et al.* (1968) recommendation, all of the indices of reliability are interpretable, regardless of per cent of intervals in which observers record a response. The level of chance agreement simply changes as the per cent of intervals in which the behavior is recorded changes.

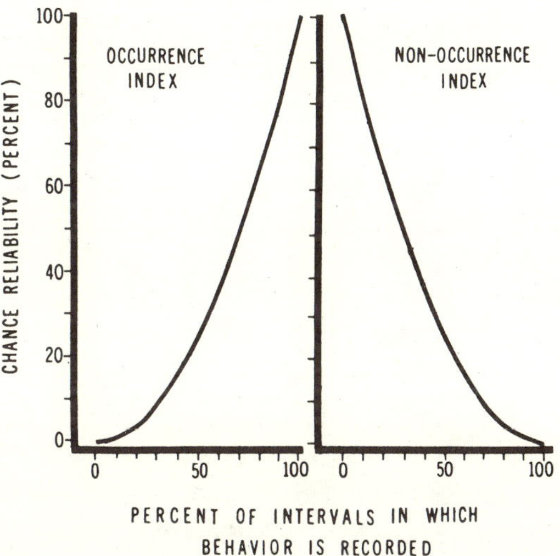

Fig. 2. Occurrence and nonoccurrence chance reliability as a function of the per cent of intervals in which a behavior is recorded as occurring.

Suppose, for example, that two observers independently record whether or not a child engages in some social interaction during each of 100, 10-sec intervals. Further suppose that each observer records the behavior as occurring in 20% of the intervals and that the empirical percentages of agreement for the two observers, as calculated by formulae (1), (2), and (3) are:

$$R_{overall} = 80\%$$
$$R_{occurrence} = 33\%$$
$$R_{nonoccurrence} = 78\%.$$

Chance agreement for these indices, as determined either by projection on Figures 1 and 2 or by calculation with formulae (4), (5), and (6) is:

$$\text{Chance } R_{overall} = 68\%$$
$$\text{Chance } R_{occurrence} = 04\%$$
$$\text{Chance } R_{nonoccurrence} = 64\%.$$

In fact, obtained reliability for all three indices is greater than would be expected by chance.

Once either the figures or the calculation formulae have been employed to determine that observations of independent observers are better than would be expected by chance, it is reasonable to question how much better. This, of course, is the kind of question for which inferential statistics might be appropriate. Several statistical procedures have been recommended for dealing with such problems. Cohen's k or kappa (Cohen, 1960) is a coefficient of interjudge agreement that excludes chance agreements. The Phi coefficient provides a measure of the correlation between the records of two different observers (Young and Veldman, 1965). Both of these descriptive statistics can be related to inferential statistics to yield an estimate of the probability that obtained reliability is superior to chance reliability. Similarly, Fisher's exact test or a Chi square can be used to compute the likelihood that agreements as good as those obtained could be attributed to chance (Siegel, 1956). However, these statistical procedures provide ambiguous answers to questions regarding how much better than chance a particular degree of reliability may be. Essentially, statistical significance increases and confidence levels decrease as sample sizes increase. Furthermore, agreement even only slightly superior to chance may become statistically significantly better than chance as sample sizes become large.

Consider again the example in which two observers record the social interactions of a child and their agreement is subsequently compared with chance agreement. Again, assume that the obtained index of overall reliability is 80% and chance overall reliability is 60%. Suppose we calculate kappa and then ask if the obtained kappa is significantly different from zero. If our data involve 100 intervals, the probability of obtaining the calculated kappa by chance is less than 0.006, while if exactly the same relationships held, but our data were based on only 10 intervals, the probability would be less than 0.23.

The other inferential statistics behave in exactly the same fashion as kappa. Unless researchers had some rule of thumb, or perhaps method based on experience, to determine what might be an acceptable level of significance for a given sample size in a particular area of research, the results of the inferential statistics provide virtually useless information. Moreover, for the large samples often involved in calculations of reliability in applied behavior analyses, the inferential statistics are particularly generous. Returning to our example, if obtained overall agreement were 80%, and if this were only slightly greater than a calculated chance agreement of 78%, kappa would still be significant at the 0.01 level if the observations were based on only 150 intervals.

At this time, there appears to be no satisfactory way to determine that obtained reliability is acceptably better than chance reliability. Therefore, the procedures for calculating chance reliability can only describe a lower boundary at which obtained reliability is unacceptable. In practice, researchers would generally demand higher degrees of interobserver reliability if the effects of independent variables are slight than if large effects were obtained, because apparent slight effects might simply be attributable to observation errors. However, there is no objective rule that allows a researcher to translate this consideration into a greater-than-chance lower limit for acceptable obtained reliability.

CONCLUSIONS

Four recommendations follow from the above considerations:

1. All publications dealing with interval data should report indices of interobserver agreement, as suggested by Bijou *et al.* (1968) and Hawkins and Dotson (1975).

2. Researchers should calculate and publish indices of random-chance interobserver agree-

ment against which obtained measures can be compared.

3. All indices (overall, occurrence, and nonoccurrence) of reliability can be interpreted regardless of the per cent of intervals in which a response is recorded. This is contrary to the recommendations of Bijou *et al.* and of Hawkins and Dotson.

4. Until other statistics are developed, researchers should postpone considerations of how much better than chance is the obtained interobserver reliability.

REFERENCES

Ayllon, T. and Roberts, M. D. Eliminating discipline problems by strengthening academic performance. *Journal of Applied Behavior Analysis,* 1974, **7,** 71-76.

Bijou, S. W., Peterson, R. F., and Ault, M. H. A method to integrate descriptive and experimental field studies at the level of data and empirical concepts. *Journal of Applied Behavior Analysis,* 1968, **1,** 175-191.

Cohen, J. A coefficient of agreement for nominal scales. *Educational and Psychological Measurement,* 1960, **20,** 37-46.

Feller, W. *An introduction to probability theory and its applications,* Vol. 1. New York: John Wiley & Sons, 1957.

Glynn, E. L. and Thomas, J. D. Effect of cueing on self-control of classroom behavior. *Journal of Applied Behavior Analysis,* 1974, **7,** 299-306.

Hawkins, R. P. and Dotson, V. A. Reliability scores that delude: an Alice in Wonderland trip through the misleading characteristics of interobserver agreement scores in interval recording. In E. Ramp and G. Semb (Eds.), *Behavior analysis: areas of research and application.* Englewood Cliffs, New Jersey: Prentice-Hall, 1975. Pp. 359-376.

Knapczyk, D. R. and Livingston, G. The effects of prompting question-asking upon on-task behavior and reading comprehension. *Journal of Applied Behavior Analysis,* 1974, **7,** 115-121.

Siegel, S. *Nonparametric statistics for the behavioral sciences.* New York: McGraw-Hill, 1956.

Young, R. K. and Veldman, D. J. *Introductory statistics for the behavioral sciences.* New York: Holt, Rinehart & Winston, 1965.

Received 14 October 1974.
(Final acceptance 15 May 1976.)

JOURNAL OF APPLIED BEHAVIOR ANALYSIS 1977, 10, 133-139 NUMBER 1 (SPRING) 1977

OBSERVER AGREEMENT, CREDIBILITY, AND JUDGMENT: SOME CONSIDERATIONS IN PRESENTING OBSERVER AGREEMENT DATA

THOMAS R. KRATOCHWILL[1] AND RALPH J. WETZEL

THE UNIVERSITY OF ARIZONA

Graphical and statistical indices employed to represent observer agreement in interval recording are described as "judgmental aids", stimuli to which the researcher and scientific community must respond when viewing observer agreement data. The advantages and limitations of plotting calibrating observer agreement data and reporting conventional statistical aids are discussed in the context of their utility for researchers and research consumers of applied behavior analysis. It is argued that plotting calibrating observer data is a useful supplement to statistical aids for researchers but is of only limited utility for research consumers. Alternatives to conventional per cent agreement statistics for research consumers include reporting special agreement estimates (*e.g.*, per cent occurrence agreement and nonoccurrence agreement) and correlational statistics (*e.g.*, Kappa and Phi).

DESCRIPTORS: observational data, methodology, observer bias, observer training, reliability, validity, experimenter calculations

---

Applied behavior analysis emphasizes collecting human behavioral data by human observers in naturalistic settings. To establish credibility of observational data, one or more calibrating observers usually verify the primary observer's data. To aid the scientific community in its judgment of the acceptability of findings, an index of observer agreement is presented along with the findings themselves. This index simplifies and relates statistically a complex series of data points from two or more observers. The derived statistic, whether per cent or correlational, functions as a "judgmental aid" (Michael, 1974). If it falls within conventional limits, the scientific community regards the primary observer's data as "basic" and "appropriate" for subsequent analysis. In this context, the index establishes the tolerance extended to measurement error.

Recently, the extent to which certain forms of statistical observer agreement aids protect against misrepresentation of error has been questioned (Hartmann, 1977; Hawkins and Dotson, 1975; Johnson and Bolstad, 1973; O'Leary and Kent, 1973). Hawkins and Dotson (1975) demonstrated that when the formula $\frac{\text{agreements}}{\text{agreements} + \text{disagreements}} \times 100$ is used to calculate an agreement coefficient from interval recording data, the resulting scores: (a) may be highly insensitive to the adequacy of response definitions, (b) may misrepresent observer competence, and (c) cannot always be relied on to assess the "believability" of the experimental effect. Of the major problems with this conventional method, the implication that it cannot always provide a safeguard against misrepresentation of experimental findings is perhaps the most salient. This is an important issue because applied behavioral researchers have conventionally provided the scientific community with data from one observer only and have relied on these data to represent experimental effects.

These and other considerations have prompted new recommendations for applied behavioral researchers. Based on problems with the conventional per cent agreement statistic, Hawkins and Dotson (1975) recommended that calibrating

---

[1]The authors thank Michael J. Subkoviak and Sidney W. Bijou, for their comments on the manuscript. Reprints may be obtained from Thomas R. Kratochwill, Department of Educational Psychology, The University of Arizona, Tucson, Arizona 85721.

observer data should be plotted along with data of the primary observer. It was argued that this assists both researcher and readers of the experimental report (*i.e.,* the consumers) to interpret more adequately the credibility of statistical observer agreement indices and to detect certain threats of internal validity (*e.g.,* observer bias).

Another recommendation calls for more sophisticated examination of the properties of the statistical scores themselves and the reporting of special observer agreement statistical aids for consumers. These suggestions involved variations on conventional per cent agreements scores (*e.g.,* occurrence and nonoccurrence) (Hawkins and Dotson, 1975) and the introduction of relatively new, for applied behavior analysts, correlation-like statistics (*e.g.,* Kappa and Phi) (Hartmann, 1977). While left unstated, statistical indices are presumed to be of benefit to both researcher and consumer.

Aids for judging observer agreement must be evaluated by the ease, efficiency, and degree of accuracy with which they permit the researcher and scientific community to judge. Observer agreement can be represented statistically or graphically by plotting both the primary and calibrating observer's data. Hawkins and Dotson (1975) suggested that graphical representations would aid not only the researcher but research readers, who could then judge for themselves the adequacy of the statistical aid's representation of observer correspondence. While we agree that both graphical and statistical aids can assist in making judgments about observer agreement, we believe that both graphical and statistical aids best serve the researcher, but that statistical aids best serve the needs of the research consumer.

The primary benefits of plotting data occur before publication of the scientific report. If plotting both sets of data reveals to researchers that only one observer recorded an experimental effect, the data should not be published, acceptable statistical representations of observer agreement notwithstanding. Clearly, the situation requires experimenters to redesign the observation technology. Plotting the calibrating observer's data makes the judgment of the acceptability of the primary observer's data individual to researchers and is in keeping with the reliance on graphical aids so pervasive in applied behavioral research.

There are several limitations in providing graphical aids (*i.e.,* both sets of data) for observer agreement judgment for research consumers. First, it will take considerable expense on the part of researchers to report such data. Second, there is already growing concern that exclusive use of visual analysis of graphical displays may lead to misrepresentation of experimental effects (*cf.* Jones, Weinrott, and Vaught, Note 1). Plotting data from two observers would further complicate the already complex conventional process of evaluating experimental effects through visual analysis.

While applied behavioral researchers have preferred to communicate data via graphical displays, and have avoided the use of statistical tests to evaluate experimental effects, they have relied almost exclusively on a statistical index to communicate observer agreement. In one respect, this has been an advantage for the scientific community. Reporting a statistical score provides a more objective judgment of the credibility of experimental data. Such objective criteria can be standardized and consumers can react to them with perfect reliability. For the researcher, statistical measures of observer agreement are also objective, in that anyone can calculate them and obtain the same result.

However, because most statistical indices of observer agreement are abbreviations, they have achieved their simplifying effects with some loss of information. The combined effects of this abbreviating process and the possible lack of understanding of the properties of some conventional scores have threatened the data base of applied behavior analysis. This paper suggests that the choice of both graphical and statistical aids must be dictated by the nature of the experiment, rather than depending on convention. First, we describe the conditions under which graphical aids provide an additional source of information that facilitates making data respectable and eventually, publicly specifiable. Second, we review some statistical aids that can increase the credibility of observational data.

Graphical Judgmental Aids

The benefits of plotting data extend beyond those of the per cent agreement index to offer researchers some additional judgmental aids over all statistical scores. Plotting the calibrating observers' data allows the researcher to detect critical behaviors that might otherwise go unnoticed, to maintain contact with the data, to evaluate absolute differences between the two observers, to detect certain threats to internal validity, and requires relatively little sophistication in statistics to evaluate any observer differences.

Detection of behavior. Clearly, one major purpose of having two or more observers is to ensure detection of behavior. We have encountered situations in which the calibrating observer detected extremely important behaviors missed by the primary observer. For example, autistic children frequently exhibit physically self-destructive behaviors. Depending on the type of recording technology used and the method of calculating agreement, a relatively high observer agreement statistic can be obtained after a "successful" program has been established and an "applied criterion" of significance (*cf.* Risley, 1970) is achieved (in this case, zero occurrence of the target behavior). A calibrating observer can detect target behaviors when the primary observer did not. Plotting both sets of data may be important, not only to detect behavior and establish its covariation with other behaviors or stimuli in the environment, but also to note temporal relationships to nonoccurrences over the duration of the treatment program. Such data displays would also allow determination of why certain behaviors are maintained despite the absence of data from the primary observer. This additional judgmental aid for behavioral occurrence allows researchers and perhaps under some conditions, the reader of the experimental report, to view the interrelationships of behavior with other behaviors displayed graphically.

Staying in touch with the data. Data presented by Hawkins and Dotson (1975) raised the possibility that some applied behavioral researchers have not understood the properties of the statistical aids used in reporting observer agreement. Such a finding gives some credibility to the argument that too heavy reliance on "statistics" can lead researchers away from basic contact with their data (*cf.* Michael, 1974). Aside from basic tabulation of raw data, plotting a calibrating observer's data involves the least amount of transformation of the observer's record forms. As a "stimulus simplifying technique" it provides a point-to-point relationship between data sets, thereby allowing visual examination of agreement. The graphical index complements a statistical index and serves as a safeguard against misrepresentation through reliance on only statistical scores.

Evaluation of absolute differences. Plotting calibrating observer data allows researchers to evaluate absolute differences between data records, and not just differences relative to total frequency or duration. For example, the conventional per cent agreement estimate and other statistical aids allow no easy visual evaluation of differences in base rates. Absolute differences can be large and may be of significance to the researcher. Consider a situation in which during baseline, a relatively high-frequency behavior is observed. Observer 1 reports 19 scored intervals and Observer 2 reports 10. During the treatment phase, differences in recorded occurrences are three and six for the two observers, respectively. While a statistical index could show an acceptable agreement level, the researcher would be unable to observe graphically the differences of nine and three, respectively.

Detection of threats to internal validity. It has not been customary for applied behavioral researchers to establish observer agreement checks on every observation session. This undoubtedly reflects availability of additional observers, cost involved in their training, and the complexity of behavior being observed. At times, researchers may obtain useful information by plotting calibrating observer data to determine the relationship between check and noncheck sessions. If the researcher found that the primary observer consistently reported more (or less) of a target behavior on check sessions relative to noncheck sessions, the hypothesis of bias could be entertained (Hawkins and Dotson, 1975).

There has been increased attention to observer bias (Hersen and Barlow, 1976; Johnson and Lotitz, 1974; McNamara and MacDonough, 1972; Reid, 1970; Scott, Burton, and Yarrow, 1967; Kass and O'Leary, Note 2) and related issues of observer feedback and drift (Hanley, 1970; Kent, O'Leary, Diament, and Dietz, 1974; O'Leary, Kent, and Kanowitz, 1975; Patterson, 1969). However, bias may occur regardless of the level of observer agreement and may similarly reflect that both observers were biased (O'Leary *et al.,* 1975). Furthermore, the response definition of the two observers could "drift" (*cf.* Hanley, 1970; O'Leary and Kent, 1973), causing both to maintain high levels of agreement but leaving a deterioration in original response definitions over the course of the study. When *both* observers are biased and drift, plotting both data sets will not serve a useful detection function.

Some authors have suggested that a third observer could be employed to detect observer drift (Bijou, Peterson, Harris, Allen, and Johnson, 1969; Hanley, 1970). Occasional checks with two regular observers would assist in determining whether either primary or calibrating observers had drifted. O'Leary and Kent (1973) noted that a third *group* of observers could be trained after several weeks of data gathering by regular observers. If comparison with regular observers demonstrated no systematic differences over the course of the experiment, it could be concluded that drift and/or bias did not occur. Plotting the third observer's (or third group of observers') data could facilitate detection of this possible threat to interval validity. A possible difficulty with the procedure is that even a third or fourth observer could be biased. There are no clear guidelines for how many such checks against bias should be employed. However, once the researcher determines the source of error, the observers could be retrained or the observational system could be redesigned.

Sophistication in statistics. A graphical representation of observer agreement data demands little sophistication in statistics. Visual examination of a graphical display of two observers' data will generally allow easy discrimination of disagreement. Researchers working with paraprofessionals, clients involved in therapy, or even children, will find that such individuals easily comprehend fully the meaning of observer agreement. Furthermore, researchers could easily establish guidelines for the amount of deviation between two observers that will be tolerated. Such tolerance could easily be "measured" rather than calculated. In addition, individuals working in applied settings could easily construct agreement graphs.

Statistical Judgmental Aids

Statistical indices have promoted ease of judgment. Yet, important judgmental information is lost in the process of abbreviation. Also, the type of information lost varies as a function of the abbreviating process (*i.e.,* the method of calculation). The major problem with the conventional per cent agreement statistic for interval recording is that it does not adequately take into account chance agreements between two observers. A thorough discussion of this problem can be found in several sources (*e.g.,* Gelfand and Hartmann, 1975; Hawkins and Dotson, 1975; Hartmann, 1977; Johnson and Bolstad, 1973). Because of this factor, some special statistical agreement indices have been proposed. These scores include per cent occurrence agreement and nonoccurrence agreement, an average of these two scores, which we will call "average agreement", and special "correlation-like" coefficients.

Special percentage scores. To circumvent problems associated with conventional per cent agreement indices, some writers have proposed that per cent occurrence agreement and nonoccurrence agreement scores could be reported (*e.g.*, Bijou *et al.*, 1969; Hawkins and Dotson, 1975; Hartmann, 1977).[2] Both occurrence agreement and nonoccurrence agreement are derived, in part, from the conventional per cent agreement formula. These scores differ in the information they use from the scoring intervals. In occurrence agreement, only intervals in which both observers recorded the presence of a behavior are scored as an agreement. Disagreements are scored in the same manner as those in the conventional method. Nonoccurrence agreement scores reflect the situation in which both observers agree on the nonoccurrence of some behavior. Disagreements are scored when one observer records the presence of a behavior and the other records its absence.

The primary basis for using these scores is that they address the issue of chance agreements that can occur at varying rates of occurrence of target behaviors (Johnson and Bolstad, 1973). Both per cent occurrence and nonoccurrence agreement can provide a great deal of information if used under conditions dictated by the nature of the data (Bijou *et al.*, 1969). Occurrence agreement should be used in a program where there is a very low rate of behavioral occurrence. Since nonoccurrence agreement can inflate the conventional per cent agreement estimate, it should not be reported under such conditions. If behavior is occurring at a very high rate, occurrence agreement can produce "high" conventional per cent agreement estimates and should not be included in calculations. In such cases, per cent nonoccurrence agreement should be calculated. With an understanding of chance agreement (see also Hartmann, 1977) and methods of calculating occurrence and nonoccurrence, these scores will provide important safeguards in reporting agreement data from interval recording. Their advantages appear to be the ease of calculation and the ease with which researchers can conceptualize information used in the scores.

Currently, there are some potential limitations in using occurrence and nonoccurrence agreement scores. Of greatest concern are the conditions under which these scores should be reported and the related issue of what level of agreement index is acceptable. We concur with Hartmann's (1977) observation that it may not be an easy task to decide under which conditions these scores should be calculated and reported when differential rates of behavior occur during an experiment. With a great deal of variability in the data, this problem is compounded.

Another problem with these scores is that the amount of information that will need to be presented in experimental reports will greatly add to the complexity of the judgmental process. For example, while Hawkins and Dotson (1975) suggested that per cent occurrence and nonoccurrence could be presented in combination, they were uncertain whether the combination should involve simply reporting the scores and/or presenting a mean of the two scores. This "average per cent agreement" score reputedly reduces the problem of dealing with variable behavior frequencies, but is not completely free of this problem under all conditions.[3] Some authors have

[2]Hartmann's (1977) effective percentage agreement statistics for occurrence and nonoccurrence are equivalent to our agreement occurrence and agreement nonoccurrence, respectively, and Hawkins and Dotson's S-I and U-I, respectively.

[3]One alternative to the "average agreement" procedure would be to establish some "rules of thumb" for acceptable occurrence and nonoccurrence agreement scores. For example, if the two observers reported more than 80% occurrence, nonoccurrence agreement could be computed and reported. Where the total number of recording intervals is 100 (N=100), a chance agreement for nonoccurrence would be 4% (probability of the first observer reporting a nonoccurrence times the probability of the second observer reporting a nonoccurrence). A nonoccurrence agreement of 75% would indicate considerable nonrandom agreement between observers. Similarly, occurrence agreement could be computed and reported when the behavior rate is less than 20%. In this case, a chance agreement for occurrence would be 4%. At an intermediate rate of behavior (*i.e.*, when behavior is occurring 50% of the time), nonoccurrence would not add much information, since chance levels are rela-

suggested that base-rate chance agreements should be computed and that differences between obtained agreement and chance agreement should be reported (Hersen and Barlow, 1976; Johnson and Bolstad, 1973). In general, if researchers decide to employ per cent occurrence and nonoccurrence agreement scores, research consumers will face a more complex judgmental process when reading scientific reports.

Special correlational statistics. Kappa and Phi statistics have been proposed as options for researchers using interval recording observational methods (Gelfand and Hartmann, 1975; Hartmann, 1977).[4] These scores, also designed to deal with chance agreements, employ all the data from the scoring intervals. Hartmann (1977) has already described the many advantages and relatively few disadvantages of these scores. The primary advantage that we perceive in the use of these scores is that only one score will have to be reported. This relative ease of judgment, coupled with the fact that these scores can be reported over varying levels of behavior change during an experiment, make them attractive.

The chief disadvantage of these scores is that their "novel" feature could cause investigators to employ them to the exclusion of simpler statistical aids that could adequately represent observer agreement. Another disadvantage is that they do require relatively greater sophistication in statistics. It remains to be seen whether they will be accepted in applied behavioral research with the current concerns on more formal reliance on statistics in general (Michael, 1974).

SUMMARY AND RECOMMENDATIONS

Applied behavioral researchers have conventionally relied on statistical judgmental aids to present observer agreement data.[5] Problems in conventional per cent agreement statistics suggest that new methods of reporting observer agreement data be used. Plotting the calibrating observer's data is useful to the researcher to ensure credibility of observational data, but requires a degree of subjectivity that could be generally unacceptable to research consumers. The reporting of special agreement estimates (per cent occurrence agreement and nonoccurrence agreement) and correlational statistics (Kappa and Phi) can greatly improve statistical judgmental aids. Correlational statistics decrease subjectivity and the degree of inference in judging agreement scores over the per cent statistics. Correlational sttaistics should be given greater attention in applied behavioral research.

To understand better the conditions under which per cent and correlational statistics promote accurate decision-making regarding the credibility of observational data, a series of simulated data series needs to be evaluated. Such a series would hopefully vary all the parameters that indicate their limitations under conditions faced by applied behavioral researchers. The current development in more refined statistical aids should be perceived as advancing the science of applied behavioral research.

tively low (*i.e.,* 25% in this case). Under these conditions, total agreement could be more easily interpreted.

[4]The reader is referred to Hartmann (1977) in this series for the method of calculation of Kappa and Phi and for a description of their statistical properties.

[5]Observer "reliability" adds an element of confusion to other terms used in conventional psychometric theory (*cf.* Johnson and Bolstad, 1973). Furthermore, it is not "reliability" in the traditional measurement sense (*cf.* Herbert and Attridge, 1975). Given these considerations, the recent work of Hawkins and Dotson (1975), and our suggestions regarding situations where plotting data from calibrating observers may be useful, we would argue that the term "observer agreement" more adequately handles the representation of observer agreement data, whether graphical or statistical.

REFERENCE NOTES

1. Jones, R. R., Weinrott, M., and Vaught, R. S. *Visual versus statistical inference in operant research.* Paper presented as a part of a symposium on the use of statistics in N=1 research at the annual meeting of the American Psychological Association, Chicago, Illinois, September 1975.
2. Kass, R. E. and O'Leary, K. D. *The effects of observer bias in field-experimental settings.* Paper

presented in a symposium, Behavior Analysis in Education, University of Kansas, Lawrence, April 1970.

REFERENCES

Bijou, S. W., Peterson, R. F., Harris, F. R., Allen, K. E., and Johnson, M. S. Methodology for experimental studies of young children in natural settings. *Psychological Record,* 1969, **19**, 177-210.

Gelfand, D. M. and Hartmann, D. P. *Child behavior analysis and therapy.* New York: Pergamon Press, 1975.

Hanley, E. M. Review of research involving applied behavior analysis in the classroom. *Review of Educational Research,* 1970, **40**, 597-625.

Hartmann, D. P. Notes on methodology: on choosing an interobserver reliability estimate. *Journal of Applied Behavior Analysis,* 1977, **10**, 103-116.

Hawkins, R. P. and Dotson, V. A. Reliability scores that delude: an Alice in Wonderland trip through the misleading characteristics of interobserver agreement scores in interval recording. In E. Ramp and G. Semb (Eds.), *Behavior analysis: areas of research and application.* Englewood Cliffs, New Jersey: Prentice-Hall, 1975. Pp. 359-376.

Herbert, J. and Attridge, C. A guide for developers and users of observational systems and manuals. *American Educational Research Journal,* 1975, **12**, 1-20.

Hersen, M. and Barlow, D. H. *Single case experimental designs. Strategies for studying behavior change in the individual.* New York: Pergamon Press, 1976.

Johnson, S. M. and Bolstad, O. D. Methodological issues in naturalistic observation: some problems and solutions for field research. In L. A. Hamerlynck, L. C. Handy, and E. J. Mash (Eds.), *Behavior change: methodology, concepts, and its practice.* Champaign, Illinois: Research Press, 1973. Pp. 7-67.

Johnson, S. M. and Lobitz, G. K. Parental manipulaion of child behavior in home observations: a methodological concern. *Journal of Applied Behavior Analysis,* 1974, **7**, 23-31.

Kent, R. N., O'Leary, K. D., Diament, C., and Dietz, A. Expectation biases in observational evaluation of therapeutic change. *Journal of Consulting and Clinical Psychology,* 1974, **42**, 774-780.

McNamara, J. R. and MacDonough, T. S. Some methodological considerations in the design and implementation of behavior therapy research. *Behavior Therapy,* 1972, **3**, 361-378.

Michael, J. Statistical inference for individual organism research: mixed blessing or curse? *Journal of Applied Behavior Analysis,* 1974, **7**, 647-653.

O'Leary, K. D. and Kent, R. N. Behavior modification for social action: research tactics and problems. In L. A. Hamerlynck, L. C. Handy, and E. J. Mash (Eds.), *Behavior change: methodology, concepts, and practice.* Champaign, Illinois: Research Press, 1973. Pp. 69-96.

O'Leary, K. D., Kent, R. N., and Kanowitz, J. Shaping data collection congruent with experimental hypotheses. *Journal of Applied Behavior Analysis,* 1975, **8**, 43-51.

Patterson, G. R. A community mental health program for children. In L. A. Hamerlynck, P. O. Davidson, and L. E. Acker (Eds.), *Behavior modification and ideal mental health services.* Calgary, Canada: University of Calgary Press, 1969. Pp. 130-179.

Reid, J. B. Reliability assessment of observation data: a possible methodological problem. *Child Development,* 1970, **41**, 1143-1150.

Risley, T. R. Behavior modification: an experimental-therapeutic endeavor. In L. A. Hamerlynck, P. O. Davison, and L. E. Acker (Eds.), *Behavior modification and ideal mental health services.* Calgary, Canada: University of Calgary Press, 1970. Pp. 103-127.

Scott, P. M., Burton, R. V., and Yarrow, M. R. Social reinforcement under natural conditions. *Child Development,* 1967, **38**, 53-63.

Received 19 June 1975.
(*Final acceptance 15 May 1976.*)

JOURNAL OF APPLIED BEHAVIOR ANALYSIS 1977, **10**, 141-150 NUMBER 1 (SPRING) 1977

ARTIFACT, BIAS, AND COMPLEXITY OF ASSESSMENT: THE ABCs OF RELIABILITY

ALAN E. KAZDIN[1]

THE PENNSYLVANIA STATE UNIVERSITY

Interobserver agreement (also referred to here as "reliability") is influenced by diverse sources of artifact, bias, and complexity of the assessment procedures. The literature on reliability assessment frequently has focused on the different methods of computing reliability and the circumstances under which these methods are appropriate. Yet, the credence accorded estimates of interobserver agreement, computed by any method, presupposes eliminating sources of bias that can spuriously affect agreement. The present paper reviews evidence pertaining to various sources of artifact and bias, as well as characteristics of assessment that influence interpretation of interobserver agreement. These include reactivity of reliability assessment, observer drift, complexity of response codes and behavioral observations, observer expectancies and feedback, and others. Recommendations are provided for eliminating or minimizing the influence of these factors from interobserver agreement.

DESCRIPTORS: methodology, observational procedures, observational code, observer bias, expectancies, feedback, reliability, artifact

---

A major feature of applied behavior analysis is the assessment of a client's overt behavior. The behavioral measures used are not usually standardized in the sense of traditional psychometric assessment; hence, one cannot rely on the consistency with which observations are made based on the assessment device itself, given uniform conditions of administration. Viscissitudes of defining target behaviors, the nature of applied settings, and conditions of observation require demonstration that behaviors are consistently recorded separately in each project. The well-known concern for consistency and accuracy of observations is expressed in the notion of "reliability" in applied behavior analysis. Reliability, as usually employed, refers to agreement between observers who independently score the same behavior of a subject. If the two observers consistently show relatively high agreement, it is assumed that the observations reflect the subject's performance relatively accurately.

Although accuracy of observations often is inferred from interobserver agreement, accuracy and agreement are not the same (*cf.* Bijou, Peterson, and Ault, 1968; Johnson and Bolstad, 1973). Accuracy usually refers to the extent to which observations scored by an observer match those of a predetermined standard for the same data. The standard is determined by other observers who reach a consensus about the data or by constructing observational material, such as videotapes or audiotapes, with predetermined behavioral samples (*e.g.,* Mash and McElwee, 1974). Interobserver agreement reflects the extent to which observers agree on scoring behavior. Usually, there is no firm basis to conclude that the one observer's data should serve as the standard, *i.e.,* is accurate.

As usually discussed, accuracy and interobserver agreement both involve comparing the

[1]The author is grateful for the comments provided by Eric J. Mash and John B. Reid on an earlier version of the manuscript. Reprints may be obtained from the author, Department of Psychology, The Pennsylvania State University, University Park, Pennsylvania 16802.

observer's data with some other source. They differ only in the extent to which the source of comparison can be entrusted to reflect the actual behavior of the subject.[2] Although accuracy and agreement are related, they need not go together. For example, an observer may observe accurately (relative to pre-established standard) but show low interobserver agreement (with another observer whose observations are quite inaccurate), or observe inaccurately (in relation to the standard) but show high interobserver agreement (with another observer who is inaccurate in an identical fashion).

Applied behavior analysis investigations usually assess interobserver agreement and assume that agreement reflects accuracy. Interobserver agreement is often considered adequate if it meets a prespecified level of agreement. Per cent agreement, one of the more commonly used measures, that reaches 70% or 80% often is considered satisfactory.[3] Yet, stressing the quantitative aspects of reliability ignores several assessment characteristics that dictate the meaningfulness of any agreement estimate. These include reactivity of reliability assessment, observer drift, complexity of the responses, information, expectancies, and feedback conveyed to the observers, and others. The present paper describes the characteristics and source of bias of reliability assessment, reviews the relevant research, and provides recommendations to minimize possible sources of bias.

[2]As with the term "reliability", "accuracy" probably is a misnomer in applied behavior analysis. The term implies that the standard of observation used as a criterion is correct and without error. Yet, consensual agreement often is used as the standard and may not reflect "true" performance.

[3]A quantitative criterion is difficult to invoke, in part, because the manner in which agreement should be defined and which of the available descriptive statistics for computing reliability should be used are unresolved (Hartmann, 1976; Hawkins and Dobes, 1975; Hawkins and Dotson, 1975.) The criterion for adequate agreement also depends on such diverse factors as the variability and rate of the observed behaviors, the number of different response codes scored, and the strength of the intervention.

Reactivity of Reliability Assessment

Nature of the problem. Interobserver agreement usually is checked periodically during an investigation. Typically, the observers are aware when their observations are checked, either because another observer enters the situation or because they observe the same client rather than different clients on these occasions. Research has shown that observer awareness of reliability assessment influences the observations.

Reid (1970) evaluated the effects of observer awareness that accuracy was being checked. Observers rated videotapes of parent-child interaction first when they were told that their observations were being compared to a standard and later when they were told that there was no standard. In fact, agreement with the standard was calculated for both sets of observations. Observers showed substantially higher accuracy when they thought that their observations were going to be checked. Indeed, when observers did not believe their observations were to be checked, their agreement with the criterion immediately dropped by approximately 25 percentage points. Although the results could have resulted from the order in which reactivity conditions were presented, subsequent studies have obtained similar findings.

Romanczyk, Kent, Diament, and O'Leary (1973) found that interobserver agreement was higher when observers believed that an individual observing with them was assessing reliability than when they believed the person was not assessing reliability. Differential accuracy of the data as a function of awareness also was suggested. Observers recorded 20% less disruptive student behavior when they were unaware, rather than aware, that interobserver agreement was assessed. Other studies also have demonstrated the influence of observer awareness that observations are being checked on accuracy and interobserver agreement (Kent, Kanowitz, O'Leary, and Cheiken, 1977; Kent, O'Leary, Diament, and Dietz, 1974; Taplin and Reid, 1973).

Awareness of whose observations serve as the standard for comparison also influences agreement. Romanczyk *et al.* (1973) found that an observer's performance was influenced by knowing who the other observer was during a reliability check. Two assessors whose observations were used as the standard were trained to score behaviors differently. For example, in scoring the category "vocalization" for a child, one assessor scored the softest vocalization possible, while the other scored only loud vocalizations. Observers were trained by and communicated with each assessor, thereby learning their idiosyncratic patterns. When the observers were checked with each assessor after training, they markedly shifted their scoring criteria.

Recommendations. The above research suggests that knowledge of reliability assessment and the identity of the reliability assessor affects interobserver agreement. Awareness of assessing agreement as a source of bias can be handled in several ways. The problem of observer awareness stems partially from conducting reliability checks under different conditions (reactive conditions) from those typically used to obtain the data (nonreactive conditions). This problem can be ameliorated in part by standardizing the conditions for reliability and nonreliability assessment. If observers believe that their behavior is not being monitored, these conditions should be maintained during reliability checks. Thus, reliability checks should be unobtrusive or covert. Alternatively, observers could be led to believe that all of their observations are being monitored. Indeed, this approach would appear advantageous because observers tend to be more accurate when they believe their agreement is assessed (Reid, 1970; Taplin and Reid, 1973).

It may be difficult to lead observers to believe that their behavior is always being checked. Covert reliability assessment may be needed. One suggestion for conducting covert reliability assessment is to have individuals score the behavior of different target subjects simultaneously in a group of subjects. In some of the intervals, the same subjects might be observed, although this would not be divulged to the observers. Comparisons of overlapping observations would provide an unobtrusive measure of reliability (O'Leary and Kent, 1973). In practice, these procedures may not be unobtrusive, due to interobserver communication or to events associated with the individual being observed. Observers may realize that they are assessing behavior of the same individuals simultaneously. Another solution is to have an experimenter covertly check reliability throughout the program, as for example, through a one-way mirror, although this may not be feasible in many naturalistic settings.

The problem of observer knowledge of identity of the reliability assessor may be resolved by controlling the communication of the assessor and observer so that they do not learn idiosyncracies of each other's recording. More elaborate solutions are available, such as conducting reliability checks from videotapes of select sections previously recorded by the observer. The assessor never has contact with the observer. Finally, several different assessors could be used so that an observer cannot readily learn the idiosyncratic patterns of any particular assessor.

Observer Drift

Nature of the problem. During training, observers usually receive extensive instruction and feedback regarding accuracy and interobserver agreement. Training is designed to ensure that observers adhere to the definitions of behavior and record behavior at a consistent level of accuracy. Once mastery is achieved, it is assumed that observers continue to apply the same definitions of behavior and record accurately. However, recent evidence suggests that observers "drift" from the original definitions of behavior (*e.g.,* Kent *et al.,* 1974, 1977; O'Leary and Kent, 1973; Reid, 1970; Reid and DeMaster, 1972; Taplin and Reid, 1973; Kent, Note 1). Drift refers to the tendency of observers to change the manner in which they apply the definitions of behavior over time.

Drift may not necessarily be reflected in interobserver agreement. If observers consistently work together and communicate, they may develop similar variations of the original response definitions (O'Leary and Kent, 1973). Thus, high levels of interobserver agreement can be maintained while accuracy has declined. In some reports, drift is revealed by comparing interobserver agreement within a given subgroup of observers who constantly work together with agreement across subgroups of observers who have not worked together (Kent *et al.*, 1974, 1977). Over time, subgroups may modify codes differently, which can be detected as differential within- and between-group interobserver agreement.

Modifications of the codes across observers may make observations from different observers incomparable. If subgroups of observers differ across experimental conditions, as might be the case for observations in a between-group design (*e.g.*, across different classrooms or homes), responses across groups cannot be meaningfully compared because they may not reflect common behavioral definitions. For within-subject designs, the data from a given set of observers or even for a single observer in one phase may not be directly comparable with data in earlier or later phases, due to observer drift.

Recommendations. Drift might be controlled by continually training all observers together as a unit throughout an investigation. Observers could periodically meet as a group, rate behavior, perhaps from videotapes, and receive immediate feedback on the accuracy of their observations relative to a predetermined standard. It is important to control drift by having access to observational data with an agreed upon standard. Otherwise, high levels of agreement might only reflect adjusting observations to meet the criteria of a familiar reliability assessor, rather than correctly applying the codes (Romanczyk *et al.*, 1973). Periodic retraining may limit the overall and differential loss of accuracy among observers. Of course, reactive retraining situations may delimit the generality of training so that behavior in the actual observation situation is not affected.

Drift might be controlled by videotaping the subject's behavior across sessions and by having observers score the tapes in a random order at the end of the study. Drift would not differentially influence data across phases. Unfortunately, taping sessions and observing behavior at the end of a project usually is time consuming and expensive. Also, ongoing data may be needed during the project to determine whether the experimental design or the intervention has to be altered in response to client behavior (Kazdin, 1977). Yet, taped samples of behavior could be compared with actual observations during select sessions partially to assess drift over time.

Drift might also be assessed or controlled by periodically bringing in newly trained observers to assess interobserver agreement during a project (O'Leary and Kent, 1973; Skindrud, 1973). Comparison of newly trained observers with observers who have continuously participated in the project can reveal whether the codes are applied differently over time. Differences between newly trained and experienced observers might simply reflect differences in the training procedures or in proficiency in applying the codes accurately, rather than modifications in applying the codes *per se.* Yet, any systematic alterations over time, including changes in proficiency, reflect observer drift.

Complexity of the Observational Coding System and Behaviors Scored

Nature of the problem. Complexity of the coding systems and behavior can refer to different characteristics of assessment. First, complexity can refer to the number of different response categories of an observational coding system. Systems with more categories are more complex than those with fewer categories. Second, complexity can refer to the number of different behaviors that are scored within a particular observational system on a given occasion. For a given observational system, more complex observations refer to those sessions in which a relatively high proportion of different codes are scored relative to all of the codes available.[4]

The influence of complexity, defined as the number of response categories of an observational system, has been investigated by Mash and McElwee (1974), who trained observers to score dyadic taped verbal interaction using either four or eight response categories. Because the interactions were preprogrammed and known in advance, observer accuracy could be assessed. Observers using the four-category system showed a higher level of accuracy than did observers using the eight-category system. Thus, the number of response categories in an observational system influences observer accuracy.

Complexity, defined as the proportion of behavioral codes that are actually recorded in a given session, also has been shown to affect agreement. Taplin and Reid (1973) and Reid (Note 4) found that interobserver agreement and the number of different (nonrepeated) codes used were negatively correlated ($r = -0.52$, $r = -0.75$, respectively). Similarly, using two sets of data, Skindrud (Note 6) found that interobserver agreement was positively related with percentage of similar (repeated) behavioral interactions ($r = +0.53$ and $+0.65$). Thus, the greater the diversity of behaviors scored within a given observational system, the lower interobserver agreement.

[4]Complexity also might be defined as the number of individuals who are observed in a given study (analogous to the number of response codes) or as the proportion of individuals who are observed on a given day relative to all those possible (analogous to the proportion of response categories used). Thus, observing several individuals might be considered more complex than observing fewer individuals. And, scoring the behavior of relatively more individuals on a given day would constitute a more complex assessment. A differential number of individuals might be scored if the observation system focuses on a particular behavior in a group situation (*e.g.,* a class) independently of who performs that behavior. The proportion of individuals observed of the total number available might be a measure of complexity. Measures of complexity based on the number of subjects observed have not been evaluated in the context of reliability assessment.

As discussed earlier, interobserver agreement and accuracy are greater when two observers are aware that their observations are being checked. Interestingly, complexity of the observations within a given observational system seems to vary systematically with observer awareness of reliability assessment. Reid (Note 3) found that complexity of observations was lower during the sessions that reliability was checked than during adjacent unchecked observation sessions (*cf.* Jones, Reid, and Patterson, 1975). Apparently, when observers overtly participate in a reliability check, they may score behaviors more conservatively than when their observations are unmonitored. Given the negative correlation between complexity of observations and interobserver agreement or accuracy, the reduced complexity of observations during monitored reliability sessions may account for the increased interobserver agreement during these sessions.

Related research has examined the influence of the predictability of behavior on accuracy. Behaviors may be performed in sequence so that they are highly predictable (one behavior tends to be followed by other behaviors), or in no particular sequence so that they are unpredictable (one behavior is not necessarily followed by other behaviors). Mash and McElwee (1974) constructed different audiotapes with verbal interactions that differed in predictability. Generally, observing predictable *versus* unpredictable behavior did not lead to differential accuracy in scoring behavior during training. However, when observing new stimulus material, a history of observing predictable behavioral sequences led to decrements in observer accuracy, whereas a history of observing unpredictable sequences led to increments in accuracy. Thus, observers trained in a given situation where behavioral codes are scored in a relatively unpredictable sequence more readily adapt to new situations than individuals exposed to predictable behavioral sequences.

Mash and Makohoniuk (1975) replicated and extended the previous study and demonstrated that observers with a history of scoring predictable rather than unpredictable responses made more of perseverative errors when scoring new observational material. Also, providing subjects with an instructional set to see a pattern in the data, *i.e.,* by noting that certain response categories are likely to follow other response categories, led to lower recording accuracy than a set specifying no pattern in the data. Looking for a pattern increased the frequency of not scoring behaviors that occurred (*i.e.,* omission errors).

There are important implications for the influence of complexity and predictability for interpreting estimates of interobserver agreement. Initially, reliability estimates of a given percentage or correlation level must be viewed in relation to the complexity of the observation system. Agreement estimates for a given category within an observation system might be influenced by the number of other categories that are scored or can be scored.

Second, observations for a given observational system may vary in complexity and predictability over time. Categories for a given observation system may be differentially utilized over time. Indeed, a larger or smaller proportion of different codes may be systematically confounded with experimental conditions. For example, as the intervention begins to affect behavior, the number of different coded entries may decrease (*e.g.,* for disruptive behaviors) or increase (*e.g.,* for prosocial behaviors). In such cases, changes in frequency of several categories and the overall proportion of different categories used would be confounded with the presentation and withdrawal of the intervention. Thus, for a given observational system in a single experiment, interobserver agreement estimates of equal magnitude for a given behavior may not be equally meaningful across phases. Even if the same number of coded entries are used across phases, behaviors may be differentially predictable. The behavior of the subject is likely to become more predictable and, indeed, more homogeneous in general during the intervention when target responses are systematically consequated than during the nonintervention phases when consequences may be allowed to vary unsystematically.

The problems of complexity and predictability may apply to the specific subjects observed. Subjects in a given experiment may vary in the complexity of behavior (*i.e.,* the number of different data entries made). Interobserver agreement based on data from a particular subject can over- or underestimate the agreement obtained from observation of another subject (Reid, Skindrud, Taplin, and Jones, Note 5).

Recommendations. Specific recommendations cannot be made for each form of complexity. Certain assessment characteristics are dictated by the nature of the investigation. For example, the number of codes employed in an observational system usually is controlled by the client's behavior and goals of the project. Similarly, complexity of observations scored within a given system are controlled by the behavior of the client. The influence of complexity within an observational system on interobserver agreement can be controlled by assessing agreement across all phases of an investigation and across all subjects, or at least a large sample of subjects, to ensure that agreement is not confounded with complexity.

Because of the consistent relationship between complexity of the observations (*i.e.,* the proportion of different codes used for a given observational system), some investigators have proposed that interobserver agreement routinely take complexity into account (Reid *et al.,* Note 5). Specifically, these investigators proposed that percentage agreement and complexity (defined as the percentage of nonrepeated code entries) should be multiplied for a given reliability session. The resulting proportion provides a *proficiency score.* Use of this score protects against obtaining high levels of interobserver agreement due to a session of relatively low complexity.

The data on complexity have clear implications for observer training. Occasionally, observers repeatedly score the same stimulus material (*e.g.,* from videotapes) until a criterion level of agreement or accuracy is achieved. Then, they are permitted to begin observations in the actual situation. During training, observers eventually may be able to predict the sequence of behaviors on the training stimuli. Accuracy or agreement obtained during training may overestimate post-training reliability when the observational samples are less familiar, more complex, and less predictable. The materials used in training observers should vary so that observations are not predictable. Also, because reliability and complexity of observations are related, high levels of interobserver agreement should be established for relatively complex observations for a given observational system. If complex observational stimuli are used during training, interobserver agreement is likely to estimate agreement conservatively during actual data collection, where complexity is allowed to vary.

Observer Expectancies and Feedback

Nature of the problem. Another potential source of bias is the expectancies of the observers regarding the subject's behavior and the feedback observers receive from the experimenter in relation to that behavior. Several studies suggest that observers who look for behavior change are more likely to find it (*e.g.*, Azrin, Holz, Ulrich, and Goldiamond, 1961; Scott, Burton, and Yarrow, 1967).

Recent investigations using behavioral assessment methods commonly employed in applied behavior analysis have examined observer expectancies. Kass and O'Leary (Note 1) told some observers that disruptive child behavior would increase and told others that it would decrease during treatment. All individuals observed the same classroom videotapes, which showed a decrease in disruptive behavior during treatment. In general, observers who expected a decrease recorded a greater reduction in some disruptive behaviors than those who expected an increase. Unfortunately, differential observer drift across groups, evident even in baseline, could have accounted for the results.

Kent *et al.* (1974) told some observers that disruptive behavior would decrease and told others that it would not change from baseline. The data on videotape in fact showed no change in disruptive behavior across phases. Overall, expectancies did not influence observer recordings. But when observers were asked to characterize the effect of the program on a questionnaire, their evaluation reflected the expectancy of the experimenter. Similarly, Skindrud (Note 6) found that informing observers of the experimental treatments did not bias the results of behavioral observations. Also, Redfield and Paul (1976) found that behaviors expected to change by observers were not influenced by these expectations on observational data. Overall, these results suggest that behavioral observations are not readily altered by observer expectancies.

Expectancies combined with feedback from the experimenter can influence observer performance. O'Leary, Kent, and Kanowitz (1975) led observers to believe that a token economy (treatment) would alter disruptive behavior on videotapes of children in a classroom. Actually, tapes of baseline and treatment were matched for disruptive behavior and no treatment was given. The experimenter provided positive comments (approval) of the observers' data if a reduction in the target behaviors was scored during the "treatment" phase, and negative comments (disappointment) if no change or an increase in the target behaviors was scored. Instructions to expect change and feedback for scoring reductions in target behaviors biased the data. Interestingly, child responses that observers were told would not change did not change during the experiment. Thus, expectancies and feedback about the effect of treatment exerted specific effects on the data.

Recommendations. The above research suggests that expectancies alone are not likely to influence behavioral observations unless some feedback also is provided. Presumably, feedback may be given by the experimenter or even be obtained by the observers from the data they are collecting. Thus, controlling expectancies and feedback may be difficult. Observers can readily detect interventions that require change in the environment (*e.g.*, delivery of tokens, use of timeout) and are alerted to the desired therapeutic effects. Observer expectancies for change might be controlled by periodically bringing in new observers who are unfamiliar with the reinforcement history of the client or behavior change that has been achieved.

Another solution might be to videotape samples of performance throughout phases of the experiment. Ratings of the tapes in random order could provide a standard against which observations used in the study could be compared. Observer accuracy could be assessed to determine whether observers in the actual situation and familiar with the clients and interventions systematically differed in their observations across phases.

The problems of providing observers with explicit feedback are somewhat more easily controlled than expectancies. Obviously, experimenters should not and probably do not usually provide feedback to observers for directional change in client behavior. Any feedback given to observers should be restricted to the accuracy of their observations, rather than for changes in the client's behavior.

Additional Influences on Reliability Assessment

The above factors do not necessarily exhaust the possible procedural influences that need to be considered when interpreting estimates of accuracy and interobserver agreement. Other variables that might influence interobserver agreement have been explored. For example, Taplin and Reid (1973) attempted to show that observer accuracy is partially determined by the status of the experimenter. Observers trained with a high-status experimenter (university professor) showed lower accuracy estimates than did observers trained by lower-status experimenters (graduate students). Regrettably, only one experimenter served in the high-status condition and, thus, individual experimenter characteristics were confounded with status. Yet, research on experimenter characteristics appears to warrant additional scrutiny.

The individuals who compute interobserver agreement may influence reliability estimates. For example, Kent *et al.* (1974) found that observer agreement tended to be higher when computed by observers than by the experimenter. Similarly, O'Leary and Kent (1973) found that higher estimates of interobserver agreement were obtained when observers were allowed to score behavior and calculate reliability without, rather than with, the supervision of an experimenter. Although calculation of data by individuals who participate in a project is not necessarily biased (Rusch, Walker, and Greenwood, 1975), as a precaution, those who compute the data should not be the same individuals as those who calculate and evaluate the data.

CONCLUSION

The above overview described major characteristics and sources of bias that need to be considered when evaluating reliability estimates. Essentially, the characteristics describe only some of the major conditions that may influence the interpretation of reliability. Interobserver agreement and accuracy can be viewed as target behaviors in their own right that are a function of a variety of variables. These include characteristics of the observational system, characteristics of the experimenter, observer, and client, methods of scoring behavior, the nature and duration of observing training, situational and instructional variables during assessment of reliability, the pattern of client behavior, concurrent observation of stimulus and consequent events, and so on. Generally, current research has only begun to evaluate these variables and supports the contention that agreement is multiply-determined.

Because the data obtained in a given investigation depend on diverse factors in addition to the specific responses of the client, some investigators (Jones *et al.*, 1974; Mash and McElwee, 1974) have advocated that the reliability of behavioral observations be conceptualized from the standpoint of generalizability theory (Cronbach, Gleser, Nanda, and Rajaratnam, 1972). Generalizability theory extends the notion of reliability so that generalizability of observations across different conditions within an investigation can be assessed. The extent to which observations in a study vary across facets or dimensions (*e.g.*, observers, occasions, phases, *etc.*) can be studied, and the generalizability of the data across different levels of these facets can be evaluated directly. An advantage of studying generalizability is that it simultaneously examines the contribution of diverse characteristics of assessment to the data. Also, the theory of generalizability emphasizes the relative nature of reliability, *viz.*, that there is no reliability for a given assessment method, but rather an infinite number of reliabilities that are a function of the range of assessment conditions.

While the research reviewed in the present paper strongly suggests that diverse sources of bias and characteristics of assessment influence reliability estimates, the generality of many of the specific conclusions must be made cautiously. Many of the investigations were laboratory analog studies and approach only some of the conditions present in naturalistic settings. For example, in some studies the duration of observer training was brief relative to the training used for many applied studies (Mash and McElwee, 1974; Reid, 1970); the observers were paid volunteers or subjects fulfilling experimental credits for a course and were not necessarily screened for their competence (Mash and McElwee, 1974; Taplin and Reid, 1973); also, the codes included multiple behaviors (*e.g.*, over 30 categories), rather than the few that are more commonly studied (Reid, 1970). Also, in a few studies, conditions are designed to maximize bias and artifact such as intentionally giving reliability assessors different behavioral definitions, permitting observers to calculate their agreement, and encouraging interobserver communication (Kent *et al.*, 1974; Romanczyk *et al.*, 1973). Yet, this area of research cannot be discounted on the grounds of frequent reliance upon analog studies for at least two reasons. First, some studies have employed observers trained for extended periods and have used observational codes evaluated in many applied investigations (*e.g.*, Romanczyk *et al.*, 1973). Second, while analog studies always raise questions about the generality of the findings, the consistency of the sources of bias revealed by the studies reviewed in the present paper presents a convincing demonstration of the importance of bias. In light of the specific characteristics and sources of bias associated with assessing interobserver agreement, any estimate of agreement must be qualified by the specific conditions of assessment. Research needs to establish the ideal conditions under which agreement can be assessed and the effects of deviation from these conditions in applied settings.

REFERENCE NOTES

1. Kass, R. E. and O'Leary, K. D. *The effects of observer bias in field-experimental settings.* Paper presented at symposium, Behavior Analysis in Education, University of Kansas, Lawrence, April 1970.
2. Kent, R. N. *Expectation bias in behavioral observation.* Unpublished doctoral dissertation. State University of New York at Stony Brook, 1972.
3. Reid, J. B. *Differences in the complexity of reliability assessment vs. adjacent non-reliability assessment observation sessions: A technical note.* Unpublished manuscript, University of Oregon, 1973. (*a*)
4. Reid, J. B. *The relationship between complexity of observer proctocol and inter-observer agreement for twenty-five reliability assessment sessions: A technical note.* Unpublished manuscript, University of Oregon, 1973. (*b*)
5. Reid, J. B., Skindrud, K. D., Taplin, P. S., and Jones, R. R. *The role of complexity in the collection and evaluation of observation data.* Paper presented at meeting of the American Psychological Association, Montreal, Quebec, September 1973.
6. Skindrud, K. *An evaluation of observer bias in experimental-field studies interaction.* Unpublished doctoral dissertation, University of Oregon, 1972.

REFERENCES

Azrin, N. H., Holz, W., Ulrich, R., and Goldiamond, I. The control of the content of conversation through reinforcement. *Journal of the Experimental Analysis of Behavior,* 1961, **4,** 25-30.

Bijou, S. W., Peterson, R. F., and Ault, M. H. A method to integrate descriptive and experimental field studies at the level of data and empirical concepts. *Journal of Applied Behavior Analysis,* 1968, **1**, 175-191.

Cronbach, L. J., Gleser, G. C., Nanda, H., and Rajaratnam, N. *The dependability of behavioral measurements: Theory of generalizability for scores and profiles.* New York: Wiley, 1972.

Hartmann, D. P. Considerations in the choice of interobserver reliability estimates. *Journal of Applied Behavior Analysis,* 1977, **10**, 103-116.

Hawkins, R. P. and Dobes, R. W. Behavioral definitions in applied behavioral analysis: Explicit or implicit. In B. C. Etzel, J. M. LeBlanc, and D. M. Baer (Eds.), *New developments in behavioral research: theory, methods, and applications. In honor of Sidney W. Bijou.* Hillsdale, New Jersey: Lawrence Erlbaum Associates, 1975.

Hawkins, R. P. and Dotson, V. A. Reliability scores that delude: an Alice in Wonderland trip through the misleading characteristics of inter-observer agreement scores in interval recording. In E. Ramp and G. Semb (Eds.), *Behavior analysis: Areas of research and application.* Englewood Cliffs, New Jersey: Prentice-Hall, 1975. Pp. 359-376.

Johnson, S. M. and Bolstad, O. D. Methodological issues in naturalistic observation: some problems and solutions for field research. In L. A. Hamerlynck, L. C. Handy, and E. J. Mash (Eds.), *Behavior change: methodology, concepts, and practice.* Champaign, Illinois: Research Press, 1973. Pp. 7-67.

Jones, R. R., Reid, J. B., and Patterson, G. R. Naturalist observation in clinical assessment. In P. McReynolds (Ed.), *Advances in psychological assessment,* Vol. 3. San Francisco: Jossey-Bass, 1975.

Kazdin, A. E. Methodology of applied behavior analysis. In T. A. Brigham and A. C. Catania (Eds.), *Handbook of applied behavior research: social and instructional processes.* New York: Irvington/Naiburg—Wiley, 1977, (*in press*).

Kent, R. N., Kanowitz, J., O'Leary, K. D., and Cheiken, M. Observer reliability as a function of circumstances of assessment. *Journal of Applied Behavior Analysis,* 1977, (*in press*).

Kent, R. N., O'Leary, K. D., Diament, C., and Dietz, A. Expectation biases in observational evaluation of therapeutic change. *Journal of Consulting and Clinical Psychology,* 1974, **42**, 774-780.

Mash, E. J. and Makohoniuk, G. The effects of prior information and behavioral predictability on observer accuracy. *Child Development,* 1975, **46**, 513-519.

Mash, E. J. and McElwee, J. Situational effects on observer accuracy: behavioral predictability, prior experience, and complexity of coding categories. *Child Development,* 1974, **45**, 367-377.

O'Leary, K. D. and Kent, R. N. Behavior modification for social action: research tactics and problems. In L. A. Hamerlynck, P. O. Davidson, and L. E. Acker (Eds.), *Critical issues in research and practice.* Champaign, Illinois: Research Press, 1973. Pp. 69-96.

O'Leary, K. D., Kent, R. N., and Kanowitz, J. Shaping data collection congruent with experimental hypotheses. *Journal of Applied Behavior Analysis,* 1975, **8**, 43-51.

Redfield, J. and Paul, G. L. Bias in behavioral observation as a function of observer familiarity with subjects and typicality of behavior. *Journal of Consulting and Clinical Psychology,* 1976, **44**, 156.

Reid, J. B. Reliability assessment of observation data: a possible methodological problem. *Child Development,* 1970, **41**, 1143-1150.

Reid, J. B. and DeMaster, B. The efficacy of the spot-check procedure in maintaining the reliability of data collected by observers in quasi-natural settings: two pilot studies. *Oregon Research Institute Research Bulletin,* 1972, **12**.

Romanczyk, R. G., Kent, R. N., Diament, C., and O'Leary, K. D. Measuring the reliability of observational data: a reactive process. *Journal of Applied Behavior Analysis,* 1973, **6**, 175-184.

Rusch, F. R., Walker, H. M., and Greenwood, C. R. Experimenter calculation errors: a potential factor affecting interpretation of results. *Journal of Applied Behavior Analysis,* 1975, **8**, 460.

Scott, P., Burton, R. V., and Yarrow, M. Social reinforcement under natural conditions. *Child Development,* 1967, **38**, 53-63.

Skindrud, K. Field evaluation of observer bias under overt and covert monitoring. In L. A. Hamerlynck, L. C. Handy, and E. J. Mash (Eds.), *Behavior change: methodology, concepts, and practice.* Champaign, Illinois: Research Press, 1973. Pp. 97-117.

Taplin, P. S. and Reid, J. B. Effects of instructional set and experimenter influence on observer reliability. *Child Development,* 1973, **44**, 547-554.

Received 6 February 1976.
(*Final acceptance 15 May 1976.*)

JOURNAL OF APPLIED BEHAVIOR ANALYSIS 1978, 11, 523-527 NUMBER 4 (WINTER 1978)

A METHOD FOR COMBINING OCCURRENCE AND NONOCCURRENCE INTEROBSERVER AGREEMENT SCORES

FRANCIS C. HARRIS AND BENJAMIN B. LAHEY[1]

UNIVERSITY OF GEORGIA

Various statistics have been proposed as standard methods for calculating and reporting interobserver agreement scores. The advantages and disadvantages of each have been discussed in this journal recently but without resolution. A formula is presented that combines separate measures of occurrence and nonoccurrence percentages of agreement, with weight assigned to each measure, varying according to the observed rate of behavior. This formula, which is a modification of a formula proposed by Clement (1976), appears to reduce distortions due to "chance" agreement encountered with very high or low observed rates of behavior while maintaining the mathematical and conceptual simplicity of the conventional method for calculating occurrence and nonoccurrence agreement.

DESCRIPTORS: reliability, interobserver agreement, combining occurrence and nonoccurrence scores, critical assessment of commonly used procedures

---

The field of applied behavior analysis currently relies heavily on data collected by human observers (Kelly, 1977). These data are typically considered reliable if two independent observers reach an "acceptable" level of agreement on the occurrence and/or nonoccurrence of a target behavior, using more-or-less standard observation methods. The demonstration of an acceptable level of interobserver agreement (and, presumably, of objectivity) is crucial to applied behavior analysis, but therein lies the problem. No current method of calculating interobserver agreement has been widely accepted, although several have been proposed. The need for a standard method by which interobserver agreement can be computed has been discussed in a recent series of articles in the *Journal of Applied Behavior Analysis* (Baer, 1977; Hartmann, 1977; Hopkins and Hermann, 1977; Kratochwill and Wetzel, 1977; Yelton, Wildman, and Erickson, 1977).

Percentage Agreement Statistics

One commonly used statistic in interval recording has been overall percentage agreement. This typically is determined by counting the number of intervals in which the observers agree on occurrences *and* nonoccurrences, dividing by the total number of observation intervals, and multiplying the quotient by 100. This statistic has face validity, in that it gives the percentage of intervals in which observers agreed that the behavior occurred and did not occur.

Overall percentage agreement generally has been considered to be susceptible to misinterpretation, however, when a relatively high or low number of intervals is scored. This can be considered to be due to the probability of "chance" agreements being high. For example, if in a 100-interval observation session each observer scored 10 occurrences, but only two in the same intervals, the overall agreement percentage would be 84% [(two agreements on occurrence + 82 agreements on nonoccurrence = 84 agreements) ÷ 100 intervals = 84%]. In this case, the high number of unscored recording intervals can be assumed to result in a high frequency of chance agreements that inflate the agreement score. In the case of high rates of recorded behavior, a high number of intervals would be marked by both observers. If the two observers

[1]Reprints may be obtained from Benjamin B. Lahey, Psychology Clinic, Dept. of Psychology, University of Georgia, Athens, GA 30602.

were randomly marking at a high rate of occurrences, a large number of intervals would be marked by *both* observers and would, therefore, be counted as agreements. If agreements on occurrences *and* nonoccurrences were included and given equal weight in the calculation of the agreement score, a high score would be obtained, even though the records of the two observers were unrelated (random). The same reasoning would apply in the case of low-rate behaviors in which the high number of chance agreements on unmarked intervals would inflate the overall agreement score (Hartmann, 1977). Hopkins and Hermann (1977) stated the same point in a different way: "The observers might be recording two entirely different but relatively high-rate behaviors, and interval by interval comparison of their records would yield many intervals of agreement simply because both are recording some response as occurring in most intervals" (p. 122).

One method of reducing the threat of such chance agreements, currently used by many behavior analysts, is to calculate the interobserver agreement for scored intervals only when the observed rate of behavior is low and for unscored intervals only when the observed rate is high. It typically is calculated by dividing the number of intervals in which the observers agree on occurrences (nonoccurrences) by the total number of intervals in which at least one observer scored an occurrence (nonoccurrence). This method may overcompensate, however, by throwing out *all* of the agreement data on unscored or scored intervals, respectively. In the example cited above, not all of the agreements on unscored intervals could be assumed to be "chance" agreements. In addition, this method is not appropriate for the many studies in which rates of observed behavior vary (Hartmann, 1977). This is due to the absence of an objective method for determining the frequency at which one score should be used instead of the other. The alternative of reporting occurrence *and* nonoccurrence agreement scores for each session would result in an unnecessary inconvenience to the research consumer (Kratochwill and Wetzel, 1977).

Recently, several investigators have suggested alternate methods for dealing with the problem of chance agreement. Hopkins and Hermann (1977) suggested that overall percentage agreement might be interpretable if it were compared to the overall agreement percentage expected by chance and presented formulas for calculating agreement scores that would be expected by chance. Minimum criterion for an acceptable level of agreement would be an obtained score greater than that expected by chance alone. In the example cited above, obtained agreement would be 84% and chance agreement would be 82% (Hopkins and Hermann, 1977). Thus, satisfactory agreement would be obtained (by a margin of 2%) even though the observers could agree on only two occurrences while they disagreed on 16. Furthermore, if, in a 100-interval session each observer scored 45 occurrences but only 21 in the same intervals, the overall percentage agreement score would be 52%, and the score expected by chance would be 51%. Thus, according to Hopkins and Hermann, adequate agreement would have been obtained even though there was only 52% overall agreement. The mathematically derived minimum criterion of chance agreement is appealing, but there is no reason to believe that it is any more *useful* to the behavior analyst than some arbitrary, but conventional level such as 80% agreement. This is similar to the clinical *versus* statistical significance issue. In the above example, the proposed statistical criterion was met, but many behavior analysts would not consider the data to be "reliable" (useful) because of the relatively low proportion of occurrence agreements.

A method of calculating occurrence (nonoccurrence) agreement that permits comparison to a score expected by chance also has been described by Hopkins and Hermann (1977). The number of intervals scored (unscored) by both observers is divided by the total number of intervals (regardless of how many were scored by either). This percentage then can be compared with the one expected by chance, with acceptable agreement being any score greater than chance. For our first example, the occurrence agreement percentage equals 2% and the chance percentage equals 1%. Thus, according to Hopkins and Hermann, adequate agreement would have been reached. This could be misleading for the same reasons that were presented for the Hopkins and Hermann overall percentage agreement statistic. Like the conventional occurrence and nonoccurrence agreement percentages, those described by Hopkins and Hermann minimize chance agreements by not considering nonoccurrence (occurrrence) agreements. They differ from the conventional agreement percentages in that the divisor is always the number of intervals in the session. This makes the possible range of the statistics dependent on the number of intervals scored. For example, a "perfect" agreement percentage could be 10% for one session and 90% for another.

Correlation-Like and Probability-Based Methods

Correlation-like measures have been proposed to minimize the chance agreement problem (Hartmann, 1977). Essentially, they express a comparison between observed and expected interobserver agreement, but in a manner that is more mathematically complicated than the formulas of Hopkins and Hermann (1977). They can assume any value between −1.0 and +1.0. Interpretation of them generally requires greater statistical sophistication than statistics that use the simple 0% to 100% scale. Kratochwill and Wetzel (1977) pointed out that another disadvantage ". . . is that their 'novel' feature could cause investigators to employ them to the exclusion of simpler statistical aids that could adequately represent observer agreement" (p. 138).

A probability-based formula that gives the exact probability of obtaining at least any given number of overall agreements has been put forth by Yelton, Wildman, and Erickson (1977). Interpretation of this statistic also requires greater statistical sophistication than does those using the 0% to 100% scale. In addition, its novelty could cause investigators to use it in lieu of simpler statistical aids, such as percentage agreement scores. Furthermore, its cumbersome mathematics make it unlikely to be adopted by many behavior analysts.

The correlation-like and probability-based methods differ from the more commonly used methods, in that they each provide a formal method of comparing an obtained agreement score with one expected by chance, rather than describing the *degree* of agreement. As with the Hopkins and Hermann (1977) method, the issue in evaluating these methods is the same as the issue of statistical *versus* clinical significance. The correlation-like and probability-based formulas tell us whether obtained interobserver agreement exceeds a mathematically determined minimum standard of "significance", rather than assessing the extent to which the degree of interobserver agreement reaches some conventional level of "usefulness". Both involve pure assumptions: one involves a mathematical model of chance agreements; the other involves a conventional standard of utility.

Combining Occurrence and Nonoccurrence Percentage Agreement Scores

The formulas suggested for calculating interobserver agreement in the Spring 1977 issue of the *Journal of Applied Behavior Analysis* seek to minimize the chance agreement problem using different, but statistically sound, procedures. Baer (1977) noted the arbitrariness of all methods of calculating interobserver agreement and suggested that the choice of a standard method be based on "(1) the avoidance of allowing the reliability of occurrence from influencing the reliability of nonoccurrence and *vice versa;* and (2) by the apparent, face meaning of the estimate's calculation technique" (p. 117). The separate calculation of conventional occurrence and nonoccurrence agreement percentages fits Baer's criteria perfectly. (1) It minimizes the likelihood of allowing occurrence agreement to influence nonoccurrence agreement, and *vice versa;* and (2) it has good face validity ". . . Two observers watching one subject, and equipped with the same definition of behavior . . . agree about its occurrence X% of the relevant intervals, and about its nonoccurrence Y% of the relevant intervals" (Baer, 1977, p. 118).

In addition to the problems with this procedure already noted, however, the interpretation of separately calculated coefficients of occurrence and nonoccurrence agreement is uncertain. We have no guidelines as to how much "weight" to give to each coefficient at differing observed rates of behavior.

If, in studies in which behavior levels vary over time, a single agreement score is required to summarize interobserver agreement and simplify the task of research consumers (Kratochwill and Wetzel, 1977), some combination of occurrence and nonoccurrence agreement scores that differentially weights each score on the basis of the observed behavior frequency would seem appropriate. Although some difficulties are associated with it, such a statistic has been proposed by Clement (1976):

$$\text{Interobserver agreement} = (A \times B) + (C \times D)$$

where

- A is the number of agreements for occurrences divided by the number of time samples marked by the "standard" observer;
- B is 1.00—(occurrences marked by the "standard" observer divided by the total number of time samples);
- C is the number of agreements for nonoccurrences divided by the number of nonoccurrences indicated by the "standard" observer; and
- D is 1.00—(nonoccurrences indicated by the "standard" observer divided by the total number of time samples).

In essence, Clement's formula provides a weighted mean of indices of occurrence and nonoccurrence agreement, with weight assigned to these two indices according to the frequency at which behavior is recorded. Proportionately greater emphasis is placed on occurrence agreement when relatively few intervals are scored and proportionately greater emphasis is placed on nonoccurrence agreement when a relatively high number of intervals is scored. This compensates for distortions due to to "chance" agreements with high- or low-rate behaviors without eliminating any data.

Clement's formula, therefore, offers a solution to the chance agreement dilemma inherent in other formulas of interobserver agreement. Two modifications of his formula are apparently needed, however, to bring it more in line with conventional thinking in applied behavior analysis. First, the A and C terms in Clement's equation provide inaccurate occurrence and nonoccurrence agreement scores. They should be calculated by dividing the number of agreements on occurrences (or nonoccurrences) by the total number of intervals marked (or left unmarked) by *either* observer, rather than by only one observer (the "standard" observer). Clement's formula overestimates agreement by providing an incomplete divisor. Second, the weighting factor should be the mean of the occurrences recorded by both observers, rather than arbitrarily designating one person as the standard observer. Since data are being combined to yield one agreement score, differentially assigning more or less weight to one observer's score is inappropriate. The modified formula for weighted agreement is therefore:

$$WA = (O \times U) + (N \times S) \times 100$$

where

- O is the occurrence agreement score, *i.e.*, the number of occurrence agreements divided by (the number of occurrence agreements + the number of occurrence disagreements);
- U is the mean proportion of unscored intervals, *i.e.*, (the proportion of intervals not scored by Observer 1 + proportion

of intervals not scored by Observer 2) divided by 2;

N is the nonoccurrence agreement score, *i.e.*, the number of nonoccurrence agreements divided by (the number of nonoccurrence agreements + the number of nonoccurrence disagreements);

S is the mean proportion of scored intervals, *i.e.*, (the proportion of intervals scored by Observer 1 + proportion of intervals scored by Observer 2) divided by two.

More simply, this formula may be conceptualized as occurrence agreement weighted by the average rate of nonoccurrence, plus nonoccurrence agreement weighted by the average rate of occurrence.

For example, if in a 100-interval observation session one observer scored 25 occurrences, the other scored 30, they agreed on occurrences 20 times and nonoccurrences 65 times, and disagreed 15 times each on occurrences and nonoccurrences:

$$\begin{aligned} WA &= \left(\frac{20}{20+15}\right)\left(\frac{0.75+0.70}{2}\right) \\ &\quad + \left(\frac{65}{65+15}\right)\left(\frac{0.25+0.30}{2}\right) \times 100 \\ &= (0.57)(0.72) + (0.81)(0.28) \times 100 \\ &= 64\% \end{aligned}$$

Note that in this example, 72% of the weight is assigned to the occurrence agreement score and 28% is assigned to the nonoccurrence score.

This formula differs from that of Clement's (1976), then, in calculating separate agreement coefficients for marked and unmarked intervals using a complete divisor (the total number of intervals marked by either observer, rather than just one observer) and by using the mean of the occurrences recorded by both observers as the weighting factor, rather than the occurrences recorded by one observer.

The score yielded by the above formula must always be between 0% and 100%, such that a convention similar to that of an adequate score being approximately 80% or greater could be adopted. The weighted agreement formula yields a single score that minimizes chance agreement and makes use of all the available interobserver agreement information by combining occurrence and nonoccurrence interobserver agreement scores. It also permits evaluation of interobserver agreement on the familiar 0% to 100% scale. It appears to be an especially useful, efficient, and convenient method for expressing interobserver agreement in studies in which the frequency of the target behavior varies considerably. Furthermore, it is only a slight departure from the widely understood and regularly used method of calculating interobserver agreement percentages. It appears, therefore, to provide a reasonable, conventional method for assessing interobserver agreement when using interval data.

REFERENCES

Baer, D. M. Reviewer's comment: just because it's reliable doesn't mean that you can use it. *Journal of Applied Behavior Analysis*, 1977, **10**, 117-119.

Clement, P. G. A formula for computing interobserver agreement. *Psychological Reports*, 1976, **39**, 257-258.

Hartmann, D. P. Considerations in the choice of interobserver reliability estimates. *Journal of Applied Behavior Analysis*, 1977, **10**, 103-116.

Hopkins, B. L. and Hermann, J. A. Evaluating interobserver reliability of interval data. *Journal of Applied Behavior Analysis*, 1977, **10**, 121-126.

Kelly, M. B. A review of the observational data-collection and reliability procedures reported in *The Journal of Applied Behavior Analysis*. *Journal of Applied Behavior Analysis*, 1977, **10**, 97-101.

Kratochwill, T. R. and Wetzel, R. J. Observer agreement, credibility, and judgement: some considerations in presenting observer agreement data. *Journal of Applied Behavior Analysis*, 1977, **10**, 133-139.

Yelton, A. R., Wildman, B. G., and Erickson, M. T. A probability-based formula for calculating interobserver agreement. *Journal of Applied Behavior Analysis*, 1977, **10**, 127-131.

Received 13 October 1977.
(Final Acceptance 28 July 1978.)

JOURNAL OF APPLIED BEHAVIOR ANALYSIS 1979, **12**, 523-533 NUMBER 4 (WINTER 1979)

A GRAPHICAL JUDGMENTAL AID WHICH SUMMARIZES OBTAINED AND CHANCE RELIABILITY DATA AND HELPS ASSESS THE BELIEVABILITY OF EXPERIMENTAL EFFECTS

JOHN C. BIRKIMER AND JOSEPH H. BROWN

UNIVERSITY OF LOUISVILLE

Interval by interval reliability has been criticized for "inflating" observer agreement when target behavior rates are very low or very high. Scored interval reliability and its converse, unscored interval reliability, however, vary as target behavior rates vary when observer disagreement rates are constant. These problems, along with the existence of "chance" values of each reliability which also vary as a function of response rate, may cause researchers and consumers difficulty in interpreting observer agreement measures. Because each of these reliabilities essentially compares observer disagreements to a different base, it is suggested that the disagreement rate itself be the first measure of agreement examined, and its magnitude relative to occurrence and to nonoccurrence agreements then be considered. This is easily done via a graphic presentation of the disagreement range as a bandwidth around reported rates of target behavior. Such a graphic presentation summarizes all the information collected during reliability assessments and permits visual determination of each of the three reliabilities. In addition, graphing the "chance" disagreement range around the bandwidth permits easy determination of whether or not true observer agreement has likely been demonstrated. Finally, the limits of the disagreement bandwidth help assess the believability of claimed experimental effects: those leaving no overlap between disagreement ranges are probably believable, others are not.

DESCRIPTORS: chance agreement, chance reliability, internal validity, interobserver agreement, observational data, observational technology, percentage agreement, reliability

---

As Kelly (1977) has indicated, research in applied behavior analysis generally produces either permanent-product data, mechanically collected data, or observational data, with the last by far the most common. When observational data are collected, a human observer watches the target individual and records instances of the behavior of interest. Sometimes simple counting of the target behavior occurs, but frequently, either interval recording, time-sampling, or trial scoring is done instead. With interval recording, the entire experimental session is divided into many brief time intervals and the observer records whether or not the behavior of interest occurs during each interval. With time-sampling, the observer either records for only some of the possible intervals during a session or records whether or not behavior is occurring at each of a prespecified subset of moments during a session (Powell, Martindale, and Kulp, 1975). With trial scoring, the observer scores "right" or "wrong" with regard to each of the subject's responses to stimulus materials.

To attempt to ensure that the data collected by the observer are similar to those that would be obtained by other competent observers, researchers arrange reliability checks. Reliability checks involve having a second observer independently record the same behavior of the same target individual through the same experimental session and then comparing the records generated by the two observers. This paper deals with several frequently used statistical procedures for summarizing the results of reliability checks. Other authors have discussed sources of bias and unreliability among observers, and procedures

Reprints of this paper are available from John C. Birkimer, Department of Psychology, University of Louisville, Louisville, Kentucky 40208.

to detect such biases and remedy them, some of this under the rubric of "generalizability theory" (Cone, 1977; Kazdin, 1977). The thrust of the current paper is, instead, toward clarifying problems which are implicit in the current commonly used procedures and toward recommending a graphical procedure which solves those problems and proves valuable as an additional tool for assessing the internal validity of behavioral research, for detecting claimed experimental effects which are not believable.

One simple reliability percentage sometimes calculated, total reliability, is simply the smaller reported frequency of occurrence of target behavior divided by the larger, the proportion then multiplied by 100. This is the only generally used agreement statistic when simple counting is the recording method, and has been correctly criticized by Hawkins and Dotson (1975) as measuring agreement on total frequencies but not on individual occurrences of target behavior. Because substantial agreement on individual occurrences is fundamental to accurate measurement, only procedures focusing on individual intervals, moments, or trials will be discussed further.

The first such procedure has been referred to as moment by moment reliability, as point by point reliability, as percentage agreement (Hartmann, 1977), and as interval by interval (I × I) reliability (Hawkins and Dotson, 1975). With this procedure the two observers' records are compared interval by interval, moment by moment, or trial by trial. The number of occasions on which the observers agree is counted, with an agreement being counted each time they agree the behavior occurred and each time they agree that it did not. The number of agreements is then divided by the total number of occasions in which they agreed and disagreed. (With this measure, the denominator equals the total number of recording occasions.) The ratio of agreements to agreements plus disagreements, when multiplied by 100, yields a percentage which is the reliability or agreement estimate. I × I reliability has been criticized by Hawkins and Dotson (1975) and Kazdin (1975), among others, with the argument that it inflates the percentage agreement estimate when response rates are low by including many cases of agreement which involve the observers agreeing the behavior has not occurred.

The second such reliability calculating procedure has been referred to as occurrence reliability, as effective percentage agreement (Hartmann, 1977), and as scored interval (S-I) reliability (Hawkins and Dotson, 1975). With this procedure, again agreements are divided by the sum of agreements plus disagreements and the ratio multiplied by 100 to yield a percentage reliability or agreement figure. With S-I reliability, however, the definition of agreement is restricted to those occasions on which the observers agree the behavior did occur. The procedure has been recommended by Hawkins and Dotson (1975) and Kazdin (1975), among others, as avoiding the inflationary effects of agreements on nonoccurrences.

The third reliability procedure sometimes used in these situations has been referred to as nonoccurrence reliability, as effective percentage agreement on nonoccurrences (Hartmann, 1977) and as unscored interval (U-I) reliability (Hawkins and Dotson, 1975), and is simply S-I reliability for agreements on nonoccurrences. Hawkins and Dotson suggested that instead of using I × I reliability, researchers should determine S-I and U-I reliabilities, reporting either each reliability or the arithmetic mean of the two. Others have made similar suggestions (Baer, 1977; Hartmann, 1977).

A PROBLEM WITH S-I AND U-I RELIABILITIES

A substantial problem exists, however, with S-I and U-I reliabilities. Observers must record on each recording occasion, scoring the presence or absence of target behavior. If the rate[1] of

[1]The use of the term "rate" here and throughout is a convenience, referring to a *percentage* of intervals,

Table 1

Effect of varying rate of behavior with constant disagreement rate on I × I, S-I, and U-I reliabilities.

Behavior Rate	*Occurrence Agreements*	*Nonoccurrence Agreements*	*Disagreements*	*I × I Reliab.*	*S-I Reliab.*	*U-I Reliab.*
90%	85%	5%	10%	90%	89%	33%
50%	45%	45%	10%	90%	82%	82%
10%	5%	85%	10%	90%	33%	89%

target behavior varies and observers' disagreement rate remains constant, these two reliabilities will vary, as Table 1 shows. In the table, disagreements are taken equally from agreements and disagreements, but the following holds, however they are distributed. I × I reliability remains constant, since it is algebraically equivalent to 100% minus the constant disagreement rate. As the target behavior rate decreases, S-I reliability divides the decreasing number of occurrence agreements by the sum of those agreements plus the constant number of disagreements, causing the reliability statistic to decrease. The opposite effect is caused similarly for U-I reliability. Only if the disagreement rate decreases proportionately to the decreasing behavior rate will S-I reliability remain constant. Such a decrease could be expected only if observers had difficulty agreeing when behavior occurred but no difficulty agreeing when it did not, a distinction rarely possible to make from typical reliability data.

Fluctuations in S-I and U-I reliabilities resulting from changes in target behavior rate, with I × I reliabilities remaining constant, could be troublesome or puzzling to researchers and, with quite low or high behavior rates, lead to obtained reliability percentages below the commonly held "acceptable" 80% to 90% range, perhaps discouraging research on such behaviors.

"CHANCE" RELIABILITIES: A PROBLEM WITH I × I, S-I, AND U-I RELIABILITIES

Hopkins and Hermann (1977), among others, have indicated that for each of these three reliability calculation procedures there are "chance" values obtainable when no true interobserver agreement exists. With observers reporting some rate of target behavior, but reporting randomly, the probabilities of agreements on occurrences, agreements on nonoccurrences, and disagreements are easily obtained (Hopkins and Hermann, 1977) and determine the "chance" values of I × I, S-I, and U-I reliabilities.

If observer 1 reports O_1 occurrences of target behavior (and N_1 nonoccurrences) while observer 2 reports O_2 occurrences and N_2 nonoccurrences, over T observation occasions, but observers report randomly, then the chance probabilities are calculated as:

$$p(\text{chance agreements on occurrences}) = \frac{O_1 \cdot O_2}{T^2}$$

$$p(\text{chance agreements on nonoccurrences}) = \frac{N_1 \cdot N_2}{T^2}$$

$$p(\text{chance disagreements}) = \frac{O_1 \cdot N_2 + N_1 \cdot O_2}{T^2}$$

and

$$I \times I \text{ chance} = \frac{O_1 \cdot O_2 + N_1 \cdot N_2}{T^2} (100)$$

moments, or trials, or a percentage of agreements on occurrences, on nonoccurrences, or a percentage of disagreements. Wording difficulties and potential confusion with the reliability percentages led us to use "rate" this way.

S-I chance =

$$\frac{O_1 \cdot O_2}{O_1 \cdot O_2 + O_1 \cdot N_2 + N_1 \cdot O_2}(100)$$

U-I chance =

$$\frac{N_1 \cdot N_2}{N_1 \cdot N_2 + O_1 \cdot N_2 + N_1 \cdot O_2}(100)$$

Our denominators for S-I chance and U-I chance differ from Hopkins and Hermann's (1977), since their use of T^2 for S-I and U-I is inconsistent with the definitions of these reliabilities.

These "chance" reliabilities explain why Hawkins and Dotson (1975) obtained substantial I × I reliabilities when observers were given different definitions of target behavior or when one observer's records were marked as showing 100% occurrences, results which led those authors to conclude I × I reliabilities were uninterpretable.

Hopkins and Hermann (1977) showed that calculating the chance values for each of the three reliabilities makes each obtained reliability interpretable. Each of the "chance" reliabilities, however, varies with the rate of target behavior, essentially as Hopkins and Hermann's figures indicate (with correction for our more appropriate S-I and U-I denominators). Thus, as behavior rates vary, the chance values of each reliability also vary. Hopkins and Hermann suggested researchers report I × I, S-I, and U-I reliabilities along with the chance values of each of these which reported rates of target behavior would have produced. Investigators would thus examine each reliability to see if it were reasonably close to 100% and also to see if it were above chance, then present all these to consumers in their research reports. While it is clearly necessary to avoid accepting reliability percentages as evidence of observer agreement which are, in fact, likely as a result of chance or random responding, elaborate tables featuring each reliability and its chance value for every reliability check would not likely be read by consumers. Presenting means and ranges for each would remove the reliability data from direct access by consumers and the implications of such measures for any particular target behavior data points would be obscure.

Some authors have proposed the use of various correlational measures to summarize interobserver agreement, and to avoid the problems described above (Hartmann, 1977; Kratochwill and Wetzel, 1977). As Baer (1977) suggests, such measures are rather far removed from the basic data they summarize and are thus counter to our tradition of basing conclusions on data as little modified as possible. Also, as Kratochwill and Wetzel (1977) note, such summarizing procedures invariably discard information in the process of summarizing. The procedure recommended below does not modify reliability data at all, preserves all the information contained in the data, and presents them all graphically (rather than in computational or tabular form), generally believed a superior way to present data whenever possible. Finally, the correlational procedures do not address the believability of claimed experimental effects as directly as the procedure we recommend.

A PROPOSED SOLUTION

We believe the problems discussed earlier can be easily solved by a simple graphical presentation of disagreement rates, on the basic graph(s) of target behavior, with substantial gain in implications for assessing the believability of claimed experimental effects. The understanding of that graphical presentation is facilitated, though, by a rearrangement of the usual formulas for I × I, S-I, and U-I reliabilities. If the calculating formula for each is subtracted from 100%, then terms are algebraically collected over the denominator of the original ratio and simplified, the nature of each measure is clearer.

$$100\% - I \times I = 100 \times \left[\frac{\text{Disagreements}}{\text{Agreements on Occurrences} + \text{Agreements on Nonoccurrences} + \text{Disagreements}}\right]$$

$$100\% - \text{S-I} = 100 \times \left[\frac{\text{Disagreements}}{\text{Agreements on Occurrences} + \text{Disagreements}} \right]$$

$$100\% - \text{U-I} = 100 \times \left[\frac{\text{Disagreements}}{\text{Agreements on Nonoccurrences} + \text{Disagreements}} \right]$$

Each measure of interobserver agreement is the inverse of disagreements divided by a denominator, but the denominators and thus the interpretations of the reliability measures differ. I × I reliability basically compares disagreements to the total number of observation occasions; S-I reliability compares disagreements to the sum of disagreements and agreements on occurrences; and U-I reliability compares disagreements to the sum of disagreements and agreements on nonoccurrences. Each focuses on disagreements, but each compares those to a different base and thus gives different information.

We believe much potential confusion for researchers and consumers can be avoided by using the disagreement rate itself as the primary measure of reliability, then examining its magnitude relative to occurrence agreements and/or to nonoccurrence agreements if desired. Thus observer error in general would be assessed, as percentage of disagreements (or as I × I reliability, if preferred), then observer error relative to agreements on occurrences and/or agreements on nonoccurrences would be examined as the ratio of disagreements to each (or as S-I and/or U-I reliability, if preferred) to see if any special implications exist. (We are not proposing a simple return to the use of I × I reliability, but present a graphical summary below we believe superior to any procedures so far discussed.)

In every case in which I × I and either S-I or U-I reliabilities are reasonable but one of the latter two is low, understanding is facilitated if researchers attend to the disagreement percentage itself as a measure of observer error and then to its magnitude relative to agreements on occurrences and/or nonoccurrences, while remembering that a constant disagreement rate produces lower S-I reliability at low response rates and lower U-I reliability at higher response rates.

GRAPHIC REPRESENTATION OF DISAGREEMENT RANGE

A simple graphic representation of disagreements aids greatly in making the recommended comparisons, conveys and summarizes all the information obtained from reliability checking, and is much simpler to present and understand than tables of obtained and chance S-I, U-I, and I × I reliabilities would be. In addition, the procedure has clear implications with respect to the believability of claimed experimental effects, as explained below.

For a given reliability check the percentage of intervals, moments, or trials that produced disagreements is found. This disagreement percentage is then graphed as a band-width or confidence interval around the primary observer's data for that day; but it is centered around the mean or the median (they are the same) of the two observers' reported rates of target behavior for that day. (Centering the disagreement range around the mean produces the properties to be described here; other ranges or other placements of the disagreement range would not.) The mean itself is not plotted, but both observers' data points are. The range is thus centered halfway between the two observers' reported rates of target behavior. The disagreement range so graphed effectively represents all the information collected by the reliability checking procedure, as explained below.[2]

The left part of Figure 1 demonstrates the use of the disagreement range for this purpose. The figure represents the results of a reliability check performed on Day 6 of an imaginary ex-

[2]Pioneering suggestions along these lines were made by Hawkins and Dotson (1975) and by Morris, Rosen, and Clinton (Note 1).

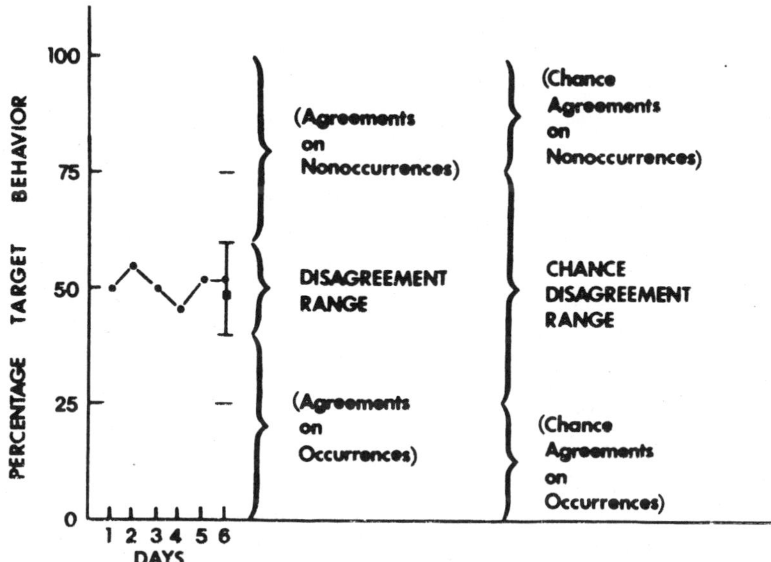

Fig. 1. Use of disagreement range to partition all observation occasions into those producing agreements on occurrences, disagreements, and agreements on nonoccurrences, and use of chance disagreement range to show chance rates of agreements on occurrences, disagreements, and agreements on nonoccurrences.

periment. On that day a reliability check was run which resulted in a disagreement percentage of 20%. Observer 1, the primary observer in this study, reported a rate of target behavior for that day of 52%, plotted as a solid circle. Observer 2, the reliability checker, reported a rate of 48%, plotted as a solid square. The mean or median of their reported rates is 50% and the disagreement range was centered around this number. This produced a disagreement range running from 40% to 60%, shown as a vertical line with horizontal limits.

The disagreement range is interpreted as follows. Both observers agreed that the behavior *occurred* on the 40% of observation occasions lying below the disagreement range. In addition, both observers agreed that the behavior *did not occur* on the 40% of observation occasions lying above the disagreement range. They disagreed on the 20% of observation occasions contained within the range.

The 20% disagreement range itself is rather substantial. Comparing it to the "agreement on occurrences" height indicates disagreements are half as great as such agreements, and comparing it to the "agreement on nonoccurrences" height also shows disagreements to be half as frequent as those agreements. With lower target behavior rates and the same disagreement rate, the disagreement range would be greater relative to agreements on occurrences and lesser relative to agreements on nonoccurrences. The opposite would be true if behavior rates were greater. Thus the graphical display of the disagreement range facilitates examination of the disagreement range, comparison of it to each of the two sorts of agreements, and identification of any special implications those comparisons might produce.

For those preferring to interpret these results in terms of the three reliability percentages, I × I reliability is the total height of the graph (100%) minus the disagreement range (20%), so equals 80%. S-I reliability is the "agreement on occurrences" height (40%) relative to that height (40%) plus the disagreement height (20%), so equals 67%. U-I reliability is the "agreement on nonoccurrences" height (40%) relative to that height (40%) plus the disagreement height (20%) so also, in this example, equals 67%.

The disagreement range thus used presents

visually all the information which would be summarized by I × I, S-I, and U-I reliability percentages, and shows clearly the relative rates of disagreement, agreements on occurrences, and agreements on nonoccurrences.

The disagreement range as used here has additional useful features. It always includes observers' reported rates of target behavior; if their reported rates were more unequal, the disagreements so produced would increase the range to include those reported rates. It always includes all disagreements, regardless of how they occurred. Graphically, the precise nature of disagreements is shown: for each observer the distance from the lower limit to the reported behavior rate is the percentage of occasions one observer reported behavior occurring and the other did not.

These points are illustrated in Table 2. In the first line of that table, while observer 1 reported a behavior rate of 52% and observer 2 a rate of 48%, the two observers disagreed on 20% of occasions, thus agreed on occurrences 40% of the time and on nonoccurrences the same. Thus observer 1 reported behavior occurring 12% of occasions on which observer 2 reported no behavior, and observer 2 reported behavior on 8% of occasions when observer 1 did not. In the second line observer 1 reports 60% occurrences, observer 2 reports 40%, and disagreements equaled 20%. Thus, on 20% of the observations observer 1 said behavior occurred while observer 2 reported it did not, and no converse cases occurred. In line three, the observers' rates differ by more than 20%, so the disagreement range must be 30% or more, with the agreements of each sort 35% or less.

GRAPHIC REPRESENTATION OF "CHANCE" DISAGREEMENT RANGE

A simple graphic summary of "chance" reliability information is also easily achieved. The "chance" disagreement percentage for two observers reporting frequencies of occurrence of target behavior O_1 and O_2, respectively, and frequencies of nonoccurrence of N_1 and N_2, across T observation occasions is given by:

$$\text{Disagreements (chance)} = 100 \times \frac{O_1N_2 + N_1O_2}{T^2}$$

If this chance disagreement percentage for each reliability check is then centered around the two observers' mean or median reported rate of target behavior for that day, the researcher and consumer can quickly see whether or not the obtained disagreement ranges are substantially smaller than "chance," smaller than random responding by observers would produce, and thus provide evidence of true observer reliability. Figure 1 illustrates the use of the chance disagreement range for this purpose. The chance disagreement range is shown by horizontal lines as limits at 75% and 25% above Day 6, explained to the right in that figure. The height below the chance disagreement range is the chance agreement on occurrences rate and the height above the chance disagreement range is the chance agreement on nonoccurrences rate. Using the imaginary data from Figure 1, the chance disagreement range calculates to equal 50% (rounded), is centered around the two observers' mean behavior rate, so ranges from 25% up to 75% in Figure 1, and leaves the

Table 2

Illustration of Additional Useful Features of Disagreement Range Used as Recommended

Reported Behavior Rate		*Disagreement Range*	*Agreements on Occurrences*	*Agreements on Nonoccurrences*
Observer 1	*Observer 2*			
52%	48%	20%	40%	40%
60%	40%	20%	40%	40%
65%	35%	30% or more	35% or less	35% or less

25% chance agreement on occurrences height below it and the 25% chance agreement on nonoccurrences height above it. If, as in Figure 1, the obtained disagreement range is smaller than the chance disagreement range, then agreements on occurrences and agreements on nonoccurrences are necessarily greater than chance, and disagreements are fewer.

Graphical representation of the chance disagreement range provides all the information contained in the three chance reliabilities Hopkins and Hermann (1977) recommended calculating. The chance level of I $\times$ I reliability is the chance disagreement range subtracted from the total height of the graph (100%; all observation occasions). Chance S-I reliability is the height below the chance disagreement range relative to that height plus the chance disagreement range itself. Similarly, chance U-I reliability is the height above the chance disagreement range relative to that height plus the chance disagreement range itself. Using the Figure 1 data and calculations, chance I $\times$ I reliability is 100% minus the 50% chance disagreement range, so equals 50%. Chance S-I reliability is the 25% chance agreement on occurrences height divided by that 25% plus the chance disagreement range of 50%, or 25%/ 25% + 50%, so equals 33%. Chance U-I reliability is the 25% chance agreement on nonoccurrences height divided by that 25% plus the chance disagreement range of 50%, so also equals 33%.

Each of the three chance reliabilities is a function of the chance disagreement range and the heights above and below it, and each of the actually obtained reliabilities is a function of the true disagreement range and the heights above and below it. Consequently, any time the true disagreement range is substantially smaller than the chance disagreement range then the obtained reliabilities will be substantially larger than their corresponding chance reliabilities. Thus, rather than examining tables of numerous reliability measures, researchers and consumers can attend to the graphical comparison of obtained and chance disagreement ranges to determine that random observer responding does not account for obtained observer agreement.

IMPLICATIONS FOR BELIEVABILITY OF EXPERIMENTAL EFFECTS

The disagreement range, when plotted as recommended here, leaves below the range all reports of target behavior on which both observers agree and leaves above the range all reports of the nonoccurrence of target behavior on which they agree. Within the range are only occasions when one observer reported the behavior and the other disagreed. Since both observers agree the behavior occurred at a rate equal to the lower limit of the disagreement range and agree it did not occur on the percentage of observation occasions above the range, then they agree only that the rate of target behavior may be anywhere within the range. (Of course, it is possible the true rate is actually outside the range and biases affecting the observers are leading them to err systematically. Assuming all efforts have been made to prevent such biases, however, our interobserver agreement only permits us to say our observers agree that the rate is probably within the disagreement range.)

Graphical presentation of the disagreement range as exemplified by Figure 1 can serve as the kind of graphical judgmental aid called for by Hawkins and Dotson (1975) and by Kratochwill and Wetzel (1977), a judgmental aid useful to consumers as well as researchers in determining whether or not, given the levels of observer agreement in a study, claimed experimental effects are believable. For experimental effects to be believable they must be substantial enough to produce no overlap between disagreement ranges resulting from reliability checks taken before and after the claimed experimental effect occurred. If overlap exists between these disagreement ranges, the apparent change in target behavior is not great enough, given the degree of observer disagreement, to permit certainty that an effect of treatment has been shown.

The use of the disagreement range to examine the believability of experimental effects is illustrated in Figure 2. Panel A of Figure 2 shows imaginary data from interval recording through a baseline phase, a treatment phase, a reversal phase, and a second treatment phase. Reliability checks are performed on Days 5, 10, 15, and 20, with each reliability check yielding a disagreement percentage of 10%. (The reliability checker's reported percentage of target behavior is shown for each reliability checking day.) The primary observer's data indicate a decreased per-

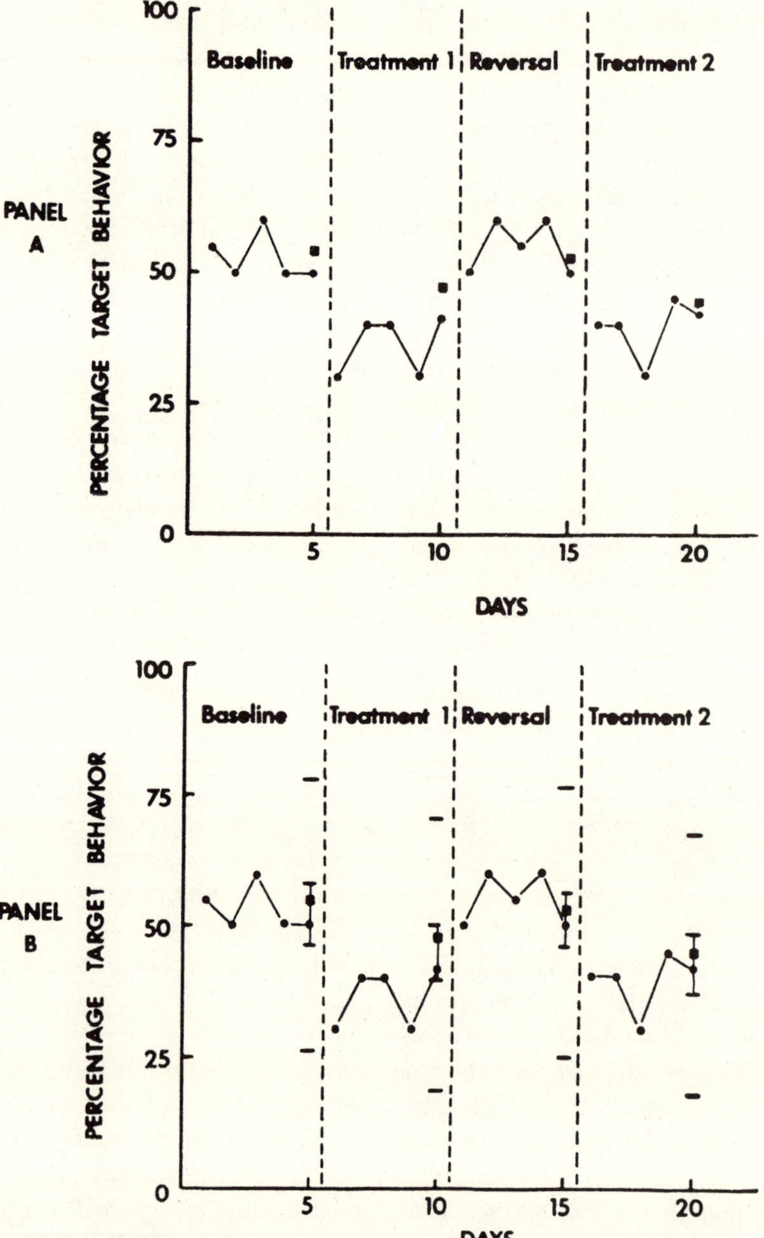

Fig. 2. Imaginary data showing primary observer's data over days and phases along with the second observer's data on reliability checking days (Panel A) and the same imaginary data with disagreement and chance disagreement ranges added (Panel B). Panel B assumes disagreement rates of 10% from each reliability check.

centage of target behavior during Treatment 1 relative to baseline, a return to baseline levels during the reversal, and a reduction back to Treatment 1 levels during Treatment 2. The reliability checker's data are consistent, showing a decrease to Treatment 1, an increase during the reversal, and a reduction back to Treatment 1 level during Treatment 2. Ninety percent I × I reliability is substantial enough to be considered generally acceptable and the agreement as to the effects of treatments and reversal shown by the reliability checker's data is the "cofunctional" reliability discussed by Goldiamond (1969), Hawkins and Dotson (1975), Kelly (1977), and by Kratochwill and Wetzel (1977). Thus the data *appear* to demonstrate a believable experimental effect.

Panel B of Figure 2 presents the same data as Panel A but shows the disagreement range and the chance disagreement range around the mean of the two observers' reported percentage of target behavior for each reliability checking day. Since the obtained disagreement ranges are consistently much smaller than the chance disagreement ranges, true observer agreement appears to have been obtained. However, comparison of the disagreement ranges across each of the four phases suggests that no believable experimental effects were demonstrated. In each case the disagreement range for the two observers is substantial enough that the true rate of target behavior may not have changed at all across these four conditions. If the true rate of target behavior was near the lower end of the range on Day 5, in the upper half of the range on Day 10, in the lower half of the range on Day 15, and in the uppermost part on Day 20, then no effects of treatments or the reversal would have occurred. Thus, with these apparent rate changes and levels of observer agreement, believable experimental effects were not obtained.

If greater effects of the treatment had been demonstrated, then with these levels of observer agreement believable experimental effects could have been demonstrated. Conversely, if greater observer agreement had been achieved, believable experimental effects might also have been shown. With the magnitude of treatment effects and the degree of observer agreement in these examples, however, neither Treatment 1 nor Treatment 2 demonstrates conclusive changes in rates of target behavior from baseline and reversal levels. The use of the disagreement range has permitted us to avoid accepting as believable experimental effects which, in fact, are not. Given that the primary observer's data and cofunctional reliability had both suggested that treatment effects had occurred, this added protection for researchers and consumers against type one errors, urged by Baer (1977), and provided by graphical presentation of the disagreement range, is strongly recommended.[3]

RECOMMENDATIONS

(1) Researchers in applied behavior analysis should attend to their obtained observer disagreement percentages as their primary measure of observer agreement, then compare it to observers' rates of agreements on occurrences and rates of agreements on nonoccurrences, recalling that lower and higher target behavior rates produce lower S-I and U-I reliabilities, respectively, with constant disagreement rates.

(2) The second observer's data should be plotted, for each reliability check, on graphs of the primary observer's data, as Hawkins and Dotson (1975) proposed.

(3) Disagreement percentages should be

[3]Early readers of this manuscript have asked how our recommendations relate to the fact that *sets* of data points within experimental conditions usually form the basis for conclusions regarding change across conditions. If the primary observer's data on reliability checking days are consistent with the data when no checks are being conducted, then the disagreement range is likely representative of what would be obtained by multiple checks within conditions, and so can be viewed as establishing a band around the data points within that condition. No overlap between such bands across conditions would then be a strong argument for believability of claimed experimental effects.

presented on graphs of the primary observer's data, centered halfway between the two observers' reported rates of target behavior. This provides all the information on observer agreement collected, in an easily understood format, and permits identification of claimed experimental effects which are not believable.

(4) Researchers should also graph the limits of chance disagreement ranges for each reliability check, thus providing all available information on chance agreement and permitting easy determination as to whether or not true observer agreement has been demonstrated.

REFERENCE NOTE

1. Morris, E. K., Rosen, H. S., and Clinton, L. P. *Reliability considerations in single-subject research.* Paper presented at meeting of the Midwestern Association for Behavior Analysis, Chicago, Illinois, May 1975.

REFERENCES

Baer, D. M. Reviewer's comment: Just because its reliable doesn't mean that you can use it. *Journal of Applied Behavior Analysis,* 1977, **10**, 117-119.

Bijou, S. W., Peterson, R. F., and Ault, M. H. A method to integrate descriptive and experimental field studies at the level of data and empirical concepts. *Journal of Applied Behavior Analysis,* 1968, **1**, 175-191.

Cone, J. D. The relevance of reliability and validity for behavioral assessment. *Behavior Therapy,* 1977, **8**, 411-426.

Goldiamond, I. Stuttering and fluency as manipulatable operant response classes. In L. Krasner and L. P. Ullman (Eds), *Research in behavior modification.* New York: Holt, Rinehart & Winston, 1969.

Hartmann, P. Considerations in the choice of interobserver reliability estimates. *Journal of Applied Behavior Analysis,* 1977, **10**, 103-116.

Hawkins, R. P. and Dotson, V. A. Reliability scores that delude: An Alice in Wonderland Trip through the misleading characteristics of interobserver agreement scores in interval recording. In E. Ramp and G. Semb (Eds), *Behavioral analysis: areas of research and application.* Englewood Cliffs, New Jersey: Prentice-Hall, 1975.

Hopkins, B. L. and Hermann, J. A. Evaluating interobserver reliability of interval data. *Journal of Applied Behavior Analysis,* 1977, **10**, 121-126.

Kazdin, A. E. *Behavior modification in applied settings.* Homewood, Illinois: Dorsey Press, 1975.

Kazdin, A. E. Artifact, bias, and complexity of assessment: The ABCs of reliability. *Journal of Applied Behavior Analysis,* 1977, **10**, 141-150.

Kelly, M. B. A review of the observation data-collection and reliability procedures reported in *The Journal of Applied Behavior Analysis, Journal of Applied Behavior Analysis,* 1977, **10**, 97-101.

Kratochwill, T. R. and Wetzel, R. J. Observer agreement, credibility and judgment: Some consideration in presenting observer agreement data. *Journal of Applied Behavior Analysis,* 1977, **10**, 133-139.

Powell, J., Martindale, A., and Kulp, S. An evaluation of time-sample measures of recording. *Journal of Applied Behavior Analysis,* 1975, **8**, 463-464.

Received 3 April 1978.
(Final Acceptance 22 January 1979.)

JOURNAL OF APPLIED BEHAVIOR ANALYSIS 1982, **15**, 477-492 NUMBER 4 (WINTER 1982)

THE INTEGRITY OF INDEPENDENT VARIABLES IN BEHAVIOR ANALYSIS

LIZETTE PETERSON, ANDREW L. HOMER, AND STEPHEN A. WONDERLICH

UNIVERSITY OF MISSOURI-COLUMBIA AND MISSOURI DEPARTMENT OF MENTAL HEALTH

Establishing a functional relationship between the independent and the dependent variable is the primary focus of applied behavior analysis. Accurate and reliable description and observation of both the independent and dependent variables are necessary to achieve this goal. Although considerable attention has been focused on ensuring the integrity of the dependent variable in the operant literature, similar effort has not been directed at ensuring the integrity of the independent variable. Inaccurate descriptions of the application of the independent variable may threaten the reliability and validity of operant research data. A survey of articles in the *Journal of Applied Behavior Analysis* demonstrated that the majority of articles published do not use any assessment of the actual occurrence of the independent variable and a sizable minority do not provide operational definitions of the independent variable. The feasibility and utility of ensuring the integrity of the independent variable is described.

DESCRIPTORS: reliability, independent variable manipulation, methodology, implementation reliability, validity

---

The primary goal of behavior analysis has been described as going beyond the simple demonstration of changes in behavior to include the demonstration that changes in the target behavior are functionally related to changes in the environment (Baer, Wolf, & Risley, 1968). This typically involves ensuring that changes in the dependent variables are due to systematic changes in the independent variable, rather than to changes in any uncontrolled extraneous variables (Sidman, 1960). Precise, demonstrated control of the independent variable and measurement of the dependent variables is therefore necessary for demonstrating the existence of a functional relationship.

In applied behavior analysis, rigorous and calibrated electromechanical recording of the dependent variable is frequently not as possible as in an animal laboratory. Thus, one of the earliest demands on applied researchers in behavior analysis was for accurate and reliable description and observation of the dependent variable (e.g., Heyns & Lippitt, 1954). The classic literature of observational technology (e.g., Arrington, 1943; Bijou, Peterson, & Ault, 1968; Rosenthal & Rosnow, 1969; Webb, Campbell, Schwartz, & Sechrist, 1966; Weick, 1968) was joined in later years by a new literature, concerned with problems of dependent variable observation such as observer reactivity (e.g., Hanley, 1970; Romanczyk, Kent, Diament, & O'Leary, 1973), observer bias (e.g., McNamara & MacDonough, 1972; O'Leary, Kent, & Kanowitz, 1975), observer drift (e.g., O'Leary & Kent, 1973; Reid, 1970), observational complexity (e.g., Kazdin, 1977*a*) and

---

This research was supported by a Summer Research Fellowship granted to the first author by the University of Missouri-Columbia Research Council. The authors are grateful to Robert J. DeRubeis, Donald P. Hartmann, Steven D. Hollon, and Steven Richards for their help in locating research examples for this paper. Appreciation is extended to Samuel M. Deitz and James Johnston for their helpful comments on past versions of this manuscript. Reprints may be obtained from Lizette Peterson, Psychology Department, 210 McAlester Hall, University of Missouri-Columbia, Columbia, Missouri 65211.

various sources of inflation of observer reliability estimates (e.g., Hartmann, 1977). The number of articles in the *Journal of Applied Behavior Analysis* (*JABA*) that contain reliability estimates of the dependent variable have steadily increased in recent years (Hayes, Rincover, & Solnick, 1980). Indeed, it is unlikely that a paper without necessary dependent variable reliability estimates would be accepted for publication in *JABA*.

In applied behavior analysis, control of the independent variable is also more difficult than in an animal laboratory. It thus may be surprising to note that the methodological rigor applied to the observation of the dependent variable may not have been applied to the independent variable. Since independent variables frequently involve human judgments, some assessment of the reliability and accuracy of the judgments may be necessary. For example, Johnston and Pennypacker (1980) stated that:

> The independent variable must be represented by some environmental event, the physical parameters of which are known, specified, and controlled to the extent required. Such a clear description of the independent variable is essential if any factually accurate statement is to issue from the experimental effort (p. 39).

Inadequate assessment of the independent variable may thus render conclusions about the functional relationship between the dependent target behavior and the independent treatment variable suspect. For example, recent reviews of experimental results from token economies (Nelson & Cone, 1979) and Differential Reinforcement of Other Behavior procedures (DRO; Homer & Peterson, 1980) complained that the independent variables are not described in sufficient detail for evaluation of the results. These and other reviews (e.g., Hobbs, Moguin, Tyroler, & Lahey, 1980) have implicated the lack of independent variable description and verification as a likely cause for poor replication of results.

The methodological gap between the observation and reporting of the dependent variable in comparison to the independent variable may have serious consequences. A variety of questions need to be answered before any definitive conclusions on this issue can be reached. First, is there anything in the literature to suggest that accurate description and observation of the independent variable is important? Second, if accurate description and observation fail to take place, does this ever result in differences between the independent variable as presented in the research report method section and the independent variable as actually applied to the subject? Third, if such differences are found, is there any significant cost to the research findings and to the field? Finally, if a cost exists, is there a cost-effective way of preventing the problem in future research? This paper proposes some answers to these questions.

Methodological Statements on Independent Variable Accuracy

First, it has already been suggested that the operant literature clearly specifies the importance of establishing a functional relationship between the dependent variable and the independent variable by *observing* that the systematic manipulation of the latter results in changes in the former (e.g., Hersen & Barlow, 1976; Johnston & Pennypacker, 1980; Sidman, 1960). Observation of the dependent variable alone will allow unambiguous conclusions about changes in the target behavior, but it will not allow conclusions about the source of those changes (Billingsley, White, & Munson, 1980).

A curious double standard has developed in operant technology whereby certain variables (e.g., social behavior, smiling, and attention) routinely have operational definitions and some measure of observer reliability when the observed behavior is the target response or dependent variable (Milby, 1970; Reisinger, 1972; and Kazdin, 1973, respectively), but no such rigor is applied to the same behaviors when they appear as antecedents or consequences to the target behavior, as independent variables (Strain, Shores, & Timm, 1977; Dorsey, Iwata, Ong, & McSween, 1980; and Hasazi & Hasazi, 1972, respectively). Either such precautions as definition and reliability of observation are necessary or they are not. The observational literature clearly suggests that they are. It is unlikely that most readers would accept the experimenter's claim that "social responding increased when the treatment variable was applied," if no data on social responding were presented to substantiate the claim. How, then, is it possible to accept the experimenter's suggestion that "social responding by the treatment agent was increased and changes in the dependent variable occurred" with no further definition or observation of social responding? The simple statement that treatment was applied as outlined in the method section or treatment manual seems insufficient (DeRubeis & Hollon, 1981).

Furthermore, although observational technology has centered on the dependent variable, all statements made concerning the observation of the dependent variable are also applicable to the observation of the independent variable. Experimenter bias (e.g., McNamara & MacDonough, 1972) may, in fact, be more likely in observing the treatment variable than the dependent variable, since the treatment variable is predefined and an informed observer might simply report observing what the therapeutic agent was supposed to do rather than what was actually done. Similarly, if the therapy agent could discriminate when observation was taking place, it is likely that the agent would adhere more closely to the assigned treatment during observational periods, demonstrating reactivity (e.g., Romanczyk et al., 1973). Finally, Hersen (1981) noted that changes can and often do develop between different treatment agents and within the same agent across time. Treatment during the first phases of a study may only approximate treatment at a later date; if observers fail to recognize such a process, the result might be both treatment and observer drift (Reid, 1970). Thus, the behavior analytic literature clearly supports the importance of independent variable definition and assessment.

Other literatures have demonstrated even greater support for independent variable definition and assessment. Stallings (1975), for example, described the effects of both open and behavioral classrooms on children's learning. Stallings carefully measured both children's in-class behavior (dependent variables) and the teachers' administration of each treatment (independent variables). Although the consistency with which the treatments were applied was generally judged to be adequate, the consistency of actual treatment variable application compared to scheduled treatment variable application *within* any one classroom ranged from $r = .30$ to .96. There was even less consistency across different classrooms. Resnick and Leinhard, when critiquing Stallings' study (cited in Stallings, 1975), noted that many of Stallings' findings would be uninterpretable without the examination of the actual (not the planned) application of the independent variable. There are many other related research areas in which investigators have urged the definition and assessment of the independent variable, including a review of interventions on children's problem solving (Urbain & Kendall, 1980) and children's psychotherapy (Hartmann, Roper, & Gelfand, 1977), behavior therapy with psychotic adults (Paul & Lentz, 1977), pharmacotherapy (Becker & Schuckit, 1978) and psychotherapy with depressed adults (Rounsaville, Weissman, & Prusoff, 1981). There have also been repeated suggestions to document the application of the independent variable within the field of program evaluation (e.g., Cook & Campbell, 1979; Donabedian, 1966; Way, Lund, & Attkisson, 1978).

Reports and Suggestions of Independent Variable Inaccuracies

There is some evidence within applied behavior analysis to suggest that the treatment described in the method section may, in fact, differ from the actual applications of the treatment. This statement of the problem should not imply that the experimenter does not retain complete flexibility to alter the treatment strategy at will. The application of the treatment variable always remains at the discretion of the experimenter. The problem occurs when the experimenter believes that the application of the independent variable has certain physical and temporal properties when, in fact, different physical and temporal properties of the independent variable apply.

Six classes of results of independent variable inaccuracies will be reviewed briefly, including: (a) cases where a difference between programmed and actual independent variable application was noted during the study, prior to the formation of any conclusions, (b) cases in which inaccuracies were noted at the end of a study, but basic conclusions remain the same, (c) cases in which inaccurate administration of the independent variable changed the conclusion, causing an ineffective treatment to appear effective, (d) cases where independent variable inaccuracies rendered an effective treatment ineffective, (e) cases where failure to replicate was caused by faulty independent variable application, and (f) cases where failures to replicate are linked to independent variable implementation inaccuracies.

First, researchers may note independent variable inaccuracies during the course of the treatment phase. A treatment agent may either become lax with timing or with effortful treatment techniques or may begin to add techniques not prescribed by the experimenter to the treatment regimen. Any case in which the treatment agent gradually alters the treatment can be termed "therapist drift." This phenomenon has been observed, recorded, and reported by behavioral investigators (e.g., Bellack, Hersen, & Himmelhock, 1980; Hollon, Mandell, Bemis, DeRubeis, Emerson, Evans, & Kriss, Note 1). Many times therapist drift results in the treatment agent's increasing use of therapeutic techniques, as opposed to becoming progressively more lax with treatment variable application (DeRubeis, Note 2).

Not all inaccuracies in independent variable application are noted prior to a study's completion, however. For example, many studies in *JABA* have overtly analyzed attempts to alter the behavior of a treatment agent, who will, in turn, alter a target subject's behavior. Thus, some reports have routinely obtained data on both the independent variable and the dependent variable, and have noted some level of inaccuracy in independent variable application which is not corrected. In one such report, teachers were to present Distar materials at either a rapid or slow rate, and the main purpose of the study was to analyze the effects of rate of presentation. Teachers received clear mechanical cues for their rate of presentation. However, observation and recording of the independent variable of Distar presentation rate demonstrated that there was a great deal of variation in the actual rate of teacher presentation; in one case the rate during a "rapid presentation" was actually slower than in the "slow presentation" sequence (Carnine, 1976). This is a particularly cogent example because many studies in applied behavior analysis use teachers or other lay therapy agents *without* mechanical cues for independent variable application and these studies typically assume that the therapy agent is accurate. Other examples from applied behavior analysis include significant inaccuracies in teacher attention (Friedling & O'Leary, 1979), proctor instruction of trainees (Mathews & Fawcett, 1977), and parent application of behavioral techniques (e.g., Porterfield, Herbert-Jackson, & Risley, 1976, found a range of 33 to 100% actual adherence to the description of the independent variable). In fact, a sizable number of the studies in *JABA* which were reviewed and found to assess independent variable application noted differences in the planned administration of the independent variable and the actual application. Again, the issue is not that the application of the independent variable must be stable but rather that when it is not stable, the method section should not describe the application as rigid and consistent. Despite the inaccurate application of treatment in the studies just cited, beneficial effects of treatment were noted (although it is unclear whether the effects were more or less beneficial than would have resulted if the experimenter's specified method had been followed). In other cases, inaccuracy in independent variable application has resulted in more serious changes in treatment variable outcome.

Baer et al. (1968) described the case in which the treatment agent allows the subject a short time period in which to respond correctly during baseline and then (through accident or intention) allows more time for responding during the experimental phase. Baer et al. noted that even with an ineffective treatment, these failures to adhere to the uniform procedures as described in the method section might result in the appearance of treatment success. Since the experimenter would be likely to be satisfied with the results, there would be little reason to question the treatment agent's adherence to the application of the independent variable. Thus, a worthless treatment would be judged to be effective and only failures to replicate the results would correct the error. Since failures to replicate are published less often than successful intervention, such errors are likely to be corrected only slowly and at great cost (Homer & Peterson, 1980), with the cost sometimes being the rejection of behavior therapy techniques by community treatment agents (Hersen & Barlow, 1976).

Other failures to adhere to the experimenter's description of independent variable implementation may harm rather than enhance treatment effectiveness. This kind of alteration may be more likely to be noted by the experimenter than is a favorable alteration, but at times the intervention is completed before the reason for the lack of treatment effectiveness is clear. Bernal, Klinnert, and Schultz (1980), for example, found that although the parent-therapists receiving behavioral training reported more child improvement than parents receiving client-centered counseling, there were no differences in observations of actual child behavior. Further assessment of the behavior of the parent-therapists demonstrated that the parents trained in behavioral techniques were not applying those techniques any more than were the counseled parents. Such findings are not limited to lay treatment agents. For example, Wodarski, Feldman, and Pedi (1974) found no effects from a behavior modification treatment program. Fortunately, the investigators had obtained data on both the professional treatment agents' behavior and the children's behavior. Analysis of these data demonstrated that the professional treatment agents had failed to apply the specified behavioral treatments (contingent time-outs, praise, directions).

In some cases of clear failure to replicate certain experimental results, lack of accurate treatment implementation has been specifically implicated as a cause. For example, Fleishman (1981) described many attempts to replicate Patterson's (1974) behavioral treatment of noxious child behaviors (yelling, aggression). He noted that the differences in results from studies which successfully replicate or which fail to replicate Patterson's results may have been due to differences in the degree to which the independent variable was implemented as described. Since treatment variable implementation had not been typically observed and reported, however, the extent to which inaccurate implementation was responsible for differences is not clear. Fleischman ended his review by noting "In any case, it suggests the need for further research on not merely the impact of social learning derived technology per se on aggressive children but also on how that technology is applied" (pp. 350-351). Similarly, other investigators have noted explicitly that their failure to replicate may have been due to inaccuracies in treatment variable application (e.g., Bornstein & Quevillon, 1976).

Cost of Inaccuracy

Despite the apparently heavy cost of independent variable inaccuracy, some operant researchers may disavow any generality in these results and will continue to argue that, in general, there is not substantial cost to independent variable inaccuracy. Several arguments might be advanced here, including the argument that "the use of steady state responding guarantees the accuracy of treatment application," "there is always some amount of 'play' in the administration of the treatment variable and that only makes the functional relationship between dependent and independent variable more robust" and " if there was substantial inaccuracy in the application of the independent variable, the experimenter would immediately be informed of it through relevant changes in the dependent variable." Each of these typical arguments against a general cost of independent variable inaccuracies must be dismissed before the generality of these results can be assumed.

First, there is the claim that in general, steady states and behavior stability of the dependent variable would provide ample demonstration of a functional relationship between the independent and dependent variable, and that observation of the dependent variable alone is sufficient for such demonstration. The argument would go like this:

1. If the stable independent variable is functionally related to the dependent variable, steady-state responding in the dependent variable will occur.

2. Steady-state responding in the dependent variable occurs.

3. Therefore, the independent variable is functionally related to the dependent variable and is responsible for the steady state.

4. Therefore, the application of the independent variable must have been stable.

This line of reasoning has been labeled the Fallacy of Affirming the Consequent (Johnston & Pennypacker, 1980). Although this logic is weak, it can be used to demonstrate behavioral control if applied repeatedly and if complete assessment is made of both the independent and dependent variables in stable states and in transition to verify all four stages of logic empirically. However, if the experimenter cannot demonstrate the state of *both* independent and dependent variables, no conclusion can be reached.

Reflection may demonstrate that there are many cases of stable states in the dependent variable that are due to carefully programmed fluctuations in the independent variable. Drug tolerance is one common example; steadily increasing dosages of some drugs (independent variables) may be required to maintain a stable drug response (dependent variables). Similarly, the animal operant literature contains several examples of complicated schedules of fluctuating contingencies designed to produce steady-state responding (e.g., Dallemagne & Richelle, 1970). Thus, a stable dependent variable does not necessarily ensure a stable independent variable.

Second, it might also be argued that the experimenter never has complete command over all the controlling variables, since there is always likely to be some degree of background noise and extraneous variables present in addition to the independent variable. However, when changes in the independent variable (even if imperfectly applied) result in changes in the dependent variable, one might argue that this demonstrates a robust functional relationship and adds strength to the conclusion of experimental control. This argument can only be made if the dependent variable changes appropriately; the imperfect application of the independent variable may result in loss of control and this would scarcely suggest a robust functional relationship. Some such failures (which are rarely published and thus shared openly with other researchers) have been documented earlier. Even if changes in the dependent variable are obtained, this does not necessarily indicate a strong functional relationship between dependent and independent variables unless the experimenter can show that the changes were due to the treatment variables and not to other variables. In other words, any "extraneous" (nonindependent) variables must be demonstrated either to be random or to have effects in the opposite direction of the effects of the independent variable. However, many of the "extraneous" variables may not be random or "countertherapeutic" at all. Indeed, as has been documented earlier, "therapist drift" to include nontreatment variables is often the result of attempts to impact the target behavior in the same manner as the independent variable attempts to impact behavior. Such extraneous variables may ride "piggyback" on the independent variable application as, for example, a treatment agent who gradually lengthens a DRO interval (described in the method section as the independent variable) while maintaining the target subject's adaptive behavior with smiles and praise (extraneous variables not described in the method section). The "extraneous variables" may even replace the ostensible independent variable as could occur with a treatment agent who used self-attributing praise to a subject (an "extraneous" variable) in combination with apparently powerful but actually inert tokens (the independent variable of record). Thus, anticipated changes in behavior when the treatment variable of record is applied do not necessarily indicate a robust functional relationship.

The example just cited also explains how the third common argument against the potential cost of independent variable inaccuracy can be shown to be false. It is often concluded that if something went "wrong" with the treatment variable application, the experimenter would immediately be aware of this because of unforeseen changes in the dependent variable. When the extraneous variables covary with the independent variable, the dependent variable may reveal only the "expected" change. It will yield no information about the cause of that change. Thus, if the treatment agent inadvertently adds to the magnitude or frequency of the independent variable or uses adjunct techniques not described in the method section, changes in the dependent variable will suggest that the treatment is more effective than it actually is. Because the experimenter will be satisfied with the obtained results, no real assessment of the true functional relationship will take place. In contrast, the experimenter sometimes becomes aware of problems in experimental methodology because the dependent variable does not change as planned. However, because this lack of effect can be due to a number of factors, including subjects' past behavioral history, reinforcer effectiveness, schedule parameters, or extraneous variables which are truly random, the experimenter may not be able to determine whether or not the lack of effect was due to insufficient administration of the independent variable. Even a powerful treatment may thus appear impotent. Such failures, especially when they are not well investigated and documented, can have very detrimental effects in the applied community where disappointment with a procedure may lead to the tendency to eliminate the procedure entirely from therapeutic programs (Hersen & Barlow, 1976).

The possibility of accepting a powerless program as strong or rejecting a powerful program as having no effect is the ultimate cost of lack of independent variable accuracy. However, it might be argued that occasionally accepting an incorrect finding may simply be the price of living in an imperfect world; the inaccuracy of the finding will be brought to light later, as a failure to replicate. This argument is far too pat and it ignores what Hersen and Barlow (1976) term the "often discouraging and sometimes painful process of clinical trial and error" (p. 355) involved in attempts to replicate. If advancement of the science is made only through direct and systematic replication (Sidman, 1960), then allowing some number of incorrect reports in the literature with no information concerning the degree to which they may be inaccurate is extremely costly.

All that can be demonstrated *in general* is a potential cost (although an extravagant one), since with the present system there is no way of gauging the level of inaccuracy or the actual cost that may exist in the current literature. However, it is possible to determine the number of studies at risk for independent variable inaccuracy. Before concluding the discussion on cost and going on to the suggestion for possible solutions, however, it would seem appropriate to assess the degree to which investigations in applied behavior analysis are at risk for inaccurate treatment variable application. If the number of at risk studies is high, perhaps that finding will influence decisions on potential cost and solutions to that cost.

METHOD

Two independent observers were responsible for rating the articles in *JABA* from 1968 (Volume 1, Number 1) to 1980 (Volume 13, Number 3). The primary observer rated every issue and the reliability observer rated one issue (25%) per year. Only experimental articles were rated; "experimental" was arbitrarily defined as any article longer than three pages of text that included a method section. This definition excluded brief reports which might have gathered independent variable data but failed to report it because of the condensed nature of the presentation, as well as technical notes and theoretical presentations.

Each experimental article was rated in terms of several categories of independent variable assessment and independent variable definition. The occurrence or nonoccurrence of these discrete categories within each article was the variable of interest, and the data are reported in terms of the percentage of articles in which at least one independent variable falls into a category. Thus, for example, if a single article had three independent variables and reported accuracy assessment on all three variables, this article would be counted as a single occurrence of independent variable accuracy reporting. Similarly, if the article defined one of the variables but failed to define the others, the article would contribute once to the category of definition and once to the category of no definition.

Ratings of independent variable assessment were divided into three categories: (A) Yes, some form of assessment of the application of the independent variable was reported. This report could be informal (e.g., "observers agreed on all but one instance of the treatment variable application"), could indicate a statistical estimate of reliability between two observers (typically either percentage agreement or a correlational statistic) or could indicate calibration (a check by the experimenter to ensure that the actual occurrence matched the true value suggested by the method section). Selection of this category required clear evidence that at least one person had observed and recorded the occurrence of at least one treatment variable. (B) No, assessment was not reported but the application of the independent variable was judged to be at low risk for inaccuracy. This category included Kelly's (1977) definitions of mechanically defined treatments (e.g., a machine that delivered a token each time the subject pressed a button) and permanent products (e.g., the experimenter painted a garbage can with school colors). In addition, this category included single behavioral interventions (e.g., the experimenter gave one set of instructions or put up a sign) or continuous application of the independent variable (e.g., each time the subject turned in a piece of garbage, he received a token). It is conceivable that an experimenter might neglect to administer a reinforcer on a one for one basis, and that error could be present in the count of permanent products or in machine delivery, but lack of accurate administration of such variables would be less likely than in other, more complex schedules (Johnston & Pennypacker, 1980) and errors would be less likely to be biased (that is, to change bidirectionally with behavior). Thus, this category was used as a conservative approach to noting treatment variables in which error was possible but less likely than in category C. (C) No, independent variable accuracy checks were not reported and they were necessary. That is, the administration of the independent variable was not exempted by any of the cases cited in category B, and the potential for error was judged to be high.

The occurrence of independent variable operational definition was similarly divided into three categories: (A) Yes, an explicit operational definition was included. (B) No, an operational definition was not included but it was unnecessary. When the treatment variable was mechanical (e.g., the light turned on or a machine gave the child one M&M), very simplistic (e.g., the experimenter wrote on the board), had been well defined previously (e.g., the experimenter "modeled" a verbal response), or had a citation to a source describing it, it was included in this category. (C) No, an operational definition was not included and it was necessary, as it was not exempted by any of the cases cited in category B. This category contained treatment variables that were almost exclusively behaviors emitted by the treatment agent; typical variables included "praise," "affection," "positive social behaviors," and "chatting." Again, only independent variables clearly requiring definition were included in category C. If the major components of the independent variable were defined but a minor component (a multicomponent study using three types of tangible reinforcers, all accompanied by "praise") was not, the variable was categorized in A or B, not in C, in order to produce a conservative estimate of the need for treatment definition.

RESULTS

Coding Reliability

The reliability of observation of both independent variable assessment and definition of the independent variable was calculated by comparing the prime observer's ratings to a second observer who rated one issue per year from 1968 to 1980. Reasonable levels of agreement were obtained (Cohen's 1960, Kappa: $K = .80$, $K = .82$, respectively).

Independent Variable Reliability

Table 1 shows the number of experimental articles published each year. Figure 1 shows the percentage of articles reporting each of the three classes of independent variable assessment. These percentages can sum to greater than 100% since papers commonly used more than one independent variable or reported more than one experiment. In 1968, for example, 68% of the articles did not report assessment when the risk of inaccuracy was high for at least one independent variable, 32% of the articles did not report independent variable assessment when the risk of inaccuracy was low, and 23% reported assessment for at least one independent variable. As can be seen in Figure 1, the majority of articles did not report independent variable assessment even when the risk of in-

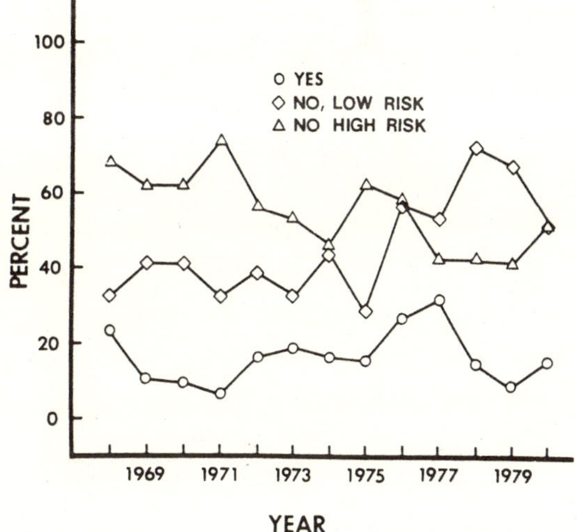

Fig. 1. Percentage of articles either presenting independent variable reliability where needed, not presenting independent variable reliability where risk of inaccuracy is high, or not presenting independent variable reliability where risk of inaccuracy is low. Percentages can sum to more than 100% because of multitreatment and multiexperiment articles.

Table 1
Number of Experimental Articles

Year	*Volume*	*Articles*
1968	1	31
1969	2	29
1970	3	34
1971	4	34
1972	5	45
1973	6	57
1974	7	56
1975	8	39
1976	9	43
1977	10	55
1978	11	36
1979	12	39
1980	13(1-3)	41

accuracy was high and there is little, if any, increase in reporting independent variable reliability over the past 12 years.

Independent Variable Operational Definition

Figure 2 shows the percentage of articles including operational definition of the independent variable. As can be seen, the majority of articles did report independent variable operational definitions when needed, although in a sizable number of cases (10%-50%) operational

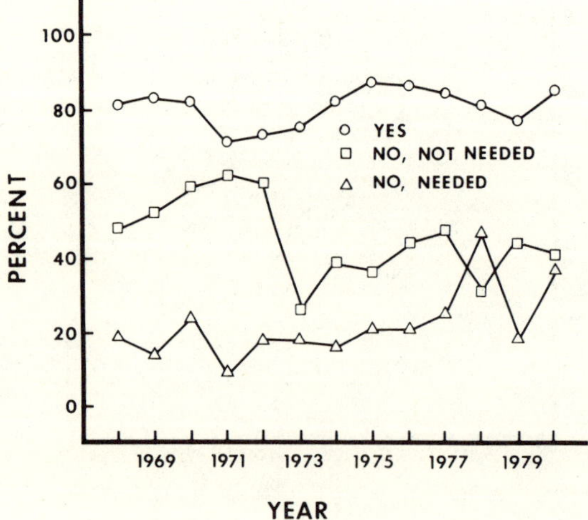

Fig. 2. Percentage of articles providing independent variable operational definitions where needed, not providing operational definitions where needed, or using independent variables not needing operational definitions. Percentages can sum to more than 100% because of multitreatment and multiexperiment articles.

definitions were not presented when necessary. There are no stable changes across time in these data, with the exception of a slight decrease in the number of independent variables not requiring operational definition in recent years.

The data on independent variable definition were collected both because definitions are often necessary for the evaluation and replication of experimental results and because the need for an operational definition can indicate the need for accuracy checks to see if the variable was used as defined. Among the surveyed studies presenting operational definitions, only an average of 16% (range 3-34%) also performed some check on the accuracy of the implementation of the independent variable.

DISCUSSION

The data document that the majority of articles published in *JABA* do not use necessary assessment of the independent variable. In addition, in a sizable minority of cases the independent variable is not operationally defined. Even when the independent variable is defined, in most cases no accuracy checks are made to see that it is used as defined. The data do not suggest any improvement in independent variable methodology since the journal was founded in 1968. Thus, the potential cost described previously would appear to be relevant to a large portion of the operant literature.

This review of the literature also revealed that there was more than one dimension of independent variable application in which inaccuracy could occur, although these were not rated separately. Inaccuracies in both the temporal and the physical dimensions of the independent variable application can be costly to the conclusions drawn from a study. For example, the temporal dimension refers to the appropriate occurrence of the independent variable in time in the ABAB or ABAC reversal sequence or in different portions of the multiple baseline design. The absence of overlap between different independent variables is important to demonstrate here. For example, if the design suggests that a parent or teacher who has been inadventently reinforcing a maladaptive response in baseline should ignore that response and reinforce alternative responses in treatment, it would be useful to identify treatment overlap reliably; that is, to show how often the maladaptive response was ignored in baseline and inadvertently reinforced in treatment. Particularly when reversals are unsuccessfully attempted, it is important to demonstrate the absence of the independent or treatment variable in the return to baseline phase. If no permanent record of the application of the independent variable exists, the experimenter may not be able to identify or exempt inaccurate treatment application from the list of causes of failure to find a functional relationship.

Another index of temporal reliability is the degree to which the treatment variable is delivered according to the schedule outlined in the method section. Since there is clear evidence with animals and some evidence with humans (e.g., Homer & Peterson, 1980) that changes in the scheduling of the independent variable can have a profound impact on responding, evidence concerning the actual delivery of reinforcement is necessary to avoid erroneous conclusions. For example, imagine a relatively untrained treatment agent applying a DRO 2-min schedule. The treatment agent begins by reliably checking his watch and delivering a food reinforcer contingent on "no tantrums" every 2 min on the dot. However, some tantrums continue and the therapist (who may have more experience with treating children than with using schedules) can tell when the child is about to have a tantrum. So he looks at his watch and says "1½ minutes, close enough" and delivers the reinforcer. Later, when the rate of tantrums is much lower, however, he may even forget a reinforcer or get it in late. When no data are collected on the treatment agent's behavior, it would not be apparent to the data collectors that any departure from the agreed on schedule had been made. Yet, the treatment agent has changed from a fixed DRO 2-min to an escalating DRO schedule and there are well-known differential effects for these two schedules (Homer & Peterson, 1980).

The physical dimension of independent variable reliability refers simply to what the treatment agent actually does, or the degree to which the description of the treatment in the method section matches the actual occurrence of treatment in practice. Again, many treatment agents are highly motivated to effect changes in behavior and may inadvertently begin to use additional treatment methods or may alter the current method to change or hasten results. For example, what if the treatment agent described above began to smile and wink at the child between reinforcers in order to maintain the withholding of tantrums? In this case, both facial expressions and food might serve as reinforcers and the actual schedule might be a DRO 15-sec rather than a DRO 2-min. Such treatment might be more likely to generalize to settings where smiles but not food was present. Similarly, the treatment agent might slowly shake his head and frown (signals for punishment in other settings) when the child had a tantrum, and thus, if effective, the actual schedule would be DRO + punishment. The above might also result in the conclusion that DRO was ineffective, if frowning served as an attentional reinforcer for tantrums. If naive observers are used, or even if experienced observers are sitting behind the treatment agent for a better view of the child, the physical reliability of the procedure cannot be determined, and the chance for results that could be reliably replicated is at risk. DeRubeis and Hollon (1981) in fact, suggest that both the therapist behaviors specified by the experimenter and the therapist-emitted behaviors not specified by the experimenter should be observed and reported as a measure of treatment variable accuracy.

Cost-Effective Solutions

Even if investigators agree that the potential for costly inaccuracy exists in independent variable methodology, there may be different reactions to this conclusion. The present authors, as well as some other investigators (e.g., Johnston & Pennypacker, 1980) feel that deliberately accepting inaccuracy in basic subject matter because it may be inconvenient to gather accurate information has no place in a science of behavior. Others may feel, however, that the potential cost of the inaccuracy must be balanced against the cost of ensuring accurate independent variable application. The cost-effectiveness of the solution would dictate whether it would be applied or not. If there were solutions which were cost-effective, then prevention of independent variable inaccuracy would be the most acceptable solution.

There are a variety of levels of solutions that might be suggested. At the lowest level of both cost and methodological completeness, this article might serve as a reminder to experimenters to ensure accurate independent variable application by rigorously training treatment agents and by periodic informal (and unreported) spot checks on the agent dispensing the independent variable. This solution might be a slight improvement on the status quo and would involve little additional cost. Since the potential for independent variable inaccuracy has rarely been explicitly discussed in the operant literature before, this discussion may spur any researchers not already engaged in such practices to more complete methodological safeguards. However, this solution leaves the possibility for continued inaccuracy. As Johnston and Pennypacker (1980) noted, when the complete description of all relevant information pertaining to a research study is not provided, the reader has only the choice of giving the author the benefit of the doubt or of making a more conservative assumption. Continuing to give the researcher the benefit of the doubt may leave a gap in acceptable behavior methodology.

A second solution might be to maintain the present practice of not assessing and reporting independent variable accuracy in cases where the risk of inaccuracy is low, but collecting and reporting data on independent variable application whenever the risk of inaccurate application is high. Thus, the reader would not be required to give the author the benefit of the doubt in cases where the doubt might be too liberal, and the researcher would retain the right to argue for or against the necessity of supplying such data. This would reduce the risk of inaccuracies in conclusions drawn from operant research at relatively low cost but it would not eliminate the risk.

A methodologically more conservative solution might be to use some measure of the accuracy of independent variable implementation routinely in much the same way the accuracy of dependent variable observation has been routinely examined, either by measuring independent variable reliability with multiple observers or by calibrating the observers against "true values" of the independent variable as specified by the researcher. If the researcher opts to take measures of independent variable reliability, the observers can simply be trained to observe the treatment variable as well as the dependent variable. Past data show that multiple variables can be reliably observed at the same time (e.g., Kent, O'Leary, Dietz, & Diament, 1979) and that data can be collected on two interacting individuals reliably (e.g., Pinkston, Reese, LeBlanc, & Baer, 1973). Some investigators have successfully observed and reported data both for the dependent and independent variables (e.g., Kazdin, 1977*b*). Simple occurrence/nonoccurrence of a crucial treatment variable can be observed in successive intervals to determine temporal reliability. Physical reliability could be determined simply by observing a category of "other therapist interaction," and then deciding whether to measure or control frequently occurring other behavior. The presentation of independent variable reliability would be a minor inconvenience for experimenters and could result in large improvements in the quality of experimental data.

Johnston and Pennypacker (1980) argue, however, that using multiple observers may not yield data relevant either to reliability or accuracy. Reliability typically refers to the extent to which an observation could be repeated to yield the same measure again, while accuracy refers to the extent to which the measure approximates the true value in nature. Simply because multiple observers agree on an observation does not automatically prove that the observation is reliable in a classic sense, since all the observers may share a bias or limitation which might systematically influence their measurement, reducing the extent to which the observation could be repeated successfully by a neutral source. Thus, simple observational reliability might not improve the actual reliability of independent variable implementation any more than multiple observer reliability can contribute conclusive information on the accuracy of dependent variable observation (Johnston & Pennypacker, 1980). A superior technique might be the method of calibration mentioned earlier, in which the data of the observer are compared with the true value in nature and inaccuracies in the observed values are then corrected. With the dependent variable, no "true" values are known, and Johnston and Pennypacker (1980) suggest a variety of methods of calibrating observers of the dependent variable including the use of bogus subjects who produce behaviors at a prearranged rate or the comparison of observed data to a permanent product or a mechanical record. Although the true value in nature of the independent variable is also an unknown, the methodology section of the research report suggests a known value that should (if the method section description is accurate) closely approximate the true value. Thus, unlike the dependent variable, on which no projection of the true value in nature is directly possible, the independent variable's true value in nature may be assumed to be the value specified by the experimenter. If the experimenter trains the observer to observe and record both independent and dependent variables, then the value of the observed independent variable can be compared to the specified value. Any difference between these values must be ascertained by the experimenter to be observational error or therapist drift. This calibration can be accomplished in the same way as dependent variable calibration, described in more detail by Johnston and Pennypacker (1980). This last method would appear to give firm assurance as to the accuracy of independent variable implementation.

Of course, there are many other cost-effective solutions to the problem of independent variable accuracy that may be used in prescribed situations. For example, correctly calibrated, mechanical methods of delivering or recording the occurrence of the independent variable which are equally effective as using human therapists and observers, might be preferred because they provide greater accuracy at lower cost. Similarly, program evaluators have suggested the routine application of process evaluation, which may consist of various means of documenting the occurrence of treatment variables (Donabedian, 1966; Way et al., 1978). Cook and Campbell (1979) suggested a variety of designs that may control for therapist drift in field settings. Finally, future investigators may engineer new, cost-effective methods to guarantee accurate independent variable application.

Thus, the observational technology used by behavior analysts suggests the need to assess the integrity of their reports of both the independent variable and the dependent variable. There are both published and anecdotal data showing that inaccuracies do occur. There is a clear potential cost for such inaccuracies, with the risk of failure to replicate and lack of generality of results being proportional to the degree of the inaccuracy. Finally, there are several cost-effective solutions to remove the risk, with perhaps the best solution being calibration of the treatment agent. The intent of the present article is not to lay down a new set of rigid requirements for behavior analysts; such rules would be antithetical to the practice of applied behavior analysis (Johnston & Pennypacker, 1980). Instead, the intent is to point out this potential methodological pitfall and to suggest some alternative strategies that may be used flexibly by behavior analysts to improve the quality of their data and the integrity of their conclusions regarding the effects of independent variables.

REFERENCE NOTES

1. Hollon, S. D., Mandell, M., Bemis, K. M., DeRubeis, R. J., Emerson, M., Evans, M. D., & Kriss, M. R. *Reliability and validity of the Young Cognitive Therapy Scale.* Unpublished manuscript, University of Minnesota, 1981.
2. DeRubeis, R. J. Personal communication, September 21, 1981.

REFERENCES

Arrington, R. E. Time sampling in studies of social behavior: A critical review of techniques and results with research suggestions. *Psychological Bulletin,* 1943, **40,** 81-124.

Baer, D. M., Wolf, M. M., & Risley, T. R. Some current dimensions of applied behavior analysis. *Journal of Applied Behavior Analysis,* 1968, **1,** 91-97.

Becker, J., & Schuckit, M. A. The comparative efficacy of cognitive therapy and pharmacotherapy in the treatment of depression. *Cognitive Therapy and Research,* 1978, **2,** 193-197.

Bellack, A. S., Hersen, M., & Himmelhock, J. M. Social skills training for depression: A treatment manual. *JSAS Catalog of Selected Documents,* 1980, **10,** 25. (MS. 2156).

Bernal, M. E., Klinnert, M. D., & Schultz, L. A. Outcome evaluation of behavioral parent training and client-centered parent counseling for children with conduct problems. *Journal of Applied Behavior Analysis,* 1980, **13,** 677-691.

Bijou, S. W., Peterson, R. F., & Ault, M. H. A method to integrate descriptive and experimental field studies at the level of data and empirical concepts. *Journal of Applied Behavior Analysis,* 1968, **1,** 175-191.

Billingsley, F., White, O. R., & Munson, R. Procedural reliability: A rationale and an example. *Behavioral Assessment,* 1980, **2,** 229-241.

Bornstein, P., & Quevillon, R. Effects of a self-instructional package on overactive preschool boys. *Journal of Applied Behavior Analysis,* 1976, **9,** 179-188.

Carnine, D. W. Effects of two teacher-presentation rates on off-task behavior, answering correctly, and participation. *Journal of Applied Behavior Analysis,* 1976, **9,** 199-206.

Cohen, J. A coefficient of agreement for nominal scales. *Educational and Psychological Measurement,* 1960, **20,** 37-46.

Cook, T. D., & Campbell, D. T. *Quasi-experimentation: Design and analysis issues for field settings.* Chicago: Rand McNally, 1979.

Dallemagne, G., & Richelle, M. Titration schedule with rats in a restraining device. *Journal of Experimental Analysis of Behavior,* 1970, **13,** 339-348.

DeRubeis, R. J., & Hollon, S. D. Behavior treatment of affective disorders. In L. Michelson, M. Hersen, & S. M. Turner (Eds.), *Future perspectives in behavior therapy.* New York: Plenum, 1981.

Donabedian, A. Evaluating the quality of medical care. *M'lbank Memorial Fund Quarterly,* 1966, **44,** 166-203.

Dorsey, M. F., Iwata, B. A., Ong, P., & McSween, T. E. Treatment of self-injurious behavior using a water mist: Initial response suppression and generalization. *Journal of Applied Behavior Analysis,* 1980, **13,** 343-353.

Fleischman, M. J. A replication of Patterson's "Intervention for boys with conduct problems." *Journal of Consulting and Clinical Psychology,* 1981, **49,** 342-351.

Friedling, C., & O'Leary, S. G. Effects of self-instruction training on second- and third-grade hyperactive children: A failure to replicate. *Journal of Applied Behavior Analysis,* 1979, **12,** 211-219.

Hanley, E. M. Review of research involving applied behavior analysis in the classroom. *Review of Educational Research,* 1970, **40,** 597-625.

Hartmann, D. P. Considerations in the choice of interobserver reliability estimates. *Journal of Applied Behavior Analysis,* 1977, **10,** 103-116.

Hartmann, D. P., Roper, B. L., & Gelfand, D. M. An evaluation of alternative modes of child psychotherapy. In B. B. Lahey & A. E. Kazdin (Eds.), *Advances in clinical child psychology,* (Vol. 1). New York: Plenum Press, 1977.

Hasazi, J. E., & Hasazi, S. E. Effects of teacher attention on digit-reversal behavior in an elementary school child. *Journal of Applied Behavior Analysis,* 1972, **5,** 157-162.

Hayes, S. C., Rincover, A., & Solnick, J. V. The technical drift of applied behavior analysis. *Journal of Applied Behavior Analysis,* 1980, **13,** 275-285.

Hersen, M. Complex problems require complex solutions. *Behavior Therapy,* 1981, **12,** 15-29.

Hersen, M., & Barlow, D. H. *Single case experimental designs.* New York: Pergamon, 1976.

Heyns, R. W., & Lippitt, R. Systematic observational techniques. In G. Lindzey (Ed.), *Handbook of social psychology,* Vol. 1. Cambridge, Mass.: Addison-Wesley, 1954.

Hobbs, S. A., Moguin, L. E., Tyroler, M., & Lahey, B. B. Cognitive behavior therapy with children: Has clinical utility been demonstrated? *Psychological Bulletin,* 1980, **87,** 147-165.

Homer, A. L., & Peterson, L. Differential reinforcement of other behavior: A preferred response elimination procedure. *Behavior Therapy,* 1980, **11,** 449-471.

Johnston, J., & Pennypacker, H. S. *Strategies and tactics of human behavioral research.* Hillsdale, N.J.: Erlbaum, 1980.

Kazdin, A. E. The effect of vicarious reinforcement on attentive behavior in the classroom. *Journal of Applied Behavior Analysis,* 1973, **6,** 71-78.

Kazdin, A. E. Artifact, bias, and complexity of assessment: The ABCs of reliability. *Journal of Applied Behavior Analysis,* 1977, **10,** 141-150. (*a*)

Kazdin, A. E. The influence of behavior preceding a reinforced response on behavior change in the classroom. *Journal of Applied Behavior Analysis,* 1977, **10,** 299-310. (*b*)

Kelly, M. B. A review of the observational data-collection and reliability procedures reported in *The Journal of Applied Behavior Analysis. Journal of Applied Behavior Analysis,* 1977, **10,** 97-101.

Kent, R. N., O'Leary, K. D., Dietz, A., & Diament, C. Comparison of observational recordings in vivo, via mirror, and via television. *Journal of Applied Behavior Analysis,* 1979, **12,** 517-522.

Mathews, R. M., & Fawcett, S. B. Community applications of instructional technology: Training low-income proctors. *Journal of Applied Behavior Analysis,* 1977, **10,** 747-754.

McNamara, J. R., & MacDonough, T. S. Some methodological considerations in the design and implementation of behavior therapy research. *Behavior Therapy,* 1972, **3,** 361-378.

Milby, J. B. Modification of extreme social isolation by contingent social reinforcement. *Journal of Applied Behavior Analysis,* 1970, **3,** 149-152.

Nelson, G. L., & Cone, J. D. Multiple-baseline analysis of a token economy for psychiatric inpatients. *Journal of Applied Behavior Analysis,* 1979, **12,** 255-271.

O'Leary, K. D., & Kent, R. N. Behavior modification for social action: Research tactics and problems. In L. A. Hamerlynck, L. C. Handy, & E. J. Mash (Eds.), *Behavior change: Methodology, concepts, and practice.* Champaign, Ill.: Research Press, 1973.

O'Leary, K. D., Kent, R. N., & Kanowitz, J. Shaping data collection congruent with experimental hypotheses. *Journal of Applied Behavior Analysis,* 1975, **8,** 43-52.

Patterson, G. R. Interventions for boys with conduct problems: Multiple settings, treatments, and criteria. *Journal of Consulting and Clinical Psychology,* 1974, **42,** 471-481.

Paul, G. L., & Lentz, R. J. *Psychological treatment for chronic mental patients: Milieu versus social learning programs.* Cambridge, Mass.: Harvard University Press, 1977.

Pinkston, E. M., Reese, N. M., LeBlanc, J. M., & Baer, D. M. Independent control of a preschool child's aggression and peer interaction by contingent teacher attention. *Journal of Applied Behavior Analysis,* 1973, **6,** 115-124.

Porterfield, J. K., Herbert-Jackson, E., & Risley, T. R. Contingent observation: An effective and acceptable procedure for reducing disruptive behavior of young children in a group setting. *Journal of Applied Behavior Analysis,* 1976, **9,** 55-64.

Reid, J. B. Reliability assessment of observational data: A possible methodological problem. *Child Development,* 1970, **41,** 1143-1150.

Reisinger, J. J. The treatment of "anxiety-depression" via positive reinforcement and response cost. *Journal of Applied Behavior Analysis,* 1972, **5,** 125-130.

Romanczyk, R. G., Kent, R. N., Diament, C., & O'Leary, K. D. Measuring the reliability of observational data: A reactive process. *Journal of Applied Behavior Analysis,* 1973, **6,** 175-184.

Rosenthal, R., & Rosnow, R. L. *Artifact in behavioral research.* New York: Academic Press, 1969.

Rounsaville, B. J., Weissman, M. M., & Prusoff, B. A. Psychotherapy with depressed outpatients: Patient and process variables as predictors of outcome. *British Journal of Psychiatry,* 1981, **138,** 67-74.

Sidman, M. *Tactics of scientific research.* New York: Basic Books, 1960.

Stallings, J. Implementation and child effects of teaching practices in Follow Through classrooms. *Monographs of the Society for Research in Child Development,* 1975, **40,** Nos. 7-8.

Strain, P. S., Shores, R. E., & Timm, M. A. Effects of peer social initiations on the behavior of withdrawn preschool children. *Journal of Applied Behavior Analysis,* 1977, **10,** 289-298.

Urbain, E. S., & Kendall, P. C. Review of social-cognitive problem-solving interventions with children. *Psychological Bulletin,* 1980, **88,** 109-143.

Way, J. R., Lund, D. A., & Attkisson, C. C. Quality assurance in human service program evaluation. In C. C. Attkisson, W. A. Hargreaves, M. J. Horowitz, & J. E. Sorensen (Eds.), *Evaluation of human service programs.* New York: Academic Press, 1978.

Webb, E. J., Campbell, D. T., Schwartz, R. D., & Sechrist, L. *Unobtrusive measures: Nonreactive research in the social sciences.* Chicago: Rand McNally, 1966.

Weick, K. E. Systematic observational methods. In G. Lindzey & E. Aronson (Eds.), *The handbook of social psychology,* Vol. 2. Menlo Park, Calif: Addison-Wesley, 1968.

Wodarski, J. S., Feldman, R. A., & Pedi, S. J. Objective measurement of the independent variable: A neglected methodological aspect in community-based behavioral research. *Journal of Abnormal Child Psychology,* 1974, **2**, 239-244.

Received October 26, 1981
Final acceptance April 6, 1982

JOURNAL OF APPLIED BEHAVIOR ANALYSIS 1999, **32**, 9–23 NUMBER 1 (SPRING 1999)

EVALUATING TREATMENT CHALLENGES WITH DIFFERENTIAL REINFORCEMENT OF ALTERNATIVE BEHAVIOR

TIMOTHY R. VOLLMER

UNIVERSITY OF FLORIDA

HENRY S. ROANE AND JOEL E. RINGDAHL

LOUISIANA STATE UNIVERSITY

AND

BETHANY A. MARCUS

EASTERN STATE HOSPITAL AND
VIRGINIA COMMONWEALTH UNIVERSITY, MEDICAL COLLEGE

In prior research, differential reinforcement of alternative behavior (DRA) has been implemented at optimal treatment values: Problem behavior is never reinforced, and alternative behavior is always reinforced. However, in application, DRA is unlikely to be conducted optimally. In this study, following a functional analysis phase and a differential reinforcement at full implementation phase, we challenged initially positive treatment effects for 3 participants by implementing DRA at less than optimal parameters. For example, some occurrences of problem behavior were reinforced, and some occurrences of alternative behavior were not reinforced. Results suggested that when exposed to DRA at full implementation, participants showed a bias toward appropriate behavior in subsequent conditions during which "mistakes" (treatment challenges) were intentionally introduced. In addition, the negative effects of treatment challenges were quickly reversible, in comparison to the positive effects of DRA, which were not quickly reversible in the face of treatment challenges.

DESCRIPTORS: functional analysis, differential reinforcement, aberrant behavior, treatment challenges

---

One of the most practical advantages of a pretreatment functional analysis is that the reinforcers that maintain problem behavior can be withheld during treatment (extinction) and presented contingent upon an alternative, more desired behavior (differential reinforcement). In general, when one behavior is placed on extinction and another behavior is reinforced, the procedure is called differential reinforcement of alternative behavior (DRA; Vollmer & Iwata, 1992). Functional communication training (FCT) is a good example of how information from a functional analysis may be applied to a DRA-based treatment: The reinforcer that maintains problem behavior can be withheld following occurrences of the problem behavior and presented following instances of communication (e.g., Carr & Durand, 1985). For example, if aberrant behavior is found to be reinforced by attention, FCT might involve placing aberrant behavior on extinction (ignoring) while providing attention contingent on appropriate mands (e.g., Hanley, Piazza, Fisher, Contrucci, & Maglieri, 1997). Similarly, if aberrant behavior is maintained by escape from instructional de-

This research was conducted when the authors were at Louisiana State University. Joel E. Ringdahl is now at the University of Iowa.

Reprint requests can be addressed to Timothy R. Vollmer, Department of Psychology, University of Florida, Gainesville, Florida 32611.

mands, aberrant behavior may be placed on extinction (e.g., working through the task) while an alternative behavior (perhaps compliance or communication) is negatively reinforced with a brief escape period (Lalli, Casey, & Kates, 1995). When escape is used as a reinforcer, the differential reinforcement application is sometimes called differential negative reinforcement of alternative behavior (DNRA; Vollmer & Iwata, 1992).

Since the emergence of functional analysis methods (e.g., Iwata, Dorsey, Slifer, Bauman, & Richman, 1982/1994), studies on differential reinforcement based on functional analyses have proliferated (e.g., Mazaleski, Iwata, Vollmer, Zarcone, & Smith, 1993; Steege, Wacker, Berg, Cigrand, & Cooper, 1990). In a DRA arrangement, appropriate and inappropriate behavior can be conceptualized as concurrent operants (Fisher & Mazur, 1997). If the reinforcement schedule favors the alternative behavior, as it should in a well-designed DRA, responding should be allocated toward appropriate behavior and away from problem behavior. Typically, in evaluations of differential reinforcement, problem behavior is never reinforced (i.e., is placed on extinction), and defined instances of the alternative behavior are reinforced to maximize the probability of response allocation in favor of the alternative behavior.

In controlled experimentation, it is important to ensure that treatments are conducted with perfect or near-perfect integrity because otherwise any noneffects may be attributed to procedural failures rather than to limitations of the treatment itself. However, in application, many DRA procedures are likely to be challenged with integrity failures. It is unlikely, for example, that all instances of alternative behavior will be reinforced or that all instances of problem behavior will fail to produce access to reinforcers. As such, both appropriate and aberrant behavior will likely produce intermittent access to reinforcers.

At one end of a continuum, a perfect integrity failure would occur if appropriate behavior was never reinforced and problem behavior was always reinforced. An analogue to such a failure is conducted in most baselines in functional analysis research: Problem behavior produces access to reinforcers and appropriate behaviors explicitly do not produce access to such reinforcers (e.g., Iwata, Pace, Kalsher, Cowdery, & Cataldo, 1990; Hanley et al., 1997; Lalli et al., 1995; Vollmer, Iwata, Zarcone, Smith, & Mazaleski, 1993). At the other end of the continuum, perfect integrity for DRA would involve reinforcement of all appropriate behaviors (or at least reinforcement would occur systematically according to a prescribed intermittent schedule) and extinction of all instances of problem behaviors. In the middle of the continuum, a therapist (or parent or teacher) might display good treatment implementation with one component (e.g., reinforcing all appropriate communication) but poor implementation with the other component (e.g., continuing to reinforce problem behavior). Recently, Shirley, Iwata, Kahng, Mazaleski, and Lerman (1997) evaluated the effects of FCT with and without extinction. The reinforcement component was conducted with 100% implementation, while no extinction component was in place. Results showed that FCT was ineffective without extinction unless FCT without extinction followed a condition in which FCT with extinction had been in place.

To date, no studies have evaluated methods for examining differential reinforcement effects along the continuum of perfect integrity failure to perfect integrity. In the study by Shirley et al. (1997), three general conditions were conducted: (a) alternative behavior was never reinforced and problem behavior was always reinforced (baseline), (b) alternative behavior was always rinforced and problem behavior was never reinforced (full treatment), and (c) both alternative and problem behaviors were always reinforced (FCT without extinction). However, it is likely that when DRA-based procedures are actually applied, the reinforcement component for either alternative will be something between all or nothing. For example, a teacher may be inclined to usually reinforce compliance with escape and sometimes (intermittently) inadvertently reinforce escape-maintained self-injurious behavior (SIB). In such cases, the actual implementation of treatment might be something like the following: Alternative behavior is reinforced 80% of the time and problem behavior is reinforced 20% of the time. In this example, the treatment is implemented "correctly" 80% of the time. The effect of such treatment implementation is not known.

Although evaluation of varying treatment integrity values has been a frequent recommendation for behavioral intervention (e.g., LeLaurin & Wolery, 1992), few studies have evaluated methods to explicitly analyze treatment at less than perfect levels of integrity. In a notable exception, Northup, Fisher, Kahng, Harrell, and Kurtz (1997) reported a method for evaluating varying levels of treatment implementation for differential reinforcement plus time-out. In that study, an appropriate behavior was reinforced 100% of the time, 50% of the time, or 25% of the time. Also, aggression or pica was followed with time-out using those same implementation values. Results showed that initial treatment effects were maintained when time-out was implemented at 50%. Thus, there is evidence supporting the use of punishment procedures at reduced levels of implementation. The effects of differential reinforcement at eroded levels of implementation have not yet been evaluated.

In the current study, we evaluated a method similar to that used by Northup et al. (1997) to study differential reinforcement procedures (reinforcement and extinction) derived directly from a functional analysis. Following a functional analysis, problem behavior and appropriate behavior were treated as concurrent operants that were reinforced all of the time, never, or some of the time, depending on the condition. The specific purposes of the study were (a) to demonstrate a methodology by which initially successful DRA effects may be evaluated in the face of treatment challenges (subsequent less than optimal implementation) and (b) to evaluate the effects of treatment challenges on appropriate and problem behavior. If a method is available to evaluate DRA at implementation strengths that may mimic actual application, researchers and clinicians may be better able to identify critical treatment values. Further, if treatment produces positive effects in the face of less than optimal implementation, the prognosis for long-term efficacy and maintenance for differential reinforcement–based interventions is improved.

In addition to being practical, the manipulation of treatment implementation values might be of conceptual interest. To date, few studies have evaluated the differential responsiveness of inappropriate and appropriate behavior to new reinforcement schedules following treatments at full implementation. It would be useful to evaluate how changes in treatment fidelity of various degrees would influence inappropriate behavior in comparison to appropriate behavior. For example, it is possible that individuals would show a bias toward inappropriate behavior as a result of relatively long reinforcement histories. If this is true, inappropriate behaviors should readily return to high rates when they are intermittently reinforced or when appropriate behavior is not reinforced frequently enough. Conversely, it is possible that biases toward appropriate behavior would emerge, for instance, if the behavior is perhaps less painful or less effortful. If this is true, appropriate behavior should be relatively slow to return to baseline levels following treatments implemented at full strength, and individuals should show a disproportional tendency to respond appropriately when reinforcement is simultaneously available for either inappropriate or appropriate behavior.

METHOD

Participants and Setting

Participants were 3 individuals who had been referred by their parents and teachers for treatment of severe behavior problems. Rachel was a 17-year-old girl who had been diagnosed with profound mental retardation and who engaged in SIB in the form of head hitting and hand biting and aggression in the form of scratching, hitting, and hair pulling. She was nonambulatory and used a wheelchair. She did not have conventional language skills and required assistance with all self-care routines. Todd was a 16-year-old boy who had been diagnosed with profound mental retardation and who engaged in SIB in the form of head hitting. He was nonambulatory and used a wheelchair. He did not use conventional language, but occasionally reached in the direction of desired items such as toys. Kyle was a 4-year-old boy who had not been formally diagnosed, but he appeared to be functioning in the severe to profound range of mental retardation. Kyle engaged in severe aggression in the form of hitting, scratching, and pulling hair. He had minimal speech and occasionally requested items by pointing or vocalizing one-word utterances. Rachel and Todd attended a school for individuals with profound handicaps. Kyle attended a noncategorical preschool program.

Sessions lasted 10 min and were conducted at the participants' schools in therapy rooms separate from their regular classrooms. Sessions were conducted three to five times per day, 3 to 5 days per week (no more than 4 days per week for Kyle, who did not attend school on Fridays). The therapy room in Rachel's and Todd's school contained a table, chairs, and items brought in by the therapist as needed for sessions. The therapy room for Kyle contained several tables and chairs and a chalkboard. It also contained books on shelves, but these were covered with sheets for sessions. Other materials were brought to the room by a therapist as needed for sessions.

Recording and Reliability

For Rachel's and Todd's sessions, observers were usually seated behind a one-way observation window but sometimes sat in the room unobtrusively. For Kyle's sessions, observers sat in a corner of the room at a table and did not interact with him. Behavior was scored using handheld computers. Inappropriate behavior included aggression and self-injury. *Aggression* was defined as hitting, pulling hair, scratching, or kicking the therapist. *Self-injury* was defined as self-hitting or self-biting (contact between the teeth and skin). Appropriate alternative behaviors were compliance (Rachel and Kyle) and mands (Todd). It is important to note that all targeted appropriate behaviors were present in the participants' repertoires prior to the study. Thus, no new alternative behaviors were shaped and no pretraining was required before entering into the differential reinforcement condition. *Compliance* was scored as completion of the requested task or task step either independently (no prompts) or following a verbal or gestural prompt. Compliance was not scored if physical guidance was used. *Mands* were scored as a reaching response with the hand and arm directed toward an item in the environment. Therapist behavior was also scored and included delivery of materials (handing a previously restricted item to the participant and allowing access for 30 ± 5 s), and delivery of escape (stating "take a break" paired with 30 ± 5 s of break from instructional activity).

During 25.5% of the functional analysis sessions, a second observer simultaneously but independently scored the participants' problem behavior. Interobserver agreement calculations were the same as those used by Shirley et al. (1997). Specifically, interobserver agreement was calculated by dividing the 10-min session into 60 10-s intervals. The frequency of a target behavior scored by one observer was compared to the frequency observed by a second observer by dividing the smaller number by the larger number in each 10-s interval and converting to a percentage. The mean percentage of agreement was then used as an overall interobserver agreement score. Interobserver agreement averaged 98.6% (range for individual sessions, 90.8% to 100%).

During 60.6% of the baseline and treatment sessions, a second observer simultaneously but independently scored the participants' appropriate and inappropriate behavior. For inappropriate behavior, interobserver agreement averaged 97.9% (range for individual sessions, 88.3% to 100%); for appropriate behavior, interobserver agreement averaged 95.2% (range for individual sessions, 81.7% to 100%).

During 31.3% of the sessions, a second observer simultaneously but independently scored therapist behavior. Using the same calculation procedures described above, interobserver agreement for delivery of reinforcers (escape or materials) averaged 97.7% (range for individual sessions, 88.3% to 100%).

Functional Analysis

Functional analysis procedures were based on those of Iwata et al. (1982/1994). Four test conditions were conducted: attention, escape, materials, and no consequence. A fifth condition was designed as a control. During the attention condition, the participant had access to various materials but did not have access to attention unless the target aberrant behavior occurred. Aberrant behavior was followed by attention for approximately 30 s using a continuous reinforcement schedule (CRF). The attention consisted of a brief reprimand and then conversation. During the escape condition, a therapist presented instructions to perform a task based on the participant's individual education plan. The instructions were presented once per 30 s using a three-prompt sequence (verbal, gestural, physical guidance, with 5 s between prompts). Contingent on aberrant behavior, a 30-s escape period was introduced (using a CRF schedule) and was signaled by saying, "take a break." During the materials condition, a therapist started a session by removing preferred materials from reach. Contingent on aberrant behavior, the materials were presented to the participant for 30 s on a CRF schedule. During the no-consequence condition, the participant had no materials or other people with which or whom to interact; also, there was no programmed consequence for aberrant behavior. A therapist was in the room but did not respond to any target behaviors. The purpose of the attention, escape, and materials conditions was to evaluate possible reinforcement effects: If differentially high rates of aberrant behavior occurred during any one of these three conditions, the tested consequence was considered to be a reinforcer (Iwata et al., 1982/1994). The purpose of the no-consequence condition was to evaluate whether aberrant behavior would persist in the absence of socially mediated reinforcement. During the control condition, the participant had continuous access to preferred materials, attention was delivered at least once every 30 s, and no instructional demands were presented. The purpose of the control condition was to evaluate whether aberrant behavior persisted when all establishing operations from the test conditions had been eliminated (i.e., no restricted access to attention or materials, no instructional demands, no austere environment).

For Kyle, the functional analysis phase was somewhat abbreviated because of an anticipated shorter time of participation. His school year was scheduled to end within a few weeks.

Baseline

During baseline, the relevant test condition from the functional analysis was replicated until aberrant behavior occurred at a relatively stable rate or was on an upward trend. For Rachel and Kyle, the escape condition from the functional analysis was used as a baseline because their behavior had been shown to be sensitive to escape as reinforcement. For Rachel, the tasks used for the instructional sessions were towel folding and utensil sorting. For Kyle, the tasks used were puzzles and sorting by color or shape. For Todd, the materials condition from the functional analysis was used as a baseline because his behavior was sensitive to materials (musical toys) as reinforcement. In all cases, the alternative behaviors (compliance, mands) produced access to reinforcers 0% of the time (extinction) and aberrant behavior produced access to reinforcers 100% of the time (CRF). This schedule arrangement is typical in functional analysis research that is designed to evaluate differential reinforcement as treatment (e.g., Shirley et al., 1997; Vollmer et al., 1993). Hereafter, baseline contingencies will be referred to as 0/100 (percentage of reinforcement for appropriate behavior/percentage of reinforcement for inappropriate behavior).

Differential Reinforcement: Full Implementation

During the first differential reinforcement conditions, treatments were based on the outcome of the functional analysis: Aberrant behavior was placed on extinction and an appropriate alternative was reinforced with 30-s access to the reinforcer on a CRF schedule. For Rachel and Kyle, whose behavior was reinforced by escape, DNRA was implemented, in which the alternative behavior was compliance and a 30-s break was made contingent on compliance. A therapist saying "take a break" and moving away from the participant signaled breaks. During breaks, work items remained on the table so that independent appropriate behaviors could occur; however, no prompting to engage with work materials was administered. For Todd, whose behavior was reinforced by materials, DRA with positive reinforcement was implemented, in which the alternative behavior was a mand (reach). In all cases, alternative behavior produced access to the reinforcer on 100% of the trials (CRF) and aberrant behavior produced the reinforcer on 0% of the trials (extinction). This schedule arrangement represents treatment schedules that are characteristic of differential reinforcement at full implementation (e.g., Shirley et al., 1997). Hereafter, full implementation contingencies will be indicated as 100/0 (percentage of reinforcement for appropriate behavior/percentage of reinforcement for inappropriate behavior).

Differential Reinforcement: Partial Implementation

During subsequent differential reinforcement phases, treatments were intentionally eroded to mimic various extremes of treatment implementation integrity failures. In other words, not all appropriate behaviors were reinforced and some aberrant behaviors were reinforced. Various partial implementation schedules were evaluated, although no attempt was made to evaluate exhaustively all possible schedule arrangements or to control for all possible order effects. The purpose of this analysis was to evaluate the effects of treatment challenges after an initially effective treatment had been implemented.

To assist with correct delivery of scheduled reinforcement, observers and therapists held cards specifying which responses should be followed by reinforcement. In the 25/75 schedule, for example, one list was a series of appropriate response instances with one out of every four randomly specified as the reinforced response, and a second list was a series of inappropriate response instances with three out of every four randomly specified as reinforced responses. On occasion, a therapist was verbally prompted by an observer or other assistant to help ensure correct reinforcer delivery.

Design

The sequence of conditions and the parameters of partial implementation were different for all participants. For all participants, baseline and full treatment were implemented first to ensure that DRA was effective.

For Rachel, the order of conditions was 0/100 (baseline), 100/0 (full treatment), 0/100, 25/75, 100/0, 50/50, and 75/25. These conditions were selected because they represented treatment at 0% strength (baseline), 100% strength (full treatment), 25% strength (25/75), 50% strength (50/50), and 75% strength (75/25). The order of conditions was selected in an attempt to evaluate lower implementation values first (other than full implementation).

For Kyle, the order of conditions was 0/100 (baseline), 100/0 (full treatment), 0/100, 100/0, 50/50, 25/75, 100/0. An attempt was made to test the same partial implementation values that were tested for Rachel, but in a different order. Because of time limitations, the 75/25 value was omitted.

For Todd, the order of conditions was 0/100 (baseline), 100/0 (full treatment), 0/100, 100/0, 20/0, 100/0, 100/100, 0/100, 100/0, 40/0, 100/0. These values were selected to evaluate a different model of partial implementation: Either one treatment component or the other (reinforcement or extinction) was always conducted with perfect integrity while the other component was implemented partially. At times in natural situations, one treatment component may be conducted perfectly while mistakes are made with the other component (e.g., always reinforcing communication but intermittently reinforcing the problem behavior, or intermittently reinforcing communication but always placing problem behavior on extinction).

RESULTS

Functional Analysis

Figure 1 shows the outcome of the functional analyses. For Todd, self-injury was observed only during the materials condition, suggesting that his behavior was sensitive to positive reinforcement in the form of materials (this outcome was summarized in a previous study by Vollmer, Marcus, Ringdahl, & Roane, 1995). For Rachel, inappropriate behavior occurred most consistently in the escape condition. For Kyle, aggression rates were highest in the escape condition, suggesting that escape reinforced the behavior.

Treatment Analysis

The upper panel of Figure 2 shows the outcome of Rachel's treatment analysis. During 0/100 (baseline), both appropriate and inappropriate behaviors occurred at high rates and increased as the condition progressed. During 100/0 (full treatment), appropriate behavior stabilized at a rate consistently higher than inappropriate behavior, which was extinguished during the final four sessions of the condition. During the return to 0/100, there appeared to be an extinction burst of appropriate behavior, which was no longer being reinforced. Inappropriate behavior was at 0 for six of the first nine sessions in the return to 0/100. During 25/75,

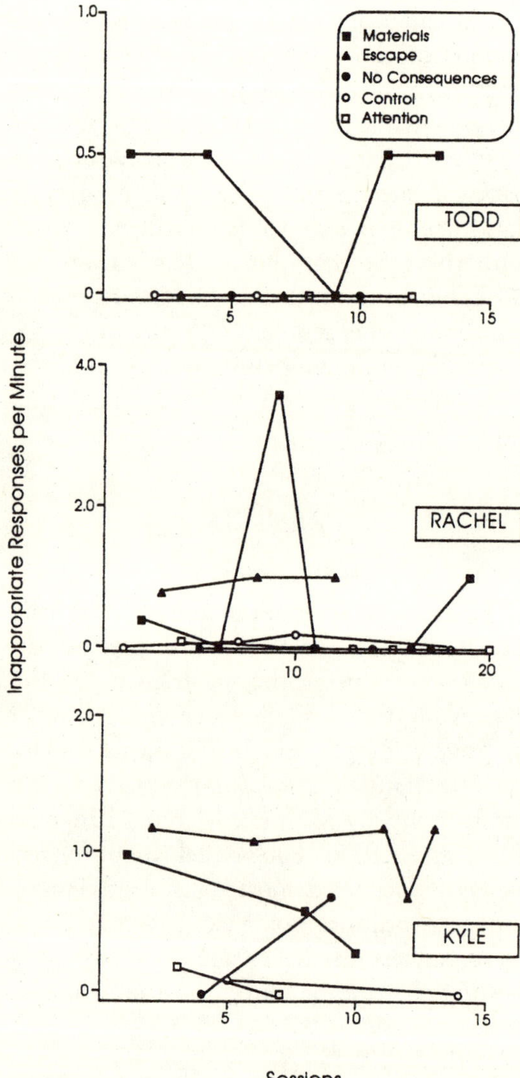

Figure 1. Results of the functional analyses for all participants. For Todd (upper panel), aberrant behavior was sensitive to positive reinforcement in the form of materials. For Rachel (center panel), aberrant behavior was sensitive to negative reinforcement. For Kyle (lower panel), aberrant behavior was sensitive to negative reinforcement.

there was an increasing trend in inappropriate behavior and a general decreasing trend in appropriate behavior. Upon returning to 100/0, inappropriate behavior never occurred and compliance occurred at a stable rate. During 50/50, compliance still occurred at a generally higher frequency than inappropriate behavior, but the effects were not as stable as had been noted at full treatment implementation. During 75/25, compliance stabilized and inappropriate behavior was at 0 during the final five sessions.

The lower panel of Figure 2 shows the response allocation of Rachel's appropriate and inappropriate behavior, plotted as a percentage of all responses (appropriate plus inappropriate). Five features of the data support a conclusion that Rachel showed a bias toward appropriate behavior. First, during baseline, appropriate behavior occurred at least as frequently as inappropriate behavior, despite the absence of escape as reinforcement for that behavior. Second, the transition from 100/0 to 0/100 yielded a very gradual change in response allocation; in fact, inappropriate behavior remained at 0 for six of the first nine sessions. Third, the transition from schedules favoring inappropriate behavior (e.g., 0/100 and 25/75) to the schedules favoring appropriate behavior (e.g., 100/0) yielded a very rapid change in response allocation; in fact, apparently because the very first instance of appropriate behavior contacted reinforcement during the second 100/0 condition, inappropriate behavior did not occur throughout the condition. Fourth, the transition from a condition in which appropriate behavior was never reinforced (0/100) to a condition in which appropriate behavior was reinforced unfavorably (25/75) produced an immediate temporary shift in response allocation toward appropriate behavior; no such immediate shift in response allocation toward inappropriate behavior was observed even in transitions to conditions in which every inappropriate behavior was reinforced and no appropriate behavior was reinforced (e.g., 0/100). Finally, when the probability of reinforcement was equal for inappropriate and appropriate behavior (i.e., 50/50), response allocation most consistently favored appropriate behavior.

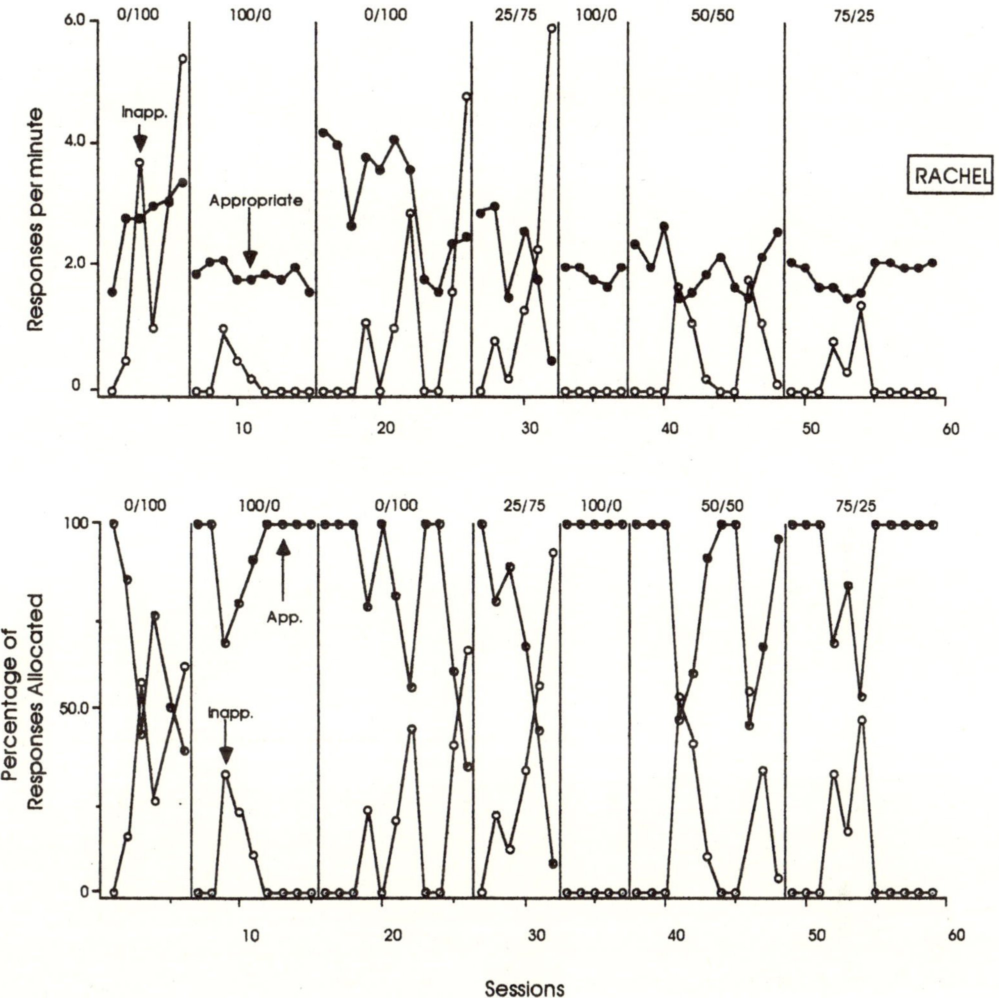

Figure 2. Results of the treatment evaluation for Rachel. Condition labels indicate the percentage of responses reinforced for both appropriate and inappropriate behavior (appropriate/inappropriate). The upper panel shows the number of responses per minute of appropriate and inappropriate behavior. The lower panel shows response allocation of appropriate and inappropriate behavior.

In the final condition (75/25), Rachel's response allocation was shifted exclusively to the appropriate behavior schedule for the final five sessions. This finding, combined with the general findings about a bias toward appropriate behavior, suggested that (a) differential reinforcement was resistant to treatment challenges, (b) treatment effects could be reobtained readily following treatment challenges, and (c) treatment probably would not need to be implemented at 100% to be successful.

The upper panel of Figure 3 shows the results of Kyle's treatment analysis. During all conditions except for the initial 0/100, appropriate behavior occurred at a higher rate than inappropriate behavior. However, the trends in the conditions that favored inappropriate responding (the second 0/100 and the 25/75) suggested that response allocation may have eventually shifted toward inappropriate behavior had the conditions been carried out longer (recall that Kyle's analysis was relatively abbreviated due to time constraints).

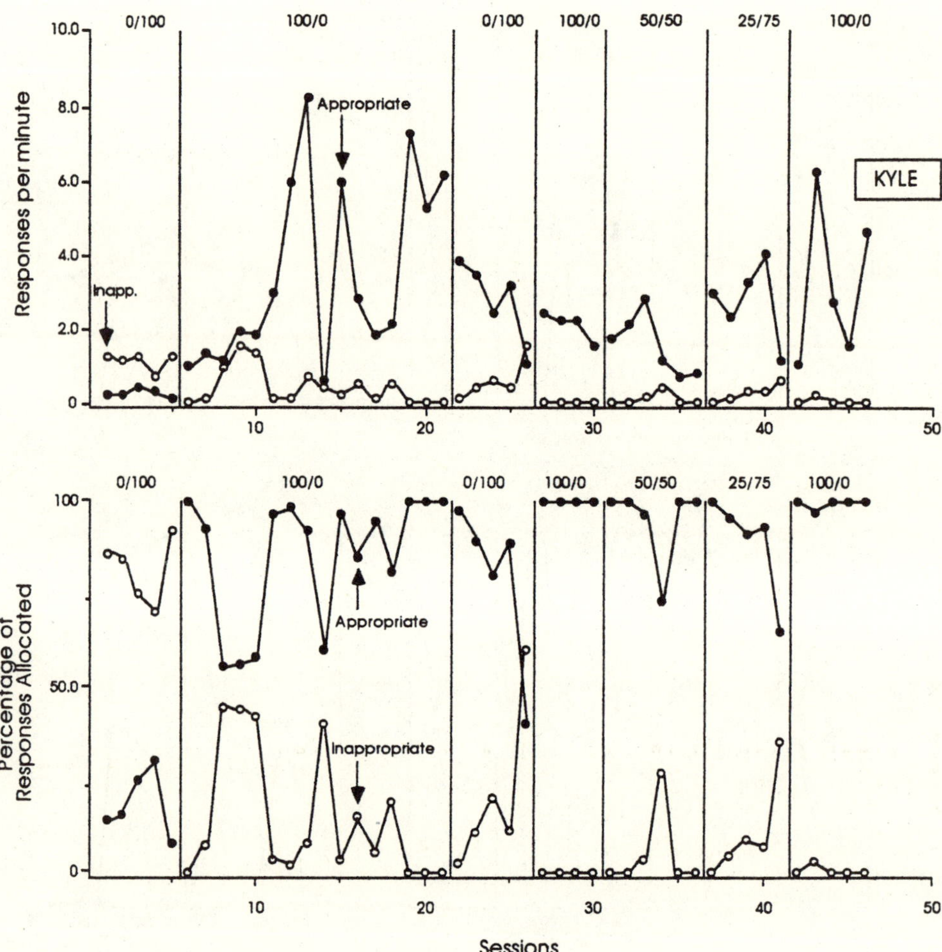

Figure 3. Results of the treatment evaluation for Kyle. Condition labels indicate the percentage of responses reinforced for both appropriate and inappropriate behavior (appropriate/inappropriate). The upper panel shows the number of responses per minute of appropriate and inappropriate behavior. The lower panel shows response allocation of appropriate and inappropriate behavior.

The lower panel of Figure 3 shows the response allocation of inappropriate and appropriate behavior as a percentage of total responses (inappropriate plus appropriate). As with Rachel, a preponderance of evidence suggested that Kyle showed a response bias toward appropriate behavior. During transitions into schedules that favored inappropriate behavior (e.g., from 100/0 to 0/100), the corresponding shifts in response allocation were gradual, whereas during transitions to schedules that favored appropriate behavior (e.g., 0/100 to 100/0), the corresponding shifts in response allocation were immediate. When the probability of reinforcement was equal (50/50), responding was allocated mainly to the appropriate behavior schedule. Given that responses were allocated primarily to appropriate behavior, DNRA was relatively resistant to implementation failures.

The upper panel of Figure 4 shows the results of Todd's treatment analysis. When treatment effects were obtained in the second 100/0 condition, all conditions that followed 100/0 conditions showed resistance to treatment challenges insofar as higher rates of appropriate behavior persisted even when the schedule favored inappropriate behavior (i.e., the third

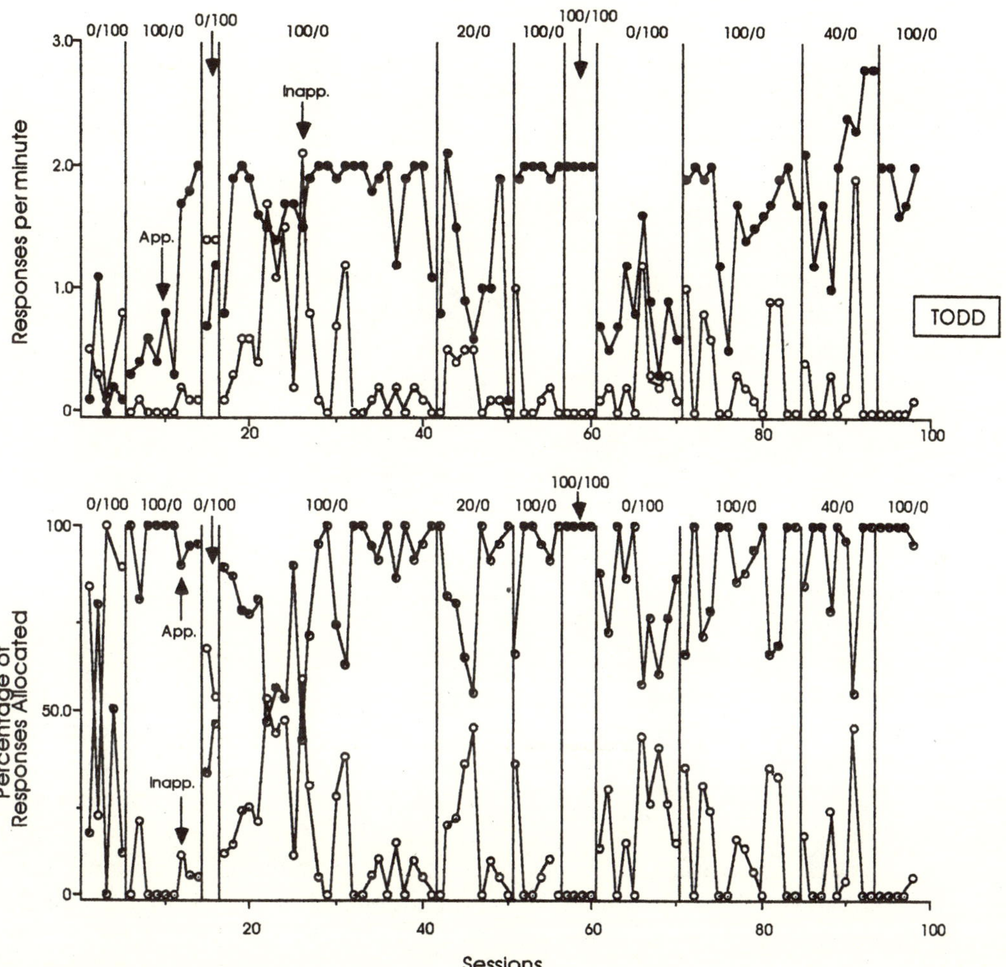

Figure 4. Results of the treatment evaluation for Todd. Condition labels indicate the percentage of responses reinforced for both appropriate and inappropriate behavior (appropriate/inappropriate). The upper panel shows the number of responses per minute of appropriate and inappropriate behavior. The lower panel shows response allocation of appropriate and inappropriate behavior.

0/100 condition). In the 20/0 and 0/100 conditions, raw rates of appropriate behavior were clearly affected by the unfavorable schedule, but the lower panel of Figure 4 shows that response allocation (plotted as a percentage of all responses) consistently favored appropriate behavior. Finally, the effects of the 100/100 condition, which followed a 100/0 condition, replicated the findings of Shirley et al. (1997) because responding was allocated exclusively to appropriate behavior following the immediately prior exposure to the 100/0 condition. Thus, although the planned arrangement was 100/100, SIB never contacted reinforcement in this condition because it never occurred. Shirley et al. had reported that FCT without extinction was effective if such a condition was preceded by FCT with extinction. For Todd, this effect was obtained because SIB did not occur at sufficient levels (i.e., anything greater than zero) to contact reinforcement.

DISCUSSION

In this study, differential reinforcement was evaluated at full implementation (all appropriate behavior was reinforced and no aberrant behavior was reinforced) and in conditions that mimicked lower levels of implementation (some appropriate behavior was not reinforced, some inappropriate behavior was reinforced, or both). Taken as a whole, results suggested the following. At full implementation of differential reinforcement, inappropriate behavior was virtually replaced by appropriate behavior; lower levels of implementation eventually reduced treatment efficacy if the schedule of reinforcement favored inappropriate behavior, but there was a general bias toward appropriate behavior.

The disproportional tendency toward appropriate behavior was an unexpected finding, given that reinforcement histories for inappropriate behavior were presumably well established. However, the more recent histories with differential reinforcement of appropriate behavior may have disposed the participants to allocate responding in that direction. Even so, it is interesting that transitions to schedules favoring appropriate behavior produced almost immediate allocation shifts and transitions to schedules favoring inappropriate behavior yielded more gradual allocation shifts: The momentum of reinforcement effects differed as a function of whether reinforcement contingencies favored appropriate or inappropriate behavior. A review of our records showed that, in many sessions, the participants first engaged in appropriate behavior (e.g., Todd manded, Rachel and Kyle complied), perhaps several times, before resorting to inappropriate behavior. Thus, if early attempts to behave appropriately were reinforced, that form of responding would then persist.

We do not suggest that the bias toward appropriate behavior is a finding generalizable to all individuals who display severe aberrant behavior. Presumably, factors such as response effort may account for differential sensitivity to reinforcement of appropriate behavior in comparison to inappropriate behavior. For example, compliance may have been a less effortful response or may have taken less time for Kyle to emit in comparison to aggression. If a response bias toward aggression is identified in future work, the experimenters may wish to consider the possibility that the inverse is true: Latency to reinforcement for aggression often may be shorter than it is for compliance if the task is relatively complex. We did not measure latency to reinforcement in this study, but it could be a focus of future manipulations of implementation strength.

Similarly, for Todd, reaching (the communicative response) had no immediate aversive consequences, whereas SIB may have hurt. The pain produced by SIB may be tolerable if no other means of obtaining reinforcers are available (e.g., in the 0/100 condition), but response allocation may be disposed to shift if reinforcement is available for an alternative response that does not hurt and requires little effort. To date, little if any research has been conducted on such conjunctive consequences. Although the presumably punishing consequence of pain may be difficult to manipulate experimentally, many behavioral procedures may contain component consequences that are both reinforcing and punishing. For example, an attention-maintained problem behavior might simultaneously produce a reprimand (reinforcement) and response cost (punishment) in the form of contingent toy withdrawal. The reprimand and response cost are components amenable to experimental manipulation.

In experimental preparations of the sort used here, response allocation should not be expected to "match" the relative probability of reinforcement in the sense of Herrnstein's (1970) matching equation. When reinforcement is delivered on concurrent ratio schedules, organisms are likely to allocate nearly all responses to the richer ratio schedule if all other factors are held constant (Herrnstein & Loveland, 1975). In Rachel's case, for example, it should not be surprising that responses were exclusively allocated to appropriate behavior in the last five sessions of 75/25, an arrangement in which appropriate behavior was reinforced three out of every four times it occurred and inappropriate behavior was on a variable-ratio 4 schedule. Any time spent responding on the inappropriate behavior schedule would have reduced the momentary probability of reinforcement. However, the clear differential sensitivity to reinforcement of appropriate behavior cannot be accounted for entirely by richer ratio schedules. For example, Rachel's response allocation was exclusive (toward appropriate behavior) after just one session of 100/0 when that condition followed either 0/100 or 25/75, whereas response allocation was still not exclusive toward inappropriate behavior after 11 sessions of 0/100 in the reversal to baseline. Similar effects were seen with the other 2 participants. Future research should evaluate differential reinforcement at various degrees of implementation using interval-based schedules. Such analyses would be more amenable to evaluation of the matching law in relation to severe aberrant behavior.

From a clinical standpoint, the finding that partial treatment implementation can be effective following exposure to full implementation suggests the possibility of intentionally thinning implementation levels prior to generalizing a treatment plan into environments in which treatment fidelity will be difficult to maintain. Given that treatment effects may eventually erode, booster sessions might be conducted periodically to reestablish 100% implementation.

A clear limitation of the current analysis was that the order of conditions did not control for sequence effects. For example, it is unknown how Kyle would have allocated responding to the desired alternative in a 50/50 condition if his only prior experimental history was with 0/100. Nonetheless, the current study can be viewed as an evaluation of one method that could be useful in identifying critical treatment values after a participant has a history with full treatment implementation. Future studies, however, should evaluate the effects of less than optimal differential reinforcement procedures for individuals who have not been exposed to full treatment implementation. In addition, more within-participant replications of the various conditions and longer exposure to each condition should provide more information about schedule effects and transitions in response allocation.

Future work should also evaluate the manipulation of other variables that constitute full or partial treatment implementation. For example, treatment errors conceivably might involve delays to reinforcement rather than reinforcement intermittency. Perfect implementation of differential reinforcement presumably entails providing reinforcers as immediately as possible after an appropriate behavior occurs (e.g., within 5 s). Treatment effects may degrade as the delay to reinforcement increases, especially if inappropriate behavior is occasionally reinforced (and perhaps more immediately). Another example of differential reinforcement parameters that could be manipulated to test the effects of treatment challenges involves the duration of reinforcer access. The relative duration of escape, attention, or access to materials as a consequence to inappropriate and appropriate behavior could be manipulated parametrically to mimic treatment implementation failures. For instance, a parent may provide several minutes of attention for an injurious response (e.g., tending to a wound) but only a few seconds attending to appropriate behavior (e.g., providing a praise statement).

Thus, the methods from the current study could be adapted and expanded upon to evaluate numerous differential reinforcement parameters. The evaluation in the current study suggests that differential reinforcement, at least when based on a prior functional analysis, can be quite resistant to treatment failures. However, the effects of recent and long-term reinforcement histories were not controlled in this study. In addition, other factors that influence response allocation (e.g., reinforcer delay, quality, duration, and magnitude) remain untested within a similar procedural format.

REFERENCES

Carr, E. G., & Durand, V. M. (1985). Reducing behavior problems through functional communication training. *Journal of Applied Behavior Analysis, 18,* 111–126.

Fisher, W. W., & Mazur, J. E. (1997). Basic and applied research on choice responding. *Journal of Applied Behavior Analysis, 30,* 387–410.

Hanley, G. P., Piazza, C. C., Fisher, W. W., Contrucci, S. A., & Maglieri, K. A. (1997). Evaluation of client preferences for function-based treatment packages. *Journal of Applied Behavior Analysis, 30,* 459–473.

Herrnstein, R. J. (1970). On the law of effect. *Journal of the Experimental Analysis of Behavior, 13,* 243–266.

Herrnstein, R. J., & Loveland, D. H. (1975). Maximizing and matching on concurrent ratio schedules. *Journal of the Experimental Analysis of Behavior, 24,* 107–116.

Iwata, B. A., Dorsey, M. F., Slifer, K. J., Bauman, K. E., & Richman, G. S. (1994). Toward a functional analysis of self-injury. *Journal of Applied Behavior Analysis, 27,* 197–209. (Reprinted from *Analysis and Intervention in Developmental Disabilities, 2,* 3–20, 1982)

Iwata, B. A., Pace, G. M., Kalsher, M. J., Cowdery, G. E., & Cataldo, M. F. (1990). Experimental analysis and extinction of self-injurious escape behavior. *Journal of Applied Behavior Analysis, 23,* 11–27.

Lalli, J. S., Casey, S., & Kates, K. (1995). Reducing escape behavior and increasing task completion with functional communication training, extinction, and response chaining. *Journal of Applied Behavior Analysis, 28,* 261–268.

LeLaurin, K., & Wolery, M. (1992). Research standards in early intervention: Defining, describing, and measuring the independent variable. *Journal of Early Intervention, 16,* 275–287.

Mazaleski, J. L., Iwata, B. A., Vollmer, T. R., Zarcone, J. R., & Smith, R. G. (1993). Analysis of the reinforcement and extinction components in DRO contingencies with self-injury. *Journal of Applied Behavior Analysis, 26,* 143–156.

Northup, J., Fisher, W., Kahng, S., Harrel, B., & Kurtz, P. (1997). An assessment of the necessary strength of behavioral treatments for severe behavior problems. *Journal of Developmental and Physical Disabilities, 9,* 1–16.

Shirley, M. J., Iwata, B. A., Kahng, S., Mazaleski, J. L., & Lerman, D. C. (1997). Does functional communication training compete with ongoing contingencies of reinforcement? An analysis during response acquisition and maintenance. *Journal of Applied Behavior Analysis, 30,* 93–104.

Steege, M. W., Wacker, D. P., Berg, W. K., Cigrand, K. K., & Cooper, L. J. (1990). The use of behavioral assessment to prescribe and evaluate treatments for severely handicapped children. *Journal of Applied Behavior Analysis, 22,* 23–33.

Vollmer, T. R., & Iwata, B. A. (1992). Differential reinforcement as treatment for behavior disorders: Procedural and functional variations. *Research in Developmental Disabilities, 13,* 393–417.

Vollmer, T. R., Iwata, B. A., Zarcone, J. R., Smith, R. G., & Mazaleski, J. L. (1993). The role of attention in the treatment of attention-maintained self-injurious behavior: Noncontingent reinforcement and differential reinforcement of other behavior. *Journal of Applied Behavior Analysis, 26,* 9–21.

Vollmer, T. R., Marcus, B. A., Ringdahl, J. E., & Roane, H. S. (1995). Progressing from brief assessments to extended experimental analyses in the evaluation of aberrant behavior. *Journal of Applied Behavior Analysis, 28,* 561–576.

Received February 2, 1998
Initial editorial decision April 10, 1998
Final acceptance October 19, 1998
Action Editor, James W. Halle

STUDY QUESTIONS

1. Explain how a differential-reinforcement-of-alternative-behavior (DRA) contingency can be conceptualized as a concurrent-operant (choice) situation. Under such an arrangement, what is the typical programmed schedule of reinforcement for the two alternatives?

2. How does the concept of "treatment integrity" relate to the importance of studying the effects of parametric variations in DRA schedules?

3. What were the dependent variables and how were they defined?

4. Describe the contingencies in effect for aberrant and alternative behavior during the baseline and DRA conditions.

5. Why were the DRA integrity values selected for Todd somewhat different than those selected for Rachel and Kyle?

6. What were the results of the treatment analysis with respect to both aberrant behavior and alternative behavior during baseline, DRA (full strength), and DRA (partial integrity) conditions?

7. What aspect of the results was somewhat surprising? Why was it surprising? What four explanations do the authors provide to account for these findings?

8. Briefly describe several ways in which one might alter this experimental arrangement to further examine the effects of less-than-perfect implementation of differential reinforcement procedures.

Questions prepared by Jana Lindberg and April Worsdell, The University of Florida

JOURNAL OF APPLIED BEHAVIOR ANALYSIS 1973, 6, 517-531 NUMBER 3 (FALL 1973)

METHODOLOGICAL AND ASSESSMENT CONSIDERATIONS IN EVALUATING REINFORCEMENT PROGRAMS IN APPLIED SETTINGS[1]

ALAN E. KAZDIN

THE PENNSYLVANIA STATE UNIVERSITY

The extensive use of reinforcement programs in applied settings has led to experimentation that often fails to consider potential problems in design. The logic of the within-subject design is reviewed and specific designs employed in reinforcement programs are discussed. For each design (ABAB, or multiple-baseline design across behaviors, individuals, or situations), effects are discussed that make that design less powerful with respect to demonstrating the effect of the experimental variable. Problems in interpreting results of experiments in this area of inquiry are evaluated from the standpoint of internal and external validity. The issue of control groups is presented with considerations as to situations that require their use. Finally, the assessment strategy for evaluating operant programs is discussed and recommendations are made for measurement of behaviors in addition to the target response.

The application of reinforcement systems to various populations in treatment and educational settings has proliferated in recent years (Bandura, 1969; Kazdin and Bootzin, 1972; O'Leary and Drabman, 1971). In spite of the apparent success of programs applying contingent social and/or token reinforcement, the evaluation of such programs, in many instances, has revealed a failure to recognize certain methodological factors that may influence the results of experiments or their interpretation. The present paper attempts to discuss certain issues of experimental design that need to be considered in evaluating behavior modification (operant conditioning) programs. The discussion is restricted in general to those studies specifically evaluating reinforcement programs because they usually employ a within-subject experimental design.

Studies have evaluated reinforcement programs in a variety of settings, including psychiatric hospitals (Ayllon and Azrin, 1965) classrooms (Wolf, Giles, and Hall, 1968), sheltered workshops (Zimmerman, Stuckey, Garlick, and Miller, 1969), institutions (Burchard, 1967), home-style treatment facilities (Phillips, 1968) the home (Wahler, 1969), and several others. The design employed in such studies is referred to as the intrasubject replication design (Sidman, 1960). A brief conspectus of the rationale behind this design will permit background for presenting methodological issues. The reader is referred to several treatises with excellent descriptions of design in this area of inquiry (Baer, 1968, 1971; Baer, Wolf, and Risley, 1968; Bijou, Peterson, and Ault, 1968; Bijou, Peterson, Harris, Allen, and Johnston, 1969; McNamara and MacDonough, 1972; Risley, 1970; Risley and Baer, 1973; Risley and Wolf, 1972; Sidman, 1960; Thoresen, 1972; Wolf and Risley, 1971).

Briefly, the basic logic of the design is to determine operations that relate functionally to the performance of behavior. The effect of a variable (*e.g.*, contingent praise) on behavior is demonstrated by the consecutive presentation, removal, and representation of the variable to a subject. Control over a behavior is demonstrated

---

[1]The author gratefully acknowledges K. Daniel O'Leary for his reading of the manuscript. Monographs of this article are available for $1.00 from the Business Office of the *Journal of Applied Behavior Analysis,* Department of Human Development, University of Kansas, Lawrence, Kansas 66044. Ask for Monograph #3.

if the behavior can be altered at will by altering the experimental operations. This research strategy is contrasted with the between-group approach, which seeks to demonstrate group differences after manipulation of the independent variable(s), usually in a single session. In this design, the data are subjected to statistical evaluation, and the focus is on mean differences instead of the behavior of individual subjects.

In the within-subject design, the effects of the experimental variables may be immediately observed on response rates. Under such circumstances, it is recommended to examine variables in an "improvised and rapidly changing design" (Skinner, 1969, p. 112), with the goal of achieving control over behavior. This approach bypasses variability due to intersubject differences which is included in the design of between-group experiments. This is a desirable feature from several standpoints. First, intersubject variability is not a feature of the behavioral process of the individual subject, but is an effect due in part to the method of study. Second, in evaluating experimental findings in traditional group designs, intersubject variability serves as a base for statistical evaluation of the results. Because of this, as Sidman (1960) noted, lawful effects of variables may be obscured. A similar problem is that averages from group data usually have no analogue in representing the behavioral process of individuals. The form or shape of the function obtained with group data does not necessarily represent the behavior change process of the individual. Several subjects in the group may be affected differently by the experimental manipulation. This is obscured in the between-group analysis. Having outlined, briefly, the rationale for the within-group approach, types of these designs used and their respective sources of problems may be identified.

Specific Designs

The first design is frequently referred to as the ABAB design (where A refers to baseline conditions, and B refers to the experimental condition). Other names for the design include reversal technique (Baer *et al.,* 1968), intrasubject replication design (Sidman, 1960), equivalent time-samples (Campbell and Stanley, 1963), and intensive design (Chassan, 1967). The design employs alternate presentations of the baseline and experimental conditions within a subject or group of subjects. Several variations may be used in this design. More than one experimental condition may be presented before the second baseline (or reversal) phase. For example, O'Leary, Becker, Evans, and Saudargas (1969) included several experimental phases in evaluating the effect of token reinforcement on classroom deportment. Separate phases included the effect of rules alone, educational structure, praise for appropriate and extinction of inappropriate behavior, and token reinforcement. After the token phase, a reversal of conditions was effected. The reversal condition (usually a return to baseline) is an essential ingredient in this design. Only such a reversal can demonstrate that behavior changes only when the experimental condition is in effect. This design is quite powerful and rules out several alternative explanations that may account for behavior change.

In spite of the usefulness and power of the design, it makes a major presupposition, namely that behavior changes made under various experimental conditions are reversible when baseline conditions are reinstated. The demonstration of a functional relationship between the presence of the experimental condition and performance requires that the changes made be transient and therefore reversible. However, the changes made in reinforcement programs might not be reversible when the experimental condition is withdrawn (*e.g.,* Surratt, Ulrich, and Hawkins, 1969). Indeed, we would hope that they are not always reversible, because this is tantamount to demonstrating only slight resistance to extinction.

If the effects of a reinforcement program are not reversible, the effect of the experimental condition(s) is not clear. For example, Hewett,

Taylor, and Artuso (1968) employed six classes in evaluating token reinforcement programs. Some classes received 17 weeks of baseline followed by 17 weeks of the program; other classes received 17 weeks of the program followed by 17 weeks of baseline (*i.e.,* no program). Two other classes were included in the design, to wit 34 weeks of the program and 34 weeks of baseline, respectively. For our purpose, it is important to note that the two groups that received the token program followed by baseline conditions failed to show a decline in target behaviors. Further, appropriate behaviors *increased* when the programs were removed. While speculations may be given to account for this (such as claiming that stimuli other than tokens in the environment have become reinforcers and maintain behavior), it is unclear that reinforcement was controlling any behavior in these two classes because no reversal occurred when the contingencies were removed. Addressing themselves to this problem, Bijou and associates (Bijou *et al.,* 1969) recommended using short experimental periods, which would facilitate obtaining a reversal of effects. This recommendation is useful when the goal is to determine short-term effects of experimental conditions. However, this design discussed (i.e., ABAB) by itself, may be inadequate when one wishes to study non-transient effects. For example, if an investigator desires to implement a condition that leads to relatively permanent changes in behavior, this is difficult to demonstrate in this design. Hence, if an investigator adds to some experimental condition, a variable that should enhance resistance to extinction, this cannot be clearly demonstrated in this design. When behavior does not reverse, other explanations for the effect remain tenable. However, variables that may result in non-transient effects can be evaluated *after* a reversal phase has been successfully employed (Kazdin and Polster, 1973).

Recently, other within-group designs have been discussed that are not susceptible to the reversibility problem outlined above. These designs are particularly useful in situations where: effecting a reversal would be undesirable because of exigencies of the situation; a reversal in responses would not be expected, as in training competence in academic skills; or where an experimental condition used is expected to inhibit a reversal of responses. The multiple-element baseline design (Sidman, 1960) or multiple-baseline design (Baer *et al.,* 1968) provides a valuable alternative to the ABAB design. In this design there is no reversal of conditions required to demonstrate the efficacy of the contingencies. Instead, data are collected across behaviors, across individuals, or across situations.

In the multiple-baseline design across behaviors, two or more behaviors are observed for the subject(s). After the behaviors have reached stable rates, the experimental condition is implemented for only one of the behaviors while baseline conditions are continued for the other(s). The behavior exposed to the experimental condition should change while the other behavior remains at baseline levels. When rates are stable for both behaviors, the second behavior is brought into the contingency. This procedure is continued until all behaviors for which multiple-baseline data were gathered are sequentially brought into the contingency. Ideally, each behavior changes only as it is included in the experimental contingency and not before. This is a powerful demonstration that the experimental condition exerts control over the behavior. The strength of the demonstration stems from the consideration that events occurring in time other than the experimental condition cannot plausibly account for the specific changes in behavior. This is demonstrated without a reversal of experimental conditions.

A major area of concern in using this design is that one must be reasonably assured beforehand that the target behaviors used are not interdependent or interrelated highly with each other. In such a situation, implementing a contingency for the performance of one behavior may be expected to alter the behavior(s) for which continued baseline data are collected. For example, in a classroom situation it may not be the most appropriate design to gather multiple-baseline data across inappropriate motor behavior, inappropriate verbalizations, and inappropriate tasks as three separate target behaviors. Although these behaviors are used as distinct categories that can be reliably observed, they are also moderately intercorrelated in terms of frequency within individual children's repertoires (Kazdin, 1973*c*).[2] Change in one of these responses may result in other response changes. An even greater demonstration of this problem of response correlations is evident from the literature on generalized imitation. In several studies, it has been shown that reinforcement for some imitative behavior leads to a generalized set for imitative behaviors. A multiple-baseline design across behaviors might not be able to demonstrate that responses are not imitated until the contingency is applied to the specific imitative behavior. As soon as some imitative behavior is reinforced, other responses would change even though not reinforced (Baer, Peterson, and Sherman, 1967; Metz, 1965; Peterson and Whitehurst, 1971), unless they are topographically dissimilar responses (Garcia, Baer, and Firestone, 1971).

The problem of intercorrelations among responses has not been evident in the few multiple-baseline studies across behaviors (*e.g.*, McAllister, Stachowiak, Baer, and Conderman, 1969; Wolf *et al.*, 1968). However, it is a consideration an investigator should make when deciding on the type of design to best demonstrate the efficacy of experimental conditions (*cf.* Buell, Stoddard, Harris, and Baer, 1968; Pendergrass, 1972).

[2]This problem stems, in part, from the definition of an operant. As a response class, any operant may include responses or elements that are part of other operants. Skinner (1953, p. 94) noted this in stating that: "In reinforcing one operant we often produce a noticeable increase in the strength of another." and "The reinforcement of a response increases the probability of all responses containing the same elements." For a discussion of problems associated with defining operants, the reader is referred to Schick (1971).

In the multiple-baseline design across individuals, baseline data are gathered for at least one behavior across several persons. After behavior stabilizes across subjects, the experimental condition is invoked for one subject while baseline conditions are continued for the other subject(s). Again, as the experimental condition is extended to include separate individuals, the response frequency changes. This demonstration shows that behavior of the subject does not change until he is included in the experimental condition.

As with the previous multiple-baseline design, one major aspect may make this design problematic. If it is possible that the alteration of the behavior of one subject will influence the behavior of other subjects, the design loses power. In this situation, implementation of the experimental condition for the first subject may dramatically alter the behavior of another subject for whom baseline conditions are continued. For example, Broden, Bruce, Mitchell, Carter, and Hall (1970) showed that altering the attentive behaviors of one subject in the classroom through contingent reinforcement changed behavior of an adjacent peer. Further, data they collected indicated that when the attentive behaviors were changed in one subject, the source of distraction and possibly social reinforcement for the other subject decreased, so he improved because there was less opportunity and peer reinforcement for inattentiveness. Similarly, Kazdin 1973*b*) demonstrated that contingent reinforcement of attentive behavior for a target subject increased attentive behavior in an adjacent subject. However, it was also shown that reinforcement of inattentive behavior in the target subject reliably *increased* attentive behavior in the non-target subject. The discriminative stimulus value of social reinforcement appeared to account for the improvement in behavior of the adjacent subject. The point of these studies is to demonstrate that introducing contingencies for some individuals in a situation may be expected to alter the behaviors of other individuals under some circumstances, *viz.*, when the behavior of one subject influences the behavior of an adjacent peer (Broden *et al.,* 1970) or when social reinforcement provides a discriminative stimulus for probable reinforcement for an adjacent peer (Kazdin, 1973*b*) or when there is a limit to the amount of reinforcement available (Sechrest, 1963). In such situations, the use of a multiple-baseline design across individuals would not effectively demonstrate the specific effects of the experimental condition on the target behavior. The implementation of the contingency for the first subject might change the behavior of others, even though the baseline conditions were continued for the other subjects.

In the multiple-baseline design across situations, data are collected for a target behavior for one or more subjects across different circumstances or situations. For example, in altering the promptness of individuals in an elementary school situation, one might collect data (number of students late and number of minutes late) across several situations (arrival to class in the morning, after recess, after lunch, after assemblies). After collecting baseline data in all situations, the experimental contingency is instituted to control the behavior in one situation. Baseline data are continued for behavior in all other situations until each is consecutively included into the contingency. As with previous multiple-baseline designs, this design is more effective when there is little or no correlation of behavior across these situations. If behavior change in one situation is expected to alter behavior in another situation, this design is a less powerful demonstration of the effects of the contingencies. For example, Hunt and Zimmerman (1969) demonstrated that contingent reinforcement for productivity in one time period increased productivity in a time period in which no reinforcement was delivered in a simulated sheltered workshop. There may be some question here as to the specific operation of the contingencies.

In the three basic types of multiple-baseline designs discussed, each has one potential weakness in powerfully demonstrating the effect of a particular experimental condition, *viz.,* concomitant changes in the areas for which baseline data are collected. Whether this is the case in the particular instance the investigator decides to use a design must be determined primarily from experience. Concomitant changes that may occur as a result of implementing a contingency for one behavior (individual or situation) have to be determined empirically. In some instances, the investigator can rely on the well-documented experience of others. For example, if one were interested in evaluating classroom deportment in a multiple-baseline design across situations or time (such as morning and afternoon class periods), there already is consistent evidence showing that changes made in one of these time periods do not appreciably alter behavior in the other (Becker, Madsen, Arnold, and Thomas, 1967; Kuypers, Becker, and O'Leary, 1968; Meichenbaum, Bowers, and Ross, 1968; O'Leary *et al.,* 1969).

The within-subject designs outlined above can be employed in most situations. In spite of the reasons outlined early in the paper as to the advantages of these designs, one must remain cognizant of the possible interaction obtained between the experimental manipulation and the design employed in determining behavior. There is evidence bearing on this from several quarters in the experimental literature. For example, in experiments varying conditioned stimulus intensity in eyelid conditioning and signal intensity in reaction time experiments, the effects of variations of the stimuli depend upon whether they are evaluated within or between groups (Grice and Hunter, 1964). Similarly, the effects of different amounts of reinforcement in discrimination learning tasks differentially affect correct responses, again, depending on whether one group is exposed to different levels of reinforcement or separate groups are used (Lawson, 1957; Schrier, 1958). These experiments and others indicate that the effects obtained may be dependent upon the design of the experiment. There is a greater lesson to be learned from this than the simple recommendation that one should not become overly dependent on one design in examining the effects of a particular operation. Since the major interest in operant work is determining how environmental manipulations functionally control behavior, it is important to be more analytic about an experimental design that, in part, dictates the results. What about the design influences behavior, and how can these influences be brought under control, minimized, or altered? When an experimental design is examined in this light, it becomes another experimental operation that exerts some functional relation to behavior. When the design does determine the result in some way, it is important to determine precisely how it accomplishes this and over what parametric levels of the experimental manipulation. Sidman (1960, pp. 334-340) recommended comparing the effects of experimental manipulations when scheduled separately or as combined with other manipulations. This is similar to recommending a closer scrutiny of the effects of our designs.

Evaluation of Results

Investigations of reinforcement programs in applied settings may introduce problems in evaluating the results. Initially, to discuss some of these problems, the distinction introduced by Campbell and Stanley (1963) on the validities of experimentation is useful. These authors refer to *internal validity* as the degree to which the results of an experiment are considered to be due to the experimental manipulation. *External validity* refers to the extent to which the findings obtained in a study may be extended or generalized to other groups and settings. Campbell and Stanley (1963) noted that the equivalent time-samples design (a version of the ABAB or reversal design) is quite strong with respect to the possible sources of threat to internal validity. In such designs, several rival hypotheses accounting for the results are ruled out. It is unlikely that events (outside of the experimental manipulation) that occur in time (history), growth or developmental processes within the subject (maturation), systematic shifts in performance over time resulting from the unreliability of measurement (*e.g.,* regression and changes in the measurement device), selective loss of subjects (mortality), repeated assessment (testing), and other factors account for the results. As for external validity, however, they list some factors that may delimit the generalizability of the results. Both these types of validity will be discussed in light of research in reinforcement programs in applied settings.

Considering internal validity, investigators must be reasonably assured that there are no factors in the design that can account for the results other than the intended manipulated operation. This statement seems so basic that it might not warrant protracted discussion. However, in several studies it is evident that there are factors that covary with implementation of the experimental operation. In some instances, the operation of these extraneous factors plausibly are causative of the changes attributed to the experimental operation. If these extraneous factor(s) could not account for the change entirely, they can interact with the experimental operation as a codeterminant of the results. Examples of extraneous factors that covary with experimental conditions are evident in several studies. One obvious factor that covaries with conditions is instructions that convey to subjects how they are supposed to perform. For example, Ayllon and Azrin (1965) instructed subjects that they could continue to work even though they would receive token reinforcement for not working (*i.e.,* a "vacation with pay", p. 366). The rapid changes noted in performance were attributed to the reinforcement contingencies. However, different instructions preceding each experimental phase appeared to contribute, in part, to the abrupt effect of contingent reinforcement. Previous work has shown that although instructions may not be sufficient to sustain performance relative to contingent operant consequences, they are effective in initiating behavior change (Ayllon and Azrin, 1964; Hopkins, 1968; Packard, 1970). Employing reinforcement contingencies alone results in behavior changes that are less dramatic than when accompanied by contingency instructions (Herman and Tramontana, 1971), although there are exceptions to this (Kazdin, 1973*c*).

The role of instructions is especially important to distinguish from that of reinforcement when the target behaviors are not apparent in the repertoire of the subjects. In this situation, the effect of reinforcement may be distinguished from initial training or practice in the reinforced responses. These are usually confounded in reinforcement studies. In one exception (Suchotliff, Greaves, Stecker, and Berke, 1970), psychiatric patients were exposed to training for grooming skills (where individuals were exposed to classes instructing them in the execution of the skills). Subsequently, a token reinforcement system was instituted to reinforce these behaviors. The results indicated that grooming behaviors did not increase during token reinforcement relative to what they were during training. Token reinforcement maintained the behaviors developed during the formal instruction period. However, the increments in performance over baseline were due to training and instruction. In several studies, the effect of instructions, in this sense, cannot be separated from the reinforcement contingencies themselves.

An additional factor when evaluating reinforcement is the possible experimental operations that are included in the effect of the contingent application of an incentive *per se.* The introduction of reinforcement for appropriate behavior includes several factors that lead to behavior change. For example, aside from an incentive function, reinforcement also serves an informational function (Bandura, 1971). Effects obtained with reinforcement may be unjustifiably attributed to the incentive function of consequating events, rather than the informational value of these events. Yet, providing feedback alone to a subject about the adequacy of his performance may affect performance dramatically. While this may demonstrate that feedback serves as reinforcement for behavior (Mathis, Cotton, and Sechrest, 1971, p. 77), this does not help when investigators wish to make conclusions about the effect of, say, token reinforcement in changing behavior. The introduction of token reinforcement includes both the effect of incentives and informative feedback. These may be reduced to at least two distinct experimental operations. For example, Zimmerman *et al.* (1969) evaluated independently the effects of feedback and token reinforcement on productivity of clients in a sheltered workshop. Before the token reinforcement phase, subjects were told that they could practise (by working well) so that they would know how to earn tokens. During this phase, subjects were told how many tokens they would have earned, if tokens were given out. Subsequently, a token reinforcement phase was instituted. Feedback alone increased production, and token reinforcement resulted in further increases. Although token reinforcement was more effective, few studies have used as a base for comparison the feedback that is implicit in token reinforcement. Hence, conclusions about the effect of token reinforcement *per se* (particularly those made about the magnitude of change) often cannot be made on the basis of the experimental manipulation.

Instructions to agents who are administering the reinforcement program may also covary with the implementation and removal of the reinforcement contingencies. For example, teachers may be told or be led to believe that certain experimental phases will result in dramatic changes in behaviors. This may change teacher behavior, which influences the target behaviors. Studies have not carefully examined this.

In considering external validity, several issues in reinforcement programs require mentioning. The question of the extent to which findings hold for other subjects and other settings than those that were included in an experiment are included in the issues discussed here.

First, there is a possibility of *multiple-treatment interference* (Campbell and Stanley,

1963), which may delimit generalization of the results. Whenever multiple phases are applied to a group, the conclusions derived from a later treatment may depend on previous phases because the effects of each are not erasable. For example, the effects of contingent reinforcement may be evaluated in a design in which it is preceded by noncontingent reinforcement, or punishment (*e.g.,* verbal reprimand by teachers). The results can only be generalized to include other individuals exposed to a similar sequence of events. Also, the conclusions may be generalized only to conditions where the reinforcement condition is introduced repeatedly, interspersed with other conditions, and not to situations in in which the reinforcement is continually present or introduced only once. For example, in two of their experiments, O'Leary and Becker (O'Leary and Becker, 1967; O'Leary *et al.,* 1969) implemented token reinforcement programs in classroom situations. In one study, instructions, praising appropriate and ignoring inappropriate behaviors along with token reinforcement, were introduced simultaneously; in the other study, these procedures were introduced sequentially in a cumulative fashion. In comparing these studies, it is evident that the simultaneous introduction of the conditions led to greater change than the sequential introduction of component parts. Thus, in generalizing the effects of token reinforcement procedures, one must be careful to specify the manner in which the component parts of the procedures (informative feedback, instructions, approval, ignoring) are introduced. The manner in which the program is introduced, as dictated by the experimental design, may have consequences as to the conclusions derived and their generalizability. In laboratory studies of punishment, for example, the manner in which the aversive event is introduced, high intensity initially or gradual approximation of high intensity, dictates the efficacy of the procedure (Azrin and Holz, 1966, p. 393).

The problem of multiple-treatment interference arises also in situations in which a baseline (or reversal) is interspersed with different experimental conditions. If different versions of a reinforcement condition are presented and preceded by a baseline condition, it is difficult to separate the effects of the particular order of conditions from the effect of the conditions. Again, any conclusions reached about a particular condition are restricted to those individuals who are exposed to the particular sequence of conditions. When multiple reversals are included in the design, it is often assumed that if behavior returns to baseline levels, that any new condition may be compared to any other condition preceded by performance because of the equivalence of performance during reversal phases. There are several problems in comparing treatments within subjects related to the sequence effects. First, equivalent performance during reversals only demonstrates an equivalence in response rates at the time the reversal phase is in effect. However, reinstating the target behavior may become easier after repeated exposure to experimental conditions. It has already been demonstrated that repeated exposure to a series of alternating conditioning and extinction trials results in a gradual decline in responding over the extinction trials (Perkins and Cacioppo, 1950). A similar phenomenon, no doubt, exists in the repetitive exposure to the reconditioning phases themselves.

A related factor that affects the external validity of experiments in applied settings has been called *reactive effect of experimental arrangements* (Campbell and Stanley, 1963). This refers to the fact that the particular experimental arrangement may preclude generalization of treatment effects across time, situations, and individuals. As this relates to reinforcement programs, several aspects delimit generalization of the effects of the program. The definition of generalization varies here depending upon the particular problem considered. Initially, the development of reinforcement procedures in applied settings is usually accomplished by having observers record target behaviors of the clients or subjects. Although the influence of observers is assumed not to affect the differential performance of, for example, school students, the presence of observers at all may constitute a reactive arrangement that delimits generalization of the findings to situations where observers are present. In classroom settings, both teacher and students are usually aware of the presence of the observers and may perform differently in situations where the observers are absent. There is only sparse evidence bearing on this point. Surratt *et al.* (1969) obtained data indicating that the presence of an observer in the classroom is a sufficient discriminative stimulus for performance of the target response. At the end of a reinforcement program designed to increase "time working" in students, two postchecks were conducted to determine to what extent the behaviors were maintained. The data from the first check were gathered by TV camera. Data for the second postcheck were gathered by an observer whose presence was previously associated with the experimental condition. "Time working" was consistently higher (in all four subjects) in the data collected by the observer. This suggests that there might be reactive effects of using observers in applied settings, particularly if the experimental conditions become associated with their presence. Subsequent introduction of an observer (S^D) may occasion the target behaviors, and the findings cannot be generalized beyond situations in which the observer is present.

A related factor not to be neglected is the effect of the investigator on the behavior of agents delivering reinforcement. The presence of the experimenter in the situation may occasion the desired response. Again, considering the classroom situation, the presence of the experimenter may serve as a reminder to the teacher to deliver reinforcement or to increase her rate of social approval. (When it is evident that observers are recording teacher behaviors, observers may also control these responses.) The major point is that the results obtained may be limited to those situations in which the experimenter is present (either in the situation itself or available for consultation). Although the presence of the experimenter has been sparsely evaluated in reinforcement programs directly, there is evidence showing that the experimenter's presence may do this in other contexts. Peterson and Whitehurst (1971) showed that systematic variation of experimenter's presence exerts functional control over imitative behavior in children.

The Use of Control Groups

In discussions of work in the functional analysis of behavior in applied settings, the matter of control groups arises infrequently. There is great justification for ignoring the use of comparative groups in most instances. Treatises on experimental design (*e.g.*, Underwood, 1957) usually recognize certain instances in which no control group is required to evaluate unambiguously the effect of the experimental manipulation. The design that fits this situation is an extended time-series design in which data are available for the subject(s) over a long period of time, or when data are available for a relatively short period, but behavior changes with the presentation and removal of the experimental variable (*i.e.*, the ABAB design discussed earlier).

Other reasons have led investigators to eschew comparison groups stemming from philosophical or presuppositional considerations rather than simply convenience or design. The use of comparison groups usually implies a statistical evaluation of the data in terms of measures of central tendency and variability. Several assumptions are required for use of various statistical techniques and risks attendant on their violation must be considered. Further, in the experimental analysis, the goal transcends obtaining mean differences between groups with exposure to an experimental operation and one that is not. Achieving functional control over behavior makes the investigator concerned with determining effective variables that will alter the individual's behavior. These variables necessarily entail within-subject manipulations. Also, examining group means does not really demonstrate that the experimenter achieved control over behavior in individual cases. There is the subject generality problem (Sidman, 1960) or representativeness of the findings. Comparisons of treated groups with untreated groups obscure a closer examination of the effect of treatment on those individuals in the experimental groups. Nevertheless, there are instances, particularly in recent years, that merit utilization of experimental groups in between- as well as within-subject comparisons. The salient instances will be presented.

Whereas the initial interest in operant work in applied settings was focused almost entirely upon examining effective experimental operations that functionally related to behavior, this interest has broadened (Staats, 1970). There is greater use of finding effective treatments that cannot easily be evaluated in single-subject or single-group designs. For example, Staats and his associates began work with reinforcement procedures on training reading skills by a careful scrutiny of the performance of individual subjects (*e.g.,* Staats and Butterfield, 1965). This led to refinement and extensions of procedures which, though modified, were evaluated (statistically) as treatments and compared with a control group (*e.g.,* Staats, Minke, and Butts, 1970). The extension of findings from an examination of single-group to between-group designs has been required in light of the greater aims of reinforcement procedures in applied settings. As a recent example of this, initial token reinforcement programs in psychiatric hospitals (*e.g.,* Ayllon and Azrin, 1965) focused on evaluating the program on within-hospital behavior rather than global measures such as discharge and readmission rates (Ayllon and Azrin, 1968, p. 27). However, as the efficacy of the procedures evolved, it became important to determine how effective reinforcement procedures were relative to traditional techniques (Birky, Chambliss, and Wasden, 1971; Marks, Sanoda, and Schalock, 1968; Hartlage, 1970) and how well they fared when compared to untreated groups in terms of follow-up success (Stayer and Jones, *unpublished*). Such comparisons, of course, imply the use of control groups.

Another situation that may require the use of comparison groups is related to the above. When different levels of variables are evaluated, the within-group design may restrict the external validity of the results. For example, if the effect of praise is evaluated and one wishes to compare that with the effect of praise and token reinforcement combined, the goal may not be achieved by merely introducing praise in one phase and adding token reinforcement in a subsequent experimental phase. The question of interest may be the effect of praise compared to that of praise-plus-token reinforcement when both are introduced initially to a group not previously exposed to any experimental phase. This requires separate groups.

In advocating the use of control groups, it is important to recognize the limitations imposed by doing research in applied settings. Even if we might envision situations in which a comparison group would provide desirable information, there are usually restrictions as to the information it can provide. With relatively rare exceptions in the literature (*e.g.,* Herman and Tramontana, 1971), subjects cannot be matched and assigned randomly to classes, hospital wards, institutional settings, or classrooms in which the procedures will be evaluated. In such instances it is desirable to select groups that will best control for the factors one is interested in controlling. For example, in a psychiatric setting, it is desirable to control for new staff, new ward facilities, and diagnostic group in evaluating the program. Some investigations in psychiatric settings have selected patients for the therapeutic program and placed them on a special ward (Heap, Boblitt, Moore, and Hord, 1970). This makes evaluation of any program ambiguous because the effect of ward change, in and of itself, may lead to behavior change (De Vries, 1968; Higgs, 1970). An excellent example of avoiding some of these problems can be found in the study by Schaefer and Martin

(1966). The patients on a ward were randomly assigned to either receiving contingent or non-contingent token reinforcement. Not only did controls receive tokens and live on the same ward as the experimental subjects, they also received contingent praise for desirable behaviors. This type of control group effectively precludes a number of factors that may account for differences between groups.

The use of controls may also be crucial when the experimenter wishes to determine whether relatively permanent effects of exposure to treatment conditions are obtained and the magnitude of these effects. For example, Wolf *et al.* (1968) evaluated the effects of token reinforcement in altering academic skills in a remedial classroom. Although the results were dramatic in within-group comparisons, the effectiveness of the program was enhanced by comparisons of students who received the program with those who did not. Over the period in which the program was evaluated (1 yr), both groups made significant gains on a standard achievement test and grades. However, the experimental group made substantial gains over and above those of controls. Clearly, a control group helped determine the magnitude of the gains made as a result of the program.

Responses Assessed in Reinforcement Programs

The selection of responses to evaluate the efficacy of procedures is usually dictated by the purpose of the study and the goals of the treatment or training institution in which the program is conducted. The use of response frequency has been employed as the most useful measure of these responses, and its use has a number of features to recommend it (see Bijou *et al.*, 1968, 1969; Ferster, 1953; Honig, 1966).

The focus on observable behaviors is perhaps one of the major advantages that accrue to behavior modification procedures in general. This assessment procedure differs markedly from traditional approaches where inferential leaps may be made in diagnosing, treating, and assessing dynamics, dispositions, or traits (Mischel, 1968; Stuart, 1970).

In spite of the advantages of this assessment approach, the observations have been restricted to the single target behavior of initial focus. While changes in target behaviors are the *raison d'être* for undertaking treatment or training programs, concomitant changes may take place as well. If so, these should be assessed. It is one thing to assess and evaluate changes in a target behavior, but quite another to insist on excluding non-target measures. It may be that investigators are short-changing themselves in evaluating the programs. Recently, other areas of behavior modification have attempted to assess behaviors that might change as a result of treatment but were not of direct therapeutic focus (*e.g.*, Bandura, Blanchard, and Ritter, 1969; Kazdin, 1973*a;* Paul, 1967). To reiterate, the use of non-target behavioral measures in reinforcement programs is to be encouraged. Yet, these measures are not to be made at the expense of the primary data on target performance.

There are several potential advantages in using measures of non-target behaviors as well as the usual target response measures. One initial advantage is that such assessment would permit the possibility of determining response generalization. If certain response frequencies are increased or decreased, it would be expected that other related operants would be influenced. It would be a desirable addition to determine generalization of beneficial response changes by looking at behaviors related to the target response. In addition, changes in the frequency of responses might also correlate with topographical alterations. For example, a reduction of inappropriate responses may result in the concomitant reduction of the severity of the responses (Burchard and Tyler, 1965; Hawkins, Peterson, Schweid, and Bijou, 1966).

As the application of reinforcement programs proliferates further, there will be increased concern with concomitant effects of such programs, aside from their obvious virtue of reliably altering the target behavior(s). Examples of this can be seen in a few studies. Mulligan, Kaplan, and Reppucci (1971) evaluated changes in "cognitive" variables made as a result of a token program for appropriate classroom behaviors and completion of tasks. The elementary school subjects in the program showed increases in IQ scores, arithmetic achievement scores, and a slight decrease in anxiety. The conclusions reached were that cognitive as well as behavioral improvement may occur in a token reinforcement program. (This particular study has methodological problems such as possibility of regression artifacts contributing to the results.) This suggests that there were important gains made outside of the obvious target response changes.

In using non-target as well as target measures to assess changes made in reinforcement programs, it is important to maintain emphasis on the target behavioral measures. It is this measure that can determine whether the program has functional control over behavior. For example, Gripp and Magaro (1971) compared schizophrenic patients on one ward exposed to token reinforcement with control wards not exposed to this treatment. Ratings were made on several indirect measures of psychotic behavior, ward atmosphere, and social behaviors. Conclusions were made on a number of dimensions relevant to psychopathology. The comparisons were determined from preprogram and postprogram ratings. The experimental ward showed greater improvement than controls in number of dimensions of gains and in degree of gains. However, because the investigation did not focus on direct behavioral targets on which the program could be evaluated, and hence could not demonstrate functional control, the conclusions are ambiguous. The effect of the program may have been due to collateral changes in staff behaviors, and a host of other factors. The use of indirect or multiple measures of treatment efficacy are only relevant when it has been demonstrated that the contingencies themselves are responsible for the direct changes in behavior. When the program has demonstrated control over behavior, it would be interesting to determine non-target correlates that may change as well.

SUMMARY

In summing up, there are several advantages in using various within-subject designs. Generally, these designs are quite powerful in demonstrating the effect of a particular experimental operation. However, there are potential weaknesses of the designs currently employed. The choice of design may be influenced by the expectation or desirability of a reversal in behavior, if the experimental condition is withdrawn. In designs without a reversal of conditions (multiple-baseline designs), other problems may arise, such as interdependence of performance (across behaviors, individuals, or situations). Although these may prove to be infrequent in future research, their occurrence in a given instance may be fatal in evaluating the results.

In interpreting results of investigations in this area, it is important to be cognizant of potential influences that may covary with the presentation and withdrawal of experimental operations. Also, various elements of the experiment may delimit generalization of the results. Salient influences relevant to internal and external validity were discussed.

The use of control groups was advocated in examining certain effects of reinforcement programs. Although the functional analysis is the major aspect of the design, the proliferation of experiments in this area has led to questions that can, in many instances, be adequately answered only by comparisons between or across groups. As a final point, the use of multiple-response measures was encouraged. Changes in target measures are the major point of undertaking reinforcement programs in applied settings. However, concomitant response changes may take place along with the target responses. If so, these should be documented.

REFERENCES

Ayllon, T. and Azrin, N. H. Reinforcement and instructions with mental patients. *Journal of the Experimental Analysis of Behavior,* 1964, **7,** 327-331.

Ayllon, T. and Azrin, N. H. The measurement and reinforcement of behavior of psychotics. *Journal of the Experimental Analysis of Behavior,* 1965, **8,** 357-383.

Ayllon, T. and Azrin, N. H. *The token economy: a motivational system for therapy and rehabilitation.* New York: Appleton-Century-Crofts, 1968.

Azrin, N. H. and Holz, W. C. Punishment. In W. K. Honig (Ed.), *Operant behavior: areas of research and application.* New York: Appleton-Century-Crofts, 1966. Pp. 380-447.

Baer, D. M. Some remedial uses of the reinforcement contingency. In J. Shlien (Ed.), *Research in psychotherapy, Volume III.* Washington, D.C.: American Psychological Association, 1968. Pp. 3-20.

Baer, D. M. Behavior modification: you shouldn't. In E. A. Ramp and B. L. Hopkins (Eds.), *A new direction for education: behavior analysis, 1971.* Lawrence, Kansas: University of Kansas Support and Development Center for Follow Through, 1971. Pp. 358-369.

Baer, D. M., Peterson, R. F., and Sherman, J. The development of imitation by reinforcing behavioral similarity to a model. *Journal of the Experimental Analysis of Behavior,* 1967, **10,** 405-416.

Baer, D. M., Wolf, M. M., and Risley, T. R. Some current dimensions of applied behavior analysis. *Journal of Applied Behavior Analysis,* 1968, **1,** 91-97.

Bandura, A. *Principles of behavior modification.* New York: Holt, Rinehart, & Winston, 1969.

Bandura, A. Vicarious- and self-reinforcement processes. In R. Glaser (Ed.), *The nature of reinforcement.* New York: Academic Press, 1971. Pp. 228-278.

Bandura, A., Blanchard, E. B., and Ritter, B. Relative efficacy of desensitization and modeling approaches for inducing behavioral, affective, and attitudinal changes. *Journal of Personality and Social Psychology,* 1969, **13,** 173-199.

Becker, W. C., Madsen, C. H., Arnold, C. R., and Thomas, D. R. The contingent use of teacher attention and praising in reducing classroom behavior problems. *Journal of Special Education,* 1967, **1,** 287-307.

Bijou, S. W., Peterson, R. F., and Ault, M. H. A method of integrate descriptive and experimental field studies at the level of data and empirical concepts. *Journal of Applied Behavior Analysis,* 1968, **1,** 175-191.

Bijou, S. W., Peterson, R. F., Harris, F. R., Allen, K. E., and Johnston, M. S. Methodology for experimental studies of young children in natural settings. *Psychological Record,* 1969, **19,** 177-210.

Birky, H. J., Chambliss, J. E., and Wasden, R. A comparison of residents discharged from a token economy and two traditional psychiatric programs. *Behavior Therapy,* 1971, **2,** 46-51.

Broden, M., Bruce, M., Mitchell, M., Carter, V., and Hall, R. V. Effects of teacher attention on attending behavior of two boys at adjacent desks. *Journal of Applied Behavior Analysis,* 1970, **3,** 199-203.

Buell, J., Stoddard, P., Harris, F., and Baer, D. M. Collateral social development accompanying reinforcement of outdoor play in a preschool child. *Journal of Applied Behavior Analysis,* 1968, **1,** 167-173.

Burchard, J. D. Systematic socialization: A programmed environment for the habilitation of antisocial retardates. *Psychological Record,* 1967, **17,** 461-476.

Burchard, J. D. and Tyler, V. O. The modification of delinquent behaviour through operant conditioning. *Behaviour Research and Therapy,* 1965, **2,** 245-250.

Campbell, D. T. and Stanley, J. C. Experimental and quasi-experimental designs for research and teaching. In N. L. Gage (Ed.), *Handbook of research on teaching.* Chicago: Rand McNally, 1963. Pp. 171-246.

DeVries, D. L. Effects of environmental change and of participation on the behavior of mental patients. *Journal of Consulting and Clinical Psychology,* 1968, **32,** 532-536.

Ferster, C. B. The use of the free operant in the analysis of behavior. *Psychological Bulletin,* 1953, **50,** 264-274.

Garcia, E., Baer, D. M., and Firestone, I. The development of generalized imitation within topographically determined boundaries. *Journal of Applied Behavior Analysis,* 1971, **4,** 101-112.

Grice, C. R. and Hunter, J. J. Stimulus intensity effects depend upon the type of experimental design. *Psychological Review,* 1964, **71,** 247-256.

Gripp, R. F. and Magaro, P. A. A token economy program evaluation with untreated control ward comparisons. *Behaviour Research and Therapy,* 1971, **9,** 137-149.

Hartlage, L. C. Subprofessional therapists' use of reinforcement versus traditional psychotherapeutic techniques with schizophrenics. *Journal of Consulting and Clinical Psychology,* 1970, **34,** 181-183.

Hawkins, R. P., Peterson, R. F., Schweid, E., and Bijou, S. W. Behavior therapy in the home: Amelioration of problem parent-child relations with the parent in a therapeutic role. *Journal of Experimental Child Psychology,* 1966, **4,** 99-107.

Heap, R. F., Boblitt, W. E., Moore, C. H., and Hord,

J. E. Behavior-milieu therapy with chronic neuropsychiatric patients. *Journal of Abnormal Psychology,* 1970, **76,** 349-354.

Herman, S. and Tramontana, J. Instructions and group *versus* individual reinforcement in modifying disruptive group behavior. *Journal of Applied Behavior Analysis,* 1971, **4,** 113-119.

Hewett, F. M., Taylor, F. D., and Artuso, A. A. The Santa Monica Project: Evaluation of an engineered classroom design with emotionally disturbed children. *Exceptional Children,* 1969, **35,** 523-529.

Higgs, W. J. Effects of gross environmental change upon behavior of schizophrenics: A cautionary note. *Journal of Abnormal Psychology,* 1970, **76,** 421-422.

Honig, W. K. Introduction. *Operant behavior: areas of research and application.* New York: Appleton-Century-Crofts, 1966.

Hopkins, B. L. Effects of candy and social reinforcement schedule learning on the modification and maintenance of smiling. *Journal of Applied Behavior Analysis,* 1968, **1,** 121-128.

Hunt, J. G. and Zimmerman, J. Stimulating productivity in a simulated workshop setting. *American Journal of Mental Deficiency,* 1969, **74,** 43-49.

Kazdin, A. E. The effect of response cost and aversive stimulation in suppressing punished and nonpunished speech disfluencies. *Behavior Therapy,* 1973, **4,** 73-82. (*a*)

Kazdin, A. E. The effect of vicarious reinforcement on attentive behavior in the classroom. *Journal of Applied Behavior Analysis,* 1973, **6,** 71-78. (*b*)

Kazdin, A. E. The role of instructions and reinforcement in behavior changes in token reinforcement programs. *Journal of Educational Psychology,* 1973, **64,** 63-71. (*c*)

Kazdin, A. E. and Bootzin, R. R. The token economy: an evaluative review. *Journal of Applied Behavior Analysis,* 1972, **5,** 343-372.

Kazdin, A. E. and Polster, R. Intermittent token reinforcement and response maintenance in extinction. *Behavior Therapy,* 1973, **4,** 386-391.

Kuypers, D. S., Becker, W. C., and O'Leary, K. D. How to make a token system fail. *Exceptional Children,* 1968, **11,** 101-108.

Lawson, R. Brightness discrimination performance and secondary reward strength as a function of primary reward amount. *Journal of Comparative and Physiological Psychology,* 1957, **50,** 35-39.

McAllister, L. W., Stachowiak, J. G., Baer, D. M., and Conderman, L. The application of operant conditioning techniques in a secondary school classroom. *Journal of Applied Behavior Analysis,* 1969, **2,** 277-285.

McNamara, J. R. and MacDonough, T. S. Some methodological considerations in the design and implementation of behavior therapy research. *Behavior Therapy,* 1972, **3,** 361-378.

Marks, J., Sonoda, B., and Schalock, R. Reinforcement *vs.* relationship therapy for schizophrenics. *Journal of Abnormal Psychology,* 1968, **73,** 397-402.

Mathis, B. C., Cotton, J. W., and Sechrest, L. *Psychological foundations of education.* New York: Academic Press, 1971.

Meichenbaum, D. H., Bowers, K., and Ross, R. R. Modification of classroom behavior of institutionalized female adolescent offenders. *Behaviour Research and Therapy,* 1968, **6,** 343-353.

Metz, J. R. Conditioning generalized imitation in autistic children. *Journal of Experimental Child Psychology,* 1965, **2,** 389-399.

Mischel, W. *Personality and assessment.* New York: Wiley, 1968.

Mulligan, W., Kaplan, R. D., and Reppucci, N. D. *Changes in cognitive variables among behavior problem elemetary school boys treated in a token economy special classroom.* Unpublished paper presented at Association for the Advancement of Behavior Therapy, Washington, D.C., September 1971.

O'Leary, K. D. and Becker, W. C. Behavior modification of an adjustment class: A token reinforcement program. *Exceptional Children,* 1967, **9,** 637-642.

O'Leary, K. D., Becker, W. C., Evans, M. B., and Saudargas, R. A. A token reinforcement program in a public school: A replication and systematic analysis. *Journal of Applied Behavior Analysis,* 1969, **2,** 3-31.

O'Leary, K. D. and Drabman, R. Token reinforcement programs in the classroom: A review. *Psychological Bulletin,* 1971, **75,** 379-398.

Packard, R. G. The control of "classroom attention": a group contingency for complex behavior. *Journal of Applied Behavior Analysis,* 1970, **3,** 13-28.

Paul, G. L. Insight versus desensitization in psychotherapy two years after termination. *Journal of Consulting Psychology,* 1967, **31,** 333-348.

Pendergrass, V. E. Timeout from positive reinforcement following persistent, high-rate behavior in retardates. *Journal of Applied Behavior Analysis,* 1972, **5,** 85-91.

Perkins, C. C. and Cacioppo, A. J. The effect of intermittent reinforcement on the change in extinction rate following successive reconditionings. *Journal of Experimental Psychology,* 1950, **40,** 794-801.

Peterson, R. F. and Whitehurst, G. J. A variable influencing the performance of generalized imitative behaviors. *Journal of Applied Behavior Analysis,* 1971, **4,** 1-9.

Phillips, E. L. Achievement Place: token reinforcement procedures in a home-style rehabilitation setting for "predelinquent" boys. *Journal of Applied Behavior Analysis,* 1968, **1,** 213-223.

Risley, T. R. Behavior modification: An experimental-therapeutic endeavor. In L. A. Hamerlynck, P. O. Davidson, and L. E. Acker (Eds.), *Behavior modification and ideal mental health services.* Calgary, Alberta, Canada: University of Calgary Press, 1970. Pp. 103-127.

Risley, T. R. and Baer, D. M. Operant behavior modification: The deliberate development of child behavior. In B. Calwell and H. Riccuiti (Eds.), *Review of child development research, Volume III: Social action,* 1973, *in press.*

Risley, T. R. and Wolf, M. M. Strategies for analyzing behavioral change over time. In J. Nesselroade and H. Reese (Eds.), *Life-span developmental psychology: methodological issues.* New York: Academic Press, 1972.

Schaefer, H. H. and Martin, P. L. Behavior therapy for "apathy" of hospitalized schizophrenics. *Psychological Reports,* 1966, **19**, 1147-1158.

Schick, K. Operants. *Journal of the Experimental Analysis of Behavior,* 1971, **15**, 413-423.

Schrier, A. M. Comparison of two methods of investigating the effects of amount of reward on performance. *Journal of Comparative and Physiological Psychology,* 1958, **51**, 725-731.

Sechrest, L. Implicit reinforcement of responses. *Journal of Educational Psychology,* 1963, **54**, 197-201.

Sidman, M. *Tactics of scientific research.* New York: Basic Books, 1960.

Skinner, B. F. *Science and human behavior.* New York: Macmillan, 1953.

Skinner, B. F. *Contingencies of reinforcement: a theoretical analysis.* New York: Appleton-Century-Crofts, 1969.

Staats, A. W. Reinforcer systems in the solution of human problems. In G. A. Fargo, C. Behrns, and P. Nolen (Eds.), *Behavior modification in the classroom.* Belmont, California: Wadsworth, 1970. Pp. 6-31.

Staats, A. W. and Butterfield, W. H. Treatment of nonreading in a culturally deprived juvenile delinquent: An application of learning principles. *Child Development,* 1965, **4**, 925-942.

Staats, A. W., Minke, K. A., and Butts, P. A token-reinforcement remedial reading program administered by black therapy technicians to problem black children. *Behavior Therapy,* 1970, **1**, 331-353.

Stayer, S. J. and Jones, F. Ward 108: *Behavior modification and the delinquent soldier.* Unpublished paper presented at Behavioral Engineering Conference, Walter Reed General Hospital, 1969.

Stuart, R. B. *Trick or treatment: how and when psychotherapy fails.* Champaign, Illinois: Research Press, 1970.

Suchotliff, L., Greaves, S., Stecker, H., and Berke, R. Critical variables in the token economy. *Proceedings of the 78th Annual Convention of the American Psychological Association,* 1970, **5**, 517-518.

Surratt, P. R., Ulrich, R. E., and Hawkins, R. P. An elementary student as a behavioral engineer. *Journal of Applied Behavior Analysis,* 1969, **2**, 85-92.

Thoresen, C. E. *The intensive design: an intimate approach to counseling research.* Unpublished paper presented at meeting of American Educational Research Association, Chicago, April, 1972.

Underwood, B. J. *Psychological research.* New York: Appleton-Century-Crofts, 1957.

Wahler, R. G. Setting generality: some specific and general effects of child behavior therapy. *Journal of Applied Behavior Analysis,* 1969, **2**, 239-246.

Wolf, M. M., Giles, D. K., and Hall, R. V. Experiments with token reinforcement in a remedial classroom. *Behaviour Research and Therapy,* 1968, **6**, 51-64.

Wolf, M. M. and Risley, T. R. Reinforcement: applied research. In R. Glaser (Ed.), *The nature of reinforcement.* New York: Academic Press, 1971. Pp. 310-325.

Zimmerman, J., Stuckey, T. E., Garlick, B. J., and Miller, M. Effects of token reinforcement on productivity in multiply handicapped clients in a sheltered workshop. *Rehabilitation Literature,* 1969, **30**, 34-41.

Received 21 March 1972.
(Revision requested 27 December 1972.)
(Final acceptance 29 January 1973.)

Comments by reviewers on following pages

METHODOLOGICAL AND ASSESSMENT CONSIDERATIONS IN APPLIED SETTINGS: REVIEWERS' COMMENTS

The large number of nonexperimental manuscripts submitted to JABA and the lack of well-defined criteria for evaluating them, has necessitated formulation of a separate editorial policy (see policy statement on page 404 of this issue). The manuscript by Alan E. Kazdin was submitted before the policy concerning nonexperimental manuscripts went into effect and was reviewed by three established researchers who have made substantial methodological contributions to the field (Montrose M. Wolf, Murray Sidman, and L. Keith Miller were Reviewers A, B, and C, respectively). On the basis of the reviewers' comments, it was decided to publish the manuscript with only minor changes. However, because of the fundamental importance of many of the issues discussed in Kazdin's paper and because of the lack of clear agreement on some of these issues, as exemplified in the reviewers' comments, these comments are presented below.

COMMENTS BY REVIEWER A

It was a pleasure to read this paper on experimental design by Alan Kazdin. The author makes many important points that JABA readers and researchers need to consider. He makes these points simply and eloquently. Kazdin's suggestion that behavior modification researchers need to consider the advantages of control group design is, I think, particularly well made and important. Also, he will do many readers a service by introducing them to the experimental design considerations of Campbell and Stanley (1963). I do have two suggestions, however, for the author to consider:

1. The paper focuses on what the author describes as "reinforcement" programs as if the only variable used in these programs was reinforcement. Then, the author describes how most behavior modification research does not attempt to analyze the role of any particular variable but instead usually involves a "package" of treatment variables such as instructions, training, practice, and reinforcement. As a result, as Kazdin points out, it is not usually possible to determine the amount of the effect that is attributable to any one of these variables. Kazdin attacks this strategy as a serious weakness in behavior modification research. It seems to me that the author himself is confounding two very important but different strategies, that of *basic-theoretical research* and of *applied research.*

In basic-theoretical research, the goal is to conduct a demonstration experiment that will support a *principle,* like the principle of reinforcement or the principle of extinction, or the principle of stimulus generalization, *etc.* This is unlike technological research, which is directed at finding a solution to a particular applied problem. In technological research, there is often no attempt to isolate the contribution of any of the variables that are applied simultaneously toward the solution of the problem. In technological research, the primary goal is to find some way to modify specific behaviors. Thus, in technological research rather than simply introducing one variable at a time and studying its effect, the investigators usually introduce multi-variable packages to see whether the whole thing has any effect. If indeed the package does have an effect and *then* if there is some *practical* or *theoretical* reason for examining the role of the individual components these roles can then be teased out. Frequently, the role of the individual components is trivial in terms of implications for either practice or theory. For example, if we find that a teacher going to a child and praising him and at the same time patting him on the shoulder increases that child's rate of doing his arithmetic, do we really care whether it was the praise statement or the pat? As long as the teacher must be next to the child anyway in order to deliver either of the consequences it may be just as easy to deliver both. The same is true for most complex behavior modification treatment packages. They may be composed of many classes of variables and each of these classes of variables may in turn be composed of a great many components. As Kazdin pointed out, in many studies it is not clear whether it is the instruction, the training, or the token reinforcement system that produces the effect. This is true. On the other hand, each of those classes of variables is made up of many, many variables. Even if it were discovered that the token system played a major role in a change, one would still not know what specific variables in the token reinforcement component were functional. It could be the color of the token, its texture, some of the things that back it up (but probably not all), *etc.* In other words, to isolate the role of every conceivable variable in a complex treatment package would take a researcher literally forever. It is only in the laboratory that we have the luxury of reasonably *pure* variables, and often even this is illusionary.

Rather than encouraging behavior modification researchers to spend more time isolating the role of each of the several variables in their treatment packages, it seems to me that they should instead be helped to consider when such component analyses would have practical or theoretical significance. For example, if an element in a treatment package is expensive or difficult to teach or to monitor, then there would be a definite practical reason for analyzing its role. Or if an element in a treatment package is novel for behavior theory, then it would be worthwhile teasing out its role so that its implications for behavior theory would be clear.

It should be pointed out even more forcefully that researchers frequently do not indicate that their treatment packages are multi-dimensional. As indeed Kazdin has pointed out, they are usually made up of more than reinforcement, and researchers often do not explicitly list the other variables like the instructions, announcements, modelling, and practice that may go into the treatment program as well as the reinforcement. Kazdin could have done us a wealth of good by prodding researchers to become more explicit in describing all of the variables of the treatment programs, thus making the descriptions of these treatment programs in JABA more likely to facilitate replication.

2. The author stated that response frequency as a dependent variable is "the most useful" in behavior modification research. However, Kazdin did not describe how he determined that this measure was "the most useful". Thus, the statement is ambiguous and should have been deleted, since there is no way to evaluate it. As a matter of fact, the Bijou *et al.* (1968) article that the author cites to support his statement does not represent an example of the use of frequency data. While Bijou sometimes uses the term "frequency", one can see by reading his procedure section that he does not use frequency as a response measure at all. Rather, he samples during each interval of a few seconds length whether or not the behavior occurs or does not occur. Thus, a response with an extremely low frequency, such as one per session, but with a long duration, such as the session length, would be noted to occur within every one of the intervals and thus would represent 100% on Bijou's graphs (which are all percentage graphs). None of Bijou's graphs display frequency.

As for the articles by Ferster (1953) and Honig (1966), which are also used to support the author's point about response frequency as "the most useful" measure, they are both animal research articles. The relevance of this animal research for contemporary applied research escapes this reviewer. The fact is, I think that frequency as a dependent variable had a great deal of use in the animal laboratory but has not generalized well to applied research. A cursory review of the response measures used in JABA articles indicates that frequency is one of the least popular dependent variables. The Bijou occurrence sampling procedure, time sampling, amount (such as pieces of litter), and per cent correct (such as in academic work) seem to be more favored than frequency as dependent variables by applied behavior analysis researchers.

Kazdin might have helped researchers and students by categorizing all of the different dependent variables that are currently used. On the other hand, the statement that frequency is "the most useful" dependent variable may mislead the casual reader.

Recommendation. This paper is potentially very important to students and JABA readers who may not be familiar with the numerous critical points made by Kazdin. I strongly recommend publication and look forward to rereading it myself soon in JABA.

COMMENTS BY REVIEWER B

This paper is a worthwhile contribution, and I recommend publication. The author might, however, consider the following points before publication:

1. Methods for assessing within-subject effects are not limited simply to reversals and multiple baselines. For example, one may also introduce quantitative variations in the variable of interest (the question of whether the complete elimination of the variable, as in the "reversal design", is simply an extreme instance of quantitative variation is not a simple problem); one may use the finding to predict other effects; the credibility of a finding can be increased by specification of the conditions under which it does *not* occur; and irreversibility may be *explainable* as a *legitimate* outcome of an experimental manipulation. Perhaps more thought should be given to these matters.

2. The problem of response and stimulus specification—as these differ between subject and experimenter—is more general than is indicated here. It is a problem in any experiment, regardless of the formal design, and it may be misleading to single out the multiple-baseline design as a specific instance.

3. Cumulative effects over time, interactions among individuals (social effects), and progressive baseline changes are all real problems in carrying out studies within a non-laboratory setting, as in a token-economy project. These effects are not a function of any particular "design". They are often unavoidable, and may either limit the generality of any study or even preclude certain kinds of investigations. Yet they do not necessarily invalidate all such studies. The question is at the nub of the distinction between laboratory and clinical research, and is responsible for the different standards in evaluating these two kinds of research. The mistake is to judge experimental and clinical research by the same criteria (although they are certainly related). I would like to have seen a more positive contribution along these lines in this paper, and not simply the critical and perhaps mistaken slant that is actually expressed.

4. With respect to internal and external validity, it would have been useful to suggest some answers to the problems the author poses. Many of the points are good, but many investigators who are already aware of them would appreciate some positive suggestions, and this would be a more meaningful contribution. The use of control groups can sometimes help, but only at the most primitive level of analysis.

COMMENTS BY REVIEWER C

I found this paper very well written, scholarly, and interesting. It presents an overview of our present research design methodology —particularly the strengths and weaknesses of the reversal and multiple baseline designs. It raises questions about some ways in which incorrect conclusions can be reached (under the rubric of internal and external validity). And it suggests that we should use both control groups and measures of supplementary behaviors more frequently. These are all extremely important considerations.

In spite of my considerable sympathy for the paper, I find it extremely difficult to review. Perhaps the major reason is that no very clear criteria have been established, or even suggested, for evaluating methodological papers. In view of this, it is essential that the reviewers explicitly state their criteria. The only unique criteria that I have been able to come up with is: "Does the manuscript specify a procedure or tool that might be useful in conducting behavioral research?" Thus, I shall review the manuscript from this point of view, by paraphrasing what the author seems to be saying in the major parts of the manuscript and providing an evaluation of each part.

PART I: Within-subject designs have important advantages over between-group designs.

These advantages are briefly described and include: (a) intersubject variability is bypassed; (b) the behavior of the individual subject is determined; (c) lawful effects of variables can be discovered; (d) individual differences are more readily observed.

Evaluation. These and other advantages are more clearly and more extensively discussed in a variety of other sources (*e.g.*, Baer, Wolf, and Risley, 1968; Bernard, 1953; Sidman, 1960).

PART II: The reversal design assumes that the experimental effect is reversible.

This is clearly an important consideration to keep in mind when evaluating the feasibility of using a reversal design in a particular setting. The author adds the further assertion that "Indeed, we would hope that they are not always reversible because this is tantamount to demonstrating only slight resistance to extinction." And, further, that behavior modification changes must be "transient" in order to use this design.

Evaluation. The general point is clearly functional in planning an experiment. One must make a guess as to whether the behavior will reverse before blindly choosing a reversal design. In my opinion, most readers of JABA already understand this point and attempt to use it in designing their experiments. The author might have made a useful contribution by suggesting guidelines for making this guess. He might have sifted through the literature, or his own experience, to select some clues for reversibility that could be translated into rules of thumb. He might have suggested some techniques whereby the chances of reversibility occurring are enhanced (the reinforcement of an alternative, incompatible response, for example). I feel that development of his theme along these lines might well have served a useful function for readers of JABA. However, his present treatment is too general and it stopped short of providing functional guides to action. It therefore does not meet my criteria of functionality.

I would like to add that his assertion that reversal designs can be used only to study transient effects is misleading. Any effect of consequences is transient once the consequences are removed unless there are other consequences to take their place. As I understand the goals of applied behavior analysis, it is to learn how to modify an environment to produce specified changes in behavior. Once the original environment is reinstated, we must ordinarily expect the behavior to revert to its original baseline rate. It is only if the original environment had a consequence that was too weak to initiate a behavioral change but that is strong enough to maintain such a response (once initiated) that the behavior should not be expected to revert (Baer and Wolf, 1970). While we may frequently work in environments with such weak consequences, we also frequently seek to discover how to engineer changes in an environment so that the changed environment will produce specified changes in some target behavior. Such an engineered environment need be in no sense transient. I would guess that Kazdin is also interested in such engineered environments; however, his phrasing could easily be misinterpreted.

PART III: The multiple-baseline design cannot be used where the dependent variables (responses, subjects, or settings) are correlated.

This is clearly an important consideration to be examined before selecting a multiple-baseline design. If an increase in one behavior will in some way increase the other behaviors of a multiple-baseline design, then no independent effect of the treatment can be established.

Evaluation. Again, this general point is functional in planning an experiment. However, it is hard for me to imagine a JABA reader who does not understand this. If there is one, he is probably neither a user nor a consumer of multiple-baseline designs.

In this case also, the author could have attempted to provide some rules of thumb for guessing whether several behaviors will be correlated. His advice on this point is not very functional, however. The author suggests that whether the dependent variables are correlated or not must be learned from experience, although in some (unspecified) instances "the investigator can rely on the well-documented experience of others". I am not clear whether the author's review of such correlations was meant to be a guide or simply a demonstration that the problem does arise. I would like to see an attempt to review known cases with the goal of providing some guidelines for predicting situations in which this problem might arise. For example, generalization is probably one source of correlation between variables. Therefore, a possible rule of thumb would be to select behaviors that are topographically as different as possible and that occur in stimulus situations that are as different as possible.

PART IV: Different experimental designs may suggest different experimental conclusions for the same questions.

Kazdin gives two examples in which the same variables are manipulated in a between-group design and a within-subject design, and in which the results suggested different conclusions for each set of data.

Evaluation. Frankly, the author already outlined a number of reasons why the results of between-group designs are questionable (*e.g.,* "lawful effects of variables may be obscured"). I agree with criticisms of group designs and feel they raise questions about the significance of this part of the manuscript. Therefore, I would first have to ask if this same type of interaction between the type of design and the results obtained from each type also applies to single-subject designs. If such an interaction seemed plausible, then I would be interested in some rules of action. How can we identify potential interactions and avoid them?

PART V: An experimental result may be caused by an unspecified component of the experimental manipulation.

Kazdin gives three examples of this problem. First, instructions to subjects are often given simultaneously with a change in contingencies. Thus, either the new contingency, the instructions, or both acting together may be the cause of any change. "In several studies, the effect of instructions . . . cannot be separated from the reinforcement contingencies themselves." Second, when some event, such as praise or tokens, is given contingent upon a response, any change might also have been caused by the "informational feedback" implicit in the delivery of the contingent event. Thus, we cannot be sure that a simple feedback system might not be just as effective as our more complicated token systems. Third, the agent who implements any experimental manipulations may change his behavior as he changes the conditions. Thus, we could not be sure that the manipulations themselves are responsible for the change—it could be the agent's behavior that is responsible for the change in the subject's behavior.

Evaluation. I cannot argue with Kazdin's points. However, they are less relevant to *applied* research than they are to *basic* research. Many authors of research articles have taken to carefully qualifying their conclusions by talking about the "package" of events that constitute the treatment. Thus, the token treatment is often taken to consist of delivering a token that can be exchanged for goodies, providing feedback about the agent's target behavior implicit in that token delivery, the social reinforcement that is necessarily involved in most token systems, and perhaps even the unspecified changes in teacher behavior induced by the token delivery (such as added attention, Mandelker, Brigham, and Bushell, 1970). By limiting their conclusions to "packages", applied researchers can present technologies that will produce a desired effect without necessarily being able to pinpoint all of the effective variables.

It would be a functional message to suggest to researchers that they limit their firm conclusions to the entire package that they used in the treatment. Another alternative is, of course, what might be called "component analysis". That is, the experimental analysis of the components of the treatment package may be separately analyzed. While Kazdin gives several examples of such analyses, his examples are more directed to pointing out the possibility of unspecified variables being responsible for experimental results. Perhaps these examples could be reworked to point out the possibility of such "component analyses". I would hope for some guidance as to when such an analysis might be important for an applied researcher. For example, when a particular component of a procedure is hard to implement or expensive to use, there may be applied reasons for evaluating the contribution of that component to the total treatment package.

PART VI: The particular experimental procedure that is selected may produce results that should not be generalized.

Kazdin gives several examples of this: first, the efficacy of shock punishment depends upon the manner in which the shock is introduced. That is, a high initial shock level will tend to eliminate responding indefinitely, while the introduction of such a level following the gradual increase of shock level may not totally eliminate the response. Second, each time a reinforcement period is followed by an extinction period, the rapidity of extinction will increase. And third, many experimental results may depend upon an observer being present in the situation and cannot be generalized to situations in which there is no observer.

Evaluation. I have difficulty finding any functional advice to draw out of this observation. Any thorough researcher, such as Azrin in his series of punishment experiments (see Azrin and Holz, 1966), might have a good chance to discover the adaptation to shock punishment as well as the effect of gradual *versus* abrupt change in the level of the shock. But what advice could be given to someone: "be thorough"? We usually hope that we are. Could that rule be specified in behavioral terms so that it translates into a procedure or tool? I cannot get to it. The second example is somewhat similar. It deals with the stable state in a multiple schedule situation. In that state, extinction will occur more quickly until some stable state is reached appropriate for the schedule of reinforcement (Ferster and Skinner, 1957). Again, what do we suggest to someone who might like to learn something from the example?

And I guess I do not agree too much with the "observer effect". If the effect depends on the observer, then by all means alter the environment by inserting a permanent observer (or if that is too costly, look for alternative treatments). But that is perfectly generalizable as a piece of behavioral engineering. Frankly, I doubt that most applied behavior analysts would agree with the assertion that "the influence of observers is assumed not to affect the differential performance of . . . school children . . .". Measuring both teacher and student behavior is the basis for any alterations that anyone can make in a classroom. How can the student be expected to behave differently if contingencies are not placed on his behavior? And, likewise, how can teachers be expected to act differently in applying those contingencies to the children, if their behavior is not observed and consequated?

PART VII: Control groups are sometimes useful.

Clearly, the use of control group sometimes provides information necessary to the practical use of a behavior modification method. If you wish to increase the rate of studying and find that some treatment will do just that, you still might want to find out if that has produced a concomitant increase in an achievement test. To evaluate the importance of the gain in the achievement test implies comparison with an untreated or "normal" group. The author gives a number of such examples.

Evaluation. Again, I cannot take exception to the general point. But I would like to see some rules or guidelines for identifying situations in which a control group should be used. It does not help me much to know that they are sometimes useful.

However, perhaps an even more important point might be to provide some guidance on how to avoid using control groups. Virtually all research on the effects of contingency management procedures in college classrooms has relied on between-groups designs. What a shame that our knowledge of the effects of such procedures is based on such a weak design. Fortunately, single-subject analyses of college teaching procedures are finally appearing (*e.g.*, Mawhinney, Bostow, Laws, Blumenfeld, and Hopkins, 1971). And even the analysis of changes in achievement test scores has now been approached through single-subject analysis (Miller and Weaver, 1972).

PART VIII: Socially important behaviors that might be modified as an incidental effect of some treatment should be measured.

Kazdin suggests several interesting samples of such a strategy. For example, the severity of inappropriate responses may decrease concomitantly with the treatment to reduce frequency of inappropriate responses. Children rewarded for appropriate behaviors also showed changes in IQ scores and arithmetic achievement levels (although I cannot figure out why Kazdin refers to these as "cognitive" variables when they are samples of the child's behavioral repertoire, and I do not know how "anxiety" was measured in this same example).

Evaluation. I thoroughly agree with Kazdin's suggestion. Supplementary behavioral observations would be a great help in understanding the effects of our environmental modifications. Why should we not know if children laugh (appropriately) as much when tokens are used as when anarchy reigns supreme? Many potential consumers of our technology wonder. Why not tell them?

Again, some guidelines for how to select such supplementary behaviors might be helpful. Perhaps asking socially relevant "judges" what they consider to be important in a situation would provide important clues to selecting such supplementary measures. The work of Wolf and his associates with "social validity" is a major step in the direction (*e.g.*, Phillips, Wolf, and Fixsen, *in press*). It may provide the most important guideline in this regard.

* * * * * * * *

Now, how do I evaluate the overall manuscript? As I see it, the manuscript as it is constructed at present fails the test that I proposed. For the most part, it does not specify procedures and tools that might be useful in conducting behavioral research. In particular, it does not provide rules for predicting when a behavior will not be reversible, when several behaviors will be intercorrelated, when to conclude that a "package" of elements is responsible for an effect or how and when to do a "component analysis" of that package, how to be thorough, when to use control groups and how to avoid their use, or how to select supplementary variables for measurement.

It should be clear that I find many of Kazdin's observations interesting and thought-provoking. There may be merit in provoking thought in JABA readers. But what are the criteria for when something is sufficiently interesting or the provoked thought worthwhile? I personally cannot formulate them. I am afraid that to get into the business of provoking thoughts at all would open a Pandora's box for JABA's editorial board. At present, we are primarily in the business of publishing sound behavioral research and secondarily in the business of publishing manuscripts that offer potentially useful research tools. This is a very narrow perspective. Let's keep it that way.

I therefore recommend that JABA not publish this very fine manuscript.

REFERENCES

Azrin, N. H. and Holz, W. C. Punishment. In W. K. Honig (Ed.), *Operant behavior: areas of research and application.* New York: Appleton-Century-Crofts, 1966. Pp. 380-477.

Baer, D. M. and Wolf, M. M. The entry in natural communities of reinforcement. In R. Ulrich, T. Stachnik, and J. Mabry (Eds.), *Control of human behavior, Volume 2.* Glenview, Illinois: Scott, Foresman and Company, 1970. Pp. 319-324.

Baer, D. M., Wolf, M. M., and Risley, T. R. Some current dimensions of applied behavior analysis. *Journal of Applied Behavior Analysis,* 1968, **1,** 91-97.

Bernard, C. *Introduction to experimental medicine.* New York: Grolier Publishing Company, 1953.

Campbell, D. T. and Stanley, J. C. Experimental and quasi-experimental designs for research and teaching. In N. L. Gage (Ed.), *Handbook of research on teaching.* Chicago: Rand McNally, 1963. Pp. 171-246.

Ferster, C. B. The use of the free operant in the analysis of behavior. *Psychological Bulletin,* 1953, **50,** 264-274.

Ferster, C. B. and Skinner, B. F. *Schedules of reinforcement.* New York: Appleton-Century-Crofts, 1957.

Honig, W. K. *Operant behavior: areas of research and application.* New York: Appleton-Century-Crofts, 1966.

Mandelker, A. V., Brigham, T. A., and Bushell, D. The effects of token procedures on a teacher's social contacts with her students. *Journal of Applied Behavior Analysis,* 1970, **3,** 169-174.

Mawhinney, V. T., Bostow, D. E., Laws, D. R., Blumenfield, G. J., and Hopkins, B. L. A comparison of students' studying-behavior produced by daily, weekly, and three-week testing schedules. *Journal of Applied Behavior Analysis,* 1971, **4,** 257-264.

Miller, L. K. and Weaver, F. H. A multiple baseline achievement test. In G. Semb (Ed.), *Behavior analysis and education—1972.* Lawrence, Kansas: Support and Development Center for Follow Through, Department of Human Development, University of Kansas, 1972. Pp. 393-399.

Phillips, E. L., Wolf, M. M., and Fixsen, D. L. Achievement Place: development of the elected manager system for administering routine tasks. *Journal of Applied Behavior Analysis, (in press).*

Sidman, M. *Tactics of scientific research.* Chicago: Basic Books, 1950.

JOURNAL OF APPLIED BEHAVIOR ANALYSIS 1975, 8, 77-82 NUMBER 1 (SPRING 1975)

DIFFERENTIAL REINFORCEMENT OF OTHER BEHAVIOR AND NONCONTINGENT REINFORCEMENT AS CONTROL PROCEDURES DURING THE MODIFICATION OF A PRESCHOOLER'S COMPLIANCE[1]

ELIZABETH M. GOETZ, MARGARET C. HOLMBERG, AND JUDITH M. LEBLANC

UNIVERSITY OF KANSAS

Differential reinforcement of other behavior (DRO) and noncontingent reinforcement were compared as control procedures during the modification of a 3-yr-old preschooler's compliance. The recorded reinforcer was teacher proximity (within 3 ft (0.9 m) of the subject for at least 5 sec) which was often accompanied by positive verbal comments that varied in content across experimental conditions. The verbal content during contingent reinforcement might have been: "Thank you for picking up the blocks"; during noncontingent reinforcement: "You're wearing a pretty dress"; and during DRO: "I don't blame you for not picking up because it isn't any fun". Contingent reinforcement increased compliance in all manipulation conditions. Noncontingent reinforcement decreased compliance during two reversal conditions. However, the behavior was variable and did not decrease to the low levels reached during the two DRO reversals.

DESCRIPTORS: compliance, DRO, noncontingent reinforcement, operant, reversals, teacher behavior

---

In addition to extinction, both noncontingent reinforcement and differential reinforcement of other behavior (DRO) have been used as control procedures for evaluating reinforcement-based behavior-modification techniques. For example, Azrin, Rubin, O'Brien, Ayllon, and Roll (1968), Buell, Stoddard, Harris, and Baer (1968), Miller and Miller (1970), Phillips (1968), Siegel, Lenske, and Broen (1969), and Wahler (1969) used noncontingent reinforcement as a reversal control procedure; Guess, Sailor, Rutherford, and Baer (1968), Osborne (1969), Reynolds and Risley (1968), and Semb (1973) used DRO for this purpose. Peterson, Cox, and Bijou (1971), after using noncontingent reinforcement to reverse the study behavior of special-education students, implemented DRO to decrease further the behavior in the reversal.

These applied studies did not compare the two procedures in terms of how rapidly the response decreased or how durable was its elimination. Although Peterson *et al.* (1971) used both noncontingent reinforcement and DRO for a reversal, they did not directly compare the two as control procedures. Instead, after a baseline and a treatment condition, they first used noncontingent reinforcement for a reversal and then immediately reduced the target behavior even further by implementing DRO. That sequence of two conditions prevents their direct comparison for efficiency, rapidity, or durability of response elimination. DRO may have seemed more effective in these ways because of its interaction with the weakening already produced by the preceding noncontingent reinforcement. That is, DRO was applied to a lower rate of behavior than was noncontingent reinforcement.

In two animal studies, response elimination during DRO was compared with that during extinction. Uhl and Garcia (1969) found that extinction eliminated the response more rapidly

---

[1]Supported in part by National Institute of Mental Health, #MH11739, and by the National Institute of Child Health and Human Development, #HD00183. We wish to thank Donald M. Baer for helping to analyze data and editing the manuscript. Ms. Susan Young's assistance in obtaining measurements was invaluable. Reprints may be obtained from Elizabeth M. Goetz, Department of Human Development, University of Kansas, Lawrence, Kansas 66045.

than did DRO, but that DRO produced greater durability of response elimination. However, Zeiler (1971) found that DRO eliminated the response more rapidly and more durably than did extinction. These studies compared free-operant responding during DRO and extinction, and may have little relationship to the present research, which dealt with a restricted operant, compliance with requests, during DRO and noncontingent reinforcement in an applied setting.

Reinforcement contingencies that increased compliance or request-following have often been investigated. Fjellstat and Sulzer-Azaroff (1973) and Zimmerman, Zimmerman, and Russell (1969) used contingent tokens; Homme, deBaca, Devine, Steinhorst, and Rickert (1963) used contingent high-probability behaviors (running, shouting, *etc.*), Burgess, Clark, and Hendee (1971) and Clark, Burgess, and Hendee (1972) used contingent theater tickets and money; Striefel and Wetherby (1973) used praise, ice cream, and physical guidance. Bucher (1973) found a direct relationship between probability of reinforcement and compliance when a competing activity was available. In general, these studies demonstrated that compliance was readily increased by reinforcement contingencies, thus providing the background from which the present treatment techniques were designed for a noncompliant preschool child.

The primary purpose of the present study was to compare the effect of two reversal control procedures on response decrement, and on reacquisition subsequent to those response-decrement procedures, for a child whose compliance was being systematically improved. One procedure was noncontingent (uncorrelated or response-independent) reinforcement; the second was differential reinforcement of other behavior (DRO). The recorded reinforcer was teacher proximity; the presence of a teacher in the vicinity of the subject. This presence was usually accompanied by positive verbal comments of the teacher that varied in content across experimental conditions. The verbal content during contingent reinforcement might have been: "Thank you for picking up the blocks", during noncontingent reinforcement: "You're wearing a pretty dress", and during differential reinforcement of other behavior: "I don't blame you for not picking up because it isn't any fun".

METHOD

Subject

Betsy was a normal, 3-yr, seven-month-old girl enrolled in a preschool class of nine boys and seven girls (aged 3 to 5 yr) at the Department of Human Development Edna A. Hill Child Development Laboratories, University of Kansas. During her first few weeks at the preschool, she exhibited little compliance to teachers' requests. For example, she would often not go outside during outdoor time, or would not sit on the floor for large group, or sit at a table for snacks, and often would not participate in clean-up.

Observation

Betsy was observed for the last 30 to 35 min of each preschool day. The activities during this time were clean-up, a group story, song, or discussion, and individual activities.

Requests given by the teacher to the subject, the subject's compliance with these requests, and teacher's presence were recorded by an observer in 10-sec intervals.

Requests were divided into four categories: (1) instruction, *e.g.,* "Do this", "It's your turn", or "We need to"; (2) direction, in which the teacher contacted the subject and physically and verbally directed her into compliance after giving the initial request; (3) suggestion, *e.g.,* "Would you like to" or "How about"; and (4) contingency, *e.g.,* "If you don't do this, you can't ____". Compliance was recorded if the subject complied within 30 sec after a request. Teacher presence (the measure used for teacher reinforcement) was recorded when the teacher was within 3 ft (0.9 m) of the subject, with no intervening person or large object (*e.g.,* a table), and remained there for five consecutive seconds of a 10-sec interval. Usually, teacher presence was accompanied by verbal statements related to compliance or noncompliance.

Two independent observers provided estimates of reliability, at least once in each condition. Average reliability across all conditions for requests was 88% (range 76 to 89%); for compliance, 89% (range 87 to 97%); and for teacher presence, 93% (range 90 to 97%). Occurrence reliability was calculated by dividing number of 10-sec intervals in which observers agreed by total number of intervals in which behavior was recorded, and multiplying by 100.

Procedure

The experiment utilized a reversal design to evaluate three basic conditions: (A) contingent teacher presence for compliance, (B) noncontingent teacher presence, and (C) contingent teacher presence for noncompliance (differential reinforcement of other behavior). These conditions were implemented in the order ABACABACA.

Contingent teacher presence. During contingent teacher presence for compliance, Betsy received verbal praise. The praise stated why the behavior was being reinforced, *e.g.,* "Thank you for helping to pick up the blocks" or "You're scrubbing the table very well". Teacher presence was recorded according to the 3-ft rule.

Noncontingent teacher presence. During noncontingent teacher presence, Betsy sometimes received verbal praise for compliance with requests in a manner similar to the other preschool children. In this condition, there were also occasions of teacher presence for noncompliance. The verbal content paired with teacher presence that occurred after compliance in this condition was the same as that during contingent teacher presence conditions. The verbal praise after compliance consisted of general pleasantries related to the subject in the preschool environment, *e.g.,* "You're wearing a pretty dress" or "Have you had your turn to feed the gerbil?". Again, teacher presence was recorded according to the 3-ft rule.

DRO. During DRO, if the subject did not comply in the alloted 30-sec time limit after a teacher's request, a teacher moved within 3 ft of her. This DRO procedure was considered a restricted-operant analogy of Reynolds' (1961) free-operant definition with an additional time base in the procedures. Usually, teachers left the subject alone if she complied. Some compliance inadvertantly received teacher presence during DRO, but this condition was characterized by more occurrences of teacher presence for noncompliance than occurred during the noncontingent reinforcement conditions. The content of verbal comments that accompanied teacher presence for noncompliance during DRO differed markedly from that given in the noncontingent and contingent conditions. Typical examples were: "I can see that you are too tired, so it's alright if you don't help" and "I don't blame you for not cleaning up because it isn't any fun".

Teacher presence was the independent variable measured during this study. However, two differences in the independent variable occurred during DRO and during the noncontingent teacher presence conditions. One was the difference in the verbal content delivered by the teacher; the other, a difference in the percentage of teacher presence delivered for noncompliance within the two conditions.

The mean number of requests per day during each condition ranged from 14 to 29. The highest number of requests was delivered during the last contingent teacher presence condition.

RESULTS

Each day's percentage of compliance was calculated by dividing the number of times Betsy complied by the number of requests she received. Figure 1 shows that Betsy's percentage of compliance to requests was higher during each contingent teacher presence condition, and decreased during noncontingent teacher presence and DRO conditions. Both DRO conditions markedly decreased compliance, whereas decreases of compliance during noncontingent

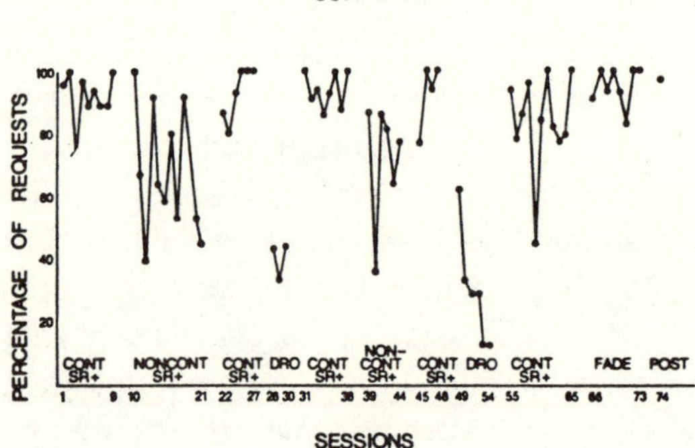

Fig. 1. The percentage of requests complied with throughout all the conditions of the study. The final data point represents the average of two postchecks.

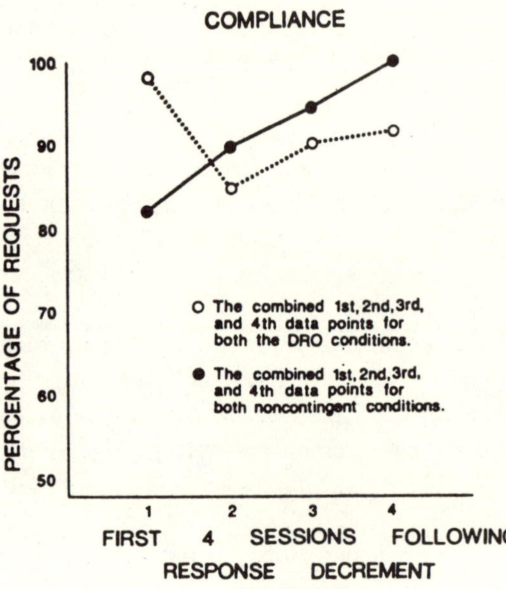

Fig. 2. The percentage of requests complied with during re-acquisitions of compliance after DRO and noncontingent conditions. The first, second, third, and fourth data points *after* both DRO conditions have been combined. The first, second, third, and fourth data points *after* both noncontingent conditions have been combined.

teacher presence decreased less and was more variable. Two postchecks (seven and 16 days after the study was completed) showed an average compliance of 97%.

There was little difference between re-acquisitions of compliance following noncontingent reinforcement and following DRO. Figure 2 compares the average of the first four sessions following each response decrement procedure.

Percentage of teacher presence for compliance was calculated by dividing the intervals of teacher presence for compliance by the total intervals of teacher presence. (A similar formula was followed to yield the noncompliance teacher-presence percentage.) As shown in Table 1, (top half) the highest percentage of teacher presence for compliance, 86%, was during the contingent conditions. The percentage of teacher presence for compliance during the DRO conditions was half that during the contingent conditions: 43%. In Table 1 (bottom half), the highest percentage of teacher presence for noncompliance was 58%, during the DRO conditions; this rate was double the percentage during the noncontingent conditions (26%) and quadruple the rate during contingent conditions (14%).

Table 1

Total intervals of teacher presence during compliance and noncompliance.*

Conditions	*Per Cent*
COMPLIANCE	
Total DRO	43%
Total Noncontingent	74%
Total Contingent	86%
NONCOMPLIANCE	
Total DRO	58%
Total Noncontingent	26%
Total Contingent	14%

*Teacher presence intervals during compliance (or noncompliance) / Total intervals of teacher presence for compliance and noncompliance = Per cent of total intervals of teacher presence during compliance (or noncompliance)

The different types of requests (instruction, direction, suggestion, and contingency) shown in Table 2 had similar ratios for each condition. The type of request given most frequently in all conditions was instruction, with direction being for the most part second highest and suggestions always higher than contingency. The percentages of each type of request across the 10 experimental conditions are shown in Table 2.

Four other children in the same classroom were observed for comparison. Each complied

Table 2

Per Cent of Each Type of Request over Total Requests per Condition of the Study

Conditions	*Instruction*	*Direction*	*Suggestion*	*Contingency*	*Total Requests*	*Number of Sessions*
Contingent SR+	59% (113)	39% (75)	1% (2)	1% (1)	191	9
Noncontingent SR+	84% (124)	14% (20)	1% (2)	1% (2)	148	12
Contingent SR+	79% (69)	18% (16)	2% (2)	0% (0)	87	6
DRO	89% (47)	4% (2)	4% (2)	4% (2)	53	3
Contingent SR+	70% (128)	28% (51)	2% (4)	0% (0)	183	8
Noncontingent SR+	83% (66)	10% (8)	9% (7)	0% (0)	80	6
Contingent SR+	87% (52)	7% (4)	7% (4)	0% (0)	60	4
DRO	92% (82)	2% (2)	6% (5)	0% (0)	89	6
Contingent SR+	75% (235)	15% (46)	10% (32)	0% (1)	315	11
Fade	66% (82)	21% (26)	11% (14)	2% (2)	124	8

with 100% of the requests given to them. However, these children received only one to three requests per day during their observations, because they voluntarily participated in the preschool schedule and activity routines, and repetitions of requests were rarely necessary.

DISCUSSION

A comparison of the two control procedures (noncontingent teacher presence and DRO), which was the primary purpose of the study, involves consideration of the following questions:

1. How much time did each need to demonstrate control?
2. How much did each reduce behavior?
3. How soon was target behavior recovered after control procedure terminated?

The DRO procedure decreased compliance faster and in fewer sessions than did noncontingent procedures. The first noncontingent condition required 12 sessions to demonstrate a stable decrease in compliance; the second required six. In comparison, DRO yielded a more immediate and dramatic decrease in target behavior.

This result confirms that of Peterson *et al.* (1971) from a stronger viewpoint, in that the DRO behavioral decrease in this instance occurred immediately after a high-rate behavior, rather than a low-rate behavior. Noncontingent procedures probably did not enhance the discrimination of which behavior was desired; both behaviors (compliance and noncompliance) were reinforced. By contrast, DRO probably enhanced the discrimination, because only one response was reinforced. Thus, a faster decrement in responding during DRO would be reasonable. Interestingly, the re-acquisition of a high-rate compliant behavior was essentially the same after both noncontingent and DRO conditions.

Since the content of the verbal remarks that sometimes accompanied teacher presence during DRO was markedly different from that in noncontingent, it is conceivable that the verbal content of attention itself had an effect on compliance. During DRO, perhaps the subject learned that it was appropriate for her not to comply. Thus, these verbal remarks possibly instructed the child to engage in only noncompliance in the future. Alternatively, during noncontingent conditions, teacher presence for compliance was not systematically accompanied by remarks instructing the child that only compliance was appropriate. This could explain why a 58% reinforcement of noncompliance during DRO could so markedly increase noncompliance (shown in Figure 1 as a decrease in compliance).

In an applied setting, neatly constructed examples of experimental conditions are extremely unlikely to occur. Ideal models of scheduling reinforcement for compliance and/or noncompliance are merely referents and are modified by the contingencies of the "real" situation. Because the teacher-experimenters had other duties in the preschool than the present experiment, he/she was not always available to deliver reinforcement contingent on the target behavior. In addition, requests were given in relation to normal demands of the ongoing preschool activities. The teaching team was not asked to limit artificially or produce a given number of requests that would not be relevant to the immediate situation. Thus, experimental conditions only approximated predetermined procedures.

The present study indicated impressive behavioral differences between DRO and noncontingent teacher presence as control techniques. The noncontingent condition resulted in a slower, more variable response reversal. The DRO condition, imperfect as it usually is in applied settings, nevertheless resulted in a more rapid and less-variable reversal. This enabled the experimenter to demonstrate control quickly and return to shaping a desirable behavior.

REFERENCES

Azrin, N., Rubin, H., O'Brien, F., Ayllon, T., and Roll, D. Behavioral engineering: postural control by a portable operant apparatus. *Journal of Applied Behavior Analysis,* 1968, **1**, 99-108.

Buell, J., Stoddard, P., Harris, F. R., and Baer, D. M. Collateral social development accompanying reinforcement of outdoor play in a preschool child. *Journal of Applied Behavior Analysis,* 1968, **1**, 167-173.

Bucher, B. Some variables affecting children's compliance with instructions. *Journal of Experimental Child Psychology,* 1973, **15**, 10-21.

Burgess, R. L., Clark, R. N., and Hendee, J. C. An experimental analysis of anti-litter procedures. *Journal of Applied Behavior Analysis,* 1971, **4**, 71-75.

Clark, R. N., Burgess, R. L., and Hendee, J. C. The development of anti-litter behavior in a forest campground. *Journal of Applied Behavior Analysis,* 1972, **5**, 1-5.

Fjellstat, N. and Sulzer-Azaroff, B. Reducing the latency of a child's responding to instructions by means of a token system. *Journal of Applied Behavior Analysis,* 1973, **6**, 125-130.

Guess, D., Sailor, W., Rutherford, G., and Baer, D. M. An experimental analysis of linguistic development: the productive use of the plural morpheme. *Journal of Applied Behavior Analysis,* 1968, **1**, 297-309.

Homme, L. E., deBaca, P. C., Devine, J. V., Steinhorst, R., and Rickert, E. J. Use of the Premack principle in controlling the behavior of nursery school children. *Journal of the Experimental Analysis of Behavior,* 1963, **5**, 544.

Miller, L. K. and Miller, O. L. Reinforcing self-help group activities of welfare recipients. *Journal of Applied Behavior Analysis,* 1970, **3**, 57-64.

Osborne, J. G. Free-time as a reinforcer with management of classroom behavior. *Journal of Applied Behavior Analysis,* 1969, **2**, 113-118.

Peterson, R. F., Cox, M. A., and Bijou, S. W. Training children to work productively in classroom groups. *Exceptional Children,* March, 1971, 491-500.

Phillips, E. L. Achievement Place: token reinforcement procedures in a home-style rehabilitation setting for "predelinquent" boys. *Journal of Applied Behavior Analysis,* 1968, **1**, 213-223.

Reynolds, G. S. *A primer of operant conditioning.* Glenview, Illinois: Scott, Foresman and Company, 1968.

Reynolds, N. J. and Risley, T. R. The role of social and material reinforcers in increasing talking of a disadvantaged preschool child. *Journal of Applied Behavior Analysis,* 1968, **1**, 253-262.

Semb, G., Hopkins, B. L., and Hursh, D. E. The effect of study questions and grades on student test performance in a college course. *Journal of Applied Behavior Analysis,* 1973, **6**, 631-642.

Siegal, G. M., Lenske, J., and Broen, P. Suppression of normal speech disfluencies through response cost. *Journal of Applied Behavior Analysis,* 1969, **2**, 265-276.

Striefel, S. and Wetherby, B. Instruction-following behavior of a retarded child and its controlling stimuli. *Journal of Applied Behavior Analysis,* 1973, **1**, 663-670.

Uhl, C. N. and Garcia, E. E. Comparison of omission with extinction in response elimination in rats. *Journal of Comparative and Physiological Psychology,* 1969, **69**, 554-562.

Wahler, R. G. Oppositional children: a quest for parental reinforcement control. *Journal of Applied Behavior Analysis,* 1969, **2**, 159-170.

Zeiler, M. D. Eliminating behavior with reinforcement. *Journal of the Experimental Analysis of Behavior,* 1971, **16**, 401-405.

Zimmerman, E. H., Zimmerman, J., and Russell, C. D. Differential effects of token reinforcement on instruction-following behavior in retarded students instructed as a group. *Journal of Applied Behavior Analysis,* 1969, **2**, 101-112.

Received 17 May 1973.
(Final acceptance 7 October 1974.)

JOURNAL OF APPLIED BEHAVIOR ANALYSIS 1976, 9, 527-532 NUMBER 4 (WINTER) 1976

THE CHANGING CRITERION DESIGN

DONALD P. HARTMANN[1] AND R. VANCE HALL

UNIVERSITY OF UTAH AND UNIVERSITY OF KANSAS

This article describes and illustrates with two case studies a relatively novel form of the multiple-baseline design called the changing criterion design. It also presents the design's formal requirements, and suggests target behaviors and circumstances for which the design might be useful.

DESCRIPTORS: multiple baseline, changing criterion design, experimental design, methodology, shaping, experimental control

The development of experimental designs to demonstrate control in individual case studies has been a crucial factor in bringing scientific status to the study of individuals. Applied behavioral research has primarily used reversal and multiple-baseline designs (Baer, Wolf, and Risley, 1968; Barlow and Hersen, 1973; Hall, Cristler, Cranston, and Tucker, 1970; Leitenberg, 1973; Wolf and Risley, 1971), although other designs suitable for individual subject research have been described by Edgington (1969, pp. 135-140), Gelfand and Hartmann (1968, p. 211), and Gottmann (1973). The advantages and limitations of these designs have been discussed by Gelfand and Hartmann (1975), Jones (1974), and McNamara and MacDonough (1972), among others. This paper describes an additional design that might be particularly useful in individual case studies when other designs are inconvenient or unsuitable, and changes in the target behavior are made in stepwise increments.

The changing criterion design, initially named by Hall (1971) and illustrated by Weis and Hall (1971), is a variation of a multiple-baseline design and is similar to a design described, but unnamed, by Sidman (1960, pp. 254-256). The design requires initial baseline observations on a single target behavior. This baseline phase is followed by implementation of a treatment program in each of a series of treatment phases. Each treatment phase is associated with a stepwise change in criterion rate for the target behavior. Thus, each phase of the design provides a baseline for the following phase. When the rate of the target behavior changes with each stepwise change in the criterion, therapeutic change is replicated and experimental control is demonstrated.

CASE I

The changing criterion design is illustrated with data from two case studies from our laboratories. The first study, taken from Hall and Fox (*in press*), used the changing criterion design to demonstrate experimental control over the num-

[1]We were independently preparing papers on the criterion change design in mid-1974. Through the *JABA* review process, we became aware of one another's work on the topic and agreed to co-author the present paper. Elements of the research and writing of this article were supported in part by National Institute of Mental Health HDMH-06914 to Donna M. Gelfand and Donald P. Hartmann, University of Utah, Salt Lake City, Utah, and by National Institute of Child Health and Human Development HD-03144 to the Bureau of Child Research, Department of Human Development and the Department of Special Education, University of Kansas. Reprints may be obtained from Donald P. Hartmann, Department of Psychology, University of Utah, Salt Lake City, Utah 84112, or from R. Vance Hall, Juniper Gardens Children's Project, 2021 North Third Street, Kansas City, Kansas 66101.

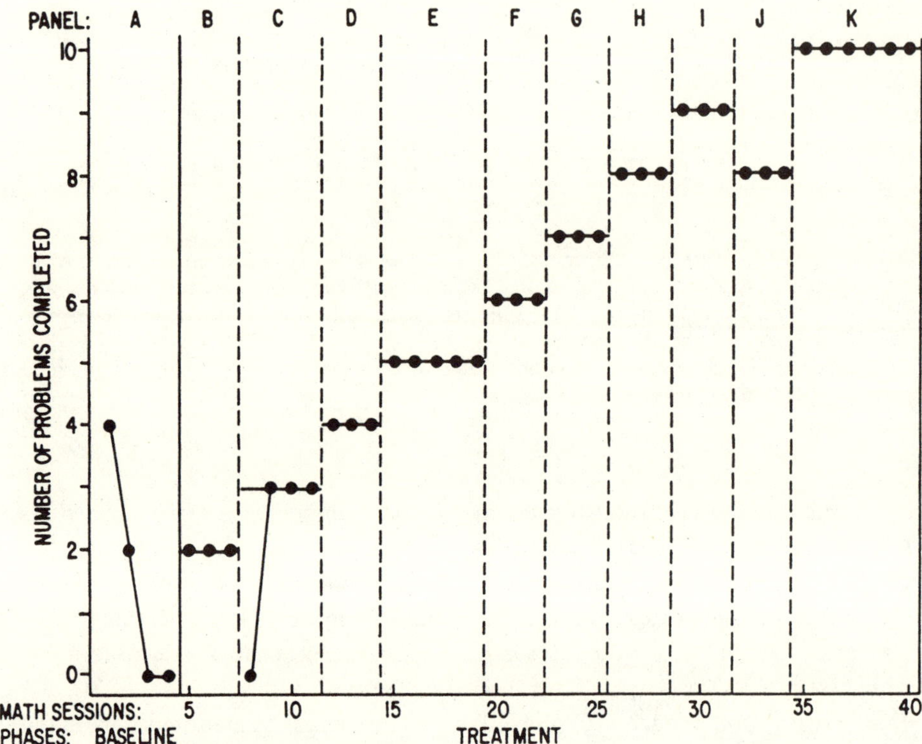

Fig. 1. A record of the number of math problems correctly solved by a behaviorally disordered boy during baseline, and when recess and the opportunity to play basketball were made contingent on changing levels of performance. Solid horizontal line segments indicate criterion for each treatment phase.

ber of math problems correctly solved by a student in a classroom for behaviorally disordered children (see Figure 1). During the baseline phase, the teacher gave the student a worksheet with nine division problems. In baseline (Panel A), the number of problems completed decreased from four during the first day to zero. In the first treatment phase (Panel B), the criterion number of problems to be worked was set at two, the next highest whole problem over the baseline mean. The consequences for correctly solving two problems on the worksheet during a 45-min work session included access to recess after the session and the opportunity to play basketball. Failure to complete two problems within the allotted time prolonged math time until the problems were correctly computed. In subsequent treatment phases, identical consequences were in effect and the criterion was advanced by one problem after three consecutive days of performing at the specified level. During the fourth treatment phase (Panel E), the problem criterion level was maintained for five rather than three consecutive days, and during the ninth treatment phase (Panel J), the criterion was dropped one problem, rather than raised one problem. Following this final worksheet phase, the subject was required to solve 10 problems in the math text correctly (Panel K) under the same contingency arrangement. During this, as well as prior treatment phases, math performance perfectly matched the criterion rate with but a single exception (Panel C).

Although these data demonstrated that the treatment package exerted control over math problem solving, they do not indicate which of the treatment components in fact exercised control. Component analysis requires additional design features, including conditions in which one or more treatment element is omitted [see, for example, Hall and Fox, Experiment III (*in press*)].

CASE II

The second study used the changing criterion design to demonstrate experimental control over smoking rate in a deceleration program (see Figure 2). The subject's baseline rate of smoking is given in Panel A; following this baseline phase, treatment was instituted. Treatment consisted of imposing a daily criterion rate of smoking and consequences for over- and under-indulgence. In the first treatment phase (Panel B), the criterion rate was set at 95% of baseline or 46 cigarettes per day. Cigarettes smoked in excess of this rate resulted in a $1.00 escalating fine ($1.00 for the forty-seventh cigarette, $2.00 for the forty-eighth cigarette, etc.). Smoking fewer than the criterion number of cigarettes resulted in a $0.10 escalating bonus. For the second (Panel C) and subsequent treatment phases, only four of 21 actually conducted being presented here (Panels D, E, F, and G), the criterion was set at 94% of the criterion rate for the previous treatment phase; identical consequences were imposed during all treatment phases.

The underlying multiple-baseline features from which the changing criterion design derives its credibility are more clearly illustrated by regraphing the smoking study data (see Figure 3). These data consist of the percentage of days within each week that four arbitrarily chosen criteria were met.[2] They indicate that the percentage of days on which the yet-to-be-applied criteria are met is low (0% to 29%), while the percentage for the current and previously applied criteria is high (invariably 100%). Furthermore, stepwise changes in percentage score (from low to high) occur only as each criterion is applied.[3] The pattern and tim-

[2]Because the data in Figure 3 are based on weekly performance, rather than daily performance as in Figure 2, Figure 3 includes data from 53 weeks, rather than from the 13 weeks presented in Figure 2.

[3]If more closely adjacent changes in the criterion had been selected for inclusion in Figure 3, the results would have been somewhat less clear than those shown, particularly for changes in the criterion instituted early in treatment, when within-phase behavioral variability was substantial. On the other hand, selection of adjacent changes in the criterion later

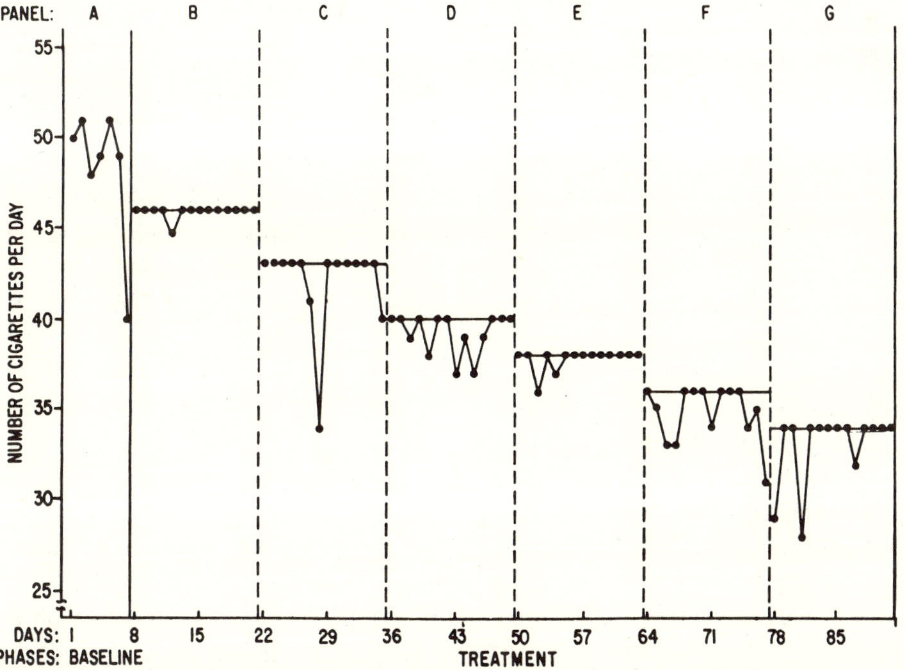

Fig. 2. Data from a smoking reduction program used to illustrate the stepwise criterion change design. Solid horizontal line segments indicate criterion for each treatment phase.

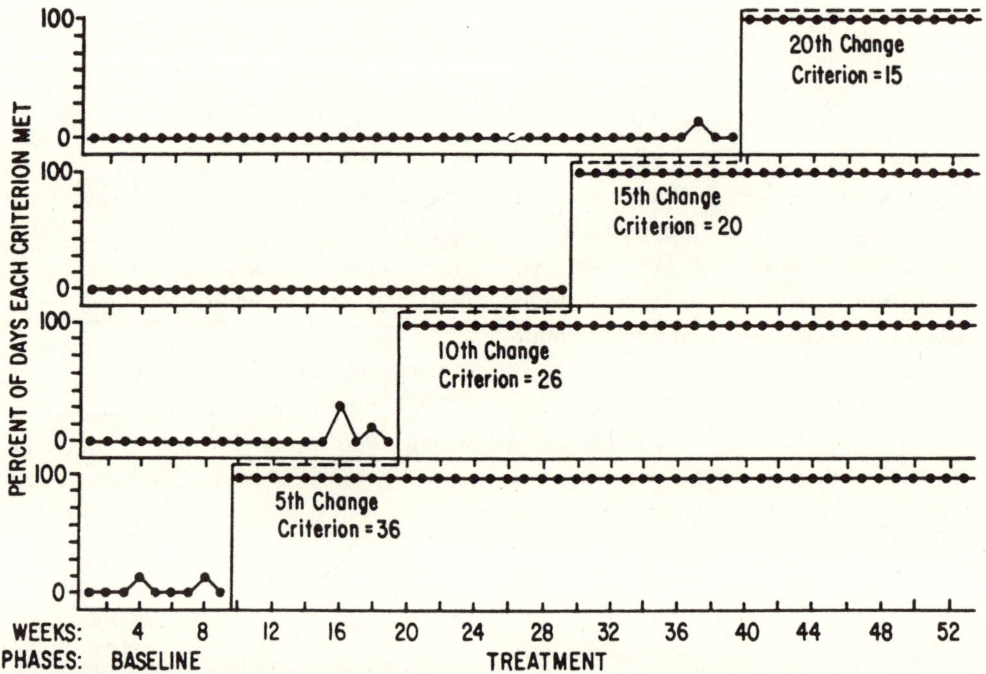

Fig. 3. Regraphing of smoking reduction program data to illustrate multiple-baseline characteristics of the changing criterion design. Note that this figure contains data from more treatment phases than does Figure 2. The data for Weeks 12 and 13 on this figure correspond to the data in Panel G of Figure 2.

ing of changes in rate resembles the pattern and timing of changes in rate expected with the successful application of a multiple-baseline design. Thus, with the changing criterion design, changes in the criterion function like the sequential changes in the behavior, situation, or person to which treatment is applied with traditional variants of the multiple-baseline design.

DISCUSSION

Successful implementation of the changing criterion design requires particular attention to three design factors: length of baseline and treatment phases, magnitude of changes in the criterion, and number of treatment phases or changes in criterion. All phases should be long enough to ensure that successive changes in a therapeutic direction are not naturally occurring due to either historical, maturational, or measurement factors (see Campbell and Stanley, 1963). In addition, treatment phases should differ in length, or if of a constant length, should be preceded by a baseline phase longer than each of the separate treatment phases. This is to ensure that stepwise changes in the rate of the target behavior are not occurring naturally in synchrony with criterion changes. The baseline data should also be stable (*e.g.*, zero slope) or should be changing in a counter-therapeutic direction. While the baseline data shown in Panel A of Figure 1 meet both of these formal design criteria, the baseline data shown in Panel A of Figure 2 unfortunately do not meet either criterion.

The length of each treatment phase and the magnitude and number of criterion changes are interdependent and should vary as a function of the total length of treatment, the variability of the target behavior, and the difference between the baseline and the anticipated terminal rate of the target behavior. Each treatment phase must be long enough to allow the rate of the

in treatment when within-phase variability was virtually zero would have produced even clearer results than those shown in Figure 3.

target behavior to restabilize at a new and changed rate; it is stability after change has been achieved, and before introduction of the next change in the criterion, that is crucial to producing a convincing demonstration of control. Thus, for example, when behavior change is slow, treatment phases must be longer to ensure stability before the criterion is again changed for the next treatment phase. In deciding the length of each treatment phase, clinician-researchers must also remain sensitive to their clients' needs and not hold clients at a criterion longer than would be wise therapeutically.

The magnitude of each stepwise change in the criterion must be large enough to ensure that the changes in the rate of the target behavior are detectable. Thus, the size of changes in the criterion employed will be largely a function of the variability of the rate of the target behavior within each treatment segment. With highly variable responses, larger changes in the criterion (and longer treatment phases) will be required to demonstrate changes in rate. Therapeutic considerations such as the difficulty of changing the rate of the problematic behavior will also determine the magnitude of changes in the criterion employed. With behavior that is difficult to change, the changes in the criterion should be small enough to be achievable, yet large enough to be clearly detectable.

Demonstration of experimental control with the changing criterion design is best shown by a visual display of the close correspondence between behavior rate and changes in the criterion. However, with data characterized by excessive variability or complex trends, a simple visual display may be unconvincing, and statistical procedures may be required. In such cases, correlational analyses (Hall and Fox, *in press*), the analysis of variance (Hartmann, 1974), or time-series analysis (Jones, Vaught, and Weinrott, *in press*) may be applied to the data from a changing criterion design. These techniques should be used with caution, however, as they either are controversial, necessitate conformity to a substantial number of statistical assumptions, or require extensive data (see, for example, Baer (*in press*); Kazdin (1976); Michael, 1974; Thoresen and Elashoff, 1974).

The number of criterion changes included is dependent on the number of replications required for a convincing demonstration of experimental control. Current practice suggests that two replications in a multiple-baseline design may be sufficient when the correspondence between changes in behavior rate and changes in condition are clear. More than two replications may be desirable when the correspondence is less clear; for example, when the rate of the target behavior regularly exceeds the criterion. When the rate of the target behavior fails to track the criteria closely, Hall and Foxx (*in press*) suggest that demonstration of control may be further strengthened by reverting temporarily either to a former criterion (see Panel J of Figure 1), or to baseline conditions (see Deitz and Repp, 1973, Experiment III). Still another technique to fortify a weak or questionable demonstration of control in a design with equal length treatment phases is to leave the criterion at an established level for a longer period than required by ordinary stability considerations (see Panel E of Figure 1).

The logic of the changing criterion design does not require counter-therapeutic behavior change, unlike the reversal design. Nor does the design require multiple independent behaviors, subjects, or situations, unlike standard multiple-baseline designs. Instead, the changing criterion design should be applicable to a wide range of treatment problems that can be modified in a stepwise manner and where reasonably prompt changes to a new, stable level are expected in response to changes in the criterion. Thus, as Hall and Fox (*in press*) suggest, the changing criterion design would be particularly suited to demonstrating the effectiveness of shaping procedures. In general, the changing criterion design should be useful for acceleration problems in which stepwise increases in accuracy, frequency, duration, latency, or magnitude are therapeutic goals; *e.g.*, increases in writing or reading rate, improvements in peer interactions, or better adherence to an exercise routine. Deceleration problems for which stepwise decreases in similar response characteristics are therapeutic goals include reductions in smoking, drinking, or overeating, and latency of compliance with instructions.

In summary, the changing criterion design is capable of providing convincing demonstrations of experimental control, seems applicable to a wide range of problematic behaviors, and should be a useful addition to applied individual-subject methodology.

REFERENCES

Baer, D. M., Wolf, M. M., and Risley, T. R. Some current dimensions of applied behavior analysis. *Journal of Applied Behavior Analysis,* 1968, **1**, 91-97.

Barlow, D. H. and Hersen, M. Single-case experimental designs. *Archives of General Psychiatry,* 1973, **29**, 319-325.

Campbell, D. T. and Stanley, J. C. *Experimental and quasi-experimental designs for research.* Chicago: Rand McNally, 1963.

Dietz, S. M. and Repp, A. C. Decreasing classroom misbehavior through the use of DRL schedules of reinforcement. *Journal of Applied Behavior Analysis,* 1973, **6**, 457-463.

Edgington, E. S. *Statistical inference: The distribution-free approach.* New York: McGraw-Hill, 1969.

Gelfand, D. M. and Hartmann, D. P. Behavior therapy with children: A review and evaluation of research methodology. *Psychological Bulletin,* 1968, **69**, 204-215.

Gelfand, D. M. and Hartmann, D. P. *Child behavior analysis and therapy.* New York: Pergamon Press, 1975.

Gottman, J. M. *N*-of-one and *N*-of-two research in psychotherapy. *Psychological Bulletin,* 1973, **80**, 93-105.

Hall, R. V. *Managing behavior: Behavior modification, the measurement of behavior.* Lawrence, Kansas: H & H Enterprises, 1971.

Hall, R. V., Cristler, C., Cranston, S. S., and Tucker, B. Teachers and parents as researchers using multiple-baseline designs. *Journal of Applied Behavior Analysis,* 1970, **3**, 247-255.

Hall, R. V. and Fox, R. G. Changing criterion designs: An alternative applied behavior analysis procedure. In B. C. Etzel, J. M. LeBlanc, and D. M. Baer (Eds.), *New developments in behavioral research: theory method and application. In honor of Sidney W. Bijou.* Hillsdale, N.J.: Erlbaum, (*in press*).

Hartmann, D. P. Forcing square pegs into round holes: some comments on "An analysis-of-variance model for the intrasubject replication design". *Journal of Applied Behavior Analysis,* 1974, **7**, 635-638.

Jones, R. R. Design and analysis problems in program evaluation. In P. O. Davidson, F. W. Clark, and L. A. Hamerlynck (Eds.), *Evaluation of behavioral programs.* Champaign, Ill.: Research Press, 1974.

Jones, R. R., Vaught, R. S., and Weinrott, M. Time-series analysis in operant research. *Journal of Applied Behavior Analysis,* (*in press*).

Kazdin, A. E. Statistical analyses for single-case experimental designs. In M. Hersen and D. H. Barlow (Eds.), *Single case experimental designs: Strategies for studying behavior change.* Oxford: Pergamon, 1976.

Leitenberg, H. The use of single-case methodology in psychotherapy research. *Journal of Abnormal Psychology,* 1973, **82**, 87-101.

McNamara, J. R. and MacDonough, T. S. Some methodological considerations in the design and implementation of behavior therapy research. *Behavior Therapy,* 1972, **3**, 361-379.

Michael, J. Statistical inference for individual organism research: mixed blessing or curse? *Journal of Applied Behavior Analysis,* 1974, **7**, 647-653.

Sidman, M. *Tactics of scientific research.* New York: Basic Books, 1960.

Thoresen, C. E. and Elashoff, J. D. "An analysis-of-variance model for intrasubject replication design": some additional comments. *Journal of Applied Behavior Analysis,* 1974, **7**, 639-641.

Weis, L. and Hall, R. V. Modification of cigarette smoking through avoidance of punishment. In R. V. Hall (Ed.), *Managing behavior: Behavior modification applications in school and home.* Lawrence, Kansas: H & H Enterprises, 1971.

Wolf, M. M. and Risley, T. R. Reinforcement: Applied research. In R. Glaser (Ed.), *The nature of reinforcement.* New York: Academic Press, 1971.

Received 16 December 1975.
(Final acceptance 22 March 1976.)

JOURNAL OF APPLIED BEHAVIOR ANALYSIS 1978, 11, 189-196 NUMBER 1 (SPRING 1978)

MULTIPLE-PROBE TECHNIQUE: A VARIATION OF THE MULTIPLE BASELINE[1]

R. DON HORNER AND DONALD M. BAER

UNIVERSITY OF KANSAS

Multiple-baseline and probe procedures are combined into a "multiple-probe" technique. The technique is designed to provide a thorough analysis of the relationship between an independent variable and the acquisition of a successive-approximation or chain sequence. It provides answers to the following questions: (1) What is the initial level of performance on each step in the training sequence? (2) What happens if sequential opportunities to perform each next step in the sequence are provided before training on that step? (3) What happens when training is applied? (4) What happens to the performance of remaining steps in the sequence as criterion is reached in the course of training each prior step? The technique features: (1) one initial probe of each step in the training sequence, (2) an additional probe of every step after criterion is reached on any training step, and (3) a series of "true" baseline sessions conducted *just* before the introduction of the independent variable to each training step. Intermittent probes also provide an alternative to continuous baseline measurement, when such measurement during extended multiple baselines (1) may prove reactive, (2) is impractical, and/or (3) a strong *a priori* assumption of stability can be made.

DESCRIPTORS: multiple baseline, multiple-probe technique, experimental design, methodology, chaining, successive approximation, experimental control

---

Multiple-baseline design is a method of establishing the reliability of an environmental intervention in altering behavior (Baer, Wolf, and Risley, 1968; Hersen and Barlow, 1976). It shows the functionality of the intervention by demonstrating that the intervention apparently produces the same kind of behavior change (1) across a variety of behaviors of the same subject within a given setting, or (2) across a variety of settings for the same behavior of a single subject, or (3) across a variety of subjects displaying the same behavior in the same setting, or (4) more controversially, various combinations of these: *e.g.,* across different subjects, each displaying a different behavior in a different setting, all of which nevertheless respond to the common intervention in a similar manner, thereby establishing Sidman's criterion of functional contiguity (1960, pp. 37-40) in a maximally systematic replication (Chapter 4) within a single design.

In essence, this family of designs examines single changes from baseline in each baseline case. Reversals are always possible, of course, and have been recommended by Kazdin and Kopel (1975); but the design then becomes a reversal design as well. The present argument is meant for designs that are only multiple-baseline designs. Without reversals, the reliability of the single changes from baseline, which constitute the multiple-baseline design, is potentiated in that design by allowing each baseline to run for a different number of points before intervening; this potential reliability then is realized if systematic behavior change in fact promptly follows on each intervention into each baseline. In that event, it appears that behavior change not only

[1]The preparation of this article was supported in part by grant OEG-0-74-2766 from the Bureau of Education for the Handicapped. However, the opinions expressed herein do not necessarily reflect the position or policy of the U.S. Office of Education, and no official endorsement should be inferred. The first author wishes to thank Ingo Keilitz, Sebastian Striefel, and Bruce Wetherby for reviewing the original version of this article. Reprints may be obtained from R. Don Horner, Bureau of Child Research, or Donald M. Baer, Department of Human Development, University of Kansas, Lawrence, Kansas 66045.

is correlated with the intervention, but in addition it can be seen that on all other baselines, within which interventions are not occurring at the same time, no similar behavior change is evident. Thus, both sides of the correlation between intervention and behavior change are observed; where intervention is applied, change occurs; where it is not, change does not occur.

Then it will be a grave weakness in any multiple-baseline design if any of the currently unchanging baselines in which interventions are not occurring (while they are occurring in some other baseline) in fact *could not* have changed at that time, intervention or no intervention. For example, consider four multiple baselines representing the addition, subtraction, multiplication, and division skills of an unskilled arithmetic student. Zero scores on the addition, subtraction, and multiplication baselines guarantee zero scores on the division baseline (short of memorization of the problems and answers presented, of course, a possibility that a competent design ought to have avoided)—generalized division ordinarily requires generalized skills of addition, subtraction, and multiplication before it can be learned. Thus, during those parts of a multiple-baseline design displaying zero ability levels in the addition, subtraction, and multiplication baselines, the inevitable zero scores on the division baseline have no real meaning: division could be nothing else than zero (or chance, depending on the test format), and there is no real point in measuring it. Such measures are *pro forma:* they fill out the picture of a multiple baseline, true, but in an illusory way. They do not so much represent zero behavior as zero opportunity for the behavior to occur, and there is no need to document at the level of well-measured data that behavior does not occur when it cannot.

This article offers a compromise between these considerations and the usual format of the multiple-baseline design. A procedure is suggested that provides a method for establishing a thorough analysis of the functional relationship between an independent variable and the acquisition of a sequence of successive approximations, or a chain. In addition, it provides an alternative to continuous measurement during extended multiple baselines. The procedure combines multiple-baseline and probe techniques and will be referred to as a "multiple-probe" technique.

Stolz (1976) pointed out the limitations of using reversal and multiple baseline techniques in applied settings. She suggested that probe procedures be used as an alternative to test the extent that behavior has become independent of treatment contingencies and responsive to natural consequences. Verhave (1966) defined a probe as "a change in conditions at some arbitrary point in an experiment made to evaluate or test for the conditions currently in control" (p. 529). This evaluation or testing function usually is maximized if the probe (1) produces responses that have no sceduled consequences, (2) is scheduled infrequently within other conditions, and (3) is relatively nonreactive.

APPLICATIONS

Application to a Chain or Successive Approximation Sequence

When applied to a chain or successive-approximation sequence, the main features of the multiple-probe technique are: (1) an initial baseline probe session conducted on each of the steps in the training sequence, (2) an additional probe session conducted on every step in the training sequence immediately after criterion is reached on any training step, and (3) a series of so-called *true* baseline sessions conducted just before each introduction of the independent variable—a series that increases by at least one session as each additional step in the sequence is trained.

Figure 1 illustrates the hypothetical application of the multiple-probe technique to the first five steps of a program designed to establish use of crutches by a mentally retarded *spina bifida* child (Horner, 1971). The figure could be continued to illustrate the use of the multiple-probe technique with all 10 steps of the sequence included. Hypothetical data (solid squares) have

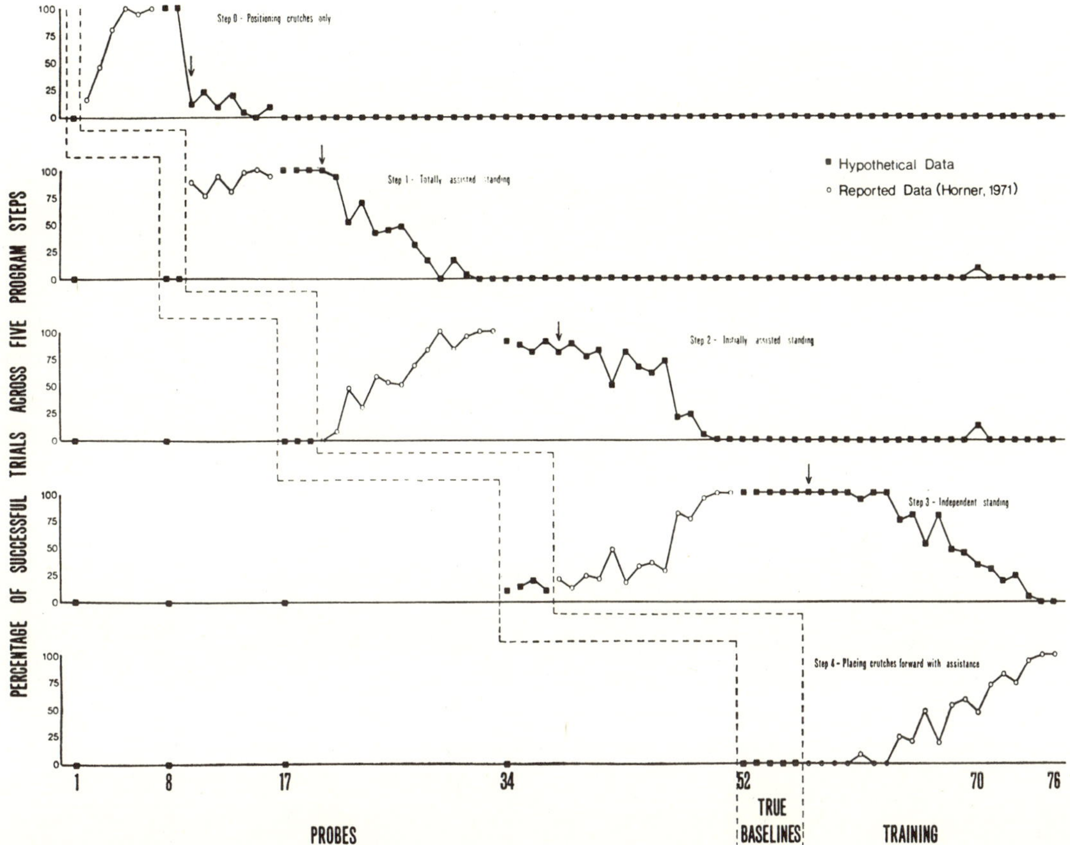

Fig. 1. Percentage of trials conforming to the definition of a correct response across the first five steps of a 10-step successive-approximation procedure designed to establish use of crutches by a mentally retarded *spina bifida* child (Horner, 1971). Hypothetical data (solid squares) have been added to the original data (open circles) to illustrate the multiple-probe technique. The arrow at each step indicates the shift of the reinforcement contingency from one step to the next.

been added to the reported data (open circles) to enhance the illustration. In the original study, there were five baseline sessions on the second step of the procedure to establish use of crutches (an additional step was added after baseline due to the zero rate on the original first step). The effectiveness of training was represented by acquisition data on each of the steps in the procedure.

The original design resembles the changing-criterion design illustrated in the first case study presented by Hartmann and Hall (1976). The design provides a procedure for demonstrating a relationship between an independent variable and a behavior subjected to progressive changes in the performance criterion. It provides data to answer one important question: what happens when training is applied?

The multiple-probe technique, if it had been applied to the use-of-crutches training sequence, would have provided measures to answer the following: (1) What is the initial level of performance on each step in the training sequence? (2) What happens if sequential opportunities to perform each next step in the sequence are provided before initiating training on that step? (3) What happens when training is applied? (4) What happens to performance of the remaining steps in the sequence, as criterion is reached in the course of training each prior step?

Probe procedure. The use of the multiple-probe technique with a chain or successive-approximation sequence requires that a probe procedure be designed to assess performance in each step of the sequence. The probe procedure for the use-of-crutches sequence would consist of sequentially setting the occasion for unassisted walking, assisted walking, unassisted standing, assisted standing, and crutch positioning. Each probe trial would proceed through the probe sequence until success at a specific step in the 10-step sequence is recorded. Since a probe trial should be as nonreactive as possible, careful consideration must be given to arranging the minimum number of trials required to determine stability of performance. One trial at each stage of the probe procedure until a success is scored, is the minimum that could be provided. The hypothetical probe data in Figure 1 are based on 10 trials at each probe session.

Training procedure. If inadequate or no performance occurs on each step in the sequence during the initial probe session, the next X sessions would consist of the application of the independent variable to the first step in the program. This would continue until a predetermined performance criterion is met. At this point, a second probe sequence would be conducted, by again providing the appropriate discriminative stimuli for each step in the sequence. Performance of the first step should reflect any influence of the prior application of the independent variable. Performance in the remaining steps of the sequence should reflect: (1) any generalization or facilitation effects on remaining steps as a result of the application of the independent variable to the first step, (2) the possibility that training of the first step in the sequence is all that is required—if all of the remaining steps are performed without the application of the independent variable, or (3) that criterion performance of the first step in the sequence has little or no effect on the performance of the remaining steps. Next, a baseline session is conducted, using that portion of the probe procedure that sets the occasion for performance of the second training step. This provides two consecutive measures in the second training step, before application of the independent variable to that step. Since performance of the second step in the chain or successive-approximation training sequence is assumed to be impossible or unlikely until the first step has been acquired, these measures provide the only *true* baseline performance of the second step in the sequence. The independent variable then is applied to the second step in the training sequence, to a predetermined performance criterion. At this point, the third probe session is conducted in the same manner as described for the first and second probes. The next two sessions are baseline sessions; they use that portion of the probe sequence designed to set the occasion for the performance of the third training step. These probes provide three consecutive measures of the third training step before application of the independent variable to that step. Since performance of the third training step also is assumed to be impossible or unlikely until the first two steps have been acquired, these three consecutive measures provide the only *true* baseline performance of the third step in the sequence. The next X sessions consist of the application of the independent variable to the third step, *etc.* until the independent variable has been applied to each step in the sequence.

The application of the multiple-probe technique to all the steps of a training sequence at one time might prove impractical. Since the training sequence designed to establish use of crutches has 10 steps, the application of the independent variable to the tenth step would be preceded by 10 consecutive true-baseline sessions. These sessions would be preceded by nine probe sessions. So large a number of baseline sessions could lead to the same difficulties encountered in the use of extended baselines in the multiple-baseline technique. When a training sequence has a large number of steps, it probably is better to break the sequence into several smaller (three- to five-step) sequences and apply the multiple-probe technique to each smaller sequence separately.

Since the data in Figure 1 are hypothetical, the absence of variability in illustrating the application of the training procedure detailed above is intentional. The hypothetical data for Steps 0 through 3 at Session 70 have introduced variability, in an attempt to illustrate how such performance would be graphed. The original data on Step 4 at this point reveal that the child independently attained a standing position and placed the crutches forward with assistance on 12 of the 25 trials (48% on Step 4). The hypothetical data at Steps 1, 2, and 3 indicate that the child progressed to independent standing on eight trials (32% on Step 3), required initial assistance in standing on three trials (12% on Step 2), and required total assistance in standing on two trials (8% on Step 1). The hypothetical data at Step 0 at this point indicate that the child did not "position crutches only" on any of the trials (0% on Step 0).

If all the data presented for the first five steps had been based on actual experimentation, the answers to the questions the multiple-probe technique is designed to answer would be as follows: (1) the initial performance on each of the first five steps in the training sequence was at a zero level, (2) sequential opportunities to perform the next step in the sequence before initiating training on that step had no effect, except that (3) the performance on Step 3 was slightly above prior performance during probe sessions, indicating some small generalization or facilitation effect, as criterion performance was attained on Step 2. Probes of performance on remaining steps (as criterion was reached on Steps 0, 1, and 3) showed no change. The data indicate that the independent variable has a reinforcing effect on these behaviors. Performance showed little or no change from probe and true-baseline levels until the independent variable was applied sequentially to each step in the sequence.

Application as an Alternative to Continuous Baseline Measurement

The multiple-probe technique also can be used to replace the continuous baseline measurement of the traditional multiple-baseline technique in those instances when measurement during extended baselines (1) may prove reactive, (2) is impractical, and/or (3) a strong *a priori* assumption of stability can be made. This type of application has been reported in the literature.

Probe procedures during baseline have been used to determine whether training certain members of a behavior class affects other (untrained) members of the same class. For example, Schumaker and Sherman (1970) used multiple baselines of probe sessions to determine when sequential training of verbs in present- and past-tense forms generalized to the production of these tenses with untrained verbs. The probe sessions followed each training session in which a criterion was met. Garcia, Baer, and Firestone (1971) used a multiple-baseline technique to introduce sequential training of imitative small-motor, large-motor, and short-vocal responses. As criterion performance on each pair of trained responses was met, a probe measured unreinforced generalization to untrained small-motor, large-motor, short-vocal, and long-vocal responses.

Probe sessions also have been used as a baseline from which to determine (later) the effects of an independent variable. Baer and Guess (1971), in a language-training program, used probes to detect any generalization of training to respond to specific comparative and superlative adjectives. Probes of superlative relationships during comparative training served as a baseline in which to determine the effects of later superlative training. Striefel and Wetherby (1973) established multiple baselines of probes across responses to different verbal instructions, to evaluate the effects of later sequential training to follow specific verbal instructions. A similar baseline was established by Striefel, Bryan, and Aikins (1974) to evaluate the effects of a stimulus-control transfer procedure. Although these applications were across behaviors, the use of intermittent probes to replace continuous baselines also could be used across individuals and settings.

Reactive baselines. The utility of the continuous baselines of the traditional multiple-baseline technique is limited when the occasion for performance of the behavior is controlled by the experimenter and may prove reactive. The absence of the antecedent or consequent events that will be used later to develop these behaviors can result in extinction or worse, especially of those behaviors that have the longest baselines. This may confound or mask the effects of the independent variable. In such cases, the independent variable must have sufficient power not only to develop behavior, but also to overcome any extinction, boredom, fatigue, or other effects introduced through the use of extended baselines. For example, in the study by Panyan, Boozer, and Morris (1970), baselines of the application of operant techniques by the staff of several institutional living units showed a dramatic drop in the percentage of training sessions conducted, as the baselines progressed. During treatment, the feedback procedure was in effect several weeks before the percentage of training sessions conducted recovered the levels of the first few weeks of baseline. In addition, the living unit with the longest baseline also required the longest time before application of the independent variable demonstrated an effect. This is not a criticism of the Panyan *et al.* study, as remediation of extinction effects was the variable under study. It serves as a possible example of the additional power required to overcome long-baseline effects. Horner and Keilitz (1975) reported an increase in irrelevant and competing behaviors, in the subject with the longest baseline, during baseline measures when the occasion for toothbrushing was set by the experimenters and otherwise did not occur. During baseline, the mentally retarded subjects engaged in such behaviors as eating toothpaste, playing in water, and spitting toothpaste foam on the mirror. These behaviors were performed increasingly by the subject with the longest baseline, as the baseline progressed. Thus, the independent variable had to have sufficient power to develop the steps in the toothbrushing program *and* decelerate irrelevant and competing behaviors as well. When the dependent variable is affected, despite a deteriorating

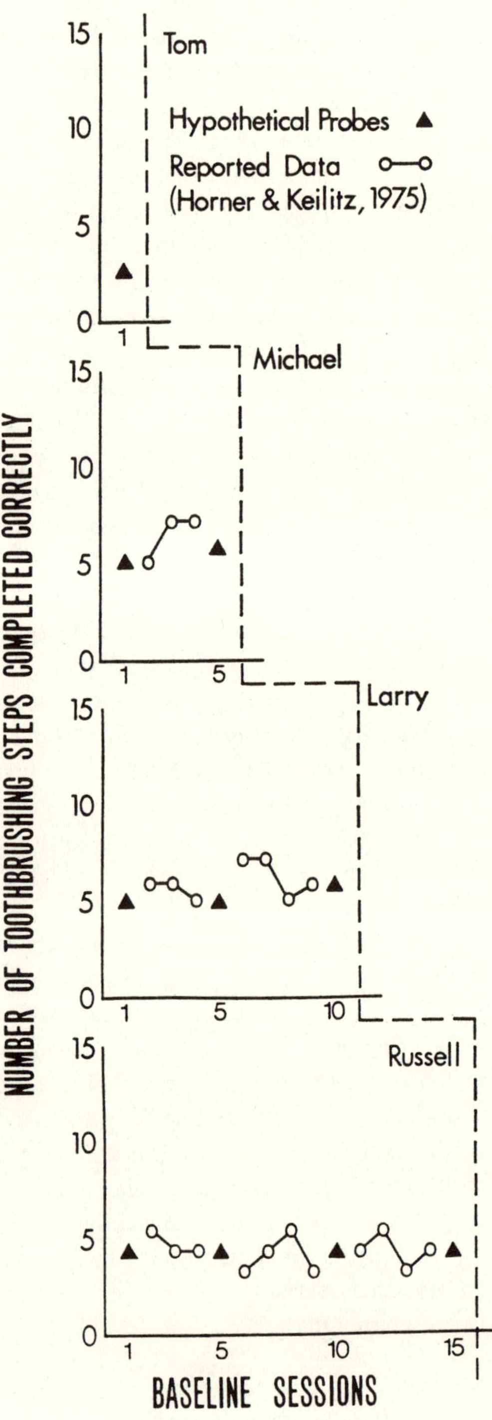

Fig. 2. Number of toothbrushing steps conforming to the definition of a correct response across four subjects. Hypothetical probe data (solid triangles) have replaced part of the original data (open circles) to illustrate the use of probes as an alternative to continuous baseline measurement.

baseline or increases in competing behaviors, it provides additional evidence of the effectiveness of the independent variable. However, if effects fail to occur under such conditions, an ambiguous situation is produced: it is not clear whether a totally inadequate treatment variable, or too adverse a baseline condition is responsible for the failure to produce a change.

Figure 2 illustrates the hypothetical use of the multiple-probe technique to establish a baseline of the number of toothbrushing steps completed correctly across four subjects (Horner and Keilitz, 1975). The hypothetical probe data (solid triangles) have replaced the original data points at Sessions 1, 5, 10, and 15. These data are separated from the reported data (open circles) to enhance the illustration. The original data represented by the open circles would not have been collected had the multiple-probe technique been used. The multiple-baseline technique provided 1, 5, 10, and 15 sessions of continuous baselines across the four subjects. The multiple-probe technique, with probes every five days, would have provided one, two, three, and five probe sessions to establish baselines across the four subjects. The multiple-probe technique probably could have provided a stable baseline with five or fewer probe sessions for the subject who had 15 days of continuous baseline in the original study. The use of the multiple-probe procedure might have precluded the increase in irrelevant and competing behaviors by this subject, because such behavior began to increase after the tenth baseline session.

Practical baselines. Bijou, Peterson, Harris, Allen, and Johnston (1969) suggested the possibility of baselines based on intermittent observations, so that limited observer time can be used more efficiently to collect data on a larger number of subjects or across a larger number of settings. These authors also provided data indicating observations of a child's frequency of verbalization to other children collected every second day differed by an average of only 3% from daily observations. Observations every third day differed by an average of only 2% from daily observations.

Stable baselines. When baselines are required for behaviors that typically improve only with training, a strong *a priori* assumption of stability as a function of time often can be made. It then becomes the task of the researcher to determine how frequently intermittent estimates of that stability will have to be provided, for the assumption of stability over time to be accepted by the research consumer.

DISCUSSION

The multiple-probe technique has an obvious limitation. The occasions for performing behaviors not yet subjected to the independent variable are less than those in the classical multiple-baseline technique. If a measure of the effects of continuous performance before introduction of an independent variable is required, the multiple-probe technique is not appropriate. When multiple probes are used as an alternative to continuous measurement, the only opportunities for performing a behavior before introduction of the independent variable are during the probe sessions. When the multiple-probe technique is applied to a chain or successive-approximation sequence, the only opportunities for performing a step before introduction of the independent variable are during the probe and true-baseline sessions. As stated above, experimenter-controlled opportunities for performance in the absence of instruction or reinforcing consequences can set the occasion for extinction. If extinction or possible punishing effects are undesirable, then the multiple-probe technique reduces the opportunity for such effects to occur. The multiple-probe technique also avoids the collection of a continuous series of ritualistic, *pro forma* zero baseline points when performance of any component of a chain of behaviors or a successive-approximation sequence is impossible or very unlikely before acquisition of its preceding component.

An additional limitation is one that also applies to the multiple-baseline design. Following the logic of Kazdin and Kopel (1975), if introduction of the independent variable to a component of a chain or successive approximation sequence results in an increase in not only that step but in the remaining untreated steps as well, interpretation is difficult. It could be due to the generalization or facilitation effects of the independent variable, or to the effects of extraneous variables. However, a different baseline exists for each step in the sequence, and each baseline represents either an additional increment in the approximation sequence or an additional behavior in the chain. In addition, a reversal could be employed to rule out extraneous effects. Thus, the recommendations for minimizing ambiguous results in the use of the multiple-baseline technique (Kazdin and Kopel, 1975) also can be applied to the multiple-probe technique.

In summary, the multiple-probe technique provides a procedure for collecting data that will permit a thorough functional analysis of the variables related to the acquisition of behavior across the components of a chain or successive-approximation sequence. In addition, intermittent probes provide an alternative method for establishing stable baselines when continuous measurement during extended multiple baselines proves impractical, unnecessary, or reactive.

REFERENCES

Baer, D. M. and Guess, D. Receptive training of adjectival inflections in mental retardates. *Journal of Applied Behavior Analysis,* 1971, **4**, 129-139.

Baer, D. M., Wolf, M. M., and Risley, T. R. Some current dimensions of applied behavior analysis. *Journal of Applied Behavior Analysis,* 1968, **1**, 91-97.

Bijou, S. W., Peterson, R. F., Harris, F. R., Allen, K. E., and Johnston, M. S. Methodology for experimental studies of young children in natural settings. *The Psychological Record,* 1969, **19**, 177-210.

Garcia, E., Baer, D. M., and Firestone, I. The development of generalized imitation within topographically determined boundaries. *Journal of Applied Behavior Analysis,* 1971, **4**, 101-112.

Hartmann, D. P. and Hall, R. V. The changing criterion design. *Journal of Applied Behavior Analysis,* 1976, **9**, 527-532.

Hersen, M. and Barlow, D. H. *Single case experimental designs: Strategies for studying behavior change.* New York: Pergamon Press, 1976.

Horner, R. D. Establishing use of crutches by a mentally retarded *spina bifida* child. *Journal of Applied Behavior Analysis,* 1971, **4**, 183-189.

Horner, R. D. and Keilitz, I. Training mentally retarded adolescents to brush their teeth. *Journal of Applied Behavior Analysis,* 1975, **8**, 301-309.

Kazdin, A. E. and Kopel, S. A. On resolving ambiguities in the multiple-baseline design: Problems and recommendations. *Behavior Therapy,* 1975, **6**, 601-608.

Panyan, M., Boozer, H., and Morris, N. Feedback to attendants as a reinforcer for applying operant techniques. *Journal of Applied Behavior Analysis,* 1970, **3**, 1-4.

Schumaker, J. and Sherman, J. A. Training generative verb usage by imitation and reinforcement procedures. *Journal of Applied Behavior Analysis,* 1970, **3**, 273-287.

Sidman, M. *Tactics of scientific research.* New York: Basic Books, 1960.

Stolz, S. B. Evaluation of therapeutic efficacy of behavior modification in a community setting. *Behaviour Research and Therapy,* 1976, **14**, 479-481.

Striefel, S. and Wetherby, B. Instruction-following behavior of a retarded child and its controlling stimuli. *Journal of Applied Behavior Analysis,* 1973, **6**, 663-670.

Striefel, S., Bryan, K. S., and Aikins, D. A. Transfer of stimulus control from motor to verbal stimuli. *Journal of Applied Behavior Analysis,* 1974, **7**, 123-135.

Verhave, T. *The experimental analysis of behavior.* New York: Appleton-Century-Crofts, 1966.

Received 7 January 1977.
(Final Acceptance 9 September 1977.)

JOURNAL OF APPLIED BEHAVIOR ANALYSIS 1979, **12**, 199-210 NUMBER 2 (SUMMER 1979)

ALTERNATING TREATMENTS DESIGN: ONE STRATEGY FOR COMPARING THE EFFECTS OF TWO TREATMENTS IN A SINGLE SUBJECT

DAVID H. BARLOW AND STEVEN C. HAYES

STATE UNIVERSITY OF NEW YORK AT ALBANY AND
UNIVERSITY OF NORTH CAROLINA AT GREENSBORO

A little used and often confused design, capable of comparing two treatments within a single subject, has been termed, variously, a multielement baseline design, a multiple schedule design, and a randomization design. The background of these terms is reviewed, and a new, more descriptive term, Alternating Treatments Design, is proposed. Critical differences between this design and a Simultaneous Treatment Design are outlined, and experimental questions answerable by each design are noted. Potential problems with multiple treatment interference in this procedure are divided into sequential confounding, carryover effects, and alternation effects and the importance of these issues vis-a-vis other single-case experimental designs is considered. Methods of minimizing multiple treatment interference as well as methods of studying these effects are outlined. Finally, appropriate uses of Alternating Treatments Designs are described and discussed in the context of recent examples.

DESCRIPTORS: Single-subject design, methodology, comparison of two treatments

---

To compare the effects of two or more treatments in applied research, each treatment is usually administered to a different group of subjects and differences are noted. Because considerable intersubject variability exists in each group (some subjects change and some do not), inferential statistics are often necessary to determine if an effect exists. This leads to problems in generalizing results from the group average to the individual subject or patient who should benefit from the research (Hersen & Barlow, 1976; Sidman, 1960). To avoid intersubject variability, an ideal solution would be to divide one subject in two and apply two different treatments simultaneously to each identical individual. This would eliminate intersubject variability and allow effects, if any, to be directly observed. Statements about other individuals could then be made through the usual process of replication and "logical generalization" (Edgington, 1966; Hersen & Barlow, 1976).

Such a procedure exists in the family of single-case experimental designs although it has been little used and often confused. It has been termed variously a *multiple schedule design* (Barlow & Hersen, 1973; Hersen & Barlow, 1976; Leitenberg, 1973), a *multielement baseline design* (Sidman, 1960; Ulman & Sulzer-Azaroff, Note 1), and a *randomization design* (Edgington, 1967). In addition, Kazdin and Hartmann (in press) use the term *Simultaneous Treatment Design* (see below). These terms were originated for somewhat different reasons, reflecting the multiple historical origins of single case research (Hersen & Barlow, 1976). Several proponents of the term *multiple schedule* (see Hersen & Barlow, 1976); Leitenberg, 1973) were associated in Vermont in the 1960s in an effort to apply operant procedures and methods to clinical problems (e.g., Agras, Leitenberg, Barlow, & Thomson, 1969). These procedures and terminology were derived directly from operant laboratories; but the term *multiple schedule* implies a distinct schedule associated with each stimulus

---

Reprint requests should be sent to David H. Barlow, Psychology Department, State University of New York, Albany, New York 12222. We would like to thank Harold Leitenberg, Mike Zeiler, and Warren Steinman for comments on an earlier draft of this manuscript.

component, and this may not always obtain in applied research, resulting in an unnecessary narrowness in the term. Ulman and Sulzer-Azaroff (1975) use Sidman's term *multielement baseline design* to describe a procedure in which different conditions or "treatments" are associated with different stimuli to establish experimental control. In fact, multielement baselines as conceived by Sidman (1960) have little parallel in applied research since the purpose is to "investigate relations between some single experimental operation and more than one behavioral baseline" (p. 326). Of more direct relevance is Sidman's term *multielement manipulation* in which the purpose is to study "the interaction between a single behavioral baseline and several qualitatively or quantitatively different experimental operations" (p. 323); in other words, a comparison of the effects of two or more treatments on one behavior. As in much basic research, however, Sidman's examples illustrate high-rate behavior brought to a point of stability before introduction of experimental operation or "treatments." Applied research, on the other hand, is more often concerned with low-rate behaviors which are unstable.

Edgington (1967, 1972), from a position outside of operant psychology, originated the term *randomization design* to describe his variation of a time series approach amenable to statistical analysis. The design differs slightly from traditional operant application in that treatments are deliberately randomized across times of application: for example, ABBABAA rather than ABAB. Treatments are repeated often enough to allow statistical comparison of A and B phases (continuing a tradition begun by R. A. Fisher (0000) who explored the abilities of a lady to discriminate tea prepared in two different ways). This frequent repetition of treatments usually requires fast alternation to obtain the necessary number of random observations, and the almost unavoidable discriminability of each condition in applied research with human (e.g., McCullough, Cornell, McDaniel, & Mueller, 1974) makes this approach procedurally similar to the two approaches described above.

The basic feature of this design, under its various names, is the fast alternation of two different treatments or conditions, each associated with a distinct and discriminative stimulus. As Leitenberg (1973) points out, this design "is based on discrimination learning principles; that is, if the same behavior is treated differently in the presence of different physical or social stimuli, it will exhibit different characteristics in the presence of these stimuli" (p. 93). Thus in the typical design, after a baseline period, two treatments (A and B) are administered, alternating with each other, and the effects on one behavior are observed. For example, A may be administered in the morning and B in the afternoon, preceded by instructions such as, "This is treatment A" and "This is treatment B." Conditions which might affect data other than treatments are counterbalanced as the experiment continues, such as time of day, therapist administering the treatment, or location of the treatment. For example, B might be given in the morning one day and the afternoon the next. The data are plotted separately for each intervention to provide a ready visual representation of the effects of each treatment. Because confounding factors such as time of administration have been neutralized (presumably) by counterbalancing, and because the two treatments are readily discriminable by subjects through instructions or other discriminative stimuli, differences in the individual plots of behavior change corresponding with each treatment should be attributable to the treatment itself, allowing a direct comparison between two (or more) treatments. [Also see Kazdin and Hartmann (in press) for a discussion of the logic of this design.]

For example, McCullough et al. (1974) described treatment of disruptive behavior in a 6-year-old boy. Following a 5-day baseline period in which cooperative behavior was measured, two treatments were introduced for a total of 4 days: (a) social reinforcement for coopera-

A CASE STUDY

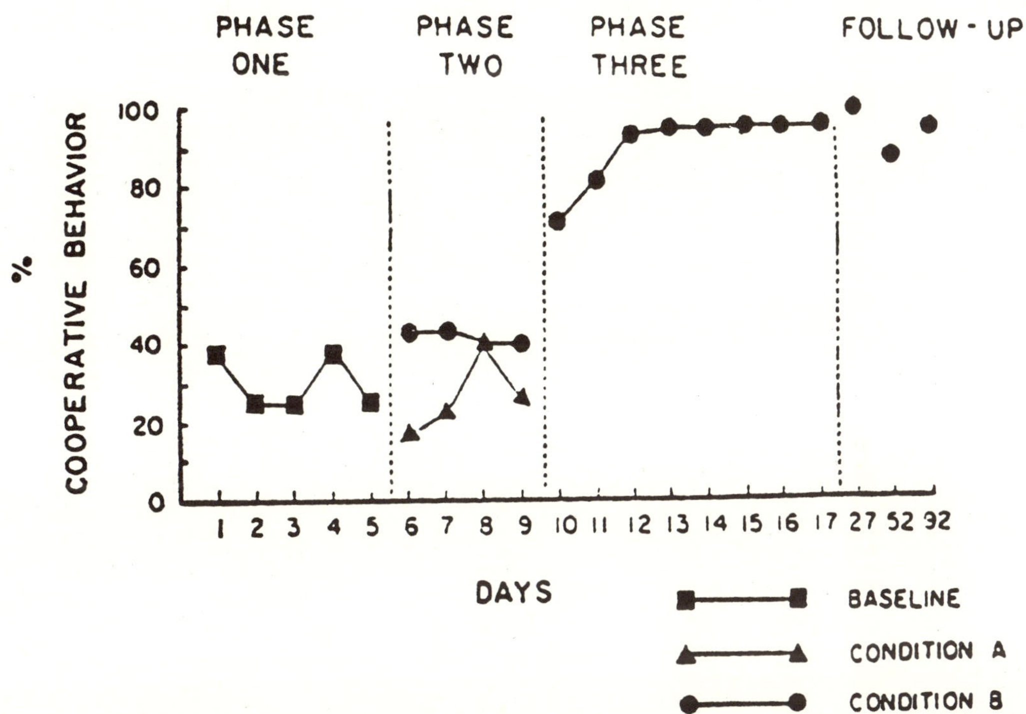

Fig. 1. Percentage of observation periods in which Cedric emitted cooperative behavior. (Reprinted from McCullough, J. P., Cornell, J. E., McDaniel, H. H., & Mueller, R. K. Utilization of the simultaneous treatment design to improve student behavior in a first-grade classroom. *Journal of Consulting and Clinical Psychology*, 1974, **42**, 288-292. Copyright 1974 by the American Psychological Association. Reprinted by permission.)

tive behavior and ignoring uncooperative behavior (labeled Treatment A), and (b) social reinforcement for cooperative behavior plus time out for uncooperative behavior, in this case removal from the classroom for 2 minutes (labeled Treatment B). A teacher (T-1) and a teacher's aide (T-2) administered the treatments with the teacher administering Treatment A the first 2 days and Treatment B the last 2 days. For purposes of this discussion, it is most important to note that a treatment was administered during both a morning session (9:00 to 11:00 a.m.) and an afternoon session (12:00 noon to 2:00 p.m.) and that treatments were *alternated* during the day so that one treatment was offered in the morning and the other in the afternoon. Across all 4 days the time of administration of a particular treatment (a.m. or p.m.) was counterbalanced. The effect of the two treatments are presented in Figure One. Treatment B increased cooperative behavior more than Treatment B in Phase 1 and therefore was continued in Phase 3.

Because none of the names mentioned above, specifically multiple schedule, multielement baseline (or more accurately multielement manipulation), and randomization design is either wholly accurate or totally suited to describe the various conditions that obtain in applied research, a new name for the design is proposed. *Alternating Treatments Design*[1] has the advan-

[1]Ulman and Sulzer-Azaroff (1975) suggested a similar name, "alternating conditions," as a possibly more descriptive substitute for multielement baseline. "Treatments" seems preferable, however, because of

tages of avoiding the inaccuracies associated with the above mentioned terms and, at the same time, describing the essential feature of this design, the fast alternation of two or more treatments in a single subject.

ALTERNATING TREATMENTS AND SIMULTANEOUS TREATMENT DESIGNS

A source of some confusion has been the similarities and differences between the Alternating Treatments Design (ATD) and its various names described above and the Simultaneous Treatment Design (STD). The STD has also been termed the concurrent schedule design in Hersen and Barlow (1976). Concurrent schedule design had the same historical origin as the term multiple schedule design described above (Barlow & Hersen, 1973; Leitenberg, 1973), but the implication that a distinct schedule of reinforcement is attached to each treatment produces the same unnecessary narrowness as in the term multiple schedule design. Browning's (1967) term, simultaneous treatment design, seems more descriptive and suitable. Nevertheless, both terms adequately describe the fundamental characteristics of this design, the concurrent or simultaneous application of two or more treatments in a single case. This contrasts with the fast alternation of two or more treatments in the ATD. Hersen and Barlow (1976) noted that only one example of the use of an STD exists in applied research, the original Browning (1967) experiment, also described in Browning and Stover (1971). This is still true.

In this experiment, as in a true concurrent schedule, the subject is able to choose the preferred schedule or treatment since those treatments were simultaneously present. But it is unlikely that the subject will be equally exposed to each treatment. In fact, the very structure of concurrent schedule ensures that the subject will not be equally exposed to all treatments because a choice is forced (except in the unlikely event that both treatments are equally preferred). The data from Browning's subject indicate a "preference" for the treatment "verbal admonishment" as indicated by frequency and duration of bragging and a decided lack of preference for ignoring. There may be instances, however, when preference for a treatment may have little relation to its effectiveness. This point will be discussed later.

Contrast this with the McCullough et al. (1974) experiment which was termed an STD by the authors and also by Kazdin and Hartmann (in press). These two experiments have much in common. Both successfully compared the effects of two or more treatments in a single case. Both used therapists as discriminative stimuli for the treatments, and, therefore, both had to counterbalance therapists to control for the effects of an individual therapist. Because it is essential that discriminations be formed, it is remarkable that each teacher was associated with a given treatment for only 2 days in McCullough et al. (1974). As each "session" lasted 2 hours, the behavior and subsequent treatment application were evidently occurring at a high rate, allowing this discrimination to occur. Both experiments also employed a Latin square statistical analysis suitable for use with a single subject (Benjamin, 1965).

But one procedure was a simultaneous treatment design with choice or preference for treatments as the method of comparing results and the other was an alternating treatment design in which the subject experienced each of the rapidly alternating treatments for an equal amount of time with the effects on behavior noted. The ATD, of course, requires a further counterbalancing of times of administration and this was evident in the McCullough et al. (1974) experiment.

its parallel in the well-accepted term "simultaneous treatment design" and the tradition of utilizing treatment to refer to a distinct, independent variable in both applied and basic research. Warren Steinman has suggested substituting "intervention" for "treatment" to avoid an overly medical or clinical connotation, but given the parallels and traditions noted above, "treatment" probably communicates more information.

This is a major procedural difference, with implications for the types of experimental questions answerable with each design as well as the nature of the data used in comparing two treatments. Thus, it would seem important to make this distinction in the case of some recent excellent examples of ATDs which have been termed STDs (e.g., Kazdin, 1977: Kazdin & Geesey, 1977). For example, it is difficult to conceive how the McCullough et al. (1974) experiment could have been administered using an STD. For this to occur, both the teacher and teacher's aide would have to be present in the classroom administering different treatments simultaneously. Furthermore, the subject would have to approach one or the other in a free operant fashion for the treatment to be administered—an unwieldy procedure at best. After the discrimination was made, the subject might continue the disruptive behavior by approaching only the therapist administering Treatment A. One would have to infer, then, that Treatment B was more effective although very few trials with Treatment B might occur because preference is being measured rather than effects on a given behavior. Of course, one can conceive of many instances where preference among several treatments would be a significant applied question.

MULTIPLE TREATMENT INTERFERENCE

Multiple treatment interference (Campbell & Stanley, 1963) or condition change interactions (Ulman & Sulzer-Azaroff, 1975) pose the question: Will the results of Treatment A in an ATD where it is juxtaposed with Treatment B be the same as when Treatment A is applied in isolation? In other words, will the results of Treatment A be generalizable from the contrived experimental situation to the natural situation. This is no small issue, since the external validity or generalizability of the result is a major portion of any experimental inquiry. It is understandable that this issue should arise in relation to an experimental design that features fast alternation of treatments or conditions as this is more unlike the real situation than the first (treatment) phase of a withdrawal design or treatment in the experimental group in a between-group comparison design. This issue must be put in perspective.

Few would question the internal validity of the ATD or the ability of the design to rule out rival hypotheses. In fact, the testing of two treatments in the same subject within the same time period produces one of the most elegant controls for most threats to internal validity. But critics who become overly concerned about external validity have, in Campbell and Stanley's (1963) view, evidenced "a recurrent reluctance to accept Hume's truism that induction or generalization is never fully justified logically" (p. 17). Because few applied behavioral researchers derive random samples, inference of results from a group to a population of individuals is not possible (Hersen & Barlow, 1976). Technically an experiment, although internally valid, is generalizable only to subjects with exactly the same set of characteristics, during the same time of day, under the same weather conditions and star constellations. Because this would get us nowhere, we often guess which factors will affect generalizability and which will not in a given experiment and proceed accordingly (Campbell & Stanley, 1963; Edgington, 1969). Perhaps we decide, based on some previous experience, that IQ will be a factor in generalizability, but star configuration will not. We would then replicate the experiment on subjects with different IQs. Campbell and Stanley (1963) note that although we should strive for as much representativeness of the natural environment as is possible while maintaining strong internal validity "we should keep in mind that the 'successful' sciences such as physics and chemistry made their strides without any attention to representativeness (but with great concern for repeatability by independent researchers)" (p. 18).

Thus, in any science, external validity takes a (temporary) back seat to internal validity, but this is particularly true with the ATD, because internal validity is so powerful and replication on additional individuals rather than statistical inference from groups to populations is the primary means of establishing external validity in our science of applied behavior analysis. Furthermore, a close look suggests that multiple treatment interference may be no more of a problem for this design than for some other designs, and may, in some instances, be less.

The "messy" area of applied research is fraught with multiple treatment interference. Unlike the splendid isolation of animal laboratories where rats are returned to their cages for 23 hours to await the next session, the children and adults who are the subjects of applied research are experiencing a variety of events before and between treatments. One subject may have recently lost a family member, another flunked an exam, a third had sexual intercourse, and a fourth was mugged on the way to a session. It is possible that these subjects responded differently to treatment than otherwise would have been the case, and these historical factors account for some of the enormous intersubject variability in between-group designs comparing two treatments. ATDs, on the other hand, attempt to control for this experience by dividing each subject in two and administering two or more treatments within the same period of time. As with all applied research, the results may be affected by interaction with events occurring in the environment which form a background (baseline) for the experiment, and the fact that single case experiments are replicable at all in view of this "multiple treatment interference" may be surprising. But, *within a single case,* ATDs handle outside interference more effectively than, say, withdrawal designs but, at the same time, introduce the issue of one *experimental* treatment interfering with another.

Ulman and Sulzer-Azaroff (1975), in an excellent discussion, divide the problem of a multiple treatment interference into sequential confounding and carryover effects. To this we would add alternation effects. Sequential confounding, of course, is the major reason why it is not possible to compare two treatments in a standard A-B-A design, or one of its variations. Because the B treatment follows the A treatment, its effects are confounded by the prior administration of A. For example, if a teacher institutes praise in a classroom and then add rules, one could say something about the effect of praise but nothing about rules except as it follows praise. To compare rules and praise in a straight A-B-A design, one would have to counterbalance the order of administration in a second subject (with several additional direct replications) using an interaction design strategy (Hersen & Barlow, 1976) to look at the separate and combined effects of each variable or treatment.[2] Later phases in the A-B-A design and its variations exist solely for purposes of internal validity. External validity must come from the first treatment phase, due to problems with sequential confounding. In an ATD, however, the effects of sequence are controlled by counterbalancing (e.g., ABBAAB). This is made possible by rapid alternation, which allows more administrations of A and B in a shorter period of time than is possible with the standard A-B-A design where phases may last days or weeks. This counterbalancing also allows statistical analysis of ATDs for those who so desire. Edgington's (1967) randomization procedure or Benjamin's (1965) special Latin square analysis (e.g., McCullough et al., 1974) have been used.

Carryover effects (or contextual effects), on the other hand, refer to the influence of one treatment on an adjacent treatment, irrespective of overall sequencing. These effects may be di-

[2]The corollary to this approach in applied group comparison research is the within subject design (e.g., Cochran & Cox, 1957), also termed a crossover or randomized block design (Edwards, 1968) among other names. In this design, the order of administration of two (or more) treatments is counterbalanced in additional groups of subjects. Overall response to treatments across the two (or more) groups is then determined and compared statistically since the counterbalancing and subsequent statistical analysis is seen as handling sequential confounding. However, the approach ignores carryover effects, which are then averaged into the group differences.

vided into contrast and induction (Reynolds, 1968; Ulman & Sulzer-Azaroff, 1975). Contrast refers to changes in behavior in a direction opposite to that expected due to a contrast with another treatment. For example, Azrin and Holz (1966) point out that comparing different magnitudes of punishment could make the lesser magnitude actually reinforcing. This is illustrated in a sequentially confounded experiment comparing 30-min versus 15-min versus 1-min time-out periods on children's disruptive behavior (White, Nielsen, & Johnson, 1972). If a 1-min time-out period was implemented first in the sequence, disruptive behavior in children was reduced; but if it followed a longer time out period in the experimental sequence, disruptive behavior actually rose above baseline, presumably due to the contrast with the much longer periods of time out which retained their suppressive effects.

Induction refers to a positive transfer between treatments with the behavior during one treatment more closely approximating the behavior during a second treatment than would occur if the treatments were applied individually. For example, if the 1-min time-out period noted above produced greater suppression following a 15-min time-out period than it did coming first in sequence, this would be induction. This phenomena emerge from basic research on components in a multiple schedule and reviews (Dunham, 1968; Freeman, 1971) suggest that the effects, although reliable, are small (Ulman & Sulzer-Azaroff, 1975).

Carryover effects in humans within the context of a multiple schedule are most often transient as treatments are relatively widely spaced, but Waite and Osborne (1972) demonstrated sustained contrast in children in a mult VI 20-sec EXT with 2-min schedule components. Nevertheless, Ulman and Sulzer-Azaroff (1975) and Sidman (1960) suggest several methods for minimizing or eliminating contrast or induction.

First, counterbalancing the order of treatments, as is necessary to control for sequential confounding so that treatments will follow one another in an unpredictable fashion, should minimize carryover effects. For example, in the White et al. (1972) experiment mentioned above, each of three time-out periods was administered to three different groups of children. In the group receiving the 1-min treatment initially, disruptive behavior was suppressed. However, 1-min time-out periods were not suppressive and perhaps even facilitative if they followed the 30-min time-out period. But each time-out period took 2 weeks with 2-week baselines interspersed. Shorter, more numerous, and unpredictable periods of treatment still separated by a reasonable period of time such as several hours (e.g., McCullough et al., 1974) might produce less contrast, particularly since O'Brien (1968) demonstrated that relatively brief periods of treatment minimize contrast effects.

Second, Powell and Hake (1971) minimized carryover effects in a study comparing two reinforcement conditions by presenting only one condition per session, a situation that usually obtains in applied research (e.g., McCullough et al., 1974; Agras et al., 1969). It is interesting to note that similar procedures have been suggested to minimize carryover effects in the traditional within-subjects group approach (Greenwald, 1976).

Finally, a third issue in studying carryover effects is the speed of alternation of treatment. For example, multiple-schedule work in basic research when carryover effects have been studied usually alternates schedules by the minute rather than once or twice a day as is now typical in applied research. This seems to heighten carryover effects, particularly contrast, as noted above (Powell & Hake, 1971; Waite & Osborne, 1972). But alternation must be frequent enough to allow a discrimination to be formed. The appropriate speed of alternation which allows discrimination learning but minimizes carryover effects in an experimental question will probably depend on the particular question asked.

With these steps and in view of the nature of applied research, including the ability of humans to discriminate quickly and efficiently, it would seem that carryover effects should not be a stumbling block to the external validity of an experiment. But, as Ulman and Sulzer-Azaroff (1975) note, "In the absence of a systematic investigation, however, such interaction remains unspecified, and any generalization based on this design should be qualified accordingly" (p. 389).

Fortunately, it is possible to assess directly the extent to which such effects are present. Sidman (1960) suggests two methods. One is termed *independent verification,* which essentially entails conducting a control experiment in which one or the other of the component treatments in the ATD are administered independently. For example, two treatments might be compared through an ATD in a direct replication across three subjects. Three more subjects might then receive baseline, followed by Treatment A, in an A-B fashion. The second treatment could be administered to a third trio of subjects in the same manner. Any differences that occur between the treatment administered in an ATD or independently could be due to carryover effects. Alternatively, these subjects could receive Treatment A alone, followed by an ATD alternating Treatments A and B, returning to Treatment A alone. An additional three subjects could receive Treatment B in the same manner. Trends and levels of behavior during either treatment alone versus the same treatment in the ATD could be compared.

A more elegant method is termed *functional manipulation* by Sidman (1960). In this procedure, the strength or intensity of one of the components is changed. For example, if comparing flooding and structured approach in the treatment of fear, the amount of time in flooding could be doubled at one point. Changes in fear behavior occurring during the second unchanged treatment (structured approach) could be attributed to carryover effects.

As Sidman (1960) observed, the study of treatment interaction can be interesting in its own right. In addition to the important step of determining the presence of carryover effects in an ATD, it is possible that some treatments juxtaposed in fast alternation could prove more effective than either component alone. That is, alternation effects, mentioned above, could prove therapeutic. For example, in some recent unpublished work, a sadistic rapist was treated by daily alternation of orgasmic reconditioning using first a sadistic fantasy and second an appropriate heterosexual fantasy. Sexual arousal to the appropriate fantasy seemed to increase more quickly during the fast alternation than during orgasmic reconditioning to the appropriate fantasy alone (Abel, Blanchard, Barlow, & Flanagan, Note 2). This may represent a contrast effect or possibly an intensification of the therapeutic effect due to a sharpening of stimulus control. Ulman and Sulzer-Azaroff (Note 1) also cite several studies reporting a possible intensification effect after multiple reversals in an A-B-A-B design. The appropriate method for studying these alternation effects would be to juxtapose a period of fast alternation with a period of slower alternation.

In summary, the unrepresentativeness of the ATD to natural situations as a threat to external validity is less of a drawback than it might be, due to the prevalent replication strategies in applied behavior analysis (as opposed to statistical inferential strategies of generalization) and the superior interval validity present in this design. Nevertheless, there are methods to minimize carryover effects as well as methods to study carryover effects which should be pursued to improve the external validity of the ATD and for possible applied value intrinsic to the fast alternation of two treatments.

USES OF ALTERNATING TREATMENT DESIGNS

ATDs have been used in two ways: (a) to compare the effect of treatment and no treatment (baseline) and (b) to compare two distinct treatments. Each of these approaches require separate comment.

Comparing Treatment with No Treatment

Several investigators have compared treatment and no treatment in an ATD. For example, O'Brien, Azrin, and Henson (1969) compared the effect of following and not following suggestions made by chronic mental patients in a group setting on the number of suggestions made by these patients. Doke and Risley (1972) alternated daily the presence of three teachers versus the usual one teacher and noted the effect on planned activities in a classroom (contingencies on individual versus groups were also compared in an ATD later in the experiment). Redd and Birnbrauer (1969) alternated reinforcement and no reinforcement, using two adult therapists as discriminative stimuli. The two adults switched treatments half way through the experiment to control for effects of person. Zimmerman, Overpeck, Eisenberg, and Garlick (1969) and Ulman and Sulzer-Azaroff (1975) also compared reinforcement and no reinforcement, although Ulman and Sulzer-Azaroff included two types of reinforcement, group versus individual. Finally, Agras, et al. (1969) studied the effects of social reinforcement in a severely claustrophobic patient by alternating social reinforcement with no reinforcement.

While data from these experiments are convincing, questions asked in the experiments mentioned above could all be answered by use of the more standard A-B-A-B withdrawal design. In the area of fear reduction, for example, the question of reinforcement versus no reinforcement and even the question of the role of relaxation in systematic desensitization have both been addressed using withdrawal designs (Agras, Leitenberg, & Barlow, 1968; Agras, Leitenberg, Barlow, Curtis, Edwards, & Wright, 1971).

The advantages of the ATD over the more usual withdrawal design have been enumerated by Ulman and Sulzer-Azaroff (1975) and Kazdin & Hartmann (in press). Clearly the major advantage of the ATD is that it does not require a withdrawal of treatment which may result in a reversal of any therapeutic gains. This allows one to proceed without concern for the ethical issue of reversing clinically relevant behavioral gains, an issue which sometimes arises in clinical research. Occasional staff resistance to withdrawal of treatment is also avoided.

A second advantage is that the comparison can be made more quickly than in a withdrawal design. McCullough et al. (1974) for example, effectively compared two treatments in 4 days. Withdrawal designs, on the other hand, require relatively stable baselines followed by at least three, and usually more, data points in each of at least three phases (A-B-A). As Ulman and Sulzer-Azaroff (1975) note, this efficiency also allows sudden termination of the experiment with the likelihood of having obtained usable data. A withdrawal design, however, must be carried through to completion.

A final advantage is the possibility of proceeding without a formal baseline phase. Ulman and Sulzer-Azaroff (1975), in considering this point, suggest that behaviors yielding chronically unstable baselines can be studied with this design. In applied research, the most common observation is behavioral improvement during baseline, which does not allow for introduction of treatment in the usual withdrawal design (Hersen & Barlow, 1976). But this does not present a problem for the ATD.

Despite these advantages, there are distinct disadvantages. Foremost among them is the as yet unknown magnitude of multiple treatment interference existing in the ATD. Until these issues are thoroughly explored experimentally, the external (or ecological) validity is uncertain since there are very few straight applied situations where a treatment is alternated with no treatment. The first time a treatment is introduced in a withdrawal design, however, does very closely resemble the applied situation because the treatment is administered in a straightforward manner. As noted above, later withdrawal and reinstatement phases occur solely for the sake of internal validity. Thus, one can assume more readily that the first treatment phase of a withdrawal design is externally valid.

One way to avoid this problem would be to administer the treatment alone in the first phase, followed by the ATD. This would still be more economical than a withdrawal design since one would not need a baseline nor the final reinstatement phase, yet one could make some estimates on the generalizability of the treatment from the first phase without the fast alternation.

A second disadvantage is that the ATD could be more cumbersome to arrange than the withdrawal design. Not only must treatments be quickly alternated, but discriminative stimuli, times, and locations (if different) must all be counterbalanced. However, increased experience with the ATD in our setting suggests that this is not a major problem.

Nevertheless, comparison of treatment with no treatment can be made with either design, and choice between the ATD and the withdrawal design will depend on the experimental questions asked and the practicalities of the experimental situation.

COMPARING TWO TREATMENTS

When the experimental question is the comparison of two treatments, there are few alternatives.[3] Indeed, the majority of ATDs published have attempted to answer this question (e.g., Corte, Wolf, & Locke, 1971; Doke & Risley, 1972; Steinman, 1970). Here the advantages of the ATD mentioned above are all relevant, and because there are few alternatives, the issue of the ATD being cumbersome is not relevant. The only remaining disadvantage is the threat to external validity posed by multiple treatment interference pending clarification of these issues. In a manner similar to those discussed above, one way to avoid this problem would be to hypothesize which of the two (or more) treatments is more effective and administer that treatment (Treatment A) alone in the first phase, followed by the ATD. As noted earlier, one could then estimate external validity from the first phase. As a check on internal validity, one should administer Treatment B followed by the ATD to a second subject to control for sequential confounding of the ATD. In any case, this threat may not be as great as it appears, for reasons discussed in the section on multiple treatment interference.

Considerations in the Use of the ATD

The most elegant examples demonstrating the correct application of the ATD comparing two treatments have appeared only recently (Kazdin, 1977; Kazdin & Geesey, 1977; McCullough, et al., 1974; Ulman & Sulzer-Azaroff, 1975). These examples are elegant because each illustrates the proper use of the ATD based on our current knowledge. Among other considerations, each design controls for sequential confounding by randomizing the order of treatment, a procedure that was not carried out, for example, in Agras et al. (1969). This is illustrated in the data advanced by McCullough et al. (1974) and presented here in Figure 1. In each of the experiments mentioned above, time of administration and location of administration were also counterbalanced if these factors were relevant to the experiment. Finally, each experiment illustrates proper use of the discriminative stimuli.

When the discriminative stimuli themselves may influence the data, as in the case of different therapists, these must also be counterbalanced.

[3]Other than the within subjects comparison (e.g., Edwards, 1968), one could address this question only by a series of withdrawal designs which administered two treatments with baseline interspersed and counterbalanced for sequence effects. For example, three subjects could receive A-B-A-C where B and C were two distinct treatments, and three could receive A-C-A-B. This design would approximate the counterbalanced within-subject group comparison with the exception of the individual analysis of the data and repeated measurement. But it would likely maximize contrast effects (White, Nielsen, & Johnson, 1972). Another possibility would be the interaction design strategy (Hersen & Barlow, 1976), but this would require that the two treatments or variables be combined at some point to examine their separate and combined effects, a strategy that would not be possible if the treatments could not be combined. An example would be flooding and desensitization.

But when the S^Ds are closer to those used in basic research (colored lights or sounds), such as cards with varying instructions posted in front of the classroom in the Ulman and Sulzer-Azaroff (1975) experiment, then interference from this source is unlikely and counterbalancing is not necessary. Because the basis of the ATD is stimulus discrimination, it is crucial that discriminations are formed. Thus, if S^Ds must be counterbalanced, this can occur only after discriminations have been made clearly, as in Agras et al. (1969). Using much shorter periods of time, successful discriminations were also made in the McCullough et al. (1974) data (see Figure 1), but if no differences had appeared in these data, one could not say if the treatments did not differ from each other or simply that the discriminations were not made. It seems best to be conservative in this instance to ensure that proper discriminations are made, but if proper discriminations are made, treatments that are topographically very similar (e.g., 5-min versus 10-min time-outs) can be compared. As noted above, this problem can be avoided by using instructions as discriminative stimuli in applied research (Kazdin & Hartmann, in press). If one is comparing 5- versus 10-min time-out periods for disruptive behavior in children, there is no reason why one would not describe the treatments as each became appropriate, particularly because someone would most likely describe these conditions in the normal use of this procedure in the natural environment.

Finally, the comparison of two treatments is not the only question answerable with an ATD. As Kazdin and Hartmann (in press), among others, point out, a comparison of the effectiveness of different therapists or of different times of treatment administration could also be carried out. This could be accomplished by collapsing data points across interventions and examining the therapeutic effects of two quickly alternating therapists. This comparison could be made more elegantly by having two or more therapists alternate quickly in the administration of a single treatment.

REFERENCE NOTES

1. Ulman, J. D., & Sulzer-Azaroff, B. *Multielement baseline design in applied behavior analysis.* Symposium presentation at the annual meeting of the American Psychological Association, Montreal, August 1973.
2. Abel, G. G., Blanchard, E. B., Barlow, D. H., & Flanagan, B. *A controlled behavioral treatment of a sadistic rapist.* Paper presentation at the ninth annual convention of the Association for Advancement of Behavior Therapy, San Francisco, December 1975.

REFERENCES

Agras, W. S., Leitenberg, H., & Barlow, D. H. Social reinforcement in the modification of agoraphobia. *Archives of General Psychiatry,* 1968, **19**, 423-427.

Agras, W. S., Leitenberg, H., Barlow, D. H., & Thomson, L. E. Instructions and reinforcement in the modification of neurotic behavior. *American Journal of Psychiatry,* 1969, **125**, 1435-1439.

Agras, W. S., Leitenberg, H., Barlow, D. H., Curtis, N., Edwards, J., & Wright, D. The role of relaxation in systematic desensitization. *Archives of General Psychiatry,* 1971, **25**, 511-514.

Azrin, N. H., & Holz, W. C. Punishment. In W. K. Honig (Ed.), *Operant behavior: Areas of research and application.* New York: Appleton-Century-Croft, 1966.

Barlow, D. H., & Hersen, M. Single case experimental designs: Uses in applied clinical research. *Archives of General Psychiatry,* 1973, **29**, 319-325.

Benjamin, L. S. A special Latin square for the use of each subject "as his own control." *Psychometrika,* 1965, **30**, 499-513.

Browning, R. M. A same-subject design for simultaneous comparison of three reinforcement contingencies. *Behaviour Research & Therapy,* 1967, **5**, 237-243.

Browning, R. M., & Stover, D. O. *Behavior modification in child treatment: An experimental and clinical approach.* Chicago: Aldine-Atherton, 1971.

Campbell, D. T., & Stanley, J. C. Experimental and quasi-experimental designs for research. In N. L. Gage (Ed.), *Handbook of research on teaching.* Chicago: Rand McNally, 1963.

Cochran, W. G., & Cox, G. M. *Experimental designs* (2nd ed.). New York: John Wiley, 1957.

Corte, H. E., Wolf, M. M., & Locke, B. J. A comparison of procedures for eliminating self-injurious behavior of retarded adolescents. *Journal of Applied Behavior Analysis,* 1971, **4**, 201-215.

Doke, L. A., & Risley, T. R. The organization of day-care environments: Required *vs.* optional activities. *Journal of Applied Behavior Analysis,* 1972, **5,** 405-420.

Dunham, P. J. Contrasted conditions of reinforcement: A selective critique. *Psychological Bulletin,* 1968, **69,** 295-315.

Edgington, E. S. Statistical inference and nonrandom samples. *Psychological Bulletin,* 1966, **66,** 485-487.

Edgington, E. S. Statistical inference from $N = 1$ experiments. *Journal of Psychology,* 1967, **65,** 195-199.

Edgington, E. S. *Statistical inference: The distribution-free approach.* New York: McGraw-Hill, 1969.

Edgington, E. S. N = 1 experiments: Hypothesis testing. *The Canadian Psychologist,* 1972, **13,** 121-135.

Edwards, A. L. *Experimental design in psychological research* (3rd ed.). New York: Holt, Rinehart & Winston, 1968.

Freeman, B. J. Behavioral contrast: Reinforcement frequency or response suppression. *Psychological Bulletin,* 1971, **75,** 347-356.

Greenwald, A. G. Within-subjects designs: To use or not to use? *Psychological Bulletin,* 1976, **83,** 314-320.

Hersen, M., & Barlow, D. H. *Single case experimental designs: Strategies for studying behavior change.* New York: Pergamon Press, 1976.

Kazdin, A. E. The influence of behavior preceding a reinforced response on behavior change in the classroom. *Journal of Applied Behavior Analysis,* 1977, **10,** 299-311.

Kazdin, A. E., & Geesey, S. Simultaneous-treatment design comparisons of the effects of earning reinforcers for one's peers versus for oneself. *Behavior Therapy,* 1977, **8,** 682-693.

Kazdin, A. E., & Hartmann, D. P. The simultaneous-treatment design. *Behavior Therapy,* in press.

Leitenberg, H. The use of single-case methodology in psychotherapy research. *Journal of Abnormal Psychology,* 1973, **82,** 87-101.

McCullough, J. P., Cornell, J. E., McDaniel, M. H., & Meuller, R. K. Utilization of the simultaneous treatment design to improve student behavior in a first-grade classroom. *Journal of Consulting and Clinical Psychology,* 1974, **42,** 288-292.

O'Brien, F. Sequential contrast effects with human subjects. *Journal of the Experimental Analysis of Behavior,* 1968, **11,** 537-542.

O'Brien, F., Azrin, N. H., & Henson, K. Increased communications of chronic mental patients by reinforcement and by response priming. *Journal of Applied Behavior Analysis,* 1969, **2,** 23-29.

Powell, J., & Hake, D. F. Positive *vs* negative reinforcement: A direct comparison of effects on a complex human response. *Psychological Record,* 1971, **21,** 191-205.

Redd, W. H., & Birnbrauer, J. S. Adults as discriminative stimuli for different reinforcement contingencies with retarded children. *Journal of Experimental Child Psychology,* 1969, **7,** 440-447.

Reynolds, G. S. *A primer of operant conditioning.* Glenview, Ill.: Scott, Foresman, 1968.

Sidman, M. *Tactics of scienctific research.* New York: Basic Books, 1960.

Steinman, W. M. The social control of generalized imitation. *Journal of Applied Behavior Analysis,* 1970, **3,** 159-167.

Ulman, J. D., & Sulzer-Azaroff, B. Multielement baseline design in educational research. In E. Ramp & G. Semb, *Behavior analysis: Areas of research and application.* Englewood Cliffs, N.J.: Prentice-Hall, 1975.

Waite, W. W., & Osborne, J. G. Sustained behavioral contrast in children. *Journal of the Experimental Analysis of Behavior,* 1972, **18,** 113-117.

White, G. D., Nielsen, G., & Johnson, S. H. Timeout duration and the suppression of deviant behavior in children. *Journal of Applied Behavior Analysis,* 1972, **5,** 111-120.

Zimmerman, J., Overpeck, C., Eisenberg, H., & Garlick, B. Operant conditioning in a sheltered workshop. *Rehabilitation Literature,* 1969, **30,** 326-334.

Received April 17, 1978
Final acceptance November 15, 1978

JOURNAL OF APPLIED BEHAVIOR ANALYSIS 1989, 22, 57–69 NUMBER 1 (SPRING 1989)

INTERACTION EFFECTS IN MULTIELEMENT DESIGNS: INEVITABLE, DESIRABLE, AND IGNORABLE

Ann Higgins Hains
UNIVERSITY OF WISCONSIN–MILWAUKEE
AND
Donald M. Baer
UNIVERSITY OF KANSAS

A single-subject design often used to compare the effectiveness of two or more independent variables (like treatment programs) is the multielement (alternating treatments or simultaneous treatments) design. Variants of this design approximate the concurrent comparison of the effects of two or more variables (or levels of variables) by programming the variables (or levels) in rapid alternation, typically across or within daily sessions. Properly combined with conventional reversal designs, these designs can also display a variety of interaction effects, some of them worrisome, others highly desirable for the future development of the field. A worrisome model is the possibility that when Treatment B alternates rapidly with Treatment C, the effects of each will not be the same as when each is the only treatment used. A desirable model is the use of the multielement design as a fast-paced component of an otherwise conventional reversal design examining contextual control of some relationship: the possibility that some behavior responds differently to Controlling Variables A and B in Context X than in Context Y. This second possibility opens single-subject designs to the more efficient examination of all interactive effects and is highly desirable, considering the prevalence and importance of interactions in determining the limits and the generality of currently understood behavioral phenomena.

DESCRIPTORS: interaction effects, multiple treatment interference, multielement design, alternating treatments design, methodology

---

THE SPECIAL USES OF MULTIELEMENT DESIGNS

The multielement design is simply a fast-paced reversal design incorporating many reversals. Like any reversal design, it can be used to compare the effects of different levels of a variable (e.g., treatment and no treatment) or different variables (e.g., Treatment 1, Treatment 2, and Treatment 3). In the latter case, the point of using the design is often to show promptly which of those treatments is best for subsequent prolonged use; thus, the design is usually called an alternating treatment or simultaneous treatment design (Barlow & Hayes, 1979; Barlow & Hersen, 1984; Hersen & Barlow, 1976; Kazdin, 1982; McReynolds & Kearns, 1983; Ulman & Sulzer-Azaroff, 1975). Even so, it is still a multielement design, in that this label denotes nothing more than relatively many, relatively fast-paced reversals: Its variables are changed sometimes every session and sometimes within every session.

The programming of relatively many, relatively fast-paced reversals has a highly specialized set of advantages. Perhaps the major advantage is the ability to compare variables within the context of uncontrolled and uncontrollable background variables that can be presumed to change more slowly or less often than the experimental variables will be made to change. This allows the relative effects of the experimental variables to be seen unconfounded with those background variables. Thus, for example, if two teaching methods can be compared daily throughout a school term, the comparison thereby escapes confoundings with such

Preparation of this article was supported in part by the National Institute of Child Health and Human Development, National Research Service Award, Public Health Service Grant 5 T32-HD-07173, by the National Institute of Mental Health Grant R01-MH-20411-14, and by the Handicapped Children's Early Education Program Grant 024BH50009.

Correspondence and requests for reprints may be sent to Ann Higgins Hains, Department of Exceptional Education, University of Wisconsin–Milwaukee, P.O. Box 413, Milwaukee, Wisconsin 53201, or to Donald M. Baer, Department of Human Development and Family Life, University of Kansas, Lawrence, Kansas 66045.

background variables as the weather, changes in curriculum topics and difficulty, changes in teachers, extracurricular activity cycles (e.g., sports, dances, field trips), and factors vaguely hypothesized as beginning-of-year and end-of-year effects.

A secondary advantage of the multielement design is that the answer to the experimental question seems to emerge very quickly; only its generality remains in question, and if the design continues, that question begins to be answered, too, at least for those background variables that will in fact change during that time.

However, those virtues also define the design's intrinsic specialization. The multielement design requires a special kind of problem to investigate: the comparison of variables that produce immediate rather than slow and cumulative effects on the behavior under study, and that, when discontinued, allow the behavior to resume promptly its prior status. Thus, multielement designs are best suited to studying effects such as stimulus control and are ill suited to a comparison of different methods that slowly and cumulatively establish new, complex skills, and might better be examined in a slow-paced reversal design with relatively few reversals.

Within that context, a further possible advantage is less certain—that multielement designs reduce the likelihood of some types of multiple treatment interference. Multiple treatment interference is "likely to occur whenever multiple treatments are applied to the same respondents, because the effects of prior treatments are not usually erasable" (Campbell & Stanley, 1963, p. 6). Sequence, carryover, and alternation effects often are mentioned as possible sources of multiple treatment interference in single-subject research (Barlow & Hayes, 1979; Barlow & Hersen, 1984; Kazdin & Hartmann, 1978; McReynolds & Kearns, 1983). These types of interaction effects are all examples of the same kinds of bias and can be addressed in the same manner.

SEQUENCE EFFECTS

Sequence effects (also known as order effects) refer to the possibility that if one treatment, say C, is examined only after another treatment, say B, has occurred, as in an A-B-C design, then some of Treatment C's effectiveness (or ineffectiveness) may be due to the fact that B preceded it. This possibility is undeniable and extremely problematic, for by the same logic we should always ask if some of B's effectiveness (or ineffectiveness) may be due to the fact that C did not precede it. And then we should also ask whether any of B's and C's effectiveness (or ineffectiveness) may be due to the fact that A preceded them, and whether any of A's effectiveness (or ineffectiveness, especially) may be due to the fact that neither B nor C preceded it. Thus, the entire domain of designs that examine different levels or forms of variables over time within the same organism is subject to the problem of sequence effects. The proper question is whether sequence effects are indeed a problem, rather than a fact of nature that we should simply let be rather than "solve."

When Sequence Is Considered a Problem

When sequence is considered a problem, it is often handled by counterbalancing. Proper counterbalancing simply administers A-B-C, A-C-B, B-A-C, B-C-A, C-A-B, and C-B-A sequences equally often. Occasionally that is done by assigning each sequence to a different subject. Such designs are committed to the assumption that A, B, and C interact similarly in all subjects, a very doubtful assumption. Sometimes that assumption is obviated by assigning each sequence to large enough, randomly selected groups of subjects. That obviates the entire point of single-subject designs.

Ulman and Sulzer-Azaroff argue that the multielement design "minimizes possible sequence effects by presenting each condition only briefly . . . rather than for a prolonged period of time" (Ulman & Sulzer-Azaroff, 1975, p. 387). They suggest that *within-subject* counterbalancing in the multielement designs is the appropriate form, and that it may co-opt the problem of sequence effects: If the generalized form of the problem is that B precedes C, then a useful design might well let it do so as briefly as possible, and also let C precede B just as often (and just as briefly) as B precedes C for that subject. That is exactly a multielement design, and it is a within-subject tactic. Because multielement designs are naturally built on some repetition of sessions, it is the sessions that can meaningfully accomplish as much counterbalancing of B-C and C-B sequences as their number allows. In addition, controllable background variables such as choice of experimenters, choice of settings, and times of day also can be counterbalanced across sessions (if there are enough sessions).

Counterbalancing *does not* eliminate sequence effects; it merely allows them (or their absence) to be seen. However, when B-C sequences show different outcomes for B and C than C-B sequences do, it requires a fair number of replications of each sequence to see that as a reliable and unambiguous difference. For example, a commonly used design is to establish a baseline, A, add the treatment conditions, say B and C, to that baseline in a multielement comparison, and then use the "better" treatment as the third and final condition:

A
A–B–C.
C

This type of design and this method for diagramming it were first illustrated by Browning in 1967. Here, baseline levels of performance, A, are assessed first in isolation for several sessions as the only condition operative across the three separate periods. Following baseline, A appears in fast-paced alternation with the interventions (a typical multielement design) for several more sessions. In the multielement phase, Treatments B and C are compared every session to each other and to A, and those comparisons can be counterbalanced, requiring six kinds of sessions: A-B-C, A-C-B, B-A-C, B-C-A, C-A-B, and C-B-A. Each of these six sequences ought to be compared to the others as often as possible, if counterbalancing is to be a serious response to a serious problem; doing so implies many sessions (12 at a bare minimum, and preferably a much larger multiple of six). Then the better of B and C, say C, can be examined in isolation during the subsequent final sessions of the study. Such a design may be represented more clearly in the sessions diagrammed below:

A A A A B B C C A A B B C C C C
A–A–B–C–A–C–A–B–B–C–A–C–A–B–C–C.
A A C B C A B A C B C A B A C C

Thus, responding to potential sequence effects with counterbalancing sacrifices much of the multielement design's supposed ability to be quickly informative.

This design does not analyze sequence effects, in that it does not relate them to more fundamental variables, but it does display some of them—as the inability to recover levels of A or C (but not B) across experimental phases where they operate in alternation and in isolation. For example, changes in levels of A can be examined across baseline, where A appears in isolation (by itself across the three sessions), and in the treatment phase, where A alternates with B and C.

Do we ever fail to recover levels of behavior, either within or across experimental phases, in this design? If we do, then the multielement design has not lived up to its advertising about minimizing sequence effects. In fact, we do. A survey of the multielement designs represented in Barlow and Hersen's classic 1984 textbook revealed 31 cases, 14 of which were unambiguous for this question. Of those 14 cases, 4 cases recovered every level examined in either a multielement comparison or in isolation (Kazdin & Geesey, 1977; Shapiro, Barrett, & Ollendick, 1980; Van Houten, Nau, MacKenzie-Keating, Sameoto, & Colavecchia, 1982; Weinrott, Garrett, & Todd, 1978); however, 10 cases failed to recover prior levels across multielement and isolation comparisons (Barrett, Matson, Shapiro, & Ollendick, 1981; Bittle & Hake, 1977; Hallahan, Lloyd, Kneedler, & Marshall, 1982; Martin, Pallotta-Cornick, Johnstone, & Celso-Goyos, 1980; O'Brien, Azrin, & Henson, 1969; Ollendick, Matson, Esveldt-Dawson, & Shapiro, 1980; Ollendick, Shapiro, & Barrett, 1981; Rojahn, Mulick, McCoy, & Schroeder, 1978; Shapiro, Kazdin, & McGonigle, 1982; Singh, Winton, & Dawson, 1982). If this small sample can be taken as at least a cautionary encounter with the still unknown general case, then multielement designs, despite their excellent face characteristics, do not reliably obviate sequence effects.

If we wish to see more of those potential sequence effects, we might in principle expand the multielement design for exactly that purpose, losing even more of its value as a quickly informative design, but gaining an appreciation of what kinds of sequence effects can appear in within-subject analyses, and how often. Following the logic of the preceding example, a more complete display of sequence effects will require the following prototype:

```
  A   A   A   A   A   A   A
A–B–B–B–C–B–A–B–B–B–C–B–A–B– . . . .
  C   C   C   C   C   C   C
```

The essence of this prototypic design is simply that every element of the design—every A, B, and C—is examined both in the characteristic fast-paced alternation of the multielement design and in isolation (and in as many sequences of that as the designer has time, curiosity, and ethical permission to pursue). This diagram assumes that when each element appears alone, it is implemented across the three sessions or time periods; likewise, it assumes that when the elements are alternated, they are counterbalanced.

CARRYOVER AND ALTERNATION EFFECTS

Carryover effects refer to "the influence of one treatment on an adjacent treatment, irrespective of overall sequencing" (Barlow & Hersen, 1984, p. 257). Alternation effects refer to multiple treatment interference resulting from the speed of alternation (rapid vs. slow) and the length of the intercomponent interval separating treatment conditions (Barlow & Hersen, 1984; McGonigle, Rojahn, Dixon, & Strain, 1987). Sequence, carryover, and alternation effects are usually discussed separately; however, they all refer to the same problem—"that one experimental treatment is interfering with the other within the experiment itself" (Barlow & Hersen, 1984, p. 257). Carryover effects are nothing but sequence effects of one component of a multielement phase preceding or following other components *within that phase.* The prototypic design above shows the possibility of both within-the-multielement-phase sequence effects and between-phases sequence effects by comparing the levels of any A, B, or C both within and between all its phases, multielement and in-isolation phases alike. Thus, there is little reason to maintain a distinction in terminology between sequence, carryover, and alternation effects. All that is at issue are sequence effects, sometimes in faster paced sequences, sometimes in slower paced sequences.

If within-the-multielement-phase sequence effects are present—if, for example, C looks as effective as it does only because it alternates so quickly with B—they will become apparent when C is examined in isolation from B, *if* C is examined at sufficient length when it is separated from B. If C looks as effective as it does in the alternation phase with A and B only because B is present, perhaps it can continue to look that effective for a few more sessions when it is examined in isolation in the next condition of the design. Then, that next condition of C-only must be a protracted one. Otherwise, these designs, instead of building a technology for improving deviant behavior, will yield a classic literature of contradictory results, specifically one in which later use of Treatment C does not match the promise shown in its initial "validation" research.

To deal with all these problems of potential sequence effects, slow- or fast-paced, the prototypic design needs even more elaboration:

```
      A               A               A
A–B–C–B–AAAAA–B–BBBBB–B–CCCCC– . . . .
      C               C               C
```

This design is a very lengthy one; indeed, it is so lengthy that in the pragmatic context of comparing two clinical treatments, it is unlikely ever to be carried out and probably should not be. This is especially so because of the obvious ethical considerations of (a) not treating subjects needful of a prompt, optimum intervention and (b) treating them as ping-pong balls, to be eternally bounced back and forth between conditions, sometimes slowly, sometimes quickly, for the sake of a complete examination of treatment–sequence interactions.

When Sequence Is Not Considered a Problem

In the pragmatic context of treatment, the Browning (1967) design is good enough, if its subsequent examination of the better treatment, say C, is protracted enough, and especially if it seems successful enough to allow its eventual end:

A
A–B–C . . . –A . . . .
C

The enabling arguments are essentially pragmatic ones. If C looks as effective as it does during the multielement phase, in part because of its fast-paced alternation with B, then that should become apparent in the subsequent protracted examination of C alone: C alone eventually will look different from C alternating rapidly with A and B. In particular, if C alone eventually seems more effective than it had during the multielement phase, we may reasonably suspect that its fast-paced alternation with A and B diluted its effectiveness then, but we will hardly care, because the design gave us the correct answer for the next clinical phase of our program. On the other hand, if C seems to lose the effectiveness that it had shown during the multielement phase, that will set the occasion for a subsequent examination of B alone, to see if it will be more effective, now that we suspect that its earlier inferiority to C was illusory (i.e., was an artifact of the multielement design).

This finding can suggest that B was always the superior treatment, but looked inferior to C only because of its fast-paced alternation with A and C. However, if B is that fragile a superior treatment—if it can become that ineffective simply by its proximity to some A or C—then perhaps that recommends against relying on it in a treatment context: How can we ensure that the uncontrolled part of our client's everyday life will not present some deleterious partner to our B in the course of treatment? In other words, we probably do not want to use Bs that sensitive to uncontrollable events.

If A alone at the end of the study seems much more effective than A alone as baseline or during the multielement phase of the design, that will simply testify to an enduring effect of treatment. We may well begin asking what natural community of support for the target behavior has been tapped by the treatment, a question that will require quite a different investigation rather than a better version of the above design.

In short, in a treatment context, we are usually not interested in the complete analysis of our target behavior's responsiveness to the sequences of the controlling variables that we can apply. Instead, we seek variables that produce useful effects *despite* their sequencing with other variables (useful or otherwise). Everyday life, as far as we know, is an ongoing, unassessable set of such sequences, some of them segregated in their effects to the settings in which they operate, some of them showing generalized effects across an unpredictable range of settings. But we can eventually restrict our focus to those variables that operate uniformly despite such sequences by examining them in reversal designs that make clear their durability or their fragility in such sequences. However, doing so will still require an ability to examine those sequence-durable effects across contexts more fundamental than the order of presentation, and for that purpose, the fast pace of the multielement design may have special usefulness, as the next section will show.

Other Approaches to the Problem

The procedures Sidman (1960) termed *independent verification* and *functional manipulation* are variations of the previously discussed prototypic designs. Sidman argues that these procedures assess the extent of any fast-paced interaction effects but do not control or prevent them. Independent verification enables the experimenter to study the "simultaneous control of behavior by a multiplicity of variables" (Sidman, 1960, p. 335) by programming each variable of interest both alone and in combination with the other variables of interest (Barlow & Hersen, 1984; McReynolds & Kearns, 1983; Shapiro et al., 1982; Sidman, 1960). A narrower definition of an independent-verification interaction design is that it follows the traditional slower paced A-B-A-B reversal design, but arranges conditions to display the ongoing additive or subtractive effects of each variable (McReynolds & Kearns, 1983); sequence effects are of course possible, but will be seen as such in a long enough design by examining the variables across conditions. Variables may appear in combination, BC, or in alternation, $\genfrac{}{}{0pt}{}{B}{C}$. For example, verbal and nonverbal reinforcement could be scheduled simultaneously or in alternation. The design sometimes adds a variable:

$$\text{A–B–BC–B–BC} \quad \text{and} \quad \text{A–B–}\genfrac{}{}{0pt}{}{\text{B}}{\text{C}}\text{–B–}\genfrac{}{}{0pt}{}{\text{B}}{\text{C}}$$

and sometimes subtracts a variable:

$$\text{A–BC–B–BC–B} \quad \text{and} \quad \text{A–}\genfrac{}{}{0pt}{}{\text{B}}{\text{C}}\text{–B–}\genfrac{}{}{0pt}{}{\text{B}}{\text{C}}\text{–B.}$$

When two variables are introduced at the same time in a package (e.g., BC), a concurrent interaction is always possible, as Sidman recognizes. For example, in an analysis of the effects of adaptive clothing on the self-injurious behavior of two blind, profoundly retarded men (Rojahn et al., 1978), a jacket (B) and a neck-brace (C) were examined separately, as a package (BC), and as fast-paced alternate conditions within a multielement phase:

$$\text{A–B–BC–}\genfrac{}{}{0pt}{}{\text{A}}{\text{BC}}\text{–}\genfrac{}{}{0pt}{}{\text{B}}{\text{C}}\text{–BC.}$$

In this design, there is probably as much possibility of interactive effects in the packaging of B and C as there is in their fast-paced alternation in the multielement comparison. The display of interaction effects is limited in this design, however, because the design does not systematically replicate isolation phases with either the packaging of BC or the alternation of $\genfrac{}{}{0pt}{}{B}{C}$. Yet, the approximation of the prototypic design seen above was an appropriate beginning and would have been even if there had not been a multielement phase.

A more complex examination of interaction effects through independent verification is seen in a study by Shapiro et al. (1982). This study was designed to examine treatment interactions within a multielement design. In addition to examining time-of-day effects (morning vs. afternoon), the design sometimes used fast-paced alternations of baseline (A), token reinforcement (B), and token reinforcement with response-cost contingencies (BC) on the on-task behavior of mentally retarded, behaviorally disturbed children:

$$\text{A–}\genfrac{}{}{0pt}{}{\text{A}}{\text{B}}\text{–}\genfrac{}{}{0pt}{}{\text{B}}{\text{BC}}\text{–}\genfrac{}{}{0pt}{}{\text{A}}{\text{B}}\text{–}\genfrac{}{}{0pt}{}{\text{B}}{\text{BC}}\text{–B.}$$

This design does not examine response-cost effects, C, in isolation; rather, it only compares response cost as a packaged treatment, BC, with the token reinforcement element, B. The examination of the response-cost system in isolation would not have been possible without some existing token system. Token reinforcement, however, was compared in alternation with baseline, $\genfrac{}{}{0pt}{}{A}{B}$, and then in alternation with the token reinforcement and response cost contingencies, $\genfrac{}{}{0pt}{}{B}{BC}$. The resultant data showed the effects of several interactions: On-task behavior during the token reinforcement condition (B) was more variable when that condition alternated rapidly with the token reinforcement and response-cost condition ($\genfrac{}{}{0pt}{}{B}{BC}$) than when it alternated with the baseline condition ($\genfrac{}{}{0pt}{}{A}{B}$). Probable sequence effects also appeared: Comparison of the initial $\genfrac{}{}{0pt}{}{A}{B}$ (fast-paced alternation of baseline and token reinforcement conditions) and its replication showed improved on-task behavior in both conditions in the replication. Furthermore, the introduction of the token reinforcement and response-cost phase apparently influenced subsequent performance in both token and baseline conditions.

An examination of the studies cited in the Barlow and Hersen (1984) text revealed that only three studies used designs that allowed some examination of interactions of treatment variables through independent verification (Bittle & Hake, 1982, and the two studies previously described). Each of these studies used an approximation to one of the prototypic independent-verification designs. In general, whenever variables appear in fast-paced alternation ($\genfrac{}{}{0pt}{}{B}{C}$) or in packages (BC) (which might be considered the ultimate case of fast pacing), their repetitive examination in isolation as well is worth considering, especially if we wish to use less ambiguous terms than the "apparently" and "probably" necessary in the above descriptions of these results. The consideration of an independent-verification design should be subject to the standard benefit-cost logic of applied research, of course. There may well be times when the benefit of being less ambiguous about those possibilities will not seem worth the cost. Furthermore, there may be situations in which the treatments compared in a multielement design could not be combined because the variables are procedurally incompatible. Similarly, situations may exist where components of a package intervention could not be tested separately.

Sidman illustrates a second method called *functional manipulation* (1960, p. 336). By systematically altering some parameter of an experimental variable, the researcher can see if those changes affect the relationship between that variable and the behavior under study.

Two studies cited by Barlow and Hersen (1984) provide examples of investigations in which important variables were examined in interaction (Corte, Wolf, & Locke, 1971; Doke & Risley, 1972). The Corte et al. (1971) study cited by Barlow and Hersen provides an elegant example of what could well be termed a superordinate multielement analysis, wherein two variables were examined in interaction, each in its own multielement design, one design within the other. That study examined the effects of food deprivation and a DRO using food reinforcement on the self-injurious behavior of an institutionalized profoundly retarded adolescent. The subject's lunch was withheld every other day, so that deprivation, D, and nondeprivation, d, conditions alternated with each daily session. Brief periods of contingent reinforcement of other behavior, R, and of noncontingent reinforcement, r, both with bites of food, occurred within each daily session; the contingent condition always preceded the noncontingent condition:

$$D^R_r - d^R_r - D^R_r - d^R_r \ldots .$$

The results showed that the lowest rates of self-injurious behavior occurred under deprivation and contingent reinforcement conditions. The highest rates of self-injurious behavior occurred during the nondeprivation and noncontingent reinforcement conditions.

The design of the Corte et al. (1971) study is a multielement design within another, slower paced multielement design. That is, contingent and noncontingent reinforcement conditions alternated within each session, and deprivation and nondeprivation conditions alternated with each successive session. That design permitted the detection of the "better" treatment procedure for eliminating self-injurious behavior, but, more important for the future of the discipline, it examined that superiority within the context of an important parameter of both treatments: The meaning of reinforcement is such that it cannot be examined except at some point on its deprivation–satiation interaction, and the meaning of contingency is such that it cannot be examined except in some contrast to a somewhat different contingency. Because these variables *must* interact, they are better studied as interactions than not, and the design just described may well be the simplest one for doing so.

If the design were extended, it might also allow an inspection of the effects of contingent and noncontingent reinforcement in isolation from each other, meaning of course only in a slower paced alternation (which is, logic suggests, all that "isolation" can mean in single-subject designs and in real life):

$$D^R_r - d^R_r - D^R_r - d^R_r - DR - dR - Dr - dr \ldots .$$

This design might offer the best of both worlds: the same relatively quick display of an interaction that the prior design offered, and an only slightly slower display of any sequence effects that might be operating within that interaction. Again, the design is obviously a costly one, and benefit-cost logic applies, as ever.

Doke and Risley (1972) provide another example of superordinate multielement analysis. This study examined the effects on preschool children's participation in activities during group versus individual dismissal from the activities; these activities were sometimes with materials (e.g., housekeeping) and sometimes without (e.g., story time). The conditions of activities with materials, M, and without materials, m, alternated within each day, always at the same times of day. The dismissal conditions alternated every few days; for a few days, children were dismissed from all of their activities as a group (as soon as all children were ready), G; then, for a few more days, they were dismissed individually (as soon as each child finished), g:

$$G^M_m - g^M_m - G^M_m - g^M_m \ldots$$

The results showed that the highest rate of participation occurred when there were materials and dismissal was individualized.

This design also permits the detection of the "better" treatment for promoting children's participation in activities; more important, it examined that superiority within the context of an important parameter, materials. All play exists at some point on a dimension of material use and availability; and all adult-managed play exists on some dimension of termination of or dismissal from that play. Thus, the study of play *ought* to be the study of at least these interactions, and again, the above design may represent the minimum design competent to begin that study. In this respect, the study differs from the Corte et al. (1971) study only in that some of the parameters for further manipulation may not be as apparent. For example, there are parameters underlying the effectiveness of activities without materials (e.g., stories) for children's participation: time of day, length of session, number of teachers present, and the complex of parameters called teacher "style." On the other hand, activities with materials (housekeeping, block, manipulative, and creative activities) are almost surely sensitive to somewhat different underlying parameters: the amount of materials available per child, the space available per child, and the range of playmates available. Thus, the design could be extended to examine the effects of individual and group dismissal within the context of availability of materials (many, 1; few, 2) for only activities with materials, M:

$$G^M_m - g^M_m - G^M_m - g^M_m - GM^1_2 - gM^1_2 - GM^1_2 - gM^1_2.$$

Then the design could be extended to allow an inspection of the effects of many and few materials in isolation from each other:

$$G^M_m - g^M_m - GM^1_2 - gM^1_2 - GM1 - gM1 - GM2 - gM2.$$

This slower extension could display any sequence effects that might be present within the interaction of the previous phase.

In the past, single-subject designs have been used in their relatively simple forms and thereby have revealed to investigators a wealth of powerful direct effects in the analysis of behavior. By the same token, they have obviated the study of contextual factors (such as deprivation, availability of materials, task difficulty) in those effects: We have learned that certain processes are very powerful, but usually have failed to learn the contextual conditions that maximize and minimize that power. Yet almost certainly, every process fundamental to the analysis of behavior is subject to exactly that kind of contextual control (cf. Kantor, 1959; Morris, Higgins, & Bickel, 1982); and almost certainly, contextual control will be found to be very powerful in modulating the generality of those apparently powerful processes. If so, it is not the final details of the analysis of behavior that have escaped investigation in the simple single-subject designs of our history; it is the fundamental statements of generality and the fundamental conditions of a *dependable* technology that await clarification.

The research paradigm for that clarification must involve a study of interactions. In its simplest form, the interaction displays the effects of several levels of Variable 1 in the context of several levels of Variable 2. For example, the effects of peer prompting of a child's social behavior may be different when certain peers do the prompting than when other peers do it, and within each of those classes, the effects may be different depending on the peer's rate of prompting. Suppose that a useful kind of peer status can be defined in terms of the subject's typical past rate of playing with that peer. Do peer status and prompt rate interact? In other words, does peer status determine the effectiveness of peer-prompt rate? Or, the same question with a somewhat different theoretical implication, does prompt rate determine the effectiveness of the prompting peer's status? The appropriate design will examine four conditions, at least (see Figure 1).

The familiar four-fold table as shown in Figure 1 has been the symbol of group-factorial designs for many years in behavioral research; in that tradition, each cell of the table has usually represented another group of subjects. Perhaps the most significant aspect of the multielement design is that it allows us to consider the same interaction (indeed, a more realistic version of it) within a single subject. If s and S represent low-status and high-status peers, respectively, and r and R represent low rates and high rates of their prompts, respectively, the following multielement within multielement designs will examine the question:

$$R^{s}_{S}-R^{S}_{s}-r^{s}_{S}-r^{S}_{s}-R^{s}_{S}-R^{S}_{s}-r^{s}_{S}-r^{S}_{s}$$

and

$$s^{R}_{r}-s^{r}_{R}-S^{R}_{r}-S^{r}_{R}-s^{R}_{r}-s^{r}_{R}-S^{R}_{r}-S^{r}_{R}.$$

The difference in these designs is primarily the difference implied in the above figure by labeling one variable TREATMENT and the other PARAMETER. That difference represents some difference in theory, no doubt; more important is the question of whether the data of the two designs would yield the same answer or two somewhat different ones.

Next, consider extending these designs to include the meaningful components examined in isolation as well. That allows the same examination of the interaction of these variables—the effects of prompt rates in the context of peer status (or vice versa)—as could be considered in the group design, and also allows an examination of whether sequence effects will operate as a consequence of examining this interaction within a single subject, and if so, to what extent.

Perhaps the most interesting case that might result from this examination is if sequence effects do appear. Some research methodologists will then argue that the group-factorial design is clearly the superior one, in that it does not allow those sequence effects to operate, and thus allows *the* interaction between rates of prompting social behavior and peer status to appear in its purest form. The point, however, is to recall Sidman's (1960) argument about such pure forms of behavioral phenomena: If they do not operate that way within the single

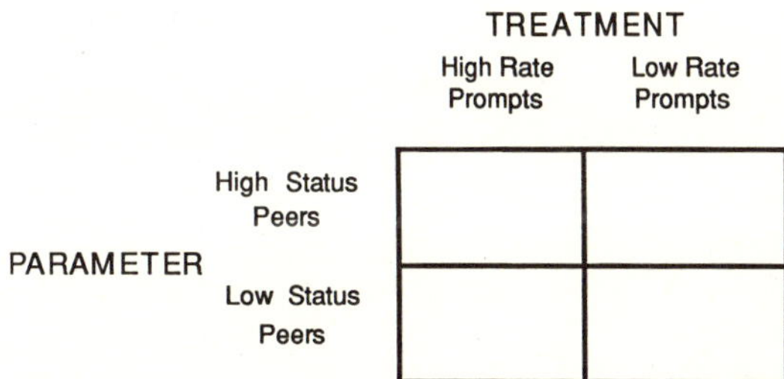

Figure 1. Examination of interactions between high-status and low-status peers and high-rate and low-rate prompts.

subject whose behavior we are trying to analyze, then no matter what their purity when freed of sequence effects through the segregation of their component variables to different subjects, they are not the analysis of *this* subject's behavior (and, indeed, perhaps not the analysis of *any* subject's behavior).

Students may encounter rapid alternations of high-status and low-status peers in their social environment, and those peers may often vary their rates of social bids. The real-world question is how those contextual parameters affect social behavior under *those* conditions of constant encounters with all levels of the variables under investigation. If the answer is that sequence effects operate within that interaction, that is the *realistic* answer to our curiosity, and we should simply let the design continue until all such effects (differences and nondifferences) seem stable. After all, that is close to what happens to students in the real world, and so that answer ought to have some real-world generality. The results of the group-factorial design, precisely because it has been purged of that sequence effect, give a purely unrealistic picture of the interaction between peer status and rate of prompting social behaviors.

These parametric manipulations are meaningful not only because they detect interactions present in a given set of data, but also because they allow the researcher to create or eliminate selected interactions through functional manipulation. In other words, when these parameters are amenable to precise enough experimental control and that control is exercised, the result is a truly systematic display of the interaction in question. For example, in the design of the Corte et al. (1971) study, we might well go on to examine various levels of deprivation,

		TREATMENT	
		Posted	Not Posted
PARAMETER	High Density		
	Low Density		

Figure 2. Examination of interactions between posted and nonposted speeds and high and low densities of police cars.

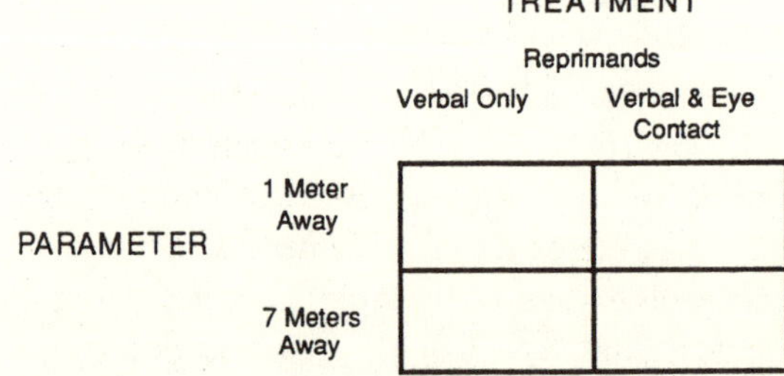

Figure 3. Examination of interactions between verbal reprimands alone and with eye contact at distances of 1 m and 7 m.

various schedules of reinforcement, and, within each of those schedules, various levels of the schedule's parameters (e.g., ratio size or interval length); knowing all those effects on self-injurious behavior might indeed give us a precise treatment technology for that problem.

Similarly, parametric manipulations could detect interactions in more applied problems. Consider two hypothetical examples. First, the speeding behavior of motorists could be examined in a multielement design wherein on some days the speed at which motorists were traveling was posted for their observation, and on other days it was not. In addition, the visible density of police cars in the area could be varied to be high, say 20 units, and low, 2 units, on a weekly basis as shown in Figure 2. (Again, which is TREATMENT and which is PARAMETER is optional.) By deliberately altering one of the components—say, the schedule of posting—changes in, or the stability of, the relationship of speeding to the other variables could be examined.

Van Houten et al. (1982) offer a second example in two separate studies. In one study, they used a multielement design to compare the effects of verbal reprimands versus a package of verbal reprimands, eye contact, and a firm grasp on the student's shoulder on student disruptive behavior. In a second study of student disruptive behavior, they compared the effects of reprimands without eye contact when the teacher was close to the student (1 m away) with reprimands given from a greater distance (7 m). Figure 3 shows how these two studies could be combined to examine the interactive effects of some of these variables. This four-fold table can be realized in multielement designs, just as were the previous examples. Perhaps any four-fold table of experimentally manipulable variables can; we need to find out. But more urgently, we need to reconsider what variables are worth the appreciable cost of these designs.

Presently, many studies using multielement designs have examined the parameters of time periods (morning vs. afternoon), settings (classroom vs. therapy session), or adults (male vs. female). These interactions are usually uninteresting; they lack both generalizability and explanation. In other words, when interactions are found between treatments and such "marker" variables (Baer, 1984), the results are nonexplanatory: If morning sessions produce better treatment effects than afternoon sessions, numerous speculations could be made regarding why this effect occurred. Sometimes the reason is eventually identified—say, differential fatigue produces the differences between sessions. Yet, even the knowledge about this factor need not identify the fundamental processes responsible for the interaction effect (why should fatigue interact with this treatment in this way?). And it need not specify the nature of its further investigation (although its management may be clinically desirable even in the absence of understanding why it occurs).

Extraneous variables can be and often are counterbalanced in multielement designs, so that their influence on different treatments will be balanced—they will have equal opportunity to influence each treatment's effectiveness. Several authors recommend additional procedures for minimizing multiple treatment interference, such as separating treatment sessions with a time interval, and using slower and/or presumably more discriminable alternations (Barlow & Hersen, 1984; Kazdin, 1982; McGonigle et al., 1987; McReynolds & Kearns, 1983). These authors carefully assert that these procedures only *minimize* multiple treatment interference (and the more prudent of these authors assert even more carefully that these procedures only *probably* minimize those effects). Even so, some studies continue to claim that they have controlled for interaction effects by using these techniques. Sequence effects, slow- or fast-paced, may or may not be eliminated by these techniques, and certainly could be present in any fast-paced alternation of treatments, counterbalanced or not. These procedures may be useful in minimizing such effects, but they do not control for them either in the sense of providing experimental evidence of when these interactions occur, or in the sense of preventing them from occurring. Further experimental manipulations are necessary to assess directly the extent to which interaction effects are present in multielement designs.

Even when precise control of marker variables is possible, the nature of their interactions quite often is specific to the individual subject (e.g., McGonigle et al., 1987). The magnitude and intricacies of such interactions usually will be idiosyncratic (i.e., not generalizable to a wide variety of conditions or subjects). Consequently, the value of experimentally investigating behavior under the interactive control of these variables will be correspondingly restricted. For these reasons, researchers should be encouraged to analyze interactions between treatments and more meaningful contextual variables rather than to counterbalance them.

Unfortunately, few researchers have been encouraged to do so. Most of the multielement designs reviewed by Barlow and Hersen (1984) did not examine interactions among variables and were not intended to do so. Only 14 of their 31 reviewed studies used multielement designs that allow some examination of interaction effects, and of these, only two—those of Shapiro et al. (1982) and Van Houten et al. (1982)—explicitly proposed to do so. The other 12 studies did not mention the extent to which interaction effects were present, and they did not evaluate the usefulness of their designs for examining interactions.

A survey of the 1975 and 1984 volumes of the *Journal of Applied Behavior Analysis* also supports the conclusion that the analytic use of multielement designs has not changed. Fourteen studies used multielement designs in the 1984 volume, whereas only seven appeared in 1975; but neither volume included studies that examined interaction effects.

CONCLUSION

When multielement designs are set within a reversal design alternating fast-paced alternations of their components with examinations of each element in isolation, as shown in the prototypic design variations above, they are capable of revealing when sequence effects operate, as described earlier by Sidman in his sketch of the methods of independent verification and functional manipulation (1960). Unfortunately, the authors of single-subject research design books usually discuss these methods only as assessing multiple treatment interference. Any interpretation of that literature as "employ the appropriate procedural controls (such as counterbalancing) and hope to minimize the effects of multiple treatment interference" seems misguided; instead, "assess many effects of potential multiple treatment interference" and "try superordinate multielement designs for the study of contextual interactions more meaningful than sequence effects" both seem more accurate and realistic. So far, researchers have often investigated the relative effectiveness of two or more treatments in alternation, but they have rarely examined whether the treatments interact, and they have not investigated the generality of their treatments' effectiveness by varying their potentially crucial contextual parameters (cf. Van Houten, 1987).

Ironically, the multielement design was introduced initially as a quickly informative design. Within very severe limits, it is. But the experience in the field of using it for that purpose now shows us that it can have a much more valuable function—the study of interactions. To serve that function, the multielement design will prove invaluable, but now it will be an expensive design: It will cost a great deal of time and careful experimental control over many conditions. In the world of experimental design, perhaps we should always doubt that a great deal of information can ever be gained in a very short design.

REFERENCES

Baer, D. M. (1984). Future directions: Or is it useful to ask, "Where did we go wrong?" before we go? In R. F. Dangel & R. A. Polster (Eds.), *Parent training: Where it's at and where it's going* (pp. 547–557). New York: Guilford Press.

Barlow, D. H., & Hayes, S. C. (1979). Alternating treatments design: One strategy for comparing the effects of two treatments in a single subject. *Journal of Applied Behavior Analysis,* **12,** 199–210.

Barlow, D. H., & Hersen, M. (1984). *Single case experimental designs: Strategies for studying behavior change* (2nd ed.). New York: Pergamon Press.

Barrett, R. P., Matson, J. L., Shapiro, E. S., & Ollendick, T. H. (1981). A comparison of punishment and DRO procedures for treating stereotypic behavior of mentally retarded children. *Applied Research in Mental Retardation,* **2,** 247–256.

Bittle, R., & Hake, D. F. (1977). A multielement design model for component analysis and cross-setting assessment of a treatment package. *Behavior Therapy,* **8,** 906–914.

Browning, R. M. (1967). A same-subject design for simultaneous comparison of three reinforcement contingencies. *Behaviour Research and Therapy,* **5,** 237–243.

Campbell, D. T., & Stanley, J. C. (1963). *Experimental and quasi-experimental designs for research.* Chicago: Rand McNally.

Corte, H. E., Wolf, M. M., & Locke, B. J. (1971). A comparison of procedures for eliminating self-injurious behavior of retarded adolescents. *Journal of Applied Behavior Analysis,* **4,** 201–213.

Doke, L. A., & Risley, T. R. (1972). The organization of day-care environments: Required vs. optional activities. *Journal of Applied Behavior Analysis,* **5,** 405–420.

Hallahan, D. P., Lloyd, J. W., Kneedler, R. D., & Marshall, K. J. (1982). A comparison of the effects of self- versus teacher-assessment of on-task behavior. *Behavior Therapy.* **13,** 715–723.

Hersen, M., & Barlow, D. H. (1976). *Single-case experimental designs: Strategies for studying behavior change.* New York: Pergamon Press.

Kantor, J. R. (1959). *Interbehavioral psychology.* Granville, OH: Principia Press.

Kazdin, A. E. (1982). *Single-case research designs: Methods for clinical and applied settings.* New York: Oxford University Press.

Kazdin, A. E., & Geesey, S. (1977). Simultaneous-treatment design comparisons of the effects of earning reinforcers for one's peers versus for oneself. *Behavior Therapy,* **8,** 682–693.

Kazdin, A. E., & Hartmann, D. P. (1978). The simultaneous-treatment design. *Behavior Therapy,* **9,** 912–922.

Martin, G., Pallotta-Cornick, A., Johnstone, G., & Celso-Goyos, A. (1980). A supervisory strategy to improve work performance for lower functioning retarded clients in a sheltered workshop. *Journal of Applied Behavior Analysis,* **13,** 183–190.

McGonigle, J. J., Rojahn, J., Dixon, J., & Strain, P. S. (1987). Multiple treatment interference in the alternating treatments design as a function of the intercomponent interval length. *Journal of Applied Behavior Analysis,* **20,** 171–178.

McReynolds, L. V., & Kearns, K. P. (1983). *Single-subject experimental designs in communicative disorders.* Baltimore: University Park Press.

Morris, E. K., Higgins, S. T., & Bickel, W. K. (1982). Comments on cognitive science in the experimental analysis of behavior. *The Behavior Analyst,* **5,** 285–290.

O'Brien, F., Azrin, N. H., & Henson, K. (1969). Increased communications of chronic mental patients by reinforcement and by response priming. *Journal of Applied Behavior Analysis,* **2,** 23–29.

Ollendick, T. H., Matson, J. L., Esveldt-Dawson, K., & Shapiro, E. S. (1980). Increasing spelling achievement: An analysis of treatment procedures utilizing an alternating treatments design. *Journal of Applied Behavior Analysis,* **13,** 645–654.

Ollendick, T. H., Shapiro, E. S., & Barrett, R. P. (1981). Reducing stereotypic behaviors: An analysis of treatment procedures utilizing an alternating treatments design. *Behavior Therapy,* **12,** 570–577.

Rojahn, J., Mulick, J. A., McCoy, D., & Schroeder, S. R. (1978). Setting effects, adaptive clothing, and the modification of head-banging and self-restraint in two profoundly retarded adults. *Behavioural Analysis and Modification,* **2,** 185–196.

Shapiro, E. S., Barrett, R. P., & Ollendick, T. H. (1980). A comparison of physical restraint and positive practice overcorrection in treating stereotypic behavior. *Behavior Therapy,* **11,** 227–233.

Shapiro, E. S., Kazdin, A. E., & McGonigle, J. J. (1982). Multiple-treatment interference in the simultaneous- or alternating-treatments design. *Behavioral Assessment,* **4,** 105–115.

Sidman, M. (1960). *Tactics of scientific research: Evaluating experimental data in psychology.* New York: Basic Books.

Singh, N. N., Winton, A. S., & Dawson, M. H. (1982). Suppression of antisocial behavior by facial screening using multiple baseline and alternating treatments designs. *Behavior Therapy,* **13,** 511–520.

Ulman, J. D., & Sulzer-Azaroff, B. (1975). Multielement baseline design in educational research. In E. Ramp & G. Semb (Eds.), *Behavior analysis: Areas of research and application* (pp. 377–391). Englewood Cliffs, NJ: Prentice-Hall.

Van Houten, R. (1987). Comparing treatment techniques: A cautionary note. *Journal of Applied Behavior Analysis,* **20,** 109–110.

Van Houten, R., Nau, P. A., MacKenzie-Keating, S. E., Sameoto, D., & Colavecchia, B. (1982). An analysis of some variables influencing the effectiveness of reprimands. *Journal of Applied Behavior Analysis,* **15,** 65–83.

Weinrott, M. R., Garrett, B., & Todd, N. (1978). The influence of observer presence on classroom behavior. *Behavior Therapy,* **9,** 900–911.

Received October 26, 1987
Initial editorial decision January 23, 1988
Revision received April 13, 1988
Final acceptance July 23, 1988
Action Editor, R. Wayne Fuqua

JOURNAL OF APPLIED BEHAVIOR ANALYSIS 1990, 23, 333–339 NUMBER 3 (FALL 1990)

APPLICATIONS OF A SEQUENTIAL ALTERNATING TREATMENTS DESIGN

David Wacker, Colleen McMahon, Mark Steege, Wendy Berg, Gary Sasso, and Kris Melloy

THE UNIVERSITY OF IOWA

We propose the use of a combined version of the alternating treatments and multiple baseline designs in situations in which a traditional baseline (no treatment) condition either does not provide an adequate contrast condition or is not feasible or practical due to clinical constraints. We refer to this design as a sequential alternating treatments design because two treatments are initially implemented in a random or counterbalanced fashion and are followed by a sequential change in one or both treatments across settings, subjects, or tasks. The effects of the independent variables are assessed first by analyzing the two series of data points representing the different treatments (relative effects) and then by assessing changes in one or both series, as application of the alternative treatment is introduced sequentially. The sequential application of treatment provides an analysis of control in the same manner as the multiple baseline design; the initial alternating treatments phase provides a contrast condition in much the same manner as a baseline condition. Applications of this design to the assessment of peer training and self-injurious behavior are described.

DESCRIPTORS: within-subject design, clinical evaluation, baseline

---

In most within-subject designs, a nontreatment or baseline phase precedes the initiation of treatment (Barlow & Hersen, 1984). The baseline phase provides a contrast condition or, as Risley and Wolf (1972) pointed out, a predictor of the target behavior if untreated. In most cases, baseline continues until stability of responding is achieved (Baer, Wolf, & Risley, 1968) so that the results of treatment can be compared directly to baseline. A number of authors (e.g., Barlow & Hersen, 1984; Johnston & Pennypacker, 1981; Kazdin, 1982) have discussed the importance of baseline for evaluating internal validity in within-subject designs.

Occasions When a Traditional Baseline Is Not Feasible or Practical

Some evaluation situations pose feasibility and pragmatic concerns regarding the inclusion of a traditional baseline (no treatment) condition in the experimental design. For example, a pragmatic concern might occur in evaluating the occurrence of social interactions between handicapped and nonhandicapped students in a classroom setting under two different conditions. In one condition, the nonhandicapped peer provides the statement, "Let's play a (specific) game"; in the other condition, the peer says, "Let me show you how to play the game." In this case, the initiating statement made by the peer is the independent variable. Some studies have suggested that social interactions will occur more often for the handicapped child if he or she is asked rather than instructed to play (Haring, Breen, Pitts-Conway, Lee, & Gaylord-Ross, 1987; Sasso, Mitchell, & Struthers, 1986). A comparison of these strategies as a research question poses several pragmatic problems relative to the inclusion of a traditional baseline condition that includes a series of observations of unprompted interactions prior to the initiating-statements condition. If a multiple baseline design across dyads is used for evaluation, the uncontrolled behavior of the peer and the target child always precedes both treatment conditions (play vs. instruct); this order could influence subsequent treatment conditions in unknown directions. In a worst-case scenario, the behavior of the peer or target child might require intervention due

---

The preparation of this manuscript was supported, in part, by the Iowa University Affiliated Facility. The authors gratefully acknowledge Agnes DeRaad for her expert editorial assistance.

Colleen McMahon is now at Georgetown University; Mark Steege is now at the University of Southern Maine.

Requests for reprints should be sent to David P. Wacker, Division of Developmental Disabilities, The University of Iowa, Iowa City, Iowa 52242.

to inappropriate behavior such as teasing, punishing statements, or the display of socially unacceptable behavior.

The inclusion of baseline also is problematic if the teacher or researcher is interested in evaluating the effects of two types of initiating statements during the *initial* contact between the students. It is not typical for children to be paired or grouped together without instructions regarding their activities. Thus, a great deal of time and effort is sometimes spent developing a baseline condition that seldom occurs in the natural context. Although a return to baseline following treatment (BAB) might be considered to evaluate control, a reversal is possible only if the effects of treatment are not maintained.

Similar concerns can arise in evaluating self-injurious behavior (SIB). For example, assume that a child in a hospital setting engages in SIB only during demanding activities (e.g., self-help skills training and physical therapy). If an activity varies on some known dimension (e.g., passive vs. active participation), it could be viewed as representing more than one treatment (type of demand). In this case, the supposition could be made that it is not demands per se, but distinct types of demands, that produce SIB. Baselines across other activities might be recorded to replicate this finding (e.g., requirements for passive vs. active participation in other activities), but one is still left with a baseline phase that is comprised of two distinct treatments.

Alternating Treatments Design Without Baseline

One solution is to use an alternating treatments design (Barlow & Hayes, 1979) that does not include a baseline phase. The major question addressed by alternating treatments designs is whether one treatment is more effective than another (Barlow & Hersen, 1984; Hains & Baer, 1989). In both examples described above, the two treatment conditions (specific statements or specific demands) may be compared directly to determine whether one treatment resulted in greater effects (higher frequency of social behavior or self-injurious behavior) relative to the other.

In some cases, the use of an alternating treatments design without a baseline phase is adequate to evaluate functional control: Treatment A is superior to Treatment B across sessions. For example, in the study reported by Steege, Wacker, Berg, Cigrand, and Cooper (1989), the use of an alternating treatments design was sufficient to demonstrate changes in self-injurious behavior across functional analysis conditions without preceding the treatment conditions with a baseline phase. The alternating treatments design, as a comparison design, is adequate for evaluating the relative effects of two or more treatments in the absence of a baseline condition (Barlow & Hersen, 1984).

Alternating Treatments Design With Baseline

In other cases, a baseline condition is necessary to evaluate the effects of treatment, especially if similar effects occurred for both treatments. For example, Wacker, Berg, Wiggins, Muldoon, and Cavanaugh (1985) used a combination multiple baseline (across subjects) with alternating treatments design to evaluate potential reinforcers. In this investigation, two or more microswitch-activated toys were evaluated as potential reinforcers for profoundly handicapped children within an alternating treatments design. Performance during baseline demonstrated that presence of the microswitches, when not connected to the toys, did not increase responding (i.e., pressing the switch). Instead, responding increased only when the microswitches activated specific toys. Of equal importance, the inclusion of some toys resulted in decreased responding relative to baseline, indicating that these toys functioned as punishers to the children. Thus, the presence of baseline provided information needed for evaluating the reinforcing effects of each toy.

A baseline condition is also useful for evaluating carryover effects. For example, Shapiro, Kazdin, and McGonigle (1982) used a baseline condition to evaluate carryover effects directly by changing the presentation of their treatments. The investigators compared response cost, token reinforcement, and a baseline condition by conducting four alternating treatment evaluations, with each dyad of treatment and baseline repeated twice. The tokens produced similar results when compared to either baseline or response cost, demonstrating minimal, if any, carryover effects. In both of the above investigations, a baseline condition, conducted either prior to treatment or counterbalanced with treatment, functioned as a contrast condition against which the results of treatment could be compared.

In the above two examples, the use of a traditional baseline condition permitted more precise evaluation of the effects of the treatment conditions by providing a contrast condition. The contrast condition, in the first example, provided more information on the absolute effects of treatment and, in the second example, provided more information on interaction effects. It is probably for this reason—the provision of additional information—that alternating treatments designs are seldom conducted without a baseline condition, even though a baseline condition is not a technical requirement (Barlow & Hersen, 1984).

Sequential Alternating Treatments Design

A paradox confronts applied researchers: In some applied situations, a naturalistic baseline is difficult to implement, yet the inclusion of a baseline or contrast condition is frequently necessary for more precise evaluations of experimental control. In these situations, improved evaluation of control might be possible by first extending the alternating treatments conditions across subjects, settings, or tasks in a staggered fashion, identical to the multiple baseline design. The alternating treatments condition then could be followed by the sequential application of one or both treatments to evaluate changes in behavior associated with each treatment. An example of this approach is provided in Figure 1. In this simulated investigation (based on a study by McMahon, Wacker, Sasso, & Melloy, 1988), the investigators assigned 2 nonhandicapped peers each to play with 3 moderately mentally retarded boys. One peer was told to approach his assigned partner and say, "Let's play ———; it's a favorite game of mine" (Play statement). The second peer was told to say, "Let me show you how to play ———" (Instruct statement). The same game was used for both peers; only the instructions changed.

In this investigation, the first condition of the design was an alternating treatments phase, with the statements made by a peer serving as the independent variable. The dependent variable was the percentage of social interactions occurring per 10-min session. The initial condition of the design was then extended sequentially across target children to form a sequential alternating treatments design. The results demonstrated good stability of responding, suggesting that social interactions were facilitated more by the play statement than by the instruct statement.

To replicate these results, one of the initiating statements (counterbalanced across children) was changed to the alternative statement; in other words, both peers asked the target child to play or both provided instruction. This was followed by a second change condition, in which both peers provided the opposite statement. The results show that (a) the statement delivered by the peer controlled responding across target children, (b) the results were reversible, and (c) changes in behavior occurred with changes in statement and not as a function of exposure to a particular peer. Extending the initial alternating treatments condition permitted evaluation of the effects of time, exposure to a given peer, practice, and other potential sources of external confounding. By changing the statement delivered by 1 peer and then by the 2nd peer, replication of control over behavior by the independent variable was evaluated.

In the above example, evaluation of experimental control by the independent variable was established through two distinct design modifications: (a) sequential modification of the treatment condition and (b) two change (or replication) conditions, each demonstrating that behavior was controlled by the peers' verbal statements. Although both design modifications are desirable for experimental control, pragmatic considerations (e.g., maintenance) may limit the use of the replication conditions (in the same way that standard reversal designs may not be possible). When replication or reversal conditions are not possible, the sequential

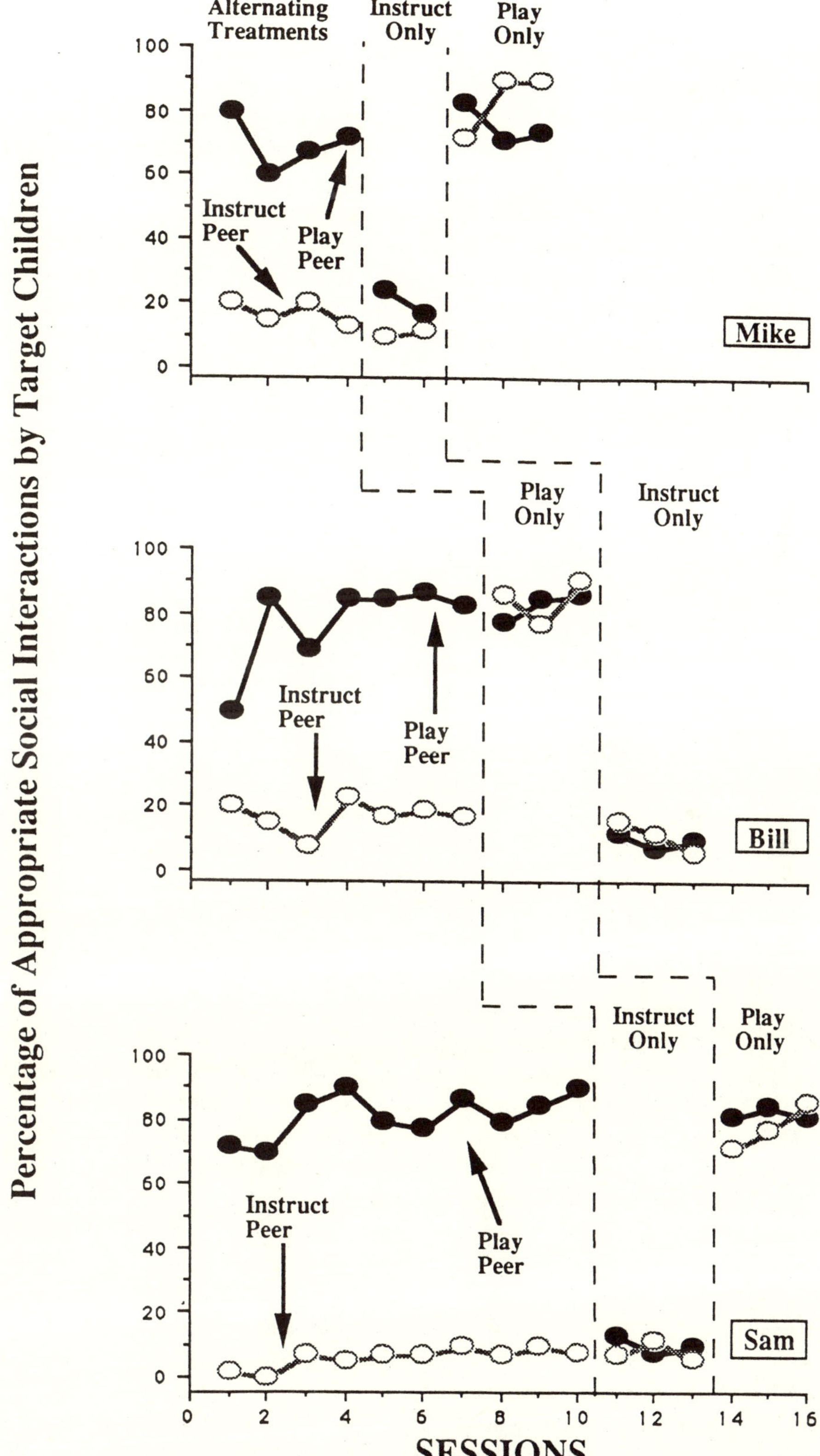

Figure 1. Example of a sequential alternating treatments design across subjects with peer training.

application of one of the treatments can still provide increased information regarding experimental control.

An example of this type of sequential alternating treatments design is provided in Figure 2. In this example, an initial assessment demonstrated that the subject, a profoundly mentally retarded child, engaged in self-injurious behavior during demanding activities. Within these activities, however, the behavior of the child was inconsistent, suggesting that different types of demands during the activities were differentially affecting behavior. To better assess whether specific types of demands had differential effects on the occurrence of self-injurious behavior, separate occurrence data were collected for both passive and active demands. The active demands were defined as prompting the child to participate partially in the activity, and the passive demands were defined as occurring when the activities were performed for the child.

During the alternating treatments condition, a greater percentage of self-injurious behavior occurred across all activities when the subject was provided with passive versus active demands (see Figure 2). However, as was the case for the first example, possible confounding effects occurred because the passive and active demands occurred in the context of the same activity. The possibility of this type of confounding effect was reduced by showing the same effects across four activities (standard alternating treatments design), but was virtually eliminated with the sequential application of active demands across the activities. Because the modification of activities occurred in a sequential fashion, the effects of practice and exposure to treatment were evaluated in the same way that these extraneous variables are evaluated within a multiple baseline across tasks design.

Applications and Limitations of the Sequential Alternating Treatments Design

The application of the sequential alternating treatments design is limited to the same situations recommended for the alternating treatments design, as discussed by Barlow and Hersen (1984) and Hains and Baer (1989): Relatively quick effects of treatment are expected with minimal carryover effects from one treatment to the next. In these situations, the greatest utility of the sequential alternating treatments design is probably in clinical or educational situations in which two or more independent variables warrant evaluation and relatively brief periods of time are available for identifying the respective effects of each independent variable. For example, in the evaluation of aberrant behavior discussed earlier, the control of behavior by one treatment over another might first be evaluated through direct comparison across situations and then confirmed through sequential changes in one or both treatments over time.

In other situations, the greatest utility might be when implementation of baseline poses pragmatic problems. For example, the applicability of a traditional baseline may be problematic in situations in which the student is receiving on-the-job training. Instead, the student might initially receive two types of instruction (e.g., picture prompts vs. time delay prompting) across work tasks to determine the relative effects of each instructional approach. Once relative differences have been identified, introduction of the preferred approach across work tasks in a staggered fashion provides the teacher with evidence of functional control in the same manner as the multiple baseline design.

In our previous research, the sequential alternating treatments design would have been useful in our evaluations of self-injurious behavior (Steege et al., 1989), picture prompts in school settings (Wacker, Berg, Berrie, & Swatta, 1985), and social behavior (Sasso & Rude, 1987).

Hains and Baer (1989) provided a thorough evaluation of alternating treatments designs and presented several options for evaluating interaction effects. We agree with Hains and Baer that evaluation of interaction effects can be important and can be best evaluated within the design options they proposed. Those options should be considered when interaction effects are of interest, because the sequential alternating treatments design is not as useful for evaluating interaction effects.

Gast and Wolery (1988) also proposed a modification of the alternating treatments design, which

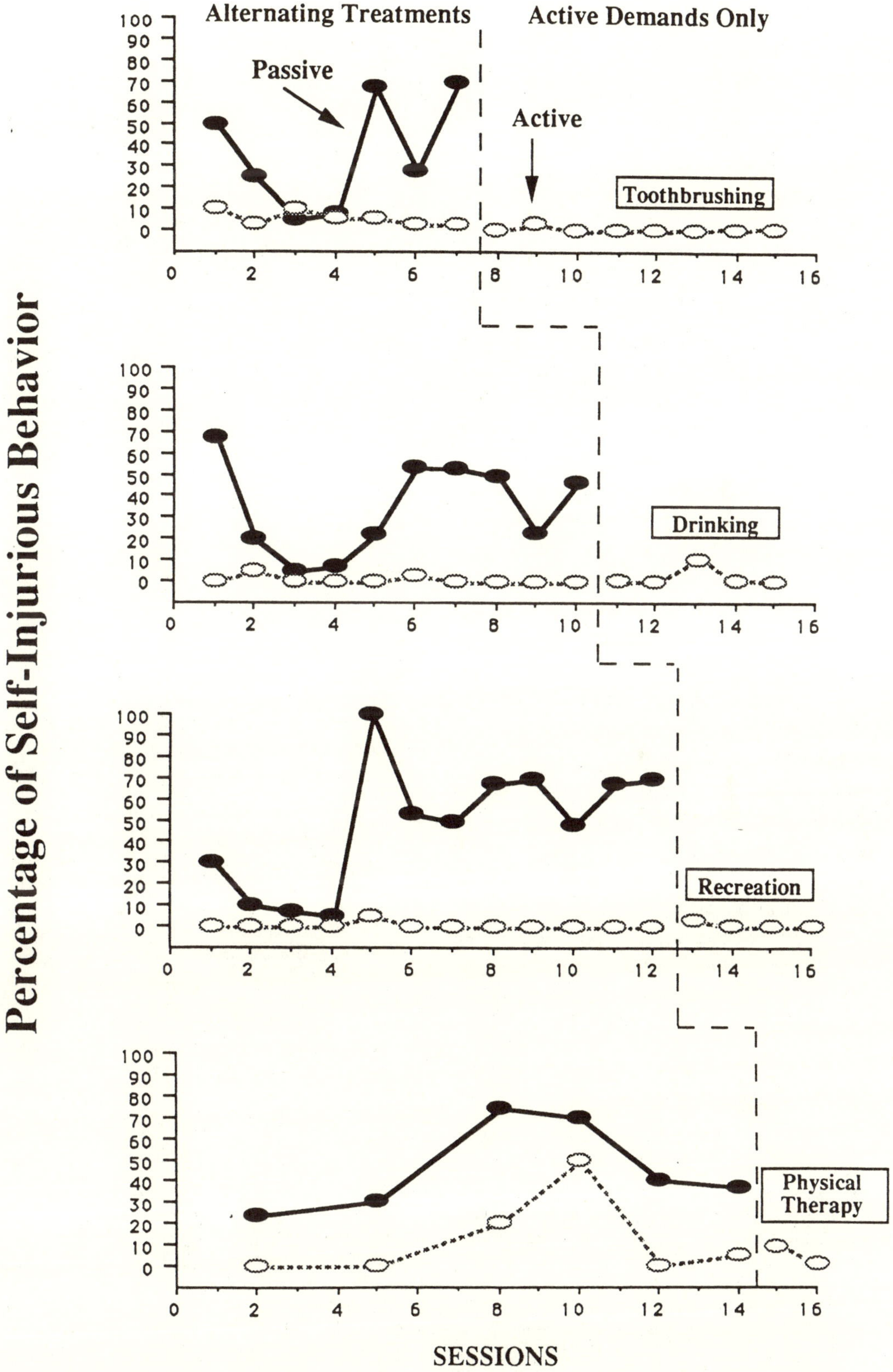

Figure 2. Example of a sequential alternating treatments design across tasks with self-injurious behavior.

they termed the parallel treatments design, for treatments that produce durable results that are not easily reversible. In situations in which two or more treatments will be compared, and both treatments are expected to produce durable results, the use of the parallel treatments design should be considered.

Summary

We suggest that the sequential alternating treatments design be considered in situations in which, for a variety of reasons, conducting a traditional baseline condition may prove to be difficult. These situations may occur most often when two or more independent variables are possible or are in effect during initial observation or assessment. In the sequential alternating treatments design, the alternating treatments condition constitutes a contrast condition within which the relative effects of each variable are evaluated. This condition is then followed by one or more change conditions, in which one treatment is sequentially applied across subjects, tasks, or settings.

The absence of a baseline phase can still be problematic with the sequential alternating treatments design. Without a baseline, for example, it is possible only to compare the relative effects of two treatments and to demonstrate the sequential control established by one or both of those treatments. In many situations, this may be adequate, as with the self-injurious behavior example. In other cases, this may not be adequate, because the central question is concerned with the absolute magnitude of effects, or with interaction effects, in addition to relative effects.

REFERENCES

Baer, D., Wolf, M., & Risley, T. (1968). Some current dimensions of applied behavior analysis. *Journal of Applied Behavior Analysis,* **1,** 91–97.

Barlow, D., & Hayes, S. (1979). Alternating treatments design: One strategy for comparing the effects of two treatments in a single subject. *Journal of Applied Behavior Analysis,* **12,** 199–210.

Barlow, D., & Hersen, M. (1984). *Single case experimental designs* (2nd ed.). New York: Pergamon Press.

Gast, D., & Wolery, M. (1988). Parallel treatments design: A nested single subject design for comparing instructional procedures. *Education and Treatment of Children,* **11,** 270–285.

Hains, A., & Baer, D. (1989). Interaction effects in multielement designs: Inevitable, desirable, and ignorable. *Journal of Applied Behavior Analysis,* **22,** 57–69.

Haring, T., Breen, C., Pitts-Conway, V., Lee, M., & Gaylord-Ross, R. (1987). Adolescent peer tutoring and special friends experiences. *Journal of the Association for Persons with Severe Handicaps,* **12,** 280–286.

Johnston, J., & Pennypacker, H. (1981). *Strategies and tactics of human behavioral research.* Hillsdale, NJ: Erlbaum.

Kazdin, A. (1982). *Single-case research designs: Methods for clinical and applied settings.* New York: Oxford University Press.

McMahon, C., Wacker, D., Sasso, G., & Melloy, K. (1988). *Instructional control of peer interactions between handicapped and nonhandicapped students.* Unpublished manuscript, University of Iowa.

Risley, T., & Wolf, M. (1972). Strategies for analyzing behavioral change over time. In J. Nesselroade & H. Reese (Eds.), *Life-span developmental psychology: Methodological issues* (pp. 175–183). New York: Academic Press.

Sasso, G., Mitchell, V., & Struthers, E. (1986). Peer tutoring versus structured interaction activities: Effects on the frequency and topography of peer initiations. *Behavioral Disorders,* **11,** 249–259.

Sasso, G., & Rude, H. (1987). Unprogrammed effects of training high-status peers to interact with severely handicapped children. *Journal of Applied Behavior Analysis,* **20,** 35–44.

Shapiro, E., Kazdin, A., & McGonigle, J. (1982). Multiple treatment interference in the simultaneous or alternating treatments design. *Behavioral Assessment,* **4,** 105–115.

Steege, M., Wacker, D., Berg, W., Cigrand, K., & Cooper, L. (1989). The use of behavioral assessment to prescribe and evaluate treatments for severely handicapped children. *Journal of Applied Behavior Analysis,* **22,** 23–33.

Wacker, D., Berg, W., Berrie, P., & Swatta, P. (1985). Generalization and maintenance of complex skills by severely handicapped adolescents following picture prompt training. *Journal of Applied Behavior Analysis,* **18,** 329–336.

Wacker, D., Berg, W., Wiggins, B., Muldoon, M., & Cavanaugh, J. (1985). Evaluation of reinforcer preferences for profoundly handicapped students. *Journal of Applied Behavior Analysis,* **18,** 173–178.

Received January 17, 1989
Initial editorial decision May 24, 1989
Revisions received August 17, 1989; April 18, 1990
Final acceptance April 20, 1990
Action Editor, Susan A. Fowler

JOURNAL OF APPLIED BEHAVIOR ANALYSIS 1972, 5, 193-198 NUMBER 2 (SUMMER 1972)

AN ANALYSIS-OF-VARIANCE MODEL FOR THE INTRASUBJECT REPLICATION DESIGN[1]

J. RONALD GENTILE, AUBREY H. RODEN, AND ROGER D. KLEIN

STATE UNIVERSITY OF NEW YORK AT BUFFALO AND UNIVERSITY OF PITTSBURGH

One- and two-way analysis-of-variance procedures are shown logically to be appropriate for testing hypotheses in successive treatment reversal designs for one-subject and N-subject experiments, respectively. The applicability of these designs is demonstrated through analyses of typical data.

The preponderance of studies conducted within the paradigm of operant behavior employ the intrasubject replication design (often called, simply, the reversal design), in which various treatments are successively applied to and removed from the same subject (Sidman, 1960). For example, the A-B-A-B design (in which A = baseline of no reinforcement for a certain response, B = the contingent availability of a reinforcing stimulus following that response) is widely used to demonstrate that if a certain reinforcer is made available contingent upon a response (treatment B), the effect is to increase the frequency of that response above operant level (condition A). Then conditions are reversed and treatment A is reinstated, during which time the response rate is expected to revert to its operant level. Finally, treatment B is re-applied and the response rate is expected once again to increase to above operant level.

Control over the behavior in question can be said to be obtained only when the B treatment provides a *significant change* in response rate over that obtained in A. In other words, changes in behavior must reliably occur as a result of these treatment changes or else the investigator cannot infer a functional relationship between the treatment and the behavior. Also, such changes in behavior as a result of changes in the treatment conditions provide the most convincing demonstration of functional relationships.

The importance of this general procedure for the experimental analysis of behavior can hardly be overemphasized. This design, or variants of it, has been the vehicle for many principles of behavior developed in the last several decades and for most of the successes of operant behavior modification procedures in practical settings. (Indeed, the general form of this argument—if A, then B; if not A, then not B—is one of the most fundamental arguments in scientific methodology.)

Nevertheless, there are some disadvantages of the reversal design (see Bandura, 1969, pp. 242-244), one of the most serious of which is the interpretive problem of how large does the behavior change from treatment to treatment have to be to be considered a significant change. As Bandura points out, interpretation is not difficult provided that large successive behavior changes occur rapidly and consistently for many subjects. The interpretive problem arises in those cases in which the behavioral changes are not dramatic or in which some individuals remain unaffected by repeated exposure to one of the treatments. Such findings are especially prevalent in situations, such as classrooms, in which laboratory controls for creating favorable experimental conditions are difficult to achieve. The problem as stated reduces to a statistical one:

---

[1]Appreciation is expressed to S. David Farr, Malcolm J. Slakter, Thomas J. Shuell, Richard Spencer and Kevin Crehan for their assistance. Reprints may be obtained from J. Ronald Gentile, Educational Psychology Dept., State University of New York, Buffalo, N.Y. 14214.

> ". . . no statistical criteria have been developed to evaluate whether the magnitude of change produced by a given treatment exceeds the variability resulting from uncontrolled factors operating while the treatment condition is not in effect." (Bandura, 1969, p. 243)

Probably the major reason for the lack of concern with statistical analyses of the data is the assumed inapplicability of statistical techniques to individual cases or small numbers of subjects. Properly conceived, however, studies that collect repeated observations on the same individual (as is typical of most operant studies using time-sampling techniques or of clinical studies collecting data on patients) are appropriate for the analysis of variance model. The purpose of the present paper is to provide the rationale behind the use of an analysis-of-variance model for the reversal design, both for the one subject case and for more than one subject.

A PROBLEM

Klein (1971) investigated the effects of teacher attention and tokens (stars, which could later be exchanged for time spent on activities during a play period) contingent upon on-task behavior, compared with tokens contingent upon task completion, on three kindergarten students. On-task behavior was defined as the student attending to the task for a specified period of time, while task completion was correctly finishing the task. One expectation was that making reinforcement contingent upon the less-demanding on-task response would increase the time these students spent in on-task behavior. The phases of the study follow:

- A_1: baseline, in which a token economy was in operation, reinforcement of five tokens being contingent upon task completion.
- B: teacher attention was made contingent upon on-task behavior, the teacher approaching the child periodically when he was working on the task and commenting favorably on his behavior. Five tokens were still received at the time of task completion.
- C_1: tokens were made contingent upon on-task behavior, the teacher approaching the child periodically as in Phase B but, in addition to supplying social reinforcement, supplying tokens. There were still five tokens per task, but they were now distributed throughout the task.
- A_2: return to baseline.
- C_2: return to condition C_1.

It is beyond the scope of this paper to go into detail on the methodology of Klein's study, since it is being discussed only as a vehicle for understanding the need for the model we present below. Suffice it to say that conditions A, B, and C constitute three experimental treatments, the independent variable. The measured result of the manipulation, the dependent variable, is a binomial distribution obtained by observers using a time-sampling procedure, *i.e.,* number of on-task responses.

The results are indicated in Table 1, and they provide some difficulties in interpretation. For instance, although there are differences as predicted among treatments A_1, B, C_1, and A_2 for James, are these differences reliable? Why did the return to condition C (Phase C_2) not have the effect of increasing the number of on-task behaviors over baseline as it had in Phase C_1? Another problem is that the same profile of results is not shown by Lynn, since on-task behavior in C_2 was increased over baseline and, more to the point, since it was increased in B over C.

Differences such as these are not easily rationalized by inspection of the data. On the other hand, 24 days of actual classroom time were involved in the collection of these data, not including the planning time, training the teacher and motivating her for the extra work, *etc.* A

Table 1

Mean proportions, standard deviations, and number of observations (recorded intervals) of on-task behavior for each phase for two students from Klein (1971).

Student		Phase A_1	B	C_1	A_2	C_2
James	Mean Proportion	0.286	0.331	0.372	0.219	0.202
	Standard Deviation	0.452	0.471	0.484	0.415	0.402
	No. of Observations	974	610	529	210	282
Lynn	Mean Proportion	0.260	0.446	0.381	0.266	0.301
	Standard Deviation	0.439	0.498	0.486	0.445	0.460
	No. of Observations	1023	480	565	90	143

statistical technique would certainly be useful to aid the experimenter in making sense of the data and to suggest whether replication would be profitable.

THE ONE-WAY ANALYSIS-OF-VARIANCE MODEL

We propose that the experiment for each subject discussed above, and other experiments similar to it, be conceived as a one-way analysis-of-variance design, with (1) treatment effects being what is traditionally considered the between-subjects effects, and (2) number of observations being considered the standard within-subjects effects. With this change in conception, the justification of which follows, traditional formulas can be used to test the hypothesis that behaviors arising from each treatment condition could have been drawn by chance from the same population.

Behavior of a single person can be conceived as a chain of response events occurring in time. Any given response of interest, adequately defined (such as the number of sneezes or vocalizations, per cent of time spent reading, *etc.*), can be viewed as occurring with some frequency per specified time period. The average number of responses over some large number of such time periods can be considered to approach the "true" frequency distribution of that response for that person. Further, each response can be considered as independent of every other response in the same class. Then, an unbiased estimate of the response belonging to the defined class, obtained by randomly sampling observation times from the population of times available on an *a priori* basis, will have a mean that approaches the true population mean for the response as the sample size increases.

The above assumptions are analogous to those that would be stated for tossing a coin repeatedly for some large number of times throughout some period of time. The "true" distribution of the results would be obtained by observing the total number of tosses. Each toss is considered to be independent of the previous toss. Unbiased estimates of the "true" mean can be obtained by randomly deciding ahead of time which tosses of the coin to observe and record.

Given this framework, it is a logical next step to suggest that an experiment could be designed to test the effects of temperature on the results of repeatedly tossing a single coin in which the following phases were defined:

A_1: the coin is tossed at room temperature for some large number of times.

B_1: the coin is tossed at absolute zero for some large number of times.

A_2: return to baseline conditions.

B_2: return to the conditions of B_1.

Since only one coin has been used, an exact control for order effects cannot be obtained.[2] Thus, a reversal design has been used in which there are actually four treatments: A_1; B_1 given A_1; A_2 given A_1 and B_1; and B_2 given A_1, B_1 and B_2. This means that any cumulative effects of prior conditions are completely confounded with treatments. Nevertheless, a reasonable estimate of the effects of room temperature *versus* absolute zero can be obtained by combining phases A_1 and A_2 and phases B_1 and B_2. This procedure yields two treatments A and B with a large number of independent observations within each. A traditional one-way analysis of variance can test the hypothesis that the two temperatures have different effects upon the coin tossing.

Returning again to the Klein problem, the analogous combined phases for A, B, and C constitute the between-subjects treatments in the one-way analysis of variance, with the observations having been determined by an *a priori* time sampling schedule.

Klein's data in Table 1 provide a vehicle to which the model can be applied. For this purpose, the data for James and Lynn can be used and they are presented in Table 2 (Phases $A_1 + A_2 =$ treatment A; $C_1 + C_2 =$ treatment C). The dependent variable is number of on-task responses.[3] A one-way analysis of variance on these data for James yielded an $F = 3.59$, $df = 2{,}2602$, $p < 0.05$. Thus, the hypothesis that the treatments did not differ in their effect on the on-task behavior of James can be safely rejected. A similar analysis could be done for Lynn's data, but we shall demonstrate that analysis in the two-way model.

Table 2

Mean proportions, standard deviations, and number of observations (recorded intervals) of on-task behavior for each treatment for two subjects from Klein (1971).

		Treatment		
		A	*B*	*C*
James	Mean Proportion	0.274	0.331	0.313
	Standard Deviation	0.446	0.471	0.464
	No. of Observations	1184	610	811
Lynn	Mean Proportion	0.262	0.446	0.364
	Standard Deviation	0.440	0.498	0.482
	No. of Observations	1113	480	708

VIOLATIONS OF THE ASSUMPTION OF INDEPENDENCE OF OBSERVATIONS

Shine and Bower (1971) proposed a one-way model in which they likewise assume "that the subject may be viewed as a response generator the responses of which to a particular stimulus are statistically independent and normally distributed about a central response value." (p. 112) Their model, however, introduces a pseudo-factor, trials, so that the model is actually a two-way design with treatments and trials as independent variables. With this design, there is only one observation per cell which, therefore, requires that the usual within-cell variance estimates cannot be used as the error term for the main effects and interaction as is standard in a fixed-effects model. Although

[2]Typical balanced designs used to control for order effects do not eliminate order effects in any case. All they do is serve to distribute such effects equally across conditions or subjects when data are pooled (see, for example, Sidman, 1960, pp. 245-256). To establish the functional relation between order of treatment and the observed behavior requires, not a balanced design, but a deliberate, systematic manipulation of sequences of treatments, the effects of which are compared with a stable baseline of performance.

[3]Although the dependent variable used here is a dichotomous measure, the F-test is robust with regard to such data (Hsu and Feldt, 1969; Lunney, 1970). Many studies for which this design would be appropriate have available the option of a continuous dependent measure. In Klein's study, for example, this could have been accomplished simply by recording the number of seconds of time on task.

Shine and Bower present a solution to this dilemma, we believe that it is entirely consistent with the assumptions of the fixed-effects analysis-of-variance model to dispense with the trials pseudo-factor *for the reversal design.*

The major objection raised to the application of analysis of variance models to single-subject experiments is that there may not be independence from observation to observation or from treatment to treatment. For example, there may be an observation to observation correlation, in which adjacent observations may be more highly correlated than nonadjacent observations. This dependency could produce problems for studies in which each treatment in succession is applied only once (although it is possible to test this assumption for any set of data). This is not a problem for the reversal design, however, for the reason that observations in adjacent treatments would, by this argument, be expected to be more highly correlated than observations in nonadjacent treatments. Thus, the correlation between observation 1 in Treatment A_1 and observation 1 in Treatment B_1 would be expected to be higher than the correlation between observation 1 in Treatment A_1 and observation 1 in Treatment A_2. Since we combine treatments A_1 with A_2 and B_1 with B_2 for the F-test, then any such correlations between observations will tend to make the treatments more similar and, therefore, reduce the size of the F-statistic. The effect of nonindependence of observations for the reversal design, in short, is to operate in the conservation direction for the F-test.[4]

THE TWO-WAY ANALYSIS-OF-VARIANCE MODEL

It is a straightforward extension of the one-way model to the two-way fixed-effects model. Treatments remain as one factor and subjects become the other. With additional subjects, each one considered a different level of a factor, subject differences can be assessed, as well as subject by treatment interaction effects. Klein's data in Table 2 again provide a vehicle for applying the model, much as we would have had we used two coins in the hypothetical temperature-coin flipping experiment described earlier.

Table 3

Analysis of Variance Summary Table

Source of Variation	*df*	*MS*	*F*	*p-level*
Subjects	1	1.2345	5.80	<0.02
Treatments	2	5.4381	25.55	<0.0001
Subjects X Treatments	2	1.5645	7.35	<0.0007
Within Cell (Error)	4900	0.2128		
Total	4905			

NOTE: This analysis was computed by Finn's (1967) Multivariance program, which accounts for unequal Ns through the least-squares method.

Table 3 presents the traditional two-way analysis-of-variance summary table for the data in Table 2. The between-subjects main effect yielded an $F = 5.80$, $df = 1{,}4900$, $p < 0.02$. This indicates that Lynn performed significantly more on-task responses than James across all treatments. The between-treatments main effect gave an $F = 25.55$, $df = 2{,}4900$, $p < 0.0001$, indicating that there were reliable differences among treatments. More interesting, perhaps, is the interaction effect, which yielded an $F = 7.35$, $df = 2{,}4900$, $p < 0.0007$. This finding provides statistical confirmation for the visual interpretation made earlier that Lynn and James were affected differently by the treatments. Thus, the apparent modest effects of the treatments can now be seen to be statistically reliable.

DISCUSSION

It should be noted that statistical confirmation that a significant difference was obtained in no

[4]In this regard, inclusion of Klein's treatment B in the analysis is not strictly appropriate, since it was presented only once. Consideration of the effects of this minor violation are beyond the scope of this paper since these data are included only as a vehicle for presenting the model.

way guarantees the psychological importance of the findings *vis-a-vis* the reversal design any more than it does in any other kind of investigation. If larger effects than those obtained are necessary to convince teachers, parents, clinicians, or experimenters that they should spend the considerable extra time to apply these procedures, then statistical significance will not constitute sufficient proof to be convincing. Rejection of the null hypothesis does, however, encourage the experimenter to continue to refine the technique in the high probability that he is not wasting his time and efforts on a nonexistent effect.

With that as a general caveat, let us turn to some specific points that might be raised about this approach. First, although the study used here as an example had widely disparate *N*s, it may be (as one reviewer stated) that "one should be quite scrupulous to avoid the problem of unequal number of observations per cell." This problem is not unique to this design, of course, and should be considered in the design of any experimental study (*e.g.,* see McNemar, 1969, pp. 118-121). A solution to the problem in the type of study under consideration here would be the use of a continuous dependent measure (as suggested in Footnote 3), collected at pre-planned intervals of equal lengths for each treatment.

A second point has to do with the generalizability of results in a fixed-effects model. Any single-subject or small-*N* study that shows significant treatment effects should be interpreted as indicating that, for the particular subject or subjects studied, the variance attributable to treatments was sufficiently larger than one might expect by chance. Generalization to other subjects must, in any case, be demonstrated by further study and not merely assumed.

Third, the data from any experimental study may be treated in many ways, and the model we propose is not exceptional in this regard. Thus, with only two treatments and one subject, it may be more appropriate to use a t-test analysis. Where order effects of treatments can be randomized, which is seldom the case in behavior analysis studies, it may be more appropriate to use Latin square arrangements. Or, as one reviewer suggested, it would be possible to consider the A_1 B_1 A_2 B_2 design for one subject (our one-way ANOVA Model) as being a two-way design: Treatments (A *vs.* B) arranged independently of Times (First *vs.* Second). For two or more subjects (our Two-Way ANOVA Model), the classification would then become three-way. In either case, one could obtain separate estimates of sequence and treatment effects, as well as their interaction.

However conceptualized, it seems to us that the analysis-of-variance models proposed here can aid in the interpretation of experimental treatment effects.

REFERENCES

Bandura, A. *Principles of Behavior Modification,* New York: Holt, Rinehart and Winston, Inc., 1969.

Finn, J. D. "Multivariance-Univariate and Multivariate Analysis of Variance and Covariance: A FORTRAN IV Program," unpublished manuscript. State University of New York at Buffalo, 1967.

Hsu, T. and Feldt, L. S. "The Effect of Limitations on the Number of Criterion Score Values on the Significance Level of the *F*-Test," *American Educational Research Journal,* 1969, **6,** 515-527.

Klein, R. D. "The Effects of a Systematic Manipulation of Contingencies Upon Overt Work Behavior in a Primary Classroom," unpublished Ph. D. dissertation, Department of Educational Psychology, State University of New York at Buffalo, 1971.

Lunney, G. H. "Using Analysis of Variance with a Dichotomous Dependent Variable: An Empirical Study," *Journal of Educational Measurement,* 1970, **7,** 263-269.

McNemar, Q. *Psychological Statistics,* New York: John Wiley & Sons, Fourth Edition, 1969.

Shine, L. C. II and Bower, S. M. "A One-Way Analysis of Variance for Single-Subject Designs," *Educational and Psychological Measurement,* 1971, **31,** 105-113.

Sidman, M. *Tactics of Scientific Research,* New York: Basic Books, 1960.

Received 29 April 1971.
(Revised 3 December 1971.)

JOURNAL OF APPLIED BEHAVIOR ANALYSIS 1973, 6, 331-332 NUMBER 2 (SUMMER 1973)

HIAWATHA DESIGNS AN EXPERIMENT[1]

MAURICE G. KENDALL

(Originally published in *The American Statistician,* Dec. 1959, Vol. 13, No. 5. Reprinted by Permission).

Hiawatha, mighty hunter,
He could shoot ten arrows upwards
Shoot them with such strength and swiftness
That the last had left the bowstring
Ere the first to earth descended.
This was commonly regarded
As a feat of skill and cunning.

One or two sarcastic spirits
Pointed out to him, however,
That it might be much more useful
If he sometimes hit the target.
Why not shoot a little straighter
And employ a smaller sample?

Hiawatha, who at college
Majored in applied statistics,
Consequently felt entitled
To instruct his fellow men on
Any subject whatsoever,
Waxed exceedingly indignant
Talked about the law of error,
Talked about truncated normals,
Talked of loss of information,
Talked about his lack of bias,
Pointed out that in the long run
Independent observations
Even though they missed the target
Had an average point of impact
Very near the spot he aimed at
(With the possible exception
Of a set of measure zero).

This, they said, was rather doubtful.
Anyway, it didn't matter
What resulted in the long run;
Either he must hit the target
Much more often than at present
Or himself would have to pay for
All the arrows that he wasted.

Hiawatha, in a temper,
Quoted parts of R. A. Fisher
Quoted Yates and quoted Finney
Quoted yards of Oscar Kempthorne
Quoted reams of Cox and Cochran
Quoted Anderson and Bancroft
Practically *in extenso*
Trying to impress upon them
That what actually mattered
Was to estimate the error.

One or two of them admitted
Such a thing might have its uses.
Still, they said, he might do better
If he shot a little straighter.

Hiawatha, to convince them,
Organized a shooting contest
Laid out in the proper manner
By experimental methods
Recommended in the textbooks
(Mainly used for tasting tea, but
Sometimes used in other cases)
Randomized his shooting order
In factorial arrangements
Used the theory of Galois
Fields of ideal polynomials,
Got a nicely balanced layout

[1]Reprints may be obtained from the author, Scientific Control Systems Limited, Sanderson House, 49-57 Berners Street, London WIP 4AQ England.

And successfully confounded
Second-order interactions.

All the other tribal marksmen
Ignorant, benighted creatures,
Of experimental set-ups
Spent their time of preparation
Putting in a lot of practice
Merely shooting at a target.

Thus it happened in the contest
That their scores were most impressive
With one notable exception
This (I hate to have to say it)
Was the score of Hiawatha,
Who, as usual, shot his arrows
Shot them with great strength and swiftness
Managing to be unbiased
Not, however, with his salvo
Managing to hit the target.
There, they said to Hiawatha
That is what we all expected.

Hiawatha, nothing daunted,
Called for pen and called for paper
Did analyses of variance
Finally produced the figures
Showing, beyond peradventure,
Everybody else was biased
And the variance components
Did not differ from each other
Or from Hiawatha's
(This last point, one should acknowledge
Might have been much more convincing
If he hadn't been compelled to
Estimate his own component
From experimental plots in
Which the values all were missing.
Still, they didn't understand it
So they couldn't raise objections.
This is what so often happens
With analyses of variance.)

All the same, his fellow tribesmen
Ignorant, benighted heathens,
Took away his bow and arrows,
Said that though my Hiawatha
Was a brilliant statistician
He was useless as a bowman.
As for variance components,
Several of the more outspoken
Made primeval observations
Hurtful to the finer feelings
Even of a statistician.

In a corner of the forest
Dwells alone my Hiawatha
Permanently cogitating
On the normal law of error,
Wondering in idle moments
Whether an increased precision
Might perhaps be rather better,
Even at the risk of bias,
If thereby one, now and then, could
Register upon the target.

JOURNAL OF APPLIED BEHAVIOR ANALYSIS 1974, 7, 627-628 NUMBER 4 (WINTER 1974)

STATISTICAL INFERENCE FOR INDIVIDUAL ORGANISM RESEARCH: SOME REACTIONS TO A SUGGESTION BY GENTILE, RODEN, AND KLEIN[1]

JACK MICHAEL

WESTERN MICHIGAN UNIVERSITY

In many of the papers published in this journal, the results of experiments are presented with little or no formal use of the logic of statistical inference. There is instead extensive reliance on relatively simple graphic presentation. Descriptive statistics such as per cents and means appear quite often but usually without an accompanying significance test or confidence interval. A recent issue of JABA, for example, (Winter, 1973) contained 13 experimental articles and only three reported any formal significance tests.

Suggesting that the major reason for this neglect is the "assumed inapplicability of statistical techniques to individual cases or small numbers of subjects" Gentile, Roden, and Klein (1972) proposed the use of an analysis-of-variance model for the analysis of data gathered with the reversal design using a single subject. Their article stimulated four further treatments of this topic that were submitted to this journal and that appear in this issue. What follows are some descriptive comments relating each of the four articles to the germinal paper by Gentile *et al.* and to each other, then each of the four papers, and finally an attempted behavioral analysis of the role of statistical methods in psychology and the implications of this analysis for the various proposals made by Gentile *et al.* and the other contributors.

All four of the follow-up articles contested the assumption made by Gentile *et al.* that successively obtained observations within a treatment condition may be considered independent of one another, a seemingly critical assumption for the valid application of the analysis-of-variance model. Kratochwill *et al.* performed an experiment in which they demonstrated the rather extreme degree of dependence seen in successively obtained observations of exactly the type analyzed by Gentile *et al.* Hartmann provides a rational analysis of the same issue using a hypothetical set of data. Thoresen and Elashoff generally support Hartmann's criticism and describe what they see as some additional weaknesses in the assumed approach of Gentile *et al.*

Finally, Keselman, though not arguing the point, also identifies the nonindependence of successively obtained observations as the critical problem not adequately dealt with by Gentile *et al.*

When the assumptions underlying a statistical inference procedure cannot be met, however, the procedure is not necessarily useless. Sometimes, the test is relatively immune to any but the most extreme types of nonconformity to assumption, in which case one can view the probability value as a rough approximation and use the procedure anyway. This situation is made even more tolerable if the failures to satisfy assumptions can be seen to cause probability errors in a known direction—for example to render the test conservative. Then, if a significant finding is obtained one can be sure that if a proper test were used, the result would be even more significant. At the end of the section dealing with violations of the independence assumption, Gentile *et al.* state exactly this point, but it appears that they were addressing themselves to a different type of

[1]This is one in a series of articles available for $1.50 from the Business Manager, *Journal of Applied Behavior Analysis,* Department of Human Development, University of Kansas, Lawrence, Kansas 66045. Ask for Monograph #4.

nonindependence than that seen as most critical by the other authors. Hartmann describes two ways in which the nonindependence of successively obtained observations within treatments would be expected to produce a positive bias, and another factor that could well produce a negative (conservative) bias if the Gentile *et al.* procedure is used; Thoresen and Elashoff agree with Hartmann's interpretation.

It would appear, then, that one of the critical assumptions underlying the analysis of variance is not usually met by the data obtained in typical JABA and JEAB experiments, and furthermore, that the effects of this failure are not easy to interpret. So, what *can* one do with such data from the point of view of statistical inference?

Keselman presents a formal rationale for the use of an analysis-of-variance model based on repeated measurements. He believes that this model is more appropriate to the type of data being considered and also more sensitive for the detection of significant treatment effects. The adequacy of his formal presentation must be assessed by someone with more statistical background than my own, but it does not seem to me that his model is free from the same assumption of independence of successively obtained observations within treatment conditions that underlies that of Gentile *et al.*

Hartmann suggests limiting the application of analysis-of-variance procedures to single-subject data that do not show sequential nonindependence. This is partially achieved by maintaining each experimental condition long enough to obtain several stable observations for that condition and then using only those data in the analysis. In addition, some statistical tests of successive dependence can be made and the analysis of variance performed only if the null hypothesis regarding dependence cannot be rejected. At the close of their paper, Thoresen and Elashoff consider Hartmann's suggestions and conclude that it will not be easy to apply them in most current single subject research.

Hartmann, Thoresen and Elashoff, and Kratochwill *et al.* all, with some enthusiasm, refer to recent developments in the area of time-series analysis as the possible solution to the problems of assessing the statistical significance of single subject data, and the latter authors also suggest the relevance of some nonparametric models.

I was left with the general impression that the procedure proposed by Gentile *et al.* is really not applicable to most single-subject data. Several alternatives seem to be available, at least for some limited experimental situations, and there is considerable optimism regarding more generally applicable methods now being developed for time-series analysis—methods that take account of the troublesome autocorrelation found in much single-subject data.

REFERENCE

Gentile, J. R., Roden, A. H., and Klein, R. D. An analysis-of-variance model for the intrasubject replication design. *Journal of Applied Behavior Analysis,* 1962, **5**, 193-198.

Received 20 August 1974.
(Published without revision.)

JOURNAL OF APPLIED BEHAVIOR ANALYSIS 1974, 7, 635-638 NUMBER 4 (WINTER 1974)

FORCING SQUARE PEGS INTO ROUND HOLES: SOME COMMENTS ON "AN ANALYSIS-OF-VARIANCE MODEL FOR THE INTRASUBJECT REPLICATION DESIGN"

DONALD P. HARTMANN[1]

UNIVERSITY OF UTAH

This paper critically examines the application of fixed-effect one-way analysis-of-variance procedures to learning data from a single subject. Procedures more appropriate for data obtained from intrasubject replication designs are briefly described.

Gentile, Roden, and Klein (1972) described an analysis-of-variance (ANOVA) model for detecting treatment effects in "noisy" single-subject reversal designs.[2] Their efforts to integrate useful elements of general psychology with operant technology are to be applauded. Nonetheless, the statistical model they recommend, a fixed-effect one-way ANOVA, deserves comment.

Briefly, Gentile *et al.* recommend collapsing the data from the four conditions of a typical reversal design (A_1, B_1, A_2, and B_2) into two treatment levels, baseline and treatment. (Preferably each condition would contain an equal number of data points.) Trials within conditions are considered replications—analogous to subject replication in a simple ANOVA. Thus, the single subject is considered to function as a random response generator; *i.e.,* the data within the two treatment cells are assumed to be statistically independent and normally distributed about the treatment means. The analysis associated with this model is summarized in Table 1.

Before examining the applicability of this model to the $N = 1$ intrasubject replication design, consider a set of idealized data (presented in Figure 1) resulting from an application of such a design to a program designed to accelerate a selected target behavior. These fictitious data have the following characteristics: baseline 1 rates are low and stable; during treatment 1, the rate of responding is positively accelerated as the subject experiences the changed contingencies, and finally reaches a stable asymptote; baseline 2 is a mirror image of treatment 1; and finally, treatment 2 is essentially a duplication of the rate displayed during treatment 1.

Table 1

Summary table for a one-way fixed effects ANOVA applied to data from an $N = 1$ reversal design.

Source	*df*	*MS*	*F*
Treatment (X_A *vs.* X_B)	1	$MS_{Treatment}$	$MS_{Treatment}/MS_{Error}$
Error (within cells)	4n−2	MS_{Error}	

NOTE—Each of the four treatment conditions, A_1, B_1, A_2, and B_2 contains *n* observations.

Data such as these are seldom if ever seen, and certainly would not require the application of statistical procedures to detect treatment effects; only with the addition of background noise would such procedures be required.

Assuming that the form of the data shown in Figure 1 (or some simple transformation) is

---

[1]I wish to thank David Dodd, Donna Gelfand, and Tom Malloy for their critical reading of an earlier draft of this paper.

This is one in a series of articles available for \$1.50 from the Business Manager, *Journal of Applied Behavior Analysis,* Department of Human Development, University of Kansas, Lawrence, Kansas 66045. Ask for Monograph #4.

[2]The critical comments made in this paper are also applicable to the application of two-way ANOVA procedures for $N > 1$, as discussed by Gentile *et al.* (1972).

prototypic of the data gathered by behavioral researchers, it can reasonably be asked how well the model suggested by Gentile *et al.* fits data of this general form. According to Hays (1963), the assumptions of the one-way fixed-effects ANOVA model include:

a. a normal distribution of error components;
b. homogeneity of variance of error components;
c. and independence of error components; *i.e.*, for any pair of observations i and j, the expected value of $r_{e_i e_j}$ must equal zero, whether e_i and e_j are selected from the same or different treatment conditions.

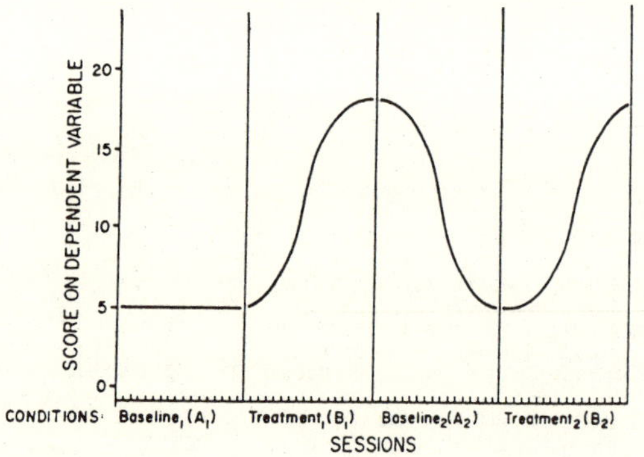

Fig. 1. Idealized data representing the application of reversal procedures to an acceleration problem.

All of these three assumptions appear to be violated with data resembling those presented in Figure 1. The distribution of error components in B_1, A_2, and B_2 would likely be more platykurtic than normal because of the large number of extreme scores in the flattened-out portions of the curves at the beginning and end of each condition except baseline 1. The error variances in A_1 and A_2 would be heterogeneous, as would be the error variances of the combined A conditions in comparison with the combined B conditions. In both cases, the heterogeneity would be due to the greater variability of scores in B_1, A_2, and B_2 in comparison with A_1.

Although these violations may be of relatively small concern (see, for example, Hays, 1963), it is violation of the third and final assumption that may provide a serious, and perhaps lethal threat to the use of the statistical model proposed by Gentile *et al.* According to Hays (1963), if the assumption of uncorrelated errors is not met (*i.e.*, if the data are sequentially dependent) "*very serious errors in inference can be made* (p. 379, author's italics)."

The within-cell dependencies that are of greatest concern are a result of the failure to consider the *systematic changes occurring across trials* within the B_1, A_2, and B_2 conditions. That is, the presence of a trial effect within conditions will result in positive serial correlations within conditions even though each trial score also has a random error component. The presence of this within-cell dependency poses a number of thorny problems for the use of the *F*-statistic. First, dependency obviously reduces the amount of independent information included in the data. This suggests that the number of degrees of freedom recommended by Gentile *et al.* is inflated and would result in a positively biased *F*-test. Second, nonindependence generally produces artificially lower variability, which also results in a positively biased *F*-test.

In addition to the problems caused by multiple violations of these assumptions, there is still another, and perhaps equally troublesome, problem with the ANOVA model proposed by Gentile *et al.* when applied to data resembling those shown in Figure 1. Again, the problem is a result of treating systematic changes within conditions as error. Thus, instead of calculating error variance in B_1, A_2, and B_2 about some linear, or, in the case of Figure 1, cubic trend, error variance in the proposed model is based on the deviation of the scores within conditions from the condition *mean, i.e.*, from the combined A and the combined B condition means respectively. This procedure greatly increases the magnitude of the MS_{Error} and consequently decreases the probability of detecting a true treatment effect. The problem is exacerbated by basing each condition mean on all data points within that condition, rather than just those obtained when asymptotic levels of performance have been reached.

SUMMARY AND RECOMMENDATIONS

In summary, the problems of increased error variance and reduced treatment variance, together with the various violations of assumptions, taken singly and in combination, suggest that the ANOVA model recommended by Gentile *et al.* should not be used with data resembling those shown in Figure 1. Its use should be restricted to data sets in which the aforementioned assumptions can be met, until such time as the nature and extent of the violations of the *F*-test are more fully examined.

If a researcher still insists on forcing square pegs into round holes by applying traditional ANOVA models to $N = 1$ data, then he should use either the relatively unexplored, but more sophisticated ANOVA model suggested by Shine and Bower (1971) and Shine (1973) or the variation of the one-way fixed-effect model described below.

This variation differs from the model suggested by Gentile *et al.* on two important points: its application is preceded by specific tests of the vexing independence assumption; and its use is restricted to data that are likely to meet both the independence assumption and the other previously noted ANOVA assumptions. The data requirements and statistical procedures for the proposed factorial model include:

1. Sufficient data so that an equal number of *stable* data points are available for each of the four treatment conditions. Thus, the analysis incorporates only the last *n* data points in each condition obtained during asymptotic responding; *i.e.,* when the regression of time on the dependent variable has zero slope. Because of the necessity to perform correlational analyses to test the independence assumptions (see below), at least 12 and preferably many more stable data points should be available for each condition.

2. Data that meet the independence assumptions. Two separate tests of independence are employed: first, on the serial correlations of at least lag one calculated on the *n* data points within each of the four conditions (see Holtzman, 1963); second, on the cross-serial correlations of at least lag zero calculated between trials across conditions, *i.e.,* $r_{A_1B_1}$, $r_{A_1A_2}$ . . . $r_{A_2B_3}$. If neither the serial correlations nor the cross-serial correlations are different from zero, it may be assumed that the data do not violate the independence assumption, and formal statistical analysis may be initiated.

3. Application of either an ANOVA set-up similar to the one summarized in Table 1 or a fixed-effects 2×2 completely randomized factorial model (summarized in Table 2) with *n* data points per condition. The data analysis procedures for both models are described in a straightforward manner in standard statistical texts. The design, as it is summarized in Table 2, allows testing of main effects due to treatments and to changes across time, and the interaction of treatment and time. For $N > 1$, a new fixed factor, subjects, would be added; the calculations and interpretations would follow those outlined for three factor factorial designs.

Table 2

Summary table for a fixed-effects 2×2 factorial ANOVA applied to data from a $N = 1$ reversal design.

Source	*df*	*MS*	*F*
Treatments (X_A *vs.* X_B)	1	MS_T	MS_T/MS_{Error}
Order (A_1+B_1 *vs.* A_2+B_2)	1	MS_O	MS_O/MS_{Error}
Treatment × Order	1	$MS_{T\times O}$	$MS_{T\times O}/MS_{Error}$
Error	$4(n-1)$	MS_{Error}	

NOTE—Each of the four treatment conditions, A_1, B_1, A_2, and B_2 contain *n* observations.

Researchers less tied to traditional ANOVA models who find it necessary to apply statistical procedures to reversal design data may want to consider a number of methods developed more specifically for time series. Foremost among these are the promising new generating-function procedures described in some detail by Gottman, McFall, and Barnett (1969). These procedures make "positive use of dependency observations (p. 302)"; they can be applied to one or more subjects, and they have associated inferential statistics to provide evaluation of both between- and within-subject effects. Additional material on time series analysis can be found in Gottman (1973) and Glass, Willson, and Gottman (1973).

REFERENCES

Gentile, J. R., Roden, A. H., and Klein, R. D. An analysis-of-variance model for the intrasubject replication design. *Journal of Applied Behavior Analysis,* 1972, **5**, 193-198.

Glass, G. V., Willson, V. K., and Gottman, J. M. *The design and analysis of time series experiments.* Boulder, Colorado: Laboratory of Educational Research Press, 1973.

Gottman, J. M. *N*-of-1 and *N*-of-2 research in psychotherapy. *Psychological Bulletin,* 1973, **80,** 93-105.

Gottman, J. M., McFall, R. M., and Barnett, J. T. Design and analysis of research using time series. *Psychological Bulletin,* 1969, **72,** 299-306.

Hays, W. L. *Statistics for psychologists.* New York: Holt, Rinehart, and Winston, 1963.

Holtzman, W. H. Statistical models for the study of change in the single case. In C. Harris (Ed.), *Problems in measuring change.* Madison: University of Wisconsin Press, 1963. Pp. 199-211.

Shine, L. C. A multi-way analysis of variance for single-subject designs. *Educational and Psychological Measurement,* 1973, **33,** 633-636.

Shine, L. C. and Bower, S. M. A one-way analysis of variance for single-subject designs. *Educational and Psychological Measurement,* 1971, **31,** 105-113.

Received 28 September 1972.
(Published without revision.)

JOURNAL OF APPLIED BEHAVIOR ANALYSIS 1974, 7, 647-653 NUMBER 4 (WINTER 1974)

STATISTICAL INFERENCE FOR INDIVIDUAL ORGANISM RESEARCH: MIXED BLESSING OR CURSE?[1]

JACK MICHAEL

WESTERN MICHIGAN UNIVERSITY

Descriptive and inferential statistics are described as judgemental aids, stimuli to which the scientist can more easily react than to his raw experimental results. The increasing emphasis on the significance test as the main judgemental aid utilized in experimental psychology is credited with several harmful effects on experimental practice. The area known as "the experimental analysis of behavior" has so far escaped most of these harmful effects, but now we see an increased interest in the development of appropriate significance tests for individual organism research. This interest is based on the view that it is not possible to effect adequate levels of experimental control with much human applied research, and that in such cases a significance test would be quite valuable as a judgemental aid, both of which points are considered to be essentially incorrect, and if accepted, potentially harmful.

Descriptive and Inferential Statistics As Judgemental Aids

The observations resulting from scientific experiments are stimuli that hopefully affect the scientist and his colleagues by producing better practical behavior, more sophisticated follow-up experiments, or better verbal behavior regarding the subject matter. These stimuli, however, may not result in any effective reaction, a fairly common reason being their complexity. Repeated observation of the same experimental condition, for example, may give rise to a set of numbers, all differing considerably from one another. This situation has occurred quite often and methods have been discovered for simplifying it to some degree. Some of the methods generate two-dimensional visual stimuli where the values of each dimension stand in a point-to-point relation to some feature of the data; a frequency polygon is such a stimulus. Another stimulus-simplifying technique results in a smaller set of numbers, each related to some important characteristic of the larger set, such as the mean and range of the raw data.

Using the term "judgement" to refer to any of the various kinds of reactions that a scientist could make to the data of his experiment, it is useful to refer to these stimulus-simplifying techniques and their products as "judgemental aids". In this sense, then, the graphing devices and the measures of central tendency, variability, *etc.* of the field of descriptive statistics are all judgemental aids. In some way they produce a stimulus to which the experimenter can react more easily than to his raw data.

The various judgemental aids do not achieve their simplifying effects without some cost, however. In the first place, they are easier to react to in part because they are abbreviations. Some stimulus aspects of the raw data are simply absent from the aid, and if one's entire reaction is based on the abbreviation, the missing feature cannot affect behavior at all. Further, the scientist must spend some time learning about them, time he might be spending in other activities relevant to his subject matter. Statistics courses displace other topics from the curriculum.

A more complex type of cost consists of the time and effort that must be expended determining the extent to which some particular aid is

---

[1]This is one in a series of articles available for $1.50 from the Business Manager, *Journal of Applied Behavior Analysis,* Department of Human Development, University of Kansas, Lawrence, Kansas 66045. Ask for Monograph #4.

appropriate to the circumstances and data of a particular experiment. Finally, just as he must accumulate experience with his subject matter by reacting to it in various ways and being affected by the relatively long-term consequences of his reactions, he must now accumulate experience in reacting to the judgemental aid and feel the long-term effects of this behavior.

With such devices as frequency polygons, means, percentages, there seems to be a relatively clear net gain. The time required to learn how to use such techniques and the time spent in determining which one to use in a particular situation is relatively small compared with the simplifying effect achieved. Furthermore, the circumstances where they apply occur often enough that the individual scientist has some chance of acquiring the necessary experience regarding the long-range effects of his reliance on such judgemental aids.

Inferential statistics are also no more nor less than techniques for simplifying a complex stimulus situation. When an experiment results in two sets of numbers, one from a control and another from an experimental condition the comparison may be quite difficult to make. It is usually easier to compare frequency polygons and means, and one's reaction to this state of affairs may be further aided in some way by performing what is called a statistical significance test or computing a confidence interval. The former is the most common inference procedure used in experimental psychology and results in a statement that the probability of such a difference (or a larger one) arising by chance when the population means are actually equal is less than or equal to some specified value.

Significance tests and confidence intervals are more expensive judgemental aids than descriptive procedures. The abbreviation is more extreme, and the time required to learn how to obtain and interpret them is much greater. Determining to what degree the judgemental aid is appropriate to the particular experiment—whether the assumptions underlying the significance test are met—is likely to require reaction to features of the situation that are fully as complex as the features that the aid is supposed to simplify.

Whether there is net gain, even with the most widely used and simplest inferential procedures depends upon the extent to which the scientist and his colleagues react more effectively with than without such judgemental aids. And although these techniques have been widely used in experimental psychology for over 30 yr it is not at all clear that this particular field is in any way more effective because of them. From an empirical point of view, it would be desirable to have some data comparing the scientific or practical results achieved when significance tests are used with those when judgements are otherwise based. I know of no information of this sort. From a rational point of view, the incorporation of statistical inference into the broader field of decision theory clarifies considerably the possible role of the significance level as a guide to action. When combined with estimates of prior probability values for null and alternative hypotheses, and with quantitative estimates of the utility to the decision maker of correct and incorrect decisions, the significance of a treatment effect may be seen as a part of a very reasonable system for making decisions (as described, for example by Raiffa, 1968, or Schmitt, 1969). There is some hope that developments within this area may eventually prove useful to the psychologist, but at present the assignment of prior probabilities and utilities seems possible in only a few applied research situations and not at all in basic research. From this decision-theoretic point of view, the significance test by itself is a very incomplete basis for any kind of judgement, and there certainly seems to be no rationale for the widespread use of any particular level of significance (0.05 is the most common) as a basis for distinguishing "real" from "chance" effects. If and when these better rationalized inference procedures become available to the psychologist, however, they will be even more expensive in terms of time spent dealing with the details of the judgemental aid itself, and a net gain will be realized only if they produce a considerable improvement in experimental effectiveness.

Some Detrimental Effects Arising from an Emphasis on Statistical Inference

Although it is not at all clear how statistical inference has helped the field of experimental psychology, it does seem closely linked with some undesirable changes in experimental practice. By the early 1930s, professional statisticians had developed significance test procedures appropriate to experiments of considerable complexity. If one was willing to rely on the result of the significance test as the main basis for reacting to an experiment, it then became possible to "control" statistically for unwanted sources of variation in a dependent variable, especially using the analysis of variance as developed by R. A. Fisher (1925). Before this development, an investigator had to discover techniques for experimentally controlling sources of irrelevant variation before he could even carry out his experiment. In the process he was likely to acquire a very valuable form of knowledge, irrespective of the ultimate value of the specific experiment. He was learning how to control his subject matter—in the case of psychology, the behavior of organisms, and even if the original reason for conducting the experiment was a poor one, something useful was likely to come of it. In addition to the reportable knowledge resulting from the effort to develop experimental control, this activity usually required a good deal of time, and so the experimenter was repeatedly exposed to the relevant contingencies of his problem area. He thus had a chance of being shaped into more effective forms of behavior regarding this subject matter even before his verbal repertoire regarding it was well developed. Also, since most problems concern more than one important independent variable, yet only one could generally be studied at a time, an investigator would usually conduct a series of separate experiments to tease out the various relationships, and was thus further exposed to the contingencies of his problem area.

The possibility of "statistical control" greatly reduced the necessity for developing experimental control. An experimenter could ask his experimental question irrespective of considerable uncontrolled variation in his dependent variable, if he could simply identify the sources of this variation. The study could then be designed in such a way that these sources were "balanced" across the various groups constituting the main comparison, and a satisfactory significance test could be computed with respect to this main comparison. These same methods of experimental design and statistical analysis also made possible the simultaneous investigation of more than one independent variable, thus further reducing experimental time and labor, but also reducing the duration and intensity of the experimenter's contact with his problem area.

At least five harmful effects of this general trend can be discerned.

1. The prolonged and intense interaction with the subject matter undertaken in order to experimentally control irrelevant sources of variation probably constituted a rich source of ideas for further experimentation. The use of statistical control deprives the experimenter of this source and he becomes more dependent upon theory, other researchers' experiments, and a form of commonsense analysis not necessarily related to his problem area as the basis for directing his research.

2. The knowledge developed in order to identify sources of variation and to select subjects in such a way as to "balance" for these sources is considerably less useful to other experimenters or for practical purposes than the knowledge required actually to control such variation.

3. Statistical control in complex experiments is easiest to accomplish by obtaining data from a large number of relatively independent behaving organisms, and such numbers generally preclude prolonged study of any one organism. Experimental situations then, are designed to maximize the efficiency with which they provide exactly the type of information relevant to the particular experimental question being asked,

and become increasingly unlike any other situations, either inside or outside of the laboratory. The results from such experiments are thus less useful for any purpose other than answering the specific question being asked in that experiment, which has the further disadvantage that they are less likely to be verified by another experimenter using the same situation to study a different problem.

4. Reliance on the significance test leading to the extensive use of statistical control and multiple-factor experiments produces an excessive dependency on the significance test, since such experiments cannot be reacted to in any other way. What started out as a supplement to other bases of judgement, has become, in the minds of many researchers an essential aspect of scientific method. Yet, as Skinner points out, "We owe most of our scientific knowledge to methods of inquiry which have never been formally analyzed or expressed in normative rules. (1972, p. 319)"

5. Since extensive preliminary study of an area is seemingly rendered unnecessary if one designs his experiment properly, and since such properly designed experiments cannot be interpreted until all the data are in and the significance tests have been performed, experiments tend to be carried out in a somewhat inflexible manner. In the type of research emphasizing experimental control, and thereby often involving prolonged study of a small number of organisms using relatively simple experimental designs, it is usually possible to change the procedure while the experiment is under way. If it appears that some previously unrecognized source of variation is causing trouble, the main manipulations can be postponed until means for controlling the interferring factor are developed. Or, if some aspect of the incoming results suggests an interesting variation the experiment can be redirected immediately.

All in all, it seems possible to argue that what might have been a moderately useful judgemental aid has ultimately had the unfortunate effect of moving psychological research methodology out of the main stream of experimental science.

Statistical Inference for Individual Organism Research: A Weak Solution to an Artificial Problem

Not all areas within experimental psychology have adopted the research methodology deplored above. One that has been relatively unaffected is the area referred to as "the experimental analysis of behavior", "operant conditioning", "Skinnerian psychology", *etc.* The shunning of significance testing by researchers with this orientation may be due, as Gentile *et al.* suggested (1972), to the unavailability of inferential techniques appropriate to typical "single subject" data. On the other hand, this type of individual organism research has been going on for well over 30 yr and it is reasonable to assume that if any strong need for such techniques was felt there would have been some concerted effort to develop them. It seems to me that the relative indifference to statistical inference is more accurately attributable to the strong emphasis on effective experimental control as a major scientific goal and as the main evidence of the scientist's "understanding" of his problem area.[2] The situation where a significance test might seem helpful is typically one involving sufficient uncontrolled variability in the dependent variable that neither the experimenter nor his readers can be sure that there is an interpretable relationship. This is evidence that the relevant behavior is not under good experimental control, a situation calling for more effective experimentation, not a more complex judgemental aid.

In any case, whether by necessity, scientific cunning, or prejudice, operant researchers, basic and applied, have made little use of statistical inference and do not seem to have suffered as a

[2]This emphasis, of course, predisposes investigators toward prolonged study of a small number of organisms, and within-subject comparisons where possible. Between-subject comparisons, however, can also be quite meaningful if behavior is under good experimental control.

result. Increasingly sophisticated methods of experimental control have developed within the area of basic research, and applied researchers have generally been able to make use of the same technology, or develop methods of experimental control appropriate to their own problem areas.

As the applied area expands, however, there seems to be an increasing tendency to present experimental results that are not easily interpreted when simply displayed in graphical form, or as a table of means or per cents. This is said to be due to the practical difficulties that the applied researcher encounters in his efforts to obtain human data in the nonlaboratory environment. It is argued that he does not have the luxury of discontinuing the experiment until he discovers and experimentally controls various sources of irrelevant or confusing variation in his data. He cannot, like the basic researcher, simply discard that pigeon and start over again with another. The opportunity for experimenting may no longer be present, a number of people may have been inconvenienced, a good deal of experimenter time may have been spent, and considerable financial as well as other resources may have been expended. One must, in a sense, make the best of the data as they stand, and this is where the significance test comes in. Faced with data that do not constitute an effective stimulus for judgement, the experimenter and his readers must do whatever is possible, and perhaps they will be able to behave somewhat more effectively if they have the judgemental aid offered by some statistical inference procedure.

This, of course, is what Gentile *et al.* are offering, and although critical of that specific solution, the other authors (Hartmann, 1974; Keselman, 1974; Kratochwill *et al.,* 1974; Thoresen and Elashoff, 1974) offer their own solutions of the same type. It is probably never appropriate to be critical of any valid knowledge-seeking activity *per se,* but one can criticize its rationale. The present interest in obtaining a proper significance test procedure for single-subject data seems based on two faulty premises. First is the belief that applied data are taken under conditions where effective experimental control cannot be expected. While workers in the field of applied behavior analysis have not been as badly affected by the experimental design and statistical significance enthusiasts as some other kinds of psychologists, they may not have escaped entirely. Peaceful coexistence with those who emphasize statistical control and multiple-factor experiments seems to have resulted in an increased tendency to plan, carry out, and then analyze the experiment all as a relatively inflexible unit of behavior—the fifth harmful effect listed earlier. When a dependent variable is not under good control—when there is considerable unexplained variability even though the independent variable being studied is at a constant value—it is not usually necessary to go ahead with the other planned manipulations. Further efforts can be made to obtain a more stable dependent variable, or to discover and eliminate some of the sources of uncontrolled variation.

If these efforts are unsuccessful and if the experiment is an expensive one in terms of time and other resources it is probably wise to abandon it at this point or recognize it as a gamble with a low probability of payoff. There are, of course, a number of "nonscientific" reasons for continuing an apparently unprofitable experiment, such as the necessity of completing a thesis or dissertation requirement, or the belief that if one does not carry out the research project that he spoke so highly of in the grant request he may have trouble getting another grant. That the significance test might be of aid in such situations and could actually further such purposes is certainly no recommendation.

The second faulty premise is that the significance test is an especially helpful judgemental aid, and therefore worth a good deal of time and inconvenience. When experimental control is emphasized and results can be portrayed in relatively simple graphical form, the probability of those results or more extreme ones given the null hypothesis is a very crude form of information, compared with the other stimulus features available to the experimenter, and is likely to be ignored if it is not consistent with the interpretation arrived at otherwise.[3] In the typical multiple-factor experiment relying heavily on statistical control, the significance value is no more informative in an absolute sense, but since the results cannot generally be reacted to in any other way, it seems more useful. This means only that one should avoid experimenting in such a way that he is forced to rely on such a weak tool.

An overvaluation of the significance test by itself is a relatively harmless misunderstanding, but it is likely to cause other changes in experimental practice that are more serious. If the significance test is valued above all other judgemental aids, experimenters are likely to try to design their experiments so that a significance test can be computed, an obvious loss in terms of experimental flexibility. Note in this connection Hartmann's (1974) suggestion that ". . . at least 12 and preferably more stable data points should be available for each condition."

Another undesirable possibility is that a good deal of time will be spent in learning about and interacting with the judgemental aid, rather than in contact with the experimental area itself. In the operant area we already have a powerful source of distraction from our primary "target", in that many experimenters often find it at least temporarily more satisfying to experiment with their behavior control equipment—electromechanical, solid state, and more recently on-line computer—than to experiment with behavior. In the case of the autoregressive techniques that seem to be "just around the corner", their understanding will surely require a good deal of graduate instruction time and their proper usage could easily become a main concern from the point of view of data analysis—clearly a case of the tail wagging the dog.[4]

If the decreased experimental flexibility and the distraction from our primary subject of interest is not sufficient reason to be unenthusiastic about this development, there is the further distinct possibility that editors confronted with results that are in an obvious sense relatively meaningless may be induced to foist these results off on the readers if they are accompanied by an appropriate significance test that reaches the 5% value.

What Gentile, Roden, and Klein, and the other authors as well, are offering researchers in the area of behavior analysis is an opportunity to adopt a practice that has had a 30-yr trial period and is still of uncertain value. It is a practice, furthermore, that seems historically almost incompatible with the emphasis on experimental control that has characterized the operant research orientation. This would seem to be an offer we can afford to refuse.

REFERENCES

Fisher, R. A. *Statistical methods for research workers.* Edinburgh: Oliver and Boyd, 1925.

Gentile, R. R., Roden, A. H., and Klein, R. D. An analysis-of-variance model for the intrasubject replication design. *Journal of Applied Behavior Analysis,* 1972, **5**, 193-198.

[3]It is possible that there are still some researchers who overvalue the significance test because they believe that the significance value reached in any particular test is equivalent to the probability that the null hypothesis is true. We cannot blame the professional statisticians for this misinterpretation, however, except that in warning us to avoid this error they have not often substituted a plausible alternative.

[4]It is often pointed out that the time spent dealing with the statistical judgemental aid can now be minimized by utilizing computer programs developed for this purpose. The experimenter can simply "plug in" his data and read out the significance value as well as some indication of the appropriateness of the particular technique to those data. This would seem to represent even further dependency upon an expertise which is beyond one's own critical scrutiny, an essentially undesirable direction to take. It can be argued, of course, that we all depend upon experts in other areas—an example is the biologist's dependency upon the optical specialists who design and construct his microscopes. We do it, however, on the basis of earned confidence, and the statisticians' contribution to experimental psychology seems quite uncertain when compared with the optical specialists' contribution to biology.

Hartmann, D. P. Forcing square pegs into round holes: some comments on 'An analysis-of-variance model for the intrasubject replication design.' *Journal of Applied Behavior Analysis*, 1974, **7**, 635-638.

Keselman, H. J. Concerning the statistical procedures enumerated by Gentile *et al.*: another perspective. *Journal of Applied Behavior Analysis*, 1974, **7**, 643-645.

Kratochwill, T., Alden, K., Demuth, D., Dawson, D., Panicucci, C., Arnston, P., McMurray, N., Hempstead, J. and Levin, J. A further consideration in the application of an analysis of variance model for the intrasubject replication design. *Journal of Applied Behavior Analysis*, 1974, **7**, 629-633.

Raiffa, H. *Decision analysis*. Reading, Mass.: Addison-Wesley, 1968.

Schmitt, S. A. *Measuring uncertainty*. Reading, Mass.: Addison-Wesley, 1969.

Skinner, B. F. *Cumulative record*. 3d ed. New York: Appleton-Century-Crofts, 1972.

Thoresen, C. E. and Elashoff, J. D. 'An analysis-of-variance model for intrasubject replication design:' some additional comments. *Journal of Applied Behavior Analysis*, 1974, **7**, 639-641.

Received 20 August 1974.
(Published without revision.)

JOURNAL OF APPLIED BEHAVIOR ANALYSIS 1977, 10, 167-172 NUMBER 1 (SPRING) 1977

"PERHAPS IT WOULD BE BETTER NOT TO KNOW EVERYTHING"[1]

DONALD M. BAER

UNIVERSITY OF KANSAS

The advent of statistical methods for evaluating the data of individual-subject designs invites a comparison of the usual research tactics of the group-design paradigm and the individual-subject-design paradigm. That comparison can hinge on the concept of assigning probabilities of Type 1 and Type 2 errors. Individual-subject designs are usually interpreted with implicit, very low probabilities of Type 1 errors, and correspondingly high probabilities of Type 2 errors. Group designs are usually interpreted with explicit, moderately low probabilities of Type 1 errors, and therefore with not such high probabilities of Type 2 errors as in the other paradigm. This difference may seem to be a minor one, considered in terms of centiles on a probability scale. However, when it is interpreted in terms of the substantive kinds of results likely to be produced by each paradigm, it appears that the individual-subject-design paradigm is more likely to contribute to the development of a technology of behavior, and it is suggested that this orientation should not be abandoned.

DESCRIPTORS: individual-subject design, group design, Type 1 error, Type 2 error, inferential statistics

---

If behavior might be different under a condition known as "A" than it is under a condition known as "B", and if it were important to find out whether that possibility was an actuality, then two basic paradigms would be available for its examination.

A number of subjects might be recruited and divided at random into two equal groups. One of these groups would be exposed to the "A" condition, and its behavior noted; the other would be exposed to the "B" condition, and its behavior similarly noted. The mean behavior of those exposed to "A" could be compared to the mean behavior of those exposed to "B". A difference in those means might be interesting.

Alternatively, a single subject might be recruited and exposed to the "A" condition for some time to behave repeatedly under its influence. Then, the "A" condition would be replaced by the "B" condition, and the ongoing behavior would continue to be monitored as before. An alternation of "A" and "B" conditions would continue, and the repeated patterns of behavior seen under the repeated "A's" would be compared to the repeated patterns of behavior seen under the repeated "B's". A consistent difference in those arrays might be interesting.

Unfortunately, in either paradigm, there are conditions under which the difference would not be interesting. Primarily, those are the conditions under which suspicion arises that the difference is a result only of chance, rather than of the intrinsic difference between "A" and "B". This suspicion is profound in behavioral scientists. It arises from a past history of discovery that behavior is subject to control by many, many variables other than "A" or "B". Any prudent inductive organism, confronted with the

[1]This comment has been attributed to Oedipus Rex, shortly after his successful investigation of a public-health problem in Thebes. The article following the comment is based largely on a symposium report presented at the meeting of the Association for the Advancement of Behavior Therapy, San Francisco, December, 1975. Reprints may be obtained from the author, Department of Human Development, University of Kansas, Lawrence, Kansas 66045.

fact that a subject matter may be affected by many, many known variables, will leap reasonably to the conclusion that the same subject matter may well be affected by even more unknown variables. Consequently, any difference in behavior will always be subject to interpretation as a product of some currently unknowable fluctuation in those unknown variables.[2] The Greeks referred to unknown variables as Barbarians; scientists refer to them as Chance.

In the individual-subject paradigm, a judicious defence against chance is available. The total array of behaviors under all the "A's" and all the "B's" is examined. Because each "A" and each "B" has yielded repeated displays of the behavior, and because the "A's" and "B's" themselves have been presented repeatedly, a potential consistency of pattern is available for inspection. If behavior repeated under the repeated "A's" is repetitively different from behavior repeated under the repeated "B's", the scientist will conclude that such consistency cannot be a product of chance. After all, it has been repeated quite repetitively. This conclusion obviously has a quantitative base, but the base is never made precise. However, a subtle recourse to the other paradigm is applied: groups of scientists are recruited to examine the same total display, and when their mean reaction is that this consistency cannot be a product of chance, then the conclusion is proclaimed a scientifically sound one. The Greeks referred to this as Democracy; scientists refer to it as Editorial Review.

In the other paradigm, a differently judicious defence against chance is available. A catechism is recited, much as follows:

What is desired is knowledge about the population of differences between "A" and "B". In particular, it is important to know whether the mean difference in the population is zero.

Unfortunately, the population of differences between "A" and "B" is too large to be available: all that is available are samples of "A-B" differences, and samples vary in their resemblance to the population from which they are drawn.

However, if the samples are drawn randomly from the population, then the likelihood that they resemble or deviate from the population to any specified degree is computable through the application of the Laws of Probability.

Unfortunately, this is true if and only if the samples are random samples from the population.[3] It is possible to sample randomly from a population, but it is extremely difficult to do so. Of course, it is always possible to consider a given sample as a random one from *some* population, but it is extremely difficult to specify from which pop-

[2]Or even some known ones unfortunately not under current experimental control.

[3]The ability to make an "if and only if" statement is both rare and wonderful in science. This one rests on an argument put forth repeatedly by statisticians. Pearson (1900), Walker and Lev (1953, pp. 10-12), and Wallis and Roberts (1956, p. 116) provide three examples of this argument.

ulation it is a random sample.

However, it is always possible to divide a sample randomly into two groups.

Unfortunately, dividing a sample randomly into two groups is not the same as randomly sampling the population of "A-B" differences.

However, it is always possible to ignore this deficiency and apply the Laws of Probability anyway. Doing so will yield an apparent probability of the sample difference having been drawn from the population, given any assumption about the population from which it was drawn.

As an act of conservatism, it may be assumed that the population of "A-B" differences has a mean of zero—in other words, that the difference between "A" and "B" is not a functional one for the behavior under study. Then, application of the Laws of Probability will produce an apparent estimate of the probability of a sample difference this large, if in fact there ordinarily would not be a difference at all. If that probability is low enough, conservatism will be abandoned; it will be concluded that the sample result is too unlikely an event, under the assumption of no functional differences between "A" and "B". Then, the assumption itself will be doubted, and will be set aside in favor of the conclusion that after all, "A" and "B" do affect this behavior differently. Usually, this will be done if the probability is as low as 0.05.

But it will always be remembered that this conclusion could be an error, and in fact, that proceeding in this manner will virtually guarantee that some 5% of all such scientific conclusions are errors. Presumably to honor this institutionalized error rate, and also because it will need to be referred to very often, it is given a title: these errors are called Type 1 errors. Of all the errors that there are to be made, these have primacy, because they are almost certain to be made. The Greeks referred to this as *hubris;* scientists refer to it as Inferential Statistics.

It should be realized immediately that Type 1 errors are not unique to the group paradigm. They occur in identical form in the individual-subject paradigm as well, for both paradigms need to defend against chance. But in the group paradigm, because of the decision to apply the laws of probability (justifiably or not), Type 1 error probabilities are computable; in the individual-subject paradigm, they are not.[4] In that paradigm, they are merely worrisome, and the basic defence against them is to consider the total array of data points available within the design with a fairly skeptical eye. That is, a difference has to be seen to be affirmed. A comparison of differences treated by skeptical examinations by eye, and by computation of the probability that they arose by chance from a zero-difference population, suggests strongly that much smaller and less consistent differences can be validated by computation than by inspection. That is, in the individual-subject paradigm, the probability of Type 1 errors is not known with any precision, but is clearly much smaller than 0.05.

Then, one might reasonably ask why Type 1 errors should be tolerated at an 0.05 probability level in the group paradigm, when they might well be reduced by relying on visual inspection rather than computation, as in the individual-subject paradigm. The answer, of course, is that there is a second type of error, fittingly known as a Type 2 error, that may be committed in

[4]Maybe. See, for example, Jones, Vaught, and Weinrott, 1977.

either paradigm, when Type 1 errors are avoided. In fact, when worrying over "A-B" differences, there are *always* two errors available: we may conclude from our sample that there is a difference, when in the population there is none (Type 1); or we may conclude from our sample that there is no difference, when in the population there is indeed one (Type 2). Furthermore, an inevitable arithmetic relates these two types of errors. That arithmetic rates a chapter in the usual textbook; here, let it suffice to remember that whenever we decrease the probability of one type of error, necessarily we increase the probability of the other. Individual-subject-design practitioners, operating at very, very low probabilities of Type 1 errors, consequently operate at very high probabilities of Type 2 errors. Group-design practitioners, able to operate at higher levels of Type 1 error probability like 0.05 (a practice difficult to match by visual inspection unaided by computation) thereby are also able to operate at somewhat lower probabilities of Type 2 errors.

In one sense, then, the advocates of each paradigm are really very similar in their scientific research practices. Both are aptly enough described by the model of inferential statistics: they are all Type 1 and Type 2 error-avoiders. It is simply that one (the individual-subject-design practitioner) usually does not calculate the probabilities of Type 1 errors, and as a result is forced to estimate them by visual inspection of the total array of data available. Consequently, the individual-subject-design practitioner makes very few Type 1 errors and very many Type 2 errors. The group-design practitioner, typically committed to calculating Type 1 error probabilities and choosing to operate at an 0.05 probability level of making them, thereby makes somewhat more Type 1 errors than does the individual-subject buff, but at the same time makes considerably fewer Type 2 errors than that imprecise person. Thus, what has sometimes been seen as a most profound difference in scientific practice, in this interpretation dissolves into a mere difference of opinion about where to set two parameters: the probabilities of Type 1 and Type 2 errors.

On the other hand, that very same difference could also be described in terms that suggest a more profound difference than a few centiles on a probability scale. This is the difference that emerges if we ask what kind of errors Type 1 and Type 2 errors are, in substantive terms.

To make a Type 1 error is to affirm that a certain variable is a functional one, when in fact it is not. Scientists who commit relatively many Type 1 errors are bound to memorize very long lists of variables that are supposed to affect diverse behaviors, some predictable proportion of which are not variables at all. By contrast, scientists who commit very few Type 1 errors have relatively short lists of variables to remember. Furthermore, and much more important, it is usually only the very robust, uniformly effective variables that will make their list. Those who will risk Type 1 errors more often will uncover a host of weak, occasional, or otherwise highly specialized variables. Unquestionably, they will know more, although some of that more is wrong, and much of it is tricky.

To make a Type 2 error is to deny that a certain variable is a functional one, when in fact it is. Thus, those who keep their probability of Type 2 errors low do not often reject an actually functional variable, relative to those whose Type 2 error probability is higher. Again, unquestionably, the practitioner with the lower probability of Type 2 errors will know more; but again, the nature of that more is seen often in its weakness, inconsistency of function, or its tight specialization.

Thus, to sum up, movement of a few centiles on a probability scale when establishing the acceptable risks of Type 1 and Type 2 errors, can alter rather importantly the character of what will be learned. Individual-subject-design practitioners, operating without calculation of the pertinent probabilities, necessarily fall into very low probabilities of Type 1 errors and very high probabilities of Type 2 errors, relative to their group-paradigm colleagues. As a result, they learn about fewer variables, but these variables are typically more powerful, general, dependable, and—very important—sometimes actionable. These are exactly the variables on which a technology of behavior might be built.[5] Thus, it is no coincidence that the individual-subject-design practitioners proved to be foremost in the development of behavioral technologies—considering the methods under which they usually operated, there was little else they could discover. Furthermore, they were comfortable in their method: their interest, when technological, was to solve social and personal problems. If a problem has been solved, you can *see* that; if you must test for statistical significance, you do not have a solution. This, after all, was the major conclusion to be made, not whether an experimental effect had been uncovered.

Currently, we are offered methods that might allow calculation of Type 1 errors in the use of individual-subject designs (*e.g.,* Gentile, Roden, and Klein, 1972; Jones, Vaught, and Weinrott, 1977). The offer is controversial, in that the data of individual-subject designs, typically consisting of the repeated behavior of an organism under sometimes similar, sometimes different conditions, do not seem to meet the independence-of-data assumptions characterizing the data around which parametric statistical methods had originally been conceived. However that controversy might be resolved, there will remain the one just sketched: if we calculate (correctly or incorrectly) the probability of Type 1 errors in our future research, will we promote ourselves out of that exquisitely valuable small corner in which we have been trapped these past years—the discovery of nothing more than a technology of behavior?

Of course, calculation of Type 1 error probability levels does not require that we set them as high as 0.05. We may set them at 0.00001. But there is a nonscientific contingency waiting for us. Results significant at the 0.05 level usually are publishable; publication is usually reinforcing, and sometimes essential; and what most of us know is what all of us publish. Thus, considering what the behavioral technology that we already know has taught us, it seems likely that if we accept this new offer, then we will be pressed to learn more about the less basic, less general, less dependable, less consistent, and less usable aspects of behavior. That is, we may have to become scholarly.

Scholarship has not usually been considered a bad value or an undesirable outcome, and even in this field, we do not ordinarily classify it with tantrums and headbanging. True, it is occasionally linked to impotence, but only in a metaphorical way. As my mother (Baer, *personal communication*) often said, "What can it hurt?" If we continue to discriminate carefully those effects that are strong, consistent, and dependable from those that are otherwise, then nothing much can be hurt. We will, of course, need more journals, or more pages, or both; but we learned to read very, very selectively long ago,[6] so that should be survivable.

On the other hand, what if we lost our old value for only the robust variables? We might, because we fell into that value rather than adopted it systematically, mainly because we were individual-subject-design practitioners.

[5]It is sometimes suggested that a technology of behavior could also be built by packaging together many variables that have weak, occasional, or otherwise specialized functions, on the premise that the resultant package will thereby contain something for everyone, and that some of the somethings will cumulate in their effectiveness and thereby become powerful. That would be interesting to see. At present, it is still a difficult problem to package the known powerful variables well enough to be universally useful. Perhaps this latter problem deserves priority over the former.

[6]We read selectively because we are not looking for experimental effects, but for useful effects. That is, we do not need to expand the list of at-least-sometimes effective variables; rather, we need to array the already known, highly effective variables into useful programs that solve problems. The occasional complaint that our indifference to new demonstrations of experimental effects leaves us nothing exciting to do, ignores the fact that we have not yet designed the *programs* of already known effective variables that will solve drug abuse, alcoholism, birth control, *etc. etc.*

Then, conceivably the offer of statistical methods for those designs could divert us from the much needed further development of that technology we almost have in hand. If it did, we would cease to be distinctive, hopeful, or useful. The Greeks referred to that as Tragedy.

REFERENCE NOTE

Baer, I. S. *Personal communications,* 1931 —.

REFERENCES

Gentile, J. R., Roden, A. H., and Klein, R. D. An analysis-of-variance model for the intrasubject replication design. *Journal of Applied Behavior Analysis,* 1972, **5,** 193-198.

Jones, R. R., Vaught, R. S., and Weinrott, M. Time-series analysis in operant research. *Journal of Applied Behavior Analysis,* 1977, **10,** 151-166.

Pearson, K. On a criterion that a given set of deviations from the probable in the case of a correlated system of variables is such that it cannot be reasonably supposed to have arisen from random sampling. *Philosophical Magazine,* 5th series, 1900, **50,** 339-357.

Walker, H. M. and Lev, J. *Statistical inference.* New York: Holt, 1953.

Wallis, W. A. and Roberts, H. V. *Statistics: a new approach.* Glencoe, Illinois: Free Press, 1956.

Received 10 May 1976.
(*Final acceptance 29 June 1976.*)

JOURNAL OF APPLIED BEHAVIOR ANALYSIS 1979, 12, 573-579 NUMBER 4 (WINTER 1979)

INCONSISTENT VISUAL ANALYSES OF INTRASUBJECT DATA

ANTHONY DEPROSPERO AND STANLEY COHEN

WESTON HOSPITAL AND WEST VIRGINIA UNIVERSITY

Visual inspection has been the method of analysis most widely employed to evaluate the functional control demonstrated by any given set of intrasubject replication data. To identify the influence of certain graphic characteristics on these evaluative behaviors, 36 "ABAB reversal" figures were constructed. They were sent to 250 reviewers of behavioral journals. Their evaluation of each figure was expressed as a rating on a 100-point scale of "experimental control." Mean interrater agreement was 0.61. In addition to this rating, a verbal description of evaluation criteria was requested. It was also found that graphic characteristics determine evaluative judgments in concert rather than singly. For example, phase mean changes had to be a pattern consistent with the hypothesized effect of the experimental variables, while degrees of mean shift and variability were less important. A description of the following evaluative criteria was presented: (a) topographic characteristics, (b) format of data presentation, (c) intra-experimental, and (d) extra-experimental circumstances.

DESCRIPTORS: visual analysis, methodology, judgmental aids, reliability, evaluative criteria

---

The main problem for analysis of intrasubject data is to determine whether changes in behavioral scores follow changes in experimental conditions with sufficient regularity to warrant the conclusion that experimental control has been demonstrated. The behavior analyst has typically employed visual inspection of the data as a means for doing so (Kazdin, 1976). Discussions of visual interpretation (Hersen and Barlow, 1976; Sidman, 1960) have identified at least four graphic features which are of interest to researchers evaluating intrasubject data. These are: (a) mean shift across phases in relation to experimental hypotheses, (b) magnitude of mean shift across phases, (c) score fluctuation or variation within phases, and (d) slope of data in relation to experimental hypotheses.

There exists evidence that visual inspection is not entirely satisfactory. Consider the work of Jones, Weinrott, and Vaught (1978) who selected a set of 58 pairs of adjacent phases from graphs depicting "nonobvious" experimental results from the *Journal of Applied Behavior Analysis*. A panel of 11 judges showed greater agreement in evaluating meaningful changes in level for adjacent phases that were not statistically reliable by time-series analysis than for phases that were statistically reliable. This "suggests that statistically reliable experimental effects may be more often overlooked by visual appraisals of data than nonmeaningful effects" (Jones *et al.*, 1978, p. 280). Over all pairs of phases, the median intercorrelation of the judges' agreement with themselves was only .39. A particular property of the data (serial dependency) was found to affect adversely the agreement of the judges.

Another example of interpretive inconsistency was found by White (1971) who demonstrated that individuals can vary widely in their interpretation of graphed data, even to the extent that some would interpret a trend as being "ac-

---

Portions of this paper were presented at the ninth annual meeting of the Association of Advancement of Behavior Therapy, New York, 1976. The authors would like to thank W. Stewart Agras for his assistance in conducting the survey and Don Hake for his careful comments and editing on an earlier draft. Reprint request should be addressed to Anthony DeProspero, Psychology Service, Weston Hospital, Weston, West Virginia 26542.

celerating" while others judged the same trend to be "decelerating." In practice, therefore, such inspection can lead to unequivocal conclusions only when the behavior change is so dramatic that no critic would disagree with its significance. While it may be desirable to have judgmental errors on the "conservative" side for some purposes (Baer, 1977), this state of affairs could conceivably result in inefficiency of experimental effort. For example, unfavorable review about nondramatic results might lead to a variable being dropped prematurely from experimentation. This purpose of the present study was to determine whether agreement in visual judgment could be reliably attributed to certain features of the graph.

METHOD

Stimulus Materials

In order to represent those characteristics thought to influence visual interpretation, a set of simulated "ABAB reversal design" graphs were constructed. Those graphs illustrated the four factors thought to represent characteristics important for visual analysis.

The first of the graphic factors (pattern of mean shift) was represented by three patterns of mean shifts across phases: (a) an "ideal" pattern of results with consistent increases in both "B" phases and an intervening return to baseline (top portion of Figure 1A), (b) "inconsistent treatment" pattern with no mean change in the first three phases, concluding with an acceleration in the last phase (middle portion of Figure 1A), and (c) an "irreversible effect" pattern of acceleration in the second phase with no subsequent mean change (bottom portion of Figure 1A).

The second characteristic was called degree of mean shift across phases. It is simply the percentage of mean change from phase X to phase X + 1. To illustrate how this was computed, consider two experimental phases, a baseline with a mean of 10.0 and a treatment period with a mean of 12.5. The difference (2.5) would be divided by the mean of the earlier phase (10.0) to yield a value of .25. All three mean shifts in an "ABAB" graph were equal, and three values were considered: (a) 1.0 (top portion of Figure 1A), (b) .50 (top portion of Figure 1B), and (c) .25 (bottom portion of Figure 1B).

The third characteristic, score fluctuation or variation within phases, was manipulated by selecting "behavior scores" with a particular relationship between mean and standard deviation. To illustrate, consider a phase with scores that have a mean of 10 and a standard deviation of 1.0. The standard deviation is divided by the mean to yield a variability coefficient of .1. Two values were represented, .1 (top portion of Figure 1A) and .25 (top portion of Figure 1C).

The final graphic characteristic was concerned with "trend," or the extent to which the data fell along a line with a given slope. Two values were represented: one-half of the graphs had zero slope in all phases (Figure 1A), and one-half had a linear slope of 30 degrees in the "positive" or "increasing" direction (bottom of Figure 1C).

These data were constructed in the following manner. First, 144 phase means were selected, four for each of the 36 "ABAB" graphs. The means were selected so that 12 pairs of phase means each illustrated the three patterns and degree of mean shift described above. This procedure resulted in four straight lines in each phase of the "ABAB" designs. For half the graphs, the "trend" was introduced by rotating these lines 30 degrees about the middle data point of each phase. To introduce the variability, a set of 1,440 deviation scores (one for each of the 10 points in each phase) was generated. These had a mean of 0, and a standard deviation of 1.0. Each behavior score was then multiplied by the deviation score and the indicated variability coefficient. These operations resulted in randomly distributed variability that had no effect on the pattern or degree of mean shift, or on the slope.

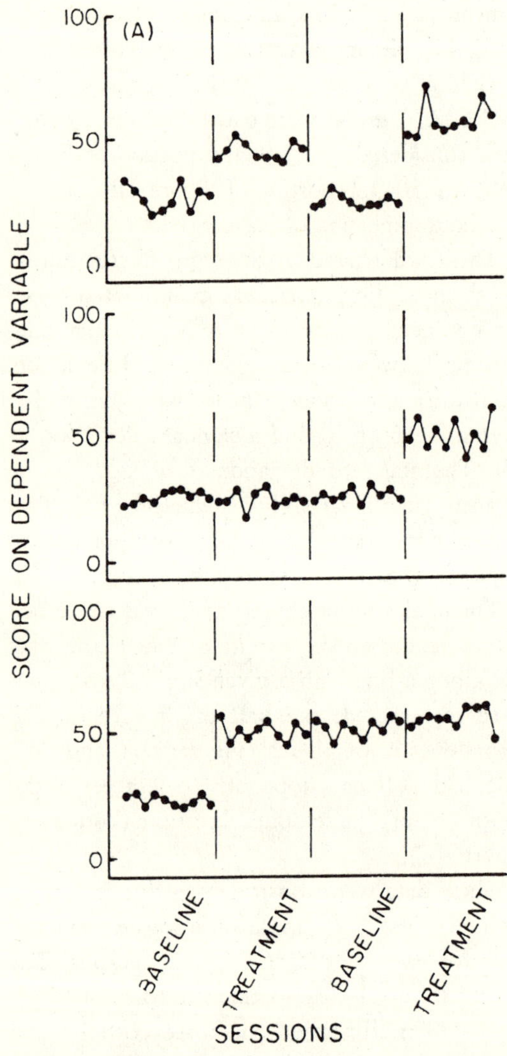

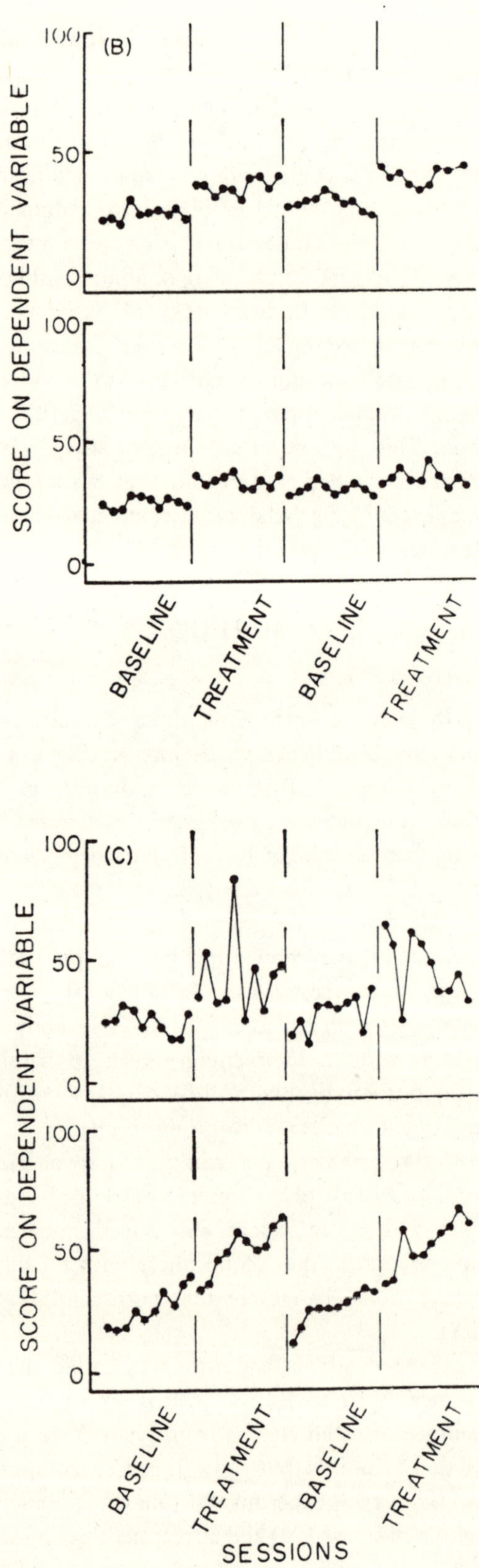

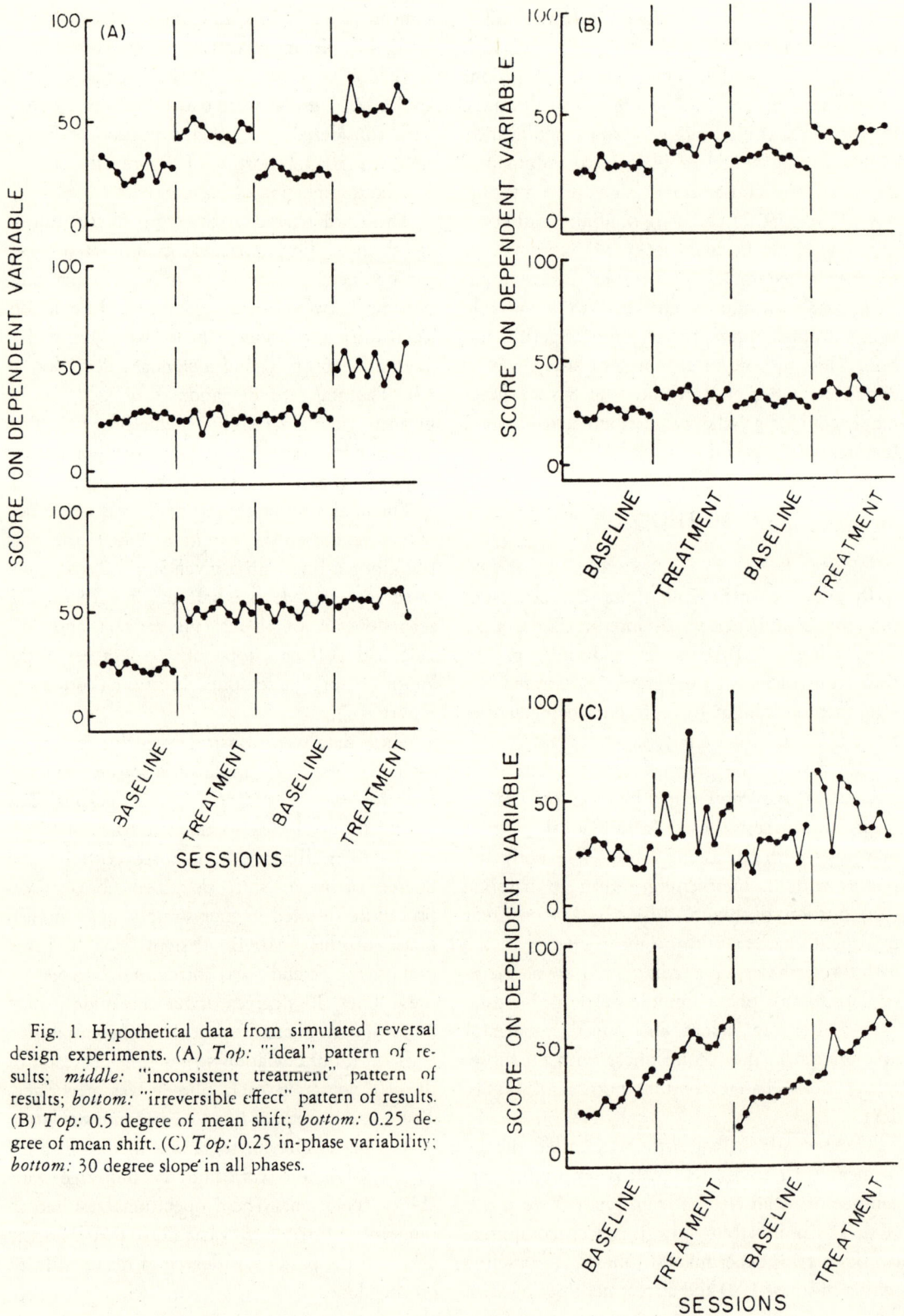

Fig. 1. Hypothetical data from simulated reversal design experiments. (A) *Top:* "ideal" pattern of results; *middle:* "inconsistent treatment" pattern of results; *bottom:* "irreversible effect" pattern of results. (B) *Top:* 0.5 degree of mean shift; *bottom:* 0.25 degree of mean shift. (C) *Top:* 0.25 in-phase variability; *bottom:* 30 degree slope in all phases.

Subjects

A pool of 250 constituted the sample, 215 members of the Board of Editors or Guest Reviewers of the *Journal of Applied Behavior Analysis* and 35 members of the Board of Editors of the *Journal of the Experimental Analysis of Behavior.* At the end of six weeks, 114 replies had been received for a response rate of 43%. Six respondents stated that they could not meaningfully answer the questions in the absence of circumstantial information, leaving a total of 108.

Procedure

The 36 graphs were divided into four sets of nine, each containing at least one sample of each of the three patterns of mean shift. One set was sent to each subject. The lower portion of the figures contained the question, "Using the following scale, how satisfactory a demonstration of experimental control do you consider this to be?" The scale was labeled "low" at the zero end and "high" at the 100 end. The average of all ratings given each figure was determined, and is hereafter referred to as mean rating. To permit the expression of idiosyncratic evaluative criteria, subjects were asked to list the factors they considered when analyzing graphic presentations of data, in general.

RESULTS

Interrater Agreement

To assess interrater agreement, the Pearson product moment correlation was calculated for each pair of raters who had reviewed the same set of graphs. The average correlation was .61, with a standard deviation of .26.

Graphic Characteristics and Evaluative Criteria

Table 1 presents graphic characteristics, size of rating sample, and the mean, standard deviation, and range of ratings for each graph. Pattern of mean shift was a critical characteristic in that mean rating fell off very rapidly for any pattern other than the "ideal." It appears that the minimum for respectable ratings was that the means of phases change in a pattern consistent with the hypothesized effect of the experimental variables. As one might expect, larger degrees of mean shift produced more favorable judgments, but the effect was not so dramatic. The bottom portion of Figure 1B has the same pattern of mean shift, variability coefficient, and a slope of trend as the top portion of Figure 1A, but the degree of mean shift is only one-fourth as large. Lower degrees of variability and the absence of trends produced more favorable judgments, but it is noted that these factors were influential only within the "ideal" pattern of mean shift; and, even here, an unfavorable combination of degree of mean shift and variability coefficient was sufficient to result in very low ratings.

It is apparent that each factor represents a source of strength in the judgment process, but it is equally apparent that the graphic factors exert their effects in concert. The mean rating for each of the 36 graphs was subjected to a four-way (pattern, degree, variability, slope) repeated measures analysis of variance. Pattern and degree of mean shift were highly significant, $F(2,935) = 154.06$, and $F(2,935) = 94.39$, respectively (in the sense of having a reliable effect upon mean rating). Together they account for only a small portion of the variance (eta squared $= .27$). Several of the interactions are significant as well, but these account for even less variance and are not reported.

Verbal Statement of Evaluative Criteria

The open-ended question about evaluative criteria prompted a comprehensive range of criteria employed by behavioral researchers. A certain amount of paraphrasing and categorization was done, but every effort was made to reflect the opinions as they were expressed, and in the appropriate context. The numbers in parentheses represent the frequency with which a given comment was made. In general, there were four "clusters" of statements.

Table 1

Relationship of Graphic Characteristics to "Demonstration of Experimental Control"

Degree of Mean Shift		*Within-Phase Variability*	*Slope of Trend*	N[a]	*Rating*		
					Mean[b]	*S.D.*	*Low/High*[b]
		"IDEAL" PATTERN OF RESULTS					
1.0	(Top, Figure 1A)	0.1	0°	32	78.6	18.7	3/100
1.0	(Bottom, Figure 1C)	0.1	+30°	28	33.1	27.8	0/89
1.0	(Top, Figure 1C)	0.25	0°	26	61.9	24.0	8/100
1.0		0.25	+30°	18	38.8	25.3	0/87
0.5	(Top, Figure 1B)	0.1	0°	18	79.5	23.1	0/100
0.5		0.1	+30°	26	27.0	24.4	0/80
0.5		0.25	0°	36	20.9	18.8	0/62
0.5		0.25	+30°	28	24.8	20.1	0/80
0.25	(Bottom, Figure 1B)	0.1	0°	27	45.1	23.5	0/87
0.25		0.1	+30°	36	11.8	11.6	0/50
0.25		0.25	0°	26	12.8	15.8	0/75
0.25		0.25	+30°	18	8.2	8.4	0/30
		"INCONSISTENT TREATMENT" PATTERN OF RESULTS					
1.0	(Middle, Figure 1A)	0.1	0°	36	17.3	15.3	0/75
1.0		0.1	+30°	28	14.4	14.5	0/57
1.0		0.25	0°	26	23.3	22.6	0/77
1.0		0.25	+30°	18	15.8	17.5	0/67
0.5		0.1	0°	18	14.4	20.1	0/85
0.5		0.1	+30°	26	11.0	10.6	0/35
0.5		0.25	0°	36	18.8	14.7	0/50
0.5		0.25	+30°	28	12.6	10.3	0/35
0.25		0.1	0°	28	14.0	17.2	0/72
0.25		0.1	+30°	36	13.3	10.8	0/43
0.25		0.25	0°	26	11.3	14.9	0/75
0.25		0.25	+30°	17	7.2	6.0	0/16
		"IRREVERSIBLE EFFECT" PATTERN OF RESULTS					
1.0	(Bottom, Figure 1A)	0.1	0°	36	23.2	18.4	0/57
1.0		0.1	+30°	28	19.3	16.2	0/59
1.0		0.25	0°	26	16.3	16.0	0/62
1.0		0.25	+30°	17	17.3	14.0	0/50
0.5		0.1	0°	18	23.5	21.0	0/85
0.5		0.1	+30°	26	12.7	8.8	0/33
0.5		0.25	0°	36	17.8	14.7	0/50
0.5		0.25	+30°	28	15.8	12.6	0/50
0.25		0.1	0°	28	18.5	17.7	0/83
0.25		0.1	+30°	36	12.5	10.6	0/40
0.25		0.25	0°	26	11.7	11.1	0/50
0.25		0.25	+30°	18	9.6	8.3	0/25

[a]N = 108
[b]Maximum score = 100

Topography of results. Most frequently mentioned were "trends" (31) or "slopes" (9), their "relation to the specific experimental hypotheses under investigation" (6), and changes in them both within (2) and between conditions. Next indicated were "means of phases" (32) and more complicated notions of "levels," (which involved judgments about "data overlap" across conditions rather than arithmetic averages). Next in frequency were the related notions of "stability" (24) and "variability" (26), both within and across conditions. At least two judges said that variability must be expressed "relative to the variability of other subjects in the same or similar studies." "Replication" of effect was also an important criteria (15), with five judges stating that the "number of" replications could be basis for this decision. Four judges indicated that "replication across subjects" was important. An interesting exclusion criterion for interpreting effects was posited by two judges, namely that there be "no evidence of (unintended) sequence or cyclical effects." Three judges simply stated that effect must be "clear," "unambiguous," and "significant."

Format of presentation. Twelve judges noted that the "labeling and scaling" of both axes must bear clear relationship to the dependent and independent variables of the study, that the graph be "easily read" and "consistent with text." Thirteen felt that the "reliability of measurement," and "scope of changes therein" must be specified for accurate interpretation. Seven considered the "number of data points in each phase" as important while one each mentioned the "presence of follow-up" and the specification of the "chronology of data gathering" as desirable practices.

Intra-experimental concerns. If data on more than one subject are under investigation, variability, effects, and mean changes are judged across subjects in a relative fashion. Other reviewers stressed that their interpretations of graphs took other factors into account. "Relation to design" was mentioned by four, "nature of experimental question under investigation" by an equal number, and one each designated "conclusions of author" and "procedures" as salient factors. Two reviewers also cited as desirable a "low probability of alternative explanations or potential confounds."

Extra-experimental concerns. Some subjects took into account information that is not strictly a part of any given experiment. Paramount among these was the well-known issue of "social" (19), "clinical" (7), and/or "applied" (4) "significance" of results. Five other reviewers indicated that the question of "frequency of research previously completed" in an area was a significant concern to them, in the sense that they would be unlikely to recommend publication of an exact replication unless the control of new variables or an "enhanced" effect was evident.

DISCUSSION

The Jones *et al.* (1978) study compared visual with statistical inference and found that visual inference of a panel of judges was not particularly reliable. The present study replicated this finding and, in addition, attempted to assess the factors contributing to reliable or unreliable visual judgment. The median interjudge agreement correlation was a modest .61. Except for the ideal pattern of results (in the hypothesized data), a wide range of ratings of effect was obtained for almost every graph. Graphic characteristics appear to determine judgments in concert rather than singly. It seems likely that raters weigh these factors differently when processing graphic information, which is quite plausible when one considers the wide range of evaluative criteria stated.

The above variability of opinions suggests that a behavioral researcher seeking corroboration on the interpretation of results would not be likely to get the same answer twice. A statistical analysis, however, produces the same result each time which could provide a "yardstick" for comparing effects from one experiment to another (which is a judgment that many reviewers now make subjectively). Such a yardstick would also be useful in single-case studies for assessing the relative contribution of variables in which the experimental goal is to isolate causes of variability or the contribution of "indvidual differences" (Hersen and Barlow, 1976). Thus, any behavioral research effort in which the information from one graph must be related to the information in another might be conducted more efficiently with a reliable judgmental aide, statistical or visual, for operationalizing effects.

REFERENCES

Baer, D. M. "Perhaps it would be better not to know everything." *Journal of Applied Behavior Analysis,* 1977, **10,** 167-172.

Hersen, M. and Barlow, D. H. *Single case experimental designs: strategies for studying behavior change.* New York: Pergamon, 1976.

Jones, R. R., Weinrott, M. R., and Vaught, R. S. Effects of serial dependency on the agreement between visual and statistical inferences. *Journal of Applied Behavior Analysis,* 1978, **11,** 277-284.

Kazdin, A. E. Statistical analysis for single case experimental designs. In M. Hersen and D. H. Barlow (Eds), *Single case experimental designs. strategies for studying behavior change.* New York: Pergamon, 1976.

Sidman, M. *Tactics of scientific research.* New York: Basic Books, 1960.

White, O. R. *Pragmatic approaches to progress in the single case.* Doctoral dissertation, University of Oregon, 1971, University Microfilms, 72-8618, Ann Arbor, Michigan.

Received 19 June 1978.
(Final Acceptance 19 July 1979.)

JOURNAL OF APPLIED BEHAVIOR ANALYSIS 1982, 15, 423-429 NUMBER 3 (FALL 1982)

A SIMPLIFIED TIME-SERIES ANALYSIS FOR EVALUATING TREATMENT INTERVENTIONS

WARREN W. TRYON

FORDHAM UNIVERSITY

Time-series analysis procedures for analyzing behavioral data are receiving increasing support. However, several authorities strongly recommend using at least 50–100 points per experimental phase. A complex mathematical model must then be empirically developed using computer programs to extract serial dependency from the data before the effects of treatment interventions can be evaluated. The present discussion provides a simple method of evaluating intervention effects that can be used with as few as 8 points per experimental phase. The calculations are easy enough to do by hand.

DESCRIPTORS: time-series analysis, statistics, statistical inference

---

Time-series analysis is a quantitative method for assisting the subjective art of data interpretation. Several studies (e.g., Gottman & Glass, 1978; Jones, Weinrott, & Vaught, 1978) have provided empirical demonstrations that visual and statistical evaluations of typical applied behavior analytic data sets often differ. Although it is not universally agreed that statistically based judgments are better than visual judgments (e.g., Baer, 1977), many authors (Hartmann, Gottman, Jones, Gardner, Kazdin, & Vaught, 1980; Jones, Vaught, & Weinrott, 1977; McCain & McCleary, 1979) have argued that it is desirable to use time-series statistics to analyze behavioral data. More confidence can be placed in data interpretations when statistical and visual analyses agree than when they disagree.

The particular time-series analysis most often suggested (e.g., Glass, Willson, & Gottman, 1975) is based on an auto-regressive integrated moving average. This procedure involves the empirical construction of a complex mathematical model that is subsequently validated against the very data from which it was constructed. The model is used to extract serial dependency from the data only after all the criteria of model construction have been met, thereby leaving an uncorrelated time series. Standard inferential statistics are used to evaluate changes in the mean level and slope of the time series due to the intervention.

A major limitation of the auto-regressive integrated moving average approach is that many data points are required for adequate model development. Hartmann et al. (1980) cited several authorities who recommended collecting at least 50 to 100 data points *per experimental phase* before attempting to use auto-regressive integrated moving average procedures. Less confidence exists in the empirically constructed model if fewer data points are used. Moreover, the power of the auto-regressive integrated moving average procedure is diminished as data are reduced, thus increasing the probability of falsely accepting the null hypothesis.

The purpose of the current discussion is to present a simple, yet elegant, method of time-series analysis that can be used on small data sets to evaluate the effects of treatment interventions. This approach can also be used to decide when responding has stabilized, i.e., when a new phase of the experiment might begin (cf. Killeen, 1978). The logic underlying the *C* statistic is the same as the logic underlying visual analysis; variability in successive data points is evaluated relative to changes in slope from one phase of the experiment to another.

Reprint requests should be sent to Warren W. Tryon, Department of Psychology, Fordham University, Bronx, New York 10458.

THE C STATISTIC

vonNeumann, Kent, Bellinson, and Hart (1941) described two orthogonal estimates of the variance of a time series. The first measure is the variance calculated as indicated in Equation 1.

$$S^2 = \frac{1}{N}\sum_{i=1}^{N}(X_i - X)^2 \qquad (1)$$

This variance of the time series increases in direct proportion to changes or trends in the mean value of the series. Consider the following data: 1, 2, 3, 4, 5. Their mean is 3 and their variance is 2.5. If this trend extends to include: 1, 2, 3, 4, 5, 6, 7, 8, 9; then their mean is 5.0 and their variance is 7.5. Hence, the presence of a trend increases both the mean and the variance. Said otherwise, the variance is inversely proportional to the stationarity of the series.

The second estimate of the variance of a time series is the Mean Square Successive Difference (*MSSD*) statistic. It is calculated as its name implies. The consecutive differences among data points are calculated, squared, and then averaged as indicated by Equation 2.

$$MSSD = D^2 = \sum_{i=1}^{N-1}\frac{(X_{i+1} - X_i)^2}{N-1} \qquad (2)$$

The *MSSD* or *D* squared statistic is independent of changes in the mean value of the time series, i.e., it is independent of the stationarity of the series. Reconsider the two brief data sets given above. The *MSSD* statistic equals 1.0 for both sets: integers 1-5 and integers 1-9. Notice that the continuing trend increased the mean squared deviation from the mean by a factor of 3 but did not alter the mean squared successive difference.

vonNeumann (1941) extensively discussed the distribution of the ratio of the *MSSD* to the variance. However, it was Young (1941) who developed this reasoning into the highly useful *C* statistic given by Equation 3.

$$C = 1 - \frac{\sum_{i=1}^{N-1}(X_i - X_{i+1})^2}{2\sum_{i=1}^{N}(X_i - X)^2} \qquad (3)$$

The numerator of the right-hand term is the sum of the $N - 1$ squared consecutive differences associated with the time series. The denominator of this same term is twice the sum of the *N* squared deviations of the time-series data points from their mean.

The standard error of the *C* statistic is easily calculated using Equation 4 and it depends entirely on the number of data points in the time series.

$$Sc = \sqrt{\frac{N+2}{(N-1)(N+1)}} \qquad (4)$$

Young (1941) has shown that the ratio of *C* to its standard error is the *Z* statistic

$$Z = \frac{C}{Sc} \qquad (5)$$

and is normally distributed for time series containing 25 or more values. Moreover, the deviation from normality is not marked even for time series containing just 8 values. Table 1 presents the 5% and 1% critical values for samples of size 8 to 25.

Characteristics of the C Statistic

Reference to Equation 3 will help illustrate the basic characteristics of the *C* statistic. The value of *C* will be zero when the sum of the squared deviations from the mean equals one-half the sum of the squared consecutive differences, because the denominator of the right-hand fraction is multiplied by 2 which makes it equal to the numerator and thus the right-hand fraction equals unity. Subtracting unit from one leaves zero. This situation is most likely to occur when the data hug the mean rather closely.

The sum of squared deviations from the mean increases more rapidly than does the sum of

Table 1

Critical values for testing the *C* statistic for selected sample sizes (*N*) at the .01 level of significance[a,b].

N	*1%*	*N*	*1%*
8	2.17	18	2.25
9	2.18	19	2.26
10	2.20	20	2.26
11	2.21	21	2.26
12	2.22	22	2.26
13	2.22	23	2.27
14	2.23	24	2.27
15	2.24	25	2.27
16	2.24	∞	2.33
17	2.25		

[a]Taken from Young (1941).

[b]The critical value for the .05 level of significance is 1.64 for all sample sizes above.

squared successive differences, given the presence of any type of trend or nonstationarity. This causes the right-hand fraction of the *C* statistic to become small, which makes the *C* statistic become large. The *C* statistic aids the investigator in evaluating how large the squared deviations from the mean are (which reflect the presence of all types of trends) relative to the sum of the squared consecutive differences (which are independent of all types of trends). The logic of this fraction is directly analogous to that of the *F* statistic.

The statistical significance of *C* is evaluated by dividing it by its standard error (cf. Equation 5). It should be noted that the standard error is entirely a function of sample size. This means that the standard error can be reduced to any value, and thus a significant *Z* can always be found given any value of *C*. Hence, the power of the test approaches infinity as the sample size approaches infinity. Entirely trivial effects can be found to the statistically significant if enough data points are collected. It should be noted that this predicament is generally true of all statistical analyses and is not a unique limitation of the *C* statistic.

Applying the C Statistic

The main logical question answered by the *C* statistic is whether or not the time series contains any trends, i.e., any systematic departures from random variation. An initial use of the *C* statistic is to evaluate the baseline data. Two outcomes are possible. Evidence of a trend will either be found or not. It is more desirable that the baseline data not contain any statistically significant trends because this allows a more powerful application of the *C* statistic by appending the first treatment series to the first baseline series and testing the ensemble or aggregate series with the *C* statistic. A significant result is evidence that the treatment series departs from the baseline series.

Two less powerful applications of the *C* statistic are available for use when the initial baseline is found to contain a trend. Both alternative procedures involve creating a comparison series and testing for a trend with the *C* statistics. The more powerful of these two alternative procedures involves calculating "difference scores from the trend in the previous phase" (Hayes, 1981, p. 201). Several methods are available for quantifying the trend in the previous phase. Standard regression techniques can be used to obtain a line of best fit. However, one or two atypical data points can severely affect both the slope and intercept values given small data sets. Velleman and Hoaglin (1981) describe how to fit a "resistant line" which passes through the medians of each third of the data. The slope and intercept values in the equation for the resistant line agree favorably with the corresponding values in the regression equation when no atypical data points are present. If a straight line does not adequately describe the trend in the previous phase, then a more complex equation is required. Perhaps a quadratic, polynomial, or trigonometric function, like a sine wave, characterizes the data more accurately. Daniel and Wood (1971) and Lewis (1960) are good sources of curve fitting procedures. The comparison series is obtained by subtracting the trend line values associated with the first baseline point from the first treatment point, then subtracting the trend line value associated with second baseline point from the second treatment point, etc., until all baseline and/or treatment values have been exhausted. Often, more treatment points will exist than baseline points. Modest extrapolation of the first phase trend line can provide a basis for adding a few more points to the comparison series, thereby enhancing the power of the test. The comparison series is tested with the *C* statistic. A significant result is evidence that the difference between the trends in the two phases contains a trend or departure of some kind. A significant *C* statistic only establishes that change has occurred. It does not guarantee that the change was due to the variable manipulated by the experimenter; it could be due to changes in an uncontrolled collateral variable. As with visual analysis, it is the overall pattern of results relative to the design used that enables a determination that the independent variable is responsible for change.

The second of the less powerful applications of the *C* statistic is the easier to use. The comparison series is obtained directly by subtracting the first baseline value from the first treatment value, etc., until all baseline and/or treatment values have been exhausted. The *C* statistic is then calculated on this comparison series. A significant result indicates that the treatment phase departs from the trend set in baseline.

Both uses of a difference series (unlike the use of raw scores when baseline is stationary) share a common limitation. The *C* statistic will not be significant when the slopes of data points in the two experimental phases under consideration are equal even when one series has been shifted up or down dramatically relative to the other series. This is because the difference series will be constant, i.e., highly stationary.

The next use of the *C* statistic might be to determine when responding has stabilized during treatment. One criterion might be to continue data collection until 10 consecutive data points are obtained for which the *C* statistic was not significant (see Killeen, 1978 for other criteria). These data would then provide a period against which the subsequent phase could be assessed. This process would continue for each successive phase. Sometimes responding may not meet the stability criteria before treatment must be reinitiated or withdrawn. The less powerful alternative procedure for using the *C* statistic could then be used.

It may seem that if values associated with a linear trend in a previous phase can be subtracted from data in a subsequent experimental phase then these values could just as well be subtracted from a linear trend line associated with the subsequent phase. Such a procedure *always* gives artificial results. It can be shown that the value of the *C* statistic is always entirely a function of the sample size when values of one linear trend line are subtracted from values of another linear trend line. That is, the value of *C* associated with all sets of, say, 15 data points will be exactly the same regardless of the data used. A different value of *C* is associated with each value of *N*. This anomaly arises because the difference between two linear trend lines is itself a linear trend line where the differences between consecutive values is constant and equal to the slope of the comparison line. However, the sum of the squared deviations from the mean associated with values on this comparison line is also a function of its slope. The ratio of the sum of the squared consecutive differences is a constant fraction of the sum of the squared deviations from the mean of such values depending only on their number.

AN EMPIRICAL EXAMPLE

Tryon and Zager (Note 1) observed the frequency of "talking-out" behavior in a class of 15 mentally retarded children aged 9-11 yr. A "talk-out" was defined as all vocalizations not authorized by the teacher. Observations were made for 1 h in the morning and for 1 h during the afternoon, Monday through Friday, yielding 10 baseline data points during the first week. These data are displayed in Figure 1.

The first question was whether some trend existed in the baseline data. The actual data are presented in Table 2 where the *C* statistic has

Table 2

Example of the Use of the C Statistic in an A-B-A Experimental Design

	Score (X)	D^2	
	28	324	First Baseline Phase:
	46	49	
	39	36	$D^2 = 1112$
	45	441	$2\ SS(X) = 1324$
First	24	16	$C = 1 - \frac{1112}{1324} = 0.160$
Baseline	20	225	
Phase	35	4	$Sc = \sqrt{\frac{8}{9(11)}} = 0.284$
	37	1	
	36	16	$Z = \frac{0.160}{0.284} = 0.563$, n.s.
	40	256	
	24	64	
	16	441	
	37	64	
	45	729	First Baseline Plus Group Tokens:
	18	1	$D^2 = 2762$
	19	1	
	18	0	$2\ SS(X) = 8227.0$
	18	25	
	13	1	$C = 1 - \frac{2762}{8227} = 0.664$
	12	9	
Group	15	4	
Tokens	13	4	$Sc = \sqrt{\frac{30}{31(33)}} = 0.171$
Phase	15	1	
	16	25	
	11	9	$Z = \frac{0.664}{0.171} = 3.883$
	14	0	$p < .001$
	14	4	
	12	1	
	13	1	
	14	9	
	17	1	Last Week of Group Tokens Plus
	16	1	First Week of Second Baseline:
	15	36	$D^2 = 353$
	21	25	$2\ SS(X) = 882$
	16	49	
	23	9	$C = 1 - \frac{353}{822} = 0.571$
Second	20	36	
Baseline	26	0	$Sc = \sqrt{\frac{18}{19(21)}} = 0.212$
Phase	26	16	
	22	49	$Z = \frac{0.571}{0.212} = 2.693$
	15	81	
	24		$p < .01$

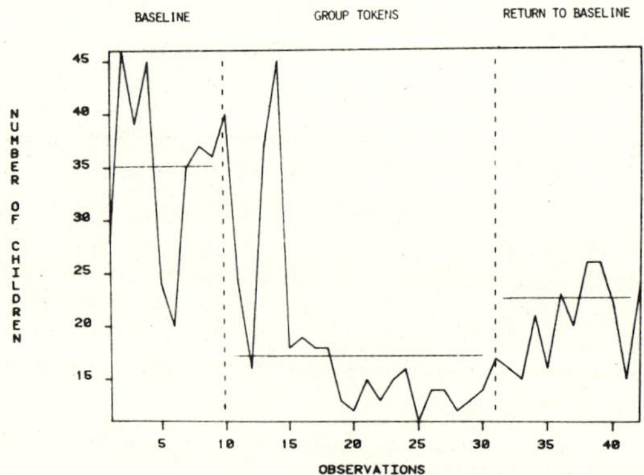

Fig. 1. The total number of children participating in all incidents of unauthorized talk-outs during baseline 1, group tokens, and baseline 2 phases.

been calculated. The value of $Z = .563$ is not statistically significant, indicating the absence of any substantial trend.

The next 11-day (22 observations) phase involved a group consequences procedure (cf. Barrish, Saunders, & Wolf, 1969; Herman & Tramontana, 1971; Packard, 1970; Schmidt & Ulrich, 1969). The teacher put a token in a glass jar on the teacher's desk at the end of every 5-min period during which no "talking-out" behavior occurred by any class member. Each student earned the number of tokens in the jar at the end of each period and tokens could be exchanged for edibles. The basic question at issue was whether the group tokens procedure had any demonstrable effect on "talking-out" behavior (see Figure 1). The data for this phase of the experiment were appended to the baseline data and tested for a trend. The resulting $Z = 3.883$, $p < .001$ confirmed the visual impression of a shift in the trend of the time series.

The next question concerned when responding under the group tokens procedure had stabilized. Inspection of the D2 column of Table 2 reveals large consecutive changes early in the intervention but leveling off shortly thereafter. An analysis of all 22 group tokens data points yielded a $Z = 2.468$, $p < .05$, confirming the visual evidence of a trend. The last 10 data points (1 wk of observation) were chosen to assess stability to compare this portion of the series with the first week of return to baseline. The value of $Z = .679$ was clearly not statistically significant, suggesting that this portion of the series was stable.

The group tokens procedure was discontinued for a 2-wk period which constituted a second baseline period. Table 2 contains the calculations associated with the last 10 data points from the intervention plus the first 10 data points from the second baseline. The resulting $Z = 2.693$, $p < .01$ indicated the presence of a trend.

Visual inspection of Figure 1 may suggest to some the presence of a trend occurring during the 2-wk second baseline period. The resulting value of $Z = .146$ is not statistically significant. This is consistent with observations (Gottman & Glass, 1978; Jones et al., 1978) that data analysis based on visual inspection and time-series analysis can disagree substantially.

DISCUSSION

The *C* statistic is a simple, yet elegant, method for quantitatively evaluating the presence of changes due to treatment interventions in serially dependent time-series data. It is an omnibus test for abrupt changes in the level of a time series as well as gradual changes in its slope. The major difference between the *C* statistic and the auto-regressive integrated moving average method is that the latter can test for abrupt changes in level separately from changes in slope while the former cannot. However, the *C* statistic can be used with much smaller data sets, does not require complex computer based model construction, and is easily calculated by hand.

The *C* statistic is best applied when responding has stabilized in the previous phase. Then the data from the subsequent phase can be appended to the previous phase and tested for any trends using the *C* statistic. Two alternate methods can be used when responding has not stabilized in the previous phase. The more powerful alternate method is to fit either a resistant or regression line to the data in the prior phase and then create a comparison series by subtracting the trend line values associated with the previous phase from the data points in the subsequent phase. This comparison series is then tested for any trends using the *C* statistic. The less powerful alternate method involves subtracting corresponding data points in the previous phase from those in the subsequent phase to create the comparison series. This series is then tested for any trends using the *C* statistic as before. Both of the less powerful methods share the limitation that they cannot test for a change in level if there has been no change in slope.

This flexible and easily calculated time-series *C* statistic should be of use to investigators who did not previously have the resources to incorporate time-series designs into their research and/or clinical practice.

REFERENCE NOTE

1. Tryon, W. W., & Zager, K. Reduction of talking-out behavior in a class of mentally retarded children through group consequences. Unpublished manuscript, 1980. (Available from Department of Psychology, Fordham University, Bronx, New York 10458.)

REFERENCES

Baer, D. M. "Perhaps it would be better not to know everything." *Journal of Applied Behavior Analysis,* 1977, **10,** 167-172.

Barrish, H. B., Saunders, M., & Wolf, M. M. Good behavior game: Effects of individual contingencies for group consequences on disruptive behavior in a classroom. *Journal of Applied Behavior Analysis,* 1969, **2,** 119-124.

Daniel, C., & Wood, F. S. *Fitting equations to data: Computer analysis of multifactor data for scientists and engineers.* New York: McGraw-Hill, 1971.

Glass, G. V., Willson, V. L., & Gottman, J. M. *Design and analysis of time series experiments.* Boulder: Colorado Associated University Press, 1975.

Gottman, J. M., & Glass, G. V. Analysis of interrupted time-series experiments. In T. R. Kratochwill (Ed.), *Single subject research: Strategies for evaluating change.* New York: Academic Press, 1978.

Hartmann, D. P., Gottman, J. M., Jones, R. R., Gardner, W., Kazdin, A. E., & Vaught, R. Interrupted time-series analysis and its application to behavioral data. *Journal of Applied Behavior Analysis,* 1980, **13,** 543-559.

Hayes, S. C. Single case experimental design and empirical clinical practice. *Journal of Consulting and Clinical Psychology,* 1981, **49,** 193-211.

Herman, S. H., & Tramontana, J. Instructions and group versus individual reinforcement in modifying disruptive group behavior. *Journal of Applied Behavior Analysis,* 1971, **4,** 113-119.

Jones, R. R., Vaught, R. S., & Weinrott, M. Time-series analysis in operant research. *Journal of Applied Behavior Analysis,* 1977, **10,** 151-166.

Jones, R. R., Weinrott, M. R., & Vaught, R. S. Effects of serial dependency on the agreement between visual and statistical inference. *Journal of Applied Behavior Analysis,* 1978, **11,** 277-283.

Killeen, P. R. Stability criteria. *Journal of Experimental Analysis of Behavior,* 1978, **29,** 17-25.

Lewis, D. *Quantitative methods in psychology.* New York: McGraw-Hill, 1960.

McCain, L. J., & McCleary, R. The statistical analysis of the simple interrupted time-series quasi-experiment. In T. D. Cook & D. T. Campbell (Eds.), *Quasi-experimentation: Design and analysis issues for field settings.* Chicago: Rand-McNally, 1979.

Packard, R. G. The control of "classroom attention": A group contingency for complex behavior. *Journal of Applied Behavior Analysis,* 1970, **3,** 13-28.

Schmidt, G. W., & Ulrich, R. E. Effects of group contingent events upon classroom noise. *Journal of Applied Behavior Analysis,* 1969, **2,** 171-179.

Velleman, P. F., & Hoaglin, D. C. *Applications, basics, and computing of exploratory data analysis.* Boston: Duxbury Press, 1981.

vonNeumann, J. Distribution of the ratio of the mean square successive difference to the variance. *Annals of Mathematical Statistics,* 1941, **12,** 367-395.

vonNeumann, J., Kent, R. H., Bellinson, H. R., & Hart, B. I. The mean successive difference. *Annals of Mathematical Statistics,* 1941, **12,** 153-162.

Young, L. C. On randomness in ordered sequences. *Annals of Mathematical Statistics,* 1941, **12,** 293-300.

Received March 9, 1981
Final acceptance January 14, 1982

JOURNAL OF APPLIED BEHAVIOR ANALYSIS 1990, 23, 341–351 NUMBER 3 (FALL 1990)

VISUAL ANALYSIS OF SINGLE-CASE TIME SERIES: EFFECTS OF VARIABILITY, SERIAL DEPENDENCE, AND MAGNITUDE OF INTERVENTION EFFECTS

THOMAS A. MATYAS AND KENNETH M. GREENWOOD

LA TROBE UNIVERSITY, VICTORIA, AUSTRALIA

Visual analysis is the dominant method of analysis for single-case time series. The literature assumes that visual analysts will be conservative judges. We show that previous research into visual analysis has not adequately examined false alarm and miss rates or the effect of serial dependence. In order to measure false alarm and miss rates while varying serial dependence, amount of random variability, and effect size, 37 students undertaking a postgraduate course in single-case design and analysis were required to assess the presence of an intervention effect in each of 27 AB charts constructed using a first-order autoregressive model. Three levels of effect size and three levels of variability, representative of values found in published charts, were combined with autocorrelation coefficients of 0, 0.3 and 0.6 in a factorial design. False alarm rates were surprisingly high (16% to 84%). Positive autocorrelation and increased random variation both significantly increased the false alarm rates and interacted in a nonlinear fashion. Miss rates were relatively low (0% to 22%) and were not significantly affected by the design parameters. Thus, visual analysts were not conservative, and serial dependence did influence judgment.

DESCRIPTORS: visual inference, data analysis, single-subject design

---

Despite the acknowledged dominance of visual analysis in single-case methodology (Kazdin, 1982) research on the performance of visual analysts is relatively sparse (DeProspero & Cohen, 1979; Furlong & Wampold, 1982; Jones, Weinrott, & Vaught, 1978; Ottenbacher, 1986; Wampold & Furlong, 1981). The published data have indicated significant problems such as poor interjudge reliability (DeProspero & Cohen, 1979; Jones et al., 1978). Some of these results (Jones et al., 1978) have been attacked for poor methodology (Huitema, 1985). Notwithstanding these problems, visual analysis has received continued advocacy (Parsonson & Baer, 1986).

The lack of evidence does not seem to have deterred claims about the likely performance of visual analysts (Kazdin, 1982; Parsonson & Baer, 1978, 1986). In particular, it is claimed that visual analysts are more likely to commit Type II errors "than those relying on statistical analyses" (Kazdin, 1982, p. 242). Similarly, Parsonson and Baer venture that: "If changes in graphed data are to be seen as such, they need to be relatively large—so large that the visual analysis of data tends to be less sensitive than statistical analysis of the same data. . . . Insensitivity ought to generate more conservative judgments that behavior has changed in correlation with experimental variables" (Parsonson & Baer, 1986, p. 158).

This however is a shallow deduction given the relationship between Type I (false alarm) and Type II (miss) errors. If visual analysts are insensitive as claimed (and this remains to be empirically demonstrated), this does not guarantee that they will rarely produce false alarms. Visual analysts may simply be more noisy detectors. That is, they may both miss and produce false alarms at a high rate. It requires a further assumption to argue that the human judge will be a detector with desired low false alarm rates and low sensitivity. This assumption is that the visual analyst will give to the control of Type I errors the same high priority that has been given to it in statistical decision theory. However, the literature has not adequately addressed the question of false alarm and miss rates in visual analysis, although a number of papers have investigated the performance of analysts (DeProspero & Cohen, 1979; Furlong & Wampold, 1982; Jones

Requests for reprints should be sent to T. A. Matyas, Department of Behavioural Health Sciences, Lincoln School of Health Sciences, La Trobe University, 625 Swanston Street, Carlton, Victoria, 3053 Australia.

et al., 1978; Ottenbacher, 1986; Wampold & Furlong, 1981).

Jones et al. (1978) investigated interobserver agreement rates and agreement between the visual and statistical interrupted time series analysis (ITSA) of published case data. They concluded that experienced judges had poor agreement rates. If their statistical analyses are taken as a yardstick, their results imply a false alarm rate of 33% and a miss rate of 48% for experienced judges, figures that should create significant concern. Unfortunately, the analysis of Jones et al. was flawed in some respects (Huitema, 1986a). Most importantly, however, the method of comparing the performance of visual analysts against statistical analysis cannot address the issue of misses and false alarms unambiguously, particularly in the absence of a power analysis. We cannot deduce that the visual analyst is wrong if the human judge declared an effect when the statistical analysis found no significant effect. An effect might have existed and the statistical analysis possessed insufficient power (sensitivity) to detect it, whereas the human judge, with unknown operating characteristics, may have detected the effect correctly. Low power was extremely likely in the results of Jones et al. because they were not only operating within the limitations of brief phases that are often imposed by case data but in addition they deliberately selected cases with "small number of data points within phases" (Jones et al., 1978, p. 278). A further problem with the study of Jones et al. is that they deliberately biased the selection of the charts to obtain, in addition to cases with brief phases, "nonobvious" experimental results, "graphs where serial dependency might be evidenced by possible non-zero trend" and "excluded large effect experiments" (p. 278). Thus, the implied estimates of false alarm and miss rates that might be deduced from their data cannot be trusted.

DeProspero and Cohen (1979) adopted the strategy of constructing ABAB charts in which they introduced effects. These were submitted to analysis by a large sample of reviewers of behavioral journals. However their results do not allow examination of the false alarm rate, because all graphs had introduced some degree of interphase differences. Further, the judges were required to rate on a 0 to 100 scale the degree of experimental control shown rather than to make a forced-choice decision; this precluded conclusions about miss rates.

Ottenbacher (1986) exposed 46 occupational therapists to five AB panels. It is not clear which charts contained an effect and which did not, thereby precluding the analysis of false alarm and miss rates. He did attempt to analyze the Type I error rate by comparing analysts' decisions with statistical analyses using White's (1974) suggestion for employing the binomial distribution on the intraphase celeration lines. Ottenbacher's approach thus suffers from the limitation discussed above in connection to Jones et al. (1978): Statistical analysis is not an acceptable yardstick for identification of "no effect" when the power is likely to be very low and no power analysis is even attempted. Ottenbacher's data (n = 8 per phase) were very likely a low power case. In any case, White's suggested method of analysis is flawed (Crosbie, 1987).

Wampold and Furlong (1981) asked graduate students to classify AB charts into groups according to the type of effects perceived. Furlong and Wampold (1982) extended this investigation to a sample of expert analysts (10 *JABA* reviewers). Unfortunately, these studies did not include no-effect charts and thus could not address the false alarm issue. However, neither do they report the miss rate, preferring to concentrate on other aspects of judge performance.

Thus, none of the empirical studies conducted to date have adequately addressed the question of false alarm and miss rates in even simple designs such as AB panels. Therefore, one aim of the present study was to examine these directly by requiring forced-choice decisions in AB panels with and without known effects. The ability to make decisions about the basic AB panel may be more fundamental than is generally acknowledged. Although the AB design is one of the weakest case designs, the AB panel represents the building block of more complex decisions in ABAB, multiple baseline, changing criterion, and other more sophisticated designs.

Another issue that has concerned visual analysis

is the possibility that serial dependence in the data may alter the accuracy of the analyst. Jones et al. (1978) concluded that visual analysis was adversely affected by increased serial dependence. However, their analysis of autocorrelation was incorrect (Huitema, 1986a). Hence their conclusion that serial dependence affects rater reliability and the degree of agreement with statistical ITSA becomes equivocal. DeProspero and Cohen's (1979) results are consistent with the notion that serial dependence matters, but the conclusion is very indirect. They manipulated the trend in data by tilting the baseline 30° from horizontal. Although they did not give calculations of autocorrelation, the tilting maneuver would have increased the amount of serial dependence in the data. They reported that the absence of trend produced higher subjective confidence of "experimental control." Because they did not calculate autocorrelation, we cannot assess its contribution in baselines that were not tilted. Further, tilting baselines by 30° was an arbitrary way of introducing trend. They offered no evidence that a 30° tilt would introduce serial dependence typical of behavioral data. Ottenbacher (1986) reported that there was only a weak relationship between serial dependence in visual charts and observer disagreement. His analysis was flawed, however, and a reanalysis of his data indicated that a strong relationship existed between serial dependence in the baseline and interjudge disagreement (Matyas & Greenwood, in press).

In summary, the empirical literature on visual analysis to date has failed to examine the adequacy of the process to the extent implicitly demanded by its advocacy as a fundamental method for case management and analysis (Barlow, Hayes, & Nelson, 1984). Although the issue of interjudge reliability has been repeatedly addressed, the basic questions of false alarm and miss rates have not been adequately investigated. The existing studies of visual analysis appear also to have been concerned directly, or indirectly, with the effect of serial dependence. However, methodological problems limit the conclusions possible from these studies. Therefore the present study aimed to quantify false alarm and miss rates, which are the fundamentals of decision making. Serial dependence in the time series was also systematically varied with reference to two surveys of the degree of autocorrelation in published data (Huitema, 1985; Matyas & Greenwood, 1985, 1990).

METHOD

Subjects

The sample comprised 37 graduate students from two groups ($n = 18$, $n = 19$) undertaking one-term courses in single-case design and analysis. The majority ($n = 25$) had obtained a bachelor's qualification with a major in psychology prior to enrollment in the course. The remainder comprised practicing health professionals (6 occupational therapists, 2 physiotherapists, 2 orthoptists, 1 neurologist, 1 podiatrist) who had typically completed only a 2-year minor in psychology. None of the subjects were experienced users of single-case designs. The investigation reported below was conducted after these students were exposed to a series of lectures on single-case design. The nature of level, trend, and other intervention effects had been discussed, as had been difficulties introduced by high variability and preexisting trend. The empirical literature on visual analysis was not reviewed until after the data collection session. Assigned readings for the course, up to the point of data collection, were from the textbooks by Hersen and Barlow (1976), Kratochwill (1978), and Kazdin (1982).

Materials

Twenty-seven AB (A = baseline, B = intervention) panels were constructed using the first order autoregressive model: $y_t = ay_{t-1} + b + d + e$, where y_t was the value at time t, y_{t-1} was the value at time $t - 1$, a was the autoregression coefficient, b was the preintervention initial level, d was the intervention effect, and e was a normally distributed random variable with a mean of 0 and standard deviation described below. Each phase comprised 10 data points, which seemed a reasonable value in the light of Huitema's (1985) survey. It should be noted that we have previously investigated the

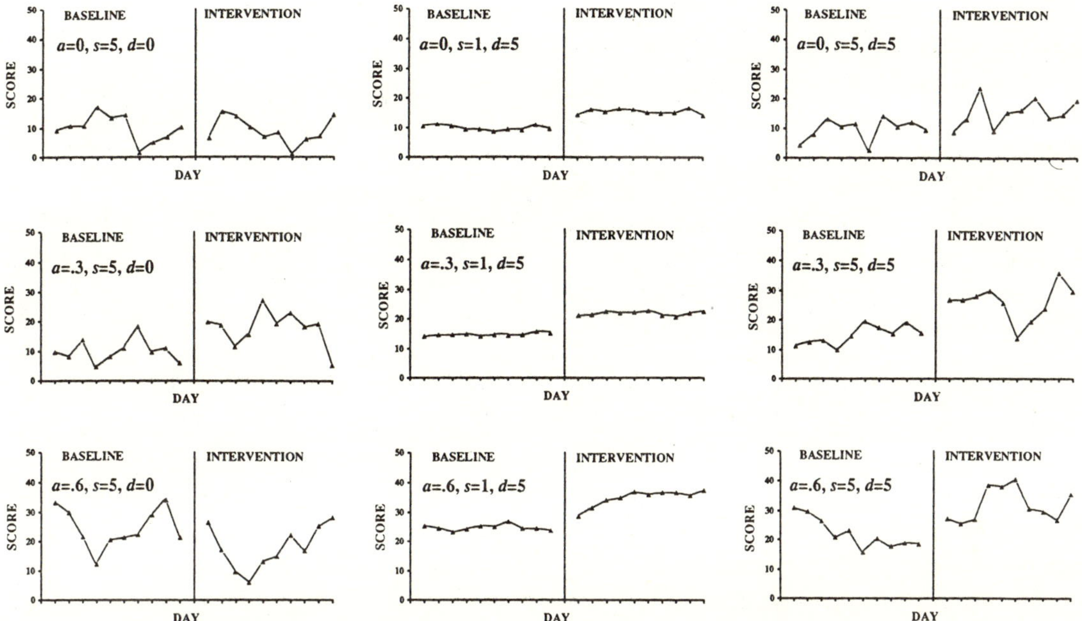

Figure 1. Nine of the AB panels used as stimuli. Information about the statistical properties (a = amount of serial dependence, s = random variability, d = magnitude of intervention effect) has been superimposed on each graph and was not presented to subjects. Subjects were instructed that the ordinate represented the client's response score, but the precise response was not described.

viability of autoregressive models for serial dependence in baseline data and found the first order model reasonable (within the power limits) for the vast majority (91%) (Matyas & Greenwood, 1985). Figure 1 illustrates some of the charts yielded by this method.

Three factors, each with three levels, were varied to obtain charts for a completely crossed factorial design. One factor was the effect of intervention that involved null and two magnitudes of treatment effect (i.e., $d = 0$, $d = 5$, $d = 10$). A second factor was the amount of random error chosen ($s = 1$, $s = 3$, $s = 5$). The third factor was the degree of serial dependence in the data. Our survey of 182 baselines published in *JABA* from 1977 to 1983 (Matyas & Greenwood, 1985), as well as that by Huitema (1985) covering a complementary period, suggested a range of first-order autocorrelation from -0.68 to 0.75, with a mean around zero. When corrected for a recently verified bias in the autocorrelation estimation procedure (Matyas & Greenwood, 1990), these data suggest a true range from -0.80 to 0.90. Because previous investigations have been primarily concerned with the effects of positive autocorrelation but have some methodological limitations, we chose to investigate three levels of true autocorrelation: $a = 0.0$, $a = 0.3$, and $a = 0.6$. These are equivalent to estimated autocorrelation of -0.1, 0, and 0.2 when $n = 10$. According to both Huitema (1985) and Matyas and Greenwood (1990), values like these are common in published time series. The effect sizes selected are best understood as the d/s ratio following Cohen (1977). Thus, the standardized effect sizes employed ranged from 1 to 10. These would be described as large to very large standardized effects by Cohen (1977), who regarded standardized effect sizes of 1 or more as representing large effects in the social/behavioral sciences. To provide an additional frame of reference for our values, time series from our *JABA* survey (Matyas & Greenwood, 1985) were analyzed according to Gottman's simplified ITSA method (Gottman, 1981) using the Gottman–Williams software suite (Williams & Gottman, 1982). A full description of this and related analyses is beyond the scope of this paper. However, the median d/s ratio obtained from 100 AB panels with $n \geq 10$ was 9.2, the 25th percentile was 4.9 and the 75th was 17.1. Thus, our standardized effect size of 1 appears to be below the 25th percentile of effect sizes published in *JABA,* and our standardized effect size of 10 appears to be just above the median effect size published in *JABA.*

Charts were produced on an Apple Macintosh Plus® computer using Microsoft Chart® software and were labeled as depicted in Figure 1, except that Figure 1 provides values for a, s, and d. Overhead transparencies were than obtained in A4 format for group presentation.

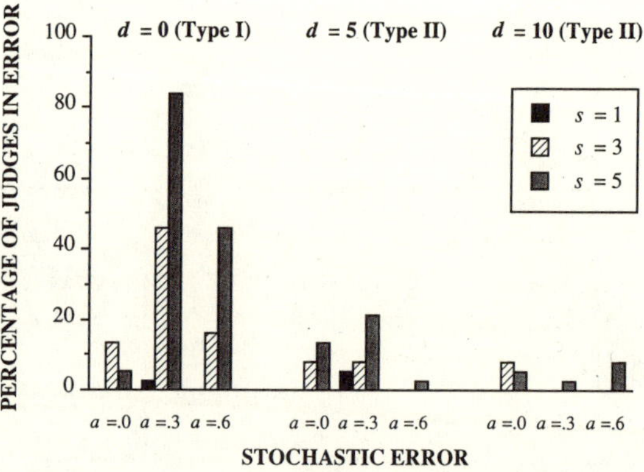

Figure 2. Type I and II error rates for each of the 27 charts as a function of the amount of serial dependence (a), random variability (s), and magnitude of intervention effect (d).

Procedure

Subjects were tested in two separate groups ($n = 18$, $n = 19$) in single 1-hr sessions. Subjects were initially instructed how to respond on a standard computer card for recording answers to multiple choice questions. The alternatives were defined as follows: A = no intervention effect; B = a level change; C = a trend change; D = combined level and trend change; and, E = other type of systematic change during intervention. A brief review of treatment effect types was conducted prior to data collection, with ideal examples from Glass, Willson, and Gottman (1975) consistent with previous lecture material on this subject.

The 27 charts were presented in a predetermined, randomized sequence. Charts were presented in a small room on a large screen. Projection clarity from all seats was established by the experimenters prior to the session. Each chart was presented for 1 min. Prior pilot data had suggested that 20 to 40 s be allowed for ample response times, depending on the individual and the chart. Thus, the test was not presented as a speed test and subjects were told to ask for additional time if required. None did. All subjects viewed and responded to all 27 charts.

RESULTS

Responses for each subject on each case chart were scored dichotomously according to whether they indicated a conclusion of effect (Alternatives B to E) or no effect (Alternative A) because the major interest was in false alarm and miss rates. These responses were then analyzed by a series of planned comparisons, employing the extension to Cochran's Q detailed by Marascuilo and McSweeney (1977). This method suited the analytic problem, not only because it deals legitimately with dichotomous data generated by a within-subject design but also because, in the planned comparison version, it permitted the phrasing of the main effect and interaction questions that arose naturally from the factorial design.

Figure 2 presents the percentage of judges who erred in each of the 27 cases comprising the experimental design: that is, three levels of autocorrelation (a = 0.0, 0.3, or 0.6) × three levels of random variability (s = 1, 3, or 5) × three levels of effect size (d = 0, 1, or 10). The figure shows that high false alarm rates occurred when variability and serial dependence increased. Error rates ranged from 16% to 84% when $s > 1$ and $a > 0$. These high false alarm rates contrasted with the relatively low miss rates, which ranged from 0% to no more than 22%. Most of the miss rates were below 10%.

The planned comparisons confirmed that the apparent general difference between miss and false alarm rates was statistically significant, $z = 2.499$, $p < .02$. The comparisons confirmed further that this difference became more accentuated as the random variation increased $z = 4.79$, $p < .001$, and as the degree of serial dependence increased, $z = 4.68$, $p < .001$.

Because the comparison designed to examine the three-way interaction between effect condition, degree of random variation, and degree of autocorrelation was significant, comparisons were constructed to investigate the two-way interaction between degree of random variation and degree of autocorrelation independently for false alarm and miss data, analogously to recommendations typical for factorial analysis of variance (Keppel, 1982). This orthogonal partitioning revealed that the false alarm rate showed a significant interaction between degree of variability and degree of serial dependence, $z = 2.657$, $p < .01$, which was also significant under the more stringent Dunn–Bonferroni criterion (Marascuilo & McSweeney, 1977). This analysis confirms the impression conveyed by Figure 2 that false alarm rates increased at $s = 3$ and more so at $s = 5$, but that these increases occurred more markedly in the presence of positive autocorrelation, particularly at $a = 0.3$. Variations in miss rates were generally of lower magnitude, and the corresponding two-way interaction comparison for these data was not significant.

In view of the significant interaction between degree of autocorrelation and degree of random variation, the effects of autocorrelation of false alarm rates were examined with six orthogonal comparisons. At $s = 1$, the averaged false alarm rates for $a = 0.3$ and $a = 0.6$ did not differ significantly from that obtained with $a = 0$. However the corresponding differences were significant at $s = 3$, $z = 2.052$, $p < .05$, and $s = 5$, $z = 5.998$, $p < .001$. Significant pairwise differences were then obtained between $a = 0.3$ and $a = 0.6$ at $s = 3$, $z = 3.005$, $p < .01$, and $s = 5$, $z = 3.824$, $p < .001$, but not at $s = 1$. All comparisons except that between the average false alarm rates at $a = 0.3$ and $a = 0.6$ against $a = 0$ at $s = 3$ were also significant under the more conservative Dunn–Bonferroni criterion for a six-comparison family. Curiously, as the figure and the comparisons both indicate, the false alarm rate was affected nonlinearly by positive autocorrelation, with stronger effects at $a = 0.3$ than at $a = 0.6$.

The simple main effects of degree of random variation on false alarm rates were also pursued, given the significant interaction between degree of autocorrelation and degree of random variation on false alarm rates, in the manner recommended for analysis of variance (see Keppel, 1982). Six pairwise contrasts were employed. At $a = 0$ the difference between false alarm rates with $s = 1$ was not significantly different from that of $s = 3$ or $s = 5$. However, at $a = 0.3$ the false alarm rate with $s = 1$ was significantly lower than with $s = 3$, $z = 4.372$, $p < .001$, and with $s = 5$, $z = 5.467$, $p < .001$. At $a = 0.6$ the false alarm rate with $s = 1$ was significantly lower than with $s = 5$, $z = 4.646$, $p < .001$, but not significantly lower than the false alarm with $s = 3$. All three significant comparisons were also significant under the Dunn–Bonferroni criterion. In general, the investigative comparisons confirmed that the interaction between degree of autocorrelation and random error was due to increases in false alarm rates obtained with higher values of random variation at $a = 0.3$ and $a = 0.6$, but not at $a = 0$, when false alarm rates were generally low.

The above analysis examined trends as a function of the experimental conditions. Individual differences in false alarm rates and miss rates were of interest in order to assess whether subjects tended to vary in their response bias. Thus, false alarms were calculated for each subject over the sample of 9 "no effect" cases. Miss rates were calculated for each subject over the 9 cases with an intervention effect of 5 units and also over the 9 cases with an intervention effect of 10 units. Pearson's correlation coefficients were calculated between false alarm and miss rates. Most interestingly, a significant inverse relationship was found between the false alarm rates and the miss rates at $d = 5$, $r = -0.43$, $p < .005$, and at $d = 10$, $r = -0.36$, $p < .02$.

DISCUSSION

The results indicate that our sample of graduate students (who were relatively inexperienced in the assessment of single-case time series), when exposed to AB panels with stochastic properties that are representative of published cases, showed generally high false alarm rates and relatively low miss rates. False alarm rates tended to increase when random variation increased, but only if positive true lag 1 autocorrelation was also present in the data. Similarly, positive autocorrelation tended to increase false alarm rates, but not if the random variation was very low. There was some evidence, however, that this increase may not progress linearly as a function of increasing positive autocorrelation. In general, positive autocorrelation and random variation tended to increase false alarm rates under a mutually potentiating interaction.

That the high false alarm rate is merely a function of the relative inexperience of the participants is possible but seems unlikely. It should be noted that our sample consisted of graduates in psychology undertaking a postgraduate course in health psychology and also included other health professionals. The sample had also received some training prior to testing. Most importantly, studies that have examined experienced judges (DeProspero & Cohen, 1979; Furlong & Wampold, 1982; Jones et al., 1978), although not able to address the false alarm issue satisfactorily, have found indications of inaccurate or unreliable decision making. Studies that have compared the performance of analysts with differing levels of experience (Furlong & Wampold, 1982; Knapp, 1983) have found no major differences in their performance indicators. In any case, the performance of relatively inexperienced judges is of significant interest, given that this may be the skill level currently representative of clinicians. Until our study is replicated in other samples and extended with other designs, it is difficult to judge fully the degree of concern that should be directed to the functioning of the wider population of clinicians who are being encouraged by the literature to adopt experimental single-case methodology. It seems reasonable at least to propose that the assumption that visual judges will be necessarily conservative does not hold for beginning practitioners employing AB designs under conditions of moderate to high variability and serial dependence.

The high false alarm rate obtained confirms the criticism suggested earlier of the position taken by some authors (e.g., Parsonson & Baer, 1986), who seem to have prematurely inferred the dominance of conservatism in human judgment of case charts. Thus, although there may be comfort in the finding that effects are not missed, as anticipated (for large effects) by Parsonson and Baer (1986), the much more serious problem of high false alarm rates, not envisaged by Parsonson and Baer, may be frustrating the valid development of single-case methodology for clinical practice. This seems to be a particularly serious issue because a fundamental argument for introducing the rigors of single case experimental method to clinical practice is to aid valid decision making. The lack of conservatism is not entirely surprising in light of other extensive literature that demonstrates several biases in human decision making (e.g., Hogarth, 1980; Slovic, Fischhoff, & Lichtenstein, 1977). The catalogue of biases includes underestimation of error and undue confidence in small samples (Kahneman & Tversky, 1972; Tversky & Kahneman, 1971), as well as unduly narrow estimation of confidence intervals (Lichtenstein, Fischhoff, & Phillips, 1977) and illusory correlation (Chapman & Chapman, 1969). This lack of conservatism, which has now also been illustrated in the context of single-case time series, indicates the potential for significant practical problems in routine clinical methodology if active clinicians have performances comparable to our sample.

Our findings contribute towards the resolution of the problem about the true effects of serial dependence on visual judgment. This problem resulted from the inadequacies in Jones et al.'s (1978) methodology, detailed in the introduction, its replication and other confounding effects that occurred in Ottenbacher's (1986) study, and the arbitrary choices of tilt in DeProspero and Cohen's (1979) studies. In our sample, positive autocorrelation in amounts that do occur in published data (Matyas & Greenwood, 1985, 1990) increased the false alarm rate, particularly when random variability was larger. These results confirm our reanalysis of Ottenbacher's (1986) study (Matyas & Greenwood, in press).

It is not immediately apparent why false alarm rates would be increased most markedly by the conjunction of positive autoregression and larger random variation. A time series that was purely random, even one with large random variation, is unlikely to demonstrate sustained drifts. Such a time series may present some difficulties in recognizing small effects but is unlikely to have sustained change suggestive of an effect when none is present. Indeed, false alarm rates at $a = 0$ were only 13.5% at $s = 3$ and only 5.4% at $s = 5$. A positive autoregressive process, however, introduces some "inertia" into the time series, such that when a large random component occurs its effects will persist, in a decaying form, through the autoregressive coefficient. Consequently, large random variance in conjunction with positive autocorrelation is more likely to create time series with a larger, apparently systematic trend or change of trend. Only relatively long baselines are likely to permit perception of the true nature of the effect: that of randomly timed but sustained change, which is both positive and negative and of variable duration. Over a relatively short phase, it is more likely than in the case of the purely random time series that the autoregressive stochastic trend will look deterministic. This raises the possibility of several effect-like appearances, such as reversal of a baseline trend or the initiation of a prolonged (or at least semiprolonged) change in the intervention phase. When random variability is low, the first-order autoregressive model has no large random components to seed the sustained change process, and fewer confusions should occur. This was indeed what we found. Our explanation seems very appealing because it simultaneously satisfies several requirements. It is consistent with the mathematical nature of the first-order autoregressive model. It is able to account for the low error rate obtained when there was low random variation and positive autoregression. It is able to account for high false alarm rate given a conjunction of positive autocorrelation and higher random variation. Finally, it is able to predict the relatively lower false alarm rate obtained when there is random variation without the inertial effect of positive autocorrelation.

The discussion so far has focused on the high false alarms obtained. However, it is worth emphasizing that the detection of effects was generally good when effects were present. The implied corollary is that interjudge reliability for cases in which an effect was present was also good. Thus, even novice analysts seem capable of detecting realistically sized effects. It is, of course, possible that the "file-drawer" effect (Rosenthal, 1979) has distorted somewhat the effect size estimates; however, the effect sizes employed are clearly representative of at least a very substantial portion of behavioral cases.

A significant inverse relationship was found between the overall false alarm and miss rates among different judges. That is, individuals with higher false alarms tended to show lower miss rates and vice versa. This suggests that in a proper signal detection analysis, response bias is likely to be of actual rather than just potential importance. Response bias should be manipulable by incentive variations or instructions, and the effect size can be altered to encompass smaller signals. Thus, we envisage that investigations of the human operator characteristics (e.g., McNicol, 1972) are readily possible as well as desirable. The extent to which the high false alarm rate can be attributed to high operator noise or to response bias has practical implications for training programs and is not merely a question of theoretical interest. In the event that the problem is simply one of response bias, there seem to be reasonable prospects for improving performance by cognitive training. In the event of high noise in the human operator, the training problem may be much more complex.

The present study allowed five categories of response: no intervention effect, level change, trend change, combined level and trend change, and other type of systematic change. It is possible that, because four of the five response categories referred to an effect type, subjects may have experienced a bias towards an increased rate of effect responses. This may have contributed to the high false alarm rate. The present categories were employed because they represent those taught in the standard literature (e.g., Kazdin, 1982), and some texts include an even more elaborate set (e.g., Glass et al., 1975). Given this, it is not at all clear whether to interpret any tendency towards a "yes" response as a bias or merely a reflection of the way in which practitioners are asked to make decisions about single-case charts. Furthermore, it is possible that multiple effect categories are the ecologically valid choice and that our response categories represent those used implicitly by practitioners. However, this is an empirical question, and no work has as yet been directed to this issue. In conclusion, it seems unlikely that the extreme false alarm rates we observed were simply a consequence of having more response categories than yes/no, and it may be unreasonable to interpret such an effect as a bias even if it did occur.

The results of the present study have a number of important implications for research aimed at the development of a valid and viable single-case methodology for routine applied practice. Clearly, the replication of the study with other populations who have different levels of experience or educational background is urgent. Studies of the human operator, which investigate the noise and response bias characteristics, as well as variables that might be able to manipulate those characteristics are also suggested. Investigations of the effects of other case data on the decision process based solely on the chart, and investigation of visual aids that might improve the chart judgment, are required. We have just completed some work on the former, and others have commenced study of the latter (Hojem & Ottenbacher, 1988; Knapp, 1983). The effect of cognitive and perceptual training on the analysis of single-case time series also appears urgent in the light of the high false alarm rate reported here and the poor interjudge reliability found by other studies.

Routine use of statistical decision aids may have to be considered. Parsonson and Baer (1986), among others, have criticized the use of statistical methods as decision aids because they might encourage the acceptance of small effects and because they are not practical in the field. However, statistical methods do control the false alarm rate, unlike our sample of performers. If the high false alarm rate proves to be more generally typical of clinicians, the use of statistical decision aids, far from holding the danger of encouraging unnecessary liberalism, may be the way to prevent the apparently natural liberal bias of human judges. Of course the probability of a miss with our data is likely to be high for statistical models operating at $\alpha = 0.05$, given the brevity of the time series. Clearly, the conjoint comparison of false alarm and miss rates in human operators and statistical models subjected to the same data is another required investigation. We believe that the impracticability argument against statistical methods is overstated in the light of the desktop computer revolution and the potential to develop user-friendly software. Perhaps more serious questions are those that relate to the valid application of statistical methodology (Huitema, 1986b), particularly in the case of brief times series, such as occur in clinical practice. However, developments in the application of ITSA with approximate models that do not require prior model identification (Gottman, 1981; Velicer & McDonald, 1984) may be able to overcome previous difficulties. This is because the objection against the application of ITSA on the grounds that correct model identification requires a large sample (Huitema, 1986b), and the objection that model identification contains complexities unlikely to be mastered by practicing clinicians (Parsonson & Baer, 1986), are both bypassed by analysis without the step of model identification. The objection concerning small effect sizes may be overcome by defining effect size indexes and developing a normative model, as indeed others are already arguing in the clinical significance debate (Christensen & Mendoza, 1986; Jacobson, Follette, & Revenstorf, 1984, 1986; Wampold & Jenson, 1986). In any case, our findings suggest that statistical models will probably be more conservative than human judges.

The visual judgment literature to date, including the present study, has been confined to AB and ABAB designs. It is true that the AB comparison is a fundamental block in the more complex decision making of full designs, including the multiple baseline design. Indeed, the basic two-phase comparison is probably even more important than previously suggested in the literature, given the context of the a posteriori method of case management in which the appearance of the chart acts as a guide to revisions of the initial case design, particularly with respect to phase duration decisions (e.g., Kazdin, 1982). However, design issues require much more research than has hitherto appeared. The effects obtained with multiple baseline, changing criterion, and other clinically useful designs remain unknown. The possibility of accurate analysis of case data, be it achieved through improved visual aids, statistical aids, or special training programs for visual analysts, is not a goal readily abandoned, given the need for effective case methodology and the improvements already introduced by time-series designs.

REFERENCES

Barlow, D. H., Hayes, S. C., & Nelson, R. O. (1984). *The scientist practitioner: Research and accountability in clinical and education settings*. New York: Pergamon Press.

Chapman, L. J., & Chapman, J. P. (1969). Illusory correlation as an obstacle to the use of valid psychodiagnostic signs. *Journal of Abnormal Psychology,* **74**, 271–280.

Christensen, L., & Mendoza, J. L. (1986). A method of assessing change in a single subject: An alteration of the RC index. *Behavior Therapy,* **17**, 305–308.

Cohen, J. (1977). *Statistical power analysis for the behavioral sciences* (rev. ed.). New York: Academic Press.

Crosbie, J. (1987). The inability of the binomial test to control type I error with single-subject data. *Behavioral Assessment,* **9**, 141–150.

DeProspero, A., & Cohen, S. (1979). Inconsistent visual analyses of intrasubject data. *Journal of Applied Behavior Analysis,* **12**, 573–579.

Furlong, M. J., & Wampold, B. E. (1982). Intervention effects and relative variations as dimensions in experts' use of visual inference. *Journal of Applied Behavior Analysis,* **15**, 415–421.

Glass, G. V., Willson, V. L., & Gottman, J. M. (1975). *Design and analysis of time-series experiments*. Boulder: Colorado Associated University Press.

Gottman, J. M. (1981). *Time-series analysis: A comprehensive introduction for social scientists*. Cambridge, England: Cambridge University Press.

Hersen, M., & Barlow, D. H. (1976). *Single case experimental designs: Strategies for studying behavior change*. Oxford, England: Pergamon Press.

Hogarth, R. (1980). *Judgement and choice: The psychology of decision*. Chichester, England: John Wiley.

Hojem, M. A., & Ottenbacher, K. J. (1988). Empirical investigation of visual-inspection versus trend-line analysis of single-subject data. *Physical Therapy,* **68**, 983–988.

Huitema, B. E. (1985). Autocorrelation in applied behavior analysis: A myth. *Behavioral Assessment,* **7**, 107–118.

Huitema, B. E. (1986a). Autocorrelation in behavioral research: Wherefore art thou? In A. Poling & R. W. Fuqua (Eds.), *Research methods in applied behavior analysis: Issues and advances* (pp. 187–208). New York: Plenum Press.

Huitema, B. E. (1986b). Statistical analysis and single-subject designs: Some misunderstandings. In A. Poling & R. W. Fuqua (Eds.), *Research methods in applied behavior analysis: Issues and advances* (pp. 209–232). New York: Plenum Press.

Jacobson, N. S., Follette, W. C., & Revenstorf, D. (1984). Psychotherapy outcome research: Methods for reporting variability and evaluating clinical significance. *Behavior Therapy,* **15**, 336–352.

Jacobson, N. S., Follette, W. C., & Revenstorf, D. (1986). Toward a standard definition of clinically significant change. *Behavior Therapy,* **17**, 308–311.

Jones, R. R., Weinrott, M. R., & Vaught, R. S. (1978). Effects of serial dependency on the agreement between visual and statistical inference. *Journal of Applied Behavior Analysis,* **11**, 277–283.

Kahneman, D., & Tversky, A. (1972). Subjective probability: A judgment of representativeness. *Cognitive Psychology,* **3**, 430–454.

Kazdin, A. E. (1982). *Single-case research designs: Methods for clinical and applied settings*. New York: Oxford University Press.

Keppel, G. (1982). *Design and analysis: A researcher's handbook* (2nd ed.). Englewood Cliffs, NJ: Prentice-Hall.

Knapp, T. J. (1983). Behavior analysts' visual appraisal of behavior change in graphic display. *Behavioral Assessment,* **5**, 155–164.

Kratochwill, T. R. (Ed.). (1978). *Single-subject research: Strategies for evaluating change*. New York: Academic Press.

Lichtenstein, S. C., Fischhoff, B., & Phillips, L. (1977). Calibration of probabilities: The state of the art. In H. Jungermann & G. de Zeeux (Eds.), *Decision making and change in human affairs* (pp. 275–324). Dordrecht, Holland: D. Reidel Publishing Company.

Marascuilo, L. A., & McSweeney, M. (1977). *Nonparametric and distribution-free methods for the social sciences*. Monterey, CA: Brooks/Cole.

Matyas, T. A., & Greenwood, K. M. (1985). *A survey of serial dependence in behavioral baselines*. Paper presented at the 8th National Conference of the Australian Behaviour Modification Association, Melbourne.

Matyas, T. A., & Greenwood, K. M. (1990). *Problems in the estimation of autocorrelation in brief time-series and some implications for behavioral data*. Manuscript submitted for publication.

Matyas, T. A., & Greenwood, K. M. (in press). The effect

of serial dependence on visual judgment of single-case charts: An addendum. *The Occupational Therapy Journal of Research.*

McNicol, D. (1972). *A primer of signal detection theory.* Sydney: Australasian Publishing Company.

Ottenbacher, K. J. (1986). Reliability and accuracy of visually analyzing graphed data from single-subject designs. *American Journal of Occupational Therapy,* **40,** 464–469.

Parsonson, B. S., & Baer, D. M. (1978). The analysis and presentation of graphic data. In T. R. Kratochwill (Ed.), *Single-subject research: Strategies for evaluating change* (pp. 101–165). New York: Academic Press.

Parsonson, B. S., & Baer, D. M. (1986). The graphic analysis of data. In A. Poling & R. W. Fuqua (Eds.), *Research methods in applied behavior analysis: Issues and advances* (pp. 157–186). New York: Plenum Press.

Rosenthal, R. (1979). The "file drawer" problem and tolerance for null results. *Psychological Bulletin,* **86,** 638–641.

Slovic, P., Fischhoff, B., & Lichtenstein, S. (1977). Behavioral decision theory. *Annual Review of Psychology,* **28,** 1–39.

Tversky, A., & Kahneman, D. (1971). The belief in the law of small numbers. *Psychological Bulletin,* **76,** 105–110.

Velicer, W. F., & McDonald, R. P. (1984). Time series analysis without model identification. *Multivariate Behavioral Research,* **19,** 33–47.

Wampold, B., & Furlong, M. (1981). The heuristics of visual inference. *Behavioral Assessment,* **3,** 79–92.

Wampold, B. E., & Jenson, W. R. (1986). Clinical significance revisited. *Behavior Therapy,* **17,** 302–305.

White, O. R. (1974). *The "split-middle" a "quickie" method of trend estimation.* Seattle: University of Washington, Experimental Education Unit, Child Development and Mental Retardation Center.

Williams, E. A., & Gottman, J. M. (1982). *A user's guide to the Gottman-Williams time-series analysis computer programs for social scientists.* Cambridge, England: Cambridge University Press.

Received January 10, 1989
Initial editorial decision June 30, 1989
Revisions received November 9, 1989; February 28, 1990
Final acceptance March 4, 1990
Action Editor, Terry J. Page

JOURNAL OF APPLIED BEHAVIOR ANALYSIS 1978, 11, 203-214 NUMBER 2 (SUMMER 1978)

SOCIAL VALIDITY: THE CASE FOR SUBJECTIVE MEASUREMENT or HOW APPLIED BEHAVIOR ANALYSIS IS FINDING ITS HEART[1]

MONTROSE M. WOLF

UNIVERSITY OF KANSAS

I apologize, but I must begin making my case for subjective measurement by recounting to you my own experiences with it over the past few years. Almost a decade ago, when the field of applied behavior analysis was beginning to expand so rapidly, we were faced with the task of putting together the *Journal of Applied Behavior Analysis.* For a period of several months Garth Hopkins, who was our managing editor, presented us with a series of unexpected decisions to make; like: What color should the paper be? And did we need a paper that would hold together for two thousand years or were we willing to live with a shelf-life of only a thousand years? And so on.

Just a couple of days before we were scheduled to go to press with our very first issue, Garth called with one more question. "What is the purpose of the *Journal of Applied Behavior Analysis?*", he asked. He said we needed to put a description of the purpose on the inside front cover, as one finds in other journals. He needed an answer almost immediately.

What was the purpose of our journal? It was a question that was clearly more important than the others I had been asked. So I decided to consult the Gods but, as usual, Don Baer, Don Bushell, Barbara Etzel, Vance Hall, Bill Hopkins, Judy LeBlanc, Keith Miller, Todd Risley, and Jim Sherman were not in their offices. However, I did find Don Baer in the hall. So I asked Don, "What is the purpose of *JABA?*" and Don said in his usual offhand but eloquent way, "It is for the publication of applications of the analysis of behavior to problems of social importance." Well, that sounded so reasonable that it had to be true. So that is what I put in the *Journal* and it went to press.

There was only one small problem; I wasn't sure what "social importance" meant or, worse still, how to measure it. And, as I am sure you can appreciate, the more I thought about this the more concerned I became.

The dictionary only added to my distress. According to my *New Webster's Vest Pocket Dictionary* (1962) importance simply meant "having value" and of course, social meant "pertaining to society". Thus, something of social importance would have to be judged by someone as having value to society.

Unfortunately, that sounded slightly subjective to me. And subjective criteria have not been very respectable in our field. We have considered ourselves a natural science, concerned about the objective measurement of natural events such as arithmetic problems worked correctly, litter picked up, sexual responses occurring, and social skills learned. We have considered ourselves to be like the other natural sciences: like physics, chemistry, and biology, which concern

[1]This manuscript was presented as an invited address to the Division of the Experimental Analysis of Behavior, American Psychological Association, Washington, D.C., September, 1976. Many valuable suggestions regarding this manuscript were made by Don Baer, Curt Braukmann, Steve Fawcett, Dean Fixsen, Bill Hopkins, Frances Horowitz, Kathi Kirigin, Jack Michael, Keith Miller, Todd Risley, Jim Sherman, and Sandra Wolf. Preparation of the manuscript was partially supported by Grants MH20030, MH13644, and MH13881 from the National Institute of Mental Health (Center for Studies of Crime and Delinquency) to the Department of Human Development and the Bureau of Child Research, University of Kansas. Reprints may be obtained from Montrose M. Wolf, Department of Human Development, University of Kansas, Lawrence, Kansas 66045.

themselves with the objective aspects of nature and profitably abandoned the subjective dimensions of natural events sometime in their primordial past.

We have considered ourselves to be distinctly purer and more objective than most of our sister social sciences. We have looked especially askance at our colleagues in sociology, anthopology, psychiatry, and humanistic psychology because they often mix into their sciences difficult-to-digest portions of subjective measurement.

But psychologists have not always been so suspicious of subjective data. For some time, and until the first decades of this century, introspection was the basic method of psychology. As you no doubt remember from your history of psychology course, introspection is defined as the observation or examination of one's own mental, emotional, or feeling states. The subjects' verbal descriptions about sensations, private events, and feelings such as pleasantness and unpleasantness had been taken to be the primary subject matter of psychology (Boring, 1950). As a reaction against introspection in psychology and in science generally, there arose positivism from Bridgeman in physics and from Comte, Mach, and Feigl in philosophy. To quote Edwin Boring (1950) about its impact:

> "The movement was positivistic. It was an attempt to get back to basic data and thus to increase agreement and diminish the misunderstandings that came about from unsuspected differences in meaning. Experience [introspection] had proved unsuccessful as the scientific ultimate." (Boring, 1950)

John Watson began page one of his book *Behaviorism* in the following manner:

> "Two opposed points of view are still dominant in American psychological thinking —introspective or subjective psychology, and behaviorism or objective psychology. Until the advent of behaviorism in 1912, introspective psychology completely dominated American university psychological life." (Watson, 1930).

B. F. Skinner, in *Science and Human Behavior* (1953), also argued forcefully against subjective measures of private events. He began by pointing out the implications of the discriminated operant model of language. He described how a community can reinforce and thus develop reliable verbal reporting of public events because both the community and the individual have access to these events. On the other hand, he pointed out that since the community cannot have access to private events, the use of psychology of introspective or subjective data leads to serious questions about reliability. Skinner continued,

> "The layman also finds the lack of a reliable subjective vocabulary inconvenient. Everyone mistrusts verbal responses which describe private events. Variables are often operating which tend to weaken the stimulus control of such descriptions, and the reinforcing community is usually powerless to prevent the resulting distortion. The individual who excuses himself from an unpleasant task by pleading a headache cannot be successfully challenged, even though the existence of the private event is doubtful."

While defining a functional analysis for us, Skinner (1953) urged us to concentrate on the objective behavioral data in our science as in the following quotation:

> "The objection to inner states is not that they do not exist, but that they are not relevant in a functional analysis. . . . In dealing with the directly observable data we need not refer to . . . the inner state. . . ."

Having been well trained in these traditions, we all agreed that in our journal, everything would be measured in objective ways. We would avoid subjective measurement—that would be a first priority. Some of the members of the

JABA Board of Editors even wanted to restrict us to using only mechanically recordable behavior in our applied research. They wanted a microswitch under every schoolroom chair and under every bed. They were even suspicious of observer measurement systems that contained reliability checks. Yet I, in a moment of haste, had committed our journal to a goal, to an ultimate criterion, to a reason for being, that was clearly and simply subjective and that we had no good way of measuring.

You can imagine what I expected. I prepared for an onslaught of abuse, invective, and ridicule from our editors and our reading audience. "Social importance? Bah! Humbug!", I thought they would say. To my surprise and relief, what happened was that people seemed pretty much to accept it. Many even seemed to know what it was. For example, *JABA* editors often referred to it in their reviews and used it as a basis for recommending or not recommending manuscripts for publication. The editors most frequently reported that the particular manuscripts that they had been asked to review didn't have very much of it. On the other hand, they reported that a few manuscripts had a moderate amount of it. And an occasional one or two had a lot of it. This made me feel somewhat better. Although I wasn't sure what it was or how to measure it objectively, it was clear that many of my colleagues had no trouble at all in recognizing it.

I was also fearful of criticism from our reading audience. And we did receive occasional complaints about social importance. But primarily they wanted to know why the research that appeared in *JABA* was not *more* socially important. That criticism was easy for me to live with. I just blamed our authors. If the readers had taken me to task for using a fuzzy subjective criterion like "social importance", then I would have had no excuse.

But the issue of subjective measurement continued to make my life complicated. One of the functions of a chief editor is to uphold the standards of the journal. And almost everyone in the field strongly suggests that these be maintained rigorously. Except, of course, in the special case of everyone's own manuscripts which, because of their unusual significance, merit special consideration. In any event, among the standards that I was entrusted to uphold was that of requiring objective, reliable data. Thus, you can appreciate the concern I began to feel when some of our most esteemed colleagues began submitting articles to *JABA* that included undisguised, blatantly subjective data.

One of the first came from, of all people, Bob Jones and Nate Azrin (1969). They had been conducting an exquisite series of experiments on the effects of rhythm and stimulus duration on stuttering behavior. They had shown, very nicely, that they could almost completely eliminate stuttering by having the stutterers synchronize their speech with a simple, regular beat. They had also developed a portable practical piece of apparatus that would present the beat tactually, and privately, thus avoiding embarrassment to the wearer. Their results indicated that they were on the verge of an important solution to stuttering. There had been one problem, however. The speech, although almost stutter-free, was complained about by listeners as sounding *artificial.* [The next sentence is to be read with a monotone with a distinct beat.] Apparently, they did not stutter, but they did not talk very naturally, either.

To deal with this problem, Jones and Azrin systematically explored various beat durations. Then,—and this was the difficult part—they asked judges to rate the "naturalness" of the speech at various beat durations. The judges reported that the speech sounded most natural to them at between two and three seconds of beat duration.

I wanted to phone Jones and Azrin and say, "Hey you guys, do you realize what you are doing to me and the journal? Do you realize what kind of precedent you will be setting with your 'naturalness'? Why, the people in our field who are not as sophisticated as you and me and who are easily influenced will begin to think that it is possible to measure how people feel about all kinds of subjective things. I know that 'naturalness' sounds innocent enough, but think about it a moment. If you publish a measure of 'naturalness' today, why tomorrow we will begin seeing manuscripts about happiness, creativity, affection, trust, beauty, concern, satisfaction, fairness, joy, love, freedom, and dignity. Who knows where it will end? Think for just a moment. What is that going to do to us and to the field of applied behavior analysis?"

But I was sure that they would have just said that they would agree that it was going to complicate our science a bit. But if those things described by subjective labels were the things that were most important to people, then those were the things, even though they might be complex, that we should become more concerned with. After all, as an applied science of human behavior, we supposedly were dedicated to helping people become better able to achieve their reinforcers.

Well, it didn't stop with Jones and Azrin. At about the same time I received a lovely manuscript from Jim McMichael and Jeff Corey (1969) in which they reported the exciting finding that college students in a Keller-type PSI (Personalized System of Instruction) course did better on the exam than the students in a traditional lecture course. This was, of course, a very important finding, as it replicated and substantiated Keller's research. The only problem was that they also asked the students in each course how much they liked their course. The students in the PSI course rated their course a great deal higher than the students in the traditional lecture sections.

"Well," I thought to myself, "What in the world am I going to do with this one? They are asking the participants in a behavioral treatment program how much they like it. Why, of course they should like it. After all, we are doing it to them for their own good aren't we? And even if they say they don't like it, we know what is best for them. Clearly, if the procedure is effective, its just not important whether anyone says they like it or not. Besides, look at the precedent that it will set. Before long, those who don't appreciate the extreme risks of subjective data will start asking for feedback from the participants in their treatment programs. Who knows where that will end?"

But I felt sure that McMichael and Corey would just say that feedback from participants is not a trivial issue: that if the participants don't like the treatment then they may avoid it, or run away, or complain loudly. And thus, society will be less likely to use our technology, no matter how potentially effective and efficient it might be.

At the same time that I was having to wrestle with the problems of subjective measurement in *JABA*, my colleagues and I in the Achievement Place Research Project were having some problems with unsolicited subjective feedback on similar issues. Colleagues, editors, and community members were asking us about the behavioral goals that we had chosen for training the teaching-parents and the youths participating in the community-based, family-style, behavioral treatment program at Achievement Place. They would ask us: "How do you know what skills to teach? You talk about appropriate skills this and appropriate skills that. How do you know that these are really appropriate?" We, of course, tried to explain that we were psychologists and thus the most qualified judges of what was best for people. Somehow, they didn't seem convinced by that logic.

In addition, the first time we tried to replicate the Achievement Place program in another community, that community gave us feedback in a most drastic manner. Before we really knew that they had complaints about our program they had "fired" us. Finally, there were those who were challenging the importance of some of the results of the training that we were reporting. "Yes," they would say, "there are changes in the behavior, but how do we know that they are really important changes?"

The message we seemed to be getting was that "social importance" was a subjective value judgement that only society was qualified to make. If our objective was, as described in *JABA,* to do something of social importance, then we needed to develop better systems and measures for asking society whether we were accomplishing this objective. The suggestion seemed to be that society would need to validate our work on at least three levels:

1. The social significance of the *goals.* Are the specific behavioral goals really what society wants?
2. The social appropriateness of the *procedures.* Do the ends justify the means? That is, do the participants, caregivers and other consumers consider the treatment procedures acceptable?
3. The social importance of the *effects.* Are consumers satisfied with the results? *All* the results, including any unpredicted ones?

We have come to refer to these as judgements of *social validity.* It seems to us that by giving the same status to social validity that we now give to objective measurement and its reliability we will bring the consumer, that is society, into our science, soften our image, and make more sure our pursuit of social relevance.

An example from our own experience in the Achievement Place Research Project is that we were told by many communities that one of the most important characteristics of teaching-parents that they wanted was "warmth". When quizzed about "warmth", the community members indicated that they wanted teaching-parents who "know how to relate to youths". For some time, our response to this request was to disagree with them. We argued, "What you really need is someone who knows how to give and take away points at the right time." But the results of our research (Braukmann, Kirigin, and Wolf, 1976) are tending to support the community's commonsense wisdom about the importance of teaching-parents being able to "relate to youths".

Thus, in order to be responsive to our communities and to our data, one of our challenges became to try to determine the behaviors that teaching-parents need in order to "relate to their youths". "What do some people have that makes kids like them? And how were we going to find out?", we asked ourselves over and over. "Relating" appeared to be such a complex behavioral puzzle of subtle social behaviors that we were not sure how to begin our behavioral analysis. We did have the Jones and Azrin example for measuring "naturalness", and we came upon another method from, of all places, the Rogerian counselling psychologists.

Haase and Tepper published an article in the *Journal of Counseling Psychology* in 1972 that was a great deal of help to us. Like so many Rogerians, Haase and Tepper were interested in "empathy". They wanted to see if they could find out what nonverbal behaviors of the counsellor were involved in empathy in order to be better able to teach and evaluate counsellors in training. They set up simulated counselling situations that contained various nonverbal components, such as level of eye contact, trunk lean (forward or backward), body orientation (toward the client or rotated away from the client), distance from the client and various levels of "empathic" verbal messages". Videotaped excerpts were then presented to experienced counsellors, who rated the amount of overall empathy presented in each excerpt. It was found that eye contact, trunk lean, distance, and verbal content were all related to the judgements of empathy. One result that really seemed to surprise the authors was that the nonverbal behaviors accounted for more than twice as much of the judgements of empathy than did the verbal behaviors. A counsellor who was saying something only moderately empathic was judged to be highly empathic if he or she were also engaging in eye contact, forward trunk lean, and were positioned close to the client.

Well, it occurred to us that this model could be used to analyze the *meaning* of all kinds of complex and subjective verbal labels. It also looked like a way to find out what some of the behaviors were that made some teaching-parents better than others in being able to "relate to youths". Alan Willner, with Curt Braukmann, Kathi Kirigin, Dean Fixsen, Lonnie Phillips, and I (Willner *et al.,* 1977) began to attempt to identify the interaction behaviors of teaching-parents in Achievement Place style group homes the youths liked and didn't like. Alan Willner had several youths look at videotaped examples of a variety of teaching-parent/youth interactions and to list the things that they liked and the things that they disliked. These comments were put into categories and then rated by the youths on an A, B, C, D, and F basis. The youths gave A's to the following teaching-parent behaviors: a calm, pleasant voice tone, offers to help, joking, fairness, explanations, concern, enthusiasm, politeness, and getting to the point. F's were given to the following teaching-parent behaviors: throwing objects, accusing, blaming statements, shouting, no opportunity provided to speak, insulting remarks, unfair point exchanges, and profanity. Willner then took some of the highest rated social behaviors, taught them to teaching-parent trainees, and found that youths rated these trainees much higher after the trainees received instruction in the youth-preferred behaviors.[2]

One important sidelight of Alan Willner's study was that he was not able to predict the behaviors of the teaching-parents that were going to be most liked by the youths. As a matter of fact, some of the behaviors that he thought would be most important to the youths were never mentioned by them. He still wasn't convinced. After all, maybe the youths just couldn't verbalize these subtle behaviors—which of course was a real possibility. In this case, however, he cross-validated the original behaviors by giving the youths more structured interviews, in which he included more detailed descriptions of the behaviors that he thought should also be important to them. The youths still rated those behaviors as much less important than the ones that they had earlier pointed out as important. This same outcome was found with youths who were not involved in the first set of interviews. It has become clear to us that we cannot predict very well what many subjective labels of complex behavioral phenomena are going to mean to our judges. Nevertheless, while the task of unravelling those social behaviors that are involved in knowing how to "relate to youths" is incomplete, Alan Willner has taken us closer to that goal.

Another example of the use of the social validation method to examine the social validity of behavioral goals is a study by Neil Minkin, with Curt Braukmann, Bonnie Minkin, Gary Timbers, Barbara Timbers, Dean Fixsen, Lonnie Phillips—and me (Minkin *et al.,* 1976). Neil Minkin wanted to determine what conversational skills of adolescent girls were relevant. He took videotapes of adolescent girls in conversations with adults and of university girls in conversations with adults. Judges from the community were then asked to rate the effectiveness of each of these girls as conversationalists. As might be expected, the community people judged the university girls to be more effective and ranked them higher. Minkin and others reviewed the videotapes of all the university and junior high-school girls several times, and determined that a composite score of three kinds of behavior correlated at the 0.84 level with

[2] Jack Michael (personal communication, 1976) has pointed out that some behaviors, identified as preferred by this method, may have acquired their reinforcing value by their usually being members of chains of behaviors. An example might be *offers to help.* It is possible that if *offers to help* were not often followed by *providing help,* the offers themselves would lose their reinforcing value. Similarly, behaviors described as showing *concern* may have the same relationship to a more complex chain of behaviors. Thus, there appears to be an important and not, as yet, well understood "sincerity" dimension that should be brought to the attention of anyone who may want to apply these findings. On the other hand, some of the behaviors identified as preferred may not be dependent on later events for their reinforcing value. Examples might be *joking* and *explanations.*

the ratings given by the community representatives. (The three behaviors were: time spent talking, conversational questions, such as "What are you taking in school?", and positive feedback behaviors such as "Uh huh", "Yeah", and "Great!") In this manner it was possible to isolate many of the behaviors that the community representatives clearly were responding to when they rated overall quality of a conversation.

Another example of the social validation of behavioral goals, conducted by the Achievement Place group, was carried out by Jack Werner, with Neil Minkin, Bonnie Minkin, Dean Fixsen, Lonnie Phillips—and me (Werner *et al.,* 1975). Police exercise a great deal of discretion in handling juvenile offenders. Less than one-fourth of those youths who come into contact with police officers and who could be taken into custody actually are taken into custody. According to Piliavin and Briar (1964), the violation *per se* is usually less influential in determining the choice of disposition than is the demeanor of the youth. It is often estimated that the social behaviors of the youths account for approximately 50% of all decisions regarding prejudicial handling of youths. Jack Werner wanted to identify some of the important behavioral components of youth-police interactions so that he could teach these to youths. Through informal interviews and then formal questionnaires, Werner and his colleagues identified several apparently important behaviors, including expression of cooperation, body orientation so that the youth was facing the officer, and politeness. Werner found that these behaviors could be reliably measured, thus partially solving the behavioral puzzle of what objectively measurable youth behaviors may influence police officers' decisions about custody.

So, rather than deciding by oneself the validity of the behavioral objectives of a treatment program, we can approach the specific consumer or representatives of the relevant community, and through interviews or ratings determine much more precisely what the socially significant problems are. And, based on the example of Jones and Azrin (1969) and the work of Haase and Tepper (1972), we find that we can establish the social importance or validity of complex classes of behavior that have subjective labels. By supplementing our traditional objective measures, we can determine the relationship between the objectively measured behaviors and the subjective labels. This procedure opens opportunities to explore all of the important goals that are described by subjective labels.

To summarize the method for determining goal behaviors, I quote from Minkin and his colleagues (1976):

> "For example, 'affection' might be considered a complex social behavior. If the goal of a behavior analyst were to teach a parent to be more affectionate towards his or her child, it would be necessary to specify the important component behaviors of affection. Some of the components might include touching, smiling, and hugging. To validate the social importance of these behaviors, four steps might be used. First, gathering sample parent-child interactions. Second, developing reliable definitions and recording specific behaviors. Third, employing relevant judges, that is, other parents or children, to rate the sample interactions and evaluate each parent as to the amount of affection shown to the child within the interaction. The evaluation instrument might be a bi-polar rating scale with the poles labelled as to the amount of affection shown. Step four would involve correlating the ratings of the judges with a composite score of the objectively measured behaviors of the parents. The subsequent correlation coefficient would indicate the level of relationship of the specified objectivity measured components of affection to the common English 'meaning' of affection as rated by the judges. Some of the important behavioral components of creativity, conversation, and affection, as well as other complex classes of social

> behaviors, could probably be identified through the use of these social validation procedures."

It is clear that a number of the most important concepts of our culture are subjective, perhaps even the most important. Martin Luther, as the story goes, was severely criticized for setting Potestant hymns to the popular melodies of songs and dances of the time. He replied, "Why should we let the devil have all the best tunes?" Well, why should we let the others have all of the best human goals and social problems?

A second kind of social validity that has impressed its importance on us is the social appropriateness (in terms of ethics, cost, and practicality) of the treatment procedures that we use. Again, behavior analysts are beginning to ask clients and care-givers systematically about the acceptability of their procedures. Foxx and Azrin (1972) found restitution procedures more acceptable to care-givers than timeout or shock punishment. These authors have also reported over-correction to be a re-education procedure that is acceptable to care-givers of the retarded.

Janet Porterfield, Emily Herbert-Jackson, and Todd Risley (1976) recently determined that "contingent observation" (that is, having to stop playing and just watch your playmates for several seconds) was not only an effective procedure for reducing the disruptive behavior of young children in a day-care setting, it was also found to be acceptable to the care-givers and to the parents of the children.

Our own data show that ratings by the youths in Achievement Place style homes of the fairness of the program and the concern of the teaching-parents correlate very highly with the number of offenses that the youths commit while they are in treatment (Braukmann, Kirigin, and Wolf, 1976). It may be that not only is it important to determine the acceptability of treatment procedures to participants for ethical reasons, it may also be that the acceptability of the program is related to effectiveness, as well as to the likelihood that the program will be adopted and supported by others.

The third dimension of social validity is the social importance of the effects of behavioral treatment. Are consumers satisfied with the results, all of the results, including those that were unplanned? Behavioral treatment programs are designed to help someone with a problem. Whether or not the program is helpful can be evaluated only by the consumer. Behavior analysts may give their opinions, and these opinions may even be supported with empirical objective behavioral data, but it is the participants and other consumers who want to make the final decision about whether a program helped solve their problems. Many behavior analysts are beginning to validate their objective data with systematic subjective measures of consumer satisfaction.

For example, Ron Kent and Dan O'Leary (1976) found the ratings by teachers and parents of child behavior also improved when their objective data showed increases in appropriate school behavior. Karen Maloney and Bill Hopkins (1973) determined that when they modified the sentence structure of stories written by elementary school children, judges' ratings of creativity also increased. This is to be contrasted with the findings of Tom Brigham, Paul Graubard, and Aileen Stans (1972), who were also attempting to improve quality of composition of school children, and found that some contingencies that increased objective dimensions had little effect on subjective ratings of quality, while other contingencies produced increases in both objective measures and subjective ratings of story quality. Steve Fawcett and Keith Miller (1975) demonstrated that an instructional package designed to enhance public-speaking behavior was effective in producing increases in both the objectively measured public-speaking behaviors and in the audience's ratings of the quality of the performance of the trainees.

We have described the Achievement Place research of Willner, Minkin, and Werner and their colleagues, where judges were used to determine socially valid dimensions of teaching-parent/youth interaction behavior, quality of conversation components, and significant elements in youth-police interaction. In each of those studies, the outcomes were also socially validated. That is, relevant judges were also used to assess the social importance of the changes in the objectively measured behaviors. And it was found that youths rated the quality of the teaching-parents higher, members of the community rated the quality of the youths' conversations higher, and police officers rated the quality of the demeanor of the youths higher as the objectively measured behaviors increased in each case.

At the treatment program level, Curt Braukmann with Dean Fixsen, Kathi Kirigin, Elaine Phillips, Lonnie Phillips—and I (1975) described how feedback from consumers can be used to provide ongoing quality control of the dissemination of the Achievement Place treatment model. The consumers of the program, that is the youths in the program, their parents, and community members and agencies, evaluate the teaching-parents by rating their effectiveness, concern, *etc.* throughout the year of training and certification, and each year thereafter. It has not been possible to demonstrate experimentally the effectiveness of this feedback system by using it with some programs and not with others because of ethical considerations. But there is one important bit of data. Since this feedback was put into effect, the Achievement Place program has not been summarily "fired" from a community, as in that first attempt at replication. Also, these consumer satisfaction ratings are often highly correlated with objective measures of effectiveness (Braukmann *et al.,* 1976).

Concern for the social validity of *objective* measures seems to be an issue in other social sciences as well. At the American Psychological Association meeting, Angus Campbell (1976) raised this issue about economics:

> "None of us doubts that economic data have admirable qualities: the question is, How well do they represent the quality of national life? How valid are they as measures of the goodness of life in this country? The history of the last 25 years is not reassuring. During this period this country has experienced an unprecedented rise in national affluence, with a spectacular increase in average family income and an associated decline in the number of families below the poverty line. During the same period we have seen a phenomenal rise in the incidence of crime, an epidemic of various forms of public violence, a greatly increased use of drugs with associated drug abuse, a continuing increase in the number of fragmented families, a sharp drop in public confidence in elected officials, and what appears to be a substantial rise in social and political alienation. [I] . . . find it hard to believe that the quality of American life has been greatly enhanced during this period."

E. F. Schumaker, in his book *Small is Beautiful: Economics as if People Mattered* (1973), raised this same issue. He urged economists to consider what he terms the *"primacy of qualitative distinctions",* rather than being so concerned with objective data like the gross national product.

Recently, the Swedish medical sociologists Levi and Anderson (1975) suggested that objective measures that habitually have been used by the United Nations to assess the quality of life be supplemented by subjective measures. They proposed that the traditional objective measures of quality of life, such as education, employment, economy, housing, nutrition, *etc.* be given equal emphasis with subjective criteria such as "happiness, satisfaction, and gratification". Thus, applied behavior analysts are not the only applied social scientists who are being asked to validate their measures by checking with society.

Well, if social validity is such a good thing, why haven't we been doing more of it all along.

Of course, the answer is that subjective data are risky data. Subjective data may not have any relationship to actual events. A program that is described by its consumers as well-liked or effective may not necessarily be either pleasant or effective. Thus, there is the danger that subjective data will seriously mislead us.

For example, Berleman, Seaberg, and Steinburn (1972) conducted a delinquency prevention experiment with carefully matched experimental and control groups, using intensive one- to two-year treatment by social workers as the intervention procedure. The evaluation of the effectiveness during the treatment period and during the eight months following treatment indicated "no positive impact" on disruptive behavior in school, police contacts, or rate of institutionalization. The untreated control group performed as well or better than the experimental group. Yet, when asked about their experience in treatment, the youths ". . . believed that their school acting-out had decreased. When asked if they would participate in a similar service again, 89 percent of the parents responded positively, as did 94 percent of the boys".

Behavioral researchers have reported many examples of a lack of correspondence between client-reported data and observer-obtained data. Patterson (*personal communication,* 1974) for example, described discrepancies between parental reports of improvements in the child's behavior, while objective data obtained by observers did not support these claims. Conrad and Wincze (1976) reported that clients undergoing orgasmic reconditioning verbally reported favorable results that were not substantiated by the objective data.

Why do these discrepancies exist? One possibility is that the contingencies of the situation create distortion. Verbal behavior, clearly, is a manipulable behavior. And we must be suspicious of it because we know that we will not always understand the contingencies operating on it. When we are asking for a verbal description of a private event, such as satisfaction with our treatment program, we must be very cautious because we have no adequate way of checking the reliability of the verbal report in an independent way. And as Skinner pointed out, verbal descriptions of private events are open to "fictional distortion" (1959).

For example, in order to influence consumer evaluations, it is conceivable that some of those being evaluated might politic their consumers for better ratings. Similarly, it is conceivable that some of those consumers giving ratings might fear that they will not remain anonymous and be afraid that those they are rating might retaliate in some manner. One can conceive of many such possibilities, but let us remember that the reliability of objective measurement systems can also be manipulated, as the excellent series of studies by O'Leary and Kent and their colleagues (O'Leary, Kent, and Kanowitz, 1975; Kent, O'Leary, Diament, and Dietz, 1972) have demonstrated. From these studies, it seems clear that the scoring behavior of observers can be affected by a variety of variables, such as experimenter feedback. We must take these into consideration whenever we design a measurement system that involves observers. Thus, we know that the reliability of objective measurement procedures can be influenced by a number of known and probably unknown variables, but we continue to use these systems because they are the only way to obtain some very important data, they often work, and we feel some confidence that we are gaining a better understanding of the conditions that may distort them.

Similarly, we know that social validity measures can be manipulated and abused, but we cannot allow this to lead us to neglect them. Rather, we must establish that set of conditions under which people can be assumed to be the best evaluators of their own treatment needs, procedural preferences, and posttreatment satisfaction. True, we know little about the proper set of conditions, but we must attempt them anyway. We can expect that they will involve education about options, lack of coercion, anonymity, and so on. We can study the effects of these conditions on subjective data, as O'Leary and Kent and their colleagues have studied their effects on objective observer-dependent measurement systems. And then we will be better able to control for them.

A second possible explanation for subjective-objective discrepancies is that the consumer is responding to changes in some behavior or condition that we are not recording with our particular objective measures. For example, the parent may say that a child has "improved", while our behavioral measure of rate of tantrums does not show a decrease. The discrepancy may be because the child has stopped cursing, which was important to the parent, but not measured by us, perhaps because it does not bother us. If this lack of appropriate measurement is one of the factors in subjective-objective discrepancies, then we must become better at setting up our measurement systems.

A third possibility, and the most serious, is that subjective measurement is impossible because humans cannot judge and report their own situation accurately enough. It may be that they don't know when they are better or worse off. It may be that to expect a human ever to be able to report accurately when something feels good or feels bad is just more than we can hope for from our confused species. But this conclusion is unacceptable if our goal is to design a responsive consumer-oriented applied social science. As Levi and Anderson (1975) argued in making their case for adding subjective measures to objective quality-of-life indicators:

> "We believe that each individual can be assumed to be the best judge of his own situation and state of well-being. The alternative is some type of 'big brother' who makes the evaluation for groups and nations. World history provides many examples of such 'expert' or 'elitist' opinions being at variance with what was expected by the man in the street."

Therefore, we may have to try to develop better ways of teaching people to observe their behavior and their conditions and to make more accurate decisions about their improvement. The opinion poll people often seem to be able to make excellent predictions about voting behavior based on verbal report. Surely we can do as well.

Undoubtedly, there will be further important studies that point out to us the shortcomings of certain social validity measures, just as has been done for observer-dependent objective measures. But we can't despair. After all, measurement has been our thing. In our field, we have developed so many ingenious measurement systems. There is no doubt that we could measure the disruptive classroom behavior of a school of fish, if need be. Surely, we will be able to develop measurement systems that will tell us better whether or not our clients are happy with our efforts and our effects.

Earlier in our history, Watson and Skinner argued forcefully against subjective measurement because they were concerned about the inappropriate causal roles that hypothetical internal variables, subjectively reported, were playing in social science. As a result, many of us concluded that all subjective measurement was inappropriate. A new consensus seems to be developing. It seems that if we aspire to social importance, then we must develop systems that allow our consumers to provide us feedback about how our applications relate to their values, to their reinforcers. This is not a rejection of our heritage. Our use of subjective measures does not relate to internal causal variables. Instead, it is an attempt to assess the dimensions of complex reinforcers in socially acceptable and practical ways. It is an evolutionary event that is occurring as a function of the contingencies of the applied research environment; contingencies that our founders would probably say they appreciate, if we had the nerve to ask them for such subjective feedback on our behavior.

REFERENCES

Berleman, W. C., Seaberg, J. R., and Steinburn, T. W. The delinquency prevention experiment of the

Seattle Atlantic Street Center: A final evaluation. *Social Science Review,* 1972, Sept., 323-346.

Boring, E. G. *A history of experimental psychology.* New York: Appleton-Century-Crofts, 1950.

Braukmann, C. J., Fixsen, D. L., Kirigin, K. A., Phillips, E. A. Phillips, E. L., and Wolf, M. M. Achievement Place: The training and certification of teaching-parents. In W. S. Wood (Ed), *Issues in evaluating behavior modification.* Champaign, Illinois: Research Press, 1975. Pp. 131-152.

Braukmann, C. J., Kirigin, K. A., and Wolf, M. M. *Achievement Place: The researchers' perspective.* Paper presented at the meeting of the American Psychological Association, Washington, D.C., September, 1976.

Brigham, T. A., Graubard, P. S., and Stans, A. Analysis of the effects of sequential reinforcement contingencies on aspects of composition. *Journal of Applied Behavior Analysis,* 1972, **5**, 421-430.

Campbell, Angus. Subjective measures of well-being. *American Psychologist,* 1976, **31**, 117-124.

Conrad, S. R. and Wincze, J. P. Orgasmic reconditioning. A controlled study of its effects upon the sexual arousal and behavior of adult male homosexuals. *Behavior Therapy,* 1976, **7**, 155-166.

Fawcett, S. B. and Miller, L. K. Training public-speaking behavior: an experimental analysis and social validation. *Journal of Applied Behavior Analysis,* 1975, **8**, 125-136.

Foxx, R. M. and Azrin, N. A. Restitution: A method of eliminating aggressive-disruptive behavior of retarded and brain damaged patients. *Behaviour Research and Therapy,* 1972, **10**, 15-27.

Hasse, R. F. and Tepper, D. T. Nonverbal components of empathetic communication. *Journal of Counseling Psychology,* 1972, **19**, 417-424.

Jones, R. J. and Azrin, N. A. Behavioral engineering: stuttering as a function of stimulus duration during speech synchronization. *Journal of Applied Behavior Analysis,* 1969, **2**, 223-230.

Kent, R. N. and O'Leary, D. K. A controlled evaluation of behavior modification with conduct problem children. *Journal of Consulting and Clinical Psychology,* 1976, **44**, 586-596.

Kent, R. N., O'Leary, K. D., Diament, C., and Dietz, A. Expectation biases in observational evaluation of therapeutic change. *Journal of Consulting and Clinical Psychology,* 1972, **42**, 774-780.

Levi, L. and Anderson, L. *Psychosocial stress: Population, environment, and the quality of life.* Holliswood, N.Y.: Spectrum Press, 1975.

Maloney, K. B. and Hopkins, B. L. The modification of sentence structure and its relationship to subjective judgements of creativity in writing. *Journal of Applied Behavior Analysis,* 1973, **6**, 425-434.

McMichael, J. S. and Corey, J. R. Contingency management in an introductory psychology course produces better learning. *Journal of Applied Behavior Analysis,* 1969, **2**, 79-84.

Minkin, N., Braukmann, C. J., Minkin, B. L., Timbers, G. D., Timbers, B. J., Fixsen, D. L., Phillips, E. L., and Wolf, M. M. The social validation and training of conversation skills. *Journal of Applied Behavior Analysis,* 1976, **9**, 127-140.

New Webster's Vest Pocket Dictionary. Ottenheimer Publishers, Inc., 1962.

O'Leary, K. D., Kent, R. N., and Kanowitz, J. Shaping data collection congruent with experimental hypotheses. *Journal of Applied Behavior Analysis,* 1975, **8**, 43-51.

Piliavin, I. and Briar, S. Police encounters with juveniles. *American Journal of Sociology,* 1964, **70**, 206-214.

Porterfield, J. K., Herbert-Jackson, E., and Risley, T. R. Contingent observation: an effective and acceptable procedure for reducing disruptive behavior of young children in a group setting. *Journal of Applied Behavior Analysis,* 1976, **9**, 55-64.

Schumaker, E. F. *Small is beautiful: economics as if people mattered.* New York: Harper & Row, 1973.

Skinner, B. F. *Science and human behavior.* New York: Macmillan Co., 1953.

Skinner, B. F. *Cumulative record.* New York: Appleton-Century-Crofts, Inc., 1959.

Watson, John B. *Behaviorism.* Chicago: The University of Chicago Press, 1930.

Werner, J. S., Minkin, N., Minkin, B. L., Fixsen, D. L., Phillips, E. L., and Wolf, M. M. Intervention package: An analysis to prepare juvenile delinquents for encounters with police officers. *Criminal Justice and Behavior,* 1975, **2**, 55-83.

Willner, A. G., Braukmann, C. J., Kirigin, K. A., Fixsen, D. L., Phillips, E. L., and Wolf, M. M. The training and validation of youth-preferred social behaviors with child-care personnel. *Journal of Applied Behavior Analysis,* 1977, **10**, 219-230.

Received 15 October 1976.
(Final Acceptance 12 August 1977.)

JOURNAL OF APPLIED BEHAVIOR ANALYSIS 1979, **12**, 581-591 NUMBER 4 (WINTER 1979)

SOCIAL VALIDATION: THE EVOLUTION OF STANDARDS OF COMPETENCY FOR TARGET BEHAVIORS

RONALD VAN HOUTEN

MOUNT SAINT VINCENT UNIVERSITY

The use of social validation procedures has become widespread in recent years. Although most researchers have used social validation procedures to select target behaviors and to evaluate whether the changes produced by a treatment program should be considered socially useful, little attention has been focused upon using the social validation process to determine the optimal levels for target behaviors. This paper suggests several ways in which social validation procedures can be employed in order to select when and how much to change target behaviors.

DESCRIPTORS: social validation, competency standards, normative data, goal selection, standard selection, response rate

---

Over the years, behavior modifiers have strived to increase the frequency of behaviors deemed desirable and to decrease the level of behaviors judged undesirable. Although considerable emphasis has been placed on evaluating the amount of change produced by experimental procedures, only recently have researchers directed their attention to assessing whether behaviors have improved sufficiently to consider a treatment socially useful (Kazdin, 1977; Wolf, 1978).

Basically, two methods have been employed to select target behaviors and to assess whether the changes produced by a treatment are of applied importance—social comparison and subjective evaluation. The first method involves comparing the performance of target subjects with that of peers who did not warrant treatment. If the client's behavior falls within the normative range of behavior, the treatment is considered successful (Patterson, 1974; Walker and Hops, 1976). The second method involves having judges with special expertise rate the behaviors of subjects before and after the treatment is implemented (Briscoe, Hoffman, and Bailey, 1975; Kent and O'Leary, 1976; Maloney, Harper, Braukmann, Fixsen, Phillips, and Wolf, 1976; Porterfield, Herbert-Jackson, and Risley, 1976; Van Houten, Morrison, Jarvis, and McDonald, 1974).

The selection of appropriate target behaviors has been identified as an important problem in applied behavior analysis (Hawkins, 1975) and variations of the two above-mentioned procedures have proven increasingly useful in solving this problem. First, in the known groups method (McFall, 1976), the behavior of individuals comprising two groups that differ in some important global dimension are compared to identify which behaviors are uniquely correlated with the more successful group. Second, in the consumer satisfaction method (Wolf, 1978), clients or other consumers of our technology are asked to judge or rate various behaviors which are suspected to be important. Both methods rely upon experimental confirmation of the importance of the selected behaviors through the use of additional social validation procedures following treatment.

Although the selection of appropriate target behaviors is a valuable and necessary application

The author would like to thank Paul Nau and George Patterson for the many valuable suggestions they made regarding this manuscript. Preparation of this manuscript was partially supported by Canada Council Grant S74-1700-R2. Reprints may be obtained from Ron Van Houten, Psychology Department, Mount Saint Vincent University, Halifax, Nova Scotia, Canada, B3M 2J6.

of social validation techniques, it is only one step in the overall assessment process. Another step which has received considerably less attention is the selection of optimal levels of performance for the behaviors chosen in the previous step. This step becomes as important as the previous step if one considers that for most behaviors there exists a range of responding within which performance is most adaptive. When the limits of this range are unknown for a particular behavior, it is possible that one could terminate treatment when performance is above or below these limits. Hence, the behavior would not be occurring within its optimal range.

Terminating treatment below the lower limit of competent performance is clearly an undesirable treatment outcome. However, social validation carried out in the traditional manner would not provide information on whether or not this type of error had actually occurred. For example, if the terminal performance is superior to baseline performance a positive social validation is likely to result. Unfortunately the evaluation would not inform the researchers that higher levels of performance would lead to even more adaptive behavior on the part of the client. Conversely if the performance is not judged to be better following treatment, it is unclear whether the behavior selected is unimportant or if it was not changed sufficiently to yield positive results.

On the other hand, if treatment is terminated after the behavior is increased beyond the upper limit of competent performance, the resulting outcome could be equally detrimental to the client. An obvious example would be an underassertive child who has been taught to make more requests. Initial increases in the frequency of requests might be considered increasingly adaptive; however, at a certain point, the behavior could begin to be considered pestering by those interacting with the child. At this point, the frequency of the behavior has surpassed its optimum value and would no longer be judged as desirable by those interacting with the child. Social validation techniques employed in the traditional manner would not inform one whether the behavior was more functional at a lower level, nor could they inform one whether negative outcomes resulted from selecting the wrong behavior as a target or from producing too little or too much change in the level of the target behavior. Similarly, there is no guarantee that normative levels represent optimal performance.

In one experiment, Willner, Braukmann, Kirigin, Fixsen, Phillips, and Wolf (1977) found that youths judged that they preferred teaching parents who engaged in various behaviors such as joking, giving explanations, or providing offers to help. Although this study identifies various important behaviors, it does not tell practitioners what level or frequency of these behaviors is optimal. Just as it is quite possible that one could engage in too few of these behaviors, one could also engage in these behaviors too much. For example, it might be possible for an adult to joke or horse around too much, or to make too many offers to help, or to overdo giving explanations. Therefore, the next step in the evaluation of teaching parents may be to determine frequency aims for these behaviors. A similar argument could be made for identifying the situations where these behaviors are judged most appropriate. Still another step in the social validation process would be to identify the various interactions between these behaviors and their influence on treatment efficacy.

Failure to identify the limits of adaptive behavior makes it difficult if not impossible to determine how much to change a particular behavior in order to obtain the best results for the client. Another problem that may result from the failure to identify the optimal range of target behaviors is that practitioners cannot tell when to change a particular behavior and when to leave it alone. Without the above-mentioned information, it would be difficult to determine whether a treatment which produces a socially validated improvement in one individual's performance would also produce such a change in another individual's performance since one would now know if that behavior is already within the optimal range.

In order to know when to initiate and terminate a treatment, practitioners require socially validated standards for which they can aim. The availability of these standards is especially important to those who are not themselves engaged in applied research, since these individuals are often not in a position to perform a complex social validation of the changes they produce because of financial or temporal constraints.

This article suggests several ways in which social validation procedures can be employed to determine these aims: normative based selection procedures and experimentally based selection procedures.

Selecting Standards of Competence through Normative Based Selection Procedures

One way of determining socially validated goals is to assess the performance of individuals who are judged to be highly competent in the area of interest. The norms obtained from these individuals can then serve as performance goals for less competent individuals. Setting norms in this manner utilizes both commonly employed methods of social validation since it involves first selecting individuals who are universally judged to be competent at a given behavior and second determining the level of their performance.

The first decision to be made involves choosing whether to obtain a single universal goal for each task from the most competent individuals we can find or to obtain separate goals from each special population such as the developmentally retarded or the handicapped. In the long run, it is probably better to select a single goal from those judged most competent within the society. Although goals obtained by this method may at first appear overly stringent for some populations, they can still serve as a yardstick against which changes produced by any treatment can be assessed. Furthermore, they possess the added advantage of serving as a challenge to develop more powerful change techniques. A failure to bring an individual's behavior within the competent range does not necessarily imply an experimental failure since it is certainly important to bring individuals as close as possible to an optimal level of performance. However, researchers will remain aware of the possibility of producing even more adaptive levels of performance. Although it is possible to avoid this issue entirely by obtaining separate competency based norms for every population, this is probably unwise since the levels of behavior which indicate competence do not change because some individuals have more difficulty obtaining them. However, it may be practical to set lower short-term goals in some instances because techniques may not presently exist to bring some individuals' performance within the component range.

An advantage of using standards based on the performance of competent individuals is that doing so does not limit potential for improvement. One objection that has been raised about using norms obtained from untreated peers as a treatment standard is that these norms themselves could be improved in many instances (Kazdin, 1977). For example, in the classroom situation it may be possible to accelerate the normative level of academic performance in most classrooms. This objection does not apply to normative data obtained from competent individuals because these data are based on the performance of the most competent individuals; and, therefore, it may be quite appropriate to accelerate the performance of an entire group to these levels. Lastly, though norms based on the performance of competent individuals lack some of the disadvantages of group norms, they should not be considered completely inflexible because additional studies may indicate higher levels of competence are possible. In fact the selection of target behavior and performance standards are both best viewed as an iterative process where repeated social validation applied to a particular problem leads to the improved delineation of important treatment goals.

Obtaining Standards from Competent Individuals

It is quite simple to obtain rate and accuracy standards for typists or stenographers. Secretarial schools have been employing such standards for many years. Merely being capable of performing a task such as typing does not demonstrate that an individual is a proficient typist. For example, one typist might be able to type 100 to 120 words per min without errors while another can only type between 30 and 40 words per min without errors. Since both students can type without errors, should we consider that they are equally proficient? In order to answer this question we must know what the term proficiency really means. Typists are proficient only when they can type at a high enough rate for their services to be useful to others or to themselves. Most individuals could type a perfect page given enough time, but that does not make them proficient typists.

If we select standards for typing proficiency by examining the performance of randomly sampled adults, it is unlikely that the standards obtained would represent maximally useful performance. Even if we randomly sampled the performance of secretaries, the resulting standards would only represent mediocre performance. Only by sampling the performance of secretaries rated as competent typists by their employers could we be sure of obtaining a standard which reflects competence, and which a powerful behavioral technology should aim to produce. Hence, one way of selecting competent individuals is to ask those who require the behavior at what level they judge it to be functional.

Similarly, standards in mathematics and reading could be easily obtained by looking at individuals who are judged to be highly competent at various mathematics and reading skills, while standards for essay writing could be obtained by looking at the performance of the best essayists. Therefore if we wished to obtain standards for adults who are learning to write essays we would get them from established writers who are judged competent by our society. These standards would then serve as goals for both adults and children who are learning to write. Again although these standards may seem overly stringent when applied to children, we should remember that a competent typist is competent regardless of age as is a competent musician, reader, or writer. The fact that there may be fewer children than adults who are competent at a particular task does not imply that the ultimate goal for children's performance is any different from that of an adult's.

For example, if we found that a competent adult could solve approximately 80 single digit multiplication problems per minute without any errors, we could set this as a goal for children and adults alike. Similarly, if we found that competent adults could read material at their reading level aloud at a rate of 150 words per min with 98% accuracy, then we could presume that children learning to read should be as competent when they meet this standard on their reading material. Although the level of the material being read may be different, the reading rate and accuracy which indicate competence may remain the same. Furthermore, it is undoubtedly true that children often become as competent as adults at specific tasks.

In both of the above examples, some individuals might have difficulty obtaining these standards, but movement in the direction of the standard would often be judged successful. Applying rigorous standards may mean we would have at least some idea of the degree to which we could approach the level of performance of a competent model, thereby revealing how much our technology needed to be improved.

If we instead derive performance standards from normative data we run the risk that the reading and mathematics performance of the "average" student is below the competent range. If we adopt these standards, we will likely terminate treatment before students are competent at a task.

The inadequacies of normative standards obtained from the overall population are excellently illustrated by the data obtained by White (1975) and Thomas, Presland, Grant, and Glynn (1978) on natural rates of teacher approval and disapproval. White measured the natural levels of approval and disapproval in sixteen classrooms. An analysis of her results indicates that the mean rate of teacher praise was .36 per min across all grades. Furthermore, teacher praise rate declined with increasing grade level so that high school teachers only praised someone every five or ten minutes. Thomas *et al.* (1978) examined the teacher praise rates of seventh grade teachers and found that the average teacher praise rate was .20 praises per min. From what is currently known about optimal rates of teacher praise (Cossairt, Hall, and Hopkins, 1973; Hall, Lund, and Jackson, 1968; McAllister, Stachowiak, Baer, and Conderman, 1969), it is unlikely that these rates would represent good standards for applied behavior analysts working with problems in the public schools. Alternatively, Nelson and Bowles (1975) suggest that normative data could be obtained from teachers described as highly competent. Although there is no guarantee that these goals will prove adequate, they can serve as a best guess in the first step of the social validation process.

By using competent behavior as a standard, we de-emphasize some of the relativity involved in norm selection because we provide goals which are judged to be functional. Furthermore, our goals are based upon estimates obtained from individuals who are performing the task at a useful level.

Selecting competent models. One problem associated with determining normative based competency standards is deciding which individuals are competent at a given task. As a first step one can ask those most often involved with rating the adequacy of the target individual's performance. We could ask teachers, parents, employers, or others who are in a position to rate an individual's performance. For example, if we wanted to establish standards for reading, we could ask the superintendent of schools in which schools students read the best. Next the teachers in these schools could be asked to identify their best readers. The resulting standards could be considered a best guess estimate of competent performance. Further research and social validations could then help to establish how good these standards really are. Again successive application of the social validation strategy should lead to more refined standards.

Selecting the correct measure. Another problem associated with determining standards of competent behavior from normative data is that we must select the most appropriate measure upon which to base our assessment. If we select an incomplete or incorrect measure, the standards obtained may not bear any relationship to the quality or social utility of the performance. For example, if in our mathematics example we had selected percentage correct alone as our standard, we would not be able to distinguish between a student who could only work 20 problems per min with no errors (100% correct) from one who could work 80 problems per min with no errors (100% correct). Clearly the addition of rate standards allows us to differentiate between a competent individual capable of working 80 problems from a less capable person who could only work 20.

Similar problems could easily arise when examining a complex task like storywriting. For example, a teacher may observe that the percentage of different adjectives used by the students is far lower than that used by competent writers. Therefore the teacher might establish a program to increase the percentage of different adjectives used. However, even if the program is successful, the teacher cannot be sure that students who increase their use of adjectives are using them in the same way as good writers. Students might string together many adjectives of the same kind, such as "the red, yellow, and blue house" rather than distributing adjectives or using different kinds of adjectives, such as the "old, deserted, grey house." It is easy to see how a general measure like the percentage of different adjectives could also be an oversimplified measure.

This does not imply that it is not possible to set objective competency standards but it does mean that we must specify our variables so that they will be related to social validation measures, which in the case of storywriting might be overall quality. If we can identify all the relevant features of good adjective usage then it will be possible to place consequences on each aspect and bring them into the normative range of competent individuals. In the case of adjective use, some important variables might be diversity in the use of different types of adjectives and the way adjectives are distributed among the various nouns. However, only when the most relevant attributes of good adjective use are clearly identified can we begin to teach students to improve systematically. A similar argument could be made about setting standards for optimal levels of teacher praise. It would be easy to conclude that frequency of praise is important when in fact a closer analysis might reveal that whether praise is descriptive or accompanied with a smile or a pat also influences whether it is effective.

Although the relevant dimensions of many behaviors may be quite complex, it is still possible to move toward the establishment of performance standards because of the iterative nature of the social validation process. Each successive study can yield a closer approximation of relevant aspects and standards.

Selecting Standards of Competence through Experimentally Based Procedures

Another way of assessing and refining socially validated goals is through two methods of empirical assessment. Using the first method, the experimenter manipulates the behavior of interest over its entire range and determines at which values the behavior is maximally useful or effective in attaining important functional goals. The aspect of this procedure that sets it apart from the more traditional application of social validation procedures is that the behavior of interest is varied over a wide range of values in order to select a range of values within which performance is optimal. Clearly this approach is quite compatible with that employed in normative based selection procedures. Social validations which experimentally vary the frequency of behaviors believed to be important because they are consistently found in the repertoire of individuals judged to be competent at a particular task can lead to the empirical validation of these behaviors. Unfortunately few researchers have performed an experimental validation of competency standards; therefore, few examples exist typifying this approach.

In one example, Warren, Rogers-Warren, and Baer (1976) taught preschool children to increase their offers to share materials with their peers. In the case of sharing, the authors concluded that offers to share were most appropriate when they were accepted, and that if a large number of offers to share were rejected, then these offers were functionally inappropriate to the children receiving them. One factor which the authors suspected might influence the likelihood that an offer would be accepted was the rate of offers to share. In two experiments the authors increased the frequency of offers to share while examining the percentage of offers accepted. They found that the percentage of offers accepted declined as the frequency of offers to share increased. These results implied that an inverted U-shaped function exists such that as offer rates increase, the percentage of offers accepted increases up to a certain point and then declines. The authors concluded that if the frequency of certain behaviors determines whether individuals will react in a positive or negative way to them, then the target rate or goal should be chosen according to these results. The results of this study illustrates how precisely treatment goals must be specified. If practitioners interested in increasing the sharing behavior of a group of children were not aware of these findings, they might teach some children who initially have effective offer rates to respond at a level which would be socially less useful than their baseline rate.

In another example, Jones and Azrin (1969) found that they could virtually eliminate stuttering by having clients synchronize their speech to a regular vibrotactual stimulus. Although this procedure markedly suppressed stuttering at beat durations less than 5 sec, the resulting speech did not always sound natural. In order to determine how beat duration influenced "naturalness" of speech, Jones and Azrin taped 1-min segments of the clients speech at nine different beat durations. These samples were then played to 12 judges who made independent judgments about the naturalness of each 1-min segment of taped speech. The results indicated that a beat duration of 1 to 3 sec produced the most natural sounding speech in all four clients. Data also indicated that the number of words read per minute were also at or near their peak value within these durations. It is interesting to note that the performances of all four clients were essentially similar. On the basis of the data obtained on stuttering, naturalness, and reading rate, it was possible for Jones and Azrin to conclude that an effective way to use a "metronome procedure as a clinical technique would be to have a stimulus duration of about 1 to 3 sec and a stimulus-off duration of 1-sec." It is interesting to note that in this example the experimental analysis of the effects of beat duration on stuttering produced compatible results on all validation measures. If all three measures had not been in such close accord, it would have been necessary to set priorities and trade each measure off against the others.

Similarly, communication skills, public speaking techniques, and other behaviors could be evaluated by their effects on their audience. For example, if researchers wanted to examine the effects of eye contact or gestures on public speakers, they could vary eye contact while keeping all other variables constant. If a particular range of durations were found to be optimally effective, clients could be taught to perform within this range. Comparable results could be easily obtained for loudness of voice and other factors which might influence the efficiency of public speakers. Subsequent analysis performed on other variables would help identify many important effects and interactions. No single researcher would be expected to vary all suspected conditions; however, over a period of time more knowledge should be accumulated through a series of systematic replications. The end results of this operation would be empirically determined performance goals. The major difficulty with determining goals in this manner is the expense in time and effort associated with varying behaviors over their entire range of occurrence. However, in the long run this problem is offset by the degree of confidence one can assign to standards obtained in this way.

The above examples illustrate how the optimal range of performance can be selected for a particular behavior by varying its frequency of occurrence over a wide range of values. A second way of evaluating the adequacy of performance standards is to examine the effects of training to various standards on the subsequent acquisition of more complex skills. Clearly this approach is relevant whenever the behavior of interest is also a prerequisite for other important behaviors which must also be acquired.

For example, Van Houten (*in press-a*) examined the relationship between the rate at which students could complete basic single digit multiplication facts (of the form 7 × 8) and their performance on long multiplication and division problems. The basic measure in this experiment was the number of long multiplication and division problems completed correctly each day on a 10-min test. During some conditions students were drilled on their basic multiplication facts at another time of the day, and during other conditions they were not. The results of this study revealed that students' performance on the long multiplication and division tests only improved during conditions when students were given drill on basic multiplication facts. Whenever multiplication drill was removed, performance on the test problems neither improved nor deteriorated but rather remained the same. It should be noted that students rarely made errors during multiplication drill from the onset of the study. Therefore, a teacher who only considered accuracy on basic multiplication tables to be important would have concluded that these students had learned their multiplication tables and therefore required no further training. However, a teacher who also examined their work rate would have noted that they could only complete between 30 and 40 problems per min at the beginning of the experiment and between 60 and 70 problems per min at the end of the experiment. This difference becomes behaviorally significant when one considers that performance on this task was positively correlated with improvement on the more complex test problems. It is possible that we could terminate training on basic number facts such as the addition or multiplication table or printing before students have obtained a performance level sufficient to allow them to improve on more complex tasks for which these skills are a prerequisite.

Haughton (1972) has suggested that a similar relationship exists between the rate at which a child can print or cursively write, and spelling and composition writing. A similar approach can be employed in the evaluation of social behaviors. For example, Ayllon and Azrin (1968) suggested that practitioners teach behaviors that would be functional for individuals in their environment when they were reintegrated into the community. In one study, Fixsen, Phillips, Phillips, and Wolf (1976) evaluated the long-term validity of the target behaviors they selected with predelinquent youths by examining subsequent effects on school performance and recidivism. Their data validated their choice of target behaviors because they produced a marked reduction in the number of police and court contacts per youth up to two years following treatment. Positive results were also obtained with various aspects of school performance.

AN EXAMPLE OF GOAL SELECTION WITH STORYWRITING

The first portion of this paper has been concerned with the general issue of selecting treatment goals or standards. The following discussion illustrates how the problems of goal selection can influence a program designed to teach children to write better stories. It also illustrates how the social validation process functions to develop standards through successive approximations.

In recent years, several articles have been published that suggest that judges give improved ratings of story quality when elementary students are taught to increase the number of different action words used in their stories (Ballard and Glynn, 1975; Maloney and Hopkins, 1973). However, Van Houten (*in press-b*) was unable to replicate these findings with elementary school children in a carefully controlled study where the number of different action words used during a 7-min story was increased from a baseline level of 4.7 to a posttreatment level of 12.1 words. When judges rated these stories on the dimension of overall quality, no differences were detected between stories written during the baseline and treatment conditions.

Similarly, Van Houten and McLellan (unpublished data) increased the number of different action words written by secondary school students during a 5-min writing period from a baseline rate of 8.9 to a posttreatment level of 19.7 words. Again, quality ratings made by experimentally naive judges revealed no changes in story quality. It is clear that these results are not in accord with the often replicated finding that increases in the number of action words written in a story are associated with increased story quality ratings.

At first it may seem confusing that changes in different action word usage were not associated with changes in judged story quality. However, if one compares these studies using an equivalent measure, a certain degree of orderliness begins to emerge. One alternative is to examine the percentage of different action words used in each story. This measure would be superior to that of rate of different action word use because it is not confounded by the number of words written. Hence students could not increase the percentage of action words used by writing more rather than by changing their writing style.

However, even when the Van Houten (*in press-b*) and Van Houten and McLellan data were corrected for overall rate, it was still clear that the treatments had an effect on action word use. For example, the percentages of different action words used during the pretreatment condition were 13% and 11.2% for the elementary and secondary students, respectively. Posttreatment percentages were 15.2% and 18.3%, respectively. Clearly the treatments produced an increase in the percentage of action words in both studies. Since changes in the percentage of different action words were not associated with increases in story quality, it would be interesting to compare these levels with normative based competence standards obtained from writers who are universally judged as competent.

Therefore random segments from established authors which were of similar length to the stories written by these students were examined. Ten excerpts were randomly selected from the short stories of renowned writers (Cline, 1952). These were Anton Chekhov, Steven Crane, Joseph Conrad, D. H. Lawrence, James Joyce, Somerset Maugham, and John Steinbeck. The length of these excerpts, 80 words, was selected in order to keep length roughly comparable to that of the elementary and secondary students' stories.

The mean percentage of different verbs used by these authors was 11.3% with a range of 10% to 13%. Clearly, the percentages calculated from the students' stories during the baseline condition fell within this range. Similarly, 80-word segments taken from award winning stories of elementary and secondary students contained 12.2% different action words. This suggests that increasing student action word rate did not produce a change in story quality because performance on this measure was already within an optimal range when the experiment began. It is also possible that in previous studies where experiments reported having improved stories by increasing the number of different action words used, students were highly repetitious in their use of action words during the baseline condition and hence were well below the percentages obtained from competent writers. If this were the case, any treatment which caused them to use action words in a way more similar to that of good writers would be associated with a judgment of improved story quality.

Unfortunately, it is impossible to compare the percentages in many of these studies because the authors did not report percentage data (Ballard and Glynn, 1975; Maloney and Hopkins, 1973) nor did they present sufficient information to allow for its computation. For example, Maloney and Hopkins (1973) gave students up to 40 min to write a 10-sentence story. Tokens were then awarded for increases in the number of different action words used per sentence. However, no information was provided on the number of words written or on sentence length, and hence it was not possible to calculate the percentage of action words per story. However, a rough comparison is possible. They reported that during the baseline condition the children used .39 different action words per sentence and during the treatment condition they used .98 different action words per sentence. If we assume that these children wrote sentences that averaged seven words or more and that this number was constant throughout the study, then the percentage of action words changed from a maximum of 6% to a maximum of 14%. If these estimates are correct, the baseline performance in this instance would be far below the norms obtained from competent writers of all ages.

In another study, it was possible to calculate the percentage of different action words directly from the experimental data (Maloney, Jacobson, and Hopkins, 1975). In this study, a teacher had third-grade students write stories that were five sentences long. During a baseline condition, action words accounted for 4% of the total; during the treatment condition (when different action word usage was reinforced) the percentage increased to 13%. Further, judges rated the stories written during the condition when different action word usage was reinforced as superior to those written during the other conditions. In this study, the authors increased the percentage of different action words from a level far below that used by competent writers to a level within the range used by competent writers and obtained improved quality ratings.

These studies illustrate how performance standards can be evolved that can help predict whether or not a student will benefit from a treatment designed to increase the level of a behavior. Although increasing the percentage of different action words in a story can clearly lead to increases in a socially validated measure (story quality) if students are below competent norms, it is not likely to benefit students who are already responding within these norms. Hence knowledge of these norms enables practitioners to determine more carefully when a treatment will have a socially validated effect.

Social Validation as an Iterative Process

The above-mentioned example illustrates why social validation is best viewed as an iterative process which when properly employed helps researchers converge on the best treatment targets along with appropriate treatment aims or levels for selected behavior. Finally, this process narrows down the specific situations in which these behaviors are most appropriate. The outcome of the social validation process is the selection of appropriate target behaviors along with competency aims expressed in terms of optimal frequency, duration, accuracy percentage, or latency, and the delineation of the most appropriate settings for these target behaviors to occur. The process is comprised of normative assessments, subjective judgments, and global short- and long-term validations. The process often begins by selecting behaviors and estimating competent levels of these behaviors through gathering normative data on the most competent individuals or by comparing the normative behavior of known groups of competent and incompetent individuals (McFall, 1976). Next researchers obtain closer and closer approximations of the best target behaviors and standards through the two types of experimental social validation procedures. First, behaviors believed to be important are varied across their natural range of occurrence and the effect on the environment and the rating behavior of judges are noted. Second, the global or long-term effects of changing specific target behaviors are noted.

The experimental aspects of the social validation process enable researchers to converge on closer approximations of guidelines specifying which behaviors are good candidates for change as well as when and how much these behaviors should be changed.

REFERENCES

Ayllon, T. and Azrin, N. *The token economy.* New York: Appleton-Century-Crofts, 1968.

Ballard, K. D. and Glynn, T. Behavioral self-management in story writing with elementary school children. *Journal of Applied Behavior Analysis,* 1975, **8**, 387-398.

Briscoe, R. V., Hoffman, D. B., and Bailey, J. S. Behavioral community psychology: training a community board to problem solve. *Journal of Applied Behavior Analysis,* 1975, **8**, 157-168.

Cline, C. L. *The Rinehart book of short stories.* New York: Holt, Rinehart & Winston, 1952.

Cossairt, A., Hall, R. V., and Hopkins, B. L. The effects of experimenter's instructions, feedback, and praise on teacher praise and student attending behavior. *Journal of Applied Behavior Analysis,* 1973, **6**, 89-100.

Fixsen, D. L., Phillips, E. L., Phillips, E. A., and Wolf, M. M. The teaching family model of group home treatment. In W. E. Craighead, A. E. Kazdin, and M. J. Mahoney (Eds), *Behavior modification: Principles, issues, and applications.* Boston: Houghton Mifflin, 1976.

Hall, R. V., Lund, D., and Jackson, D. Effects of teacher behavior on study behavior. *Journal of Applied Behavior Analysis,* 1968, **1**, 1-12.

Hawkins, R. P. Who decided that was the problem? Two stages of responsibility for applied behavior analysts. In J. S. Wood (Ed), *Issues in evaluating behavior modification.* Champaign, Illinois: Research Press, 1975.

Haughton, E. Aims growing and sharing. In J. Jordan and L. Robbins (Eds), *Let's try doing something else kind of thing: behavioral principals and the exceptional child.* Reston, Virginia: The Council for Exceptional Children, 1972.

Jones, R. J. and Azrin, N. H. Behavioral engineering: stuttering as a function of stimulus duration during speech synchronization. *Journal of Applied Behavior Analysis,* 1969, **2,** 223-229.

Kazdin, A. E. Assessing the clinical or applied importance of behavior change through social validation. *Behavior Modification,* 1977, **1,** 427-452.

Kent, R. N. and O'Leary, K. D. A controlled evaluation of behavior modification with conduct problem children. *Journal of Consulting and Clinical Psychology,* 1976, **44,** 586-596.

Maloney, D. M., Harper, T. M., Braukmann, C. J., Fixsen, D. L., Phillips, E. L., and Wolf, M. M. Teaching conversation-related skills to pre-delinquent girls. *Journal of Applied Behavior Analysis,* 1976, **9,** 371.

Maloney, K. B. and Hopkins, B. L. The modification of sentence-structure and its relationship to subjective judgments of creativity in writing. *Journal of Applied Behavior Analysis,* 1973, **6,** 425-433.

Maloney, K. B., Jacobson, C. R., and Hopkins, B. L. An analysis of the effects of lectures, requests, teacher praise, and free time on the creative writing behaviors of third-grade children. In E. Ramp and G. Semb (Eds), *Behavior analysis: Areas of research and application.* Englewood Cliffs, New Jersey: Prentice-Hall, 1975.

McAllister, L. W., Stachowiak, J. G., Baer, D. M., and Conderman, L. The application of operant conditioning techniques in a secondary school classroom. *Journal of Applied Behavior Analysis,* 1969, **2,** 227-285.

McFall, R. M. Behavioral training: A skill acquisition approach to clinical problems. In J. T. Spence, R. C. Carson, and J. W. Thibaut (Eds), *Behavioral approaches to therapy.* Morristown, New Jersey: General Learning Press, 1976.

Nelson, R. O. and Bowles, P. E. The best of two worlds-observation with norms. *Journal of School Psychology,* 1975, **13,** 3-9.

Patterson, G. Interventions for boys with conduct problems: multiple settings, treatments and criteria. *Journal of Consulting and Clinical Psychology,* 1974, **42,** 471-481.

Porterfield, J. K., Herbert-Jackson, E., and Risley, T. R. Contingent observation: an effective and acceptable procedure for reducing disruptive behavior of young children in a group setting. *Journal of Applied Behavior Analysis,* 1976, **9,** 55-64.

Thomas, J. D., Presland, I. E., Grant, M. D., and Glynn, T. L. Natural rate of teacher approval and disapproval in grade-7 classrooms. *Journal of Applied Behavior Analysis,* 1978, **11,** 91-94.

Van Houten, R. *Learning through feedback.* New York: Human Sciences Press, *in press.* (*a*)

Van Houten, R. The performance feedback system: Generalization of effects across time. *Child Behavior Therapy, in press.* (*b*)

Van Houten, R., Morrison, E., Jarvis, R., and McDonald, M. The effects of explicit timing and feedback on compositional response rate in elementary school children. *Journal of Applied Behavior Analysis,* 1974, **7,** 547-555.

Walker, H. M. and Hops, H. Use of normative peer data as a standard for evaluating classroom treatment effects. *Journal of Applied Behavior Analysis,* 1976, **9,** 159-168.

Warren, S. F., Rogers-Warren, A., and Baer, D. M. The role of offer rates in controlling sharing by young children. *Journal of Applied Behavior Analysis,* 1976, **9,** 491-497.

White, M. A. Natural rates of teacher approval and disapproval in the classroom. *Journal of Applied Behavior Analysis,* 1975, **8,** 367-372.

Willner, A. G., Braukmann, C. J., Kirigin, K. A., Fixsen, D. L., Phillips, E. L., and Wolf, M. M. The training and validation of youth-preferred social behaviors with child-care personnel. *Journal of Applied Behavior Analysis,* 1977, **10,** 219-230.

Wolf, M. M. Social validity: the case for subjective measurement or how applied behavior analysis is finding its heart. *Journal of Applied Behavior Analysis,* 1978, **11,** 203-214.

Received 31 July 1978.
(*Final Acceptance 20 July 1979.*)

JOURNAL OF APPLIED BEHAVIOR ANALYSIS 1991, 24, 189–204 NUMBER 2 (SUMMER 1991)

SOCIAL VALIDITY ASSESSMENTS: IS CURRENT PRACTICE STATE OF THE ART?

ILENE S. SCHWARTZ AND DONALD M. BAER
UNIVERSITY OF KANSAS

The use of evaluative feedback from consumers to guide program planning and evaluation is often referred to as the assessment of social validity. Differing views of its role and value in applied behavior analysis have emerged, and increasingly stereotyped assessments of social validity are becoming commonplace. This paper argues that current applications of social validity assessments are straying from the point originally proposed for them. Thus, several suggestions for improving current social validity assessment are proposed, including (a) expanding the definition of consumers to acknowledge the variety of community members able and likely to affect a program's survival, (b) increasing the psychometric rigor of social validity assessments, (c) extending assessment to heretofore underrepresented populations, (d) implementing widespread application of well-designed social validity assessments, (e) increasing meaningful consumer involvement in the planning and evaluation of behavioral programs, and (f) educating consumers to make better informed programming decisions.

DESCRIPTORS: social validation, assessment, methodology, dissemination

---

In 1978, Wolf formally introduced the issue of social validity to the field of applied behavior analysis. Essentially, he noted how rarely the consumers of behavior-analytic programs had been queried about their acceptance of a program's procedures, goals, and personnel; he warned from experience that nonacceptance could precede disastrous consumer rejection of the programs; and he recommended careful future assessment of consumer satisfaction from that point of view (Wolf, 1978). Applied behavior analysis has progressed extensively since 1978 and, indeed, social validity has often been of paramount interest to scholars tracing the field's history and predicting its future.

Opinion about the contribution of social validity to the discipline, however, is far from unanimous. Social validity has been heralded by some as an important guide for the future of the field (e.g., Baer, Wolf, & Risley, 1987) and denounced by others as a detraction from the scientific nature of our research practice (e.g., Barrett, 1987). Despite these differences, social validity measures are becoming almost commonplace in the behavioral literature.

This paper discusses the current practice of social validity assessment, proposes elements that should be included in any state-of-the-art procedure for assessing social validity, offers a propaedeutic taxonomy of consumers to guide the construction and circulation of these assessments, and suggests strategies that may help shape current practice to produce more accurate assessments of the behaviors associated with social validity.

WHAT IS SOCIAL VALIDITY?

The purpose of social validity assessments is to evaluate the acceptability or viability of a programmed intervention. Most often, social validity assessment is accomplished by asking people other than the program planners or experimenters to complete some type of questionnaire (Kazdin, 1977; Wolf, 1978). The point of these assessments is to anticipate rejection of a program before that happens; therefore, the assessments should involve all

Preparation of this article was supported in part by grants from the U.S. Department of Education (HO24J80003) and the National Institute of Child Health and Human Development (HD03144).

Appreciation is extended to Julie Cross Hoko and Mary Todd for their assistance in preparation of this manuscript, and to Susan A. Fowler, Kathryn K. Ramp, Montrose M. Wolf, Edward K. Morris, and Deborah Altus for their helpful comments on earlier versions of this paper. Requests for reprints should be addressed to Ilene S. Schwartz, Juniper Gardens Children's Project, 1614 Washington Blvd., Kansas City, Kansas 66102, or to Donald M. Baer, Department of Human Development, University of Kansas, Lawrence, Kansas 66045.

relevant consumers of the program. The consumers should be queried about the acceptability of the program goals, methods, personnel, outcomes, and ease of integration of program components into the consumers' current life-style. Then, this information should be used immediately, as well as in future program planning, implementation, and evaluation. Thus, social validity assessments are not meant to be, and indeed are not, primary dependent measures; logically, they can only supplement the objective measures of behavior that are the primary dependent measures (cf. Barrett, 1987; Dietz, 1978; Michael, 1980; Pierce & Epling, 1980; Scheirer, 1978).

Social validity assessment is ideally a two-part process: first an accurate and representative sample of the consumers' opinions is collected; then that information is used to sustain satisfactory practices or effect changes in the program to enhance its viability in the community. Failure to implement either part of this process undermines the social validity concept, and often will also discredit the social validity assessment. A useful social validity assessment should not (a) assess the opinions of a limited (or the wrong) community, (b) incorrectly assess the opinions of the relevant community, or (c) assess the opinions of the relevant community correctly, but not use that information to change the program and/or its consumers' opinion about it. In short, it is as inappropriate to sample criticism and praise and not respond to it as it is to respond to it without investigating its sources and its correlates (i.e., its accuracy).

Canvassing consumers for feedback on proposed and ongoing programs may establish closer ties between the community and the program; this may give a program's audience a sense of shared control, which in turn may circumvent complaints and program attrition (Baer et al., 1987; Giordano, 1977; Lebow, 1982). It is vital, though, to make this input functional by incorporating the feedback in future programming and telling consumers how the feedback process works (Wartel, Maloney, & Blase, 1981). Repeatedly soliciting feedback without explaining how it will be used, and without implementing any of the suggestions, may teach consumers that their feedback is not useful and the solicitors are deceptive. This may invalidate future attempts to assess social validity and in turn threaten program viability (i.e., consumers' program participation and adoption).

What is Social Invalidity?

Social invalidity is not simply the absence of positive evaluations by the consumers and relevant community when they are asked; it is not simply the failure to ask; it is not simply asking and then ignoring what you hear; and it is not simply the inverse of social validity. Baer (1987) described social invalidity as the behaviors of consumers who not only disapprove of some component in the ongoing program but are going to do something about their disapproval. That something may include withdrawing from the program, encouraging others to do the same, complaining to community officials and the media, or, more subtly, not implementing some or all of the program's procedures after the program consultant leaves, despite positive responses on questionnaires.

Discontented consumers are not members of a homogeneous group; there is great variation in the causes and displays of discontent (Aaker & Day, 1971). That is, some will do something more about their displeasure, some will not; and, of those who do something more, their demonstrations of disapproval can vary widely. Therefore, cases of social invalidity should be evaluated individually to trace the source to specific program or environmental variables and to explore what will happen next, if anything, if the program is changed in response to that feedback and also if it is not.

Social invalidity is difficult to predict from the results of typical social validity assessments. The most consistent finding across reviews of the consumer satisfaction literature in mental health services, medical services, and behavior therapy is that consumers generally rate treatment programs in an overall positive manner (Bornstein & Rychtarik, 1983; Fuqua & Schwade, 1986; Lebow, 1982; McMahon & Forehand, 1983; Ware, Davies-Avery, & Stewart, 1978). Consumers, even when given the opportunity to complain, seem acquiescent, especially with medical and mental health services (Lebow, 1982; Ware, 1978). Yet, common experience suggests that despite positive ratings, some of those programs are rejected. Some are rejected crudely, and many more subtly, especially in the form of discontinuing program procedures when program personnel leave the scene. Thus, that verbal acquiescence was less than accurate and, hence, less than valid; calling it social validity is frivolous, and relying on it handicaps the prediction of social invalidity.

The prediction of social validity and invalidity requires assessments that evoke truthful reporting of what consumers like and dislike about a program. The first goal of social validity assessments should be to gather accurate and useful information about possible trouble, not to encourage false praise from consumers. Discontented consumers should be urged to complain, and complain early, to key program personnel. Indeed, it may be that consumers who make their complaints public are often more satisfied with the resolution of the problem than consumers who complain privately or not at all (Bearden & Oliver, 1985). Positive responses to social validity assessments do reinforce the program personnel and sometimes please or appease regulatory or funding agencies, but if they do so at the cost of leaving silent a discontented consumer, the initial reinforcement implicit in noncomplaining consumers may be replaced with the punishment of program failure (Bornstein & Rychtarik, 1983).

What Social Validity and Invalidity Are Not

The variety of meanings attributed to social validity has burgeoned beyond usefulness and into confusion. Its original meaning was, and still is, simple: When applying programs in real-life settings, assess early how acceptable those programs will be to their relevant audience. Social validity assessment is a defensive technique. It is oriented toward detecting unacceptability in any of the three major sources—the program's goals, its methods, and its personnel.

But almost immediately after the introduction of this concept, quite different applications of social validity assessments emerged, and in recent years, their variety has flourished. The fear that behavior analysts would substitute the obviously subjective social validity measures for the obviously objective measures of program outcome is one of the oldest criticisms of this methodology. But, this was never intended to be a purpose of social validity assessments. In fact, social validity assessments were always proposed on the assumption that a behavioral program had target behaviors other than statements of liking or disliking the program's goals, procedures, and personnel. It was always supposed that those target behaviors would be measured as directly, behaviorally, objectively, and reliably as possible, and that social validity would be assessed as an important second issue, one relevant not to the program's effectiveness but to its viability (cf. Kazdin, 1977; Wolf, 1978).

Yet, ironically, an implicit contingency to produce positive measures of social validity, as if they were target behaviors, apparently did arise almost immediately. Program developers seemed to assume that an important criterion for publication of their program was a positive social validity assessment. It is not clear what this imputed contingency may have done to the accuracy of those social validity assessment attempts. Of course, a program that accomplishes its goals thoroughly and cost effectively, and is also liked by its consumers, is indeed the ultimate goal of applied behavior analysis. However, the point of social validity assessment is to identify, from all the programs accomplishing their target behaviors thoroughly and cost effectively and also from all the programs not that successful, which ones are liked by their consumers less than others. The dual points of social validity assessment are:

1. It is important to the advancement and survival of applied behavior analysis to know in advance which programs are liked and which are disliked, and thus publication of negative social validity assessments is certainly as valuable and important as publication of positive ones; and

2. It is important to begin the analysis of *why* some programs are liked and others disliked, so eventually social validity assessment can become a

calculated prediction rather than an empirically assessed early warning or endorsement. Without publication of a rich sample of the negative instances to compare with the positive ones, this second goal is not likely to be achieved.

If the experience of behavior analysis is indeed that all its programs seem socially valid, which is what could be concluded from its literature so far, then almost certainly social validity is often being assessed in a spurious manner. Applied behavior analysis simply cannot be that good. It is more likely that current techniques of assessing social validity are too often themselves socially and psychometrically invalid. They are implicitly demanding their consumers to answer their short, simple, bland, undemanding 7-point scales positively. We are encouraging consumers to "fake good," in the terminology of the test-development researchers who have been plagued by similar problems for at least five decades.

In a recent ABA panel discussion of current uses of social validity assessments, Cataldo (personal communication, May 1990) noted a quite similar contingency: The need to rebut for program sponsors, funders, and any other attentive audience the often-heard criticism that behavior-analytic programs are disliked by modern consumers. Indeed, both the media and our conceptual competitors often suggest that behavioral programs are not congruent with the contemporary Zeitgeist of mentalism, personal autonomy, and the need to analyze every social problem to find its origin in the failings of its clients. Confronted by such a need, positive social validity assessments may well seem to be a useful defense. But, as in the prior case, the nature of that contingency is to reinforce positive assessments and punish negative ones and thereby degrade the accuracy of those social validity techniques. Thus, it is a contingency destructive to the original function of yielding early warnings of program rejection by the program's consumers.

In the same ABA panel discussion, Geller (personal communication, May 1990) suggested that social validity assessments are sometimes seen now as techniques for discovering the new, important social goals that behavior-analytic (and other) programs ought to target and for reaffirming the social importance of certain past goals not yet achieved on a societal scale. If social validity assessments are indeed to be used for this purpose, two problems will arise immediately:

1. If the point of social validity assessments is to detect program rejection (by those capable of it and likely to), then sampling should be aimed at representing just those populations. So far that is a relatively easy and inexpensive thing to do in our current small scale of research and application. But, if social importance is the point, then any concept of social importance deriving from the wishes of the society itself will require a random sample of the society as a whole, and this is an extraordinarily difficult and expensive thing to do.

2. However, many concepts of social importance are orthogonal to, and sometimes antithetical to, the momentary wishes of the society as a whole. The true liberation of women and the functional equality of racial, ethnic, and religious minorities are examples of program goals that would have shown little social validity when they began and still show less than unanimous support. Yet, who could now declare them socially unimportant goals? Thus, social importance tends to be, and perhaps always ought to be, resolved by the usual political process of a democratic or even partially democratic society, rather than by anything akin to social validity assessments.

Assessing Social Validity

Identifying Program Consumers

What to ask your audience, who constitutes your audience, and how to assess your audience reliably are key questions in social validity assessments. Reviews of this literature show general agreement on the questions to be asked; however, the questions of who should be asked and how to ask them are not so clear (e.g., Fuqua & Schwade, 1986; McMahon & Forehand, 1983). Three types of questions to ask were summarized succinctly by Wolf (1978):

1. Are the goals of the procedures important and relevant to the desired life-style changes?

2. Are the techniques used acceptable to the consumers and the community, or do they cost too much (e.g., in terms of effort, time, discomfort, ethics, or the like)?

3. Are the consumers satisfied with the outcome, both with the predicted behavior change and with any unpredicted side effects?

Once the questions to assess social validity are chosen, the more difficult issue arises: whom to ask? There is general consensus that the "consumers of the program" should be asked (Bornstein & Rychtarik, 1983; Kazdin, 1977; Larsen, Attkisson, Hargreaves, & Nguyen, 1979; Lebow, 1982; Wolf, 1978). The problem, however, lies in identifying these consumers, especially the consumers who control the viability, either directly or indirectly, of the program. Currently, the consumers most often are simply the recipients of the program. But it could well be true that the persons or agencies who hired the program and certain members of the larger community are also consumers, especially if the criterion is control of the program's viability. For example, the next-door neighbors of a group home program for adults with developmental disabilities become its audience, and they can complain to the larger community if they do not like it. The spouses of factory workers can be a supportive audience of a factory safety program, if they like it, or can be destructive critics of the procedure if they do not. The peers of an aggressive or socially withdrawn child can become part of a program to change the child's behaviors or can sabotage it as soon as the program personnel are absent. Are not taxpayers consumers of all programs supported by public funding?

The key characteristics of these examples are that many people other than the program recipients are passive consumers of treatment programs, and if they decide to become active consumers they can be supportive or critical of the program. We have at present almost no analysis of what turns nonrecipients into active consumers and what makes these consumers program supporters or critics.

In the business world, a consumer is anyone who purchases goods or services or causes them to be purchased (Engel, Kollat, & Blackwell, 1973; Troelstrup, 1974). The breadth of this definition is appropriate to both business and the application of behavioral programs, but the terms *consumer* and *purchase* need more development before they can contribute to the increased accuracy of social validity assessments. For this purpose, it may be helpful to categorize consumers as direct consumers, indirect consumers, members of the immediate community, and members of the extended community. Membership might be determined by the following criteria:

Direct consumers. Direct consumers are the primary recipients of the program intervention. They may have purchased or "hired" the program or may have been referred by someone else. (Thus, a child with developmental disabilities is often the direct consumer, yet rarely "hires" the program.) These consumers can affect program viability directly and at any moment, by participating or by selective or generalized refusals to participate. Examples of direct consumers include parents in a parent-training program, peer monitors and point-earners in a peer-monitoring classroom program, motorists who are referred to a driver-safety program due to their record of traffic violations, and customers in a restaurant participating in a program to increase consumers' selection of low-fat entrees.

Indirect consumers. Indirect consumers purchase or hire the program for someone else or are strongly affected by the behavior change targeted in the intervention, but they are not its recipients. Indirect consumers may directly affect program viability through continuing to purchase more of it, or refusing to do so, and indirectly affect it by behaving as satisfied customers, spouses, or friends of the direct consumers and thus as an advertisement for the program. Examples of indirect consumers include the parents of a child with developmental disabilities who learns to dress independently, the administrators of a company that commissions a program to improve safety conditions in a factory, and the family members of participants in a home-weatherization program.

Members of the immediate community. The immediate community are those people who interact with the direct and indirect consumers on a regular basis, usually through close proximity during work, school, or social situations. These consumers can affect program viability indirectly, through interaction (or lack of interaction) with the direct and indirect consumers. Examples of members of the immediate community include neighbors of a group home for juvenile offenders, the regular bus driver on the route used by adults with developmental disabilities, and children who occasionally play at the same playground as a child whose severe aggressive behavior was targeted for treatment.

Members of the extended community. The extended community includes those people who probably do not know or interact with the direct and indirect consumers but who live in the same community. Examples include newspaper editors who may find treatment programs newsworthy as either human interest or bad social policy and their swayed or angry readers; supermarket cashiers who may find adults with developmental disabilities using newly acquired shopping skills either heartwarming or troublesome; taxpayers who may protest paying for a program or demand more of it and less of another; Mothers Against Drunk Driving and similar organizations; and legislators and bureaucrats who may regulate the program into or out of existence.

The following example was designed to illustrate these abstract classes of consumers, their roles as purchasers, and the interrelationships among the different roles:

An insurance company contacts one of its clients, the owners of an open-pit mining company, and tells them that unless they implement a safety program for their employees in the mine and document a decrease in the rate of industrial accidents, their insurance rates will quadruple and their policy may be canceled. The mine owners respond by contracting with safety consultants to implement and document an ongoing safety program for the miners (see Fox, Hopkins, & Anger, 1987). The direct consumers are the employees who work at the mine, including miners, janitors, and clerical staff. These consumers, however, did not purchase the program. The program purchasers are the mine owners; therefore, the mine owners are one group of indirect consumers. Another group of indirect consumers consists of the families and friends of the direct consumers who benefit indirectly from the increased safety of their loved ones and breadwinners and may also benefit from any incentive system the safety program uses. The insurance company, although it provided the impetus for the program, is neither a direct nor an indirect consumer. It is a member of the immediate community; it is affected only monetarily by the outcome of the program and may have no other involvement with the program or its participants. The extended community includes taxpayers, who may benefit from fewer workers collecting disability payments, and the merchants who benefit from workers spending both their extra pay and their cash incentives for following the safety guidelines.

This example of consumer classes, despite their somewhat indefinite membership, provides a logic of determining whom to include when assessing social validity. Simply recognizing the existence of different groups of consumers and their possible stakes in program outcomes shows that program adoption or program rejection cannot be predicted safely from a restricted sample of only direct consumers (cf. Mathews & Fawcett, 1979). In this case, the immediate and extended community represent consumers who can truly control program survival, and this case is not unrepresentative.

Conducting Social Validity Assessments

Once the questions of whom and what to ask in a social validity assessment are decided, the next difficult question is how to collect information in a valid, reliable, and cost-efficient manner. This question poses special problems for behavior analysts. Most social validity assessments rely on the use of interviews, questionnaires, or surveys administered by the experimenter (e.g., Fuqua & Schwade, 1986; McMahon & Forehand, 1983; Schwartz, 1991). The subjective nature of this type of information, paired with the possible confounding variables of social contingencies provided by the experimenter (often referred to in other disciplines as "demand characteristics"), often make these data difficult to interpret (see Azrin, Holz, & Goldiamond, 1961, for an empirical case in point).

Subjective data can be of value to behavior analysis. Skinner (1953, 1963) acknowledged the importance of private behavior in the study of human behavior; indeed, he differentiated public and private behaviors by their accessibility to observation, not by the extent to which they are lawful phenomena. Even so, any predictable or uniform labeling of feelings is unlikely. For example, many social validity assessments ask respondents to answer questions by describing (e.g., on a 7-point scale) how satisfied they are. "Satisfaction" describes a state controlled by a vast range of different stimulus conditions for different people. For some individuals, "satisfied" may be an average rating, for others it may be extraordinary. The challenge, as Skinner noted long ago, is to seek the public accompaniments of private behavior.

Answers on social validity questionnaires are certainly public; the question becomes one of determining when they are early accompaniments of the behaviors that truly determine program viability and when are they the false positives that may endanger it. Some methods to assess social validity have emerged that cite a wider range of observable behavior but ask the same types of questions as the more commonly used subjective measures. These techniques include (a) use of operationally defined affect rating scales to assess a child's "emotional" behavior while engaged in the target intervention (e.g., Dunlap, 1984; Dunlap & Koegel, 1980), (b) allowing consumers to choose the intervention after being exposed to two or more interventions designed to address the same target behavior (e.g., Harris, 1986), (c) experimentally assessing different rates of the target behavior in the natural environment to determine the optimal rate and using this information to determine the goal of intervention (e.g., Jones & Azrin, 1969; Warren, Rogers-Warren, & Baer, 1976), (d) asking competent performers of the target behavior to judge the adequacy of permanent-product examples produced by the direct consumers of the intervention (e.g., Schepis, Reid, & Fitzgerald, 1987), and (e) asking peer and expert judges to compare photographed or videotaped pre- and postintervention behavior samples (e.g., Friman & Hove, 1987).

Although these procedures encourage applied behavior analysts to use social validity measures that rely on wider sampling of observable and probably relevant behaviors, they represent the minority of procedures used. Sound social validity assessment consists of asking the right questions, to the right people, in an appropriate manner. Before attempting to chart a course for future directions in the area of social validity assessment, we should assess the current practices of the field. We should know (a) who is assessing social validity; (b) who, what, and how they are asking; and (c) what they are doing with the information. Schwartz (1991) attempted to answer these questions in a review of the frequency and variety of social validity assessments reported in one year's output of seven behavioral journals. She found that 29% of the 139 articles reviewed reported some form of social validity assessment (but note that in *JABA* 41% of the 34 articles reported some measure of social validity). However, these articles used inconsistent methods to collect their social validity data and inconsistent conceptual language to describe them. Although an encouraging number of interesting and innovative methods to assess social validity were reported, most of the studies questioned only the direct or indirect consumers and relied solely on the use of questionnaire data to assess social validity.

Future Directions

These results suggest three future directions for improving social validity assessments: (a) More researchers and practitioners should conduct and respond to social validity assessments and begin reporting the apparent results of doing so, negative as well as positive, even if only as anecdotes; (b) a greater breadth of consumers and community members should be sampled, and again the apparent results of doing so should be reported, even if only as anecdotes; and (c) research should target the discovery of more objective, more reliable precursors of social invalidity than are available at present—perhaps at first by scanning those emerging anecdotes for interesting commonalities.

Each of these areas will be discussed individually, even though improvements in each area may well affect the others, and even though improvements in either of the first two will probably not substantially reduce the present risk of proceeding inappropriately. For example, if researchers currently reporting social validity assessments found more reliable ways to predict social validity and social invalidity, applied behavior analysis would be a better discipline for the knowledge, but only a small proportion of current programs would benefit. On the other hand, if all behavioral researchers began to use the current assessments of unknown validity, the field would be no closer to its goal of solving important problems with effective *and* socially acceptable methods.

Increasing Reports of Social Validity

The first problem is the current rate of using social validity assessments. Is there a case for making social validity assessments as routine in program application and evaluation as measurement reliability assessment is in our current research practices? We believe there is. The results of research programs are not considered credible or replicable without assessing the reliability and validity of their measurement procedures. In the case of application programs, it is not the credibility of their outcomes but the programs themselves that are at risk when they proceed without a reliable assessment of social validity. Perhaps it is just that shift in where to look for validity and reliability that accounts for present consistent attention to measurement reliability and minimal attention to social validity. So far, most of the field's practitioners who report in journals were trained as researchers rather than as practitioners; most of them learned application on the job. If most of their applications have survived so far, at least as long as they were directly involved, they may not even question the viability of their programs. Thus, neither their professional socialization nor their current experience has consistently punished an absence of social validity assessments—at least not with the same vigor as any absence of measurement reliability was punished.

We may solve this disparity by waiting for the inevitabilities of the future, or, perhaps, we may use verbal behavior now to change enough professional behavior to avoid some of them. One technique that may facilitate this change in our professional behavior is to establish criteria for conducting and reporting social validity measures that must be met for publication in behavioral journals. These criteria exist for other methodological issues; perhaps it is time to extend them to social validity assessment.

The field of applied behavior analysis has done much toward demonstrating the lawfulness of human behavior and developing a technology for behavior change. It has been considerably less successful in marketing and disseminating itself and its technology (e.g., Geller, 1989, 1990; Morris, 1985; Pennypacker, 1986; Seekins & Fawcett, 1984). It is at least possible that the widespread use of *accurate* social validity assessments would improve some of that condition, if only by showing program consumers that behaviorists care about what they think rather than about controlling their thoughts (as suggested by the opposition).

Perhaps social validity assessments will become standard procedure when practitioners and researchers stop using social validity assessments as nothing more than compliance with the law (Community Mental Health Centers Amendment, PL 94-63) and as an inexpensive method of assuaging the concerns of vocal program participants and community members. However, the problem may prove to be remarkably similar to that of many health-education programs: Students learn what is taught about preserving or maintaining their health but do not begin to practice what they have learned until they have seen enough peers suffer the consequences of not doing so. Unfortunately for that analysis, program invalidity and its subsequent disasters are rarely reported as journal, convention, or media reports, and so program developers learn about them, and their rates, only through chance anecdotes. Would a program obituary column in every issue of every relevant journal prove salutary?

Even accurate social validity assessments will be of little use to program viability unless they are conducted prescriptively rather than remedially. The social validity of program goals, methods, and anticipated outcomes needs to be known prior to the beginning of the program, and should be assessed periodically throughout implementation. However, if consumers are asked to complete frequent satisfaction questionnaires, doing so had better benefit the consumer in tangible ways: Either any disliked components should be made better, or an excellent and credible reason for not following consumer recommendations should be offered. Otherwise the consumer learns that the social validity assessments are not only useless but in fact are in some sense fraudulent, and thereby the assessment procedure becomes one more element in the program's social invalidity. The evaluation component of the Teaching-Family Model offers an excellent example of the positive side of that relation: It includes an ongoing consumer evaluation system that is steadily responsive to consumers, either with changes or explanations (Blase, Fixsen, & Phillips, 1984; Phillips, Phillips, Fixsen, & Wolf, 1972; Warfel et al., 1981).

Expanding Consumer Participation

Just as it may be difficult to encourage practitioners to conduct social validity assessments more frequently, it may also be difficult to move program developers to sample their consumers more broadly. The extended community has rarely been represented in social validity assessments, and when they have been included they are most likely asked about the acceptability of program objectives, although they are likely to have equally strong interests in the program's methods and outcomes (Schwartz, 1991). Applied behavior analysts, who are usually not in direct control of the viability of their programs, can hardly be considered *applied* without soliciting and using community feedback (Baer, Wolf, & Risley, 1968).

Some researchers are already meeting this challenge. The Teaching-Family Model offers an example for conducting consumer-satisfaction interviews with people with developmental disabilities (Strouse, 1988). Fawcett and his colleagues (e.g., Seekins, Fawcett, & Mathews, 1987; Seekins, Mathews, & Fawcett, 1984; Whang, Fawcett, & Mathews, 1984) validated community-based interventions with panels of experts from the community. For example, the judges of a leadership-training program were two political scientists, an organizational development consultant, an urban planner, and a communications consultant (Seekins et al., 1984); the judges for a job-related social-skills training program were local business people (Whang et al., 1984); and judges of a program teaching consumer-advocacy skills were a local politician and a public administrator (Seekins et al., 1987).

As behavior analysts begin to include a broader spectrum of consumers in social validity assessments, the issue of differentially weighting feedback from various groups of consumers, especially when that feedback is conflicting, must be addressed. The purpose of social validity assessments is to provide information to help ensure program survival. Therefore, the information from consumers most directly related to program viability should be given the most weight. The question of what group of consumers most directly affects program viability is empirical; however, the data necessary to answer these questions are not yet available. So, behavior analysts should begin to collect these data by including members of all four classes of consumers (i.e., direct, indirect, members of the immediate community, and members of the extended community) in social validity assessments and by relating consumer satisfaction and dissatisfaction in each group to program longevity.

The Accuracy of Social Validity Assessments

The accuracy of social validity assessments is the core issue for future work. Social validity is intrinsically an adjunctive measure; its function is not to evaluate program effectiveness but program acceptability and viability. Similarly, its purpose is not to compare programs but to safeguard programs against rejection or sabotage. Rather than attempting to compare the acceptability of programs or program components, perhaps we should review the assessed components of programs and compile a menu of elements of different programs rated favorably by consumers and a parallel menu of those rated unfavorably. Then we can examine these program components to determine whether they have anything in common that would explain their similar ratings, despite the dissimilarity of the programs in which they operated. It is the similarities in the highly regarded program components (and in the unfavorably rated ones) that may provide answers of how to provide acceptable and effective behavior-change interventions.

Improved construction of social validity assessments is an important goal for applied behavior analysis. Researchers should consider basic rules of test construction and statistics when developing social validity assessments (Baer, 1987). Questionnaires about program acceptability should (a) use scales that invite a workably wide variation in consumers' responses (e.g., a 7-point rather than a 3-point scale), (b) require differential responding by the consumer (i.e., they should require even the most satisfied consumer to use the entire range of the rating scale) (Cone, 1981), (c) specify the period of time being rated (e.g., ask consumers to rate only the services provided during the last 3 months, rather than all services) (McMahon, 1984), (d) address all the dimensions pertinent to the acceptability and viability of a program (e.g., if you are interested in the consumers' opinions about observers in the classroom, ask directly), and (e) be as specific as possible, because increased specificity may increase the usefulness of information collected from social validity questionnaires (Mash & Terdal, 1981).

If, in addition, more objective techniques for assessing social validity are developed, these assessments might well prove even more useful. Four classes of techniques could be expanded to assess social validity more functionally: (a) proof that a program's goals and outcomes are themselves valid, (b) unobtrusive measurement, (c) identification and measurement of the behavioral precursors of the kinds of satisfaction and dissatisfaction culminating in program rejection, and (d) providing the consumers with experiences with different program options, then allowing them to choose the most satisfactory option.

Goals and outcomes. Asking about a program's goals and outcomes is the most frequently assessed form of social validity (Schwartz, 1991). Van Houten (1979) suggested that the behavior of normal models and competent performers be used to help identify target behaviors and determine the standards of competent performance. Identifying competent performers, however, invokes difficult ethical issues. For example, who are the competent models for people living in a state institution? Should we set community standards for these consumers, because we assume they will get there, or do we pose lower standards appropriate to their present environment, because we assume they are staying? If the former, then future-environment surveys (Anderson & Schwartz, 1986; Fowler, 1982) can answer these questions. These surveys identify the clients' next environment and set behavioral goals to levels appropriate to the subsequent setting. This technique can ease clients' transitions across programs (e.g., from a residential facility to living at home, or from a specialized preschool to regular kindergarten).

The behavior of community members can be used as models to set intervention goals. Junior high school and college students can model the appropriate levels of conversational skills to teach delinquent and predelinquent teenagers (Minkin et al., 1976). Normal peers in preschool classrooms can be observed to determine desirable within-classroom transition skills and rates of verbal interaction (Osnes, Guevremont, & Stokes, 1986; Sainato, Strain, Lefebvre, & Rapp, 1987). Judges can score the fluency, "naturalness," and speech rates of college students treated for stuttering (Jones & Azrin, 1969). The optimum rate for preschoolers to make share offers to peers is taken to be the rate most often accepted by those peers; the peers become the experts simply by consistently responding more often to some rates than to others (Kohler & Fowler, 1985; Warren et al., 1976). Teachers and peers can rate the social status of their students or friends and then identify target skills for those rated lowest. Subsequent to the establishment of those skills, teachers or peers can rate the students or friends again, to see if those skills were indeed crucial to improving their status with those judges (Hoier & Cone, 1987; Plienis et al., 1987).

When selecting community members to serve as experts, however, we need to demonstrate that they are in fact appropriate experts for the target intervention (Greenwood, 1990). Community membership alone does not qualify someone to serve as a model for appropriate behavior or to judge the outcome of an intervention. In general, the original complainer or buyer (i.e., the indirect consumer who hired the program) can validate the goals and the behavioral targets as almost no one else can, especially if that person is the only complainer (Baer, 1986). If it is their complaint that defines the problem, then the program applied has social validity if their complaint is satisfied by it—they are the "community" defining validity for this problem. If, however, the problem is defined by a larger community, we must identify representative and appropriate members of that community to assist in assessing the social validity of the proposed solution.

Unobtrusive measurement. Obtrusive measurement is often its own threat to social validity, because so many people dislike having their behavior rated. Thus, the development of unobtrusive measures can occasionally be crucial to the social validity of a program acceptable in every other dimension. Unobtrusive measurement occurs when the subject is unaware of ongoing observations or target behavior (Kazdin, 1979). However, this type of measurement rarely is ethical and often is illegal (American Psychological Association, 1979). And when it is ethical and legal, it often generates some logistic issues of how to do it, especially outside of laboratory settings. Still, some forms of unobtrusive measurement can escape these handicaps: for example, the use of archival records. Documents can be searched to retrieve data on rates of recidivism, complaints (see Baer, 1988), industrial accidents, energy consumption (Winett, Neale, & Grier, 1979), and the like. It is important to remember, however, that although data from archival sources escape many difficulties in the realm of social validity, their validity as outcome data is often doubtful. For example, reduced recidivism of juvenile offenders may reflect increased criminal skill, decreased police behavior, changed judicial standards, or overloaded record-keeping instead of decreased criminal activity (Kazdin, 1979). Similarly, increased recidivism by children with autism in residential treatment facilities may reflect a breakdown in family systems rather than a lack of generalization and maintenance of children's behavioral gains (Anderson, Christian, & Luce, 1986).

Behavioral correlates of satisfaction. The most basic technique crucial to accurate social validity assessments, however, remains the identification and measurement of observable behaviors that correlate with program satisfaction or rejection. The behaviors that clearly show support for a program include continued participation in it, regular attendance and prompt arrival for program sessions, recommending it to friends, earning many of whatever points its incentive system may offer, defense of the program against attack by others, and pleasant affect and high enthusiasm during program sessions. The behaviors that clearly show the social invalidity of a program include withdrawal, demands that the program personnel leave (e.g., the program buyer "firing" the program), complaining to friends, officials, and the media, poor attendance and/or chronic tardiness at program sessions, refusal to participate or poor performance in whatever incentive system the program may offer, generalized or selective noncompliance with program routines, and negative affect and low enthusiasm during program sessions.

Many of these indices of social validity are relatively easy to measure and, in fact, may already be included in ongoing data collection systems. Their disadvantage, which can often outweigh their validity, is their lateness in emerging. By the time these signs of social validity or invalidity appear, especially in the case of social invalidity, it is often too late to respond adaptively to them.

Even so, these measures may have some utility

in programs for people with developmental disabilities, because many do not require much verbal ability, and people with disabilities often express their displeasure with a program quite early in its development, often in just these ways. Indeed, it is more often the developmentally able consumers who are burdened with a courtesy that keeps them from troubling program appliers with their complaints until those complaints are quite severe. For example, Koegel and his colleagues (e.g., Dunlap & Koegel, 1980; Koegel & Egel, 1979) have developed a reliable coding system for assessing affect and enthusiasm in children with autism. These overt measures of satisfaction are potentially relevant to measuring the social validity of programs serving people with severe developmental disabilities. Note again that this measurement system is an adjunctive measure, not an evaluation of program effectiveness.

A prerequisite for measuring behaviors correlated with program satisfaction or dissatisfaction is the identification of these behaviors. Researchers may be able to identify behavioral correlates of satisfaction by studying successful treatment programs (see Fuoco & Christian, 1986; Paine, Bellamy, & Wilcox, 1984, for descriptions of successful programs). Identifying correlates of dissatisfaction, especially early and perhaps predictive correlates, is more elusive. One reason may be that researchers do not disseminate information about program failures or dissatisfied consumers. Perhaps applied behavior analysts should act as epidemiologists and conduct careful post mortem analyses on unsuccessful programs. Prior to program implementation, behavior analysts conduct thorough need assessments, and throughout an intervention they systematically evaluate program effectiveness. This type of thorough assessment should be extended to dissatisfied consumers and program failures, and the results of these assessments should be disseminated through professional journals and conference presentations. Careful study of elements common to program failures may lead to more effective program planning and more sensitive social validity assessments.

Choice offering. The ultimate measure of a program's social validity is the range of alternatives a consumer will reject in order to choose the program. Choosing a program over a number of alternatives is the fundamental behavioral definition of preference, and what is more socially valid than that? Arranging such a measure of social validity, however, is simple only in logic: Give the consumers experience with two or more programs and let them choose. The probability of their later rejecting what they have chosen against a range of alternatives should be low, to the extent that the range is wide. However, as new alternatives to their current choice become available—as the range widens—the choice must be offered again to ensure the stability of their preference and the durability of the social validity assessed earlier.

The validity of choice is strong and the logic of choice is simple, but the implementation of choice is not. Valid choice requires that the consumer have extensive, nearly concurrent experience with all the alternatives, that all the alternatives are equally effective, and that all alternatives are easily available. Additionally, evaluators must carefully select the treatment options, so not to bias the assessment by offering the target program posed against much less desirable alternatives. Arranging those conditions will prove expensive in time, effort, resources, and sophistication, especially if the number of choices exceeds two. And although all of these barriers are formidable, time may be especially problematic. The function of social validity assessments is to provide an *early* warning of program rejection in any of its forms; thus, any measure requiring a great deal of time to be valid may be useless.

As a consequence, we are always tempted to search instead for quick, cheap, easy, and gracefully repetitive measures that will predict social validity or invalidity early, and our intrinsic problem is the suspicion that the quicker, cheaper, easier, earlier, and more graciously repetitive these measures are, the lower their correlation with the actual events that make up social validity and invalidity. In other words, easily and early-stated verbal preference and later, actual behavioral choices do not always correlate highly, even with nonimpaired adults (e.g., Lockhart, 1979), and perhaps especially with nonimpaired adults. Still, it may be worth recommending studies of the correlation between various forms of verbal preference, some of them much like the methods currently in use, to see if any of them correlate especially well with the very expensive choice techniques.

Offering choices, however, is not an impossible technique, especially if we do not insist on perfection in its execution. It has been used with college students to assess different teaching methods (Lockhart, 1979), among adults with severe mental retardation to assess task preference in vocational settings (Mithaug & Hanawalt, 1978; Mithaug & Mar, 1980), among students with learning disabilities to select preferred instructional strategies (Harris, 1986), and with students demonstrating high rates of self-stimulatory behavior to assess their preference for more appropriate forms of stimulation (Buyer, Berkson, Winnega, & Morton, 1987). So far, we have not learned that any of those less-than-perfect applications proved disastrously misleading.

Although the logic of choice as the most valid method of making social validity assessment is well developed (e.g., Fuqua & Schwade, 1986; McMahon & Forehand, 1983), methods for implementing choice in more natural settings need work to facilitate integration into program evaluations. Additionally, choice making is not an appropriate assessment technique with all programs. Not all programs permit side-by-side comparisons with alternative programs, but for selected programs this technique may be an efficient and objective technique to assess social validity.

Conclusions

The concept of assessing the social validity of behavioral programs, and then using these data in programmatic decisions, has been controversial since it was introduced (Wolf, 1978). Yet, rather than disappearing, social validity assessments are becoming more common in behavioral research and practice. Changes in the current practice of social validity assessment are needed, however, before these assessments can be used as accurate and reliable predictors of program success or failure. As behavior analysts, we require procedures relevant to behavior-change programs to be thoroughly specified and defined (Baer et al., 1968); we should judge techniques to assess social validity by the same criteria. Most current social validity assessment procedures do not meet those criteria fully enough to be considered a technological tool used to secure the maintenance of applied programs and advance the state of our science.

The procedures for conducting social validity assessments should include the following guidelines:

1. Social validity assessments should be a standard part of program application and applied research methodology. Inclusion of a thorough social validity assessment should be a minimum requirement, similar to assessment of interobserver reliability, in all applied behavioral research and practice.

2. Social validity assessments should be conducted prospectively and throughout an intervention, as well as at the end. Otherwise, consumers' concerns about the program cannot be answered in ways that defend the consumers, the program, and the discipline.

3. Applied behavior analysts need to recognize that there are more relevant and powerful consumers than they have identified and queried so far. Thus, a wider spectrum of consumers should be included in ongoing social validity assessment, with special consideration to consumers who control the viability of community programs. When consumers cannot respond to standard forms of social validity assessments (e.g., people with developmental disabilities), special techniques must be developed for them.

4. Social validity assessments, though not program-outcome measures, nevertheless deserve the same psychometric rigor as any behavioral measure. Rigor is not the same as standardization, but striving for valid and reliable measurement would probably lead to a more uniform methodology than characterizes the current practice of social validity assessment. Better attention to validity and reliability would make these measures better predictors of program acceptance or rejection.

5. If the fourth recommendation is to be achieved,

the field will require the development of some objective, clearly valid measures of social validity and social invalidity (i.e., program acceptance and rejection). It follows that we shall have to study actual program acceptance and rejection, painful as that will be, in order to know something about its truly reliable and valid antecedents. When we have identified valid and reliable precursors of program acceptance and rejection, we can then study how well these questionnaire techniques relate to them, or, more characteristic of us, how well they *can be made to* relate to them. Objective procedures to measure social validity (e.g., observations, reports of program adoption rates) will invariably be more expensive to conduct than the standard subjective measures (e.g., questionnaires). This expense, however, is minimized if viewed in the context of accurately predicting program viability.

6. Finally, applied behavior analysts should offer their consumers and relevant community members more education about the ongoing treatment programs, potential treatment programs, and other treatment options. This information will probably represent a mix of what we discover our consumers want to know and what we believe they need to know. This information should not be used as propaganda. We are not usually and not properly in the business of shaping our consumers' values; instead, we need to know what information is required to enable the consumers to make informed decisions. In behavior analysis, this task is especially important. Behavior analysis is often misrepresented in the popular and scientific media (Morris, 1985; Todd & Morris, 1983); we had better not intensify the problem. Consumers are entitled to accurate information presented in a clear and intelligible manner. They should not be asked to make choices about any services without adequate information about them and about all relevant, available treatment options.

Since the introduction of social validity, applied behavior analysis has moved further toward Wolf's (1978) implicit prescription—the search for its heart. The use of social validity assessments in behavioral research has increased, and researchers and practitioners alike (at least sometimes) try to improve its technique. Better social validity assessments are vital to the survival of applied behavior analysis; however, they are not the discipline, only a defensive tool of it. We still need to be applied, behavioral, analytic, technological, conceptual, effective, and in as generalized a way as the problem requires (Baer et al., 1968, 1987). State-of-the-art social validity assessment should address all seven of those dimensions, and when it does, the discipline will be another step closer to finding its heart.

REFERENCES

Aaker, D. A., & Day, G. S. (1971). Introduction: A guide to consumerism. In D. A. Aaker & G. S. Day (Eds.), *Consumerism: Search for the consumer interest* (pp. 1–19). New York: Free Press.

American Psychological Association. (1979). *Ethical standards of psychologists.* Washington, DC: American Psychological Association.

Anderson, S. R., Christian, W. P., & Luce, S. C. (1986). Transitional programming for autistic individuals. *Behavior Therapist,* **9**, 205–211.

Anderson, S. R., & Schwartz, I. S. (1986). Transitional programming. In F. J. Fuoco & W. P. Christian (Eds.), *Behavior analysis and therapy in residential programming* (pp. 76–100). New York: Van Norstrand Reinhold.

Azrin, N. H., Holz, W., & Goldiamond, I. (1961). Response bias in questionnaire reports. *Journal of Consulting Psychology,* **25**, 324–326.

Baer, D. M. (1986). In application, frequency is not the only estimate of the probability of behavioral units. In T. Thompson & M. D. Zeiler (Eds.), *Analysis and integration of behavioral units* (pp. 117–136). Hillsdale, NJ: Erlbaum.

Baer, D. M. (1987, March). *A behavior-analytic query into early intervention.* Paper presented at the Banff International Conference on Behavioral Science, Banff, Canada.

Baer, D. M. (1988). If you know why you're changing a behavior, you'll know when you've changed it enough. *Behavioral Assessment,* **10**, 219–223.

Baer, D. M., Wolf, M. M., & Risley, T. R. (1968). Some current dimensions of applied behavior analysis. *Journal of Applied Behavior Analysis,* **1**, 91–97.

Baer, D. M., Wolf, M. M., & Risley, T. R. (1987). Some still-current dimensions of applied behavior analysis. *Journal of Applied Behavior Analysis,* **20**, 313–327.

Barrett, B. H. (1987). Drifting? Course? Destination?: A review of *Research in applied behavior analysis: Issues and advances. The Behavior Analyst,* **10**, 253–276.

Bearden, W. O., & Oliver, R. L. (1985). The role of public and private complaining in satisfaction with problem resolution. *Journal of Consumer Affairs,* **19**, 222–240.

Blase, K., Fixsen, D., & Phillips, E. (1984). Residential treatment for troubled children: Developing service delivery systems. In S. C. Paine, G. T. Bellamy, & B. Wilcox (Eds.), *Human services that work: From innovation to standard practice* (pp. 149–166). Baltimore: Paul Brookes.

Bornstein, P. H., & Rychtarik, R. G. (1983). Consumer satisfaction in adult behavior therapy: Procedures, problems, and future perspectives. *Behavior Therapy,* **14,** 191–208.

Buyer, L. S., Berkson, G., Winnega, M. A., & Morton, L. (1987). Stimulation and control as components of stereotyped body rocking. *American Journal of Mental Deficiency,* **91,** 543–547.

Cone, J. (1981). Psychometric considerations. In M. Hersen & A. S. Bellack (Eds.), *Behavioral assessment: A practical handbook* (pp. 38–68). New York: Pergamon.

Deitz, S. M. (1978). Current status of applied behavior analysis: Science vs. technology. *American Psychologist,* **33,** 805–814.

Dunlap, G. (1984). The influence of task variation and maintenance tasks on the learning and affect of autistic children. *Journal of Experimental Child Psychology,* **37,** 41–64.

Dunlap, G., & Koegel, R. L. (1980). Motivating autistic children through stimulus variation. *Journal of Applied Behavior Analysis,* **13,** 619–627.

Engel, J. F., Kollat, D. T., & Blackwell, R. D. (1973). *Consumer behavior.* New York: Holt, Rinehart, & Winston.

Fowler, S. A. (1982). Transition from preschool to kindergarten for children with special needs. In K. E. Allen & E. M. Goetz (Eds.), *Early childhood education: Special problems, special solutions* (pp. 309–334). Rockville, MD: Aspen.

Fox, D. K., Hopkins, B. L., & Anger, W. K. (1987). The long-term effects of a token economy on safety performance in open-pit mining. *Journal of Applied Behavior Analysis,* **20,** 215–224.

Friman, P. C., & Hove, G. (1987). Apparent covariations between child habit disorders: Effects of successful treatment for thumb sucking on untargeted chronic hair pulling. *Journal of Applied Behavior Analysis,* **20,** 421–425.

Fuoco, F. J., & Christian, W. P. (Eds.). (1986). *Behavior analysis and therapy in residential programs.* New York: Van Nostrand Reinhold.

Fuqua, R. W., & Schwade, J. (1986). Social validation of applied behavioral research: A selective review and critique. In A. Poling & R. W. Fuqua (Eds.), *Research methods in applied behavior analysis: Issues and advances* (pp. 265–292). New York: Plenum.

Geller, E. S. (1989). Applied behavior analysis and social marketing: An integration for environmental preservation. *Journal of Social Issues,* **45,** 17–36.

Geller, E. S. (1990). Behavior analysis and environmental protection: Where have all the flowers gone? *Journal of Applied Behavior Analysis,* **23,** 269–273.

Giordano, P. (1977). The client's perspective in agency evaluation. *Social Work,* **22,** 34–39.

Greenwood, C. R. (1990, October). Social validity. In S. Warren (Chair), *Innovations in research standards and methods.* Symposium presented at the Annual Meeting of the Division of Early Childhood, Council for Exceptional Children, Albuquerque, NM.

Harris, K. R. (1986). Self-monitoring of attentional behavior versus self-monitoring of productivity: Effects on on-task behavior and academic response rate among learning disabled children. *Journal of Applied Behavior Analysis,* **19,** 417–423.

Hoier, T. S., & Cone, J. D. (1987). Target selection of social skills for children: The template-matching procedure. *Behavior Modification,* **11,** 137–163.

Jones, R. J., & Azrin, N. H. (1969). Behavioral engineering: Stuttering as a function of stimulus duration during speech synchronization. *Journal of Applied Behavior Analysis,* **2,** 223–229.

Kazdin, A. E. (1977). Assessing the clinical or applied importance of behavior change through social validation. *Behavior Modification,* **1,** 427–452.

Kazdin, A. E. (1979). Unobtrusive measures in behavioral assessment. *Journal of Applied Behavior Analysis,* **12,** 713–724.

Koegel, R. L., & Egel, A. L. (1979). Motivating autistic children. *Journal of Abnormal Psychology,* **88,** 418–426.

Kohler, F. W., & Fowler, S. A. (1985). Training prosocial behaviors to young children: An analysis of reciprocity with untrained peers. *Journal of Applied Behavior Analysis,* **18,** 187–200.

Larsen, D. L., Attkisson, C., Hargreaves, W. A., & Nguyen, T. D. (1979). Assessment of client/patient satisfaction: Development of a general scale. *Evaluation and Program Planning,* **2,** 197–207.

Lebow, J. (1982). Consumer satisfaction with mental health treatment. *Psychological Bulletin,* **91,** 244–259.

Lockhart, K. A. (1979). Behavioral assessment of human preference. *The Behavior Analyst,* **2,** 20–29.

Mash, E. J., & Terdal, L. G. (1981). Behavioral assessment of childhood disturbances. In E. J. Mash & L. G. Terdal (Eds.), *Behavioral assessment of childhood disorders* (pp. 3–76). New York: Guilford.

Mathews, R. M., & Fawcett, S. B. (1979). Assessing dissemination capability: An evaluation of an exportable training package. *Behavior Modification,* **3,** 49–62.

McMahon, R. J. (1984). Behavioral checklists and rating scales. In T. H. Ollendick & M. Hersen (Eds.), *Child behavioral assessment: Principles and procedures* (pp. 80–105). New York: Pergamon.

McMahon, R. J., & Forehand, R. L. (1983). Consumer satisfaction in behavioral treatment of children: Types, issues, and recommendations. *Behavior Therapy,* **14,** 209–225.

Michael, J. (1980). Flight from behavior analysis. *The Behavior Analyst,* **3,** 1–22.

Minkin, N., Braukman, C. J., Minkin, B. L., Timbers, G. D., Timbers, B. J., Fixsen, D. L., Phillips, E. L., & Wolf, M. M. (1976). The social validation and training of conversational skills. *Journal of Applied Behavior Analysis,* **9,** 127–139.

Mithaug, D. E., & Hanawalt, D. A. (1978). The validation of procedures to assess prevocational task preferences in retarded adults. *Journal of Applied Behavior Analysis,* **11,** 153–162.

Mithaug, D. E., & Mar, D. K. (1980). The relation between choosing and working prevocational tasks in two severely retarded young adults. *Journal of Applied Behavior Analysis,* **13,** 177–182.

Morris, E. K. (1985). Public information, dissemination, and behavior analysis. *The Behavior Analyst,* **8,** 95–110.

Osnes, P. G., Guevremont, D. C., & Stokes, T. F. (1986). If I say I'll talk more, then I will: Correspondence training to increase peer-directed talk by socially withdrawn children. *Behavior Modification,* **10,** 287–299.

Paine, S. C., Bellamy, G. T., & Wilcox, B. (Eds.). (1984). *Human services that work: From innovation to standard practice.* Baltimore: Paul Brookes.

Pennypacker, H. S. (1986). The challenge of technology transfer: Buying in without selling out. *The Behavior Analyst,* **9,** 147–156.

Phillips, E. L., Phillips, E. A., Fixsen, D. L., & Wolf, M. M. (1972). *The teaching-family handbook.* Lawrence, KS: Bureau of Child Research.

Pierce, W. D., & Epling, W. F. (1980). What happened to analysis in applied behavior analysis. *The Behavior Analyst,* **3,** 1–9.

Plienis, A. J., Hansen, D. J., Ford, F., Smith, S., Stark, L. J., & Kelly, J. A. (1987). Behavioral small group training to improve the social skills of emotionally-disordered adolescents. *Behavior Therapy,* **18,** 17–32.

Sainato, D. M., Strain, P. D., Lefebvre, D., & Rapp, N. (1987). Facilitating transition times with handicapped preschool children: A comparison between peer-mediated and antecedent prompt procedures. *Journal of Applied Behavior Analysis,* **20,** 285–292.

Scheirer, M. (1978). Program participants' positive perceptions: Psychological conflict of interest in social program evaluation. *Evaluation Quarterly,* **2,** 53–70.

Schepis, M. M., Reid, D. H., & Fitzgerald, J. R. (1987). Group instruction with profoundly retarded persons: Acquisition, generalization, and maintenance of a remunerative work skill. *Journal of Applied Behavior Analysis,* **20,** 97–105.

Schwartz, I. S. (1991). *A review of current practice of methods used to assess social validity.* Manuscript submitted for publication.

Seekins, T., & Fawcett, S. B. (1984). Planned diffusion of social technologies for community groups. In S. C. Paine, G. T. Bellamy, & B. Wilcox (Eds.), *Human services that work: From innovation to standard practice* (pp. 247–260). Baltimore: Paul Brookes.

Seekins, T., Fawcett, S. B., & Mathews, R. M. (1987). Effects of self-help guides on three consumer advocacy skills: Using personal experiences to influence public policy. *Rehabilitation Psychology,* **32,** 29–38.

Seekins, T., Mathews, R. M., & Fawcett, S. B. (1984). Enhancing leadership skills for community self-help organizations through behavioral instruction. *Journal of Community Psychology,* **12,** 155–163.

Skinner, B. F. (1953). *Science and human behavior.* New York: Free Press.

Skinner, B. F. (1963). Behaviorism at fifty. *Science,* **140,** 951–959.

Strouse, M. C. (1988). The client satisfaction evaluation. In J. A. Sherman, J. B. Sheldon, & M. C. Strouse (Eds.), *Evaluation programs using the Teaching-Family Model for people with developmental disabilities* (pp. 1–36). Topeka, KS: Kansas Planning Council on Developmental Disabilities.

Todd, J. T., & Morris, E. K. (1983). Misconceptions and miseducations: Presentations of radical behaviorism in psychology textbooks. *The Behavior Analyst,* **6,** 153–160.

Troelstrup, A. W. (1974). *The consumer in American society.* New York: McGraw Hill.

Van Houten, R. (1979). Social validation: The evolution of standards of competency for targets. *Journal of Applied Behavior Analysis,* **12,** 581–591.

Ware, J. E. (1978). Effects of acquiescent response set on patient satisfaction ratings. *Medical Care,* **16,** 327–336.

Ware, J. E., Davies-Avery, A., & Stewart, A. L. (1978). The measurement and meaning of patient satisfaction. *Health and Medical Care Services Review,* **1,** 1–15.

Warfel, D. J., Maloney, D. M., & Blase, K. (1981). Consumer feedback in human service programs. *Social Work,* **26,** 151–156.

Warren, S. F., Rogers-Warren, A., & Baer, D. M. (1976). The role of offer rates in controlling sharing by young children. *Journal of Applied Behavior Analysis,* **9,** 491–497.

Whang, P. L., Fawcett, S. B., & Mathews, R. M. (1984). Teaching job-related social skills to learning disabled adolescents. *Analysis and Intervention in Developmental Disabilities,* **4,** 29–38.

Winett, R. A., Neale, M. S., & Grier, H. C. (1979). Effects of self-monitoring and feedback on residential electricity consumption. *Journal of Applied Behavior Analysis,* **12,** 173–184.

Wolf, M. M. (1978). Social validity: The case for subjective measurement, or how behavior analysis is finding its heart. *Journal of Applied Behavior Analysis,* **11,** 203–214.

Received August 8, 1990
Initial editorial decision January 7, 1991
Revision received February 12, 1991
Final acceptance February 17, 1991
Action Editor, E. Scott Geller

JOURNAL OF APPLIED BEHAVIOR ANALYSIS 1991, 24, 235–239 NUMBER 2 (SUMMER 1991)

SOCIAL VALIDITY: A NOTE ON METHODOLOGY

STEPHEN B. FAWCETT

UNIVERSITY OF KANSAS

Applied researchers hope that the behavioral goals they select for study are significant, that the procedures they develop are appropriate, and that the effects produced are important for clients and society. Social validation (Wolf, 1978) offers an explicit tactic for assessing whether these applied research goals are met and an implicit strategy for helping ensure their attainment.

In the process of social validation, representatives of constituencies who control important consequences for targets and program developers (known as consumer judges) provide information about the social acceptability of goals, procedures, and effects. The relevance of this assessment procedure to determining clinical significance has been noted (Kazdin, 1977). Despite limitations of this methodology (Fuqua & Schwade, 1986), its adoption as a standard for applied behavioral research has been swift and widespread (Baer, Wolf, & Risley, 1987).

Social validation is also being used as a strategy to program for or help ensure selection of socially important goals, development of socially acceptable procedures, and attainment of socially important effects. Although some researchers (e.g., Wolf & Ramp, 1991) use social validation for this purpose, most reported uses of social validity are confined to assessment. Similarly, the dominant form of social validity is consumer satisfaction (social validation of procedures), with only modest use in validating the importance of effects, and even less attention to validating the significance of goals. Despite advances in articulating the methodology of social validity assessment (Schwartz & Baer, 1991), these procedures may not be sufficiently explicit to permit their adoption and adaptation by scientist-practitioners in this and other related fields.

The purpose of this brief commentary is to outline considerations in assessing (and programming for) social validity that may increase chances for attaining results valued by relevant client audiences. The next section provides a brief introduction to the objectives and contexts of the several types of social validation. The main section outlines the general procedures involved in conducting a social validation. Questions addressed by researchers in assessing (and attempting to program for) social validity are noted, and necessary variations in this general procedure are described.

OBJECTIVES AND CONTEXTS OF SOCIAL VALIDATION

Validating the Social Significance of Goals

The social significance of goals may be assessed (and programmed for) at several levels: broad social goals, behavioral categories, and discrete responses within categories of behavior. At the level of broad social goals, social validation procedures may be used to involve consumers in setting an agenda for action (Fawcett, Seekins, Whang, Muiu, & Suarez de Balcazar, 1982), establishing a research agenda (Fawcett, 1990), and creating information for decision makers about the importance of particular social goals according to their constituents (Fawcett, Seekins, & Jason, 1987).

To assess the social importance of goals, the researcher must be precise about the goals of the behavior change effort at the levels of (a) the broad social goal (e.g., improved parenting, enhanced social skills, improved cardiovascular health, increased independence), (b) the categories of behavior hypothesized to be related to the broad goal (e.g., parenting—providing instructional feedback, providing positive reinforcement, using time out, etc.), and/or (c) the responses that comprise the

I am grateful to Mont Wolf for sharing his insights on this topic in many informal conservations. Thanks also to Bill Hopkins, who helped shape some of these ideas in a course that we taught together. Reprints may be obtained from the author, Department of Human Development, University of Kansas, Lawrence, Kansas 66045.

behavioral category of interest (e.g., Using time-out—directing the child to a location away from other people, instructing the child to "sit out" for a specified duration, etc.). Social validation may be conducted for any of these levels of goals.

Validating the Social Appropriateness of Procedures

The appropriateness of behavioral interventions may be validated at several levels: comprehensive treatment programs, treatment packages or components of a program, and specific behavioral procedures or components of treatment packages. To assess the social appropriateness of the procedures, the researcher must provide a clear description of the behavior-change program at the levels of (a) the existing or planned comprehensive treatment program (e.g., group home for adults with developmental disabilities), (b) the treatment package(s) or components that are part of the existing or planned comprehensive program (e.g., academic skills program, social skills program, self-government program, motivational system), and/or (c) the specific procedures that comprise the existing or planned treatment package or component (e.g., performance feedback, social reinforcement, time-out). Social validation of procedures may be conducted at any of these levels.

Validating the Social Importance of the Effects

The social importance of the effects of behavioral interventions may be assessed at several levels: proximal effects, intermediate effects, and distal effects or outcomes. The process requires a precise description of the observed effects of the behavior-change effort at the levels of (a) proximal effects (e.g., increased occurrence of social skills, increased rate of exercise), (b) intermediate effects that appear to be related to the main effects (e.g., social skills—increased contacts with friends and neighbors; exercise—reduced blood pressure), and (c) distal effects or outcomes (e.g., social skills—increased size of the social network; for a group of adults who exercise—reduced incidence of cardiovascular disease). Social validation should take into account all of the levels for which results are available.

General Procedures of Social Validation

This section outlines 10 operations commonly involved in conducting a social validation. Variations for each type of social validity are noted.

1. Consider how samples of the phenomenon will be obtained and arranged for review by experts. To assess the social validity of goals, a sample of broad goals for the health concern of cardiovascular disease, for example, might consist of a list of potential health objectives such as increased physical exercise, smoking cessation, or lowered intake of dietary fat. A sample of behavioral categories for a planned resource conservation program, for example, might consist of a list of home energy-conserving activities such as caulking windows, putting weather stripping on doors, and setting the temperature back at night. At the level of responses for a particular category of behavior, a sample for the parental activity of providing corrective feedback, for example, might consist of an audiotape capturing the discrete activities involved in this interaction.

To assess the social appropriateness of procedures, a sample for a comprehensive treatment program, such as a group home for people with psychiatric disabilities, might consist of a description of the treatment approach and a day-long visit to one or more actual group homes. At the level of a particular intervention or procedure, a sample might consist of a written product such as a manual or an actual or videotaped demonstration of the procedure.

To assess the social importance of effects, researchers must specify the preintervention and postintervention samples to be used. Ideally, these samples will include levels of performance of the specified behaviors that might be labeled as *ideal* (i.e., representing the best performance available), *normative* (i.e., representing commonly occurring performance levels), and *deficient* (i.e., representing the worst performance available). A sample for a particular category of behavior, such as the parental activity of providing corrective feedback, might consist of a videotape composed of teaching interactions selected randomly from those obtained before and after the intervention.

2. Identify consumer judges (sometimes called "clients" or "experts") who should assess the social validity of goals, procedures, and/or effects. Those consumers who control consequences for the target, client, and/or program developer may be particularly appropriate reviewers. Researchers should consider recruiting the following types of consumer judges: (a) other similar targets, clients, or consumers (e.g., low-income youths, customers, residents of treatment programs), (b) people most affected by the targets' problems (e.g., spouses of abusing partners, parents of adolescents who abuse drugs), (c) mediators, program implementers, natural and professional helpers (e.g., teachers, direct-care staff, police officers, friends), (d) administrators and funding agents (e.g., school principals, agency directors, foundation officials), (e) journalists, appointed and elected officials, consumer advocates (e.g., newspaper editors, city council members, citizen lobbyists), and (f) researchers and knowledge experts (e.g., public health researchers, criminal justice officials).

3. Specify the qualitative or evaluative dimensions on which assessments of social validity should be based. Qualitative dimensions refer to distinguishing attributes of the phenomenon, such as its significance or fairness, that cannot be measured in quantitative terms. These dimensions would normally be identified in reviews of the literature, informal interviews with experts, and follow-up surveys.

To assess the social significance of goals or effects, potentially relevant qualitative dimensions are captured by such descriptive labels as "significant," "important," "complete," or "representative" for the level of broad goals. To determine the social significance of effects at the level of behavioral category, other more specific qualitative dimensions are used, such as "enthusiastic," "knowledgeable," or "sincere" (for the skill of public speaking, for example).

To assess the appropriateness of procedures, more global qualitative dimensions include "overall satisfaction," "willingness to use," or "willingness to recommend the intervention to others." More specific dimensions include "efficient," "practical," "easy to use," "simple," "inexpensive," "fair," "humane," "effective," "robust," "suitable," and "compatible with local values."

4. Select a rating scale to obtain consumer judgments about these qualitative dimensions in quantitative terms. Common forms of rating scales include semantic differential (with extreme values anchoring each end) or Likert-type items (with each point anchored by a particular descriptor) of either 5 or 7 points. An example of a 7-point Likert-type rating scale used to evaluate the appropriateness of a procedure follows: "How easy was the program to learn?" 1, very difficult; 2, moderately difficult; 3, slightly difficult; 4, neither easy nor difficult; 5, slightly easy; 6, moderately easy; 7, very easy.

5. Prepare instructions for consumer judges to minimize potential sources of experimenter bias and measurement artifact. Instructions can influence how expert judges rate samples of behavioral goals, procedures, and effects. Potential bias can be minimized by preparing written instructions that avoid descriptions of the researchers' expectations about rating results. Similarly, measurement artifacts can be reduced by arranging the samples in random order. Protecting the confidentiality of consumer judges can also help ensure the honest assessment of samples of goals, procedures, and effects.

6. If the results of the social validation are likely to be challenged, obtain and present evidence regarding the validity and reliability of the assessment. When the results of the social validation affect important consequences for clients, the results may be challenged as invalid or unreliable. Challenges to validity may be countered with assertions of face validity or data showing interitem correlations for related dimensions of the behavior. Similarly, measures of test–retest reliability for scores of the same rater may be obtained to suggest the reliability of the assessment instrument.

7. Summarize the rating data and compare them with direct observational data for the same samples. Rating data are usually summarized by presenting the mean and range for each type of consumer judge for each experimental condition. Data may also be reported by types of samples (e.g., participants representing ideal, normative, or deficient levels of behavior).

To assess the social importance of effects, mean

ratings for dimensions are compared with data from direct observations for preintervention and postintervention samples of behavior. For a public speaking training program, for example, rating data on "enthusiasm" might be compared with data on the percentage of intervals in which a gesture was made by the speaker. Correlation coefficients are often computed to show relationships between composite scores. To assess the social appropriateness of procedures, ratings of acceptability for the featured intervention may be compared to those of other similar interventions that may be used as standards for comparison.

8. Obtain information about the behaviors of targets/clients, implementers, or consumers that suggest social validity. To assess the social significance of goals, consider evidence of public protests about the issue, formal complaints about the problem, accounts of attempts to solve the problem, and other actions that suggest their importance to society. To assess the appropriateness of procedures, consider information about demonstrated preference for the procedures over similar others, adoption of the program, and recommendations to others that they use the program. To assess the social importance of the effects, consider the existence of public testimonials about successes, media reports by journalists, and widespread adoption by those for whom the effects may be important.

9. Obtain information about the outcomes or consequences for targets/clients, implementers, or consumers that suggest social validity. To assess the social significance of goals, consider consequences of the problem for targets including low levels of positive events (e.g., social attention, money, or life opportunities) and high levels of aversive events (e.g., unemployment, substance abuse, or diseases and injuries). Epidemiological data, information on the incidence and prevalence of undesirable outcomes such as disease and behaviors related to the problem, may be particularly useful in making this point (e.g., the work of Winett, Moore, & Anderson, 1991).

To assess the appropriateness of procedures, consider possible consequences of the program's implementation, including reduced complaints about targets' behaviors, social attention to adopters and implementers, and reduced costs for service. Social marketing techniques, such as the use of focus groups to involve potential consumers in reviewing prototypes of programs and products, may be helpful in obtaining such information (see Winett et al., 1991).

To assess the social importance of the effects, consider evidence that the observed changes in behavior are linked to important social, health, or developmental outcomes. Data from formative and summative evaluations can be used to suggest that observed levels of behavior change may be related to broader outcomes.

10. If expert ratings are not sufficiently high, consider what else might be done to program for social validity. Despite the best efforts, assessments may show that research goals are regarded by consumer judges as insignificant, intervention procedures as unacceptable, or results as unimportant.

To program further for social validity, consider changing (a) the procedures (based on pilot or formative research), (b) the goals (based on experience with the problem and/or intervention), (c) the rating scale or instructions, and/or (d) the ratings (by educating the community of consumer judges about the significance of the goals, acceptability of the procedures, or importance of the effects). Recognize, however, that it is improper to program for social validity by attempting to manipulate the verbal behavior or ratings of a particular panel of judges. Rather, after changes in the content and presentation of the program are made, similar assessments may be conducted with a new panel of judges to assess the value of the revised program.

Conclusion

This brief commentary has outlined considerations in assessing (and programming for) social validity. Making explicit these procedures may contribute to their wider adoption and adaptation by behavior analysts as well as by those outside the discipline. This may, in turn, contribute to the field's mission of enhancing understanding of behavior–environment relations and improving attainment of goals valued by clients and the broader culture.

REFERENCES

Baer, D. M., Wolf, M. M., & Risley, T. R. (1987). Some still-current dimensions of applied behavior analysis. *Journal of Applied Behavior Analysis*, **20**, 313–327.

Fawcett, S. B. (1990). Some emerging standards for community research and action. In P. Tolan, C. Keys, F. Chertok, & L. Jason (Eds.), *Researching community psychology: Issues of theory and methods* (pp. 64–75). Washington, DC: American Psychological Association.

Fawcett, S. B., Seekins, T., & Jason, L. A. (1987). Policy research and child passenger safety legislation: A case study and experimental evaluation. *Journal of Social Issues*, **43**, 133–148.

Fawcett, S. B., Seekins, T., Whang, P. L., Muiu, C., & Suarez de Balcazar, Y. (1982). The concerns report method: Involving consumers in setting local improvement agendas. *Social Policy*, **13**, 36–41.

Fuqua, R. W., & Schwade, J. (1986.) Social validation of applied behavioral research: A selective review and critique. In A. D. Poling & R. W. Fuqua (Eds.), *Research methods in applied behavior analysis: Issues and advances* (pp. 265–292). New York: Plenum Press.

Kazdin, A. E. (1977). Assessing the clinical or applied importance of behavior change through social validation. *Behavior Modification*, **1**, 427–451.

Schwartz, I. S., & Baer, D. M. (1991). Social validity assessments: Is current practice state of the art? *Journal of Applied Behavior Analysis*, **24**, 189–204.

Winett, R. A., Moore, J. F., & Anderson, E. S. (1991). Extending the concept of social validity: Behavior analysis for disease prevention and health promotion. *Journal of Applied Behavior Analysis*, **24**, 215–230.

Wolf, M. M. (1978). Social validity: The case for subjective measurement or how applied behavior analysis is finding its heart. *Journal of Applied Behavior Analysis*, **11**, 203–214.

Wolf, M. M., & Ramp, K. K. (1991). *Consumer feedback and the Teaching-Family Model: On the auld art of keeping dragons away*. Unpublished manuscript, Department of Human Development, University of Kansas, Lawrence.

Received February 27, 1991
Initial editorial decision March 1, 1991
Revision received March 4, 1991
Final acceptance March 7, 1991
Action Editor, E. Scott Geller

JOURNAL OF APPLIED BEHAVIOR ANALYSIS 1977, 10, 349-367 NUMBER 2 (SUMMER) 1977

AN IMPLICIT TECHNOLOGY OF GENERALIZATION[1]

TREVOR F. STOKES AND DONALD M. BAER

THE UNIVERSITY OF MANITOBA AND THE UNIVERSITY OF KANSAS

Traditionally, discrimination has been understood as an active process, and a technology of its procedures has been developed and practiced extensively. Generalization, by contrast, has been considered the natural result of failing to practice a discrimination technology adequately, and thus has remained a passive concept almost devoid of a technology. But, generalization is equally deserving of an active conceptualization and technology. This review summarizes the structure of the generalization literature and its implicit embryonic technology, categorizing studies designed to assess or program generalization according to nine general headings: Train and Hope; Sequential Modification; Introduce to Natural Maintaining Contingencies; Train Sufficient Exemplars; Train Loosely; Use Indiscriminable Contingencies; Program Common Stimuli; Mediate Generalization; and Train "To Generalize".

DESCRIPTORS: generalization, treatment-gain durability, followup measures, maintenance, postcheck methodology

---

Traditionally, many theorists have considered generalization to be a *passive* phenomenon. Generalization was not seen as an operant response that could be programmed, but as a description of a "natural" outcome of any behavior-change process. That is, a teaching operation repeated over time and trials inevitably involves varying samples of stimuli, rather than the same set every time; in the same way, it inevitably evokes and reinforces varying samples of behavior, rather than the same set every time. As a consequence, it is predictable that newly taught responses would be controlled not only by the stimuli of the teaching program, but by others somewhat resembling those stimuli (Skinner, 1953, p. 107ff.). Similarly, responses resembling those established directly, yet not themselves actually touched by the teaching procedures, would appear as a result of the teaching (Keller and Schoenfeld, 1950, p. 168ff.). Thus, generalization was something that happened, not something produced by procedures specific to it.

If generalization seemed absent or insignificant, it was simply to be assumed that the teaching process had managed to maintain unusually tight control of the stimuli and responses involved, allowing little sampling of their varieties. This assumption was strongly supported by the well-known techniques of discrimination: by differential reinforcement (in general, by *any* differential teaching) of certain stimuli relative to others, and/or certain responses relative to others, generalization could be programmatically restricted and diminished to a very small range. Thus, it was *discrimination* that was understood as an active process, and a technology of its procedures was developed and practiced extensively. But generalization was considered the natural result of failing to practice discrimination's technology adequately, and thus remained a passive concept almost devoid of a technology. Nevertheless, in educational practice, and in the development of theories aimed at serving both practice and a better understanding of human functioning, generalization is equally as important as dis-

[1]Preparation of this paper was supported in part by PHS Training Grant 00183, Program Project Grant HD 00870, and Research Grant MH 11739. Reprints may be obtained either from T. F. Stokes, Department of Psychology, University of Manitoba, Winnipeg, Manitoba, Canada R3T 2N2, or D. M. Baer, Department of Human Development, University of Kansas, Lawrence, Kansas 66045.

crimination, and equally deserving of an active conceptualization.

Generalization has been and doubtless will remain a fundamental concern of applied behavior analysis. A therapeutic behavioral change, to be effective, often (not always) must occur over time, persons, and settings, and the effects of the change sometimes should spread to a variety of related behaviors. Even though the literature shows many instances of generalization, it is still frequently observed that when a change in behavior has been accomplished through experimental contingencies, then that change is manifest where and when those contingencies operate, and is often seen in only transitory forms in other places and at other times.

The frequent need for generalization of therapeutic behavior change is widely accepted, but it is not always realized that generalization does not automatically occur simply because a behavior change is accomplished. Thus, the need actively to *program* generalization, rather than passively to expect it as an outcome of certain training procedures, is a point requiring both emphasis and effective techniques (Baer, Wolf, and Risley, 1968). That such exhortations have often been made has not always ensured that researchers in the field have taken serious note of and, therefore, proceeded to analyze adequately the generalization issues of vital concern to their programs. The emphasis, refinement, and elaboration of the principles and procedures that are meant to explain and produce generalization when it does not occur "naturally" is an important area of unfinished business for applied behavior analysis.

The notion of generalization developed here is an essentially pragmatic one; it does not closely follow the traditional conceptualizations (Keller and Schoenfeld, 1950; Skinner, 1953). In many ways, this discussion will sidestep much of the controversy concerning terminology. Generalization will be considered to be the occurrence of relevant behavior under different, non-training conditions (*i.e.,* across subjects, settings, people, behaviors, and/or time) without the scheduling of the same events in those conditions as had been scheduled in the training conditions. Thus, generalization may be claimed when no extratraining manipulations are needed for extratraining changes; or may be claimed when some extra manipulations are necessary, but their cost or extent is clearly less than that of the direct intervention. Generalization will not be claimed when similar events are necessary for similar effects across conditions.

A technology of generalization programming is almost a reality, despite the fact that until recently, it had hardly been recognized as a problem in its own right. Within common teaching practice, there is an informal germ of a technology for generalization. Furthermore, within the practice of applied behavior analysis (especially within the past 5 yr or so), there has appeared a budding area of "generalization-promotion" techniques. The purpose of this review is to summarize the structure of that generalization literature and its implicit embryonic technology. Some 270 applied behavior analysis studies relevant to generalization in that discipline were reviewed.[2] A central core of that literature, consisting of some 120 studies, contributes directly to a technology of generalization. In general, techniques designed to assess or to program generalization can be loosely categorized according to nine general headings:

1. Train and Hope
2. Sequential Modification
3. Introduce to Natural Maintaining Contingencies
4. Train Sufficient Exemplars
5. Train Loosely
6. Use Indiscriminable Contingencies
7. Program Common Stimuli

[2]Ninety per cent of the literature reviewed was from five journals: *Behaviour Research and Therapy; Behavior Therapy; Journal of Applied Behavior Analysis; Journal of Behavior Therapy and Experimental Psychiatry;* and *Journal of Experimental Child Psychology.* Seventy-seven per cent of the literature reviewed has been published since 1970.

8. Mediate Generalization
9. Train "To Generalize".

This review characterizes each category, and describes some examples of research that illustrate the generalization analyses or programming involved in each category. Obviously, all the relevant references cannot be discussed in this review.[3] The nine categories listed above were induced from the literature; they are not *a priori* categories. Consequently, studies do not always fit neatly into these categories. It should also be noted that not all studies reviewed were thorough experimental analyses of generalization. Often inferences were necessary to categorize the research. However, the following discussion still may provide a useful organization and conceptualization of generalization and its programming.

1. *Train and Hope*

In applied behavior analysis research, the most frequent method of examining generalization, so far, may be labelled *Train and Hope.* After a behavior change is effected through manipulation of some response consequences, any existent generalization across responses, settings, experimenters, and time, is concurrently and/or subsequently documented or noted, but not actively pursued. It is usually hoped that some generalization may occur, which will be welcomed yet not explicitly programmed. These hopeful probes for stimulus and response generalization characterize almost half of the applied literature on generalization. The studies have considerable importance, for they begin to document the extent and limits of generalization of particular operant intervention techniques. While not being examples of the programming of generalization, they are a sound first step in any serious analysis of generalization. When generalization is desired, but is shown to be absent or deficient, programming procedures can then be instituted.

For example, useful generalization across settings was documented by Kifer, Lewis, Green, and Phillips (1974). In an experimental classroom setting, parent-child pairs were taught to negotiate in conflict situations. During simulated role-playing, instructions, practice, and feedback were used to teach the negotiation behaviors of fully stating one's position, identifying the issues of conflict, and suggesting options to resolve the conflict. The data showed increased use of negotiation behaviors and the reaching of agreements in actual parent-child conflict situations at home.

An assessment of generalization across experimenters was described by Redd and Birnbrauer (1969), who demonstrated that control over the cooperative play of retarded children did not generalize from an adult who dispensed contingent edible reinforcement to five other adults who had not participated in training.

Studies that are examples of Train and Hope across time are those in which there was a change from the intervention procedures, either to a less intensive but procedurally different program, or to no program or no specifically defined program. Data or anecdotal observations were reported concerning the maintenance of the original behavior change over the specified time intervening between the termination of the formal program and the postchecks. An example of a followup evaluation was the study by Azrin, Sneed, and Foxx (1973). An intensive training program involving reinforcement of correct toileting and positive practice procedures promptly decreased bedwetting by 12 retarded persons. The reduced rate of accidents was maintained during a three-month followup assessment.

Perhaps there are many more studies in the Train and Hope category than would have been expected (about 135, of which 65% are across Time). However, despite its obvious value, this research is frequently characterized by a lack of

[3]Complete reference lists and detailed tables describing subjects, procedures, and generalization of *all* studies reviewed are deposited with the National Auxiliary Publications Service (NAPS). For copies, order NAPS Document #02873. Order from ASIS/NAPS Co., C/O Microfiche Publications, 305 East 46th Street, New York, New York 10017. Remit with order for each copy $3.00 for microfiche or $19.50 for photocopies. Make checks payable to Microfiche Publications.

comprehensiveness and depth of the generalization analysis. Even though generalized behavior change was frequently reported, extensive, wide-ranging, and practical generalization was not often noted or even sought. The continued development of behavior analysis almost surely will demand more extensive collection of generalization data than is presently the fashion. The extent and limits of applied behavioral interventions may be well documented and understood if measurement is extended over longer periods of time, over more than one circumscribed part of the day, with more than one related response, and with more than a restricted part of the social and physical environment. It is as important for the field to formalize the conditions of the nonoccurrence of generalization as it is to document the conditions associated with the display of unprogrammed generalization.

Most of the Train-and-Hope research described successful generalization—approximately 90% of Train-and-Hope studies. By definition, there was no further need to program generalization in those studies where generalization had been exhibited within the Train-and-Hope paradigm—presuming, of course, that the generalization exhibited was considered sufficient to meet the therapeutic goals of the various modification programs (not necessarily a valid presumption in the Train-and-Hope research). This preponderance of positive data may simply reflect the tendency of some researchers not to report their generalization data if measurement procedures were instituted to probe for any generalized behavior changes, but generalization was shown to be absent. Some researchers may view nongeneralization as reflecting a deficiency or ineffectiveness of their procedures to develop a desirable generalized performance. Behavior analysts, nevertheless, should encourage their fellow researchers to document and to *analyze* experimentally their apparent failures, rather than allowing them to slide into oblivion. A detailed and systematic understanding of generalization and its programming could result. Alternatively, researchers might view their generalization baselines as being essentially independent of the modified baseline; thus, to report nongeneralization would serve no useful purpose, for its nonoccurrence would be expected. Again, any such documentation contributes to our understanding of the extent and limits of generalization, as well as serving as an indication of the frequent necessity of generalization-programming techniques.

There is another reason for the predominance of positive results in this section: if nongeneralization was clearly evident, and the modification of this state was important, then a form of limited programming was frequently instituted. Examples of this research will be discussed in the next category, "Sequential Modification".

2. *Sequential Modification*

These studies exemplify a more systematic approach to generalization than the Train-and-Hope research. Again, a particular behavior change is effected, and generalization is assessed. But then, if generalization is absent or deficient, procedures are initiated to accomplish the desired changes by systematic sequential modification in every nongeneralized condition, *i.e.,* across responses, subjects, settings, or experimenters. The possibility of unprogrammed generalization typically was not examined in these sequential modification studies, because after the initial demonstration of nongeneralization, all other baselines were exhausted. That is, after changes had been produced directly in all baselines, generalization to nonrecorded responses, subjects, settings, and experimenters may have occurred, but could not be examined.

For example, Meichenbaum, Bowers, and Ross (1968) reported an absence of generalization of behavior changes from an afternoon intervention period to the morning period in a classroom for institutionalized female adolescent offenders. Money dispensed contingent on on-task behaviors effected desired behavior changes during the afternoon, but generalization to the morning period required that the same manipulations be applied there as well (sequential modification across settings). Similarly, generalization across settings of the disruptive and oppositional behavior of two children was investigated by Wahler (1969). He demonstrated control of these behaviors in the home by using differential attention and timeout operations. When generalization to the children's school behavior was not evidenced, similar contingency operations were employed to accomplish changes in that setting as well.

The category of Sequential Modification characterizes much of the actual practice of many behavior analysts. Sequential modification is merely a systematized experimental procedure that formalizes and allows evaluation of these typical therapeutic endeavors. The tactic of scheduling behavior-change programs in every condition to which generalization is desired is frequently employed. The rationale for these procedures is as follows. If a desired generalization is not likely to be exhibited after changing a behavior in a particular condition, or a number of conditions, *e.g.*, settings, then the researcher or practitioner works to effect changes across conditions as a matter of course, rather than as an outcome of the display or nondisplay of generalization. Thus, a behavior analyst is likely to advise the scheduling of consequences in every relevant condition in preference to the dispensing of consequences in only one or a few conditions, while hoping for generalization, but likely not seeing it.

3. *Introduce to Natural Maintaining Contingencies*

Perhaps the most dependable of all generalization programming mechanisms is one that hardly deserves the name: the transfer of behavioral control from the teacher-experimenter to stable, natural contingencies that can be trusted to operate in the environment to which the subject will return, or already occupies. To a considerable extent, this goal is accomplished by choosing behaviors to teach that normally will meet maintaining reinforcement after the teaching (Ayllon and Azrin, 1968).

Baer and Wolf (1970) reported a study by Ingram that illustrated the mechanism of "trapping", where a preschool child was taught an entry response that exposed the child to the natural contingencies of peers in the preschool environment. Preschool teachers modified the low rate of skillful interaction of the child by priming others to interact with the subject and reinforcing appropriate interactions. The data showed that over time the teachers lost control of the interaction behavior, which remained high; it was assumed that the group's natural consequences for interaction had taken control of the subject's behavior. Thus, to program generalization, the child perhaps needed only to be introduced adequately to the natural reinforcers inherent in active preschool play and interaction. Some early analyses of preschool children's behavior have stressed that if the child can be so introduced (through the operation of differential attention from teachers) to a reinforcing preschool natural environment, then the behaviors eventually do not need to be maintained by continued contrived modification of the environment. For example, Hall and Broden (1967) modified the manipulative play, climbing, and social interaction of three subjects through social reinforcement operations. Behavior changes were shown to be durable and successful followup data at three months were described.

Buell, Stoddard, Harris, and Baer (1968) demonstrated the collateral development of appropriate social behavior (*e.g.*, touching, verbalizing, and playing with other children) accompanying the reinforcement of increased use of outdoor play equipment by a 3-yr-old girl. This entry response to the natural reinforcement community was tactically sound because the child's motor behavior was modified in a setting where the resulting behavior would tend automatically to increase social contact with other children, and this natural social environment could maintain the child's new skills, but indeed may also be expected to sharpen and refine them, and add entirely new ones as well.

Most of the research concerning natural maintaining contingencies has involved children, perhaps because such techniques seem particularly suitable, especially to their social behavior. Research would profit by determining what natural reinforcement communities exist for various behaviors and subjects, and what economical means may be employed to ensure entry to these behavioral traps.

Unfortunately, in some instances there may be no natural reinforcement operating to develop and maintain skills. For example, in the case of retarded and institutionalized persons whose dependency has become a stable fact in the lives of their caretakers, some re-arrangement of the natural environment may be necessary. A few studies have introduced subjects to semicontrived or redesigned "natural" reinforcement communities. A simple but meaningful example was provided by Horner (1971), who taught a 5-yr-old institutionalized retarded boy to walk on crutches in an experimental setting. The child was then prompted to generalize the new walking skill to other settings and activities to which he previously had been taken in a wheelchair by solicitous caretakers, by enlisting those caretakers to refrain from offering this help. Within 15 days after treatment was concluded, the child walked on crutches to all those activities and settings, eventually extending his ambulation skills to any part of his world. Stolz and Wolf (1969) trained a 16-yr-old, "blind" retarded male to discriminate visual stimuli. Then, the environment was so structured that assistance was not given in situations where it had previously been given as a matter of course. When the boy was required to use visual cues to help himself in a cafeteria line, he soon emitted the necessary behaviors. However, these studies did not establish the functionality of their procedures in the maintenance of behavior changes.

Another significant example was provided by Seymour and Stokes (1976). In their study, institutionalized delinquent girls were taught to solicit reinforcement (*cf.* Graubard, Rosenberg, and Miller, 1971) from their natural community, the staff of their residential institution. In their case, the staff had rarely displayed any systematic attempts at reinforcing desirable behavior shown by the girls, perhaps on the presumption that the girls were "bad" and not reinforcible in any case. However, the experimenters were able to teach the girls that when their work was objectively good, and when staff persons were nearby, a simple skill of calling these adults' attention to their good work would result in fairly consistent reinforcement. Thus, this was a case in which experimental reinforcement was used to develop a response in the subjects that would tap and cultivate the available but dormant natural community. In theory, this new skill should have obviated the need for further experimental reinforcement, for the praise evoked should have functioned to maintain both the girls' work and cueing, and the cueing, in turn, should have functioned to maintain staff praise. The Seymour and Stokes' study could not be continued long enough to establish whether this would happen, and so it remains a logically appealing but still unexplored method of enhancing generalization: teaching the subject a means of *recruiting* a natural community of reinforcement to maintain that generalization. Perhaps an even greater advantage of such procedures is a change in the locus of control: the subjects can become more prominent agents of their own behavior change, rather than being hapless pawns of more-or-less random environmental contingencies.

Restructuring the environment thus becomes a target of research aimed at extending the generalization of newly taught skills; even though, at a technical level, this operation may not be considered generalization, but rather transfer of control from one reinforcement contingency to another. In any event, it is a much neglected topic of experimental research, although widely recognized as a desirable, and even essential characteristic of any rehabilitative effort.

Some natural contingencies are inevitably at work contributing to the maintenance of inappropriate behavior. For example, peer-group control of inappropriate behavior has often been suspected and sometimes documented (Buehler, Patterson, and Furniss, 1966; Gelfand, Gelfand, and Dobson, 1967; Solomon and Wahler, 1973).

It would seem reasonable, then, that if the pattern of reinforcement of inappropriate behavior is modified, the observed outcome may erroneously, but happily be attributed to generalization. For example, Bolstad and Johnson (1972) presented data that showed that both experimental and control subjects in the same classroom were all affected (although not to the same extent) by experimental manipulation of the reinforcement contingency for the experimental subjects, whereas control subjects in a different classroom were not so affected. The authors presented data that may account for these differences. The control subjects in the experimental classroom, who were also disruptive students, had fewer disruptive interactions with the experimental subjects during the treatment phases than during baseline. This possible generalization effect may be due to the disruption of the natural contingencies operating in that environment. That is, other disruptive students previously supported some of the disruptive behavior of the control subjects, but during treatment these experimental subjects did not support the disruptive behavior of their peers and, thus, a "generalized" decrease in disruptive behavior by the control subjects resulted.

4. *Train Sufficient Exemplars*

If the result of teaching one exemplar of a generalizable lesson is merely the mastery of the exemplar taught, with no generalization beyond it, then the obvious route to generalization is to teach another exemplar of the same generalization lesson, and then another, and then another, and so on until the induction is formed (*i.e.,* until generalization occurs sufficiently to satisfy the problem posed). Examples of such programming techniques will be described in this category of training sufficient exemplars, perhaps one of the most valuable areas of programming. Certainly it is the generalization-programming area most prominent and extensive in the present literature.

In the research discussed previously under the categories of Train and Hope and Sequential Modification, the typical analysis of generalization concerned the measurement of generalization to only a few (and often only one) extraexperimental responses, subjects, settings, experimenters, or times. When the absence of generalization was noted, sometimes it was accomplished by further direct intervention in every nongeneralized condition (*i.e.,* Sequential Modification). Having completed such modifications, the possibility of more extensive generalized effects (*i.e.,* beyond the two or three modified baselines) was not examined. In the training of sufficient exemplars, generalization to untrained stimulus conditions and to untrained responses is programmed by the training of *sufficient* exemplars (rather than all) of these stimulus conditions or responses.

A systematic demonstration of programmed generalization and measurement of generalized effects beyond intervention conditions was reported by Stokes, Baer, and Jackson (1974). They established that training and maintenance of retarded childrens' greeting responses by one experimenter was not usually sufficient for the generalization of the response across experimenters. However, high levels of generalization to over 20 members of the institution staff (and newcomers as well) who had not participated in the training of the response were recorded, after a second experimenter trained and maintained the response in conjunction with the first experimenter. Thus, when generalization did not prevail after the training of one stimulus exemplar, it was programmed by training a greater diversity of stimulus (trainer) conditions. Similarly, Garcia (1974) taught a conversational speech form to two retarded children, and, upon discovering a lack of stable generalization across experimenters after one training input, programmed generalization across experimenters by having a second experimenter teach the same responses.

A sufficient-stimulus-exemplars demonstration of programmed generalization across settings has been described by Allen (1973). Allen modified the bizarre verbalizations of an 8-yr-old boy by differential attention procedures. Ignoring bizarre verbalizations and praise for appropriate interaction reduced bizarre verbalizations during evening camp activities. However, there was no generalization to three other camp settings. After additional training in a second setting, some generalization to the unmanipulated settings was noted. This generalization was further enhanced by intervention in the third setting. Unfortunately, the experimental procedures did not allow sufficient time to document the full extent of generalization after training in two settings, but generalization after training in two settings was clearly evident. Griffiths and Craighead (1972) similarly programmed generalization across settings. A 30-yr-old retarded woman received praise and tokens for correct articulation in speech therapy. Generalization to a residential cottage was not observed until the same procedures were instituted there. Following training in these two stimulus exemplars, generalization to a third nontraining setting (a classroom) was observed.

Very little research concerned with generalization programming has dealt with the training of sufficient stimulus exemplars. The infrequent research that has been published is characterized largely by programming across experimenters. This work has been promising, for after a modest number of training inputs, generalization apparently will occur with persons not involved in training—unquestionably a valuable and inexpensive outcome. However, the present implication of these studies is limited because of the restricted nature of the type of subjects and responses analyzed. Further work is also needed to give direction to the optimal conditions whereby the most extensive generalization will be achieved with a minimal training expenditure. Nevertheless, it is optimistic to note how frequently a sufficient number of exemplars is a small number of exemplars. Frequently, it is no more than two. In particular, there may well be reason to suspect that the use of two trainers will yield excellent results in terms of generalization. This possibility, obviously an economical one, certainly merits systematic study of its potential and limits.

Although very little research has been reported, the analysis of generalization programming by training in a number of settings is a virtually untapped area of far-reaching value. However, consistent optimism should follow examination of the studies showing generalization after training in only a few settings. Unfortunately, behavior analysts seem too often satisfied with the modification of a single, well-defined behavior in one setting, *e.g.*, a laboratory preschool. Discriminated programs are often acceptable, and sometimes even desirable. When generalization is a valid concern, but researchers and practitioners do not act as if this were so, the discriminated behavior of researchers is most probably inhibitory to the development of an effective generalization technology.

Over the past 10 yr, there has developed an extensive literature discussing the programmed generalization of responses through the training of sufficient response exemplars. A response class has been operationally defined to describe the fact that some responses are organized such that operations applied to a subset of responses in the class affect the other members of that class in the same manner. For example, Baer, Peterson, and Sherman (1967) reinforced various motor imitations by retarded children. They found that as long as reinforcement followed some imitative responses, other imitations continued to be performed without training or reinforcement.

A topographical analysis of generalized imitation has been made by Garcia, Baer, and Firestone (1971). Four retarded children were trained to imitate three different topographical types of response: small motor, large motor, and short vocal. These subjects were also probed for their imitation of other unreinforced responses: short motor, long motor, short vocal, and long vocal. Generalized imitation was observed with each subject, but this generalization reflected the particular dimensions of the topographical response currently being trained or having previously received training. Thus, generalization may occur within well-defined classes and may not generalize to other classes unless some special training (generalization programming) occurs within that class as well. These data depict one possible limitation of the generality of generalized imitation, as well as pointing to the need to train response exemplars that will adequately reflect the diversity of the generalization being programmed.

Children's grammatical development has been another prominent area of research dealing with generalized behavior. The concept of response class is again pivotal in these studies, which conceptualize the rules of morphological grammar as equivalent to response class phenomena. For example, Guess, Sailor, Rutherford, and Baer (1968) developed the generative correct use of plurals by a retarded girl. After teaching a number of exemplars of the correct plural response, the girl appropriately labelled new objects in the singular or plural without further direct training relevant to those objects. Plural usage had become a generalized response class; the morphological rule had been established. Schumaker and Sherman (1970) rewarded three retarded children for the correct production of past- and present-tense forms of verbs. As past- and present-tense forms of verbs within an inflectional class were modified, there occurred a generalized usage of untrained verbs to similar tense forms.

There has been considerable research to establish the importance of the training of sufficient response exemplars. A survey of these (approximately 60) studies shows that the number of exemplars found to be "sufficient" for a desirable level and durability of generalization varies widely, probably determined primarily by the nature of the task and the subject's prior skills relevant to it. Most of this research was concerned with the development of motor and vocal imitations, and the beginning development of grammar and syntax. The development of question-asking and instruction-following is also well represented.

In conclusion, examination of the sufficient exemplar research points to a significant (and long-familiar) generalization-programming procedure: a number of stimulus and/or response exemplars should undergo training. That is, to program the generalized performance of certain responses across various setting conditions or persons, training should occur across a (sufficient) number of setting conditions and/or with various persons. In a similar manner, generalization across responses can be programmed reliably by the training of a number of responses. Diversity of exemplars seems to be the rule to follow in pursuit of the maximum generalization. Sufficient diversity to reflect the dimensions of the desired generalization is a useful tactic. However, diversity may also be our greatest enemy: too much diversity of exemplars and not enough (sufficient) exemplars of similar responses may make potential gains disproportional to the investment of training effort. The optimal combination of sufficient exemplars and sufficient diversity to yield the most valuable generalization is critically in need of analysis. Is the best procedure to train many exemplars with little diversity at the outset, and then expand the diversity to include dimensions of the desired generalization? Or is it a more productive endeavor to train fewer exemplars that represent a greater diversity, and persist in the training until generalization emerges?

5. *Train Loosely*

One relatively simple technique can be conceptualized as merely the negation of discrimination technique. That is, teaching is conducted with relatively little control over the stimuli presented and the correct responses allowed, so as to maximize sampling of relevant dimensions for transfer to other situations and other forms of the behavior. A formal example of this most often informal technique was provided by Schroeder and Baer (1972), who taught vocal imitation skills to retarded children in both of two ways, one emphasizing tight restriction of the vocal skills being learned at the moment (serial training of vocal imitations), and the other allowing much greater range of stimuli within the current problem (concurrent training of imitations). The latter method was characterized repeatedly by greater generalization to as-yet-untaught vocal imitation problems, thus affirming "loose" teaching techniques as a contributor to wider generalization.

It will be appreciated that the literature of the field contains very few examples of this type. Researchers always have attempted to maintain thorough control and careful restriction and standardization of their teaching procedures, primarily to allow easy subsequent interpretation of the nature of their (successful) teaching techniques. Yet the import of this technique is that careful management of teaching techniques to a precisely repetitive handful of stimuli or formats may, in fact, correspondingly restrict generalization of the lessons being learned. The ultimate force of this recommendation remains to be seen. What seems required is programmatic research aimed at assessing the generalization characteristics of lessons taught under careful, restricted conditions, relative to similar lessons taught under looser, more variable conditions.

6. *Use Indiscriminable Contingencies*

Intermittent schedules of reinforcement have been shown repeatedly to be particularly resistant to extinction, relative to continuous schedules (Ferster and Skinner, 1957). Resistance to extinction may be regarded as a form of generalization—generalization across time subsequent to learning. The essential feature of intermittent schedules may be their unpredictability—the impossibility of discriminating reinforcement occasions from nonreinforcement occasions until after the fact. Thus, if contingencies of reinforcement or punishment, or the setting events that mark the presence or absence of those contingencies, are made indiscriminable, then generalization may well be observed.

In generalization, behavior occurs in settings in which it will not be reinforced, just as it does in settings in which it will be reinforced. Then, the analogue to an intermittent schedule, extended to settings, is a condition in which the subject cannot discriminate in which settings a response will be reinforced or not reinforced. A potential approximation to such a condition was presented in a study by Schwarz and Hawkins (1970). In that experiment, the behavior of a sixth-grade child was videotaped during math and spelling classes. Later, after each school day had ended, the child was shown the tape of the math class and awarded reinforcers according to how often good posture, absence of face-touching, and appropriate voice-loudness were evident on that tape. Although reinforcers were awarded only on the basis of behaviors displayed during the math class, desirable improvements were observed during the spelling class as well. In that reinforcement was delayed, this technique must have made it difficult for the child to discriminate in which class the behaviors were critical for earning reinforcement. In other words, the generalized success of the study may well be attributable to the partly indiscriminable nature of the reinforcement contingency.

In general, it may be suspected that delayed reinforcement often will have the advantage of making the times and places in which the contingency actually operates indiscriminable to the subject. However, this advantage is an advantage, by hypothesis, primarily for the goal of generalization. Otherwise, delayed reinforcement would often be considered an inefficient technique, most especially so for the initial development of a new skill. Indeed, it may be exactly in the realm of disadvantaged persons such as retarded children that the usual inefficiency of delayed reinforcement may seem the most severe handicap to its use. However, its potential for fostering generalization suggests strongly that further research be invested in this procedure (and any others that make reinforcement contingencies properly indiscriminable), to develop methods of applying it perhaps only after the initial development of a new skill, in the interests of promoting generalization.

Less than a dozen studies of generalization interpretable as cases of indiscriminable reinforcement contingencies can be found in the literature. Kazdin (1973), for example, showed that teacher attention to one retarded child was responded to by another child as if it were reinforcement for on-task behavior. Indeed, the onlooker reacted with increased on-task behavior, even when the teacher attended to the target child's off-task behavior. Possibly, prior experience with reinforcement contingent on the peers' on-task behavior was sufficient to make all future praise (contingent or not) discriminative for on-task behavior. In other words, with sufficient prior experience, the onlooker may have stopped observing the contingency in which the reinforcement operated and responded only to the reinforcing stimulus' presence, making the contingency functionally indiscriminable.

Generalization across subjects has similarly been reported by Broden, Bruce, Mitchell, Carter, and Hall (1970) in a classroom of culturally disadvantaged children. When positive teacher attention was given for one child's attention to academic work, the attending of a peer also increased. This generalization was also a probable function of the cueing properties of teacher reinforcement. However, the generalization observed may also have been due to the manipulation of natural social consequences received by the nontarget child through peer attention, or may have been caused by a slight increase in the amount of teacher attention to the nontarget child. These effects deserve further systematic evaluation because of their relevance to the classroom practices of many teachers who strive to instruct effectively but are unable to devote extensive time to individual children.

Pendergrass (1972) showed that timeout could be employed to decrease the destructive behavior of two retarded children. With one subject, decreased rates were also observed with another response (self-biting) which was sometimes chained to the destructive behavior, but not itself subjected to contingent timeout. However, with the second subject, generalization to a second response (autistic jerking movement) was not observed. Analysis of the data revealed that the two behaviors occurred simultaneously more frequently with the subject with whom generalization was evidenced. Thus, with this subject, punishment of the generalization response occurred more frequently when destructive behavior was punished. Unfortunately, it was not determined how often the self-biting occurred at times not simultaneous with the destructive behavior. Therefore, the schedule of punishment for self-biting was not established, *i.e.,* whether biting occurred only when destructive behavior occurred and, therefore, always met the timeout contingency. In this example (which was not intended to be a careful analysis of the indiscriminable reinforcement concept), not only was the reinforcement contingency somewhat difficult to discriminate, but the two behaviors (destructive and self-destructive responses) also may well have been only somewhat differentiated by the subject.

Thus, preventing the ready discrimination of contingencies is a generalization-programming technique worthy of application and research. Perhaps a random or haphazard delivery of reinforcement will (if luck or good judgement prevails) function to modify targetted behavior as well as behavior occurring in proximal time or space. Even noncontingent reinforcement, delivered at the outset of an intervention program, may retard initial effects, but may work to later advantage in generalization outcomes.

Finally, Kazdin and Polster (1973) showed once again the usefulness of intermittent schedules to delay subsequent extinction, relative to continuous schedules of reinforcement. Social interaction by two retardates was reinforced with tokens. After establishing social interaction, one subject received continuous reinforcement and the other, intermittent reinforcement. During extinction, only the subject who received intermittent reinforcement continued to interact socially with peers. However, these results may simply reflect different extinction rates by two subjects. The research was essentially a group study where $N = 1$. Adequate single-subject experimental control was lacking. Therefore, replication of these procedures would be desirable.

7. *Program Common Stimuli*

The passive approach to generalization described earlier need not be a completely impractical one. If it is supposed that generalization will occur, if only there are sufficient stimulus components occurring in common in both the training and generalization settings, then a reasonably practical technique is to guarantee that common and salient stimuli will be present in both. One predictor of the salience of a stimulus to be chosen for this role is its already established function for other important behaviors of the subject.

Children's peers may represent peculiarly suitable candidates for a stimulus common to both training and generalization settings. An example has been provided by Stokes and Baer (1976). In their study, two children exhibiting serious learning disabilities were recruited to learn several word-recognition skills. One child was taught these skills and concurrently shown how to teach them to the other child, thus acting as a peer-tutor. It was found that both children reliably learned the skills, but that neither generalized them reliably or stably to somewhat different settings in which the other child usually was absent. However, when the peer-tutor was brought into those settings, then each child similarly showed greatly increased and stabilized generalization, even though there were never any consequences for generalization. Similar demonstrations have been provided by Johnston and Johnston (1972) for the skill of speech articulation. In that study, peers were rewarded for correct monitoring of the subjects' articulation. Generalization of correct articulation occurred only when the "monitoring" peer was present. Unfortunately, it was not determined clearly whether generalization was evidenced because of the discriminative properties of the peers' presence in both settings, or whether the peers actively continued their monitoring in the generalization setting.

Rincover and Koegel (1975) have also incorporated functional training stimuli into the generalization setting. Autistic children were rewarded for imitation and instruction-following in a training setting. Four of their 10 subjects then did not exhibit generalization to a different setting. Therefore, to program for this generalization, various aspects of the training procedures (*e.g.,* hand movement by therapist) or physical training environment (*e.g.,* table and chairs) were systematically introduced to the generalization setting to control generalization. Making the experimental setting more closely resemble the regular classroom (generalization setting) was the programming procedure employed by Koegel and Rincover (1974). They decreased the teacher-to-student ratio in the experimental setting from 1-to-1 to 1-to-8. After these special programming conditions were instituted, there was increased performance on previously learned and new behaviors learned in the classroom. Walker and Buckley (1972) programmed generalization of the effects of remedial training of social and academic classroom behavior by establishing common stimuli between the experimental remedial classroom and the childrens' regular classroom by using the same academic materials in both classrooms.

The literature of this field shows only a handful of studies deliberately making use of a common stimulus in both training and generalization settings. Obviously, this is a technological dimension urgently in need of thorough development. The use of peers as the common stimulus has much to recommend it as a practical and natural technique. To what extent peers need to participate in the training setting has not yet been determined, although the absence of generalization sometimes shown when peers are present in nontraining settings, suggests that peers not involved in a training setting will not likely acquire sufficient discriminative function to control generalized responding. The use of common physical stimuli is in even greater need of systematic research. A common stimulus approach to generalization would encourage the incorporation into training settings of (naturally occurring) physical stimuli that are frequently prominent or functional in nontraining environments. If these stimuli are well chosen, and can be made functional and salient in the training procedures, then generalization may thereby be programmed.

8. *Mediate Generalization*

Mediated generalization is well known as a theoretical mechanism explaining generalization of highly symbolic learnings (Cofer and Foley, 1942). In essence, it requires establishing a response as part of the new learning that is likely to be utilized in other problems as well, and will constitute sufficient commonality between the original learning and the new problem to result in generalization. The most commonly used mediator is language, apparently. However, the deliberate application of language to accomplish generalization is rare in the literature reviewed, and correspondingly little is known about what aspects of a language response make for best mediation.

A sophisticated analysis of mediated generalization was conducted by Risley and Hart (1968), who taught preschool children to report at the end of play on their play-material choices. Mention of a given choice was reinforced with snacks, which produced increased mentioning of that choice, but no change in the children's actual use of that play-material. When reinforcement was restricted to *true* reports of play-material choices, however, the children then changed their play behavior (the next day) so that when queried about that play, they could truthfully report on their use of the specified play material and earn reinforcement. Control over any choice of play materials proved possible with this technique, which placed teaching contingencies not on the play, but on a potential mediator (verbal report) of that play behavior. That the reports were only potential mediators was apparent in the early stages of the study, when the children readily reported (untruly) their use of play materials with no corresponding actual behavior with those materials; at that stage, they earned reinforcement even so. When the reinforcement was restricted to true reports, the reports then became mediators of play behavior. The lesson generalized, such that after several sequential experiences with these procedures, the children then used reports about play as mediators, even without reinforcement being restricted to only true reports. Israel and O'Leary (1973) used essentially the same paradigm to compare the effects of having children report first what they would play with later, in contrast to having them report after play what they had done (the Risley and Hart method); they found that reinforcing postreports (when they were true) produced more actual behavior (the next day) than reinforcing the actual behavior when it agreed with the earlier promise to perform it. This technique has been extended subsequently to the case of social skills, specifically sharing and praising between young children (Rogers-Warren and Baer, 1976). In that case, modelling was added, such that the young children would have a thorough chance to learn the nature of the relatively complex responses at issue.

Obviously, verbal mediation can easily fail, most especially in those situations in which the verbal mediators have little meaning (*i.e.,* tightly restricted discriminative value) for the subjects. It is commonplace to find children agreeing to a query (*e.g.,* about whether they praised or shared) without any knowledge of what that must entail in actual behavior. In the case of retarded children, it might be particularly true that the ability to use verbal responses as mediators would lag behind that of normal children using the same language responses. It may be reasonable to suggest that in the development of language-training programs, systematic attention be given to the training of language skills sufficiently well elaborated to function as mediators of nonverbal behavior. Language is a response, of course; it is also, equally obviously, a stimulus to the speaker as well as to the listener. Thus, it meets perfectly the logic of a salient common stimulus, to be carried from any training setting to any generalization setting that the child may ever enter. It also perfectly exemplifies the essence of the active generalization approach recommended earlier.

The mediation of generalization is also exemplified in the behavior analysis research of self-control and self-management procedures. That is, self-control procedures such as self-recording, taught as part of an intervention program, may function to promote generalization: such techniques are easy to transport and may be employed readily to facilitate responding under generalization conditions. Some research that has employed any or all of the various tactics of self-assessment, self-recording, self-determination of reinforcement, and/or self-administration of reinforcement (Glynn, Thomas, and Shee, 1973), has also displayed maintenance and generalization of behavior change; however, the correlation is not perfect.

Broden, Hall, and Mitts (1971) reported that after an eighth-grade girl experienced self-recording of study behavior and teacher praise for improved study, her study behavior maintained at a high level for a recorded three weeks. Although the individual effects of the self-recording and praise were not determined, it is possible that the self-recording procedures contributed significantly to this generalization.

Drabman, Spitalnik, and O'Leary (1973) taught disruptive children to match their teacher's evaluations of their appropriate classroom behavior. Tokens were dispensed for appropriate classroom behavior and accurate matching. Disruptive classroom behavior decreased and was maintained at low levels during a 12-day phase when tokens were not dispensed for self-recording accuracy. Generalized behavior improvement was also evident during a 15-min no-token period within the experimental hour. These changes were possibly a function of the close temporal proximity of the token periods, which frequently immediately preceded or followed the generalization period.

The role of self-control procedures in mediating generalization has often been proposed. Research would do well to examine the contribution of self-control tactics in generalization and maintenance, especially when formal intervention manipulations have ceased to operate. The effects of accompanying procedures should be experimentally separated from self-control effects, and the role of each of the various self-control tactics (Glynn *et al.,* 1973) should be individually analyzed. The potential of self-mediated generalization is apparent, but its implications and practical utility still remain to be assessed.

9. *Train "To Generalize"*

If generalization is considered as a response itself, then a reinforcement contingency may be placed on it, the same as with any other operant. Informally, teachers often do this when they urge a student who has been taught one example of a general principle to "see" another example as "the same thing". (In principle, they are also attempting to make use of language as a mediator of generalization, relying on the supposed characteristics of words like "same" to accomplish the generalization.) Common observation suggests that the method often fails, and that when it does succeed, little extrinsic reinforcement is offered as a consequence. A more formal example of the technique was seen in a study by Goetz and Baer (1973), in which three preschool children were taught to generalize the response of making block forms (in blockbuilding play). Descriptive social reinforcement was offered only for every different form the child made, *i.e.,* contingent on every first appearance of any blockbuilding form within a session, but not for any subsequent appearances of that form. Thus, the child was rewarded for moving along the generalization gradient underlying blockform inventions, and never for staying at any one point. In general, the technique succeeded, in that the children steadily invented new block forms while this contingency was in use. Thus, there exists the possibility of programming reinforcement specifically, perhaps *only,* for movement along the generalization gradient desired.

In largely unspecified ways, perhaps two other studies exemplify this logic. Herbert and Baer

(1972), for example, taught two mothers of deviant children to give social reinforcement only to their children's appropriate behaviors, but taught the mothers from the outset to judge all behavior according to criteria they helped to develop, rather than attack only a few specified child responses. These mothers learned a generalized skill because they applied correct social contingencies to categories that included virtually all appropriate child behavior likely to occur. Behavior changes were maintained at 20 and 24 weeks after completion of formal training. Similarly, Parsonson, Baer, and Baer (1974) taught two teachers of retarded children to apply generalized correct social contingencies to all likely appropriate and inappropriate behaviors of preschool retarded children. These effects were also durable over several months. Apparently generalized changes were produced in these studies by Herbert and Baer and Parsonson *et al.*, but the extent and quality of that generalization was not quantified as such.

Very few studies of this type are found in the literature of applied behavior analysis, probably because of the preference of behaviorists to consider generalization as an outcome of behavioral change, rather than as a behavior itself. Ultimately, this behavioristic stance may well prove durable and consistent. Meanwhile, it is worth hypothesizing that "to generalize" may be treated as if it were an operant response, and reinforced as such, simply to see what useful results occur.

Consequently, one other technique deserves discussion: the systematic use of instructions to facilitate generalization. Thus, if a behavior is taught and generalization is not displayed, the least expensive of all techniques is to tell the subject about the possibility of generalization and then ask for it. If that generalization then occurs, it may well be referred to as "instructed generalization". If the effects of that instruction are themselves to become generalized (yielding a "generalized generalizer"?), then reinforcement of the generalized behavior, on a suitable schedule, might well be prudent, at least at first. Perhaps it is simply a very elaborate version of this technique that is being practiced when a client is taught to relax in a somewhat anxiety-arousing situation, and reinforced (socially) for doing so; and then is instructed to relax in a somewhat more powerful anxiety-arousing situation, *etc.* That is, systematic desensitization to a heirarchy of stimuli may be analyzed as reinforcing not just relaxation, but also generalization along an already constructed generalization gradient (*cf.* Yates, 1970, p. 64ff.).

CONCLUSION

The structure of the generalization literature and its implicit embryonic technology has been summarized. The most frequent treatments of generalization are also the least analytical—those described as *Train and Hope* and *Sequential Modification.* Included in the category of Train and Hope were those studies where the potential for generalization had been recognized, its presence or absence noted, but no particular effort was expended to accomplish generalization. By contrast, some limited programming was implemented in the Sequential Modification research. In these studies, given an absence of reliable generalization, procedures to effect changes were instituted directly in every nongeneralized condition. Although contributing significantly to our understanding of the generalization of behavior-change programs, these studies are not examples of the programming of generalization.

Seven categories were discussed that directly relate to a technology of generalization. First, the potential role of *Natural Maintaining Contingencies* was discussed. According to this tactic, generalization may be programmed by suitable trapping manipulations, where responses are introduced to natural reinforcement communities that refine and maintain those skills without further therapeutic intervention. The *Training of Sufficient Exemplars* is numerically the most extensive area of programming: generalization to untrained stimulus conditions and to untrained responses is programmed by the training of sufficient exemplars of those stimulus conditions or responses. *Train Loosely* is a programming technique in which training is conducted with relatively little control over the stimuli and responses involved, and generalization is thereby enhanced. To invoke the tactic of *Indiscriminable Contingencies,* the contingencies of reinforcement or punishment, or the setting events marking the presence or absence of those contingencies, are deliberately made less predictable, so that it becomes difficult to discriminate reinforcement occasions from nonreinforcement occasions. *Common Stimuli* may be employed in generalization programming by incorporating into training settings social and physical stimuli that are salient in generalization settings, and that can be made to assume functional or obvious roles in the training setting. *Mediated Generalization* requires establishing a response as part of new learning that is likely to be utilized in other problems as well, and thus result in generalization. The final technique, *Train "To Generalize",* involves reinforcing generalization itself as if it were an explicit behavior. These programming techniques should be researched further and usefully applied in programs in which generalization is relevant.

This list of generalized tactics conceals within itself a much smaller list of specific tactics. These specific tactics can be presented as a small picture of the generalization technology in its present most pragmatic form, not only to offer a set of what-to-do possibilities, but also to emphasize how very small the current technology is and how much development it requires:

1. Look for a response that enters a natural community; in particular, teach subjects to cue their potential natural communities to reinforce their desirable behaviors.
2. Keep training more exemplars; in particular, diversify them.
3. Loosen experimental control over the stimuli and responses involved in training; in particular, train different examples concurrently, and vary instructions, S^Ds, social reinforcers, and backup reinforcers.
4. Make unclear the limits of training contingencies; in particular, conceal, when possible, the point at which those contingencies stop operating, possibly by delayed reinforcement.
5. Use stimuli that are likely to be found in generalization settings in training settings as well; in particular, use peers as tutors.
6. Reinforce accurate self-reports of desirable behavior; apply self-recording and self-reinforcement techniques whenever possible.
7. When generalizations occur, reinforce at least some of them at least sometimes, as if "to generalize" were an operant response class.

There are many examples of generalization and nongeneralization of behavior changes. The fact that apparently unprogrammed generalization has been demonstrated (particularly across time) is valuable. It heralds a practicality desirable in any technology of behavior: that every one of a subjects' responses, in every setting, with every experimenter, and at every conceivable time does not need to meet specific treatment consequences for that program to accomplish and maintain important behavior changes. Alternatively, the fact that generalization is not always observed and durability is not inevitable means that there is hope for behavior modification: behavior can always be modified and changes are not necessarily irreversible. That is, once behavior has been modified, there is still the possibility of reconditioning if changes are undesirable or inappropriate, or if new inappropriate behaviors develop. If both appropriate and inappropriate behavior changes were to persist and prove irreversible, it would presage the demise of any technology of behavioral intervention. This occurrence of nongeneralization also underlines the need to develop a technology of generalization, so that programming will be a fundamental component of any procedures when durability and generalization of behavior changes are desirable.

A most important question is prompted by an examination of the previous research: does generalization ever occur without programming? In the above research, generalization was not always evident. In fact, the highly discriminated effects of some operant programs were sometimes documented. We have seen that the behavior analysis literature describes various programs that have shown that generalization may be promoted or programmed by particular intervention techniques. It seems reasonable to suggest, then, that many of the successful Train-and-Hope examples cited above may be undiagnosed instances of informal or inadvertent programming techniques, rather than an absence of programming techniques. It cannot be discounted, and is indeed possible, that these generalization examples may simply depict successful programmed generalization, and neither the authors of those papers, nor the present authors have recognized or hypothesized the programming technique.

Perhaps the most pragmatic orientation for behavior analysts is to assume that generalization does not occur except through some form of programming. Thus, the best course of action seems to be that of systematic measurement and analysis of variables that may have been functional in any apparently unprogrammed generalization. These analyses should be included as part of all research where "unprogrammed" generalized behavior changes are evidenced, for discriminated behavior changes may well be the rule if generalization is not specifically programmed. Such analyses, if successful, will contribute to a technology of generalization by further developing the understanding of critical variables that function to produce generalization, and would further emphasize the need always to be concerned not only with generalization issues, but with the various techniques that accomplish generalization.

In other words, behavioral research and practice should act as if there were no such animal as "free" generalization—as if generalization never occurs "naturally", but always requires programming. Then, "programmed generalization" is essentially a redundant term, and should be descriptive only of the active regard of researchers and practitioners.

REFERENCES

Allen, G. J. Case study: Implementation of behavior modification techniques in summer camp settings. *Behavior Therapy,* 1973, **4**, 570-575.

Ayllon, T. and Azrin, N. H. *The token economy.* New York: Appleton-Century-Crofts, 1968.

Azrin, N. H., Sneed, T. J., and Fox, R. M. Dry-bed: A rapid method of eliminating bedwetting (enuresis) of the retarded. *Behaviour Research and Therapy,* 1973, **11**, 427-434.

Baer, D. M., Peterson, R. F., and Sherman, J. A. The development of imitation by reinforcing behavioral similarity to a model. *Journal of the Experimental Analysis of Behavior,* 1967, **10**, 405-416.

Baer, D. M. and Wolf, M. M. The entry into natural communities of reinforcement. In R. Ulrich, T. Stachnik, and J. Mabry (Eds), *Control of human behavior: Volume II.* Glenview, Illinois: Scott, Foresman, 1970. Pp. 319-324.

Baer, D. M., Wolf, M. M., and Risley, T. R. Some current dimensions of applied behavior analysis. *Journal of Applied Behavior Analysis,* 1968, **1**, 91-97.

Bolstad, O. D. and Johnson, S. M. Self-regulation in the modification of disruptive behavior. *Journal of Applied Behavior Analysis,* 1972, **5**, 443-454.

Broden, M., Hall, R. V., and Mitts, B. The effect of self-recording on the classroom behavior of two eighth-grade students. *Journal of Applied Behavior Analysis,* 1971, **4**, 191-199.

Broden, M., Bruce, C., Mitchell, M. A., Carter, U., and Hall, R. V. Effects of teacher attention on attending behavior of two boys at adjacent desks. *Journal of Applied Behavior Analysis,* 1970, **3**, 199-203.

Buehler, R. E., Patterson, G. R., and Furniss, J. M. The reinforcement of behavior in institutional settings. *Behaviour Research and Therapy,* 1966, **4**, 157-167.

Buell, J., Stoddard, P., Harris, F. R., and Baer, D. M. Collateral social development accompanying reinforcement of outdoor play in a preschool child. *Journal of Applied Behavior Analysis,* 1968, **1**, 167-173.

Cofer, C. N. and Foley, J. P. Mediated generalization and the interpretation of verbal behavior: I. Prolegomena. *Psychological Review,* 1942, **49**, 513-540.

Drabman, R. S., Spitalnik, R., and O'Leary, K. D. Teaching self control to disruptive children. *Journal of Abnormal Psychology,* 1973, **82**, 10-16.

Ferster, C. B. and Skinner, B. F. *Schedules of reinforcement.* New York: Appleton-Century-Crofts, 1957.

Garcia, E. The training and generalization of a conversational speech form in nonverbal retardates. *Journal of Applied Behavior Analysis,* 1974, **7,** 137-149.

Garcia, E., Baer, D. M., and Firestone, I. The development of generalized imitation within topographically determined boundaries. *Journal of Applied Behavior Analysis,* 1971, **4,** 101-112.

Gelfand, D. M., Gelfand, S., and Dobson, W. R. Unprogrammed reinforcement of patients behavior in a mental hospital. *Behaviour Research and Therapy,* 1967, **5,** 201-207.

Glynn, E. L., Thomas, J. D., and Shee, S. M. Behavioral self-control of on-task behavior in an elementary classroom. *Journal of Applied Behavior Analysis,* 1973, **6,** 105-113.

Goetz, E. M. and Baer, D. M. Social control of form diversity and the emergence of new forms in children's blockbuilding. *Journal of Applied Behavior Analysis,* 1973, **6,** 105-113.

Graubard, P. S., Rosenberg, H., and Miller, M. B. Student applications of behavior modification to teachers and environments or ecological approaches to social deviancy. In E. A. Ramp and B. L. Hopkins (Eds), *A new direction for education: behavior analysis.* Lawrence, Kansas: Support and Development Center for Follow Through, 1971. Pp. 80-101.

Griffiths, H. and Craighead, W. E. Generalization in operant speech therapy for misarticulation. *Journal of Speech and Hearing Disorders,* 1972, **37,** 485-494.

Guess, D., Sailor, W., Rutherford, G., and Baer, D. M. An experimental analysis of linguistic development: the productive use of the plural morpheme. *Journal of Applied Behavior Analysis,* 1968, **1,** 297-306.

Hall, R. V. and Broden, M. Behavior changes in brain-injured children through social reinforcement. *Journal of Experimental Child Psychology,* 1967, **5,** 463-479.

Herbert, E. W. and Baer, D. M. Training parents as behavior modifiers: self-recording of contingent attention. *Journal of Applied Behavior Analysis,* 1972, **5,** 139-149.

Horner, R. D. Establishing use of crutches by a mentally retarded *spina bifida* child. *Journal of Applied Behavior Analysis,* 1971, **4,** 183-189.

Israel, A. C. and O'Leary, K. D. Developing correspondence between children's words and deeds. *Child Development,* 1973, **44,** 575-581.

Johnston, J. M. and Johnston, G. T. Modification of consonant speech-sound articulation in young children. *Journal of Applied Behavior Analysis,* 1972, **5,** 233-246.

Kazdin, A. E. The effect of vicarious reinforcement on attentive behavior in the classroom. *Journal of Applied Behavior Analysis,* 1973, **6,** 71-78.

Kazdin, A. E. and Polster, R. Intermittent token reinforcement and response maintenance in extinction. *Behavior Therapy,* 1973, **4,** 386-391.

Keller, F. S. and Schoenfeld, W. N. *Principles of psychology.* New York: Appleton-Century-Crofts, 1950.

Kifer, R. E., Lewis, M. A., Green, D. R., and Phillips, E. L. Training predelinquent youths and their parents to negotiate conflict situations. *Journal of Applied Behavior Analysis,* 1974, **7,** 357-364.

Koegel, R. L. and Rincover, A. Treatment of psychotic children in a classroom environment: I. Learning in a large group. *Journal of Applied Behavior Analysis,* 1974, **7,** 45-59.

Meichenbaum, D. H., Bowers, K. S., and Ross, R. R. Modification of classroom behavior of institutionalized female adolescent offenders. *Behaviour Research and Therapy,* 1968, **6,** 343-353.

Parsonson, B. S., Baer, A. M., and Baer, D. M. The application of generalized correct social contingencies by institutional staff: an evaluation of the effectiveness and durability of a training program. *Journal of Applied Behavior Analysis,* 1974, **7,** 427-437.

Pendergrass, V. E. Timeout from positive reinforcement following persistent high-rate behavior in retardates. *Journal of Applied Behavior Analysis,* 1972, **5,** 85-91.

Redd, W. H. and Birnbrauer, J. S. Adults as discriminative stimuli for different reinforcement contingencies with retarded children. *Journal of Experimental Child Psychology,* 1969, **7,** 440-447.

Rincover, A. and Koegel, R. L. Setting generality and stimulus control in autistic children. *Journal of Applied Behavior Analysis,* 1975, **8,** 235-246.

Risley, T. R. and Hart, B. M. Developing correspondence between the nonverbal and verbal behavior of preschool children. *Journal of Applied Behavior Analysis,* 1968, **1,** 267-281.

Rogers-Warren, A. and Baer, D. M. Correspondence between saying and doing: teaching children to share and praise. *Journal of Applied Behavior Analysis,* 1976, **9,** 335-354.

Schroeder, G. L. and Baer, D. M. Effects of concurrent and serial training on generalized vocal imitation in retarded children. *Developmental Psychology,* 1972, **6,** 293-301.

Schumaker, J. and Sherman, J. A. Training generative verb usage by imitation and reinforcement procedures. *Journal of Applied Behavior Analysis,* 1970, **3,** 273-287.

Schwarz, M. L. and Hawkins, R. P. Application of delayed reinforcement procedures to the behavior of an elementary school child. *Journal of Applied Behavior Analysis,* 1970, **3,** 85-96.

Seymour, F. W. and Stokes, T. F. Self-recording in training girls to increase work and evoke staff praise in an institution for offenders. *Journal of Applied Behavior Analysis,* 1976, **9,** 41-54.

Skinner, B. F. *Science and human behavior.* New York: Macmillan, 1953.

Solomon, R. W. and Wahler, R. G. Peer reinforcement control of classroom problem behavior. *Journal of Applied Behavior Analysis,* 1973, **6**, 49-56.

Stokes, T. F. and Baer, D. M. Preschool peers as mutual generalization-facilitating agents. *Behavior Therapy,* 1976, **7**, 549-556.

Stokes, T. F., Baer, D. M., and Jackson, R. L. Programming the generalization of a greeting response in four retarded children. *Journal of Applied Behavior Analysis,* 1974, **7**, 599-610.

Stolz, S. B. and Wolf, M. M. Visually discriminated behavior in a "blind" adolescent retardate. *Journal of Applied Behavior Analysis,* 1969, **2**, 65-77.

Wahler, R. G. Setting generality: some specific and general effects of child behavior therapy. *Journal of Applied Behavior Analysis,* 1969, **2**, 239-246.

Walker, H. M. and Buckley, N. K. The use of positive reinforcement in conditioning attending behavior. *Journal of Applied Behavior Analysis,* 1968, **1**, 245-250.

Yates, A. J. *Behavior therapy.* New York: John Wiley and Sons, 1970.

Received 22 December 1975.
(Final acceptance 3 June 1976.)

JOURNAL OF APPLIED BEHAVIOR ANALYSIS 1981, 14, 327-338 NUMBER 3 (FALL 1981)

SETTING EVENTS IN APPLIED BEHAVIOR ANALYSIS: TOWARD A CONCEPTUAL AND METHODOLOGICAL EXPANSION

ROBERT G. WAHLER AND JAMES J. FOX

UNIVERSITY OF TENNESSEE AND VANDERBILT UNIVERSITY

The contributions of applied behavior analysis as a natural science approach to the study of human behavior are acknowledged. However, it is also argued that applied behavior analysis has provided limited access to the full range of environmental events that influence socially significant behavior. Recent changes in applied behavior analysis to include analysis of side effects and social validation represent ways in which the traditional applied behavior analysis conceptual and methodological model has been profitably expanded. A third area of expansion, the analysis of setting events, is proposed by the authors. The historical development of setting events as a behavior influence concept is traced. Modifications of the basic applied behavior analysis methodology and conceptual systems that seem necessary to setting event analysis are discussed and examples of descriptive and experimental setting event analyses are presented.

DESCRIPTORS: setting events, correlational analyses, stimulus control, molar units of measurement

The application and adaptation of natural science methods to the study of human behavior have greatly increased our knowledge of some of the environmental conditions which influence behavior. A particularly successful instance of this application to socially significant behavior is applied behavior analysis, or ABA. In the dozen years since its formal inception, ABA proponents have investigated such diverse and important behaviors as aggression, energy consumption, social withdrawal, sexual functioning, self-injury, and academic performance. Certainly, much more is now known about how we can change certain environmental conditions to have desirable impact upon these and other behaviors. Also, by focusing on observable behavior and by analyzing the functional relationships between these behaviors and other observable events in the natural environment, ABA has helped to further a science of human behavior.

The basic model upon which these achievements rest was most explicitly and concisely stated by Baer, Wolf, and Risley (1968). Seven dimensions or criteria for applied behavior analysis were described. Briefly, ABA was to concern itself only with the actual behaviors of an individual, behaviors that were both socially important and objectively measured. Changes in these specific behaviors were to be related to deliberate and specifically described changes in social and nonsocial environmental events through experimental analyses. Behavioral techniques were effective if they produced "large enough effects to have practical value" (Baer et al., 1968), and more so if the effects were durable or generalized. Finally, behavioral procedures were to be related to a particular model or set of general principles. Though this requirement was simply that ABA be conceptually systematic to avoid collecting a grab bag of tricks and no particular model was explicitly called for, there seemed to be an implication that the model of preference was an operant one.

However, despite its obvious accomplishments, ABA has provided limited coverage and

Reprints may be obtained from Robert G. Wahler, Child Behavior Institute, University of Tennessee, 1720 Lake Avenue, Knoxville, Tennessee 37916.

understanding of human behavior and of its ecological context. Indeed, in recent years there have been proposals, both from outside and within ABA, to expand the scope of inquiry. One quite obvious example was Willems' (1974) call for behavior analysts to assume a more ecological systems approach to the study of applied problems by examining the potential "side effects" or unintended effects of behavioral intervention. This was to be accomplished by including the measurement of behaviors, persons, or situations other than those to which an intervention had been applied. Research on side effects has largely justified Willems' concerns and indicated the scientific and pragmatic utility of expansion in this area. That is, the occurrence of side effects has been repeatedly documented (Epstein, Doke, Sajwaj, Sorrell, & Rimmer, 1974; Nordquist, 1971; Sajwaj, Twardosz, & Burke, 1972; Wahler, Sperling, Thomas, Teeter, & Luper, 1970) and it has also been shown that behavioral interventions can have both negative (Sajwaj et al., 1972; Wahler & Fox, 1980) and positive (Koegel, Firestone, Kramme, & Dunlap, 1974; Strain, Shores, & Kerr, 1976; Wahler & Fox, 1980) side effects.

A more recent argument for expansion of ABA has come from within its ranks. Wolf (1978) has argued for the subjective measurement and evaluation of behavior change, i.e., social validation. Like side effects research, social validation studies did and continue to constitute an extremely small percentage of behavior analytic research. Yet, again the expansion of ABA to include this type of subjective measurement promises benefits. Social validation research indicates that reliable, subjective measurement can be achieved (Minkin, Braukman, Minkin, Timbers, Timbers, Fixsen, Phillips, & Wolf, 1976; Twardosz, Schwartz, Fox, & Cunningham, 1979), that it can be related to observable behavior and used to analyze complex social behaviors further (Minkin et al., 1976, Twardosz et al., 1979) and that it can be used to demonstrate that socially significant behavior change has been accomplished (Fawcett & Miller, 1975; Minkin et al., 1976).

In the above tradition we suggest that ABA can benefit from further conceptual and methodological expansion. In contrast to previous proposals, our suggestions focus upon expanding the other side of the functional analysis equation. That is, we propose that behavior analysts should increase the range of environmental phenomena that they seek to manipulate and relate to the changes in socially important behaviors. We would paraphrase Kantor's (1970) friendly critique of the experimental analysis of behavior and argue that the operant conceptual model so dominant in ABA research has resulted in an undue emphasis on the relatively simple and temporally proximate conditions of behavior influence, i.e., the immediate antecedents and consequences of behavior. One can easily conceive of more complex and temporally distant behavior—environment interactions that potentially influence behavior. There also appears to be a developing data base to support such conjecture (e.g., Krantz & Risley, 1977; Wahler, 1980; Wahler, Leske, & Rogers, 1979). In short, we contend that behavior analysts can profitably investigate the relationship of these "setting factors" (Kantor, 1959, 1970) to human behavior change through both descriptive and experimental analyses.

Setting Factors and the Analysis of Behavior

If setting factors are to be included in the analysis of behavior, then it is necessary to distinguish between setting factors and other behavior influence concepts. Although setting factors have been given relatively less research emphasis than other concepts, some behavioral philosophers and researchers have discussed and attempted to research the effects of setting factors.

In his presentation of an "interbehavioral psychology," Kantor (1959) described "setting factors" as part of an interbehavioral field which also included stimulus functions, response functions, historical processes, and the media of contact between an organism and its environment. Briefly, he defined setting factors as those "immediate circumstances" that influenced which of the various stimulus-response relationships (already built up through past organism-environment interactions) would occur. Kantor (1959) further identified setting factors in the following way:

> Such setting factors as the hungry or satiated condition of the organism, its age, hygienic or toxic condition, as well as the presence or absence of certain environing objects clearly influence the occurrence or non-occurrence of interbehavior.... (p. 95)

Clearly, setting factors were considered distinct from stimulus events that were simple, discrete, immediate events or objects. That is, setting factors consisted of more complex conditions such as food deprivation, or durational events such as the presence (or absence) of another person. Temporally, setting factors preceded and overlapped with the occurrence of a particular stimulus and response function. Finally, the effect of setting events was to facilitate or to inhibit the occurrence of existing stimulus and response functions that followed the setting event.

Later, Bijou and Baer (1961) discussed the concept of setting events in the context of a child's developing psychological environment, referring the reader to Kantor's earlier (1959) work. Like Kantor, Bijou and Baer distinguished between two classes of antecedent events: setting events and stimulus events. Setting events were again described as environmental conditions or events that were more complex than the simpler more discrete stimulus events. Also, Bijou and Baer's illustrative examples, like Kantor's, included allusions to deprivation or satiation conditions and the presence or absence of certain events or objects (e.g., verbal statements such as instructions).

However, Bijou and Baer (1961) also introduced a dimension of setting events that had not been explicitly stated previously and that has received little emphasis since. Setting events were defined in the following way:

> .... But, in contrast to stimulus events, setting events are more complicated than the simple presence, absence or change of a stimulus (such as turning on a light, a sudden drop in temperature, or a smile from mother). Instead, a setting event is a stimulus-response interaction, which simply because it has occurred will affect other stimulus-response relationships which follow it. (p. 21)

Those authors went on to illustrate the stimulus-response interaction aspect of setting events with the hypothetical example of an infant whose nap in his crib is typically followed by vigorous but appropriate play in his playpen. However, when outdoor noises prevented the infant from napping in his crib and instead he remained awake and active, the child later cried and protested upon being placed in his playpen. Thus, the crib-awake interaction served as a setting event for the playpen-crying behavior which occurred at a later point in time.

This definition and illustration of setting events seems crucial in two respects. First, they indicate that at least some setting events are composed not simply of a durational condition or event but of both an environmental event and the person's response to that event. Secondly, the definition of setting events as the interaction of a stimulus and a response, particularly in the infant example, admits into consideration setting events which occur wholly separate in space and time from the other, succeeding stimulus-response relationships which they influence. That is, unlike deprivation or presence-of-object setting events, the onset and offset of some stimulus-response setting events may occur well before, yet still facilitate or inhibit, the occurrence of later interbehavioral relationships.

This interactional, temporally distant dimension of setting events seems to be what Kantor (1970) intended for the experimental analysis of behavior to investigate in addition to reward conditions. In discussing the "conditions of behavior", he stated the following:

> .... For psychological behavior in general there are obviously many other conditions localizable in and around the organism and its stimuli. For example, the hygiene of the organism, its habituation or past behavioral history, *what behavioral circumstances it has recently or just previously passed through,* the presence or absence of confining objects and numerous others. (p. 107)

If, conceptually, setting events have undergone a metamorphosis from being defined simply as durational events or conditions to the inclusion of antecedent and temporally distinct stimulus-response interactions, what do those studies in which setting events have been analyzed tell us about their definition and charactertics?

A review of such research reveals several things. First, the 1968-1977 cumulative index of the Journal of Applied Behavior Analysis, surely the major publication organ of ABA, contains only three explicit references under the descriptor "setting events," while the cumulative index for the same journal during the period 1978-1979 contains no references to setting events. Obviously then, setting events, per se, constitute an almost negligible proportion of applied behavior analytic research although they continue to be described philosophically as important components of behavioral fields by behavior analysts (Bijou, 1976; Bijou & Baer, 1961, 1965).

Secondly, our review of the setting event research literature indicates that setting events have been predominantly investigated in terms of the presence or absence of complex events rather than stimulus-response interactions. A series of studies examining generalized imitation have described such setting events as instructions not-to-imitate (Steinman, 1970a, 1970b); experimenter presence/absence (Peterson, Merwin, Mayer, & Whitehurst, 1971; Rosenbaum & Breiling, 1976) as well as experimenter hand movements, prompting statements, and the presence of specific pieces of furniture (Rincover & Koegel, 1975).

Some researchers have investigated what appear to be setting events of the temporally distinct, stimulus-response interaction type. For example, Krantz and Risley (1977) have reported that in a kindergarten class an antecedent period of vigorous activity set the occasion for reduced attention to the teacher and more disruptive behavior during a subsequent story reading activity. Interestingly enough, manipulation of this type of setting event (i.e., by providing, instead, a rest period antecedent to the story reading period) was as effective as the introduction of contingency management procedures in the control of inappropriate behavior.

Another more recent example of the stimulus-response interaction setting event has been provided by Wahler (1980) who reports that low-income parents who experience particular kinds of interactions with certain members of their functional community are unlikely to maintain the benefits of a previously successful behavioral treatment package (see Wahler & Fox, 1980) applied to their children's oppositional actions. More specifically, the children of parents whose daily contacts consist primarily of aversively rated interchanges with relatives and community helping agency personnel did not maintain reductions in their oppositional and rule violating behavior during follow-up assessment, i.e., when the treatment consultant has reduced his or her contact with the family. These parents' community interactions during baseline and follow-up conditions seemed to set the occasion for increased aversive interchanges between parents and their children, because on those days in which parents experienced fewer aversive kinfolk/helping agency contacts, their later interchanges with their children that same day were less aversive.

A third implication of the small but existing setting event literature is that setting events do not appear to be fixed activities; rather, they must be empirically and individually defined and identified. A particular setting event may be functional for some subjects or response relationships and not for others (Kantor, 1959, 1970). Thus, Peterson et al. (1971) found that the presence of the experimenter was a setting event for generalized imitation behavior in normal children, whereas Rincover and Koegel (1975) found that each of four autistic children in another generalized imitation training study was only responsive to one of four different setting events.

It appears that although a rather definite conceptual framework for setting events exists within behavioral psychology (Kantor, 1959, 1970; Bijou, 1976; Bijou & Baer, 1961, 1965) and their importance has been verbally acknowledged, setting events have only infrequently been included in a descriptive (Bijou, Peterson, & Ault, 1968) or functional (Baer et al., 1968) analysis of behavior. The concept of setting events includes complex antecedent conditions, events and stimulus-response interactions which may overlap with or entirely preceded subsequent behaviors that they affect. Most research to date, with a few exceptions, that has examined directly setting events as conditions of behavior influence has focused on deprivational or presence/absence-of-object types of setting events. The analysis of setting events appears crucial to practical methods of behavior change both in terms of effective, initial behavior change (e.g., Krantz & Risley, 1977) and in terms of generalization (e.g., Peterson et al., 1971; Rincover & Koegel, 1975; Steinman, 1970a, 1970b) and maintenance of behavior change (Wahler, 1980).

Given this state of affairs, it seems a rather glaring omission that behavior analysts have not yet devoted more effort to the analysis of setting events. Yet, we find it somewhat difficult to criticize our colleagues for this omission because it is only recently that we have pursued our own interest in this area. Too, this interest has largely resulted from our own qualified success (or failure?) within the typical contingency management paradigm (e.g., Wahler and Moore, Note 1) and the reports of similar difficulty by others (Ferber, Keeley, & Shemberg, 1974; Keeley, Shemberg, & Carbonel, 1976). Thus, it has only been apparent in more recent years that additional investigation into setting events was necessary. Finally, it seems, too, that some adjustment of the methodological model of ABA will be necessary if we are to understand more precisely the role of setting events in the ecology of behavior. Next, we would like to present briefly our impressions of what such expansion will involve.

TOWARD A METHODOLOGICAL EXPANSION

If setting events are to be considered in a functional analysis of behavior, some departures from standard ABA methodology will be necessary. We believe that these departures center on three methodological features: the *measurement unit, temporal relationships* among these units, and mode of *unit analysis*.

The Measurement Unit

Applied behavior analysis has always followed a pragmatic bent in its emphasis on concrete, molecular units of measurement. Units such as smiling, verbal approval, prompts, and disapproval are practical from a psychometric viewpoint (i.e., observer reliability) as well as from an applied perspective. In the latter case, a technology for behavioral and environmental change virtually requires its targeted units to be concrete or tangible. But, one must also realize that a focus on the fine-grained composition of an ecological field is bound to yield a limited access to that field—both in terms of assessment and change. For example, one can obtain a highly useful understanding of a child's classroom reading performance by monitoring that behavior along with a description of the reading material and social contingencies for the child's performance. However, it is also possible that some or all of that child's social and work interactions during the hour previous to reading will add variance to the obtained reading measure.

Although these behavior-environment interchanges could also be monitored in fine-grained fashion, there will come a limit to the time, money, and effort that one can expend on such setting events. A more prudent course of action would entail the initial study of these events as *global* entities—those monitored through molar units of measurement. Given that a broadly and dependably defined unit can be shown to bear functional relationships to the targeted stimulus-response interaction, *then* the more costly fine-grained analysis of that setting event would appear warranted. Through this strategy it should prove feasible to segment and categorize much of an ecological field. If some of these segments do in fact serve a setting event function, an inspection of their functional properties as global categories would seem a reasonable first step in methodology.

Time Relationships among the Units

In the search for functional relationships among chosen stimulus and response units, applied behavior analysts are likely to hold a conceptual bias about time. Stimulus control conceptions typically imply brief temporal associations between likely stimuli and their socially relevant targeted responses. Thus, notions concerning parent influences on child behavior are apt to steer one's attention to the things a parent does and says contiguous with those child behaviors of designated interest. And, if these parental stimuli are not viewed as contiguous, they are almost certain to be removed briefly as immediate antecedents and/or consequences of the child behaviors. We believe that Baer et al. (1968) refer to this bias in their argument that applied behavior analysis is best advanced through *conceptually systematic* guidelines. There can be little doubt that advances thus far have been promoted by reinforcement principles designating the crucial temporal relationships described above.

We think it only reasonable to put aside such temporal guidelines in fostering the study of setting event phenomena. Obviously there are no a priori assumptions concerning ideal or even necessary time spans between a suspected setting event and a particular target behavior. Thus, Krantz and Risley's (1977) demonstration of quiet play as a setting event for preschoolers had little to do with the temporal properties of reinforcement principles. These investigators showed that child attention during a group activity could be substantially and dependably increased by scheduling a quiet play period prior to the group activity. The quiet play activity—a globally conceived child-environment interchange—clearly functioned as a setting event for the same children's attending behavior at some later time. Although this "later time" was only a few minutes in duration, it is conceivable that time separations amounting to hours could be functional in setting event operations. Perhaps the most striking new evidence behind this latter contention is seen in the adverse treatment side effects reported by Forehand, Breiner, McMahon, and Davies (1981). These investigators monitored the home and school behaviors of 16 children referred for help with their oppositional behaviors in the home setting. When a parent training program was then shown to produce therapeutic effects in the home settings, an opposite trend occurred with these children in their school settings. The multiple regression model using home therapeutic change scores and pretreatment levels of school oppositional behavior accounted for 70% of the variance in the oppositional changes at school! Thus, the home-based treatment program, at least several hours removed from the children's school settings, appeared to function as a setting event for their oppositional actions in this second location.

Mode of Unit Analysis

Perhaps the most convincing property of any study is its *experimental* demonstration of causality. The "believability" of a procedure is tremendously augmented if one can offer experimental proof of its impact. No doubt the widespread use of procedures derived from applied behavior analysis is due to the experimental tests so commonly associated with ABA—tests in which the procedures are subjected to systematic manipulations as their expected effects are monitored.

Such a functional analysis of units obviously depends on the investigator's capability to manipulate the units in some fashion. And, if the units in question are global in size, one's capability to alter their presence and absence systematically will be reduced. For example, Wahler's (1980) recent study of mother-child problem interchanges focused on the mothers' extra-family social contacts as possible setting events for these within family problems. The suspected setting events were defined as mother self-reported contacts with friends, relatives, and helping agency representatives, along with mother ratings of these contacts as positive, neutral, and negative. As discussed earlier, these contacts could have been studied in fine-grained, molecular units as were the mother-child interchanges. However, because there was little basis to assume that these contacts would affect the mother-child interactions, the cost and time required to conduct such an assessment seemed prohibitive. Instead, the relatively simple process of collecting mother reports on occurrences and valences of these contacts was initiated each time a mother-child home observation was conducted. Results showed statistically significant correlations between friendship contacts and the mother-child problems; on days marked by increments in number of friend contacts, mother-child problems were lower in frequency, and vice versa. This finding is hardly a convincing demonstration of the setting event function of mother friendship contacts, but it offers an empirical look at a heretofore speculative relationship. In other words, the ecological field encompassing family operations was described more completely through this relatively inexpensive correlational analysis.

In addition to cost and time considerations, there is yet another reason to consider correlational analyses as a part of ABA methodology. Some likely setting events may not be manipulable because of ethical and procedural problems. For example, the day-to-day operations of a school may vary enough to permit a correlational inspection of their impact on relevant behaviors of the children and school personnel. Some of these operations, such as a single teacher's classroom routine, could and have been manipulated experimentally. Others, such as the number of hours school is in session, could not be readily manipulated because the control lies outside the cooperation of a single individual. Likewise, a mother's aversive interchanges with members of her extended family might prove to correlate with her childrearing problems—yet these kinfolk and/or the mother may refuse to cooperate in a proposal to change the quality of such interchanges. In both examples, quantitative analyses of important stimulus-response relationships could still be made available for the scrutiny of all concerned. The interpretation of these relationships would certainly be more subdued than ABA researchers are accustomed to handling; nevertheless, it would seem that a step well beyond speculation could be attained through the obtained correlation coefficients.

If we are to maintain our positions as behavioral scientists, then some analysis of potential setting events that are not directly manipulable is necessary. As Kantor (1970) has noted, the purpose of any science is to get knowledge and then to use it. Consequently, we must recognize experimental analysis as simply one of many tools in answering questions that we pose about behavior. Simply because some specific aspect of the interbehavioral field is currently uncontrollable (in the sense of being directly manipulable by the scientist) this does not diminish such an event's effects upon behavior or its importance in an analysis of behavior. Actually, the mixture and complementarity of descriptive analyses were pointed out previously by behavior analysts (Bijou et al., 1968) and we are simply suggesting that the study of some (not all) setting events may necessitate the use of this complementary methodology. Indeed, it may occur that positive results of descriptive setting event analyses may set the occasion for later experimental analyses.

If ABA researchers proceed with the above methodological guidelines, we would anticipate an initial period of theoretical confusion. Imagine, for example, a consistent body of studies documenting strong and replicable correlations between some aspects of an individual's behavior and setting events far removed (temporally) from that behavior. What, then, if even a small portion of such environment-behavior relationships are shown via experimental manipulations to have causal properties? Because scientists, clinicians, and most every category of people for that matter seem to quest for theoretical understanding (Kuhn, 1970), such an array of data is apt to promote conceptual notions beyond the observable relationships. Operant and respondent concepts have been valuable guidelines for ABA because they are comprised solely of observable factors and their observable temporal and sequential relationships. Some setting event findings are simply not going to be "understandable" within these concepts. The temptation to introduce unobservable factors by way of "stretching" the operant-respondent concepts or the postulation of other hypothetical processes will be overpowering. One must keep in mind, however, that operant and respondent concepts "make sense" in a paradigmatic way only because we are familiar with day-to-day documented examples. When setting event phenomena are equally common, old shoe illustrations of environment-behavior relationships, we would predict reductions in the frantic building of hypothetical constructs.

HYPOTHESIS GENERATION: SOME LIKELY FRUITS OF THE METHODOLOGICAL EXPANSION

It is obvious that the three proposals just presented encompass some of the very objections ABA has voiced against standard psychological research. For example, the choice of molar measurement units and correlational analyses were virtual signposts of the "personality trait" era of research—an essentially nonproductive approach to human problems. Of course, much of this standard research strategy also emphasized both laboratory study and a focus on groups rather than individuals. Our proposals are to be understood in a strategic context fostering naturalistic study of individuals. With this perspective, we believe that the ABA movement could generate new research questions in a largely inductive fashion.

As the last statement might imply, our intent behind the three proposals is to formulate a means of viewing new problems for ABA. In the long run, one must eventually conduct *experimental* analyses dealing with *molecular* units comprising the chosen problem. If one is to provide technological solutions to applied problems, these mainstay strategies of ABA are essential. Thus, we see the proposed methodological expansion as a set of *preliminary* guidelines that might well stimulate the inductive process of question asking. Like most "new" proposals, there are already published examples of this process. Environmental settings considered in these examples include home or family settings, group homes, and school classrooms.

Recent home setting data by Patterson (1978) provide some fascinating correlational analyses of normal children and aggressive problem children as well as their parents. Unlike nonproblem children, the latter youngsters tended to increase the likelihood of aggressive actions when such behaviors were followed by parent disapproval. In fact, these "acceleration" tendencies were shown to correlate positively with the children's overall rates of in house aggression—the parent defined problem. Based on these statistically significant correlations, one might guess that a parent training intervention would be most successful if the focus of change were geared to these parent disapproval-linked bursts of aggressive behavior, rather than just *any* instance of child aggression. In other words, if the acceleration bursts were stopped, might such a change affect the overall rates of child aggression?

The Patterson data suggest the potential value of correlational analyses applied to a fine-grained picture of parent-child interchanges. Wahler and Moore (Note 1) provided a broader picture in their correlational analyses of similar childhood problems. These researchers discovered inverse correlations between the problem children's observed solitary toy play and parent global reports of the children's aggression at other times of the day at home. Later, Wahler and Fox (1980) conducted the experimental analyses suggested by these data. When four aggressive children were reinforced for increments in their solitary play activities at home, clear (but, unfortunately, temporary) reductions were observed in observer-recorded and parent-recorded instances of aggression and opposition. Although this was not a highly practical finding, a setting event function of each child's solitary play was clearly demonstrated.

More recent correlational analyses of setting event phenomena have been reported by the Achievement Place research group (Wolf, 1978). These investigators have thus far completed a series of three correlational studies, each leading inductively to the next. In the first of these studies (Kirigin, Braukman, Atwater, and Wolf, in press), two global measures of delinquent boys' behavior in group homes and the surrounding communities were intercorrelated: Official records of youth delinquency were tracked as a possible function of these boys' self-reported satisfaction with the group home treatment program. Across all homes studied, a correlation of —.65 was obtained between these measures. Next, the investigators' review of the observational literature in normal and delinquency prone families suggested that family living satisfaction (and potential delinquency) may be related to the sheer frequency of prosocial interactions between the children and their parents. Thus, Solnick, Braukman, Bedlington, Kirigin, and Wolf (Note 2) directly observed proximity and talking between group home delinquent youth and their teaching parents. These fine-grained measures were then correlated with the youths' self-reported delinquency, yielding across home correlations between the delinquency measure and talk-proximity of —.95 and —.81, respectively. Unfortunately, this potential setting event function of talk-proximity was not supported through similar correlations for the individual youths. Nevertheless, the grouped data correlations were encouraging enough to lead the researchers into a third correlational study: an attempt to analyze components of the talk-proximity predictor variable (Bedlington, Solnick, Schumaker, Braukman, Kirigin, and Wolf, Note 3). Once again it proved possible to predict self-reported delinquency—this time through inverse relationships between this measure and the sheer frequency of parent teaching behaviors such as modeling, praise, and feedback. If this inductively guided correlational search continues to yield setting event predictors, there is little doubt that the Achievement Place investigators will soon be ready to conduct some suggested experimental analyses.

Descriptive analyses in elementary and secondary school classroom settings have led to some equally interesting questions regarding teacher-child interchanges. White (1975), Heller and White (1975), and Thomas, Presland, Grant, and Glynn (1978) all measured the teachers' natural rates of verbal approval and disapproval during their teaching exchanges with students. Findings showed that the majority of teachers used disapproval more frequently than approval. Because the three studies covered a fairly large range and number of classrooms, it would seem reasonable to conclude that these rate differences reflect an "average" mode of classroom teaching in public schools. The findings are reminiscent of Patterson's (1978) previously discussed results indicating that "normal" children are more apt to change their actions following parent disapproval than are aggressive problem children. One might suspect that adult disapproval could function as an important teaching-parenting factor for the average child—an hypothesis for future research work in ABA.

A particularly illustrative example of setting event phenomena in schools was documented by

Fowler and Baer (1981). Their concern with increasing preschool children's interpersonal sharing focused on the impact of temporally remote reinforcement contingencies. The investigators first obtained reinforcement control over sharing in a morning play setting of the preschool by use of point rewards delivered immediately after the conclusion of morning play. In addition, observers monitored the same children's sharing in an afternoon free play setting of the preschool. Once the sharing contingent points were shown to increase sharing in the morning setting, the delivery of these reinforcers was then delayed to day's end. Following this operation, the children's sharing increased markedly in the afternoon setting, even though the points were not contingent upon sharing in this setting. Experimental variations in procedure clearly showed that these latter increments in sharing depended on the previously described reinforcement operations in the morning setting. Once completed, this setting operation had a peculiar functional impact on the now delayed point deliveries. Although these points bore no contingent relationship to the children's afternoon sharing, the children acted as if such a relationship existed. As long as sharing in the morning was consistently reinforced and its point reinforcers delayed to day's end, the temporally remote afternoon sharing could be maintained at rates well above baseline.

The foregoing examples of descriptive and experimental research have illustrated implementation of some or all of the three proposals outlined earlier. Obviously, the question-asking productivity of our proposed methodology expansion cannot be evaluated on the basis of these examples. It does seem to us, however, that a rough set of guidelines is now available to promote future searches for setting event phenomena. To do so, we have outlined two proposed changes in methodology and one conceptual change in the time concept. The studies we reviewed also suggest some initial directions concerning what aspects of the ecosystem are apt to serve setting event functions. Obviously, this question of "what" must be considered in the same strategic sense as prior searches for reinforcers—these are often idiosyncratic and require post hoc definition. But, just as ABA has documented gross categories of likely nomothetic reinforcers (e.g. social approval), there may also be such categories of setting events. An overview of the previous studies would strongly suggest that specific sorts of behavior-environment interactions would be a profitable initial locus of the "what" question. Krantz and Risley (1977), Fowler and Baer (1981), and Solnick et al. (Note 2) indicate that episodes of positive reinforcement are likely to serve a setting event function for these reinforced behaviors in later time frames ranging from minutes to hours. Wahler (1980), Forehand et al. (1981), and Patterson (1978) point to aversive contingency episodes as also serving such a function for the aversively consequated behaviors—once again in later time frames ranging from minutes to hours. Suppose then that one wished to explore the possibility that mother-child coercive disputes were under setting event control—in addition to the possible reinforcement control exercised by each of these people. Accordingly, one might wish to look at those antecedent segments of time in which either mother or child was involved in similar sorts of environment-behavior interactions. These episodes could be between mother and child, mother and father, child and father, mother and extended family members, for instance; and, as the previous studies show, these antecedent episodes need not be in the setting where the targeted mother-child disputes occur. Following our methodological recommendations, the antecedent episodes could be recorded as global "aversive interchange" categories, per haps through self-recording by the participants. Then, after tabulating these categories over days, one could conduct correlational analyses of score distributions made up of the setting event categories and the observed mother-child coercive disputes. It would not be difficult to imagine similar setting event quests for other socially significant behavioral interchanges such as child-teacher instructional work, child-peer cooperative play, and other positive or desirable facets of adult and child interactions.

Notice that our preceding guideline examples start with some particular behavior-environment interaction. Our arguments in specifying such a start are purely pragmatic: (a) If that socially important behavior is not *largely* controlled by its temporally close stimulus associations, a setting event search ought to be initiated. Thus, when an ABA researcher manipulates these stimuli and finds no change, or highly variable change, the control locus may lie at more temporally distant points. As argued earlier, setting events appear to influence behavior via their functional impact on the temporally immediate stimulus contingencies for that behavior. (b) If that socially important behavior occurs in settings that are not readily influenced by the ABA researcher, setting event possibilities should be considered. Perhaps the most apparent of these instances concerns generalization of therapeutic treatment effects across settings. For example, many child behavior problems, such as stealing, fighting, truancy, and property destruction occur in settings outside the scope of most any contingency intervention program. Certainly one often can, and should, attempt to program such across setting effects by direct control of their stimulus contingencies. But, when this strategy is simply not feasible, it might well be possible to alter the function of these temporally remote stimuli through setting event operations (e.g., Fowler and Baer, 1981).

As we noted earlier, the study of setting events has thus far comprised a very small portion of ABA research efforts. We have presented a set of guidelines pointing to a means of including such phenomena within the subject matter of ABA. Although the guidelines are certainly different from those usually associated with this research movement, we do believe these proposals preserve the essential integrity of ABA—an empirical focus on observable environment-behavior relationships.

REFERENCE NOTES

1. Wahler, R. G., & Moore, D. M. *School-home behavior change procedures in a high risk community.* Unpublished manuscript, Child Behavior Institute, University of Tennessee, Knoxville, 1975.
2. Solnick, J. V., Braukman, C. J., Bedlington, M. M., Kirigin, K. A., & Wolf, M. M. *The relationship between parent-youth interaction and delinquency in group homes.* Unpublished manuscript, Department of Human Development, University of Kansas, Lawrence, 1980.
3. Bedlington, M. M., Solnick, J. V., Schumaker, J., Braukman, C. J., Kirigin, K. A., & Wolf, M. M. *Evaluating group homes: The relationship between parenting behaviors and delinquency.* Unpublished manuscript, Department of Human Development, University of Kansas, Lawrence, 1978.

REFERENCES

Baer, D. M., Wolf, M. M., & Risley, T. R. Some current dimensions of applied behavior analysis. *Journal of Applied Behavior Analysis,* 1968, **1**, 91-97.

Bijou, S. W. *Child development III: Basic stage of early childhood.* Englewood Cliffs, N.J.: Prentice-Hall, 1976.

Bijou, S. W., & Baer, D. M. *Child development I: A systematic and empirical theory.* Englewood Cliffs, N.J.: Prentice-Hall, 1961.

Bijou, S. W., & Baer, D. M. *Child development II: Basic stage of infancy.* Englewood Cliffs, N.J.: Prentice-Hall. 1965.

Bijou, S. W., Peterson, R. F., & Ault, M. H. A method to integrate descriptive and experimental field studies at the level of data and empirical concepts. *Journal of Applied Behavior Analysis,* 1968, **1**, 175-191.

Epstein, L. H., Doke, L. A., Sajwaj, T. E., Sorrell, S., & Rimmer, B. Generality and side effects of overcorrection. *Journal of Applied Behavior Analysis,* 1974, **7**, 385-390.

Fawcett, S. B., & Miller, L. K. Training public speaking behavior: An experimental analysis and social validation. *Journal of Applied Behavior Analysis,* 1975, **8**, 125-134.

Ferber, H., Keeley, S. M., & Shemberg, K. M. Training parents in behavior modification: Outcome of problems encountered in a program after Patterson's work. *Behavior Therapy,* 1974, **5**, 415-419.

Forehand, R., Breiner, J., McMahon, R. J., & Davies, G. Predictors of cross setting behavior change in the treatment of child problems. *Journal of Child Clinical Psychology,* 1981. In press.

Heller, M. S., & White, M. A. Teacher approval and disapproval on ability grouping. *Journal of Educational Psychology,* 1975, **67**, 796-800.

Fowler, S. A., & Baer, D. M. "Do I have to be good all day?" The timing of delayed reinforcement as a factor in generalization. *Journal of Applied Behavior Analysis,* 1981, **14,** 13-24.

Kantor, J. R. *Interbehavioral psychology.* Granville, Ohio: Principia Press, 1959.

Kantor, J. R. An analysis of the experimental analysis of behavior (TEAB), *Journal of the Experimental Analysis of Behavior,* 1970, **13,** 101-108.

Keeley, S. M., Shemberg, K. M., & Carbonell, J. Operant clinical intervention: Behavioral management or beyond? Where are the data? *Behavior Therapy,* 1976, **7,** 292-305.

Kirigin, K. A., Braukman, C. J., Atwater, J., & Wolf, M. M. An evaluation of the Achievement Place teaching-family model of group home treatment for delinquent youths. *Journal of Applied Behavior Analysis.* In press.

Koegel, R., Firestone, P. B., Kramme, K. W., & Dunlap, G. Increasing spontaneous play by suppressing self-stimulation in autistic children. *Journal of Applied Behavior Analysis,* 1974, **7,** 521-528.

Krantz, P. J., & Risley, T. R. Behavioral ecology in the classroom. In S. G. O'Leary & K. D. O'Leary (Eds.), *Classroom management: The successful use of behavior modification.* New York: Pergamon Press, Inc., 1977.

Kuhn, T. S. *The structure of scientific revolutions.* (2nd ed.). Chicago: University of Chicago Press, 1970.

Minkin, N., Braukman, C. J., Minkin, B. L., Timbers, G. D., Timbers, B. J., Fixsen, D. L., Phillips, E. L., & Wolf, M. M. The social validation and training of conversational skills. *Journal of Applied Behavior Analysis,* 1976, **9,** 127-139.

Nordquist, V. M. The modification of a child's enuresis: Some response-response relationships. *Journal of Applied Behavior Analysis,* 1971, **4,** 241-247.

Patterson, G. R. A performance theory for coercive family interactions. In R. Cairns (Ed.), *Social interactions: Methods, analysis and illustrations.* Chicago: University of Chicago Press, 1978.

Peterson, R. F., Merwin, M. R., Mayer, T. J., & Whitehurst, G. J. Generalized imitation: The effects of experimenter absence, differential reinforcement, and stimulus complexity. *Journal of Experimental Child Psychology,* 1971, **12,** 114-128.

Rincover, A., & Koegel, R. L. Setting generality and stimulus control in autistic children. *Journal of Applied Behavior Analysis,* 1975, **8,** 235-247.

Rosenbaum, M. S., & Breiling, J. The development and functional control of reading comprehension behavior. *Journal of Applied Behavior Analysis,* 1976, **9,** 323-335.

Sajwaj, T., Twardosz, S., & Burke, M. Side effects of extinction procedures in a remedial preschool. *Journal of Applied Behavior Analysis,* 1972, **2,** 177-182.

Steinman, W. M. The social control of generalized imitation. *Journal of Applied Behavior Analysis,* 1970, **3,** 159-167(a).

Steinman, W. M. Generalized imitation and the dissemination hypothesis. *Journal of Experimental Child Psychology,* 1970, **10,** 79-99(b).

Strain, P. S., Shores, R. E., & Kerr, M. M. An experimental analysis of "spill-over" effects on the social interaction of behaviorally handicapped preschool children. *Journal of Applied Behavior Analysis,* 1976, **9,** 31-40.

Thomas, J. D., Presland, I. E., Grant, M. D., & Glynn, T. L. Natural rates of teacher approval and disapproval in grade 7 classrooms. *Journal of Applied Behavior Analysis,* 1978, **11,** 91-94.

Twardosz, S., Schwartz, S., Fox, J., & Cunningham, J. L. Development and validation of a system to measure affectionate behavior. *Behavioral Assessment,* 1979, **1,** 177-190.

Wahler, R. G. The insular mother: Her problems in parent-child treatment. *Journal of Applied Behavior Analysis,* 1980, **13,** 207-219.

Wahler, R. G., & Fox, J. J. Solitary toy play and time-out: A family treatment package for aggressive and oppositional children. *Journal of Applied Behavior Analysis,* 1980, **1,** 23-39.

Wahler, R. G., Leske, G., & Rogers, E. S. The insular family: A deviance support system for oppositional children. In L. A. Hamerlynck (Ed.), *Behavioral systems for the developmentally disabled: I. School and family environments.* New York: Brunner/Mazel, Inc., 1979.

Wahler, R. G., Sperling, K., Thomas, M., Teeter, N., & Luper, H. The modification of childhood stuttering: Some response-response relationships. *Journal of Experimental Child Psychology,* 1970, **9,** 411-428.

White, M. A. Natural rates of teacher approval and disapproval in the classroom. *Journal of Applied Behavior Analysis,* 1975, **8,** 367-372.

Willems, E. P. Behavioral technology and behavioral ecology. *Journal of Applied Behavior Analysis,* 1974, **7,** 151-166.

Wolf, M. M. Social validity: The case for subjective measurement or how applied behavior analysis is finding its heart. *Journal of Applied Behavior Analysis,* 1978, **11,** 203-214.

Received May 5, 1980
Final acceptance December 16, 1980

JOURNAL OF APPLIED BEHAVIOR ANALYSIS 1987, 20, 361–378 NUMBER 4 (WINTER 1987)

NEGATIVE REINFORCEMENT IN APPLIED BEHAVIOR ANALYSIS: AN EMERGING TECHNOLOGY

BRIAN A. IWATA

UNIVERSITY OF FLORIDA

Although the effects of negative reinforcement on human behavior have been studied for a number of years, a comprehensive body of applied research does not exist at this time. This article describes three aspects of negative reinforcement as it relates to applied behavior analysis: behavior acquired or maintained through negative reinforcement, the treatment of negatively reinforced behavior, and negative reinforcement as therapy. A consideration of research currently being done in these areas suggests the emergence of an applied technology on negative reinforcement.

DESCRIPTORS: aversive stimulation, avoidance, escape, negative reinforcement

---

Research published in the *Journal of Applied Behavior Analysis* (*JABA*) has, for 20 years now, demonstrated how knowledge about environment–behavior interactions, particularly those involving response-contingent events and correlated stimuli, may be used for the benefit of individuals and the larger society. In doing so, applied research has also made significant contributions to the general science of behavior by providing extension and external validation of experimental findings from the basic research laboratory (Baer, 1978).

Along with the development of the applied field and its expansion into a number of areas in which the outcome of an experiment often has immediate social implications (e.g., business and industry, developmental disabilities, education, medicine, mental health, public affairs), there has been growing concern of a widening gap between basic and applied behavior analysis. Critics (Deitz, 1978; Pierce & Epling, 1980) have indicated that the emphasis of contemporary applied behavior analysis has shifted away from the study of conditions that produce change to the production of change per se, and that "relevance to basic principle," a supposed characteristic of applied behavior analysis (cf. Baer, Wolf, & Risley, 1968), is reflected less and less in the research that journals such as *JABA* publish. The general accuracy of these criticisms, as well as their basis and implications, will continue to be the subject of periodic debate (Baer, 1981; Cullen, 1981; Michael, 1980). Nevertheless, it is possible at this point in the development of our field to identify specific and well-established areas of basic research for which little parallel exists in the applied literature, and vice versa.

The thesis of this article is that research on negative reinforcement provides one of the clearest and most immediately relevant examples of a case in which consideration, replication, and extension of basic research would benefit the applied area. Along with positive reinforcement and punishment, negative reinforcement has long been considered one of the elementary principles of behavior. A voluminous amount of research on negative reinforcement exists in the basic literature (see reviews by Bolles, 1970; Herrnstein, 1969; Hineline, 1977, 1981, 1984; Hoffman, 1966; Schoenfeld, 1969; Sidman, 1966), and its inclusion as a distinct topic in texts on experimental analysis (e.g., Honig & Staddon, 1977) justifies its status as a major organizing principle. For example, acquisition, maintenance, extinction, and stimulus control all have been studied using negative reinforcement as the operant mechanism of interest.

Sandler and Davidson (1973) reviewed some of this basic research and discussed its relevance to the

Appreciation is expressed to Ed Malagodi, Jack Michael, Gary Pace, Terry Page, and Terri Rodgers, whose work or helpful suggestions assisted in the preparation of this article. Support was provided by Grant HD16052 from the National Institute of Child Health and Human Development.

Reprints may be obtained from Brian A. Iwata, Department of Psychology, University of Florida, Gainesville, Florida 32611.

development and treatment of pathological human behavior. They concluded that "... the escape and avoidance paradigms are still plagued by a number of unresolved issues ..." (p. 254) that they hoped would be clarified by additional basic research and extension to the world of humans. Since that time, a number of investigations on negative reinforcement with humans have been conducted, yet a systematic and comprehensive body of applied research still does not exist. Consider the two most recent texts on aversive control with humans (Axelrod & Apsche, 1983; Matson & DiLorenzo, 1984). Both provide thorough discussion of topics such as positive reinforcement, extinction, time-out, response cost, and contingent aversive stimulation. Thus, one might expect that these texts would be the most likely sources of information on negative reinforcement as well, but this is not the case. One text (Axelrod & Apsche, 1983) devotes less than a half dozen of over 300 pages to the topic of avoidance, and the discussion always is limited to avoidance as a side effect of punishment. No mention is made of escape or avoidance as directly produced performances. The second (Matson & DiLorenzo, 1984) describes the hypothetical features of escape and avoidance training on two pages but does not cite any applied references.

The relative absence of integrated material on negative reinforcement with humans raises several questions concerning generality and utility. Is human behavior relatively insensitive to contingencies of negative reinforcement? Are naturalistic human situations typically characterized by the absence of stimuli that can function as negative reinforcers, or opportunities to escape from or avoid these stimuli? What types of performances are likely to be acquired through negative reinforcement? Finally, do procedures based on the application of negative reinforcement, unlike those based on positive reinforcement and punishment, have little therapeutic or pragmatic value?

For the past few years my students, colleagues, and I have been conducting a series of investigations in two areas—self-injurious behavior and pediatric feeding disorders. Curiously, these very different problems have brought us into direct contact with situations involving the use of negative reinforcement and have forced us to consider more generally the relevance of negative reinforcement in applied behavior analysis. Our experience and our examination of the basic and applied research suggest that the answer to each of the above questions is "No." In fact, it appears that negative reinforcement plays a central role in the development of many behaviors, appropriate as well as inappropriate, and that its application in a number of studies has not been formally acknowledged. In what follows, I will describe three aspects of negative reinforcement as it relates to the applied situation: first, undesirable behavior acquired or maintained through negative reinforcement; second, the treatment of negatively reinforced behavior; and third, negative reinforcement as therapy. This organization departs somewhat from that used in reviews of the basic research literature and has been adopted here to highlight the relevance of particular issues to the applied researcher. Much of the research included here has been done with the developmentally disabled population because there is a high prevalence of significant behavioral disorders in this group and because it provides a narrow but adequate focus for discussion.

CURRENT CONCEPTUALIZATION OF NEGATIVE REINFORCEMENT

Before proceeding, it may be helpful to clarify terminology and to delineate the defining features of negative reinforcement. The purpose of this digression is to show that the task of determining whether a given contingency is an example of negative reinforcement may not always be a simple one. Although there has been little confusion regarding the effect of negative reinforcement, describing its operations has posed a challenge to many beyond the level of the beginning student.

The process of negative reinforcement typically involves the removal, reduction, postponement, or prevention of stimulation; these operations strengthen the response on which they are contingent (Hineline, 1977). Removal and reduction of ongoing stimulation typically produce behavior that is called "escape," whereas postponement and prevention of stimulus presentation produce behavior that is called "avoidance." "Typically" is used as a qualifier throughout because the terms negative reinforcement, escape, and avoidance are subject to confusion under certain conditions, as the following will illustrate.

In commenting on the distinction between positive and negative reinforcement, Michael (1975) reviewed a number of historical points related to terminological usage. More important, he noted that some stimulus changes associated with an increase in behavior are difficult to classify as "presentation" (positive reinforcement) versus "removal" (negative reinforcement), and that the use of either description may be nothing more than an arbitrary and incomplete abbreviation for the static "prechange" and "postchange" stimulus conditions as well as for what transpires in between. For example, is a change in temperature more accurately characterized as the presentation of cold (heat) or the removal of heat (cold)? Problems such as this led Michael to suggest that "The distinction between two types of reinforcement [positive vs. negative], based in turn upon the distinction between presentation and removal simply can be dropped" (p. 44). An additional basis for distinguishing between positive and negative reinforcement was suggested first by Catania (1973) and later by Hineline (1984), who noted that ". . . if a stimulus or situation is to be reducible or removable by some response, that response must occur in its presence. In contrast, positively reinforced responses necessarily occur in the absence of the stimuli upon which reinforcement is based" (pp. 496–497). Such a distinction is not without its own problems, as can be seen in the previous example. Is responding prior to a temperature change more accurately described as responding in the presence versus the absence of heat (cold)? Another problem with this distinction is encountered when one considers the difference between escape (responding in the presence of stimulation), and avoidance (responding in the absence of stimulation), both of which are examples of negative reinforcement.

In many applied situations, it is possible to identify unambiguously a stimulus change as one involving presentation (e.g., of physical contact) or removal (e.g., of a token) and to determine whether or not the response of interest occurs in the presence or the absence of stimulation. However, because research outside of the laboratory is subject to greater variation of and less control over a multitude of potentially relevant stimuli, the motivational features of some stimulus changes are difficult to specify. Consider, as a case in point, Osborne's (1969) "Free-time as a reinforcer in the management of classroom behavior," which examined the out-of-seat behavior of six students. During the baseline condition, the students worked for approximately 4 hours daily without recess, and data showed that the target behavior occurred frequently. During treatment, students could earn 5 min of free time at the end of every 15-min work period by remaining in their seats, and the data showed a decrease in out-of-seat. It is interesting to note the target behavior. Defined and recorded as "out-of-seat," free time was made available for its absence; this type of contingency usually is described as differential reinforcement of other behavior (DRO). However, the instructions given to students specified that they were to remain *in* their seats, suggesting "in-seat" as the functional target. If so, free time was made available for the occurrence of in-seat behavior; this type of contingency is not considered an example of DRO. Depending on how one characterizes "free time," (i.e., the availability of preferred activities vs. the termination of nonpreferred activities), we would label the contingency as one involving positive or negative reinforcement for in-seat behavior. Osborne suggested both of these possibilities in his discussion and perhaps this is why he did not place an adjective in front of the term "reinforcer" in the title of the article.

As a field, we have not attended carefully to the important distinction that Osborne drew. His study is regarded as a seminal piece of research in the applied literature for expanding our notion of what constitutes a reinforcing event and for demonstrating very nicely the effects of group contingencies, although the exact nature of the contingency is still unclear. A number of interesting replications and extensions have appeared in *JABA* (e.g., Aaron & Bostow, 1978; Baer, Rowbury, & Baer, 1973; Barrish, Saunders, & Wolf, 1969; Harris & Sherman, 1973, 1974; Long & Williams, 1973; Maloney & Hopkins, 1973; Medland & Stachnik, 1973), but none have included further discussion or analysis of free time contingencies as positive versus negative reinforcement. Although such analyses may have little or no impact on outcome (i.e., in either case, behavior will have been increased), our general tendency to overlook a negative reinforcement interpretation may lead to undue emphasis on the numerous forms that free time may take at the expense of considering important features of the environment that free time replaces. That is, if free time serves as negative reinforcement, its only essential component may be alteration or termination of the preceding aversive situation.

In a more general sense, the complete analysis and specification of conditions in effect prior and subsequent to responding was the primary basis underlying Michael's (1975) suggestion to eliminate the distinction between positive and negative reinforcement. It appears unlikely that the terms "positive" and "negative" will be deleted from our technical vocabulary in the near future; nevertheless, researchers should be cognizant of the fact that the two are potentially interchangeable and that failure to consider both possibilities may have a limiting effect on experimental procedure, interpretation, and subsequent application.

UNDESIRABLE BEHAVIOR ACQUIRED AND MAINTAINED BY NEGATIVE REINFORCEMENT

Hineline (1977) noted that a typical negative reinforcement paradigm includes three features: the presence of aversive stimulation, the availability of a response, and a suitable contingency between the response and the stimulation. Any behavior thus developed or maintained, including a variety of disruptive, destructive, aggressive, self-injurious, and otherwise problematic acts, could be considered "normal" or "adaptive" in that it is the orderly outcome of specific conditioning operations. The term "undesirable" is used here only as a means of classifying behaviors that are considered inappropriate given the usual social context.

An initial question of particular interest to those working in applied areas relates to factors that determine the form of the response. Acquisition of negatively reinforced behavior has been a subject of interest to basic researchers as well because it has been found that some topographies are more readily produced than others. For example, the treadle-press and shuttle responses of pigeons are more easily controlled by negative reinforcement than is the key peck, which is highly responsive to positive reinforcement (Ferrari, Todorov, & Graeff, 1973; Foree & LoLordo, 1970; MacPhail, 1968; Rachlin & Hineline, 1967; Smith & Keller, 1970). Similar data based on the study of different species have provided some support for the hypothesis that negative reinforcement involves selective control over preexisting "species-specific defense reactions" to aversive stimulation (Bolles, 1970, 1971). This account, however, does not provide adequate explanation for the wide range of human behaviors that apparently is succeptable to negative reinforcement. A more likely explanation is that aversive stimulation initially produces one or more of a variety of responses characteristic of both human and nonhuman subjects, including flinching, freezing, jumping, visual scanning, and related and diffuse motor activity (see reviews by Davis, 1979; Hutchinson, 1977; Myer, 1971), and that the eventual and more elaborate form of the behavior is determined by the individual's previous history and the prevailing contingency.

Thus, many of the serious behavioral disorders that are seen in, for example, mentally retarded individuals may be a function of negative reinforcement applied to a particular behavioral repertoire and shaped over time. It is possible that certain instructional sequences (e.g., requests or even the appearance of specific training materials or the instructor) become discriminative for aversive stimulation in the form of physical contact, which is a common element in many teaching routines. At first, the stimulation and its associated cues may produce behaviors similar to those noted above. If, however, other behaviors have been successful in eliminating similar types of stimulation in the past, their eventual occurrence should not be surprising. Tantrums, attempts to flee, or destruction of materials are examples of such behavior, particularly if the individual is unskilled at more subtle or socially acceptable forms of escape. Although disruptive, these behaviors usually are not considered insurmountable barriers to instruction. A number of informal and formal interventions (e.g., proceeding in spite of the tantrum, "scooting" the individual's chair under a table and backing both against a wall, bolting the materials to the table, etc.) are successful in managing disruptive behavior in some cases. In other cases, the interventions may provide a means for shaping more serious forms of escape. The immediate result of aggression for the individual toward whom it is directed suggests that physically harmful acts could serve as very effective escape behaviors, and their ability to terminate aversive instruction is most likely a function of the relative size and strength of client and trainer. Finally, self-injurious behavior, if severe enough, will quickly terminate any situation.

Data relevant to a negative reinforcement hypothesis for the development of behavior disorders in the mentally retarded exist in retrospective form only because it would be unethical to produce pathological behavior in humans when it does not already exist. Nevertheless, support for such a hypothesis can be found in several studies. Carr and Durand (1985) and Weeks and Gaylord-Ross (1981) showed that several different topographies of inappropriate behavior occurred more frequently during a "difficult task" condition when compared to an "easy task" condition, suggesting that the former condition contained aversive properties and that the resulting behavior was escape- or avoidance-motivated. Carr, Newsom, and Binkoff (1976) examined variables that apparently exerted stimulus control over the self-injurious behavior of a psychotic boy. In one of their experiments, they presented the boy with three alternating situations: a free-play period, a condition in which the experimenter spoke descriptive sentences to the child (e.g., "The sky is blue")—this was called the "tact" condition, and a third condition in which the experimenter spoke instructions to the child—this was called the "mand" condition. Higher levels of self-injurious behavior were associated with the mand condition. Carr, Newsom, and Binkoff (1980) conducted a similar analysis of aggressive behavior in two boys, showing that aggression was more likely to occur when demands were present than when they were absent. Finally, Iwata, Dorsey, Slifer, Bauman, and Richman (1982) described a general methodology that allowed one to differentiate self-injury associated with positive versus negative reinforcement. In one of the conditions, self-injury was followed by adult attention; in another, self-injury produced brief escape from adult demands. Some subjects consistently exhibited self-injury during the latter condition, suggesting that their behavior was more sensitive to and maintained by negative reinforcement.

It is important for us to identify how environments that we create may provide negative reinforcement for undesirable behaviors. When faced with situations in which our students and clients are disruptive, we should immediately examine the antecedent as well as the consequent conditions to determine if the difference between the two provides reduction of aversive stimulation, keeping in mind that negative reinforcers may be just as idiosyncratic as positive ones. If we conclude that our clients and students exhibit bizarre and potentially dangerous behaviors to terminate instruction, we might question whether or not our well-intentioned efforts to teach are in our clients' best interest; at the very least, we must question one or more aspects of our teaching technique. Perhaps most important from the standpoint of contingencies, our ability to identify negative reinforcement as a maintenance variable for undesirable behavior may directly influence treatment selection and outcome. This is particularly true with respect to extinction and time-out. Their use typically calls for one or more therapist responses (e.g., turning away from the client, removing stimuli from immediate access, removing the client from the setting, etc.) that terminate the ongoing situation. Studies conducted with nonhuman (Appel, 1963; Azrin, 1961; Thompson,

1964) and human (Plummer, Baer, & LeBlanc, 1977; Solnick, Rincover, & Peterson, 1977) subjects, however, indicate that the effects of time-out are highly dependent on features of the "time-in" environment. Thus, although time-out might be an effective means of extinguishing most positively reinforced behavior, it might directly strengthen negatively reinforced behavior.

TREATMENT OF NEGATIVELY REINFORCED BEHAVIOR

A number of procedures based on the application of extinction, differential reinforcement, and punishment have been evaluated as treatments for problematic behavior of unspecified origin. Their use with behavior maintained by negative reinforcement will be discussed in this section, along with an additional procedure involving stimulus fading.

Extinction

Traditional time-out will not provide for the extinction of behavior that has been maintained by negative reinforcement, but other procedures might. One rather obvious possibility is elimination of the supposed aversive stimulation and its related cues, which should produce a reliable decrease in escape or avoidance behavior (Boren & Sidman, 1957; Shnidman, 1968). However, as Hineline (1977) has noted, this procedure may not be a true extinction operation. The complete removal of aversive stimulation during extinction of negatively reinforced behavior can be considered analogous to the continuous presence of, for example, food during extinction of positively reinforced behavior. Both procedures amount to noncontingent reinforcement, which removes the basis for responding and indirectly reduces the frequency of behavior. That is, if food is always present during extinction of food-maintained behavior, there is no basis for responding; a similar situation exists if shock is always absent during extinction of shock-avoidance behavior. Following these procedures, food removal or, alternatively, reappearance of the shock should immediately produce the target response (see Michael, 1982, for an extended discussion of this topic).

A more appropriate extinction procedure would entail continued presentation of the aversive stimulus or its cue and elimination of the consequence that was provided formerly (i.e., avoidance or escape). In this manner, the basis for responding (aversive stimulation) remains, but reinforcement does not (Bankart & Elliott, 1974; Coulson, Coulson, & Gardner, 1970; Davenport, Coger, & Spector, 1970; Schiff, Smith, & Prochaska, 1972). Techniques derived from this type of extinction actually have been used for a number of years in the treatment of clinical phobias and provide the major theoretical basis for interventions collectively known as "implosion therapies" (Levis, 1979).

An example of extinction for negatively reinforced behavior was reported recently by Heidorn and Jensen (1984). After noting that demand-related situations were associated with an increase in their subject's self-injurious behavior, a treatment was developed that included the following: (a) continued presentation of demands, (b) physical guidance to complete the requested performance contingent on the occurrence of self-injury, (c) termination of the session contingent on compliance, and (d) gradual increase in performance criteria across sessions. Positive reinforcement in the form of praise, food, and physical contact also was provided, but its role as an active component of treatment may have been minimal. A similar procedure was used in one of the experiments reported by Carr et al. (1980) on the treatment of aggression. Extinction consisted of belting the subject in a chair to prevent escape while a therapist wearing protective gear sat across a table from him. The intervention differed from that used by Heidorn and Jensen in that no attempt was made to deliver instructions during extinction sessions; instead, demands were introduced after aggressive behavior was eliminated almost completely.

As with extinction of positively reinforced behavior, it is possible to foresee situations in which extinction of negatively reinforced behavior might not be in the immediate best interest of either the client (as in the case of severe self-injury) or the therapist (as in the case of aggression). Extinction procedures may be compromised further by the potential effects of what procedurally may resemble noncontingent aversive stimulation (see earlier discussion on acquisition of avoidance responding). To the extent that these "elicited" responses occur during the extinction of negatively reinforced behavior in applied situations, attempts to increase alternative behaviors, as well as to reduce the target behavior, may be disrupted. Finally, research showing that time-based delivery of aversive stimulation can maintain (Powell & Peck, 1969) and even increase (Kelleher, Riddle, & Cook, 1963; Sidman, Herrnstein, & Conrad, 1957) the rates of avoidance behavior suggests that schedule-related variables and the subject's previous history may be important considerations in the use of extinction.

Differential Reinforcement

Applications of reinforcement to decrease a target behavior (differential reinforcement of other behavior [DRO], differential reinforcement of incompatible behavior [DRI], etc.) are well documented in the applied literature, although the maintaining variable for the target behavior rarely is noted. The reinforcement contingency itself typically involves the use of positive reinforcement, and discussion here will be similarly confined. Applications of negative reinforcement will be addressed separately.

An experiment designed to examine the suppressive effects of differential reinforcement on negatively reinforced behavior may take several forms. First, access to an appetitive reinforcer (e.g., food) could be made contingent on the absence of the target behavior (DRO) while the escape/avoidance contingency is still operative. Although this approach might be considered unusual, it may resemble very closely situations in the natural environment in which DRO is implemented without attempting to identify the behavior-maintaining contingency. To my knowledge, this study has not been reported in the basic literature, probably due to difficulties associated with equating reinforcement. It is possible that this type of study has been reported in the applied literature but that it was not explicitly identified.

A second approach might involve appetitive reinforcement for a competing behavior (DRI) with the escape/avoidance contingency again operative. Ruddle, Bradshaw, Szabadi, and Foster (1982) studied human operant performance (button pressing) using exactly this procedure. They presented subjects with concurrent avoidance/positive reinforcement schedules, and obtained matched responding when the schedules were equated (this was made possible by using points exchangeable for money). Performance shifts were correlated with schedule shifts roughly in a manner predicted by Herrnstein's (1961) matching law. Our assessment research on self-injury (Iwata et al., 1982) provides an approximation to the Ruddle et al. methodology. During one condition, we presented to subjects a series of instructional demands. Compliance was followed by praise and physical contact from the experimenter, whereas the occurrence of self-injury produced a 30-s time-out. Data gathered during that study, as well as those collected since, indicate that both responses are likely to occur; in other words, positive reinforcement for compliance alone does not suppress avoidance-motivated self-injury. Another example of differential reinforcement was reported by Kelley, Jarvie, Middlebrook, McNeer, and Drabman (1984). They provided token reinforcement (stars) for reductions in the pain behavior (screaming, interfering, etc.) of two children undergoing open burn treatment. The procedure was moderately effective in that reductions in pain behavior averaged less than 50%. The findings of Iwata et al. and Kelley et al. are consistent with those of Ruddle et al., indicating that positively reinforced behavior competes with but does not suppress avoidance or escape responding that is reinforced concurrently. In contrast, Carr et al. (1980) were able to obtain almost complete elimination of aggression in one of their subjects by introducing positive reinforcement to an existing demand situation. They did note, however, that their second subject was not responsive to the positive reinforcement and that a different treatment (see previous discussion of extinction) was used.

A third experiment might examine reinforcement, as described in either of the above examples, combined with extinction (continued presentation of aversive stimuli and prevention of escape). The Heidorn and Jensen (1984) study on self-injury, described previously, is an example of this approach. From an applied perspective, their procedures represent optimal treatment because contingencies were provided for the inappropriate as well as the appropriate behavior. However, here the effects of reinforcement are inseparable from those of extinction, and a clearer interpretation would require comparative analysis (reinforcement plus extinction vs. reinforcement alone vs. extinction alone).

The studies described here remain prototypical for the most part because very little research has been reported on the use of differential (positive) reinforcement with escape and avoidance behavior. On purely ethical grounds, and for the purposes of establishing and strengthening alternative behaviors, the use of positive reinforcement seems critically important. On the other hand, its therapeutic effects as primary treatment for negatively reinforced behavior have yet to be demonstrated. Based on the small amount of data available, one might expect that positive reinforcement is more likely to produce beneficial results if the negatively reinforced behavior is extinguished concurrently or if the density of positive reinforcement is noticeably greater than that of the negative reinforcement.

Punishment

Contingent aversive stimulation for negatively reinforced behavior is the functional complement of DRO for positively reinforced behavior, in that prevention of aversive stimulation (negative reinforcement) is contingent on the absence of responding. Procedural curiosities aside, we know very little about the effects of punishment on human escape and avoidance, in spite of the many applied studies on punishment published to date. For example, the literature on self-injury, in which most of the current applied research on punishment can be found, contains only two studies reporting the use of punishment for behavior described as avoidance motivated. One of the elements in the Heidorn and Jensen (1984) multiple-treatment approach consisted of physical guidance to complete a requested performance, contingent on the occurrence of self-injury. It is interesting to note that the particular form of stimulation used as punishment may have been exactly the same aversive stimulation whose prior removal served as negative reinforcement; if so, the treatment amounted to a perfect reversal of the maintaining contingency. Borreson (1980) also reported a case study of multiple treatment for avoidance-motivated self-injury; however, the punishing stimulus—"forced running" up and down a stairway—appeared to be unrelated to the prior function of the behavior.

Punishment of negatively reinforced behavior presents significant complexities not found with positively reinforced behavior because it involves aversive stimulation following responses for which such stimulation already plays an important role as an eliciting, discriminative, and motivating event (for extensive reviews of this topic, see Davis, 1979; Fowler, 1971; Hineline, 1981; and Morse & Kelleher, 1970, 1977). The major issues are summarized here. First, the eliciting properties of aversive stimulation, described previously with respect to acquisition and extinction, are relevant in the case of punishment. Although elicited behavior may not necessarily compromise the use of punishment, it may have a deleterious effect on the overall treatment program. Second, punishment with the same stimulus used during escape or avoidance training may acquire discriminative properties for responding as a result of reinstating the conditions under which escape originated, thereby occasioning the very behavior being punished. For example, several studies have shown response maintenance and even facilitation when shock-preventing behavior was followed by the presentation of shock (e.g., Appel, 1960; Sandler, Davidson, & Malagodi, 1966). Third, schedule-related variables can determine whether contingent stimulation serves as either punishment or reinforcement. Kelleher and Morse (1968) and McKearney (1972) found that responding developed as avoidance behavior was suppressed under dense schedules of punishment but facilitated under thinner schedules. Finally, it has been noted that punishment intensity and the presence or absence of avoidance contingencies may have an interactive effect on behavior. Sandler, Davidson, Greene, and Holzschuh (1966) imposed high-, intermediate-, and low-intensity shock as punishment for ongoing avoidance behavior and found greater response persistence under the high-intensity condition. However, when the avoidance contingency was later removed (i.e., responding produced shock but no longer prevented it), the high-intensity condition produced the most rapid response suppression.

The use of punishment should always be considered very carefully, and even greater caution should be taken when there is reason to believe that the target behavior has been maintained by negative reinforcement. Findings from the basic research literature suggest, although in a very tentative manner, that a stimulus different from that associated with prior avoidance should be used, that the schedule of punishment should be a continuous one, and that "mildly aversive" stimuli may produce greater response suppression than more intense stimulation when the prevailing avoidance contingency remains operative. On the other hand, data from the Heidorn and Jensen (1984) study indicated that, within the context of their multiple-treatment approach, the relationship between stimulation used as negative reinforcement and punishment may not be an important one.

Stimulus Fading

In contrast to approaches in which a contingency is directly manipulated, fading consists of altering one or more features of stimuli that occasion the target behavior. Various types of stimulus fading have been used for many years in the treatment of clinical fears and phobias, dating back to the work of Jones (1924). Contemporary formulations differ greatly along procedural dimensions (actual vs. representational stimulus presentation, the presence or absence of reinforcement and punishment) as well as on underlying theory (respondent vs. operant conditioning). The operant model of stimulus fading to reduce escape or avoidance behavior involves (a) initial identification of response-producing stimuli, (b) stimulus alteration to the point where responding does not occur, (c) presentation of the altered stimuli with a gradual return to their original state, and (d) extinction of escape behavior.

Approximations to the stimulus fading approach can be found in two studies previously discussed. Heidorn and Jensen (1984) decreased and then gradually increased the frequency with which response-producing stimuli (demands) were presented, although they did not withdraw them entirely at the beginning of treatment. In contrast, Carr et al. (1976) were able to reduce self-injury by embedding demands within entertaining stories, although the stories were never faded out nor were additional demands faded in. The results of both studies suggest that more complete evaluations of treatment based on fading are warranted. One potential advantage of fading over extinction and punishment might be the complete elimination of escape behavior from the outset of treatment.

NEGATIVE REINFORCEMENT AS THERAPY

I have noted previously that free-time contingencies might function as negative reinforcement, although that possibility has been seldom acknowledged. Free time also may be one of the few contingencies in the applied literature that represents pure escape in that the stimulation (work) is relatively continuous and can be reduced or terminated but not avoided. A great majority of applications make use of time- or trial-based presentation of stimuli preceded by cues, which produces avoidance behavior. Examples of negative reinforcement used to strengthen desirable behavior will be discussed in this section, grouped according to similarities in either procedure or problem.

Behavioral Engineering

The earliest examples of negative reinforcement to develop or maintain appropriate behavior published in *JABA* made use of apparatus-delivered stimulation. Azrin and his colleagues conducted two such studies. The first (Azrin, Rubin, O'Brien, Ayllon, & Roll, 1968) established automated measurement and control over postural slouching. An apparatus built into a shoulder harness operated closure of a circuit when slouching occurred. This action produced an audible click, followed 3 s later by a 55-db tone. The contingency was an ingenious one in that it included aspects of both free-operant and discriminated avoidance plus escape. Maintenance of correct posture (free-operant) avoided the click, postural correction (discriminated) during the 3 s following the click avoided the tone, and correction during the tone provided escape. Subjects consisted of 25 adults, all of whom showed reductions in slouching while the device was worn. When the contingency was reversed for two of the subjects, both showed increases in slouching. In a later study, Azrin and Powell (1969) evaluated an apparatus to increase pill taking in six subjects. The pill dispenser produced a 50-db tone every 30 min, an arbitrary between-pill interval. The tone could be turned off by pushing a knob on the case, which also delivered two pills. One might expect that this arrangement would produce escape behavior initially, followed by free-operant avoidance, although data to that effect were not presented. A third study involving apparatus-delivered negative reinforcement was conducted by Greene and Hoats (1969). Their subject was an adult male assigned to a correctional unit whose task was to sort computer cards, for which he earned cigarettes. He also was allowed to watch TV while performing the task. During the treatment condition, if the subject did not complete a task cycle within a specified interval of time (avoidance), visual and auditory output from the TV were distorted and remained that way until the work cycle was completed (escape).

Toilet Training and Incontinence

The presence or absence of elimination is more than the occurrence or nonoccurrence of a response. Sphincter contraction as well as relaxation is involved, and negative reinforcement has been used in the management of both behaviors. Hansen (1979) incorporated escape and avoidance contingencies in the treatment of nocturnal enuresis in two children. When a device placed in the bed detected urination, an apparatus located 4 ft away produced a 70-db tone, which was followed in 7 s by a 95-db tone. By remaining dry, the child could avoid the first tone; if the child urinated, he or she could escape the first tone and avoid the second by immediately getting out of bed and turning the unit off. O'Brien, Ross, and Christophersen (1986) recently used negative reinforcement to produce elimination. As part of an overall treatment program for four encopretic children, the authors wanted to establish morning control over bowel movements. To do so, parents had the children sit on the toilet each morning for 5 min; failure to defecate a minimum equivalent of one-fourth of a cup during that time was followed immediately by insertion of a suppository. A second administration was given if the first did not produce the desired outcome.

Overcorrection

Originally designed as a means for eliminating accidents during toilet training (Azrin & Foxx, 1971), overcorrection consists of a group of techniques whose common feature is repetitive performance of motor activity. Overcorrection is one of the most thoroughly studied and frequently used methods for reducing the frequency of a wide range of undesirable behaviors (see Foxx & Bechtel, 1983, for a review). The procedures are considered to be derivatives of punishment and are applied contingent upon the occurrence of a target behavior. At the same time, overcorrection can serve as negative reinforcement in at least two ways. First, because the procedure calls for performance of activities that apparently are aversive, a therapist always is at hand to ensure compliance through continued instruction and, if necessary, physical guidance. Thus, the client can avoid repeated instructions and potentially intrusive physical contact through continued performance of the required activity. Avoidance behavior is also produced when overcorrection is applied contingent upon the absence of a desirable response. For example, Foxx (1977) showed that 5 min of functional movement training, involving the practice of varying head positions, was superior to food and praise in developing and maintaining eye contact in three retarded children. Examination of the overcorrection literature yields a number of instances in which the procedure was used to increase rather than decrease behaviors, including class attendance (Foxx, 1976), repetitive tasks (Carey & Bucher, 1983), sharing (Barton & Osborne, 1978), speech (Matson, Esveldt-Dawson, & O'Connell, 1979), and spelling accuracy (Foxx & Jones, 1978; Ollendick, Matson, Esveldt-Dawson, & Shapiro, 1980).

Error Correction During Instruction

Rodgers and Iwata (1987) recently conducted a survey whose initial focus was on response prompting as an adjunct during behavioral acquisition. We quickly determined that most prompting occurs following an error and expanded the analysis to include all events that can be made contingent on incorrect responses. Negative reinforcement was not a subject of interest at the outset, but some of the techniques that were found suggest that it plays a much more prominent role in the instructional process than is currently acknowledged.

The most dramatic example is a study by Kircher, Pear, and Martin (1971) entitled "Shock as *punishment* [emphasis added] in a picture-naming task with retarded children." In one experiment, two children were exposed to the following two treatments: (a) token reinforcement for correct picture-naming responses, and (b) token reinforcement for correct responses *plus* shock for either errors or a response latency greater than 5 s. The shock condition produced superior results. Because the token reinforcement remained constant across the two conditions and because, regardless of how one defines the target behavior (i.e., errors vs. correct responses, inattention vs. attention), the desirable performance was a correct picture name, the procedure clearly represents an avoidance contingency in that correct responses made within 5 s of the cue prevented the delivery of the shock.

The Kircher et al. (1971) study represents a rather extreme use of negative reinforcement to increase desirable behavior, one that cannot be defended on ethical grounds today. However, less dramatic but analogous situations are quite common in the literature on instructional technology. It has become standard practice to follow errors with statements of disapproval (Dunlap & Johnson, 1985; Rincover & Newsom, 1985; Schreibman, 1975), physical guidance (Haring, 1985; Luyben, Funk, Morgan, Clark, & Delulio, 1986; Sprague & Horner, 1984), session-lengthening procedures consisting of either time-out (Barrera & Sulzer-Azaroff, 1983; O'Brien & Azrin, 1972) or remedial learning trials (Nutter & Reid, 1978; Page, Iwata, & Neef, 1976; Richman, Reiss, Bauman, & Bailey, 1984), and so on. Thus, in addition to producing positive reinforcement in the form of experimenter praise, correct responses also may function to avoid aversive social and physical stimulation and to effectively reduce the duration of training sessions (this latter point is potentially significant, for it has been shown that complex setting events or stimulus situations, and not just discrete stimuli, can function as negative reinforcers [Krasnegor, Brady, & Findley, 1971], and that reduction of avoidance-session durations can itself serve as negative reinforcement [Mellitz, Hineline, Whitehouse, & Laurence, 1983]).

Behavioral Replacement Strategies

Given that aversive stimuli are ubiquitous and that escape is highly adaptive in their presence, it is usually the form, rather than the function, of escape and avoidance behavior that presents a problem. This raises the possibility of eliminating inappropriate forms of escape by negatively reinforcing appropriate alternatives; in essence, replacing one behavior with another but not eliminating the function of the original. The concept is rather straightforward in principle and is analogous to lever switching by nonhuman subjects following a change in reinforcement schedule (e.g., De Villiers, 1974).

Carr and Durand (1985) recently provided an example of this strategy by teaching three children, who had tantrums when faced with difficult tasks, how to request help from the teacher. When a child exhibited the appropriate response ("I don't understand"), brief escape was provided in the form of teacher assistance.

Another example is drawn from our work on feeding disorders. While attempting to increase the oral acceptance of food in four children, Riordan, Iwata, Finney, Wohl and Stanley (1984) found that one child, who was fed through a gastrostomy tube, did not respond well to positive reinforcement because her baseline rate of acceptance was virtually nonexistent. She also had resisted a number of forced feeding regimens; these practices were aversive and it appeared that her success in defeating them constituted negative reinforcement. Her treatment consisted of the following components: (a) the presentation of a redundant cue—"Take a bite"—immediately followed by (b) the presentation of food on a spoon. If acceptance of food did not occur within 3 s, (c) her mouth was held open and the food was deposited. This procedure thus resembled very closely a discriminated avoidance contingency in which one avoidance behavior (active food refusal) was replaced with another (opening the mouth and accepting food) by allowing it to prevent forced feeding.

Other Examples

In addition to the Kircher et al. (1971) study on academic performance described earlier, one can find instances in which negative reinforcement has been used—in a highly intrusive manner—to increase appropriate social behaviors. Lovaas, Schaeffer, and Simmons (1965) used escape and avoidance in training two autistic children to approach adults. Prior to treatment, the children frequently engaged in stereotypic behavior and showed no social responsivity or appropriate play. Treatment consisted of presenting the instruction, "Come here," followed by shock delivered through a floor grid. The shock was terminated when the child moved toward the therapist (escape). Both children quickly learned to approach the adult in response to the verbal instruction (avoidance). In defense of their use of electric-shock avoidance, the authors presented data indicating that increases in approach behavior were accompanied by more frequent displays of affection and decreases in stereotypy and aggression.

A less intrusive but similar procedure was used by Fichter, Wallace, Liberman, and Davis (1976) in an attempt to improve the social skills of a chronic and withdrawn schizophrenic male. The researchers targeted three aspects of his conversational behavior: voice loudness, duration of verbal responding, and keeping his hands on the armrests of his chair while speaking. A therapist approached the client, called his name, and asked him to converse about one of several predetermined topics. During treatment, the staff member continuously monitored the target behaviors; if any failed to meet criterion, the staff member would nag loudly one or more of the following: "Longer!," "Louder!," or "Put your hands on the armrests of the chair!," and would continue to nag at 3-s intervals until the target behavior occurred. Although effective, it should be noted that the contingencies used by Fichter et al. would not be considered typical consequences for social interaction; in fact, it is entirely possible that the appearance of the therapist would become discriminative for withdrawal. Data similar to those provided by Lovaas et al. (1965) showing that social behavior (e.g., conversations initiated by the subject or his response to approach by a therapist) improved outside of treatment sessions would have been informative with respect to this question. One can only assume that there was no generalized improvement, based on a comment made by the authors:

> ". . . his [the subject's] last interaction before . . . [being discharged from the] . . . unit was to tell one staff member how much he disliked the unit and the staff" (Fichter et al., 1976, pp. 384–385).

SUMMARY

In this article I have attempted to point out a number of ways in which negative reinforcement is relevant to behavioral development and its subsequent modification in the applied situation. My review has been a selective one in that I made no attempt to summarize the large and varied literature on aversion, implosion, and desensitization therapies often used in the treatment of alcoholism, smoking, phobic reactions, sexual disorders, and related clinical problems. Still, the applied examples represent a thorough cross section of research published in *JABA* over the past 20 years, and a number of general conclusions and implications can be drawn from the work described here.

Historically, applied analyses of behavior have failed to acknowledge escape and avoidance as potentially common and powerful sources of reinforcement. Evidence of this can be found in work on severe behavioral disorders such as self-injury, in which discussions of etiology have focused primarily on attentional factors rather than on those related to escape; in research on contingencies such as free time, in which free time as negative reinforcement has not been a subject of analysis; in studies in which avoidance contingencies have been inaccurately described as punishment; and in research on instructional processes, in which a variety of avoidance contingencies have been used but not evaluated or even described as such.

A second and more optimistic conclusion supportable by work described here is that an applied technology of negative reinforcement is emerging. The work is somewhat scattered at present and little is known in some areas. Nevertheless, under each of the topics included in the present discussion—behavioral development, treatment of negatively reinforced behavior, and therapeutic uses of negative reinforcement—research activity has increased in recent years, and we are beginning to see investigations of common procedures to the point where categorization is both possible and useful. This evidence of growing interest suggests that negative reinforcement may be one of the most significant areas of applied research during the coming years. Having made that prediction, what remains is to offer some prompts to help ensure its accuracy.

The area of behavioral development is particularly problematic because applied researchers often are faced with situations in which the behavior of interest has a long, complex, and unknown history. In fact, the most important difference between laboratory- and field-based research, at least from a behavioral standpoint, is the lack of control over history that is characteristic of applied research. In some cases (perhaps even most), behavioral history may be irrelevant if a sufficiently powerful contingency can be found. In other cases, however, implementation of treatment without consideration of developmental factors, or treatment selection based on a consideration of topography alone, may produce a number of unnecessary failures and subsequently may limit our ability to determine the basis for differential outcome.

Laboratory researchers solve problems related to history by controlling its course in a naive animal. Although applied researchers rarely can exercise this option, they can make a unique contribution by developing methods for "unravelling" behavioral history, to the extent that it is possible. Our realization that behavioral development through negative reinforcement can produce the same topography as that resulting from positive reinforcement, time and time again, may provide the impetus for continued refinement in the analysis of behavioral function. For example, a number of researchers have concluded that unitary accounts of severe behavioral disorders in the developmentally disabled are unsatisfactory and have begun to establish methodologies for identifying the functional properties (one being negative reinforcement) of disorders such as pica (Mace & Knight, 1986), self-injury (Carr & Durand, 1985; Iwata et al., 1982), and stereotypy (Durand & Carr, 1987). Most recently, Bailey (1987) has proposed the term "behavioral diagnostics" to describe a general strategy for isolating the bases of problematic behavior. Continued work in this area and extension of the relevant methodologies to other human problems are essential if we are to develop a mature technology of behavior. In the meantime, researchers should be encouraged (perhaps by editors) to seek out and include more detail on subjects' behavioral histories. In addition to the usual demographics offered (e.g., age, sex, grade or functioning level, etc.), which provide little information relevant to a behavioral analysis, it would be helpful to provide some account of factors related to behavioral development and maintenance. As evidence supporting a negative reinforcement interpretation accumulates, we will be increasingly compelled to formalize our anecdotal observations and to confirm these observations through manipulation.

Because applied research often is concerned with a problem as it actually exists, the treatment of negatively reinforced behavior will provide perhaps the greatest opportunity for creative work. For example, research on the extinction of positively reinforced behavior has included variation and extension (e.g., time-out, exclusion, seclusion, contingent observation, time-out ribbon, movement suppression), parametric analysis (e.g., duration, delay, schedule, changeover requirement), and comparison (e.g., with differential reinforcement, response cost, and punishment). None of these questions have been addressed adequately in applied research on the extinction of negatively reinforced behavior, and a similar situation exists with respect to differential reinforcement and punishment.

Research on the treatment of negatively reinforced behavior will require consideration of issues that are different than those relevant to the treatment of positively reinforced behavior. These issues have been noted previously, and some have been the focus of laboratory research for several years. Stimulus selection, schedules, and intensity, for example, may differentially affect the outcome of contingent aversive stimulation for ongoing avoidance behavior. Therefore, it will be important for applied researchers to become acquainted with basic findings on negative reinforcement. As a result, we may find that methodologies and procedures developed in the laboratory can be extended to the applied situation so as to facilitate analysis and treatment.

Research on the use of negative reinforcement may take several interesting directions. First, negative reinforcement may provide an alternative means for establishing behavior when attempts to use positive reinforcement fail (e.g., as in the case of Riordan et al., 1984, in which a child's operant level of eating was nonexistent). If so, we will want to know the behaviors for which specific contingencies are useful and the conditions under which they should be applied. Second, it appears that the acquisition of adaptive behavior in our training programs is at least partially a function of negative reinforcement. Future research must evaluate the roles of escape and avoidance within the training context so that (a) we will have a proper estimate of the effectiveness of commonly used positive reinforcers (the results of this estimate may indicate that more potent reinforcers are needed), (b) we can determine whether procedures such as remedial trials, physical assistance, and so on, serve any useful function and if that function is one of negative reinforcement, and (c) we can base future training successes on the planned rather than the accidental use of negative reinforcement. A third promising application involves further elaboration of behavioral replacement strategies. If we are willing to entertain the assumption that it is impossible to eliminate all sources of aversive stimulation, the use of such stimulation to alter the topography of escape and avoidance behavior, from an undesirable one to a tolerable one, makes eminent sense from a clinical standpoint.

A final cautionary note. Some of the applied research included in this review was selected specifically to show that negative reinforcement can form the basis of highly intrusive intervention. In at least one sense, negative reinforcement might be considered more intrusive than punishment because, with negative reinforcement, presentation of the aversive stimulus is contingent on the absence, rather than the occurrence, of behavior. Therefore, as with punishment, we should conduct research on negative reinforcement with great care and under the appropriate conditions to determine how it might be used effectively and humanely, its limitations, and its proper role within the larger realm of currently available treatment.

REFERENCES

Aaron, B. A., & Bostow, D. E. (1978). Indirect facilitation of on-task behavior produced by contingent free-time for academic productivity. *Journal of Applied Behavior Analysis,* **11**, 197.

Appel, J. B. (1960). Some schedules involving aversive control. *Journal of the Experimental Analysis of Behavior,* **3**, 349–359.

Appel, J. B. (1963). Aversive aspects of a schedule of positive reinforcement. *Journal of the Experimental Analysis of Behavior,* **6**, 423–430.

Axelrod, S., & Apsche, J. (1983). *The effects of punishment on human behavior.* New York: Academic Press.

Azrin, N. H. (1961). Time-out from positive reinforcement. *Science,* **133**, 382–383.

Azrin, N. H., & Foxx, R. M. (1971). A rapid method of toilet training the institutionalized retarded. *Journal of Applied Behavior Analysis,* **4**, 89–99.

Azrin, N. H., & Powell, J. (1969). Behavioral engineering: The use of response priming to improve prescribed self-medication. *Journal of Applied Behavior Analysis,* **1**, 99–108.

Azrin, N., Rubin, H., O'Brien, F., Ayllon, T., & Roll, D. (1968). Behavioral engineering: Postural control by a portable operant apparatus. *Journal of Applied Behavior Analysis,* **2**, 39–42.

Baer, A. M., Rowbury, T., & Baer, D. M. (1973). The development of instructional control over classroom activities of deviant preschool children. *Journal of Applied Behavior Analysis,* **6**, 289–298.

Baer, D. M. (1978). On the relation between basic and applied research. In A. C. Catania & T. A. Brigham (Eds.), *Handbook of applied behavior analysis: Social and instructional processes* (pp. 11–17). New York: Irvington.

Baer, D. M. (1981). A flight of behavior analysis. *The Behavior Analyst,* **4**, 85–91.

Baer, D. M., Wolf, M. M., & Risley, T. R. (1968). Some current dimensions of applied behavior analysis. *Journal of Applied Behavior Analysis,* **1**, 91–97.

Bailey, J. S. (1987, May). *Behavioral diagnostics: New tools for applied behavior analysis.* Presented as an invited address at the Association of Behavior Analysis Convention, Nashville, TN.

Bankart, B., & Elliott, R. (1974). Extinction of avoidance in rats: Response availability and stimulus presentation effects. *Behaviour Research and Therapy,* **12**, 53–56.

Barrera, R. D., & Sulzer-Azaroff, B. (1983). An alternating treatment comparison of oral and total communication training programs with echolalic autistic children. *Journal of Applied Behavior Analysis,* **16**, 379–394.

Barrish, H. H., Saunders, M., & Wolf, M. M. (1969). Good behavior game: Effects of individual contingencies for group consequences on disruptive behavior in a classroom. *Journal of Applied Behavior Analysis,* **2**, 119–124.

Barton, E. S., & Osborne, J. G. (1978). The development of classroom sharing by a teacher using positive practice. *Behavior Modification,* **2**, 231–250.

Bolles, R. G. (1970). Species-specific defense reactions and avoidance learning. *Psychological Review,* **77**, 32–48.

Bolles, R. G. (1971). Species-specific defense reactions. In F. R. Brush (Ed.), *Aversive conditioning and learning* (pp. 183–233). New York: Academic Press.

Boren, J. J., & Sidman, M. (1957). A discrimination based on repeated conditioning and extinction of avoidance behavior. *Journal of Comparative and Physiological Psychology,* **50**, 18–22.

Borreson, P. M. (1980). The elimination of a self-injurious avoidance response through a forced running consequence. *Mental Retardation,* **18**, 73–77.

Carey, R. G., & Bucher, B. (1983). Positive practice overcorrection: The effects of duration of positive practice on acquisition and response reduction. *Journal of Applied Behavior Analysis,* **16**, 101–109.

Carr, E. G., & Durand, M. V. (1985). Reducing behavior problems through functional communication training. *Journal of Applied Behavior Analysis,* **18**, 111–126.

Carr, E. G., Newsom, C. D., & Binkoff, J. A. (1976). Stimulus control of self-destructive behavior in a psychotic child. *Journal of Abnormal Child Psychology,* **4**, 139–153.

Carr, E. G., Newsom, C. D., & Binkoff, J. A. (1980). Escape as a factor in the aggression of two retarded children. *Journal of Applied Behavior Analysis,* **13**, 101–117.

Catania, A. C. (1973). The nature of learning. In J. A. Nevin & G. S. Reynolds (Eds.), *The study of behavior: Learning, motivation, emotion, and instinct* (pp. 31–68). Glenview, IL: Scott, Foresman.

Coulson, G., Coulson, V., & Gardner, L. (1970). The effect of two extinction procedures after acquisition on a Sidman avoidance contingency. *Psychonomic Science,* **18**, 309–310.

Cullen, C. (1981). The flight to the laboratory. *The Behavior Analyst,* **4**, 81–83.

Davenport, D. G., Coger, R. W., & Spector, O. J. (1970). The redefinition of extinction applied to Sidman free-operant avoidance responding. *Psychonomic Science,* **19**, 181–182.

Davis, H. (1979). Behavioral anomolies in aversive situations. In J. D. Keehn (Ed.), *Psychopathology in animals: Research and clinical implications* (pp. 197–222). New York: Academic Press.

Deitz, S. M. (1978). Current status of applied behavior anlaysis: Science versus technology. *American Psychologist,* **33**, 805–814.

De Villiers, P. A. (1974). The law of effect and avoidance: A quantitative relationship between response rate and shock-frequency reduction. *Journal of the Experimental Analysis of Behavior,* **21**, 223–235.

Dunlap, G., & Johnson, J. (1985). Increasing the independent responding of autistic children with unpredictable supervision. *Journal of Applied Behavior Analysis,* **18**, 227–236.

Durand, V. M., & Carr, E. G. (1987). Social influences on "self-stimulatory" behavior. *Journal of Applied Behavior Analysis,* **20**, 119–132.

Ferrari, E. A., Todorov, J. C., & Graeff, F. G. (1973). Nondiscriminated avoidance of shock by pigeons pecking a key. *Journal of the Experimental Analysis of Behavior,* **19**, 211–218.

Fichter, M. M., Wallace, C. J., Liberman, R. P., & Davis, J. R. (1976). Improving social interaction in the chronic psychotic using discriminated avoidance ("nagging"): Experimental analysis and generalization. *Journal of Applied Behavior Analysis,* **9**, 367–386.

Foree, D., & LoLordo, V. (1970). Signalled and unsignalled free-operant avoidance in the pigeon. *Journal of the Experimental Analysis of Behavior,* **13**, 283–290.

Fowler, H. (1971). Suppression and facilitation by response contingent shock. In R. F. Brush (Ed.), *Aversive conditioning and learning* (pp. 537–604). New York: Academic Press.

Foxx, R. M. (1976). Increasing a mildly retarded woman's

attendance at self-help classes by overcorrection and instruction. *Behavior Therapy,* **6**, 390–396.

Foxx, R. M. (1977). Attention training: The use of overcorrection avoidance to increase the eye contact of autistic and retarded children. *Journal of Applied Behavior Anlaysis,* **10**, 488–499.

Foxx, R. M., & Bechtel, D. R. (1983). Overcorrection: A review and analysis. In S. Axelrod & J. Apsche (Eds.), *The effects of punishment on human behavior* (pp. 133–220). New York: Academic Press.

Foxx, R. M., & Jones, J. R. (1978). A remediation program for increasing spelling achievement of elementary and junior high school students. *Behavior Modification,* **2**, 211–230.

Greene, R. R., & Hoats, D. L. (1969). Reinforcing capabilities of television distortion. *Journal of Applied Behavior Analysis,* **2**, 139–141.

Hansen, G. D. (1979). Enuresis control through fading, escape, and avoidance training. *Journal of Applied Behavior Analysis,* **12**, 303–307.

Haring, T. G. (1985). Teaching between-class generalization of toy play behavior to handicapped children. *Journal of Applied Behavior Analysis,* **18**, 127–139.

Harris, V. W., & Sherman, J. A. (1973). Use and analysis of the "good behavior game" to reduce disruptive classroom behavior. *Journal of Applied Behavior Analysis,* **6**, 405–417.

Harris, V. W., & Sherman, J. A. (1974). Homework assignments, consequences, and classroom performance in social studies and mathematics. *Journal of Applied Behavior Analysis,* **7**, 505–519.

Heidorn, S. D., & Jensen, C. C. (1984). Generalization and maintenance of the reduction of self-injurious behavior maintained by two types of reinforcement. *Behavior Research and Therapy,* **22**, 581–586.

Herrnstein, R. J. (1961). Relative and absolute strength of response as a function of frequency of reinforcement. *Journal of the Experimental Analysis of Behavior,* **4**, 267–272.

Herrnstein, R. J. (1969). Method and theory in the study of avoidance. *Psychological Review,* **76**, 49–69.

Hineline, P. N. (1977). Negative reinforcement and avoidance. In W. K. Honig & J. E. R. Staddon (Eds.), *Handbook of operant behavior* (pp. 364–414). Englewood Cliffs, NJ: Prentice-Hall.

Hineline, P. N. (1981). Several roles of stimuli in negative reinforcement. In P. Harzem & M. D. Zeiler (Eds.), *Advances in analysis of behavior: Vol. 2. Predictability, correlation, and contiguity* (pp. 203–246). Chichester, England: Wiley.

Hineline, P. N. (1984). Aversive control: A separate domain? *Journal of the Experimental Analysis of Behavior,* **42**, 495–509.

Hoffman, H. S. (1966). The analysis of discriminated avoidance. In W. K. Honig (Ed.), *Operant behavior: Areas of research and application* (pp. 499–530). New York: Appleton.

Honig, W. K., & Staddon, J. E. R. (Eds.). (1977). *Handbook of operant behavior.* Englewood Cliffs, NJ: Prentice-Hall.

Hutchinson, R. R. (1977). By-products of aversive control. In W. K. Honig & J. E. R. Staddon (Eds.), *Handbook of operant behavior* (pp. 415–431). Englewood Cliffs, NJ: Prentice-Hall.

Iwata, B. A., Dorsey, M. F., Slifer, K. J., Bauman, K. E., & Richman, G. S. (1982). Toward a functional analysis of self-injury. *Analysis and Intervention in Developmental Disabilities,* **3**, 1–20.

Jones, M. C. (1924). Elimination of children's fears. *Journal of Experimental Psychology,* **7**, 382–390.

Kelleher, R. T., Riddle, W. C., & Cook, L. (1963). Persistent behavior maintained by unavoidable shocks. *Journal of the Experimental Analysis of Behavior,* **6**, 507–517.

Kelleher, R. T., & Morse, W. H. (1968). Schedules using noxious stimuli, III: Responding maintained with response-produced electric shocks. *Journal of the Experimental Analysis of Behavior,* **11**, 819–838.

Kelley, M. L., Jarvie, G. J., Middlebrook, J. L., McNeer, M. F., & Drabman, R. S. (1984). Decreasing burned children's pain behavior: Impacting the trauma of hydrotherapy. *Journal of Applied Behavior Analysis,* **17**, 147–158.

Kircher, A. S., Pear, J. J., & Martin, G. L. (1971). Shock as punishment in a picture-naming task with retarded children. *Journal of Applied Behavior Analysis,* **4**, 227–233.

Krasnegor, N. A., Brady, J. V., & Findley, J. D. (1971). Second-order optional avoidance as a function of fixed-ratio requirements. *Journal of the Experimental Analysis of Behavior,* **15**, 181–187.

Levis, D. J. (1979). The infrahuman avoidance model of symptom maintenance and implosive therapy. In J. D. Keehn (Ed.), *Psychopathology in animals: Research and clinical implications* (pp. 257–277). New York: Academic Press.

Long, J. D., & Williams, R. W. (1973). The comparative effectiveness of group and individual contingent free time with inner-city junior high school students. *Journal of Applied Behavior Analysis,* **6**, 465–474.

Lovaas, O. I., Schaeffer, B., & Simmons, J. Q. (1965). Building social behavior in autistic children by use of electric shock. *Journal of Experimental Research in Personality,* **1**, 99–109.

Luyben, P. D., Funk, D. M., Morgan, J. K., Clark, K. A., & Delulio, D. W. (1986). Team sports for the retarded: Training a side-of-the-foot soccer pass using a maximum-to-minimum prompt reduction strategy. *Journal of Applied Behavior Analysis,* **19**, 431–436.

Mace, F. C., & Knight, D. (1986). Functional analysis and treatment of severe pica. *Journal of Applied Behavior Analysis,* **19**, 411–416.

MacPhail, E. M. (1968). Avoidance responding in pigeons. *Journal of the Experimental Analysis of Behavior,* **11**, 629–632.

Maloney, K. B., & Hopkins, B. L. (1973). The modification of sentence structure and its relationship to subjective judgments of creativity in writing. *Journal of Applied Behavior Analysis,* **6**, 425–433.

Matson, J. L., & DiLorenzo, T. M. (1984). *Punishment*

and its alternatives: A new perspective for behavior modification. New York: Springer.

Matson, J. L., Esveldt-Dawson, K., & O'Connell, D. (1979). Overcorrection, modeling, and reinforcement procedures for reinstating speech in a mute boy. *Child Behavior Therapy,* **1,** 363–371.

McKearney, J. W. (1972). Maintenance and suppression of responding under schedules of electric shock presentation. *Journal of the Experimental Analysis of Behavior,* **17,** 425–432.

Medland, M. B., & Stachnik, T. J. (1973). Good behavior game: A replication and systematic analysis. *Journal of Applied Behavior Analysis,* **6,** 45–51.

Mellitz, M., Hineline, P. N., Whitehouse, W. G., & Laurence, M. T. (1983). Duration-reduction of avoidance sessions as negative reinforcement. *Journal of the Experimental Analysis of Behavior,* **40,** 57–67.

Michael, J. (1975). Positive and negative reinforcement: A distinction that is no longer necessary; Or a better way to talk about bad things. *Behaviorism,* **3,** 33–44.

Michael, J. (1980). Flight from behavior analysis. *The Behavior Analyst,* **3,** 1–24.

Michael, J. (1982). Distinguishing between discriminative and motivational functions of stimuli. *Journal of the Experimental Analysis of Behavior,* **37,** 149–155.

Morse, W. H., & Kelleher, R. T. (1970). Schedules as fundamental determinants of behavior. In W. N. Schoenfeld (Ed.), *The theory of reinforcement schedules* (pp. 139–185). New York: Appleton.

Morse, W. H., & Kelleher, R. T. (1977). Determinants of reinforcement and punishment. In W. K. Honig & J. E. R. Staddon (Eds.), *Handbook of operant behavior* (pp. 174–200). Englewood Cliffs, NJ: Prentice-Hall.

Myer, J. S. (1971). Some effects of noncontingent aversive stimulation. In R. F. Brush (Ed.), *Aversive conditioning and learning* (pp. 469–536). New York: Academic Press.

Nutter, D., & Reid, D. H. (1978). Teaching retarded women a clothing selection skill using community norms. *Journal of Applied Behavior Analysis,* **11,** 475–487.

O'Brien, F., & Azrin, N. H. (1972). Developing proper mealtime behaviors of the institutionalized retarded. *Journal of Applied Behavior Analysis,* **5,** 389–399.

O'Brien, S., Ross, L. V., & Christophersen, E. R. (1986). Primary encopresis: Evaluation and treatment. *Journal of Applied Behavior Analysis,* **19,** 137–145.

Ollendick, T. H., Matson, J. L., Esveldt-Dawson, K., & Shapiro, E. S. (1980). Increasing spelling achievement: An analysis of treatment procedures utilizing an alternating treatments design. *Journal of Applied Behavior Analysis,* **13,** 645–654.

Osborne, J. G. (1969). Free-time as a reinforcer in the management of classroom behavior. *Journal of Applied Behavior Analysis,* **2,** 113–118.

Page, T. J., Iwata, B. A., & Neef, N. A. (1976). Teaching pedestrian skills to retarded persons: Generalization from the classroom to the natural environment. *Journal of Applied Behavior Analysis,* **9,** 433–444.

Pierce, W. D., & Epling, W. F. (1980). What happened to analysis in applied behavior analysis? *The Behavior Analyst,* **3,** 1–10.

Plummer, S., Baer, D. M., & LeBlanc, J. M. (1977). Functional considerations in the use of timeout and an effective alternative. *Journal of Applied Behavior Analysis,* **10,** 689–705.

Powell, R. W., & Peck, S. (1969). Persistent shock-elicited responding engendered by a negative reinforcement procedure. *Journal of the Experimental Analysis of Behavior,* **12,** 1049–1062.

Rachlin, H., & Hineline, P. N. (1967). Training and maintenance of keypecking in the pigeon using negative reinforcement. *Science,* **157,** 954–955.

Richman, G. S., Reiss, M. L., Bauman, K. E., & Bailey, J. S. (1984). Teaching menstrual care to mentally retarded women: Acquisition, generalization, and maintenance. *Journal of Applied Behavior Analysis,* **17,** 441–451.

Rincover, A., & Newsom, C. D. (1985). The relative motivational properties of sensory and edible reinforcers in teaching autistic children. *Journal of Applied Behavior Analysis,* **18,** 237–248.

Riordan, M. M., Iwata, B. A., Finney, J. W., Wohl, M. K., & Stanley, A. E. (1984). Behavioral assessment and treatment of chronic food refusal in handicapped children. *Journal of Applied Behavior Analysis,* **17,** 327–341.

Rodgers, T. A., & Iwata, B. A. (1987, September). Analysis of error correction procedures during behavioral acquisition. In J. S. Bailey (Chair), *Training research in mental retardation.* Symposium presented at the Florida Association for Behavior Analysis Convention, Sarasota.

Ruddle, H. V., Bradshaw, C. M., Szabadi, E., & Foster, T. M. (1982). Performance of humans in concurrent avoidance/positive-reinforcement schedules. *Journal of the Experimental Analysis of Behavior,* **38,** 51–61.

Sandler, J., & Davidson, R. S. (1973). *Psychopathology: Learning theory, research and applications.* New York: Harper & Row.

Sandler, J., Davidson, R. S., Greene, W. E., & Holzschuh, R. D. (1966). Effects of punishment intensity on instrumental avoidance behavior. *Journal of Comparative and Physiological Psychology,* **61,** 212–216.

Sandler, J., Davidson, R. S., & Malagodi, E. F. (1966). Durable maintenance of behavior during concurrent avoidance and punished-extinction conditions. *Psychonomic Science,* **6,** 105–106.

Schiff, R., Smith, N., & Prochaska, J. (1972). Extinction of avoidance in rats as a function of duration and number of blocked trials. *Journal of Comparative and Physiological Psychology,* **81,** 356–359.

Schoenfeld, W. N. (1969). "Avoidance" in behavioral theory. *Journal of the Experimental Analysis of Behavior,* **12,** 669–674.

Schreibman, L. (1975). Effects of within-stimulus and extra-stimulus prompting on discrimination learning in autistic children. *Journal of Applied Behavior Analysis,* **8,** 91–112.

Shnidman, S. R. (1968). Extinction of Sidman avoidance behavior. *Journal of the Experimental Analysis of Behavior,* **11,** 153–156.

Sidman, M. (1966). Avoidance behavior. In W. K. Honig

(Ed.), *Operant behavior: Areas of research and application* (pp. 448–498). New York: Appleton.

Sidman, M., Herrnstein, R. J., & Conrad, D. G. (1957). Maintenance of avoidance behavior by unavoidable shocks. *Journal of Comparative and Physiological Psychology,* **50,** 553–557.

Smith, R., & Keller, F. (1970). Free-operant avoidance in the pigeon using a treadle response. *Journal of the Experimental Analysis of Behavior,* **13,** 211–214.

Solnick, J. V., Rincover, A., & Peterson, C. R. (1977). Some determinants of the reinforcing and punishing properties of timeout. *Journal of Applied Behavior Analysis,* **10,** 410–424.

Sprague, J. R., & Horner, R. H. (1984). The effects of single instance, multiple instance, and general case training on generalized vending machine use by moderately and severely handicapped students. *Journal of Applied Behavior Analysis,* **17,** 273–278.

Thompson, D. M. (1964). Escape from S^D associated with fixed-ratio reinforcement. *Journal of the Experimental Analysis of Behavior,* **7,** 1–8.

Weeks, M., & Gaylord-Ross, R. (1981). Task difficulty and aberrant behavior in severely handicapped students. *Journal of Applied Behavior Analysis,* **14,** 449–463.

Received August 25, 1987
Initial editorial decision August 30, 1987
Revision received September 14, 1987
Final acceptance September 15, 1987
Action Editor, Jon S. Bailey

JOURNAL OF APPLIED BEHAVIOR ANALYSIS 1994, 27, 739–760 NUMBER 4 (WINTER 1994)

SHAPING IN THE 21ST CENTURY: MOVING PERCENTILE SCHEDULES INTO APPLIED SETTINGS

GREGORY GALBICKA

WALTER REED ARMY INSTITUTE OF RESEARCH

The present paper provides a primer on percentile reinforcement schedules, which have been used for two decades to study response differentiation and shaping in the laboratory. Arranged in applied settings, percentile procedures could be used to specify response criteria, standardizing treatment across subjects, trainers, and times to provide a more consistent training environment while maintaining the sensitivity to the individual's repertoire that is the hallmark of shaping. Percentile schedules are also valuable tools in analyzing the variables of which responding is a function, both inside and outside the laboratory. Finally, by formalizing the rules of shaping, percentile schedules provide a useful heuristic of the processes involved in shaping behavior, even for those situations that may not easily permit their implementation. As such, they may help further sensitize trainers and researchers alike to variables of critical importance in behavior change.

DESCRIPTORS: shaping, response differentiation, percentile schedules, reinforcement density, operant conditioning

---

In behavior analysis, it is often desirable to take a behavioral repertoire and mold it into something different. In developmental disabilities, self-care, social, and vocational skills often need to be trained; in sports psychology, more skilled performance is a frequent goal; and education itself is nothing but the modification of behavioral repertoires. When dealing with operant behavior, this change is generally effected via a process termed *shaping,* a shorthand for differential reinforcement of successive approximations to a terminal response (see Skinner, 1953). Organisms and environments continuously shape the behavior of other organisms by providing consequences differentially following particular responses demonstrating certain criterion characteristics. A response (e.g., adding some wine to the spaghetti sauce) followed by a positive reinforcer (e.g., a better tasting sauce that wins the approval of your dinner companions) will increase in frequency over one provided no consequences, changing the response distribution to include relatively more responses similar to the type reinforced. Extinction, on the other hand, not only decreases response frequency but also temporarily increases the variability in responding, thereby increasing the probability that a response from the reinforced class will occur. Shaping occurs when reinforcement and extinction are used in combination with a systematically changing set of response criteria to reinforce responding differentially (i.e., to reinforce responses exhibiting some criterional attribute while not reinforcing noncriterional responses). Thus, the successful shaper must carefully ascertain characteristics of an individual's present response repertoire, explicitly define characteristics the final behavior will have at the end of training, and plot a course between reinforcement and extinction that will bring the right responses along at the right time, fostering the final behavioral sequence while never losing responding altogether.

For such a prevalent technique, shaping is subject to considerable variation between subjects, between trainers, and even with a single subject–trainer pair at different times. The "rules" of shaping are typically qualitative in nature only, with little empirical data on the effects of quantitative variation. As such, the rules constitute more an art form than a science, and the attitude is often that shaping is something you can only learn by doing—it is con-

I thank Timothy F. Elsmore, Carol Pilgrim, G. Jean Kant, and members of the Physiology and Behavior Branch for comments on an earlier version of this report. The views of the authors do not purport to reflect the position of the Department of the Army or the Department of Defense (para 4-3, AR 360-5).

Request reprints from the author, Department of Medical Neurosciences, WRAIR, Washington, D.C. 20307-5100.

tingency shaped, not rule governed. The contingencies that shape effective shaping are themselves found in the effectiveness of interactions between trainer and client, and will necessarily vary with a change in either or both of the individuals. Hence, developing a quantitative science of shaping may seem, if not beyond reach, at least difficult to the point of having little applied relevance.

The present paper argues against this view. It presents a primer on the workings of percentile reinforcement schedules, procedures that have been used in laboratory studies of response differentiation and shaping for over two decades. Percentile schedules disassemble the process of shaping into its constituent components, translate those components into simple, mathematical statements, and then use these equations, with parameters specified by the experimenter or trainer, to determine what presently constitutes a criterional response and should therefore be reinforced.

Percentile schedules, however, do more than automate shaping. In addition, they make explicit and objective the criteria that define responses as criterional or noncriterional throughout acquisition and maintenance, providing explicit prior control over reinforcement density as well as criterional response probability. Because of this, they provide almost complete independence from trainer- and subject-related variables. This allows all subjects to be trained in a specified manner despite changes in the trainer or the subject, or at different points in the differentiation.

Shaping's Golden Rules

As a prelude to presenting the mechanics of percentile schedules, it may be helpful to consider the verbal "rules" of shaping as they have been distilled from experience, and as they are generally presented to students and trainers when teaching the fundamentals of shaping. This presentation is explicitly rudimentary, in that it attempts to provide a common starting point for the discussion of how to transform the verbal rules into more explicit, quantitative ones. A review of these rules clarifies the operation of percentile schedules by providing a point of correspondence between what we already know verbally about shaping and what percentile schedules provide in the form of equations.

Shaping involves differential reinforcement of operant behavior. Because a behavior must occur prior to being reinforced, the first rule of shaping is generally some variant of "Start where the subject is"—set the initial reinforcement criterion at a value within the subject's current repertoire. That is, the current repertoire will be characterized by a distribution of responses varying across some range of values. Requiring values completely outside this distribution at the beginning of training transforms shaping into extinction, because all responses emitted will fail to meet the reinforcement criterion and thus will not produce reinforcement.

The next rule is generally of the form "Clearly define the terminal response." This ensures that we know when the differentiation has been successful and also often helps to define important behavioral dimensions and potential intermediate steps. Rule 1 provides a clear understanding of the subject's initial behavioral distribution. Rule 2 specifies characteristics of the ultimate distribution once shaping is complete. By comparing attributes of the initial and terminal responses for the ways in which they differ, an idea of the kinds of response characteristics that should be measured will emerge. For example, suppose I am interested in becoming a long-distance runner. Given my previous interest in running (zero), it seems to be a good idea to establish explicit reinforcement contingencies external to the joy of running per se to shape running. Setting aside questions of finding a suitable reinforcer and someone to deliver them appropriately, the main problem is to develop a program of differential reinforcement contingencies that will result in my ultimately emitting the terminal response of completing a marathon. I can probably dispense immediately with measuring sit-ups and concentrate on running, because the dimension of interest has something to do with running. I also need not concern myself with running speed, only stamina (i.e., I am not foolish enough to want to *win* my first marathon, only to finish it). Further, focusing on the terminal response helps to define the response unit as "running 26 miles and 385 yards," emphasizing that distance is the functional aspect of a running episode being differentiated, not other possible aspects or units (e.g., number of strides). Other units could be shaped without necessarily achieving the terminal response of completing a marathon (e.g., number of strides can increase with little change in distance if strides shorten). Emphasizing the difference in distance between the initial and terminal runs forces that dimension to be the functional unit of behavior. Finally, by noting the difference between the current level and the goal, a number of finite criteria can be defined that increase the required distance run in fixed arithmetic or exponential increments (i.e., adding or multiplying a constant to each level to generate a series of intermediate values). All this follows as a consequence of specifying in advance where responding is (Rule 1) and where it will end (Rule 2).

The third rule is "Use small steps." To use the running example again, this rule indicates that the smaller the increment in the reinforcement criterion (i.e., distance run) at each criterion change, the less likely it will be that responding will reach a point at which the variation from instance to instance will not include enough reinforceable values to maintain a fair degree of behavior. Compare two training regimens, one of which increases the reinforcement criterion in increments of half a mile and the other of which increases it by 5 miles at each criterion shift. With each change in the criterion, the natural variation in running stamina all but guarantees that the new criterion will be met by a run in the near future under the former regimen, whereas requiring a more substantial change (the latter regimen) decreases the probability that the criterion will be met following each change.

The last rule, not always taught explicitly, is "Reinforce movement, not position." Criteria established in terms of the *change* they generate will more likely result in behavior change than those anchored to some static quality or product. For the running example, this rule suggests that reinforcement contingent on a specified *increase in distance* from the previous run (i.e., *x* miles *farther*) will be more successful in increasing running than are criteria set to specific distances. Criteria that emphasize behavior change may increase the probability that behavior will change when the criterion is again shifted, increasing the likelihood that subsequent criteria will also be met.

Shaping's Foundations

These rules work because of the manner in which reinforcement and extinction, the component processes of differential reinforcement, work. In Skinner's (1938) earliest writings on operant behavior, he noted that reinforcement increased the rate of a class of responses, not the rate of a particular response. Members of this class vary with respect to the exact distribution of any of a number of measurable response characteristics (e.g., location, intensity, duration, topography, etc.), but are invariant with respect to their function—they all produce the consequence in question. If that consequence reinforces the operant, similar responses will more likely recur.

Extinction is often presented as the opposite of reinforcement, but it is very much more. No longer reinforcing an operant ultimately does decrease the rate of the response class. If this was the only effect of extinction, however, learning would be very constrained. Because reinforcement typically generates responses similar to those previously reinforced, some other mechanism must generate novel behaviors in response to a changing criterion. That mechanism is extinction. Removing reinforcement initially generates variability in behavior (see Galbicka, 1988, for a review of the experimental literature). As the patterns previously learned begin to extinguish, they recombine with other response units occasioned by the same environment; oftentimes previously trained units reemerge (e.g., Epstein, 1983) or other, previously ineffective, sources of control generate novel responses. This variability is important because it increases the probability that a response meeting the new criteria will be emitted. When we check into the hotel for a convention and are confronted by a bathroom fixture we have never seen before, we first behave in a fashion appropriate to the one at home. Turn the handle, or twist the dial—but if none of those work, we slowly start trying other responses. Where do they come from? They are

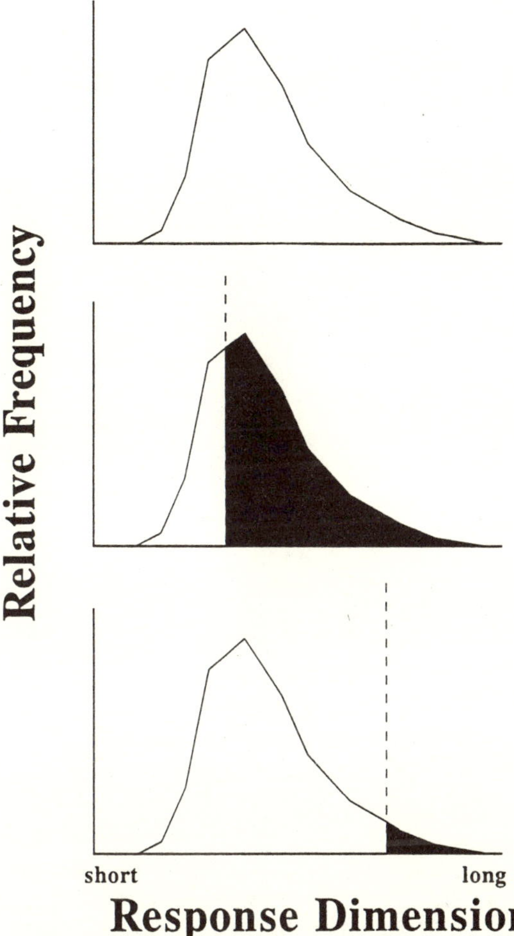

Figure 1. Illustration of how different criteria (the vertical lines in the bottom two panels) applied to a single response distribution establish different overall reinforcement densities and differences in the degree to which reinforcement is correlated with extreme values.

extinction-induced variations in responding that relate to our past histories with respect to buttons, levers, dials, and so forth. Push it, punch it, turn it, just keep varying—sooner or later something will work. Reinforcement, then, generates responses that are identical in function and similar in appearance to those preceding it. Extinction, for a while at least, is an aid to learning, because it generates a local high rate of variable behavior that can come under control of the changing contingencies that define a differentiation. However, if this transient increase in variability does not successfully induce a member of the new criterion class, extinction ultimately will eliminate responding.

The temporary nature of this effect is the conceptual basis of Rule 3. Step size determines the probability of a criterional response, which in turn determines when reinforcers are presented. Suppose that the top distribution in Figure 1 refers to the current distribution of a behavior, and suppose that we wish to generate longer values. (The actual response as well as the values represented along the response dimension are irrelevant for now; we simply want to increase the frequency of "longer" values and thereby shift the entire distribution to the right.) As a first step towards this end, we could decide to impose the criteria indicated by the vertical line in the middle panel and then reinforce only responses longer than that value (i.e., the shaded portion). Alternatively, the criterion could be set at the value indicated by the dashed line in the lower panel. The criterion in the middle panel is relatively lax, in that a majority of responses observed during the baseline would exceed the criterion. If behavior does not change (i.e., if the distribution of behavior remains constant), most responses will still produce reinforcement (the shaded portion of the distribution). The lower panel shows a much more stringent criterion; much longer values are required for reinforcement, and if the distribution remains constant only a small proportion of responses are reinforced. Which step size will lead to the most rapid shaping? There are advantages and disadvantages of either selection. The criterion in the middle panel protects against the complete elimination of behavior by all but guaranteeing a relatively high reinforcement density after the criterion is put into effect. However, that protection comes at the expense of differential reinforcement—the range of values reinforced is very large and includes many relatively short and medium values as well as long ones. As such, it is not likely that very long values will soon begin to predominate. The advantage of highly differential reinforcement resides with the stricter criterion depicted in the lower panel. Because only relatively large-valued responses produce reinforcement, similar large-valued ones will more likely recur once reinforced. The disadvantage is that responding could extinguish altogether before a criterional response occurs.

Deciding between these two alternatives is the crux of shaping; establishing criteria that provide sufficient but not excessive reinforcement is central to the success of the procedure. Less often appreciated is the importance of shifting criteria at the right time. Assume for the moment that we somehow solve the dilemma and set the criterion at the point denoted by the dashed vertical line in the top panel of Figure 2. If all baseline responses were reinforced, then imposing the criterion will result in an immediate substantial decrease in the density of reinforcement (i.e., only the initially small proportion of responses above the criterion will produce reinforcement). This partial extinction is important in producing the local effects noted above, ultimately generating greater values that will exceed the criterion and be reinforced. After exposure to the criterion for some period of time, responding might come to resemble the distribution depicted in the middle panel. After even further exposure, it might resemble that shown in the lower panel. The criterion (i.e., the vertical line) remains unchanged in each panel, but, because of the progressive change in the distribution, more responses meet criterion with extended exposure (approximately one half of the distribution meets criterion in the middle panel, whereas practically all responses exceed the criterion in the lower panel). When should the next level be imposed? That is, when should the criterion be shifted towards even greater values?

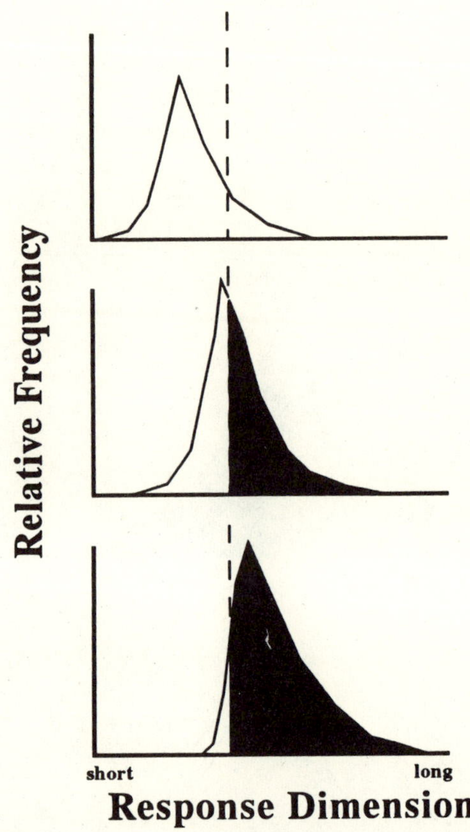

Figure 2. Three hypothetical distributions illustrating responding under baseline (top) and after exposure to a particular differential reinforcement criterion (i.e., responses longer than the value indicated by the vertical line produce reinforcement) for a moderate period (middle panel) or for a more extended period (lower panel).

The conservative approach might be to provide the client with substantial training and ensure a high probability of long responses before increasing the criterion. However, consider what happens to reinforcement frequency each time the criterion is changed. Because the criterion by definition includes only a portion of the current distribution, imposing a new criterion is always associated with a decrease in reinforcement density. Only by shifting the distribution of responses emitted to even longer values can the reinforcement density be returned to its former level. A plot of reinforcement density across time would reveal a pattern like a sawtooth; with each change in the criterion, reinforcement density drops abruptly, but as behavior gradually changes to include more and more criterional responses, reinforcement density gradually increases until the cycle repeats with the next criterion change. This cyclic change in reinforcement density is more pronounced following extended training. That is, reinforcement density can fall from a maximum probability of about .5 if the criterion is changed when the distribution of responding resembles that shown in the middle panel of Figure 2. Extended training provides a higher reinforcement probability (almost 1.0; see the lower panel of Figure 2) prior to the criterion shift, and hence a greater potential reduction in reinforcement frequency from that value once the criterion changes.

This discussion suggests a corollary to Rules 1 and 3, namely that criteria should be adjusted often to remain sensitive to current behavior and keep reinforcement differential and intermittent. Consistently intermittent reinforcement is essential to successful differentiation because it generates persistence in the face of extinction. The experimental and applied literatures are both replete with demonstrations that a prior history of intermittent reinforcement generates far more responding during extinction than does a history of continuous reinforcement. Hence, rather than wait for most responses to meet criterion and then drastically reducing reinforcement frequency by shifting criteria infrequently, it is better to change criteria frequently to maintain both a relatively *constant* reinforcement density and an *intermittent* one. Both characteristics decrease the likelihood of losing control over responding prior to the acquisition of the terminal response.

Percentile Schedules: Formalized Shaping

The preceding discussion suggests that any attempt to formalize these rules into a procedure should include the following characteristics: (a) It should set criteria relative to current behavior and change them rapidly as behavior changes. (b) It should establish criteria in such a way that some sufficiently large proportion of responses is reinforced, but that proportion cannot be so large as to dilute the differential nature of the contingency. (c) It should provide reinforcement consistently and intermittently, despite any changes in behavior upon which that reinforcement ultimately depends. (d) Finally, it should provide some terminal response definition.

The third characteristic is the most problematic in formalizing shaping; the procedure must provide a consistent, intermittent density of reinforcement. The traditional view of shaping holds that responding is a *dependent* variable subject to change and not an independent one that can be controlled prior to its occurrence. Yet, reinforcing only responses in the criterion zone (required by the second characteristic above) while keeping reinforcement density constant at some specified intermittent value seemingly requires prior knowledge of, and control over, the proportion of criterional responses. For example, if the desired probability of reinforcement is .25, and all criterional responses are reinforced, then the criterion must be set so that 25% of all responses exceed the criterion. This is contrary to the role normally attributed to responding in a shaping procedure, where changes in the probability of criterional responses define the effectiveness of a differentiation rather than being subject to experimental control.

How can responding be characterized so that the probability of criterional and noncriterional responses could be specified in advance? The percentile solution, developed and expanded by Platt (1973) and colleagues, is momentarily to abandon the exact physical characteristics of the response and treat it as an ordinal quantity. Ordinal quantities are values that carry only an associated rank, as opposed to the more typical means of quantifying observations by assigning a cardinal number and a standard unit. For example, height can be cardinally measured as 6 ft 8 in., or it can be ordinally measured by comparing two people and placing the taller one on the left.

We generally prefer to use the cardinal method because it provides more detailed information. However, there are times when measuring things ordinally has its advantages. Suppose the horizontal line in the top panel of Figure 3 represents a dimension along which a particular response of interest may vary. Using the running example again, the response is an episode of running and the dimension is the distance run. The probability that the next response (a run) will fall somewhere along this dimension is 1 (all runs have some distance). Suppose that the first run sampled falls at Point A, depicted in the second panel of the figure. How likely is it that the next run will be less than A, and how likely is it to exceed A? Intuition may suggest that the next run is equally likely to fall above or below the single observation at A, and that is in fact the case. Suppose the next run has the value represented by the point labeled B in the third line. With what probability will the run after that fall into each of the three intervals bounded by the two observations (i.e., below A, between A and B, and above B)? Now intuition suggests that values less than A or greater than B should be observed proportionately more often than ones between A and B, because the interval AB is smaller than the other two intervals. In fact, a subsequent response will again fall into each interval with equal probability, or one third of the time. Adding a third observation, at C in the fourth panel, generates four intervals by splitting the interval from A to B into the intervals AC and CB. Although these two intervals are clearly not the same size, the probability of the next observation falling into each interval bounded by C, and the other two intervals as well, is one fourth.

The generalization derived from the above example is that m previous observations create $m + 1$ intervals, one of which must contain the next observation. This fact alone is insufficient to derive percentile procedures. A single, simple constraint must be attached: Observations must be sampled randomly and independently from the population of values. This means that knowing the value of the current response cannot help to predict the occurrence of a later one. If these two conditions are met, the probability of a criterional response can actually be predicted and controlled (i.e., specified in advance). Even when this assumption is clearly violated, some steps discussed below can be taken to maintain control over reinforcement probability.

The counterintuitive notion that intervals of different sizes are equally likely to contain the next observation arises because the line represents a *cardinal* scale, but the question of which interval will contain the next observation relates to the *ordinal* properties of the observations. For the moment, ignore the fact that there are physical values attached to any of these observations, and treat them solely in terms of their ranks. In any distribution of values, there is one and only one value ranked 1st, 2nd, 3rd, and so forth. The question of interest is not "What is the expected value of the next observation (i.e., what distance will next be run)?" but rather is "Where will the next observation rank?" If the assumption of independence is met, it will be as likely to rank first or last or anywhere in between, depending on the number of prior observations. The probability that it will rank between 1 and $m + 1$ is 1 (i.e., it must fall somewhere on the line). This also equals the sum of the probabilities that it falls into each of the intervals defined by each observation. That is, the bottom line is segmented into four parts by the three prior observations A, B, and C. If the next observation fell below A, it would receive a rank of 1st (lowest); if it fell between A and C it would net a rank of 2nd lowest, between C and B a rank equal to 3rd lowest, and above B a rank of 4th lowest. Each of these rankings is equally likely by definition. Further, the sum of the probabilities of ranking 1st, 2nd, 3rd, or 4th must equal 1 (i.e., no other ranks exist). Hence, each rank will occur with a probability equal to the reciprocal of the number of intervals available to contain the next response. Thus, given any distribution of m prior observations, the probability the next observation will fall into each one of the $m + 1$ intervals bounded by

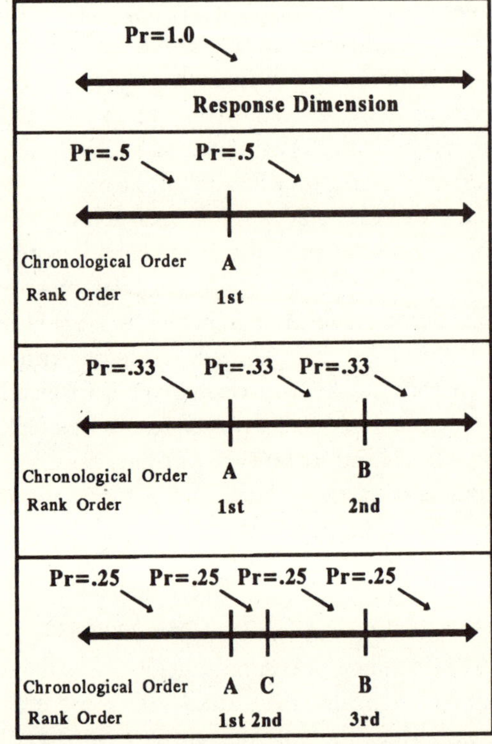

Figure 3. Illustration of the how successive observations (denoted A, B, etc.) divide a dimension into intervals having equal probabilities of containing the next response. See text for details.

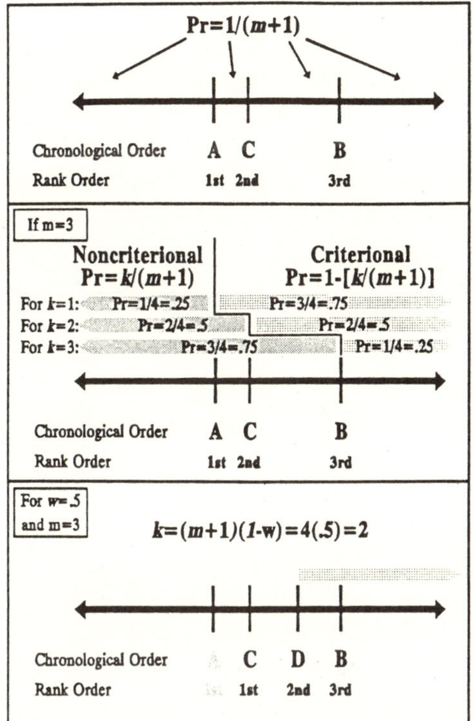

Figure 4. Upper panel: generalization of the effect illustrated in Figure 3. Middle panel: illustration of how criteria can be established in terms of exceeding particular ranks, and the resulting effects on the probability of observing a criterional response. Lower panel: inversion of the middle panel, demonstrating the percentile equation, which determines the rank (k) that must be exceeded in the current distribution of m responses to observe a criterional response with the specified probability w.

these observations is $1/(m + 1)$, as shown for $m = 1$, 2, or 3 in the bottom three panels of Figure 3, respectively, or for the generalized case in the top panel of Figure 4.

The relevance to shaping depends on understanding one implication of the above. If the probability that the next observation will be ranked in any one interval defined by m observations is $1/(m + 1)$, the probability that it will fall into any two of those intervals is twice that, or $2/(m + 1)$, the probability that it falls into any three would be $3/(m + 1)$, and so on. Hence, the probability that the next observation will fall into any one of k intervals defined by m observations is k times the probability of falling into each interval, or $k/(m + 1)$. This extension suggests the step taken in the second panel of Figure 4—establishing a criterion at the kth rank. That is, rather than setting the criterion at a particular fixed, physical value, the criterion can specify that the next observation, to meet criterion, must rank higher than the value currently ranked k. The middle panel of Figure 4 illustrates the effects of establishing criteria at different values of k. When $k = 1$, responses will be considered criterional if they exceed the response currently ranked 1st (A). The probability of not meeting criterion equals the probability of falling into the one interval below A, which is $k/(m + 1) = 1/(3 + 1) = .25$. The probability of a criterional response (denoted w) is the complement, or $w = 1 - [k/(m + 1)] = .75$. Setting the criterion (k) so that the 2nd rank (C) must be exceeded raises the probability of not meeting criterion to the sum of the two intervals below C, or $2/(m + 1) = 2/4 = .5$. The probability of meeting it is again the complement, or $w = 1 - .5 = .5$. If all observations must be exceeded (i.e., $k = 3$), then the probability of a criterional response will be $w = 1 - [k/(m + 1)] = 1 - 3/4 = .25$. Thus, as the criterion is made more stringent (i.e., as k is increased), the probability of observing a criterional response decreases accordingly, as intuition would suggest.

Notice that the rank and the chronological order of the observations are independent. In the sample shown in the figure, the chronological order has been indicated by the letters A, B, and C, whereas the ranks are specified 1st, 2nd, or 3rd. Hence, Observation C occurred after Observation B, but would be ranked before it, because relative values along the response dimension define ranks, not the temporal order of occurrence.

The equation above can be rearranged to specify the rank that must serve as the criterion (k) in order that criterional events occur with a specified probability w. If $w = 1 - [k/(m + 1)]$, then subtracting 1 from both sides and reversing signs yields $1 - w = k/(m + 1)$, and multiplying both sides of the equation by $m + 1$ yields $k = (m + 1)(1 - w)$. This expression, the basic percentile equation, provides the criterion rank order k that must be exceeded to witness a criterional response with a trainer-specified probability w, given a sample of m prior observations. For example, to observe a criterion response half the time (i.e., $w = .5$) given three prior observations (i.e., $m = 3$), the rank order to be exceeded would be set to $k = (3 + 1)(1 - .5) = 2$. A response would be considered criterional if it exceeded the value represented by the 2nd rank (C) in the middle panel of Figure 4.

By specifying a criterion relative to a distribution of behavior rather than relative to some fixed physical value, the probability of a criterional response on the next trial is determined not by the client, but by the trainer. But what of subsequent trials? That is, suppose the next response occurs at the value denoted by D in the bottom panel of Figure 4. How should the criterion for the next response be evaluated? One possibility would be to add each new observation to the list of previous values, increasing the value of m in the above equation. However, this strategy does not distinguish current observations from more remote ones. Although above I noted that chronological order was unimportant in ranking observations, we must at some point recognize that as observations become more and more remote, they may no longer adequately characterize the population of values likely to be observed now. An alternative that overcomes this problem is to update the distribution of observations by replacing the oldest observation in the distribution (A) with the newest (D). Doing so maintains the number of comparison observations (m) constant, such that with a constant w the required value of k is unaltered. For example, to observe a criterion response with a probability of .5, it is again necessary that the next response exceed two of the three observations. This would now mean that the criterion would be set at the value represented by D, because the comparison distribution now consists of Observations B, C, and D, with the latter ranked 2nd of the three (see the bottom of Figure 4). Note that the current response becomes part of the comparison memory only after all decisions concerning its criterional status have been made. The current response is never compared to itself, given that, by definition, it can never exceed itself.

Updating the comparison distribution with each response explicitly does what skilled shapers do. Although we start differentiating responding where the subject is, as the comparison distribution changes, the criterion changes with it to keep the overall probability of a criterion response relatively constant. Percentile schedules set the criterion at a fixed rank to control overall criterional response probability, and then let changes in the physical values of the responses comprising the comparison distribution determine where the physical criterion will fall. Note that only the physical value of the criterion changes; the rank order (i.e., k) of that physical value remains constant. Hence, behavior is differentiated only in the sense that physical values change; the criterion remains constant at a particular rank order, providing a constant probability of criterional responses. In this way, percentile schedules concurrently shape behavior (changing values along a physical dimension) while controlling the probability of criterional responses (defined ordinally).

At this point, it may be helpful to consider a hypothetical example of how a percentile schedule might be programmed in an applied setting. In posing any particular example, I ask the reader's indulgence in granting me a degree of latitude sufficient to illustrate the workings of the schedule without tackling the myriad additional problems that make applied work especially challenging, but that are not uniquely relevant to the use of percentile schedules (e.g., defining responses, observing and recording strategies, patient compliance, etc.). Failure to mention these important aspects of behavior analysis should not be taken as an admission of ignorance or disregard. They represent complex problems that must always be addressed, independent of the exact procedure used, and for this reason are not germane to a discussion of percentile schedules per se.

To illustrate how a percentile schedule might be used to help define response criteria in an applied setting, consider an example involving "task engagement." Assume I wish to increase the time a developmentally disabled client devotes to a vocational task while at the work station. I might

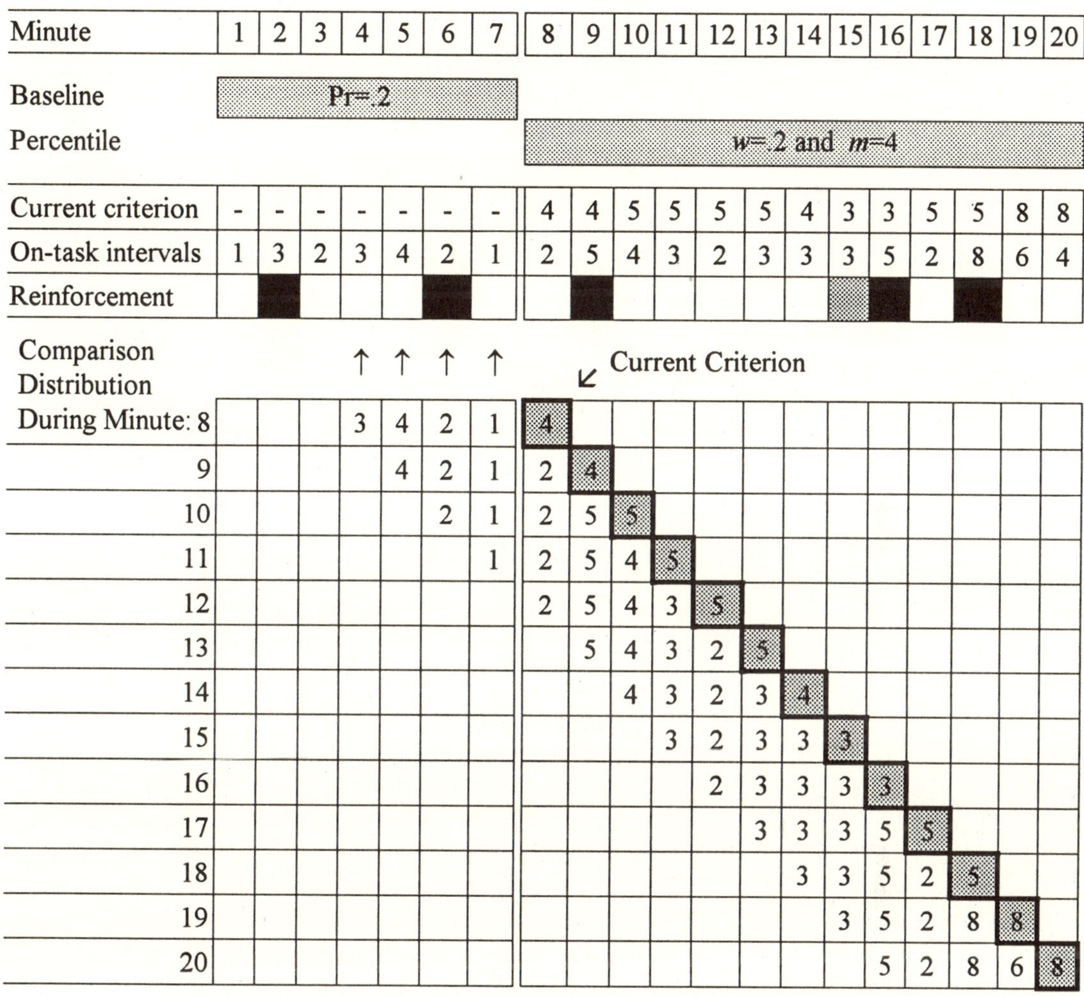

Minute	1	2	3	4	5	6	7	8	9	10	11	12	13	14	15	16	17	18	19	20
Baseline	Pr=.2																			
Percentile								w=.2 and m=4												
Current criterion	-	-	-	-	-	-	-	4	4	5	5	5	5	4	3	3	5	5	8	8
On-task intervals	1	3	2	3	4	2	1	2	5	4	3	2	3	3	3	5	2	8	6	4
Reinforcement		■				■			■						▒	■		■		

Comparison Distribution During Minute:	1	2	3	4	5	6	7	8	9	10	11	12	13	14	15	16	17	18	19	20
8				3	4	2	1	4												
9					4	2	1	2	4											
10						2	1	2	5	5										
11							1	2	5	4	5									
12								2	5	4	3	5								
13									5	4	3	2	5							
14										4	3	2	3	4						
15											3	2	3	3	3					
16												2	3	3	3	3				
17													3	3	3	5	5			
18														3	3	5	2	5		
19															3	5	2	8	8	
20																5	2	8	6	8

Figure 5. Hypothetical example illustrating the operation of percentile schedules.

decide to divide each minute into 5-s intervals and record whether the client remained "on task" during the entire interval. (Other recording techniques might be preferable; this example has been chosen to provide a moderate range of observable values.) This regimen generates a score each minute ranging between 0 (no intervals on task) and 12 (consistently on task). Presume further that a reinforcer has previously been identified for this client. The first decision required is how often to provide reinforcement. Assume that my previous history with this client suggests that, on average, a reinforcer delivered every 5 min should suffice.

Although technically not required, a baseline condition would probably be conducted first. This serves two functions: (a) It provides an indication of the current level of behavior, and (b) it provides a comparison for the effects of intermittent reinforcement alone. The baseline provides the same reinforcement frequency as the percentile procedure but does not make it contingent on the degree of task engagement. This can be accomplished by presenting a reinforcer at the end of each 1-min interval with a random probability of .2 (i.e., on the average, every 5th min).

Suppose this procedure generates the behavior shown for the first 7 min in Figure 5. The row labeled "current criterion" contains no value under baseline, because it is by definition undefined (i.e., reinforcement is not contingent on task engagement). Reinforcement (denoted by the darkened square in the row labeled "reinforcement") is delivered by the prearranged random probability after Minutes 2 and 6. The mean number of on-task intervals during baseline is approximately 2.3 per minute, and the mean number of intervals engaged prior to reinforcer delivery is 2.5. The correspondence between these values indicates that reinforcement is nondifferential (i.e., the degree of task engagement does not influence reinforcement delivery).

Instituting a percentile procedure involves first substituting .2 for w in the equation above, such that $k = (m + 1)(1 - .2) = .8(m + 1)$. Next, a value must be assigned to m (i.e., how many prior observations will be used as comparison values?). This is not a completely arbitrary decision, as will be discussed shortly. For purposes of the current example, however, setting m to 4 yields a value for $k = .8(5) = 4$. Hence, to observe criterional responses with a probability equal to .2 (w), the current score should be compared to the score from the most recent four intervals (m), and if it exceeds the fourth rank-ordered value (k) in the list of prior scores, it is criterional. If criterional and only criterional responses are reinforced, the probability of reinforcement and the probability of criterional responses will be equal (i.e., .2).

The most recent four scores during Minute 8 are those from Minutes 4 through 7. As such, they define the initial comparison distribution for the percentile condition. During that time, my client was on task for three, four, two, and one interval(s), respectively. Ordering these observations from lowest to highest associates one, two, three, and four intervals with Ranks 1 through 4, respectively. Hence, the current criterion score is 4 (the 4th-ranked value). The score during Minute 8 is actually 2. Because this does not meet the criterion, no reinforcement is delivered. For the next minute, the comparison distribution is changed by replacing the most remote score with the most recent one. The comparison distribution now comes from Minutes 5 through 8, or four, two, one, and two intervals on task, which when ordered becomes 1, 2, 2, and 4. Thus, the criterion score remains 4. During this minute, the number of intervals engaged in the task (five) exceeds the criterion and reinforcement is delivered. During the next 4 min, the 4th-ranked value in the comparison distribution is always five, the current score never exceeds the criterion, and no reinforcement is provided. In Minute 14, the 4th rank in the distribution falls back to 4, and in the next minute it falls back to 3, because the current distribution now contains three, two, three, and three intervals engaged. This illustrates how percentile schedules, while maintaining contingencies to differentiate "more" engagement (i.e., the largest value in the comparison distribution sets the criterion), also allow the definition of "more" to slide back towards a lower score if behavior consistently moves in that direction. During Minute 15, the number of engaged intervals equals the criterion, raising the question of how to treat ties. Classifying all ties as criterional overestimates the expected probability, whereas classifying them as noncriterional underestimates it. The problem is magnified as ties become more frequent. If a sequence of 20 observations all tied, treating all as criterional or noncriterional would result in a reinforcement probability of 1 or 0, respectively, across those observations, and not the .2 probability programmed. The simplest solution is to select ties with a random probability equal to w and call them criterional. Here, the observation is not classified as criterional and as a result does not generate a reinforcer (that this is a function of a tie decision is indicated by the gray shading in the figure). Continuing through Minute 20 results in two more criterional scores, a score of 5 in Minute 16, when the criterion was 3, and eight intervals engaged 2 min later when the criterion was 5. As a result, three criterional responses are observed during the 13 min of the percentile procedure, for an obtained probability of .23, within the sampling error of the probability programmed. The mean score during this time was 3.8, whereas the mean score preceding reinforcement was 6.0. This difference defines the differential nature of the reinforcement contingency.

The above equation defining the basic percentile schedule provides a fixed, specified probability of a criterional response at all times during the course of shaping. If reinforcers follow only criterional responses, as is most likely in applied settings, the probability of reinforcement will also equal w, and reinforcement will be maximally differential. That is, reinforcers will be delivered only after responses that are relatively closer to the terminal response along the dimension being differentiated (e.g., "more" time on task). Criteria are always set relative to current behavior, so not only does training start with the client, it stays and ends with the client. Criteria are updated with each response, remaining most responsive to changes in behavior. Finally, the probability of a criterional response can be specified to be whatever works best for that particular client–response–reinforcer combination, maximizing the differential nature of the contingency (i.e., reinforcing only instances of "more" engagement, as defined by the current distribution) but providing reinforcement consistently and intermittently in order to maximize persistence and decrease the probability of the frustration, aggression, emotional responses, and response elimination associated with extinction. Determining the optimal criterional response probability is not a problem unique to percentile schedules, but rather is an empirical question faced with each new procedure and/or response. Unlike other procedures, percentile schedules allow an empirical answer to this question by directly controlling reinforcement parameters independent of behavior.

Percentile schedules appear to meet all the requirements for a viable procedure to formalize shaping except the last—they do not specify a terminal response. The criterion is never specified as an absolute; rather, it is described only in relative fashion (i.e., exceed the kth rank). Yet, even here, percentile schedules help to focus our understanding of shaping. There is only one terminal response of all shaping—to do better on the next trial than on previous trials. This is what percentile schedules program, where "better" is defined as exceeding the kth rank and "previous trials" is given by the most recent m observations. Because criteria are evaluated relative to ongoing behavior, there is never a need to stop shaping. Once acquisition is complete and behavior stabilizes, the percentile schedule can still be used to select the same overall proportion of responses for reinforcement. And if an external event should disrupt responding, the criteria automatically adjust to take this into account and shape responding back to previous levels while ensuring a constant reinforcement density.

Implementing Percentile Schedules in Applied Settings

Percentile schedules make two requirements not found in traditional operant conditioning procedures. First, they require a continuously updated record of the most recent m responses that, second, can at least be partially ranked. Modern computers of all sizes are fast enough to program percentile contingencies with no discernible delays between responses and reinforcers. But computers are not a prerequisite to the implementation of percentile contingencies. Selecting particular pairs of criterional response probabilities and comparison distribution sizes makes it possible to program percentiles with a pencil and paper.

An updated list of the last m responses can easily be kept on a device similar to that shown in Figure 6. A roll of paper like that used in event recorders, adding machines, and cardiac monitors is threaded through a window with lines demarcating each comparison observation. Each new response is recorded in a slot marked "current response," located just below the window. Once recorded, the paper is advanced one observation out the top of the device, such that the latest observation (at the bottom) replaces the oldest one (at the top) in the list. An adjustable shutter slides vertically to vary the number of prior observations (m) visible, as noted by the numbers along the right side. In this way, the most recent m responses will always show in the window to provide the current comparison memory.

Ranking the observations is a more difficult, but surmountable, task. Even in the laboratory we do not spend the time required to rank all observations and then determine where the physical value of rank k is. Rather, the computer code compares the current value to every value in the comparison distribution. If the current value exceeds the comparison value, a counter is incremented. As soon as that counter exceeds k, the response is considered to be criterional. If, after all comparisons have been made, the counter still does not exceed k, the response is noncriterional. This procedure is faster than sorting, but is still of little help to someone lacking a computer.

An alternative approach is illustrated in the top panel of Figure 4. The expected probability that the next response will fall into each interval is given by $1/(m + 1)$. Although it is difficult to sort through a whole list of values, it is relatively easy to scan a list and determine the largest value. If we always set the criterion to the largest value in the comparison distribution, criterional responses will be observed with a probability equal to $1/(m + 1)$. To observe a particular probability w of a criterional response, therefore, m can be set to the value given by $m = (1/w) - 1$. For example, to obtain a criterion probability of .2, $m = (1/.2) - 1 = 5 - 1 = 4$ observations are needed. This was the approach used in the task-engagement example above. The suggestion of the sliding window in the above device now may be more understandable. By using this calculation to determine the memory size, and then adjusting the window to the appropriate number of values, it is necessary only to determine whether the current value is longer than any currently in view. If so, it is a criterional response, and will occur with the probability given by w.

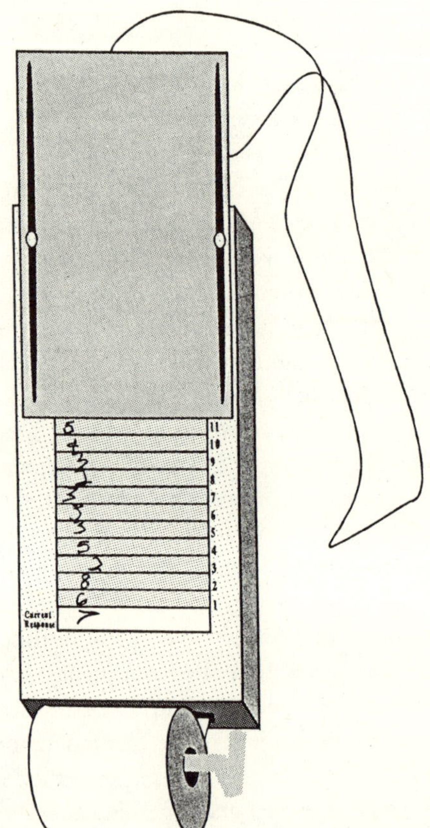

Figure 6. Illustration of a recording device designed to facilitate the programming of percentile contingencies in the absence of computers. Response values are recorded on the strip of paper in the slot at the bottom of the window. Prior to each new trial or response, the paper is advanced one response up, such that only the most recent responses are visible. The vertical shutter can be used to adjust the number of previous observations visible at any time (m). See text for further description of use.

Limitations on Applying Percentile Procedures

There are only two formal assumptions involved in deriving the percentile schedule equation: (a) Behavior must be measured in such a way that ordinal ranks can be assigned, and (b) those ranks must not be sequentially related (i.e., successive observations must represent random and independent samples from the population of response values). Dealing with the second limitation first, the degree to which responses are sequentially related increasingly affects the operation of percentile schedules as the comparison distribution size (m) decreases. Consider a situation that violates the assumption that observations occur randomly and independently. Suppose that each response has a .8 probability of being followed by an even longer value (i.e., four out of every five times, the next value is longer). Suppose further that the programmed probability of a criterional response (w) is .5. Using the shortcut suggested above, this probability is plugged into the equation for m to solve for the memory size that will yield the appropriate

Minute	1	2	3	4	5	6	7	8	9	10	11	12	13	14	15	16	17	18	19	20
Percentile	w=.5 and m=1																			
Current criterion	-	1	2	3	4	5	1	2	3	4	5	1	2	3	4	5	1	2	3	4
On-task Intervals	1	2	3	4	5	1	2	3	4	5	1	2	3	4	5	1	2	3	4	5
Reinforcement																				

Comparison Distribution ↑ ↙ Current Criterion

During Minute:	1	2	3	4	5	6	7	8	9	10	11	12	13	14	15	16	17	18	19	20
2	1	1																		
3		2	2																	
4			3	3																
5				4	4															
6					5	5														
7						1	1													
8							2	2												
9								3	3											
10									4	4										
11										5	5									
12											1	1								
13												2	2							
14													3	3						
15														4	4					
16															5	5				
17																1	1			
18																	2	2		
19																		3	3	
20																			4	4

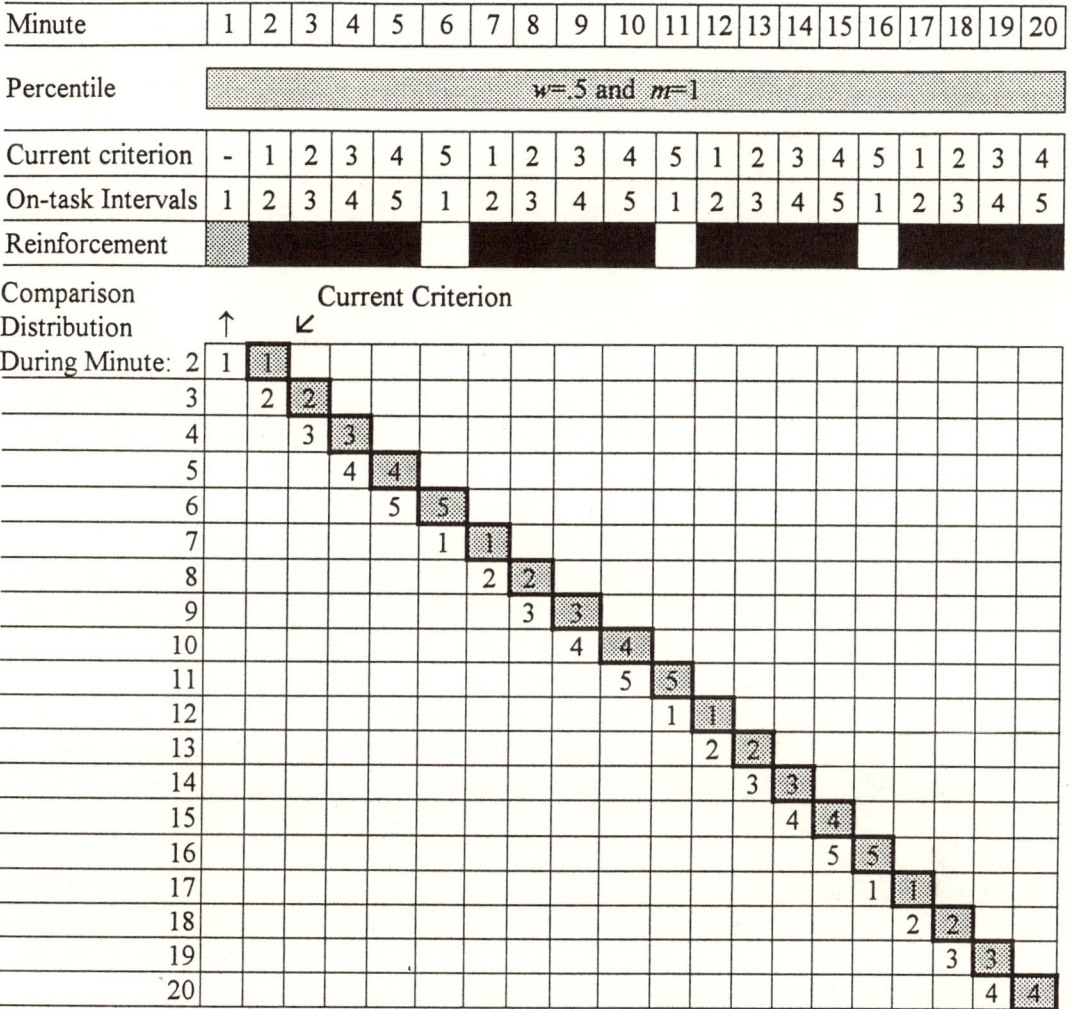

Figure 7. Effects of nonrandom observations on a percentile schedule with $w = .5$ and $m = 1$.

probability if the current value exceeds the longest comparison observation. This value is $m = (1/w) - 1 = 1/.5 - 1 = 1$. Hence, using only the most recent response as a comparison value, we begin programming the percentile schedule.

Figure 7 presents an illustrated case in which $m = 1$ and $w = .5$. To satisfy the requirement of a .8 probability of a longer subsequent observation, the score (using the task-engagement example again) repeats a cycle of values 1, 2, 3, 4, and 5. Because the first value observed has no comparison, suppose we arbitrarily call it criterional with a probability of .5. This is denoted in the reinforcement square by gray shading. During Minute 2, the criterion is one and two intervals are scored as engaged, so the response meets criterion and is reinforced, as indicated by the dark square in the row labeled "reinforcement." In the next minute the criterion is two and the score is 3, so again reinforcement is delivered. The criterion in the next 2 min is three and four, respectively, and the number of intervals engaged is four and five, so reinforcement is provided on each occasion. In Minute 6, when the cycle begins again, the criterion is five but only one on-task interval is scored, so reinforcement is not delivered. During Minutes 2 through 6, four of five scores are considered criterional and are reinforced. This represents a substantial departure from the .5 probability nominally programmed by the percentile schedule. Further, there is no indication

Minute	1	2	3	4	5	6	7	8	9	10	11	12	13	14	15	16	17	18	19	20
Percentile	w=.5 and m=3																			
Current criterion	-	-	-	2	3	4	4	2	2	3	4	4	2	2	3	4	4	2	2	3
On-task Intervals	1	2	3	4	5	1	2	3	4	5	1	2	3	4	5	1	2	3	4	5
Reinforcement																				

Comparison Distribution ↑ ↑ ↑ ↙ Current Criterion

Comparison Distribution During Minute:																				
4	1	2	3	2																
5		2	3	4	3															
6			3	4	5	4														
7				4	5	1	4													
8					5	1	2	2												
9						1	2	3	2											
10							2	3	4	3										
11								3	4	5	4									
12									4	5	1	4								
13										5	1	2	2							
14											1	2	3	2						
15												2	3	4	3					
16													3	4	5	4				
17														4	5	1	4			
18															5	1	2	2		
19																1	2	3	2	
20																	2	3	4	3

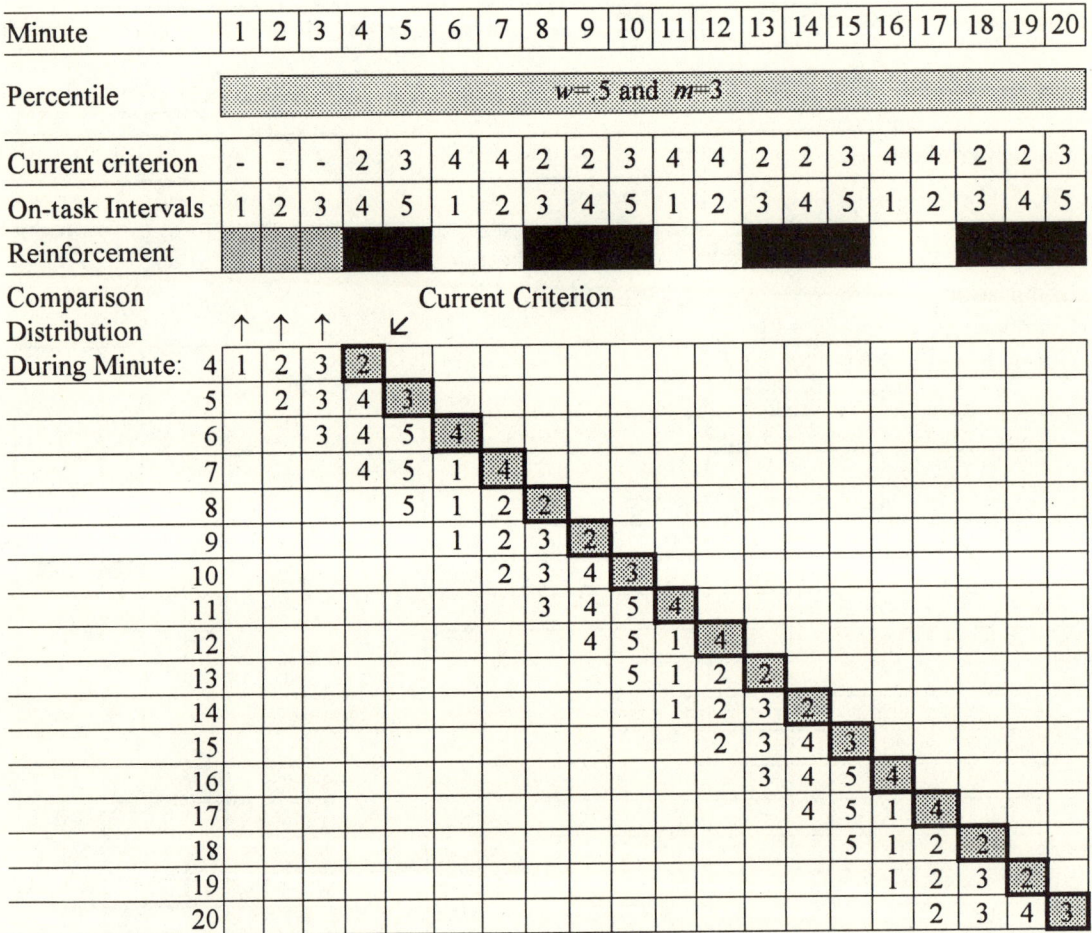

Figure 8. Effects of nonrandom observations on a percentile schedule with w = .5 and m = 3.

that this probability will decrease with further sampling—each time the cycle repeats, four out of every five scores are considered criterional. This is because percentile schedules are based on the presumption that the next observation is as likely to be ranked lowest as highest—that each interval has an equal likelihood of claiming the next response. Yet in this example, responses are falling on the high side of the last observation 80% of the time. This asymmetry defines a sequential dependency. Knowing the most recent response allows prediction of the next one's value (i.e., 80% of the time the next response will be longer than the current one, rather than the expected 50% that it will fall either above or below).

Although sequential dependencies diminish the ability of percentile schedules to control criterional response probability, their effects can be minimized by increasing the comparison distribution size. Consider the same scenario, but with a memory size of three. From the percentile equation above, $k = (m + 1)(1 - w) = (4)(.5) = 2$; the current response will be considered criterional if it exceeds two of the three most recent values. Figure 8 illustrates this case. Reinforcement is randomly assigned with a probability of .5 after each of the first 3 min, because of the lack of sufficient comparison observations. In Minute 4, the criterion is two and the score obtained is 4, so reinforcement is delivered. In the next minute the criterion is three and the client remains on task for five intervals. During both Minutes 6 and 7 the criterion is four, but only one or two intervals are judged as being on task; hence, no reinforcement occurs. In the next minute the criterion is two, and three on-task intervals are scored, resulting in reinforcement. The cycle then repeats. Adding two additional observations to the comparison distribution increases the correspondence between programmed and obtained criterional response probability over that generated with only a single comparison value. Where the obtained probability of criterional responses had been .8 when $m = 1$, here it is only .6, which is much closer to the nominally programmed value of .5. Task engagement continues to show strong sequential dependencies, in that scores during 4 out of every 5 min are longer than their immediate predecessor. However, these scores are no longer guaranteed to be criterional because it is not sufficient to exceed only the last score; rather, the current score must exceed two of the three most recent responses. Because more than a single score is used as a comparison, the effects of local variation, and hence sequential dependencies, are diminished.

Although not always eliminated, the effects of sequential dependencies are greatly limited by increasing the comparison distribution size. This property allows percentile schedules to be used even in situations in which the formal assumptions underlying their derivation are violated. However, their use in these circumstances would likely be limited to those involving computer control, because comparisons would have to be made to more than the largest comparison value.

The other "limitation," that responding be ordinally rankable, could actually aid application of percentile schedules. In the laboratory, percentiles have been used exclusively to shape responding along a single dimension—to shape longer or shorter interresponse times (e.g., Alleman & Platt, 1973; Arbuckle & Lattal, 1992; Galbicka & Platt, 1986; Kuch & Platt, 1976), response durations (e.g., Platt, 1984; Platt, Kuch, & Bitgood, 1973), run lengths (e.g., Galbicka, Fowler, & Ritch, 1991; Galbicka, Kautz, & Jagers, 1993; Galbicka, Kautz, & Ritch, 1992), different spatial response locations (e.g., Davis & Platt, 1983; Galbicka & Platt, 1989; Scott & Platt, 1985), or variable response sequences (Machado, 1989). Although there may be applications that could easily be envisioned as changing a single dimension of behavior (e.g., the running or task-engagement regimens described earlier), it is more likely that behaviors to be shaped in both research and applications with human subjects will involve behavioral change along multiple dimensions. Although to this point changes along single dimensions have been emphasized, the fact that percentile schedules do not deal directly with physical aspects of behavior, but only their ranking relative to prior behavior, implies that the number of response dimensions involved is immaterial. Any behavioral sequence, from any identified starting point to any terminal response, can be subjected to the workings of a percentile schedule to the extent that each response in the sequence can reasonably be ranked relative to every other response. This is not a burden unique to percentile schedules because all shaping requires some means of attributing directional change (and hence some crude ranking) to behavior across many dimensions. Percentile schedules actually remove some of the burden by identifying steps that require a modified response definition.

To illustrate, suppose we wish to train a developmentally disabled client to drink fluid though a straw. Prior observation of the behavior leads the shaper to suggest that the following five behaviors might be involved: (1) holds glass, (2) directs glass toward mouth, (3) holds straw with other hand, (4) directs straw into mouth, and (5) sucks on straw. These five behaviors can easily be ranked 1 to 5, with 1 being furthest from the terminal response and 5 being closest. A percentile schedule could be imposed by recording the response value (i.e., 1 through 5) on each trial. Whether our conception of the response matches the subject's will be evident in the relative frequency of each of the different rankings. For example, if after collecting substantial data an analysis revealed that Step 3 (i.e., holds straw with other hand) was never recorded, but instead the client progressed directly from Step 2 to Step 4 by holding the glass and manipulating it to position the straw in his or her mouth, then Step 3 probably represents an overly specific or functionally irrelevant response category for this subject. On the other hand, if some other step showed a disproportionately high frequency of occurrence, it is possible that further definition may be required to distinguish functionally the multiple response classes that are likely being included under this heading. The interesting thing about percentile schedules is that making such modifications on line does not alter their effectiveness. Refining response definitions by adding or removing particular classes at any time during shaping has no effect because the *number* of response classes is irrelevant to the operation of percentile schedules; the only requirement is that these response classes must easily be ordinally rankable with respect to all other responses. By allowing behavior to be the ultimate arbitrator in deciding where response classes "naturally fracture," the potential ramifications of misjudging these classes are limited. More classes can be added as they are identified with experience, and superfluous ones can either be dropped or retained.

The Shape of Things to Come?

I have argued that percentile schedules represent a formalization of the rules of shaping. I have tried to present the derivation of the equations that define percentile schedules in such a way as to make this relation clear. Finally, I have tried to demonstrate that little instrumentation is necessary to program these procedures. The applied utility of percentile schedules ultimately rests in the hands of the applied community. I only wish to note that percentile schedules do not impose any additional constraints and may actually remove some of those that limit application of other behavioral procedures. The ever-present problems of observation and measurement in applied settings will obviously affect application of percentile schedules as well. However, because percentile schedules use only ordinal response values, many problems associated with traditional procedures may be circumvented.

The research potential of these procedures is equally far-reaching. I have treated the probability of criterional responses and of reinforcement as equivalent throughout most of this paper, but this is true only if all criterional and only criterional responses are reinforced. This is generally the case in applied settings because these conditions most rapidly change behavior. However, a research setting holds one further level of complication. The more general scenario characterizing all attempts at response differentiation is represented in Figure 9. Training involves two independent decisions on the part of the experimenter: (a) whether the response is criterional or not, as indicated by whether it falls into rows indicated W and $\overline{\text{W}}$, and (b) subsequently whether or not to reinforce that response. This second decision is independent of the first and determines whether the response falls into the two columns labeled Z and $\overline{\text{Z}}$. Responses falling in Cell *a* are criterional responses that were followed by reinforcement, and those in Cell *b* are criterional responses that were not reinforced. Similarly, responses in Cell *c* are noncriterional reinforced responses, and those in Cell *d* are noncriterional nonreinforced responses. These cells describe all potential joint occurrences of responding and reinforcement. The percentile equation specifies segregation by criterional response probability only (i.e., it specifies whether the current response falls in the upper row or the lower one); it technically does not speak to whether that response, criterional or not, is reinforced.

Two additional parameters are needed to define the conditional probability of reinforcement for criterional and noncriterional responses, termed u and v, respectively (e.g., Galbicka & Platt, 1986, 1989; Scott & Platt, 1985). These specify the probability, given the prior occurrence of a criterional (or noncriterional) response, that a consequence also occurs. As the conditional probabilities of reinforcement increase, the relative proportion of responses on the left side of the appropriate row increases. Thus, increasing u increases the proportion of criterional responses falling into Cell *a* (i.e., without changing the total number of responses in the top row, increasing u shifts responses from Cell *b* to Cell *a*). Increasing v increases the proportion of noncriterional (bottom row) responses falling into Cell *c*. Each of these probabilities is independently specifiable, from each other and from the probability of a criterion response (w).

The matrix in Figure 9 represents an extensive

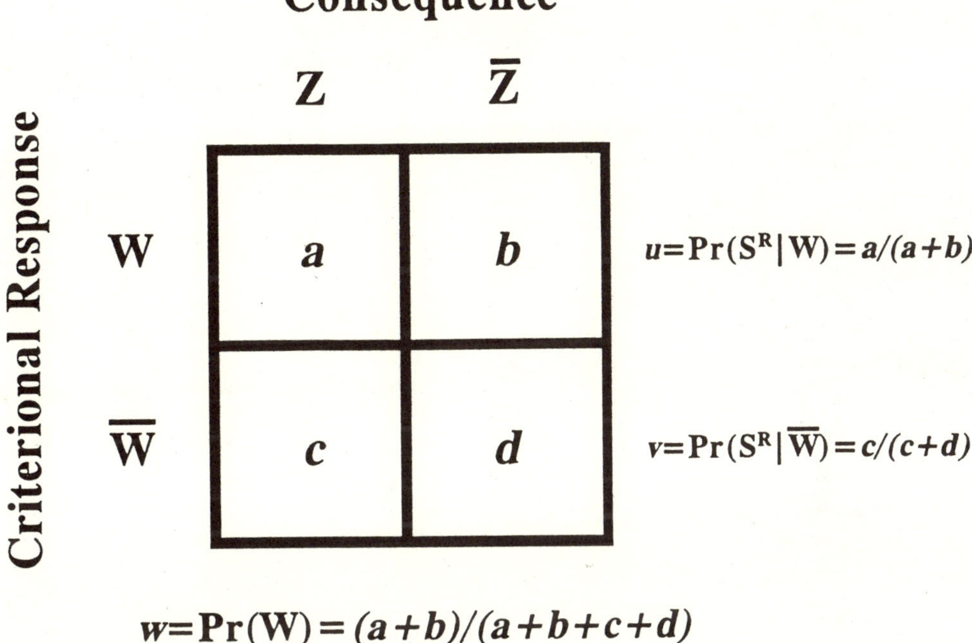

Figure 9. Two-by-two table showing the joint effects of specifying the probability of a criterional response (w) and the conditional probabilities of reinforcement for criterional (u) and noncriterional (v) responses. See text for details.

research program. By using the percentile equation to generate a specific probability w of a criterional response, the experimenter gains control over how responses get segregated into the two rows of the matrix. Specifying particular values of u and v allows researchers to specify further how events in each of those two rows are distributed with respect to reinforcement. Combining these two operations for the first time allows researchers to dictate *in advance* the expected frequencies of each of the four cells, and hence to control the relation between criterional responding and reinforcement. This prompts a number of previously unanswerable questions. For example, what happens to shaping as u increases? as v increases? as w increases? In general, we might expect that increasing u (reinforcement of criterional responses) would facilitate shaping, whereas increasing v (reinforcement of noncriterional responses) would impede it. But what of the effect of w? The answer here is less clear. The suggestion offered by Rule 3 is that optimal shaping will occur when the probability of a criterional response is not so small that contingent reinforcement is too infrequent, but not so large as to be virtually nondifferential. Hence, modifying w may produce an inverted U-shaped function with respect to response differentiation. How might this interact with the relations above? That is, given that increasing u enhances acquisition and increasing v retards it, how are these effects quantitatively modified by the proportion of responses considered criterional? In other words, what happens to the slope of these functions as w changes? Finally, is there a way we can put all these effects together into some general index that will correlate with the degree of shaping under a particular set of parameters? For example, if increasing u and decreasing v each enhance acquisition, then acquisition is differentially correlated with increasing values in Cells a and d relative to Cells b and c in Figure 9. Several measures of statistical contingency also increase with such changes and might be used as metrics of the relation between reinforcement and criterional responses that map to the changes in behavior produced (see Galbicka & Platt, 1986, 1989; Scott & Platt, 1985, for examples of such efforts involving nonhuman subjects).

Percentile schedules represent a radical departure

from traditional methods in the degree of experimental control they afford. They represent the next step in the experimental control of variables that are critical to the modification of behavior; thus, they could potentially revolutionize our methods as well as our models of behavior change. Specific examples of applications presented here can serve only to focus attention unduly on particular behaviors or populations in the applied realm, at the expense of other, potentially more relevant behaviors or populations. But with that caveat in mind, percentile schedules might, for example, provide for replacement of vague qualitative labels for "cognitive abilities" with more extensive, quantitative formulations of learning and learning disabilities. A diagnostic video game could be devised that repeatedly requires the client to select from a ring of keys the one that unlocks the door barring entrance into the next passage. The keys differ along a number of dimensions, but the one of interest is key length. Selecting a particular key is considered criterional if it is closer to some target length, chosen by the experimenter, than 80% of the previous *m* key selections. This is an example of a targeted percentile in which responding is shaped to a particular value instead of in a particular direction. Targeted percentile schedules are programmed as two separate percentile schedules. One operates when the current response is short of the target (i.e., when the key selected is less than the target value) and differentially reinforces values *longer* than the 80th percentile of all recent previous selections that were also short of the target. The other operates when the current response is above the target and differentially reinforces responses *shorter* than 80% of all responses above the target. These two, simultaneously operating percentile schedules control the overall probability of criterional responses above and below the target value, but reinforce only the closest 20% of all responses, causing the distribution to peak in the area of the target (see Galbicka et al., 1993, for an example of targeted percentile shaping).

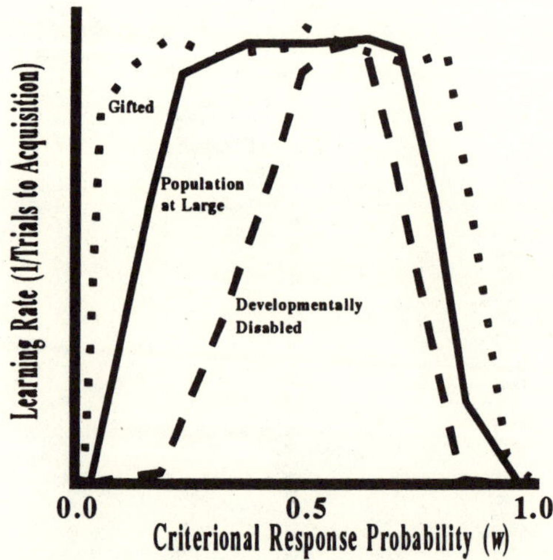

Figure 10. Hypothetical results showing the rate of learning (1/number of trials to acquisition) as a function of manipulating the probability of a criterional response (w) under a percentile schedule. The solid curve shows potential results from the population at large, the dashed curve illustrates potential results from a population of developmentally disabled clients, and the dotted line depicts results from a population of gifted individuals.

The rate of acquisition of this task under a variety of different values of w, u, and v could be used to increase the precision of behavioral "diagnoses" of different populations. For example, certain developmental disabilities might be associated with generally slower acquisition than other populations, under all values of w, when u and v are constant at 1.0 and 0. Or the relation may be more complex, such as that shown in Figure 10. The possibility exists that the degree of learning demonstrated under different w values by different populations could be used to categorize a range of behavioral populations. The solid curve suggests that, in general, the population at large may shape well under a relatively wide range of w values, with learning falling off at the extremes when w is relatively low, and hence reinforcement density is low, or when it is relatively high; consequently, criterional responses can be diverse at any particular time. Developmentally disabled clients might demonstrate a more restricted range of effective parameters (shown by the dashed line) indicating a greater sensitivity to sparse reinforcement (i.e., low w values) and a greater difficulty coming under control of the dimension of responding being shaped at higher w values. On the other hand, gifted populations might be defined by the production of functions similar to those shown by the dotted line, with learning spread across a range of w values broader than that for the population at large.

These hypothetical examples are presented only to illustrate the potential quantitative analysis of learning that could be derived using percentile procedures. Percentile schedules provide a better platform from which to develop such "diagnostics," because they greatly reduce differences arising from the different behavioral repertoires each subject brings to the task. Traditional operant procedures specify behaviors with particular physical characteristics (responses with particularly defined topographies, forces, durations, etc.). The variable nature of operant behavior, in conjunction with the variable histories of reinforcement each subject brings to the training environment, all but guarantee that different subjects will respond with different frequencies of responses meeting the fixed physical criteria. As a result, each subject's behavior will interact uniquely with the contingencies of reinforcement. Percentile schedules remove the obstacle posed by individual behavioral differences by defining all response criteria relative to each subject's own repertoire. All subjects share exactly the same probability of emitting a response closer than half the responses emitted recently, independent of how close those recent responses were. This holds not only across subjects but also across time within the same subject.

In addition to providing a potential diagnostic tool, percentiles could be used to assess the effects of variables such as alcohol consumption and drug administration, sleep deprivation, or aging. They may also serve to categorize the degree of behavioral disruption induced by reinforcement for noncriterional responses (i.e., "distraction") or by lack of reinforcement for criterional responses (i.e., "short attention span"). Not only could these be used as diagnostic tools, they also could serve as therapeutic aids by providing a consistent probability of reinforcement while encouraging continued development towards some targeted value.

Finally, percentile schedules may help revive interest in programmed texts (e.g., Holland & Skinner, 1961) and associated personalized systems of instruction. Programmed texts enjoyed a certain popularity for a period of time in the 1960s and 1970s, but have recently declined in popularity. Students often complained that these texts were boring. Because step size could not be individualized in a printed text, it was often set at a size almost everyone could achieve, but one most students found extremely small.

The advent of computer-based instruction (e.g., McDade & Goggans, 1993) provides a means of presenting varying stimulus frame sequences, and percentile schedules could provide a mechanism for coupling that presentation to performance. Numerous multiple choice questions could be developed to illustrate each key concept in successive organizational units of the program. Units of the program would be ranked relative to other units to establish a progression through the course. The lowest ranked unit would present questions on fundamental concepts, shaping a transition from introductory or lay concepts to those required by the subject matter. Subsequent units would be ranked relative to the degree to which correct responses in this unit depend on the acquisition of textual behavior in some prior unit. Each correct response would generate a rank appropriate to the level of that question, and achieving some number of consecutive correct questions at one level would be prerequisite to moving on to the next. Incorrect answers would generate ranks associated with the prior unit in which material relevant to that answer was first presented. For example, in a text on behavior analysis, a question dealing with an example of negative reinforcement might include an answer that makes reference to a decrease in response rate. Selecting this option would constitute a lower ranked response because the more fundamental verbal operant that reinforcement is always associated with an increase in the frequency of an operant is not evident in the repertoire. By ranking this response with the level in which the general concept of reinforcement was introduced, this error would not only force return to a prior level, it would specifically return to the level associated with the misunderstanding leading to the inappropriate selection of that answer. Specific deficits could then be corrected while adjusting the criterion automatically to generate a relatively constant frequency of reinforcement.

The application of percentile procedures may prove to be difficult in the extreme, or the definition and transduction of multidimensional response classes too cumbersome to be practically useful. Even so, the present discussion still serves the heuristic function of explicitly dissecting the fundamental components of shaping. Increasing familiarity with percentile schedules leads to the recognition that a variety of contingencies in daily life are arranged, not necessarily with any conscious awareness, in much the same way as percentile schedules. As social organisms selected to select behavior, we often act as organic ranking machines. We maintain continuously updated lists of our companions' recent accomplishments and provide reinforcement with respect to some relatively constant upper proportion of this list. We judge our children not with respect to some fixed standard, but relative to their development (i.e., the degree of change in the behavioral distribution). Once responses become commonplace, they no longer merit reinforcement. Rather, the relatively rarer exceptional response that may yet be quite far from target but still qualifies as criterional because it is *closer* wins our attention. As people mature, behavior changes but the criterion remains qualitatively the same—do better, be in the upper tail of the distribution, be exceptional, relative to what you have been recently. When those around us get sick or old, we relax the criterion by increasing the probability of a criterional response or more often by noting that the current distribution of responding has regressed.

Understanding percentile schedules may increase our understanding of the complex social and nonsocial dynamics that shape behavior. They allow us to treat clients similarly, and to define response criteria to which each subject can relate in a similar manner. They allow unprecedented control over experimentally relevant stimuli in operant conditioning and differentiation procedures and provide a seemingly endless horizon against which to cast our sights for extensions and applications. However, like all operant behavior, the benefits accruing from the use of percentile procedures can be delivered only after a response has been emitted. I trust that, relative to your recent history, you may find their operation reinforcing.

REFERENCES

Alleman, H. D., & Platt, J. R. (1973). Differential reinforcement of interresponse times with controlled probability of reinforcement per response. *Learning and Motivation, 4,* 40–73.

Arbuckle, J. L., & Lattal, K. A. (1992). Molecular contingencies in schedules of intermittent punishment. *Journal of the Experimental Analysis of Behavior, 58,* 361–375.

Davis, E. R., & Platt, J. R. (1983). Contiguity and contingency in the acquisition and maintenance of an operant. *Learning and Motivation, 14,* 487–512.

Epstein, R. (1983). Resurgence of previously reinforced behavior during extinction. *Behaviour Analysis Letters, 3,* 391–397.

Galbicka, G. (1988). Differentiating *The Behavior of Organisms. Journal of the Experimental Analysis of Behavior, 50,* 343–354.

Galbicka, G., Fowler, K., & Ritch, Z. (1991). Control over response number by a targeted percentile schedule: Reinforcement loss and the acute effects of *d*-amphetamine. *Journal of the Experimental Analysis of Behavior, 56,* 205–215.

Galbicka, G., Kautz, M., & Jagers, T. (1993). Response acquisition under targeted percentile schedules: A continuing quandary for molar models of operant behavior. *Journal of the Experimental Analysis of Behavior, 60,* 171–184.

Galbicka, G., Kautz, M., & Ritch, Z. (1992). Reinforcement loss and behavioral tolerance to *d*-amphetamine: Using percentile schedules to control reinforcement density. *Behavioural Pharmacology, 3,* 535–544.

Galbicka, G., & Platt, J. R. (1986). Parametric manipulation of interresponse-time contingency independent of reinforcement rate. *Journal of Experimental Psychology: Animal Behavior Processes, 12,* 371–380.

Galbicka, G., & Platt, J. R. (1989). Response-reinforcer contingency and spatially defined operants: Testing an invariance property of phi. *Journal of the Experimental Analysis of Behavior, 51,* 145–162.

Holland, J. G., & Skinner, B. F. (1961). *The analysis of behavior.* New York: McGraw-Hill.

Kuch, D. O., & Platt, J. R. (1976). Reinforcement rate and interresponse time differentiation. *Journal of the Experimental Analysis of Behavior, 26,* 471–486.

Machado, A. (1989). Operant conditioning of behavioral variability using a percentile reinforcement schedule. *Journal of the Experimental Analysis of Behavior, 52,* 155–166.

McDade, C. E., & Goggans, A. (1993). Computer-based precision learning: Achieving fluency with college students. *Education and Treatment of Children, 16,* 290–305.

Platt, J. R. (1973). Percentile reinforcement: Paradigms for experimental analysis of response shaping. In G. H. Bower (Ed.), *The psychology of learning and motivation: Vol. 7. Advances in theory and research* (pp. 271–296). New York: Academic Press.

Platt, J. R. (1984). Motivational and response factors in temporal differentiation. In J. Gibbon & L. Allan (Eds.), *Timing and time perception* (pp. 200–210). New York: New York Academy of Sciences.

Platt, J. R., Kuch, D. O., & Bitgood, S. C. (1973). Rats' lever-press durations as psychophysical judgments of time. *Journal of the Experimental Analysis of Behavior, 19,* 239–250.

Scott, G. K., & Platt, J. R. (1985). Model of response-reinforcer contingency. *Journal of Experimental Psychology: Animal Behavior Processes, 11,* 152–171.

Skinner, B. F. (1938). *The behavior of organisms.* New York: Appleton-Century-Crofts.

Skinner, B. F. (1953). *Science and human behavior.* New York: MacMillan.

Received July 6, 1993
Initial editorial decision October 3, 1993
Revisions received January 4, 1994; March 2, 1994; April 22, 1994
Final acceptance May 10, 1994
Action Editor, F. Charles Mace

JOURNAL OF APPLIED BEHAVIOR ANALYSIS 1995, **28**, 237–241 NUMBER 2 (SUMMER 1995)

THE APPLIED IMPORTANCE OF RESEARCH ON THE MATCHING LAW

W. David Pierce and W. Frank Epling

UNIVERSITY OF ALBERTA

In this essay, we evaluate the applied implications of two articles related to the matching law and published in the *Journal of the Experimental Analysis of Behavior,* May 1994. Building on Mace's (1994) criteria for increasing the applied relevance of basic research, we evaluate the applied implications of basic research studies. Research by Elsmore and McBride (1994) and Savastano and Fantino (1994) involve an extension of the behavioral model of choice. Elsmore and McBride used rats as subjects, but arranged a multioperant environment that resembles some of the complex contingencies of human behavior. Savastino and Fantino used human subjects and extended the matching law to ratio and interval contingencies. These experiments contribute to a growing body of knowledge on the matching law and its relevance for human behavior.

DESCRIPTORS: choice, matching law, application, concurrent schedules

The May issue of the *Journal of the Experimental Analysis of Behavior* (*JEAB*) included a position paper by Mace (1994) pointing to the need for basic research with greater ecological and external validity in relation to human behavior. Building on previous commentary and analysis, Mace recommended a three-step approach to increase the applied relevance of basic research. The approach includes the development of animal models of important human problems, extending the modeled relations to humans (i.e., experimental analysis of human behavior), and testing the generality of these relations with human problems in everyday settings. At the present time, it is difficult to find examples of Mace's three-step approach in the behavior analysis literature (but see Pierce & Epling, 1994, for activity anorexia, and McDowell, 1988, for the matching law).

Mace's suggestions may, however, be slightly modified and then used to evaluate the practical importance of basic research. In this essay, we evaluate the applied implications of two articles published in *JEAB,* May 1994, that focused on the matching law. These criteria offer a strategy for judging the practical importance of basic research. It seems plausible that the practical importance of any basic experiment increases as it fulfills more and more of these criteria.

Matching and Response Allocation

Mace (1994) points to the applied relevance of research on response allocation and the matching law (Baum, 1974; Herrnstein, 1961). Two articles in the May issue of *JEAB* have implications for the analysis and modification of human choice behavior in everyday life. Elsmore and McBride (1994) and Savastano and Fantino (1994) both raise questions about the generality of the matching law. In order to assess the applied importance of these articles, it is necessary to place them in the context of other related experiments.

There is strong evidence that pigeons (and other nonhuman organisms) presented with concurrent variable-interval schedules (VI VI) of reinforcement allocate behavior in accord with the distribution of reinforcement. In this situation, relative rate of response matches (equals) relative rate of reinforcement (Davison & McCarthy, 1988; de Villiers, 1977). In terms of application, concurrent schedules of reinforcement model complex environments in which humans are faced with choosing between

Address correspondence to W. David Pierce, Center for Experimental Sociology, University of Alberta, Edmonton, Alberta T6G 2H4, Canada.

alternative courses of action. For example, Conger and Killeen (1974) assessed human performance in a group discussion situation. Talking was reinforced by two listeners on a concurrent VI VI schedule with brief positive words or phrases. Relative time spent talking to a listener matched relative rate of social reinforcement from that listener. This study and others (e.g., McDowell, 1988) showed that the basic research on concurrent schedules and matching with nonhumans generalizes to everyday human behavior.

In terms of generality, the matching law is a good description of human behavior on concurrent VI VI schedules in laboratory settings (Pierce & Epling, 1983). McDowell (1988) showed that matching theory generalizes to natural human environments and has implications for the modification of human behavior (see also Myerson & Hale, 1984). At the present time, a few applied studies have found that the matching law predicts socially important behavior on concurrent variable-ratio (VR VR) schedules (Mace, McCurdy, & Quigley, 1990) and on concurrent VI VI schedules (Conger & Killeen, 1974; Martens & Houk, 1989; Martens, Lochner, & Kelly, 1992), although recent studies suggest limitations. For example, students in a special education program approximated matching on concurrent VI VI schedules, but only when timers signaled the intervals on the operating schedules or were used in preliminary training (Neef, Mace, & Shade, 1993; Neef, Mace, Shea, & Shade, 1992). Also, departures from matching may be expected in applied settings when quality of, and delayed access to, reinforcement are varied (Neef et al., 1993).

Although basic research on concurrent schedules and matching is relevant to human problems, researchers continue to question the generalizability of basic animal experiments (Mace, 1994; Pierce & Epling, 1991). For example, Neef et al. (1992) and Mace (1994) note that most of the laboratory research with pigeons and humans uses symmetrical-choice procedures. Mace indicates that "the vast majority of research on concurrent schedules has involved symmetrical choices . . . between alternatives that differ only in the rate of reinforcement each alternative produces, while the reinforcers, response manipulanda, and delays to reinforcement are held constant" (1994, p. 533). In everyday settings, humans are faced with alternatives that arrange qualitatively different reinforcers and that require different forms of response after varying delays. For example, a person may choose among television channels offering qualitatively different programs that schedule entertaining events on a random-interval basis. Experiments that introduce procedures that depart from standard concurrent VI VI food reinforcement schedules test the matching law in novel situations. To the extent that variation in the experimental procedures models the complexity of human environments, the relevance of matching as a description of human behavior is potentially increased.

Matching in a Multioperant Environment

Elsmore and McBride (1994) reported two experiments on the matching law. These experiments introduce new procedures that begin to model the complexity of the natural environment. Rats were required to search for food in an eight-arm radial maze. The maze consisted of a central platform with eight straight arms that extend from the central area. Standard pellet feeders were connected to the end of each arm, and the rats could choose to enter any of the arms to obtain food. Food was available on eight independent concurrent interval schedules—fixed-interval schedules in Experiment 1 and random-interval schedules in Experiment 2. Rates of reinforcement for the eight schedules varied between 65 and 5 reinforcers per hour. Some conditions were run with a changeover delay (COD) contingency in effect, and others omitted this contingency.

In terms of procedure, Elsmore and McBride (1994) present a situation that begins to contact some of the features found in human environments. People typically are able to choose among many alternative sources of reinforcement that require a change in location in order to obtain reinforcement. In a library, a person chooses among many different books located in different places of the building. In terms of application, this research implies that the architecture and physical arrangement of objects and materials will be important determinants of behavior allocation. Also, human situations seldom set up contingencies like the COD; it is therefore interesting to find out what happens when this requirement is eliminated in a complex environment. Finally, the researchers measured searching for (number of entries into an arm of the maze) and procurement of (both time spent in an arm and responses for food) reinforcement. This is similar to finding the locations of clothing stores in a shopping mall. Each store is a different arm of the maze, and the shopper is free to go from one store to another. Once in the store, reinforcing items are found on an intermittent schedule. Elsmore and McBride's experiment raises the question of whether these two performances (finding the location vs. shopping for items) are regulated by the same principles.

In general, results from these experiments support the extension of the matching law to situations involving many alternative sources of reinforcement. In the absence of the COD, responses for reinforcement (procurement) were well described by Baum's (1974) generalized matching equation. This indicates that relative rate of reinforcement determines behavior in complex settings, even when procedures are eliminated that favor matching.

This overall conclusion is tempered by the finding that searching for reinforcement was not as well described by the matching law as was behavior that directly produced reinforcement (procurement). Apparently, behavior that is closer to reinforcement is more sensitive to relative rate of reinforcement than responses that are more distant. As a speculation, a shopper's entries into clothing stores may not be as sensitive to relative rates of reinforcement as when the shopper is selecting items on different racks within the store.

Human Matching on a Concurrent Interval-Ratio Schedule

Savastano and Fantino (1994) also investigated the matching law, but in a situation that favored optimal performance. Economic theories of choice (maximization) often assume that humans are rational actors who consciously attempt to minimize cost and maximize benefits. Behavioral theories (including the matching law) emphasize the role of contingencies of reinforcement as a determinant of choice behavior. Savastano and Fantino asked whether human performance is best described by matching or by maximizing.

Matching occurs when a person distributes behavior in accord with the relative rates of reinforcement. Maximizing requires that an individual shift between alternative sources of reinforcement in a way that yields the greatest overall payoff (optimal performance). In order to evaluate the experimental question, Savastano and Fantino arranged a situation in which matching relative rates of reinforcement would lower the overall payoff. That is, a person who distributed behavior in terms of the matching law would necessarily behave in a suboptimal manner.

Undergraduate students faced a panel and pressed a button to change from one schedule of monetary reinforcement to another. The schedules of reinforcement were similar to VI and VR schedules, but controlled for rate of response. When given a choice between different values of VI and VR schedules of reinforcement, a person would obtain the maximum payoff by spending most of the time on the ratio alternative and occasionally sampling the interval schedule. This maximizing strategy takes advantage of the fact that the interval schedule continues to advance even when the person is spending time on the ratio alternative. In contrast, the ratio schedule pays off only when the person spends time on that schedule. A person who distributed behavior in accord with the relative rates of reinforcement (matching) would spend more time on the interval alternative than is predicted by maximization.

Results showed that, in general, human performance is not well described by a maximization account of behavior. Human subjects spent more time on the interval schedule than was required to obtain the maximum overall payoff. The performance of humans was more in accord with the matching law. Baum's (1974) generalized matching equation was applied to the time spent on the ratio and interval alternatives. The grouped data for all subjects approximated matching of time spent to the relative rates of reinforcement. These results, however, should be interpreted with caution because the data showed considerable between-subject variability.

Savastano and Fantino's (1994) experiment supports the applied significance of the matching law as presented by Myerson and Hale (1984). Myerson and Hale considered the implications of schedule control of target behavior when the maintenance schedule for that behavior is unknown. One part of their analysis concerned a situation in which the target behavior is maintained by unidentified ratio contingencies (i.e., the ratio requirement is unknown). In an applied setting, the target behavior often occurs at high frequency and is considered to be a problem. In order to reduce the probability of a response, Myerson and Hale suggest programming reinforcement for alternative behavior on an interval schedule. According to the matching law, the target behavior must be reduced because of the shift in relative rate of reinforcement; this analysis is supported by Savastano and Fantino's experiment. Of course, a ratio schedule for alternative behavior could also be used, but it may not work, because the richer alternative, on a concurrent ratio schedule, captures all the behavior in the situation (exclusive preference). The intervention will be a total success if the ratio schedule for alternative behavior is richer than the maintenance schedule, but the intervention will be a complete failure if it is not.

Evaluation of Applied Importance

The applied importance of the experiments by Elsmore and McBride (1994) and Savastano and Fantino (1994) may be assessed according to the criteria suggested in the first section this paper. Both experiments involve an extension of the behavioral model of choice. Elsmore and McBride used rats, but arranged a multioperant environment that more closely models the contingencies of human behavior. Savastino and Fantino used human subjects and extended the matching law to ratio and interval contingencies. Again, this experiment begins to model the operating schedules in everyday settings.

Both experiments contribute to a growing body of knowledge on the matching law and its relevance for human behavior (Davison & McCarthy, 1988; de Villiers, 1977; Pierce & Epling, 1983). In this regard, any one experiment has less applied importance than the body of research to which it contributes. As more and more basic research confirms and extends the generality of the matching law, applied behavior analysts can have greater confidence that behavioral theories of choice strongly determine human behavior. This observation implies that behavior analysts weigh the applied relevance of any experiment within the context of other research.

The two experiments highlighted in this paper have increased importance for applied behavior analysis because a few studies have used the matching law for modification of problem behavior. For example, McDowell (1981, 1982) reported the use of matching theory to treat a mildly retarded man's aggression, noncompliance, and temper tantrums. Token reinforcement was arranged for unrelated alternative behavior, which resulted in a substantial reduction in oppositional behavior. Since these early reports, other studies have used the matching law to analyze and modify on-task and disruptive behavior of a retarded girl (Martens & Houk,

1989) and students' academic behavior (Martens et al., 1992; Neef et al., 1992). These studies show that the matching law is useful in applied settings and suggest that basic research extensions of the law may contribute to more powerful applications.

REFERENCES

Baum, W. M. (1974). On two types of deviation from the matching law: Bias and undermatching. *Journal of the Experimental Analysis of Behavior, 22,* 231–242.

Conger, R., & Killeen, P. (1974). Use of concurrent operants in small group research. *Pacific Sociological Review, 17,* 399–416.

Davison, M., & McCarthy, D. (1988). *The matching law: A research review.* Hillsdale, NJ: Erlbaum.

de Villiers, P. A. (1977). Choice in concurrent schedules and a quantitative formulation of the law of effect. In W. K. Honig & J. E. R. Staddon (Eds.), *Handbook of operant behavior* (pp. 233–287). Englewood Cliffs, NJ: Prentice-Hall.

Elsmore, T. F., & McBride, S. A. (1994). An eight-alternative concurrent schedule: Foraging in a radial maze. *Journal of the Experimental Analysis of Behavior, 61,* 331–348.

Herrnstein, R. J. (1961). Relative and absolute strength of response as a function of frequency of reinforcement. *Journal of the Experimental Analysis of Behavior, 4,* 267–272.

Mace, F. C. (1994). Basic research needed for stimulating the development of behavioral technologies. *Journal of the Experimental Analysis of Behavior, 61,* 529–550.

Mace, F. C., McCurdy, B., & Quigley, E. (1990). A collateral effect of reward predicted by matching theory. *Journal of Applied Behavior Analysis, 23,* 197–205.

Martens, B. K., & Houk, J. L. (1989). The application of Herrnstein's law of effect to disruptive and on-task behavior of a retarded adolescent girl. *Journal of the Experimental Analysis of Behavior, 51,* 17–27.

Martens, B. K., Lochner, D. G., & Kelly, S. Q. (1992). The effects of variable-interval reinforcement on academic engagement: A demonstration of matching theory. *Journal of Applied Behavior Analysis, 25,* 143–151.

McDowell, J. J. (1981). On the validity and utility of Herrnstein's hyperbola in applied behavior analysis. In C. M. Bradshaw, E. Szabadi, & C. F. Lowe (Eds.), *Quantification of steady-state operant behaviour* (pp. 311–324). Amsterdam: Elsevier/North-Holland.

McDowell, J. J. (1982). The importance of Herrnstein's mathematical statement of the law of effect for behavior therapy. *American Psychologist, 37,* 771–779.

McDowell, J. J. (1988). Matching theory in natural human environments. *The Behavior Analyst, 11,* 95–108.

Myerson, J., & Hale, S. (1984). Practical implications of the matching law. *Journal of Applied Behavior Analysis, 17,* 367–380.

Neef, N. A., Mace, F. C., & Shade, D. (1993). Impulsivity in students with serious emotional disturbances: The interactive effects of reinforcer rate, delay, and quality. *Journal of Applied Behavior Analysis, 26,* 37–52.

Neef, N. A., Mace, F. C., Shea, M. C., & Shade, D. (1992). Effects of reinforcer rate and reinforcer quality on allocation of academic behavior. *Journal of Applied Behavior Analysis, 25,* 657–664.

Pierce, W. D., & Epling, W. F. (1983). Choice, matching and human behavior: A review of the literature. *The Behavior Analyst, 6,* 57–76.

Pierce, W. D., & Epling, W. F. (1991). Can operant research with animals rescue the science of human behavior. *The Behavior Analyst, 14,* 129–132.

Pierce, W. D., & Epling, W. F. (1994). Activity anorexia: An interplay between basic and applied behavior analysis. *The Behavior Analyst, 17,* 7–24.

Savastano, H. I., & Fantino, E. (1994). Human choice in concurrent ratio-interval schedules of reinforcement. *Journal of the Experimental Analysis of Behavior, 61,* 453–463.

Received October 28, 1994
Initial editorial decision November 14, 1994
Revisions received November 24, 1994; March 21, 1995; March 23, 1995
Final acceptance March 23, 1995
Action Editor, F. Charles Mace

JOURNAL OF APPLIED BEHAVIOR ANALYSIS 1995, **28,** 583–590 NUMBER 4 (WINTER 1995)

MAKING LIFE EASIER WITH EFFORT: BASIC FINDINGS AND APPLIED RESEARCH ON RESPONSE EFFORT

PATRICK C. FRIMAN

FATHER FLANAGAN'S BOYS' HOME

CREIGHTON UNIVERSITY SCHOOL OF MEDICINE

AND

ALAN POLING

WESTERN MICHIGAN UNIVERSITY

Early basic research showed that increases in required response effort (or force) produced effects that resembled those produced by punishment. A recent study by Alling and Poling determined some subtle differences between the two behavior-change strategies, but also confirmed that increasing required effort is an effective response-reduction procedure with enduring effects. In this paper we summarize basic research on response effort and explore the role of effort in diverse applied areas including deceleration of aberrant behavior, attention deficit hyperactivity disorder, oral habits, health care appointment keeping, littering, indexes of functional disability, and problem solving. We conclude that renewed interest in response effort as an independent variable is justified because of its potent effects and because the political constraints imposed on punishment- and reinforcement-based procedures have yet to be imposed on procedures that entail manipulations of response effort.

DESCRIPTORS: response effort, response force, response requirement, punishment

"Life is hard and then you die." A primary goal of applied behavior analysis is to render the first half of this bumper sticker slogan untrue, or at least less true (Baer, Wolf, & Risley, 1968). A logical candidate for research focused on this goal is response effort, yet the relevant literature is surprisingly limited and involves mostly basic research. In this paper we present a brief review of basic research on response effort as an independent variable, highlighting a recent *JEAB* paper by Alling and Poling (1995). We then review applied research in some diverse areas, specify applied implications for others, and advocate increased research exploring the applied benefits of effort-based interventions. We conclude with a brief discussion of types of effort and suggestions for future research.

The authors gratefully acknowledge Cheryl Pollock for manuscript preparation and Susan Thibadeau for conceptual inspiration.

Address correspondence and requests for reprints to Patrick C. Friman, Youthcare Building, Boys Town, Nebraska 68010.

BASIC RESEARCH ON RESPONSE EFFORT

Approximately 50 years ago, several studies investigated the effects in nonhumans of increasing the physical effort required to emit a designated operant response (e.g., Mowrer & Jones, 1943; Skinner, 1938, 1950; Solomon, 1948). Basic studies of response effort (or force) as an independent variable appeared occasionally in the intervening years. In brief, those studies demonstrated that (a) response rates decrease as force requirements increase (Adair & Wright, 1976; Chung, 1965; Mowrer & Jones, 1943; Skinner, 1950), (b) increasing the force requirement in the second component of a two-component chain schedule decreases response rates in the first component (Miller, 1970), (c) extinction is more rapid as force requirements increase (Capehart, Viney, & Hulicka, 1958; Mowrer & Jones, 1943), (d) subjects will escape from situations that require particularly effortful responding (Miller, 1968a, 1968b), and (e) subjects prefer lower effort responding to higher effort responding (Perone & Baron, 1980). These findings have led some investigators to suggest that increasing the effort required to obtain reinforcement is similar to adding an aversive consequence (i.e., arranging punishment) for the response (e.g., Blough, 1966; Chung, 1965; Miller, 1968b, 1970; Solomon, 1948).

The extent to which increasing minimum force requirements produces effects similar to those of punishment was addressed in a recent study that altered lever-press force requirements for rats responding under multiple fixed-ratio (FR) schedules of food delivery (Alling & Poling, 1995). The first experiment arranged an FR 15 in both components, maintained a constant force requirement (0.25 N, or 25 g) in one component, and varied force requirements in the other component (i.e., 0.25, 0.50, 1.00, or 2.00 N). The second experiment also arranged multiple FR 15 schedules and maintained the 0.25-N force requirement in one component. The force requirement in the other component was sometimes increased from 0.25 to 2.00 N for five consecutive responses at the beginning, middle, and end of each ratio. The third experiment reduced the number of required responses in each component from 15 to 5 to 1 while varying force requirements in one component (from 0.25 to 2.00 N) and keeping them constant (0.25 N) in the other. In all experiments, as required response force increased, response rates characteristically decreased, whereas interresponse times and postreinforcement pause times typically increased. These findings agree with those of prior investigations and suggest that the effects of increasing response effort resemble those of punishment in some respects.

In three noteworthy respects, however, the effects of increasing response force differed from those of punishment. One difference is that response suppression produced by mild punishment (e.g., low-intensity shock) often diminishes over time (Azrin, 1956, 1959, 1960; Hake & Azrin, 1963; Rachlin, 1966), but no such recovery of responding occurred when response force was increased. Also, adding punishment to one component of a multiple schedule frequently leads to rate increases in the other unpunished component (punishment contrast) (e.g., Azrin, 1956; Lattal & Griffin, 1972). Comparable effects were not observed with increases in response force. Finally, the suppressive effects of punishment under FR schedules are strongly influenced by the point in the schedule at which the punishment is arranged; earlier introduction produces greater suppression (Dardano, 1970; Dardano & Sauerbrunn, 1964). In contrast, Alling and Poling found that the rate reductions associated with increased force requirements differed little, regardless of whether the increase was arranged at the beginning, middle, or end of the FR.

INCREASED RESPONSE EFFORT AS AN APPLIED INTERVENTION

The basic research reviewed above indicates that increasing required effort is an effective response-reduction procedure with enduring effects. Manipulating response effort may, in some cases, be a viable alternative to other behavior-change techniques used in applied settings, and may have certain advantages relative to those alternatives, especially punishment. A few studies, selectively reviewed below, have demonstrated that manipulating response effort can be useful for modifying troublesome human behaviors. Moreover, there appears to be growing recognition of the potential importance of response effort as a determinant of human behaviors. For example, recent articles on response efficiency (Horner & Day, 1991; Mace, Neef, Shade, & Mauro, in press; Neef, Shade, & Miller, 1994) have emphasized that behavior is always imbedded in an economic matrix that involves its costs and benefits, which are based on response effort as well as reinforcer rate, quality, and delay. Manipulating any of these variables, including effort, may be effective in producing desired rates and temporal patterns of responding.

Effort-Based Alternatives to Punishment

One of the most divisive issues in psychology in recent years is the controversy over punishment procedures that employ response-contingent aversive stimulation (Mulick, 1990). Although there are radical constituents of the nonaversive position who appear to oppose any application that has a reductive effect on human behavior (cf. Mudford, 1995), most people seem to accept effective response-deceleration interventions that

> (a) do not involve the delivery of physical pain, (b) do not produce effects that require medical attention, and (c) are subjectively judged to be within typical norms of how people in our society should treat each other. (Horner, 1990, pp. 166–167)

Aberrant behavior in individuals with delays. Although critics of punishment are probably opposed to its use with any population, the focus of their criticisms has mostly been on individuals with intellectual delays who exhibit severe behavior problems (Mulick, 1990). A small number of studies have shown that increasing required response effort can be an effective alternative to punishment in programs for these persons. For example, Van Houten (1993) demonstrated that placing 0.68-kg weights on the wrists of an adolescent boy with developmental delays and autistic features essentially eliminated self-injurious face slapping. Van Houten noted that "the instant reduction in self-injury, following the application of the weights, suggested that they may have reduced face slaps primarily through the increased response effort required" (p. 198). Interestingly, he made no mention of basic studies that have documented the rapid and enduring rate reductions associated with increasing required response effort.

In other studies, behavior has been reduced not by increasing the effort associated with the target response but by making an effortful response contingent upon the occurrence of the target response (cf. Miller, 1970). For example, changing from a simple to a more difficult task contingent upon tantrums reduced them to near-zero levels in an institutionalized 9-year-old girl (Sailor, Guess, Rutherford, & Baer, 1968). As a second example, mild exercise contingent upon aggressive behavior reduced it to near-zero levels in 2 boys with severe disabilities (Luce, Delquadri, & Hall, 1980). As a third example, brief contingent arm movements were more successful than reinforcement procedures in reducing aggression and self-biting in an 11-year-old boy with severe disabilities (Luiselli, 1984).

These studies demonstrate the potent influence that response-contingent increases in response effort can have on inappropriate behavior in individuals with disabilities. Moreover, the procedures used appear to fit Horner's (1990) criteria for acceptable response-reduction interventions. None of the procedures caused pain or required medical attention, nor did they contrast with societal norms. For instance, coaches often require disobedient players to run laps, and drill instructors make misbehaving recruits do push-ups. Future research, however, should investigate ways to decrease the seeming arbitrariness of the effortful responses that are required contingent on undesired behavior (cf. Sailor et al., 1968). Also, it is important to recognize that extremely effortful responding may, in a functional sense, be aversive, insofar as organisms will respond to escape or avoid situations in which effortful responding is required (Miller, 1968a, 1968b).

Hyperactivity in children. Response-reduction procedures based on increased effort could also reduce misbehavior in children with normal intellectual development. For example, one of the most reported, discussed, and treated problems in children is attention deficit hyperactivity disorder (ADHD) (Friman & Christophersen, 1983). A hallmark of the condition is high-rate switching between activities, which leads teachers to respond with interventions that range from verbal disapproval to classroom expulsion and medical referral. An early (and unfortunately isolated) demonstration of the applied benefits of increased response effort showed that requiring preschool children to complete a "switching task" prior to moving from one activity area to another substantially reduced the number of switches the children made (Jacobsen, Bushell, & Risley, 1969). Whether similar benefits could be obtained for children with ADHD by manipulating response effort is a question worthy of investigation.

Oral habits in children. Another example involves an even more common problem, prolonged pacifier and thumb sucking in children. One method for treatment involves application of an aversive taste solution to the thumb or pacifier (Friman, Barone, & Christophersen, 1986). Although highly effective, aversive taste treatment is also controversial (Friman, Barone, & Christophersen, 1987; MacKenzie, 1987). An early uncontrolled case study described how gradually shortening pacifiers reduced their use, presumably because of the increased effort necessary for children to hold the pacifiers in their mouths (McReynolds, 1972). Further study of similar interventions is warranted.

Other Effort-Based Interventions

Not all interventions involving changes in effort can be categorized as an alternative to punishment. For example, decreasing the effort associated with an appropriate response may increase its frequency and thereby decrease the rate of an inappropriate alternative. There are other possibilities. In the section that follows, we provide examples of effort-based interventions whose effects resemble processes other than punishment.

Broken health care appointments. Broken health care appointments are a notorious problem in medicine. Between 10% and 30% of health care appointments are broken, and patients obviously cannot benefit from health care that is not received (Barron, 1980). Among the reasons identified for broken appointments are several that involve the effort of keeping them. A small series of studies showed that by mailing a reminder and a parking pass to make remembering the appointment and parking at a pediatric clinic easier, broken appointments were decreased approximately 20% (Friman, Finney, Rapoff, & Christophersen, 1985; Friman, Glasscock, Finney, & Christophersen, 1987; Ross, Friman, & Christophersen, 1993). Although these results were obtained in one site with idiosyncratic conditions, the effort of responding is a generic variable, universally present in human behavior. Keeping a health care appointment involves a chain of responses, each requiring effort and each presenting opportunities for reduction thereof. For example, clinics are sometimes difficult to find; therefore, clearer directions would reduce the effort needed to attend them. Occupying children during long waiting times at pediatric clinics is often difficult. Reducing waiting times or supplying child play areas could reduce the effort needed to manage the children and thereby increase appointment keeping.

Littering. Littering is an enormous, costly, and unsightly problem in the United States. A common strategy for attempting to reduce littering is to threaten to fine those who are caught. Reducing the effort necessary for litter control may be an effective alternative intervention. As an example of this strategy, a recent series of studies showed that reducing response effort by increasing proximity to ashtrays at four separate entrances to a university medical school substantially increased the extent of their use (Friman, 1995). Similarly, a recent study showed that increasing container proximity increased recycling of office paper from 28% to above 85% (Brothers, Krantz, & McClannahan, 1994).

The research on manipulating response effort to improve litter control is sparse but promising and, consistent with the theme of this paper, shows that manipulating response effort has applied implications for a widespread, important problem.

Indexes of functional disability for the aged or ill. The importance of measuring physical disability increases with each life-extending medical breakthrough. As persons live longer, the number of disabling conditions (e.g., chronic diseases, age-related infirmities) increases (Feinstein, Josephy, & Wells, 1986). Measurements of functional disability are critical to compensation determinations, program planning, residential options, critical care estimates, and changes in status for these persons. There are currently more than 1,000 "clinimetric" indexes available for use in assessing various dimensions of disability (Feinstein, 1982; Feinstein et al., 1986; Feinstein, Wells, Joyce, & Josephy, 1985). A common omission in these indexes is a measure of patient effort or collaboration with others. Yet both variables can dramatically influence the degree of an individual's disability. For example, the helpful presence of another person during mundane tasks of daily life (e.g., dressing) substantially reduces the effort required for task completion and thereby reduces related disability. As a second example, some people with angina may bring on an attack merely by walking to the store. If they rode a motorized cart, however, their trip probably would be symptom free. As a third example, a person with infirm legs would require much less effort to pursue the tasks of daily living in a ranch-style house than in a multistory dwelling. Other related examples are numerous (see White, Paine-Andrews, Mathews, & Fawcett, 1995), yet related measures are typically unaccounted for in disability assessments. Feinstein et al. (1986) conjecture that the reason effort and collaboration are so frequently omitted from disability assessments is a prevailing belief that they are complex psychological phenomena that are difficult to measure, interpret, and incorporate into strictly physical ratings. Yet patient effort and collaboration are readily observable and therefore measurable variables. They are also much easier to interpret than variables such as motivation that are often included in disability indexes (Feinstein et al., 1986). Incorporating measures of response effort into indexes of functional disability is a task that is well suited to the commitments and methods of applied behavior analysis (Baer et al., 1968). The task is important and timely because of the dramatic increase in physical disability in the industrialized world.

There are several other examples of effective procedures in the applied literature that could be construed in terms of response-effort manipulations (e.g., Blank, 1985; Chapman, Smith, & Layden, 1971; Epstein, Miller, & Webster, 1976; Schulman, 1986; Stuart & Davis, 1976; Van Houten, Nau, & Merrigan, 1981). Whether it is profitable to conceptualize them in this fashion is, however, an important issue that merits consideration.

CONCLUDING COMMENTS

Laboratory studies of response force or effort characteristically involve a manipulandum (e.g., lever or key) with clearly specified physical requirements for successful operation. With such arrangements, four distinct types of force can be measured and manipulated: (a) isotonic forces, (b) isometric forces, (c) forces proportional to displacement, and (d) forces proportional to velocity (for discussion of these forces, see Fowler, 1987; Notterdam & Minz, 1965). In the study by Alling and Poling (1995), as in most other studies with nonhumans, response effort was defined and measured in simple physical units (i.e., Newtons). Such precise quantification of effort is difficult in applied settings, although some exceptions are evident. For example, Schulman (1986) reduced speeding by making it harder to operate the gas pedal of an automobile at speeds above the legal limit, and the exact operating characteristics of the pedal at various speeds were specified precisely. Less precision was possible in a study by Van Houten (1993), who compared rates of self-injury under conditions in which wrist weights were and were not used with a self-injurious adolescent. Nonetheless, the increased effort in this study is clearly physically similar to the increased effort in the study by Alling and Poling (1995), and the comparability of the independent variables in the two investigations is evident.

In other studies that we have considered, however, effort was manipulated in a rather different way. For example, in a study that required youths to solve math problems, Neef et al. (1994) indicated that

> Response effort refers to the relative ease with which problems from the respective sets of problems could be completed, as determined by pretest performance on samples of problems ranging from 1-digit addition and subtraction to 4-digit multiplication and division with regrouping operations. Problems completed at the highest rate with the highest accuracy and confirmed by the classroom teacher as "review" or "fluency" targets were designated as low effort. Problems that were completed at a lower rate with at least 50% accuracy and that were confirmed by the teacher as "acquisition" or "mastery" targets were designated as high effort. (p. 578)

Here, rate and accuracy of responding, rather than response force, defined effort. In other studies, effort was indexed in terms of duration or probability of responding; a response that did not occur when a person was not required to perform it was assumed to be effortful. For instance, Luiselli (1984) demonstrated that requiring a boy to engage in arm movements contingent on aggressive or self-injurious behavior reduced those responses. The arm movements almost never occurred in the absence of the intervention, hence, requiring their emission increased response effort. Although this analysis is reasonable, an equally tenable explanation can be made in terms of the Premack principle (Premack, 1959): Forcing an organism to engage in a lower probability behavior contingent on a higher probability behavior punishes (i.e., reduces the rate of) the higher probability behavior.

Whether anything is gained by construing the study by Luiselli (1984) in terms of a response-effort manipulation is open to debate. Moreover, the extent to which results from laboratory studies in which response effort is indexed in terms of physical units of force will generalize to situations in which effort is measured in other ways remains to be determined. The results of several applied studies, summarized previously, are consistent with the findings of Alling and Poling (1995) and earlier basic research that increasing response force produces rapid and enduring decreases in behavior. Important tasks for future research include determination of the range of procedures that can be meaningfully considered to involve response-effort manipulations in basic and applied settings and delineation of similarities and differences in the effects of those procedures. Renewed interest in response effort as an independent variable appears to be justified because of the scope of its potential applications (as indicated by the diverse examples described above). It is also justified because the political constraints imposed on punishment- and reinforcement-based procedures, due to an imbalance between effectiveness and social validity (cf. Bernstein, 1990; Mulick, 1990), have yet to be imposed on procedures that entail manipulations of response effort. Finally, it is justified because, for many persons, life is hard, and increased study of response effort just might make it a little easier.

REFERENCES

Adair, E. R., & Wright, B. A. (1976). Behavioral thermoregulation in the squirrel monkey when response effort is varied. *Journal of Comparative and Physiological Psychology, 90,* 179–184.

Alling, K., & Poling, A. (1995). The effects of differing response-force requirements on fixed-ratio responding of rats. *Journal of the Experimental Analysis of Behavior, 63,* 331–346.

Azrin, N. H. (1956). Some effects of two intermittent schedules of immediate and nonimmediate punishment. *Journal of Psychology, 42,* 3–21.

Azrin, N. H. (1959). Punishment and recovery during fixed ratio performance. *Journal of the Experimental Analysis of Behavior, 2,* 301–305.

Azrin, N. H. (1960). Sequential effects of punishment. *Science, 131,* 605–606.

Baer, D. M., Wolf, M. M., & Risley, T. R. (1968). Some current dimensions of applied behavior analysis. *Journal of Applied Behavior Analysis, 1,* 91–98.

Barron, W. M. (1980). Failed appointments: Who misses them, why they are missed, and what can be done. *Primary Care, 7,* 563–574.

Bernstein, D. J. (1990). Of carrots and sticks: A review of Deci and Ryan's *Intrinsic Motivation and Self-Determination in Human Behavior. Journal of the Experimental Analysis of Behavior, 54,* 323–332.

Blank, H. (1985). Funding of day care and public policy. In *Daycare, report of the 16th Ross Round Table on critical approaches to common pediatric problems* (pp. 31–37). Columbus OH: Ross Laboratories.

Blough, D. S. (1966). The study of animal sensory processes by operant methods. In W. K. Honig (Ed.), *Operant behavior: Areas of research and application* (pp. 345–379). New York: Appleton-Century-Crofts.

Brothers, K. J., Krantz, P. J., & McClannahan, L. E. (1994). Office paper recycling: A function of container proximity. *Journal of Applied Behavior Analysis, 27,* 153–160.

Capehart, J., Viney, W., & Hulicka, I. M. (1958). The effect of effort on extinction. *Journal of Comparative and Physiological Psychology, 51,* 505–507.

Chapman, R. F., Smith, J. W., & Layden, T. A. (1971). Elimination of cigarette smoking by punishment and self-management training. *Behavior Research and Therapy, 9,* 255–264.

Chung, S. (1965). Effects of effort on response rate. *Journal of the Experimental Analysis of Behavior, 8,* 1–7.

Dardano, J. F. (1970). Fractional punishment of fixed ratio performance. *Journal of the Experimental Analysis of Behavior, 14,* 185–198.

Dardano, J. F., & Sauerbrunn, D. (1964). Selective punishment of fixed-ratio performance. *Journal of the Experimental Analysis of Behavior, 7,* 255–260.

Epstein, L. H., Miller, P. M., & Webster, J. S. (1976). The effects of reinforcing concurrent behavior on self-monitoring. *Behavior Therapy, 7,* 89–95.

Feinstein, A. R. (1982). The Jones criteria and the challenges of clinimetrics. *Circulation, 66,* 1–5.

Feinstein, A. R., Josephy, B. R., & Wells, C. K. (1986). Scientific and clinical problems in indexes of functional disability. *Annals of Internal Medicine, 105,* 413–420.

Feinstein, A. R., Wells, C. K., Joyce, C. M., & Josephy, B. R. (1985). The evaluation of sensibility and the role of patient collaboration in clinimetric indexes. *Transatlantic Association of American Physicians, 98,* 146–149.

Fowler, S. C. (1987). Force and duration of operant responses as dependent variables in behavioral pharmacology. In T. Thompson, P. B. Dews, & J. E. Barrett (Eds.), *Neurobehavioral pharmacology* (pp. 83–127). Hillsdale, NJ: Erlbaum.

Friman, P. C. (1995). *Proximity and ashtray usage: An experimental demonstration of the role of response requirement.* Unpublished raw data.

Friman, P. C., Barone, V. J., & Christophersen, E. R. (1986). Aversive taste treatment of finger- and thumb-sucking. *Pediatrics, 78,* 174–176.

Friman, P. C., Barone, V. J., & Christophersen, E. R. (1987). Reply to Mackenzie. *Pediatrics, 79,* 485–486.

Friman, P. C., & Christophersen, E. R. (1983). Behavior therapy and hyperactivity: A brief review of therapy for a big problem. *The Behavior Therapist, 6,* 175–176.

Friman, P. C., Finney, J. W., Rapoff, M. A., & Christophersen, E. R. (1985). Improving pediatric appointment keeping: Cost effectiveness and social validation of reminders and reduced response requirement. *Journal of Applied Behavior Analysis, 18,* 315–323.

Friman, P. C., Glasscock, S. G., Finney, J. W., & Christophersen, E. R. (1987). Reducing effort with reminders and a parking pass to improve appointment keeping for patients of pediatric residents. *Medical Care, 25,* 83–86.

Hake, D. F., & Azrin, N. H. (1963). An apparatus for delivering pain-shock to monkeys. *Journal of the Experimental Analysis of Behavior, 6,* 297–298.

Horner, R. (1990). Ideology, technology, and typical community setting: Use of severe aversive stimuli. *American Journal on Mental Retardation, 95,* 166–168.

Horner, R. H., & Day, H. M. (1991). The effects of response efficiency on functionally equivalent competing behaviors. *Journal of Applied Behavior Analysis, 24,* 719–732.

Jacobsen, J. M., Bushell, D., & Risley, T. (1969). Switching requirements in a Head Start classroom. *Journal of Applied Behavior Analysis, 2,* 43–47.

Lattal, K. A., & Griffin, M. A. (1972). Punishment contrast during free-operant avoidance. *Journal of the Experimental Analysis of Behavior, 18,* 509–516.

Luce, S. C., Delquadri, J., & Hall, R. V. (1980). Contingent exercise: A mild but powerful procedure for suppressing inappropriate verbal and aggressive behavior. *Journal of Applied Behavior Analysis, 13,* 583–594.

Luiselli, J. K. (1984). Therapeutic effects of brief contingent effort on severe behavior disorders in children with developmental disabilities. *Journal of Clinical Child Psychology, 13,* 257–262.

Mace, F. C., Neef, N. A., Shade, D., & Mauro, B. C. (in press). Effects of problem difficulty and reinforcer quality on time allocated to concurrent arithmetic problems. *Journal of Applied Behavior Analysis.*

MacKenzie, E. P. (1987). Thumb sucking debate. *Pediatrics, 79,* 485–486.

McReynolds, W. T. (1972). A procedure for the withdrawal of an infant oral pacifier. *Journal of Applied Behavior Analysis, 5,* 65–66.

Miller, L. K. (1968a). The effect of response force on avoidance rate. *Journal of the Experimental Analysis of Behavior, 11,* 809–812.

Miller, L. K. (1968b). Escape from an effortful situation. *Journal of the Experimental Analysis of Behavior, 11,* 619–628.

Miller, L. K. (1970). Some punishing effects of response force. *Journal of the Experimental Analysis of Behavior, 13,* 215–220.

Mowrer, O. H., & Jones, H. (1943). Extinction and behavior variability as a function of effortfulness of task. *Journal of Experimental Psychology, 58,* 341–347.

Mudford, O. C. (1995). Review of the gentle teaching data. *American Journal on Mental Retardation, 99,* 345–355.

Mulick, J. A. (1990). The ideology and science of punishment in mental retardation. *American Journal of Mental Retardation, 95,* 142–181.

Neef, N. A., Shade, D., & Miller, M. S. (1994). Assessing influential dimensions of reinforcers on choice in students with serious emotional disturbance. *Journal of Applied Behavior Analysis, 27,* 575–583.

Notterdam, J. M., & Minz, D. E. (1965). *Dynamics of response.* New York: Wiley.

Perone, M., & Baron, A. (1980). Reinforcement of human observing behavior by a stimulus correlated with extinction or increased effort. *Journal of the Experimental Analysis of Behavior, 34,* 239–261.

Premack, D. (1959). Toward empirical behavior laws: 1. Positive reinforcement. *Psychological Review, 66,* 219–233.

Rachlin, H. (1966). Recovery of responses during mild punishment. *Journal of the Experimental Analysis of Behavior, 9,* 251–263.

Ross, L. V., Friman, P. C., & Christophersen, E. R. (1993). A component analysis of an effort reducing appointment keeping package. *Journal of Applied Behavior Analysis, 26,* 461–469.

Sailor, W. S., Guess, D., Rutherford, G., & Baer, D. M. (1968). Control of tantrum behavior by operant techniques during experimental verbal training. *Journal of Applied Behavior Analysis, 1,* 237–244.

Schulman, R. (1986). *Deaccelerator: Behavioral control of highway speeding.* Paper presented at the meeting of the Association for Behavior Analysis, Milwaukee.

Skinner, B. F. (1938). *The behavior of organisms.* New York: Appleton-Century-Crofts.

Skinner, B. F. (1950). Are theories of learning necessary? *Psychological Review, 57,* 193–216.

Solomon, R. L. (1948). Effort and extinction rate: A confirmation. *Journal of Comparative and Physiological Psychology, 41,* 93–101.

Stuart, R. B., & Davis, B. (1976). *Slim chance in a fat world.* Champaign, IL: Research Press.

Van Houten, R. (1993). The use of wrist weights to reduce self-injury maintained by sensory reinforcement. *Journal of Applied Behavior Analysis, 26,* 197–203.

Van Houten, R., Nau, P. A., & Merrigan, M. (1981). Reducing elevator energy use: A comparison of posted feedback and reduced elevator convenience. *Journal of Applied Behavior Analysis, 14,* 377–387.

White, G. W., Paine-Andrews, A., Mathews, R. M., & Fawcett, S. B. (1995). Home access modifications: Effects on community visits by people with physical disabilities. *Journal of Applied Behavior Analysis, 28,* 457–463.

Received August 31, 1995
Revision received September 11, 1995
Final acceptance September 20, 1995
Action Editor, Nancy A. Neef

JOURNAL OF APPLIED BEHAVIOR ANALYSIS 1996, **29**, 213–230 NUMBER 2 (SUMMER 1996)

RECENT REINFORCEMENT-SCHEDULE RESEARCH AND APPLIED BEHAVIOR ANALYSIS

KENNON A. LATTAL AND NANCY A. NEEF

WEST VIRGINIA UNIVERSITY AND
UNIVERSITY OF PENNSYLVANIA

Reinforcement schedules are considered in relation to applied behavior analysis by examining several recent laboratory experiments with humans and other animals. The experiments are drawn from three areas of contemporary schedule research: behavioral history effects on schedule performance, the role of instructions in schedule performance of humans, and dynamic schedules of reinforcement. All of the experiments are discussed in relation to the role of behavioral history in current schedule performance. The paper concludes by extracting from the experiments some more general issues concerning reinforcement schedules in applied research and practice.

DESCRIPTORS: reinforcement schedules, behavioral history, verbal behavior, dynamic schedules, application of basic processes

---

We selected three areas of contemporary reinforcement-schedule research as the topic of our article for this series on the potential applications of recent developments in the experimental analysis of behavior: the effects of behavioral history on reinforcement schedule performance, the role of instructions in schedule performance of humans, and dynamic schedules of reinforcement. These areas share several interesting similarities, beyond representing some current research directions in schedules of reinforcement. First, all of the research bears directly on human behavior, which is a strong trend in the experimental analysis of behavior (Hyten & Reilly, 1992). Even the nonhuman animal (hereafter, animal) experiments on behavioral history that we discuss are rooted in earlier investigations of behavioral history effects with humans. Second, the research in each area illustrates how the immediate schedule circumstances interact with other variables to control behavior. These variables may be thought of broadly as historical ones, whether they involve what happened on the preceding cycle in the case of dynamic schedules, in preceding conditions in the case of history effects, or in the person's verbal repertoire, which often is considered another kind of history. Third, the research in each area comments on and qualifies the reinforcement process, albeit in different ways.

We begin by discussing the definitions and roles of reinforcement schedules in contemporary behavior analysis. This is followed by a review of some representative experiments in each area mentioned above and a discussion of their potential relevance for applied behavior analysis. We conclude with some more general issues concerning basic research involving schedules of reinforcement in relation to applied behavior analysis.

REINFORCEMENT SCHEDULES IN BEHAVIOR ANALYSIS

Reinforcement schedules have been defined as prescriptions for arranging rein-

---

Lattal thanks Mark Reilly for many helpful discussions about progressive reinforcement schedules.

Reprints can be obtained from Kennon A. Lattal, Department of Psychology, West Virginia University, Morgantown, West Virginia 26506-6040 (E-mail: lattal@wvnvm.wvnet.edu) or from Nancy A. Neef, Graduate School of Education, University of Pennsylvania, 3700 Walnut Street, Philadelphia, Pennsylvania 19104-6216 (E-mail: nancyn@nwfs.gse.upenn.edu).

forcers in time and in relation to responses, as the rules used to present reinforcing stimuli (Zeiler, 1977), or as "specification(s) of the criteria by which responses become eligible to produce reinforcers" (Catania, 1992, p. 394). Such definitions are useful in specifying the form or structure of the schedule, but they fall short in other domains. First, they are mute on the dynamic interplay between the initial prescription or rule and subsequent behavior. This dynamic nature of at least some reinforcement schedules affects the subsequent arrangement between time, responses, and reinforcers that in turn leads to changes in performance. Second, they do not consider how schedule-controlled performance may be tempered by such factors as prior history or the operation of other contextual factors such as, in the case of humans, instructions that may either compete with or complement the rules specified by the schedule. Third, the definitions understate the role of schedules in natural settings where they also may be presumed to operate, but not always in a manner prescribed or imposed by an agent or specified by an a priori rule, as the definitions imply.

The ubiquity of schedules has made them a focal point of behavior analysis. They sometimes have been labeled the "amino acids of behavior" and often have been discussed as fundamental determinants of behavior (Morse & Kelleher, 1977). Reinforcement schedules are central in the experimental analysis of behavior because of what can be learned about the reinforcement process from them *and* because they serve as useful baselines for the study of other behavioral processes (Zeiler, 1984). Reinforcement schedules serve similar purposes in applied behavior analysis and also, either directly or indirectly, are embedded in most treatment programs.

CURRENT SCHEDULE PERFORMANCE AND SCHEDULE HISTORY

An assumption of behavior analysis is that operant behavior is controlled by current reinforcement schedules. Recent investigations with both animal and human subjects have systematically explored how previous experiences also influence current schedule-controlled behavior. The experiments illustrate techniques for establishing functional relations between explicitly arranged past experiences, offer a broader context for discussing reinforcement schedule performance, and raise important issues for applied behavior analysts concerning how historical variables are conceptualized and studied in relation to applied problems.

Historical variables have been examined in basic research by establishing different baseline histories of responding under separate schedules and evaluating subsequent performance under a common third schedule as a function of prior schedule experience. For example, Freeman and Lattal (1992) examined behavioral history effects in three experiments with pigeons. In the first experiment, subjects initially were exposed daily to a fixed-ratio (FR) schedule during one session and to a differential-reinforcement-of-low-rate (DRL) schedule during the other session, each under different stimulus conditions. Each schedule was presented for 50 or more sessions, and established a history of responding at a rate that was about 4.5 times higher under the FR than under the DRL schedule. Subsequently, identical fixed-interval (FI) schedules were implemented under the respective stimulus conditions during both of the sessions for 60 days. Response rates in the former FR condition remained higher than response rates in the former DRL condition, and they tended to converge only after prolonged (approximately 15 to 40 sessions) exposure to the FI schedule. Similar results were obtained in a second experiment that examined the effects of high-rate (FR schedule) and low-rate (DRL schedule) histories of responding on subsequent performance under a variable-interval (VI) schedule of reinforcement, except that the effects of history were not as persistent. These results were replicated in a third experiment using a multiple schedule to generate high and low response rates within individual baseline sessions.

These studies demonstrated that if behavior has been established under stimulus control in the past, then that past schedule performance affects current responding in the presence of the stimuli. They also suggest that certain histories of reinforcement can be relatively persistent (e.g., DRL on subsequent FI performance). Does an intervening history mitigate the persistence in behavior of more remote histories? LeFrancois and Metzger (1993) compared rates of bar presses by two groups of rats under FI schedules. For both groups, responses first were conditioned under a DRL schedule, but for one group, exposure to an FR schedule preceded the FI schedule. Performance under the FI schedule was affected by immediate history, and DRL schedule histories did not affect FI performance for subjects with an intervening FR schedule history.

Humans past the age of 5 or 6 years often differ from animals in patterns of responses and control by schedules of reinforcement. For example, whereas the scalloped or "break-and-run" pattern predicted by FI schedules readily occurs with rats and pigeons (i.e., postreinforcement pause followed by positively accelerated response rates), human performance, particularly human performance that is instructed (e.g., Catania, Matthews, & Shimoff, 1982), is resistant to control by the temporal variables that are implicit in those schedules. Thus, one could expect some history effects (e.g., those reported by Freeman & Lattal, 1992) to be even more persistent or to manifest differently with humans. This in turn has led to other investigations of variables related to behavioral history that might account for such differences.

For example, it has been hypothesized that, for humans, variable-ratio (VR) schedules that generate high-rate responding could interfere with subsequent FI performance (Wanchisen, Tatham, & Mooney, 1989); however, the results of a study by Baron and Leinenweber (1995) suggested that such a VR history does not by itself account for FI performance differences between humans and other animals. That study examined performance of 18 rats under an FI 30-s schedule, half of whom had a conditioning history of high-rate responding under single or compound VR schedules. As in previous studies, the high response rates initially established in the rats exposed to VR schedules progressively diminished with continued exposure to the FI schedule. Of particular note, however, was that the pattern of responding within each FI was similar for subjects with and without a VR history. That is, subjects with and without a prior VR history showed similar development of the characteristic FI scallop and postreinforcement pauses that are indicative of temporal control by FI schedules. Thus, although history effects for rats with prior exposure to VR schedules were evident in high overall response rates under the FI schedule, within-interval response rates were similar to those of rats without a VR history. Regardless of history, then, rats' responding was controlled by the schedule in a way that is not always characteristic of adult human performance.

That a history of responding established under certain schedules affects current performance under a different reinforcement schedule for some period of time after the original conditions have changed has also been observed in applied studies with human subjects. For example, in a study of concurrent schedule reinforcement of academic behavior, Mace, Neef, Shade, and Mauro (1994) reported that "changes in the concurrent VI schedules failed to generate patterns of time allocation that matched the relative rates of reinforcement. Instead subjects generally tended to persist in their allocation patterns of the previous schedule condition" (p. 593).

Considering that the control of current schedule performance by past experiences appears to be a robust finding in basic research, it is somewhat surprising that the residual or carryover effects of prior experiences have not been observed more often in applied studies. It may be that carryover effects are more common than it would appear from the literature. For example, because multiple baseline and reversal designs that are common in applied research require immediate changes in behavior to demonstrate experimental control, studies in which behavior patterns persist from one condition to the next may not be submitted, or may be rejected, for publication.

Another possibility for the absence of history effects in applied studies is that changes in independent variables in these studies are often correlated with unique discriminative stimuli, which may mitigate the effects of behavioral history. This is supported by the results of studies by Freeman and Lattal (1992) indicating stimulus control of history effects, and by Hanna, Blackman, and Todorov (1992) showing that discriminated responding following changes in concurrent VI schedules occurred sooner in pigeons when each schedule was uniquely correlated with a discriminative stimulus (although see Mace et al., 1994, for an exception).

The extent to which history effects persist with humans cannot be predicted with certainty from those involving animals, as the results of Baron and Leinenweber's (1995) experiment illustrate. Perone, Galizio, and Baron (1988) discussed a number of differences between human and animal studies that may contribute to the differences in schedule performance as a function of schedule history. Specifically, in the case of differences in behavioral history effects, unlike the animal subjects' relatively simple and brief (e.g., 2 months or less) "simulated" histories, the behaviors of individuals treated by applied behavior analysts often have a history of many years' duration. The duration of a history might affect its persistence and may, for example, partially account for Lovaas' finding that the success of even prolonged intensive treatment for autism was related to the age of the child (Lovaas, 1993).

The results of LeFrancois and Metzger (1993) indicating that current performance is affected more by immediate history than by remote history have implications for applied research on functional analysis. In a sense, functional analyses involve efforts to determine the effects of immediate history by identifying the contingencies that maintain current responding. But doing so involves implementing contingencies and schedules of reinforcement that also create immediate histories for those behaviors. It is possible that the behaviors measured may come to be controlled more by the intervening histories arranged by the functional analysis than by the histories the functional analysis is designed to assess, especially if the analysis is prolonged.

Although the above studies indicate the control of current performance by previous schedules, they also demonstrate the diminishment of this control as experience under other schedules increases. History effects therefore can be conceptualized as transition states (Sidman, 1960). Indeed, the assumption that history effects, for the most part, will not persist indefinitely as behavior adapts to the present environment is the raison d'être for applied behavior analysis. It underlies our successes as well as our treatment failures such as relapse (Lerman, Iwata, Smith, Zarcone, & Vollmer, 1994).

Paradoxically, applied behavior analysts have regarded the role of behavioral history as both paramount and irrelevant. On the one hand, a tenet of behavior analysis is that history profoundly affects human behavior. In fact, it could be argued that for applied behavior analysts, arranging conditions to alter subsequent behavior is itself a matter, and goal, of generating a different history that will produce durable changes in the targeted behavior. On the other hand, until the development of functional analysis methods (Iwata, Dorsey, Slifer, Bauman, & Richman, 1982/1994), behavior analysts generally disregarded the historical conditions under which behavior developed. The relative lack of emphasis on the history that subjects bring to the situation is, in part, what distinguishes our field (e.g., from psychoanalytic models). One reason was practical: We can never know with certainty the history that led to the development of a particular problem behavior because we were not able to observe it (nor, obviously, to change it). We therefore relegated history to the role of an inevitable source of behavior variability, recognizing that "any difference in behavior will always be subject to interpretation as a product of some currently unknowable fluctuation in those unknown variables" (Baer, 1977, p. 168).

Another reason for disregarding behavioral history was a belief that history is irrelevant, either because the problem behavior, when we encounter it, might be affected by different conditions than those that contributed to its development, or because the arrangement of different conditions (immediate or proximal history) can override the effects of prior conditions (remote or distal history). As noted by Iwata et al. (1982/1994), "behavioral researchers and clinicians generally have dismissed the importance of etiology, since the conditions that are necessary to develop or maintain a response may be totally unrelated to the conditions that are sufficient to alter or eliminate it" (p. 198). It may be inconsistent or arbitrary to assume, however, that the relevance of history depends on whether or not we have arranged it. For example, sometimes we seek to establish a history that will render a desired behavior insensitive to immediate contingencies (as implied by the definition of generalization) so that it will be maintained in the natural environment. If we can arrange treatment conditions for desirable behavior to persist in the presence of disruptive events, then we also must appreciate that other conditions in the natural environment create a history in which problem behavior is resistant to change by our treatment conditions. By understanding how and under what conditions history affects schedule-controlled behavior, applied behavior analysts may be able to design interventions that mitigate or optimize those influences.

HUMAN VERBAL BEHAVIOR AND SCHEDULE PERFORMANCE

The studies just discussed illustrate that schedule performance is not determined exclusively by contemporary requirements for reinforcement. Human schedule performance also may be affected by typically long-standing histories of verbal behavior.

Hackenberg and Joker (1994) examined choices of adult humans when the correspondence between instructions and contingencies was made progressively less accurate by gradual shifts in the schedule of reinforcement. The purposes of their investigation were to examine instructional control under conflicting schedule requirements, the transition from instructional to schedule control, and the effects of a history of inaccurate instructions on compliance. The procedure involved presenting two different stimuli on a computer screen, one of which was associated with a fixed-time (FT) schedule and the other with a progressive-time (PT) schedule. Neither schedule required a response; the reinforcers were simply delivered at the end of the scheduled time period. After each successive reinforcer, subjects selected one or the other schedule, which then remained in effect throughout that trial. If a subject initially selected the stimulus associated with the PT schedule, a point was delivered immediately (0 s), and each successive choice of the PT schedule gradually increased the time to point delivery in fixed increments. If a subject initially selected the stimulus associated with the FT schedule, a point was delivered after 60 s and the PT schedule was reset to 0 s.

Subjects were given the same set of instructions throughout the experiment. Under the first experimental condition, the instructions accurately characterized the sequence of PT and FT choices that would produce the most reinforcement (i.e., the schedule and the instructions were identical). The size of the increments (step size) in the PT schedule was altered gradually across successive experimental conditions (in ascending and then descending order), such that the same instructions gradually became less (and then more) accurate in describing the optimal choice sequence. This unique procedure permitted examination of the transition from instructional to schedule control on a continuum of changing stimulus conditions, and examination of schedule control as a function of history.

Instructional control was established quickly in the first condition, in which instructions accurately described the schedules. However, conformity with instructions necessarily constrained the range of behavior (choice patterns), thereby both precluding contact with changes in the schedule and reducing subsequent control of responding. Choices continued to be controlled by instructions as the PT step size increased across several experimental conditions. As the instructions became progressively more inaccurate, however, choice patterns became more variable and produced more reinforcement, resulting in an abrupt transition from instructional to schedule control. The extent to which choices were controlled by the schedule contingencies as PT step sizes decreased (in the descending sequence) varied according to the point at which instructional control first broke down in the ascending sequence, suggesting that the history of consequences for following inaccurate instructions can have enduring effects on behavior.

The schedules in Hackenberg and Joker's (1994) experiment are analogous to many situations in the natural environment in which conditions gradually change (e.g., the progression of an illness, potency of a drug, the economy) such that instructions from others (e.g., physicians, financial advisers) that initially described the schedule become progressively less accurate. Hackenberg and Joker's results suggest that the history and degree of correspondence between instructions and consequences of behavior may affect the extent to which choices are determined by those changing conditions or continue to be controlled by instructions. In some situations, instructional control and weak control by changing schedule conditions are desirable because they increase the probability that a response will persist despite short-term punishers, extinction, or increasing work requirements (e.g., a physician's instructions when a medical program takes time to work). In other situations, control by instructions is maladaptive (albeit not always for the person giving them). Scam artists, for example, strengthen instructional control by initially arranging consequences that support their instructions (such as ensuring that the victim receives "profits" for a period of time) so that instructions will continue to control escalated investments in a bogus operation in which the effectiveness of the instructions depends on the victim's behavior becoming insensitive to the changing consequences (e.g., when the profits no longer arrive).

One direct implication of Hackenberg and Joker's (1994) findings for applied behavior analysts involves interventions to decrease noncompliance, one of the most pervasive childhood behavior problems (e.g., Neef, Shafer, Egel, Cataldo, & Parrish, 1983; Parrish, Cataldo, Kolko, Neef, & Egel, 1986). Establishing a history of following adult instructions may also have the disadvantage of reducing the direct schedule control of the behavior of children. For example, Parrish et al. (1986) found that reinforcing compliant behavior produced collateral reductions in inappropriate behavior (e.g., aggression, disruption) for which there were no scheduled consequences. Similarly, Neef et al. (1983) demonstrated that reinforcing compliance to a subset of instructions increased compliance with instructions of similar types of requests ("do" or "don't") that were not reinforced. The demonstration of generalized response classes (i.e., that reinforcement of instruction following had collateral effects on unreinforced behaviors) in both of these studies necessarily also shows that the unreinforced members were not controlled by the reinforcement schedule. Although these particular results had obvious advantages, such histories might also have long-term disadvantages if they produce rigid rule following that is not regulated by environmental contingencies.

Such rigidity effects were demonstrated in a recent study by Wulfert, Greenway, Farkas, Hayes, and Dougher (1994) on the effects of instructional histories and measures of behavioral rigidity on sensitivity to schedule contingencies. In the first experiment, the responding of subjects who were given accurate, specific instructions under a multiple DRL FR schedule of reinforcement showed more persistence when the condition was changed to extinction than did the responding of subjects who were not given specific instructions. Persistence was most pronounced for subjects who previously had been classified as "rigid."

In a second experiment, subjects were given accurate, specific instructions with an FR schedule in effect. When the schedule was changed to DRL, half of the subjects were instructed accurately and the other half were instructed inaccurately. All subjects who had been given accurate instructions responded accordingly. When instructions were inaccurate, all subjects initially responded according to the instructions (which described the previous FR schedule), but the subjects who had previously been characterized as rigid persisted in this pattern of behavior; responses of most of the "nonrigid" subjects eventually conformed to the schedule.

Some recent research suggests that self-generated rules may control nonverbal behavior similarly to instructions from others (e.g., Rosenfarb, Newland, Brannon, & Howey, 1992). For example, in some preliminary work on matching by Neef and colleagues, a student whose completion of different sets of math problems was reinforced on a concurrent VI 30-s VI 60-s schedule devoted her time exclusively to one set of problems, saying, "I should finish what I start before doing something else." Obviously in many situations control of behavior by that rule (or the history that is reflected in the rule) would be adaptive in obtaining reinforcers that are associated with successful task completion. But because that rule competed with the optimal response strategy in this situation, her behavior could not come into contact with the programmed contingencies. Her exclusive responding to a single alternative that yielded a relatively low rate of reinforcement persisted over numerous sessions until adjunct procedures were added (e.g., modeling, count-down timers) that nonverbally described the contingencies. Similarly, the extent to which faulty or imprecise rules may have been generated by other subjects in studies on matching by Neef, Mace, and Shade (1993), Neef, Mace, Shea, and Shade (1992), and Mace et al. (1994) could have contributed to the initial lack of control of their responding by concurrent VI schedules until adjunct procedures were used to establish matching.

The effects of self-generated rules on schedule performance was also examined by Horne and Lowe (1993) in a series of six experiments with 30 adults. Because matching had been reported in a number of studies with humans by Bradshaw, Szabadi, and Bevan (1976, 1977, 1979), Horne and Lowe used a similar procedure. Two computer keys could be pressed for points (exchangeable for money) on concurrent VI schedules. On one key, six different-valued VI schedules were randomly rotated every 10 min separated by 5-min rest periods; responses to the other key were reinforced on the same VI schedule throughout. Each VI schedule was correlated with a different stimulus (e.g., geometric shape). At the end of each experiment, subjects completed a questionnaire asking them to describe the schedules that had been in effect and the factors that had influenced their choices. These performance rules then were compared to the subjects' schedule performance. The choices of only 13 of the 30 subjects conformed to the generalized matching equation and approximated the typically reported performance of animal subjects. Significantly, actual performance of 29 of the subjects corresponded closely to their descriptions of the performance rules they had generated, whether or not those rules accurately described the reinforcement schedules (see also Rosenfarb et al., 1992).

These data suggest that adult humans' own verbal behavior may influence their behavior in the presence of reinforcement schedules, although in other studies the relation between subjects' descriptions and accompanying verbal responses has been less clear (Hackenberg & Axtell, 1993; Jacobs & Hackenberg, 1996). The relation between verbal description and schedule performance may be represented as a continuum. On the one hand, it is likely that schedule performance influences the verbal description. On the other, schedules might control performance only indirectly, to the extent that they affect individuals' verbal behavior in the form of rules that govern behavior. This latter observation has interesting implications for treatment. For example, naturally existing reinforcement schedules are often ambiguous, and even in treatment settings it is difficult to arrange them with the consistency and precision that are characteristic of laboratory research. To the extent that individuals formulate and follow faulty rules, nonverbal behavior that is controlled by those rules may be maladaptive or restricted such that it does not come into contact with schedules that might lead to other rules. In counseling situations, for example, clients are often encouraged to articulate their covert verbal behavior so that inaccurate contingency descriptions can be observed and challenged; the therapist can then shape more appropriate performance rules or prompt clients to follow testable rules that will contact contingencies that support alternative behaviors.

Early applied research addressed the role of verbal behavior directly in relations between verbal and nonverbal correspondence (e.g., Deacon & Konarski, 1987; also see Israel, 1978, for a review) or indirectly in self-instruction training (Meichenbaum & Goodman, 1971). However, there have been few studies in *JABA* on the role of verbal behavior over the past decade. For the most part, behavior analysts have treated verbal behavior and pretreatment history similarly: Because neither history nor covert verbal behavior can be directly observed, and reports of those events cannot be presumed to be reliable or valid, these variables are often considered to be incidental to prediction and management of behavior. In fact, in a seminal article that continues to define our field, Baer, Wolf, and Risley (1968) stated that applied research

> usually studies what subjects can be brought to do rather than what they can be brought to say. . . . Accordingly, a subject's verbal description of his own nonverbal behavior usually would not be accepted as a measure of his actual behavior unless it were independently substantiated. Hence, there is little applied value in the demonstration that an impotent man can be made to say that he is no longer impotent. The relevant question is not what he can say, but what he can do. (p. 93)

Although the focus of behavior analysis appropriately remains on what an individual does, the research by Horne and Lowe (1993) and others (e.g., Catania et al., 1982; Hayes, Brownstein, Zettle, Rosenfarb, & Korn, 1986) suggests that behavior analysts need to consider that "what subjects can be brought to do" may, in many situations, be a function of "what they can be brought to say." It seems that the analysis of verbal behavior in relation to reinforcement schedules may warrant a more central role in applied behavioral research.

DYNAMIC REINFORCEMENT SCHEDULES

Much of the research in the areas described above concerns the role of distal experiences, either those with previous reinforcement schedules or aspects of a history of rule following, on current schedule performance. The control of schedule performance by more contemporary, or proximal, events is more characteristic of behavior-analytic research.

Reinforcement schedules typically involve repetitive, basically static, arrangements whereby the same requirements for reinforcement are in effect on successive cycles. With an FR schedule, for example, after every reinforcer the same fixed response requirement is repeated. But even here, there may be an interaction between schedule performance at a given point in a session and subsequent performance in that session. For example, during an FR schedule, reinforcement rate is determined by response rate such that more rapid responding yields a higher rate of reinforcement than does lower rate responding. Similar relations have been described for other schedules (e.g., Baum, 1973, 1989; Nevin, 1984). Such effects may be considered on the same continuum as those in the previously cited studies of historical influence on schedule performance, the difference being the time scale over which the prior experience is measured. The interaction of humans' rules and schedules also illustrates dynamic schedule effects. For example, if a rule and the requirements of a schedule are in conflict, over time the subject's behavior may conform to the schedule even though it was initially controlled by the rule (Galizio, 1979). Self-generated rules, if and when they occur, might interact in a similar way with schedule-controlled behavior to change the latter from time to time. As the person's rules change, within or between sessions, behavior changes, which leads to further changes in the rules and so on.

Dynamic reinforcement schedules provide a procedure for explicitly studying the types of interactions suggested in the preceding paragraphs. With these dynamic schedules, the requirements for reinforcement change after each reinforcer, or some sequence of reinforcers, as a function of either an a priori algorithm or some aspect of the organism's previous performance on the schedule. Theoretically, such dynamic schedules are of interest because of the insights they may reveal into the adaptation of behavior to rapidly changing circumstances. They also may be of interest to applied behavior analysts because they represent an attempt by basic researchers to address complex situations without dissecting them into more elemental schedules. Such dissection in fluid, applied settings sometimes is undesirable, difficult, or even impossible. We note too that we do not wish to proliferate an already complex taxonomy of schedules. Thus, the distinctions that we describe below are only for didactic purposes. We do not propose these terms as substitutes for descriptions of schedules that we believe are adequate (e.g., Lattal, 1991).

Algorithm-Based Dynamic Schedules

One dynamic arrangement occurs when the requirements for reinforcement are changed according to an algorithm. When an algorithm is used, the requirements change independently of behavior. Progressive schedules of reinforcement involve systematic, gradually incrementing response requirements for reinforcement in the case of progressive-ratio (PR) schedules, or time between reinforcement availability for a response in the case of progressive-interval (PI) schedules. The most common algorithms for incrementing the schedule requirements are arithmetic (i.e., a constant amount is added to each successive interval) and geometric (i.e., each successive interval is increased by a constant proportion of the preceding one) progressions. Because the changes in schedule requirements occur after each reinforcer (or block of reinforcers) and do so without regard to the organism's behavior, they exemplify an algorithm-driven dynamic reinforcement schedule.

Dougherty, Cherek, and Roache (1994) investigated PI schedule performance of human subjects. Subjects were seated at a console and earned points by pushing a button according to a chained PI *t*-s FI 20-s schedule. In the presence of the letter A on the computer screen, the first response after *t* s on a button changed the stimulus on the screen to B, indicating that an FI 20-s schedule was in effect. The first response after 20 s was reinforced in the presence of B. The FI schedule remained in effect until five reinforcers (points on a counter that were exchangeable for money) were earned. At that time, the letter A reappeared on the screen and the PI *t*-s schedule was incremented. This A-B cycle repeated throughout each 1-hr session. The size of *t* was 20 s, 40 s, 80 s, or 160 s in different conditions of the experiment. Increments in *t* were made according to either geometric or arithmetic progressions in different conditions. Human PI performance was characterized by diminishing response rates and increasing postreinforcement pause durations as a function of progressively increasing interval requirements. Postreinforcement pauses tended to increase arithmetically under the arithmetic progressions and geometrically under the geometric ones. Under both types of progressions, response rates decreased across increasing PI requirements. These results were similar to those reported by Harzem (1969), with rats as subjects. In a second experiment, Dougherty et al. used PI schedules to assess temporal control of behavior in humans as a function of different doses of marijuana. The findings of that second study are less important to the present theme than the fact that the investigators first analyzed a schedule with unknown effects on human behavior and then were able to use the schedule to assess another behavioral process: temporal control under a drug.

In PR schedules, it is customary to continue increasing the ratio requirement for reinforcement until responding ceases for a preestablished time period (e.g., 10 min, but the actual duration varies from one experiment to another), described as the break point (but see also Thompson, 1972, and Keesey & Goldstein, 1968, for other criteria). Break points have not been studied with PI schedules, raising a question about how PR and PI schedules compare in terms of engendering response persistence. Lattal, Reilly, and Kohn (1996) compared PI and PR performance directly by yoking PR and PI schedules such that, in successive pairs of sessions, a PR schedule in one session was followed by a PI schedule with a matched (yoked) distribution of reinforcers to the PR schedule. In each of 4 birds in almost every pair of sessions, PI responding continued beyond the point at which the break point had been reached on the PR schedule.

A progressive reinforcement schedule can be likened to an applied setting in which the level of difficulty of material being taught increases independently of the subject's behavior, as when instructor-paced changes in material are used. That is, regardless of the individual student's performance, according to a specified set of rules, objectives, or plans (often based on some performance measure based on group averages or modes), the requirements for reinforcement (successful task completion) increase systematically. Such progressions occur in many educational systems, and it is not uncommon under these conditions for a student's performance to deteriorate as the difficulty level or work requirements increase. Conversely, the difficulty level may remain constant but the subject's performance improves over time. The traditional negatively accelerated learning curve expresses the latter relation.

Progressive-ratio schedules also have been used to assess response persistence (Stewart, 1975). For example, Hodos (1961) showed a correlation between food deprivation and the break point on PR schedules. Mace et al. (1988, 1990) have provided a valuable series of experiments and thoughtful conceptual analyses that have elucidated the issues surrounding the resistance of targeted behavior to change in applied settings. Performance on PR schedules could be a useful complement to other measures of resistance to change in applied settings.

Interactive Dynamic Schedules

Another dynamic schedule arrangement is one in which the requirements for upcoming reinforcers change directly as a function of the organism's current or past behavior. The last schedule described by Ferster and Skinner (1957) was an adjusting schedule in which the response requirement of a ratio schedule was increased or decreased after each reinforcer as a function of how long the animal paused before responding after each reinforcement. These adjusting procedures sometimes have been described as titration procedures (e.g., Lea, 1976; Weiss & Laties, 1959).

Hackenberg and Axtell (1993) used an interactive dynamic reinforcement schedule to study the control of human behavior by long- and short-term consequences. They provided human subjects with choices between a PI schedule and an FI schedule that also, in some conditions, reset the PI schedule to 0 s. We will limit our description to the first of their three experiments, because it contained the features critical to the present discussion and yielded findings that were replicated and elaborated on in the subsequent experiments. On each of a series of trials, subjects chose one of two schedules (the unchosen schedule at the start of each trial was rendered ineffective for the remainder of the trial), each correlated with a distinct stimulus on a computer monitor. All operant responses were made on a computer keyboard space bar and, according to the schedules described below, yielded points that could be exchanged for money. Each trial started immediately after the preceding reinforcer with the simultaneous presentation of a red and a blue stimulus on the monitor. The red stimulus was correlated with an FI schedule, and the blue stimulus was correlated with a PI schedule that increased by 5 s after each point was delivered on that schedule. In different phases of the experiment, the FI was 15, 30, or 60 s. Two conditions were compared in each phase. In a no-reset condition, "PI requirements were independent of FI choices, escalating with successive PI choices" (Hackenberg & Axtell, 1993, p. 448). In a reset condition, choices of the FI schedule allowed a point to be produced by the operant response and reset the PI schedule to 0 s.

All but 1 subject switched between the schedules more frequently during the reset than during the no-reset condition. During the reset conditions, the subjects switched more frequently between the schedules when the FI value was shorter. Hackenberg and Axtell (1993) then asked whether the switching patterns were better predicted by taking into account only the immediately preceding PI interval, or whether they were better predicted by taking into account some aggregate of previous PI intervals. This was done by comparing the data to predictions derived from an optimality model (Charnov, 1976) and from a model based on the cumulative effects of one or more delays (PIs) to reinforcement. Based on these comparisons, they concluded that choice in diminishing returns situations (i.e., PI schedules) is determined by an aggregate of reinforcers in time over multiple trials, and not only by the immediately preceding PI value.

The shaping of a response through the differential reinforcement of successive approximations is a simpler example of a dynamic interactive schedule. Shaping involves systematic and progressive changes in the requirements for reinforcement as the subject meets successive behavioral objectives in relation to the target behavior. As the behavior more and less closely approximates the target response, the conditions necessary for reinforcement are adjusted. Thus, the subject's behavior alters the scheduling of reinforcers. The optimal relation between behavior and changing requirements for reinforcement (i.e., the schedule) during shaping has been a matter of considerable speculation but limited experimentation.

There is general agreement that the contingencies should be changed "gradually," but the shaping of new behavior largely remains an art. One exception to this latter observation is the work of Eckerman, Hienz, Stern, and Kowlowitz (1980), who quantified the shaping process and suggested that large, rapidly changing requirements for reinforcement led to the fastest shaping of a key-peck response of a pigeon to a particular location on a 10-in. wide response strip. Similar conclusions about the dynamic changes in shaping have been reached by Platt and his colleagues (e.g., Alleman & Platt, 1973; Kuch & Platt, 1976) in the shaping of interresponse times. Galbicka (1994) recently discussed some of the applied implications of Platt's shaping procedures.

The control of human behavior by long- and short-term consequences is another example of an interactive dynamic schedule, in that what a person does in the present may either positively or negatively affect future reinforcers. In Hackenberg and Axtell's (1993) experiment, the value of the PI schedule, and the subsequent overall rate of reinforcement, depended on the choices of either of two schedules over trials. Applied behavior analysis historically has emphasized the immediate consequences of behavior, but further development of the type of analysis and theory derived from Hackenberg and Axtell's analysis of a dynamic interactive schedule illustrates how one might conceptualize and assess the effects of longer term consequences (e.g., reinforcement rate over extended time periods) on both individual and group (systems) behavior.

In terms of individual behavior, one example, which has been of considerable controversy among applied behavior analysts, is the use of aversive (shock) procedures as a means of controlling self-injurious behavior (e.g., Iwata, 1988). Some have argued that the short-term benefits of reduced maladaptive behavior are not compensated for by the long-term negative effects of shock on the child. Although Hackenberg and Axtell's (1993) study of dynamic reinforcement schedules obviously does not bear directly on this issue, it offers a framework for placing the problem of competing outcomes of individual behavior or individual treatment programs on a continuum with other problems that involve the analysis of short- and long-term consequences.

The same framework described above can be useful in behavior-analytic applications involving aggregates of people. In a business, for example, changing to a new system for providing a service may produce short-term losses of revenue that result from the time that must be devoted to employee training, but these losses may be more than compensated for in the long run by having employees who are better trained to deliver the services offered by the business.

It is perhaps too much of a stretch to claim that experiments like that of Hackenberg and Axtell (1993) are precisely analogous to the complex examples described in the preceding two paragraphs; however, their experiment, and others related to it, are valuable in providing a bridge between applied behavior analysts and basic researchers that allows the use of similar descriptions and techniques to account for human behavior through reinforcement schedule analyses.

CONCLUDING COMMENTS

We conclude by extracting from the experiments reviewed above some more general observations about reinforcement schedules and their relation to issues in applied behavior analysis.

1. Often, the term *contingency* (or contingencies) is used in applied work or in talking about naturally occurring behavior to describe the interrelations among stimuli, responses, and reinforcers. The term *schedule* is used less often, perhaps because the latter term has come to connote greater precision than *contingencies.* Nonetheless, it is important to recognize that, in the noted uses, the two terms describe the same phenomena. Sometimes contingency is used to describe the fact that the reinforcer depends on a response, but one of us has suggested that *dependency* is preferable for that use (Lattal, 1995; Lattal & Poling, 1981). Terms are important, lest applied behavior analysts consider that they are not studying or using reinforcement schedules. They are—perhaps not with the precise specification of the laboratory, but the schedules are operative nonetheless. This latter observation reinforces our initial observation and the theme of this paper that basic research on reinforcement schedules, even the esoteric ones, is a rich vein for applied behavior analysts to mine.

2. Most basic reinforcement-schedule research has involved and continues to almost exclusively involve positive reinforcement. Positive reinforcement procedures have been meticulously honed over many years by many investigators. Such a history gives behavior analysts a powerful research tool, as the reviewed studies illustrate. At least in part because positive reinforcement procedures are so thoroughly analyzed, reliable, and of such proven value, there has been relatively little study of the aversive control of behavior, involving schedules of negative reinforcement and schedules of punishment. This is an unfortunate omission from the standpoint of applied behavior analysis because the controversies that surround the use

of aversive control in applied settings invite a better basic understanding of aversive control and its by-products (e.g., Iwata, 1987).

3. Reinforcement schedules have not generated the same enthusiasm in applied work as they have at some points in the history of the experimental analysis of behavior. Indeed, many complex schedules have been avoided or regarded as esoteric or even useless by a number of applied behavior analysts. Similarly, Zeiler (1984) reserved his strongest criticism of schedule research for basic researchers who are caught up in the minutiae of schedules. Although these criticisms have merit, each research problem described in the preceding sections suggests exciting adaptations of reinforcement schedules to interesting problems for applied behavior analysts: elucidating the role of behavioral history in current performance, gleaning insights into the relation between verbal and direct contingency control of behavior, and disentangling the dynamic processes that often operate in applied settings.

The questions regarding schedules and schedule use need to be framed functionally and pragmatically rather than structurally: How can the schedule be used to address an important applied question? We earlier noted that at least part of the utility of schedules may result from how the schedule concept is used. Applied, or basic, situations and problems need not, and do not, always reduce down to single, simple schedules. They often can be conceptualized usefully, however, along the lines suggested in some of the experiments on dynamic reinforcement schedules.

4. Reinforcement schedule performance is essential to discussions about mechanisms of reinforcement. For example, in a VR schedule, do high response rates occur because of the differential reinforcement of short interresponse times or because higher response rates increase the overall reinforcement rate? The former position is characterized as molecular and the latter as molar, and each has strong proponents (e.g., Baum, 1973, 1989; Peele, Casey, & Silberberg, 1984). One purpose of Hackenberg and Axtell's (1993) experiment was to determine whether reinforcers operate over extended, molar time frames or whether reinforcement effects are more local.

The body of evidence and the arguments concerning the merits and limitations of each position are beyond the scope of this paper (see Williams, 1983, for an informative critique of the debate), but one general point about the debate is important in relation to applied work. The debate about the mechanisms of reinforcement may be separated from the practical issues of using reinforcement. In applied work, the appropriate level of analysis might be selected on practical grounds alone: One selects a level of analysis that yields the behavioral control necessary to achieve the behavior change. If a molecular approach leads to behavioral control, it should be used. If a molar approach does so, then use it. This is not to undermine the importance and value of understanding reinforcement mechanisms, but only to iterate the idea that many things work even when the precise mechanism of their operation cannot be isolated. For example, Darwin (1859/1964) articulated the theory of natural selection in the absence of any evidence of the genetic mechanisms that make such selection possible.

5. Discussions of both reinforcement schedule performance in the basic literature and reinforcement theory increasingly utilize quantitative description and analysis. Such analyses and their advantages have been summarized succinctly by Nevin (1984) and Shull (1991). Applied behavior analysis has not yet been strongly affected by these developments in the experimental analysis of behavior. Research on the matching law (e.g., McDowell, 1988) and on behavioral momentum (Nevin, Mandell, & Atak,

1983) is grounded in quantitative analysis, but both have been imported into applied behavior analysis primarily at a conceptual level, largely in the absence of the quantitative framework in which they developed.

6. The study of human behavior in the laboratory has largely, but, of course, not exclusively, been a matter of studying schedule control of behavior. Issues of prior histories, both in and out of the immediate experimental situation, and of the role of verbal behavior are common themes in this research. The question of how to study and account for the effects of self-generated rules on human schedule performance is important. It does, however, raise some knotty issues, for if this source of control is acknowledged, we must rethink some fundamental assumptions behavior analysts have made about the ways in which behavior is controlled.

Questions of similarities and differences between human and animal behavior abound. Some attribute much of the difference to procedural differences between human and animal research procedures (Perone et al., 1988), but others view the differences as being more fundamental. The role of rules and instructions in the schedule control of behavior is a critical issue for both basic researchers and applied behavior analysts. Similarly, the more general question of the relation between the controlling variables of animal and human operant behavior cuts to the quick of the relevance of basic research in the experimental analysis of behavior to applied problems.

There was a time in our early history when the study of reinforcement schedules could be considered a distinct area of research, and their elaboration and development was of general concern to many basic researchers. Although research designed to elucidate the effects of schedules of reinforcement still appears regularly in the *Journal of the Experimental Analysis of Behavior,* schedule research is more often conceptualized around other problems than those posed by the reinforcement schedule per se. For example, Hackenberg and Axtell (1993) used a complex schedule to analyze the effects of diminishing returns on behavior, and several investigators have used different schedules as a way of studying problems related to behavioral history. Despite the changed role of schedules in basic research, reinforcement schedules are woven deeply into the fabric of the experimental analysis of behavior. In applied behavior analysis, reinforcement schedules have not sustained the degree of interest that they have among basic researchers. Nonetheless, we hope that our discussion will bring applied behavior analysts to realize that "a student of any problem in psychology . . . ignores the consequences of the precise scheduling arrangements of his experiments [or, we would add, applications] at his peril" (Dews, 1963, p. 148).

REFERENCES

Alleman, H. D., & Platt, J. R. (1973). Differential reinforcement of interresponse times with controlled probability of response per reinforcement. *Learning and Motivation, 4,* 40–73.

Baer, D. M. (1977). Perhaps it would be better not to know everything. *Journal of Applied Behavior Analysis, 10,* 167–172.

Baer, D. M., Wolf, M. M., & Risley, T. R. (1968). Some current dimensions of applied behavior analysis. *Journal of Applied Behavior Analysis, 1,* 91–97.

Baron, A., & Leinenweber, A. (1995). Effects of a variable-ratio conditioning history on sensitivity to fixed-interval contingencies in rats. *Journal of the Experimental Analysis of Behavior, 63,* 97–110.

Baum, W. M. (1973). The correlation-based law of effect. *Journal of the Experimental Analysis of Behavior, 20,* 137–153.

Baum, W. M. (1989). Quantitative prediction and molar description of the environment. *The Behavior Analyst, 12,* 167–176.

Bradshaw, C. M., Szabadi, E., & Bevan, P. (1976). Behavior of humans in variable-interval schedules of reinforcement. *Journal of the Experimental Analysis of Behavior, 26,* 135–141.

Bradshaw, C. M., Szabadi, E., & Bevan, P. (1977). Effect of punishment on human variable-interval performance. *Journal of the Experimental Analysis of Behavior, 27,* 275–279.

Bradshaw, C. M., Szabadi, E., & Bevan, P. (1979). The effect of punishment on free-operant choice behavior in humans. *Journal of the Experimental Analysis of Behavior, 31,* 71–81.

Catania, A. C. (1992). *Learning* (3rd ed.). New York: Prentice Hall.

Catania, A. C., Matthews, B. A., & Shimoff, E. (1982). Instructed versus shaped human verbal behavior: Interactions with nonverbal responding. *Journal of the Experimental Analysis of Behavior, 38,* 233–248.

Charnov, E. L. (1976). Optimal foraging: The marginal value theorem. *Theoretical Population Biology, 9,* 129–136.

Darwin, C. (1964). *On the origin of species.* Cambridge, MA: Harvard University Press. (Original work published 1859)

Deacon, J. R., & Konarski, E. A., Jr. (1987). Correspondence training: An example of rule-governed behavior? *Journal of Applied Behavior Analysis, 20,* 391–400.

Dews, P. B. (1963). Behavioral effects of drugs. In S. M. Farber & R. H. L. Wilson (Eds.), *Conflict and creativity* (pp. 138–153). New York: McGraw Hill.

Dougherty, D. M., Cherek, D. R., & Roache, J. D. (1994). The effects of smoked marijuana on progressive-interval schedule performance in humans. *Journal of the Experimental Analysis of Behavior, 62,* 73–87.

Eckerman, D. A., Hienz, R. D., Stern, S., & Kowlowitz, V. (1980). Shaping the location of a pigeon's peck: Effect of rate and size of shaping steps. *Journal of the Experimental Analysis of Behavior, 33,* 299–310.

Ferster, C. B., & Skinner, B. F. (1957). *Schedules of reinforcement.* New York: Appleton-Century-Crofts.

Freeman, T. J., & Lattal, K. A. (1992). Stimulus control of behavioral history. *Journal of the Experimental Analysis of Behavior, 57,* 5–15.

Galbicka, G. (1994). Shaping in the 21st century: Moving percentile schedules into applied settings. *Journal of Applied Behavior Analysis, 27,* 739–760.

Galizio, M. (1979). Contingency-shaped and rule-governed behavior: Instructional control of human loss avoidance. *Journal of the Experimental Analysis of Behavior, 31,* 53–70.

Hackenberg, T. D., & Axtell, S. A. M. (1993). Humans' choices in situations of time-based diminishing returns. *Journal of the Experimental Analysis of Behavior, 59,* 445–470.

Hackenberg, T. D., & Joker, V. R. (1994). Instructional versus schedule control of humans' choices in situations of diminishing returns. *Journal of the Experimental Analysis of Behavior, 62,* 367–383.

Hanna, E. S., Blackman, E. E., & Todorov, J. C. (1992). Stimulus effects on concurrent performance in transition. *Journal of the Experimental Analysis of Behavior, 58,* 335–347.

Harzem, P. (1969). Temporal discrimination. In R. M. Gilbert & N. S. Sutherland (Eds.), *Animal discrimination learning* (pp. 299–334). New York: Academic Press.

Hayes, S. C., Brownstein, A. J., Zettle, R. D., Rosenfarb, I., & Korn, Z. (1986). Rule-governed behavior and sensitivity to changing consequences of responding. *Journal of the Experimental Analysis of Behavior, 45,* 237–256.

Hodos, W. (1961). Progressive ratio as a measure of reward strength. *Science, 134,* 943–944.

Horne, P. J., & Lowe, C. F. (1993). Determinants of human performance on concurrent schedules. *Journal of the Experimental Analysis of Behavior, 59,* 29–60.

Hyten, C., & Reilly, M. P. (1992). The renaissance of the experimental analysis of human behavior. *The Behavior Analyst, 15,* 109–114.

Israel, A. C. (1978). Some thoughts on correspondence between saying and doing. *Journal of Applied Behavior Analysis, 11,* 271–276.

Iwata, B. A. (1987). Negative reinforcement in applied behavior analysis: An emerging technology. *Journal of Applied Behavior Analysis, 20,* 361–378.

Iwata, B. A. (1988). The development and adoption of controversial default technologies. *The Behavior Analyst, 11,* 149–157.

Iwata, B. A., Dorsey, M. F., Slifer, I. J., Bauman, K. E., & Richman, G. S. (1994). Toward a functional analysis of self-injury. *Journal of Applied Behavior Analysis, 27,* 197–209. (Reprinted from *Analysis and Intervention in Developmental Disabilities, 2,* 3–20, 1982)

Jacobs, E. A., & Hackenberg, T. D. (1996). Humans' choices in situations of time-based diminishing returns: Effects of fixed-interval duration and progressive-interval step size. *Journal of the Experimental Analysis of Behavior, 65,* 5–19.

Keesey, R. E., & Goldstein, M. D. (1968). Use of progressive fixed ratio procedures in the assessment of ICS reinforcement. *Journal of the Experimental Analysis of Behavior, 11,* 293–301.

Kuch, D. O., & Platt, J. R. (1976). Reinforcement rate and interresponse time differentiation. *Journal of the Experimental Analysis of Behavior, 26,* 471–486.

Lattal, K. A. (1991). Scheduling positive reinforcers. In I. H. Iversen & K. A. Lattal (Eds.), *Techniques in the behavioral and neural sciences: Vol. 6. Experimental analysis of behavior* (Part 1, pp. 87–134). Amsterdam: Elsevier.

Lattal, K. A. (1995). Contingency and behavior analysis. *The Behavior Analyst, 18,* 209–224.

Lattal, K. A., & Poling, A. D. (1981). Describing response-event relations: Babel revisited. *The Behavior Analyst, 4,* 143-152.

Lattal, K. A., Reilly, M. P., & Kohn, J. P. (1996). *Separating temporal and response requirements for reinforcement in progressive schedules.* Manuscript submitted for publication.

Lea, S. E. G. (1976). Titration of schedule parameters by pigeons. *Journal of the Experimental Analysis of Behavior, 25,* 43–54.

LeFrancois, J. R., & Metzger, B. (1993). Low-response-rate conditioning history and fixed-interval responding in rats. *Journal of the Experimental Analysis of Behavior, 59,* 543–549.

Lerman, D. C., Iwata, B. A., Smith, R. G., Zarcone, J. R., & Vollmer, T. R. (1994). Transfer of behavioral function as a contributing factor in treatment relapse. *Journal of Applied Behavior Analysis, 27,* 357–370.

Lovaas, O. I. (1993). The development of a treatment research project for developmentally disabled and autistic children. *Journal of Applied Behavior Analysis, 26,* 617–630.

Mace, F. C., Hock, M. L., Lalli, J. S., West, B. J., Belfiore, P., Pinter, E., & Brown, D. K. (1988). Behavioral momentum in the treatment of noncompliance. *Journal of Applied Behavior Analysis, 21,* 123–141.

Mace, F. C., Lalli, J. S., Shea, M. C., Lalli, E. P., West, B. J., Roberts, M., & Nevin, J. A. (1990). The momentum of human behavior in a natural setting. *Journal of the Experimental Analysis of Behavior, 54,* 163–172.

Mace, F. C., Neef, N. A., Shade, D., & Mauro, B. C. (1994). Limited matching on concurrent-schedule reinforcement of academic behavior. *Journal of Applied Behavior Analysis, 27,* 585–596.

McDowell, J. J. (1988). Matching theory in natural human environments. *The Behavior Analyst, 11,* 95–109.

Meichenbaum, D., & Goodman, J. (1971). Training impulsive children to talk to themselves: A means of developing self-control. *Journal of Abnormal Psychology, 77,* 115–126.

Morse, W. H., & Kelleher, R. T. (1977). Determinants of reinforcement and punishment. In W. K. Honig & J. E. R. Staddon (Eds.), *Handbook of operant behavior* (pp. 174–200). New York: Prentice Hall.

Neef, N. A., Mace, F. C., & Shade, D. (1993). Impulsivity in students with serious emotional disturbance: The interactive effects of reinforcer rate, delay, and quality. *Journal of Applied Behavior Analysis, 26,* 37–52.

Neef, N. A., Mace, F. C., Shea, M., & Shade, D. (1992). Effects of reinforcer rate and reinforcer quality on time allocation: Application of matching theory to educational settings. *Journal of Applied Behavior Analysis, 25,* 691–699.

Neef, N. A., Shafer, M. S., Egel, A. L., Cataldo, M. F., & Parrish, J. M. (1983). The class specific effects of compliance training with "do" and "don't" requests: Analogue analysis and classroom application. *Journal of Applied Behavior Analysis, 16,* 81–99.

Nevin, J. A. (1984). Quantitative analysis. *Journal of the Experimental Analysis of Behavior, 42,* 421–434.

Nevin, J. A., Mandell, C., & Atak, J. R. (1983). The analysis of behavioral momentum. *Journal of the Experimental Analysis of Behavior, 39,* 49–59.

Parrish, J. M., Cataldo, M. F., Kolko, D. J., Neef, N. A., & Egel, A. L. (1986). Experimental analysis of response covariation among compliant and inappropriate behaviors. *Journal of Applied Behavior Analysis, 19,* 241–254.

Peele, D. B., Casey, J., & Silberberg, A. (1984). Primacy of interresponse-time reinforcement in accounting for rate differences under variable-ratio and variable-interval schedules. *Journal of Experimental Psychology: Animal Behavior Processes, 10,* 149–167.

Perone, M., Galizio, M., & Baron, A. (1988). The relevance of animal-based principles in the laboratory study of human operant conditioning. In G. Davey & C. Cullen (Eds.), *Human operant conditioning and behavior modification* (pp. 59–85). London: Wiley & Sons.

Rosenfarb, I. S., Newland, M. C., Brannon, S. E., & Howey, D. S. (1992). Effects of self-generated rules on the development of schedule-controlled behavior. *Journal of the Experimental Analysis of Behavior, 58,* 107–121.

Shull, R. L. (1991). Mathematical description of operant behavior: An introduction. In I. H. Iversen & K. A. Lattal (Eds.), *Techniques in the behavioral and neural sciences: Vol. 6. Experimental analysis of behavior* (Part 2, pp. 243–282). Amsterdam: Elsevier.

Sidman, M. (1960). *Tactics of scientific research.* New York: Basic Books.

Stewart, W. J. (1975). Progressive reinforcement schedules: A review and evaluation. *Australian Journal of Psychology, 27,* 9–22.

Thompson, D. M. (1972). Enhancement of progressive ratio performance by chlordiazepoxide and phenobarbital. *Journal of the Experimental Analysis of Behavior, 18,* 287–293.

Wanchisen, B. A., Tatham, T. A., & Mooney, S. E. (1989). Variable-ratio conditioning history produces high- and low-rate fixed-interval performance in rats. *Journal of the Experimental Analysis of Behavior, 52,* 167–179.

Weiss, B., & Laties, V. (1959). Titration behavior on various fractional escape programs. *Journal of the Experimental Analysis of Behavior, 2,* 227–248.

Williams, B. A. (1983). Revising the principle of reinforcement. *Behaviorism, 11,* 63–85.

Wulfert, E., Greenway, D. E., Farkas, P., Hayes, S. C., & Dougher, M. J. (1994). Correlation between self-reported rigidity and rule-governed insensitivity to operant contingencies. *Journal of Applied Behavior Analysis, 27,* 659–671.

Zeiler, M. D. (1977). Schedules of reinforcement: The controlling variables. In W. K. Honig & J. E. R. Staddon (Eds.), *Handbook of operant behavior* (pp. 201–232). New York: Prentice Hall.

Zeiler, M. D. (1984). Reinforcement schedules: The sleeping giant. *Journal of the Experimental Analysis of Behavior, 42,* 485–493.

Received February 6, 1996
Initial editorial decision February 8, 1996
Final acceptance February 16, 1996
Action Editor, David P. Wacker

JOURNAL OF APPLIED BEHAVIOR ANALYSIS 1996, **29**, 345–382 NUMBER 3 (FALL 1996)

DEVELOPING A TECHNOLOGY FOR THE USE OF OPERANT EXTINCTION IN CLINICAL SETTINGS: AN EXAMINATION OF BASIC AND APPLIED RESEARCH

DOROTHEA C. LERMAN

JOHNS HOPKINS UNIVERSITY SCHOOL OF MEDICINE AND THE KENNEDY KRIEGER INSTITUTE

AND

BRIAN A. IWATA

THE UNIVERSITY OF FLORIDA

Extinction of operant behavior, which involves terminating the reinforcement contingency that maintains a response, is important to the development, generalization, and reduction of behavior in clinical settings. We review basic and applied research findings on variables that influence the direct and indirect effects of extinction and discuss the potential value of a general technology for the use of extinction. We suggest that current research findings are not sufficient for the development of a comprehensive, applied technology of extinction and provide extensive guidelines for further studies on factors that may affect the course of extinction in clinical settings.

DESCRIPTORS: extinction, behavior disorders, reinforcement

Extinction of operant behavior involves terminating the reinforcement contingency that maintains a response, which results in a reduction in the behavior's occurrence over time.[1] Results of basic research (e.g., Ferster & Skinner, 1957; Skinner, 1938) have revealed much about its direct and indirect effects, including a number of variables that influence the general course of responding during extinction. These findings have important implications for the use of extinction in applied settings, in which behavior is often acquired and eliminated through procedures involving extinction. In fact, the efficacy of many procedures used as treatment for severe behavior disorders may depend on the inclusion of extinction (e.g., W. Fisher et al., 1993; Mazaleski, Iwata, Vollmer, Zarcone, & Smith, 1993; Wacker at al., 1990; Zarcone, Iwata, Smith, Mazaleski, & Lerman, 1994).

Recent improvements in methodologies for identifying the reinforcement contingencies that maintain a number of behavior disorders have facilitated the use of extinction in applied settings. However, further progress in the treatment of behavior disorders, as well as in the development of adaptive behavior, could be achieved through the development of a comprehensive, general technology for the use of extinction. The objective of this paper is to extend the most recent review on the use of extinction to treat behavior disorders (Ducharme & Van Houten, 1994) by providing a broader overview of basic research findings; discussing the relevance of extinction to the acquisition, main-

We thank Marc Branch, Timothy Hackenberg, Cecil Mercer, and Betty Capaldi for their helpful comments on an earlier draft of this manuscript.

Reprints may be obtained from Dorothea C. Lerman, Department of Behavioral Psychology, Triad Technology Bldg., 333 Cassell Drive, Suite 4200, Baltimore, Maryland 21224.

[1] Although there is some disagreement as to whether extinction involves termination of the response–reinforcer contingency per se versus termination of the contingency plus nondelivery of the reinforcer (Catania, 1992; Rescorla & Skucy, 1969), the majority of studies reviewed in this paper used the latter procedure to examine extinction. Thus, for the purposes of this paper, we consider extinction to include both termination of the contingency and nondelivery of the reinforcer.

tenance, and generalization of behavior; and presenting detailed suggestions for future research.

At first glance, the voluminous basic literature on extinction appears to provide a solid foundation for technological development; in fact, many texts and chapters on application cite basic research findings when discussing extinction (e.g., Grant & Evans, 1994; Kazdin, 1994). However, a careful examination of this research indicates that it may not provide a sufficient basis for direct translation into an applied technology. Although hundreds of basic studies on extinction have been conducted during the past 5 decades, most were designed to support or refute particular theoretical positions and, as a result, did not thoroughly examine variables relevant to application. In fact, a number of important research findings appeared to depend on the use of specific laboratory preparations. For these reasons, translation of basic findings into an applied technology of extinction requires both replication with and extension to human behavior in clinical settings.

The need for additional research on extinction has gone relatively unnoticed in applied behavior analysis. Studies have focused almost exclusively on the utility of extinction in treating maladaptive behavior, often ignoring more detailed but equally practical examinations of the basic process. In particular, the role of extinction in the development (e.g., response shaping) and generalization of adaptive behavior has received little attention in applied research. The lack of applied research on extinction may be due, at least in part, to the seemingly comprehensive collection of basic research studies and the assumption that results of these studies are completely generalizable to applied problems.

Initially, research on the use of extinction to treat behavior disorders was impeded by difficulties in identifying the source of reinforcement to be withheld. Prior to the development of assessment procedures based on functional analysis methodology, the design and implementation of extinction as treatment for problem behavior often emphasized procedural form (e.g., ignoring inappropriate behavior) rather than function (i.e., withholding maintaining reinforcers). These practices most likely resulted in numerous investigations of procedures erroneously described as extinction because they involved withholding irrelevant reinforcers while failing to disrupt the existing contingency between responding and reinforcement. Procedural variations of extinction that are not matched to behavioral function (e.g., ignoring behavior that is not maintained by attention) are generally ineffective in reducing maladaptive behavior, whereas properly designed extinction procedures can produce robust treatment effects (Iwata, Pace, Cowdery, & Miltenberger, 1994; Repp, Felce, & Barton, 1988). Admonitions against the use of extinction, still commonly found in some textbooks and articles on the treatment of problem behavior (e.g., LaVigna & Donnellan, 1986), may be based on the results of incorrect applications of extinction that occurred in early applied work (for reviews of this literature, see Ducharme & Van Houten, 1994; W. Johnson & Baumeister, 1981). Advances in functional analysis technology during the past 10 years have permitted a clearer distinction between procedural and functional variations of extinction, which has led to more effective treatment (e.g., Iwata et al., 1994).

CHARACTERISTICS OF RESPONDING DURING EXTINCTION

Basic research studies have delineated several characteristics of behavior exposed to extinction, including the extinction burst, general pattern of responding, indirect effects, spontaneous recovery, and disinhibition. Although some of these characteristics have also been demonstrated in applied research, few studies have systematically examined these phenomena. Because most of these characteristics can be altered by changes in variables associated with the acquisition, maintenance, and extinction of behavior (e.g., reinforcement schedules, intertrial intervals), the generality of basic findings to behavior in applied settings may be limited.

Extinction Burst

Basic (Nonclinical) Research

Results of basic research with both humans and nonhumans indicate that responding during extinction is often characterized by an initial increase in response frequency (Alessandri, Sullivan, & Lewis, 1990), duration (Margulies, 1961), amplitude (Holton, 1961), and variability (Antonitis, 1951). Initial increases in the variability of a response during extinction can occur in terms of its duration (Trotter, 1957), location (Antonitis, 1951), interresponse time (Millenson & Hurwitz, 1961), latency (Stebbins & Lanson, 1962), and amplitude (Morris, 1968). Extinction has also been associated with an increase in the variability of response sequences (e.g., Schwartz, 1980, 1981, 1982). For example, Schwartz (1982) demonstrated that college students who received points (exchangeable for money) for pressing two keys in any order exhibited a particular response sequence on almost every trial by the end of acquisition training. However, exposure to extinction was immediately associated with a decrease in subjects' dominant response sequences and an increase in the number of novel sequences.

Applied Research and Implications

The extinction burst is the most frequently noted characteristic of extinction in applied texts and literature reviews (e.g., Ducharme & Van Houten, 1994; Kazdin, 1994; Martin & Pear, 1992) and has been observed as a temporary increase in response frequency in a number of clinical studies (e.g., France & Hudson, 1990; Iwata, Pace, Kalsher, Cowdery, & Cataldo, 1990; Laws, Brown, Epstein, & Hocking, 1971; Neisworth & Moore, 1972; Salend & Meddaugh, 1985). In nearly all of these cases, the burst was relatively brief (lasting a few sessions) and caused no notable problems. Clinicians are often cautioned to expect bursting during treatment (e.g., Cooper, Heron, & Heward, 1987; Drabman & Jarvie, 1977), advised about ways to ensure the safety of the individual and others while continuing treatment (e.g., Ducharme & Van Houten, 1994), and urged to implement alternative treatments when potential bursts are considered unmanageable (e.g., Benoit & Mayer, 1974). However, the extinction burst may not be as common as previously assumed. Lerman and Iwata (1995) recently examined the prevalence of the extinction burst in applied research by analyzing 113 sets of extinction data and found that initial increases in response frequency occurred in only 24% of the cases. Further studies should directly examine the extinction burst, particularly characteristics other than increases in response frequency (e.g., increases in amplitude and variability), the prevalence of bursts during the treatment of problem behavior, and the potential association of bursts with acquisition procedures that involve extinction (e.g., shaping and differential reinforcement).

Although most applied researchers have emphasized the negative aspects of bursting, extinction bursts might be desirable in certain situations. While establishing behavior via response shaping (i.e., differentially reinforcing successive approximations to a target response), extinction might induce the desired rates, amplitudes, or topographies of appropriate behavior. For example, withholding reinforcement for appropriate behavior that occurs at a low amplitude (e.g., speech loudness) could induce instances of higher amplitude behavior, which then could be maintained through reinforcement. Several studies have examined the use of extinction to increase behavioral variability (e.g., Carr & Kologinsky, 1983; Duker & van Lent, 1991; Lalli, Zanolli, & Wohn, 1994). For example, Duker and van Lent increased the number of different gesture requests exhibited by 6 individuals with developmental disabilities by withholding reinforcement for high-rate requests. The experimenters first identified two or three requests that subjects exhibited most frequently during a baseline condition in which all gesture requests were reinforced. They then continued to reinforce all but these high-rate requests, and results demonstrated increases in different gesture requests for all subjects. During the treatment of problem behavior, extinction-induced variability may sometimes lead to increases in alternative, more appropriate responses, and clinicians should be prepared to detect and reinforce these appropriate behaviors as soon as they occur. Further studies should examine the practical aspects of extinction bursts during both the acquisition and the reduction of behavior.

General Course of Responding

Basic (Nonclinical) Research

With the exception of bursting, extinction produces a relatively gradual change in responding compared to that observed during the initial acquisition of the behavior (Skinner, 1938). However, reductions in response rate do not always follow a monotonic function; instead, individuals exposed to extinction tend to respond sporadically during the sessions, gradually pausing for longer periods of time (e.g., Herrick, 1965; Hurwitz, 1962; Warren & Brown, 1943). That is, they tend to allocate less and less time to the response, but when they engage in the behavior, they do so at rates similar to those in acquisition. Skinner (1933a, 1933b, 1938), who first noted this characteristic of extinction by describing the typical extinction curve as "wave like," speculated that these fluctuations were due to intervening emotional reactions, which eventually "adapt out" across the extinction period. However, Miller and Stevenson (1936), who obtained similar waves in the response curves of rats exposed to extinction of a runway response, found no relationship between these waves and measures of agitated (i.e., emotional) behavior.

Applied Research and Implications

Few applied studies have examined within-session patterns of responding during exposure to extinction. In a notable exception, Dorsey, Iwata, Reid, and Davis (1982) examined the response patterns of a subject's self-injurious behavior (SIB) that was effectively treated with the continuous application of protective equipment. Cumulative records of within-session responding, which showed the typical wave-like pattern of the extinction curves obtained in basic studies, suggested that the reduction in SIB was due to an extinction effect. Many texts and articles simply describe extinction as an extremely gradual reduction in behavior (e.g., W. Johnson & Baumeister, 1981; Miron, 1973; Romanczyk, Kistner, & Plienis, 1982) and recommend that extinction not be used as the sole intervention if rapid treatment effects are desired (e.g., Favell et al., 1982; R. D. Horner & Barton, 1980; Muttar, Peck, Whitlow, & Fraser, 1975). Results of many early studies supported the contention that extinction was a relatively inefficient treatment procedure (e.g., Duker, 1975; Jones, Simmons, & Frankel, 1974; Lovaas & Simmons, 1969; Wright, Brown, & Andrews, 1978). Jones et al. (1974), for example, found that the extinction of an autistic girl's SIB required more than 160 2-hr treatment sessions during which thousands of nonreinforced responses occurred. By contrast, data from other studies have shown fairly rapid extinction of problem behavior (e.g., Forehand, 1973; Iwata et al., 1990; Pinkston, Reese, LeBlanc, & Baer, 1973; Repp et al., 1988; Rincover, Cook, Peoples, & Packard, 1979). These numerous exceptions suggest that the inefficiency of extinction as treatment for severe behavior disorders may be overemphasized. For example, Iwata et al. (1990) observed that the SIB of 3 subjects was decreased to near-zero levels by the fifth 15-min session of extinction. It is possible that specific factors present during the acquisition, maintenance, or extinction of behavior are responsible for the varied resistance to extinction found in applied research. These variables, which will be described in some detail, have received surprisingly little attention in the literature.

Indirect Effects

Basic (Nonclinical) Research

Several apparent side effects of extinction have been identified in both human and nonhuman subjects. These include increases in other behaviors, such as aggression and previously learned responses, and increases in the target behavior in contexts unassociated with extinction.

Aggression. An increase in aggressive responses (called *extinction-induced aggression*) has been observed during extinction following contingent or noncontingent reinforcement (e.g., Azrin, Hutchinson, & Hake, 1966; Frederiksen & Peterson, 1974; J. F. Kelly & Hake, 1970; Todd, Morris, & Fenza, 1989), as well as during discrimination learning (Rilling, 1977). Researchers have suggested that removal of reinforcement constitutes an aversive event, which elicits an emotional reaction in the form of aggression similar to that seen in the presence of shock, intense heat, and physical blows (Azrin et al., 1966).

Levels of extinction-induced aggression generally are highest at the beginning of the extinction period (often following an initial burst in the frequency of the previously reinforced response) and gradually decrease across the extinction session (Azrin et al., 1966; Thompson & Bloom, 1966; Todd et al., 1989). In addition, this indirect effect can continue to occur despite repeated exposure to alternating periods of reinforcement and extinction.

Agitated or emotional behavior. Extinction also has been associated with an increase in nonaggressive responses, often called *agitated behaviors* (e.g., Zeiler, 1971). In nonhumans, these behaviors include escape responses (Davis & Donenfeld, 1967); increases in general activity, such as sniffing, ambulating, and whisker cleaning (e.g., Gallup & Altomari, 1969); and increases in responses that are topographically similar to those undergoing extinction (I. Mackintosh, 1955). This increase in activity has been interpreted as frustration associated with exposure to extinction rather than as the resurgence of previously reinforced behavior. In humans, this behavior includes crying, pouting, fussing, rocking, and leaving or attempting to escape the experimental situation (e.g., Baumeister & Forehand, 1971; Rovee-Collier & Capatides, 1979; Sullivan, Lewis, & Alessandri, 1992; Verplanck, 1955).

Previously reinforced responses. Few studies with nonhumans and no studies with humans have systematically examined the resurgence of previously reinforced behavior during extinction. Epstein (1983) followed the reinforcement and extinction of a pigeon's key-peck response with the reinforcement and extinction of an alternative, incompatible response (wing raising, turning). During extinction of the alternative response, the pigeons suddenly began to peck the key following a decrease in the frequency of the alternative response. Absence of responding on an available control key indicated that the resumption of responding was not the result of frustration (Amsel, 1958) or an increase in the variability of the behavior (Antonitis, 1951).

Behavioral contrast. Many studies with humans and nonhumans have shown a relation between extinction and a phenomenon called *behavioral contrast.* Exposure to extinction (or less favorable conditions of reinforcement) in the presence of one stimulus can lead to an increase in the occurrence of behavior in the presence of a different stimulus associated with continued reinforcement of the response. This occurs when the two schedules are available concurrently (Catania, 1969; Rachlin, 1973) or alternated successively (Reynolds, 1961). For example, studies have found that when a multiple variable-interval (VI) VI schedule is switched to a multiple extinction (EXT) VI schedule, the response rate in the altered component (EXT) decreases, and the response rate in the unaltered component (VI) increases (e.g., Fagen, 1979; McSweeney & Melville, 1993). This effect, called *positive contrast,* is relatively persistent across time. Although the amount of contrast is greatest when the time interval between components of a multiple schedule is small (N. Mackintosh, Little, & Lord, 1972), the effect has been obtained when the components are separated by as much as 23 hr (Bloomfield, 1967). Positive contrast has even been obtained with nonhumans when different reinforcing stimuli and different response topographies were associated with the two components of a multiple or concurrent schedule (e.g., Beninger & Kendall, 1975; Premack, 1969).

Applied Research and Implications

Despite the potential problems associated with the use of extinction in applied settings, few studies have examined its varied indirect effects, and the prevalence of effects such as extinction-induced aggression and behavioral contrast is unknown. Some have suggested that, due to the potential occurrence of adverse indirect effects, extinction should not be used as treatment for severe behavior disorders (e.g., LaVigna & Donnellan, 1986). However, such admonitions are premature in the absence of thorough investigations on the prevalence and severity of these problems. Although several studies that have implemented extinction during acquisition procedures or as treatment for problem behavior have anecdotally noted increases in inappropriate behavior, such as aggression (e.g., Herbert, Pinkston, Cordua, & Jackson, 1973; Rekers & Lovaas, 1974; P. Scott, Burton, & Yarrow, 1967), crying (E. Fisher, 1979), complaining (McDowell, Nunn, & McCutcheon, 1969), and leaving or requesting to leave the experimental setting (e.g., Lambert, 1975), few studies have presented data that clearly link these types of behavior with exposure to extinction. Three notable exceptions in the applied literature include Goh and Iwata (1994), who demonstrated increases in aggression during extinction of SIB; Lovaas, Freitag, Gold, and Kassorla (1965), who obtained increases in SIB during extinction of appropriate behavior (clapping and singing); and Sajwaj, Twardosz, and Burke (1972), who showed that increases in both appropriate and inappropriate behaviors (cooperative play and disruption) were associated with removal of reinforcement for student–teacher interactions. These indirect effects could be attributed to either the occurrence of extinction-induced frustration behavior or the resurgence of previously reinforced behavior. In each of the three studies, the inappropriate behavior was eliminated with continued exposure to extinction (Goh & Iwata, 1994; Lovaas et al., 1965) or the application of an additional treatment procedure (Sajwaj et al., 1972). It is somewhat surprising that extinction-induced aggression, which is usually listed among the disadvantages of extinction in texts and articles on application, has rarely been reported in applied research.

Another potential indirect effect of extinction, behavioral contrast, has received even less attention in the applied literature. Results of basic research suggest that problem behavior exposed to extinction in only some contexts (e.g., in certain settings or with certain therapists) might worsen in contexts associated with continued reinforcement of the response, even if the contexts are separated by large amounts of time (Bloomfield, 1967). The possibility of contrast effects is particularly important because extinction often is not implemented in all situations. For example, teachers sometimes implement treatment for problem behavior at school, even though caregivers or parents are unwilling or unable to implement the procedure at home. Results of several studies show some evidence of contrast effects during the treatment of problem behavior (Forehand et al., 1974; S. Johnson, Bolstad, & Lobitz, 1976; J. A. Kelly & Drabman, 1977; Wahler, 1975). However, it is unclear if extinction was included in any of these treatment procedures. Koegel, Egel, and Williams (1980), for example, implemented a time-out procedure to reduce an autistic child's aggression at school. The child was placed in isolation time-out for 20 s contingent on each occurrence of aggression on the school playground. Findings showed that treatment-related reductions in aggression at school were associated with increases in aggression at a day-care center, where the time-out procedure was not implemented. Additional research is necessary to determine if extinction is associated with behavioral contrast in applied settings, the characteristics of contrast effects (e.g., persistence across time), and the specific factors responsible for the occurrence of such effects (Gross & Drabman, 1981).

Although clinicians and caregivers should be wary of various indirect effects when implementing extinction during the acquisition and reduction of behavior, these effects sometimes may be desirable, particularly if they are associated with increases in appropriate behavior (e.g., France & Hudson, 1990; Sajwaj et al., 1972). Various strategies to promote such positive indirect effects could be incorporated into an extinction technology. Prior to extinguishing problem behavior, for example, caregivers could reinforce an alternative response that occurs consistently, if not frequently, using the same consequence that maintains the problem behavior. This procedure might increase the efficacy of subsequent treatment (e.g., extinction combined with differential reinforcement of alternative behavior [DRA]) if it results in the resurgence of the previously reinforced alternative response. As another example, teachers might induce higher frequencies of a child's appropriate behavior (e.g., saying "please" before a request) that occurs rarely at school but frequently at home by asking the parent to terminate reinforcement for the behavior at home. The potential occurrence of these desirable indirect effects, however, is hypothetical in the absence of supportive research data.

Spontaneous Recovery

Basic (Nonclinical) Research

After extinction of a behavior appears to be completed (i.e., it does not occur for a specified period of time), responding can temporarily reappear. Such spontaneous recovery can occur in both humans and nonhumans from a few minutes (e.g., Sheppard, 1969) to more than 1 month (Youtz, 1938) following extinction. Although as much as 50% of the initial response strength may return during the first instance of spontaneous recovery, this amount appears to depend on particular characteristics of acquisition and the length of time that passes between the last extinction session and the test for recovery (Kimble, 1961). Continued exposure to extinction during periods of spontaneous recovery results in similar but smaller extinction curves relative to the original response curve (Skinner, 1938). This phenomenon, which has not been found to occur with differential reinforcement of other behavior (DRO) (Topping & Ford, 1974; Zeiler, 1971) or punishment (Holz & Azrin, 1963), appears to be exclusively associated with extinction.

Applied Research and Implications

Detailed investigations of the characteristics and prevalence of spontaneous recovery in applied settings are nonexistent. Although spontaneous recovery is frequently described in texts and reviews (e.g., Ducharme & Van Houten, 1994; Kazdin, 1994; Malott, Whaley, & Malott, 1991; Martin & Pear, 1992), few studies have reported its occurrence (e.g., Forehand, 1973; Jones et al., 1974; Wolf, Birnbrauer, Williams, & Lawler, 1965). For example, C. Williams (1959) and Durand and Mindell (1990) noted the reoccurrence of infants' bedtime tantrums after the parents successfully extinguished the behavior. However, recovery of behavior in both studies was associated with the presence of an adult who had not previously implemented extinction, suggesting that the tantrums reoccurred because treatment effects failed to generalize across caregivers. Few studies that reported the reoccurrence of behavior after successful treatment have provided information about events that occurred prior to or following instances of this recovery. Thus, it is unclear if these cases actually involved spontaneous recovery as demonstrated in basic research or if other variables (e.g., lack of generalization, program inconsistency) could account for treatment relapse.

Although most authors emphasize the potential occurrence of spontaneous recovery during treatment of inappropriate behavior, recovery could also be problematic during acquisition procedures. For example, topographies of behavior that previously met the reinforcement criterion during response shaping could reappear and disrupt performance. Potential problems associated with spontaneous recovery in applied settings should be examined in future research.

Disinhibition

Basic (Nonclinical) Research

In a manner somewhat similar to spontaneous recovery, responding during extinction can temporarily increase when a novel (extraneous) stimulus is introduced into the setting. Stimuli that have occasioned this increase in responding (called *disinhibition*) include buzzers, lights, white noise, and electric shock (e.g., Baumeister & Hawkins, 1966; Brimer, 1970a; Horns & Heron, 1940). Disinhibition is relatively transient and has not been observed consistently with either humans or nonhumans (cf. Skinner, 1936; Spradlin, Fixsen, & Girardeau, 1969; Warren & Brown, 1943). However, its occurrence may depend on a number of factors, including the type (Horns & Heron, 1940), duration (Brimer, 1970a), and novelty (Yamaguchi & Ladioray, 1962) of the stimulus and the length of time the behavior has been exposed to extinction prior to the introduction of the stimulus (Brimer, 1970a). Research on disinhibition is relatively limited, and conditions that reliably produce this phenomenon have not yet been identified.

Applied Research and Implications

Disinhibition is rarely discussed in texts or articles on application, and no studies have reported its occurrence. Although results of basic research suggest that some types of stimuli produce disinhibition, this phenomenon may not be prevalent in applied settings. Future studies should attempt to determine which stimuli (if any) produce disinhibition and if it occurs consistently across subjects in particular situations. Although transient increases in behavior characteristic of disinhibition may be relatively innocuous, caregivers may want to limit an individual's exposure to unusual or novel stimuli if disinhibition is found to be a common phenomenon during the acquisition and reduction of behavior. At the least, caregivers should be prepared for possible increases in extinguished behavior when extraneous stimuli (e.g., loud noises, new staff members) are introduced into the setting.

DETERMINANTS OF BEHAVIORAL ACQUISITION AND MAINTENANCE THAT INFLUENCE RESPONDING DURING EXTINCTION

Results of basic research indicate that a number of variables that are present during the acquisition or maintenance of behavior can influence the extinction process. These factors include amount, magnitude, delay, and schedule of reinforcement; variation in the conditions associated with acquisition and maintenance (e.g., presence of certain environmental stimuli); and exposure to aversive stimulation. As part of an extinction technology, these variables could be manipulated prior to extinction to improve the efficacy of treatment aimed at both behavioral acquisition and reduction. For example, factors that minimize resistance to extinction, response bursts, or spontaneous recovery could be incorporated into treatment programs for problem behavior. This strategy would also be useful when reinforcing and extinguishing appropriate behavior during response shaping procedures. Alternatively, variables that increase resistance could be manipulated to enhance response maintenance and stimulus generalization, which can be weakened by extinction effects. Techniques that comprise the current generalization technology (see Stokes & Baer, 1977, for a review) already incorporate some of these variables (e.g., delayed reinforcement, variable acquisition conditions), suggesting that this technology could be expanded to include a variety of factors that alter resistance to extinction. In fact, a similar mechanism may account for both resistance to extinction and the occurrence of certain types of generalization. In basic research, the effects of variables on resistance often have been explained in terms of the similarity between reinforcement and extinction conditions (N. Mackintosh, 1974), or the extent to which the individual can discriminate the transition from reinforcement to extinction. In a similar manner, articles on application often emphasize the use of procedures designed to alter discrimination or stimulus control when generalization across nontraining conditions (stimulus generalization) or time (maintenance) is desired (Stokes & Baer, 1977; Stokes & Osnes, 1988).

Although these variables appear to have important implications for the acquisition, maintenance, generalization, and reduction of behavior, few applied studies have directly examined their effects on responding during extinction. Such investigations are imperative due to the limited generality of basic research findings and the complexity of variables that tend to operate in the natural environment. Most applied strategies involve manipulating preexisting variables prior to extinction, an operation that has been examined infrequently in basic studies. In addition, the effects of these variables on many characteristics of extinction, including response bursting, extinction-induced aggression, and spontaneous recovery, have received limited attention in basic research.

Number of Reinforcers

Basic (Nonclinical) Research

Studies with humans and nonhumans have shown that more reinforcers or trial presentations may alter the course of extinction in several ways. First, lengthier acquisition training or the presentation of response-independent reinforcers during acquisition has been found to increase resistance to extinction (e.g., Nevin, Tota, Torquato, & Shull, 1990; Perin, 1942; Siegel & Foshee, 1953). Although these findings generally suggest that the increase in resistance does not continue beyond 100 reinforcers (i.e., the increase in resistance reaches an asymptote), some studies have obtained increases in resistance with up to 1,000 reinforcers (e.g., Furomoto, 1971).[2]

Reinforcement number also may affect the occurrence and intensity of the extinction burst, behavioral contrast, spontaneous recovery, and disinhibition. Results of several studies suggest that exposure to a larger number of reinforcers during acquisition may increase the magnitude of the extinction burst (e.g., Holton, 1961), spontaneous recovery (e.g., Homme, 1956), and disinhibition (e.g., Brimer, 1970b), but may decrease the likelihood of contrast effects (Gutman, 1978).

Applied Research and Implications

The effects of reinforcement number on responding during extinction are particularly relevant in applied settings, where inappropriate behavior often has a long history of reinforcement. Although many texts and articles on application have stated that resistance to extinction will increase as the number of reinforcers (or length of time a behavior has been reinforced) increases (e.g., Cooper et al., 1987; Grant & Evans, 1994; Kazdin, 1994; Mercer & Snell, 1977), no studies have examined this variable, and the generality of basic research findings is somewhat limited. In particular, the specific reinforcement parameters compared in most basic studies (e.g., 50 vs. 100 reinforcers; 5-min vs. 15-min acquisition phases) may not be relevant to responses that have been reinforced for several months or even years. In fact, results of basic research indicate that resistance may fail to change beyond a certain number of reinforcers. For example, behavior that has been maintained for several years may be no more resistant to extinction than behavior that has been maintained for several weeks.

Future studies should examine the effects of reinforcement number by manipulating the length of acquisition or maintenance phases, as well as the presentation of additional reinforcement (either noncontingently or for alternative responses) during maintenance. Results of a study by Nevin et al. (1990) suggest that additional reinforcement (e.g., DRA, noncontingent reinforcement [NCR]) during response maintenance can lead to an increase in resistance to extinction. This finding has an important applied implication because clinicians sometimes implement treatment programs for problem behavior without first identifying and terminating the reinforcement contingency that maintains the behavior. Such a strategy (i.e., implementing DRO, DRA, or NCR without extinction) is not only unlikely to produce substantial treatment effects (cf. Mazaleski et al., 1993) but may produce further treatment difficulties if the problem behavior is subsequently exposed to extinction.

If research findings suggest that reinforcement number is positively related to resistance across a broad range of parameters, behavior disorders should be exposed to extinction in a timely manner, and treatment with DRO, DRA, or NCR should not be implemented prior to extinction. During response shaping, changes in the reinforcement criteria should proceed fairly rapidly so

[2] In some cases, resistance to extinction may actually decrease with extended acquisition training, a phenomenon called the *overtraining extinction effect* (see N. Mackintosh, 1974, and Sperling, 1965, for reviews). This effect may have limited relevance to application because it has been demonstrated with temporal measures of responding only (i.e., latency, duration, or speed).

that resistance to extinction does not hinder the acquisition of new response topographies. Alternatively, reinforcement number could be manipulated when increased resistance to extinction is the desired outcome. For example, acquisition programs for adaptive behavior could be conducted during extended training conditions to promote response maintenance and stimulus generalization. In addition, maintenance conditions could be combined with procedures that involve delivery of additional reinforcement (e.g., NCR, DRA). Although these alternative sources of reinforcement probably would decrease response rates during acquisition, they might in turn enhance response persistence (cf. Nevin et al., 1990). The effects of reinforcement number on other characteristics of extinction (e.g., bursting, behavioral contrast, spontaneous recovery) should also be examined in future studies and the results incorporated into the developing extinction technology.

Magnitude of Reinforcement

Basic (Nonclinical) Research

Results of basic research with humans and nonhumans suggest that reinforcement magnitude during acquisition or maintenance conditions can influence resistance to extinction. However, the precise nature of this relationship appears to depend on the manner in which reinforcement magnitude is defined and altered. For example, increases in the number of food pellets or cigarettes or the weight of food have been inversely associated with resistance (e.g., Ellis, 1962; Lamberth & Dyck, 1972; Skjoldager, Pierre, & Mittleman, 1993; Wagner, 1961). That is, smaller reinforcement magnitudes produced more resistance to extinction than larger magnitudes.[3] By contrast, other studies in which reinforcer intensity (e.g., level of sucrose concentration in water) rather than its physical amount was manipulated reported that a larger reinforcement magnitude was associated with more resistance to extinction than was a smaller magnitude (e.g., Barnes & Tombaugh, 1970; Lewis & Duncan, 1957).

Applied Research and Implications

Many texts on application have suggested that the use of large reinforcement magnitudes during acquisition or maintenance increases resistance to extinction (e.g., Grant & Evans, 1994; Kazdin, 1994), although results of basic research in this area have been inconsistent. In fact, results of the only applied study in which responding during extinction was examined following different reinforcement magnitudes showed an inverse relationship between magnitude and resistance (E. Fisher, 1979). In this study, 13 psychiatric patients received either one token or five tokens for brushing teeth during weekly phases that were alternated with extinction phases in a reversal design. Results showed that 11 subjects exhibited more brushing during extinction after receiving the smaller magnitude of reinforcement (one token) than after receiving the larger magnitude (five tokens). The effect was demonstrated twice for each subject, with the larger reinforcement magnitude always presented prior to the smaller magnitude. Although this design failed to control for possible sequence effects, the author obtained consistent results across repeated presentations of reinforcement and extinction. These findings also replicate those of basic studies that defined reinforcement magnitude as the number of reinforcers delivered for each response.

Future studies should examine the effects of this variable on all characteristics of responding during extinction and assess the utility of altering reinforcement magnitude

[3] This relationship depends on the use of a continuous schedule of reinforcement during acquisition. The interaction between reinforcement schedule and reinforcement magnitude will be discussed below.

prior to extinction. This research should incorporate a variety of behaviors, reinforcers, and reinforcement magnitudes. In particular, reinforcement magnitude should be manipulated across a number of dimensions (e.g., duration, number, intensity). For example, the magnitude of social reinforcement (praise) could be increased by lengthening the duration of each interaction or by enhancing the intensity of the interaction (e.g., praising more enthusiastically). These various dimensions of magnitude may influence responding during extinction in different ways. For example, results of basic studies appear to indicate that lengthy durations of social interaction may reduce resistance to extinction, whereas high-intensity praise may produce the opposite effect (cf. Barnes & Tombaugh, 1970; Wagner, 1961).

In some cases, reduction in magnitude per se might be associated with a decrease in responding due to a concomitant decrement in reinforcer potency, as exemplified in a study by Lawton, France, and Blampied (1991), who treated night wakings in 6 children. They instructed parents to gradually decrease the duration of attention delivered contingent on night wakings from baseline levels to zero across 28 days. This procedure, which the authors termed *graduated extinction,* produced decreases in night wakings for 3 subjects. Treatment effects were obtained before reinforcement for night wakings was completely eliminated, and data for 2 of the 3 subjects showed evidence of bursting (i.e., initial increases in the frequency of night wakings). These results suggest that even slight reductions in reinforcement magnitude could reduce the efficacy of reinforcing stimuli. Although this effect may be beneficial during treatment of problem behavior, it would be problematic for studies that examine basic processes or behavioral acquisition or maintenance.

If results of further studies indicate that reinforcement magnitude influences responding in predictable ways, this variable could be altered prior to extinction. For example, reinforcement magnitudes that are likely to increase resistance to extinction could be provided when establishing appropriate behavior, a strategy that might enhance response maintenance and stimulus generalization. In addition, the efficacy of treatment for problem behavior might be increased by altering the magnitude of its maintaining reinforcer prior to extinction. If behavior is maintained by escape, for example, the duration of escape could be increased (or decreased) to reduce resistance to extinction or the likelihood of other undesirable indirect effects. If the behavior is maintained by social positive reinforcement, the intensity or duration of contingent attention could be manipulated prior to extinction.

Delay of Reinforcement

Basic (Nonclinical) Research

Numerous studies with nonhumans have reported that reinforcement delay during acquisition can increase resistance to extinction (e.g., Capaldi & Bowen, 1964; Crum, Brown, & Bitterman, 1951; Fehrer, 1956; Logan, Beier, & Kincaid, 1956; E. Scott & Wike, 1956; Tombaugh, 1966). Results of these studies suggest that the reinforcement delay should be at least 20 s to 30 s long and should occur intermittently (partial reinforcement delay) rather than following every response (constant reinforcement delay). In fact, a number of studies examining constant reinforcement delay have reported *decreases* in resistance (e.g., Nevin, 1974, Experiment IV; Renner, 1965; Tombaugh, 1970; Wike, Mellgren, & Cour, 1967). For example, Tombaugh (1970) compared the effects of no reinforcement delay (i.e., immediate reinforcement) to both constant and partial delays on the extinction of bar pressing in rats. Results demonstrated that partial delays were positively related to resistance, whereas constant delays were negatively related to resistance.

Applied Research and Implications

The effects of reinforcement delay have important implications for the use of extinction in schools and institutional settings, where low staff-to-client ratios often result in delayed consequences for inappropriate behavior. If a parent or caregiver is not present when problem behavior occurs, the maintaining consequences may be provided at a later time. For example, parents may receive reports about the occurrence of inappropriate behavior at school and deliver reinforcement (e.g., attention in the form of verbal reprimand) when the child returns home from school.

Results of several applied studies suggest that delayed reinforcement may increase resistance to extinction and promote stimulus generalization (e.g., Fowler & Baer, 1981; Mayhew & Anderson, 1980). For example, Mayhew and Anderson compared the effects of immediate and delayed reinforcement on the appropriate work behavior of 2 individuals with developmental disabilities. The two reinforcement conditions were alternated with extinction within a reversal design, and each extinction phase was terminated when behavior had decreased to 50% of the previous baseline level. During immediate reinforcement, the subjects received tokens on a VI 30-s schedule for appropriate work behavior in a math class. During delayed reinforcement, the subjects were videotaped during math class but received no tokens. Immediately following class, they viewed the recording while receiving tokens on a VI 30-s schedule for engaging in appropriate behavior on the videotape. Both subjects required more sessions to reach the extinction criterion following delayed reinforcement than following immediate reinforcement. However, sequence effects could partially account for their findings because delayed reinforcement was implemented first. In addition, exposure to the videotape during the delayed reinforcement condition could have influenced resistance to extinction.

Further research is needed to demonstrate the reliability and generality of these findings. In particular, studies should investigate the effects of both consistent and intermittent delays, which have been found to produce opposite effects on resistance. If delayed reinforcement increases resistance to extinction or the likelihood of undesirable indirect effects, parents or clinicians could deliver more immediate reinforcement for problem behavior prior to treatment with extinction. Alternatively, reinforcer delivery could be systematically delayed when long-term maintenance (i.e., increased resistance) is the desired outcome. Comparable but opposite strategies involving constant reinforcement delay could be implemented if further research suggests that this variable decreases resistance.

Schedule of Reinforcement

Basic (Nonclinical) Research

Exposure to intermittent or partial schedules of reinforcement can increase resistance to extinction, a phenomenon that has been termed the *partial reinforcement extinction effect* (PREE; see Lewis, 1960; N. Mackintosh, 1974, for reviews). A target response is maintained by partial reinforcement (PRF) if only some instances of the response are followed by a reinforcer; by contrast, every occurrence of the response is followed by a reinforcer under a continuous reinforcement (CRF) schedule. In general, the amount of resistance to extinction, as measured by response rate, number of responses, or time to meet a prespecified extinction criterion, is positively related to the intermittence of the reinforcement schedule (Ferster & Skinner, 1957). The PREE has been demonstrated using a variety of subjects, responses, and reinforcers, as well as with both free-operant and discrete-trial procedures, although almost always with between-subject designs. By contrast, many attempts to replicate the effect using within-subject designs have failed (e.g., Adams, Nemeth, & Pavlik, 1982; Pittenger & Pavlik, 1988, 1989; but see Hearst, 1961, for a notable exception).

The effect of reinforcement schedules on resistance to extinction is somewhat complex. Most investigations of the PREE manipulated the percentage of reinforced responses or trials during acquisition and demonstrated that resistance was inversely related to these percentages. However, results of studies with both humans and nonhumans, conducted primarily by Capaldi and colleagues, suggest that resistance to extinction is determined by other factors related to reinforcement schedules, such as the number of consecutive nonreinforced trials preceding a reinforced trial (N length), the number of different N lengths, and the number of each N length (e.g., Capaldi, 1964; Halpern & Poon, 1971; Litchfield & Duerfeldt, 1969; Meyers & Capaldi, 1970). In addition, the PREE is more likely to occur when PRF is combined with other variables, including lengthy acquisition training (Uhl & Young, 1967), large reinforcement magnitudes (Amsel, Hug, & Surridge, 1968), delayed reinforcement (L. Peterson, 1956), and massed acquisition trials (Sheffield, 1949). Reinforcement schedules also can influence the effect of reinforcement magnitude on resistance to extinction. Specifically, results of studies in which amount of reinforcement (e.g., number of food pellets) was manipulated showed that large reinforcement magnitudes increased resistance following PRF schedules but decreased resistance following CRF schedules (e.g., Wagner, 1961).

Recent research findings also suggest that the effects of PRF schedules on resistance to extinction may depend on the particular measure used to reflect resistance. In most studies, resistance is measured by calculating response rate or total number of responses during extinction, or the amount of time to meet an extinction criterion (e.g., no responses for 5 min). Results of these studies generally demonstrated greater resistance to extinction following PRF than following CRF schedules. However, others have argued that data on the PREE should be transformed to adjust for differences in response rates associated with different schedules of reinforcement (e.g., Nevin, 1988). Rate of responding under PRF schedules is generally much higher than rate of responding under CRF, a difference in response rates that will carry over into the subsequent extinction phase. As such, Nevin argued that traditional measures of resistance (e.g., response rate, number of responses) should not be compared following baselines with PRF and CRF schedules because response rates are necessarily much higher during extinction following PRF schedules than following CRF. Instead, data on the PREE should be expressed as a proportion of the response rate during baseline or during the initial extinction sessions, and rate of decrease in responding (i.e., slopes of extinction curves) should be examined. Using this measure of resistance, Nevin reanalyzed data from previous studies on the PREE and found greater resistance following CRF than following PRF schedules (i.e., a reversed PREE).[4]

Results of other research on the PREE have also been inconsistent with both humans and nonhumans. Findings suggest that implementing a period of CRF following a period of PRF might decrease resistance to extinction (Dubanoski & Weiner, 1978; Moreland, Stalling, & Walker, 1983; Pittenger, Pavlik, Flora, & Kontos, 1988), increase

[4] Nevin (1988, 1992) suggested that the reversed PREE will occur when the CRF schedule produces a higher rate of reinforcement than the PRF schedule, which may often be the case in the natural environment.

resistance (H. Jenkins, 1962; Shigley & Guffey, 1978), or have no effect (E. Quartermain & Vaughan, 1961; Sutherland, Mackintosh, & Wolfe, 1965). Numerous procedural differences among these studies make comparisons difficult. Results of studies that have examined the effects of switching from CRF to PRF schedules prior to extinction have been more consistent, demonstrating increases in resistance compared to acquisition training with CRF only (e.g., Nation & Boyajian, 1980; Pittenger et al., 1988).

Reinforcement schedules may influence characteristics of extinction other than resistance. For example, the extinction burst is less likely to occur during extinction following PRF compared to CRF schedules (Keller, 1940; Skinner, 1938). In addition, the response curves of behavior maintained by PRF often fail to show the wave-like character during extinction (W. Jenkins & Rigby, 1950; Skinner, 1938). Although the occurrence of spontaneous recovery appears to be unrelated to reinforcement schedules during acquisition (e.g., Lewis, 1956), results of several studies suggest that reinforcement intermittency is positively related to levels of disinhibition (e.g., Baumeister & Hawkins, 1966; Brimer, 1970b).

Applied Research and Implications

Although behavior is often maintained on PRF schedules in the natural environment, few applied studies have examined the effects of this variable on responding during extinction. Results of basic studies suggest that certain characteristics of extinction, such as the response burst, may be less likely to occur in the natural environment if behavior has been maintained on PRF rather than on CRF schedules. In addition, reinforcement schedules may increase the likelihood or amount of other characteristics of responding, including resistance to extinction and disinhibition, and may alter the effects of reinforcement magnitude on resistance. Nevertheless, only a few applied studies have examined the PREE (e.g., R. Baer, Blount, Detrich, & Stokes, 1987; Kazdin & Polster, 1973; Koegel & Rincover, 1977), and each contains some potential limitations that prevent clear interpretation of the data (see Lerman, Iwata, Shore, & Kahng, 1996, for a detailed discussion of these problems).

For example, Kazdin and Polster (1973), who reinforced the social interactions of 2 men diagnosed with mild retardation during three daily break periods at a sheltered workshop, compared the effects of two reinforcement schedules on response maintenance during extinction. Reinforcement conditions were alternated with extinction conditions within a reversal design. Initially, both subjects received tokens immediately following each break period (continuous reinforcement) for conversing with peers. They were then exposed to extinction for 3 weeks, and the social interactions of both subjects decreased to near-zero levels by the 2nd week. Following extinction, 1 subject received tokens on the CRF schedule for conversing with peers, and the other subject received tokens after either one or two of the three break periods (intermittent reinforcement). Both subjects then were exposed to extinction for 5 weeks. The subject who had received tokens on the CRF schedule exhibited few social interactions by the 2nd week of extinction, whereas the subject who had received tokens on the PRF schedule showed no reduction in behavior across the 5 weeks of extinction. These results provide one of the few demonstrations of the PREE in applied research. It is possible, however, that results may have been partially a function of reinforcement delay, another variable that was included in the procedure (i.e., the subjects received reinforcement after the break period rather than immediately following each interaction). When combined with PRF schedules, reinforcement delay can enhance the PREE (L. Peterson, 1956).

A recent study by Lerman et al. (1996) examined the PREE with severe behavior disorders using two different experimental designs and measures of resistance recommended by Nevin (1988). After sources of reinforcement that were maintaining 3 subjects' self-injury, aggression, or disruption were identified via functional analyses, the individuals were exposed to extinction following baseline conditions with CRF or PRF schedules alternated within reversal or multielement designs. Responding during extinction following the two reinforcement conditions was compared by examining response rate expressed as a proportion of baseline. Results suggested that problem behaviors may *not* be more difficult to treat with extinction if they have been maintained on PRF rather than CRF schedules and replicated basic research findings by showing that reinforcement schedules can produce different effects on responding during extinction, depending on the particular measure of resistance.

Further studies should investigate the relationship between reinforcement intermittency and resistance to extinction and potential interactions of other variables that commonly occur in the natural environment (e.g., different reinforcement magnitudes, delays, acquisition lengths). In addition, the effects of PRF on other characteristics of responding during extinction (e.g., bursting, aggression) should be examined. Results might indicate various strategies for altering reinforcement schedules prior to treatment with extinction. However, such strategies should be examined in further studies because results of basic research in this area have been inconsistent (cf. H. Jenkins, 1962; Theios & McGinnis, 1967).

Although several applied studies have attempted to examine the benefits of altering reinforcement schedules while treating problem behavior (e.g., Foxx & McMorrow, 1983; Neisworth, Hunt, Gallup, & Madle, 1985; Schmid, 1986), conclusions about the effects of switching from PRF to CRF schedules prior to extinction cannot be formed on the basis of their findings. In these studies, the contingencies that were maintaining subjects' inappropriate behavior (stereotypy) were not identified, and it was assumed that the behavior was maintained by PRF schedules of automatic reinforcement. Because sources of automatic reinforcement are difficult to manipulate, arbitrary reinforcers (e.g., food items) were delivered following each occurrence of stereotypy (i.e., on a CRF schedule) and then removed in an attempt to decrease the behavior. Results suggested that the procedure produced short-term reductions in stereotypy for some of the subjects. However, these studies demonstrated the effects of introducing and removing an arbitrary reinforcer on behavior maintained by an unidentified reinforcer, not the effects of switching reinforcement schedules prior to extinction. Studies in this area must involve identification of the maintaining reinforcers for inappropriate behavior and a comparison of responding during extinction following delivery of the relevant reinforcer on PRF schedules versus a switch from PRF to CRF schedules. Lerman et al. (1996), who implemented this strategy with 1 subject, found that switching from a PRF to a CRF schedule prior to extinction lowered the total number of responses exhibited during extinction. However, this outcome was attributed to the differences in baseline response rates associated with the different reinforcement conditions (responding under the CRF schedule was much lower than responding under the PRF schedule).

Other Types of Variation in Acquisition

Basic (Nonclinical) Research

Irregularity of training conditions per se, including changes in the response topography required for reinforcement, presence of environmental stimuli, and variables related to reinforcement (e.g., location, delay, quantity), appear to increase resistance to extinction in nonhumans. The effects of both single and multiple sources of variability on resistance to extinction have been investigated (e.g., Logan et al., 1956; McNamara & Wike, 1958; Tombaugh, 1970). For example, McNamara and Wike, who examined a large number of varied components (e.g., specific stimuli associated with the alley, reinforcement delay, target response, reinforcement schedule, deprivation level, type of reinforcer), found that the greater the irregularity in training conditions, the greater the resistance to extinction under constant conditions.

Applied Research and Implications

Although behavior in applied settings probably is often exposed to variable acquisition and maintenance conditions, their potential influence on responding during extinction is rarely mentioned in texts and articles on application, and no applied studies have systematically investigated these factors. However, results of several studies examining generalization techniques categorized by Stokes and Baer (1977) as "train loosely" and "train sufficient exemplars" suggest that variability in training conditions could increase resistance to extinction. In these studies, subjects exposed to varied conditions (i.e., different settings, times, experimenters, or other environmental stimuli) during the acquisition of behavior showed both stimulus generalization and response maintenance in situations that were not associated with reinforcement (e.g., Dunlap & Johnson, 1985; Sprague & Horner, 1984; Stokes, Baer, & Jackson, 1974).

In a study by Stokes et al. (1974), for example, generalization and maintenance of a greeting response in children diagnosed with severe or profound retardation were facilitated by altering the number of experimenters associated with the training procedure. For some subjects, initial training with a single experimenter failed to produce maintenance of the greeting response (i.e., hand wave) in the presence of individuals who did not implement the procedure. When the training procedure was implemented by two experimenters, the subjects' behavior generalized and was maintained across more than 20 other members of the institution staff who did not participate in training. Further, the subjects continued to exhibit the wave for up to 6 months. Although variable training might account for initial generalization and maintenance, natural reinforcement contingencies provided by the staff may be responsible for the extended response maintenance obtained in this study. As discussed by the authors, the subjects' greeting response may have contacted these social consequences more frequently after training. That is, the behavior may have been introduced to a "natural shaping environment" (p. 609) as a result of variable training.

Further research specifically designed to examine the effects of variation on resistance to extinction and other characteristics of responding, such as the extinction burst, extinction-induced aggression, behavioral contrast, and spontaneous recovery, might suggest strategies that could be incorporated into an extinction technology. Prior to treating problem behavior with extinction, for example, clinicians could attempt to reduce sources of variation related to reinforcement delivery (e.g., reinforcement magnitude, schedule, delay) and environmental stimuli correlated with reinforcement delivery (e.g., specific location or caregiver associated with reinforcement). Conversely, variation could be manipulated to promote maintenance and generalization of appropriate behavior.

Exposure to Aversive Stimuli

Basic (Nonclinical) Research

Results of studies with both humans and nonhumans suggest that exposure to punishment or noncontingent aversive stimulation during acquisition can increase resistance to extinction (e.g., Brown & Wagner, 1964; Chen & Amsel, 1982; Deur & Parke, 1970). For example, Brown and Wagner found that rats exposed to both a CRF reinforcement schedule (contingent food) and an intermittent punishment schedule (contingent shocks) during acquisition of a runway response were more resistant to extinction than were rats exposed to reinforcement alone. However, this effect of punishment or noncontingent aversive stimulation on resistance has not been consistently demonstrated (e.g., Dyck, Mellgren, & Nation, 1974; Haddad & Mellgren, 1976; Halevy, Feldon, & Weiner, 1987).

Applied Research and Implications

The effects of previous exposure to punishment or noncontingent aversive stimulation on responding during extinction have not been examined in applied research, and this variable is rarely discussed in texts and literature reviews on extinction. However, this factor may be particularly relevant to the use of extinction in clinical settings. Behavior disorders are often exposed to a plethora of treatment interventions, including punishment, before an effective program is identified (e.g., Bird, Dores, Moniz, & Robinson, 1989). In addition, parents, caregivers, and teachers may inadvertently deliver both reinforcement and punishment following inappropriate behavior (Katz, 1971). For example, parents may deliver verbal reprimands followed by comforting statements contingent on the child's disruptive behavior. When the reinforcers that are maintaining problem behavior eventually are identified and withheld, previous exposure to punishment may influence treatment efficacy. However, additional studies are necessary due to the inconsistent findings of basic research.

DETERMINANTS OF BEHAVIOR REDUCTION THAT INFLUENCE RESPONDING DURING EXTINCTION

Results of basic research suggest that some characteristics of behavior that is exposed to extinction, particularly resistance, can be altered when variables are manipulated during extinction. These variables include stimulus change, response effort, intertrial-interval (ITI) length, and the use of other behavior reduction procedures and should be considered when developing and implementing acquisition procedures or treatment programs in applied settings.

Stimulus Change

Basic (Nonclinical) Research

Resistance to extinction is positively related to the similarity between conditions of reinforcement and extinction, a phenomenon that may be responsible for the effect of other variables (e.g., reinforcement magnitude, delay, and schedule) on resistance to extinction (N. Mackintosh, 1974). During acquisition and maintenance, a variety of events or features of the environment can acquire stimulus control properties due to their contiguity with reinforcement delivery. These stimuli can then occasion responding during extinction. Thus, resistance will decrease if these discriminative stimuli are altered or removed simultaneously with the introduction of extinction. Studies directly investigating this variable have manipulated ITI length (e.g., Teichner, 1952), the subject's drive level (e.g., Hatton, 1965), and other stimuli associated with reinforcement, such as goal box color (e.g., Bitterman, Feddersen, & Tyler, 1953; May & Beauchamp,

1969; Morris, 1968). This variable may also be responsible for the efficacy of a procedure called *errorless discrimination learning,* in which stimuli associated with nonreinforcement are initially made as distinct as possible from stimuli associated with reinforcement (e.g., Terrace, 1963).

Instead of changing the parameters of a single variable (e.g., ITI length), some studies have manipulated the proportion of stimuli that are common to both acquisition and extinction (e.g., Hulicka, Capehart, & Viney, 1960). However, the stimuli in these studies may have altered resistance because they were established as conditioned reinforcers rather than as discriminative stimuli during acquisition. For example, Viney, Hulicka, Bitner, Raley, and Brewster (1968) manipulated the number of stimuli that were common to both acquisition and extinction conditions with 60 kindergarten children who were taught a two-choice discrimination task. When a subject responded correctly in acquisition, delivery of the reinforcer (a marble) was accompanied by an audible click, a red light, a blue light, a bell, and a buzzer. During extinction, different groups of subjects were exposed to varying numbers of these stimuli following occurrences of the target response. They reported that subjects' persistence on this task was a direct function of the number of stimuli that were common to both acquisition and extinction. In a similar study, however, N. Johnson (1973) varied the number of stimuli present during acquisition and extinction while keeping the number of stimuli constant across the two phases for individual subjects (i.e., no stimulus change); results showed that resistance was positively related to the number of stimuli present during extinction, which supports a conditioned reinforcement interpretation for the findings of Viney et al. Most likely, both processes (stimulus control and conditioned reinforcement) can operate to enhance resistance when identical stimuli are present during acquisition and extinction.

Applied Research and Implications

Although this variable may be one of the most prominent factors that influence resistance to extinction, few applied studies have systematically manipulated stimulus change during extinction, and this variable is rarely mentioned in texts and articles on application. However, results of studies that have examined a generalization technique classified by Stokes and Baer (1977) as "program common stimuli" are consistent with the findings of basic studies suggesting that stimulus change might alter resistance to extinction. For example, results of several studies demonstrated that adaptive behavior persisted longer during extinction or was more likely to generalize to a setting associated with extinction when the therapist who implemented the acquisition procedure was present in the environment rather than absent (e.g., Peterson, Merwin, Moyer, & Whitehurst, 1971; Stokes & Baer, 1976). Further, results of studies by Redd (1970) and Cameron, Luiselli, McGrath, and Carlton (1992) showed that responding was less likely to occur in the therapist's presence when other stimuli paired with reinforcement delivery, such as the container holding the reinforcers, were removed from the setting.

In an interesting study by Rincover and Koegel (1975), 4 autistic children who were taught to follow simple instructions (e.g., "touch your nose") did not respond correctly when a new therapist delivered the instructions in a novel setting. After certain stimuli that had been present during acquisition were introduced into the generalization setting (e.g., therapist's hand movement, touch prompts, table and chairs), correct responding suddenly occurred and was maintained across repeated extinction trials. Stimulus change might also explain the results of studies demonstrating that variation in acquisition can enhance response maintenance and stimulus generalization (e.g., Sprague & Horner, 1984; Stokes et al., 1974). By exposing subjects to a variety of exemplars during behavioral acquisition, the experimenters increased the likelihood that similar stimuli were present in both the training and the generalization settings.

Results of these studies suggest that behavior may be difficult to extinguish when the transition from reinforcement to extinction involves no change in the stimulus conditions other than termination of the response–reinforcer contingency, which is frequently the case in applied settings. For example, teachers and caregivers often implement treatment with extinction by simply ignoring problem behaviors that have been maintained by attention, or by continuing ongoing instructional activities if the behaviors have been maintained by escape from these activities. Instead, various strategies designed to increase or decrease stimulus change could be implemented when behavior is exposed to extinction. Certain features of the environment, such as the therapist's appearance, ITI length, and color or texture of task materials, could be altered or removed during treatment of problem behavior. When response maintenance or stimulus generalization is the desired outcome, stimuli associated with reinforcement should remain unchanged (cf. Rincover & Koegel, 1975), and resistance may be further enhanced by pairing additional stimuli with reinforcement and introducing them during extinction (cf. Viney et al., 1968). Further studies should investigate the efficacy of these strategies as well as the effects of stimulus change on other characteristics of the extinction process.

Response Effort

Basic (Nonclinical) Research

The amount of physical exertion or effort required to complete a response has been shown to influence resistance to extinction in some studies with nonhumans (e.g., Applezweig, 1951; Mowrer & Jones, 1943). For example, Mowrer and Jones trained groups of rats to press a weighted lever with varying loads (0.5 g, 42.5 g, or 80 g) and then extinguished the response with just one load. They found that resistance was inversely related to the weight of the lever during extinction. Similar results have been demonstrated by altering runway inclines (e.g., N. Johnson & Viney, 1970) and jumping distance (e.g., Solomon, 1948); however, other studies have failed to demonstrate this effect (e.g., Haralson, Gillman, & Ralph, 1965; Maatsch, Adelman, & Denny, 1954; D. Quartermain, 1965). Procedural differences probably account for these inconsistent findings; results of several studies suggest that variables that are present during acquisition, including response effort, reinforcement number, and reinforcement schedule, can influence the effects of response effort during extinction (e.g., Aiken, 1957; Young, 1966). For example, Aiken (1957) manipulated the weight of a swinging door during both acquisition and extinction and found that rats that were switched from low effort in acquisition to high effort in extinction demonstrated less resistance to extinction than rats that were exposed to high effort in both conditions. Rats that were switched from high effort in acquisition to low effort in extinction demonstrated greater resistance to extinction than rats that were exposed to low effort in both conditions. Further, resistance was similar for the groups of rats that were exposed to either high or low effort in both conditions.

Results of studies on response effort also may be difficult to interpret because procedures designed to manipulate effort may simultaneously influence other important variables. For example, subjects exposed to a weighted bar during acquisition tend to exhibit many partial responses, which alter the reinforcement schedule (Eisenberger, 1992).

If these partial responses are not counted during extinction, heavy bar weights necessarily appear to produce less resistance to extinction than do light bar weights. In a study by Applezweig (1951), for example, the effect of effort on resistance was less significant when these partial responses were included in the analysis. Other variables that may change when effort is manipulated include reinforcement number, reinforcement delay, and complexity of the target response (Maatsch et al., 1954).

Applied Research and Implications

Results of basic research suggest that procedures designed to manipulate response effort could be combined with extinction to increase or decrease resistance. Although no applied studies on extinction have examined this variable, several studies have obtained extinction-like decrements in behavior by increasing response effort without terminating the response–reinforcement contingency (e.g., R. H. Horner & Day, 1991; Luiselli, 1991; Schroeder, 1972; Van Houten, 1993). Van Houten, for example, placed soft wrist weights on a subject who engaged in self-injurious face slapping after results of a functional analysis had indicated that the behavior was maintained by sensory (automatic) reinforcement. Results showed an immediate decrease in self-injury during treatment sessions with the wrist weights, as well as a gradual reduction in self-injury during the 5 min immediately preceding and following treatment sessions. R. H. Horner and Day (1991) obtained decreases in appropriate behavior (signing and complying to instructions) by reducing response efficiency (i.e., increasing the work requirement for reinforcement, delaying reinforcement delivery) while reinforcing problem behavior on a CRF schedule. The process responsible for these findings may be somewhat similar to those involved in ratio strain, a decrease in responding that is sometimes observed when behavior is exposed to relatively thin intermittent reinforcement schedules.

These findings suggest that, when combined with extinction, procedures designed to increase response effort might improve the efficacy of extinction. However, further research is necessary to clarify the relationship between effort and resistance and to examine potential interactions with other variables that may influence behavior in the natural environment (e.g., PRF schedules, long maintenance conditions).

Response effort could be manipulated in a variety of ways, depending on the type of response under investigation and the precise definition of the term *effort.* For example, effort could refer to the level of physical exertion that is required to complete a response, as well as the complexity of a particular task (e.g., one requiring relatively fine discriminations) (cf. Eisenberger & Leonard, 1980). In terms of physical exertion, responses could be made more effortful by attaching weights to relevant appendages like legs or wrists (cf. Van Houten, 1993) or by partially restraining movement in some manner. If the response involves movement of objects in the environment (e.g., task materials), features of these items could be altered so that they are more difficult to grasp or move (e.g., by attaching a weight to the object, removing the handles from an object that must be carried). Alternatively, effort could be reduced by physically assisting the individual to complete the response or by manipulating features of an object that must be moved or carried. In terms of task complexity, effort could be manipulated by providing or removing extra prompts and cues.

Results of this research might suggest various strategies for implementing extinction in applied settings. Basic research findings indicate that response effort should be relatively minimal during reinforcement but high during extinction when a rapid decrease in behavior is the desired outcome. Thus, treatment programs for problem behavior could be combined with procedures that increase response effort during extinction. Conversely, responding during extinction should be relatively effortless compared to responding during acquisition when resistance to extinction is desirable. Prior to tests for response maintenance and stimulus generalization, for example, therapist prompts and cues could be removed from the situation. When the contingency between responding and reinforcement is eventually terminated, these prompts and cues could be reintroduced into the setting, thereby decreasing response effort.

Length of Intertrial or Intersession Interval

Basic (Nonclinical) Research

Results of studies with nonhumans generally have found that massed trials (i.e., short ITI lengths) during extinction will reduce resistance to extinction (e.g., Birch, 1965; Krane & Ison, 1971; Teichner, 1952).[5] Capaldi, Berg, and Sparling (1971), who examined ITI lengths ranging from 3 min to 24 hr, further demonstrated that the PREE can be eliminated by switching from spaced trials during acquisition to massed trials during extinction, an effect that was not entirely attributable to stimulus change (the performance of subjects exposed to massed trials during acquisition but spaced trials during extinction was similar to that of subjects exposed to spaced trials in both conditions). Kurke (1956) examined the effect of manipulating the interval between practice sessions (rather than trials) on the extinction of free-operant bar pressing in rats. Subjects received extinction sessions spaced 22, 46, or 70 hr apart after receiving training sessions spaced 24 hr apart. In general, he found that resistance to extinction was positively related to the amount of time between extinction sessions.

In addition to influencing resistance, ITI or intersession interval length may affect other characteristics of responding during extinction, particularly spontaneous recovery. Results of some studies have demonstrated that spontaneous recovery was greater when more time elapsed between the first and second extinction periods (e.g., Ellson, 1938; Lewis, 1956; Skinner, 1938).

Applied Research and Implications

Behavior in the natural environment often occurs during discrete time periods rather than continuously throughout the day. That is, opportunities to reinforce and extinguish both appropriate and inappropriate behavior may be restricted to specific settings or activities, or may be determined by the presence of certain individuals (e.g., parents, teachers, etc.). Results of basic research on ITI (or intersession interval) lengths suggest that massing trials within sessions or decreasing the time between sessions might decrease resistance to, or attenuate the undesirable indirect effects associated with, extinction. If so, various strategies could be incorporated into treatment programs for problem behavior. During extinction of escape behavior, for example, the therapist could deliver the aversive stimuli (e.g., instructions) using fairly short ITI lengths. In addition, treatment sessions could be implemented frequently throughout the day. When opportunities to respond appropriately are restricted to discrete trials (e.g., following delivery of "Do . . ." instructions), resistance to extinction might be enhanced if the trials are separated by relatively large amounts of time. In this case, however, similar ITI lengths probably should be implemented during both acquisition and extinction, because simply altering this variable when switching from rein-

[5] At least one exception should be noted due to its potential relevance to application. Massed trials during extinction may not decrease resistance when the response is exposed to both PRF and massed trials during acquisition (cf. Capaldi, Berg, & Sparling, 1971).

forcement to extinction could decrease resistance (e.g., Teichner, 1952). Thus, an appropriate ITI length should be selected and implemented prior to extinction if resistance to extinction is the desired outcome.

Combining Extinction with Other Procedures

Basic (Nonclinical) Research

Results of studies in which extinction was implemented in conjunction with alternative procedures (e.g., NCR, DRO, DRA) indicate, with some exceptions, that the use of alternative procedures decreases resistance to extinction and the likelihood of certain indirect effects. The effects of NCR have been examined by providing reinforcement (e.g., free food) either continuously or intermittently throughout the extinction session. In general, results of these studies have demonstrated that continuous availability of response-independent reinforcement decreased responding during extinction (e.g., Enkema, Slavin, Spaeth, & Neuringer, 1972). On the other hand, delivery of NCR on fixed or variable-time schedules often increased resistance to extinction or produced resurgences in responding when the reinforcement was introduced after extinction of the behavior appeared to be completed (e.g., Baker, 1990; Lattal, 1972; Neuringer, 1970; Rescorla & Skucy, 1969; Spradlin, Girardeau, & Hom, 1966). Results of these studies suggested that response-independent reinforcement increased resistance because the reinforcer adventitiously followed responding (e.g., Neuringer, 1970) or because the reinforcer acquired stimulus control properties during acquisition (e.g., Baker, 1990; Rescorla & Skucy, 1969). Results of several studies also indicated that intermittent delivery of NCR during extinction reduced the likelihood of behavioral contrast (e.g., Boakes, 1973; Halliday & Boakes, 1971).

Results of studies in which DRA was implemented during extinction have consistently demonstrated that DRA eliminates the response burst and reduces resistance to extinction (e.g., Leitenberg, Rawson, & Bath, 1970; Timmons, 1962; Vyse, Rieg, & Smith, 1985). Results of a study by Leitenberg, Rawson, and Mulick (1975) further demonstrated that the effectiveness of DRA depended on the reinforcement schedule for the alternative response. Specifically, a relatively lean schedule (i.e., VI 4 min vs. VI 30 s) failed to decrease resistance to extinction.

On the other hand, studies that examined the effects of DRO during extinction have reported somewhat mixed findings with both human and nonhuman subjects. Although results of some studies demonstrated that DRO attenuated the response burst, decreased resistance to extinction, enhanced generalization, and reduced the likelihood of behavioral contrast and spontaneous recovery (e.g., Moss, Ruthven, Hawkins, & Topping, 1983; Nevin, 1968; Topping & Ford, 1974; Zeiler, 1971), others demonstrated quicker reduction in behavior when extinction was implemented without DRO (e.g., Cross, Dickson, & Sisemore, 1978; Uhl, 1973). Some authors have suggested that delivery of the reinforcer for not responding during extinction can occasion the target behavior due to the stimulus control properties of the reinforcer. However, results of a recent study by Rieg, Smith, and Vyse (1993) demonstrated that the effectiveness of DRO relative to extinction depended on the relationship between two contingencies involved in DRO procedures, the response–reinforcement interval and the reinforcement–reinforcement interval. The response–reinforcement interval is the amount of time that reinforcement delivery is postponed after each occurrence of the target response, whereas the reinforcement–reinforcement interval is the time between each reinforcement delivery if no responses occur. Rieg et al. found that DRO was more effective than extinction when the response–reinforcement interval was longer than the reinforcement–reinforcement interval.

Studies that examined the effects of punishment during extinction have consistently reported that punishment decreases resistance (e.g., Azrin & Holz, 1961; D. Baer, 1966; Boe & Church, 1967; Weiner, 1964). Although results suggested that the effectiveness of the punishing stimuli, which included electric shock, point loss, and time-out from positive reinforcement, was directly related to the intensity level, combining extinction with punishment reduced the number of responses even with the mildest intensity level examined.

Applied Research and Implications

Although many texts and articles on application suggest that combining extinction with other procedures, such as NCR, DRA, and DRO, decreases resistance to extinction and the likelihood of other undesirable indirect effects (e.g., Ducharme & Van Houten, 1994; Kazdin, 1994; Martin & Pear, 1992), few applied studies have directly compared the effects of extinction with and without alternative procedures. Nevertheless, results of these studies have replicated those of basic research, suggesting that combining extinction with NCR, DRA, DRO, or punishment can decrease resistance to extinction. In most cases, the reinforcing stimuli delivered as part of the alternative procedures were those that had maintained the target response prior to treatment.

Several studies have examined the effects of NCR by delivering reinforcers either continuously or periodically throughout the extinction session. Results of studies that examined the continuous delivery of NCR demonstrated a reduction in responding compared to extinction alone. For example, Mason and Iwata (1990) provided continuous social interaction (e.g., praise, pats on the head or back) as part of treatment for SIB that was maintained by attention. NCR was alternated with an extinction-only condition in which a therapist was present but did not interact with the subject. Results showed immediate suppression of SIB during the NCR condition. On the other hand, levels of responding remained similar to those during baseline (reinforcement) when extinction alone was implemented prior to and following treatment with NCR. The authors concluded that the presence of the therapist during the extinction sessions was discriminative for SIB and that continuous delivery of attention reduced the motivation to engage in the behavior.

Two studies have examined the effects of escape extinction with and without instructional fading on SIB maintained by escape from instructions (Pace, Iwata, Cowdery, Andree, & McIntyre, 1993; Zarcone et al., 1993). For the fading procedure, all instructions were initially removed from the session and later were faded into the sessions by gradually increasing the rate of instructions across the treatment condition. This procedure is somewhat analogous to NCR because subjects are provided with noncontingent access to escape, which is gradually eliminated as more instructions are introduced into the sessions. Pace et al. compared the effects of extinction combined with fading to those of extinction alone using a reversal design during the initial stages of treatment for 1 subject. In the study by Zarcone et al., subjects were exposed to both treatment procedures alternated within a multielement design. Results of these studies demonstrated an immediate suppression of SIB with the introduction of the fading procedure. In addition, fewer self-injurious responses were exhibited in the extinction-plus-fading condition than in the extinction-only condition. Zarcone et al. further demonstrated that implementing extinction in conjunction with fading eliminated the extinction burst for 2 subjects. It is important to note, however, that the subjects in both studies were frequently exposed to instructions during the negative reinforcement baseline; results of basic studies suggest that if individuals successfully avoid most instructions during baseline, responding may continue to persist during the initial stages of instructional fading (cf. Malloy & Lewis, 1988; Solomon, Kamin, & Wynne, 1953). For these individuals, extinction without instructional fading may be the treatment of choice.

Results of studies in which NCR was delivered continuously rather than intermittently replicated the findings of basic research by demonstrating increases in resistance. For example, Waxler and Yarrow (1970) exposed groups of nursery school children to extinction with or without NCR (praise) after reinforcing imitative responses during a storytelling session. They examined the data for male and female subjects separately. Imitative responses extinguished more slowly for the group of male subjects exposed to the NCR-plus-extinction condition than for the group of male subjects exposed to the extinction-only condition. This finding, however, was not replicated with the female subjects, who responded similarly in the two conditions. The authors did not offer possible explanations for the increased resistance associated with NCR or the different outcomes for male and female subjects. The male subjects exposed to NCR may have demonstrated an increase in resistance because the reinforcer adventitiously followed responding during the storytelling sessions. On the other hand, results of this between-group comparison could simply reflect different extinction rates for the two groups of male subjects.

Findings of another study suggest that NCR may enhance resistance because the reinforcer can acquire stimulus control functions during acquisition and subsequently occasion responding during extinction. Koegel and Rincover (1977) presented response-independent reinforcers periodically after the appropriate behaviors of 2 children diagnosed with autism failed to be maintained in settings that were not associated with the treatment contingencies. When the children no longer responded correctly to "Do . . ." instructions in the absence of contingent reinforcement, the therapist delivered a piece of candy and then continued to present additional instructional trials. Results for both subjects showed temporary but significant increases in correct responding immediately following NCR presentations. In another component of this study, 2 other subjects received a piece of candy every 20 consecutive extinction trials regardless of their previous responding. Their performance was compared to that of 2 subjects who were exposed to extinction without NCR. For the 2 subjects in the extinction-plus-NCR condition, correct responding was maintained for 540 and 450 trials before extinguishing. On the other hand, correct responding of the other 2 subjects was extinguished within 100 trials. The authors concluded that the discriminative stimulus functions of reinforcement were responsible for the enhanced response maintenance demonstrated in this study. However, adventitious reinforcement or different extinction rates among the children could also account for the findings in the second part of the study.

To summarize, results of both basic and applied studies have demonstrated that continuous delivery of NCR can decrease resistance to extinction, whereas delivery of NCR on intermittent schedules can increase resistance. These findings suggest that treatment of problem behavior with NCR should involve, at least initially, nearly continuous presentation of reinforcement. The amount of response-independent reinforcement eventually could be faded as treatment progresses. In two recent studies (Hagopian, Fisher, & Legacy, 1994; Vollmer, Iwata, Zarcone, Smith, & Mazaleski, 1993), delivery of NCR during extinction was gradually thinned from almost continuous (fixed-time [FT] 10-s) to FT 5-min schedules while low levels of self-injury were maintained. The effects of combining extinction with NCR using arbitrary reinforcers could also be examined in further studies. Delivery of arbitrary reinforcers on intermittent schedules should not occasion responding during extinction, because no previous contingency existed between the target response and the reinforcer. (This procedure could nevertheless result in adventitious reinforcement during extinction.) The relative effectiveness of this NCR procedure compared to extinction alone probably will depend on the identification of reinforcers that substitute for those that were previously maintaining the target response. When response maintenance and stimulus generalization are desirable, however, intermittent delivery of response-independent reinforcement could be used to enhance resistance to extinction.

Several studies have implemented DRA in conjunction with extinction and compared the effects to a baseline condition in which extinction was implemented alone. Results of these studies consistently demonstrated that DRA reduced resistance to extinction, replicating basic research findings. In a study by Carr and Durand (1985), 5 children were taught to exhibit a verbal response to receive the same reinforcer that previously maintained their disruptive behavior (i.e., either attention or escape from instructions), and treatment with DRA was alternated with a baseline condition in a reversal design. During baseline, the therapist provided no consequences for either disruptive or verbal responses. Results showed immediate suppression of disruption during the DRA condition, whereas high to moderate levels of disruption persisted when extinction was implemented without DRA. In a similar study, Steege et al. (1990) implemented treatment for SIB maintained by negative reinforcement (escape from grooming activities) using a procedure that combined escape extinction with DRA. Two children who had been diagnosed with profound mental retardation were provided a brief (10-s) escape from grooming activities for pressing a microswitch that activated the prerecorded message "Stop." For 1 subject, treatment was alternated with a baseline condition in which neither response (SIB or microswitch press) produced escape. For the other subject, DRA with and without extinction were compared using a multiple baseline across tasks design. Results for both subjects showed lower levels of SIB in the extinction-plus-DRA condition than in the extinction-alone condition. The specific effects of DRA on SIB were not clear, however, because treatment also included a contingent guided compliance component that was not implemented during baseline (extinction alone).

Although results of these studies showed that DRA decreased resistance, a similar outcome was not obtained in a study that directly examined the effects of DRO on responding during extinction. Following a functional analysis indicating that the SIB of 2 subjects was maintained by attention, Mazaleski et al. (1993) compared the effects of extinction with and without DRO by alternating the treatment procedures with a baseline (reinforcement) condition in a reversal design. The order of the treatment conditions was counterbalanced across the subjects, and results demonstrated similar reductions in SIB during the extinction-plus-DRO and extinction-only conditions. As suggested by the findings of Rieg et al. (1993), however, a different reinforcement schedule might have increased the relative efficacy of treatment with DRO. The DRO schedule used by Mazaleski et al. involved identical response–reinforcement and reinforcement–reinforcement intervals (both were 15 s). DRO may have been more effective than extinction if the response–reinforcement interval had been longer than 15 s.

Although relatively few applied studies have compared the effects of extinction alone to extinction combined with alternative sources of reinforcement, results have consistently demonstrated that responding during extinction was reduced substantially when NCR or DRA was implemented in conjunction with extinction. Lerman and Iwata (1995) examined the prevalence of the extinction burst in 113 sets of data and further noted that the occurrence of bursting was reduced when extinction was combined with other treatment components. These findings suggest that treatment with extinction should be implemented in conjunction with NCR, DRA, or DRO as recommended by various authors (e.g., Ducharme & Van Houten, 1994; Kazdin, 1994). On the other hand, these results also indicate that reinforcement delivery should be withheld if maintenance of appropriate behavior during extinction is the desired outcome. That is, behavior may rapidly extinguish when the reinforcer that previously maintained the target response is delivered noncontingently or for other responses.

Not surprisingly, results of several studies have also demonstrated that punishment can decrease resistance to extinction. In a study by W. Fisher et al. (1993), the disruptive behavior of 2 individuals who had been diagnosed with profound mental retardation persisted during treatment with extinction (1 subject) or extinction combined with DRA (the other subject). For both subjects, combining extinction with punishment (either contingent effort or contingent restraint) produced immediate decreases in disruptive behavior. Results of three studies that examined extinction of SIB with and without punishment (contingent electric shock) also demonstrated the superiority of punishment combined with extinction relative to extinction alone as treatment for problem behavior (Baroff & Tate, 1968; Lovaas & Simmons, 1969; D. Williams, Kirkpatrick-Sanchez, & Iwata, 1993). These findings suggest that extinction combined with punishment may be the treatment of choice when behavior is extremely resistant to extinction. However, the prevalence of such cases may be reduced dramatically with the development of a comprehensive technology for the use of extinction in applied settings.

CONCLUSIONS

Results of basic research indicate that a number of variables may influence responding during extinction. In general, behavior that is exposed to aversive stimuli, variable maintenance conditions, and large, intermittent, delayed reinforcers may be highly resistant to extinction. This resistance may be further enhanced if extinction is implemented with spaced trials or sessions and a reduction in response effort, if the transition from reinforcement to extinction involves minimal stimulus change, and if extinction is not combined with alternative procedures such as NCR, DRA, and DRO.

These findings are based, in large part, on experiments done in laboratory settings with nonhuman subjects, yet they suggest that problem behavior, which is often exposed to factors like intermittent reinforcement in the natural environment, may be difficult to treat with extinction. Such a conclusion appears to be incongruent with results of numerous applied studies during the past 10 years that have demonstrated that extinction can produce fairly immediate, large, and durable reductions in problem behavior if the procedure involves withholding relevant (maintaining) reinforcers (e.g., Iwata et al., 1994). However, the baseline (reinforcement) and extinction conditions implemented in most applied studies incorporated (either by design or accident) variables that were associated with reduced resistance. For example, behavior typically was maintained by continuous, immediate reinforcement under constant (nonvarying) conditions prior to treatment, and the extinction procedures often included relatively massed trials and delivery of the relevant reinforcer for either nonresponding or the occurrence of alternative responses.

The present analysis of basic and applied research indicates the potential value of a comprehensive technology of extinction, provides a number of guidelines for future research, and suggests strategies that might facilitate the acquisition, maintenance, and reduction of behavior in applied settings. In the case of problem behavior, for example, treatment efficacy might be enhanced if caregivers or therapists alter several variables prior to extinction. Specifically, the therapist could switch from a PRF to a CRF schedule, shorten the latency between the occurrence of a response and reinforcer delivery, alter the reinforcement magnitude (the direction may depend on the reinforcer and how this variable is modified), and eliminate any variation in the conditions associated with reinforcement. If a target response is maintained by escape from instructional activities, for example, the therapist could deliver escape immediately following each occurrence of problem behavior while ensuring that the maintenance conditions are fairly consistent (e.g., the setting, therapist, task materials, and other stimuli associated with reinforcement delivery remain unchanged). Future research should determine if, in fact, these procedures increase the clinical efficacy of extinction.

With the transition from reinforcement to extinction, ITI length could be shortened, response effort could be increased, a variety of environmental stimuli could be modified, and additional procedures (e.g., DRO, DRA) could be incorporated into the treatment program. During escape extinction, for example, the therapist could conduct numerous instructional sessions throughout the day, alter a variety of environmental stimuli (e.g., appearance of the setting), increase response effort by modifying the task materials, and provide escape from instructions for alternative behaviors such as compliance. Treatment of problem behavior could also be combined with methods designed to facilitate the occurrence of desirable indirect effects that are associated with extinction (e.g., increases in appropriate behavior due to behavioral contrast or the resurgence of previously reinforced responses).

Parallel strategies could be constructed to facilitate generalization and long-term maintenance of appropriate behavior. Applied behavior analysts generally agree that a pragmatic approach to therapeutic behavior change incorporates strategies designed to promote change across time, people, and settings (Stokes & Baer, 1977). Procedures that strengthen resistance to extinction are appropriate when response maintenance and stimulus generalization may be undermined by extinction effects. After a response is acquired, the probability of long-term maintenance might be increased if the reinforcement schedule, delay, and magnitude are altered; other stimuli associated with reinforcement delivery are varied (e.g., different therapists and settings are incorporated into maintenance sessions); response effort is reduced; and the relevant reinforcer is delivered for alternative responses or independent of behavior.

The development of an applied technology of extinction will require thorough examination of these variables (singly and in combination), their potential effects on other characteristics of responding during extinction (e.g., extinction-induced aggression, spontaneous recovery, disinhibition), and the efficacy of the numerous strategies outlined in this paper. However, the benefits of this technology should be considered in relation to the costs of conducting this research and of implementing such complex strategies in applied settings (along with the formidable task of identifying the maintaining variables of problem behavior). In particular, this technology may be largely superfluous if other interventions can reduce problem behavior without the use of extinction.

Results of numerous studies have, in fact, demonstrated that a variety of reinforcement and punishment procedures can effectively treat problem behavior (see reviews by Cooper et al., 1987; Favell et al., 1982; Matson & DiLorenzo, 1984). However, procedures such as DRO, DRA, and punishment typically include an implicit extinction component, and the potential contribution of extinction to the utility of these alternative treatments is generally overlooked. In fact, results of several recent studies indicate that the effects of reinforcement-based interventions may be limited unless extinction is included as part of the treatment (e.g., W. Fisher et al., 1993; Mazaleski et al., 1993; Williamson, Coon, Lemoine, & Cohen, 1983; Zarcone, Iwata, Mazaleski, & Smith, 1994). In addition, data from a number of studies suggest that even restrictive interventions (implemented without extinction), such as time-out, water mist, manual restraint, verbal reprimands, mouthwash, and the noncontingent application of protective equipment, can be less effective than properly designed extinction procedures (e.g., Dorsey et al., 1982; Iwata et al., 1994; Luiselli, 1988).

These research findings suggest that extinction, which is rarely recommended as a single intervention, may be a critical component in the treatment of severe behavior disorders. Further, extinction appears to play an influential role in the development and generalization of adaptive behavior. In light of the potential contribution of an extinction technology to such a broad array of applied problems, it seems that time would be well spent conducting both comparative and component analyses to identify key factors that affect the course of extinction in applied settings.

REFERENCES

Adams, J. F., Nemeth, R. V., & Pavlik, W. B. (1982). Between- and within-subjects PRE with sucrose incentives. *Bulletin of the Psychonomic Society, 20,* 261–262.

Aiken, E. G. (1957). The effort variable in the acquisition, extinction, and spontaneous recovery of an instrumental response. *Journal of Experimental Psychology, 53,* 47–51.

Alessandri, S. M., Sullivan, M. W., & Lewis, M. (1990). Violation of expectancy and frustration in early infancy. *Developmental Psychology, 26,* 738–744.

Amsel, A. (1958). The role of frustrative nonreward in noncontinuous reward situations. *Psychological Bulletin, 55,* 102–119.

Amsel, A., Hug, J. J., & Surridge, C. T. (1968). Number of food pellets, goal approaches, and the partial reinforcement effect after minimal acquisition. *Journal of Experimental Psychology, 77,* 530–534.

Antonitis, J. J. (1951). Response variability in the white rat during conditioning, extinction, and reconditioning. *Journal of Experimental Psychology, 42,* 273–281.

Applezweig, M. H. (1951). Response potential as a function of effort. *Journal of Comparative and Physiological Psychology, 44,* 225–235.

Azrin, N. H., & Holz, W. C. (1961). Punishment during fixed-interval reinforcement. *Journal of the Experimental Analysis of Behavior, 4,* 343–347.

Azrin, N. H., Hutchinson, R. R., & Hake, D. F. (1966). Extinction-induced aggression. *Journal of the Experimental Analysis of Behavior, 9,* 191–204.

Baer, D. M. (1966). Effect of withdrawal of positive reinforcement on an extinguishing response in young children. In T. Verhave (Ed.), *The experimental analysis of behavior: Selected readings* (pp. 171–179). New York: Appleton-Century-Crofts.

Baer, R. A., Blount, R. L., Detrich, R., & Stokes, T. F. (1987). Using intermittent reinforcement to program maintenance of verbal/nonverbal correspondence. *Journal of Applied Behavior Analysis, 20,* 179–184.

Baker, A. G. (1990). Contextual conditioning during free-operant extinction: Unsignaled, signaled, and backward-signaled noncontingent food. *Animal Learning & Behavior, 18,* 59–70.

Barnes, W., & Tombaugh, T. N. (1970). Effects of sucrose rewards on the overtraining extinction effect. *Journal of Experimental Psychology, 86,* 335–359.

Baroff, G. S., & Tate, B. G. (1968). The use of aversive stimulation in the treatment of chronic self-injurious behavior. *Journal of the American Academy of Child Psychiatry, 7,* 454–470.

Baumeister, A. A., & Forehand, R. (1971). Effects of extinction of an instrumental response on stereotyped body rocking in severe retardates. *Psychological Record, 21,* 235–240.

Baumeister, A. A., & Hawkins, W. F. (1966). Extinction and disinhibition as a function of reinforcement schedule with severely retarded children. *Journal of Experimental Child Psychology, 3,* 343–347.

Beninger, R. J., & Kendall, S. B. (1975). Behavioral contrast in rats with different reinforcers and different response topographies. *Journal of the Experimental Analysis of Behavior, 24,* 267–280.

Benoit, R. B., & Mayer, G. R. (1974). Extinction: Guidelines for its selection and use. *Personnel and Guidance Journal, 52,* 290–295.

Birch, D. (1965). Extended training extinction effect under massed and spaced extinction trials. *Journal of Experimental Psychology, 70,* 315–322.

Bird, F., Dores, P. A., Moniz, D., & Robinson, J. (1989). Reducing severe aggressive and self-injurious behaviors with functional communication training. *American Journal on Mental Retardation, 94,* 37–48.

Bitterman, M. E., Feddersen, W. E., & Tyler, D. W. (1953). Secondary reinforcement and the discrimination hypothesis. *American Journal of Psychology, 66,* 456–464.

Bloomfield, T. M. (1967). Some temporal properties of behavioral contrast. *Journal of the Experimental Analysis of Behavior, 10,* 159–164.

Boakes, R. A. (1973). Response decrements produced by extinction and by response-independent reinforcement. *Journal of the Experimental Analysis of Behavior, 19,* 293–302.

Boe, E. E., & Church, R. M. (1967). Permanent effects of punishment during extinction. *Journal of Comparative and Physiological Psychology, 63,* 486–492.

Brimer, C. J. (1970a). Disinhibition of an operant response. *Learning and Motivation, 1,* 346–371.

Brimer, C. J. (1970b). Inhibition and disinhibition of an operant response as a function of the amount and type of prior training. *Psychonomic Science, 21,* 191–192.

Brown, R. T., & Wagner, A. R. (1964). Resistance to punishment and extinction following training with shock or nonreinforcement. *Journal of Experimental Psychology, 68,* 503–507.

Cameron, M. J., Luiselli, J. K., McGrath, M., & Carlton, R. (1992). Stimulus control analysis and treatment of noncompliant behavior. *Journal of Developmental and Physical Disabilities, 4,* 141–150.

Capaldi, E. J. (1964). Effect of N-length, number of different N-lengths, and number of reinforcements on resistance to extinction. *Journal of Experimental Psychology, 658,* 230–239.

Capaldi, E. J., Berg, R. F., & Sparling, D. (1971). Trial spacing and emotionality in the rat. *Journal of Comparative and Physiological Psychology, 76,* 290–299.

Capaldi, E. J., & Bowen, J. N. (1964). Delay of reward and goal box confinement time in extinction. *Psychonomic Science, 1,* 141–142.

Carr, E. G., & Durand, V. M. (1985). Reducing behavior problems through functional communication training. *Journal of Applied Behavior Analysis, 18,* 111–126.

Carr, E. G., & Kologinsky, E. (1983). Acquisition of sign language by autistic children II. Spontaneity and generalization effects. *Journal of Applied Behavior Analysis, 16,* 297–314.

Catania, A. C. (1969). Concurrent performances: Inhibition of one response by reinforcement of another. *Journal of the Experimental Analysis of Behavior, 12,* 731–744.

Catania, A. C. (1992). *Learning.* Englewood Cliffs, NJ: Prentice Hall.

Chen, J., & Amsel, A. (1982). Habituation to shock and learned persistence in preweanling, juvenile, and adult rats. *Journal of Experimental Psychology: Animal Behavior Processes, 8,* 113–125.

Cooper, J. O., Heron, T. E., & Heward, W. L. (1987). Applied behavior analysis. Columbus, OH: Merrill.

Cross, S. M., Dickson, A. L., & Sisemore, D. A. (1978). A comparison of three response-elimination procedures following VR training with institutionalized, moderately retarded individuals. *Psychological Record, 28,* 589–597.

Crum, J., Brown, W. L., & Bitterman, M. E. (1951). The effect of partial and delayed reinforcement on resistance to extinction. *American Journal of Psychology, 64,* 228–237.

Davis, H., & Donenfeld, I. (1967). Extinction induced social interaction in rats. *Psychonomic Science, 7,* 85–86.

Deur, J. L., & Parke, R. D. (1970). Effects of inconsistent punishment on aggression in children. *Developmental Psychology, 2,* 403–411.

Dorsey, M. F., Iwata, B. A., Reid, D. H., & Davis, P. A. (1982). Protective equipment: Continuous and contingent application in the treatment of self-injurious behavior. *Journal of Applied Behavior Analysis, 15,* 217–230.

Drabman, R. S., & Jarvie, G. (1977). Counseling parents of children with behavior problems: The use of extinction and time-out techniques. *Pediatrics, 59,* 78–85.

Dubanoski, R. A., & Weiner, H. R. (1978). Resistance to extinction: A test of the discrimination hypothesis. *Psychological Reports, 42,* 91–97.

Ducharme, J. M., & Van Houten, R. (1994). Operant extinction in the treatment of severe maladaptive behavior. *Behavior Modification, 18,* 139–170.

Duker, P. (1975). Behaviour control of self-biting in a Lesch-Nyhan patient. *Journal of Mental Deficiency Research, 19,* 11–19.

Duker, P. C., & van Lent, C. (1991). Inducing variability in communicative gestures used by severely retarded individuals. *Journal of Applied Behavior Analysis, 24,* 379–386.

Dunlap, G., & Johnson, J. (1985). Increasing the independent responding of autistic children with unpredictable supervision. *Journal of Applied Behavior Analysis, 18,* 227–236.

Durand, V. M., & Mindell, J. A. (1990). Behavioral treatment of multiple childhood sleep disorders. *Behavior Modification, 14,* 37–49.

Dyck, D. G., Mellgren, R. L., & Nation, J. R. (1974). Punishment of appetitively reinforced instrumental behavior: Factors affecting response persistence. *Journal of Experimental Psychology, 102,* 125–132.

Eisenberger, R. (1992). Learned industriousness. *Psychological Review, 99,* 248–267.

Eisenberger, R., & Leonard, J. M. (1980). Effects of conceptual task difficulty on generalized persistence. *American Journal of Psychology, 93,* 285–298.

Ellis, N. R. (1962). Amount of reward and operant behavior in mental defectives. *American Journal of Mental Deficiency, 66,* 595–599.

Ellson, D. G. (1938). Quantitative studies of the interaction of simple habits. I. Recovery from specific and generalized effects of extinction. *Journal of Experimental Psychology, 23,* 339–358.

Enkema, S., Slavin, R., Spaeth, C., & Neuringer, A. (1972). Extinction in the presence of free food. *Psychonomic Science, 26,* 267–268.

Epstein, R. (1983). Resurgence of previously reinforced behavior during extinction. *Behaviour Analysis Letters, 3,* 391–397.

Fagen, J. W. (1979). Behavioral contrast in infants. *Infant Behavior and Development, 2,* 101–112.

Favell, J. E., Azrin, N. H., Baumeister, A. A., Carr, E. G., Dorsey, M. F., Forehand, R., Foxx, R. M., Lovaas, O. I., Rincover, A., Risley, T. R., Romanczyk, R. G., Russo, D. C., Schroeder, S. R., & Solnick, J. V. (1982). The treatment of self-injurious behavior. *Behavior Therapy, 13,* 529–554.

Fehrer, E. (1956). Effects of amount of reinforcement and of pre- and postreinforcement delays on learning and extinction. *Journal of Experimental Psychology, 52,* 167–176.

Ferster, C. B., & Skinner, B. F. (1957). *Schedules of reinforcement.* New York: Appleton-Century-Crofts.

Fisher, E. B., Jr. (1979). Overjustification effects in token economies. *Journal of Applied Behavior Analysis, 12,* 407–415.

Fisher, W., Piazza, C., Cataldo, M., Harrell, R., Jefferson, G., & Conner, R. (1993). Functional communication training with and without extinction and punishment. *Journal of Applied Behavior Analysis, 26,* 23–36.

Forehand, R. (1973). Teacher recording of deviant behavior: A stimulus for behavior change. *Journal of Behavior Therapy and Experimental Psychiatry, 4,* 39–40.

Forehand, R., Sturgis, E. T., McMahon, R. J., Aguar, D., Green, K., Wells, K. C., & Breiner, J. (1974). Parent behavioral training to modify child noncompliance: Treatment generalization across time and from home to school. *Behavior Modification, 3,* 3–25.

Fowler, S. A., & Baer, D. M. (1981). "Do I have to be good all day?" The timing of delayed reinforcement as a factor in generalization. *Journal of Applied Behavior Analysis, 14,* 13–24.

Foxx, R. M., & McMorrow, M. J. (1983). The effects of continuous and fixed ratio schedules of external consequences on the performance and extinction of human stereotyped behavior. *Behaviour Analysis Letters, 3,* 371–379.

France, K. G., & Hudson, S. M. (1990). Behavior management of infant sleep disturbance. *Journal of Applied Behavior Analysis, 23,* 91–98.

Frederiksen, L. W., & Peterson, G. L. (1974). Schedule-induced aggression in nursery school children. *Psychological Record, 24,* 343–351.

Furomoto, L. (1971). Extinction in the pigeon after continuous reinforcement: Effects of number of reinforced responses. *Psychological Reports, 28,* 331–338.

Gallup, G. G., Jr., & Altomari, T. S. (1969). Activity as a postsituation measure of frustrative nonreward. *Journal of Comparative and Physiological Psychology, 68,* 382–384.

Goh, H., & Iwata, B. A. (1994). Behavioral persistence and variability during extinction of self-injury maintained by escape. *Journal of Applied Behavior Analysis, 27,* 173–174.

Grant, L., & Evans, A. (1994). *Principles of behavior analysis.* New York: Harper Collins.

Gross, A. M., & Drabman, R. S. (1981). Behavioral contrast and behavior therapy. *Behavior Therapy, 12,* 231–246.

Gutman, A. (1978). The effect of extended baseline training on positive behavioral contrast: Reversible and preventable retardation. *Psychological Record, 28,* 399–404.

Haddad, N. F., & Mellgren, R. L. (1976). Effects of magnitude of reward and intensity of intermittent punishment on resistance to extinction. *Bulletin of the Psychonomic Society, 7,* 449–451.

Hagopian, L. P., Fisher, W. W., & Legacy, S. M. (1994). Schedule effects of noncontingent reinforcement on attention-maintained destructive behavior in identical quadruplets. *Journal of Applied Behavior Analysis, 27,* 317–325.

Halevy, G., Feldon, J., & Weiner, I. (1987). Resistance to extinction and punishment following training with shock and non-reinforcement: Failure to obtain cross-tolerance. *Quarterly Journal of Experimental Psychology, 39B,* 147–160.

Halliday, M. S., & Boakes, R. A. (1971). Behavioral contrast and response independent reinforcement. *Journal of the Experimental Analysis of Behavior, 16,* 429–434.

Halpern, J., & Poon, L. (1971). Human partial reinforcement extinction effects: An information-processing development from Capaldi's sequential theory. *Journal of Experimental Psychology, 89,* 207–227.

Haralson, J. V., Gillman, C. B., & Ralph, G. S. (1965). Interaction between effort and partial reinforcement in free-operant response of rats and fish. *Psychological Reports, 16,* 761–768.

Hatton, G. I. (1965). Drive shifts during extinction: Effects on extinction and spontaneous recovery of bar-pressing behavior. *Journal of Comparative and Physiological Psychology, 59,* 385–391.

Hearst, E. (1961). Resistance to extinction functions in the single organism. *Journal of the Experimental Analysis of Behavior, 4,* 133–144.

Herbert, E. W., Pinkston, E. M., Cordua, G., & Jackson, C. (1973). Adverse effects of differential parental attention. *Journal of Applied Behavior Analysis, 6,* 15–30.

Herrick, R. M. (1965). Lever displacement under a fixed-ratio schedule and subsequent extinction. *Journal of Comparative and Physiological Psychology, 59,* 263–270.

Holton, R. B. (1961). Amplitude of an instrumental response following the cessation of reward. *Child Development, 32,* 107–116.

Holz, W. C., & Azrin, N. H. (1963). A comparison of several procedures for eliminating behavior. *Journal of the Experimental Analysis of Behavior, 6,* 399–406.

Homme, L. E. (1956). Spontaneous recovery and statistical learning theory. *Journal of Experimental Psychology, 51,* 205–212.

Horner, R. D., & Barton, E. S. (1980). Operant techniques in the analysis and modification of self-injurious behavior: A review. *Behavior Research of Severe Developmental Disabilities, 1,* 61–91.

Horner, R. H., & Day, H. M. (1991). The effects of response efficiency on functionally equivalent competing behaviors. *Journal of Applied Behavior Analysis, 24,* 719–732.

Horns, H. L., & Heron, W. T. (1940). A study of disinhibition in the white rat. *Journal of Comparative Psychology, 30,* 97–102.

Hulicka, I. M., Capehart, J., & Viney, W. (1960). The effect of stimulus variation on response probability during extinction. *Journal of Comparative and Physiological Psychology, 53,* 79–82.

Hurwitz, H. M. B. (1962). Periodicity of response in operant extinction following continuous and fixed ratio reinforcement. *Quarterly Journal of Experimental Psychology, 14,* 1–7.

Iwata, B. A., Pace, G. M., Cowdery, G. E., & Miltenberger, R. G. (1994). What makes extinction work: An analysis of procedural form and function. *Journal of Applied Behavior Analysis, 27,* 131–144.

Iwata, B. A., Pace, G. M., Kalsher, M. J., Cowdery, G. E., & Cataldo, M. F. (1990). Experimental analysis and extinction of self-injurious escape behavior. *Journal of Applied Behavior Analysis, 23,* 11–27.

Jenkins, H. M. (1962). Resistance to extinction when partial reinforcement is followed by regular reinforcement. *Journal of Experimental Psychology, 64,* 441–450.

Jenkins, W. O., & Rigby, M. K. (1950). Partial (periodic) versus continuous reinforcement in resistance to extinction. *Journal of Comparative and Physiological Psychology, 43,* 30–40.

Johnson, N. A. (1973). Effect of number of secondary reinforcers on resistance to extinction in children. *Journal of Experimental Psychology, 100,* 375–379.

Johnson, N., & Viney, W. (1970). Resistance to extinction as a function of effort. *Journal of Comparative and Physiological Psychology, 71,* 171–174.

Johnson, S. M., Bolstad, O. D., & Lobitz, G. K. (1976). Generalization and contrast phenomena in behavior modification with children. In E. Marsh & L. Hamerlynck (Eds.), *Behavior modification in families* (pp. 123–145). New York: Brunner/Mazel.

Johnson, W. L., & Baumeister, A. A. (1981). Behavioral techniques for decreasing aberrant behaviors of retarded and autistic persons. In R. M. Eisler, M. Hersen, & P. M. Miller (Eds.), *Progress in behavior modification* (Vol. 12, pp. 119–170). New York: Academic Press.

Jones, F. H., Simmons, J. Q., & Frankel, F. (1974). An extinction procedure for eliminating self-destructive behavior in a 9-year-old autistic girl. *Journal of Autism and Childhood Schizophrenia, 4,* 241–250.

Katz, R. C. (1971). Interactions between the facilitative and inhibitory effects of a punishing stimulus in the control of children's hitting behavior. *Child Development, 42,* 1433–1446.

Kazdin, A. E. (1994). *Behavior modification in applied settings* (5th ed.). Pacific Grove, CA: Brooks/Cole.

Kazdin, A. E., & Polster, R. (1973). Intermittent token reinforcement and response maintenance in extinction. *Behavior Therapy, 4,* 386–391.

Keller, F. S. (1940). The effect of sequence of continuous and periodic reinforcement upon the "reflex reserve." *Journal of Experimental Psychology, 27,* 559–565.

Kelly, J. A., & Drabman, R. S. (1977). Generalizing response suppression of self-injurious behavior through an overcorrection punishment procedure: A case study. *Behavior Therapy, 8,* 468–472.

Kelly, J. F., & Hake, D. F. (1970). An extinction-induced increase in an aggressive response with humans. *Journal of the Experimental Analysis of Behavior, 14,* 153–164.

Kimble, G. A. (1961). *Hilgard and Marquis' conditioning and learning* (2nd ed.). New York: Appleton-Century-Crofts.

Koegel, R. L., Egel, A. L., & Williams, J. A. (1980). Behavioral contrast and generalization across settings in the treatment of autistic children. *Journal of Experimental Child Psychology, 30,* 422–437.

Koegel, R. L., & Rincover, A. (1977). Research on the difference between generalization and maintenance in extra-therapy responding. *Journal of Applied Behavior Analysis, 10,* 1–12.

Krane, R. V., & Ison, J. R. (1971). Positive induction in differential instrumental conditioning: Effect of the interstimulus interval. *Journal of Comparative and Physiological Psychology, 75,* 129–135.

Kurke, M. I. (1956). Extinction rate as a function of distribution of practice and of practice sessions. *Journal of Comparative and Physiological Psychology, 49,* 158–161.

Lalli, J. S., Zanolli, K., & Wohn, T. (1994). Using extinction to promote response variability in toy play. *Journal of Applied Behavior Analysis, 27,* 735–736.

Lambert, J. (1975). Extinction by retarded children following discrimination learning with and without errors. *American Journal of Mental Deficiency, 80,* 286–291.

Lamberth, J., & Dyck, D. G. (1972). Reward magnitude and sequence of magnitudes as determinants of resistance to extinction in humans. *Journal of Experimental Psychology, 96,* 280–286.

Lattal, K. A. (1972). Response-reinforcer independence and conventional extinction after fixed-interval and variable-interval schedules. *Journal of the Experimental Analysis of Behavior, 18,* 133–140.

LaVigna, G. W., & Donnellan, A. M. (1986). *Alternatives to punishment: Solving behavior problems with non-aversive strategies.* New York: Irvington.

Laws, D. R., Brown, R. A., Epstein, J., & Hocking, N. (1971). Reduction of inappropriate social behavior in disturbed children by an untrained paraprofessional therapist. *Behavior Therapy, 2,* 519–533.

Lawton, C., France, K. G., & Blampied, N. M. (1991). Treatment of infant sleep disturbance by graduated extinction. *Child and Family Behavior Therapy, 13,* 39–55.

Leitenberg, H., Rawson, R. A., & Bath, K. (1970). Reinforcement of competing behavior during extinction. *Science, 169,* 301–303.

Leitenberg, H., Rawson, R. A., & Mulick, J. A. (1975). Extinction and reinforcement of alternative behavior. *Journal of Comparative and Physiological Psychology, 88,* 640–652.

Lerman, D. C., & Iwata, B. A. (1995). Prevalence of the extinction burst and its attenuation during treatment. *Journal of Applied Behavior Analysis, 28,* 93–94.

Lerman, D. C., Iwata, B. A., Shore, B. A., & Kahng, S. (1996). Responding maintained by intermittent reinforcement: Implications for the use of extinction with problem behavior in clinical settings. *Journal of Applied Behavior Analysis, 29,* 153–171.

Lewis, D. J. (1956). Acquisition, extinction, and spontaneous recovery as a function of percentage of reinforcement and intertrial intervals. *Journal of Experimental Psychology, 51,* 45–53.

Lewis, D. J. (1960). Partial reinforcement: A selective review of the literature since 1950. *Psychological Bulletin, 57,* 1–28.

Lewis, D. J., & Duncan, C. P. (1957). Expectation and resistance to extinction of a lever-pulling response as functions of percentage of reinforcement and amount of reward. *Journal of Experimental Psychology, 52,* 115–120.

Litchfield, P. M., & Duerfeldt, P. H. (1969). Resistance to extinction in children as a function of N-lengths and number of different N-lengths. *Psychonomic Science, 14,* 299–300.

Logan, F. A., Beier, E. M., & Kincaid, W. D. (1956). Extinction following partial and varied reinforcement. *Journal of Experimental Psychology, 52,* 65–70.

Lovaas, O. I., Freitag, G., Gold, V. J., & Kassorla, I. C. (1965). Experimental studies in childhood schizophrenia: Analysis of self-destructive behavior. *Journal of Experimental Child Psychology, 2,* 67–84.

Lovaas, O. I., & Simmons, J. Q. (1969). Manipulation of self-destruction in three retarded children. *Journal of Applied Behavior Analysis, 2,* 143–157.

Luiselli, J. K. (1988). Comparative analysis of sensory extinction treatments for self-injury. *Education and Treatment of Children, 11,* 149–156.

Luiselli, J. K. (1991). Behavioral-pharmacological treatment of severe self injury in an adult with dual sensory impairment. *Journal of Behavior Therapy and Experimental Psychiatry, 22,* 233–238.

Maatsch, J. L., Adelman, H. M., & Denny, M. R. (1954). Effort and resistance to extinction of the bar-pressing response. *Journal of Comparative and Physiological Psychology, 47,* 47–50.

Mackintosh, I. (1955). Irrelevant responses during extinction. *Canadian Journal of Psychology, 9,* 183–189.

Mackintosh, N. J. (1974). *The psychology of animal learning.* New York: Academic Press.

Mackintosh, N. J., Little, L., & Lord, J. (1972). Some determinants of behavioral contrast in pigeons and rats. *Learning and Motivation, 3,* 148–161.

Malloy, P., & Lewis, D. J. (1988). A laboratory demonstration of persistent human avoidance. *Behavior Therapy, 19,* 229–241.

Malott, R. W., Whaley, D. L., & Malott, R. W. (1991). *Elementary principles of behavior* (2nd ed.). Englewood Cliffs, NJ: Prentice Hall.

Margulies, S. (1961). Response duration in operant level, regular reinforcement, and extinction. *Journal of the Experimental Analysis of Behavior, 4,* 317–321.

Martin, G., & Pear, J. (1992). *Behavior modification: What it is and how to do it* (4th ed.). Englewood Cliffs, NJ: Prentice Hall.

Mason, S. A., & Iwata, B. A. (1990). Artifactual effects of sensory-integrative therapy on self-injurious behavior. *Journal of Applied Behavior Analysis, 23,* 361–370.

Matson, J. L., & DiLorenzo, T. M. (1984). *Punishment and its alternatives: New perspectives for behavior modification.* New York: Springer.

May, R. B., & Beauchamp, K. L. (1969). Stimulus change, previous experience and extinction. *Journal of Comparative and Physiological Psychology, 68,* 607–610.

Mayhew, G. L., & Anderson, J. (1980). Delayed and immediate reinforcement: Retarded adolescents in an educational setting. *Behavior Modification, 4,* 527–545.

Mazaleski, J. L., Iwata, B. A., Vollmer, T. R., Zarcone, J. R., & Smith, R. G. (1993). Analysis of the reinforcement and extinction components in DRO contingencies with self-injury. *Journal of Applied Behavior Analysis, 26,* 143–156.

McDowell, E. E., Nunn, L. K., & McCutcheon, B. A. (1969). Comparison of a programed method of beginning reading instruction with the look-and-say method. *Psychological Record, 19,* 319–327.

McNamara, H. J., & Wike, E. L. (1958). The effects of irregular learning conditions upon the rate and permanence of learning. *Journal of Comparative and Physiological Psychology, 51,* 363–366.

McSweeney, F. K., & Melville, C. L. (1993). Behavioral contrast for key pecking as a function of component duration when only one component varies. *Journal of the Experimental Analysis of Behavior, 60,* 331–343.

Mercer, C. D., & Snell, M. E. (1977). *Learning theory research in mental retardation: Implications for teaching.* Columbus, OH: Merrill.

Meyers, L. S., & Capaldi, E. J. (1970). Resistance to extinction as a function of sequence of events in partial reinforcement. *Psychonomic Science, 19,* 199–200.

Millenson, J. R., & Hurwitz, H. M. B. (1961). Some temporal and sequential properties of behavior during conditioning and extinction. *Journal of the Experimental Analysis of Behavior, 4,* 97–106.

Miller, N. E., & Stevenson, S. S. (1936). Agitated behavior of rats during experimental extinction and a curve of spontaneous recovery. *Journal of Comparative Psychology, 21,* 205–231.

Miron, M. B. (1973). Therapy of self-injurious behavior in institutions. *Current Psychiatric Therapies, 13,* 197–206.

Moreland, J. W., Stalling, R. B., & Walker, L. C. (1983). The effect of interpolated continuous reinforcement on persistence in extinction: A replication demonstrating reversibility. *Behaviour Analysis Letters, 3,* 149–156.

Morris, J. P. (1968). Changes in response force during acquisition and extinction in retarded children. *American Journal of Mental Deficiency, 73,* 384–390.

Moss, J. D., Ruthven, A. J., Hawkins, W. M., & Topping, J. S. (1983). The relative effects of three response-elimination procedures in severely/profoundly and trainable retarded individuals. *Psychological Record, 33,* 231–236.

Mowrer, O. H., & Jones, H. M. (1943). Extinction and behavior variability as functions of effortfulness of task. *Journal of Experimental Psychology, 33,* 269–285.

Muttar, A. K., Peck, D., Whitlow, D., & Fraser, W. (1975). Reversal of a severe case of self-mutilation. *Journal of Mental Deficiency Research, 19,* 3–9.

Nation, J. R., & Boyajian, L. G. (1980). Continuous before partial reinforcement: Effect on persistence training and resistance to extinction in humans. *American Journal of Psychology, 93,* 697–710.

Neisworth, J. T., Hunt, F. M., Gallup, H. R., & Madle, R. A. (1985). Reinforcer displacement: A preliminary study of the clinical application of the CRF/EXT effect. *Behavior Modification, 9,* 103–115.

Neisworth, J. T., & Moore, F. (1972). Operant treatment of asthmatic responding with the parent as therapist. *Behavior Therapy, 3,* 95–99.

Neuringer, A. J. (1970). Superstitious key pecking after three peck-produced reinforcements. *Journal of the Experimental Analysis of Behavior, 13,* 127–134.

Nevin, J. A. (1968). Differential reinforcement and stimulus control of not responding. *Journal of the Experimental Analysis of Behavior, 11,* 715–726.

Nevin, J. A. (1974). Response strength in multiple schedules. *Journal of the Experimental Analysis of Behavior, 21,* 389–408.

Nevin, J. A. (1988). Behavioral momentum and the

partial reinforcement effect. *Psychological Bulletin, 103,* 44–56.

Nevin, J. A. (1992). An integrative model for the study of behavioral momentum. *Journal of the Experimental Analysis of Behavior, 57,* 301–316.

Nevin, J. A., Tota, M. E., Torquato, R. D., & Shull, R. L. (1990). Alternative reinforcement increases resistance to change: Pavlovian or operant contingencies? *Journal of the Experimental Analysis of Behavior, 53,* 359–379.

Pace, G. M., Iwata, B. A., Cowdery, G. E., Andree, P. J., & McIntyre, T. (1993). Stimulus (instructional) fading during extinction of self-injurious escape behavior. *Journal of Applied Behavior Analysis, 26,* 205–212.

Perin, C. T. (1942). Behavior potentiality as a joint function of the amount of training and the degree of hunger at the time of extinction. *Journal of Experimental Psychology, 30,* 93–113.

Peterson, L. P. (1956). Variable delayed reinforcement. *Journal of Comparative and Physiological Psychology, 49,* 232–234.

Peterson, R. F., Merwin, M. R., Moyer, T. J., & Whitehurst, G. J. (1971). Generalized imitation: The effects of experimenter absence, differential reinforcement, and stimulus complexity. *Journal of Experimental Child Psychology, 12,* 114–128.

Pinkston, E. M., Reese, N. M., LeBlanc, J. M., & Baer, D. M. (1973). Independent control of a preschool child's aggression and peer interaction by contingent teacher attention. *Journal of Applied Behavior Analysis, 6,* 115–124.

Pittenger, D. J., & Pavlik, W. B. (1988). Analysis of the partial reinforcement extinction effect in humans using absolute and relative comparisons of schedules. *American Journal of Psychology, 101,* 1–14.

Pittenger, D. J., & Pavlik, W. B. (1989). Resistance to extinction in humans: Analysis of the generalized partial reinforcement effect. *Learning and Motivation, 20,* 60–72.

Pittenger, D. J., Pavlik, W. B., Flora, S. R., & Kontos, J. (1988). Analysis of the partial reinforcement extinction effect in humans as a function of sequence of reinforcement schedules. *American Journal of Psychology, 101,* 371–382.

Premack, D. (1969). On some boundary conditions of contrast. In J. T. Tapp (Ed.), *Reinforcement and behavior* (pp. 120–145). New York: Academic Press.

Quartermain, D. (1965). Effect of effort on resistance to extinction of the bar-pressing response. *Quarterly Journal of Experimental Psychology, 17,* 63–64.

Quartermain, E., & Vaughan, G. M. (1961). Effect of interpolating continuous reinforcement between partial training and extinction. *Psychological Reports, 8,* 235–237.

Rachlin, H. (1973). Contrast and matching. *Psychological Review, 80,* 217–234.

Redd, W. H. (1970). Generalization of adult's stimulus control of children's behavior. *Journal of Experimental Child Psychology, 9,* 286–296.

Rekers, G. A., & Lovaas, O. I. (1974). Behavioral treatment of deviant sex-role behaviors in a male child. *Journal of Applied Behavior Analysis, 7,* 173–190.

Renner, K. E. (1965). Delay of reinforcement and resistance to extinction: A supplementary report. *Psychological Reports, 16,* 197–198.

Repp, A. C., Felce, D., & Barton, L. E. (1988). Basing the treatment of stereotypic and self-injurious behaviors on hypotheses of their causes. *Journal of Applied Behavior Analysis, 21,* 281–289.

Rescorla, R. A., & Skucy, J. C. (1969). Effect of response-independent reinforcers during extinction. *Journal of Comparative and Physiological Psychology, 67,* 381–389.

Reynolds, G. S. (1961). Behavioral contrast. *Journal of the Experimental Analysis of Behavior, 4,* 57–71.

Rieg, T. S., Smith, N. F., & Vyse, S. A. (1993). Differential reinforcement of other behavior and response suppression. *Psychological Record, 43,* 271–288.

Rilling, M. (1977). Stimulus control and inhibitory processes. In W. K. Honig & J. E. R. Staddon (Eds.), *Handbook of operant behavior* (pp. 432–480). Englewood Cliffs, NJ: Prentice Hall.

Rincover, A., Cook, R., Peoples, A., & Packard, D. (1979). Sensory extinction and sensory reinforcement principles for programming multiple adaptive behavior change. *Journal of Applied Behavior Analysis, 12,* 221–233.

Rincover, A., & Koegel, R. L. (1975). Setting generality and stimulus control in autistic children. *Journal of Applied Behavior Analysis, 8,* 235–246.

Romanczyk, R. G., Kistner, J. A., & Plienis, A. (1982). Self-stimulatory and self-injurious behavior: Etiology and treatment. In J. J. Steffan & P. Karoly (Eds.), *Advances in child behavior analysis and therapy* (pp. 189–254). Lexington, MA: Lexington Books.

Rovee-Collier, C. K., & Capatides, J. B. (1979). Positive behavioral contrast in 3-month-old infants on multiple conjugate reinforcement schedules. *Journal of the Experimental Analysis of Behavior, 32,* 15–27.

Sajwaj, T., Twardosz, S., & Burke, M. (1972). Side effects of extinction procedures in a remedial preschool. *Journal of Applied Behavior Analysis, 5,* 163–175.

Salend, S. J., & Meddaugh, D. (1985). Using a peer-mediated extinction procedure to decrease obscene language. *The Pointer, 30,* 8–11.

Schmid, T. L. (1986). Reducing inappropriate behavior of mentally retarded children through interpolated reinforcement. *American Journal of Mental Deficiency, 91,* 286–293.

Schroeder, S. (1972). Parametric effects of reinforcement, frequency, amount of reinforcement, and required response force on shelter workshop behavior. *Journal of Applied Behavior Analysis, 5,* 431–442.

Schwartz, B. (1980). Development of complex, stereotyped behavior in pigeons. *Journal of the Experimental Analysis of Behavior, 33,* 153–166.

Schwartz, B. (1981). Reinforcement creates behavioral units. *Behaviour Analysis Letters, 1,* 33–41.

Schwartz, B. (1982). Reinforcement-induced behavioral stereotypy: How not to teach people to discover rules. *Journal of Experimental Psychology, 111,* 23–59.

Scott, E. D., & Wike, E. L. (1956). The effect of partially delayed reinforcement and trial-distribution on the extinction of an instrumental response. *American Journal of Psychology, 69,* 264–268.

Scott, P. M., Burton, R. V., & Yarrow, M. R. (1967). Social reinforcement under natural conditions. *Child Development, 38,* 53–63.

Sheffield, V. F. (1949). Extinction as a function of partial reinforcement and distribution of practice. *Journal of Experimental Psychology, 39,* 511–525.

Sheppard, W. C. (1969). Operant control of infant vocal and motor behavior. *Journal of Experimental Child Psychology, 7,* 36–51.

Shigley, R. H., & Guffey, J. (1978). Resistance to extinction as a function of partial reinforcement before and after continuous reinforcement in a human operant task. *Journal of General Psychology, 99,* 257–261.

Siegel, P. S., & Foshee, J. G. (1953). The law of primary reinforcement in children. *Journal of Experimental Psychology, 45,* 12–14.

Skinner, B. F. (1933a). On the rate of extinction of a conditioned reflex. *Journal of General Psychology, 8,* 114–127.

Skinner, B. F. (1933b). "Resistance to extinction" in the process of conditioning. *Journal of General Psychology, 9,* 420–429.

Skinner, B. F. (1936). A failure to obtain "disinhibition." *Journal of General Psychology, 14,* 127–135.

Skinner, B. F. (1938). *The behavior of organisms: An experimental analysis.* Acton, MA: Copley Publishing Group.

Skjoldager, P., Pierre, P. J., & Mittleman, G. (1993). Reinforcer magnitude and progressive ratio responding in the rat: Effects of increased effort, prefeeding, and extinction. *Learning and Motivation, 24,* 303–343.

Solomon, R. L. (1948). Effort and extinction rate: A confirmation. *Journal of Comparative and Physiological Psychology, 41,* 93–101.

Solomon, R. L., Kamin, L. J., & Wynne, L. C. (1953). Traumatic avoidance learning: The outcomes of several extinction procedures with dogs. *Journal of Abnormal and Social Psychology, 48,* 291–302.

Sperling, S. E. (1965). Reversal learning and resistance to extinction: A review of the rat literature. *Psychological Bulletin, 63,* 281–297.

Spradlin, J. E., Fixsen, D. L., & Girardeau, F. L. (1969). Reinstatement of an operant response by the delivery of reinforcement during extinction. *Journal of Experimental Child Psychology, 7,* 96–100.

Spradlin, J. E., Girardeau, F. L., & Hom, G. L. (1966). Stimulus properties of reinforcement during extinction of a free operant response. *Journal of Experimental Child Psychology, 4,* 369–380.

Sprague, J. R., & Horner, R. H. (1984). The effects of single instance, multiple instance, and general case training on generalized vending machine use by moderately and severely handicapped students. *Journal of Applied Behavior Analysis, 17,* 273–278.

Stebbins, W. C., & Lanson, R. N. (1962). Response latency as a function of reinforcement schedule. *Journal of the Experimental Analysis of Behavior, 5,* 299–304.

Steege, M. W., Wacker, D. P., Cigrand, K. C., Berg, W. K., Novak, C. G., Reimers, T. M., Sasso, G. M., & DeRaad, A. (1990). Use of negative reinforcement in the treatment of self-injurious behavior. *Journal of Applied Behavior Analysis, 23,* 459–467.

Stokes, T. F., & Baer, D. M. (1976). Preschool peers as mutual generalization-facilitating agents. *Behavior Therapy, 7,* 549–556.

Stokes, T. F., & Baer, D. M. (1977). An implicit technology of generalization. *Journal of Applied Behavior Analysis, 10,* 349–367.

Stokes, T. F., Baer, D. M., & Jackson, R. L. (1974). Programming the generalization of a greeting response in four retarded children. *Journal of Applied Behavior Analysis, 7,* 599–610.

Stokes, T. F., & Osnes, P. G. (1988). The developing applied technology of generalization and maintenance. In G. Dunlap, R. H. Horner, & R. L. Koegel (Eds.), *Generalization and maintenance: Life-style changes in applied settings* (pp. 5–19). Baltimore: Paul H. Brookes.

Sullivan, M. W., Lewis, M., & Alessandri, S. M. (1992). Cross-age stability in emotional expressions during learning and extinction. *Developmental Psychology, 28,* 58–63.

Sutherland, N. S., Mackintosh, N. J., & Wolfe, J. B. (1965). Extinction as a function of the order of partial and consistent reinforcement. *Journal of Experimental Psychology, 69,* 56–59.

Teichner, W. H. (1952). Experimental extinction as a function of the intertrial intervals during conditioning and extinction. *Journal of Experimental Psychology, 44,* 170–178.

Terrace, H. S. (1963). Discrimination learning with

and without "errors." *Journal of the Experimental Analysis of Behavior, 6,* 1–27.

Theios, J., & McGinnis, R. W. (1967). Partial reinforcement before and after continuous reinforcement. *Journal of Experimental Psychology, 73,* 479–481.

Thompson, T., & Bloom, W. (1966). Aggressive behavior and extinction-induced response-rate increase. *Psychonomic Science, 5,* 335–336.

Timmons, E. O. (1962). Weakening verbal behavior: A comparison of four methods. *Journal of General Psychology, 67,* 155–158.

Todd, J. T., Morris, E. K., & Fenza, K. M. (1989). Temporal organization of extinction-induced responding in preschool children. *The Psychological Record, 39,* 117–130.

Tombaugh, T. N. (1966). Resistance to extinction as a function of the interaction between training and extinction delays. *Psychological Reports, 19,* 791–798.

Tombaugh, T. N. (1970). A comparison of the effects of immediate reinforcement, constant delay of reinforcement, and partial delay of reinforcement on performance. *Canadian Journal of Psychology, 24,* 276–288.

Topping, J. S., & Ford, T. W. (1974). Response elimination with DRO and extinction: A within-subject comparison. *Psychological Record, 24,* 563–568.

Trotter, J. R. (1957). The timing of bar-pressing behaviour. *Quarterly Journal of Experimental Psychology, 9,* 78–87.

Uhl, C. (1973). Eliminating behavior with omission and extinction after varying amounts of training. *Animal Learning & Behavior, 1,* 237–240.

Uhl, C. N., & Young, A. G. (1967). Resistance to extinction as a function of incentive, percentage of reinforcement, and number of nonreinforced trials. *Journal of Experimental Psychology, 73,* 556–564.

Van Houten, R. (1993). The use of wrist weights to reduce self-injury maintained by sensory reinforcement. *Journal of Applied Behavior Analysis, 26,* 197–203.

Verplanck, W. S. (1955). The control of the content of conversation: Reinforcement of statements of opinion. *Journal of Abnormal and Social Psychology, 51,* 668–676.

Viney, W., Hulicka, I., Bitner, J., Raley, C. L., & Brewster, P. (1968). Effect of stimulus variation upon resistance to extinction in kindergarten children. *Journal of Comparative and Physiological Psychology, 65,* 539–541.

Vollmer, T. R., Iwata, B. A., Zarcone, J. R., Smith, R. G., & Mazaleski, J. L. (1993). The role of attention in the treatment of attention-maintained self-injurious behavior: Noncontingent reinforcement and differential reinforcement of other behavior. *Journal of Applied Behavior Analysis, 26,* 9–21.

Vyse, S., Rieg, R. S., & Smith, N. F. (1985). Reinforcement-based response elimination: The effects of response-reinforcement interval and response specificity. *Psychological Record, 35,* 365–376.

Wacker, D. P., Steege, M. W., Northup, J., Sasso, G., Berg, W., Reimers, T. L., Cooper, L., Cigrand, K., & Donn, L. (1990). A component analysis of functional communication training across three topographies of severe behavior problems. *Journal of Applied Behavior Analysis, 23,* 417–429.

Wagner, A. R. (1961). Effects of amount and percentage of reinforcement and number of acquisition trials on conditioning and extinction. *Journal of Experimental Psychology, 62,* 234–242.

Wahler, R. G. (1975). Some structural aspects of deviant child behavior. *Journal of Applied Behavior Analysis, 8,* 27–42.

Warren, A. B., & Brown, R. H. (1943). Conditioned operant response phenomena in children. *Journal of General Psychology, 28,* 181–207.

Waxler, C. Z., & Yarrow, M. R. (1970). Factors influencing imitative learning in preschool children. *Journal of Experimental Child Psychology, 9,* 115–130.

Weiner, H. (1964). Response cost effects during extinction following fixed-interval reinforcement in humans. *Journal of the Experimental Analysis of Behavior, 7,* 333–335.

Wike, E. L., Mellgren, R. L., & Cour, C. A. (1967). Delayed reward, delay-box confinement, and instrumental performance: A within-type design. *Psychological Reports, 21,* 857–862.

Williams, C. D. (1959). The elimination of tantrum behavior by extinction procedures. *Journal of Abnormal and Social Psychology, 59,* 269.

Williams, D. E., Kirkpatrick-Sanchez, S., & Iwata, B. A. (1993). A comparison of shock intensity in the treatment of longstanding and severe self-injurious behavior. *Research in Developmental Disabilities, 14,* 207–219.

Williamson, D. A., Coon, R. C., Lemoine, R. L., & Cohen, C. R. (1983). A practical application of sensory extinction for reducing the disruptive classroom behavior of a profoundly retarded child. *School Psychology Review, 12,* 205–211.

Wolf, M. M., Birnbrauer, J. S., Williams, T., & Lawler, J. (1965). A note on apparent extinction of the vomiting behavior of a retarded child. In L. P. Ullmann & L. Krasner (Eds.), *Case studies in behavior modification* (pp. 364–366). New York: Holt, Rinehart, & Winston.

Wright, D. F., Brown, R. A., & Andrews, M. E. (1978). Remission of chronic ruminative vomiting through a reversal of social contingencies. *Behaviour Research and Therapy, 16,* 134–136.

Yamaguchi, H. G., & Ladioray, G. L. (1962). Disinhibition as a function of extinction trials and stimulus intensity. *Journal of Comparative and Physiological Psychology, 55,* 572–577.

Young, A. G. (1966). Resistance to extinction as a function of number of nonreinforced trials and effortfulness of response. *Journal of Experimental Psychology, 72,* 610–613.

Youtz, R. E. P. (1938). Reinforcement, extinction, and spontaneous recovery in a nonpavlovian reaction. *Journal of Experimental Psychology, 22,* 305–318.

Zarcone, J. R., Iwata, B. A., Mazaleski, J. L., & Smith, R. G. (1994). Momentum and extinction effects on self-injurious escape behavior and noncompliance. *Journal of Applied Behavior Analysis, 27,* 649–658.

Zarcone, J. R., Iwata, B. A., Smith, R. G., Mazaleski, J. L., & Lerman, D. C. (1994). Reemergence and extinction of self-injurious escape behavior during stimulus (instructional) fading. *Journal of Applied Behavior Analysis, 27,* 307–316.

Zarcone, J. R., Iwata, B. A., Vollmer, T. R., Jagtiani, S., Smith, R. G., & Mazaleski, J. L. (1993). Extinction of self-injurious escape behavior with and without instructional fading. *Journal of Applied Behavior Analysis, 26,* 353–360.

Zeiler, M. D. (1971). Eliminating behavior with reinforcement. *Journal of the Experimental Analysis of Behavior, 16,* 401–405.

Received January 25, 1996
Initial editorial decision March 25, 1996
Revision received April 9, 1996
Final acceptance May 13, 1996
Action Editor, Joseph E. Spradlin

JOURNAL OF APPLIED BEHAVIOR ANALYSIS 1996, **29,** 409–431 NUMBER 3 (FALL 1996)

NAMING, THE FORMATION OF STIMULUS CLASSES, AND APPLIED BEHAVIOR ANALYSIS

ROBERT STROMER AND HARRY A. MACKAY

EUNICE KENNEDY SHRIVER CENTER AND NORTHEASTERN UNIVERSITY

AND

BOB REMINGTON

UNIVERSITY OF SOUTHAMPTON

The methods used in Sidman's original studies on equivalence classes provide a framework for analyzing functional verbal behavior. Sidman and others have shown how teaching receptive, name-referent matching may produce rudimentary oral reading and word comprehension skills. Eikeseth and Smith (1992) have extended these findings by showing that children with autism may acquire equivalence classes after learning to supply a common oral name to each stimulus in a potential class. A stimulus class analysis suggests ways to examine (a) the problem of programming generalization from teaching situations to other environments, (b) the expansion of the repertoires that occur in those settings, and (c) the use of naming to facilitate these forms of generalization. Such research will help to clarify and extend Horne and Lowe's recent (1996) account of the role of verbal behavior in the formation of stimulus classes.

DESCRIPTORS: naming, stimulus classes, stimulus equivalence, generalization, application of basic research

---

Sidman's early research on stimulus equivalence in individuals with mental retardation is viewed by many as a prototype for the behavioral analysis of rudimentary language and reading skills (e.g., Baer, 1982; Browder & Lalli, 1991; Mackay, 1991; McIlvane, 1992; Singh & Singh, 1986; Stromer, 1991; Stromer, Mackay, & Stoddard, 1992). Sidman (1971), for example, established new oral reading and comprehension skills, not by direct training, but via expansion of receptive and expressive language skills that the participant had acquired before the experiment. Sidman's work (see summary and discussion by Sidman, 1994) has provided the methodological and conceptual bases for a growing number of studies with implications for applied analyses (e.g., Clarke, Remington, & Light, 1986, 1988; Cowley, Green, & Braunling-McMorrow, 1992; de Rose, de Souza, & Hanna, in press; Haring, Breen, & Laitinen, 1989; Kennedy, Itkonen, & Lindquist, 1994; Lynch & Cuvo, 1995; Maydak, Stromer, Mackay, & Stoddard, 1995; Remington & Clarke, 1993a, 1993b; Stromer & Mackay, 1992, 1993; Stromer, Mackay, Howell, McVay, & Flusser, 1996).

Sidman's research has also raised theoretical issues about the nature of the relationship between verbal behavior and the formation of equivalence classes (Dugdale & Lowe, 1990; Mackay & Sidman, 1984; Sidman & Tailby, 1982; Sidman, Willson-Morris, & Kirk, 1986). For example, suppose that a participant is taught to match pictures and printed words to dictated words, and

This paper was prepared with support from the National Institute of Child Health and Human Development (Grants HD25995 and HD32506) and the Massachusetts Department of Mental Retardation (Contract 100220023SC). We are grateful to Dermot Barnes, Julio de Rose, Bill Dube, Murray Sidman, and Joe Spradlin for their helpful comments on versions of the manuscript.

Correspondence should be addressed to Robert Stromer, Behavioral Sciences Division, Eunice Kennedy Shriver Center, 200 Trapelo Road, Waltham, Massachusetts 02254 (E-mail: RStromer@Shriver.org).

then proves to be capable of (a) matching pictures and printed words and (b) orally naming either the pictures or the printed words. Few would disagree with the suggestion that the emergent matching could have resulted from active or implicit naming (Sidman, Cresson, & Willson-Morris, 1974). In a recent article, however, Horne and Lowe (1996) argue that virtually all such demonstrations of the formation of equivalence classes can be accounted for by the participant's verbal (naming) repertoire, despite some contradictory evidence (e.g., Green, 1990; Lazar, Davis-Lang, & Sanchez, 1984; Sidman et al., 1974, 1986).

The current debate about the role of verbal behavior in equivalence class formation (Horne & Lowe, 1996; commentaries and reply) occasioned the present reconsideration of the practical significance of Sidman's original studies (Sidman, 1971; Sidman & Cresson, 1973; Sidman et al., 1974) and other relevant work on equivalence and verbal behavior. Within that context, we focus on Eikeseth and Smith's (1992) study of naming and equivalence in children with autism because it has both direct and broader implications for applied research. Finally, we consider in detail the issues raised by Horne and Lowe's account of class formation and examine its relevance for applied behavior analysis.

Matching to Sample and Class Formation

Consider the practical objective of establishing all of the educationally relevant behaviors depicted in Figure 1 (Panel 1). Arrows connect the sample stimuli to the comparison stimuli of matching-to-sample tasks (Tasks 1, 3, 5, and 6) and connect these same stimuli to the verbalizations produced by the student (Tasks 2, 4, and 7). On (spoken) name-picture trials (Task 1) with the sample "dog," a response to the picture of a dog is reinforced; when the sample is "cat," a response to the picture of a cat is rein-

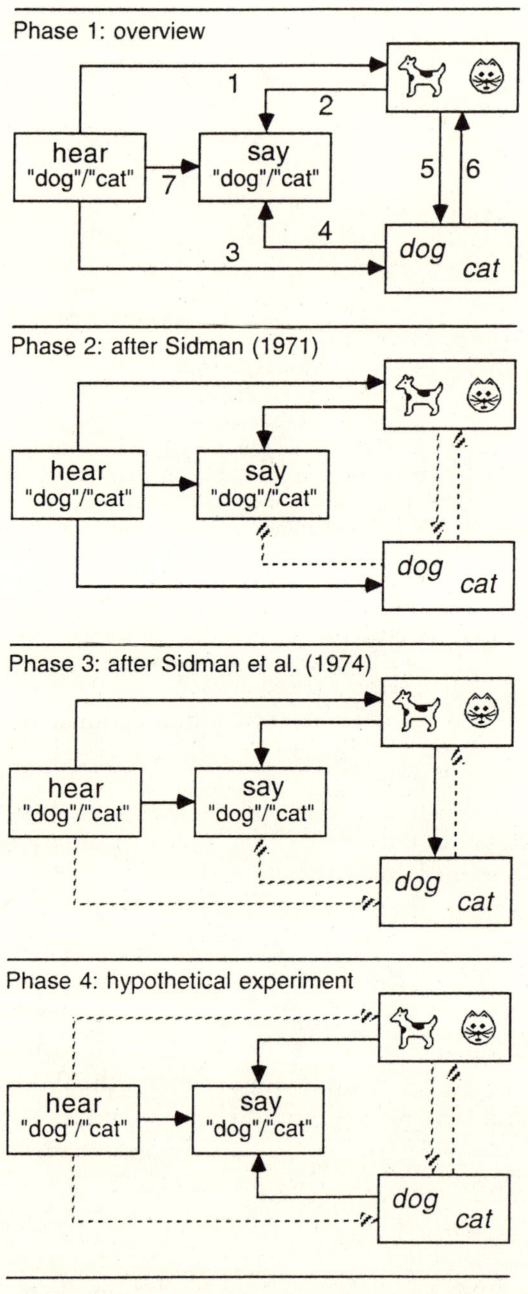

Figure 1. Diagrams representing networks of matching-to-sample and oral naming performances. Arrows connect the sample to comparison stimuli of the matching tasks, and the stimuli to their oral names. Solid arrows represent tasks used during training; broken arrows represent tasks used during testing.

forced. On name-word trials (Task 3), the comparison words *dog* and *cat* are matched to the corresponding "dog" and "cat" samples. In picture-word matching (Task 5), the comparisons *dog* and *cat* are matched to the pictures of the dog and cat, respectively; likewise, in word-picture matching (Task 6), the pictures of the dog and cat are matched to the word samples *dog* and *cat,* respectively. Other tasks involve naming aloud the pictures (Task 2) and printed words (Task 4) and repeating (imitating) the dictated names (Task 7) used during matching trials. Following Skinner's (1957) definitions, Task 2 is tacting and Task 7 is echoic responding (see also the discussion of verbal behavior and matching to sample by Michael, 1985). According to Horne and Lowe (1996), Tasks 2 and 7, together with Task 1 (receptive speech), are the components that, when integrated as a higher order bidirectional relation, constitute naming (see below).

Except for Task 7 (vocal imitation), the tasks involve arbitrary relations between the physically dissimilar stimuli involved in the conditional, selection-based discriminations or between the discriminative stimuli and vocal response topographies of the oral naming tasks. The stimuli in Tasks 1 to 6 could be members of *arbitrary stimulus classes.* Here, we concentrate on the kinds of arbitrary classes articulated in Sidman's (1994) reformulation of *stimulus equivalence classes.* The reader is referred to Sidman's book and other sources (e.g., Hall & Chase, 1991; Horne & Lowe, 1996; R. Saunders & Green, 1992) for discussions of the formal definition of equivalence, the distinction between functional and equivalence classes, and related matters. Arbitrary stimulus classes may be distinguished from *feature stimulus classes* in which the stimuli share physical attributes (McIlvane, Dube, Green, & Serna, 1993; see also the discussion of similarity- and nonsimilarity-based concepts by Wasserman & DeVolder, 1993). In the case of vocal imitation, for example, the stimuli produced by the imitator are physically similar to the stimuli heard. The question, then, is how spoken names, whether heard or said, may participate in arbitrary classes that also involve visual stimuli like pictures and printed words. Because the classes of interest involve spoken names, heard and said, vocal imitation is obviously important and deserves special consideration.

Although Skinner (1957) emphasized the importance of the echoic repertoire, imitation was not prominent in Sidman's original writings (Sidman, 1971, 1977; Sidman & Cresson, 1973; Sidman et al., 1974). Subsequently, Baer (1982, pp. 290–298) recognized that the emergent matching *and* naming in Sidman's original studies were likely because the participants were vocally imitative, and, moreover, the words heard and said may have functioned as members of classes (p. 294). More recently, Sidman (1994, pp. 115–116, see also pp. 305–307) also considered the possibility that the relationship between names that are heard and said may be a reflection of a unitary process involving the repertoires of an individual as speaker and listener (cf. Lee, 1981; Skinner, 1957). As Sidman put it, "it is not far-fetched to propose that in order to be a speaker, one must first become a listener" (p. 116) or, as Horne and Lowe (1996) put it, "the child's listener achievements are . . . a vital stepping stone in the acquisition of verbal behavior . . . [making the transition] from being a listener to the verbal productions of others to becoming a speaker-listener in her own right" (p. 196). We stress that one's long-term and more immediate history of reinforcement will determine whether what is heard is subsequently repeated, and whether what is heard when one speaks then also functions as a stimulus that controls behavior. In contrast, there are circumstances in which listener behavior gives rise to speaker behavior in vocally imitative individuals.

Again, however, the interdependence or bidirectionality of listener and speaker behavior will require an appropriate learning history (for a discussion of relations among visual discrimination and production tasks, see Mackay, 1991).

Sidman's research demonstrated two ways in which a network of naming and matching performances might be established. Sidman's (1971) participant entered the experiment able (a) to match pictures to their dictated names, (b) to name the pictures orally (tact), and (c) to imitate vocally (Figure 1, Panel 2). After being taught to match printed words to the same dictated names, the participant matched pictures and words to one another, and named the words orally (all at about 80% accuracy). Sidman and Cresson (1973) replicated these results with participants who were less proficient on name-picture matching and picture naming (roughly 50% to 75% correct on pretests). Nonetheless, after name-picture and name-word matching were trained, new matching and naming performances emerged (about 67% to 90% correct). Sidman et al. (1974) extended these studies using a different procedure (Figure 1, Panel 3). For example, 1 vocally imitative participant received initial training on name-picture matching. A subsequent picture naming test showed only intermediate accuracy (around 75% correct). Picture-word matching then was taught, and additional tests showed increases in accuracy on word-picture (near 100% correct) and name-word (75% correct) matching tasks. During final tests, word naming also increased over initial levels (about 50% correct).

The emergent matching in these studies permitted the inference of classes of equivalent stimuli, each consisting of a dictated name, a picture, and a printed word. Besides the matching-to-sample training given during the studies, the success of both Sidman's (1971) and Sidman and Cresson's (1973) participants at naming words can probably be attributed to the highly accurate picture naming learned before the experiment began. In general, such outcomes are more likely when stimulus classes that are established by training relate to existing receptive and expressive repertoires. Indeed, Sidman's findings have been replicated across a variety of procedures with participants who possess such entry skills despite considerable variation in developmental status and hearing acuity (e.g., Hollis, Fulton, & Larson, 1986; Joyce & Wolking, 1989; Mackay, 1985; Mackay & Sidman, 1984; Osborne & Gatch, 1989; Stromer, 1996a). Sidman's (1971) and Sidman and Cresson's (1973) name-referent (e.g., picture, word, and symbol) matching procedures have also been used with young children without developmental disorders (Sidman, Kirk, & Willson-Morris, 1985; Sidman & Tailby, 1982; Sidman et al., 1986) and persons with mental retardation (Green, 1990; Sidman et al., 1986). Notably, however, although the participants in these latter studies formed classes, a few of the young children and more than half of the participants with mental retardation did not produce common names for the stimuli during testing. For practical purposes it would be useful to be able to account for why the procedures often failed to yield much oral naming, although it should be mentioned that the studies by Sidman (Sidman et al., 1985, 1986; Sidman & Tailby, 1982) and Green (1990) were not explicitly designed to achieve this outcome. Indeed, the influence of oral naming was minimized; only posttests were conducted because the experiments aimed to demonstrate class formation in the absence of the use of common oral names.

Referent Naming and Class Formation: Eikeseth and Smith (1992)

Figure 1 (Panel 4) illustrates a hypothetical study that examines another way in which a network of matching and naming performance might be established. In this case, naming is directly taught to the participant using imitative vocal prompts. Tests following such training would then assess any changes in the individual's listener behavior using name-picture and name-word matching, in addition to establishing whether printed word-picture (visual) matching had developed. The emergence of the visual matching would permit the inference that the "auditory and visual stimuli [are] related by equivalence" (Sidman, 1994, p. 62).

Eikeseth and Smith's (1992) study lends empirical support to this possibility. In addition, their study tested the generality of several demonstrations of the formation of equivalence classes using only visual stimuli (e.g., Lazar et al., 1984; Stromer & Osborne, 1982; Wetherby, Karlan, & Spradlin, 1983). The analysis of such classes is relevant to educational concerns because the tasks resemble the selection-based visual tasks often used to teach appropriate use of symbols on communication boards (e.g., Remington, 1994; Shafer, 1993) rather than topography-based speech or signing tasks. Eikeseth and Smith's study is also important because the data are relevant to Horne and Lowe's (1996) contention that teaching referent naming may be a "powerful determinant of subsequent performance on equivalence tests" (p. 224).

Overview. Eikeseth and Smith (1992) examined whether children with autism would form classes consisting only of visual stimuli, and, if not, whether a naming intervention might facilitate class formation. The children were aged 3 years 6 months (Trey), 3 years 10 months (Joe), 5 years 6 months (Danny), and 4 years 5 months (Rory). Prior treatment sessions had established generalized identity matching, generalized vocal imitation, and oral naming skills. Age-equivalent scores on the Peabody Picture Vocabulary Test were 2 years 6 months (Trey), 2 years 8 months (Joe), 3 years 7 months (Danny), and <2 years 4 months (Rory), reflecting proficiency in name-picture matching.

Phase 1. Phase 1 examined whether matching-to-sample training with visual stimuli would establish classes. To highlight the potential for teaching functional communication skills, we describe Eikeseth and Smith's (1992) procedure as if they had used pictures of everyday items, printed words, and oral names rather than the abstract Greek symbols actually employed as stimuli. The dog class consists of a picture of a dog and the printed words *dog* and *seb,* and the cat class consists of a picture of a cat and the words *cat* and *tip*. Figure 2 (top left) thus would depict the initial training tasks, matching visual samples and visual comparisons in a two-choice arrangement. Some trials were like matching the words *dog* and *cat* to their respective pictures, whereas others were like matching the words *seb* and *tip* to the same pictures. After the training, blocks of 10 test trials assessed the maintenance of the trained tasks as a baseline, symmetry of the baseline relations (i.e., interchangeability of samples and comparisons), and derived matching (e.g., word-word matching, as in a combined test for symmetry and transitivity; see Sidman & Tailby, 1982). Although oral naming was not assessed on a trial-by-trial basis (e.g., as in Tasks 2 and 4; Figure 1), spontaneous unprompted vocalization that occurred during testing was recorded.

Figure 3 presents test data. Phase 1 began with four blocks of trials that assessed derived matching; all children did poorly, with accuracy ranging from 40% to 60%. Note, however, that Joe's accuracy was 90% for the first block of trials and then declined. On symmetry tests, Trey and Joe passed (scores of 80% to 100% correct), whereas Rory's scores varied from 70% to 90% correct, and Danny's were all 40% correct. In final tests of derived matching, the children performed

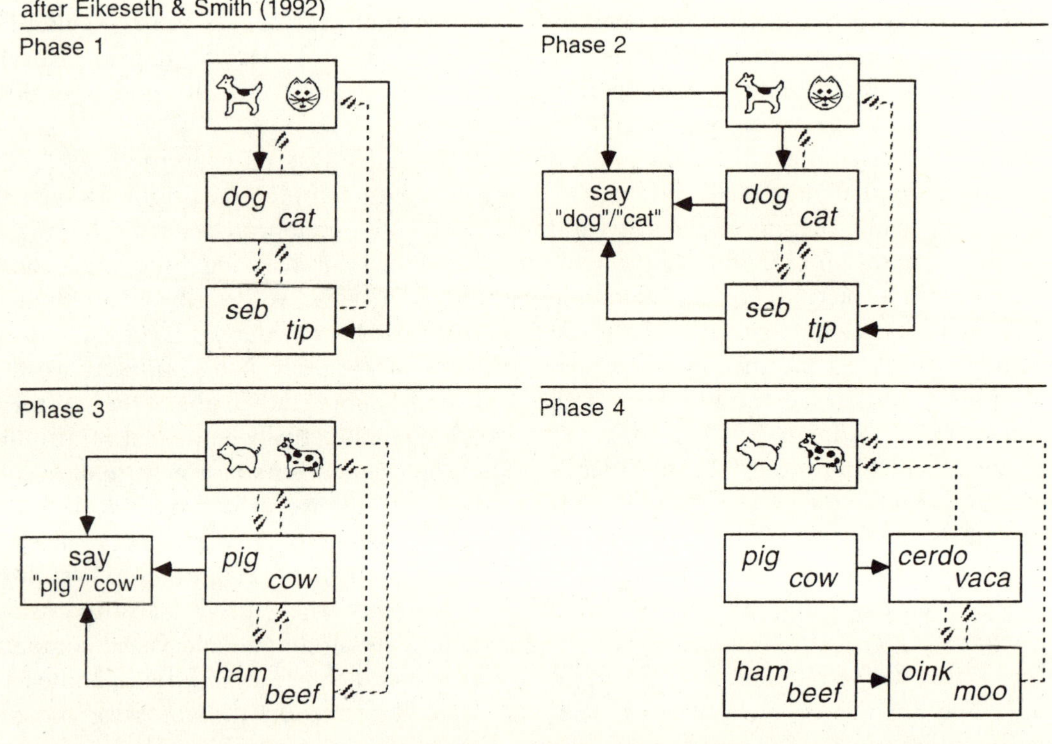

Figure 2. Diagrams representing Eikeseth and Smith's (1992) procedures. Arrows connect the sample to comparison stimuli of the matching-to-sample tasks, and the stimuli to their oral names. Solid arrows represent tasks used during training; broken arrows represent tasks used during testing.

as they did earlier. The lack of background shading for the groups of bars in Phase 1 indicates that none of the children spontaneously produced an audible common name for the stimuli in a potential class while performing the matching tasks during testing. The figure does not include the children's baseline performances that were nearly perfect throughout the study.

Phase 2. Phase 2 involved two training conditions. First, the children were taught to respond to the question "What is it?" by naming orally (tacting) the stimuli used during Phase 1 (Figure 2, top right). The children learned to produce one common name (e.g., "dog") for each of the three stimuli assigned to one potential class (e.g., the picture of a dog and the printed words *dog* and *seb*), and another name (e.g., "cat") for each of the three stimuli assigned to the other class (e.g., the picture of a cat and the words *cat* and *tip*). Next, the children were required to name each stimulus as it was presented for the baseline matching tasks. (Presumably, the cue "What is it?" was dropped during the matching trials.) Blocks of test trials then assessed the baseline (e.g., picture-word matching) and derived matching (e.g., word-word matching). Trey, Joe, and Danny passed the tests of derived matching, but Rory scored only 40% (Figure 3). Although none of the children was required to name the stimuli, all but Danny did so (indicated by background shading on Figure 3). Note, however, that Rory named the stimuli spontaneously and correctly but did poorly on these tests of matching.

Phase 3. In Phase 3, new stimuli (pig and cow classes, Figure 2, bottom left) were used to assess whether teaching a common name

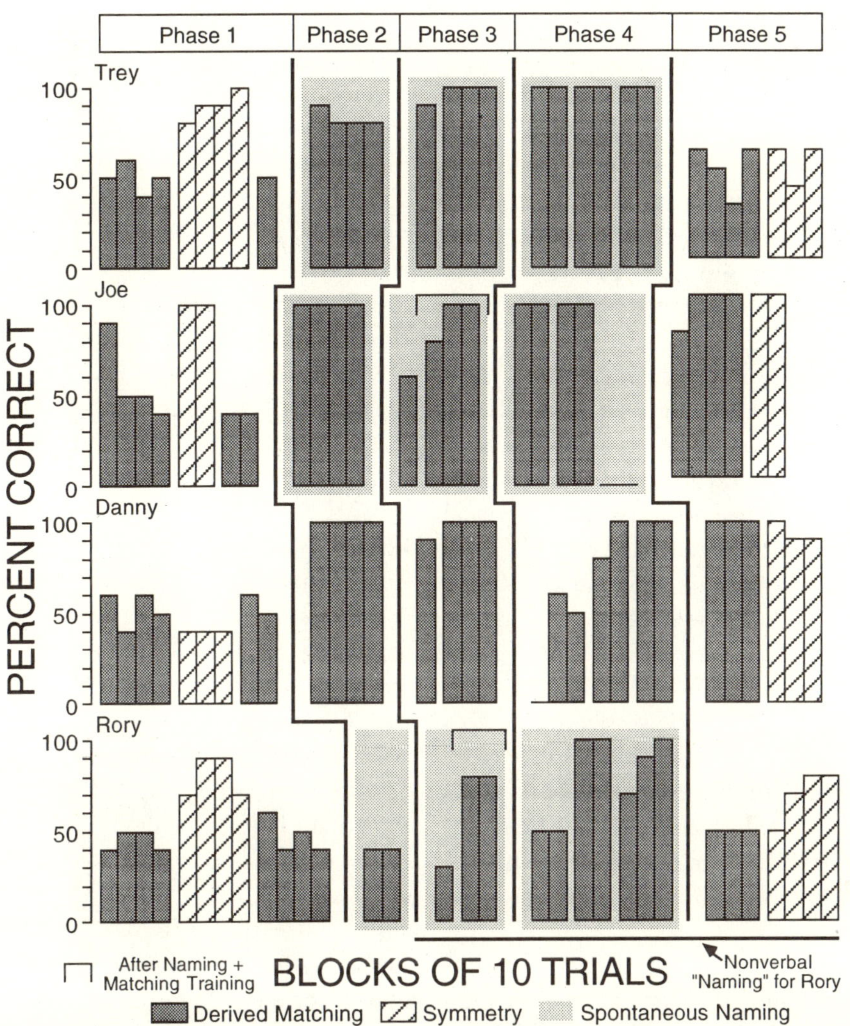

Figure 3. Data based on Eikeseth and Smith's (1992) study. Each bar represents the percentage of correct trials out of 10 given in consecutive blocks of test trials across Phases 1 through 5 (listed at the top). Performances assessed included those on derived matching (solid bars) and symmetry (striped bars) trials. The bracketed bars for Joe and Rory in Phase 3 reflect test performances after training with matching to sample was added to the naming. In Phases 3, 4, and 5, Rory's naming response involved block constructions common to each class of stimuli, instead of the oral names used previously. The background shading denotes that names were produced spontaneously by the child during testing; a white background denotes that names were not produced.

for the stimuli in each potential class would establish the classes. The training involved teaching referent naming (Figure 1), then testing picture-word and word-word matching. Note that because of unsuccessful test results in Phase 2, Rory now tacted the stimuli nonvocally by constructing one of two possible patterns of blocks. In addition, after the initial block of test trials for derived matching, 2 children (Joe and Rory) received additional training before further tests were conducted. This involved adding a matching-to-sample baseline like that used in Phase 2.

Only Trey and Danny unequivocally formed classes following training with common names, as suggested by perfect scores on tests of derived matching (Figure 3). However, as in Phase 2, Joe and Rory received direct training on the visual-visual matching baseline before they passed the tests of derived matching. Also as in Phase 2, Trey and Joe displayed oral naming during testing, Danny did not, and Rory exhibited spontaneous tacting (different block constructions).

Phase 4. Phase 4 (Figure 2, bottom right) assessed whether the stimulus classes established in Phase 3 could be expanded by adding two new stimuli to each class. The procedure involved teaching two new visual matching tasks. For example, one task was like using the words *pig* and *cow* as samples and the new words *cerdo* and *vaca* as the respective correct comparisons. The other task was like using *ham* and *beef* as samples with *oink* and *moo* as the respective correct comparisons. Two kinds of tests for derived matching were conducted: (a) matching *cerdo* and *vaca* and *oink* and *moo* to their corresponding pictures (pig and cow), and (b) matching *oink* and *moo* and *cerdo* and *vaca* to one another.

Only Trey clearly passed all tests for class expansion in Phase 4 (Figure 3). Joe was perfect on the tests that resembled matching *cerdo* and *vaca* to the corresponding pictures of pig and cow and matching *oink* and *moo* to the same pictures. Joe's 0% scores occurred on tests like matching *oink* and *moo* and *cerdo* and *vaca* to one another. In contrast, Danny's low scores occurred on trials like matching *cerdo* and *vaca* and *oink* and *moo* to their corresponding pictures. Note that the 0% scores on some of these tests reflect perfect conditional stimulus control; the children selected the incorrect comparison stimulus on every trial. Danny was the only child who did not name the stimuli during testing, as in Phases 2 and 3.

Phase 5. Phase 5 was like Phase 1, except sets of novel stimuli were used to assess the generality of the performance established earlier. As a result of their experience (i.e., previous history of reinforcement) of common naming, would children now form visual equivalence classes in the absence of explicitly programmed naming? Joe and Danny passed the tests for derived matching and symmetry (Figure 3). Scores for Trey and Rory never reached passing levels, although Rory's symmetry test scores increased from 50% to 80% across four test blocks. No child produced names spontaneously during these tests.

Discussion. Although the 4 children learned the visual matching baselines during Phase 1, all failed the subsequent tests for equivalence. Naming procedures were used in Phases 2, 3, and 4 and, in general, the matching of all children improved. Phase 5 repeated the Phase 1 procedures, and 2 of the 4 children now passed the tests for equivalence. The findings led Eikeseth and Smith (1992) to conclude that "naming may remediate failures to develop untrained conditional relations, some of which are indicative of stimulus equivalence" (p. 123). We agree with this appraisal. The results of Phase 3 support the possibility raised earlier that a speaker's naming may yield relations of equivalence among visual stimuli given the same name. As Sidman (1994) suggests, naming—or any other procedure that produces a partition, classification, or categorization of stimuli—may involve equivalence relations (pp. 416–421). The success of Trey and Danny on the tests for emergent matching in Phase 3 demonstrates such a partition, thus supplying a basis for inferring that the stimuli with the same names were related by equivalence. These findings support the recommendation that stimulus classes should be at the center of future analyses of teaching methods that seek to establish generative and functionally useful expressive verbal skills.

The results of Phase 1 are interesting because the children's naming skills prior to the study might have predicted better performance on the tests of equivalence, despite the unfamiliarity and abstract nature of the Greek letters actually used as stimuli (cf. Horne & Lowe, 1996, p. 224). This notion gains some support from a study by Devany, Hayes, and Nelson (1986), in which young children with mental retardation, who were clinically judged to be "language-able," demonstrated equivalences among visual stimuli with procedures similar to those of Eikeseth and Smith (1992). Further research is needed to determine whether differences between Eikeseth and Smith's and Devany et al.'s findings can be attributed to the nature of the children's disability or to the procedures. Eikeseth and Smith's methods may not have been optimal for class formation (Dube & McIlvane, in press; Stromer & Mackay, in press). For example, positive outcomes might have occurred in Phase 1 if the trained performances had been maintained during posttests, thereby providing a concurrent rather than a remote history of reinforcement with these tasks. The discrepancies between scores on tests for symmetry and derived matching (Trey, Joe, and Rory) and the loss of appropriate stimulus control (Joe) suggest that such procedural refinements may be needed (e.g., Galizio, 1996).

Analysis of the conditions that promote integration of previous and new learning has major educational implications. Eikeseth and Smith (1992) have shown one way in which naming might accomplish such integration, and their results are in general agreement with others involving individuals with mental retardation (K. Saunders & Spradlin, 1990, 1993) and young children (Dugdale & Lowe, 1990). As research clarifies how naming results in positive effects, the nature of tacting responses involved in the formation of stimulus classes may be important (cf. Mackay, 1985). For example, tacting via speech, sign, or even the block constructions used by Rory (and for examples with nonhumans see Manabe, Kawashima, & Staddon, 1995; McIntire, Cleary, & Thompson, 1987) may have an advantage over selection-based tasks because training establishes discriminative control of topographically distinct behaviors by the stimuli that are prospective members of a class (see Mackay, Stromer, & Serna, in press; Stromer & Mackay, in press; Sundberg & Sundberg, 1990).

The naming procedure used in Phase 2 (and in Phase 3 for Joe and Rory) provided two bases for the derived matching that occurred during testing: The comparison stimuli were each related to a common visual sample *and* to a common spoken name. Although the concurrent relationship makes it difficult to identify the source of emergent outcomes, equivalence did not emerge for any of the children in Phase 1 when only visual stimuli were used. Thus, the naming intervention used in Phase 2 may have played an important role in the formation of equivalence classes. The possible facilitative effects of naming identified by Eikeseth and Smith (1992) have practical benefits (see Sidman, 1994, pp. 413–414). For example, as our everyday examples using pictures and words suggest, functionally useful behaviors that typically are viewed as conceptual (e.g., Wasserman & DeVolder, 1993) may be readily established. Further, as suggested previously (see Figure 1, Panel 4), one could examine whether, and when, supplementary training using names would also give rise to new name-referent matching performances. Because an important educational objective is to establish a flexible, bidirectional verbal repertoire (Hayes, 1991; Horne & Lowe, 1996), it would be important to know how receptive and expressive skills can become functionally related to one another. Ample data suggest that such skills may on occasion function independently (e.g., Anderson & Spradlin, 1980; Guess & Baer, 1973; and see reviews by Goldstein, 1993; Stromer & Mackay, in press).

Phase 3 showed that common names alone may provide sufficient basis for the emergence of classes of visual stimuli (Trey and Danny). If the listener (name-referent matching) and speaker (referent naming or tacting) behaviors of these children were functionally interdependent, that might explain both the facilitation effects observed and the emergence of the stimulus classes based solely on a common name (Phase 3). In addition, congruent with these facilitation effects are observations that training with name-referent matching (e.g., Sidman, 1971; Sidman & Cresson, 1973) may be more likely to produce equivalence in children with mental retardation than would training that is entirely visual (Green, 1990; Sidman et al., 1986).

The attempt in Phase 4 to expand current stimulus classes via the use of common names met with mixed success. Only Trey's test results were as expected. The matching displayed by Joe and Danny was particularly interesting because these results were opposite to expectation. These data suggest that the teaching procedure established relations that were incompatible with the formation of the desired classes (e.g., relations between samples and negative rather than positive comparisons; Carrigan & Sidman, 1992). As Sidman (1987) suggested, undesirable sources of stimulus control may be especially likely when two-choice matching procedures are used, as in Eikeseth and Smith (1992). Part of the remedy, then, may lie in the use of three or more comparison stimuli instead of just two.

Spoken names were potential members of the stimulus classes established in Phases 2, 3, and 4 but not in Phases 1 and 5. No naming occurred in Phases 1 and 5. In contrast, Trey, Joe, and Rory always supplied class-consistent names for the stimuli during the tests in Phases 2, 3, and 4, even though the contingencies did not require it. Such spontaneous common naming has been viewed as one (but not the only) basis for success on tests of equivalence by Horne and Lowe (1996, pp. 217–218; and see Stromer & Mackay, in press). However, the relationship clearly was not perfect: There were several instances during Phases 2, 3, and 4 in which Joe and Rory named the stimuli but did not match them in ways that were consistent with the expected classes. Furthermore, Danny succeeded on tests of equivalence in Phases 3 and 5 without overtly naming the stimuli during testing. Likewise, Joe passed the tests in Phase 5 without overt naming. These data are relevant to the supposition that overt common naming is both necessary and sufficient for class formation.

Further Analyses of Stimulus Classes

The stimulus class framework outlined here may be used to examine other functional relations involving verbal events. This section examines (a) how a stimulus class analysis might contribute to the study of ways to promote behavioral generality, particularly (b) how naming and class formation may advance the study of mediated generalization, and (c) how classes may be established by forms of incidental learning.

Feature classes, arbitrary classes, and treatment generalization. Feature stimulus classes often are said to provide the basis for programming the generalization of the effects of intervention (e.g., Albin & Horner, 1988; Horner, Bellamy, & Colvin, 1984; Stokes & Baer, 1977). In contrast, arbitrary classes in general and equivalence classes in particular are mentioned only rarely in this respect (e.g., Goldstein, 1993; Kirby & Bickel, 1988; Mackay et al., in press; Spradlin, 1989; Stromer, 1991). Not surprisingly, therefore, the potential interplay between arbitrary and feature classes has received little attention in discussions of generalization (but see Barnes & Keenan, 1993; Cowley et al., 1992; Fields, Reeve, Adams, & Verhave, 1991; Haring et al., 1989).

The development of feature classes may ensure that stimulus control is not restricted to the particular stimuli used to establish arbitrary matching. For example, Sidman (1971) and Sidman and Cresson (1973) took precautions against producing narrow outcomes by training with several different variations of each of 20 pictures (e.g., pictures of cars included a VW and an MG) in the stimulus set (e.g., Constantine & Sidman, 1975; Sidman et al., 1974). Other research also suggests that the use of multiple instances or sufficient exemplars (Stokes & Baer, 1977) of a potential feature class during training makes the formation of that class much more likely (e.g., Albin & Horner, 1988; Karsh, Repp, & Lenz, 1990; Repp, Karsh, & Lenz, 1990).

Both feature and arbitrary classes are needed for a complete analysis of behavioral generality. For example, consider Sidman's (1971) study in terms of the different preexperimental and experimental situations involved (and see Mackay et al., in press; Stromer et al., 1996, p. 40): Recall that, as a result of an unrecorded history, the student entered the study able to match pictures to dictation and to name the pictures. Because these performances were present on pretests in the experimental setting, it is possible to infer two sets of feature classes. One set included the words dictated by tape recorder, which the participant clearly treated identically to those spoken by people outside the laboratory. The other set of feature classes involved the pictures; the drawings on the response keys were treated as corresponding to their object and picture counterparts outside the laboratory. Without these two sets of feature classes, the student could not have matched and named the stimuli accurately on pretests.

Sidman's (1971) study demonstrates how arbitrary stimulus classes may derive from different learning situations (Stromer, 1991). Recall that after name-word matching was taught, picture-word and word-picture matching emerged in the experimental setting. Similarly, studies by Remington and his associates (e.g., Clarke et al., 1986; and see summary by Duker & Remington, 1991) have shown how preexisting receptive speech (name-picture matching) accelerates the development of expressive signing (referent-signing performance). These studies suggest that the analysis of arbitrary classes may be relevant to the practical concerns of getting novel behaviors to occur appropriately in different settings. Consider the example depicted in Figure 4, in which there are three different settings: Tabletop activities (top) are responsible for teaching name-picture matching and picture naming (e.g., matching the apple and pear to dictation and tacting these stimuli). In addition, a computer located elsewhere (middle) is used to teach the student to match the words *apple* and *pear* to dictation. Given the development of feature and arbitrary classes, the performances acquired in the two settings could give rise to new ones in some other setting, like a store. For example, the student might be able to gather items already written on a shopping list and even ask a store clerk for assistance by reading the names of items on the list. Moreover, if the computer were used to teach anagram spelling (Dube, McDonald, McIlvane, & Mackay, 1991) rather than matching, the student might learn to write the shopping list that is used in the novel matching and naming tasks required at the store (Mackay, 1985; Mackay & Sidman, 1984; Stromer et al., 1996).

The preceding discussion illustrates just a few applications of a framework that involves feature and arbitrary stimulus classes in the analysis of verbal behavior. As additional examples, we note that the notion of equivalence has been given importance in discussions of methods to teach receptive

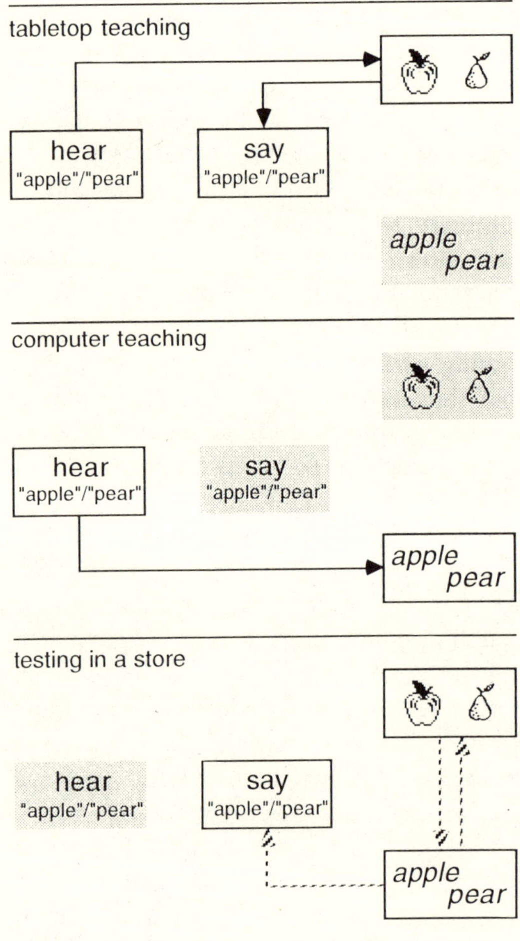

Figure 4. Diagrams representing a hypothetical experiment based on Sidman's (1971) study. Arrows connect the sample to comparison stimuli of the matching-to-sample tasks, and the stimuli to their oral names. Solid arrows represent tasks used during tabletop and computer teaching; broken arrows represent tasks used during testing in a store.

and expressive speech (Goldstein, 1993), augmentative and alternative forms of nonvocal communication (Remington, 1994; Shafer, 1993), and picture reading skills (Lignugaris/Kraft, McCuller, Exum, & Salzberg, 1988) designed to establish adaptive behaviors such as cooking (Johnson & Cuvo, 1981) and cleaning (Wacker, Berg, Berrie, & Swatta, 1985). Clarifying the role of both feature and arbitrary stimulus classes in such instructional pursuits will likely facilitate the development of methods of programming generalization (Albin & Horner, 1988; Kirby & Bickel, 1988; Stokes & Baer, 1977).

Stimulus classes established incidentally. There are major practical benefits when the performances prerequisite for class formation are not taught directly but instead come about incidentally. In one example noted earlier, the reinforcement contingencies in Phase 2 of Eikeseth and Smith's (1992) study permitted two bases for class formation: The comparison stimuli were related to common visual sample stimuli and to the names spoken and heard by the children. Rather than restricted control by one of these stimulus aspects, and even though the reinforcement contingencies did not require it, the visual samples and the spoken names, said and heard, could come to exert discriminative control over comparison selection (cf. Maguire, Stromer, Mackay, & Demis, 1994; Remington & Clarke, 1993a, 1993b). When the procedure engenders such performance, the separate elements of the complex stimuli may function as interchangeable stimuli in classes. Research supporting this possibility has involved college students (Stromer & Stromer, 1990), young children without disabilities (Maguire, Stromer, & Mackay, 1995; Schenk, 1993; Smeets & Striefel, 1994), children with mental retardation (Clarke et al., 1986, 1988), and individuals with autism (Maguire et al., 1994; Remington & Clarke, 1983).

Suppose that a teacher engages students in tabletop activities that are designed to teach children about food groups. One kind of teaching activity involves complex sample stimuli (e.g., saying the word "apple" while holding up a picture of an apple on some trials and saying "carrot" while holding up a picture of a carrot on other trials). The comparisons in both instances are the printed words *apple* and *carrot.* Such procedures may produce broad learning outcomes because each element of each sample may come to exert the same discriminative control. These potential separate outcomes include matching words to dictation and to pictures. In addition, the procedure may give rise to name-picture matching and picture naming.

A second example of incidental learning is based on work showing that differential consequences may become members of classes that include the samples and comparisons to which they have been related (e.g., Dube, McIlvane, Mackay, & Stoddard, 1987; Wolery et al., 1991). For example, students might be taught to match the pictures of apple, pear, carrot, and celery to their corresponding dictated names. Now, in addition to praising correct picture selections, the teacher differentially adds the category name of each food: "Good, the apple is a fruit" or "Good, the carrot is a vegetable." If such consequences were common across training with several stimuli in each category, they could provide the basis for the formation of superordinate classes. Thus, tests would demonstrate that students might match the pictures of apple and pear to "fruit" and the pictures of carrot and celery to "vegetable" without further training. Emergent naming based on the categories might also be possible.

This example suggests how equivalence classes that involve pictures of foods and their printed and spoken names may be brought under the contextual control of category names. The conceptual framework for examining such behaviors already exists (Sidman, 1986), and its potential for addressing applied concerns awaits programmatic study (for a review of some of the laboratory work see Stromer, McIlvane, & Serna, 1993).

A third example is based on the possibility that observational learning may provide the bases for class formation (MacDonald, Dixon, & LeBlanc, 1986). Again, such learning may occur without the support of explicit contingencies. To illustrate, consider a teacher working with a pair of students. One student is taught to match the printed words *apple* and *carrot* and their respective pictures to the dictated names "apple" and "carrot" while a 2nd student merely observes. The 2nd student is then given similar training but with different stimuli (e.g., *pear* and *celery*) while the 1st student observes. The question, of course, is whether each student will demonstrate new performances suggesting that relations among the stimuli were established through the observation of training given to another individual.

Precurrent behavior. Eikeseth and Smith's (1992) data suggest that naming may facilitate the formation of equivalence classes. In principle, this may happen because naming may ensure that the named stimuli function concurrently as discriminative stimuli. Another possibility is that sample naming may function as a mediating response. Indeed, the transfer of behavior trained in the classroom to the community, as exemplified above, may be more likely if a participant learns to use naming as mediating behavior. Such naming is a form of *precurrent* behavior (Skinner, 1968), which is indirectly related to the relevant prevailing contingencies because its occurrence increases the likelihood that some other *current* behavior will be reinforced (e.g., Parsons, Taylor, & Joyce, 1981; Torgrud & Holborn, 1989). The behavioral effects of a mediator, however, may transcend the circumstances of direct training to mediate generalization. Stokes and Baer (1977) suggested that such generalization involved "establishing a response as part of the new learning that is likely to be utilized in other problems as well, and will constitute sufficient commonality between the original learning and the new problem to result in generalization" (p. 361; cf. Kirby & Bickel, 1988, p. 123). Stokes and Baer suggested that verbal behavior has unique properties as a potential mediator, making it easily transported "from any training setting to any generalization setting" (p. 361).

Potential mediators include names that are spoken (Constantine & Sidman, 1975; Gutowski, Geren, Stromer, & Mackay, 1995), signed (Bonta & Watters, 1981, 1983), and written (Stromer et al., 1996). Laboratory studies of such mediators have used delayed matching-to-sample procedures. In delayed matching, the sample stimuli are not presented at the time that responses to the comparison stimuli occur, unlike simultaneous matching, in which the sample stimuli *are* presented at the time that comparisons are selected. For example, in Constantine and Sidman's (1975) study, participants with mental retardation could name pictures, match them to dictation, and match pictures to one another in simultaneous matching tasks. They could also match pictures to dictation in delayed matching. Given the same delay intervals, however, they did not match pictures to pictures. These matching performances then improved dramatically after instructions were given to name each of the picture samples aloud. Without the instructions, accuracy returned to baseline levels. Participants were thus capable of producing mediators that might have bridged the delays and resulted in correct matching. At issue is how to get participants to engage in such naming in the absence of instructions. This does occur (Gutowski et al., 1995), but the learning histories that reliably produce such precurrent behavior are unknown.

Stimulus Equivalence and the Naming Hypothesis: Horne and Lowe (1996)

Applied behavior analysts will find Horne and Lowe's (1996) paper, the commentaries, and reply informative and controversial. Their work is informative largely because it blends data and concepts from theory and research both within and outside the tradition of behavior analysis to chart the course of development of the early naming repertoire of infants and young children without disabilities. It is controversial because Horne and Lowe's appraisal of much of the research on equivalence differs markedly from the views of Sidman (1994) and many other researchers: Horne and Lowe provocatively suggest that some of the methods used to study equivalence are artificial in the sense that they are irrelevant to understanding either the normal development of verbal behavior or the processes by which stimulus classes are normally formed.

Horne and Lowe (1996; see also Dugdale & Lowe, 1990) argue that an individual's naming skills are necessary and may be sufficient for the kinds of performances that emerge in learning situations like those examined by Sidman (1971) and Eikeseth and Smith (1992). Their key contribution is an account in behavior-analytic terms of the development in infancy and early childhood of a "naming relation" that is subsequently responsible for the formation of all equivalence classes, including those involving exclusively visual stimuli. The naming relation represents a synthesis of various expressive *and* receptive abilities, including tacting (Task 2 in Figure 1), echoic responding (Task 7), and receptive speech (Task 1) that are acquired through natural reinforcement processes during the first 24 months of life (see also Dugdale & Lowe, 1990; Hayes, 1991, 1994; Hayes & Hayes, 1992). Horne and Lowe suggest that naming, once fully developed, functions as a higher order bidirectional relation and that "naming *is* stimulus-classifying behavior" (p. 227). Naming relations thus make possible the formation of arbitrary classes, including equivalence classes. Receptive tasks may give rise to what we earlier called feature classes (pp. 195–196). However, in contrast to Sidman (1994), neither receptive nor expressive tasks alone are viewed as the basis of arbitrary classes that involve equivalence relations.

Horne and Lowe (1996, pp. 207–208) describe several tests that might be used to decide whether someone is capable of naming relations. Two of the tests examine the bidirectionality of the relationship between receptive and expressive performances after instances of both are in a child's repertoire. In one such test, new referent naming relations are established directly and then the corresponding name-referent relations are assessed. A second test involves a kind of observational learning or simple pairing procedure (as discussed above) in which, for example, a teacher displays a referent and states its name but no explicit contingencies require any response. Whether the child is then able to perform name-referent matching or referent naming is assessed. Other tests stem from the preceding two and involve stimulus classes, like the feature and arbitrary classes described earlier. An individual who succeeds on such tests has, presumably, satisfied some of the critical behavioral requirements of the naming relation.

Horne and Lowe (1996) adopt the view that the naming involved in mediating stimulus equivalence either may be overt and can be reliably measured as the outcome of a naming test (as for some of the participants in Eikeseth & Smith, 1992), or may remain covert and thus unmeasurable except via self-report or supplementary talk-aloud procedures (Hayes, 1986). Whether overt or covert, verbal behavior is viewed as the critical determinant in the formation of equivalence classes. Horne and Lowe propose that naming may involve the use of common names for members of a stimulus class, as in Eikeseth and Smith, or intraverbal naming (Skinner, 1957), as when a participant provides separate names for each member of the potential stimulus class and then learns a verbal sequence that links them, such as "pig, ham, oink."

For most behavior analysts, the appeal to inner covert processes as an explanation of equivalence class formation raises serious concerns. Consistent with the tenets of behavior analysis, the experimental analysis of the determinants of naming and equivalence relations should emphasize "the environment–behavior relations, such as the contingencies of reinforcement, that give rise to the stimulus control involved" (Stromer, 1996b, p. 250; and see Skinner, 1974, pp. 16–18; Baer, 1982, p. 278). Putative inner causes are normally avoided as explanations, and this approach has often benefited both the practitioner and the scientist because the determinants of behavior, and the methods used to study them, are typically readily accessible to teachers, clinicians, and others for application.

Horne and Lowe's (1996) position, however, is that naming—including covert naming—is indeed the product of a history of reinforcement that is observable, at least in principle, but that once acquired, this repertoire has some transcendent properties. Although many behavior analysts have traditionally preferred to ignore the role of a covert verbal repertoire in modulating operant behavior, Skinner has written extensively on the topic (e.g., Skinner, 1957, especially chap. 19; 1969, 1989). In one sense, Horne and Lowe are arguing that for a verbally competent human, the typical stimulus equivalence task is a problem-solving situation that can be approached through the construction of verbal rules involving the names of stimuli (see Skinner, 1969, for a detailed discussion of rule-governed behavior and problem solving).

What Horne and Lowe (1996, pp. 222–227) term "key tests" of their argument for the necessity of such naming relations are framed here as general experimental questions: (a) Will nonhuman organisms fail tests of stimulus equivalence? (b) Will humans who lack the prerequisite naming skills (naming relations) fail tests of stimulus equivalence? (c) Will teaching participants particular name relations that involve the stimuli used in matching-to-sample procedures be a powerful determinant of subsequent performance on equivalence tests? Horne and Lowe suggest that the existing data so strongly support a positive answer to each question that they propose to fully explain all instances of equivalence with their naming hypothesis, thus disposing of equivalence as an analytic framework. As noted in many of the commentaries on the Horne and Lowe article, this proposal may be premature.

There is general agreement that the search for equivalence, as demonstrated by humans, has eluded most researchers working with nonhumans. The best data to date come from Schusterman and Kastak's (1993) study with a sea lion. Horne and Lowe (1996, pp. 223–224) hypothesize procedural artifacts that may have led to that animal's success on tests of equivalence (but see R. Saunders & Green, 1996) and properly suspend judgment pending replication of the results. However, it is their opinion that it would not be very informative even if such results did hold up in nonhumans because the processes involved would necessarily be contingency shaped rather than verbally mediated, that is, rule governed. The data therefore would be irrelevant to questions concerning the role of verbal behavior in human equivalence. There are at least two possible responses to this position. First, the value of fundamental research in both field and laboratory settings would be diminished if we did not continue to acknowledge the potential relevance of basic behavioral processes that are common across species (Sidman, 1960, pp. 54–56). Second, we should not neglect the possibility that processes that underlie any robust demonstration of equivalence in nonhuman animals may be of importance in understanding the contingencies that actually give rise to rule-governed and other verbal behavior in humans. Moreover, we concur with Mace's (1994) suggestion that the study of equivalence and other kinds of stimulus classes is one of the areas of inquiry that will profit from a wide range of research efforts that include process-oriented laboratory work with both humans and nonhumans as well as intervention studies that attempt to establish socially adaptive behaviors (see also Epling & Pierce, 1986; Hake, 1982). This approach has been just as profitable for behavior analysis as for many other sciences, and, given the complexity and importance of the subject matter, seems most likely to clarify the origins of equivalence and other complex learning phenomena.

Eikeseth and Smith's (1992) data are germane to the proposition of a general relationship between naming skills and performance on tests of equivalence. Horne and Lowe's (1996) position suggests that the children's insufficiently developed verbal skills may have been related to their initial failures on the tests given in Phase 1. However, the nature of those presumed deficits is not at all clear. Nor is it clear what verbal skills were acquired during the naming interventions that might have led to the successful outcomes only for Joe and Danny in Phase 5. Apparently the verbal skills of Trey and Rory were still insufficient. For Trey, this was true even after several sessions of highly accurate matching during the naming interventions. Although there is some evidence that children with mental retardation and autism fail to use available naming skills unless verbally prompted (Clarke et al., 1988; Constantine & Sidman, 1975; Kellas, Ashcraft, & Johnson, 1973), this in itself raises questions about what additional conditions beyond the ability to name are necessary before equivalence emerges. Thus, although the general proposition of a positive relationship between verbal behavior and equivalence is intuitively reasonable and is supported by some findings (e.g., Devany et al., 1986; Horne & Lowe, 1996, p. 224), and although it may serve as a useful guide for applied study, it does not replace the need for fine-grained behavioral analyses of developmental processes and educational and clinical practices.

With respect to potential interventions, Horne and Lowe (1996) stated that Eikeseth and Smith's (1992) study "as a whole shows that common naming can be a powerful intervention in bringing about equivalence even in autistic children" (p. 225). Later, they concluded, "The possibility that naming is both necessary *and* sufficient for success on equivalence tests is supported by evidence, collected from several studies, that naming interventions are highly effective in bringing about such success" (Lowe & Horne, 1996, pp. 332–333). In contrast, the data in Figure 3 suggest that (a) Eikeseth and Smith's results were not robust, showing differences across children; (b) alternative explanations of the improvements in test performances have not been ruled out (e.g., Carr & Blackman, 1996; Galizio, 1996; McIlvane & Dube, 1996); and (c) the nature of the naming skills that may be involved in passing the tests for equivalence require further clarification (e.g., Fields, 1996; Lowenkron, 1996; Pilgrim, 1996; Remington, 1996; K. Saunders & Spradlin, 1996; Stromer, 1996b).

Part of the clarification requires the recognition that the use of common names is but one form of verbal behavior upon which equivalence may be based (e.g., Horne & Lowe, 1996, pp. 218–219; and see Stoddard & McIlvane, 1986). Horne and Lowe's discussion of intraverbal naming, particularly when considered in the context of an analysis of feature and arbitrary classes, suggests interesting applied and basic research possibilities that would extend the few studies that have used participants with developmental disabilities (Braam & Poling, 1983; Luciano, 1986; Watkins, Pack-Teixteira, & Howard, 1989). For example, a child who, when asked to name "school things," says "bus, chalkboard, globe" may be exhibiting intraverbals (Braam & Poling, 1983). The complexities and payoffs of analyses of intraverbals grow when one considers Sidman's (1986, 1994) discussions of higher order classes. As noted earlier, for example, first-order equivalence classes involving pictures, words, and names of foods might be brought under the contextual or second-order control of category names ("fruit" and "vegetable"). The range of emergent naming performances could include item naming as well as category or intraverbal naming. Examples here include saying "apple, pear, orange" when asked to "name some fruit," and saying "carrot, celery, broccoli" when asked to "name some vegetables." Studies using higher order procedures are important because they highlight the relevance of equivalence for applied and basic research on category learning (e.g., Rosch, Mervis, Gray, Johnson, & Boyes-Braem, 1976) and suggest ways of analyzing contextually controlled verbal repertoires (e.g., Hall & Chase, 1991; Mackay et al., in press; Silverman, Anderson, Marshall, & Baer, 1986).

Horne and Lowe (1996) accept that naming alone is not a panacea for difficulties a participant might have on tests of equivalence: "Whether or not naming is established in ways that facilitate the passing of equivalence tests is dependent on the particular training procedure used" (p. 217). They also said that "intraverbal naming can work for or against success on tests of stimulus equivalence depending on whether or not the intraverbal sequences that are formed before such testing are congruent with experimenter-defined classes" (p. 226). These conclusions are consistent with the thematic focus of the present paper: whether the names heard or said participate in classes will require a relevant prior and current history with contingencies of reinforcement. As shown by Eikeseth and Smith (1992), for example, a naming intervention may fail to facilitate class formation as often as it succeeds (and see Stromer & Mackay, in press), justifying the conclusion that naming may or may not suffice, depending on other, unknown factors. With respect to such considerations, Horne and Lowe's commitment to a hypothesis that ascribes special status to covert verbal events has theoretical significance, but its practical utility remains to be clarified. Postulating a functional role for covert naming in matching performances that show equivalence offers no simple, immediate, or complete solutions to the practical problems of designing effective educational intervention procedures. From a broader perspective, however, a better understanding of the acquisition of naming as a developmental process has important implications for the remediation of language deficits. In addition, Horne and Lowe's analysis implies that educational interventions may be more effective if delivered in a structured sequence, with entry to higher levels based on appropriate testing for prerequisite lower level skills, of which naming is the most critical.

In keeping with the idea that naming is a necessary prerequisite of equivalence, Lowe and Horne (1996) write, "If it could be shown that any nonverbal human (e.g., young infant) or other human subject who did not, for some reason, name stimuli or use verbal rules during a study could pass Sidman's tests, then this alone would show that verbal behavior was not necessary for success" (pp. 331–332). In fact, one could comfortably argue that such evidence already exists (e.g., R. Saunders & Green, 1996; Sidman, 1990; Stromer, 1996b; Stromer & Mackay, in press), at least if only overt naming is taken into account. For example, Joe and Danny in Eikeseth and Smith's (1992) study passed the tests for equivalence among visual stimuli (Phase 5) without supplying oral names. Also, reconsider the 4 participants in Sidman et al. (1986) and the 5 participants in Green (1990), all with mental retardation, who learned the name-referent matching baseline and eventually succeeded on tests of equivalence. Only 4 of these 9 participants passed the referent naming tests. For the other 5, listener behavior (name-referent matching) brought about equivalence classes apparently in the absence of the corresponding speaker behavior (referent naming). Moreover, there is little if any empirical foundation to suggest that individuals with autism and mental retardation would have been able, if tested appropriately, to supply a verbal rule that accounted for their emergent matching. For example, it is unlikely that intraverbal naming exists in the repertoires of participants with autism and mental retardation without being explicitly taught (Braam & Poling, 1983; Luciano, 1986; Watkins et al., 1989; see also Sidman, 1990).

To uphold the theory that naming is necessary for positive results on tests of equivalence, Horne and Lowe (1996) might respond to Sidman et al.'s (1986) and Green's (1990) data by questioning whether the tests used to measure naming produced false-negative outcomes. To the suggestion that participants with autism or mental retardation lacked intraverbal skills, Horne and Lowe might point out that the intraverbals required need be no more than repeated name pairs and that what is important "is not that all performance on matching-to-sample tests is necessarily self-instructed or verbally controlled but that, incontrovertibly, at least some is" (Lowe & Horne, 1996, p. 329). Furthermore, Horne and Lowe might emphasize that studies with very young children (p. 224) and those with the most severe language impairments (e.g., Barnes, McCullagh, & Keenan, 1990; Devany et al., 1986; Eikeseth & Smith, 1992) have, so far, almost always failed to find evidence of equivalence relations (cf. Stromer & Mackay, in press).

What is incontrovertible is that the publication of Horne and Lowe's (1996) article has set the stage for much-needed further analysis of stimulus classes that involve verbal events. Important contributions to the analysis will come from researchers who are working on the practical concerns of establishing rudimentary language and communication skills in individuals with severe intellectual limitations. Both basic and applied science will benefit from the thorough study of the conditions under which naming—whether spoken, signed, written, or constructed—participates in the formation and elaboration of feature and arbitrary stimulus classes.

REFERENCES

Albin, R. W., & Horner, R. H. (1988). Generalization with precision. In R. H. Horner, G. Dunlap, & R. L. Koegel (Eds.), *Generalization and maintenance: Lifestyle changes in applied settings* (pp. 99–120). Baltimore: Brookes.

Anderson, S. R., & Spradlin, J. E. (1980). The generalized effects of productive labeling training involving common object classes. *Journal of the Association for the Severely Handicapped, 5,* 143–157.

Baer, D. M. (1982). Applied behavior analysis. In G. T. Wilson & C. M. Franks (Eds.), *Contemporary behavior therapy: Conceptual and empirical foundations* (pp. 277–309). New York: Guilford.

Barnes, D., & Keenan, M. (1993). A transfer of functions through derived arbitrary and nonarbitrary stimulus relations. *Journal of the Experimental Analysis of Behavior, 59,* 61–81.

Barnes, D., McCullagh, P. D., & Keenan, M. (1990). Equivalence class formation in non-hearing-impaired children and hearing-impaired children. *The Analysis of Verbal Behavior, 8,* 19–30.

Bonta, J. L., & Watters, R. G. (1981). Use of manual signs in delayed matching-to-sample with developmentally disordered, speech deficient children. *Behavior Research of Severe Developmental Disabilities, 2,* 51–66.

Bonta, J. L., & Watters, R. G. (1983). Use of manual signs by developmentally disordered speech-deficient children in delayed auditory-to-picture matching-to-sample. *Analysis and Intervention in Developmental Disabilities, 3,* 295–309.

Braam, S. J., & Poling, A. (1983). Development of intraverbal behavior in mentally retarded individuals through transfer of stimulus control procedures: Classification of verbal responses. *Applied Research in Mental Retardation, 4,* 279–302.

Browder, D. M., & Lalli, J. S. (1991). Review of research on sight word instruction. *Research in Developmental Disabilities, 12,* 203–228.

Carr, D., & Blackman, D. E. (1996). Equivalence relations, naming, and generalized symmetry [commentary]. *Journal of the Experimental Analysis of Behavior, 65,* 245–247.

Carrigan, P. F., & Sidman, M. (1992). Conditional discrimination and equivalence relations: A theoretical analysis of control by negative stimuli. *Journal of the Experimental Analysis of Behavior, 58,* 183–204.

Clarke, S., Remington, B., & Light, P. (1986). An evaluation of the relationship between speech skills and expressive signing. *Journal of Applied Behavior Analysis, 19,* 231–239.

Clarke, S., Remington, B., & Light, P. (1988). The role of referential speech in sign learning by mentally retarded children: A comparison of total communication and sign-alone training. *Journal of Applied Behavior Analysis, 21,* 419–426.

Constantine, B., & Sidman, M. (1975). Role of naming in delayed matching-to-sample. *American Journal of Mental Deficiency, 79,* 680–689.

Cowley, B. J., Green, G., & Braunling-McMorrow, D. (1992). Using stimulus equivalence procedures to teach name-face matching to adults with brain injuries. *Journal of Applied Behavior Analysis, 25,* 461–475.

de Rose, J. C., de Souza, D. G., & Hanna, E. S. (in press). Teaching reading and spelling: Exclusion and stimulus equivalence. *Journal of Applied Behavior Analysis.*

Devany, J. M., Hayes, S. C., & Nelson, R. O. (1986). Equivalence class formation in language-able and language-disabled children. *Journal of the Experimental Analysis of Behavior, 46,* 243–257.

Dube, W. V., McDonald, S. J., McIlvane, W. J., & Mackay, H. A. (1991). Constructed-response matching to sample and spelling instruction. *Journal of Applied Behavior Analysis, 24,* 305–317.

Dube, W. V., & McIlvane, W. J. (in press). Some implications of a stimulus control topography analysis for emergent behavior and stimulus classes. In T. R. Zentall & P. M. Smeets (Eds.), *Stimulus class formation in humans and animals.* Amsterdam: North-Holland.

Dube, W. V., McIlvane, W. J., Mackay, H. A., & Stoddard, L. T. (1987). Stimulus class membership established via stimulus-reinforcer relations. *Journal of the Experimental Analysis of Behavior, 47,* 159–175.

Dugdale, N., & Lowe, C. F. (1990). Naming and stimulus equivalence. In D. E. Blackman & H. Lejeune (Eds.), *Behaviour analysis in theory and practice: Contributions and controversies* (pp. 115–138). Hove, UK: Erlbaum.

Duker, P., & Remington, B. (1991). Manual sign-based communication for individuals with severe or profound learning difficulties. In B. Remington (Ed.), *The challenge of severe mental handicap: A behaviour analytic approach* (pp. 167–187). Chichester, England: Wiley.

Eikeseth, S., & Smith, T. (1992). The development of functional and equivalence classes in high-functioning autistic children: The role of naming. *Journal of the Experimental Analysis of Behavior, 58,* 123–133.

Epling, W. F., & Pierce, W. D. (1986). The basic importance of applied behavior analysis. *The Behavior Analyst, 9,* 89–99.

Fields, L. (1996). The evidence for naming as a cause or facilitator of equivalence class formation [commentary]. *Journal of the Experimental Analysis of Behavior, 65,* 279–282.

Fields, L., Reeve, K. F., Adams, B. J., & Verhave, T. (1991). Stimulus generalization and equivalence classes: A model for natural categories. *Journal of the Experimental Analysis of Behavior, 55,* 305–312.

Galizio, M. (1996). Methodological issues in the study of naming [commentary]. *Journal of the Experimental Analysis of Behavior, 65,* 286–288.

Goldstein, H. (1993). Structuring environmental input to facilitate generalized language learning by children with mental retardation. In A. P. Kaiser & D. B. Gray (Eds.), *Enhancing children's communication* (Vol. 2, pp. 317–334). Baltimore: Brookes.

Green, G. (1990). Differences in development of visual and auditory-visual equivalence relations. *American Journal on Mental Retardation, 95,* 260–270.

Guess, D., & Baer, D. M. (1973). An analysis of individual differences in generalization between receptive and productive language in retarded children. *Journal of Applied Behavior Analysis, 6,* 311–329.

Gutowski, S. J., Geren, M., Stromer, R., & Mackay, H. A. (1995). Restricted stimulus control in delayed matching to complex samples: A preliminary analysis of the role of naming. *Experimental Analysis of Human Behavior Bulletin, 13,* 18–24.

Hake, D. F. (1982). The basic-applied continuum and the possible evolution of human operant social and verbal research. *The Behavior Analyst, 5,* 21–28.

Hall, G. A., & Chase, P. N. (1991). The relationship between stimulus equivalence and verbal behavior. *The Analysis of Verbal Behavior, 9,* 107–119.

Haring, T. G., Breen, C. G., & Laitinen, R. E. (1989). Stimulus class formation and concept learning: Establishment of within- and between-set generalization and transitive relationships via conditional discrimination procedures. *Journal of the Experimental Analysis of Behavior, 52,* 13–25.

Hayes, S. C. (1986). The case of the silent dog—verbal reports and the analysis of rules: A review of Ericsson and Simon's *Protocol Analysis: Verbal Reports as Data. Journal of the Experimental Analysis of Behavior, 45,* 351–363.

Hayes, S. C. (1991). A relational control theory of stimulus equivalence. In L. J. Hayes & P. N. Chase (Eds.), *Dialogues on verbal behavior* (pp. 19–40). Reno, NV: Context Press.

Hayes, S. C. (1994). Relational frame theory: A functional approach to verbal events. In S. C. Hayes, L. J. Hayes, M. Sato, & K. Ono (Eds.), *Behavior analysis of language and cognition* (pp. 9–30). Reno, NV: Context Press.

Hayes, S. C., & Hayes, L. J. (1992). Verbal relations and the evolution of behavior analysis. *American Psychologist, 47,* 1383–1395.

Hollis, J. H., Fulton, R. T., & Larson, A. D. (1986). An equivalence model for vocabulary acquisition in profoundly hearing-impaired children. *Analysis and Intervention in Developmental Disabilities, 6,* 331–348.

Horne, P. J., & Lowe, C. F. (1996). On the origins of naming and other symbolic behavior. *Journal of the Experimental Analysis of Behavior, 65,* 185–241.

Horner, R. H., Bellamy, G. T., & Colvin, G. T. (1984). Responding in the presence of nontrained stimuli: Implications of generalization error patterns. *Journal of the Association for Persons with Severe Handicaps, 9,* 287–295.

Johnson, B., & Cuvo, A. (1981). Teaching mentally retarded adults to cook. *Behavior Modification, 5,* 187–202.

Joyce, B. G., & Wolking, W. D. (1989). Stimulus equivalence: An approach for teaching beginning reading skills to young children. *Education and Treatment of Children, 12,* 109–122.

Karsh, K. G., Repp, A. C., & Lenz, M. W. (1990). A comparison of task demonstration model and the standard prompting hierarchy in teaching word identification to persons with moderate retardation. *Research in Developmental Disabilities, 11,* 395–410.

Kellas, G., Ashcraft, M. H., & Johnson, N. S. (1973). Rehearsal processes in the short-term memory performance of mildly retarded adolescents. *American Journal of Mental Deficiency, 77,* 670–679.

Kennedy, C. H., Itkonen, T., & Lindquist, K. (1994). Nodality effects during equivalence class formation: An extension to sight-word reading and concept development. *Journal of Applied Behavior Analysis, 27,* 673–683.

Kirby, K. C., & Bickel, W. K. (1988). Toward an explicit analysis of generalization: A stimulus control interpretation. *The Behavior Analyst, 11,* 115–129.

Lazar, R. M., Davis-Lang, D., & Sanchez, L. (1984). The formation of visual stimulus equivalences in children. *Journal of the Experimental Analysis of Behavior, 41,* 251–266.

Lee, V. L. (1981). Prepositional phrases spoken and heard. *Journal of the Experimental Analysis of Behavior, 35,* 227–242.

Lignugaris/Kraft, B., McCuller, G. L., Exum, M., & Salzberg, C. L. (1988). A review of research on picture reading skills of developmentally disabled individuals. *Journal of Special Education, 22,* 297–329.

Lowe, C. F., & Horne, P. J. (1996). Reflections on naming and other symbolic behavior. *Journal of the Experimental Analysis of Behavior, 65,* 315–340.

Lowenkron, B. (1996). Joint control and word-object bidirectionality [commentary]. *Journal of the Experimental Analysis of Behavior, 65,* 252–255.

Luciano, M. C. (1986). Acquisition, maintenance, and generalization of productive intraverbal behavior through transfer of stimulus control procedures. *Applied Research in Mental Retardation, 7,* 1–20.

Lynch, D. C., & Cuvo, A. J. (1995). Stimulus equivalence instruction of fraction-decimal relations. *Journal of Applied Behavior Analysis, 28,* 115–126.

MacDonald, R. P. F., Dixon, L. S., & LeBlanc, J. M. (1986). Stimulus class formation following observational learning. *Analysis and Intervention in Developmental Disabilities, 6,* 73–87.

Mace, F. C. (1994). Basic research needed for stimulating the development of behavioral technologies. *Journal of the Experimental Analysis of Behavior, 61,* 529–550.

Mackay, H. A. (1985). Stimulus equivalence in rudimentary reading and spelling. *Analysis and Intervention in Developmental Disabilities, 5,* 373–387.

Mackay, H. A. (1991). Stimulus equivalence: Implications for the development of adaptive behavior. In R. Remington (Ed.), *The challenge of severe mental handicap: An applied behaviour analytic approach* (pp. 235–259). Chichester, England: Wiley.

Mackay, H. A., & Sidman, M. (1984). Teaching new behavior via equivalence relations. In P. H. Brooks, R. Sperber, & C. MacCauley (Eds.), *Learning and cognition in the mentally retarded* (pp. 493–513). Hillsdale, NJ: Erlbaum.

Mackay, H. A., Stromer, R., & Serna, R. W. (in press). Emergent behavior and intellectual functioning: Stimulus classes, generalization, and transfer. In S. Soraci & W. J. McIlvane (Eds.), *Perspectives on fundamental processes in intellectual functioning.* Norwood, NJ: Ablex.

Maguire, R. W., Stromer, R., & Mackay, H. A. (1995). Delayed matching to complex samples and the formation of stimulus classes in children. *Psychological Reports, 77,* 1059–1076.

Maguire, R. W., Stromer, R., Mackay, H. A., & Demis, C. A. (1994). Matching to complex samples and stimulus class formation in adults with autism and young children. *Journal of Autism and Developmental Disorders, 24,* 753–772.

Manabe, K., Kawashima, T., & Staddon, J. E. R. (1995). Differential vocalization in budgerigars: Towards an experimental analysis of naming. *Journal of the Experimental Analysis of Behavior, 63,* 111–126.

Maydak, M., Stromer, R., Mackay, H. A., & Stoddard, L. T. (1995). Stimulus classes in matching to sample and sequence production: The emergence of numeric relations. *Research in Developmental Disabilities, 16,* 179–204.

McIlvane, W. J. (1992). Stimulus control analysis and nonverbal instructional methods for people with intellectual disabilities. In N. W. Bray (Ed.), *International review of research in mental retardation* (Vol. 18, pp. 55–109). New York: Academic Press.

McIlvane, W. J., & Dube, W. V. (1996). Naming as a facilitator of discrimination [commentary]. *Journal of the Experimental Analysis of Behavior, 65,* 267–272.

McIlvane, W. J., Dube, W. V., Green, G., & Serna, R. W. (1993). Programming conceptual and communication skill development: A methodological stimulus class analysis. In A. P. Kaiser & D. B. Gray (Eds.), *Enhancing children's communication* (Vol. 2, pp. 242–285). Baltimore: Brookes.

McIntire, K. D., Cleary, J., & Thompson, T. (1987). Conditional relations in monkeys: Reflexivity, symmetry and transitivity. *Journal of the Experimental Analysis of Behavior, 47,* 279–285.

Michael, J. (1985). Two kinds of verbal behavior plus a possible third. *The Analysis of Verbal Behavior, 3,* 2–5.

Osborne, J. G., & Gatch, M. B. (1989). Stimulus equivalence and receptive reading by hearing-impaired preschool children. *Language, Speech, and Hearing Services in Schools, 20,* 63–75.

Parsons, J. A., Taylor, D. C., & Joyce, T. M. (1981). Precurrent self-prompting operants in children: "Remembering." *Journal of the Experimental Analysis of Behavior, 36,* 253–266.

Pilgrim, C. (1996). Can the naming hypothesis be falsified? [commentary]. *Journal of the Experimental Analysis of Behavior, 65,* 284–286.

Remington, B. (1994). Augmentative and alternative communication and behavior analysis: A productive partnership? *Augmentative and Alternative Communication, 10,* 3–13.

Remington, B. (1996). The evolution of naming—just so! [commentary]. *Journal of the Experimental Analysis of Behavior, 65,* 243–245.

Remington, B., & Clarke, S. (1983). Acquisition of expressive signing by autistic children: An evaluation of the relative effects of simultaneous communication and sign-alone training. *Journal of Applied Behavior Analysis, 16,* 315–328.

Remington, B., & Clarke, S. (1993a). Simultaneous communication and speech comprehension. Part I: Comparison of two methods of teaching expressive signing and speech comprehension skills. *Augmentative and Alternative Communication, 9,* 36–48.

Remington, B., & Clarke, S. (1993b). Simultaneous communication and speech comprehension. Part II: Comparison of two methods of overcoming selective attention during expressive sign training. *Augmentative and Alternative Communication, 9,* 49–60.

Repp, A. C., Karsh, K. G., & Lenz, M. W. (1990). Discrimination training for persons with developmental disabilities: A comparison of the task demonstration model and the standard prompting hierarchy. *Journal of Applied Behavior Analysis, 23,* 43–52.

Rosch, E., Mervis, C. B., Gray, W. D., Johnson, D. M., & Boyes-Braem, P. (1976). Basic objects in natural categories. *Cognitive Psychology, 8,* 382–439.

Saunders, K. J., & Spradlin, J. E. (1990). Conditional discrimination in mentally retarded adults: The development of generalized skills. *Journal of the Experimental Analysis of Behavior, 54,* 239–250.

Saunders, K. J., & Spradlin, J. E. (1993). Conditional discrimination in mentally retarded subjects: Programming acquisition and learning set. *Journal of the Experimental Analysis of Behavior, 60,* 571–585.

Saunders, K. J., & Spradlin, J. E. (1996). Naming and equivalence relations [commentary]. *Journal of the Experimental Analysis of Behavior, 65,* 304–308.

Saunders, R. R., & Green, G. (1992). The nonequivalence of behavioral and mathematical equivalence. *Journal of the Experimental Analysis of Behavior, 57,* 227–241.

Saunders, R. R., & Green, G. (1996). Naming is not (necessary for) stimulus equivalence [commentary]. *Journal of the Experimental Analysis of Behavior, 65,* 312–314.

Schenk, J. J. (1993). Emergent conditional discrimination in children: Matching to compound stimuli. *Quarterly Journal of Experimental Psychology, 46B,* 345–365.

Schusterman, R. J., & Kastak, D. (1993). A California sea lion (*Zalophus californianus*) is capable of forming equivalence relations. *Psychological Record, 43,* 823–839.

Shafer, E. (1993). Teaching topography-based and selection-based verbal behavior to developmentally disabled individuals: Some considerations. *The Analysis of Verbal Behavior, 11,* 117–133.

Sidman, M. (1960). *Tactics of scientific research: Evaluating experimental data in psychology.* New York: Basic Books.

Sidman, M. (1971). Reading and auditory-visual equivalences. *Journal of Speech and Hearing Research, 14,* 5–13.

Sidman, M. (1977). Teaching some basic prerequisites for reading. In P. Mittler (Ed.), *Research to practice in mental retardation: Vol. 2. Education and training* (pp. 353–360). Baltimore: University Park Press.

Sidman, M. (1986). Functional analysis of emergent verbal classes. In T. Thompson & M. D. Zeiler (Eds.), *Analysis and integration of behavioral units* (pp. 213–245). Hillsdale, NJ: Erlbaum.

Sidman, M. (1987). Two choices are not enough. *Behavior Analysis, 22,* 11–18.

Sidman, M. (1990). Equivalence relations: Where do they come from? In D. Blackman & H. Lejeune (Eds.), *Behaviour analysis in theory and practice: Contributions and controversies* (pp. 93–114). Hove, UK: Erlbaum.

Sidman, M. (1994). *Equivalence relations and behavior: A research story.* Boston: Authors Cooperative.

Sidman, M., & Cresson, O., Jr. (1973). Reading and crossmodal transfer of stimulus equivalences in severe retardation. *American Journal of Mental Deficiency, 77,* 515–523.

Sidman, M., Cresson, O., Jr., & Willson-Morris, M. (1974). Acquisition of matching to sample via mediated transfer. *Journal of the Experimental Analysis of Behavior, 22,* 261–273.

Sidman, M., Kirk, B., & Willson-Morris, M. (1985). Six-member stimulus classes generated by conditional-discrimination procedures. *Journal of the Experimental Analysis of Behavior, 43,* 21–42.

Sidman, M., & Tailby, W. (1982). Conditional discrimination vs. matching-to-sample: An expansion of the testing paradigm. *Journal of the Experimental Analysis of Behavior, 37,* 5–22.

Sidman, M., Willson-Morris, M., & Kirk, B. (1986). Matching-to-sample procedures and the development of equivalence relations: The role of naming. *Analysis and Intervention in Developmental Disabilities, 6,* 1–19.

Silverman, K., Anderson, S. R., Marshall, A. M., & Baer, D. M. (1986). Establishing and generalizing audience control of new language repertoires. *Analysis and Intervention in Developmental Disabilities, 6,* 21–40.

Singh, N. N., & Singh, J. (1986). Reading acquisition and remediation in the mentally retarded. In N. R. Ellis & N. W. Bray (Eds.), *International review of research in mental retardation* (Vol. 14, pp. 165–199). New York: Academic Press.

Skinner, B. F. (1957). *Verbal behavior.* New York: Appleton-Century-Crofts.

Skinner, B. F. (1968). *The technology of teaching.* New York: Appleton-Century-Crofts.

Skinner, B. F. (1969). *Contingencies of reinforcement:*

A theoretical analysis. New York: Appleton-Century-Crofts.

Skinner, B. F. (1974). *About behaviorism.* New York: Knopf.

Skinner, B. F. (1989). The behavior of the listener. In S. C. Hayes (Ed.), *Rule-governed behavior: Cognition, contingencies and instructional control* (pp. 85–96). New York: Plenum.

Smeets, P. M., & Striefel, S. (1994). Matching to complex stimuli under nonreinforced conditions: Errorless transfer from identity to arbitrary matching tasks. *Quarterly Journal of Experimental Psychology, 47B,* 39–62.

Spradlin, J. E. (1989). Model of generalization. In L. McReynolds & J. E. Spradlin (Eds.), *Generalization strategies in the treatment of communication disorders* (pp. 132–146). Toronto: Decker.

Stoddard, L. T., & McIlvane, W. J. (1986). Stimulus control research and developmentally disabled individuals. *Analysis and Intervention in Developmental Disabilities, 6,* 155–178.

Stokes, T. F., & Baer, D. M. (1977). An implicit technology of generalization. *Journal of Applied Behavior Analysis, 10,* 349–367.

Stromer, R. (1991). Stimulus equivalence: Implications for teaching. In W. Ishaq (Ed.), *Human behavior in today's world* (pp. 109–122). New York: Praeger.

Stromer, R. (1996a). *On the benefits of direct teaching of spelling in children's language arts instruction.* Manuscript submitted for publication.

Stromer, R. (1996b). On the experimental analysis of naming and the formation of stimulus classes [commentary]. *Journal of the Experimental Analysis of Behavior, 65,* 250–252.

Stromer, R., & Mackay, H. A. (1992). Spelling and emergent picture-printed word relations established with delayed identity matching to complex samples. *Journal of Applied Behavior Analysis, 25,* 893–904.

Stromer, R., & Mackay, H. A. (1993). Delayed identity matching to complex samples: Teaching students with mental retardation spelling and the prerequisites for equivalence classes. *Research in Developmental Disabilities, 14,* 19–38.

Stromer, R., & Mackay, H. A. (in press). Naming and the formation of stimulus classes. In T. R. Zentall & P. M. Smeets (Eds.), *Stimulus class formation in humans and animals.* Amsterdam: North-Holland.

Stromer, R., Mackay, H. A., Howell, S. R., McVay, A. A., & Flusser, D. (1996). Teaching computer-based spelling to individuals with developmental and hearing disabilities: Transfer of stimulus control to writing tasks. *Journal of Applied Behavior Analysis, 29,* 25–42.

Stromer, R., Mackay, H. A., & Stoddard, L. T. (1992). Classroom applications of stimulus equivalence technology. *Journal of Behavioral Education, 2,* 225–256.

Stromer, R., McIlvane, W. J., & Serna, R. W. (1993). Complex stimulus control and equivalence. *Psychological Record, 43,* 585–598.

Stromer, R., & Osborne, J. G. (1982). Control of adolescents' arbitrary matching-to-sample by positive and negative stimulus relations. *Journal of the Experimental Analysis of Behavior, 37,* 329–348.

Stromer, R., & Stromer, J. B. (1990). The formation of arbitrary stimulus classes in matching to complex samples. *Psychological Record, 40,* 51–66.

Sundberg, C. T., & Sundberg, M. L. (1990). Comparing topography-based verbal behavior with stimulus selection-based verbal behavior. *The Analysis of Verbal Behavior, 8,* 31–41.

Torgrud, L. J., & Holborn, S. W. (1989). Effectiveness and persistence of precurrent mediating behavior in delayed matching to sample and oddity matching with children. *Journal of the Experimental Analysis of Behavior, 52,* 181–191.

Wacker, D. P., Berg, W. K., Berrie, P., & Swatta, P. (1985). Generalization and maintenance of complex skills by severely handicapped adolescents following picture prompt training. *Journal of Applied Behavior Analysis, 18,* 329–336.

Wasserman, E. A., & DeVolder, C. L. (1993). Similarity- and nonsimilarity-based conceptualization in children and pigeons. *Psychological Record, 43,* 779–793.

Watkins, C. L., Pack-Teixteira, L., & Howard, J. S. (1989). Teaching intraverbal behavior to severely retarded children. *The Analysis of Verbal Behavior, 7,* 69–81.

Wetherby, B., Karlan, G. R., & Spradlin, J. E. (1983). The development of derived stimulus relations through training in arbitrary-matching sequences. *Journal of the Experimental Analysis of Behavior, 40,* 69–78.

Wolery, M., Doyle, P. M., Ault, M. J., Gast, D. L., Meyer, S., & Stinson, D. (1991). Effects of presenting incidental information in consequent events on future learning. *Journal of Behavioral Education, 1,* 79–104.

Received April 22, 1996
Initial editorial decision April 25, 1996
Revision received May 16, 1996
Final acceptance May 17, 1996
Action Editor, David P. Wacker

JOURNAL OF APPLIED BEHAVIOR ANALYSIS 1996, **29,** 535–547 NUMBER 4 (WINTER 1996)

THE MOMENTUM OF COMPLIANCE

JOHN A. NEVIN

UNIVERSITY OF NEW HAMPSHIRE

Compliance with demanding requests that are normally ineffective may be increased by presenting a series of easy or high-probability (high-*p*) requests before the more demanding requests. Mace and his colleagues have discussed the effectiveness of the high-*p* procedure in relation to behavioral momentum—the tendency for behavior, once initiated and reinforced, to persist in the face of a challenge. The high-*p* procedure differs in several ways from that employed in laboratory research on momentum, and the methods and findings of basic research may not be relevant to applied work on compliance. This article reviews some laboratory procedures used in research on behavioral momentum, summarizes the major findings of that research, and discusses its relevance to the high-*p* procedure and its outcomes. Increased compliance with demanding requests following the high-*p* procedure can be understood in relation to the procedures and findings of basic research, but some questions arise in the process of translating research into application via the metaphor of momentum. These questions suggest some new directions for both experimental and applied behavior analysis.

DESCRIPTORS: behavioral momentum, response rate, resistance to change, compliance, high-*p* procedure

---

The metaphor of behavioral momentum gives us a way to talk about two independent dimensions of behavior that are of immediate concern to applied behavior analysis: the rate of responding that is established and maintained by the contingencies of reinforcement, and its resistance to change when responding is challenged or disrupted in some way. The metaphor identifies these two aspects of behavior with the velocity and mass of a moving body, respectively. The product of the velocity-like and mass-like dimensions of behavior is *behavioral momentum,* a compound dependent variable that captures the outcome of training conditions that influence response rate and its persistence when those conditions are altered.

The goals of applied behavior analysis include the establishment of desirable, adaptive behavior through interventions that also insure the persistence of that behavior when the intervention ends. Persistence requires that the behavior in question be sufficiently resistant to change so that it continues during the transition from treatment contingencies to the natural contingencies of everyday life. In terms of the momentum metaphor, a successful intervention endows the behavior in question with a high level of momentum. For example, an intervention designed to establish compliance with requests is successful if compliance occurs rapidly and reliably during training (high velocity) and persists effectively, after explicit training has been discontinued, in the classroom, workplace, and other social settings in which compliance is appropriate (high mass). However, if compliance deteriorated rapidly when the intervention ended (low mass), we would not be fully satisfied with the outcome regardless of the rate of compliance

---

This paper was prepared while the author was an Erskine Visiting Professor at the University of Canterbury. I thank the University of Canterbury for its hospitality and support, and especially Anthony McLean of the Psychology Department for many stimulating discussions and comments on a draft of this paper. The treatment of differential reinforcement of low rate in relation to resistance to change and the characterization of the velocity of noncompliance are based in part on his insights.

Address correspondence to John A. Nevin, RR#2, Box 162, Vineyard Haven, Massachusetts 02568 (E-mail: tnevin@worldnet.att.net).

during the intervention. Conversely, if compliance occurred only infrequently during intervention (low velocity), we would not regard it as firmly established in the person's repertoire even if that low rate also occurred outside the intervention conditions. This latter observation might suggest that *non*compliance was highly resistant to change, perhaps because of an extensive history of reinforcement by escape from task demands. The therapist's problem is to overcome that history with interventions that establish a high rate of compliance during treatment and that make compliance likely to persist when treatment ends—in brief, to maximize the momentum of compliance.

This article begins by reviewing some laboratory research on behavioral momentum, conducted for the most part with pigeons as subjects, and summarizes its main findings, including their generality to people. It then discusses a procedure for establishing compliance in clinical settings that was developed by Mace et al. (1988), based in part on an extension of the momentum metaphor. Known as the high-probability (high-*p*) procedure, it differs from basic research on momentum in several ways, but its effectiveness can be understood within the context of that research.

A RESEARCH REVIEW

Methods and Measures

First, it is important to understand that momentum is a property of a *discriminated operant*—a three-term unit comprised of an antecedent or current stimulus situation, a specified response class, and the contingencies of reinforcement in that situation (Skinner, 1969). Interest focuses on the asymptotic response rate and the resistance to change of that response rate within that stimulus situation. Because the absolute value of resistance to change depends on the nature and value of the disrupter (e.g., amount of prefeeding or duration of extinction sessions), research has concentrated on resistance to change in a given stimulus situation relative to that in one or more other situations involving different reinforcement contingencies.

A particularly convenient experimental paradigm for evaluating the resistance to change of one discriminated operant relative to another is a multiple schedule of reinforcement, in which the experimenter presents two (or more) distinctive stimuli successively, in regular or irregular alternation, for predetermined durations. Different contingencies or schedules of reinforcement for a designated response (or responses) are arranged in the presence of these stimuli to define two (or more) discriminated operants, commonly termed the *components* of the multiple schedule. The components may be separated by time-out periods to minimize interaction between them. The component performances are trained until response rates appear to be stable to establish a reliable baseline, and then their relative resistance is evaluated by disrupting asymptotic performance in some way that applies equally to both components—for example, by prefeeding (giving access to food in the home cage shortly before an experimental session). The disrupter is usually arranged for a brief period (one or a few sessions) to minimize long-term effects of interaction between the disrupter and the baseline conditions of reinforcement. Resistance to change is measured most directly by comparing response rate under disruption with the immediately preceding baseline response rate, separately for each component. Equivalently, it may be estimated from the slope of a function relating response rate under disruption, on a logarithmic scale, to the value of the disrupter. The component performance that exhibits the smaller change relative to baseline, or the shallower slope, is judged to be the more resistant to change. Because comparisons are made within subjects and sessions, they are usually quite reliable.

An Experimental Example

Nevin, Tota, Torquato, and Shull (1990, Experiment 2) arranged a three-component multiple schedule that illustrates several of the major findings of research on behavioral momentum. They employed food-deprived pigeons as subjects in a two-key chamber. In one component (designated Component C in their article and signaled by lighting both keys white), a standard variable-interval (VI) 60-s schedule provided 60 food reinforcers per hour of time in that component for right-key pecks; left-key pecks were not reinforced. A second component (B, both keys lighted red) provided 15 reinforcers per hour for right-key pecks; again, left-key pecks were not reinforced. Thus, comparisons of baseline response rate and resistance to change for responding on the right key in Components B and C would evaluate the effects of different reinforcer rates for that response. A third component (A, both keys lighted green) arranged concurrent VI VI schedules that provided 15 reinforcers per hour for right-key pecks as in Component B and 45 reinforcers per hour for left-key pecks, providing a total of 60 reinforcers per hour as in Component C. Thus, comparisons of baseline response rate and resistance to change for responding on the right key in Components A and B would evaluate the effects of alternative reinforcement for the competing left-key response in Component A, and similar comparisons for Components A and C would evaluate the effects of the distribution of reinforcers across keys with a constant total. Components alternated irregularly with a time-out period between them. The paradigm is illustrated in Figure 1.

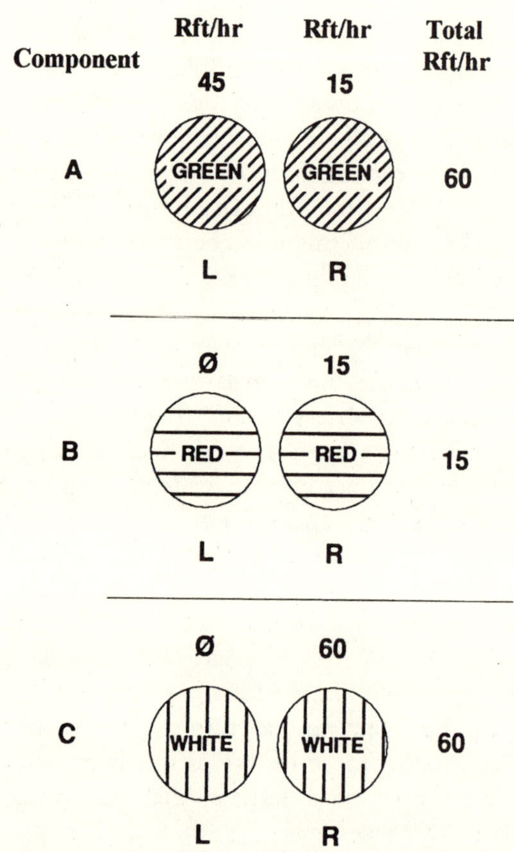

Figure 1. The three-component multiple-schedule paradigm employed in Experiment 2 of Nevin et al. (1990).

After response rates had stabilized, baseline performances were disrupted by allowing satiation in a long continuous session, by prefeeding in the home cage immediately before a session, and by extinction (i.e., termination of all reinforcers), with baseline recovery between disruptions. For all 3 subjects, right-key response rates in baseline were high in Component C, slightly lower in Component B, and substantially lower in Component A, reflecting the ordering of absolute reinforcer rate (60 per hour in C vs. 15 per hour in B) and relative reinforcer rate (1.0 in B vs. .25 in A) within components. However, right-key responding in Component A was substantially more resistant to change than in Component B. Likewise, right-key responding in Component C was more resistant than in Component B and was similar to that in Component A. These results are illustrated for extinction in Figure

2. Note especially that right-key response rate in Component B started above that in Component A and fell below it as extinction progressed. This pattern of results held for all birds and all three resistance tests.

The C-B comparison shows that resistance to change of right-key responding was directly related to the reinforcer rate for that response signaled by the component stimuli, consistent with a number of previous studies (see Nevin, 1992b, for review). However, the B-A and C-A comparisons suggest that resistance to change was directly related to the total reinforcer rate signaled by the component stimuli, independently of whether all reinforcers were contingent on the right-key response and independently of its baseline rate. Similar results were reported by Nevin et al. (1990, Experiment 1) using additional noncontingent reinforcers in one component rather than reinforcers that were explicitly contingent on a second alternative response as in Component A of Experiment 2. Nevin et al. (1990) concluded that the stimulus–reinforcer relation was the critical determiner of resistance to change. An important implication for applied work is that although alternative reinforcers (e.g., left-key reinforcers in Component A) reduce the rate of a target response, they also increase the resistance to change of that response rate because they are presented in the same stimulus situation (see discussion by Mace et al., 1990).

The Relativity of the Stimulus–Reinforcer Relation

The specification of the stimulus–reinforcer relation was refined by Nevin (1992a) in an experiment that arranged a constant reinforcer rate in one component of a two-component multiple schedule while the reinforcer rate in the alternated component was varied across successive conditions, with pigeons as subjects. Resistance to prefeeding and resistance to extinction in the constant component were inversely related to rein-

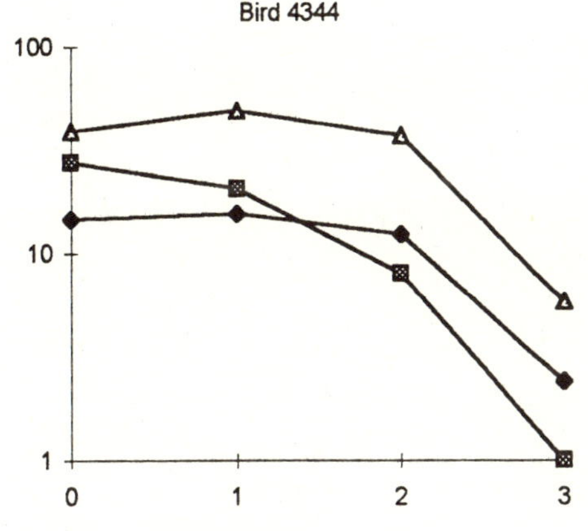

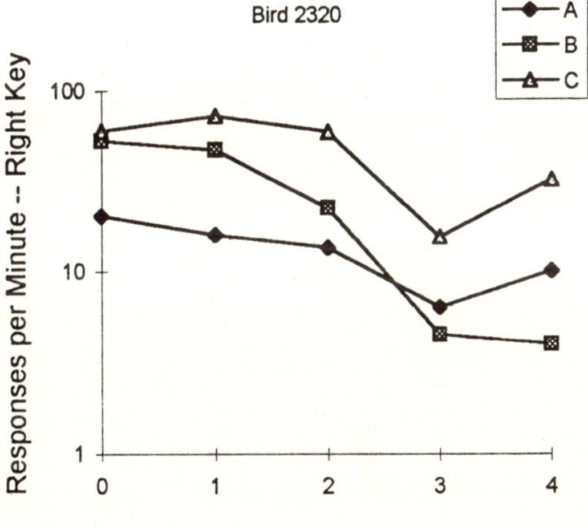

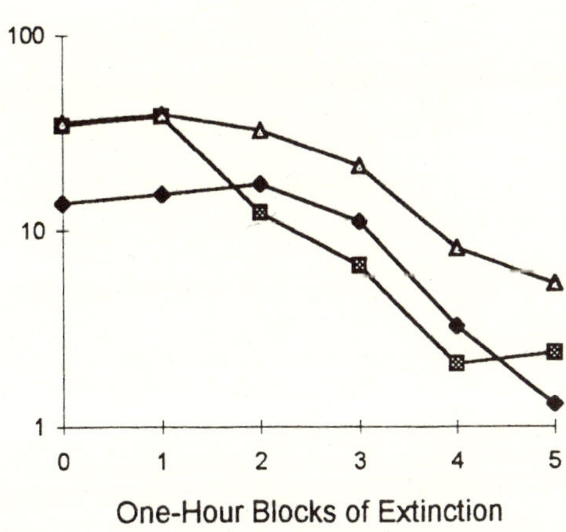

Figure 2. The course of responding on the right key in each of the three components of Experiment 2 of Nevin et al. (1990) during consecutive 1-hr blocks of extinction. Right-key response rates in the baseline session immediately preceding extinction are shown over 0, and the response-rate scale is logarithmic. Adapted from Nevin et al. (1990).

forcer rate in the alternated component. Nevin concluded that resistance to change depended on the relative rather than the absolute reinforcer rate in the presence of a stimulus, and Nevin (1992b) showed that a *contingency ratio* characterizing the reinforcer rate in a component relative to the overall average reinforcer rate in the experimental context accounted well for all of the resistance data obtained in his laboratory. For applied work, the implication is that resistance to change in the therapy setting depends on the reinforcer rate outside that setting as well as within it.

Generality to Other Species

Pigeons are notorious for pecking at lighted keys that are paired with food regardless of the response–reinforcer contingency, as shown in research on autoshaping (see Schwartz & Gamzu, 1977, for review). Thus, it is important both for interpretation and for applied analysis that pigeon data be replicable with humans who are engaged in arbitrary tasks. Experiment 1 by Nevin et al. (1990) has been replicated by Mace et al. (1990) with adults with mental retardation in a group home engaged in a sorting task, and by Cohen (1996) with college students engaged in a typing task. Experiment 2 has been replicated with rats by Mauro and Mace (1996), with visual but not with auditory stimuli. It has not yet been repeated with humans, to my knowledge, but the present status of cross-species replication suggests that the results reported by Nevin et al. (1990) do not depend on a species-specific propensity to direct responses at signals paired with reinforcers.

Summary and Conclusions

The following conclusions appear to be quite general:

1. The resistance to change of a discriminated operant depends directly on the rate of reinforcement obtained by the target response class.

2. The resistance to change of a discriminated operant maintained by a given rate of reinforcement increases if additional reinforcers are allocated to an alternative concurrent response, or are provided independently of responding.

3. The resistance to change of a discriminated operant maintained by a given rate of reinforcement is inversely related to the rate of reinforcement obtained by other, successive discriminated operants.

These three conclusions are consistent with determination of resistance to change by stimulus–reinforcer relations. Evidence reviewed by Nevin (1992b) suggests that these conclusions hold for reinforcer magnitude as well as reinforcer rate. His review also suggests that:

4. The resistance to change of a discriminated operant is independent of the steady-state baseline rate of the target response.

Taken together, these four conclusions comprise what has come to be known as behavioral momentum theory. In fact, they are not theoretical statements but are generalizations from experimental data, and as such are perpetually open to revision. Applied researchers may predict or interpret the effects of various interventions in relation to these conclusions, but should be careful to equate the relevant variables in applied settings with those that have been identified in basic research. A more rigorous and quantitative expression of these conclusions in relation to the metaphor of behavioral momentum is presented in the Appendix.

Some Qualifications

Harper and McLean (1992) challenged the generality of the foregoing conclusions in an experiment that varied the reinforcer rate equally in two multiple-schedule components with different reinforcer magnitudes. They found that variations in reinforcer rate produced equal proportional changes relative to baseline in the two components, a result that contrasted with their own finding (and several others; e.g., Nevin, 1974, Experiment 3) that responding was more resistant to change in the component with the larger reinforcer when free food was given during time-out periods between components. Accordingly, they distinguished between external disrupters such as intercomponent food or prefeeding that leave the component contingencies intact, and internal disrupters such as schedule changes that alter those contingencies, where the latter may not reliably confirm Conclusion 1. However, a change in the schedule for a large reinforcer may be a greater disrupter than a comparable change for a small reinforcer, as shown by Harper (1996). This difference might counteract the expected difference in resistance to change. Moreover, the usual effects of extinction (an internal disrupter) on multiple-schedule performances are entirely in accord with those of external disruptors (e.g., Shettleworth & Nevin, 1965). Complete characterization and scaling of effective disrupters remain to be achieved.

Cohen, Riley, and Weigle (1993) also challenged the generality of the foregoing conclusions by showing that resistance to change does not depend on the reinforcer rate for single-schedule performances that were trained and maintained for a number of consecutive sessions. For example, they found that resistance to prefeeding on fixed-ratio (FR) 40 did not differ from that on FR 160, regardless of the order of exposure to these single schedules. This result is contrary to the expectation that resistance to change is positively related to reinforcer rate, which was higher for the FR 40 performance. When they arranged the same schedules as components of a multiple schedule, however, they confirmed Conclusion 1, with one exception: When free food was provided during (not between) components (an internal disrupter) there was no systematic difference in the resistance of component performances with different reinforcer rates. These findings, which held for both rats and pigeons, suggest that the relation between resistance to change and baseline reinforcer rate may depend on the use of two or more signaled schedules that alternate within sessions. However, some single-schedule results exhibit a positive relation between resistance to change and reinforcer rate (for review, see Nevin, 1979, 1988), and the critical factors that distinguish single-schedule studies that confirm and disconfirm the positive relation remain to be identified.

Finally, different contingencies between responding and reinforcement in two components that establish different response rates may influence resistance to change even when stimulus–reinforcer relations are the same. For example, Lattal (1989) arranged a tandem FR VI schedule in one component and a tandem differential-reinforcement-of-low-rate (DRL) VI schedule in a second component with pigeons as subjects. He found that the low-rate tandem DRL performance was more resistant to disruption by free food between components than was the high-rate tandem FR performance, relative to their baselines, even though reinforcer rates were equated. Lattal's findings suggest that different sorts of contingencies may establish behavioral classes that are differentially susceptible to disruption. For example, disruption of DRL performance may lower the tendency to refrain from responding immediately after a response as well as the overall tendency to engage in the DRL performance itself, resulting in a smaller net reduction in responding. However, when comparable response classes are established in both components, as in multiple VI VI schedules, there is no correlation between response rate and resistance to change.

THE HIGH-*P* PROCEDURE AND COMPLIANCE WITH REQUESTS

An Example of the Procedure and Results

Mace et al. (1988) invoked the metaphor of behavioral momentum in relation to a method for increasing compliance with requests in adults with mental retardation who lived in a group home. Their procedure was designed to enhance compliance with requests such as "clear the table" or "take a shower," which were termed low-*p* requests because the clients rarely complied with them. To enhance low-*p* compliance, Mace et al. presented a series of three high-*p* requests with which the clients readily complied and appeared to enjoy doing, such as "give me five" or "show me your pipe," and then presented a low-*p* request. When the low-*p* request followed shortly after the high-*p* series, there was a striking increase in the probability of or a decrease in the latency to low-*p* compliance.

Compliance is a discriminated operant, in which the immediate stimulus is a request, the response class is an action that conforms to the request, and the consequence is at least intermittent social reinforcement, which is correlated with the overall stimulus situation in which compliance occurs. Accordingly, the findings of research on the momentum of discriminated operant behavior should be relevant. In the terms of the momentum metaphor, the high-*p* series may be viewed as establishing a high velocity of the response class "compliance." At the same time, reinforcers for compliance during the high-*p* sequence, whether explicit or implicit, increase the mass-like aspect of compliance. The resulting momentum serves to make compliance more resistant to the challenge of a low-*p* request.

The high-*p* procedure may not always be sufficient to enhance compliance. For example, Zarcone, Iwata, Mazaleski, and Smith (1994) failed to obtain enhanced compliance using this procedure with children who engaged in self-injurious behavior (SIB) unless it was coupled with extinction of SIB, possibly because SIB disrupted compliance during the high-*p* sequence. Conversely, the high-*p* procedure may not be necessary to enhance compliance. Carr, Newsom, and Binkoff (1976) observed a substantial improvement in compliance (and a reduction of SIB, which was their principal concern) when they told amusing stories to a child with mental retardation in the compliance-request setting. However, the high-*p* procedure has been used successfully with different clients in a variety of settings (e.g., Davis, Brady, Hamilton, McEvoy, & Williams, 1994; Davis, Brady, Williams, & Hamilton, 1992; Ducharme & Worling, 1994), and it is unquestionably a valuable addition to the repertoire of behavioral interventions for addressing problems of noncompliance. The issue here is the interpretation of the high-*p* procedure in relation to behavioral momentum.

Some Procedural Issues

The high-*p* procedure differs in a number of ways from the procedures that are employed in basic research. First, although there is a well-defined stimulus situation—the physical setting and the presence of the therapist—there is no well-defined alternated situation with different conditions of reinforcement that is analogous to an alternated component of a multiple schedule. Second, there is no steady-state baseline response rate against which to evaluate the effect of a disrupter, for two reasons: (a) The compliance response class is not a free operant, but is prompted by a discrete request and indeed is defined by correspondence between the request and the action; and (b) the high-*p* sequence is too brief to establish a reliable baseline. Third, the disrupter involves the presentation of a more demanding request rather than an orthogonal variable that is independent of the contingencies that maintain compliance. Collectively, these differences may seem to rule out the application of principles based on the disruption of free-operant behavior in multiple schedules. I will consider these differences in order.

The single-stimulus situation. As noted previously, Cohen et al. (1993) showed that alternated exposure to two or more schedule components that involve different schedules of reinforcement within a fairly short period, such as an experimental session, may be necessary for demonstrating a positive relation between resistance to change and rate of reinforcement. Thus, there may not be a positive relation between low-*p* compliance and the contingencies arranged by the high-*p* procedure within the single-stimulus situation of a therapy session. However, it is surely the case that a client experiences other stimulus situations and their correlated reinforcement contingencies for compliance, or noncompliance, or unrelated behavior, in the course of daily life. These situations and the uncontrolled or extraneous reinforcers available within them constitute the conditions that alternate successively with therapy sessions. The additional reinforcers arranged during therapy sessions by the high-*p* procedure could be effective in differentially enhancing the persistence of compliance within that setting, construed as one component of a client's life.

Response measures. Because compliance is by definition a response to a request, its rate of occurrence cannot exceed the rate of requests. Accordingly, its velocity-like aspect must be evaluated by its latency from the request, or its probability of occurrence within a brief period after a request. By contrast, virtually all research on resistance to change has employed the rate of a free operant as its dependent variable. I am aware of only two published exceptions. Fath, Fields, Malott, and Grossett (1983) measured both latency to the first response and response rate in each component of a multiple schedule and found similar changes in these measures when responding was disrupted. Elsmore (1971) showed that the probability of completing a fixed ratio within a brief trial period decreased to a lesser extent on trials that signaled a high probability of reinforcement than on trials that signaled a low probability of reinforcement when the ratio value was abruptly increased. This result parallels the usual finding that resistance to change is directly related to reinforcer rate in a component, suggesting that probability of responding in a discrete signaled period may be functionally similar to response rate. Thus, there is no reason to question the relevance of momentum research on the basis of the measures used in the high-*p* procedure. Moreover, Elsmore's disrupter (an abrupt increase in the response requirement) may be analogous to a low-*p* request.

The need for a stable baseline. Basic research on behavioral momentum has routinely established stable baseline response rates before evaluating resistance to change. In this way, it combines the interest in steady-state performance that characterizes modern research on operant behavior with a more traditional emphasis on behavior in transition during acquisition or extinction. Although a steady-state baseline is necessary for quantitative analyses (see the Appendix), it is possible to make ordinal comparisons of resistance to change without a stable baseline response rate. For example, Furomoto (1971) explored the effects of number of reinforcers on resistance to extinction in a parametric between-group experiment with pigeons as subjects. One of her groups received a reinforcer after each of three consecutive responses, and a pretraining control group received none. She found that the three-reinforcer group made about seven times more responses than the zero-reinforcer control group during a subsequent period of extinction (actually, a continuation of nonreinforcement for the control group). This comparison did not require a stable preextinction baseline, which in any case was precluded by the brevity of training. Analogously, the effects of prompting and reinforcing compliance with three high-*p* requests on low-*p* compliance can be compared with low-*p* compliance in the absence of the high-*p* series without establishing a stable high-*p* baseline.

The nature of the disrupter. The majority of momentum research has employed disrupters such as prefeeding or free food during periods between components that leave the baseline contingencies unchanged. The high-*p* procedure differs in that its disrupter—a low-*p* request—is simply a more demanding instance of compliance that has already been made probable by the high-*p* sequence. In this sense, it may be more like Harper and McLean's (1992) schedule change, which they characterized as an internal disrupter and, as noted previously, had no differential effects on component performances maintained by different reinforcer magnitudes. However, as described above, Elsmore (1971) employed a demanding ratio as an internal disrupter and obtained results that were entirely in accord with expectations based on momentum research with external disrupters. In summary, the procedures and measures of momentum research can be interpreted as relevant to the effects of the high-*p* procedure on low-*p* compliance.

Some Conceptual Issues

When low-*p* compliance occurs reliably after the high-*p* sequence, is this the result of the velocity of compliance, the mass of compliance, or both (momentum)? This may seem like a scholastic question concerning angels on pinheads, but it is important because of what we know (and don't know) about the separate determiners of the velocity-like and mass-like aspects of behavior.

First, if the high-*p* sequence increases the mass of compliance, it presumably does so through the correlation of reinforcers with the stimulus situation. But as described previously, reinforcement for one class of behavior increases the mass of all behavior that is maintained by the same reinforcer within the situation, including competing responses (as in Component A of Experiment 2 by Nevin et al., 1990). Thus, paradoxically, reinforcing high-*p* compliance may also increase the mass of *non*compliance—whatever the client normally does in response to a low-*p* request in the same situation. At one level, this is not a problem: Because the high-*p* sequence is structured to guarantee that noncompliance does not occur, its local velocity within the high-*p* situation is zero, and its momentum is therefore zero regardless of its mass. However, if noncompliance does occur in the therapy situation, there is a problem of interpretation. Let's assume that compliance is positively reinforced, whereas noncompliance is likely to be negatively reinforced (e.g., by escape from task demands). The question, then, is whether positive reinforcement of one class of behavior also increases the mass of an incompatible class that is maintained by negative reinforcement. No research, to my knowledge, has addressed this question. If future research suggests that both positively and negatively reinforced response classes gain similarly in mass when additional reinforcers are given for the former, a momentum account would have to argue that compliance wins out over noncompliance when a low-*p* request is presented after a high-*p* sequence because the high-*p* sequence selectively increases the velocity of compliance. Future applications of the high-*p* sequence would therefore concentrate on response–reinforcer contingencies that maximize the velocity of compliance. However, if it turns out that positive reinforcers have a selective effect on the mass of positively reinforced behavior, low-*p* compliance would be construed as evidence of the mass of compliance as well as its velocity, and future applications would emphasize situation–reinforcer relations.

Second, the high-*p* series may not be necessary for increasing low-*p* compliance. Although Mace et al. (1988, Experiments 2 and 4) conducted attention controls that included the presentation of pleasant comments with no evidence of enhanced low-*p* compliance, Carr et al. (1976) improved compliance by telling amusing stories in the therapy setting, and Kennedy, Itkonen, and Lindquist (1995) obtained comparable levels of low-*p* compliance by presenting the high-*p* series and by making pleasant comments in separate conditions. These findings appear to be problematic for a momentum account because there is no obvious source of velocity in the absence of the high-*p* sequence. However, they may be understood in relation to the foregoing argument. If amusing stories and pleasant comments are construed as response-independent positive reinforcers, they should increase the mass of compliance in much the same way as the high-*p* sequence reinforcers do. In both studies, compliance had a history of reinforcement in the therapy setting before amusing stories or pleasant comments were introduced. Therefore, the mass of compliance with low-*p* requests might be enhanced by response-independent positive reinforcers, leading to the observed result. (Note that this interpretation works only if such reinforcers did not equally increase the mass of noncompliance, as argued above.) An optimal method for enhancing low-*p* compliance might present explicit response-contingent positive reinforcers in the high-*p* series to establish the velocity and mass of compliance, and also provide response-independent reinforcers in the treatment situation to enhance its mass.

Third, Mace et al. (1988, Experiment 3) did not observe an enhancement in low-*p* compliance when the interval between the high-*p* series and the low-*p* request was increased from 5 s to 20 s. How might a momentum account interpret this transience of low-*p* compliance? One approach is to conceptualize the delay between the high-*p* series and the low-*p* request as an independent disrupter, in addition to the disruptive challenge posed by the low-*p* request itself. Perhaps the delay after the high-*p* series allows other competing behavior to intervene and disrupt compliance; but whatever the interpretation of the delay effect, it should be reduced by any procedure that increases the mass of compliance. For example, response-independent positive reinforcers could be provided in addition to the high-*p* series reinforcers. If the mass-like aspect of compliance is enhanced by such reinforcers, low-*p* compliance should be more resistant to disruption and persist over longer delays. To make more direct contact with the multiple-schedule paradigm, this sort of analysis might profitably be conducted in two physically different settings with two different therapists, one providing response-independent reinforcers in conjunction with the high-*p* series and the other using the high-*p* series alone. Resistance of low-*p* compliance to delay after the high-*p* series could then be compared between settings.

CONCLUSION

In summary, the effectiveness of the high-*p* procedure and its variants can be understood and, perhaps, advanced within the framework of the momentum metaphor from which it developed. However, translating the terms of the metaphor into the high-*p* procedure, or indeed any other application, encounters some uncertainties and entails a fair amount of speculation; thus, alternative accounts are surely possible. Basic research can address these uncertainties, but the direct application of laboratory findings to clinical work with people whose histories and environments are complex and uncontrolled will always involve a certain amount of faith. On the basis of research on resistance to change, I have considerable faith in the power of stimulus–reinforcer relations to influence the persistence of discriminated operant behavior in a wide variety of settings.

My faith is based to some extent on the appeal of the metaphor of behavioral momentum, which continues to guide much of my research. Metaphors can be dangerous if they are extrapolated beyond the domain in which their terms have unambigious referents, but they can also be helpful in communicating scientific ideas. Most important, they may foster innovation because they can interact unpredictably with the repertoires of scientists, as exemplified by the development of the high-*p* procedure.

REFERENCES

Carr, E. G., Newsom, C. D., & Binkoff, J. A. (1976). Stimulus control of self-destructive behavior in a psychotic child. *Journal of Abnormal Child Psychology, 4,* 139–153.

Cohen, S. L. (1996). Behavioral momentum of typing behavior in college students. *Journal of Behavior Analysis and Therapy, 1,* 36–51.

Cohen, S. L., Riley, D. S., & Weigle, P. A. (1993). Tests of behavioral momentum in simple and multiple schedules with rats and pigeons. *Journal of the Experimental Analysis of Behavior, 60,* 255–291.

Davis, C. A., Brady, M. P., Hamilton, R., McEvoy, M. A., & Williams, R. E. (1994). Effects of high-probability requests on the social interactions of young children with severe disabilities. *Journal of Applied Behavior Analysis, 27,* 619–637.

Davis, C. A., Brady, M. P., Williams, R. E., & Hamilton, R. (1992). Effects of high-probability requests on the acquisition and generalization of responses to requests in young children with behavior disorders. *Journal of Applied Behavior Analysis, 25,* 905–916.

Ducharme, J. M., & Worling, D. E. (1994). Behavioral momentum and stimulus fading in the acquisition and maintenance of child compliance in the home. *Journal of Applied Behavior Analysis, 27,* 639–647.

Elsmore, T. F. (1971). Effects of response effort on discrimination performance. *Psychological Record, 21,* 17–24.

Fath, S. J., Fields, L., Malott, M. K., & Grossett, D. (1983). Response rate, latency, and resistance to change. *Journal of the Experimental Analysis of Behavior, 39,* 267–274.

Furomoto, L. (1971). Extinction in the pigeon after continuous reinforcement: Effect of number of reinforced responses. *Psychological Reports, 28,* 331–338.

Harper, D. N. (1996). Response-independent food delivery and behavioral resistance to change. *Journal of the Experimental Analysis of Behavior, 65,* 549–560.

Harper, D. N., & McLean, A. P. (1992). Resistance to change and the law of effect. *Journal of the Experimental Analysis of Behavior, 57,* 317–337.

Herrnstein, R. J. (1970). On the law of effect. *Journal of the Experimental Analysis of Behavior, 13,* 243–266.

Kennedy, C. H., Itkonen, T., & Lindquist, K. (1995). Comparing interspersed requests and social comments as antecedents for increasing student compliance. *Journal of Applied Behavior Analysis, 28,* 97–98.

Lattal, K. A. (1989). Contingencies on response rate and resistance to change. *Learning and Motivation, 20,* 191–203.

Mace, F. C., Hock, M. L., Lalli, J. S., West, B. J., Belfiore, P., Pinter, E., & Brown, D. K. (1988). Behavioral momentum in the treatment of noncompliance. *Journal of Applied Behavior Analysis, 21,* 123–141.

Mace, F. C., Lalli, J. S., Shea, M. C., Lalli, E. P., West, B. J., Roberts, M., & Nevin, J. A. (1990). The momentum of human behavior in a natural setting. *Journal of the Experimental Analysis of Behavior, 54,* 163–172.

Mauro, B. F., & Mace, F. C. (1996). Differences in the effect of Pavlovian contingencies on behavioral momentum using auditory versus visual stimuli. *Journal of the Experimental Analysis of Behavior, 65,* 389–399.

McLean, A. P., Campbell-Tie, P., & Nevin, J. A. (1996). Resistance to change as a function of stimulus–reinforcer and location–reinforcer contingencies. *Journal of the Experimental Analysis of Behavior, 66,* 169–191.

Nevin, J. A. (1974). Response strength in multiple schedules. *Journal of the Experimental Analysis of Behavior, 21,* 389–408.

Nevin, J. A. (1979). Reinforcement schedules and response strength. In M. D. Zeiler & P. Harzem (Eds.), *Advances in analysis of behaviour: Vol. 1. Reinforcement and the organization of behavior* (pp. 117–158). Chichester, England: Wiley.

Nevin, J. A. (1984). Pavlovian determiners of behavioral momentum. *Animal Learning & Behavior, 12,* 363–370.

Nevin, J. A. (1988). Behavioral momentum and the partial reinforcement effect. *Psychological Bulletin, 103,* 44–56.

Nevin, J. A. (1992a). Behavioral contrast and behavioral momentum. *Journal of Experimental Psychology: Animal Behavior Processes, 18,* 126–133.

Nevin, J. A. (1992b). An integrative model for the study of behavioral momentum. *Journal of the Experimental Analysis of Behavior, 57,* 301–316.

Nevin, J. A., Mandell, C., & Atak, J. R. (1983). The analysis of behavioral momentum. *Journal of the Experimental Analysis of Behavior, 39,* 49–59.

Nevin, J. A., Smith, L. D., & Roberts, J. (1987). Does contingent reinforcement strengthen operant behavior? *Journal of the Experimental Analysis of Behavior, 48,* 17–33.

Nevin, J. A., Tota, M. E., Torquato, R. D., & Shull, R. L. (1990). Alternative reinforcement increases resistance to change: Pavlovian or operant contingencies? *Journal of the Experimental Analysis of Behavior, 53,* 359–379.

Schwartz, B., & Gamzu, E. (1977). Pavlovian control of operant behavior. In W. K. Honig & J. E. R. Staddon (Eds.), *Handbook of operant behavior* (pp 53–97). New York: Prentice Hall.

Shettleworth, S., & Nevin, J. A. (1965). Relative rate of response and relative magnitude of reinforcement in multiple schedules. *Journal of the Experimental Analysis of Behavior, 8,* 199–202.

Skinner, B. F. (1969). *Contingencies of reinforcement.* New York: Appleton-Century-Crofts.

Tota-Faucette, M. (1991). *Alternative reinforcement and resistance to change.* Unpublished doctoral dissertation, University of North Carolina at Greensboro.

Williams, B. A., & Wixted, J. T. (1986). An equation for behavioral contrast. *Journal of the Experimental Analysis of Behavior, 45,* 47–62.

Zarcone, J. R., Iwata, B. A., Mazaleski, J. L., & Smith, R. G. (1994). Momentum and extinction effects on self-injurious escape behavior and noncompliance. *Journal of Applied Behavior Analysis, 27,* 649–658.

Received April 29, 1996
Initial editorial decision June 19, 1996
Revision received July 10, 1996
Final acceptance July 17, 1996
Action Editor, David P. Wacker

APPENDIX

The momentum metaphor links behavioral mass to resistance to change by invoking Newton's second law, which states that the change in velocity of a moving body is inversely related to its mass when a given external force is imposed. More formally,

$$\Delta v = f/m, \tag{1}$$

where Δv is the change in velocity (i.e., acceleration) over the period of force application, f is the imposed force, and m is the inertial mass of the body. For behavioral applications, Nevin, Mandell, and Atak (1983) proposed that Δv be expressed as the logarithm (base 10) of response rate during disruption (B_X) relative to baseline response rate (B_O):

$$\log(B_X/B_O) = f/m, \tag{2}$$

where f is the value of the disrupter and m is behavioral mass. When a given disrupter (f) is applied equally to Components 1 and 2 of a multiple schedule, Equation 2 is written separately for each and the resulting expressions are divided, giving

$$\log(B_{X1}/B_{O1})/\log(B_{X2}/B_{O2}) = m_2/m_1. \tag{3}$$

That is, the ratio of behavioral masses is inversely proportional to the ratio of the logarithms of responding under disruption relative to baseline in the two components. This computation gives a point estimate of the mass ratio, which may be unreliable. If the disrupter value is varied systematically over a series of tests or is defined by a series of consecutive sessions with a given disrupter (e.g., extinction), the ratio of behavioral masses may be estimated more reliably by calculating the slopes of functions that relate response rates under disruption to the value of the disrupter, and quantifying the mass ratio by the inverse slope ratio.

Nevin (1992b) used the inverse-slope analysis to summarize results from a wide variety of procedures employing two-component multiple schedules, multiple chain schedules, and serial schedules that differed in reinforcer rate, magnitude, and contingency between the target response and the reinforcer, with disrupters including free reinforcers between components, signaled concurrent reinforcement, prefeeding, and extinction. He found that the ratio of masses was a power function of a contingency ratio characterizing reinforcer rate or magnitude in one component relative to that in another component, where each was expressed relative to the overall average reinforcer rate or magnitude in the experimental session. In effect, the contingency ratio quantifies the stimulus–reinforcer relation, which has been shown above to be a powerful determiner of resistance to change. Its value can be altered experimentally by changing the reinforcer rate in a target component, the reinforcer rate in an alternated component, or the length of time-out periods between components (which affects the overall average reinforcer rate for a session). Nevin (1992a) showed that these different ways of changing the contingency ratio had similar effects on mass ratios.

The foregoing material addresses the quantification and determiners of behavioral mass. We turn now to velocity, measured as baseline response rate in a multiple-schedule component. Baseline response rate in single schedules is described by Herrnstein's (1970) well-known hyperbolic equation:

$$B = kR/(R + R_E), \tag{4}$$

where B represents response rate, R represents reinforcer rate, R_E represents the rate of extraneous reinforcers, and k represents the asymptotic response rate as reinforcer rate increases indefinitely. Herrnstein (1970) modified the equation to account for interactions in multiple schedules:

$$B_N = kR_N/(R_N + mR_A + R_E), \tag{5}$$

where B_N represents response rate in the target Component N, R_N represents reinforcer rate in that component, and R_A represents reinforcer rate in the alternated component; m, which ranges from 1.0 to 0, represents the degree of interaction between components; and k and R_E remain defined as above. Equation 5 provides an adequate account of response rate in many experiments, but it makes some incorrect predictions and has logical shortcomings. Williams and Wixted (1986) proposed an equation that resolves these difficulties:

$$B_N = sR_N/(R_N + pR_{N-1} + fR_{N+1})/(1 + p + f) + C, \tag{6}$$

where B_N is response rate and R_N is reinforcer rate in the target Component N, R_{N-1} is the reinforcer rate in the preceding component, and R_{N+1} is the reinforcer rate in the following component; p and f reflect the degree of interaction with the preceding and following components, respectively; C represents the inhibitory effects of all reinforcers in the situation; and s is a scaling constant. Equation 6 describes steady-state response rate in a variety of multiple-schedule procedures quite well. If f is greater than p, the equation also accounts for the fact that response rate is lower in the presence of a component with a given reinforcer rate if it precedes a component with a richer schedule than if it precedes a component with a leaner schedule.

Equations 4, 5, and 6 all predict that response rate maintained by a rich schedule will be more resistant to change than that maintained by a lean schedule. This is because a given increase in R_E or C, characterizing the disruptive effect of an external variable (force in the momentum metaphor), will have a relatively smaller impact on B_N if R_N is large than if it is small. This aspect of the equations for asymptotic response rate suggests that a single formulation, such as Equation 6, may be able to describe resistance data as well as response rate, obviating the need for a separate formulation of the relation between behavioral mass and the stimulus–reinforcer contingency. However, these equations cannot handle some aspects of the Nevin et al. (1990) results (see their article for discussion), and they predict the opposite of some data on resistance to change. For example, Nevin (1992a) disconfirmed the predictions of Equations 4, 5, and 6 as extrapolated to resistance to change in a standard two-component multiple schedule when the reinforcer rate in the alternated component varied between conditions. In addition, Equation 6 predicts that both response rate and resistance to change will be greater in a target component with a given reinforcer rate that is preceded or followed by a leaner component schedule than in an identical target component that is preceded or followed by a richer component schedule. However, Nevin (1984) and Nevin, Smith, and Roberts (1987) found that resistance in a target component was greater when it was followed by a richer component, and Tota-Faucette (1991) found that resistance was similarly enhanced regardless of whether the richer schedule preceded or followed the target component.

The results of Nevin (1984), Nevin et al. (1987), and Tota-Faucette (1991) are consistent with the conclusion that behavioral mass depends directly on the stimulus–reinforcer contingency ratio, because their constant target components were embedded within a serial compound defined by a repeating stimulus sequence that was correlated with a distinctive situational cue such as the location of a lighted key. Nevin (1992b; see also McLean, Campbell-Tie, & Nevin, 1996) argued that, for serial schedules, the contingency ratio is the joint product of the reinforcer rate in the target component, relative to the overall session average, and the reinforcer rate in the serial compound within which the target component is embedded, again relative to the overall session average. Nevin (1992b) showed that when the resistance data of serial schedules were analyzed in this way, target-component mass ratios were related to contingency ratios by the same power function as for conventional two-component multiple schedules. Collectively, these analyses suggest that resistance to change in a target component is directly related to the rate of reinforcement obtained in a distinctive stimulus situation, regardless of whether those reinforcers are obtained during, before, or after the target component, and regardless of whether they are allocated to the target response, contingent on an alternative response, or noncontingent.

The conclusion is that steady-state response rate is determined by the rate of reinforcement for a target response, relative to all reinforcers in the experimental situation, as described by Equations 4, 5, 6, or related forms, whereas resistance to change is determined by the rate of reinforcement that is correlated with a target component, irrespective of its source and independent of response rate in that component, as described by a power function relating resistance to a contingency ratio that characterizes the stimulus–reinforcer relation. The independence and separate determination of response rate and resistance to change parallel the independence and separate determination of velocity and mass in classical mechanics, which gave rise to the metaphor of behavioral momentum.

JOURNAL OF APPLIED BEHAVIOR ANALYSIS 1997, **30,** 343–375 NUMBER 2 (SUMMER 1997)

ANTECEDENT INFLUENCES ON BEHAVIOR DISORDERS

RICHARD G. SMITH
UNIVERSITY OF NORTH TEXAS

AND

BRIAN A. IWATA
UNIVERSITY OF FLORIDA

The influence of antecedent events on behavior disorders has been relatively understudied by applied behavior analysts. This lack of research may be due to a focus on consequences as determinants of behavior and a historical disagreement on a conceptual framework for describing and interpreting antecedent variables. We suggest that antecedent influences can be described using terms derived from basic behavioral principles and that their functional properties can be adequately interpreted as discriminative and establishing operations. A set of studies on assessment and treatment of behavior disorders was selected for review based on their relevance to the topic of antecedent events. These studies were categorized as focusing on assessment of antecedent events, antecedent treatments for behavior disorders maintained by either positive or negative reinforcement, and special cases of antecedent events in behavior disorders. Some directions for future research on antecedent influences in the analysis and treatment of behavior disorders are discussed.

DESCRIPTORS: antecedent events, behavior disorders, establishing operations, functional analysis

---

In a seminal article published over 25 years ago, Baer, Wolf, and Risley (1968) proposed several dimensions of applied behavior analysis. These characteristics were to be guideposts for the study of socially significant behavior and are largely accepted as standards for the conduct of applied research. One dimension of applied behavior analysis is its relation to a conceptual system. That is, procedures and interpretations in research should be derived from basic principles in order to establish and maintain a conceptually coherent applied science. The extent to which research published in journals such as the *Journal of Applied Behavior Analysis* reflects adherence to this standard has been the subject of ongoing discussion (e.g., see the special section entitled "Science, Theory, and Technology," Vol. 24, No. 3). In fact, a criticism of applied behavior analysis is a perceived failure to relate the many procedures generated for changing socially significant behavior to basic behavioral principles.

A conceptual issue that has received relatively little attention in applied research is the influence of antecedent events on problematic behavior. A recent review of research on behavior disorders indicates that only 11.1% of subjects treated for maladaptive behavior received treatment primarily based upon manipulation of antecedent variables (Lennox, Miltenberger, Spengler, & Erfanian, 1988).[1] At least two factors might ac-

Development of this paper was supported in part by a grant from the Florida Department of Health and Rehabilitative Services and a grant from the Texas Higher Education Coordinating Board. Richard Smith also acknowledges support from the Denton State School during the development of this manuscript. We thank Marc Branch and Timothy Hackenberg for their comments on an earlier draft of this manuscript.

Correspondence regarding this paper should be directed to Richard G. Smith, Department of Behavior Analysis, P.O. Box 13438, University of North Texas, Denton, Texas 76203 (E-mail: Rsmith@scs.unt.edu).

[1] The percentage of subjects who had received antecedent-based treatments was derived by dividing the number of subjects who had received antecedent-based treatments (61) by the number of subjects surveyed

count for this lack of emphasis on antecedent control. First, a primary goal of applied research is socially significant behavior change. A central thesis of behavior analysis is that operant behavior occurs (or does not occur) as a function of its consequences. The most direct method to produce changes in behavior is to manipulate its consequences. The search for interventions, then, naturally focuses on well-established consequent operations, such as reinforcement and punishment, rather than on antecedent events, whose influence on behavior is often considered to be both secondary to and derived from consequences.

In addition, there is a lack of consensus at the theoretical level on how best to describe or classify antecedent variables (Catania, 1993; Marr, 1993; Michael, 1993b; Morris, 1993). At least three theoretical frameworks currently exist: Skinner's operant theory (Skinner, 1953), Kantor's interbehavioral account of setting events (Kantor, 1970), and Michael's system of evocative functions (Michael, 1982). Although the latter accounts are derived from and are consistent with operant theory, they represent significant extensions of Skinner's original account, and the relative contributions and limitations of each for improving our understanding of antecedent events remain unclear. Thus, attempts to relate the outcomes of antecedent manipulations in applied work to behavioral principles find little in the way of a unifying system of interpretation.

The objectives of this article are to describe the major accounts of antecedent processes in operant behavior, to offer a conceptual review of applied research on antecedent events in behavior disorders, and, finally, to identify some promising areas for future investigation.

SKINNER

Although Skinner's account of behavior is often characterized primarily as *reinforcement theory*, with major emphasis on consequences as determinants of behavior (e.g., Roediger, Capaldi, Paris, & Polivy, 1991), his writings contained extensive consideration of the environmental conditions under which behavior may occur. These antecedent influences include such processes as discrimination, deprivation and satiation, emotion, and aversive stimulation.

Discriminative Stimuli

Skinner defined the discriminative contingency as "the occasion upon which a response . . . is followed by reinforcement" (Skinner, 1953, p. 108). That is, stimulus control[2] over behavior is developed through differential reinforcement of responding in the presence of discriminative stimuli (S^Ds). Skinner emphasized the probabilistic nature of the behavior that resulted and contrasted this with the one-to-one relationship between eliciting stimuli and behavior in the respondent paradigm.

Skinner claimed that virtually all operant behavior falls under stimulus control, asserting that "if all behavior were equally likely

(548) and multiplying the result by 100. The number of subjects who had received antecedent-based treatment was derived by summing the total number of subjects treated by procedures categorized as environmental change (n = 13), antecedent control (n = 7), instructions (n = 23), role play (n = 14), and satiation (n = 4); this estimate may artificially inflate the actual number of antecedent-based interventions, because it is unclear that categories such as "environmental change," "instructions," and "role play" represent antecedent interventions exclusively.

[2] The term *stimulus control* is used here and throughout this article to describe conditions under which behavior is altered due to a correlation between responses and consequences. This usage is consistent with the commonplace characterization of stimulus control operations as "signaling" occasions on which responses will result in particular consequences (Catania, 1992, p. 21). Thus, stimulus control is viewed as equivalent to *discriminative control*, and the terms are used interchangeably throughout this article.

to occur on all occasions, the result would be chaotic" (Skinner, 1953, p. 108). He believed that a description of the discriminated operant was incomplete without specification of the conditions under which responding was likely to result in reinforcement, the response requirement, and the reinforcing event; these were major organizing principles of operant behavior. However, he suggested that discrimination may be irrelevant for behavior maintained independent of the extrinsic environment (i.e., behavior that is "automatically reinforced by the organism's own body without respect to external circumstances," Skinner, 1953, p. 108), presumably because no conditions are *differentially* correlated with these consequences.

Discrimination describes a specific functional relationship among antecedent events, behavior, and consequences that applies to a wide range of circumstances. However, discriminative stimuli do not always evoke relevant responses. Apparently, variables that are unrelated to the availability of reinforcement may also affect the likelihood that behavior will occur. Skinner proposed several processes to account for such variability in the discriminated operant.

Deprivation and Satiation, Emotional Stimuli, and Other Antecedent Variables

Skinner suggested that, with access to reinforcement held constant, operant behavior could be increased or decreased through deprivation or satiation, respectively. If an organism is sufficiently deprived of a given reinforcer, responses maintained by that reinforcer will be emitted at the first opportunity. By contrast, satiation will reduce responding even when the reinforcer is freely available. Although the adaptive significance of these operations is most evident in the consumption of substances necessary to sustain life (i.e., food, water, etc.), Skinner (1953) suggested that deprivation also could strengthen behaviors such as physical exercise, social interaction, and sexual activity.

Skinner's account of emotions and emotional stimuli suggests a similar effect, stating that "we define an emotion—insofar as we wish to do so—as a particular state of strength or weakness in one or more responses induced by any one of a class of operations" (Skinner, 1953, p. 166). Emotions such as rage, love, fear, anger, joy, sorrow, frustration, and phobic responses share common features in that they (a) are induced by some environmental condition, (b) are typically accompanied by reflex responses, and (c) alter the probability of a class of behaviors distinguished by a "common consequence" (Skinner, 1953, p. 166). Emotional behavior thus appears to be primarily operant in nature; emotional stimuli simultaneously elicit reflex responses and evoke responses that belong to a specific functional class.

Other events can similarly alter response probabilities; classic examples of the ways in which drinking may be increased, including induction of sweating through heat or exercise, increased excretion through the ingestion of salt, or the loss of blood, all take their effects independent of the availability of water (Skinner, 1953). That is, given continuous access to water, the probability of drinking can be changed through these procedures.

Thus, deprivation and satiation, emotions, and certain other events can have effects on behavior that cannot be described in terms of discriminative control. Although Skinner recognized a common "motivational" aspect among all these operations, the precise mechanisms of control were not stated. These antecedent influences were defined according to their *structural* rather than their *functional* properties. This absence of unifying function forced independent consideration of the formal variants of antecedent influence, producing overlap among classes of variables and categorization of unusual cases, by default, as "other variables" that have effects "similar to . . . deprivation or satiation" (Skinner, 1953, p. 158).

Aversive Stimuli

Another way in which antecedent conditions can influence behavior is through aversive stimulation. Skinner introduced the term *negative reinforcement* to describe response-contingent termination or avoidance of aversive stimulation. *Aversiveness* was a property defined by its effects on behavior rather than by its power to induce pain, discomfort, or annoyance; thus, a stimulus that strengthens behavior through its contingent withdrawal, postponement, or reduction is, by definition, aversive.

Although aversive stimuli share characteristics with discriminative stimuli in that their presence as antecedent conditions alters the probability of responding, aversive stimulation is not necessarily correlated with response-contingent reinforcement (as in the case of inescapable shock). Therefore, the evocative functions of aversive and discriminative stimuli seem more structurally than functionally similar. Skinner noted similarities between antecedent aversive stimulation and "a sudden increase in deprivation" (Skinner, 1953, p. 172) and acknowledged an apparent relationship between aversive stimulation and emotional responding (e.g., Skinner, 1953, pp. 172, 174, 176); however, the exact nature of this relationship is unclear (Skinner's argument that emotional responses generated by aversive stimulation may interfere with operant conditioning suggests that these were considered to be separate but correlated processes). Although antecedent aversive stimulation shares properties with discriminative stimuli, deprivation, and emotional responding, Skinner apparently viewed it a separate process, warranting independent analysis of its effects.

Skinner's analysis of antecedent events included a functional account of the discriminated operant; however, events such as satiation and deprivation, emotions, aversive stimulation, and other antecedent variables were described in terms of observed stimulus–response relations. Conspicuously absent was an account of the relationship between these antecedent conditions and the consequences that maintain operant behavior. Whereas the discriminative stimulus derives control over responding through a special historical relationship with behavioral consequences, Skinner's account of other antecedents suggests a different source of influence between some antecedent stimuli and behavior. Thus, although no internal contradictions exist in a Skinnerian account of antecedent influences, further theoretical extension is necessary.

KANTOR

J. R. Kantor's 1959 book, *Interbehavioral Psychology: A Sample of Scientific System Construction,* introduced a theoretical system that ostensibly accounted for complexities in human behavior beyond those explained by Skinner. In his analysis of the experimental analysis of behavior (TEAB), Kantor criticized limitations in its scope. He asserted that the customary methods of behavior analysis could not extend to complex human behavior and that "the needs of a general naturalistic psychology require such elaboration of the TEAB analytic procedure as to greatly multiply the number of factors searched for and described" (Kantor, 1970, p. 105). Wahler supported this view and suggested that although operant and respondent concepts had been "valuable guidelines," certain behavioral events "simply are not going to be 'understandable' within these concepts" (Wahler & Fox, 1981, p. 334).

Analysis of alternative approaches proposed by Kantor (1970) reveals a "structure-bound" conceptual system in which it is inferred that, because certain elements comprising the behavioral field are formally distinguishable from discrete stimuli, the mechanisms by which they affect behavior must also be distinct. For example, he argued that the behavioral field was comprised of many setting events; antecedent (and concurrent) factors whose influence extended apart from those of simple, discrete stimulus events and included conditions of deprivation or satiation, age, hygienic condition, the presence or absence of important events or objects (e.g., other people, etc.), and previously or recently experienced behavioral interactions. However, as Skinner pointed out as early as 1935, defining stimuli and responses merely as parts of environment and behavior ignores the "natural lines of fracture along which behavior and environment break" (Skinner, 1935, p. 40). For Skinner, any environmental event or combination of events, regardless of temporal or physical extension, may meet the definition of a stimulus. He proposed that relevant features of the environment could be identified through progressive restrictions of behavioral preparations until maximum consistency is observed between independent and dependent variables. Skinner's argument was that more is gained by isolating relevant versus irrelevant variables and identifying classes of relations that may then be extended to complex cases than by presuming that complex cases operate outside of those classes.

Kantor similarly criticized behavior analysts for not probing deeply enough into the nature of stimuli, asserting that the traditional behavior-analytic definition of stimulus is an "object or condition that determines a response" (Kantor, 1970, p. 106). He argued that stimulus and response functions are not inherent but are mutually corresponsive "interbehavioral" functions. Few behavior analysts would disagree with those assertions; in fact, Skinner offered similar descriptions of the processes by which stimuli acquire behavioral functions in several writings (e.g., Skinner, 1931, 1935, 1945, 1953, 1969). One must remember that environmental and behavioral functions are not resident properties of responses or stimuli but are dynamic and mutually interactive; however, this also is compatible with traditional behavioral theory, which long has eschewed simplistic explanations of stimulus–response relations.

Claiming that "though anyone can claim semantic license to refer to every kind of behavior condition by the word 'reinforcement,' this is certainly not the advantage of behavioral analysis" (Kantor, 1970, p. 107), Kantor also criticized a putative emphasis on "rewards" to the exclusion of other events present during behavioral episodes. These were setting events, and enumerated among them were "the hygiene of the organism, its habituation or past behavioral history, what behavioral circumstances it has recently or just previously passed through, the presence or absence of confining objects, and numerous others. In human situations, of course, there are such circumstances as rivalry, compliance, and competition, as well as the unique needs and desires of the behaving individual" (Kantor, 1970, p. 107). Although Kantor identified a range of possible influences on behavior, the mechanisms of influence again were not clear. Setting events may exert stimulus control over behavior, or they may be motivating influences, or both; further, their effects are likely to be idiosyncratic. Thus, the benefits of classifying these influences according to formal features are unclear.

The concept of the behavioral field nevertheless may contribute to our understanding of antecedent events. Although Skinner's definition of the stimulus included no formal restrictions, much behavioral research has focused on simple and discrete stimulus events. The fact that temporally remote, extended, and compound events can also possess stimulus properties may have special relevance for applied research, in which stimulus properties typically are not established but are brought to the experimental situation. That is, in applied research the functional properties of many stimuli have been established prior to the experimental situation by idiosyncratic and often unknown histories. Whereas Kantor's account encourages an expanded search for relevant antecedent variables through recognition of the potential stimulus properties of temporally and spatially extended events, the most promising framework for interpreting these events remains in the purview of operant theory; it is not clear that additional concepts are necessary to describe the *fundamental* relationships between these variables and behavior.

Kantor charged the field of behavior analysis several times with providing merely a superficial explanation of the influences over behavior; however, the alternative system he proposed is also conceptually incomplete pending more exhaustive analysis of functional relationships. Thus, regardless of how one views or defines classes of antecedent events (using either Skinner's or Kantor's nomenclature), the functional properties of these events require further analysis.

MICHAEL

Although the term *establishing operation* (EO) was first introduced by Keller and Schoenfeld (1950), recent work by Michael has provided the clearest and most thorough articulation of this process (Michael, 1982, 1983, 1988, 1993a, 1993b). Defined as a variable that momentarily alters the reinforcing effectiveness of some other object or event (Keller & Schoenfeld, 1950), the establishing operation provides a framework for interpreting the effects of many variables whose functional properties were not fully described by either Skinner or Kantor.

The above definition imposes only one formal restriction on the EO: that of temporary effects. Thus, EOs are dynamic influences whose effects are motivational in nature. They do not derive their functional properties through prior pairings with reinforcer availability (as with discriminative stimuli); rather, their presence or absence mediates the effectiveness of stimuli as effective consequences and alters the momentary frequency of responses that have previously produced those consequences. These effects are, in turn, mediated by the presence of other establishing and discriminative conditions. Further, although the term *establishing operation* suggests directionality, EOs can either increase or decrease the potency of a given form of reinforcement.

Deprivation provides perhaps the most obvious illustration of an EO. For example, the effects of water deprivation are (a) to increase the reinforcing effectiveness of water and (b) to strengthen all conditioned and unconditioned responses associated with water consumption (Skinner, 1953). These are defining characteristics of an EO.

A less immediately obvious but equally appropriate example of an EO is aversive stimulation, which produces an increase in the probability of behavior that has been previously reinforced through the termination of such stimulation. Although some have suggested that aversive stimulation is a discriminative stimulus for escape responding (e.g., Carr, Newsom, & Binkoff, 1976; Touchette, MacDonald, & Langer, 1985), Michael pointed out two important differences that favor an EO interpretation. First, aversive stimulation is not necessarily correlated with the availability of response-contingent escape, which is a requirement for discriminative control. Michael aptly states the case:

> Being in pain is not systematically correlated with being able to remove pain, sad but true, except in the sense that if there were no pain there would be no pain to remove. In other words, the presence of pain is a necessary but not sufficient condition for its removal, just as food or water deprivation is necessary but not sufficient for food or water reinforcement. . . . Just because an organism is hungry doesn't mean that food is likely to be available, as would be pointed out by many currently hungry organisms. Similarly with painful stimulation: It is not differentially correlated with the availability of some way to reduce the pain. (Michael, 1988, p. 4)

A second difference between aversive stimulation and stimulus control is the mechanism that is responsible for low levels of responding (or nonresponding). Responding in the presence of a discriminative stimulus is due to the correlation between the stimulus and reinforcement; nonresponding in the absence of the stimulus is due to extinction. By contrast, nonresponding in the absence of aversive stimulation is not due to extinction; escape responses do not occur in the absence of aversive stimulation simply because there is no reason (i.e., motivation) to do so. Just as food presentation has no reinforcing function for the satiated organism, the absence of aversive stimulation as a consequence will not maintain responding in the absence of (at least a history of) antecedent aversive stimulation.

Emotional variables provide a third general example of EOs. As previously noted, Skinner viewed emotions as "a particular strength or weakness in one or more responses induced by any one of a class of operations" (Skinner, 1953, p. 166). Further, the operant concept of the emotion contained three defining characteristics: (a) induction via environmental stimulation, (b) the simultaneous occurrence of reflex responses, and (c) an alteration in the probability of a class of behaviors distinguished by a common consequence. It is the third feature of emotions that places them directly in the realm of EOs. Emotional stimuli do not derive their evocative functions via differential access to reinforcement, as do discriminative stimuli; rather, they fit nicely within the paradigm of EOs because they (a) momentarily alter the effectiveness of certain forms of reinforcement and (b) alter the frequency of conditioned and unconditioned responses associated with those reinforcers. The "felt" aspects of the emotional event are considered to be, as in Skinner's account, covariants with rather than causes of emotional behavior.

Skinner spoke of a number of other events whose effects are similar to those of deprivation but are difficult to classify within his theoretical system due to disparate formal characteristics. The effects of salt ingestion, blood loss, or perspiration on drinking, of aphrodisiacs on sexual behavior, of psychoactive drugs in general, and a host of other examples all were discussed in loosely motivational terms. Yet Skinner did not propose a common process underlying these similar effects. Because each of these variables alters the probability that operant behavior will occur independent of a special correlation with consequences, their influences seem amenable to an EO account.

The concept of the EO offers a parsimonious framework for classifying a broad range of motivational variables. The appeal of the EO is that it can assimilate the effects of deprivation, emotions, setting events, and related antecedent variables based on functional relations among environmental conditions and behavior. Its scope may be evaluated through conceptual review of existing literature as well as through empirical research.

The following is a review of selected research on behavior disorders, focusing on interpretation of antecedent operations. We have attempted to develop a set of general guidelines to distinguish discriminative from establishing operations and, given adequate procedural and historical information, to classify antecedent variables according to behavioral function. When it is necessary to infer information in order to classify variables, inference has been noted and interpretations are qualified. Classification of discriminative control requires the demonstration of control over behavior by antecedent events that are differentially correlated with consequences. That is, when behavior was altered as a function of the presence or absence of variables associated with different behavioral outcomes (as reported in the Subjects or Methods sections of reviewed studies), then those variables are classified as discriminative events.

Antecedent variables are classified as EOs if, given constant contingencies between behavior and consequences, behavior was altered by the presence or absence of antecedent variables. Thus, when antecedent conditions vary independent of the probability of reinforcement or punishment, behavioral effects are described in terms of EOs.

When it is not possible to specify sufficiently the conditions under which antecedent events influence behavior, alternative interpretations in terms of discriminative and establishing operations are explored, and the tentative nature of these accounts is noted. When future research might clarify unresolved issues, potential strategies are discussed.

It should be noted that the EO concept was not well articulated or widely understood when many of the studies we reviewed were conducted. Therefore, our interpretations have the advantage of a perspective informed by conceptual developments that may not have been available to the original investigators. In addition, the conceptual framework upon which our interpretations are based has not been universally adopted in our discipline, and so some of our accounts may be at odds with, or seem critical of, other explanations. Although our interpretations are sometimes inconsistent with those of the authors, the importance of these studies and their contributions to the applied literature are not diminished.

ASSESSMENT OF ANTECEDENTS

One approach to the assessment of antecedent variables that are associated with problem behaviors is to identify and catalogue the range of environmental conditions that are correlated with undesirable behaviors in the natural environment (e.g., Berkson & Davenport, 1962; Bijou, Peterson, & Ault, 1968; Davenport & Berkson, 1963; Wahler & Fox, 1981). Wahler argued that "conceptual and methodological expansion" was necessary to evaluate influences beyond the "relatively simple and temporally proximate conditions" typically studied by applied behavior analysts (Wahler & Fox, 1981, p. 328). Thus, he developed a methodology for assessing setting events, emphasizing dynamic interrelations among variables as well as an increased breadth and scope of analysis. Such methods, sometimes termed *ecological assessment,* attempt to form a comprehensive picture of environmental influences on problem behavior. For example, Wahler (1975) described an observational coding system that was used to identify environmental and behavioral covariations for 2 boys referred for treatment of behavior disorders. Using interval-based measures in the home and school settings, Wahler derived several "clusters" of intercorrelated behavior categories (e.g., a cluster for 1 child in the school setting included sustained schoolwork, self-stimulation, object play, and noninteraction) that were considered to be indicative of possible response classes. However, within-session analyses of temporal relations between clusters and environmental events revealed no consistent antecedents or consequences for any cluster. Without empirical evidence of common maintaining variables, interpretation of correlated behavior categories as response classes is limited. Another interesting outcome of this study was that each child showed setting-specific behavior clusters; that is, clusters in the school settings were different from clusters in the home settings. Further, planned changes in behavior brought about by intervention in one of the settings were accompanied by additional unplanned changes in the second setting. For example, 1 child's increases in classroom schoolwork were associated with increased self-stimulation and decreased social interactions with adults in the home. Wahler's assertion that the operant model may inadequately describe the organization of behavior repertoires and environments (p. 28) suggests that theoretical extension may be required to account for such effects. Alternatively, these secondary changes may have been due to undocumented environmental or social changes that were associated with the treatments.

Another representative analysis of ecological conditions related to problem behavior described a program for the treatment of self-injurious behavior (SIB), including the use of data collected via "ecological interval recording." Using a variation of Wahler's recording system (Wahler, 1975; Wahler, House, & Stambaugh, 1976), Schroeder et al. (1982) scored the occurrence of 29 categories of behavior. Results indicated that variables such as the pace of staff-initiated interactions, presence of a disruptive client, time of day, staff-client ratios, presence of "self-protective devices," and presence of toys all appeared to affect rates of SIB and other maladaptive behaviors. Although these data may have general implications for the design of environments for persons with behavior disorders, several interpretive limitations exist. First, although some general relationships between broadly defined environmental variables and target behaviors are suggested, these findings may not be representative of the functional relationships affecting the behavior of any one individual. Also, because of the dynamic nature of the naturalistic context, it is difficult to isolate relevant variables. For example, Schroeder et al. found a correlation between time of day and maladaptive behavior; however, it is unlikely that this variable directly evoked or maintained problem behavior. Rather, some other correlated variables, such as the timing of medication regimes, activity or meal schedules, staffing shift changes, or other temporal changes, may have been relevant. Finally, this method does not permit analysis of the functional relationships involved, even when relevant conditions are identified. That is, although it may be the case that the presence of a disruptive client occasions increases in SIB among some individuals, it is not possible to determine the mechanisms that underlie this change. The disruptive client may represent an aversive stimulus, thus serving as an EO for escape behavior. Alternatively, the disruptive person may serve as a model for attention-maintained maladaptive behavior if staff members differentially attend to this behavior (the interaction between staff and the disruptive client being discriminative for the availability of attention for maladaptive behavior).

In another setting-event assessment, Repp, Singh, Karsh, and Deitz (1991) examined the effects of overt task demands (i.e., when a staff member worked directly with a student), covert task demands (i.e., when a student had been given a task demand but no staff member worked directly with the student), and no task demands within six settings (leisure, prevocational, gym, academic, home living, and lunch) on the stereotypy of 12 individuals with developmental disabilities. Data were examined both within and across subjects. Group data showed little difference in stereotypy across settings but revealed higher correlations between stereotypy and demand conditions relative to no-demand conditions. Individual subjects' data showed idiosyncratic correlations between stereotypic behavior and environmental antecedents, with several subjects' data indicating relationships opposite to those reported for the group. Although the individual data provided information about the general conditions under which stereotypy was likely to occur in a given subject, identification of the mechanisms underlying stereotypy was not possible because these potentially important variables were not experimentally manipulated. For example, the observation that a subject's stereotypy increases as a function of demands may indicate that stereotypy is maintained by escape from demands (Iwata, Pace, Kalsher, Cowdery, & Cataldo, 1990), but may also suggest that the presence of demands is discriminative for attention contingent upon stereotypy (Vollmer, Iwata, Smith, & Rodgers, 1992), among other possibilities. The authors were appropriately cautious in concluding that "the functional relationship between maladaptive behaviour and environmental events may have to be assessed at a much greater molecular level than has been the case in the past to ensure appropriate and effective intervention" (p. 426); thus, they acknowledged that this observational method permits only an initial search for potentially relevant antecedent conditions and that greater focus and control are necessary to identify the functional relationships that form the basis of observed correlations between environmental events and occurrences of a given behavior.

Berkson and Mason (1963) examined the effects of molar antecedent variables more directly, placing their subjects in several settings (the dayroom and dining area of their residence, a hospital room, a barren room, and an outdoor playground) and measuring levels of stereotypy, self-manipulation, environment manipulation, and locomotion. They found that stereotypy and self-manipulation occurred at higher levels in a novel, restricted environment than in familiar contexts in which alternative activities, such as manipulation of the environment and locomotion, were possible. The authors interpreted these findings as suggesting that stereotypy and self-manipulation were "self-stimulation" that was reinforced by sensory consequences. However, the strength of this interpretation is limited to the extent that consequences for stereotypy and self-manipulation may have varied across experimental situations. A more definitive analysis might have been possible if consequences for all relevant behaviors (including environment manipulation and locomotion) had been held constant.

Kennedy and Itkonen (1993) performed setting-event analyses of the maladaptive behaviors of 2 female students with developmental disabilities. Awakening late was found to be correlated with increases in problem behavior later at school for 1 student; the use of a city street route versus a highway route on the way to school was associated with later problem behavior for the other student. Eliminating these setting events resulted in decreases in maladaptive behavior for both students; however, in each case the behavioral operations that were involved in these decreases remain unclear. Because no analysis of the reinforcement contingencies that maintained problem behaviors occurred, it is not possible to determine the discriminative or establishing functions of the setting events. Further, although getting up late or taking a given route to school may have been correlated with the occurrence of problem behaviors, it is quite possible that these events had no direct influence on those behaviors. Rather, they may have initiated a long and complex chain of environment–behavior interactions, potentially including both establishing and discriminative events that culminated in target responses, *and* some unknown type of reinforcement. Thus, the functional elements that were responsible for maintaining the students' problem behavior, as well as those that were responsible for subsequent behavior reduction, are unknown. And, as was the case with the Berkson and Mason (1963) study, the definition of setting variables does not permit specification of relevant versus irrelevant events. Kennedy and Itkonen suggested that

> future research should more stringently control for immediate antecedents and consequences that occur along with problem behavior to avoid possible confounding effects among events. Also, the need to ascertain directly the positively and/or negatively reinforcing consequences that maintain behavior and the relation of the setting event to the maintaining variable(s) is critical. (p. 327)

Another method for assessing the effects of ecological variables was developed by Touchette et al. (1985). These investigators devised a scatter plot for data collection and display that showed the temporal distribution of problem behaviors. Personnel in the subjects' home and training environments were instructed to make marks on a grid of consecutive half-hour intervals when subjects engaged in target behaviors. Time intervals were represented on the data sheet in horizontal rows, and consecutive days were represented in columns. After several days, patterns on the data sheet, when juxtaposed with a schedule of daily activities, revealed correlations between the occurrence of 2 subjects' maladaptive behaviors and certain daily activities. Although the authors interpreted these correlations as evidence of stimulus control by certain antecedent events over problem behavior, limitations on inferences about function based on correlation weaken this account. For example, 1 subject's scatter plot indicated that his self-hitting occurred more frequently in the presence of one attending aide than in the presence of a second aide. However, it was unclear whether this outcome was due to differential consequences or specific antecedent activities that were associated with each aide. Thus, the behavioral functions associated with different levels of problem behavior were unclear.

Several researchers have systematically controlled specific antecedents to analyze their effects on maladaptive behavior. The methodology described by Iwata, Dorsey, Slifer, Bauman, and Richman (1982/1994) is an example of a procedure in which antecedent and consequent conditions were designed to simulate those that may evoke and maintain problem behavior in natural environments. By arranging conditions under which SIB produced either attention from therapists, escape from task demands, or no social consequences, and by comparing rates of SIB among these conditions (and a control condition), possible reinforcement functions of SIB could be assessed (i.e., social positive reinforcement, social negative reinforcement, and automatic reinforcement [either positive or negative], respectively). Although the primary purpose of this assessment is to identify maintaining or consequent variables, antecedent conditions are also designed to evoke behavior thus maintained. For example, in the attention condition, which assesses behavior maintained by social positive reinforcement, the therapist provides attention (e.g., statements of concern, mild reprimands) as a consequence for SIB. The condition also utilizes deprivation from attention to establish its reinforcing effects (i.e., the therapist ignores the subject unless SIB occurs) and the presence of a therapist as a discriminative stimulus for attention. In the demand condition, training trials are presented on a fixed-time schedule and are terminated contingent on SIB to assess whether SIB is maintained by social negative reinforcement. The training trials represent establishing stimuli for escape responses, which could not (by definition) occur in the absence of aversive stimulation. In the alone condition, which is designed to assess whether SIB is maintained by automatically produced stimulation, no social consequences for SIB are delivered. In addition, sessions are conducted in a deprived environment to simulate conditions that may establish self-stimulation as reinforcement (it is noteworthy that this condition will not identify the exact maintaining variable, because the automatically produced consequences of SIB are not controlled; thus, automatic reinforcement is inferred rather than analyzed). A play condition is also included in this assessment as a control. In this condition, toys are present and social interaction is delivered on a time-based schedule; these procedures should function as "abolishing operations" both for attention and automatic reinforcement, thus reducing motivation for SIB that is maintained by those variables. The establishing conditions for escape—task demands—are not presented in this condition. Thus, little or no SIB should be seen in this condition unless SIB is maintained by an idiosyncratic reinforcer or by some other process.

Antecedent analyses may be used to identify specific discriminative conditions after the variables that maintain problem behavior have been identified. Taylor, Sisson, McKelvey, and Trefelner (1993) used an assessment similar to that described by Iwata et al. (1982/1994) to assess the aggressive scratching of an adolescent girl with developmental disabilities. This assessment revealed that scratching was maintained by attention from adults; however, during a baseline phase conducted in her classroom in which the teacher was instructed to interact with other students and to attend to the subject only when scratching occurred, no scratching was observed. Casual observation indicated that the subject scratched only when the teacher interacted with other adults, and a baseline condition in which another adult was present was juxtaposed with the original baseline condition to assess this effect. The subject's scratching was shown to vary reliably as a function of the presence of another adult with the teacher, and this condition was the context for a differential-reinforcement-of-other-behavior treatment. The authors attributed the relationship between the presence of adults and scratching to discriminative control; although this is a reasonable interpretation, the conditions of this experiment did not permit a definitive conclusion. It is possible that the presence of other adults was not historically correlated with reinforcement for scratching, but that it somehow altered the reinforcing effectiveness of attention from the teacher. Thus, the primary contribution of this study was to show that manipulating antecedent conditions while maintaining a constant reinforcement contingency for maladaptive behavior can identify the specific context in which treatment should occur.

In some experimental analyses, there have been attempts to identify maintaining contingencies through manipulation of antecedent events exclusively. For example, Carr et al. (1976) investigated the effects of mands in the apparent absence of an escape contingency for their subject's SIB and found that the presentation of mands per se evoked high rates of SIB. That is, even though SIB had no programmed consequence (i.e., had no effect on ongoing task requirements), mands set the occasion for SIB. Comparison conditions consisted of free-time activities and the presentation of simple declarative statements (tacts) to control for the general effects of therapist verbalizations; SIB almost never occurred in these conditions. The finding that SIB was maintained at high rates in the mand condition is somewhat surprising, given that it did not result in escape. The failure of this response to be extinguished was likely a result of rapid condition changes, with no more than four consecutive 10-min mand sessions in any phase of analysis.

In a later phase of the experiment the investigators conducted four mand sessions in which a "marker stimulus" was presented at the end of the session. In one condition, the therapist said "OK, let's go," a statement that had previously been correlated with session termination. In a second condition, the therapist said, "The sky is blue," a statement that had never previously occurred at the end of sessions. Observers continued to record data for 1 min following the marker stimulus. Results showed that SIB decreased to zero in the "OK, let's go" condition but continued to occur during the 1-min interval in the "The sky is blue" condition. This effect is consistent with that of the reflexive conditioned EO, in which a stimulus correlated with environmental changes (e.g., improvement or worsening) acquires motivational properties relative to that correlation (for a detailed description of conditioned EOs, see Michael, 1993a). The "OK, let's go" stimulus was correlated with improvement (session termination), so responses that may have interfered with such improvement (e.g., SIB) may have been suppressed. Alternatively, "OK, let's go" may simply have been discriminative for the absence of further aversive stimulation, and negatively reinforced behavior may thus have been decreased.

Durand and colleagues conducted a series of studies in which experimental analyses involved the manipulation of antecedent conditions exclusively (Carr & Durand, 1985; Durand & Carr, 1987, 1992; Durand & Crimmins, 1987, 1988). This assessment paradigm involves the systematic arrangement of establishing conditions associated with hypothesized functions of maladaptive behavior while no programmed consequences are provided for maladaptive behavior. In a representative example of this procedure (Durand & Carr, 1992), an assessment of challenging behavior was conducted across three conditions; sessions in each condition were 10 min in duration and were divided into 60 10-s intervals. In the baseline condition, easy tasks (identified previously as tasks that occasioned 100% correct responses) were presented, and prompts to complete these tasks were issued approximately every 30 s, or during 33% of intervals. A variable-ratio 3 schedule of social reinforcement for correct responses resulted in the occurrence of praise approximately every 30 s, or during 33% of intervals. Neutral comments were delivered in the remainder of intervals, resulting in the presentation of some form of attention from therapists in 100% of intervals during baseline. This was a control condition, in which attention-maintained behavior would not be expected to occur due to satiation (i.e., elimination of the EO for attention-maintained behavior), and behavior maintained by escape would not be expected to occur due to the absence of difficult tasks (i.e., the EO for escape).

The attention condition was designed to assess "changes in the participants' challenging behavior as a function of changing the distribution of verbal attention" (Durand & Carr, 1992, p. 780). Tasks and the total amount of attention delivered were identical to baseline. However, in this condition, the temporal distribution of attention was changed from 100% to 33% of intervals. Thus, the trainer presented a task demand, praise, and a neutral comment approximately every 30 s instead of every 10 s. The presumed establishing effect of the absence of social interaction during 66% of intervals was expected to evoke behavior maintained by contingent attention.

The demand condition assessed the effects of a more difficult task on challenging behavior. The distribution of attention was the same as in baseline (100% of intervals); however, tasks were selected for which the individual previously exhibited approximately 33% correct responses. To maintain task-consequent praise in 33% of intervals, a schedule of continuous reinforcement was in place. Accuracy percentages were monitored during sessions, and demands were changed as necessary to maintain correct responses in 33% of intervals. The increased level of difficulty in this condition was expected to establish the reinforcing effectiveness of escape and to evoke behavior thus maintained.

Results of this experiment showed low rates of challenging behavior in baseline and demand conditions and increases in challenging behavior during attention conditions for 16 subjects. The authors concluded that the maladaptive behavior of these subjects was maintained by attention from adults, and successful treatments based upon these findings provided further support for this interpretation. Other studies by this research group have implicated escape, the presentation of materials, and sensory reinforcement in the maintenance of challenging behavior (Carr & Durand, 1985; Durand & Carr, 1987; Durand & Crimmins, 1987, 1988).

Although Durand and colleagues report positive outcomes using this method of assessment, its reliance on subtle antecedent manipulations to differentiate functional classes of challenging behavior raises certain issues. For example, it is surprising that providing social interaction on a fixed-time (FT) 30-s schedule (compared to a 10-s schedule) represents sufficient deprivation to establish attention as a reinforcer for maladaptive behavior. Conditions that were designed to assess escape, tangible, and sensory functions appear to raise similar issues. In addition, providing antecedents that were presumed to evoke but not consequences that were presumed to maintain maladaptive behavior should result in extinction in all cases except that of a sensory function. Although some of the procedures seem to be inconsistent with reinforcement principles and the EO manipulations used to produce differentiation are subtle, Durand and colleagues have employed this methodology with positive results in a number of studies and have found it useful for prescribing effective treatment.

In a study designed to identify EOs for negatively reinforced behavior, the effects of various antecedent conditions were assessed in an arrangement in which SIB always produced escape (Smith, Iwata, Goh, & Shore, 1995). After first conducting experimental analyses showing their subjects' SIB to be maintained by escape, the investigators manipulated antecedent variables including task novelty, session duration, and rate of task trials. Subjects were able to escape task trials throughout all sessions, so the investigators attributed changes in patterns of SIB to EO effects. Outcomes suggested that each of these variables may have EO properties for escape behavior. Using a similar approach, O'Reilly (1995) showed that sleep deprivation increased the maladaptive escape behavior of 1 subject. Although sleep deprivation was not directly manipulated, an escape contingency for problem behavior was maintained throughout the analysis, suggesting an EO effect. The isolation of such variables by maintaining a consistent reinforcement contingency for problem behaviors may provide a general method for assessing EOs for behavior maintained by positive as well as by negative reinforcement.

We suggest that analysis of conditions (both antecedent and consequent) associated with behavior disorders ideally should contain four elements: (a) conditions that establish the form of reinforcement suspected of maintaining the behavior, (b) conditions that are discriminative for reinforcement contingent upon the target behavior, (c) a contingency between the target behavior and reinforcement, and (d) control over (a), (b), and (c) by the experimenter. The ability of antecedent conditions, both establishing and discriminative, to reliably evoke behavior is inextricably linked with response-contingent reinforcement. Thus, it seems that each of these conditions (establishing, discriminative, and consequent) is necessary, and none is sufficient for an experimental analysis of operant behavior (although it may be argued that discrimination is irrelevant if no condition exists under which reinforcing consequences are not delivered contingent upon responding). Thus, analysis of antecedent variables requires (at least) specification of behavioral consequences, and vice versa. Further, scientific skepticism dictates that experimenters demonstrate functional relations by controlling the controlling variables, as in (d) above. That is, our certainty about functional relations is increased when we are able to manipulate relevant variables and observe orderly changes in behavior. Naturalistic observations of ecological conditions fail to meet criterion (d), and experimental analyses that manipulate only antecedents fail to meet criterion (c) immediately and criterion (b) eventually.

Naturalistic observation procedures may provide some initial insight into variables that may later be included in an experimental analysis. As more complex interrelationships among operant elements in behavior disorders are studied, naturalistic observations may help to identify potentially important variables (e.g., Mace & Lalli, 1991; Repp et al., 1991). Thus, as a screening tool and as a method to identify variables that otherwise may be neglected, ecological assessment can be useful. However, the level of control required to reveal the basic principles that underlie behavior disorders (both generally and case specifically) dictates the use of experimental analyses to identify relevant antecedent and consequent relations.

TREATMENT

Behavior Maintained by Positive Reinforcement

Very few studies have systematically manipulated only antecedent events to reduce problem behaviors maintained by social positive reinforcement. An early study in which establishing conditions were altered to reduce problem behavior was conducted by Ayllon and Michael (1958). For 4 psychiatric patients whose magazine hoarding had been targeted for reduction, a satiation intervention, consisting of flooding the psychiatric ward with magazines, was combined with extinction, in which social interaction relative to hoarding was withheld. This treatment resulted in decreases in hoarding for all subjects. Because no assessment of the variables that maintained hoarding was conducted (i.e., hoarding may have been maintained by viewing the magazines or by social reinforcement from ward staff), and because both components of treatment were introduced simultaneously, the relative effectiveness of each component is unclear. However, this experiment is commonly cited as the first published study in applied behavior analysis, and the use of an EO-based intervention shows a very early recognition of the potential importance of such events in modifying maladaptive behavior.

In a similar but more recent EO intervention, Vollmer, Iwata, Zarcone, Smith, and Mazaleski (1993) examined the role of satiation in reducing problem behavior maintained by attention. Following a functional analysis revealing that the SIB of 3 subjects was maintained by contingent attention, a schedule of noncontingent reinforcement (NCR) was arranged in which attention was initially provided in 100% of 10-s intervals, and then was faded systematically to an FT 5-min schedule. The effects of NCR were attributed to a combination of extinction of SIB and elimination of the reinforcing effectiveness of attention. Extinction may have occurred because, as the schedule of NCR was gradually thinned, responses that occurred during interreinforcement intervals were not followed by attention. Hagopian, Fisher, and Legacy (1994) contrasted initial effects of lean (FT 5-min) versus dense (FT 10-s) NCR schedules and found that each reduced the maladaptive behavior of 3 of 4 subjects, but that dense schedules were more effective prior to fading, suggesting a combined EO and extinction effect. Results of a similar procedure used by Mace and Lalli (1991) to reduce bizarre vocalizations of an individual with mental retardation that were maintained by contingent disapproval, however, did not provide support for multiple treatment functions. Following conditions in which aberrant speech was reduced using extinction plus scheduled attention, the experimenters were able to maintain low rates of aberrant speech using a variable-time 90-s schedule of attention, although contingent social disapproval was reinstated. Results of these studies suggest that, although extinction *may* be necessary for initial NCR effects, it may not be critical for maintenance of a successful NCR intervention.

A component analysis of the NCR procedure, in which the contingency between maladaptive behavior and attention remains intact as the NCR schedule is thinned, would help to separate the relative effects of extinction and satiation. It is possible that the abolition of attention's effectiveness suppresses responding when attention is delivered on a rich schedule, but that extinction takes effect as scheduled attention is faded. In this case, the effectiveness of NCR without extinction would break down at some critical value of the reinforcement schedule, requiring that extinction be arranged for further fading of time-based reinforcement. In any event, the possibility that combining NCR with extinction may ameliorate the typical extinction burst that is associated with extinction alone makes this an attractive combination of antecedent and consequent strategies for behavior reduction.

A related treatment for behavior maintained by positive reinforcement (both socially mediated and automatically produced) is environmental enrichment (e.g., Berkson & Davenport, 1962; Berkson & Mason, 1963, 1965; Horner, 1980). This treatment involves noncontingent access to a range of potentially reinforcing items and activities that may compete effectively with maladaptive behavior. For example, Berkson and colleagues conducted a series of studies investigating variables such as the presence and nature of objects in the environment, social stimulation, and forced versus nonforced contact with objects and stimuli on the stereotypic and other behaviors of groups of subjects with profound developmental disabilities (Berkson & Davenport, 1962; Berkson & Mason, 1963, 1965). The results showed a variety of correlations, most notably that stereotypy was inversely correlated with object manipulation. Although analysis of the mechanisms underlying group differences was not possible, these findings set the occasion for the future development of the enriched environment approach to the treatment of stereotypic behavior.

It is possible that successes thus obtained are a function of reductions in the effectiveness of attention through an EO of some sort; however, due to the general nature of the intervention (i.e., a variety of stimuli are present), it is not possible to isolate the effective elements of treatment. An interesting point arises from the possibility that the availability of dissimilar forms of reinforcement may reduce socially maintained problem behavior: If making alternative reinforcers available can reduce the effectiveness of the reinforcer that maintains problem behaviors (i.e., if alternative reinforcers are substitutable for the maintaining variable; Green & Freed, 1993), then it may be possible to construct effective treatments without identifying maintaining variables. Further, presentation of substitutable stimuli may have effects that endure temporarily following withdrawal of those stimuli (similar to satiation with the maintaining variable). This would have potentially powerful implications for treatment of automatically reinforced behavior, because the maintaining reinforcer is often unknown or inaccessible to manipulation. However, research on substitution functions *would* require analysis of the variables that maintain the behavior problem, as well as presentation of stimuli that are formally dissimilar from the maintaining variable, in order to distinguish substitutability from NCR. Manipulations of the availability and response requirements associated with each alternative would further illuminate substitutability relations.

Antecedent interventions designed specifically for maladaptive behavior maintained by nonsocial or automatic positive reinforcement typically involve a manipulation of putative establishing events to reduce the motivation to engage in the behavior. This is accomplished through the noncontingent provision of stimulation similar to that suspected of maintaining maladaptive behavior or by providing a generally enriched environment (e.g., Horner, 1980).

Favell, McGimsey, and Schell (1982) used an NCR approach to reduce three topographies of SIB in 6 subjects. The hand mouthing of 1 subject decreased when toys that could be mouthed were made available, the eye poking of 2 other subjects decreased when an alternative form of visual stimulation was presented, and the pica (ingestion of inedible objects) of 3 subjects decreased when alternative edible items were present. These outcomes may have been a function of satiation with respect to the reinforcers maintaining SIB, evidence for which was seen in differential effects of stimulation similar to that suspected to maintain SIB versus less similar forms of stimuli. In all cases, similar forms of self-stimulation were most effective in suppressing SIB. Also, because sensory extinction was not attempted, the confidence with which the results of this study can be attributed to EOs is increased (i.e., the absence of extinction in the Favell et al. study permits the isolation of NCR as the sole treatment variable).

Another possible example of the manipulation of an EO is the use of satiation techniques to reduce chronic vomiting or rumination. Rast, Johnston, and colleagues conducted a series of studies investigating the finding that consumption of large quantities of food can suppress rumination in some subjects (Johnston, Greene, Rawal, Vazin, & Winston, 1991; Rast, Johnston, & Drum, 1984; Rast, Johnston, Drum, & Conrin, 1981; Rast, Johnston, Ellinger-Allen, & Drum, 1985; Rast, Johnston, Lubin, & Ellinger-Allen, 1988). It was posited that the reductive effect of the satiation diet may be due to biochemical variables (i.e., nutritive effects), mechanical variables (i.e., volume of stomach contents and stomach distension), satiation of oropharyngeal and esophageal stimulation, or some combination of these variables. These researchers conducted parametric and component analyses of the potential behavioral and physiological mechanisms that might be responsible for this effect. Results of this series of studies suggest that each of the variables mentioned may contribute to the therapeutic effects of increased food consumption. Changes in caloric intake appear to have greater effects on ruminating than do changes in stomach distension or in oropharyngeal and esophageal stimulation; however, increases in each of these variables were shown to produce moderate decreases in rumination. Of current interest is the possibility that oropharyngeal and esophageal stimulation were automatically reinforcing consequences that contributed to the maintenance of rumination and that the food-satiation procedure constitutes NCR, reducing the reinforcing effectiveness of these stimuli. Rast et al. (1988) showed that providing premeal oropharyngeal stimulation through gum chewing produced moderate reductions in rumination without changes in caloric intake or stomach distension. Their analysis provides support for an automatic reinforcement component to rumination and suggests that EOs may account for part of the therapeutic effects of the satiation diet.

Few attempts to isolate discriminative effects in behavior disorders that are maintained by positive reinforcement have been made. This paucity of empirical research is probably due to the relationship between discriminative stimuli and behavioral consequences. Discrimination occurs only as a function of the correlation between antecedent stimuli and the availability of certain consequences contingent upon behavior. Thus, stimulus control treatments to control maladaptive behavior necessarily involve either manipulation of that correlation to alter the discriminative relation or elimination of the effective discriminative stimulus from the environment. The effectiveness of these procedures depends primarily on consequences rather than on antecedents of behavior; in the first case, responding in the presence of the stimulus is extinguished, and in the second case, extinction must be applied when the stimulus is absent. Thus, because stimulus control over behavior is developed as a function of differential reinforcement, it is impossible to completely separate discriminative from consequent effects.

Azrin and Powell (1968) arranged a novel stimulus control intervention in which clearly discriminable periods of extinction were juxtaposed with reinforcer availability to reduce cigarette smoking. These researchers provided each subject with a cigarette container that automatically locked for a prespecified period after removal of a cigarette. Each container was fitted with a timer, a clock dial face, a ratchet-type clicker, and a narrow rod that could be projected 0.25 in. from the top of the container. During extinction (i.e., when the container was locked) the clock dial face showed how many minutes remained until the container could be opened. At the moment following an interval of extinction, the clicker sounded for 0.5 s and the narrow rod projected from the case. Smoking was reduced by slowly increasing the extinction intervals. Although discriminative control was systematically arranged in this study, its importance to the success of the intervention is unclear. That is, gradually increasing periods of extinction alone may produce similar results. In fact, making the conditions of this study so clearly discriminable may have increased the number of cigarettes smoked by establishing strong stimulus control over reaching for a cigarette at the end of extinction intervals. The authors noted that the number of cigarettes smoked was primarily a function of their availability and that latencies to removal of cigarettes from containers following extinction intervals were short. Perhaps arranging a schedule of reinforcement in which components are not differentially associated with exteroceptive stimuli (i.e., a mixed rather than a multiple schedule) would have produced longer latencies to cigarette withdrawal and, thus, fewer cigarettes smoked. However, the general strategy of fading reinforcement of problem behavior using differential reinforcement of diminishing rates schedules presents an approach to treatment that may minimize the negative side effects that are associated with extinction, especially when combined with reinforcement for alternative behavior or omission of problem behavior (it should be noted that the use of fading or extinction as the sole strategy for reducing behavior would be proscribed in cases in which the behavior is maintained by life-sustaining reinforcers such as food or water).

Another study showed that treatment effects for cigarette butt pica could be maintained by pairing an arbitrary stimulus with treatment conditions and then presenting the stimulus in nontreatment contexts (Piazza, Hanley, & Fisher, 1996). Following a response-interruption treatment for the cigarette butt pica of an individual with mental retardation, a stimulus control assessment was conducted in which presentation of a purple card was associated with treatment conditions. After the participant received training with the card, the card continued to exercise stimulus control over pica even when treatment contingencies were not in place and in nontreatment environments. This study is significant in showing that stimulus control procedures can be used to maintain and generalize treatment effects under conditions in which it is not possible to implement actual treatment contingencies. No follow-up data were presented, so the durability of such procedures is unclear. Further research will be necessary to determine the conditions under which such effects can be maintained for long periods of time.

Behavior Maintained by Negative Reinforcement

Negatively reinforced problem behaviors present a unique opportunity for a high level of control over antecedent events; the researcher typically presents the stimuli that occasion escape responses. Several methods have been developed for the manipulation of antecedents to reduce problem behaviors maintained by escape. Perhaps the most obvious and direct method of reducing escape behavior involves elimination of aversive events from the environment—an effective, if sometimes impractical, strategy. Although no studies have investigated this effect per se, it can be seen in a range of studies in which no-demand conditions are contrasted with conditions containing demands during assessment (e.g., Carr et al., 1976; Iwata et al., 1982/1994).

A similar strategy is noncontingent escape (NCE), in which aversive stimuli are systematically introduced into the environment but are withdrawn on a time-based schedule (Vollmer, Marcus, & Ringdahl, 1995). By initially providing noncontingent escape almost immediately following presentation of task demands and subsequently increasing the duration of demands, subjects were able to tolerate up to 10 min of continuous instruction without exhibiting maladaptive escape behavior. During treatment phases of the study, maladaptive behavior did not produce escape, so, as with NCR, the relative effects of EOs versus extinction remain unclear.

A related approach for reducing behavior maintained by social negative reinforcement is the elimination and then systematic reintroduction of aversive stimulation into the environment. This approach is distinguished from NCE in that presentation rather than termination of aversive stimulation is determined according to a time-based schedule. Pace, Iwata, Cowdery, Andree, and McIntyre (1993) showed that low rates of escape behavior (in this case, SIB) could be maintained when escape extinction was combined with a gradual fading in of the frequency of demand presentations. A subsequent study by Zarcone, Iwata, Vollmer, et al. (1993) showed that instructional fading could enhance the effects of extinction by reducing the bursts of responding associated with extinction in the absence of fading. Results of another component analysis of this treatment in which instructional fading was implemented without extinction (Zarcone, Iwata, Smith, Mazaleski, & Lerman, 1994) showed that initial suppression of SIB was not maintained as the frequency of task demands was increased. Extinction was required to complete the fading procedure for each of 3 subjects. These results suggest a shift in the functional aspects of treatment, from an initial abolition of escape as a reinforcing consequence to extinction of the escape response as increases in demand rates produced increases in self-injurious escape behavior (presumably due to the reestablishment of the reinforcing effectiveness of escape). However, a recent case study reported that demand fading alone was effective in reducing escape-maintained obscene verbalizations in a psychiatric patient. Thus, under certain conditions, fading may have durable escape-abolishing effects (Pace, Ivancic, & Jefferson, 1994).

It may be possible to use fading along dimensions other than demand frequency. For example, Weeks and Gaylord-Ross (1981) used errorless learning procedures (Touchette & Howard, 1984) to fade along the dimension of task difficulty. Eventually, stimuli that had evoked incorrect responses and maladaptive behavior came to evoke correct responses and no inappropriate behavior. Because the authors did not explicitly state the contingency for maladaptive behavior, it may be assumed that no change in procedures occurred as a consequence of target behaviors (i.e., extinction was in effect for these responses). Thus, the relative importance of extinction versus EO effects is unknown.

In a similar study, Cameron, Luiselli, McGrath, and Carlton (1992) showed that the noncompliant behavior of their subject (defined as falling to the ground, throwing his walker and eyeglasses, body thrashing), associated with a request to exit a van in front of his school, could be reduced by reinforcing approximations to the target response (walking from the van into the school without noncompliance) using a backward chaining procedure. After establishing the presentation of a ball as a conditioned reinforcer by pairing it with preferred activities (gym activities and music), walking to the gym from the classroom, then from outside the building, and finally from the van and through the building were shaped using the ball to reinforce initial responses in the chain (the chain always ended in reinforcement with gym activities). As in the Weeks and Gaylord-Ross (1981) study, the subject ultimately was required to comply (i.e., to enter the building from the van) throughout the study; thus, extinction of escape-maintained noncompliance may have contributed to treatment (presuming that noncompliance was maintained by escape, which was not clearly shown). However, in an interesting stimulus control analysis of this procedure, it was shown that when stimuli correlated with reinforcing gym activities (i.e., participating staff and the ball) were not present, noncompliance increased over treatment levels. That is, decrements in compliance were observed when participating staff met the subject at his van without the ball and when nonparticipating staff met the subject at his van with or without the ball. This stimulus control over correct responding suggests that positive reinforcement for correct responses might have altered the reinforcing effectiveness of escape (i.e., contact with positive reinforcers in the school diminished the aversiveness of that setting); when discriminative stimuli for compliance were absent, responses that were presumably maintained by escape increased.

A component analysis of the motivational and extinction effects of the errorless learning and backward chaining procedures would be especially interesting because it is possible that these procedures could produce direct changes in EOs. That is, if the effect of errorless learning is to establish in the subject's repertoire correct responses to tasks that previously evoked incorrect responses, then the escape-establishing function of those task demands may be directly altered. Put another way, tasks that can be completed successfully may not be aversive, and if a difficult task can be transformed into an easy task using errorless training, the reinforcing effects of escape may be diminished to a point where escape behavior is not evoked. Similarly, pairing compliance with requests with reinforcement by requiring only the performance of terminal components of a task (as in backward chaining) may alter the escape-establishing function of the task. These effects may contrast with those of fading along the dimension of frequency, which may not fundamentally alter the EO function of demands; however, successful demonstrations of demand fading without extinction (e.g., Pace et al., 1994) suggest that mere exposure to a task in small, incremental steps might have durable effects with some individuals.

In a similar approach, Cameron, Ainsleigh, and Bird (1992) modified an aspect of a task that had been shown to evoke aggression and noncompliance in their subject. These behaviors reliably occurred when the subject was handed a bar of soap and was prompted to wash himself. In probe sessions, the trainer presented the subject with a liquid rather than a solid form of soap, and maladaptive responding was immediately eliminated. The authors termed this a "stimulus control analysis" of the subject's aggression and noncompliance; however, their explanation of the evocative effects of bar soap was that "the requirement of holding onto a wet bar of soap increased the level of difficulty of the bathing routine and set the occasion for behaviors that would allow [the subject] to successfully escape from the demand" (p. 337). This account suggests that their procedure was an assessment of establishing rather than discriminative operations. Despite this interpretive limitation, the study shows a simple method for reducing escape-maintained maladaptive behavior by making a minor modification in the nature of the task demand. Further, by utilizing a probe design to assess the effects of their procedure, they were able to limit the possibility that escape extinction (compliance with the bathing routine was required throughout the study) was responsible for differences in maladaptive responding. Throughout treatment, liquid soap probes were interspersed among sessions in which bar soap was presented; bar soap sessions continued to evoke maladaptive behavior whereas liquid soap sessions did not. This study differed from those previously described in that no return to the conditions that originally evoked problem behavior was attempted or necessary. This procedure demonstrated a pragmatic approach in which the goals of training could be achieved and maladaptive behavior could be eliminated merely by modifying a formal property of the task.

Dunlap, Kern-Dunlap, Clarke, and Robbins (1991) implemented a molar antecedent intervention called curricular revision to reduce the motivation for disruptive behavior and inappropriate vocalizations in an adolescent girl with developmental disabilities. This intervention included (a) a decrease in the duration of fine-motor activities, (b) interspersing fine- with gross-motor activities, (c) arranging activity content so that it was "interesting . . . and [led] to a concrete and preferred outcome" (p. 392), and (d) permitting the subject to choose activities from a menu of options when possible. Significant reductions in maladaptive behaviors and increases in appropriate responding were shown. However, neither the elements of the intervention package responsible for the treatment effect nor the mechanisms of change can be identified, because all were simultaneously implemented. Further, although the consequences for maladaptive behaviors during baseline were task termination and seclusion time-out, the contingencies for maladaptive behavior during treatment were not described. Unless the contingencies of baseline remained in place during treatment, the possible role of extinction in producing treatment effects must be considered.

Other methods of reducing the motivation to escape have also been investigated, including embedding demands in pleasant stories (Carr et al., 1976) or in the context of easy tasks (Horner, Day, Sprague, O'Brien, & Heathfield, 1991). Carr et al. interpreted the effectiveness of these procedures in terms of discriminative operations, suggesting that demands exerted stimulus control over their subject's SIB and that pleasant stories were discriminative for behavior that was incompatible with SIB. The drawbacks of a stimulus control account of antecedent aversive stimulation have been stated earlier and will not be repeated here. The effects of embedded requests may be better explained as resulting from an EO because the presentation of pleasant stories was not discriminative for escape; the correlation between SIB and task termination was unchanged by this manipulation, and that correlation was zero in this example because no contingencies were programmed for SIB. A definitive determination of motivational versus discriminative control would require examination of the effects of embedded demands while reinforcement for SIB (escape) remained in place.

In an inventive antecedent manipulation, Mace and Belfiore (1990) used high-probability demand sequences to establish compliance in treating stereotypy maintained by escape. After first presenting a series of requests that were highly likely to evoke compliance and unlikely to evoke stereotypy, they presented demands that were previously associated with stereotypy and a low likelihood of compliance. The results of this study showed increases in compliance accompanied by decreases in stereotypy. The authors interpreted these findings in terms of behavioral momentum (Nevin, Mandell, & Atak, 1983), in which behavioral persistence is a function of the product of response rate and reinforcement rate. By increasing both response and reinforcement rates through the presentation of high-probability sequences, compliance with low-probability demands would be predicted due to the persistence of the response class of compliance. Several possible mechanisms were suggested to explain reductions in stereotypy, including topographical or functional incompatibility between compliance and stereotypy and an inverse relation between concurrent operants. Each of these accounts suggests a change in the relative reinforcing efficacy of escape; stereotypy is reduced because the presence of alternative reinforcers, performance of other responses, or both alter the extent to which aversive stimulation evokes escape responses, rather than because of differential availability of escape for those responses. However, as in several previous examples, escape was not contingent on the target response during treatment, raising the possibility that extinction was at least partially responsible for reductions in stereotypy.

In a subsequent component analysis, the effects of high-probability sequences were replicated when escape was not contingent upon SIB; however, the procedures were ineffective when SIB produced escape (Zarcone, Iwata, Hughes, & Vollmer, 1993). These results suggest that escape extinction may be necessary for the success of high-probability sequences, at least when they are applied as treatment for escape behavior. In fact, these investigators reported that demands that were initially associated with high probabilities of compliance and low probabilities of SIB came to evoke SIB and lower rates of compliance when the high-probability sequence was presented and SIB continued to produce escape. This result resembles that of the reflexive conditioned EO (Michael, 1993a). The high-probability sequence reliably preceded the presentation of a low-probability demand and was thus correlated with "worsening" of conditions. Eventually, the high-probability sequence began to evoke escape responding, as would be predicted by the model of the reflexive conditioned EO. This was the opposite of the intended effect; the expected outcome of the relationship between high-probability sequences and low-probability demands was to reduce or eliminate the escape-establishing function of low-probability demands.

A discriminative stimulus for negative reinforcement is correlated with the availability of an effective escape response in the presence of aversive stimulation. Thus, as with positively reinforced behavior, the reduction of negatively reinforced behavior using discriminative control is necessarily a matter of consequences. That is, treatments based on stimulus control involve an alteration of the correlation between the discriminative stimulus and escape (requiring extinction of responses that occur in the presence of the stimulus), the removal of that stimulus from the environment (requiring extinction of responses occurring in the absence of the stimulus), or transfer of stimulus control (requiring differential reinforcement across two or more stimulus conditions). We know of no studies reporting antecedent treatments for escape behavior that may be properly interpreted as specific manipulations of discriminative operations. Further, the pursuit of such treatments may be contraindicated because they involve (by definition) the maintenance or establishment of a condition in which maladaptive responding maintained by negative reinforcement is correlated with escape.

Antecedent interventions designed to reduce maladaptive behavior that is maintained by automatic negative reinforcement are conspicuously absent in applied research. Automatic negative reinforcement involves the nonsocially mediated termination or avoidance of aversive stimulation contingent upon a given response. This typically involves either physical withdrawal from the source of stimulation (as in pulling one's hand away from a fire) or behavior that directly attenuates private aversive stimulation (as in scratching at itchy skin). The second example often involves contact between afflicted and nonafflicted body parts, which, when excessive, may result in tissue damage. Thus, most maladaptive behavior maintained in this way would be characterized as self-injurious. That is, behavior disorders that arise from automatic negative reinforcement will, by definition, be self-directed, and their classification as undesirable will most likely be based on detrimental effects to the behaver.

The most straightforward antecedent intervention for SIB thus maintained is to treat the condition associated with pain or discomfort. Examples of this approach would be the application of topical creams on rashes and infected areas to reduce scratching, administration of analgesics to reduce head hitting maintained by attenuation of headaches, dental intervention to reduce jaw hitting maintained by attenuation of toothaches, and treatment of allergy conditions that may motivate self-scratching. Although each of these procedures is commonplace in the provision of services to persons with developmental disabilities, none is documented in the applied literature on behavior disorders. The effects of such procedures can be explained as the abolition of escape from aversive stimulation as a reinforcing event by providing noncontingent reinforcement. This approach is directly analogous to the reduction of social escape behavior by eliminating aversive demands from the environment. It is unclear how discriminative control could be used to decrease maladaptive behavior maintained by automatic negative reinforcement.

Special Cases

In certain cases, antecedent interventions do not correspond directly to specific maintaining variables. That is, the effects of manipulating antecedent variables may not always depend upon a known relationship with consequences for problem behavior. One possible example of this is the enriched environment approach, in which noncontingently available reinforcers may substitute for the reinforcement that maintains problem behavior. Thus, knowledge of the specific reinforcer that maintains problem behavior may not be necessary for the success of this treatment. However, the enriched environment approach may be best suited to the treatment of positively reinforced behavior. Based upon current research, it is unclear whether substitutability occurs across types of reinforcement contingencies (i.e., whether a positive reinforcer is substitutable for a negative reinforcer). Thus, because studies on environmental enrichment are typically conducted in nondemand contexts, and because the relevance of this approach to negatively reinforced behavior is not obvious, the effects of enriching the environment were discussed in the context of behavior maintained by social and automatic positive reinforcement.

Several studies have investigated the effects of antecedent exercise in the treatment of behavior disorders (Allison, Basile, & MacDonald, 1991; Bachman & Fuqua, 1983; Bachman & Sluyter, 1988; Baumeister & MacLean, 1984; Kern, Koegel, & Dunlap, 1984; Kern, Koegel, Dyer, Blew, & Fenton, 1982; Powers, Thibadeau, & Rose, 1992). These interventions typically involve participation by subjects in aerobic exercise routines (e.g., jogging or dance) and have resulted in subsequent decreases in maladaptive behaviors such as self-injury (Baumeister & MacLean), aggression (Allison et al.), and stereotypy (Kern et al.).

Research has shown a positive correlation between exercise intensity and its effectiveness as intervention (Bachman & Fuqua, 1983; Baumeister & MacLean, 1984); however, a study reporting a physiological measure of exertion (pulse rate) showed no correlation between heart rate during exercise and subsequent maladaptive behavior (Allison et al., 1991). It is possible that this outcome was a function of their subject's relatively high heart rate throughout treatment (rates during exercise never fell below 59% of maximum, even during less intensive exercise), suggesting a threshold of intensity above which effects are asymptotic. Indeed, a subsequent study (Levinson & Reid, 1993) showed a relationship between heart rate just after exercise and effects of antecedent exercise when the low-intensity exercise generated increases in heart rate between 30% to 45% over resting rates. The use of physiologic measures of exertion is a promising method for research on antecedent exercise, because it may permit more definitive parametric analyses of the effects of different levels of exertion as well as controlled assessments of the effects of variables such as the type of activity (i.e., by controlling for level of exertion, it may be determined whether the type of movement involved in antecedent exercise has a differential effect on subsequent behavior).

These preliminary data on antecedent exercise suggest an EO account of its effects. Because no manipulation of the availability of reinforcement occurs, the effects of antecedent exercise seem to be most consistent with a change in the reinforcing efficacy of the consequences that maintain maladaptive behavior. However, several issues remain unresolved. For example, what specific components of antecedent exercise are responsible for its effectiveness? As suggested above, analyses of the effects of exertion and different types of exercise may reveal important clues about the mechanisms that underlie this effect. If exertion is found to be the most important variable in reducing maladaptive behavior, then a general "fatigue" effect may be implicated. However, both empirical data and anecdotal evidence suggest that this may be an untenable account. Fatigue would be expected to produce a general suppression of behavior; however, several studies have reported increases in appropriate responding as a result of antecedent exercise (Kern et al., 1982), and others have noted the absence of drowsiness or other symptoms of fatigue in their subjects (Baumeister & MacLean, 1984; Kern et al., 1982; Tarnowski & Drabman, 1985). These outcomes are inconsistent with a fatigue account of antecedent exercise.

Analyses of the effects of various forms of exercise (controlling for exertion) might reveal relationships between the movements of exercise and levels of maladaptive behavior and, thus, may suggest particular interpretations about the effects of antecedent exercise. For example, if the movements involved in a particularly effective form of exercise are similar to those of the maladaptive behavior itself (e.g., highly repetitive aerobic exercises and stereotypic rocking), then satiation of the reinforcer that maintained the maladaptive behavior may be suspected. Levinson and Reid (1993) showed data suggesting that motor stereotypies may be differentially sensitive to antecedent exercise relative to vocal/oral or other forms of stereotypy. These effects were inconsistent, however, and the authors recommended further research to examine the possibility of functional relationships between exercise movements and topographical characteristics of stereotypy.

Another important direction for investigations of the effects of antecedent exercise is the integration of functional analysis methodology into this research. Analysis of the variables that maintain maladaptive behavior would provide a stronger basis for interpreting the functional properties of antecedent exercise and might provide important prescriptive information. For example, if antecedent exercise is especially effective for behavior maintained independently of social consequences, then functional analysis results could be important for determining when it should be used as treatment. Such an outcome would be consistent with a satiation account of the effects of antecedent exercise, especially if the topographies of exercise and maladaptive behaviors were similar.

The specificity of the effects of antecedent exercise (i.e., its suppressive effects seem to be specific to maladaptive behaviors) is puzzling; the class of behaviors reduced by these procedures is characterized only by social unacceptability and includes a wide range of behavioral topographies that are presumably maintained in idiosyncratic ways. It is unclear why the effects of antecedent exercise generalize across these behaviors, yet are also specific to them. The results of functional analyses of problem behaviors treated by antecedent exercise might clarify the basis for these effects if the functional properties of maladaptive behaviors are found to be differentially correlated with treatment effectiveness.

A special case in which the consequences for problem behavior may be irrelevant to the effectiveness of antecedent control is the use of restraint. The literature on the treatment of severe behavior disorders is replete with examples of the use of restraint or protective devices to control problem behaviors (Favell, McGimsey, & Jones, 1978; Favell, McGimsey, Jones, & Cannon, 1981; Foxx & Dufrense, 1984; Isley, Kartsonis, Mc-

Curley, Eager Weisz, & Roberts, 1991; Pace, Iwata, Edwards, & McCosh, 1986; Paul & Romanczyk, 1973; Rojahn, Mulick, McCoy, & Schroeder, 1978; Silverman, Watanabe, Marshall, & Baer, 1984). Clearly, the effectiveness of procedures that render maladaptive responding impossible is independent of the contingencies that maintain problem behavior. Responding is automatically eliminated. Restraint thus represents a special case of stimulus control in which the reinforcer previously contingent upon maladaptive responding is unavailable only because it is no longer possible to emit the previously reinforced response. When restraint is applied, no response will be reinforced because no reinforceable response can occur; the decrease in responding is a result of neither a change in consequences nor a change in the reinforcing function of those consequences. Thus, the effects of restraint are properly interpreted as resulting from a discriminative relationship between restraint and the absence of a response–reinforcement contingency.

Although restraint is unquestionably effective in reducing maladaptive behaviors, serious side effects, including the development of a preference for restraint (i.e., self-restraint; Favell et al., 1978) and reductions in social interactions and appropriate behaviors (Rojahn, Schroeder, & Mulick, 1980) may result from its use. The development of methods to investigate and reduce these side effects has produced data showing some interesting relationships between restraint and maladaptive behaviors. For example, several researchers have shown that it is possible to modify the form of restraint while maintaining control over it. Foxx and Dufrense (1984) were able to fade the size of held objects and the form of protective devices while controlling the self-injury of a subject, even though self-injury was possible when the restraints were in their final form. Similarly, Pace et al. (1986) faded rigid arm tubes to wrist bands and faded the air pressure in air splints while maintaining control over the SIB of their subjects. These examples, in which control is transferred from a stimulus that physically prevents responding to a stimulus that does not, present an interesting interpretive dilemma. Although it is tempting to interpret these results in terms of discriminative control, reinforcement is available contingent upon maladaptive behavior when symbolic restraint is used. Typically, when an antecedent event alters behavior but is unrelated to the availability of reinforcement contingent upon that behavior, its effects are interpreted in terms of EOs. However, because it likely that the effectiveness of symbolic restraint is a direct function of its historic relationship with functional restraint, symbolic restraint may represent a generalization of stimulus control based upon the gradual and systematic transformation of the stimulus (Touchette, 1968). Thus, the ultimate success of treatments that employ symbolic control may depend upon their integration with other treatments to reduce the likelihood of relapse due to recontact with the contingencies that originally maintained problem behavior.

Other research on restraint has shown that restraint may itself become a positive reinforcer and that some subjects will actively engage in self-restraint (Favell et al., 1981). Investigators have noted that self-restraint typically results in decreases in maladaptive behavior (usually SIB), and that self-restraint often seems "designed to prevent" maladaptive responding (Silverman et al., 1984, p. 545). Smith, Iwata, Vollmer, and Pace (1992) conducted an analysis of the variables that maintain self-restraint and found evidence that idiosyncratic contingencies may be operative. That is, for different individuals, self-restraint may be maintained by reducing SIB, by variables similar to those that maintain SIB, or by contingencies unrelated to those that maintain SIB. Thus, conditions associated with SIB may establish the reinforcing effectiveness of self-restraint (as when self-restraint is maintained by reductions in SIB), or self-restraint may displace SIB in a reinforcer substitutability relation, as in the latter two cases.

Another way in which stimulus control over problem behavior may be important, independent of maintaining consequences, occurs when antecedent stimuli are differentially paired with punishment. Results of a study by Corte, Wolf, and Locke (1971) indicated that contingent electrical stimulation was effective in reducing their subjects' SIB. However, reductions in SIB came under discriminative control of stimuli associated with the delivery of shock. For example, the reductive effects of shock were specific to both the settings in which sessions took place and the therapists who delivered shocks. Only when generalization was actively programmed, by increasing the number of settings and therapists associated with shock (i.e., by making the conditions under which shock was contingent on SIB less predictable), was the specificity of effects reduced.

In another study, SIB was brought under discriminative control of a stimulus that could be constantly present in the subjects' environment. Linscheid, Iwata, Ricketts, Williams, and Griffin (1990) showed that wearing a device that had previously delivered electrical stimulation contingent upon SIB was discriminative for low rates of SIB. Specifically, following experience with the punishment contingency, merely placing the inactive device on the subject produced decreases in the SIB of 3 of 5 subjects. However, in all but 1 of these subjects, the decrease was temporary, with SIB returning to previous levels within several sessions. That is, when the device was no longer differentially correlated with the delivery of shock contingent upon SIB, the behavior reemerged, consistent with the abolition of discriminative control. It is possible that systematic fading procedures may produce a more durable generalization effect. Alternatively, a device that could deliver contingent aversive stimulation, but whose presence is undetectable (i.e., very small devices), might facilitate generalization by virtue of low correlations with any particular environmental conditions.

SOME DIRECTIONS FOR FUTURE RESEARCH

Much remains to be investigated about the influence of antecedent events on problem behaviors. Although antecedents are often manipulated (or at least controlled) in the assessment and treatment of behavior disorders, few studies have done so in a manner that permits the systematic identification of antecedent classes, and fewer still have attempted to relate the effects of antecedents to basic principles of behavior. A primary goal of research on antecedent variables in behavior disorders should be the development of research methods that permit experimentally sound analyses of antecedent effects and that produce a conceptually coherent understanding of these effects.

Although it is tempting to leap forward into analyses of complex relationships among antecedent, response, and consequence variables, an overview of the current state of the applied literature suggests that the field has not yet reached the point at which such analyses are productive. Research that shows correlations among broadly defined classes of variables brings a measure of scope to the search for environmental determinants of behavior. However, greater control is required for the demonstration of functional relations, and careful arrangements are necessary to reveal the mechanisms of behavior change. Even proponents of the setting-events approach to applied behavior analysis suggest the need for greater precision in the analysis and control of antecedent events (e.g., Kennedy & Itkonen, 1993). Whenever broad classes of antecedent variables are defined in terms of formal properties (e.g., setting events), the likelihood of producing effects based upon changes in the class increases, even as the likelihood of correctly identifying relevant versus irrelevant variables decreases. Thus, setting-event analyses may cloud more issues than they clarify.

How, then, might applied behavior analysts proceed to disentangle the complex antecedent relations that are involved in the production of maladaptive behavior? To deny the influence of temporally distant or extended events or to discount the effects of interrelationships among prior environmental and behavioral events would be naive; indeed, the greatest contribution of the setting-events literature is to prompt consideration and investigation of such variables. However, analyses of these events must proceed using sound scientific practice. A suggested approach to the examination of contextual variables is to build context by first examining the effects of isolated antecedent variables and then studying the effects of various combinations and arrangements on resultant behavior.

Functional analysis of antecedents first requires identification of the contingency that maintains problem behavior. Then, while systematically controlling relevant consequences, the effects of antecedent events may be investigated. Following demonstrations of functional relationships between isolated antecedent events and behavior, antecedents could be combined in various ways to determine the effects of complex stimuli. This approach requires tedious and eventually complex experimentation, but the relationships thus identified would provide both functional and operational definitions of context and would allow component analyses of the elements comprising context.

Some specific areas for future research can be identified. Little research exists on discriminative control of problem behavior maintained by positive reinforcement. Bringing difficult behavior under discriminative control and then systematically restricting the occurrence of the S^D (Azrin & Powell, 1968) may reduce the negative side effects of extinction; however, the effects of discrimination per se in this treatment remain unclear pending a component analysis. EOs that are associated with positively reinforced behavior disorders present a wide range of research opportunities. Studies could investigate deprivation effects on behavior disorders maintained by attention by varying periods of isolation prior to sessions in which attention is contingent upon maladaptive behavior. Conversely, the effects of satiation on maladaptive behavior could be shown by arranging a time-based schedule of attention (e.g., NCR) while maintaining a contingency between maladaptive behavior and attention. Similarly, effects of deprivation from stimuli similar to those suspected of maintaining automatically reinforced behavior problems (e.g., the effects of food deprivation on pica) might increase the confidence of interpretations about these contingencies. Also, as was suggested previously, the possibility that substitutable reinforcers may alter the effectiveness of the form of reinforcement that maintains problem behavior suggests a potential program of research. Topics such as the identification of reinforcers that are likely to serve as successful substitutes and the conditions under which reinforcer substitution is more or less probable could be examined (e.g., can reinforcer substitutability be enhanced by using varied substitutes, by imposing deprivation from substitutes, or by imposing satiation with respect to the substituted reinforcer?).

Many possibilities exist for extending research on antecedent events in negatively reinforced behavior. As with positively reinforced behavior, analyses of discriminative events in negative reinforcement are rare. One possible approach to integrating stimulus control into the treatment of escape behavior might be to perform a manipulation similar to that described by Azrin and Powell (1968) to treat positively reinforced behavior. That is, by bringing escape behavior under stimulus control, and then restricting the S^D, it may be possible to limit the negative side effects of escape extinction.

The influence of EOs on escape behavior currently represents the most developed topic on antecedent effects in behavior disorders, yet much remains to be learned. Component analyses of aspects of the demand context that are associated with problem behavior might identify common dimensions of aversiveness that may then facilitate the development of generally effective treatments (Smith et al., 1995). Also, continued research into the extrademand conditions (context variables) that influence the reinforcing effects of escape will improve the ability of trainers to educate their students with a minimum of problem behavior. Similarly, further investigations of procedures that alter features of tasks to make them less aversive, such as errorless learning (Weeks & Gaylord-Ross, 1981) and backward chaining (Cameron et al., 1992), may also lead to the improvement of training techniques.

The analysis and treatment of escape behavior maintained by automatic reinforcement is an area in which almost no research data exist. As with all automatically reinforced behavior, the identification of maintaining variables is difficult, and it may be necessary to base preliminary interpretations on indirect evidence. However, one promising area of investigation is the use of medical treatment in a noncontingent reinforcement approach to reduce the reinforcing effectiveness of maladaptive escape behavior. If simple and straightforward treatments, such as topical creams and solutions for dermatological disorders and analgesic medication for headache and other pain, produce decreases in self-injury, then a negative reinforcement account of this problem behavior is tenable. A series of studies linking specific treatments to specific topographies of SIB (and, perhaps, the preexistence of specific medical conditions) could provide a rationale for basing treatment upon the form of SIB when automatic negative reinforcement is suspected.

Special cases of antecedent control also provide research opportunities. Careful studies that relate the effects of environmental enrichment to various functions of maladaptive behavior could produce information about the conditions under which reinforcer substitution is likely to occur. For example, the effects of environmental enrichment have not been investigated in cases of negatively reinforced behavior. Studies on this topic may reveal whether positive reinforcers may be substitutable for negative reinforcers.

Further investigation might also be productive in the use of restraint to reduce maladaptive behavior. The conditions under which restraint may be faded, and the conditions that promote continued symbolic control by faded forms of restraint over problem behavior, remain to be clarified. Future research might investigate how treatment components may combine to improve the likelihood of successful treatment using restraint fading.

Future research might also provide information about the relationship between SIB and self-restraint. As was previously suggested, self-restraint maintained by contingencies similar to those that maintain problem behavior or by independent contingencies may reduce maladaptive behavior through reinforcer substitutability. This possibility might be further investigated by manipulating the cost of engaging in one of these responses while monitoring changes in the other response. Also, continued refinement of a technology for functional analysis of the variables that maintain self-restraint may be important for the above analyses.

Another potentially important area of future research involves the enhancement of punishment effects using stimulus control procedures. Punishment is typically seen as the alternative of last resort in the treatment of behavior disorders, and it seems prudent to investigate ways in which its effects can be enhanced to limit the necessity of its continued use. Evidence exists that pairing response-contingent punishment with antecedent stimuli may establish a discriminative function of those stimuli, at least temporarily. Identifying the conditions under which this stimulus function can be maintained may result in an increase in the effectiveness of punishment contingencies and reduce the total amount of aversive stimulation necessary to produce and maintain significant decreases in problem behaviors.

The topic of antecedent events in behavior disorders offers a wide range of potentially important research directions. One of the major contributions of developing an array of antecedent-based treatments is to provide alternatives to the use of aversive consequences for problem behavior. If the EOs that establish maladaptive behavior as reinforcing can be controlled, or if the conditions under which maladaptive behavior is likely to be reinforced can be limited, then it may be possible to avoid using aversive consequences or producing negative side effects attendant to extinction-based treatments. Careful study of the antecedent variables that affect maladaptive behavior may not only result in an expansion of treatment alternatives but also may contribute to a fundamental understanding of the mechanisms of antecedent control. By first identifying and controlling functional relations among isolated antecedents and subsequent behavioral events, it may be possible to build experimental models of setting events and behavioral fields. These models would have a distinct advantage over current research in that the functional properties of the elements that comprise these constructs already would be known. Potential special relations among these variables, such as synergism (enhanced effects of variables as a function of their combination) or antagonism (reduced effects of variables as a function of their combination), could be analyzed systematically. Thus, it is clear that much work remains to be conducted, and although the existence of difficult and complex human behavior disorders establishes the reinforcing effects of elaborate explanatory schemes, there is no substitute for a solid base of data as stimulus control over effective interpretation.

REFERENCES

Allison, D. B., Basile, V. C., & MacDonald, R. B. (1991). Brief report: Comparative effects of antecedent exercise and lorazepam on the aggressive behavior of an autistic male. *Journal of Autism and Developmental Disorders, 21,* 89–94.

Ayllon, T., & Michael, J. (1958). The psychiatric nurse as behavioral engineer. *Journal of the Experimental Analysis of Behavior, 2,* 323–334.

Azrin, N. H., & Powell, J. (1968). Behavioral engineering: The reduction of smoking behavior by a conditioning apparatus and procedure. *Journal of Applied Behavior Analysis, 1,* 193–200.

Bachman, J. E., & Fuqua, R. W. (1983). Management of inappropriate behaviors of trainable mentally impaired students using antecedent exercise. *Journal of Applied Behavior Analysis, 16,* 477–484.

Bachman, J. E., & Sluyter, D. (1988). Reducing inappropriate behaviors of developmentally disabled adults using antecedent aerobic dance exercises. *Research in Developmental Disabilities, 9,* 73–83.

Baer, D. M., Wolf, M. M., & Risley, T. R. (1968). Some current dimensions of applied behavior analysis. *Journal of Applied Behavior Analysis, 1,* 91–97.

Baumeister, A. A., & MacLean, W. E. (1984). Deceleration of self-injurious and stereotypic responding by exercise. *Applied Research in Mental Retardation, 5,* 385–393.

Berkson, G., & Davenport, R. K. (1962). Stereotyped movements of mental defectives. I. Initial survey. *American Journal of Mental Deficiency, 66,* 849–852.

Berkson, G., & Mason, W. A. (1963). Stereotyped movements of mental defectives. III. situational effects. *American Journal of Mental Deficiency, 68,* 409–412.

Berkson, G., & Mason, W. A. (1965). Stereotyped movements of mental defectives. IV. The effects of toys on the character of the acts. *American Journal of Mental Deficiency, 70,* 511–524.

Bijou, S. W., Peterson, R. F., & Ault, M. H. (1968). A method to integrate descriptive and experimental field studies at the level of data and empirical concepts. *Journal of Applied Behavior Analysis, 1,* 175–191.

Cameron, M. J., Ainsleigh, S. A., & Bird, F. L. (1992). The acquisition of stimulus control of compliance and participation during an ADL routine. *Behavioral Residential Treatment, 7,* 327–340.

Cameron, M. J., Luiselli, J. K., McGrath, M., & Carlton, R. (1992). Stimulus control analysis and treatment of noncompliant behavior. *Journal of Developmental and Physical Disabilities, 4,* 141–150.

Carr, E. G., & Durand, V. M. (1985). Reducing behavior problems through functional communication training. *Journal of Applied Behavior Analysis, 18,* 111–126.

Carr, E. G., Newsom, C. D., & Binkoff, J. A. (1976). Stimulus control of self-destructive behavior in a psychotic child. *Journal of Abnormal Child Psychology, 4,* 139–153.

Catania, A. C. (1992). *Learning.* Englewood Cliffs, NJ: Prentice Hall.

Catania, A. C. (1993). Coming to terms with establishing operations. *The Behavior Analyst, 16,* 219–224.

Corte, H. E., Wolf, M. M., & Locke, B. J. (1971). A comparison of procedures for eliminating self-injurious behavior of retarded adolescents. *Journal of Applied Behavior Analysis, 4,* 201–213.

Davenport, R. K., & Berkson, G. (1963). Stereotyped movements of mental defectives. II. Effects of novel objects. *American Journal of Mental Deficiency, 67,* 879–882.

Dunlap, G., Kern-Dunlap, L., Clarke, S., & Robbins, F. R. (1991). Functional assessment, curricular revision, and severe behavior problems. *Journal of Applied Behavior Analysis, 24,* 387–397.

Durand, V. M., & Carr, E. G. (1987). Social influences on "self-stimulatory" behavior: Analysis and treatment application. *Journal of Applied Behavior Analysis, 20,* 119–132.

Durand, V. M., & Carr, E. G. (1992). An analysis of maintenance following functional communication training. *Journal of Applied Behavior Analysis, 25,* 777–794.

Durand, V. M., & Crimmins, D. B. (1987). Assessment and treatment of psychotic speech in an autistic child. *Journal of Autism and Developmental Disorders, 17,* 17–28.

Durand, V. M., & Crimmins, D. B. (1988). Identifying the variables maintaining self-injurious behavior. *Journal of Autism and Developmental Disorders, 18,* 99–117.

Favell, J. E., McGimsey, J. F., & Jones, M. L. (1978). The use of physical restraint in the treatment of self-injury and as positive reinforcement. *Journal of Applied Behavior Analysis, 11,* 225–242.

Favell, J. E., McGimsey, J. F., Jones, M. L., & Cannon, P. R. (1981). Physical restraint as positive reinforcement. *American Journal of Mental Deficiency, 85,* 425–432.

Favell, J. E., McGimsey, J. F., & Schell, R. M. (1982). Treatment of self-injury by providing alternate sensory activities. *Analysis and Intervention in Developmental Disabilities, 2,* 83–104.

Foxx, R. M., & Dufrense, D. (1984). "Harry": The use of physical restraint as a reinforcer, timeout from restraint, and fading restraint in treating a self-injurious man. *Analysis and Intervention in Developmental Disabilities, 4,* 1–13.

Green, L., & Freed, D. E. (1993). The substitutability of reinforcers. *Journal of the Experimental Analysis of Behavior, 60,* 141–158.

Hagopian, L. P., Fisher, W. W., & Legacy, S. M. (1994). Schedule effects of noncontingent reinforcement on attention-maintained destructive behavior in identical quadruplets. *Journal of Applied Behavior Analysis, 27,* 317–325.

Horner, R. D. (1980). The effects of an environmental "enrichment" program on the behavior of institutionalized profoundly retarded children. *Journal of Applied Behavior Analysis, 13,* 473–491.

Horner, R. H., Day, H. M., Sprague, J. R., O'Brien, M., & Heathfield, L. T. (1991). Interspersed requests: A nonaversive procedure for reducing aggression and self-injury during instruction. *Journal of Applied Behavior Analysis, 24,* 265–278.

Isley, E. M., Kartsonis, C., McCurley, C. M., Eager Weisz, K., & Roberts, M. S. (1991). Self-restraint: A review of etiology and applications in mentally retarded adults with self-injury. *Research in Developmental Disabilities, 12,* 87–95.

Iwata, B. A., Dorsey, M., Slifer, K., Bauman, K., & Richman, G. (1994). Toward a functional analysis of self-injury. *Journal of Applied Behavior Analysis, 27,* 197–209. (Reprinted from *Analysis and Intervention in Developmental Disabilities, 2,* 3–20, 1982)

Iwata, B. A., Pace, G. M., Kalsher, M. J., Cowdery, G. E., & Cataldo, M. F. (1990). Experimental analysis and extinction of self-injurious escape behavior. *Journal of Applied Behavior Analysis, 23,* 11–27.

Johnston, J. M., Greene, K. S., Rawal, A., Vazin, T., & Winston, M. (1991). Effects of caloric level on ruminating. *Journal of Applied Behavior Analysis, 24,* 597–603.

Kantor, J. R. (1959). *Interbehavioral psychology: A sample of scientific system construction.* Granville, OH: Principia Press.

Kantor, J. R. (1970). An analysis of the experimental analysis of behavior (TEAB). *Journal of the Experimental Analysis of Behavior, 13,* 101–108.

Keller, F. S., & Schoenfeld, W. N. (1950). *Principles of psychology.* New York: Appleton-Century-Crofts.

Kennedy, C. H., & Itkonen, T. (1993). Effects of setting events on the problem behavior of students with severe disabilities. *Journal of Applied Behavior Analysis, 26,* 321–327.

Kern, L., Koegel, R. L., & Dunlap, G. (1984). The influence of vigorous versus mild exercise on autistic stereotyped behaviors. *Journal of Autism and Developmental Disorders, 14,* 56–67.

Kern, L., Koegel, R. L., Dyer, K., Blew, P. A., & Fenton, L. R. (1982). The effects of exercise on self-stimulation and appropriate responding in autistic children. *Journal of Autism and Developmental Disorders, 12,* 399–419.

Lennox, D. B., Miltenberger, R. G., Spengler, P., & Erfanian, N. (1988). Decelerative treatment practices with persons who have mental retardation: A review of five years of the literature. *American Journal of Mental Retardation, 92,* 492–501.

Levinson, L. T., & Reid, G. (1993). The effects of exercise intensity on the stereotypic behaviors of individuals with autism. *Adapted Physical Activity Quarterly, 10,* 255–268.

Linscheid, T. R., Iwata, B. A., Ricketts, R. W., Williams, D. E., & Griffin, J. C. (1990). Clinical evaluation of the Self-Injurious Behavior Inhibiting System (SIBIS). *Journal of Applied Behavior Analysis, 23,* 53–78.

Mace, F. C., & Belfiore, P. (1990). Behavioral momentum in the treatment of escape-motivated stereotypy. *Journal of Applied Behavior Analysis, 23,* 507–514.

Mace, F. C., & Lalli, J. S. (1991). Linking descriptive and experimental analyses in the treatment of bizarre speech. *Journal of Applied Behavior Analysis, 24,* 553–562.

Marr, M. J. (1993). Contextualistic mechanism or mechanistic contextualism: The straw machine as tar baby. *The Behavior Analyst, 16,* 59–65.

Michael, J. (1982). Distinguishing between the discriminative and motivational functions of stimuli. *Journal of the Experimental Analysis of Behavior, 37,* 149–155.

Michael, J. (1983). Evocative and repertoire-altering effects of an environmental event. *Analysis of Verbal Behavior, 6,* 3–9.

Michael, J. (1988). Establishing operations and the mand. *Analysis of Verbal Behavior, 6,* 3–9.

Michael, J. (1993a). *Concepts and principles of behavior analysis.* Kalamazoo, MI: Society for the Advancement of Behavior Analysis.

Michael, J. (1993b). Establishing operations. *The Behavior Analyst, 16,* 191–206.

Morris, E. K. (1993). Behavior analysis and mechanism: One is not the other. *The Behavior Analyst, 16,* 25–43.

Nevin, J. A., Mandell, C., & Atak, J. R. (1983). The analysis of behavioral momentum. *Journal of the Experimental Analysis of Behavior, 39,* 49–59.

O'Reilly, M. F. (1995). Functional analysis and treatment of escape-maintained aggression correlated with sleep deprivation. *Journal of Applied Behavior Analysis, 28,* 225–226.

Pace, G. M., Ivancic, M. T., & Jefferson, G. (1994). Stimulus fading as treatment for obscenity in a brain injured adult. *Journal of Applied Behavior Analysis, 27,* 301–305.

Pace, G. M., Iwata, B. A., Cowdery, G. E., Andree, P. J., & McIntyre, T. (1993). Stimulus (instructional) fading during extinction of self-injurious escape behavior. *Journal of Applied Behavior Analysis, 26,* 205–212.

Pace, G. M., Iwata, B. A., Edwards, G. L., & McCosh, K. C. (1986). Stimulus fading and transfer in the treatment of self-restraint and self-injurious behavior. *Journal of Applied Behavior Analysis, 19,* 381–389.

Paul, H. A., & Romanczyk, R. G. (1973). The use of air splints in the treatment of self-injurious behavior. *Behavior Therapy, 4,* 320–321.

Piazza, C. C., Hanley, G. P., & Fisher, W. W. (1996). Functional analysis and treatment of cigarette pica. *Journal of Applied Behavior Analysis, 29,* 437–449.

Powers, S., Thibadeau, S., & Rose, K. (1992). Antecedent exercise and its effects on self-stimulation. *Behavioral Residential Treatment, 7,* 15–22.

Rast, J., Johnston, J. M., & Drum, C. (1984). A parametric analysis of the relationship between food quantity and rumination. *Journal of the Experimental Analysis of Behavior, 41,* 125–134.

Rast, J., Johnston, J. M., Drum, C., & Conrin, J. (1981). The relation of food quantity to rumination behavior. *Journal of the Experimental Analysis of Behavior, 14,* 121–130.

Rast, J., Johnston, J. M., Ellinger-Allen, J. A., & Drum, C. (1985). Effects of nutritional and mechanical properties of food on ruminative behavior. *Journal of the Experimental Analysis of Behavior, 44,* 195–206.

Rast, J., Johnston, J. M., Lubin, D., & Ellinger-Allen, J. A. (1988). Effects of premeal chewing on ruminative behavior. *American Journal of Mental Retardation, 93,* 67–74.

Repp, A. C., Singh, N. N., Karsh, K. G., & Deitz, D. E. D. (1991). Ecobehavioural analysis of stereotypic and adaptive behaviours: Activities as setting events. *Journal of Mental Deficiency Research, 35,* 413–429.

Roediger, H. L., III, Capaldi, E. D., Paris, S. G., & Polivy, J. (1991). *Psychology.* New York: Harper Collins.

Rojahn, J., Mulick, J. A., McCoy, D., & Schroeder,

S. R. (1978). Setting effects, adaptive clothing, and the modification of head-banging and self-restraint in two profoundly retarded adults. *Behavior Analysis and Modification, 2,* 185–196.

Rojahn, J., Schroeder, S. R., & Mulick, J. A. (1980). Ecological assessment of self-protective devices in three profoundly retarded adults. *Journal of Autism and Developmental Disorders, 10,* 59–66.

Schroeder, S. R., Kanoy, R. C., Mulick, J. A., Rojahn, J., Thios, S. J., & Stephens, M. (1982). Environmental antecedents which affect management and maintenance of programs for self-injurious behavior. In J. H. Hollis & C. E. Meyers (Eds.), *Life threatening behavior: Analysis and intervention* (pp. 105–159). Washington, DC: American Association on Mental Deficiency (Monograph 5).

Silverman, K., Watanabe, K., Marshall, A. M., & Baer, D. M. (1984). Reducing self-injury and corresponding self-restraint through the strategic use of protective clothing. *Journal of Applied Behavior Analysis, 17,* 545–552.

Skinner, B. F. (1931). The concept of the reflex in the description of behavior. *The Journal of General Psychology, 5,* 427–458.

Skinner, B. F. (1935). The generic nature of the concepts of stimulus and response. *The Journal of General Psychology, 12,* 40–65.

Skinner, B. F. (1945). The operational analysis of psychological terms. *Psychological Review, 52,* 270–277.

Skinner, B. F. (1953). *Science and human behavior.* New York: Macmillan.

Skinner, B. F. (1969). *Contingencies of reinforcement: A theoretical analysis.* New York: Appleton-Century-Crofts.

Smith, R. G., Iwata, B. A., Goh, H. L., & Shore, B. A. (1995). Analysis of establishing operations for self-injury maintained by escape. *Journal of Applied Behavior Analysis, 28,* 433–445.

Smith, R. G., Iwata, B. A., Vollmer, T. R., & Pace, G. M. (1992). On the relationship between self-injurious behavior and self-restraint. *Journal of Applied Behavior Analysis, 25,* 515–535.

Tarnowski, K. J., & Drabman, R. S. (1985). The effects of ambulation training on the self-stimulatory behavior of a multiply handicapped child. *Behavior Therapy, 16,* 275–285.

Taylor, J. C., Sisson, L. A., McKelvey, J. L., & Trefelner, M. F. (1993). Situation specificity in attention-seeking problem behavior. *Behavior Modification, 17,* 474–497.

Touchette, P. E. (1968). The effects of graduated stimulus change on the acquisition of a simple discrimination in severely retarded boys. *Journal of the Experimental Analysis of Behavior, 11,* 39–48.

Touchette, P. E., & Howard, J. S. (1984). Errorless learning: Reinforcement contingencies and stimulus control transfer in delayed prompting. *Journal of Applied Behavior Analysis, 17,* 175–188.

Touchette, P. E., MacDonald, R. F., & Langer, S. N. (1985). A scatter plot for identifying stimulus control of problem behavior. *Journal of Applied Behavior Analysis, 18,* 343–351.

Vollmer, T. R., Iwata, B. A., Smith, R. G., & Rodgers, T. A. (1992). Reduction of multiple aberrant behaviors and concurrent development of self-care skills with differential reinforcement. *Research in Developmental Disabilities, 13,* 287–299.

Vollmer, T. R., Iwata, B. A., Zarcone, J. R., Smith, R. G., & Mazaleski, J. L. (1993). The role of attention in the treatment of attention-maintained self-injurious behavior: Noncontingent reinforcement and differential reinforcement of other behavior. *Journal of Applied Behavior Analysis, 26,* 9–21.

Vollmer, T. R., Marcus, B. A., & Ringdahl, J. E. (1995). Noncontingent escape as treatment for self-injurious behavior maintained by negative reinforcement. *Journal of Applied Behavior Analysis, 28,* 15–26.

Wahler, R. G. (1975). Some structural aspects of deviant child behavior. *Journal of Applied Behavior Analysis, 8,* 27–42.

Wahler, R. G., & Fox, J. J. (1981). Setting events in applied behavior analysis: Toward a conceptual and methodological expansion. *Journal of Applied Behavior Analysis, 14,* 327–338.

Wahler, R. G., House, A. E., & Stambaugh, E. E. (1976). *Ecological assessment of child problem behavior.* New York: Pergamon Press.

Weeks, M., & Gaylord-Ross, R. (1981). Task difficulty and aberrant behavior in severely handicapped students. *Journal of Applied Behavior Analysis, 14,* 449–463.

Zarcone, J. R., Iwata, B. A., Hughes, C. E., & Vollmer, T. R. (1993). Momentum versus extinction effects in the treatment of self-injurious escape behavior. *Journal of Applied Behavior Analysis, 26,* 135–136.

Zarcone, J. R., Iwata, B. A., Smith, R. G., Mazaleski, J. L., & Lerman, D. C. (1994). Reemergence and extinction of self-injurious escape behavior during stimulus (instructional) fading. *Journal of Applied Behavior Analysis, 27,* 307–316.

Zarcone, J. R., Iwata, B. A., Vollmer, T. R., Jagtiani, S., Smith, R. G., & Mazaleski, J. L. (1993). Extinction of self-injurious escape behavior with and without instructional fading. *Journal of Applied Behavior Analysis, 26,* 353–360.

Received August 8, 1996
Initial editorial decision October 16, 1996
Final acceptance February 5, 1997
Action Editor, Wayne W. Fisher

JOURNAL OF APPLIED BEHAVIOR ANALYSIS 1997, **30**, 387–410 NUMBER 3 (FALL 1997)

BASIC AND APPLIED RESEARCH ON CHOICE RESPONDING

WAYNE W. FISHER

KENNEDY KRIEGER INSTITUTE AND
JOHNS HOPKINS UNIVERSITY SCHOOL OF MEDICINE

AND

JAMES E. MAZUR

SOUTHERN CONNECTICUT STATE UNIVERSITY

Choice responding refers to the manner in which individuals allocate their time or responding among available response options. In this article, we first review basic investigations that have identified and examined variables that influence choice responding, such as response effort and reinforcement rate, immediacy, and quality. We then describe recent bridge and applied studies that illustrate how the results of basic research on choice responding can help to account for human behavior in natural environments and improve clinical assessments and interventions.

DESCRIPTORS: basic research, choice, matching theory, concurrent schedules

---

How one response is affected by consequences associated with concurrently available responses has been the topic of a considerable amount of basic behavior analysis research over the last few decades (see Williams, 1994 for a review). In addition, a number of discussion articles have been written on the potential applied significance of basic laboratory research on choice responding and the related theoretical accounts, most notably matching theory (e.g., McDowell, 1988, 1989; Meyerson & Hale, 1984; Pierce & Epling, 1995). Articles on this topic published in the 1980s had but a few available exemplars of clinical investigations that used the matching equation to account for, assess, or treat aberrant behavior (e.g., Carr & McDowell, 1980; Conger & Killeen, 1974; Martens & Houk, 1989). Since that time, however, the number of studies that have examined matching phenomena or choice responding with human participants in more natural settings has steadily increased. The primary goals of the current article are to describe and discuss (a) the variables that affect choice responding under laboratory and natural conditions with both nonhumans and humans, (b) the application of choice methods to the identification and assessment of reinforcers among individuals with developmental disabilities, and (c) the application of choice methods to analyzing and improving the effects of clinical interventions designed to reduce problem behavior. Before discussing the basic and applied studies on choice responding, it may be helpful to briefly describe how we categorized those investigations.

This investigation was supported in part by Grant MCJ249149-02 from the Maternal and Child Health Service of the U.S. Department of Health and Human Services and by Grant MH 38357 from the National Institute of Mental Health. We thank Rachel H. Thompson, Cathleen C. Piazza, Dorothea Lerman, and Bridget Shore for their helpful comments on this manuscript.

Requests for reprints should be addressed to Wayne W. Fisher, Neurobehavioral Unit, Kennedy Krieger Institute, 707 N. Broadway, Baltimore, Maryland 21205.

CATEGORIZING STUDIES ALONG THE BASIC–APPLIED CONTINUUM

Behavior-analytic investigations on choice responding and other phenomena vary along a continuum from basic to applied studies (for discussion of the basic–applied continuum, see Hake, 1982; Wacker, 1996). For heuristic purposes, it may be useful to segment that continuum into three broad categories: basic, applied, and bridge studies. A basic investigation on choice responding is one in which the primary goal is to elucidate the variables that determine how individuals allocate their responding or time across available options. By contrast, an applied investigation on choice responding is one in which the primary goal is to employ the principles derived from (or methods used in) basic investigations on choice to achieve a better clinical outcome (e.g., to identify more potent reinforcers or to produce more rapid or complete reductions in aberrant behavior). Finally, a bridge study is one in which the primary goal is to determine the extent to which the variables that affect choice responding under laboratory conditions in basic research operate in a similar manner with either clinical or normal populations under more naturalistic conditions.

Basic and applied studies are important because they improve our understanding of behavioral phenomena and help to solve real human problems, respectively. Bridge studies are also important because they help to determine the extent to which the behavioral phenomena observed in laboratory experiments (and the resultant explanations of those phenomena) also occur in and are applicable to natural human environments. Bridge studies that replicate laboratory findings may reveal novel and potentially useful applications of basic principles (e.g., Neef, Shade, & Miller, 1994). In addition, bridge studies that fail to replicate findings from basic research may raise new and important questions that could be a focus of subsequent laboratory research (Wacker, 1996). In the remainder of this article, we discuss the major findings from laboratory research on matching and choice responding and the related applied and bridge studies that illustrate how the results of basic research can help to account for human behavior in natural environments.

VARIABLES THAT INFLUENCE CHOICE RESPONDING IN BASIC INVESTIGATIONS

Studying Choice and Preference Using Concurrent-Operants Arrangements

The variables that influence choice responding are generally studied in a concurrent-operants arrangement in which two or more responses are simultaneously available (e.g., two keys in an operant chamber) and each is correlated with an independent schedule of reinforcement. One advantage of a concurrent arrangement is that it allows the experimenter to evaluate how manipulations of the three-term contingency (usually of the consequence) for one response affects the probability of other concurrently available responses. Said another way, a concurrent arrangement allows the experimenter to study choice (i.e., whether and why an individual emits one response over one or more alternatives at a given point in time). This has obvious significance to clinical behavior analysis because there are almost always multiple response options available to individuals in natural human environments.

A second advantage of a concurrent-operants arrangement (over a single-operant arrangement) is that it provides a much more sensitive method of assessing an individual's preference for one reinforcer over another. That is, when two reinforcers are concurrently available, the individual must choose between them. By contrast, when two reinforcers are compared using a single-operant arrangement, each one is available at different points in time, and thus the individual is not required to choose between them.

In a concurrent arrangement, two reinforcers are in direct competition, and individuals allocate or distribute their responding in accordance with how much they value each reinforcer. That is, choice responding provides an excellent measure of an individual's preferences for concurrently available reinforcers. An individual's preference for a given reinforcer is determined by how much responding is allocated to that reinforcer relative to the amount of responding allocated to other available reinforcers, a measure called relative response rate. That is, the relative rate of a response is its rate in proportion to the other concurrently available responses (e.g., the rate of Response A divided by the combined rate of Responses A and B in a two-operant arrangement). By contrast, the absolute rate of a response is its frequency (e.g., number per session) divided by some unit of time (e.g., the number of minutes in the session).

A clear preference for one reinforcer over another may be identified through differences in relative response rates observed in a concurrent arrangement, even when the two consequences produce equal absolute response rates in a single-operant arrangement. In general, relative response rate is a more sensitive measure of preference than is absolute response rate. For example, suppose that an individual with developmental disabilities did piecework in a sheltered workshop. On Mondays the individual could sort nuts for Company A, who paid 6 cents per bag; on Tuesdays the individual could sort nuts for Company B, who paid 7 cents per bag; and on Wednesdays the individual could sort for either Company A or B, or do some amount of both. A comparison of the work rates on Mondays and Tuesdays represents a single-operant arrangement (i.e., one response option and reinforcer was available on each day). A comparison of the work rates for Company A (6 cents per bag) and Company B (7 cents per bag) on Wednesdays, when both response options and corresponding reinforcers were simultaneously available, represents a concurrent-operants arrangement. The work rates on Mondays (6 cents per bag) and Tuesdays (7 cents per bag) might be similar, which would lead to the conclusion that the individual values each of the two consequences (6 or 7 cents per bag) about the same. However, a comparison of the work rates for Company A (6 cents) and Company B (7 cents) on Wednesdays, when both consequences were concurrently available, might clearly show that the individual preferred to earn 7 cents per bag rather than 6 cents per bag. This example is analogous to laboratory studies with both nonhuman and human participants that typically have found exclusive preference for the "better" of two concurrent ratio schedules (e.g., Herrnstein & Loveland, 1975; Shah, Bradshaw, & Szabadi, 1989).

Most basic investigations on choice responding have focused on how an individual's allocation of responding is affected by variables like response effort and reinforcement rate, magnitude, quality, and immediacy. In some cases, manipulations of these response and reinforcement parameters produce a phenomenon called matching, where response allocation matches the rate of reinforcement obtained from each available response option. In other cases, changes in these variables produce deviations from matching.

Matching Between Rate of Responding and Reinforcement

In basic investigations in which two or more responses are each correlated with independent reinforcement schedules, the rate or amount of reinforcement available on each schedule is often different (e.g., a variable-interval [VI] 30-s schedule for Response A and a VI 60-s schedule for Response B). When two concurrent VI schedules are in effect, individuals usually switch back and forth between the two schedules, emitting one of the responses for a while and then the other (e.g., Herrnstein, 1961). Only by frequently switching between the alternatives can an individual obtain all or almost all of the reinforcers available from both VI schedules. Over time (e.g., over several sessions), individuals often learn to distribute their responding such that the relative rate of a response will approximately equal its relative rate of reinforcement (e.g., with concurrent VI 30-s VI 60-s schedules, two thirds of the responses and reinforcers will occur on the VI 30-s schedule and one third of responses and reinforcers will occur on the VI 60-s schedule). The distribution of responding in proportion to the amount of reinforcement obtained from each response option during concurrent arrangements is called matching (Herrnstein, 1961).

When two concurrent-ratio schedules are in effect (e.g., a variable-ratio [VR] 100 for Response A and a VR 20 for Response B), there is no benefit to switching back and forth between the two response options. Over time, individuals typically learn to allocate all or almost all of their responding to the schedule that produces a higher rate of reinforcement (e.g., the VR 20 schedule). The matching equation holds for VR schedules, because when an individual learns to respond exclusively on the denser schedule, all responding is allocated to and all reinforcement is obtained from this schedule.

Deviations from Matching in Symmetrical and Asymmetrical Arrangements

Baum (1974, 1979) described three ways in which relative response rates may deviate from the predictions of the matching equation, which he called overmatching, undermatching, and bias.

Overmatching. The term *overmatching* is used to describe situations, like those observed by Baum (1982), in which the relative rate of the more frequent response is consistently greater than its relative rate of reinforcement (e.g., Response A accounts for 70% of responding but produces 60% of the reinforcers; Response B accounts for 30% of responding but produces 40% of the reinforcers). Overmatching occurs when relative response rates (Response A, 70%; Response B, 30%) are further away from the midpoint (50%) than are the corresponding relative reinforcement rates (Reinforcer A, 60%; Reinforcer B, 40%). Overmatching is sometimes observed when there is a substantial penalty for switching between alternatives. For example, Baum (1982) found that pigeons allocated increasingly more responding to the denser of two VI schedules than would be predicted by the matching equation as the response effort involved in switching between the two schedules was increased (by placing a barrier and hurdle between the two response keys).

Undermatching. Although overmatching is observed occasionally in basic investigations, undermatching is considerably more common. Undermatching describes situations in which the relative rate of the more frequent response is consistently lower than its relative rate of reinforcement (e.g., Response A accounts for 60% of responding but produces 70% of the reinforcers; Response B accounts for 40% of responding but produces 30% of the reinforcers). Undermatching occurs when relative response rates (Response A, 60%; Response B, 40%) are closer to the midpoint (50%) than are the corresponding relative reinforcement rates (Reinforcer A, 70%; Reinforcer B, 30%). One common explanation for undermatching is that individuals switch back and forth more frequently than would be predicted by matching because switching may be reinforced accidentally. This explanation is supported by the finding that undermatching can be reduced by including a changeover delay (COD), which prevents reinforcement until a fixed amount of time has elapsed after a switch from one response to the other.

CODs are therefore included in most laboratory studies with concurrent VI schedules.

Bias. The term *bias* is used to describe situations in which the individual consistently emits one response more than would be predicted by simple matching (e.g., 70% of responding occurs on the right key when it produces 60% of the reinforcers, whereas 50% of responding occurs on the left key when it produces 60% of the reinforcers). For example, Baum and Rachlin (1969) found that the pigeons in their study had a consistent bias for the right side of the operant chamber.

Symmetrical and asymmetrical arrangements. McDowell (1989) pointed out that deviations from matching are much more likely when concurrent arrangements are asymmetrical rather than symmetrical. He referred to concurrent arrangements as being symmetrical when identical response options (pecking Key A vs. Key B) produce qualitatively identical reinforcers (e.g., 2 s of access to food). By contrast, asymmetrical concurrent arrangements are ones in which either the responses (e.g., communication vs. aggression) or the type of reinforcers (e.g., a toy vs. attention) are different. In natural human environments, the response options available to an individual are often qualitatively different (e.g., mow the lawn vs. watch television), as are the reinforcers associated with each response. As a result, individuals may often allocate responding in ways that deviate from matching. Although deviations from matching may be more likely in asymmetrical concurrent arrangements, significant deviations from matching also may occur under symmetrical ones.

BRIDGE STUDIES ON CHOICE

One major purpose of bridge studies on choice is to determine the extent to which the variables that affect response allocation in basic studies with nonhumans (e.g., reinforcement rate and immediacy) produce similar effects with humans under more naturalistic conditions.

Matching and Self-Control Choice with Humans

A number of laboratory experiments with concurrent VI schedules have been conducted with human subjects, and some have obtained results that closely conform to the predictions of the matching law. For example, Schroeder and Holland (1969) instructed subjects to watch four dials on a panel and to try to detect as many needle deflections as possible. Needle deflections on the two dials on the left were programmed by one VI schedule, and needle deflections on the two right dials were programmed by a second VI schedule. Subjects were told to press one of two buttons whenever they saw a needle deflection. However, the operant responses in this task were the subject's eye movements, which were recorded by a camera throughout the experiment. Each subject was exposed to two or more conditions with different pairs of VI schedules. Schroeder and Holland found that their subjects' eye movements varied considerably depending on whether there was a COD. With no COD, there was substantial undermatching, but with a 2.5-s COD, the results were well described by the matching law: The percentage of eye movements toward the left dials was approximately equal to the percentage of needle deflections on the left dials. In a similar study, subjects played a video game in which they could detect and destroy two types of enemy missiles by pressing two response keys, and their key-press percentages closely matched the percentages of the two types of missiles (Baum, 1975).

Other studies with human subjects have also obtained close approximations to matching. Bradshaw and his colleagues conducted several experiments in which the operant responses were pressing levers or response keys and the reinforcers were points that could later be exchanged for money (e.g., Bradshaw, Ruddle, & Szabadi, 1981; Bradshaw, Szabadi, & Bevan, 1976). By using different lights on the control panel as discriminative stimuli for different VI schedules, Bradshaw and colleagues were able to present as many as five different pairs of VI schedules in a single session. In general, their results were similar to those obtained with nonhuman subjects, with some subjects exhibiting approximate matching, some undermatching, and some overmatching.

By contrast, some studies with human subjects using concurrent VI schedules have obtained results that did not conform to the matching law. For example, Horne and Lowe (1993) conducted studies that were patterned after Bradshaw's research, but some of their subjects displayed response patterns that deviated greatly from the matching law. Some subjects exhibited near indifference for two different VI schedules, whereas others showed exclusive preference for whichever VI schedule delivered more reinforcers. Lowe and Horne (1985) suggested that the approximate matching observed by Bradshaw and colleagues may have been the result of a fortuitous arrangement of the stimulus lights associated with the different VI schedules. The lights were arranged in a row, and the ordinal position of a light corresponded to the richness of the VI schedule. Therefore, subjects could have learned to distribute their choice responses according to a simple rule such as, "The further the light is to the right, the more I should respond on the right button." By questioning their own subjects about their response strategies, Horne and Lowe (1993) provided evidence that the participants' choices were influenced by the verbal rules they had formulated about how to respond. For example, a subject who showed extreme undermatching stated that random responding was the best strategy, and a subject who responded exclusively on one key said that he decided he could earn the most points by responding only on the key that delivered points more frequently. Based on such verbal reports, Horne and Lowe concluded that human choice is largely rule governed rather than contingency shaped. For this reason, human choice may frequently differ from nonhuman choice and thus from the principles derived from research with nonhumans, such as the matching law.

It should be noted that the results of Horne and Lowe (1993) are not as different from those of Bradshaw and colleagues as they may appear. Although some of Horne and Lowe's subjects showed gross departures from matching, others exhibited approximate matching. Nevertheless, Horne and Lowe presented evidence that there is often a strong correspondence between a human subject's verbal rules and his or her actual performance in choice situations. Perhaps the safest conclusion that can be drawn at this time is that both the current reinforcement contingencies and a subject's verbal rules can influence behavior in choice situations. The factors that determine which of these two sources of behavioral control will dominate in any particular choice situation are not well understood.

Another popular procedure in laboratory research on choice is the so-called *self-control choice* situation, in which subjects must choose between a small, fairly immediate reinforcer and a larger but more delayed reinforcer. Subjects are said to exhibit self-control if they choose the larger, more delayed reinforcer, and they are sometimes called impulsive if they choose the smaller, more immediate reinforcer. Numerous studies have shown that nonhuman subjects will frequently make the impulsive choice under these circumstances (e.g., Ainslie, 1974; Rachlin & Green, 1972), and several experiments have shown that humans often do so as well. Solnick, Kannenberg, Eckerman, and Waller (1980) had college students work on math problems in the presence of an aversively loud noise, and on each trial they could choose (a) an immediate 60-s period of silence followed by a 120-s period of noise or (b) a 90-s period of noise followed by a 90-s period of silence. In some conditions of this experiment, the students chose the immediate period of silence on nearly every trial, even though this meant that they would be exposed to more noise in the long run. In an experiment by Logue and King (1991), college students who had not eaten for several hours were given repeated choices between (a) a small amount of fruit juice after a 1-s delay and (b) a larger amount after a 60-s delay. Logue and King found large individual differences, with some subjects choosing the small immediate option and others the large delayed option. Eight of their 19 subjects chose the small immediate option on more than half of the trials. Other studies have obtained similar results with a variety of different reinforcers that could be delivered in small or large amounts, including snack items (Schweitzer & Sulzer-Azaroff, 1988), slides of sports and entertainment personalities (Navarick, 1986), and opportunities to play video games (Millar & Navarick, 1984).

Not all experiments with human subjects have found preference for the smaller, more immediate reinforcer. For example, in some studies in which the reinforcers were points that could be exchanged for money at the end of the session, subjects showed strong preferences for the larger, delayed reinforcer, and by doing so they increased the total amount of money they earned during the session (Logue, Forzano, & Tobin, 1992; Logue, Peña-Correal, Rodriguez, & Kabela, 1986). Why do human subjects exhibit self-control in some studies and impulsive choices in others? Some writers have suggested that an important variable is whether primary or conditioned reinforcers are used (Flora & Pavlik, 1992). The hypothesis is that impulsive choices are more likely to occur with primary reinforcers that can be consumed or used as soon as they are delivered. By contrast, when the large and small alternatives are conditioned reinforcers, such as points or tokens that can be exchanged for money or other tangible items only at the end of the session, subjects may consistently choose the larger, delayed alternative. This strategy seems reasonable because there is no advantage in choosing an immediate but smaller quantity of tokens that cannot be redeemed until the end of the session. This distinction between primary and conditioned reinforcers is certainly not the only factor that can affect whether a person will choose a small immediate reinforcer or a larger delayed one, but it may be an important factor.

The research on self-control choice has several potential implications for applied work with clinical populations. First, it suggests that if it is possible to impose a delay of just a few seconds before the delivery of a more preferred reinforcer (e.g., attention) for maladaptive behavior (e.g., self-injury), the subject's preference may switch to a less preferred reinforcer (e.g., a toy) that is delivered immediately for appropriate behavior (e.g., task completion). Second, there is some evidence that children can be taught to avoid making impulsive choices that are not in their best long-term interests. With preschool children who were identified by their teachers as impulsive, Schweitzer and Sulzer-Azaroff (1988) used a training procedure in which the delay for the larger of two reinforcers was gradually lengthened over many sessions. Five of the six children showed significant increases in the amount of time they chose to wait for the larger reinforcer. Third, children's choices in self-control situations might be useful as an assessment or screening measure, because choices in such situations change systematically as children get older (Sonuga-Barke, Lea, & Webley, 1989). In addition, several studies have found that impulsive choices are more likely in children with attention deficit hyperactivity disorder (ADHD; e.g., Schweitzer & Sulzer-Azaroff, 1995; Sonuga-Barke, Taylor, Sembi, & Smith, 1992). Therefore, it may be particularly important to develop treatments that are designed to train individuals with ADHD to choose larger, delayed reinforcers over smaller, more immediate reinforcers. Teaching individuals to respond more to quantity of reinforcement and less to immediacy of reinforcement is an effect that can often require many trials, but it may be time and effort well spent, especially for individuals who are particularly prone to impulsive responding.

Choice Responding and Matching in Natural Settings and Clinical Populations

A number of investigators have examined the extent to which the parameters that affect response allocation in basic experiments (e.g., response effort, reinforcement rate, delay, and quality) also do so in natural settings or with distinct clinical populations. For example, Conger and Killeen (1974) reported that college students in a group discussion spent more time talking to a confederate group member who frequently delivered positive statements (e.g., "good point") than to another confederate who issued such statements much less frequently. In fact, by the end of the group discussion, the proportion of time spent talking to each confederate closely matched the proportion of positive statements each delivered to the participant.

Neef, Mace, and colleagues have conducted a series of investigations on the effects of response effort and reinforcement rate, quality, and delay on students' time allocation to concurrently available sets of math problems (Mace, Neef, Shade, & Mauro, 1994, 1996; Neef, Mace, & Shade, 1993; Neef, Mace, Shea, & Shade, 1992; Neef et al., 1994). Neef et al. (1992) examined how special education students allocated their time across two concurrently available sets of math problems in relation to the rate and quality of reinforcement correlated with each set. A unique discriminative stimulus (a distinctly colored math sheet) and an independent VI schedule (i.e., concurrent VI 30-s VI 120-s schedules) were associated with each set of math problems. The experimenters included a prebaseline training condition in which kitchen timers were used to signal the time remaining until reinforcement was available on each VI component. This was done to increase the participants' sensitivity to the rates of reinforcement associated with each schedule. Interestingly, matching between the time allocation and reinforcement rates occurred only after the kitchen timers were added, but matching persisted in subsequent phases after they were removed.

In the formal experimental phases, Neef et al. (1992) alternated between phases in which the quality of the reinforcers delivered were equal (either program money or nickels on both schedules) or unequal (program money on the VI 30-s schedule and nickels on the VI 120-s schedule). Time allocation closely matched reinforcement rates (e.g., approximately 80% of responding on the VI 30-s schedule) when the quality of reinforcement associated with each schedule was the same. However, time allocation shifted toward the leaner schedule when it was associated with a higher quality reinforcer (nickels). That is, each participant displayed a preference for nickels over program money, which resulted in a deviation from matching in which the effects of reinforcer quality overrode the effects of reinforcement rate (time allocation was biased toward the higher quality reinforcer).

In subsequent studies, these investigators

have used similar methods to evaluate the effects of (a) reinforcement delay, which (consistent with basic investigations) shifted responding away from matching toward more immediate reinforcement (Neef et al., 1993); (b) problem difficulty, which did not result in a deviation from matching (i.e., time allocation matched rate of reinforcement independent of problem difficulty; Mace et al., 1996); and (c) a variety of adjunctive procedures (changeover delays, demonstrations, limited holds, and timers), which were necessary to produce matching as the relative rates of reinforcement available from two concurrent VI schedules were systematically manipulated (Mace et al., 1994). These investigations are noteworthy in that the effects of response and reinforcement parameters on matching and deviations from matching were evaluated with a clinical population (students with severe emotional, learning, and behavioral disabilities) using a socially meaningful target response as the dependent variable (math problems).

APPLIED RESEARCH ON REINFORCER IDENTIFICATION

Recent applied investigations have begun to examine ways in which the principles and methods used in basic investigations to evaluate and influence choice responding may be used to improve clinical assessments and interventions. In the next three sections, we discuss how choice arrangements have been used (a) to improve stimulus preference assessments, (b) to compare reinforcer effects, and (c) to analyze and improve clinical interventions.

Choice and Stimulus Preference Assessments

One method of assessing an individual's preference for potential reinforcers is to present stimuli in pairs (e.g., Fisher et al., 1992). This method of assessing client preferences for potential reinforcers has been called a forced- or paired-choice assessment in the literature on developmental disabilities (e.g., DeLeon & Iwata, 1996; Fisher et al., 1992). For example, Stimulus A (e.g., a Slinky™) is presented with Stimulus B (e.g., a bite of pizza), and the client is asked to choose one stimulus over the other. Then Stimulus A is similarly presented with Stimuli C, D, E, and so on. This process continues until each stimulus has been presented with every other stimulus one or more times.

The basic approach of presenting stimuli in pairs has been used for years in other areas of psychology and in other disciplines. For example, this method has been used in psychophysiological research and neurological examinations to assess perception (e.g., measuring just noticeable differences; Fechner, 1860/1966). Presenting stimuli in pairs also has been used to quantify human judgments (e.g., the method of paired comparisons; Thurstone, 1927).

Fisher et al. (1992) applied the method of presenting stimuli in pairs to the stimulus preference assessment developed by Pace, Ivancic, Edwards, Iwata, and Page (1985). Fisher et al. (1992) compared the single-stimulus and paired-choice methods of assessing preference. The paired-choice assessment resulted in greater differentiation among the stimuli than did the single-stimulus method and better predicted which items functioned as more effective reinforcers when presented contingently in a concurrent-operants arrangement. Northup, George, Jones, Broussard, and Vollmer (1996) similarly found that the accuracy of children's verbal reports regarding their preferences were improved by presenting stimuli in pairs rather than singly (e.g., "Would you rather get _ or _?" rather than "Do you like _ a little, a lot, or not at all?"). In addition, Piazza, Fisher, Hagopian, Bowman, and Toole (1996) found that reinforcer effectiveness varied proportionally with the preference values derived from a paired-choice assessment; high-preference stimuli were more effective reinforcers than moderately preferred stimuli, which, in turn, were more effective than those assessed as low preference by the paired-choice assessment.

Increasing the efficiency of preference assessments. Several recent investigations have focused on further improving the efficiency of preference assessments. Two recent investigations by Windsor, Piche, and Locke (1994) and DeLeon and Iwata (1996) are particularly noteworthy in this regard. Windsor et al. assessed whether individuals with developmental disabilities could choose from a larger array of concurrently available stimuli (six stimuli at a time rather than two). The obvious advantage of presenting six or more stimuli at a time rather than two is that the stimuli can be presented in fewer trials and less time. However, Windsor et al. found that the paired-choice assessment produced more distinct rankings than did the multiple-stimulus method. In addition, the paired-choice assessment produced more stable preference rankings over repeated administrations.

DeLeon and Iwata (1996) hypothesized that the advantages of the paired-choice assessment (better differentiation and stability of preference rankings) may have been due to the fact that, with the multiple-stimulus method, an individual's highest preference stimuli were available during each trial. Thus, an individual might choose only one or a few stimuli during the entire assessment. Based on this hypothesis, DeLeon and Iwata developed a variation of the multiple-stimulus method that retained its efficiency (i.e., fewer trials and less time) but also included a component that required the individual to choose among lesser preferred stimuli, thus allowing better differentiation among these items. During the first trial, seven stimuli were present, and the individual was allowed to choose and have access to just one. On the second trial, the stimulus chosen on the first trial was omitted from the array of available stimuli (e.g., the highest preference stimulus from the first trial was not present during the second trial). On each subsequent trial, the stimuli that had been chosen on previous trials were omitted until the individual stopped choosing or chose between the last two stimuli. They called the procedure *multiple stimulus without replacement* (MSWO). The MSWO was more efficient than the paired-choice assessment (30 or fewer trials completed in about 22 min for the MSWO, 105 trials completed in about 53 min for the paired-choice assessment).

The most important clinical advancement offered by the MSWO may not be that the entire procedure was completed in about 22 min, but rather that an abbreviated version of the procedure could be used on an ongoing basis to select one or two potential reinforcers from an array of seven or more prior to each training session. Mason, McGee, Farmer-Dougan, and Risley (1989) used an abbreviated version of the paired-choice assessment prior to each training session and reported that preferences frequently changed from one session to the next. Thus, it may be beneficial to reassess an individual's preferences as frequently as possible.

Choice and Reinforcer Assessments

The purpose of a reinforcer assessment is to evaluate stimuli that have been identified as being preferred to determine whether they actually function as reinforcers (i.e., verifying reinforcer function). The ultimate goal for both stimulus preference and reinforcer assessments is to identify effective reinforcers that subsequently can be used in typical training situations.

Based in part on the supposition that it may be important to evaluate the effects of a given reinforcer relative to other competing reinforcers, Fisher et al. (1992) assessed preferred stimuli in a concurrent-operants arrangement. Two free-operant responses (e.g., sitting in Chair A vs. Chair B) were each correlated with different consequent stimuli. For example, when in-seat behavior was the dependent measure, the stimuli associated with Chair A were available to the participant as long as he or she remained in that chair; the stimuli associated with Chair B were available as long as the participant remained in that chair. Thus, the reinforcers were presented on concurrent fixed-ratio (FR) 1 schedules, but a reinforcement interval continued as long as the individual remained in a chair. For 3 of 4 participants with severe to profound mental retardation, clear preferences were established in the very first concurrent-operants session. Using similar procedures, Piazza, Fisher, Hagopian, Bowman, and Toole (1996) and Fisher, Piazza, Bowman, and Amari (1996) also found that this method showed fairly rapid and clear differences in relative reinforcement value. Taken together, these results suggest that this method was a rapid and sensitive means of establishing the relative reinforcement value of different stimuli among individuals with severe to profound mental retardation.

Behavioral economics and reinforcer assessments. One potential limitation of both the single and the concurrent arrangements described by Pace et al. (1985) and Fisher and colleagues, respectively, was the use of simple, free-operant responses (e.g., reaching, in-seat behavior) as dependent measures (Piazza, Fisher, Hagopian, Bowman, & Toole, 1996). A second and perhaps related limitation was that the schedule requirements for reinforcement delivery were low (e.g., FR 1 schedules; Tustin, 1994). Although use of simple responses and schedules permits comparisons of the effects of reinforcers in an efficient manner, their use may limit the generality of the results (i.e., efficiency at the expense of validity). A stimulus that has been shown to function as a reinforcer for a simple free-operant response during a reinforcer assessment may not increase or maintain more complex or socially meaningful responses in typical training situations. Similarly, a stimulus that maintains a response on a dense schedule (e.g., FR 1) may not do so on a leaner schedule (e.g., FR 20). Responding may decrease during leaner schedules not only because of increases in the ratio of responses to reinforcers but also because the amount of time that elapses between reinforcer deliveries is extended.

The extent to which reinforcement effects obtained with a simple free-operant response generalize to more complex and socially meaningful responses is an empirical question that remains largely untested. However, two recent applied investigations (DeLeon, Iwata, Goh, & Worsdell, 1997; Tustin, 1994) based on principles of behavioral economics illustrate how schedule density may affect an individual's preferences for two concurrently available reinforcers.

Within a behavioral economics framework, reinforcement is viewed as a transaction in which responding (or work) is exchanged for reinforcement (or payment; Tustin, 1994). Tustin used progressive FR schedules to determine whether an individual's preferences for two concurrently available reinforcers changed as the price (i.e., the number of responses per reinforcer) of one or both of them was systematically increased. The participants were adult men with moderate to severe mental retardation, autism, or both. The reinforcers were brief attention from the experimenter or computer-generated visual patterns and musical tones, either alone or in combination. Two reinforcers were available at a time, and each was correlated with a different response (two buttons on a joystick) and an independent FR schedule. In one arrangement, one of the reinforcers (e.g., visual) was always correlated with an FR 5 schedule, while the schedule for the other reinforcer (e.g., attention) varied between an FR 1 and an FR 20. As would be expected from a behavioral economics framework, the individual's preferences were a function of both the type of stimulus (i.e., reinforcer quality) and the cost (i.e., number of responses per reinforcer) associated with each option. For example, during one assessment, the participant showed a clear preference for attention when its cost was less than or equal to the visual stimulus. But the individual's preference shifted away from attention and toward the visual stimulus in a linear fashion as the price of attention increased.

In another arrangement in the Tustin (1994) investigation, the schedules for both stimuli varied together between an FR 1 and an FR 20 (i.e., the two schedules varied but were always equal to one another). Surprisingly, the participant had a slight preference for one stimulus (constant color over combined visual patterns and musical tones) when the schedule requirements for both stimuli were low (i.e., an FR 1). However, his preference reversed (combined over constant color) as the schedule requirements increased. In fact, the individual showed a near-exclusive preference for the combined stimulus when the price of both stimuli was 10 responses per reinforcer (FR 10) or higher.

Given that this arrangement (concurrent and equal progressive-ratio schedules) was implemented with only 1 of the participants in the Tustin (1994) investigation, it would be easy to discount this unusual finding as spurious or idiosyncratic. However, DeLeon et al. (1997) have similarly shown that an individual's preference for one item over another may be readily apparent when schedule requirements are relatively high (e.g., concurrent FR 10 schedules) but not when they are low (e.g., concurrent FR 1 schedules). In addition, they found that this effect (i.e., a shift from no apparent preference to a clear preference as schedule requirements increased) occurred with both participants when similar reinforcers were concurrently available (two food items) but not when dissimilar items were compared (a food and a leisure item).

Based on these findings, DeLeon et al. (1997) suggested that increased schedule requirements may magnify small differences in preference between similar but not dissimilar stimuli. This is because stimuli that share physical characteristics (e.g., food items) are more likely to share functional properties as well (e.g., hunger reduction). An individual can exclusively consume the more preferred (or less costly) item without experiencing deprivation when two concurrently available stimuli serve the same function (e.g., either food item reduces hunger). By contrast, when two stimuli serve separate functions, exclusive consumption of one reinforcer results in deprivation of the other (e.g., sustenance but no fun or leisure). If each function is important or valued, the individual will continue to allocate responding to both options as schedule requirements increase.

Given that the DeLeon et al. (1997) investigation involved just 2 participants, their findings and the accompanying explanation should be viewed as tentative. Further, it should be noted that these investigators specifically selected reinforcers for which the individuals showed no apparent preference under concurrent FR 1 schedules, which may be an uncommon occurrence. Fisher and colleagues have generally found that individuals with developmental disabilities show clear preferences on concurrent FR 1 schedules (Fisher et al., 1992, 1996; Piazza, Fisher, Hagopian, Bowman, & Toole, 1996). Nevertheless, stimuli that maintain responding as schedule requirements increase may be more likely to function as reinforcers when they are used as consequences in more typical training situations. Thus, it may be beneficial to assess potential reinforcers using schedule requirements similar to those the individual is likely to encounter in his or her training activities. The investigations by DeLeon et al. and Tustin (1994) are important because they illustrate how basic findings and principles from the field of behavioral economics can be relevant to clinical populations and how they may be used to improve assessments designed to identify potent reinforcers.

Choice as reinforcement. Up to this point, we have discussed choice in terms of (a) how individuals distribute responding among concurrently available reinforcers and (b) how knowledge of choice responding may improve our ability to predict and assess the effects of stimuli used as reinforcers. However, providing individuals with choice-making opportunities may actually produce reinforcement effects that are relatively independent of the consequences associated with each response option.

Catania and Sagvolden (1980) showed that pigeons displayed a small but consistent preference for a condition in which they could produce reinforcement through responding on any of three available keys (choice) over one in which only a single response key produced reinforcement (no choice), even though the programmed reinforcement (i.e., food pellets on equal fixed-interval [FI] schedules) was the same for the choice and no-choice conditions. Similarly, clinical investigations have shown that providing choice-making opportunities to individuals with developmental disabilities can result in marked increases in appropriate behavior or decreases in aberrant behavior (e.g., Dyer, Dunlap, & Winterling, 1990; Mason et al., 1989; Parsons, Reid, Reynolds, & Bumgarner, 1990). However, in most clinical investigations on this topic, the consequences in the choice and no-choice conditions were not equated. Thus, it is possible that the effects were partially or completely due to the fact that the stimuli available in the choice condition were more highly preferred than those presented in the no-choice condition. The investigations by Lerman et al. (1997) and Fisher, Thompson, Piazza, Crosland, and Gotjen (1997) are noteworthy because they equated the consequences delivered in the choice and no-choice conditions; however, one study used a single-operant arrangement (Lerman et al.) and the other used a concurrent arrangement (Fisher et al.).

Lerman et al. (1997) and Fisher et al. (1997) equated the consequences in the choice and no-choice conditions by yoking the reinforcers selected by the therapist in the no-choice condition to selections that had been previously made by the participant in the choice condition. In the choice condition, simple free-operant responses (e.g., stamping the date on paper, switch pressing) were reinforced on FR schedules (usually an FR 1 schedule). When the response requirement was completed, the therapist presented two reinforcers, and the participant was allowed to choose and consume one of them. The no-choice condition was similar to the choice condition except that the therapist selected the reinforcers for the participant (i.e., on a schedule that was yoked to choices the participant had made in the previous session).

Lerman et al. (1997) did not find an effect of choice (i.e., the rates of responding were equivalent in the two conditions). By contrast, Fisher et al. (1997) found a clear effect of choice, perhaps because a concurrent-operants arrangement was used. That is, participants showed almost exclusive responding on the option that allowed them to choose the reinforcers when the consequences in the choice and no-choice conditions were equated.

The participants in the Fisher et al. (1997) study were higher functioning than those in the Lerman et al. (1997) study, and this may have contributed to the differential findings. Thus, it is unclear whether a concurrent arrangement would have detected an effect of choice among the participants of the Lerman et al. investigation. On the other hand, it is doubtful that Fisher et al. would have detected an effect of choice with their participants had they used a single-operant arrangement, because choice affected relative but not absolute rates. As previously mentioned, relative response rates are often a more sensitive measure of reinforcement value than are absolute response rates. In a concurrent arrangement, relative response rates allow detection of a difference in reinforcement value above and beyond that which is necessary to maintain a response in a single-operant arrangement. In a concurrent arrangement, the relative response rates shift toward the response option associated with the more favorable outcome even when absolute response rates remain unchanged (because of a ceiling effect or other factors).

Assessing client preferences for different treatments. Schwartz and Baer (1991) suggested that allowing individuals to choose among concurrently available behavioral programs may be the most valid method of assessing the social acceptability of those programs. However, most investigations on the social acceptability of behavioral treatments used with persons with developmental disabilities have employed indirect measures (e.g., rating scales; Miltenberger, 1990). In addition, these tools have generally been used to assess caregiver (e.g., parents, teachers) rather than client preferences for the treatment. An investigation by Hanley, Piazza, Fisher, Contrucci, and Maglieri (1997) provided an example of how a modification of a concurrent-chains procedure can be used to directly assess a client's preference for one treatment over another.

A chain schedule consists of two or more simple schedules combined together in a fixed sequence (e.g., VI 30 s followed by VI 90 s). Each simple schedule is correlated with a unique discriminative stimulus (e.g., a VI 30-s schedule correlated with a green light followed by a VI 90-s schedule correlated with a red light). The first schedule in the chain is called the initial link, and the last one is called the terminal link. In a concurrent-chains procedure, two or more concurrent responses are each correlated with an independent chain schedule (e.g., a VI 30-s VR 10 chain schedule on the right key, and a VI 30-s FR 10 chain schedule on the left key).

Concurrent-chains procedures have been used to evaluate an individual's preferences for different schedules of reinforcement (e.g., do individuals prefer variable over fixed schedules?). This is done by making the initial links in each chain identical (both VI 30-s schedules) and presenting the schedules of interest in the two terminal links (VR 10 vs. FR 10 schedules). If the individual prefers one terminal-link schedule over the other (e.g., prefers a VR 10 to an FR 10), then more responding will occur on the initial link that produces the preferred schedule (cf. Herrnstein, 1964).

Hanley et al. (1997) used a variation of a concurrent-chains procedure to evaluate preferences for three different treatments developed to decrease the problem behavior of 2 individuals with developmental disabilities: functional communication training with extinction (FCT+EXT), noncontingent reinforcement with extinction (NCR+EXT), and extinction alone (EXT). All three treatments were based on the results of a functional analysis (Iwata, Dorsey, Slifer, Bauman, & Richman, 1982/1994), which indicated that the participants' problem behaviors were maintained by attention. During all three treatments, the contingency between problem behavior and attention was discontinued (i.e., extinction). In addition, attention was delivered contingent on an appropriate communication response during FCT and on a time-based schedule during NCR. In the initial links of the concurrent-chains procedure, three independent FR 1 schedules were each correlated with separate responses (pressing one of three switches) and with unique discriminative stimuli (three colors). Pressing one switch resulted in 2 min of FCT+EXT, pressing a second switch produced 2 min of NCR+EXT, and pressing the third led to 2 min of EXT. Differential rates of responding in the initial links demonstrated that both participants had a clear preference for FCT+EXT over either NCR+EXT or EXT alone.

The variation of a concurrent-chains procedure described by Hanley et al. (1997) represents a unique method of assessing social acceptability, one that allows individuals to have input into the selection of the behavioral treatments they receive, even if they are unable to express their preferences verbally. It also provides a means of assessing specific treatment components (differential reinforcement of other vs. alternative behavior) to determine which ones have the largest effect on an individual's preferences.

CLINICAL INTERVENTIONS THAT INVOLVE CHOICE ARRANGEMENTS

The focus of the clinical investigations reviewed thus far has been on assessing an individual's preferences for various stimuli or evaluating the reinforcing effects of a stimulus relative to the effects of other concurrently available stimuli. In the following section, we discuss studies that have incorporated choice arrangements into clinical interventions designed to reduce problem behavior.

Choice and Functional Communication Training

A number of behavior analysts have conceptualized the treatment of aberrant behavior using functional communication training (FCT) or similar differential reinforcement treatments in terms of concurrent operants (e.g., Carr, 1988; Fisher et al., 1993; R. H. Horner & Day, 1991; Mace & Roberts, 1993). FCT is designed to reduce problem behavior, is based on the results of a functional analysis, and is used primarily when the functional analysis determines that the aberrant behavior is maintained by social contingencies (e.g., attention, escape from demands). During FCT, the reinforcer that is responsible for behavioral maintenance is delivered contingent on an alternative (communicative) response. In most cases, FCT has been combined with extinction (i.e., discontinuation of reinforcement for aberrant behavior; e.g., Lalli, Casey, & Kates, 1995), but in other cases it has not (concurrent reinforcement of communication and aberrant behavior; e.g., Fisher et al., 1993; R. H. Horner & Day, 1991). There are certain clinical situations in which placing aberrant behavior on extinction is impractical or even dangerous (cf. Pace, Ivancic, & Jefferson, 1994; Piazza, Moes, & Fisher, 1996). In these cases, it may be critical to find alternative responses and corresponding reinforcers that compete effectively with aberrant behavior and its correlated reinforcer. The major goal of conceptualizing differential reinforcement procedures in terms of concurrent operants is to help to "stack the deck" in favor of the appropriate alternative response by making it less effortful and correlating it with denser, more immediate, or higher quality reinforcement (see Mace & Roberts, 1993, for a more in-depth discussion of how response effort and reinforcement rate, immediacy, and quality can affect treatment selection).

An investigation by R. H. Horner and Day (1991) provides a nice example of how a concurrent-operants arrangement may help to evaluate how response effort and reinforcement rate and immediacy can influence the effectiveness of differential reinforcement procedures like FCT. The participants were 3 individuals with severe to profound mental retardation; one also had cerebral palsy and another also had autism. In each of three experiments, participants received a break from work (e.g., 30-s break from toothbrushing) or assistance with the task (e.g., the therapist pointing to the correct answer) contingent on an appropriate mand (e.g., signing "break") or problem behavior.

In Experiment 1, the amount of effort required for the FCT response was systematically manipulated. In two experimental conditions, the individual could escape the work task for approximately 30 s to 45 s through either aggression or an appropriate mand (i.e., concurrent FR 1 FR 1 schedules). However, in one condition, the appropriate mand was a single word (signing "break") and, in the other, it was a longer sentence that required more effort (signing "I want to go, please"). The participant allocated his responding almost exclusively to problem behavior when the choice was between an effortful communication response and aggression. By contrast, when the less effortful mand was available, the individual allocated his responding almost exclusively to this option, and aggression was maintained at near-zero levels. These results differ from those obtained by Chung (1965), who manipulated response effort with pigeons by systematically altering the amount of physical force required to complete a key-peck response, and by Mace et al. (1996), who manipulated response effort by systematically altering the difficulty level of two concurrently available sets of math problems. This difference may be partially due to the fact that these latter two investigations used concurrent VI schedules, whereas ratio schedules were in effect in the R. H. Horner and Day (1991) study. The more effortful response (signing a complete sentence) in the Horner and Day investigation probably took more time to complete than the less effortful one (signing a single word), which probably lowered the rate of reinforcement, given that concurrent-ratio schedules were used.

In Experiment 2 of the R. H. Horner and Day (1991) study, the rate of reinforcement for the alternative mand was manipulated (FR 1 vs. FR 3), and predictable effects were obtained; responding was allocated to self-injurious behavior (SIB) when the schedule for the mand was an FR 3 and was allocated toward the mand when the schedule was an FR 1. Finally, in Experiment 3, the effects of shorter versus longer reinforcement delays for the FCT response (a break after 1 s vs. 20 s) were compared while problem behavior continued to produce immediate reinforcement in each condition. As expected, the rates of problem behavior were much higher when the alternative mand was associated with the longer delay than when it was associated with a shorter delay.

Peck et al. (1996) extended the findings of R. H. Horner and Day (1991) by showing that their participants displayed high rates of the FCT response and low rates of problem behavior when the former response was correlated with a better outcome (i.e., a higher quality reinforcer that was presented for a longer duration). Piazza et al. (1997) similarly found that participants allocated their responding toward compliance when it produced higher quality reinforcement than was produced by problem behavior. However, as the schedule of reinforcement for compliance was gradually thinned from an FR 1 to schedules more typical of most training situations (e.g., FR 10), it was necessary to include both higher quality reinforcement for compliance (e.g., escape plus attention) and extinction for aberrant behavior in all three cases.

Choice and Aberrant Behavior Maintained by Automatic Reinforcement

Certain aberrant behaviors (e.g., pica, stereotypies, some forms of SIB) persist in the absence of apparent social or environmental contingencies. One operant hypothesis for this phenomenon is that these behaviors produce their reinforcement automatically (Skinner, 1953; see Vollmer, 1994, for a review). For example, it has been suggested that pica and rumination may sometimes be maintained by the oral stimulation that is produced by these responses (Favell, McGimsey, & Schell, 1982; Rast, Johnston, Lubin, & Ellinger-Allen, 1988). Similarly, it has been hypothesized that blind individuals display SIB involving the eyes more often than do other populations because pressure to the eyes (e.g., through eye pressing or eye poking) can stimulate the visual cortex (Hyman, Fisher, Mercugliano, & Cataldo, 1990; Kennedy & Souza, 1995).

One approach to treating behavior hypothesized to be maintained by automatic reinforcement is to provide a way for the individual to obtain the putative reinforcer through a more appropriate response. For example, Favell et al. (1982) hypothesized that the pica of 3 clients was maintained by the oral stimulation it produced. They then provided the participants with materials that could be used to produce benign but similar forms of oral stimulation (popcorn and toys that could be mouthed and chewed but not swallowed). Consistent with the automatic reinforcement hypothesis, pica decreased when oral stimulation was available with these alternative materials. In addition, if the alternative materials produced additional forms of reinforcement (e.g., a higher quality reinforcement due to the taste of the popcorn), this may have increased the likelihood of switching from the aberrant to the more appropriate target behaviors.

A second approach to the treatment of aberrant behavior that persists in the absence of social consequences is to provide the individual with one or more alternative forms of stimulation that might effectively compete with the putative reinforcer for aberrant behavior. Viewed from a choice perspective, responding should shift toward an alternative form of stimulation if it produces a higher quality form of reinforcement than does the aberrant behavior (given that both forms of stimulation are available immediately and continuously and require similar amounts of effort). For example, Berkson and Mason (1965) showed that stereotypic behavior decreased when the participants were given toys and attention. R. D. Horner (1980) developed a similar treatment for aberrant behavior called *environmental enrichment* wherein multiple toys and objects were available noncontingently. Vollmer, Marcus, and LeBlanc (1994) showed that environmental enrichment more effectively reduced aberrant behavior that persisted in the absence of social contingencies when the toys and objects presented were ones that had been identified by a choice assessment (Fisher et al., 1992) as highly preferred relative to ones that were less preferred. Thus, a choice assessment may be used to identify high-quality reinforcers that may be more likely to compete with the putative automatic reinforcement associated with aberrant behavior.

Several recent investigations have examined the extent to which stimuli evaluated during a preference assessment effectively competed with aberrant behavior that persisted in the absence of social contingencies (Derby et al., 1995; Piazza, Fisher, Hanley, Hilker, & Derby, 1996; Ringdahl, Vollmer, Marcus, & Roane, 1997). In each investigation, there was one dependent measure (e.g., approach responses, duration of interaction) that was designed to assess the participants' preferences for the various stimuli presented. In addition, each investigation measured the level of aberrant behavior that occurred each time a stimulus or group of stimuli was presented. In most cases, the stimuli associated with high levels of interaction and low levels of SIB were more effective than other stimuli when used during treatment. However, an investigation by Shore, Iwata, DeLeon, Kahng, and Smith (1997) illustrates how relative response rates during a free-operant arrangement may not always predict the effects of differential reinforcement contingencies.

In the first of a three-experiment investigation, Shore et al. (1997) showed that SIB persisted in the absence of social contingencies and also that object manipulation competed with SIB when both were freely and continuously available. However, in Experiment 2, contingent access to the objects was not effective reinforcement for the absence of SIB during a differential-reinforcement-of-other-behavior (DRO) intervention, even when the length of the DRO interval was small (absence of SIB for 5 s) relative to the length of the reinforcement interval (60 s of access to the object). The authors then completed a third experiment that helped to clarify why a relatively large amount of a more preferred activity (60 s of object manipulation) did not function as reinforcement for the brief absence (5 s) of a less preferred response (SIB). In this experiment, both responses were concurrently and continuously available, but the amount of effort required to obtain the object was systematically manipulated while the response effort associated with SIB remained constant. This was accomplished by tying the object to a string, anchoring the other end of the string in front of the individual, and then systematically altering the length of the string. The length of the string determined how far the individual had to bend over in order to manipulate the object (i.e., the shorter the string, the more the individual had to bend). The results showed that just a small increment in response effort required to obtain the object resulted in a shift in preference away from object manipulation toward SIB.

It is worth noting that the results obtained by Shore et al. (1997) in Experiment 2 are inconsistent with the predictions of Premack's principle (1962) and the response deprivation hypothesis. Each of these theoretical formulations predicts reinforcement effects based on the relative rates of two concurrently available responses observed in a free-operant assessment (i.e., no programmed contingency for either response). This was also the approach used by Derby et al. (1995), Piazza, Fisher, Hanley, Hilker, and Derby (1996), and Ringdahl et al. (1997). However, relative response rates during a free-operant assessment may not predict the effects of treatments that involve manipulation of other response and reinforcement parameters (e.g., reinforcement delay, response effort).

Choice arrangements may be useful not only for identifying stimuli that effectively compete with aberrant behavior that persists in the absence of social consequences but also for identifying the specific source of automatic reinforcement. Piazza, Hanley, and Fisher (1996) conducted a series of analyses to indirectly assess whether a young man's pica of cigarette butts was maintained by the effects of nicotine consumption. A functional analysis showed that the response was maintained without social consequences. Using a choice assessment, the authors confirmed that the participant preferred tobacco over the other components of the cigarettes (e.g., paper, filter, butts with herbs instead of tobacco). This assessment also helped to rule out the alternative hypothesis that his pica was maintained by the oral stimulation it produced, because the herbal butts would have served this function equally well. Finally, a treatment that was designed to interrupt the hypothesized response–reinforcer relationship reduced pica.

CONCLUDING COMMENTS

Basic studies have produced both conceptual and mathematical formulations of how several key variables (e.g., reinforcement rate, immediacy, quality) influence choice responding under laboratory conditions. The extent to which these formulations can be used to predict or control human responding in natural settings has been the topic of some debate (e.g., Fuqua, 1984; Horne & Lowe, 1993; Meyerson & Hale, 1984).

Fuqua (1984) argued that there are a number of differences between laboratory settings and natural human environments that limit the relevance of findings from basic research on matching to applied settings. For example, Fuqua contended that CODs are often necessary to produce matching but are rarely present in applied settings. However, the results of more recent applied and bridge studies suggest that the effects and necessity of CODs for matching to occur under laboratory and natural conditions may be more similar than Fuqua suggested. CODs have often (but not always) been required to produce matching, but their necessity does not seem to depend on whether (a) the participants are human or nonhuman (cf. Conger & Killeen, 1974; Herrnstein, 1961; Schroeder & Holland, 1969; Rachlin & Baum, 1972), (b) the setting is a laboratory or a natural human environment (cf. Baum, 1975; Conger & Killeen, 1974), or (c) the target response is contrived or more socially meaningful (cf. Horne & Lowe, 1993; Mace et al., 1994).

In basic and bridge studies on matching, CODs and other adjunctive procedures (e.g., instructions, timers) are often used to facilitate discrimination of the relative reinforcement rates that are associated with concurrent VI schedules or to penalize adventitious reinforcement of switching from one response to the other. CODs have similarly been used during applied studies on FCT with extinction to prevent adventitious reinforcement of problem behavior (e.g., Lalli et al., 1995). When problem behavior is treated with FCT, participants will sometimes rapidly switch from the inappropriate (e.g., SIB) to the appropriate (e.g., signing "break") target response, and a response chain consisting of these two responses may be adventitiously reinforced if a COD is not used (e.g., Fisher et al., 1993). CODs are usually unnecessary in both basic and applied studies when the schedules associated with each concurrent response are easily discriminated by the participants. For example, Fisher et al. (1997) used concurrent VI schedules to evaluate preferences for choice over no-choice conditions, and a COD was not necessary (presumably because the contingencies associated with each response were clear to the participants). Thus, based on currently available data, it appears that the arrangement (e.g., concurrent schedules that are not readily discriminated) rather than the setting (laboratory vs. natural), participant (human vs. nonhuman), or type of response (contrived vs. socially meaningful) determines whether CODs or other adjunctive procedures are necessary.

Fuqua (1984) also argued that the applied relevance of matching theory may be limited because the concurrent responses evaluated in basic studies were almost always topographically identical and mutually exclusive. By contrast, humans often allocate their time among different response topographies and can emit multiple responses and consume the corresponding reinforcers simultaneously (e.g., carry on a conversation while listening to music). However, in the majority of the applied investigations reviewed above, participants allocated their responding to one of two topographically distinct response options even though it was possible for both responses to occur simultaneously (e.g., R. H. Horner & Day, 1991; Piazza et al., 1997; Shore et al., 1997; Vollmer et al., 1994). Thus, it appears that there may be many situations in which matching theory is applicable to concurrent arrangements in natural human settings even when the target responses are dissimilar and not mutually exclusive.

Fuqua (1984) also pointed out that the reinforcers and corresponding schedules that maintain responding in applied settings may not be easily identified, thus making it difficult to apply the quantitative formulations of matching theory. As a result, Fuqua suggested that basic research on concurrent responses may have greater applicability on a qualitative rather than on a quantitative level. In fact, only a few of the studies reviewed above included mathematical analyses of the extent to which relative response rates matched relative reinforcement rates, and those that did were specifically designed to test the applicability of the matching equation to human responding (e.g., Horne & Lowe, 1993; Mace et al., 1994). Instead, most of the applied studies reviewed here used matching and choice principles on a more qualitative level. In general, the goals of these investigations were to identify preferred stimuli (e.g., DeLeon & Iwata, 1996; Piazza, Fisher, Hagopian, Bowman, & Toole, 1996), to evaluate reinforcer and schedule preferences or effects (e.g., Fisher et al., 1997; Hanley et al., 1997), or to treat problem behavior (e.g., R. H. Horner & Day, 1991; Shore et al., 1997). The application of matching or choice principles on a qualitative level clearly facilitated accomplishment of these goals; whether a more quantitative approach would have provided additional benefit remains uncertain.

There are undoubtedly many ways in which laboratory analogues fail to capture all of the complexities of human choice responding in more natural settings, and Fuqua's (1984) general admonition regarding the need to exercise caution when applying matching theory outside of the laboratory remains prudent. In fact, even in the applied studies reviewed above, choice responding was evaluated under analogue conditions in which the experimenters programmed specific reinforcers and schedules for each target response (e.g., DeLeon et al., 1997; Fisher et al., 1997). Thus, the extent to which the concurrent arrangements used in these applied studies accurately mimicked the schedules that maintained the target responses in the participants' natural environments remains unknown. Nevertheless, the applied and bridge studies reviewed above provide considerable empirical evidence regarding the applied relevance of choice and matching formulations of responding. More specifically, the results of these studies suggest that the variables that affect choice responding with nonhumans in the laboratory (i.e., response effort and reinforcement rate, immediacy, and quality) often operate in a similar manner in applied settings and with socially meaningful human responses. Thus, although Fuqua's concerns regarding factors that distinguish laboratory conditions from applied settings are quite reasonable, the data now available suggest that what could be, in principle, important differences between the two settings are, in practice, often not serious problems.

The applied literature on choice responding and matching is still relatively small in comparison with the corresponding basic literature on this topic. As the principles derived from basic research receive additional field testing in natural human environments, the applied technology of choice responding that develops will in some ways be similar to and in other ways be different from the basic knowledge base on this topic. We hope that the similarities will lead to more accurate and effective clinical procedures, and that the differences will spark additional basic and bridge studies that further our understanding of human choice responding.

REFERENCES

Ainslie, G. (1974). Impulse control in pigeons. *Journal of the Experimental Analysis of Behavior, 21,* 485–489.

Baum, W. M. (1974). On two types of deviation from the matching law: Bias and undermatching. *Journal of the Experimental Anlaysis of Behavior, 22,* 231–242.

Baum, W. M. (1975). Time allocation in human vigilance. *Journal of the Experimental Analysis of Behavior, 23,* 45–53.

Baum, W. M. (1979). Matching, undermatching, and overmatching in studies of choice. *Journal of the Experimental Analysis of Behavior, 32,* 269–281.

Baum, W. M. (1982). Choice, changeover, and travel. *Journal of the Experimental Analysis of Behavior, 38,* 35–49.

Baum, W. M., & Rachlin, H. C. (1969). Choice as time allocation. *Journal of the Experimental Analysis of Behavior, 12,* 861–874.

Berkson, G., & Mason, W. A. (1965). Stereotyped movements of mental defectives: 4. The effects of toys and the character of the acts. *American Journal of Mental Deficiency, 70,* 511–524.

Bradshaw, C. M., Ruddle, H. V., & Szabadi, E. (1981). Studies of concurrent performances in humans. In C. M. Bradshaw, E. Szabadi, & C. F. Lowe (Eds.), *Quantification of steady-state operant behaviour* (pp. 79–90). Amsterdam: Elsevier/ North Holland Biomedical Press.

Bradshaw, C. M., Szabadi, E., & Bevan, P. (1976). Human variable-interval performance. *Psychological Reports, 38,* 881–882.

Carr, E. G. (1988). Functional equivalence as a mechanism of response generalization. In R. Horner, R. L. Koegel, & G. Dunlap (Eds.), *Generalization and maintenance: Life-style changes in applied settings* (pp. 221–241). Baltimore: Paul H. Brookes.

Carr, E. G., & McDowell, J. J. (1980). Social control of self-injurious behavior of organic etiology. *Behavior Therapy, 11,* 402–409.

Catania, A. C., & Sagvolden, T. (1980). Preference for free choice over forced choice in pigeons. *Journal of the Experimental Analysis of Behavior, 34,* 77–86.

Chung, S. (1965). Effects of effort on response rate. *Journal of the Experimental Analysis of Behavior, 8,* 1–7.

Conger, R., & Killeen, P. (1974). Use of concurrent operants in small group research. *Pacific Sociological Review, 17,* 399–416.

DeLeon, I. G., & Iwata, B. A. (1996). Evaluation of a multiple-stimulus presentation format for assessing reinforcer preferences. *Journal of Applied Behavior Analysis, 29,* 519–533.

DeLeon, I. G., Iwata, B. A., Goh, H., & Worsdell, A. S. (1997). Emergence of reinforcer preference as a function of schedule requirements and stimulus similarity. *Journal of Applied Behavior Analysis, 30,* 439–449.

Derby, K. M., Wacker, D. P., Andelman, M., Berg, W., Drew, J., Asmus, J., Prouty, A., & Laffey, P. (1995). Two measures of preference during forced-choice assessments. *Journal of Applied Behavior Analysis, 28,* 345–346.

Dyer, K., Dunlap, G., & Winterling, V. (1990). Effects of choice making on the serious problem behaviors of students with severe handicaps. *Journal of Applied Behavior Analysis, 23,* 515–524.

Favell, J. E., McGimsey, J. F., & Schell, R. M. (1982). Treatment of self-injury by providing alternate sensory activities. *Analysis and Intervention in Developmental Disabilities, 2,* 83–104.

Fechner, G. T. (1966). *Elements of psychophysics.* (H. E. Adler, D. H. Howes, & E. G. Boring, Eds.). New York: Holt, Rinehart & Winston. (Original work published in 1860)

Fisher, W. W., Piazza, C. C., Bowman, L. G., & Amari, A. (1996). Integrating caregiver report with a systematic choice assessment. *American Journal on Mental Retardation, 101,* 15–25.

Fisher, W., Piazza, C. C., Bowman, L. G., Hagopian, L. H., Owens, J. C., & Slevin, I. (1992). A comparison of two approaches for identifying reinforcers for persons with severe and profound disabilities. *Journal of Applied Behavior Analysis, 25,* 491–498.

Fisher, W., Piazza, C., Cataldo, M., Harrell, R., Jefferson, G., & Conner, R. (1993). Functional communication training with and without extinction and punishment. *Journal of Applied Behavior Analysis, 26,* 23–26.

Fisher, W. W., Thompson, R. H., Piazza, C. C., Crosland, K., & Gotjen, D. (1997). On the relative reinforcing effects of choice and differential consequences. *Journal of Applied Behavior Analysis, 30,* 423–438.

Flora, S. R., & Pavlik, W. B. (1992). Human self-control and the density of reinforcement. *Journal of the Experimental Analysis of Behavior, 57,* 201–208.

Fuqua, R. W. (1984). Comments on the applied relevance of the matching law. *Journal of Applied Behavior Analysis, 17,* 381–386.

Hake, D. F. (1982). The basic-applied continuum and the possible evolution of human operant social and verbal research. *The Behavior Analyst, 5,* 21–28.

Hanley, G. P., Piazza, C. C., Fisher, W. W., Contrucci, S. A., & Maglieri, K. A. (1997). Evaluation of client preference for function-based treatment packages. *Journal of Applied Behavior Analysis, 30,* 459–473.

Herrnstein, R. J. (1961). Relative and absolute strength of response as a function of frequency of reinforcement. *Journal of the Experimental Analysis of Behavior, 4,* 267–272.

Herrnstein, R. J. (1964). Aperiodicity as a factor in choice. *Journal of the Experimental Analysis of Behavior, 7,* 179–182.

Herrnstein, R. J., & Loveland, D. H. (1975). Maximizing and matching on concurrent ratio schedules. *Journal of the Experimental Analysis of Behavior, 24,* 107–116.

Horne, P. J., & Lowe, C. F. (1993). Determinants of human performance on concurrent schedules. *Journal of the Experimental Analysis of Behavior, 59,* 29–60.

Horner, R. D. (1980). The effects of an environmental "enrichment" program on the behavior of institutionalized profoundly retarded children. *Journal of Applied Behavior Analysis, 13,* 473–491.

Horner, R. H., & Day, M. D. (1991). The effects of response efficiency on functionally equivalent competing behaviors. *Journal of Applied Behavior Analysis, 24,* 719–732.

Hyman, S. L., Fisher, W., Mercugliano, M., & Cataldo, M. F. (1990). Children with self-injurious behavior. *Pediatrics, 85,* 437–441.

Iwata, B. A., Dorsey, M. F., Slifer, K. J., Bauman, K. E., & Richman, G. S. (1994). Toward a functional analysis of self-injury. *Journal of Applied Behavior Analysis, 27,* 197–209. (Reprinted from *Analysis and Intervention in Developmental Disabilities, 2,* 3–20, 1982)

Kennedy, C. H., & Souza, G. (1995). Functional analysis and treatment of eye poking. *Journal of Applied Behavior Analysis, 28,* 27–37.

Lalli, J. S., Casey, S., & Kates, K. (1995). Reducing escape behavior and increasing task completion with functional communication training, extinction, and response chaining. *Journal of Applied Behavior Analysis, 28,* 261–268.

Lerman, D. C., Iwata, B. A., Rainville, B., Adelinis, J., Crosland, K., & Kogan, J. (1997). Effects of reinforcement choice on task responding in individuals with developmental disabilities. *Journal of Applied Behavior Analysis, 30,* 411–422.

Logue, A. W., Forzano, L. B., & Tobin, H. (1992). Independence of reinforcer amount and delay: The generalized matching law and self-control in humans. *Learning and Motivation, 23,* 326–342.

Logue, A. W., & King, G. R. (1991). Self-control and impulsiveness in adult humans when food is the reinforcer. *Appetite, 17,* 105–120.

Logue, A. W., Peña-Correal, T. E., Rodriguez, M. L., & Kabela, E. (1986). Self-control in adult humans: Variation in positive reinforcer amount and delay. *Journal of the Experimental Analysis of Behavior, 46,* 159–173.

Lowe, C. F., & Horne, P. J. (1985). On the generality of behavioural principles: Human choice and the matching law. In C. F. Lowe, M. Richelle, D. E. Blackman, & C. M. Bradshaw (Eds.), *Behaviour analysis and contemporary psychology* (pp. 97–115). London: Erlbaum.

Mace, F. C., Neef, N. A., Shade, D., & Mauro, B. C. (1994). Limited matching on concurrent-schedule reinforcement of academic behavior. *Journal of Applied Behavior Analysis, 27,* 585–596.

Mace, F. C., Neef, N. A., Shade, D., & Mauro, B. C. (1996). Effects of problem difficulty and reinforcer quality on time allocated to concurrent arithmetic problems. *Journal of Applied Behavior Analysis, 29,* 11–24.

Mace, F. C., & Roberts, M. L. (1993). Factors affecting selection of behavioral interventions. In J. Reichle & D. P. Wacker (Eds.), *Communicative alternatives to challenging behavior: Integrating functional assessment and intervention strategies* (pp. 113–133). Baltimore, MD: Paul H. Brookes.

Martens, B. K., & Houk, J. L. (1989). The application of Herrnstein's law of effect to disruptive and on-task behavior of a retarded adolescent girl. *Journal of the Experimental Analysis of Behavior, 51,* 17–27.

Mason, S. A., McGee, G. G., Farmer-Dougan, V., & Risley, T. R. (1989). A practical strategy for ongoing reinforcer assessment. *Journal of Applied Behavior Analysis, 22,* 171–179.

McDowell, J. J. (1988). Matching theory in natural human environments. *The Behavior Analyst, 11,* 95–109.

McDowell, J. J. (1989). Two modern developments in matching theory. *The Behavior Analyst, 12,* 153–166.

Meyerson, J., & Hale, S. (1984). Practical implications of the matching law. *Journal of Applied Behavior Anlaysis, 17,* 367–380.

Millar, A., & Navarick, D. J. (1984). Self-control and choice in humans: Effects of video game playing as a positive reinforcer. *Learning and Motivation, 15,* 203–218.

Miltenberger, R. G. (1990). Assessment of treatment acceptability: A review of the literature. *Topics in Early Childhood Special Education, 10,* 24–38.

Navarick, D. J. (1986). Human impulsivity and choice: A challenge to traditional operant methodology. *Psychological Record, 36,* 343–356.

Neef, N. A., Mace, F. C., & Shade, D. (1993). Impulsivity in students with serious emotional disturbance: The interactive effects of reinforcer rate, delay, and quality. *Journal of Applied Behavior Analysis, 26,* 37–52.

Neef, N. A., Mace, F. C., Shea, M. C., & Shade, D. (1992). Effects of reinforcer rate and reinforcer quality on time allocation: Extensions of matching theory to educational settings. *Journal of Applied Behavior Analysis, 25,* 691–699.

Neef, N. A., Shade, D., & Miller, M. S. (1994). Assessing influential dimensions of reinforcers on choice in students with serious emotional disturbance. *Journal of Applied Behavior Analysis, 27,* 575–583.

Northup, J., George, T., Jones, K., Broussard, C., & Vollmer, T. R. (1996). A comparison of reinforcer assessment methods: The utility of verbal and pictorial choice procedures. *Journal of Applied Behavior Analysis, 29,* 201–212.

Pace, G. M., Ivancic, M. T., Edwards, G. L., Iwata, B. A., & Page, T. J. (1985). Assessment of stimulus preference and reinforcer value with profoundly retarded individuals. *Journal of Applied Behavior Analysis, 18,* 249–255.

Pace, G. M., Ivancic, M. T., & Jefferson, G. (1994). Stimulus fading as treatment for obscenity in a brain-injured adult. *Journal of Applied Behavior Analysis, 27,* 301–305.

Parsons, M. B., Reid, D. H., Reynolds, J., & Bumgarner, M. (1990). Effects of chosen versus assigned jobs on the work performance of persons with severe handicaps. *Journal of Applied Behavior Analysis, 23,* 253–258.

Peck, S. M., Wacker, D. P., Berg, W. K., Cooper, L. J., Brown, K. A., Richman, D., McComas, J. J., Frischmeyer, P., & Millard, T. (1996). Choice-making treatment of young children's severe behavior problems. *Journal of Applied Behavior Analysis, 29,* 263–290.

Piazza, C. C., Fisher, W. W., Hagopian, L. H., Bowman, L. B., & Toole, L. (1996). Using a choice assessment to predict reinforcer effectiveness. *Journal of Applied Behavior Analysis, 29,* 1–9.

Piazza, C. C., Fisher, W. W., Hanley, G. P., Hilker, K., & Derby, K. M. (1996). A preliminary procedure for predicting the positive and negative effects of reinforcement-based procedures. *Journal of Applied Behavior Analysis, 29,* 137–152.

Piazza, C. C., Fisher, W. W., Hanley, G. P., Remick, M. L., Contrucci, S. A., & Aitken, T. A. (1997). The use of positive and negative reinforcement in the treatment of escape-maintained destructive behavior. *Journal of Applied Behavior Analysis, 30,* 279–298.

Piazza, C. C., Hanley, G. P., & Fisher, W. W. (1996). Functional analysis and treatment of cigarette pica. *Journal of Applied Behavior Analysis, 29,* 437–450.

Piazza, C. C., Moes, D. R., & Fisher, W. W. (1996). Differential reinforcement of alternative behavior and demand fading in the treatment of escape-maintained destructive behavior. *Journal of Applied Behavior Analysis, 29,* 569–572.

Pierce, W. D., & Epling, W. F. (1995). The applied importance of research on the matching law. *Journal of Applied Behavior Analysis, 28,* 237–241.

Premack, D. (1962). Reversibility of the reinforcement relation. *Science, 136,* 255–257.

Rachlin, H., & Baum, W. M. (1972). Effects of alternative reinforcement: Does the source matter? *Journal of the Experimental Analysis of Behavior, 18,* 231–241.

Rachlin, H., & Green, L. (1972). Commitment, choice, and self-control. *Journal of the Experimental Analysis of Behavior, 17,* 15–22.

Rast, J., Johnston, J. M., Lubin, D., & Ellinger-Allen, J. (1988). Effect of premeal chewing on ruminative behavior. *American Journal on Mental Retardation, 93,* 67–74.

Ringdahl, J. E., Vollmer, T. R., Marcus, B. A., & Roane, H. S. (1997). An analogue evaluation of environmental enrichment: The role of stimulus preference. *Journal of Applied Behavior Analysis, 30,* 203–216.

Schroeder, S. R., & Holland, J. G. (1969). Reinforcement of eye movement with concurrent schedules. *Journal of the Experimental Analysis of Behavior, 12,* 897–903.

Schwartz, I. S., & Baer, D. M. (1991). Social validity assessments: Is current practice state of the art? *Journal of Applied Behavior Analysis, 24,* 189–204.

Schweitzer, J. B., & Sulzer-Azaroff, B. (1988). Self-control: Teaching tolerance for delay in impulsive children. *Journal of the Experimental Analysis of Behavior, 50,* 173–186.

Schweitzer, J. B., & Sulzer-Azaroff, B. (1995). Self-control in boys with attention deficit hyperactivity disorder: Effects of added stimulation and time. *Journal of Child Psychology and Psychiatry and Allied Disciplines, 36,* 671–686.

Shah, K., Bradshaw, C. M., & Szabadi, E. (1989). Performance of humans in concurrent variable-ratio variable-ratio schedules of monetary reinforcement. *Psychological Reports, 65,* 515–520.

Shore, B. A., Iwata, B. A., DeLeon, I. G., Kahng, S., & Smith, R. G. (1997). An analysis of reinforcer substitutability using object manipulation and self-injury as competing responses. *Journal of Applied Behavior Analysis, 30,* 21–41.

Skinner, B. F. (1953). *Science and human behavior.* New York: Macmillan.

Solnick, J. V., Kannenberg, C. H., Eckerman, D. A., & Waller, M. B. (1980). An experimental analysis of impulsivity and impulse control in humans. *Learning and Motivation, 11,* 61–77.

Sonuga-Barke, E. J., Lea, S. E. G., & Webley, P. (1989). The development of adaptive choice in a self-control paradigm. *Journal of the Experimental Analysis of Behavior, 51,* 77–85.

Sonuga-Barke, E. J., Taylor, E., Sembi, S., & Smith, J. (1992). Hyperactivity and delay aversion: I. The effect of delay on choice. *Journal of Child Psychology and Psychiatry and Allied Disciplines, 33,* 387–398.

Thurstone, L. L. (1927). A law of comparative judgment. *Psychological Review, 34,* 273–286.

Tustin, R. D. (1994). Preference for reinforcers under varying schedule arrangements: A behavioral economic analysis. *Journal of Applied Behavior Analysis, 27,* 597–606.

Vollmer, T. R. (1994). The concept of automatic reinforcement: Implications for behavioral research in developmental disabilities. *Research in Developmental Disabilities, 15,* 187–207.

Vollmer, T. R., Marcus, B. A., & LeBlanc, L. (1994). Treatment of self-injury and hand mouthing following inconclusive functional analyses. *Journal of Applied Behavior Analysis, 27,* 331–344.

Wacker, D. P. (1996). Behavior analysis research in *JABA*: A need for studies that bridge basic and applied research. *Experimental Analysis of Human Behavior Bulletin, 14,* 11–14.

Williams, B. A. (1994). Reinforcement and choice. In N. J. Mackintosh (Ed.), *Animal learning and cognition* (pp. 81–108). San Diego, CA: Academic Press.

Windsor, J., Piche, L. M., & Locke, P. A. (1994). Preference testing: A comparison of two presentation methods. *Research in Developmental Disabilities,* 15, 439–455.

Received April 23, 1997
Initial editorial decision April 28, 1997
Final acceptance May 16, 1997
Action Editor, David P. Wacker

JOURNAL OF APPLIED BEHAVIOR ANALYSIS 1997, **30,** 533–544 NUMBER 3 (FALL 1997)

BEHAVIORAL CUSPS: A DEVELOPMENTAL AND PRAGMATIC CONCEPT FOR BEHAVIOR ANALYSIS

JESÚS ROSALES-RUIZ

UNIVERSITY OF NORTH TEXAS

AND

DONALD M. BAER

UNIVERSITY OF KANSAS

Most concepts of development explain certain behavior changes as products or markers of the invariable succession of emerging periods, stages, refinements, or achievements that define and order much of an individual's life. A different but comparable concept can be derived from the most basic mechanisms of behavior analysis, which are its environmental contingencies, and from its most basic strategy, which is to study behavior as its subject matter. From a behavior-analytic perspective, the most fundamental developmental questions are (a) whether these contingencies vary in any systematic way across the life span, and thus make behavior change in a correspondingly systematic way; and (b) whether some of these contingencies and their changes have more far-reaching consequences than others, in terms of the importance to the organism and others, of the behavior classes they change. Certain behavior changes open the door to especially broad or especially important further behavior change, leading to the concept of the behavioral cusp. A behavioral cusp, then, is any behavior change that brings the organism's behavior into contact with new contingencies that have even more far-reaching consequences. Of all the environmental contingencies that change or maintain behavior, those that accomplish cusps are developmental. Behavior change remains the fundamental phenomenon of development for a behavior-analytic view; a cusp is a special instance of behavior change, a change crucial to what can come next.

DESCRIPTORS: development, developmental stages, pivotal behaviors, behavior traps, behavior analysis, behavior change

---

Conceptualizing the development of behavior over the life span has been an enduring problem in psychology. Organismic theories postulate an invariable succession of emerging stages, periods, achievements, differentiations, refinements, or products; they suppose that much behavior develops in obedience to that sequence. And, because the sequence is invariant, it requires an explanatory logic, which most often takes the form of its apparent goal, as if the sequence were self-organizing: The individual is seen as traveling epigenetic roads to uniquely adult stages of development, much like a train stopping at various stations before it reaches its final, always scheduled destination, or a butterfly passing through the embryo-larva-pupa-imago stages to the inevitable fluttering forth (see Overton & Reese, 1973; Reese, 1991; Reese & Overton, 1970; Spiker, 1966). Whereas the teleological sequence implied in such approaches is that an embryo is just a butterfly's way of making another butterfly, it is equally plausible to

The authors are grateful to Sigrid Glenn, Joel Greenspoon, Hayne Reese, Wendy Roth, and John Wright for sympathetic, critical, careful, competent, detailed, and constructive argument; but they should not be held responsible for the arguments advanced here. The authors are also grateful to the National Institute of Child Health and Human Development for research support (HD 18955).

Address correspondence to Jesús Rosales-Ruiz at the Department of Behavior Analysis, University of North Texas, P.O. Box 13438, Denton, Texas 76203 (E-mail: Rosales@scs.unt.edu) or to Donald M. Baer at the Department of Human Development and Family Life, University of Kansas, Lawrence, Kansas 66045-2133.

argue that a butterfly is just an embryo's way of making another embryo. Perhaps the concept of "development" is sometimes a way to ignore an arbitrary half of the evolutionary process.

Behavior analysis is different; it has no comparable guiding metaphor to explain patterns of behavior change throughout the life span. At least, none is intrinsic to its present logic. Of course, one or several such metaphors might be added. But that addition would seem apt only if it were done in the natural-science style that has guided the development of behavior analysis so far. That means it must be more than a metaphor; the premises justifying it should be verifiable.

Behavior analysis currently offers its well-known behavior-shaping contingencies as its basic analytical processes; and it offers them, so far, without specifying any distinctive, reliable patterning of them over the life span. If a concept of development is to be added, that concept must posit a reliable pattern of how these contingencies are applied over the life span. Stated this way, the possibility of a reliable pattern of behavior-change processes over the life span becomes a matter of facts to be determined rather than as a theory to be imposed. We can ask whether the application of these contingencies, by nature and by people, varies in any systematic way. We can ask whether the behaviors to which they are applied vary in any systematic way, and if so, whether that is by nature or by idiosyncratic societal convention. Discerning those kinds of systematic patterns of contingencies across the life span appears to be an implicit theme of two recent texts that describe development from a behavior-analytic perspective (Novak, 1996; Schlinger, 1995). These texts are oriented toward undergraduate readers; their mission is to show how traditional developmental topics are amenable to a behavior-analytic interpretation. But we can also ask whether some of the resultant behavior changes have more far-reaching consequences than others. Here, we address that question by describing the concept of developmental "cusps" (Rosales-Ruiz & Baer, 1996) and suggesting some criteria for "far-reaching."

A PRAGMATIC CONCEPT OF DEVELOPMENT FOR BEHAVIOR ANALYSIS

Consider a cusp as a behavior change that has consequences for the organism beyond the change itself, some of which may be considered important. That requires us to develop the criteria of importance. To approach those criteria, we must expand the definition of cusp: We take as axiomatic that any behavior change results from changes in the interaction between the organism and its environment. What makes a behavior change a cusp is that it exposes the individual's repertoire to new environments, especially new reinforcers and punishers, new contingencies, new responses, new stimulus controls, and new communities of maintaining or destructive contingencies. When some or all of those events happen, the individual's repertoire expands; it encounters a differentially selective maintenance of the new as well as some old repertoires, and perhaps that leads to some further cusps.

Consider, for example, what can happen as a result of learning to crawl. The baby suddenly has increased access to the environment and its contingencies. Now the baby can get to toys, family, and other things more easily, or can stumble into obstacles, all of which produce interactions that will further shape the baby's behavior. Some of these interactions initiate the shaping of other behaviors that will soon contribute to walking, others will shape responsiveness to visual cliffs (e.g., Campos, Bertenthal, & Kermoian, 1992), and still others will produce a variety of parental contingencies, some delighted, some dismayed, that will further shape how much more and how much less of the physical and social environment will be open to the child's further interaction. Thus, if walking, safety, and the immediate next direction of socialization are important for that baby at that time, crawling is a cusp.

This argument does not deny the development of the many small, sequential skills that culminate in crawling. Perhaps each of them is a prerequisite for the next, and thus for crawling. But the important point here is that none of these skills alone suddenly open the child's world to new contingencies that will develop many new, important behaviors. Instead, each of them opens the child's world only to the next skill. Their end point, crawling, is a cusp.

By contrast, consider a child who has all the prerequisites for walking, yet continues to crawl; an early study by Harris, Johnston, Kelley, and Wolf (1964) dealt with such a case. They systematically shaped walking in a preschool girl who almost always crawled. Walking made it possible for her to participate in the upright, fast-moving games her peers played, which was most of their games. A host of new interactions typically will follow from walking. If leg strength and participation in peer socialization were important to that girl at that time, walking was a cusp for her. Or perhaps it was a cusp for her parents and teachers: Perhaps the girl's behavior showed that walking and peer games had little importance for her at that time; it was her parents and teachers who believed that leg strength, coordination, and peer participation would have consequences that would be important to her later.

Teach a child to read accurately and fluently, and suddenly and systematically a vast amount of further development, and a new, drastically more efficient method of teaching, are operative. If any of that is important to the child or to the child's future, then accurate, fluent reading is a cusp. Teach a child with developmental disabilities generalized imitation, and future expansion of the child's repertoire can suddenly and systematically be as explosive as the social environment cares to make it, simply by modeling new skills, not necessarily intentionally. If any of that is important, to the child or to those responsible for the child, generalized imitation is a cusp. Teach an infant to discriminate between positive parent attention and disapproving parent attention, and you end the paradoxical reinforcement of inappropriate child behavior, which suddenly and systematically will alter the child's and the parents' futures, especially their joint futures. If gentle social guidance is important to the child at that time, then coming under the conventional stimulus controls used naturally by almost every parent (and almost every subsequent teacher) is a cusp. Give young adults the first sizable, dependable, disposable income of their lives, and suddenly, systematically, and enduringly, new sources of teaching will emerge that may alter and expand some of their criteria for and some of their practice of what constitutes food, housing, transportation, entertainment, travel, family, and responsibility. If any of that is important to the young people, to their society, or to its economy, disposable income is a cusp. (The parallel argument for elderly people who can retire with a disposable income is obvious.)

These examples show that the concept of cusp always depends on the phrase, "If that is important . . .," as if the audience must decide if that is important. We suggest that in these arguments, importance most often is indeed a social phenomenon. In biology, perhaps importance is unquestionably survival. In development, survival is rarely clear, so importance is very often a matter of something else, usually social validity. A cusp may unquestionably open new environments for a child, and we may view what those new environments will produce as being important; but if we inquire, we often will find that others do not. More than one preschool teacher has told parents that their child is a social isolate and that the teacher can remediate that, only to be told by the parents that they prefer their child to be a social isolate, because the parents think that isolation is important to the child's artistic, intellectual, or political development.

Not all new cusps need be seen as positive or desirable. Introducing a child to an addiction is an obvious example of a terrible cusp (for the great majority of us); teaching a child that the correct first response to any new problem is to seek help rather than to persist in independent tries is a more subtle example (for many of us).

Sometimes changing only one behavior will create a cusp; sometimes it will be necessary to change a class of behaviors. A cusp may be easy to accomplish, or it may be difficult, tedious, subtle, or otherwise problematic; yet if the cusp is not achieved, little or no further change is possible in its realm (and perhaps in several other realms). But, when the cusp is achieved, a set of subsequent changes, important to someone, suddenly becomes easy or highly probable. And when that cusp brings the developing organism into contact with other, subsequent contingencies crucial to further, more complex, or more refined development in a thereby steadily expanding, steadily more interactive realm, that will connote the conventional label of *developmental.* In traditional theory, the connotations of increased complexity or refinement often are put forward as causal and explanatory, in a teleological sense. The cusp explains in a different way. It points out that certain behavior changes cause subsequent broad or important behavior changes, in the sense of making those subsequent changes available. If we want to explain those subsequent changes, we need to know the contingencies that shape them and the cusp that makes them available for that shaping.

The logic of cusps is implicit in earlier discussions by Baer and Wolf (1970) and Baer, Rowbury, and Goetz (1976), who considered behavioral "traps" and the responses that enter such traps (cf. Martin & Pear, 1978; Stokes & Baer, 1977). A behavioral trap is a community of reinforcement in the natural environment that could maintain and potentially shape much new behavior of its members. Preschools, universities, and other social organizations are traps waiting for new members to enter and so, probably, to be shaped. To the extent that these traps shape behavior beyond the entry responses, and to the extent that those behaviors are important to someone at some time, the entry responses are cusps. For example, a child's rudimentary social skills could be trapped in the natural community of peers' social reinforcement by reinforcing responses that result in proximity to other children. The contingencies practiced by those peers on the behavior of anyone in steady contact with them will differentiate, discriminate, schedule, and maintain a much larger, more refined, and more complex set of social skills (e.g., Allen, Hart, Buell, Harris, & Wolf, 1964). In this example, the cusp is the behavior change of being proximate to the group. That is a very small behavior change and relatively easy to program; but it is also a cusp because of the extent and importance of what happens next.

Some arguments by the Koegels and their colleagues (Koegel & Frea, 1993; Koegel & Koegel, 1988; Koegel, Koegel, & Schreibman, 1991) embody the cusp concept. They call "pivotal" any behavior changes that "result in collateral changes of other behaviors as well" (Koegel & Frea, 1993, p. 369). They suggest that many children with autism do not persevere in problems as do typically developing children. But programming more reinforcement across a variety of problem-solving opportunities can remediate that, and thereby increase the children's repertoires; when that happens, it widens the range of situations that evoke teaching from the teachers. The result is new and improved skills not specifically targeted by the initial program; Koegel and Koegel (1988) cite tying shoes, buttoning clothes, and restaurant skills as examples. Similarly, Koegel and Frea (1993) report that effectively teaching students eye contact and appropriate facial expressions may decrease some abnormal behavior and increase effective conversation. To the extent that these collateral behavior changes prove to be important or introduce the organism to new shaping environments that prove to be important, they are cusps as well as pivotal behaviors. If, for example, the collateral behavior changes seem to be only brief, stereotypic conversations about very few topics, they remain collateral behavior changes, but their importance to the child or to others seems problematic, and thus they may not be cusps. Cusps are behavior changes that systematically lead to either widespread further changes or to important further changes.

Again, the criteria for importance are usually situational. Most often, they hinge on what the behavior changes are and on what their consequences are for that organism, not in their own right, but relative to what that organism wants, what its caretakers, advocates, and teachers want for it, and what a disinterested audience sees as significant for that organism, or for any organism in their society or species. These "wantings" may be pragmatic, or they may reflect an allegiance, even an implicit one, to some theory about what is important to any developing organism. Behavior analysis is not such a theory, apart from its usual endorsement of evolution as an inevitable process and of survival as a near-universal reinforcer of exceptional importance. That is, behavior analysis is a theory about how behavior is changed, not about how it should be changed. That it can be changed by procedures that are so prevalent in the natural world, and that are so easily open to social intervention, probably reflects great survival value.

Thus, cusps are behavior changes, sometimes simple, sometimes complex, that systematically cause other, further, not formally programmed behavior changes that are significant either because of their breadth or because of their importance to the organism or its species. That importance is seen sometimes by the organism, or by parties concerned for that organism, or by its relevance to the selection pressures of the environment, or all of those. Cusps often accomplish that kind of extensive or important collateral behavior change because they increase the organism's exposure to the relevant teaching contingencies.

Restated, the importance of cusps is judged by (a) the extent of the behavior changes they systematically enable, (b) whether they systematically expose behavior to new cusps, and (c) the audience's view of whether these changes are important for the organism, which in turn is often controlled by societal norms and expectations of what behaviors should develop in children and when that development should happen. Most of that is ultimately judged by survival, but "ultimately" is a long time and is extremely difficult to predict in advance. It is the third criterion, including our guesses about survival, that often prompts us to see only certain behavior changes as developmental.

The cusp concept is focused on understanding the importance of what happens after any behavior change, in order to define development. Other approaches, by contrast, define development by asking what new level of ability or complexity the behavior change represents. Yet, cusps can be simple: Access to other environments sometimes requires only a simple response, like dialing the critical number, or keyboarding the critical address, or extending the stimulus control of an existing response. They can also be as complex as the task analysis of conservation, seriation, transitivity, or self-instruction. In other approaches, the ability to read might be valued as developmental because of the time required to teach it, the extensive skill it represents, or the mental functions it is inferred to represent. However, if teaching reading were to have little effect beyond the achievement of reading, it would, for this behavior-analytic view of development, be irrelevant to development; it would not be a cusp. It would be typical of modern applied behavior analysts to ask how to repair an environment in which reading did not lead to broad further changes. (It might be typical of near-future applied behavior analysts to ask what behavior change—what media skill?—is, in that future world, better than reading for producing those broad further changes.)

As mentioned, cusps can range from quite large to quite small behavior changes. An obvious example of a large cusp is generalized imitation. An example of a small cusp is seen in an anecdote from a parent rearing a child with profound retardation: Teaching this child to manipulate the door latches that separated her from the outside fenced yard transformed her from a child who asked often all day (and often unsuccessfully) for doors to be opened for her into a child who could manage them herself. The child's new skill greatly expanded her opportunities for learning and activity from mainly indoor ones. It obviously enhanced her control over some of her daily life. It transformed her family's perception of her as an eternal problem to a learner whose skill acquisitions could improve everyone's life—from someone to be managed into someone who now could be taught more independence. A cusp whose size is less easy to assess is chaining the elements of verbal behavior (e.g., teaching the chunking of verbal messages; cf. Case, 1987). At the least, it transforms a listener from one who must be spoken to with slow-paced, one-word messages into one who can respond correctly to ordinary sentences, which may not be seen as a very important change. But, given enough of other related skills—of other cusps passed—it can also transform that listener into an efficient student.

Normal children get through many cusps to what follows in their various worlds, usually by extensive if casual teaching (e.g., imitation and spoken language), and aided by various skills acquired through prior cusps that made them increasingly better at self-teaching (e.g., self-regulation). Less fortunate, less endowed, less skilled, and less well-taught children do not get through as many of those cusps and become problems that attract diagnostic labels and remedial teaching.

The point of these examples is that cusps can vary in size, particularly in the length or intensity of their teaching programs, yet have similarly important consequences for what can happen next. It is not their management, their complexity, or the complexity of the behavior they target but their behavior-change outcomes that define their importance. Thus, cusp transcendence is pragmatic, but pragmatics do not change the laws of behavior or the principles of behavior management. However, they may well change management tactics, because the nature of cusps is that the developing organism's situation changes in systematically important ways.

SMALL CONVERGENCES OF TRADITIONAL AND BEHAVIOR-ANALYTIC VIEWS

Organisms are always doing something and are always doing new things; there are no holes in the stream of behavior (Bijou & Baer, 1961; Schoenfeld & Farmer, 1970; Skinner, 1953; Watson, 1926). The question has always been whether that stream has a structure. Some developmentalists organize it as a progression of stages, often according to what they call the complexity of behavior. They describe how behavior increases, not in amount but in complexity, during certain parts of the life span, from early and simple to late and complex. In most arguments, that sequence is predictable and uniform. Thus, a stage of development is a portion of the organism's life, qualitatively different from the preceding or subsequent stages, whose content is often (but not necessarily) described as a mental structure that guides action and is said to be universal, and is relevant to many outcomes, especially emotional, cognitive, and moral ones. Its timing is seen as modifiable, but only a little; and its sequence is seen as even more resistant to change (e.g., Bickhard, Cooper, & Mace, 1985; Flavell, 1982; Glasersfeld & Kelly, 1982; Lerner, 1986; Overton & Reese, 1973; Reese & Overton, 1970; Wohlwill, 1973).

Stage concepts of development are often challenged, even within the scientific community that generated them. Piaget's stages of cognitive development (1971), Freud's stages of psychosexual development (1905), Kohlberg's stages of moral development (Kohlberg, Levine, & Hewer, 1983), and Erikson's stages of psychosocial development (1950)—four prominent examples—have been criticized on many grounds, most of which reflect the vagueness of three sets of criteria: those that define a stage; those that tell the theorist how many stages are needed to explain development; and those that define the transition from one stage to the next (see Brainerd, 1978, for a heuristic example of these unresolved questions). These are criticisms not of the stage strategy but of its topical tactics. In effect, these criticisms assume and applaud the stage strategy by asking that it find better tactical criteria.

Some modern theories of development do not postulate a stage-specific mental structure that explains all developmental phenomena. Some theorists now see cognitive development, for example, as highly diverse and seamlessly continuous: Individuals use multiple rules, strategies, hypotheses, and so forth, changing them from one kind of problem to the next; these structures range simultaneously from simple to complex; the competence of each one may change at any time; and each one is more likely to be specific to a small domain (e.g., speech perception, reading, arithmetic, language, categorization, or reasoning) rather than to be generalized across them all (see Case, 1987; Fisher, 1980; Flavell, 1982, 1992; Howe & Pasnak, 1993; and Siegel, 1991, for reviews of this shift in conceptualization).

The general stage concept is still used, even so. For example, Flavell postulates developing capacities to process information and to resist interference, which, if they exist, should allow more complex cognition across all relevant domains (see Flavell, 1982). Within a domain, though, it is levels of skill competence rather than stages of qualitative changes that are assumed to proceed in an orderly sequence (Fisher, 1980; Fisher & Silvern, 1985; Siegler, 1981).

The thesis that developing an ability or competence will open a much larger realm to improvement is not new; like most theoretical overreaches, it has seen its waves of endorsement and rejection. As the 20th century began, educational psychologists often supposed that training any specific skill (e.g., matching colored sticks) would educate the senses and make them hospitable to many untrained discriminations, just as studying any small discipline (e.g., Latin, mathematics) would improve reasoning in general. Later, that thesis was refined: Not *any* training or study would lead to generalized results; only *certain* kinds of training or studies would do that. A specific ability would benefit a larger domain (mathematics would improve reasoning) only if both contained sufficient common elements (see Thorndike, 1903). That was the logic of *transfer* (e.g., Grose & Birney, 1963). It automatically recommended training in larger categories, so as to sample more of the elements that are operative in the larger domains to be benefited. It also warned the teacher that the benefited domain would be no larger than the common elements justified. Clearly, the concept had moved behavior-ward. But it was still as vague as any stage theory in offering criteria for identifying "common elements."

Thus, it was not long before a psychologist like Ferguson (1954, 1956), apparently following Spearman (1927) and Thurstone (1938), would see little use in constructs as general as intelligence. These constructs could only denote subsets of more real abilities, which in turn were properties of the ultimate reality, behavior. So Ferguson's concept of development was to list the skill masteries that together would justify the term *ability* and to catalog their transfer functions (generalizability) at different stages of learning and at different ages. The developmental question had become: What prior learned abilities transfer to what untaught abilities, and how, and under what conditions? The converse question became: What new abilities alter prior abilities, and in what ways?

Forty years later, cognitive scientists would be asking: What prior abilities, learned or otherwise, lead to what changes in development? They would answer the question of how by inferring cognitive mediators such as memory access, information organization, inference itself, and strategizing (Glaser, 1992, p. 249); they would answer the question of under what conditions by inferring developing levels of function for those inferred mediators.

From a behavior-analytic point of view, the small domain to which these relatively new cognitive-analysis tactics were applied was admirable. Smaller arenas of analysis allow a much more intimate interaction between research and data and allow more of the data to be experimental. More important, smaller domains of analysis allow, and almost insure, at least a partial intersection of the logic of behavior analysis and cognitive analysis: (a) We all analyze behavior, even when it is not the fundamental unit of our theory; (b) behaviors are readily changed by environmental contingencies; and (c) we know any behavior can contact different environmental contingencies than other behaviors do. These three points tell us that different behaviors can come under different control (even though some theories need some very similar behaviors to be under similar control). To the extent that even similar behaviors do come under different control, then an overarching stage-like organization of great quantities of behavior is improbable, although not impossible to program. Our research ought to look first for regularity in much smaller domains, then seek experimental control of as much of that regularity as proves to be possible (and ethical), and then ask if that control can be extended (experimentally) to a domain large enough to justify a stage concept.

For behavior analysis, behavior classes as large as "intelligence" have never seemed useful, or even real. Response classes have been defined by the experimenter's ability to prove that all members of the putative class are in fact under the same control (antecedent, consequent, or both) and have been understood by the experimenter's ability to make them. Similar response classes that result from similar histories of programming then have been seen as possible events in natural development.

In behavior analysis, the stage concept seems neither essential nor explanatory, but it is still heuristic. Bijou (1993, p. 46) argues that it can guide analysis; he sketches a sequence of foundational, basic, and societal stages, much as Kantor proposed in 1959 (see Bijou, 1989, 1993). When the changes described by a stage concept show great generality across behaviors and contexts, for many children and for a specific period of the life span, then, and only then, does the concept of stage become correspondingly heuristic.

But, when a discipline knows, or thinks it knows, how to diminish or disassemble or how to create or intensify some of the generality described by the stage concept, and when a discipline can do so by fairly straightforward environmental interventions (as has been done for at least some cases like conservation skills, Kuhn, 1974, and generalized imitation, Baer, Peterson, & Sherman, 1966), then the concept of stage becomes correspondingly more fragile and arbitrary. Behavior analysis has always at least asked if its processes could create or intensify or diminish or disassemble that kind of generality, and has succeeded often enough to make this argument viable.

In fact, learning to manage the detailed composition of stages may soon prove to be more interesting than the generalities the stages describe. For stage theory, those generalities are described rather than experimentally analyzed. By contrast, the management of their components is almost always experimentally analyzed; that is what management means in behavior analysis. Then why not shift interest to the often dramatic changes in behavior that become possible with experimental mastery of those components? For example, one way in which children expand their vocabularies is the disambiguation effect described as part of the mutual-exclusivity bias (Merriman & Bowman, 1989). Around 2½ years of age, most children begin to learn new words when presented with a novel name in the presence of a novel object (one whose name has not been learned) and a familiar object (one whose name has been learned). These children typically select the novel object and thus learn the name of the novel object. Before the age of 2½, children usually select the object whose name already controls their behavior. However, children as young as 2 years also have demonstrated the disambiguation effect when correction and reinforcement procedures are used. In behavior analysis, this phenomenon has been experimentally investigated in persons with mental retardation, with both spoken and visual stimuli and with visual stimuli in matching tasks (cf. Dixon, 1977; McIlvane & Stoddard, 1981, 1985). It has been demonstrated that learning by exclusion permits an economical way of expanding the repertoire of individuals—a way that the teaching community could use to produce almost error-free behavior changes, even when other teaching methods have failed (e.g., de Rose, de Souza, & Hanna, 1996). Learning by exclusion is a cusp that along with other cusps may lead us to an understanding of the behavior changes and the environments that are required to produce the vocabulary explosion typically seen at around 18 months of age (Smith, 1926).

Studies looking for cusps will eventually produce a long list of organism–environment interactions, some of small importance for what can happen next, others of great importance for what can happen next, and still others of importance conditional on what other cusps have been attained. Thus a cusp may be universal, but it need not and rarely will be. Similarly, a cusp may have wide generality, but need not. One child's cusp may be another child's waste of time.

In metaphor, cusps often are steps in an orderly path. Perhaps more often they are like the branches of a tree: They stem from an earlier branch or trunk, and new branches may stem from them, where their structure in conjunction with the environment allows for that. But their mutual order, size, and probability of twigs are not very thoroughly predetermined. Sequences, whether necessary or merely societal, can be essential to this concept; but it is the cusps that need to be analyzed first. As we come to understand them, we will then be in a better position to learn when their sequences are crucial or conditional.

As behavior changes that proved to be cusps for one child or another, or many, are listed, any reader is free to chunk that list according to the reader's criteria, which may be a predetermined notion of complexity, sequence, or growth. Some readers no doubt will chunk them exactly that way; others will find a variety of alternative logics. However, a list of cusps, defined as they are here, is a list of teachable behaviors, a set of teaching procedures that accomplish them, a shaping community of reinforcement, and a description of the systematic consequences of doing so, including the consequences of the consequences. Teachable cusps are susceptible to experimental analysis, and experimental analysis allows us to identify their consequences. Nonteachable cusps are susceptible only to correlational analysis; correlational analysis allows us to say only what their accompaniments are. A truly developmental analysis needs more certainty about what causes what. An illustrative example of such analysis is the case of the "disappearing" stepping reflex. Newborns held upright with their feet on a surface display well-coordinated step-like movements; these responses disappear within the first few months and are seen again towards the end of the first year. These changes have been explained as correlates of the maturation of the voluntary cortical centers. We could suppose that those centers first inhibited subcortical or reflexive movements and later facilitated them at higher levels of control (McGraw, 1943). After all, inhibition is what a center should do to make one of its skills disappear, and facilitation is what it should do to make that skill reappear. This explanation remained unchallenged for 40 years until Thelen and Fisher (1982) demonstrated experimentally that the disappearance of this reflex was due to an increase in the baby's weight and to the changing mechanical demands of its posture. They restored the stepping reflex by submerging infants in torso-deep warm water and inhibited it again by adding weights. Once again, the value of an inferred central control had varied inversely with the application of experimental analysis.

The cusp concept defined here is most powerful when it is limited to those changes that can be experimentally taught and the consequences of which can be experimentally verified. Correlational analyses that look for the sequelae of a cusp will not easily separate cause and effect; experimental control will be required to meet the definition. A stage theory may be as unverifiable as the theorist wishes; then it can be made to embrace everything the theorist needs to explain. By contrast, to the extent that cusp assessment must be verifiable, cusp-based development will automatically be a set only of already-tested facts and procedures. This cusp concept will not embrace everything that a developmental theory needs to explain, because ethics and practicality bar experimental analysis from many parts of that domain. Teaching reading to see its consequences fits the cusp concept; awaiting complete myelinization of the nervous system to see its consequences does not. But if myelinization should ever become experimentally manageable and ethically acceptable to manage, it might then be tested for its cusp qualities.

REFERENCES

Allen, K. E., Hart, B. M., Buell, J. C., Harris, F. R. & Wolf, M. M. (1964). Effects of social reinforcement on isolate behavior of a nursery school child. *Child Development, 35,* 511–518.

Baer, D. M., Peterson, R. F., & Sherman, J. A. (1966). The development of imitation by reinforcing behavioral similarity to a model. *Journal of the Experimental Analysis of Behavior, 10,* 405–416.

Baer, D. M., Rowbury, T., & Goetz, E. (1976). Behavioral traps in the preschool: A proposal for research. In A. D. Pick (Ed.), *Minnesota symposia on child psychology* (Vol. 10, pp. 3–27). Minneapolis, MN: University of Minnesota Press.

Baer, D. M., & Wolf, M. M. (1970). The entry into natural communities of reinforcement. In R. Ulrich, T. Stachnik, & J. Mabry (Eds.), *Control of human behavior: From cure to prevention* (Vol. 2, pp. 319–324). Glenview, IL: Scott, Foresman.

Bickhard, M., Cooper, R., & Mace, P. (1985). Vestiges of logical positivism: Critiques of stage explanations. *Human Development, 28,* 240–258.

Bijou, S. W. (1989). Behavior analysis. In R. Vasta (Ed.), *Annals of child development: Six theories of child development: Revised formulations and current issues* (pp. 61–83). Greenwich, CT: JAI Press.

Bijou, S. W. (1993). *Behavior analysis of child development.* Reno, NV: Context Press.

Bijou, S. W., & Baer, D. M. (1961). *Child development I: A systematic and empirical theory.* New York: Appleton-Century-Crofts.

Brainerd, C. J. (1978). The stage question in cognitive-developmental theory. *Behavioral and Brain Sciences, 2,* 173–213.

Campos, J. J., Bertenthal, B. I., & Kermoian, R. (1992). Early experience and emotional development: The emergence of wariness of heights. *Psychological Science, 3*(1), 61–64.

Case, R. (1987). Neo-Piagetian theory: Retrospect and prospect. *International Journal of Psychology, 22,* 773–791.

de Rose, J. C., de Souza, D. G., & Hanna, E. S. (1996). Teaching reading and spelling: Exclusion and stimulus equivalence. *Journal of Applied Behavior Analysis, 29,* 451–469.

Dixon, L. S. (1977). The nature of control by spoken words over visual stimulus selection. *Journal of the Experimental Analysis of Behavior, 27,* 433–442.

Erikson, E. (1950). *Childhood and society.* New York: Norton.

Ferguson, G. A. (1954). On learning and human ability. *Canadian Journal of Psychology, 8,* 95–112.

Ferguson, G. A. (1956). On transfer and the abilities of man. *Canadian Journal of Psychology, 10,* 121–158.

Fisher, K. W. (1980). A theory of cognitive development: The control and construction of hierarchies of skills. *Psychological Review, 87,* 477–531.

Fisher, K. W., & Silvern, L. (1985). Stages and individual differences in cognitive development. *Annual Review of Psychology, 36,* 613–648.

Flavell, J. H. (1982). Structures, stages, and sequences in cognitive development. In W. A. Collins (Ed.), *The concept of development: The Minnesota symposia on child psychology* (pp. 1–28). Hillsdale, NJ: Erlbaum.

Flavell, J. H. (1992). Cognitive development: Past, present, future. *Developmental Psychology, 28*(6), 998–1005.

Freud, S. (1905). *Three essays on the theory of sexuality.* London: Hogarth Press.

Glaser, R. (1992). Learning, cognition, and education: Then and now. In H. L. Pick, P. V. D. Broek, & A. D. C. Knill (Eds.), *Cognition: Conceptual and methodological issues* (pp. 239–265). Washington, DC: American Psychological Association.

Glasersfeld, E., & Kelly, M. (1982). On the concepts of period, phase, stage, and level. *Human Development, 25,* 152–160.

Grose, R., & Birney, R. (Eds.). (1963). *Transfer of learning.* Princeton, NJ: Van Nostrand.

Harris, F. R., Johnston, M. K., Kelley, C. S., & Wolf, M. M. (1964). Effects of positive social reinforcement on regressed crawling of a nursery-school child. *Journal of Educational Psychology, 55,* 35–41.

Howe, M., & Pasnak, R. (1993). Shifting conceptions of cognitive development. In M. L. Howe & R. Pasnak (Eds.), *Emerging themes in cognitive development: Vol. 1. Foundations* (pp. 267–276). New York: Springer-Verlag.

Kantor, J. R. (1959). *Interbehavioral psychology.* Bloomington, IN: Principia Press.

Koegel, R., & Frea, W. (1993). Treatment of social behavior in autism through the modification of pivotal social skills. *Journal of Applied Behavior Analysis, 26,* 369–377.

Koegel, R., & Koegel, L. (1988). Generalized responsivity and pivotal behaviors. In R. H. Horner, G. Dunlap, & R. L. Koegel (Eds.), *Generalization and maintenance: Life-style changes in applied settings* (pp. 41–66). Baltimore: Paul H. Brookes.

Koegel, R., Koegel, L., & Schreibman, L. (1991). Assessing and training parents in teaching pivotal behaviors. In R. J. Prinz (Ed.), *Advances in behavioral assessment of children and families* (Vol. 5, pp. 65–82). London: Jessica Kingsley.

Kohlberg, L., Levine, C., & Hewer, A. (1983). *Moral stages: A current formulation and a response to critics.* Basel, Switzerland: Karger.

Kuhn, D. (1974). Inducing development experimentally: Comments on a research paradigm. *Developmental Psychology, 10*(5), 590–600.

Lerner, R. M. (1986). *Concepts and theories of human development* (2nd ed.). New York: Random House.

Martin, G., & Pear, J. (1978). *Behavior modification: What it is and how to do it.* Englewood Cliffs, NJ: Prentice Hall.

McGraw, M. B. (1943). *The neuromuscular matura-*

tion of the human infant. New York: Columbia University Press.

McIlvane, W. J., & Stoddard, L. T. (1981). Acquisition of matching-to-sample performances in severe mental retardation: Learning by exclusion. *Journal of Mental Deficiency, 25,* 33–48.

McIlvane, W. J., & Stoddard, L. T. (1985). Complex stimulus relations and exclusion in severe mental retardation. *Analysis and Intervention in Developmental Disabilities, 5,* 307–321.

Merriman, W. E., & Bowman, L. L. (1989). The mutual exclusivity bias in children's word learning. *Monographs of the Society for Research in Child Development, 54* (3–4, Serial No. 220).

Novak, G. (1996). *Developmental psychology: Dynamical systems and behavior analysis.* Reno, NV: Context Press.

Overton, W., & Reese, H. (1973). Models of development: Methodological implications. In J. R. Nesselroade & H. W. Reese (Eds.), *Life-span developmental psychology: Methodological issues* (pp. 65–86). New York: Academic Press.

Piaget, J. (1971). *Biology and knowledge.* Chicago: University of Chicago Press.

Reese, H. (1991). Contextualism and developmental psychology. In H. W. Reese (Ed.), *Advances in child development and behavior* (Vol. 23, pp. 187–230). New York: Academic Press.

Reese, H., & Overton, W. (1970). Models of development and theories of development. In L. R. Goulet & P. B. Baltes (Eds.), *Life-span developmental psychology: Research and theory* (pp. 115–145). New York: Academic Press.

Rosales-Ruiz, J., & Baer, D. M. (1996). A behavior-analytic view of development. In E. Ribes & S. W. Bijou (Eds.), *Recent approaches to behavioral development* (pp. 155–180). Reno, NV: Context Press.

Schlinger, H. (1995). *A behavior analytic view of child development.* New York: Plenum Press.

Schoenfeld, W. N., & Farmer, J. (1970). Reinforcement schedules and the "behavior stream." In W. N. Schoenfeld (Ed.), *The theory of reinforcement schedules* (pp. 215–245). New York: Appleton-Century-Crofts.

Siegel, L. (1991). On the maturation of developmental psychology. In F. S. Kessel, M. H. Borstein, & A. J. Sameroff (Eds.), *Contemporary constructions of the child: Essays in honor of William Kessen* (pp. 251–264). Hillsdale, NJ: Erlbaum.

Siegler, R. (1981). Developmental sequences within and between concepts. *Monographs of the Society for Research in Child Development, 46*(2), 1–13.

Skinner, B. F. (1953). *Science and human behavior.* New York: Free Press.

Smith, M. E. (1926). An investigation of the development of the sentence and the extent of vocabulary in young children. *University of Iowa Studies in Child Welfare, 3,* 5.

Spearman, C. (1927). *The abilities of man: Their nature and measurement.* London: Macmillan.

Spiker, C. C. (1966). The concept of development: Relevant and irrelevant issues. In H. W. Stevenson (Ed.), Concept of development: A report of a conference commemorating the 40th anniversary of the Institute of Child Development, University of Minnesota (pp. 40–54). *Monographs of the Society for Research in Child Development, 31* (5, Serial No. 107).

Stokes, T. F., & Baer, D. M. (1977). An implicit technology of generalization. *Journal of Applied Behavior Analysis, 10,* 349–367.

Thelen, E., & Fisher, D. M. (1982). Newborn stepping: An explanation for a "disappearing reflex." *Developmental Psychology, 18,* 760–775.

Thorndike, E. L. (1903). The psychology of learning. In *Educational psychology* (Vol. 2, pp. 357–464). New York: Teachers College, Columbia University.

Thurstone, L. (1938). *Primary mental abilities.* Chicago: University of Chicago Press.

Watson, J. B. (1926). What the nursery has to say about instincts. In C. Murchison (Ed.), *Psychologies of 1925* (pp. 1–35). Worcester, MA: Clark University Press.

Wohlwill, J. H. (1973). *The study of behavioral development.* New York: Academic Press.

Received August 9, 1996
Initial editorial decision September 27, 1996
Final acceptance April 3, 1997
Action Editor, David P. Wacker

JOURNAL OF APPLIED BEHAVIOR ANALYSIS 1992, 25, 83–88 NUMBER 1 (SPRING 1992)

SHOULD WE TRAIN APPLIED BEHAVIOR ANALYSTS TO BE RESEARCHERS?

RICHARD W. MALOTT

WESTERN MICHIGAN UNIVERSITY

Should we continue the tradition of training nearly all our masters and doctoral students to be research scientists, or should we provide different training for those who wish to be practitioners? In searching for an answer to this question, the present paper involves informal use of two general approaches of behavioral systems analysis: front-end analysis and feasibility analysis.

BEHAVIORAL SYSTEMS ANALYSIS

To do a behavioral systems analysis, the practitioner should systematically perform the following steps: Do a front-end analysis of the behavioral system. Specify the goals of the system. Design the system. Implement it. Evaluate it. And recycle through the preceding steps until the goals are obtained (Malott, 1974; Mechner & Cook, 1988; Redmon, 1991).

> [In a behavioral system] the principal components are organisms, usually human beings, working together to accomplish some set of ultimate goals or objectives. Organizations are behavioral systems—for example, a factory, a hospital, a school, a city government. But there are some behavioral systems that, by convention, we do not usually call organizations—for example, on a large scale, an entire country; on an intermediate scale, a department or division of an organization; on a smaller scale, a family; and on a tiny scale, we may consider individual people as behavioral systems, though not as organizations. In this latter case, the system's components might consist of various tasks the individual does. (Malott & Garcia, 1987, p. 128)

We do the front-end analysis before designing and implementing our intervention. It includes a goal analysis and a task analysis. The goal analysis helps us select the goals for our system (Mager, 1984; Malott & Garcia, 1987). Therefore, in designing an instructional system to train applied behavior analysts, our goal analysis might involve both a market analysis and a needs analysis. Furthermore, Malott and Garcia (1987) argued that all systems should have the well-being of humanity as their ultimate goal and that intermediate goals should be selected so that they lead to the ultimate goal. This suggests that in our goal analysis we should consider formally the relation between our training of behavior analysts and the needs of humanity; we should not take that relation for granted.

Recently, several behavior analysts have suggested, either directly or indirectly, that we include a market analysis when we do a front-end analysis to insure that people will use our products once we have produced them. Geller (1991a) pointed to the importance of market analysis by noting that W. Edwards Deming, credited with revolutionizing Japan's quality control systems, stressed the importance of front-end market research in his 4-day seminar on quality enhancement.

Redmon (1991) also illustrated the need for market analysis, suggesting that interventions are maintained only to the extent that their maintenance benefits the decision makers in an organization and to the extent that the benefits are apparent to those decision makers. As examples, he cited the failure of management to maintain a refuse packaging program that apparently benefited the garbage pickup crew but not the managers. Similarly, a utility company failed to maintain a pro-

Address correspondence to the author at the Department of Psychology, Western Michigan University, Kalamazoo, Michigan 49008-5052.

gram that successfully reduced electricity use, possibly because there were no apparent benefits for the company, even though that program might have benefited society in general.

Bailey (1991) also supported the need for front-end market analysis, suggesting that much consumer resistance to behavior analysis has occurred because "We did not do the front-end analysis with potential consumers to discover exactly what they were looking for, what form it should take, how it should be packaged and delivered, and so forth" (p. 446).

In discussions of social validity, behavior analysts have argued for the importance of doing front-end goal-directed needs analyses. Wolf (1978) stressed the importance of subjective evaluations of the social significance of intervention goals. However, Geller (1991b) implied that the consumer's subjective evaluations of appropriate goals and procedures might not always be our best guide: "In the domain of road safety, for example, most consumers would prefer increased speed limits and no enforcement of safety belt use laws. In the industrial setting, most workers would vote to eliminate requirements to wear uncomfortable and inconvenient personal protective equipment (e.g., safety glasses, hard hats, ear plugs, and face shields)" (p. 182). Geller (1991b) further suggested that we should not rely on "personal (or celebrity) opinion to determine allocation of priorities [in goal selection]. . . . Surely it would be more appropriate to determine a priority ranking of socially significant problems [goals] by systematically applying epidemiological statistics, cost-benefit ratios, and intervention effectiveness data, as well as information about the availability of pertinent resources and socially valid solutions" (pp. 183–184). In other words, Geller recommended a behavioral systems approach to goal selection prior to intervention.

In addition to a goal analysis (market analysis and needs analysis), a front-end analysis can include a task analysis to determine the tasks and supporting skills needed to achieve the goals. Mager (1988) said, "Task analysis is the name given to a collection of techniques used to help make the components of competent performance visible. . . . Every job is made up of a collection of tasks. . . . A *task* is a series of steps leading to a meaningful outcome. . . . A *step* in a task . . . would be something like tighten a nut [or] pick up a scalpel" (pp. 29–30). For each task, the analysis specifies the occasion for the task, the steps in the task, and the criteria for successful completion of the task. In turn, an analysis of the steps and of the student's entering repertoire suggests the skills the training program should establish. Although applied behavior analysts use detailed task analyses in the design of programs to train workers in industry and even programs to train the developmentally disabled, they seem to make little use of such analyses in the design of programs to train other applied behavior analysts.

Finally, the importance of feasibility analyses is just beginning to receive formal recognition by behavior analysts. This is the essence of Geller's (1991b) recommendation that our efforts be guided by "cost-benefit ratios and intervention effectiveness data, as well as information about the availability of pertinent resources" (p. 184). In some senses we might consider such a feasibility analysis to be part of a front-end analysis—something done before the intervention; however, most often we must have some data from an intervention before we can reasonably assess the feasibility of continuing that intervention or implementing similar ones in the future.

Front-End Analysis

Goal Analysis

We can now use these concepts from behavioral systems analysis to consider whether programs to train applied behavior analysts should emphasize the training of research skills.

Market analysis. To get a rough idea of the job market for behavior analysts, I used a printout of the nonstudent membership of the Association for Behavior Analysis. The practitioners constituted 38% of the PhDs, 52% of the EdDs, and 86% of the MAs, although the sample may be biased in favor of university teachers and researchers, who may join and maintain memberships more often than practitioners. (By practitioner, I mean anyone other than a professor or researcher.)

This preliminary market analysis implies that a large percentage of behavior-analyst alumni of our graduate programs work mainly as practitioners, not as teachers and researchers. So what should we teach the large percentage of our graduate students who will become practitioners so that they can better contribute to the well-being of humanity?

Needs analysis. We already have many effective applied behavior analysis procedures, but few non-behavior analysts use them. Perhaps our main problem is getting children and parents, students and teachers, employees and employers, clients and therapists, and the governed and the government to use what we already know. As Stoltz (1981) pointed out, "Applied researchers develop useful innovative technologies experimentally, and yet few of these technologies enjoy widespread adoption by our society" (p. 491). Here is an infamous example: The national education establishment failed to adopt the technology of direct instruction, although "the largest experiment in history on instructional methods" had shown it to be dramatically superior to eight other popular methods of instruction in elementary education" (Watkins, 1988, p. 10). As another example, Reid (1991) pointed out,

> Even in the field of developmental disabilities, . . . the actual impact of behavior analysis is well below its potential impact. There is a serious gap in typical service settings between state-of-the-art services, as represented in the professional literature, versus existing services. Indeed, most people who work in developmental disabilities are not very well skilled, or skilled at all, in applied behavior analysis. (p. 438)

So we might spread the use of behavioral technology more reliably by simply increasing the number of practitioners we graduate rather than the number of researchers who generate more technology.

Traditionally, we train even our applied graduate students to be research scientists rather than the staff managers and program administrators that many, if not most, will become. We train them to value research highly and to value those who produce it. Then the new graduates get jobs as practitioners or as managers and administrators and find themselves poorly trained to do the job they were not taught to value. In other words, most of the people paying the pipers are calling for one set of tunes, but the graduate schools are teaching their students to play and value a different set. Furthermore, the graduate schools often fail to teach such an invaluable skill as behavioral systems analysis.

Conclusions of the goal analysis. This analysis suggests we should train fewer scientists and more practitioners. But this does not mean practitioners and managers should not empirically evaluate their work and the systems they manage, nor does it mean they should not make their decisions as data-based as possible. It only means applied settings need a special sort of program evaluation and systems analysis research, and this systems evaluation and research is rarely of the sort that meets the standards of novelty and experimental control properly required for publication in prestigious research journals.

Task Analysis

One useful rule of thumb from behaviorally oriented trainers in industry is to teach only the repertoires essential to the job and the empirically demonstrated prerequisites for acquiring those repertoires. How many nonessential, and thus easily lost, repertoires are we teaching our graduate students in the name of science or in the name of the scientist/practitioner model or in the name of education (as opposed to training)? For instance, experienced task analysts suggest we look skeptically at the history and theory parts of most curricula.

Advocates of training practitioners as scientists argue that the scientist's critical, data-based, empirical analysis skills transfer to decision making in the professional and personal lives of science-trained practitioners. My frequent but informal observations suggest that most scientists show little evidence of their scientific training when making decisions outside their areas of expertise.

Another common argument is that scientific training will allow the practitioner to read professional journals and stay abreast of the latest empirically based behavioral technology. Again, my informal observations suggest otherwise; I think, at most, practitioners usually only skim a few behavior analysis textbooks or handbooks when searching for a new technique—a more efficient technique than scouring and critically evaluating the professional journals. Even if practitioners do read scholarly journals, it may not be cost effective for them to be trained as scientists for the purpose of weeding out poorly conducted and analyzed research; the journal editors have had much more experience doing that.

The sorts of systems analyses and program evaluations appropriate to applied settings often depart greatly from typical research methodology: The scientist carefully manipulates an independent variable to measure its effects on a dependent variable. The practitioner must use intervention or treatment packages to force the dependent variable into an acceptable range as quickly as possible, with little concern for isolating the crucial values of the independent variables.

So before designing our curriculum, we need to analyze what tasks practitioners should do, as well as what they actually do. Those tasks are the essentials. In stressing these essentials, we might reduce the emphasis on history, theory, and methods of science, as well as experimental theses and dissertations for most practitioners. We could then stress areas such as basic quantitative concepts, program evaluation, empirical behavioral systems analysis, social skills, accounting, computer use, project management, management information systems, public speaking, marketing (Bailey, 1991; Lindsley, 1991; Schwartz, 1991) and behavior analysis. Johnston (1991) made a related argument:

> We should make a clear distinction between technological research and technological application. . . . Technological application should not have to focus on asking experimental questions at all, although these will sometimes arise when procedures fail to produce the desired effects. . . . We should represent the different needs of applied research versus practice in how we accept students into graduate programs, how we train them, and how they are employed. . . . It might even be argued that practitioners should receive training that is more service oriented than research oriented. The scientist-practitioner philosophy we seem to have uncritically borrowed from clinical psychology . . . may be counter-productive for this new model. . . . Few careers fit its assumptions very well. Not only are most holders of the doctorate in psychology apparently uninterested in being both researchers and practitioners, it is difficult to do both well. . . . As a general approach to training practitioners the scientist-practitioner model is easy to argue against. . . . The model I have suggested . . . should be seen as enhancing rather than diminishing the role of practitioners. . . . We would no longer need to define their value by such academic credentials as research publications. (pp. 426–427)

Feasibility Analysis

I suggested some issues involved in deciding what we should teach. That was part of an informal front-end analysis. Now we might consider what we can feasibly teach. Even if we should train most practitioners to be scientists, can we do so?

How Feasible Is It to Train Successful Publishers?

How well do we train practitioner/scientists? An applied student of behavior analysis might spend the equivalent of 2 to 4 years learning to be a scientist—a heavy investment for all concerned. What concrete returns does this investment produce? Should such extensive training result in graduates publishing frequently in our most important journal, *Journal of Applied Behavior Analysis* (*JABA*)? It does not. During *JABA*'s second decade, only 26 people published five or more articles there—one article every 2 years.

Of the 784 applied behavior analysts at the doctoral level in the Association for Behavior Analysis, only 2% are frequent publishers in *JABA*. I took *JABA* to be the journal of first choice for publication of experimental work by applied behavior analysts, although that may not always be the case. However, even if considering frequent publication of empirical research in other prestigious journals tripled this estimate, the percentage of frequent publishers of experimental work would be only 6%. We invest much effort in training applied behavior analysts to be scientists; but applied behavior analysts seem to have a low rate of generating research of a type or quality adequate for publication in *JABA*.

Who Can Train Experimental Scientists?

To acquire reliably the complex and subtle repertoire of a productive experimental scientist, the student may need to apprentice with a teacher who is a productive experimental scientist; book and classroom learning may not be nearly enough. In this regard, who did the frequent publishers of *JABA*'s second decade study with? At least 50% (13 of 26) studied with people who themselves were frequent publishers in either *JABA*'s first or second decade. And, if I may use a double standard for productive research, at least two others studied with a major research publisher, although he was not a frequent publisher in *JABA*. Of course, several confounding factors can contribute to these results; but in any event, the odds are low that someone who is not a productive researcher will train a student who will become a productive researcher. And 22 of the 26 frequent publishers were university professors; so only 22 professors had the skills for productive research in their active repertoire during *JABA*'s second decade. If my criterion is too restrictive, we could triple the number and still there would be only 66 such professors. So what about the great majority of the professors of applied behavior analysis?

If It Is Not Feasible for Most of Us to Train Scientists, Who Can We Train?

Many poor scientists may be excellent practitioners (and of course many excellent scientists may be poor practitioners). We should recognize the value of our practitioner, teacher, and administrator skills and teach those skills, without apologizing and without cloaking them in the guise of scientific research. These are the skills most of our graduates will be paid to use. If we cannot practice what we preach, at least we should preach what we practice.

This is not an antiintellectual, antiscience argument. It is merely an argument that we should leave the training of scientists to those who have science skills in their currently active repertoires; the rest of us should concentrate on training practitioners in whatever areas we effectively practice, whether it be education, industry, the clinic or other areas. (One of the reviewers of this manuscript raised the following point: "Do we need practitioner skills in our repertoires to teach this? Some of my colleagues have *neither* practitioner nor research skills at the exemplary levels of excellence advocated here.")

THESES AND DISSERTATIONS

As part of this preliminary front-end analysis, we have glanced at our goals and a few of the relevant tasks needed to achieve those goals. We have also considered the feasibility of teaching the various repertoires. Now we examine the implications of this analysis for theses and dissertations.

Applied students need high-quality training leading to the acquisition and demonstration of professionally relevant repertoires, for example, the skills of doing behavioral systems analysis in applied settings. However, in many programs, when students attempt to do applied theses and dissertations, they must distort their practical intentions to create the illusion of science.

Proponents of the experimental dissertation often argue that the PhD degree is a degree for scholars, not practitioners. Therefore the dissertation must demonstrate scholarship, not practical skills. These proponents of the experimental dissertation seem to imply that if students want to be mere practitioners, then let them get PsyD degrees. But the PhD is no longer just a degree for people who will become professional scholars. I suspect most PhDs in applied behavior analysis do not become professional researchers and scholars. And even if the PsyD degree had the status of a PhD, few universities offer PsyD degrees in applied behavior analysis. Perhaps this should change, at least according to this preliminary needs analysis.

In considering the curricula for practitioners, one reviewer referred to Redmon's (1991) suggestion that interventions are maintained only to the extent that their maintenance benefits the decision makers in an organization: "Teachers and researchers only want to train future teachers and researchers because of the benefits to them (e.g., publishing partners)."

CONCLUSION

The present analysis suggests that those few who are successfully training productive scientists should be encouraged to train even more. But the rest of us should take pride in concentrating on teaching whatever useful skills we now possess (e.g., college teaching, one-on-one clinical practice, behavioral systems analysis, or departmental administration). The rest of us should redesign our thesis and dissertation requirements to help our students acquire skills more relevant to practice rather than skills more relevant to publication.

REFERENCES

Bailey, J. S. (1991). Marketing behavior analysis requires different talk. *Journal of Applied Behavior Analysis,* **24**, 445–448.

Geller, E. S. (1991a). Is applied behavior analysis technological to a fault? *Journal of Applied Behavior Analysis,* **24**, 401–406.

Geller, E. S. (1991b). Where's the validity in social validity? *Journal of Applied Behavior Analysis,* **24**, 179–184.

Johnston, J. M. (1991). We need a new model of technology. *Journal of Applied Behavior Analysis,* **24**, 425–427.

Lindsley, O. R. (1991). From technical jargon to plain English for application. *Journal of Applied Behavior Analysis,* **24**, 449–458.

Mager, R. F. (1984). *Goal analysis.* Belmont, CA: David S. Lake Publishers.

Mager, R. F. (1988). *Making instruction work.* Belmont, CA: David S. Lake Publishers.

Malott, R. W. (1974). A behavioral-systems approach to the design of human services. In D. Harshbarger & R. F. Maley (Eds.), *Behavior analysis and systems analysis: An integrative approach to mental health programs* (pp. 319–342). Kalamazoo, MI: Behaviordeila.

Malott, R. W., & Garcia, M. E. (1987). A goal directed model approach for the design of human performance systems. *Journal of Organizational Behavior Management,* **9**, 125–159.

Mechner, F., & Cook, D. A. (1988). Performance analysis. *Youth Policy,* **10**(7), 36–42.

Redmon, W. K. (1991). Pinpointing the technological fault in applied behavior analysis. *Journal of Applied Behavior Analysis,* **24**, 441–444.

Reid, D. H. (1991). Technological behavior analysis and societal impact: A human services perspective. *Journal of Applied Behavior Analysis,* **24**, 437–439.

Schwartz, I. S. (1991). The study of consumer behavior and social validity: An essential partnership for applied behavior analysis. *Journal of Applied Behavior Analysis,* **24**, 241–244.

Stoltz, S. B. (1981). Adoption of innovations from applied behavioral research: "Does anybody care?" *Journal of Applied Behavior Analysis,* **14**, 491–505.

Watkins, C. L. (1988). Project Follow Through: A story of the identification and neglect of effective instruction. *Youth Policy,* **10**(7), 7–11.

Wolf, M. M. (1978). Social validity: The case for subjective measurement, or how behavior analysis is finding its heart. *Journal of Applied Behavior Analysis,* **11**, 203–214.

Received June 28, 1991
Initial editorial decision October 10, 1991
Revision received November 19, 1991
Final acceptance December 2, 1991
Action Editor, E. Scott Geller

JOURNAL OF APPLIED BEHAVIOR ANALYSIS 1992, 25, 89–92 NUMBER 1 (SPRING 1992)

TEACHER PROPOSES, STUDENT DISPOSES

DONALD M. BAER

THE UNIVERSITY OF KANSAS

Malott proposes a problem in behavioral-science training and an attractive solution. The problem is that we need many practitioners and few researchers; the solution is to teach very many of the very many people who want to be practitioners to be practitioners, and teach the very few people who want to be researchers to be researchers.

This problem is urgent only for those audiences who have not noticed that its solution is already a widespread reality: That is what we are doing right now and have been doing for some time. We simply have not been admitting that we do, as if that solution to the problem had no social validity. In fact, it is socially invalid only within a very small community, but this community is one of our most vocal and often gets taken as Our opinion. Thus Malott's argument is functional and valuable.

Unfortunately, it is also more elegant than the issue requires. Malott devotes some interestingly conceptualized effort to empirical proof of his facts, but in my opinion not convincingly. For example, if we want to know what proportions of the world's probable 5,000 behavior analysts are researchers, practitioners, teachers, and administrators, we ought not to sample the 2,000 members of ABA, because, as Malott notes, ABA probably attracts, supports, and maintains membership from these categories differentially. Then why proceed with an ABA-based market analysis? The only fact wanted is that very many of our students after graduation fill roles other than researcher or research teacher. I recommend simply asserting that fact; it is so obvious to us that it needs no survey, and its credibility may even be damaged by an obviously inaccurate one. Similarly, if we want to know how many of the people we thought we had taught to publish applied behavior-analytic work actually do, we will not find that out by surveying *JABA*. It publishes roughly a quarter of what it receives, and it receives a lot less than exists, probably because many authors see that their work is not much like what *JABA* has published previously. Behavior analysis is published in at least 26 journals. If we want to know how few behavior analysts publish behavior analysis, we should survey all of those journals. But if the only fact wanted is that relatively few behavior analysts publish it, again I recommend simply asserting that fact, because it is obvious to us.

Malott proposes that behavior analysis might become better accepted in our society if we trained very many behavior-analytic practitioners. If very many of the students whom we intended to train as researchers behave immediately after graduation as practitioners, then apparently we *are* training very many practitioners, whatever topography we may claim for that training.

Are we burdening too many of our graduates with the wrong skills by pretending to train them as researchers when in fact they will behave as practitioners and administrators? That needs proof before we begin to mend our ways. I found no proof in Malott's argument or references. My own experience does not support the hypothesis. Most of what my students and I discuss is how behavior works, and some of what we discuss is how we could prove that. We do not often discuss whether they will spend their lives proving that, or whether the department and I want them to, or whether that is all they can extract from their graduate training program.

However, my students quite often do say that not me and not the department, but something called ABA and something called *JABA* are quite contemptuous of mere practice and mere practitioners and complain constantly about the poor status of behavior analysis in our society. Those

Reprints may be obtained from the author, Department of Human Development, University of Kansas, Lawrence, Kansas 66045.

students agree with Malott, as do I: If you are contemptuous of what your society needs, your society will be contemptuous of you and will give you excellent occasion to complain about it.

Of course, neither ABA nor *JABA* is a behaving organism; neither is capable of contempt or complaint. My students are describing only the behaviors of only a few of the people who behave in ABA and *JABA*. Perhaps those people are the most obvious, the most vocal, the most repetitive, or the most official; ABA and *JABA* are not the culprits but only overgeneralizations from them—synecdoches.

The point is only that Malott has chosen the wrong target. Perhaps our graduate training programs do not need reform: They may be very pretentious about what they supposedly do, but in fact they actually do train a large number of practitioners and administrators. Perhaps it is only the contempt that some people feel for those roles that should be published less frequently, if ever.

If our training programs were honest about what they actually do, could they become more efficient at doing it? That too needs a proof, and I did not find one in Malott's paper. It may be true, of course, but my opinion is that training programs are not nearly as effective in altering student behavior as students are in taking from the programs only what they want while humoring the useless requirements at their minimal levels (which are *quite* minimal). Because our students are very diverse, it is a good thing that our training programs are diverse enough to train a small number of researchers and research teachers and a large number of practitioners and administrators—just about what Malott recommends—no matter what we say about our mission.

It is again the wrong target to impute to some collective Us the belief that shaping shrewd science behaviors will yield a generalized set of shrewd rest-of-the-world behaviors, or that practitioners must know how to read journal articles critically, or indeed any other beliefs that supposedly justify research teaching or distinguish it from practice teaching. It does not matter whether these beliefs are true or false, or who espouses them: The functional question is whether our training programs are producing a few researchers and a lot of practitioners; obviously they are, no matter what their faculty say those programs are doing.

This problem in choice of target arises in the opening question of Malott's manuscript: "Should we continue" research training with our students, or turn to practice training? First, those labels are not the terms of an intrinsically either/or proposition; second, and more important, is the subtlety of the "we continue" theme. ("*We* continue?" When the Lone Ranger, seeing too many hostile Indians, said to Tonto, "We're done for, old friend," Tonto replied, "What you mean 'we,' white man?") Perhaps Malott's graduate program offers only one MA and one PhD, both dedicated to extensive research training. Kansas offers four MA and two PhD tracks, and in my opinion one of the two doctoral tracks harbors two subtracks that for some of us are not worth distinguishing administratively and for others of us are administratively worth not distinguishing. Among the several differences that do distinguish these six or seven training programs is the proportion of emphasis given to research and practice training. Students choose freely among them and move freely among them.

To generalize: Behavioral-science doctoral programs have many components in common and many components not in common across Western societies; this paper is, after all, only a proposal that behavior-analytic programs shift a large part of the research training component from their "in common" category to their "not in common" category. My point in resisting Malott's "continue" theme is simply to note that a great deal of the core of research training already has been moved to the "not in common" category by the actions of quite a few doctoral programs, some of them behavior analytic. Sometimes that was done ostentatiously with a change in the name of the degree (e.g., PsyD); more often it was done quietly by an internal change in the definition of "research" that a faculty adopted.

In my opinion, the change Malott recommends has already been made in all but name and on a massive scale outside of behavior-analytic programs and to a lesser extent within them. Especially outside of our programs (but increasingly within them, I submit), the research required of a very large number of behavioral-science PhDs is nothing more than to cite a theory, correlate two strangely chosen scales in a small sample representative of no one knows whom, explain away the slightness of the correlation that results, and then recommend the redesign of society that the chosen theory will continue to imply whether or not those scales correlate. I do not call that research. It follows that the majority of our society's behavioral-science PhDs graduate quite untroubled by what I can call research training. Topographically, Malott's recommendation may seem revolutionary within some communities of verbal behavior about graduate training; functionally, it is commonplace.

Yet I prefer to expose even future practitioners and administrators to a certain fairly brief version of a certain type of research training, not because I am confident that they can cheerfully ignore it while they extract what they really want from our training programs, but because I suspect that they will not ignore it because it is part of what they really want from our training programs.

For me, the essence of research training is (a) to understand as fully as possible the stimulus controls our community establishes and supports for the response class of saying that something is true or false, (b) to contrast those stimulus controls with a few other communities' stimulus controls for saying that something is true or false, and (c) to consider the related verbal behavior (the justification) each of those communities offers in support of its stimulus controls rather than those of some other community. Given that, a choice response usually occurs, or is imposed, that determines some of the character of the student's future research behavior, *and some of their practice and administration behavior, too,* at least for a while. If I am wrong in supposing that practice and administration students will want this, then I still rest confident in their ability to ignore all but the quite minimal amount of it necessary to pass.

Unfortunately, exposure to a variety of communities' stimulus controls for saying that something is true or false does not happen in many research training programs. Instead, many research "methods" are taught, either in a single community's stimulus controls, or, more often, as ritual. I do not see that as a good use of time, and although I agree with the central them of Malott's thesis, it is mainly for other reasons: I do not see that kind of research training as a good use of time quite apart from the question of how many of our students are going to extract practice training and how many research training from us. In my opinion, if we understand a lot about the conditions under which we will say that something is true or false, we will reliably invent the necessary technique whenever we need it, if we do not already know it. Thus, I do not recommend teaching a lot of technique; I recommend teaching the logic of experimental control. I see that as a good use of time: I want researchers to know a lot about the conditions that control when We will say that something is true or false, and how dependably We can say it is true or false in a contextual universe, because than I expect them to choose or fall into a set of conditions that will control when *they* will say that.

I see practitioners not as persons who are to produce new knowledge, begin to explore its dependability, and convince us of the results, but as persons who are to use reasonably dependable old knowledge to change those behaviors that will solve problems. I want them to have examined a few communities' stimulus controls for only four classes of statements about what is true or false: (a) preintervention statements that the target behavior is indeed a problem, (b) midintervention statements that the target behavior is changing, (c) postintervention statements that the change is because of what they did, and (d) final statement that these changes do reduce the referring problem. I very often settle for the first three; I call that a good use of time. I suspect that the students do too. But even if they do not, the necessary proportions of researchers and practitioners will continue to extract what they see as their relevant training from our programs.

Thus, in my opinion, the best responses to Malott's thesis are (a) to agree that we should train a few researchers and many practitioners; (b) to note that we already do and always have; (c) to understand that our students are not conscripts for an army, and will choose what profession they want to extract from our training program, even when we arrogantly attempt to impose one on them and speak and write as if we succeed in doing so; (d) to note that our programs already vary what they call research training and practice training, as well as the time devoted to what they call research training and practice training; (e) to conclude that therefore the best debate is at the level of detail, not principle, and should be based on studies that measure what happens when we experimentally vary those times and contents (and perhaps on studies of what happens when we are honest about it as well); and (f) therefore to note that those studies have not been done.

Received November 7, 1991
Final acceptance November 18, 1991
Action Editor, E. Scott Geller

JOURNAL OF APPLIED BEHAVIOR ANALYSIS 1992, 25, 93–96 NUMBER 1 (SPRING 1992)

MANAGING OUR OWN BEHAVIOR: SOME HIDDEN ISSUES

J. M. Johnston
AUBURN UNIVERSITY

Malott's paper seems less a thorough argument about his titled theme than a casual stroll through a minefield of issues embedded in almost any discussion of graduate training in behavior analysis. It is easy to find premises and conclusions to disagree with, and developing such critiques might be an educational exercise. In the interest of facilitating discussion, I would like to highlight a few hidden issues and, in the process, offer some additional arguments.

A Call for Disciplinary Research

Malott may be criticized for offering too few empirical facts as a basis for some of his statements, but he had little choice. There is almost no empirical data base describing the graduates that behavior analysis training programs produce, the training that produced them, the careers these graduates build, and how well their training prepared them for what they actually wind up doing. There is also little formal evidence about the changing needs of the employment markets that new graduates face and the things they will be called on to do once they have jobs.

Unlike other established disciplines, we have not yet developed a regular program of disciplinary research. We are just now beginning to define the minima that constitute a training program in behavior analysis (Hopkins, 1991). As a result, we do not even know how many masters and doctoral degrees are earned each year, much less the details of a graduate's competencies. We also do not know much about the kinds of baccalaureate training our students bring to graduate school or why they choose the career directions they do. Neither have we studied the personnel needs of the discipline or its employment markets.

Reprints may be obtained from the author, Department of Psychology, Auburn University, Auburn, Alabama 36849.

The question of whether behavior analysis needs proportionally more researchers or practitioners cannot be answered until we know what we are producing now. If these data were available, however, we could still not answer this question. We would also have to figure out how we wanted the field to develop over the next decade or so. In addition, we would have to study the potential employers of graduates and the annual demand they create for different kinds of behavior analysts. This might show us conflicts between how we want the discipline to develop and the needs of its users (e.g., we might want more applied researchers even when certain markets need more practitioners). These data, in turn, would challenge us to decide how behavior analysis might manage its production of graduate degrees. These are new problems for us, and we have a lot to talk about.

The collection of these data is too important to leave to the vagaries of individual research motivations; they should be one of the routine functions of the Association for Behavior Analysis (ABA). ABA should support the continuing collection of data concerning graduate training and employee demand, supplemented by particular projects designed to answer specific questions.

Graduate Training Models

Malott's thesis calls for us to discuss graduate training as being partly a matter of producing a product; this idea may not be comfortable for many of us. We are probably more accustomed to talking about an apprenticeship model of graduate training than considering a manufacturing metaphor. Some graduate programs enthusiastically embrace a very open approach to graduate training in which most of a student's experiences result solely from his or her interests, which may often depend on who serves as a major professor. Others make no apologies for requiring a common core of course work for all students, if not a selection of specific advanced program tracks. The characteristics of such requirements may sometimes have more to do with local resources and politics than the needs of the discipline or employers, however.

The apprenticeship model certainly has its strengths, especially for doctoral study, but it is not incompatible with the notion of managing the scope and direction of graduate training. Many of today's senior faculty were trained at a point in the field's development when there was simply much less material than is now available that could be considered a proper foundation for a masters or doctoral degree in behavior analysis. Similarly, today's jobs, whether academic or applied, may also require a range of competencies that a "pure" apprenticeship training history may sometimes fail to satisfy.

The idea that we can manage certain features of degree production may be new for behavior analysis, but the notion that students are free to choose the directions of graduate training should prompt an easy critique from a radical behavioristic perspective (Skinner, 1971). Conceptual issues aside, graduate faculty know that most students have only very general and ill-formed interests when they begin graduate training and that their eventual career interests tend to adapt to the training and experiences they are offered. In any case, educational philosophy notwithstanding, graduate programs do produce trained students, who can be usefully viewed as one of our products if we want to worry about how good a job we are doing for the students, their employers, and the discipline.

ABA's new accreditation program may encourage graduate programs to address some issues concerning exactly what we ought to be doing in the name of graduate education. The accreditation standards approved by the ABA Executive Council include a number of specific "curriculum topics" that must be taught to or mastered by all students in accredited programs. This is the first time the field of behavior analysis has attempted to influence the education of its personnel, and it should prompt us to consider more carefully than in the past the criteria that guide our future management decisions.

Doctoral, Master's, and Bachelor Programs

One of the issues that Malott did not address clearly, and that the field will have to weigh in considering its training output in relation to the demands of the job market, is the proportion of its graduates produced at different degree levels. According to ABA's *Graduate Training in Behavior Analysis* (1990), graduate programs in behavior analysis offer the customary mix of graduate degree options. In addition, each grouping of behavior-analytic faculty has the potential to offer some undergraduate training in behavior analysis, although local considerations may often preclude offering a clear sequence of courses.

Although the actual number of graduates at each degree level is unknown, it is easy to guess that the market's needs are inversely related to the degree of training. That is, all markets considered, the greatest number of jobs are probably available for those holding the bachelors degree and the smallest number for the doctorate. If true, one problem with this relationship is that coherent programs of instruction in behavior analysis are most highly developed only at the graduate level. At the undergraduate level, whether in psychology or education departments, behavior analysis is not usually represented as a well-identified program of study. Furthermore, the course offerings at this level are likely to be quite limited, and extracurricular experiences (e.g., practica) are probably uncommon, if not rare.

A related problem concerns our understanding of how educational experiences should differ at each degree level. It is clear that graduates holding the BA degree will be employed in service delivery settings, but how well do we know what skills are necessary for effective employment with different service populations and settings? Although MA graduates are also likely to work in applied settings as practitioners, do we know what positions and responsibilities are typical and how students should be prepared for them? There is also a potential conflict between the everyday demands of employment markets and the curricular emphasis of psychology MA programs that require a substantial core of mainstream psychology course work and a research thesis. However, many departments offering doctoral training are reluctant to offer a terminal nonthesis MA degree that is professionally oriented. In these cases, are we merely offering a junior version of a doctoral degree that is poorly matched to career needs, or is there something about the effects of traditional core requirements and a thesis that justifies the time required?

Applied Research Versus Service Delivery

One issue Malott highlighted clearly has long been quite familiar to clinical psychology. It involves a confrontation that behavior analysis is increasingly facing. Although doctoral training has an honored tradition as a research degree, for many students it is merely a ticket that must be purchased before they can depart on a career as a practitioner. Clinical psychology has yet to develop a consensus on this issue. Instead, it has either pretended to pursue a scientist-practitioner model in which students are supposedly trained to do everything, or it has admitted the interests if not the needs of its students and offered an alternative PsyD model.

Although the evidence is unclear, it seems that most doctoral graduates in behavior analysis do not intend to become researchers and do not conduct or publish archival research as part of their jobs. If this is so, behavior analysis will be able to avoid the consequences of clinical psychology's confusion only if we do a better job of addressing this problem.

I have recently described one approach to this issue (Johnston, 1991, in press) and will not repeat the details here. In brief, embedded in this old problem is an important issue that goes to the heart of how we define applied behavior analysis in particular and behavior analysis overall. The present conception of applied behavior analysis embodies the confusion that clinical psychology has struggled with—a failure to distinguish honestly between research and service delivery at a number of levels. In our case, the confusion has pervaded our conception of the discipline by intermingling applied research and service interests in such a way that a distorted model of applied research has resulted. One result is an unnecessarily weak though large applied research literature that is overly subservient to service delivery needs. Research problems are often conceptualized in terms of the need for immediate, practical solutions, and methodological compromises are frequently resolved in favor of applied interests.

As we come to grips with some of these issues, I believe we must revise our conception of applied behavior analysis in such a way that we greatly strengthen applied research in quantity, focus, and methodology. One part of this challenge must involve a better appreciation of how applied research should be defined. Clearly distinguishing it from service delivery will be a crucial step, and the distinction will have unavoidable implications for graduate education. Beyond a common core, I suspect we should train practitioners somewhat differently than we train applied researchers, although I am not sure exactly what the differences should be. Unfortunately, Malott's paper seems to be reaching this conclusion prematurely by failing to consider the larger issues, of which graduate training curricular are but one consequence.

In Summary

I disagree with a number of points in Malott's commentary. For reasons that I have not attempted to articulate, I disagree that we need to train "few scientists and many practitioners." I am especially troubled with the proposal of such a laissez faire approach to developing graduate training curricula (i.e., we should each teach what we do best). I am certainly not comfortable with the status quo in applied behavior analysis at any level. In other words, it is not difficult to quibble with some of his data, arguments, and conclusions.

Nevertheless, Malott's proposal is useful in calling for us to debate a variety of issues concerning how we train behavior analysts at all degree levels. In particular, for the sake of our field's future, we must begin to manage our training and production of behavior analysts with the same behavioral skills we bring to other applied problems. This will mean collecting data that help define the issues and guide policies. These policies must address the future development of the entire discipline by leading to contingencies that will appropriately influence professional behavior. We especially need to build support for coordinated action. It will not matter how effective behavior analysis can be in the areas of research and service if it does not produce sufficient numbers of graduates at all levels who are well prepared to serve both the discipline and its users.

REFERENCES

Association for Behavior Analysis. (1990). *Graduate training in behavior analysis.* Kalamazoo, MI: Author.

Hopkins, B. L. (1991, May). *Accreditation of graduate training programs in behavior analysis.* Symposium conducted at the meeting of the Association of Behavior Analysis, Atlanta.

Johnston, J. M. (1991). We need a new model of technology. *Journal of Applied Behavior Analysis,* **24**, 425–427.

Johnston, J. M. (in press). A model for developing and evaluating behavioral technology. In S. Axelrod & R. Van Houten (Eds.), *Effective behavioral treatment: Issues and implementation.* New York: Plenum.

Skinner, B. F. (1971). *Beyond freedom and dignity.* New York: Knopf.

Received November 20, 1991
Final acceptance December 3, 1991
Action Editor, E. Scott Geller

JOURNAL OF APPLIED BEHAVIOR ANALYSIS 1992, 25, 97–99 NUMBER 1 (SPRING 1992)

THE NEED TO TRAIN MORE BEHAVIOR ANALYSTS TO BE BETTER APPLIED RESEARCHERS

DENNIS H. REID

WESTERN CAROLINA CENTER, MORGANTON, NORTH CAROLINA

Malott's paper is a provocative and welcomed contribution to the behavior analysis literature. He has addressed the important topic reflected in his title in a seemingly forthright, albeit controversial, manner. The focus and effectiveness of graduate programs in applied behavior analysis have received relatively little attention in the behavioral literature; however, attention is currently warranted in light of the larger issue of the status of the education system in general in the United States. Hence, the main thrust of Malott's points warrants serious consideration. Such consideration could lead to responsive action, resulting in important changes in the graduate education of applied behavior analysts.

To suggest that Malott's paper should help set the occasion for changes in graduate programs in applied behavior analysis of course implies agreement with his summary of the primary problem with these programs (i.e., the low success rate of teaching productive researchers in applied behavior analysis). In this regard, I am in agreement with his summary. However, I am not in total agreement with his recommended corrective actions. I suggest that graduate programs in applied behavior analysis should not discontinue training as many students to be researchers, as Malott recommends, but rather should make changes in order to do a more effective job of teaching students how to be successful researchers in nonacademic settings. The rationale for why such teaching should occur is summarized in the following paragraphs, followed in turn by suggestions on how to improve the teaching.

Appreciation is expressed to Marsha Parsons for sharing her thoughts on the topic of this commentary and to Mary Keller for assistance in preparing the manuscript. Requests for reprints should be addressed to Dennis H. Reid, Western Carolina Center, Morganton, North Carolina 28655.

Why Graduate Programs Should Teach Students to Be (Better) Researchers

Malott cogently responds to, and negates to a large degree, traditional reasons for training practitioners in research methodology and related skills. However, there are other important reasons for teaching research skills not addressed by Malott. Some of the reasons have been discussed in depth previously (Reid, 1987), and a few will be only briefly described here. First, research skills in applied behavior analysis can be important for assisting practitioners in critically evaluating the validity and efficacy of new developments in the human services, which is the primary area of employment of behavior analysts in nonacademic settings. Human services in general, and education in particular, are replete with recommendations supposedly stemming from research that have led to changes in policy and practice over the years. Unfortunately, much of the research (where research exists) is conducted very poorly, and resulting conclusions are of limited value at best for practitioners. Relatedly, practitioners are rarely sufficiently trained to evaluate research critically. Many practitioners often assume new developments popularized in the professional literature, workshops, and so on are useful because the recommendations reportedly stem from research (which to many human services personnel simply means there is some reference to statistics). Practitioners trained in critically evaluating research can be invaluable for controlling (or at least impeding enthusiastic adoption of) ineffectual procedural changes based on research of questionable quality. In this regard, perhaps consideration is warranted regarding Malott's point that it is cost ineffective to train practitioners in research skills in order to allow the practitioners to be able to detect poorly conducted and/or analyzed research presented in scholarly behavioral journals. However, good research skills are useful for critically evaluating those journals and related sources that are not so scholarly or scientifically rigid, from which invalid conclusions are likely to be drawn. At least someone (i.e., a behavior analyst skilled in research) should be in every human services agency to help prevent the agency from responding to misguided information that can result in ineffective and even counterproductive changes in service provision.

Another advantage of training behavior analyst practitioners in research skills not emphasized by Malott is that if practitioners successfully conduct research, the applied research process can improve an agency's service provision as well as the human services field in general (see Reid, 1987, for elaboration). Also, by successfully involving a behavioral researcher's agency colleagues in collaboration on applied research, the service provision skills of these colleagues can be enhanced. The skill enhancement results from participating in various professional activities related to conducting successful research, such as reading relevant professional literature, attending conferences, and responding to requests for consultation. Such professional activity is otherwise frequently lacking among many personnel in human services settings.

The end result of the processes just summarized is a small but important increase in the awareness and corresponding application (i.e., adoption) of behavior analysis technology in applied settings. When considered in this vein, more applied behavior-analytic researchers are needed in applied settings, not fewer—assuming, of course, that the researchers are skilled and successful at conducting applied research.

Improving the Success of Graduate Programs in Teaching Students to Be Productive Researchers in Applied Behavior Analysis

As alluded to earlier, Malott makes a rather striking case regarding the ineffectiveness of many graduate programs at teaching students to be successful researchers in applied behavior analysis. He subsequently concludes that most graduate faculty should consider deemphasizing the teaching of scientific research, because most faculty members do not perform such teaching very well. Based on the premise just noted that applied behavior analysis research is important in human services settings, I would argue not to deemphasize teaching research skills in graduate programs but, as indicated previously, to change the teaching focus somewhat and do a more effective job of teaching. If graduate programs were more successful at teaching research skills (and this point seems at least implicitly reflected in Malott's comments) then the question of whether the programs should teach such skills becomes much less of an issue.

Applied behavior analysis as a field has grown enormously since the 1960s, with many specialty areas of research and application having developed. Some of the specialty areas are amenable to research undertakings in nonacademic settings, and some are not. If most behavior analysts will eventually work in applied settings as Malott indicates, then the focus of their research training should be on the former specialty areas. To illustrate, research on applied behavior analysis technology—its development, application, refinement, and adoption—is often amenable to incorporation into existing human services settings and practices, whereas theoretical research is not amenable in this respect. Technological research can be problem solving in nature, and every human services agency has problems to be solved.

In addition to the selected focus of applied research, the eventual success of a research program is affected significantly by *how* the research is conducted in relation to a respective setting's resources and routine practices. The latter issue pertains to research skills typically not addressed in academic research curricula. Such skills include, for example, (a) establishing a research agenda based on the goals of the agency and interests of agency staff in contrast to the researcher's particular research interests, (b) selecting experimental designs acceptable to agency staff and flexible to compensate for day-to-day work contingencies, and (c) finding and applying available agency staff resources to assist with the research. Actually, the latter skills could be addressed through a systems analysis approach, as described by Malott, and be incorporated into graduate training curricula.

One suggestion for improving the applied research skills of students offered by Malott that seems especially interesting is for students to complete a research internship under the tutelage of a successful researcher working in an applied setting. As a practitioner, and perhaps responding selfishly, I strongly support such an idea. I also believe many agency executives, at least in the human services with which I am familiar, would seriously welcome such an arrangement—provided it was clear to all involved that the research would be applied in nature and in accordance with respective agency missions. A related suggestion I offer is for faculty members responsible for teaching applied research methodology to fulfill periodically a sabbatical-type role in an applied setting and conduct research while in that role, under the supervision of a successful practitioner/researcher. Many contingencies operating on a faculty member's research behavior are different than the contingencies operating on a practitioner's research behavior. The type of sabbatical arrangement suggested here could serve to increase a faculty person's awareness of the latter contingencies as well as the countercontrol types of skills often necessary for conducting research in an applied services setting. In essence, this process could function in the same manner as more traditional postdoctoral training for practitioners, but in this case for university teachers, and could have a number of educational benefits (cf. Bailey, 1981) that would subsequently be incorporated into graduate training programs in applied behavior analysis.

In summary, Malott identifies an important and problematic issue warranting attention. Although I disagree in large part with his recommended solutions, I sincerely commend his willingness to raise the issue so cogently. Indeed, a problem is unlikely to be solved if the problem is not well identified. Malott's pointed articulation of the problem in current graduate programs is likely to draw considerable professional attention to the issue, attention that is seriously needed if significant improvements are going to occur in the training of productive researchers in applied behavior analysis.

REFERENCES

Bailey, J. S. (1981). Wanted: A rational search for the limiting conditions of habilitation in the retarded. *Analysis and Intervention in Developmental Disabilities*, **1**, 45–52.

Reid, D. H. (1987). *Developing a research program in human service agencies: A practitioner's guidebook.* Springfield, IL: Charles C Thomas.

Received October 16, 1991
Final acceptance November 12, 1991
Action Editor, E. Scott Geller

JOURNAL OF APPLIED BEHAVIOR ANALYSIS 1992, 25, 513–515 NUMBER 2 (SUMMER 1992)

FOLLOW-UP COMMENTARY ON TRAINING BEHAVIOR ANALYSTS

RICHARD W. MALOTT

WESTERN MICHIGAN UNIVERSITY

I recommend that we decrease our ineffective efforts to train prominent researchers (Malott, 1992). So I am honored that three of our most prominent researchers have critically evaluated those recommendations (Baer, 1992; Johnston, 1992; Reid, 1992). One of those researchers leads the elite list of 26 scholars who authored at least five articles in the *Journal of Applied Behavior Analysis* (*JABA*) during its second decade. He published 16 articles! And he is not a college professor! Another of those researchers *is* a college professor and is responsible for having trained more of *JABA*'s authors than perhaps anyone else in the world.

However, among these critics I find no nonresearcher/author—no main-line behavior-analytic practitioner: the sort of professional I recommend we should be training more of. Whether this reflects editorial bias or the low frequency with which practitioners publish, the criticisms of my recommendations hardly come from a representative sample. Nonetheless, I am still honored that these three scholars were willing to respond, although often negatively.

Before addressing the individual critiques, I present one general clarification: I do not argue that there should be less high-quality research in applied behavior analysis. More would be fine. I do argue that we should stop training nearly all applied behavior analysts as if they were going to be researchers, when most will not.

Please address requests for reprints to Richard W. Malott, Department of Psychology, Western Michigan University, Kalamazoo, Michigan 49008-5052.

Editor's Note. This rebuttal to commentary in the Spring 1992 issue of *JABA* is published with the author's original discussion paper and the three reviews in the *JABA* Monograph 7 that features discussion and commentary on education (*The Education Crisis: Issues, Perspectives, Solutions*).

IN RESPONSE TO BAER (1992)

In Defense of the Status Quo?

Baer essentially supports the status quo. He argues, "If very many of the students whom we intended to train as researchers behave immediately after graduation as practitioners, then apparently we *are* training very many practitioners, whatever topography we may claim for that training" (p. 89). That reminds me of what physicians in Montevideo tell me about the practice of medicine there: The medical school trains more MDs than there are desirable positions to fill. Therefore, many MDs become taxi drivers. Does Baer's logic suggest the more appropriate name for the overly productive medical school should be the Uruguay National Medical School and Taxi Driver Institute? That trained researchers become practitioners does not mean they were trained to become practitioners. They became practitioners in spite of their training.

However, *if* the status quo were Don Baer, I would certainly join its defense. I know of no one who matches his rate of graduating high-quality researchers. In his case, I consider the effective practitioner/administrators he graduates as an added benefit, not as a justification for others adopting his practices.

Inculcating Proresearcher, Antipractitioner Values

Baer is right; I do not have much formal data. And he may not often tell his students they should become researchers. And he may be among the rare professors who do not find it especially reinforcing to clone themselves. Or he may define the clone more generally than most—perhaps successful clones are alumni who are properly data based in whatever endeavor they take on. But, despite what we professors say, we do train our graduate students in environments in which so much emphasis is placed on research that the winning professors are defined as those with the most or best publications and the losers, including those who do not get tenure, are those with the fewest or worst publications. It is hard to imagine our graduate students successfully modeling their professors without acquiring those values to some extent. In other words, I take it as unexceptional that I heard a Kansas alumnus complain that the developmental disabilities center where he worked as a practitioner/administrator did not support research.

Student and Teacher: Conflicting Interests?

Baer believes that "Training programs are not nearly as effective in altering student behavior as students are in taking from them what they want" (p. 90). He almost seems to offer this as defense for teaching whatever that professor finds reinforcing or expedient to teach. What the professor tries to teach does not matter because hidden within the professor's course will be ample training for the student to do whatever the student ends up doing. Furthermore, the cunning and resourceful student will be able to extract that useful training from the mass of irrelevancies the course contains. Does this seem optimistic?

In Defense of Pseudoscience?

Baer seems to suggest that a quiet increase in the frequency of worthless correlation studies is evidence that many people know research training is irrelevant for practitioners, so they do easy pseudoscience dissertations. Why not do worthwhile behavioral systems analysis and interventions of the sort students need practice doing for their later careers? Of course such work might not help the advisors get tenure, a serious concern I do not demean.

I did not hope my recommendations would be "revolutionary" within any "communities of verbal behavior about graduate training" (p. 91). But I did hope my recommendation for a functional, job-based, goal-driven curriculum would be discriminated from a recommendation for more useless "functionally . . . commonplace" (p. 91) pseudoscientific research.

Can We Reliably Train Strategies?

I do not argue against the value of training our students to tell if something is "true or false" (p. 91). And I do not argue with Baer's observation that this "does not happen in many research-training programs" (p. 91). Also, I do not argue with Baer's suggestion that "if we understand a lot about the conditions under which we will say that something is true or false, we will reliably invent the necessary technique whenever we need it, if we do not already know it" (p. 91). But one of the most outstanding researchers in behavior analysis lamented that many students from his graduate course in truth and falsehood showed no evidence of ever having read Johnston and Pennypacker or Sidman at dissertation time. Perhaps he failed to teach "the logic of experimental control" (p. 91). However, my 25 years experience in teaching graduate students has been that it is depressingly hard for students to acquire general abstract strategies they can transfer across disparate problems. I have not quit; I still try. But my experience and the training literature suggest that the more specific and concrete the training, the more likely it will alter the student's repertoire in usable ways. Along the same lines, I see little evidence that most scholars, including behavior analysts, are much better judges of truth and falsity outside their own specialty areas than are taxi drivers, especially if the scholars have a vested interest.

Can We Justify the Status Quo?

Baer seems to suggest that no matter who we train and no matter what the market needs, everything will adjust appropriately. That seems a Panglossian justification for the status quo. Also, the absence of experimental data does not seem to be an adequate justification for our current expensive, restrictive status quo.

IN RESPONSE TO REID (1992)

Should We Try Harder to Produce Productive Practitioner/Researchers?

Reid agrees that we have a low rate of producing productive researchers; however, he suggests the goal of producing productive practitioner/researchers justifies trying harder. Then these practitioner/researchers could tell the false from the true when they read nonrigorous applied literature. Our past failure in large-scale science training offers little support for this optimistic perspective. Wouldn't it be more cost effective for the Association for Behavior Analysis (ABA) to publish an annual review of the best and the worst from the literature outside *JABA*?

Instead of encouraging more *JABA*-type research, why not train behavior analysts to involve everyone in behavioral systems analyses and interventions? This would directly enhance the achievement of the agency's mission as well as produce the side benefits of enhancing service provision skills of the participants and increasing their general professional activities. In other words, I think we can accomplish Reid's objectives more cost effectively than by trying harder at continuing variations of the scientist/practitioner model.

Would It Suffice to Try Harder in Training Practitioner/Researchers?

If we could teach science more reliably, then it would be less wasteful to continue to try to do so. We should train our graduates to solve agency problems; that is the essence of behavioral systems analysis. But usually it will not be cost effective to solve the problem and also establish the truth about what intervention, if any, was responsible for the removal of the problem.

For those few graduates who will try to emulate Reid's model of productive publishing in an applied setting, his training program is exemplary: (a) train skills directly related to doing research in applied settings *where you live and get paid*; (b) have students do research internships in such settings with a master researcher (I recommend Reid); (c) have the faculty do sabbaticals in such settings with a master researcher (I recommend Reid). But the major problem is that there are not enough Reids to begin to meet the need (I recommend that students and faculty start queuing at Reid's door). In short, I agree that those faculty and departments with a fighting chance of success should try harder, but trying harder is not a practical solution for most graduate training programs. Furthermore, a plan to try harder is not an excuse for continuing the mediocre efforts of most faculty and departments at training would-be scientists or scientist/practitioners.

IN RESPONSE TO JOHNSTON (1992)

Data?

I agree with Johnston: We should do an analysis of the system. (a) What are we producing in what proportions (scientists, practitioners, BAs, MAs, PhDs)? (b) What needs to be produced? Furthermore, ABA might be the agency responsible to address these questions. We probably need much more emphasis on training BAs and MAs in applied behavior analysis, with coherent programs to do so. But I am less optimistic than Johnston is about the likelihood that data will have any significant control over our current institutional and professional behavior.

My impression is that Johnston's main concern with my recommendations is that I did not address all of the related issues he raised. True, I did not; but I do agree with essentially everything he said regarding those issues. My recommendation that we should all teach whatever we do best was only a compromise; I consider that a big improvement over most of us teaching what we do worst.

REFERENCES

Baer, D. M. (1992). Teacher proposes, student disposes. *Journal of Applied Behavior Analysis*, **25**, 89–92.

Johnston, J. M. (1992). Managing our own behavior: Some hidden issues. *Journal of Applied Behavior Analysis*, **25**, 93–96.

Malott, R. W. (1992). Should we train applied behavior analysts to be researchers? *Journal of Applied Behavior Analysis*, **25**, 83–88.

Reid, D. H. (1992). The need to train more behavior analysts to be better applied researchers. *Journal of Applied Behavior Analysis*, **25**, 97–99.

Received February 7, 1992
Final acceptance February 25, 1992
Action Editor, E. Scott Geller

JOURNAL OF APPLIED BEHAVIOR ANALYSIS 1990, 23, 491–495 NUMBER 4 (WINTER 1990)

TRENDS IN BEHAVIOR ANALYSIS IN EDUCATION

BETH SULZER-AZAROFF AND ALEX GILLAT

UNIVERSITY OF MASSACHUSETTS, AMHERST

The preparation of the *Journal of Applied Behavior Analysis Reprint Series: Behavior Analysis in Education* (1988) provided an opportunity to survey and analyze trends in the field, as reflected by publications in the journal. Apparently, the large volume of behavior-analytic papers on educational topics has been declining and its contents undergoing some interesting but not uniformly welcome shifts. Although the intense concern with classroom conduct has diminished somewhat, that topic continues to be heavily emphasized. Simultaneously, reports of social skills and language studies have accelerated, but analyses of academic performance have progressively declined. Explanations for the findings remain speculative, but behavior analysts are encouraged to address these areas of essential social need.

DESCRIPTORS: education, classrooms, schools

Tomorrow's world will be in the hands of today's youth. How their actions will affect the future depends in great measure upon how effectively they have been educated. The field of applied behavior analysis has made major contributions toward educational improvement throughout its publication history and has the potential of tendering considerably more.

The preparation of the *JABA* reprint series, *Behavior Analysis in Education* (1988), that occurred coincident with the journal's 20th anniversary, provided a unique opportunity to examine the *Journal of Applied Behavior Analysis*'s coverage of this topic. The charge of the ad hoc editors was to identify and classify all the papers on education published in the journal since its inception and to nominate a model set to be reproduced in the volume. Participating in the process of assembling the reprint volume has permitted the authors to gain a broad perspective on the trends related to the proportion of papers devoted to educational topics and their content over the years. In this report these findings are shared with readers who are interested in where educational behavior analysis has been for the past 19 years and the directions in which it seems to be headed.

The authors wish to express their appreciation to the ad hoc editors of *Behavior Analysis in Education* (1988), whose assistance was essential to the preparation of this report.

Correspondence and reprint requests may be addressed to Beth Sulzer-Azaroff, Department of Psychology, University of Massachusetts, Amherst, Massachusetts 01003.

METHOD

Participants

Five accomplished scholars of behavior analysis in education agreed to participate as editors: Ronald S. Drabman, Douglas Greer, R. Vance Hall, Brian A. Iwata, and Susan G. O'Leary. Each was asked to assume responsibility for reviewing three or four volumes to (a) identify articles in education and suggest categories for classifying them and (b) to nominate papers for inclusion in the reprint volume by using criteria of quality, representativeness of the state of the art, and utility for school personnel. Later all were asked to review the entire proposed set and "advocate for any articles you feel absolutely must be included as reprints."

Procedure

For purposes of the volume and this analysis, papers on education were defined as those whose research was set in the classroom or those that had as their objective instruction in specific academic skills for students or educational personnel. We omitted articles dealing with one-to-one instruction of developmentally disabled students because *JABA* had published a reprint volume on developmental disabilities in 1986.

Several steps were taken to assure that educational papers were identified and classified as to content and level: (a) The lists of titles were compiled by each reviewer and (b) independently by

Table 1
Definitions of Categories (Levels)

- Preschool: subject population or setting identified as preschool or prekindergarten.
- Special Education: separate instructional groups consisting of students identified as having special needs. Included were programs serving students with developmental, perceptual, motoric, language, and other special disabilities.
- Elementary: subject population or setting identified as elementary (usually kindergarten through fourth or sixth grade).
- Middle/College: subject population or setting identified as middle (usually Grades 4 through 8), junior high school (usually Grades 7 through 9), high school (usually Grades 8 or 9 through 12), and college/university. (These groups were combined due to the small representation of each group and the common focus on academic skills.)
- Professional: formal training of management and/or instructional skills, including in-service training for teachers and/or other professional or paraprofessional personnel.

Table 2
Definitions of Categories (Content)

Defined as having targets of change or focus of intervention based on:

- Conduct: management of classroom deportment and attending (e.g., out of seat, on-task, hyperactivity, disruption, aggression).
- Social: social skills training, such as teaching adaptive skills (e.g., play, sharing, taking turns, helping, recruiting reinforcement).
- Academic: performance on academic subjects (e.g., reading, math, social studies, printing, and writing).
- Language: oral communication (e.g., increasing rates of speaking, labeling objects, elaborating sentences, using adjectives, and so on).
- Health/safety: skills related to physical well-being (e.g., nutrition, safe playground play, street crossing, and school bus and home safety).
- Teaching: skills for teaching and managing the classroom (e.g., using praise, attending, and organizing the classroom environment).

each of the two authors of this paper. (c) The reviewers also suggested ways to classify the educational level and content of each article. (d) Based on these suggested classifications, the two authors of this paper jointly finalized sets of categories related to level and content and defined each (see Tables 1 and 2). (e) Then the two authors independently assigned a level and category for each article. (f) Next we compared the two lists and discussed the few (less than 10%) differences until both agreed as to the most appropriate designation. (No formal interscorer reliability scores were determined because the classifications ultimately were determined collaboratively.) In cases of overlap of categories, such as multiple grade level or content, we assigned the article to the category that it represented most closely. The special education category spanned all grade levels, because chronological age usually was not the basis on which students were assigned to classes.

RESULTS

The list used for the analysis included 347 educational research articles, 70 of which were nominated as reprints. In addition, four discussion/review papers (Baer, Wolf, & Risley, 1968; Bijou, 1970; Keller, 1968; Stokes & Baer, 1977) with important conceptual messages were reprinted. These were excluded from the analyses to follow.

Number and Proportion of Papers in Education

Figure 1 displays the total number of papers published in *JABA* during each of its first 19 years and distribution of the 347 reports on education by year. The number of articles published in the journal per volume ranged from the 30s to over 90, peaking in Volume 10 (1977). The count focusing on education also peaked in that volume and in Volumes 7 (1974) and 9 (1976). In contrast with other topics, the proportion of papers on education showed a clearly diminishing trend from the first to the second decade. About twice as many educational papers were published during the first 10 years as in the second. In Volumes 3, 5, 6, 7, and 9, over half the articles dealt with education. This proportion has not been repeated since.

Populations Served

What educational populations have been served by behavior analysis? Primarily, populations at the elementary level have been emphasized (39.4%), with special education (19.9%), and preschool

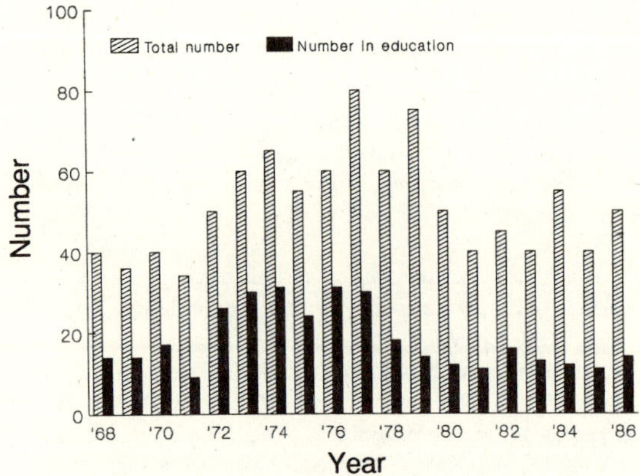

Figure 1. Total number of papers published in the *Journal of Applied Behavior Analysis* and total number published on the topic of education.

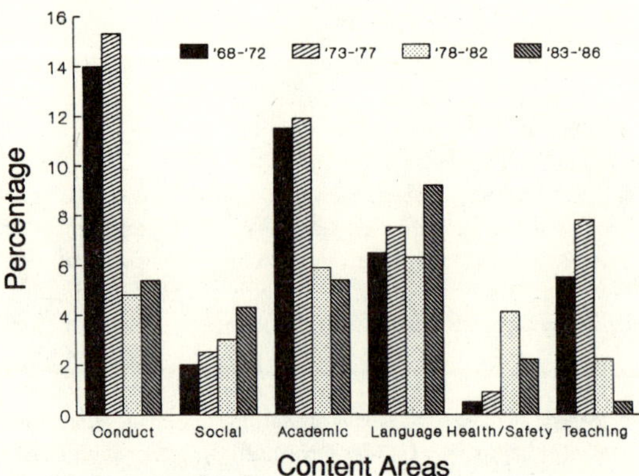

Figure 2. Percentage of each problem area addressed in studies of educational topics included in the *Journal of Applied Behavior Analysis* across 5-year blocks (except the last block, which covers only 4 years).

(18.4%) groups falling in second and third place. By contrast, so few papers involved students at the middle or junior high school, high school, or college level, that these populations were combined for the analysis (15.3%). Professional and paraprofessional educators accounted for the remaining 6.9% of the subject populations.

Problem Areas Addressed

Aggregating content areas across all volumes revealed that the topic of classroom conduct, such as being off-task, disruptive, or aggressive, led the way (29%). Other emphasized topics have been academic skills (25%) and language (20%). Skills for instructional personnel (i.e., teaching) (12%), pupil social skills (8%), and health and safety (5.5%) were emphasized less.

Has the relative emphasis changed for each of these topics over the years? Figure 2 displays the way in which the content areas have distributed themselves among the educational papers published in *JABA* in 5-year (or 4-year) blocks. (Specific distributions by content and level for each volume may be obtained from the authors.) The focus on conduct, although relatively high in the first decade, has fallen somewhat during the second. The proportion of the papers on social skills has risen gradually, whereas the proportion of papers on language has risen more substantially. Health and safety and teaching began to rise but declined during the last block of years, and studies of academic performance have shown a steady decline.

Although papers on education continue to be published in *JABA,* their absolute and relative number has fallen substantially. In the absence of experimental evidence, why this has happened can only be a matter of conjecture. One possibility is that the gradual expansion of applied behavior analysis into other realms (e.g., clinical, community, organizational, health, and safety behavior) might be crowding educational studies out of the journal. Yet a skimming of *JABA*'s content areas suggests that this hypothesis lacks support. In fact, in the past few years papers dealing with the developmentally disabled are heavily represented, whereas those on the other topics listed seem to be included increasingly in specialty journals of their own.

In a symposium on this topic at the 1988 annual meeting of the Association for Behavior Analysis, the Editor, Jon Bailey, reported that *JABA* was not receiving a heavy flow of articles on education. Functional analyses of the efficacy of important methodologies, such as precision teaching, direct instruction, the personalized system of instruction, computer-assisted instruction, educational leadership, organizational and systems studies, and the many innovative successes in the field of school psychology were essentially lacking from recent issues.

Research needs to be undertaken to determine

whether or not this is because reports are being submitted elsewhere, model papers have been absent from *JABA* for a while, authors have been punished by rejection of their papers, the papers have lacked the rigorous methodology demanded by the journal's editorial board, sufficient behavior-analytic research in these areas is not occurring, or if other unknown reasons are influencing submissions. To address these possibilities, *JABA*'s archives might be inspected to determine how many education articles were submitted on what topic and the editorial decision for each. Surveys could be sent to sample groups, such as previous authors of papers on education, to determine whether or not they continue to perform behavior analyses of educational topics; if so, where they submit their results, and if not, why they have discontinued this line of research.

Those who participate in setting or implementing public funding and policy may need to examine their practices as well. Similar to studies of the type undertaken by Braddock, Hemp, and Fujiura (1987), who investigated trends in public spending for mental retardation and developmental disabilities, trends in public support of educational research also need investigation to determine how behavior-analytic work has been faring. Perhaps the behavior of grant reviewers from within applied behavior analysis can be studied to determine whether or not they are applying overly rigorous or inflexible standards in judging the proposals or reports on education topics of their behavior-analytic peers.

In terms of focus, as the proportion of papers emphasizing classroom misconduct has diminished, the area of social skills has received growing consistent attention. From our perspective, this is a healthy sign, implying that researchers are emphasizing the promotion of constructive, adaptive skills in preference to the reduction of unwanted behavior. The upward trend in the percentage of studies of language shows a similar focus on skill development. Perhaps some of the upsurge in that area may be explained by the contemporary fascination with cognitive development.

Of special concern is the relative neglect of students at the middle-school through university level. During its first several years, *JABA* published a number of articles on the personalized system of instruction (Keller, 1968) and others on college instruction; however, the proportion rapidly diminished when the *Journal of Personalized Instruction* emerged. Unfortunately, although the latter is no longer in operation, papers on college teaching have not reappeared in *JABA*. Does this mean that behavior-analytic research on the education of adolescents and adults has diminished? Or are such studies being published elsewhere?

Certainly major educational topics merit behavior-analytic investigations. Data-based decision making in science education, remedial reading, creative problem solving, mathematical concepts, computer and job skills, foreign language instruction, and sex and health education are topics critical to society.

The hundreds of educational reports in *JABA* and the thousands published elsewhere demonstrate that behavior analysis has yielded exciting results of relevance to educational improvement (see Sulzer-Azaroff & Mayer, 1986, for an extensive coverage of this topic). The redesign of educational environments stemming from the established findings of behavioral educators promises to improve the future of our society. It is hoped that the number of high-quality papers on this topic will proliferate in *JABA* once again.

REFERENCES

Baer, D. M., Wolf, M. M., & Risley, T. R. (1968). Some current dimensions of applied behavior analysis. *Journal of Applied Behavior Analysis,* **1**, 91–97.

Bijou, S. W. (1970). What psychology has to offer education—now. *Journal of Applied Behavior Analysis,* **3**, 65–71.

Braddock, D., Hemp, R., & Fujiura, G. (1987). National study of public spending for mental retardation and developmental disabilities. *American Journal of Mental Deficiency,* **92**, 121–133.

Journal of Applied Behavior Analysis. (1986). Behavior analysis in developmental disabilities 1968–1985. Reprint Series (Vol. 1).

Journal of Applied Behavior Analysis. (1988). Behavior

analysis in education 1968–1987. Reprint Series (Vol. 3).

Keller, F. S. (1968). "Good-bye teacher . . ." *Journal of Applied Behavior Analysis,* **1,** 79–89.

Stokes, T. F., & Baer, D. M. (1977). An implicit technology of generalization. *Journal of Applied Behavior Analysis,* **10,** 349–367.

Sulzer-Azaroff, B., & Mayer, G. R. (1986). *Achieving educational excellence.* Fort Worth, TX: Holt, Reinhart & Winston.

Received November 17, 1988
Initial editorial decision April 12, 1989
Revisions received September 18, 1989; March 13, 1990
Final acceptance May 23, 1990
Action Editor, Susan A. Fowler

JOURNAL OF APPLIED BEHAVIOR ANALYSIS 1993, 26, 513–525 NUMBER 4 (WINTER 1993)

TAKING STOCK: THE FIRST 25 YEARS OF THE JOURNAL OF APPLIED BEHAVIOR ANALYSIS

VICTOR G. LATIES

UNIVERSITY OF ROCHESTER

AND

F. CHARLES MACE

UNIVERSITY OF PENNSYLVANIA

Some aspects of the performance of the *Journal of Applied Behavior Analysis* (*JABA*) are described on the occasion of the journal's 25th anniversary. Comparative circulation data are presented. *JABA*'s influence on the scientific community is measured by examining the citation history of articles that it has published, with attention to both frequency and source of the citations. The influence that other journals have on *JABA*'s authors is assessed through an analysis of citations made by those authors in this journal's reference lists. The citation history indicates clearly that *JABA* has made substantial contributions toward producing methods useful in coping with a wide variety of problem behaviors, from profound developmental disabilities (such as autism) to the simpler behavioral problems that interfere with normal functioning in home and at school. Recently, the journal has devoted many issues and parts of issues to special topics, in a concerted effort to reflect the increasing breadth of applied behavior analysis.

DESCRIPTORS: *Journal of Applied Behavior Analysis,* publication history, applied behavior analysis

---

The *Journal of Applied Behavior Analysis* (*JABA*), whose first issue appeared in 1968, is celebrating its 25th birthday. The story of *JABA*'s founding by the Society for the Experimental Analysis of Behavior (SEAB) was briefly recounted in a special section of the *Journal of the Experimental Analysis of Behavior* (*JEAB*) that celebrated SEAB's and *JEAB*'s 30th anniversaries (Hineline & Laties, 1987; Laties, 1987; see also Bailey, 1987; Wolf, 1993; Wright, 1993). About 5 years ago, several authors helped celebrate *JABA*'s 20th anniversary by considering the outlook for this journal in light of some of its major contributions and possible shortcomings during the preceding two decades (Baer, 1987; Baer, Wolf, & Risley, 1987; Hopkins, 1987; Iwata, 1987; Kunkel, 1987; Wolf, Braukmann, & Ramp, 1987). Recent articles by others have examined other aspects of the journal's progress. For example, Kennedy (1992) presented a content analysis of the use of social validity measures by *JABA* authors, and Northup, Vollmer, and Serrett (1993) discuss in this issue trends in the characteristics of *JABA* articles.

What follows is a summary of some data on *JABA*'s performance along a few objectively measured dimensions: its success in attracting subscribers, its influence on other journals, and the influence that other journals have on it.

Circulation

JABA was born at a propitious time for behavioral science and immediately attracted an impressive number of subscribers. About 1,500 subscriptions were sold before the first (Spring) issue was mailed in mid-April 1968. By the time the Summer issue appeared, circulation had doubled to 3,000. At the end of the first year, paid subscriptions totaled 4,271, consisting of 761 institutions (mostly libraries) plus 1,558 individual and 1,952 student subscribers.

For 1992, *JABA* had a total circulation of 4,636,

Address correspondence concerning this article to Victor G. Laties, Department of Environmental Medicine, Box EHSC, University of Rochester Medical Center, Rochester, New York 14642.

Table 1
Comparative Data on Journal Circulation (1992)

Journal (publisher)	Paid circulation
American Journal on Mental Retardation (AAMR)(U)	11,600
Behavior Modification (Sage)	1,322
Behavior Therapy (AABT)	2,731
Behavioral Assessment (Pergamon)(SPD)[a]	1,200
Behaviour Research & Therapy (Pergamon)(U)[b]	4,300
Child & Family Behavior Therapy (Haworth)(SPD)	532
Cognitive Therapy & Research (Plenum)	1,023
Education & Training in Mental Retardation (CEC)(U)	9,100
Journal of Abnormal Psychology (APA)	6,745
Journal of Applied Behavior Analysis (SEAB)	**4,636**
Journal of Applied Psychology (APA)	5,647
Journal of Behavior Therapy & Experimental Psychiatry (Pergamon)(SPD)	2,000
Journal of Behavioral Medicine (Plenum)	1,740
Journal of Consulting & Clinical Psychology (APA)	10,488
Journal of Counseling Psychology (APA)	7,454
Journal of Educational Psychology (APA)	4,838
Journal of Experimental Psychology: Learning, Memory & Cognition (APA)	3,503
Journal of Mental Deficiency Research (Blackwell)(U)	1,100[c]
Journal of the Association for Persons with Severe Handicaps (TASH)(SPD)[d]	7,600
Journal of the Experimental Analysis of Behavior (SEAB)	2,357
Psychological Assessment (APA)	5,917
Psychological Bulletin (APA)	7,572
Psychological Record (Kenyon College)	1,180
Research in Developmental Disabilities (Pergamon)(SPD)	600

Note. AABT: Association for the Advancement of Behavior Therapy; AAMR: American Association on Mental Retardation; APA: American Psychological Association (see *American Psychologist*, 1992, *47*, 968); CEC: Council for Exceptional Children; NASP: National Association of School Psychologists; SEAB: Society for the Experimental Analysis of Behavior; SPD: *Standard Periodical Directory* (16th ed.), 1993; TASH: The Association for Persons with Severe Handicaps; U: *Ulrich's International Periodicals Directory* (31st ed.), 1992–1993. Circulation data are from 1992 statements of ownership in the journals, except for those labeled "U" or "SPD."

[a] Merged into *Behaviour Research & Therapy* in 1993.
[b] This number has remained unchanged since the 1980 edition.
[c] Renamed *Journal of Intellectual Disability Research* in 1991.
[d] Controlled circulation; sent to all TASH members.

made up of 1,923 institutions, 1,927 individuals, and 786 students—almost three times as many institutions, about the same number of individuals, but many fewer students. Table 1 contains 1992 paid circulation data for some of the journals that cite *JABA* often or are cited heavily by *JABA*, as well as for other well-established journals that are useful as benchmarks in assessing our performance.

However, presenting only the figures for 1968 and 1992 omits both the delightful circulation peaks reached during the 1970s and the depressing downturn of the subsequent years, the latter an experience shared by all publishers as support for research and graduate education, particularly in the social sciences, eroded. *JABA*'s total circulation reached 7,097 in 1975 but then declined.

JABA's total circulation for 1992 was off by 26% from its 1979 figure of 6,290. In comparison, *Behavior Therapy* (*BT*) dropped from 3,276 to 2,731 (14%), *Behavior Modification* (*BM*) from 2,232 to 1,322 (41%), *JEAB* from 3,062 to 2,357 (23%), and *Psychological Bulletin* (*PB*) from 9,887 to 7,572 (23%). However, *Journal of Applied Psychology* (*JAP*) was down only 9%, from 6,153 to 5,647, and *Journal of Consulting and Clinical Psychology* (*JCCP*) actually rose from 9,741 to 10,488. *JABA*'s institutional subscriptions peaked at 2,344 in 1979. Since then, the erosion of library budgets has caused the loss of about 400 institutional subscribers.

JABA's 1992 institutional circulation of 1,923 approximated that of some of the journals published by the American Psychological Association (e.g., *Developmental Psychology,* 2,223; *Journal of Counseling Psychology,* 2,305; *Journal of Experimental Psychology: Learning, Memory and Cognition,* 1,893. But it fell short of matching *PB,* 2,778; *JAP,* 2,726; *JCCP,* 2,599; *Journal of Educational Psychology,* 2,912; or *Journal of Abnormal Psychology,* 2,935. These numbers are a good estimate of the probable maximums that can be reached for journals in psychology. *Psychological Assessment,* founded quite recently in 1989, had only 895 institutions in 1992, a figure that testifies to how difficult it has become to convince librarians to add new journals.

JABA*'s Influence on the Scientific Community*

Citation frequency and impact: JABA*'s relative standing among social science journals.* The extent to which a scientific contribution has been cited in the literature is one measure of its influence (Garfield, 1972). Citation analysis has been made feasible by the extensive compilations of the citation histories of both individual papers and the journals in which they appear by the Institute for Scientific Information (ISI). Since 1974, annual volumes of *Journal Citation Reports* (*JCR*) have documented the standing of journals on highly relevant performance measures, including *times cited* and *impact factor. Times cited* is a cumulation of the number of times that articles from a particular journal have been cited during a year. *Impact factor,* on the other hand, measures citations per published article and therefore tries to diminish the influence of journal size. It is a ratio of the citations and the number of citable articles published, and is usually based on the frequency with which articles that appeared in the immediately prior 2 years have been cited during a particular year (e.g., total citations during 1988 to articles published in the journal during 1986 and 1987, divided by the number of articles the journal published during those 2 years).

Table 2 presents these measures for *JABA* plus 24 others of interest, including most that cite or are cited in *JABA* frequently. The data, which apply to journal performance during 1988, are presented in three ways: as raw scores, as ranks within the relevant SSCI databases (N = 1,382 journals for times cited, 1,370 for impact factor), and of those ranks converted into percentiles. Expressing these ranks in percentiles shows more clearly that *JABA,* as well as several of the behavioral journals that cite it or are heavily cited within it (e.g., *BT, JEAB*), stand well within the top group of social and behavioral science journals on both measures. An impact factor of 0.50 translates into about the 58th percentile, 1.00 the 83rd, 1.50 the 90th, 2.00 the 95th, and 2.50 the 97th percentile. (Impact factors for 1992 are given for the journals that most frequently cite *JABA* in the far left column of Table 4.)

JABA's impact factor has varied between 0.98 and 2.07 over the years in a somewhat haphazard fashion since it was first made available in 1975, when it was 1.20. Since 1977, it has been 2.07, 1.85, 1.79, 1.60, 1.84, 1.62, 1.16, 1.36, 0.98, 1.26, 1.44, 1.39, 1.04, 1.15, 1.24, and 1.46. The associated percentiles of the impact factors between 1977 and 1992 were between 82 and 97 (M = 90.6; median = 90.5). A similar analysis for times cited yielded percentiles between 95 and 98 (M = 96.8; median = 97).

Citation frequency and impact: Comparisons among ISI "clinical psychology" journals. One could argue that comparing journals such as *JABA* with the whole SSCI data base is foolish because the data base contains many journals from much smaller fields where a few hundred citations per year would be the equivalent of a few thousand for journals in larger fields. (In 1988, only 242 of the 1,382 journals in the data base were cited more than 500 times.) *JABA* is classified under clinical psychology by *JCR* when it places journals into subject categories. Although far from a perfect fit, our presence there makes possible comparisons with a somewhat more homogeneous reference group.

In 1988, *JABA* was 8th of 42 journals listed in that category and ranked by impact factor. (No ranking by times cited was presented.) It had been cited 1,486 times during that year. Because 122

Table 2

Journal Performance Measures: Times Cited and Impact Factor (*Journal Citation Reports,* 1988)

Journal	Times cited			Impact factor		
	Cites	Rank	%[a]	IF	Rank	%[a]
American Journal of Mental Retardation	1,310	84	94	0.89	283	79
Behavior Modification	352	327	76	0.64	428	69
Behavior Therapy	1,314	82	94	1.44	119	91
Behavioural Psychotherapy	93	839	39	0.60	463	66
Behaviour Research & Therapy	1,596	62	96	1.73	76	94
Clinical Psychology Review	324	356	74	1.29	146	89
Cognitive Therapy & Research	784	140	90	1.30	143	90
Education & Training in Mental Retardation	199	527	62	0.32	795	42
Exceptional Children	989	112	92	2.62	29	98
Journal of Applied Behavior Analysis	**1,486**	**73**	**95**	**1.39**	**134**	**90**
Journal of Applied Psychology	3,426	19	99	2.13	49	96
Journal of the Association for Persons with Severe Handicaps	199	27	62	1.23	154	89
Journal of Consulting & Clinical Psychology	5,895	8	99	2.01	57	96
Journal of Behavior Therapy & Experimental Psychiatry	427	278	80	0.45	624	54
Journal of Autism & Developmental Disorders	682	162	88	1.21	160	88
Journal of the Experimental Analysis of Behavior	2,125	41	97	1.48	109	92
Journal of Experimental Child Psychology	1,181	90	94	0.97	248	82
Journal of Learning Disabilities	1,003	108	92	1.04	217	84
Journal of Speech & Hearing Disorders	908	123	91	0.76	345	75
Journal of Speech & Hearing Research	1,559	68	95	1.06	211	85
Journal of Special Education	346	334	76	0.48	584	57
Mental Retardation	371	317	77	0.48	584	57
Psychological Bulletin	6,321	6	99	4.55	7	99
Psychological Record	348	330	76	0.51	551	60
School Psychology Review	295	385	72	0.93	261	81

[a] % = % below.

of those citations had been to the 88 articles published during 1986 and 1987, its impact factor was 1.39. Some of the journals above us were *Psychological Medicine* (first, impact factor of 2.21), *Journal of Clinical and Experimental Neuropsychology* (second, 2.14), *Journal of Clinical Psychiatry* (third, 2.02), *JCCP* (fourth, 2.01), *Journal of Abnormal Psychology* (*JAbP*; fifth, 1.87) and *BT* (seventh, 1.44). Among those below were *BM* (21st, 0.64), *Behavioural Psychotherapy* (*BP*; 22nd, 0.60), and *Journal of Behavior Therapy and Experimental Psychiatry* (*JBTEP*; 33rd, 0.45).

Whereas the impact factor is useful in estimating the average citability of a journal's articles, it is also important to consider the total number of citations attracted by a journal. Times cited figures for 1988 for some of the journals mentioned above have already been given in Table 2. Even within this smaller category, we are dealing with a very wide range of sizes, from *JCCP,* which in 1988 attracted 5,895 citations (and that year published 141 articles) to *JABA* and *BT* with 1,486 and 1,314 citations (and 41 and 48 articles, respectively) down to journals with fewer than 500 citations.

In 1992, we ranked 9th of 44 journals by impact factor. Above us were *JCCP,* this time first with 2.83, plus all the others that preceded us in 1988 as well as *Clinical Psychology Review* (third, 2.56), and *BT* (seventh, 1.78). Below were *BM* (23rd, 0.75), *JBTEP* (33rd, 0.40), and *BP* (36th, 0.32).

Citation histories of individual JABA *papers.* The rapidity with which *JABA* established its place in the sun is shown in Figure 1. The early citation history of the 10 articles comprising the journal's first issue (the graph shows their progress through 1980) testifies to the scholarly influence of these classic papers: Two were cited at least 100 times through 1973 and continued to accelerate for almost a decade, two more hit that mark the following year, and another two achieved it 2 years later. Two of the remaining four (the ones just below 100 in 1980) reached that number about 5 years later. Citations of one more, Ayllon and Azrin (1968a), which described a way to increase the efficacy of reinforcement within the context of a token economy that had been established in a mental hospital, were undoubtedly overshadowed by the appearance later in the same year of Ayllon and Azrin (1968b), the influential monograph on the token economy that itself has received over 700 citations.

This history of *JABA*'s initial issue is continued in Table 3, which lists the 29 *JABA* papers that were cited 125 or more times through 1986; these data come from an unpublished study by ISI that listed the most highly cited papers appearing in each of the journals covered in the *Social Science Citation Index* (*SSCI*). These 29 papers give a good picture of how the journal has contributed to the progress of behavior analysis, with most areas within the field being represented. The top six papers from the first issue can be found among them. We have added data from subsequent volumes of *SSCI,* and the far right column gives cumulative citations through 1992. Some papers that appeared 20 or more years ago continued to be actively cited. Taken together, the 10 papers of the first issue were cited about 2,500 times through 1992. This early burst of intellectual energy is congruent with an observation made by Garfield (1987) who, in commenting on citation classics in the social and behavioral sciences, noted that "many classics were published in the first volumes of a specialty journal associated with the emergence of the then new field" (p. xii). Authors of most of these highly cited papers were invited by ISI to submit reminiscences concerning the circumstances surrounding their contributions to the "Citation Classics" section of the weekly editions of *Current Contents.* Many of them did so, and references to the essays are included in the Appendix.

One more fact, courtesy of the enormously helpful technical staff at ISI: Slightly more than one

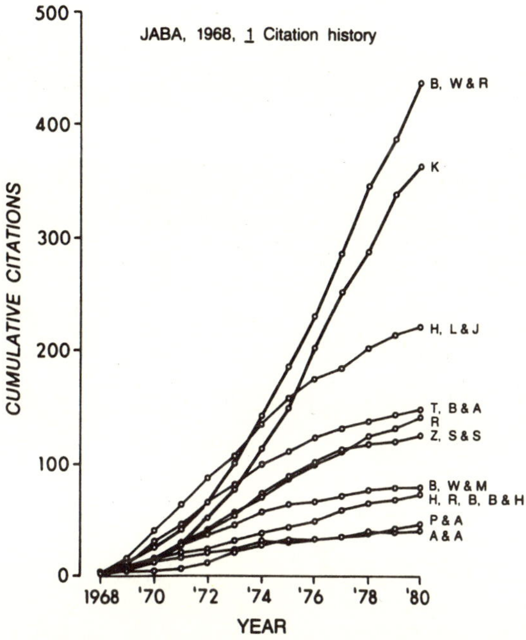

Figure 1. Citation history, 1968 through 1980, of the articles from the first issue of the *Journal of Applied Behavior Analysis.* Complete references for the top six curves (Baer, Wolf, & Risley; Keller; Hall, Lund, & Jackson; Thomas, Becker, & Armstrong; Risley; and Zielberger, Sampen, & Sloane) are in Table 3. Azrin and Ayllon is listed among the general references. The remaining reference is Powell, J., & Azrin, N. H. (1968). The effects of shock as a punisher for cigarette smoking. *1,* 63–71. The figure is reprinted from Laties (1987).

third of the approximately 1,200 papers published by *JABA* were cited 25 or more times through 1992.

Sources of citations to JABA *articles.* Which journals publish the articles that cite papers in *JABA*? First and foremost is *JABA* itself, whose authors cite other *JABA* articles frequently. Table 4 shows the principal sources of citations to *JABA* during the 5-year period of 1988 through 1992. Of the grand total of 7,054 recent citations to *JABA* articles, 1,341 originated within the journal itself (19%). The yearly *self-cited* rates (*JABA* author citations of papers published in *JABA* expressed as a percentage of the total number of citations received by the journal) varied from 11% to 28%, the latter figure for 1992 being relatively high. In 1974, the first year for which data are available, 143 references to *JABA* papers made up

Table 3

Most Often Cited Papers from the *Journal of Applied Behavior Analysis*

Rank		Citations through 1986	Citations through 1992
1	Bear, D. M., Wolf, M. M., & Risley, T. R. (1968). Some current dimensions of applied behavior analysis. *1,* 91–97.	762	916
2	Stokes, T. F., & Baer, D. M. (1977). An implicit technology of generalization. *10,* 349–367.	458	717
3	Wolf, M. M. (1978). Social validity: The case for subjective measurement or how applied behavior analysis is finding its heart. *11,* 203–214.	314	527
4	Keller, F. S. (1968). "Good-bye, teacher. . ." *1,* 79–89.	375	427
5	Kazdin, A. E., & Bootzin, R. R. (1972). The token economy: An evaluative review. *5,* 343–372.	280	299
6	Hartmann, D. P. (1977). Considerations in the choice of interobserver reliability estimates. *10,* 103–116.	191	289
7	Hall, R. V., Lund, D., & Jackson, D. (1968). Effects of teacher attention on study behavior. *1,* 1–12.	263	281
8	Madsen, C. H., Becker, W. C., & Thomas, D. R. (1968). Rules, praise, and ignoring: Elements of elementary classroom control. *1,* 139–150.	255	268
9	Lovaas, O. I., & Simmons, J. Q. (1969). Manipulation of self-destruction in three retarded children. *2,* 143–157.	228	263
10	Foxx, R. M., & Azrin, N. H. (1973). The elimination of self-stimulatory behavior by overcorrection. *6,* 1–14.	239	260
11	Lovaas, O. I., Koegel, R., Simmons, J. Q., & Long, J. S. (1973). Some generalization and follow-up measures on autistic children in behavior therapy. *6,* 131–166.	208	250
12	Risley, T. R. (1968). The effects and side-effects of punishing the autistic behaviors of a deviant child. *1,* 21–34.	209	228
13	O'Connor, R. D. (1969). Modification of social withdrawal through symbolic modeling. *2,* 15–22.	179	196
14	O'Leary, K. D., Becker, W. C., Evans, M. B., & Saudargas, R. A. (1969). A token reinforcement program in a public school: A replication and systematic analysis. *2,* 3–13.	185	194
15	Phillips, E. L. (1968). Achievement Place: Token reinforcement procedures in a home-style rehabilitation setting for "pre-delinquent" boys. *1,* 213–223.	181	194
16	Thomas, D. R., Becker, W. C., & Armstrong, M. (1968). Production and elimination of disruptive classroom behavior by systematically varying teacher's behavior. *1,* 35–45.	177	190
17	Bijou, S. W., Peterson, R. F., & Ault, M. H. (1968). A method to integrate descriptive and experimental field studies at the level of data and empirical concepts. *1,* 175–191.	157	179
18	Barrish, H. H., Saunders, M., & Wolf, M. M. (1969). Good behavior game: Effects of individual contingencies for group consequences on disruptive in a classroom. *2,* 119–124.	165	178
19	Azrin, N. H., & Foxx, R. M. (1971). A rapid method of toilet training the institutionalized retarded. *4,* 89–99.	149	165
20	Broden, M., Hall, R. V., & Mitts, B. (1971). The effect of self-recording on the classroom behavior of two eighth-grade students. *4,* 191–199.	146	163
21	Wahler, R. G. (1969). Setting generality: Some specific and general effects of child behavior therapy. *2,* 239–246.	149	160

Table 3
(*Continued*)

Rank		Citations through 1986	Citations through 1992
22	Phillips, E. L., Phillips, E. A., Fixsen, D. L., & Wolf, M. M. (1971). Achievement Place: Modification of the behaviors of pre-delinquent boys within a token economy. *4,* 45–59.	140	152
23	Zeilberger, J., Sampen, S. E., & Sloane, H. N. (1968). Modification of a child's problem behaviors in the home with the mother as therapist. *1,* 47–53.	148	150
24	Ayllon, T., Layman, D., & Kandel, H. J. (1975). A behavioral-educational alternative to drug control of hyperactive children. *8,* 137–146.	131	149
25	Wahler, R. G. (1969). Oppositional children: A quest for parental reinforcement control. *2,* 159–170.	136	147
26	Winett, R. A., & Winkler, R. C. (1972). Current behavior modification in the classroom: Be still, be quiet, be docile. *5,* 499–504.	137	146
27	Budzynski, T. H., & Stoyva, J. M. (1969). An instrument for producing deep muscle relaxation by means of analog information feedback. *2,* 231–237.	139	145
28	Bolstad, O. D., & Johnson, S. M. (1972). Self-regulation in the modification of disruptive classroom behavior. *5,* 443–454.	128	142
29	Lovitt, T. C., & Curtiss, K. A. (1969). Academic response rate as a function of teacher- and self-imposed contingencies. *2,* 49–53.	125	131

60% of the total 239 citations of *JABA* articles. The contribution of internal citations to total citations decreased rapidly as outside citations increased. In 1975, it was 42% (288 of 688), and in 1977, it was 18% (361 of 1,978). During the 1980s, it varied between 8% (153 of 1,795 in 1984) and 15% (284 of 1,896 in 1982).

In 1988, the last year for which data from *SSCI* are readily available for all journals, *JABA* had a self-cited rate of 11%. Some other journals' rates that year were: *Journal of Applied Psychology*: 15%; *BM*: 6%; *BP*: 17%; *BRT*: 14%; *BT*: 7%; *JCCP*: 6.9%; *Journal of Autism and Developmental Disabilities*: 30%; *Journal of the Association for Persons with Severe Handicaps*: 30%.

The 5,713 citations of *JABA* articles during the 1988 to 1992 period that did *not* come from within *JABA* came from a wide variety of other journals: in 1988, 168 others; in 1989, 171; in 1990, 180; in 1991, 175; and, in 1992, 166. Because the 32 journals listed in Table 4 accounted for about 3,690 citations over the 5 years, the remaining journals contributed slightly more than 2,000.

Although there is great year-to-year variability in citations from any particular journal, the major portion of citations, about 40%, comes from the journals devoted to the general field of behavioral psychology: *JABA* itself, *BM, BT, CFBT, TBA, BP, CPR, JPTEP,* and *JEAB.* The specialty journals in the developmental disabilities cite *JABA* next most frequently, contributing about 25% of the total.

Citations to a single year of JABA. The journals that showed the most evidence of influence by *JABA* were determined in a second way by counting citations to all articles published in *JABA* for the single year of 1985. This serves as a check on the applicability of the Table 4 data, which reflect the whole 25-year life of the journal, to its more recent history. Citations were counted in volumes of *SSCI* through 1992 and are shown in the far right column of Table 4. A total of 84 other journals cited 1985 *JABA* articles at least once. The journals in the table are now listed in order of their mean citations per year to articles published at any time in *JABA*. That order would not have to be changed much to match the order of citations to the 1985 volume of *JABA*.

Table 4

Sources of Recent Citations to the *Journal of Applied Behavior Analysis*

Impact factor 1992	Citing journal	Citations 1988	1989	1990	1991	1992	Times cited per year	Citations of 1985 *JABA*[a]
1.46	***Journal of Applied Behavior Analysis***	**157**	**135**	**246**	**408**	**395**	**268**	**113**
0.61	*Research in Developmental Disabilities*	47	25	74	101	127	75	31
0.56	*Education & Training in Mental Retardation*	41	96	63	47	37	57	24
0.75	*Behavior Modification*	63	55	34	38	84	55	12
0.76	*Journal of the Association for Persons with Severe Handicaps*	46	85	55	35	21	48	44
0.79	*School Psychology Review*	87	18	16	36	39	39	9
0.72	*American Journal on Mental Retardation*	47	43	34	30	18	34	10
0.56	*Mental Retardation*	67	16	37	20	19	32	7
1.78	*Behavior Therapy*	35	50	26	18	11	28	13
0.64	*Journal of Special Education*	21	14	13	76	16	28	6
0.93	*Behavioral Assessment*[b]	39	33	24	11	23	26	1
0.93	*Journal of Autism & Developmental Disorders*	25	28	32	19	19	25	17
0.31	*Child & Family Behavior Therapy*	<6	34	48	24	10	24	1
0.73	*Exceptional Children*	30	8	23	30	24	23	6
0.73	*The Behavior Analyst*	35	16	38	11	12	22	7
0.32	*Behavioural Psychotherapy*	21	16	26	12	18	19	6
2.56	*Clinical Psychology Review*	<6	15	33	29	8	18	6
0.40	*Journal of Behavior Therapy & Experimental Psychiatry*	44	<6	12	21	9	18	3
0.20	*Psychology in the Schools*	10	16	<6	41	15	17	3
0.70	*Journal of Mental Deficiency Research*[c]	18	<6	19	23	15	16	8
1.55	*Journal of the Experimental Analysis of Behavior*	7	30	20	<6	11	15	4
0.28	*Psychological Reports*	15	14	15	26	<6	15	2
0.74	*Topics in Early Childhood Special Education*	<6	<6	17	24	20	13	8
0.76	*Journal of Speech & Hearing Disorders*	<6	31	14	<6	8	12	7
0.36	*Psychological Record*	13	9	10	<6	24	12	2
0.41	*Journal of School Psychology*	<6	8	18	12	9	10	1
2.83	*Journal of Consulting & Clinical Psychology*	15	12	<6	7	11	10	1
0.78	*Journal of Experimental Child Psychology*	32	<6	<6	<6	<6	9	1
0.27	*Topics in Language Disorders*	31	<6	<6	<6	<6	9	3
0.93	*Journal of Speech & Hearing Research*	<6	<6	<6	25	8	8	0
0.30	*Irish Journal of Psychology*	29	<6	<6	<6	<6	8	0
4.96	*Psychological Bulletin*	<6	<6	6	25	<6	8	5
2.00	*Advances in Child Development and Behavior*	<6	26	<6	<6	<6	8	1
	Summary							
	Citations						Total	
	from *JABA*	157	135	246	408	395	1,341	
	from the 32 other journals listed	842	722	730	762	634	3,690	
	from other journals	487	390	411	377	358	2,023	
	Total citations	1,486	1,247	1,387	1,547	1,387	7,054	

Table 5
Journals That Cited *JABA* Relatively Frequently

JABA's rank among cited journals	Citing journal	*JABA*'s percentage	Comments
1	*Behavior Modification*	6.7	2nd: *BT* & *JCCP*, 6.1% each
	Topics in Language Disorders	3.3	2nd: *JEdP*, 3.2%
	Irish Journal of Psychology	5.4	2nd: *AJMR*, 3.5%
2	*Research in Developmental Disabilities*	6.9	1st: *AJMR*, 10.9%
	The Behavior Analyst	6.4	1st: *JEAB*, 15.9%
	Journal of the Association for Persons with Severe Handicaps	5.2	1st: self, 6.8%
	Journal of Psychopathology & Behavioral Assessment	3.8	1st: *JCCP*, 5.7%
	School Psychology Review	4.1	1st: self, 4.9%
	Behavioural Psychotherapy	3.3	1st: *BRT*, 6.0%
	American Journal on Mental Retardation	2.7	1st: self, 13%
3	*Journal of Behavior Therapy & Experimental Psychiatry*	6.2	1st: self, 8.7%; 2nd: *BRT*, 8.6%
	Education & Training in Mental Retardation	5.1	1st: *AJMR*, 8.3%; 2nd, *EC*, 5.6%
	Mental Retardation	2.2	1st: self, 8.6%; 2nd, *AJMR*, 7.4%
	Journal of Special Education	2.8	1st: *EC*, 5.1%; 2nd: *AJMR*, 4.1%

Note. AJMR: *American Journal on Mental Retardation*; *BRT*: *Behaviour Research and Therapy*; *BT*: *Behavior Therapy*; *EC*: *Exceptional Children*; *JCCP*: *Journal of Consulting and Clinical Psychology*; *JEdP*: *Journal of Educational Psychology*; *JEAB*: *Journal of the Experimental Analysis of Behavior*.

These are *JABA*'s ranks among cited journals by each citing journal listed. The relative importance of *JABA* to each journal is measured by comparing that journal's citations to *JABA* during 1988 with the total 1988 citations it made to all journals. The absolute numbers of citations to *JABA* during 1988 already appear in Table 4, except for the *Journal of Psychopathology & Behavioral Assessment*, which cited *JABA* 23 times that year. All figures were derived from the *SSCI* citing behavior tables for these journals in Garfield (1989).

The journals that contributed citations were placed into five categories: behavioral psychology (e.g., *JABA, BT, BM*); general psychology (e.g., *JCCP, Psychological Bulletin*); education (e.g., *School Psychology Review, Journal of Educational Psychology*); developmental disabilities (e.g., *AJMR, RDD, MR*); and rehabilitation/speech/medicine (e.g., *International Journal of Rehabilitation Research, Journal of Speech and Hearing Disorders*). The citation percentages for these categories were, in the order given above, 39%, 13%, 7%, 36%, and 6%.

Relative importance of JABA *to other behavioral journals.* Table 4 presented the absolute numbers of citations for those journals that cite *JABA* most frequently. In order to determine the relative importance of *JABA* to a particular journal, to at least approach the question of what proportion of its intellectual product is influenced by what our authors write, we have expressed citations to *JABA* as a percentage of the citations made in the citing journal to all other journals, doing this for all journals that cited *JABA* 15 or more times during 1988. *JABA* was an important target of citations from the journals listed in Table 5. Not surprisingly, this analysis reaffirms the importance of the

←

Note. This table includes all sources that cited *JABA either* 10 or more times per year *or* 25 or more times in at least 1 of the 5 years. The 1988 data are from *SSCI Journal Citation Reports* (1989, p. 498). The rest, including the impact factor data in the far left column, were obtained directly from the Institute for Scientific Information, Philadelphia (Linda Corson, June 17, 1993). Precise data are not available if fewer than six citations were made; in such cases, estimates of three citations were used to calculate means.

[a] Citations, 1986 through 1992, to *JABA*, 1985, Vol. 18.

[b] Merged into *Behaviour Research & Therapy* in 1993.

[c] Name changed to *Journal of Intellectual Disabilities Research* in 1992.

Table 6
Journals Frequently Cited in Recent *JABA* Reference Lists

Cited journal	Citations 1988	1989	1990	1991	1992	Times cited per year
Journal of Applied Behavior Analysis	**157**	**135**	**246**	**408**	**395**	**268**
Journal of the Experimental Analysis of Behavior	12	<6	22	27	83	29
Journal of the Association for Persons with Severe Handicaps	8	7	25	42	43	25
American Journal on Mental Retardation	11	14	15	16	33	18
Behavior Therapy	19	16	18	21	13	17
Analysis & Intervention in Developmental Disabilities[a]	14	10	20	23	18	17
Behavior Modification	15	6	16	22	26	17
Journal of Autism & Developmental Disorders	11	7	14	13	28	15
Behavioural Analysis & Modification[b]	<6	<6	6	36	24	14
Education & Training in Mental Retardation	7	8	<6	8	32	12
Journal of Organizational Behavior Management	<6	<6	<6	6	45	12
American Psychologist	8	<6	6	17	19	11
Mental Retardation	6	<6	8	18	12	9
Applied Research in Mental Retardation[a]	5	11	<6	10	10	8
Behavioral Assessment[c]	<6	<6	11	12	12	8
Journal of Behavior Therapy & Experimental Psychiatry	6	9	12	9	<6	8
Behaviour Research & Therapy	7	8	10	7	<6	7
Journal of Experimental Child Psychology	<6	8	<6	10	10	7
Psychological Bulletin	<6	<6	9	8	6	6
Total citations to all journals	664	579	967	1,655	1,980	
JABA text pages published	430	456	544	804	918	

Note. Fewer than six citations were coded as three in computing means.
[a] Combined to form *Research in Developmental Disabilities* in 1987.
[b] Ceased publication in 1981.
[c] Merged into *Behaviour Research & Therapy* in 1993.

citation sources that have been revealed in several other ways already. The only surprise was to find that *JABA* had, for one brief moment, become the most important source of enlightenment for the *Irish Journal of Psychology.*

Citations by JABA *Authors: Which Journals Publish Articles That Influence Them?*

The references listed by *JABA* authors reveal some of the sources of their own writing behavior. As Moore (1992) noted, "from a functional perspective, the importance of the articles is reflected in the extent to which they function as discriminative stimuli for the subsequent behavior of those who read them" (p. 1). Table 6 presents data on the recent citation behavior of those writing for this journal. Early in the life of the journal, *self-citing* (i.e., citations of *JABA* papers as a percentage of all papers cited in *JABA*) was quite high; it was 39% in 1974 and 34% in 1975. During the 1980s, it varied between 20% and 26% and, from 1988 through 1992, it averaged 23%. The proliferation of behavioral journals in the 1970s and 1980s probably accounts for the downward drift in self-citations (cf. Wyatt, Hawkins, & Davis, 1986).

About 77% of citations by *JABA* authors during the 5-year period were spread among other sources, including books as well as journals. (The largest number of such sources was 657 in 1992.) There is an understandably strong relationship between citation patterns from and to a journal, the processes

Table 7
Cumulative Percentage of Citations Given by Journal Authors Who Published in 1988 to Articles Appearing During Years Indicated (Abbreviations As Given in the Text)

	1988	1987	1986	1985	1984	1983	1982	1981	1980	1979	Citing half-life
BM	0.3	2.5	8.8	15.4	22.8	32.7	37.9	44.6	48.8	55.0	9.1
BRT	1.9	10.7	21.5	30.8	37.9	46.4	52.4	59.2	63.7	68.6	6.5
BT	1.9	8.1	15.9	23.6	31.6	39.1	46.9	54.1	60.3	65.8	7.4
JABA	1.2	6.7	16.7	23.0	32.5	40.0	48.2	55.0	62.0	67.5	7.2
JCCP	1.2	5.9	15.5	25.7	35.3	43.9	50.9	57.4	62.8	67.5	6.8
RIDD	0.6	3.2	11.6	22.3	30.2	38.3	47.3	54.9	62.2	67.8	7.3

being quite dependent upon one other. The apparent discrepancy between the relative importance of *Research in Developmental Disabilities* as a source of citations to *JABA* (see Table 4) and its absence among the journals of Table 6 that were targets of citations from *JABA* is due to its appearance on the scene with that name only in 1987, being the product of a merger of two other journals that do appear in Table 6: *Analysis and Intervention in Developmental Disabilities* and *Applied Research on Mental Retardation.*

Year-by-year variability among which journals were cited obviously reflected variation in subject matter. Particularly wide fluctuations, such as the sudden appearance of the *Journal of Organizational Behavior Management* with 45 citations by *JABA* authors during 1992, were due to two special sections in the Fall issue on "Performance Management for Business and Industry" and "Performance Management for Sports and Exercise." These sections were also partially responsible for the sharp increase in citations of *JEAB* papers, several authors drawing inspiration from basic research on such topics as behavioral momentum and the matching law.

Note that the large increases in citations given by *JABA* authors for 1991 and 1992 were mainly the product of an increase in the number of text pages published those years. However, citations per page did increase over this period, from 1.5 per page in 1988 to 2.2 per page in 1992.

Table 7 provides information on the citing practices of authors from various journals, indicating how they distributed their citations through time. The data show little difference in citing behavior among the subset of applied journals, most having a *citing half-life* of about seven years, meaning that was the number of years going backwards through time that would account for half of the citations made by authors.

Discussion

It seems clear that this journal has been successful in contributing methods useful in coping with problem behavior at many levels. *JABA*'s authors have addressed questions on a wide variety of problem behaviors, ranging from such profound developmental disabilities as autism all the way to less intrusive behavioral problems that may interfere with normal functioning at home or in the schoolroom.

The contributions applied behavior analysis has made to the field of developmental disabilities have been tremendous. But there are many new frontiers for behavior analysis to enter. This journal will continue to play a key role in advancing behavioral solutions to many of our culture's most pressing social problems. Many of the advances in behavioral technology, known generically as behavior therapy, behavior modification, and behavioral teaching, have their origins in the pages of *JABA*. Techniques and programs such as differential social reinforcement, token economies, prompt hierarchies, self-management, and effective and nonintrusive forms of time-out, have produced lasting changes in the delivery of psychological and educational services.

Recent developments, such as functional analysis methodologies, are changing the fundamental character of behavioral intervention, giving it a more analytic flavor and grounding it more closely within basic behavioral principles.

The current vision of *JABA*'s future, apparent in the behavior of the two most recent editors, Scott Geller and Nancy Neef, has been one of diversification. Applying behavior analysis to new arenas has been a goal realized during the past few years in several issues that contained sections devoted to specialized topics. These sections have considered subjects as diverse as road safety, community intervention, the education crisis, social validity, sports and exercise, improving social competence, performance management for business and industry, and the interrelationships among science, theory, and technology. This trend towards diversity continues in the present issue with a section on behavioral pediatrics. Two additional topics, school psychology and the integration of basic and applied research, will be addressed in 1994.

Behavioral journals have proliferated over the past 30 years; chronologically, *JABA* was the *third* such journal established of the 25 identified by Wyatt et al. (1986). The contents of them all attest to the impact that behavioral solutions to social problems have had so far. *JABA*'s masthead states that it is "primarily for the original publication of reports of experimental research involving applications of the experimental analysis of behavior to problems of social importance." That broad mission is one that everyone associated with *JABA* proudly embraces. Was there ever a better reason to publish a journal?

REFERENCES

Ayllon, T., & Azrin, N. H. (1968a). Reinforcer sampling: A technique for increasing the behavior of mental patients. *Journal of Applied Behavior Analysis, 1,* 13–20.

Ayllon, T., & Azrin, N. H. (1968b). *The token economy: A motivational system for therapy and rehabilitation.* New York: Appleton-Century-Crofts.

Baer, D. M. (1987). Weak contingencies, strong contingencies, and many behaviors to change. *Journal of Applied Behavior Analysis, 20,* 335–337.

Baer, D. M., Wolf, M. M., & Risley, T. R. (1987). Some still-current dimensions of applied behavior analysis. *Journal of Applied Behavior Analysis, 20,* 313–327.

Bailey, J. S. (1987). The editor's page. *Journal of Applied Behavior Analysis, 20,* 305–307.

Garfield, E. (1972). Citation analysis as a tool in journal evaluation. *Science, 178,* 471–479.

Garfield, E. (1987). Preface. In *Contemporary classics in the social and behavioral sciences,* compiled by N. J. Smelser (pp. xi–xv). Philadelphia: ISI Press.

Garfield, E. (1989). *SSCI journal citation reports, 1988 annual.* Philadelphia: Institute for Scientific Information.

Hineline, P. N., & Laties, V. G. (Eds.). (1987). Anniversaries in behavior analysis. *Journal of the Experimental Analysis of Behavior, 48,* 439–514.

Hopkins, B. L. (1987). Comments on the future of applied behavior analysis. *Journal of Applied Behavior Analysis, 20,* 339–346.

Iwata, B. A. (1987). Negative reinforcement in applied behavior analysis: An emerging technology. *Journal of Applied Behavior Analysis, 20,* 361–378.

Kennedy, C. H. (1992). Trends in the measurement of social validity. *The Behavior Analyst, 15,* 147–156.

Kunkel, J. H. (1987). The future of *JABA*: A comment. *Journal of Applied Behavior Analysis, 20,* 329–333.

Laties, V. G. (1987). Society for the Experimental Analysis of Behavior: The first thirty years (1957–1987). *Journal of the Experimental Analysis of Behavior, 48,* 495–512.

Moore, J. (1992). Editorial. The function of journals. *The Behavior Analyst, 15,* 1.

Northup, J., Vollmer, T. R., & Serrett, K. (1993). Publication trends in 25 years of the *Journal of Applied Behavior Analysis. Journal of Applied Behavior Analysis, 26,* 527–537.

Smelser, N. J. (1987). *Contemporary classics in the social and behavioral sciences.* Philadelphia: ISI Press.

Wolf, M. M. (1993). Remembrances of issues past: Celebrating *JABA*'s 25th anniversary. *Journal of Applied Behavior Analysis, 26,* 543–544.

Wolf, M. M., Braukmann, C. J., & Ramp, K. A. (1987). Serious delinquent behavior as part of a significantly handicapping condition: Cures and supportive environments. *Journal of Applied Behavior Analysis, 20,* 347–359.

Wright, M. L. (1993). How time flies! *Journal of Applied Behavior Analysis, 26,* 559–561.

Wyatt, W. J., Hawkins, R. P., & Davis, P. (1986). Behaviorism: Are reports of its death exaggerated? *The Behavior Analyst, 9,* 101–105.

APPENDIX

Essays by authors on "Citation Classics" that were published in the *Journal of Applied Behavior Analysis*

Hall, R. V., Lund, D., & Jackson, D. Effects of teacher attention on study behavior. (1968). *1,* 1–12. [*Current Contents in the Social and Behavioral Sciences*/Number 5, p. 10, 1/29/79]

Keller, F. S. "Good-bye, teacher . . ." (1968). *1,* 79–89. (*CC*/Number 43, p. 22, 10/22/90]

Baer, D. M., Wolf, M. M., & Risley, T. R. Some current dimensions of applied behavior analysis. (1968). *1,* 91–97. [*CC*/Number 46, p. 14, 11/15/82]

Phillips, E. L. Achievement Place: Token reinforcement procedures in a home-style rehabilitation setting for "predelinquent" boys. (1968). *1,* 213–223. [*CC*/Number 30, p. 20, 7/25/83]

Barrish, H. H., Saunders, M., & Wolf, M. M. Good behavior game: Effects of individual contingencies for group consequences on disruptive behavior in the classroom. (1969). *2,* 119–124. [*CC*/Number 18, p. 16, 5/3/82]

Kazdin, A. E., & Bootzin, R. R. The token economy: An evaluative review. (1972). *5,* 343–372. [*CC*/Number 39, p. 22, 9/29/80]

Foxx, R. M., & Azrin, N. H. The elimination of autistic self-stimulatory behavior by overcorrection. (1973). *6,* 1–14. [*CC*/Number 22, p. 18, 5/30/83]

Stokes, T. F., & Baer, D. M. An implicit technology of generalization. (1977). *10,* 349–367. [*CC*/Number 10, p. 24, 3/7/83]

O'Leary, K. D., Becker, W. C., Evans, M. B., & Saudargas, R. A. A token reinforcement program in a public school—A replication and systematic analysis. (1969). *2,* 3–13. [*CC*/Number 40, p. 8, 10/7/91]

Wolf, M. M. Social validity—The case for subjective measurement. (1978). *11,* 203–214. [*CC*/Number 2, p. 8, 1/14/91]

Winett, R. A., & Winkler, R. C. Current behavior modification in the classroom: Be still, be quiet, be docile. (1972). *5,* 499–504. [*CC*/Number 35, p. 20, 9/2/85]

Note. All but four of these essays (Keller, O'Leary et al., Wolf, and Winett & Winkler) were reprinted in Smelser (1987).

JOURNAL OF APPLIED BEHAVIOR ANALYSIS 1993, 26, 527–537 NUMBER 4 (WINTER 1993)

PUBLICATION TRENDS IN 25 YEARS OF THE JOURNAL OF APPLIED BEHAVIOR ANALYSIS

JOHN NORTHUP, TIMOTHY R. VOLLMER, AND KAREN SERRETT
LOUISIANA STATE UNIVERSITY

All articles published in the first 25 years of *JABA* (1968 to 1992) were reviewed to classify the percentage of articles published in the following categories: (a) type of article, (b) subjects, (c) setting, (d) behavior-change agent, (e) target behavior, (f) use of basic principles, and (g) miscellaneous procedures. Overall percentages and trends are reported in each category. Results indicate an increase in the percentage of articles with participants and target behaviors in developmental disabilities and a decrease in the percentage of studies targeting academic behavior, verbal behavior, and other child behavioral excesses. The most frequent setting continues to be a school; however, there is a clear trend towards community and other naturalistic settings. Results also highlight the increasing complexity and multicomponent nature of *JABA* interventions. Potential implications for future applications are discussed.

DESCRIPTORS: survey, publication trends, subjects, settings, target behaviors, procedures

The *Journal of Applied Behavior Analysis* (*JABA*) is a unique professional journal. In contrast to many professional journals, *JABA* is not dedicated solely to any particular problem area, population, procedure, or setting. Rather, *JABA* is dedicated to the application of behavioral principles to problems of social importance (*JABA*, Statement of Purpose). However, topographical considerations are also implicit in a definition of social importance, and determining the generality of behavioral principles requires application across a diversity of problem areas, participants, and settings. In addition, many professional positions and interests are commonly defined by topography, that is, by problem areas, settings, and subjects. It is probable that these parameters are often important controlling conditions for many professional behaviors, including journal reading and manuscript submission.

Topography also has presented a special problem for applied behavior analysis, because the field has often been criticized for the subjects or settings that are (or perceived to be) most frequently represented. Kunkel (1987) characterized this criticism as the study of "simple problem activities of children and mental patients in institutional settings" (p. 329). The emphasis in applied behavior analysis on developmental disabilities has also been a topic of concern (e.g., Schwartz & Lacey, 1982). Some have suggested that behavior analysts should focus more on other areas of social importance (e.g., Hopkins, 1987), whereas others have stressed the importance of repeated refinement of specific areas of research (e.g., Baer, 1987).

The purpose of this paper is to provide a review of the most frequent topographies (subjects, settings, target behaviors, etc.) represented in the first 25 years of *JABA*. It is suggested that a data-based review of where applied behavior analysis has been (as represented in the pages of *JABA*) may provide an important context for future directions.

All articles published in the first 25 years of *JABA* (1968 through 1992) were reviewed to classify the percentage of articles in the following categories: (a) type of article, (b) subjects, (c) setting, (d) behavior-change agent, (e) target behavior, (f) use of basic principles, and (g) miscellaneous procedures. Multiple subcategories were included within each general category. The range and scope of *JABA* literally defied classification. As a result, the present survey includes only the broadest of potential categories and a selected few that were perceived by the authors to be of interest. In all, 67 categories were included in the complete review.

The authors thank Kevin Jones, Joel Ringdahl, and Lisa Bridwell for their assistance with data collection.

Requests for reprints should be sent to John Northup, Department of Psychology, Audubon Hall, Louisiana State University, Baton Rouge, Louisiana 70803.

Table 1
Definitions of Reported Categories

Type of article

Research article: An experimental study that demonstrated the effect of an independent variable on some dependent variable (usually behavior).

Methodological study: A study that was designed solely to improve research methods, such as demonstrating observational procedures, comparing sampling methods, research equipment demonstrations, etc.

Review/discussion: A paper that was not designed to present new experimental data, but functions as a literature review or discussion of a topic area.

Other: Does not fit one of the above categories.

Participants

Developmental disabilities: Individuals who were reported as having a diagnosis for some type of developmental disability such as autism (childhood schizophrenia) or mental retardation. Individuals who exhibit some specific learning disability or isolated deficit do not fit this category. If no diagnosis was reported, indicators such as IQ score < 70 placed individual in this category.

Psychiatric: Individuals who were diagnosed as having a psychiatric disorder such as schizophrenia (but not childhood schizophrenia), psychoses, etc. If no diagnosis was reported, behavior and setting could serve as prompt to score this category (i.e., hallucinations or psychiatric facility).

Other children: Individuals under the age of 18 who do not fall into one of the above categories.

Other adults: Individuals who do not fall into one of the above categories. Individuals who were targeted due to factors related to aging were not scored in this category.

Geriatric: Individuals who were targeted due to factors related to aging.

Behavior-change agents

Experimenter: The independent variables of interest were manipulated directly by the author of the study or by research assistants designated solely for that task. If the experimenter happened to serve another role (such as college teacher) in the study that role was scored instead.

Teacher: Independent variables of interest were manipulated by an individual responsible for the academic education of the subject. Teachers for individuals with developmental disabilities were scored in another (unreported) category.

Self: Independent variables of interest were manipulated by the subject.

Parent: Independent variables of interest were manipulated by the subject's parent(s).

Setting

School: Regular education environment. State schools for individuals with developmental disabilities were not scored in this category if the school was actually the subject's residence.

DD residential: The study took place at the residence of an individual with developmental disabilities.

Analogue setting: Analogue or laboratory setting arranged explicitly for the purposes of experimentation.

Medical setting: Included doctor's office, dentist's office, nonpsychiatric or DD hospital.

Home: Residence other than group living environment.

Community: Applications in public settings other than those described above, such as cities, stores, restaurants, highways, neighborhoods, etc.

Target behavior

DD skill acquisition: The procedure was explicitly designed to increase at least one desired behavior for an individual with developmental disabilities. This category contained a number of subcategories not reported in this paper (e.g., DD academic, DD social skills).

DD language: A subcategory of DD skill acquisition. Verbal behavior displayed by individuals with DD.

Other academic: Traditional academic behavior such as math, reading, spelling, or college course work with target population other than DD.

Other language: Verbal behavior (including manual, gestural, imitative, etc.) displayed by individuals other than DD.

DD behavioral excess: The procedure was explicitly designed to decrease at least one undesired behavior for an individual with developmental disabilities. This category contained a number of subcategories (e.g., DD aggression, self-injury, stereotypy, etc.).

Other child behavioral excess: The procedure was explicitly designed to decrease at least one undesired behavior for an individual other than DD.

Substance abuse: The study focused on variables influencing substance abuse including drugs, alcohol, and cigarettes.

Child abuse: The study focused on variables influencing the verbal or physical mistreatment or neglect of children.

Table 1
(*Continued*)

SIB: A subcategory of DD behavioral excess (all articles scored in this category also were scored in the larger category). The study focused on variables influencing behavior that results in self-injury displayed by individuals with developmental disabilities.

Behavioral procedures

Positive reinforcement: A consequence was delivered that resulted in an increased probability of behavior.

Negative reinforcement: The removal of stimulation as a consequence of behavior resulted in an increased probability of behavior.

Punishment: A consequence of behavior was delivered that resulted in a decreased probability of behavior. Also, the removal or withdrawal of a stimulus as a consequence of behavior resulted in a decreased probability of behavior (i.e., response cost and time-out).

Verbal instruction: Written or vocal information was presented to the subject regarding either the contingencies in effect or the behavior that was desired/undesired.

Tokens: A medium of exchange was delivered as a consequence to behavior and resulted in an increased probability of behavior (and was therefore also scored as positive reinforcement). If the tokens were removed contingent on undesired behavior, the article was also scored as response cost/time-out.

Modeling: An individual (behavior-change agent) engaged in antecedent behavior that was intended to match the target behavior topographically along some dimension.

Generalization: Data were presented to demonstrate a success or failure of behavior to generalize across settings, situations, contexts, new topographies, etc.

Follow-up: Measures of the target behavior were reported from at least 6 months following the initial implementation of an intervention.

METHOD

The general categories of type of article, subjects, setting, behavior-change agent, target behavior, and use of basic principles and specific procedures were selected by the authors as representing the most basic defining features of a *JABA* article. Subcategories were selected on both an empirical and a rational basis. Initially, five volumes were selected at random. All articles in these five volumes were reviewed and for each the type of article, subjects, setting, behavior-change agent, target behavior, use of basic principles, and general procedures were recorded. Categories that occurred most frequently were identified and included in the complete review. Additional subcategories were included on the basis of potential interest to *JABA* readers (e.g., academic behavior), potential practice implications (e.g., use of reinforcer assessments), and for comparison to prevalence in the general population (e.g., geriatric issues, substance abuse). (A list of all 67 categories is available from the authors.) Operational definitions of all reported categories are presented in Table 1. Some categories are not reported either because the results did not produce any particular trends or because of low interrater agreement.

All articles published in *JABA* between 1968 and 1992 were reviewed and the total number of each category was tallied. These data were converted to a percentage of total research articles for each volume (year). In addition, some volumes contained abstracts. Abstracts were scored for their content and were tallied as research articles. Categories were not mutually exclusive. For example, interventions could occur at both school and home and be implemented by both teachers and parents. Thus, most category totals exceed 100%.

Interrater agreement was assessed separately for each dependent measure by having two of the authors independently score the same five volumes (20% of total volumes). For each volume scored by two raters, the smaller number of articles scored in a category was divided by the larger number of articles scored in that category for each year. An average agreement score was first obtained for each category, and overall agreement was calculated by obtaining an average of all categories. The five volumes used to assess interrater agreement were randomly dispersed throughout the 25 volumes.

Table 2
Number of Research Articles

1968	30
1969	31
1970	34
1971	33
1972	47
1973	61
1974	61
1975	46
1976	57
1977	69
1978	47
1979	38
1980	50
1981	42
1982	40
1983	31
1984	46
1985	33
1986	48
1987	30
1988	38
1989	31
1990	40
1991	51
1992	53

Agreement was assessed early in the investigation so that we could identify definitional nuances and correct the scoring method. At times, we made notes on our data sheets so that we could later come to a consensus on which category a topic fit (e.g., is an older student a peer?). We did not score such notes as disagreements (Sulzer-Azaroff & Gillat, 1990). Overall average agreement across all reported categories for the five volumes was 86.6%. The lowest agreement score for any single reported category was 76.9% (analogue setting), and the highest agreement score was 99.7% (research article).

RESULTS

Results are reported as a percentage of the total number of research articles rather than as the numbers of articles within each category. Although changes in the number of articles within a given category for any given year could be obscured by a percentage measure as a function of the total number of research articles, our results indicate that there is no trend in the total number of research articles. Thus, overall trends would be similar. Table 2 shows the total number of research articles, including abstracts, by year.

Type of Article

Review and discussion articles have been a small but consistent contribution to *JABA*. They represent an average of 12% of all articles, with no observable trend. Methodological studies have been similarly consistently represented, but are a smaller percentage (4%); there has been a small decrease in frequency since 1980. Of all *JABA* articles, 74% are experimental research articles.

Participants

Figure 1 (upper panel) shows the percentage of research articles in which individuals with developmental disabilities (DD), other children, other adults, and psychiatric patients were participants. From 1968 until approximately 1977, other children were clearly the most frequent participants. Recently, individuals with developmental disabilities have become the most frequent participants, and there was an upward trend from 1989 to 1992. A crossover between the percentage of other children and the percentage of individuals with DD occurred at about 1980. Other adults have been consistently and frequently represented in *JABA*, and have been the second most frequent participants in recent years. Psychiatric patients were consistently represented as participants during the earlier years of *JABA*, but have been rare since about 1980. Although older individuals (geriatric) are not represented in Figure 1, our data show few articles in which they were participants (with the exception of a special issue in 1986).

Behavior-Change Agent

Figure 1 (lower panel) shows that experimenters (authors) have been responsible for implementing the experimental procedures for the majority of *JABA* studies. This percentage would be higher if students and unidentified "trainers" or "therapists" were included as experimenters. If an author also served in an additional capacity (e.g., teacher), that capacity was scored rather than the role of exper-

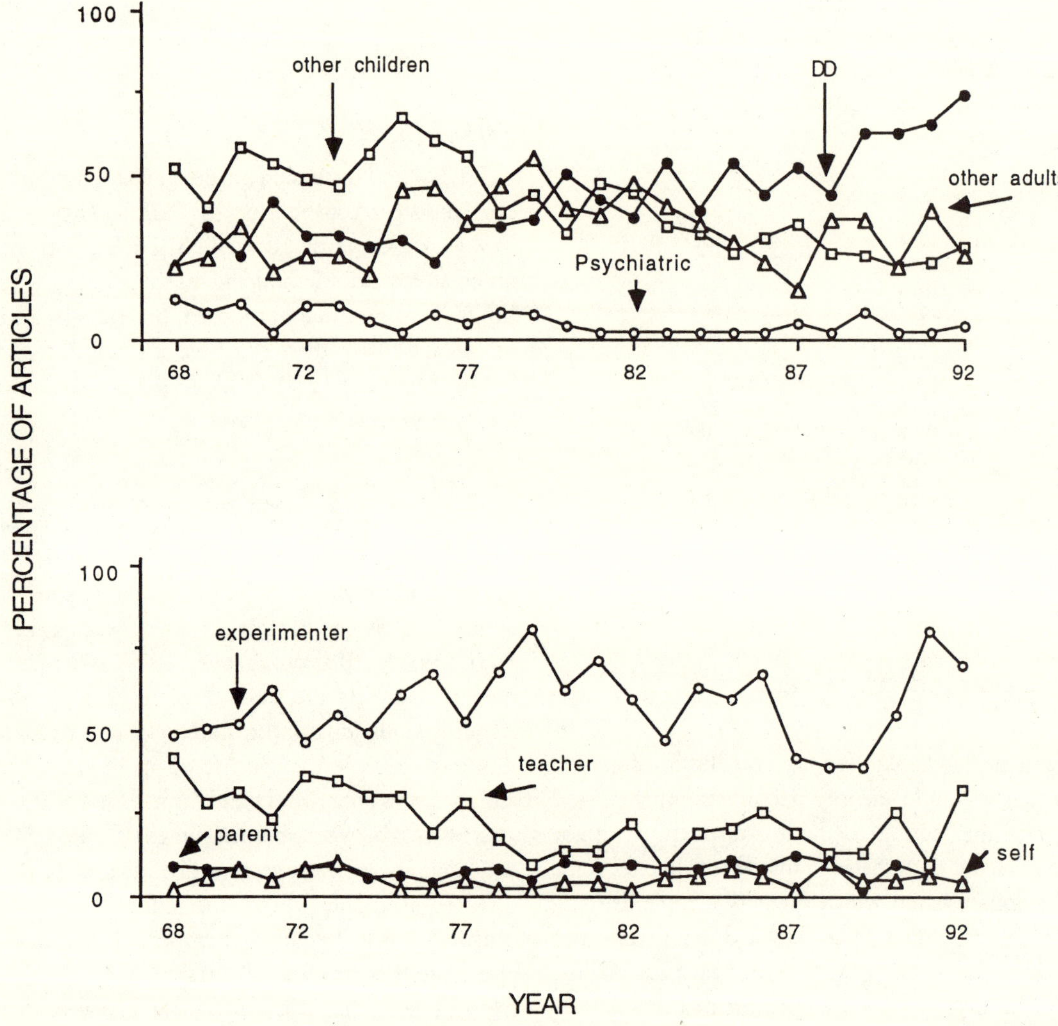

Figure 1. Percentage of articles across 25 years of *JABA* by participants (upper panel) and behavior-change agents (lower panel).

imenter. The percentage of experimenters who were the behavior-change agents increased throughout the 1970s, decreased from 1979 to 1989, and has again increased since that time. The percentage of teachers (not including those in developmental disabilities) acting as the behavior-change agent steadily decreased from 1968 to 1983, and has been variable since that time. The direct involvement of parents and peers has increased slightly. The percentage of developmental disabilities staff and teachers (not shown in Figure 1) showed little change, despite the substantial increase in participants with developmental disabilities. Few applications have involved participants as agents of their own behavior change. The other recorded categories remained relatively constant.

Setting

Figure 2 shows that the school setting is the most frequently used setting for *JABA* studies; this has changed little in 25 years. In 1968, approximately 47% of all studies were conducted in a school setting, and in 1992 it was 49%. In comparison, residential facilities have not been a frequent setting. Figure 2 also contrasts applications in analogue settings with those in community set-

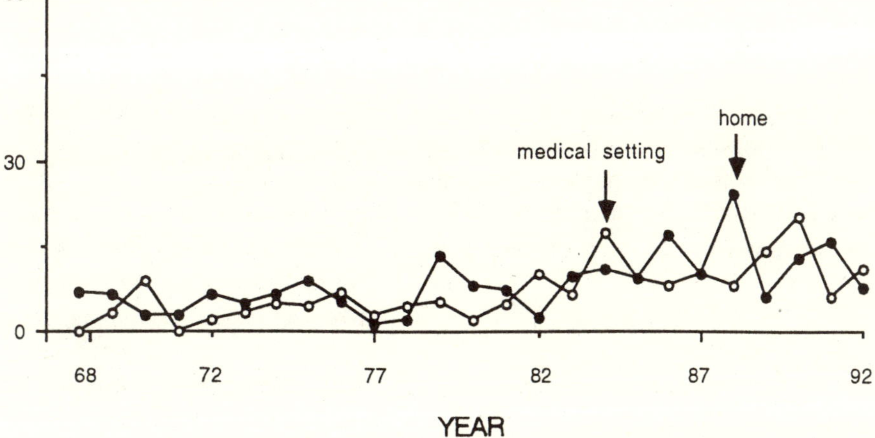

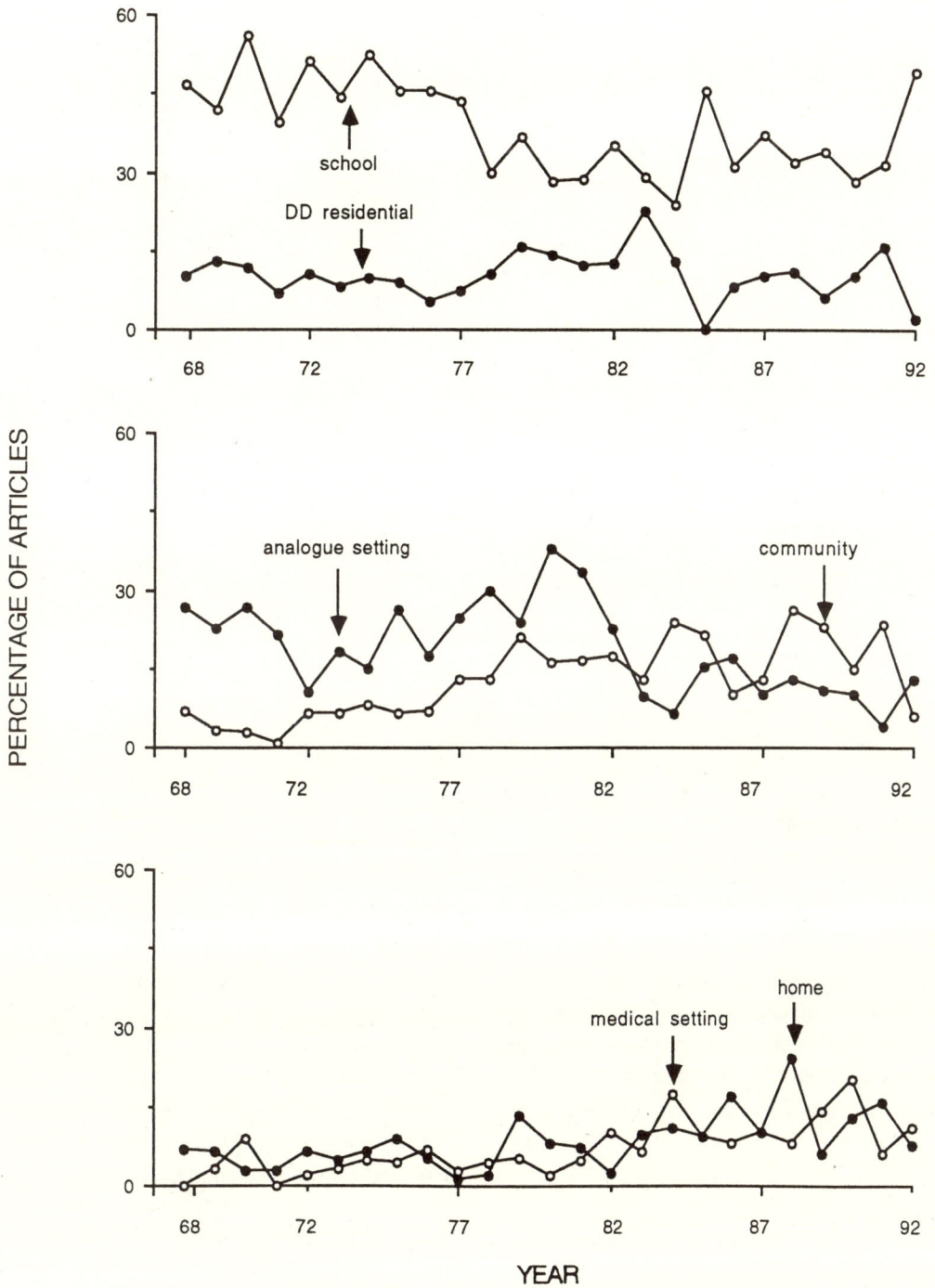

Figure 2. Percentage of articles across 25 years of *JABA* by setting (all three panels).

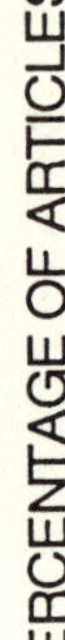

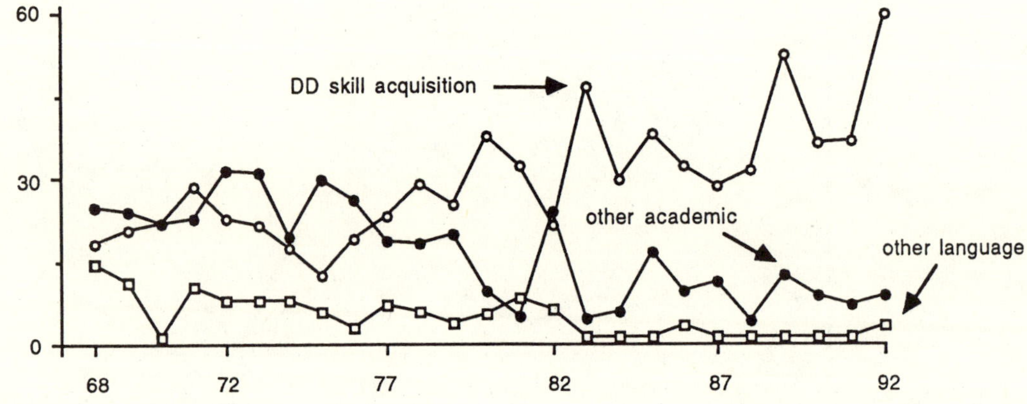

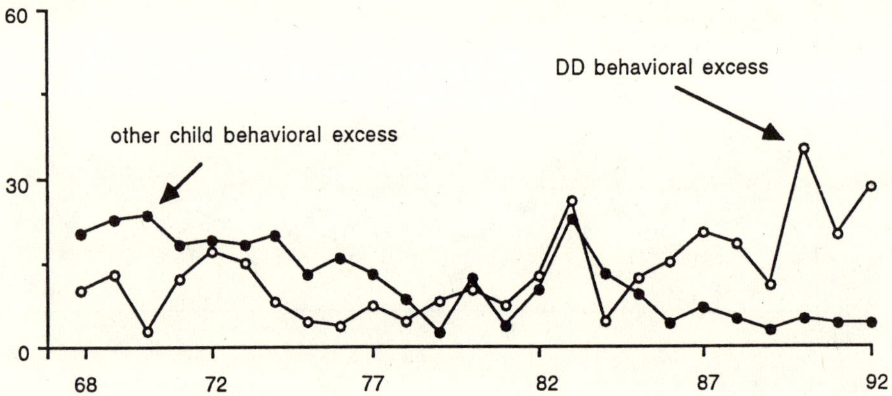

Figure 3. Percentage of articles across 25 years of *JABA* by target behavior (both panels).

tings (center panel) and displays the results for home and medical settings (lower panel). The use of analogue settings has declined since 1982 and has been generally less frequent than applications in the community. Overall, there has been since that time an upward trend in community, home, and medical settings.

Target Behavior

Figure 3 shows the progressive increase in the percentage of articles that include skill acquisition in developmental disabilities as target behaviors (upper panel). In contrast, investigations of academic behavior and other language skills (non-DD participants) have declined. Academic behavior was one of the most frequent topics until about 1976; it declined steeply from a high of 32% in 1972 to 3% in 1981. Since then, it has increased slightly, averaging 8% of all articles. The study of language in other children and adults was also a frequent and consistent topic from the first issue of *JABA* until 1983 (14% of all articles). However, in contrast to the same area in developmental disabilities, these studies have been quite rare since that time. Studies of language and communication in developmental disabilities (not shown in Figure 3) have remained at an average of approximately 7% of all articles for 25 years.

The lower panel of Figure 3 shows an increase in studies that include DD behavioral excess as a target behavior and a corresponding decrease in behavioral excesses by other children as target behaviors. The category of behavioral excesses by other children was also a frequent topic in the early years of *JABA,* but progressively decreased until 1979; it has remained relatively constant in recent years at approximately 3% to 4% of all articles.

Compared to other socially important problem areas, articles targeting substance abuse or child abuse have been quite rare. Articles addressing substance abuse were found in only seven volumes and were always a very small percentage (1% to 6%). Child abuse was represented in only two volumes and totaled 3% and 4% of the articles. Studies involving self-injury (in DD) as the dependent variable have been a small but constant topic in *JABA*; however, they have increased substantially since 1989 (11% of all articles from 1989 through 1992).

Overall, other target behaviors (those that did not fit any of the 17 categories surveyed) represented 26% of all articles and was at times the single largest category (in 8 years). It is difficult to convey the scope of these articles; for example, they ranged from responding by a comatose patient and fetal monitoring to the driving skills of pizza delivery drivers and hitting curveballs.

Principles and Procedures

Figure 4 (upper panel) shows the frequent and constant inclusion of positive reinforcement in *JABA* articles. The status of positive reinforcement as the most basic and essential principle of applied behavior analysis is reflected in this survey. The overwhelming majority of studies in *JABA* describe, define, and explicitly program positive reinforcement. Studies of negative reinforcement, on the other hand, have been rare, although they have increased substantially in the past 5 years. The use of extinction procedures was not scored in this survey, primarily because of a perceived difficulty with accurate identification. For example, differential reinforcement procedures imply an extinction procedure that was often not stated. Anecdotally, it was noted that the explicit description of extinction procedures was rare.

Figure 4 also shows the percentage of articles that included punishment (response cost/time-out or other punishment). The effects of punishment have been a consistent, but declining, topic of study in *JABA*. Overall, studies that included some type of explicit punishment procedure represented 19% of all articles. It should be noted that these results are obtained for all participants, settings, and target behaviors. For example, studies of public safety interventions conducted in the community were particularly likely to include a punishment component (i.e., a fine).

Anecdotally, we noted that many of the interventions in *JABA* consisted of multiple components. Although positive reinforcement was the single most frequent component, a common intervention was actually a treatment package consisting of multiple components. The general model, perhaps most typical, might be characterized as: instruct, model, prompt, practice, feedback, and praise.

Explicit verbal instruction has been a frequent and consistent component of *JABA* interventions (38% of all articles; range, 15% to 53%). Although verbal instruction was a frequent component of intervention packages, it was itself rarely the independent variable of interest. Modeling has also frequently been a component of interventions in *JABA,* particularly since about 1975. (The average for all 25 years was 23% of articles; range, 0 to 36%.) However, we noted that modeling has itself more frequently been the independent variable of interest. Interestingly, the use of token reinforcement was quite frequent in the early years of *JABA* (M = 33% between 1970 and 1973), but has progressively declined and is currently relatively rare (M = 2% between 1988 and 1992).

The bottom panel of Figure 4 shows the percentage of articles including generalization and at least 6-month follow-up data. An increased concern with generalization is clearly reflected by an increase in the percentage of articles that included generalization data. Although maintenance per se was not addressed in this survey, the number of articles that included at least a 6-month follow-up was tallied. Overall, the percentage of articles with 6-month follow-up data has increased slightly.

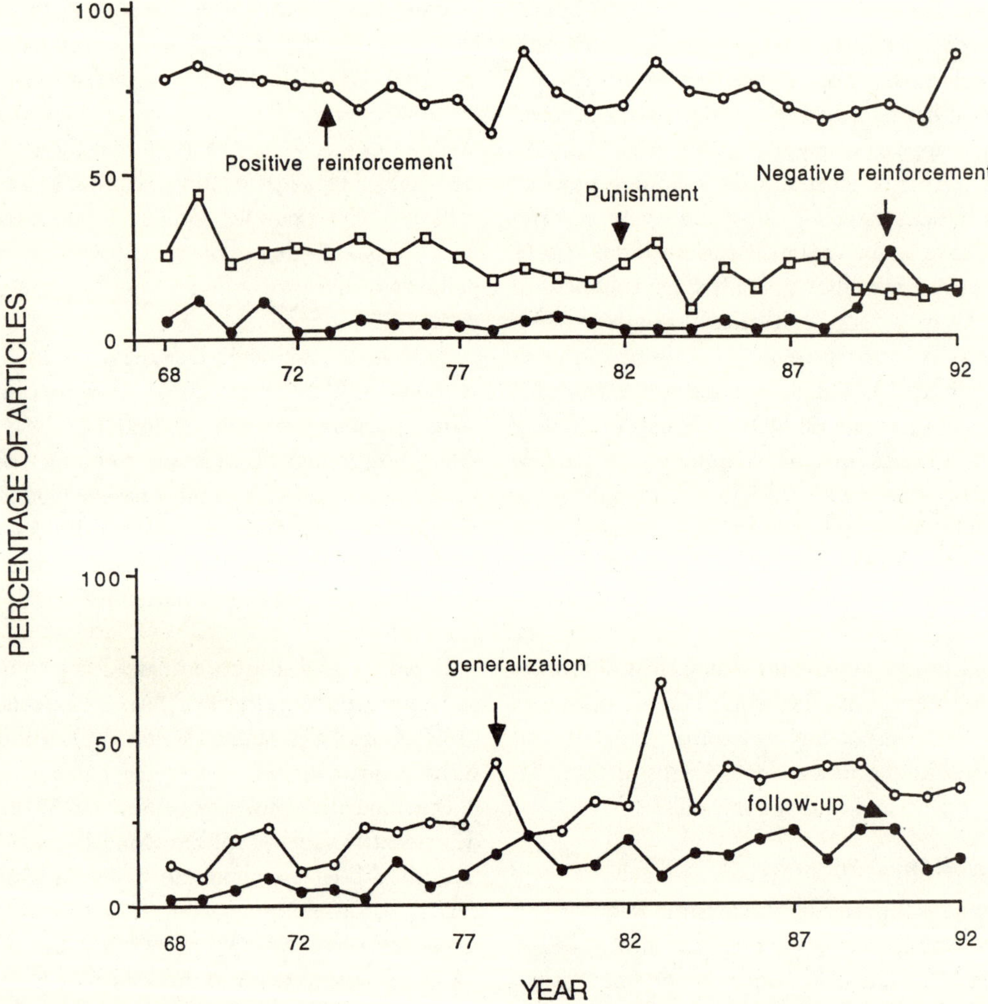

Figure 4. Percentage of articles across 25 years of *JABA* by behavioral process (upper panel) and maintenance issues (lower panel).

DISCUSSION

Over the course of its first 25 years, many of the topographies characterizing *JABA* articles have changed, and many have stayed the same. Perhaps most notable is the relative increase in the percentage of articles in developmental disabilities, especially between 1988 and 1992. Skills acquisition and behavioral excess in developmental disabilities have recently been the most frequent target behaviors. There has also been a corresponding decrease in studies targeting academic behavior, verbal behavior, and behavioral excesses of other children. Although these developments may have been apparent to even a casual reader, the magnitude and trend of the changes may not have been so readily observed. It should be emphasized that these trends are not a result of editorial policies; in fact, there have been recent efforts to promote submissions involving diverse populations (Geller, 1990; Neef, 1993). Recent special issues have addressed a wide range of topics outside of developmental disabilities.

Although schools continue to be the most frequent setting, the trend towards community and other naturalistic settings is clear and robust. Community settings are also perhaps the antithesis to analogue experimental settings, which are declining in prevalence. Furthermore, residential institutions have never been the most frequent setting in *JABA,* which in some ways refutes a common stereotype. The increasing trends in home and medical settings are also encouraging.

The relative infrequency or absence of a number of topics of unquestioned social importance (e.g., substance abuse, geriatrics) supports suggestions that applied behavior analysis should continue to expand its focus to other socially important topics (e.g., Geller, 1990; Hopkins, 1987). The discrepancy between the number of studies on developmental disabilities and those on other topics is enhanced when one considers the incidence and prevalence of various socially important problems in the general population. The relative proliferation of articles in developmental disabilities must be seen as unusual, given that only about 1% of the general population is diagnosed with mental retardation (American Psychiatric Association, 1987). An analysis of the variables maintaining research and practice in developmental disabilities might prove instructive for other areas of application. For example, the topography of behavior (e.g., self-injury) in developmental disabilities research is often incidental to an investigation of more basic principles (e.g., extinction). In practice, behavioral applications have been somewhat uniquely incorporated within a variety of state and federal regulations involving developmental disabilities.

Other trends may also be relevant to the topic of social importance. Studies of all types of verbal behavior (e.g., language, academic skills) have declined. It has long been recognized that complex verbal repertoires can alter the effects of other behavior–environment relations. The study of child behavior excesses, particularly of nondisabled children in schools, was well represented in the early years of *JABA*. Yet surveys consistently report that discipline in the schools is a primary concern for both teachers and parents. *JABA*'s rich literature in this area remains in need of continued refinement and synthesis, particularly in the areas of technology transfer and adoption (Hopkins, 1987), as well as more accurate identification of the true nature of the complaint (Witt, 1990). Other areas that are currently identified with applied behavior analysis appear to be relatively neglected or largely unexplored (e.g., pharmacological evaluations, rule-governed behavior).

Although it is not surprising that the majority of applications have been implemented by the experimenters, the overall frequency was somewhat unexpected. That the experimenters remain predominantly responsible for implementing the procedures of applied behavior analysis may be related to the problems the field is experiencing with effective transfer and large-scale dissemination and adoption. In general, models of effective technology transfer have been very rare. Although a controlled examination of procedures is an imperative for applied behavior analysis and is often a prerequisite to transfer, experimenter-implemented interventions may be especially susceptible to a neglect of the larger context and system in which an application occurs.

The current results suggest that the generality of behavioral applications has not been as widely demonstrated as might be expected. Positive reinforcement is, of course, the exception, and perhaps the model. Positive reinforcement effects have been demonstrated across the spectrum of populations, settings (cultures), problem behaviors, and use by potential consumers. However, the effects of few other behavioral principles have been so widely demonstrated. For example, the majority of studies including negative reinforcement have been with participants with developmental disabilities, primarily those with severe behavior problems. However, the increase in applications of negative reinforcement in recent years corresponds closely to an increase in functional assessment and demonstrations of the role of negative reinforcement in maintaining severe behavior disorders (e.g., self-injury). As functional analyses are conducted with other target behaviors, applications of negative reinforcement may expand further (Iwata, 1987). Many other specific applications, although perhaps also demonstrated in the field of developmental disabilities, have not been widely extended to other populations, behaviors, and settings.

Frequency is, of course, a poor measure of the range of both the kinds of applications and the socially important topics that have been addressed by *JABA*. Perhaps the most auspicious finding of this survey is that the range and scope of *JABA* articles are so broad that it is impossible to accurately classify them all. It was repeatedly observed that *JABA* contains numerous exemplary studies that appear as "one of a kind," with little, if any, subsequent follow-up. This rich data base is promising for the future development of the field. It is also encouraging that none of the categories included in this survey have yet come to define a *JABA* article.

REFERENCES

American Psychiatric Association. (1987). *Diagnostic and statistical manual of mental disorders* (3rd ed. rev.). Washington, DC: Author.

Baer, D. M. (1987). Weak contingencies, strong contingencies, and many behaviors to change. *Journal of Applied Behavior Analysis, 20,* 335–337.

Geller, E. S. (1990). The editor's page. *Journal of Applied Behavior Analysis, 23,* 143–145.

Hopkins, B. L. (1987). Comments on the future of applied behavior analysis. *Journal of Applied Behavior Analysis, 20,* 339–346.

Iwata, B. A. (1987). Negative reinforcement in applied behavior analysis: An emerging technology. *Journal of Applied Behavior Analysis, 20,* 361–378.

Kunkel, J. H. (1987). The future of *JABA*: A comment. *Journal of Applied Behavior Analysis, 20,* 329–333.

Neef, N. A. (1993). Editorial. *Journal of Applied Behavior Analysis, 26,* 3–4.

Schwartz, B., & Lacey, H. (1982). *Behaviorism, science, and human nature.* New York: Norton.

Sulzer-Azaroff, B., & Gillat, A. (1990). Trends in behavior analysis in education. *Journal of Applied Behavior Analysis, 23,* 491–495.

Witt, J. C. (1990). Complaining, precopernican thought and the univariate linear mind: Questions for school based behavioral consultation research. *School Psychology Review, 19,* 367–377.

COMPLETE BIBLIOGRAPHY, 1968–1999

The Nature of Applied Behavior Analysis

Baer, D. M., Wolf, M. M., & Risley, T. R. (1968). Some current dimensions of applied behavior analysis. *1,* 91–97.

Baer, D. M., Wolf, M. M., & Risley, T. R. (1987). Some still-current dimensions of applied behavior analysis. *20,* 313–327.

Hopkins, B. L. (1986). Comments on the future of applied behavior analysis. *20,* 339–346.

Kunkel, J. H. (1987). The future of applied behavior analysis: A comment. *20,* 329–333.

Science, Theory, and Technology

Baer, D. M. (1991). Tacting "to a fault." *24,* 429–431.

Bailey, J. S. (1991). Marketing behavior analysis requires different talk. *24,* 445–448.

Hayes, S. C. (1991). The limits of technological talk. *24,* 417–420.

Hayes, S. C., Rincover, A., & Solnick, J. V. (1980). The technical drift of applied behavior analysis. *13,* 275–285.

Iwata, B. A. (1991). Applied behavior analysis as technological science. *24,* 421–424.

Johnston, J. M. (1991). We need a new model of technology. *24,* 425–427.

Lindsley, O. R. (1991). From technical jargon to plain English for application. *24,* 449–458.

Mace, F. C. (1991). Technological to a fault or faulty approach to technology development? *24,* 433–435.

Morris, E. K. (1991). Deconstructing "Technological to a fault." *24,* 411–416.

Redmon, W. K. (1991). Pinpointing the technological fault in applied behavior analysis. *24,* 441–444.

Reid, D. H. (1991). Technological behavior analysis and societal impact: A human services perspective. *24,* 437–439.

Measurement

Aitchison, R. A. (1972). A low-cost, rapid delivery point system with "automatic" recording. *5,* 527–528.

Alevizos, P., DeRisi, W., Liberman, R., Eckman, T., & Callahan, E. (1978). The Behavior Observation Instrument: A method of direct observation for program evaluation. *11,* 243–257.

Azrin, N. H., Bugle, C., & O'Brien, F. (1971). Behavioral engineering: Two apparatuses for toilet training the retarded. *4,* 249–253.

Baker, J. G., & Whitehead, G. (1972). A portable recording apparatus for rating behavior in free-operant situations. *5,* 191–192 (Technical Note).

Barlow, D. H., Becker, R., Leitenberg, H., & Agras, W. S. (1970). A mechanical strain gauge for recording penile circumference change. *3,* 73–76 (Technical Note).

Bass, R. F. (1987). Computer-assisted observer training. *20,* 83–88.

Bernal, M. E. (1971). A device for automatic audio tape recording. *4,* 151–156.

Bijou, S. W., Peterson, R. F., & Ault, M. H. (1968). A method to integrate descriptive and experimental field studies at the level of data and empirical concepts. *1,* 175–191.

Boer, A. P. (1968). Application of a simple recording system to the analysis of free-play behavior in autistic children. *1,* 335–340.

Branch, R. C., & Sulzbacher, S. I. (1968). Rapid computation of rates with a simple nomogram. *1,* 251 (Technical Note, plus erratum, p. 334).

Brasted, W. S., & Callahan, E. J. (1984). An evaluation of the electronic fetal monitor as a feedback device during labor. *17,* 261–266.

Brechner, K. C., Linder, D. E., Meyerson, L., & Hayes, V. L. (1974). A brief report on a device for unobtrusive visual recording. *7,* 499–500.

Carroll, P. J. (1977). A durable recording and feedback system. *10,* 339–340.

Cleary, A., & Packham, D. (1968). A touch detecting teaching machine with auditory reinforcement. *1,* 341–345.

Coleman, A. D., & Boren, J. J. (1969). An information system for measuring patient behavior and its use by staff. *2,* 207–214.

Craighead, W. E., Mercatoris, M., & Bellack, B. (1974). A brief report on mentally retarded residents as behavioral observers. *7,* 333–340.

Crist, R., Delabastita, H., & Eelen, P. (1971). A device for presenting blurred visual stimuli. *4,* 333–336.

Critchfield, T. S. (1999). An unexpected effect of recording frequency in reactive self-monitoring. *32,* 389–391.

Dinoff, M., Finch, A. J., Jr., & Skelton, H. M. (1972). A circuit for video-tape interviewing and its recording reliability. *5,* 203–207.

Doran, J., & Holland, J. G. (1971). Eye movements as a function of response contingencies measured by blackout technique. *4,* 11–17.

Drash, P. W., Ray, R. P., & Tudor, R. M. (1989). An inexpensive event recorder. *22,* 453.

Edleson, J. L. (1978). An inexpensive instrument for rapid recording of "in vivo" observations. *11,* 502 (Communication).

Edwards, K. A. (1978). An index for assessing weight change in children: Weight/height ratios. *11,* 421–429.

Fargo, G., & Behrns, C. (1969). Rapid computation

and pupil self-recording of performance data. *2,* 264 (Technical Note).

Farkas, G. M., & Tharp, R. G. (1980). Observation procedure, observer gender, and behavior valence as determinants of sampling error in a behavior assessment analogue. *13,* 529–536.

Filipczak, J., Archer, M. B., Neale, M. S., & Winett, R. A. (1979). Issues in multivariate assessment of a large-scale behavioral program. *12,* 593–613.

Fitzsimmons, J. R. (1978). A behavioral tachometer. *11,* 438 (Communication).

Foster, S. L., & Ritchey, W. L. (1979). Issues in the assessment of social competence in children. *12,* 625–638.

Foxx, R. M., & Martin, P. L. (1971). A useful portable timer. *4,* 60 (Technical Note).

Frankel, F., & Weber, D. (1978). A portable low-cost multichannel timing apparatus for collection of observational duration data. *11,* 522 (Communication).

Frederikson, L. W., Martin, J. E., & Webster, J. S. (1979). Assessment of smoking behavior. *12,* 653–664.

Green, S. B., & Alverson, L. G. (1978). A comparison of indirect measures for long-duration behaviors. *11,* 530 (Abstract).

Greenwood, C. R., Walker, H. M., Todd, N. M., & Hops, H. (1979). Selecting a cost-effective screening measure for the assessment of preschool social withdrawal. *12,* 639–652.

Guitar, B., & Andrews, G. (1977). An inexpensive cumulative counter. *10,* 530 (Communication).

Harris, F. C., & Ciminero, A. R. (1978). The effect of witnessing consequences on the behavioral recordings of experimental observers. *11,* 513–521.

Harrop, A., & Daniels, M. (1986). Methods of time sampling: A reappraisal of momentary time sampling and partial interval recording. *19,* 73–77.

Harrop, A., & Daniels, M. (1993). Further reappraisal of momentary time sampling and partial-interval recording. *26,* 277–278.

Hartmann, D. P. (1975). A brief report clarifying the effects of distributional shifts on standardized test statistics. *8,* 349–350.

Hawkins, R. P. (1979). The function of assessment: Implications for selection and development of devices for assessing repertoires in clinical, educational, and other settings. *12,* 501–516.

Hay, L. R., Nelson, R. O., & Hay, W. M. (1977). The use of teachers as behavioral observers. *10,* 345–348.

Hay, L. R., Nelson, R. O., & Hay, W. M. (1980). Methodological problems in the use of participant observers. *13,* 501–504.

Haynes, S. N., & Wackwitz, J. H. (1975). Digitek coding and computer analysis of behavior observation data. *8,* 475–477.

Helweg, J. J., Johns, J. C., Norman, J. E., & Cooper, J. O. (1976). The measurement of manuscript letter strokes. *9,* 231–236.

Henson, D. E., Rubin, H. B., & Henson, C. (1979). Analysis of the consistency of objective measures of sexual arousal in women. *12,* 701–711.

Johnson, S. M., & Bolstad, O. D. (1975). Reactivity to home observation: A comparison of audio recorded behavior with observers present or absent. *8,* 181–185.

Johnson, S. M., Christensen, A., & Bellamy, G. T. (1976). Evaluation of family intervention through unobtrusive audio recordings: Experiences in "bugging" children. *9,* 213–219.

Johnston, J. M. (1970). Universal behavior graph paper. *3,* 271–272 (Technical Note).

Kahng, S., & Iwata, B. A. (1998). Computerized systems for collecting real-time observational data. *31,* 253–261.

Katz, R. C. (1973). A procedure for concurrently measuring elapsed time and response frequency. *6,* 719–720 (Technical Note).

Kazdin, A. E. (1979). Unobtrusive measures in behavioral assessment. *12,* 713–724.

Kelly, M. B. (1976). A review of academic permanent-product data collection and reliability procedures in applied behavior analysis research. *9,* 211 (Abstract).

Kelly, M. B. (1977). A review of the observational data-collection and reliability procedures reported in the *Journal of Applied Behavior Analysis. 10,* 97–101.

Kent, R. N., O'Leary, K. D., Deitz, A., & Diament, C. (1979). Comparison of observational recordings in vivo, via mirror, and via television. *12,* 517–522.

Klein, R. D. (1975). A brief research report on accuracy and academic performance. *8,* 121–122.

Kubaney, E. S., & Sloggett, B. B. (1973). Coding procedure for teachers. *6,* 339–344.

Lehrer, P., Schiff, L., & Kris, A. (1970). The use of a credit card in a token economy. *3,* 289–291 (Technical Note).

Lindsley, O. R. (1968). A reliable wrist counter for recording behavior rates. *1,* 77–78 (Technical Note).

Logan, D. L. (1970). "Paper money" system as a recording aid in institutional settings. *3,* 183–184 (Technical Note).

Macht, J. (1971). Operant measurement of subjective visual acuity in non-verbal children. *4,* 23–36.

Martinez-Diaz, J. A., & Edelstein, B. A. (1979). Multivariate effects of demand characteristics on the analogue assessment of heterosocial competence. *12,* 679–689.

Mattos, R. L. (1968). A manual counter for recording multiple behaviors. *1,* 130 (Technical Note).

McKenzie, T. L., Sallis, J. F., Nader, P. R., Patterson, T. L., Elder, J. P., Berry, C. C., Rupp, J. W., Atkins, C. J., Buono, M. J., & Nelson, J. A. (1991).

BEACHES: An observational system for assessing children's eating and physical activity behaviors and associated events. *24,* 141–151.

Milby, J. B., Jr., Willcutt, H. C., Hawk, J. W., Jr., MacDonald, M., & Whitfield, K. (1973). A system for recording individualized behavioral data in a token system. *6,* 333–338.

Milone, M. N., Jr., Cloninger, C. J., & Cowardin, J. L. (1979). Computer graphed data for behavioral research. *12,* 362 (Communication).

Miltenberger, R. G., Rapp, J. T., & Long, E. S. (1999). A low-tech method for conducting real-time recording. *32,* 119–120.

Mudford, O. C., Beale, I. L., & Singh, N. N. (1990). The representativeness of observational samples of different durations. *23,* 323–331.

Nordquist, V. M. (1971). A method for recording verbal behavior in free play settings. *4,* 327–331.

Ozbek, I. N., Russo, D. C., & Cataldo, M. F. (1978). A device for training and maintaining fixed-interval behaviors in the nontime-telling population. *11,* 430 (Communication).

Porter, J., Herson, J. L., III, & Payne, J. S. (1972). A portable observation-experimental booth. *5,* 379–380 (Technical Note).

Powell, J., Martindale, A., & Kulp, S. (1975). An evaluation of time-sample measures of behavior. *8,* 463–469.

Powell, J., Martindale, B., Kulp, S., Martindale, A., & Bauman, R. (1977). Taking a closer look: Time sampling and measurement error. *10,* 325–332.

Powell, J., & Rockinson, R. (1978). On the inability of interval time sampling to reflect frequency of occurrence data. *11,* 531–532 (Abstract).

Prinz, R. J., Foster, S., Kent, R. N., & O'Leary, K. D. (1979). Multivariate assessment of conflict in distressed and nondistressed mother-adolescent dyads. *12,* 691–700.

Quilitch, H. R. (1972). A portable programmed, audible timer. *5,* 18 (Technical Note).

Repp, A. C., Karsh, K. G., Felce, D., & Ludewig, D. (1989). Further comments on using hand-held computers for data collection. *22,* 336–337.

Repp, A. C., Roberts, D. M., Slack, D. J., Repp, C. F., & Berkler, M. S. (1976). A comparison of frequency, interval, and time-sampling methods of data collection. *9,* 501–508.

Rosenbaum, M. S., & Drabman, R. S. (1979). Goniometry in behavior modification: A useful assessment technique. *12,* 354 (Communication).

Rusch, F. R., Walker, H. M., & Greenwood, C. R. (1975). Experimenter calculation errors: A potential factor affecting interpretation of results. *8,* 460 (Abstract).

Sanders, R. M., Hopkins, B. L., & Walker, M. B. (1969). An inexpensive method for making data records of complex behaviors. *2,* 221–222 (Technical Note).

Sanson-Fisher, R. W., Poole, A. D., & Dunn, J. (1980). An empirical method for determining an appropriate interval length for recording behavior. *13,* 493–500.

Saudargas, R. A., & Zanolli, K. (1990). Momentary time sampling as an estimate of percentage time: A field validation. *23,* 533–537.

Saunders, R. M., & Paine, F. (1972). Time lapse automation. *5,* 110 (Technical Note).

Schnelle, J. F. (1974). A brief report on the invalidity of parent evaluations of behavior change. *7,* 341–343.

Schroeder, S. R. (1972). Automated transduction of sheltered workshop behaviors. *5,* 523–525.

Shriberg, L. D. (1971). A system for monitoring and conditioning modal fundamental frequency of speech. *4,* 337–339.

Skrtic, T. M., & Sepler, H. J. (1982). Simplifying continuous monitoring of multiple-response/multiple-subject classroom interactions. *15,* 183–187.

Strang, H. R., & George, J. R. (1975). Clowning around to stop clowning around: A brief report on an automated approach to monitor, record, and control classroom noise. *8,* 471–474.

Stuart, R. B. (1970). A cueing device for acceleration of positive interactions. *3,* 257–260 (Technical Note).

Suen, H. K., Ary, D., & Covalt, W. (1991). Reappraisal of momentary time sampling and partial interval recording. *24,* 803–804.

Tate, B. G. (1968). An automated system for reinforcing and recording retardate work behavior. *1,* 347–348 (Technical Note).

Thompson, C., Holmberg, M., & Baer, D. M. (1974). A brief report on a comparison of time-sampling procedures. *7,* 623–626.

Touchette, P. E., MacDonald, R. F., & Langer, S. N. (1985). A scatter plot for identifying stimulus control of problem behavior. *18,* 343–351.

Trant, L. (1977). Pictoral token card. *10,* 548 (Communication).

Van Houten, R. (1978). Normative data: A comment. *11,* 110 (Communication).

White, G. D. (1977). The effects of observer presence on the activity levels of families. *10,* 734 (Abstract).

Whittaker, R. (1973). A note on a multi-movement, on-line behavior recorder. *6,* 721–723 (Technical Note).

Williams, A. M. (1979). The quantity and quality of marital interaction related to marital satisfaction: A behavioral analysis. *12,* 665–678.

Willis, J., & Crowder, J. (1972). A portable device for group modification of classroom attending behavior. *5,* 199–202.

Wintre, M. G., & Webster, C. D. (1974). A brief report on using a traditional social behavior scale with disturbed children. *7,* 345–348.

Worthy, R. C. (1968). A miniature, portable timer and audible signal-generating device. *1,* 159–160 (Technical Note).

Interobserver Agreement

Baer, D. M. (1977). Reviewer's comment: Just because it's reliable doesn't mean you can use it. *10,* 117–119.

Birkimer, J. C., & Brown, J. H. (1979). Back to basics: Percentage agreement measures are adequate, but there are easier ways. *12,* 535–543.

Birkimer, J. C., & Brown, J. H. (1979). A graphical judgmental aid which summarizes obtained and chance reliability data and helps assess the believability of experimental effects. *12,* 523–533.

Boykin, R. A., & Nelson, R. O. (1981). The effects of instructions and calculation procedures on observers' accuracy, agreement, and calculation correctness. *14,* 479–489.

Cone, J. D. (1979). Why the "I've got a better agreement measure" literature continues to grow: A commentary on two articles by Birkimer and Brown. *12,* 571.

Deitz, S. M. (1988). Another's view of observer agreement and observer accuracy. *21,* 113.

Farkas, G. M. (1978). Correction for bias in an interobserver agreement formula. *11,* 188 (Communication).

Harris, F. C., & Lahey, B. B. (1978). A method for combining occurrence and nonoccurrence interobserver agreement scores. *11,* 523–527.

Hartmann, D. P. (1977). Considerations in the choice of interobserver reliability estimates. *10,* 103–116.

Hartmann, D. P. (1979). A note on reliability: Old wine in a new bottle. *12,* 298 (Communication).

Hartmann, D. P., & Gardner, W. (1979). On the not so recent invention of interobserver reliability: A commentary on two articles by Birkimer and Brown. *12,* 559–560.

Hartmann, D. P., & Gardner, W. (1982). A cautionary note on the use of probability values to evaluate interobserver agreement. *15,* 189–190.

Hawkins, R. P., & Fabry, B. D. (1979). Applied behavior analysis and reliability: A commentary on two articles by Birkimer and Brown. *12,* 545–552.

Hopkins, B. L. (1979). Proposed conventions for evaluating observer reliability: A commentary on two articles by Birkimer and Brown. *12,* 561–564.

Hopkins, B. L., & Hermann, J. A. (1977). Evaluating interobserver reliability of interval data. *10,* 121–126.

Kazdin, A. E. (1977). Artifact, bias, and complexity of assessment: The ABCs of reliability. *10,* 141–150.

Kent, R. N., Kanowitz, J., O'Leary, K. D., & Cheiken, M. (1977). Observer reliability as a function of circumstances of assessment. *10,* 317–324.

Kratochwill, T. R. (1979). Just because it's reliable doesn't mean it's believable: A commentary on two articles by Birkimer and Brown. *12,* 553–557.

Kratochwill, T. R., & Wetzel, R. J. (1977). Observer agreement, credibility, and judgment: Some considerations in presenting observer agreement data. *10,* 133–139.

Lewin, L. M., & Wakefield, J. A., Jr. (1979). Percentage agreement and phi: A conversion table. *12,* 299–301.

Martin, J. E., & Epstein. L. H. (1977). An inexpensive technique for establishing the reliability of blood-pressure measurement. *10,* 508 (Communication).

Meighan, M. (1977). Confidence intervals and reliability coefficients. *10,* 530 (Communication).

O'Leary, K. D., Kent, R. N., & Kanowitz, J. (1975). Shaping data collection congruent with experimental hypotheses. *8,* 43–51.

Repp, A. C., Deitz, D. E. D., Boles, S. M., Deitz, S. M., & Repp, C. F. (1976). Differences among common methods for calculating interobserver agreement. *9,* 109–113.

Romanczyk, R. G., Kent, R. D., Diament, C., & O'Leary, K. D. (1973). Measuring the reliability of observational data: A reactive process. *6,* 175–184.

Yelton, A. R. (1979). Reliability in the context of the experiment: A commentary on two articles by Birkimer and Brown. *12,* 565–569.

Yelton, A. R., Wildman, B. G., & Erickson, M. T. (1977). A probability based formula for calculating interobserver agreement. *10,* 127–131.

Treatment Integrity

Gresham, F. M., Gansle, K. A., & Noell, G. H. (1993). Treatment integrity in applied behavior analysis with children. *26,* 257–263.

Peterson, L., Homer, A. L., & Wonderlich, S. A. (1982). The integrity of independent variables in behavior analysis. *15,* 477–492.

Vollmer, T. R., Roane, H. S., Ringdahl, J. E., & Marcus, B. A. (1999). Evaluating treatment challenges with differential reinforcement of alternative behavior. *32,* 9–23.

Experimental Design

Barlow, D. H., & Hayes, S. C. (1979). Alternating treatments design: One strategy for comparing the effects of two treatments in a single subject. *13,* 199–210.

Goetz, E. M., Holmberg, M. C., & LeBlanc, J. M. (1975). Differential reinforcement of other behavior and noncontingent reinforcement as control procedures during the modification of a preschooler's compliance. *8,* 77–82.

Hartmann, D. P., & Hall, R. V. (1976). The changing criterion design. *9,* 527–532.

Higgins Hains, A., & Baer, D. M. (1989). Interaction effects in multielement designs: Inevitable, desirable, and ignorable. *22,* 57–69.

Horner, R. D., & Baer, D. M. (1978). Multiple-probe technique: A variation on the multiple baseline. *11,* 189–196.

Kazdin, A. E. (1973). Methodological and assessment considerations in evaluating reinforcement programs in applied settings (including reviewers' comments). *6,* 517–539.

McGonigle, J. J., Rojahn, J., Dixon, J., & Strain, P. S. (1987). Multiple treatment interference in the alternating treatments design as a function of the intercomponent interval length. *20,* 171–178.

Pechacek, T. F. (1978). A probabilistic model of intensive designs. *11,* 357–362.

Rusch, F. R., & Kazdin, A. E. (1981). Toward a methodology of withdrawal designs for the assessment of response maintenance. *14,* 131–140.

Van Houten, R. (1987). Comparing treatment techniques: A cautionary note. *20,* 109–110.

Wacker, D., McMahon, C., Steege, M., Berg, W., Sasso, G., & Melloy, K. (1990). Applications of a sequential alternating design. *23,* 333–339.

Data Analysis

Baer, D. M. (1977). "Perhaps it would be better not to know everything." *10,* 167–172.

Bailey, D. B. (1984). Effects of lines of progress and semilogarithmic charts on ratings of charted data. *17,* 359–365.

Blumberg, C. J. (1984). Comments on "A simplified time-series analysis for evaluating treatment interventions." *17,* 539–542.

Carr, J. E., & Burkholder, E. O. (1998). Creating single-subject design graphs with Microsoft Excel. *31,* 245–251.

DeProspero, A., & Cohen, S. (1979). Inconsistent visual analyses of intrasubject data. *12,* 573–579.

Furlong, M. J., & Wampold, B. E. (1982). Intervention effects and relative variation as dimensions in experts' use of visual inference. *15,* 415–421.

Gentile, J. R., Roden, A. H., & Klein, R. D. (1972). An analysis-of-variance model for the intrasubject replication design. *5,* 193–198.

Hantula, D. A. (1995). Disciplined decision making in an interdisciplinary environment: Some implications for clinical applications of statistical process control. *28,* 371–377.

Hartmann, D. P. (1974). Forcing square pegs into round holes: Some comments on "An analysis-of-variance model for the intrasubject replication design." *7,* 635–638.

Hartmann, D. P., Gottman, J. M., Jones, R. R., Gardner, W., Kazdin, A. E., & Vaught, R. S. (1980). Interrupted time-series analysis and its application to behavioral data. *13,* 543–559.

Hopkins, B. L. (1995). Applied behavior analysis and statistical process control? *28,* 379–386.

Jones, R. R., Vaught, R. S., & Weinrott, M. (1977). Time-series analysis in operant research. *10,* 151–166.

Jones, R. R., Weinrott, M. R., & Vaught, R. S. (1978). Effects of serial dependency on the agreement between visual and statistical inference. *11,* 277–283.

Kendall, M. G. (1973). Hiawatha designs an experiment. *6,* 331–332.

Kennedy, C. H. (1989). Selecting consistent vertical axis scales. *22,* 338–339.

Keselman, H. J., & Leventhal, L. (1974). Concerning the statistical procedures enumerated by Gentile et al.: Another perspective. *7,* 643–645.

Kratochwill, T., Alden, K., Demuth, D., Dawson, D., Panicucci, C., Arnston, P., McMurray, N., Hempstead, J., & Levin, J. (1974). A further consideration in the application of an analysis of variance model for the intrasubject replication design. *7,* 629–633.

Matyas, T. A., & Greenwood, K. M. (1990). Visual analysis of a single-case time series: Effects of variability, serial dependence, and magnitude of intervention effects. *23,* 341–351.

Michael, J. (1974). Statistical inference for individual organism research: Mixed blessing or curse? *7,* 647–653.

Michael, J. (1974). Statistical inference for individual organism research: Some reactions to a suggestion by Gentile, Roden, and Klein. *7,* 627–628.

Pfadt, A., Cohen, I. L., Sudhalter, V., Romanczyk, R. G., & Wheeler, D. J. (1992). Applying statistical process control to clinical data: An illustration. *25,* 551–560.

Pfadt, A., & Wheeler, D. J. (1995). Using statistical process control to make data-based clinical decisions. *28,* 349–370.

Thoresen, C. E., & Elashoff, J. D. (1974). "An analysis-of-variance model for intrasubject replication design": Some additional comments. *7,* 639–641.

Tryon, W. W. (1982). A simplified time-series analysis for evaluating treatment interventions. *15,* 423–429.

Tryon, W. W. (1984). "A simplified time-series analysis for evaluating treatment interventions": A rejoinder to Blumberg. *17,* 543–544.

Social Validity

Baer, D. M., & Schwartz, I. S. (1991). If reliance on epidemiology were to become epidemic, we would need to assess its social validity. *24,* 231–234.

Fawcett, S. B. (1991). Social validity: A note on methodology. *24,* 235–239.

Finney, J. W. (1991). On further development of the concept of social validity. *24,* 245–249.

Hawkins, R. P. (1991). Is social validity what we are interested in? Argument for a functional approach. *24,* 205–213.

Kazdin, A. E. (1980). Acceptability of alternative

treatments for deviant child behavior. *13,* 259–273.

Schwartz, I. S. (1991). The study of consumer behavior and social validity: An essential partnership for applied behavior analysis. *24,* 241–244.

Schwartz, I. S., & Baer, D. M. (1991). Social validity assessments: Is current practice state of the art? *24,* 189–204.

Van Houten, R. (1979). Social validation: The evaluation of standards of competency for target behaviors. *12,* 581–591.

Walker, H. M., & Hops, H. (1976). Use of normative peer data as a standard for evaluating classroom treatment effects. *9,* 159–168.

Winett, R. A., Moore, J. F., & Anderson, E. S. (1991). Extending the concept of social validity: Behavior analysis for disease prevention and health promotion. *24,* 215–230.

Wolf, M. M. (1978). Social validity: The case for subjective measurement or how applied behavior analysis is finding its heart. *11,* 203–214.

Conceptual Issues

Balsam, P. D., & Bondy, A. S. (1983). The negative side effects of reward. *16,* 283–296.

Balsam, P. D., & Bondy, A. S. (1985). Reward induced response covariation: Side effects revisited. *18,* 79–80.

Cataldo, M. F., & Brady, J. V. (1994). Deriving relations from the experimental analysis of behavior. *27,* 763–770.

Catania, A. C., Shimoff, E., & Matthews, B. A. (1987). Correspondence between definitions and procedures: A reply to Stokes, Osnes, and Guevremont. *20,* 401–404.

Chandler, L. K., Lubeck, R. C., & Fowler, S. A. (1992). Generalization and maintenance of preschool children's social skills: A critical review and analysis. *25,* 415–428.

Cone, J. D. (1973). Assessing the effectiveness of programmed generalization (including reviewers' comments). *6,* 713–718.

Epstein, R. (1985). The positive effects of reinforcement: A commentary on Balsam and Bondy (1983). *18,* 73–79.

Fisher, E. B., Jr. (1979). Overjustification effects in token economies. *12,* 407–415.

Fisher, W. W., & Mazur, J. E. (1997). Basic and applied research on choice responding. *30,* 387–410.

Foster, W. S. (1978). Adjunctive behavior: An underreported phenomenon in applied behavior analysis? *11,* 545–546.

Friman, P. C., & Poling, A. (1995). Making life easier with effort: Basic findings and applied research on response effort. *28,* 583–590.

Fuqua, R. W. (1984). Comments on the applied relevance of the matching law. *17,* 381–386.

Galbicka, G. (1994). Shaping in the 21st century: Moving percentile schedules into applied settings. *27,* 739–760.

Hayes, S. C., & Hayes, L. J. (1993). Applied implications of current *JEAB* research on derived relations and delayed reinforcement. *26,* 507–511.

Hineline, P. N., & Wacker, D. P. (1993). *JEAB,* November '92: What's in it for the *JABA* reader? *26,* 269–274.

Houlihan, D., & Brandon, P. K. (1996). Compliant in a moment: A commentary on Nevin. *29,* 549–555.

Hughes, C., Harmer, M. L., Killian, D. J., & Niarhos, F. (1995). The effects of multiple-exemplar self-instructional training on high school students' generalized conversational interactions. *28,* 201–218.

Israel, A. C. (1978). Some thoughts on the correspondence between saying and doing. *11,* 271–276.

Iwata, B. A. (1986). Negative reinforcement in applied behavior analysis: An emerging technology. *20,* 361–378.

Iwata, B. A., & Michael, J. L. (1994). Applied implications of theory and research on the nature of reinforcement. *27,* 183–193.

Kagel, J. H., & Winkler, R. C. (1972). Behavioral economics: Areas of cooperative research between economics and applied behavioral analysis. *5,* 335–342.

Karlan, G. R., & Rusch, F. R. (1982). Correspondence between saying and doing: Some thoughts on defining correspondence and future directions for application. *15,* 151–162.

Kazdin, A. E., & Bootzin, R. R. (1972). The token economy: An evaluative review. *5,* 343–372.

Kirby, K. C., & Bickel, W. K. (1995). Implications of behavioral pharmacology research for applied behavior analyses: *JEAB*'s special issue celebrating the contributions of Joseph V. Brady (March 1994). *28,* 105–112.

Lalli, J. S., & Mauro, B. C. (1995). The paradox of preference for unreliable reinforcement: The role of context and conditioned reinforcement. *28,* 389–394.

Lattal, K. A., & Neef, N. A. (1996). Recent reinforcement-schedule research and applied behavior analysis. *29,* 213–230.

Lerman, D. C., & Iwata, B. A. (1996). Developing a technology for the use of operant extinction in clinical settings: An examination of basic and applied research. *29,* 345–382.

Mace, F. C. (1996). In pursuit of general behavioral relations. *29,* 557–563.

Mace, F. C., & Wacker, D. P. (1994). Toward greater integration of basic and applied behavioral research: An introduction. *27,* 569–574.

Matthews, B. A., Shimoff, E., & Catania, A. C. (1987). Saying and doing: A contingency-space analysis. *20,* 69–74.

Myerson, J., & Hale, S. (1984). Concurrent schedules and matching in applied settings: A reply to Fuqua. *17,* 387–389.

Myerson, J., & Hale, S. (1984). Practical implications of the matching law. *17,* 367–380.

Nevin, J. A. (1996). The momentum of compliance. *29,* 535–547.

Nevin, J. A., & Mace, F. C. (1994). The ABCs of *JEAB,* September 1993. *27,* 561–565.

Pierce, W. D., & Epling, W. F. (1995). The applied importance of research on the matching law. *28,* 237–241.

Pigott, H. E., Fantuzzo, J. W., & Gorsuch, R. L. (1987). Further generalization technology: Accounting for natural covariation in generalization assessment. *20,* 273–278.

McGill, P. (1999). Establishing operations: Implications for the assessment, treatment, and prevention of problem behavior. *32,* 393–418.

Poling, A., & Normand, M. (1999). Noncontingent reinforcement: An inappropriate description of time-based schedules that reduce behavior. *32,* 237–238.

Rosales-Ruiz, J., & Baer, D. M. (1997). Behavioral cusps: A developmental and pragmatic concept for behavior analysis. *30,* 533–544.

Shull, R. L., & Fuqua, R. W. (1993). The collateral effects of behavioral interventions: Applied implications from *JEAB,* January, 1993. *26,* 409–415.

Smith, R. G., & Iwata, B. A. (1997). Antecedent influences on behavior disorders. *30,* 343–375.

Spradlin, J. E. (1996). Comments on Lerman and Iwata. *29,* 383–385.

Stokes, T. (1992). Discrimination and generalization. *25,* 429–432.

Stokes, T. F., & Baer, D. M. (1977). An implicit technology of generalization. *10,* 349–367.

Stokes, T. F., Osnes, P. G., & Guevremont, D. C. (1987). Saying and doing: A commentary on a contingency-space analysis. *20,* 161–164.

Stromer, R., Mackay, H. A., & Remington, B. (1996). Naming, the formation of stimulus classes, and applied behavior analysis. *29,* 409–431.

Vollmer, T. R. (1999). Noncontingent reinforcement: Some additional comments. *32,* 239–240.

Wahler, R. G., & Fox, J. J. (1981). Setting events in applied behavior analysis: Toward a conceptual and methodological expansion. *14,* 327–338.

Research, Training, and Professional Practice

Axelrod, S. (1992). Disseminating an effective educational technology. *25,* 31–35.

Azrin, N. H. (1978). Toward a solution: A critique. *11,* 175.

Baer, D. M. (1987). Weak contingencies, strong contingencies, and many behaviors to change. *20,* 335–337.

Baer, D. M. (1992). The reform of education is at least a four-legged program. *25,* 77–79.

Baer, D. M. (1992). Teacher proposes, student disposes. *25,* 89–92.

Baer, D. M. (1993). A brief, selective history of the Department of Human Development and Family Life at the University of Kansas: The early years. *26,* 569–572.

Bijou, S. W. (1970). What psychology has to offer education now. *3,* 65–71.

Birnbrauer, J. S. (1978). Better living through behaviorism? *11,* 176–177.

Carnine, D. (1992). Expanding the notion of teachers' rights: Access to tools that work. *25,* 13–19.

Communidad Los Horcones. (1992). Natural reinforcement: A way to improve education. *25,* 71–75.

Fantuzzo, J., & Atkins, M. (1992). Applied behavior analysis for educators: Teacher centered and classroom based. *25,* 37–42.

Fawcett, S. B., Mathews, R. M., & Fletcher, R. K. (1980). Some promising dimensions for behavioral community technology. *13,* 505–518.

Fixsen, D. L., & Blase, K. A. (1993). Creating new realities: Program development and dissemination. *26,* 597–615.

Geller, E. S. (1993). Thinking big. *26,* 555–559.

Goldiamond, I. (1978). The professional as a double agent. *11,* 178–184.

Hawkins, R. P., Chase, P. N., & Scotti, J. R. (1993). Applied behavior analysis at West Virginia University: A brief history. *26,* 573–582.

Holland, J. G. (1978). Behaviorism: Part of the problem or part of the solution? *11,* 163–174.

Holland, J. G. (1978). Toward a solution: A rejoinder. *11,* 185–187.

Jacobs, H. E. (1991). Ya shoulda, oughta, wanna, or, laws of behavior and behavioral community research. *24,* 641–644.

Jason, L. A., & Crawford, I. (1991). Toward a kinder, gentler, and more effective behavioral approach in community settings. *24,* 649–651.

Johnston, J. M. (1992). Managing our own behavior: Some hidden issues. *25,* 93–96.

Kazdin, A. E. (1975). The impact of applied behavior analysis on diverse areas of research. *8,* 213–229.

Keller, F. S. (1968). "Goodbye teacher. . ." *1,* 79–89.

King, L. (1981). Comment on "Adoption of innovations from applied behavioral research: 'Does anybody care?'" *14,* 507–511.

Krantz, D. L. (1971). The separate worlds of operant and nonoperant research. *4,* 61–70.

Kratochwill, T. R., & Martens, B. K. (1994). Applied behavior analysis and school psychology. *27,* 3–5.

Laties, V. G., Preston, R. A., Inglis, G. B., & Pittelli, R. L. (1996). *JEAB* and *JABA* on the World Wide Web: A report to readers. *29,* 435–436.

Lindsley, O. R. (1992). Why aren't effective teaching tools widely adopted? *25,* 21–26.

Lloyd, M. E. (1990). Gender factors in reviewer recommendations for manuscript publication. *23,* 539–543.

Lovaas, O. I. (1993). The development of a treatment-research project for developmentally disabled and autistic children. *26,* 617–630.

Lovitt, T. C. (1993). A brief history of applied behavior analysis at the University of Washington. *26,* 563–567.

Malott, R. W. (1992). Follow-up commentary on training behavior analysts. *25,* 513–515.

Malott, R. W. (1992). Should we train applied behavior analysts to be researchers? *25,* 83–88.

McClannahan, L. E., & Krantz, P. J. (1993). On systems analysis in autism intervention programs. *26,* 589–596.

McGimsey, J. F., Greene, B. F., & Lutzker, J. R. (1995). Competence in aspects of behavioral treatment and consultation: Implications for service delivery and graduate training. *28,* 301–315.

Michael, J. (1993). A brief overview of the history of Western Michigan University's behavioral programs. *26,* 587–588.

Miller, L. K. (1991). Avoiding the countercontrol of applied behavior analysis. *24,* 645–647.

Myers, D. L. (1995). Eliminating the battering of women by men: Some considerations for behavior analysis. *28,* 493–507.

Nordyke, N. S., Baer, D. M., Etzel, B. C., & LeBlanc, J. M. (1977). Implications of the stereotyping and modification of sex role. *10,* 553–557.

Peterson, L., & Calhoun, K. (1995). On advancing behavior analysis in the treatment and prevention of battering: Commentary on Myers. *28,* 509–514.

Poling, A., Alling, K., & Fuqua, R. W. (1994). Self- and cross-citation in the *Journal of Applied Behavior Analysis* and the *Journal of the Experimental Analysis of Behavior:* 1983–1992. *27,* 729–731.

Reid, D. H. (1992). The need to train more behavior analysts to be better applied researchers. *25,* 97–99.

Rubin, H. B., & Cuvo, A. J. (1993). The Behavior Analysis and Therapy Program at Southern Illinois University at Carbondale. *26,* 583–586.

Sajwaj, T. (1977). Issues and implications of establishing guidelines for the use of behavioral techniques. *10,* 531–540.

Sherman, J. A., & Sheldon, J. B. (1991). Values for community research and action: Do we agree where they guide us? *24,* 653–655.

Sherman, J. G. (1992). Reflections on PSI: Good news and bad. *25,* 59–64.

Stolz, S. B. (1977). Why no guidelines for behavior modification? *10,* 541–547.

Stolz, S. B. (1981). Adoption of innovations from applied behavioral research: "Does anybody care?" *14,* 491–505.

Sulzer-Azaroff, B. (1992). Is back to nature always best? *25,* 81–82.

Willems, E. P. (1974). Behavioral technology and behavioral ecology (including rejoinder by D. M. Baer and reviewers' comments). *7,* 151–170.

Winett, R. A. (1991). Caveats on values guiding community research and action. *24,* 637–639.

Winett, R. A., & Winkler, R. C. (1972). Current behavior modification in the classroom: Be still, be quiet, be docile (including rejoinder by K. D. O'Leary and reviewers' comments). *5,* 499–515.

Winkler, R. C. (1977). What types of sex-role behavior should behavior modifiers promote? *10,* 549–552.

Trends in Applied Behavior Analysis

Dunlap, G., Clarke, S., & Reyes, L. (1998). An analysis of trends in *JABA* authorship. *31,* 497–500.

Laties, V. G., & Mace, F. C. (1993). Taking stock: The first 25 years of the *Journal of Applied Behavior Analysis. 26,* 513–525.

Mathews, R. M. (1997). Editors as authors: Publication trends of articles authored by *JABA* editors. *30,* 717–721.

Northup, J., Vollmer, T. R., & Serrett, K. (1993). Publication trends in 25 years of the *Journal of Applied Behavior Analysis. 26,* 527–537.

Pelios, L., Morren, J., Tesch, D., & Axelrod, S. (1999). The impact of functional analysis methodology on treatment choice for self-injurious and aggressive behavior. *32,* 185–195.

Sulzer-Azaroff, B., & Gillat, A. (1990). Trends in behavior analysis in education. *23,* 491–495.